REA

The Nonprofit Handbook: Management

WILEY NONPROFIT LAW, FINANCE, AND MANAGEMENT SERIES

The Art of Planned Giving: Understanding Donors and the Culture of Giving by Douglas E. White
Beyond Fund Raising: New Strategies for Nonprofit Investment and Innovation by Kay Grace
Budgeting for Not-for-Profit Organizations by David Maddox
Charity, Advocacy, and the Law by Bruce R. Hopkins
The Complete Guide to Fund Raising Management by Stanley Weinstein
The Complete Guide to Nonprofit Management by Smith, Bucklin & Associates
Critical Issues in Fund Raising edited by Dwight Burlingame
Developing Affordable Housing: A Practical Guide for Nonprofit Organizations, Second Edition by Bennett L. Hecht
Faith-Based Management: Leading Organizations that are Based on More than Just Mission by Peter Brinckerhoff
Financial and Accounting Guide for Not-for-Profit Organizations, Sixth Edition by Malvern J. Gross, Jr., Richard F. Larkin, Roger S. Bruttomesso,
    John J. McNally, PricewaterhouseCoopers LLP
Financial Empowerment: More Money for More Mission by Peter Brinckerhoff
Financial Management for Nonprofit Organizations by Jo Ann Hankin, Alan Seidner, and John Zietlow
Financial Planning for Nonprofit Organizations by Jody Blazek
The First Legal Answer Book for Fund-Raisers by Bruce R. Hopkins
The Second Legal Answer Book for Fund-Raisers by Bruce R. Hopkins
The Fund Raiser's Guide to the Internet by Michael Johnston
Fund-Raising: Evaluating and Managing the Fund Development Process, Second Edition by James M. Greenfield
Fund-Raising Fundamentals: A Guide to Annual Giving for Professionals and Volunteers by James M. Greenfield
Fundraising Cost Effectiveness: A Self-Assessment Workbook by James M. Greenfield
Fund-Raising Regulation: A State-by-State Handbook of Registration Forms, Requirements, and Procedures by Seth Perlman and Betsy Hills Bush
Grantseeker's Toolkit: A Comprehensive Guide to Finding Funding by Cheryl S. New and James A. Quick
Grant Winner's Toolkit: Project Management and Evaluation by James A. Quick and Cheryl S. New
High Performance Nonprofit Organizations: Managing Upstream for Greater Impact by Christine Letts, William Ryan, and Allen Grossman
Intermediate Sanctions: Curbing Nonprofit Abuse by Bruce R. Hopkins and D. Benson Tesdahl
International Fund Raising for Nonprofits by Thomas Harris
International Guide to Nonprofit Law by Lester A. Salamon and Stefan Toepler & Associates
Joint Ventures Involving Tax-Exempt Organizations, Second Edition by Michael I. Sanders
The Law of Fund-Raising, Second Edition by Bruce R. Hopkins
The Law of Tax-Exempt Healthcare Organizations by Thomas K. Hyatt and Bruce R. Hopkins
The Law of Tax-Exempt Organizations, Seventh Edition by Bruce R. Hopkins
The Legal Answer Book for Nonprofit Organizations by Bruce R. Hopkins
A Legal Guide to Starting and Managing a Nonprofit Organization, Second Edition by Bruce R. Hopkins
Starting and Managing a Nonprofit Organization: A Legal Guide, Third Edition by Bruce R. Hopkins
Managing Affordable Housing: A Practical Guide to Creating Stable Communities by Bennett L. Hecht, Local Initiatives Support Corporation,
    and James Stockard
Managing Upstream: Creating High-Performance Nonprofit Organizations by Christine W. Letts, William P. Ryan, and Allen Grossman
Mission-Based Management: Leading Your Not-for-Profit In the 21st Century, Second Edition by Peter Brinckerhoff
Mission-Based Management: Leading Your Not-for-Profit In the 21st Century, Second Edition, Workbook by Peter Brinckerhoff
Mission-Based Marketing: How Your Not-for-Profit Can Succeed in a More Competitive World by Peter Brinckerhoff
Nonprofit Boards: Roles, Responsibilities, and Performance by Diane J. Duca
Nonprofit Compensation and Benefits Practices by Applied Research and Development Institute International, Inc.
The Nonprofit Counsel by Bruce R. Hopkins
The Nonprofit Guide to the Internet, Second Edition by Michael Johnston
Nonprofit Investment Policies: A Practical Guide to Creation and Implementation by Robert Fry, Jr.
The Nonprofit Law Dictionary by Bruce R. Hopkins
Nonprofit Compensation, Benefits, and Employment Law by David G. Samuels and Howard Pianko
Nonprofit Litigation: A Practical Guide with Forms and Checklists by Steve Bachmann
The Nonprofit Handbook, Third Edition: Volume I—Management by Tracy Daniel Connors
The Nonprofit Handbook, Third Edition: Volume II—Fund Raising by James M. Greenfield
The Nonprofit Manager's Resource Dictionary by Ronald A. Landskroner
Nonprofit Organizations' Business Forms: Disk Edition by John Wiley & Sons, Inc.
Planned Giving: Management, Marketing, and Law, Second Edition by Ronald R. Jordan and Katelyn L. Quynn
Private Foundations: Tax Law and Compliance by Bruce R. Hopkins and Jody Blazek
Program Related Investments: A Technical Manual for Foundations by Christie I. Baxter
Reengineering Your Nonprofit Organization: A Guide to Strategic Transformation by Alceste T. Pappas
Reinventing the University: Managing and Financing Institutions of Higher Education by Sandra L. Johnson and Sean C. Rush,
    PricewaterhouseCoopers LLP
The Second Legal Answer Book for Nonprofit Organizations by Bruce R. Hopkins
Social Entrepreneurship: The Art of Mission-Based Venture Development by Peter Brinckerhoff
Special Events: Proven Strategies for Nonprofit Fund Raising by Alan Wendroff
Strategic Communications for Nonprofit Organizations: Seven Steps to Creating a Successful Plan by Janel Radtke
Strategic Planning for Nonprofit Organizations: A Practical Guide and Workbook by Michael Allison and Jude Kaye, Support Center for
    Nonprofit Management
Streetsmart Financial Basics for Nonprofit Managers by Thomas A. McLaughlin
A Streetsmart Guide to Nonprofit Mergers and Networks by Thomas A. McLaughlin
Successful Marketing Strategies for Nonprofit Organizations by Barry J. McLeish
Successful Corporate Fund Raising: Effective Stra tegies for Today's Nonprofits by Scott Sheldon
The Tax Law of Charitable Giving, Second Edition by Bruce R. Hopkins
The Tax Law of Colleges and Universities by Bertrand M. Harding
Tax Planning and Compliance for Tax-Exempt Organizations: Forms, Checklists, Procedures, Third Edition by Jody Blazek
The Universal Benefits of Volunteering: A Practical Workbook for Nonprofit Organizations, Volunteers and Corporations by Walter P. Pidgeon, Jr.
The Volunteer Management Handbook by Tracy Daniel Connors
Trade Secrets for Every Nonprofit Manager by Thomas A. McLaughlin
Values-Based Estate Planning: A Step-by-Step Approach to Wealth Transfers for Professional Advisors by Scott Fithian

Also by Tracy Daniel Connors:
The Volunteer Management Handbook

The Nonprofit Handbook: Management

Third Edition

Edited by
Tracy Daniel Connors

John Wiley & Sons, Inc.

NEW YORK / CHICHESTER / WEINHEIM / BRISBANE / SINGAPORE / TORONTO

Copyright © 2001 by John Wiley & Sons, Inc.

Library of Congress Cataloging in Publication Data:

The nonprofit handbook. Management/edited by Tracy Daniel Connors.—3rd ed.
      p. cm.—(Wiley nonprofit law, finance, and management series)
    Includes bibliographical references and index.
    ISBN 0-471-39799-7 (cloth: alk. paper)
      1. Nonprofit organizations—Management—Handbooks, manuals, etc. 2. Nonprofit organizations—Finance—Handbooks, manuals, etc. 3. Total quality management—Handbooks, manuals, etc. I. Title: Management. II. Connors, Tracy Daniel. III. Series.

HD62.6 .N662 2001
658'.048—dc21   00-061960

For:
Andrew Jeffrey Henson
Catherine Cottrell Henson
Marie Danielle Henson
Joshua Warren McCarns

SUBSCRIPTION NOTICE

This Wiley product is updated on a periodic basis with supplements to reflect important changes in the subject matter. If you purchased this product directly from John Wiley & Sons, Inc., we have already recorded your subscription for this update service.

If, however, you purchased this product from a bookstore and wish to receive (1) the current update at no additional charge, and (2) future updates and revised or related volumes billed separately with a 30-day examination review, please send your name, company name (if applicable), address, and the title of the product to:

Supplement Department
John Wiley & Sons, Inc.
One Wiley Drive
Somerset, NJ 08875
1-800-225-5945

For customers outside the United States, please contact the Wiley office nearest you:

Professional & Reference Division
John Wiley & Sons Canada, Ltd.
22 Worcester Road
Rexdale, Ontario M9W 1L1
CANADA
(416) 675-3580
1-800-567-4797
Fax (416) 675-6599

Jacaranda Wiley Ltd.
PRT Division
P.O. Box 174
North Ryde, NSW 2113
AUSTRALIA
(02) 805-1100
Fax (02) 805-1597

John Wiley & Sons, Ltd.
Baffins Lane
Chichester
West Sussex, P019 1UD
UNITED KINGDOM
(44) (243) 779777

John Wiley & Sons (SEA) Pte. Ltd.
37 Jalan Pemimpin
Block B # 05-04
Union Industrial Building
SINGAPORE 2057
(65) 258-1157

About the Editor

Tracy Daniel Connors is President of the BelleAire Institute, a management communications and publishing organization (http://www.belleaire.com). For the past 20 years, Mr. Connors has served as executive editor for six of the best-selling, most comprehensive handbooks for leaders and managers of nonprofit organizations. In addition, he has served in a variety of management positions in business, government, and philanthropy. He retired from the U.S. Navy in 1999. Voluntarily recalled to active duty frequently since 1985, most recently Captain Connors served on the staff of the Secretary of the Navy as Director of Systems Integration/Quality of Life Broadcast Network for LIFELines; as director of Congressional & Public Affairs for the Space and Naval Warfare Systems Command and the Naval Sea Systems Command in Washington, DC; as Deputy Director of the Navy's Command Excellence and Leader Development Program; and as the first Total Quality Leadership Public Affairs Officer for the Chief of Naval Operations. Other private and public sector positions have included Director of Satellite Learning Services for the U.S. Chamber of Commerce; chief of staff for a senior member of Congress; corporate communications manager for a major electronics corporation; vice president of a national publishing corporation; and as an officer, board member, or professional staff director of numerous not-for-profit organizations. He attended Jacksonville University, graduated from the University of Florida, and earned a Master of Arts degree from the University of Rhode Island. He is also the editor of *The Volunteer Management Handbook, Nonprofit Management Handbook, Operating Policies & Procedures, Nonprofit Organization Handbook, Financial Management for Nonprofit Organizations,* the *Dictionary of Mass Media and Communication,* and *Flavors of the Fjords: The Norwegian Holiday Cookbook.*

▼ Contributors

Jody Blazek, CPA, is a partner in Blazek & Vetterling, LLP, a Houston CPA firm focusing on tax and financial planning for exempt organizations and the individuals who create, fund, and work with them. Blazek & Vetterling serves over 200 not-for-profit organizations, providing financial reports and tax compliance and planning services. Blazek serves on the Tax-Exempt Organizations Committee of the American Institute of Certified Public Accountants, the national editorial board of Tax Analysts' *The Exempt Organization Tax Review,* and the Volunteer Service Committee of the Houston Chapter of Certified Public Accountants. She is the author of *Tax Planning and Compliance for Tax-Exempt Organizations,* 3rd edition, and *Financial Planning for Nonprofit Organizations;* she is co-author of *Private Foundations: Tax Law and Compliance.*

Jeanne H. Bradner is a nationally known author, speaker, trainer, and consultant in volunteer management, board development, and leadership. She is the author of *Leading Volunteers for Results* (Conversation Press, 1999), *The Board Member's Guide: A Beneficial Bestiary* (Conversation Press, 1995), and *Passionate Volunteerism* (Conversation Press, 1993). She served as Midwest Regional Director of ACTION, as Executive Director of the Illinois Commission on Community Service, and as Director of the Illinois Governor's Office of Voluntary Action.

Jeffrey L. Brudney, PhD, is a professor of political science and director of the doctor of public administration program at the University of Georgia. He has published extensively on volunteer programs and is a member of the editorial boards of leading journals in nonprofit sector studies. His book, *Fostering Volunteer Programs in the Public Sector: Planning, Initiating, and Managing Volunteer Activities,* received the John Grenzebach award for outstanding Research in Philanthropy for Education.

Joseph E. Champoux, PhD, is professor of management at the Robert O. Anderson Schools of Management of the University of New Mexico. His research activities have included total quality management, the organization and management effects of modern manufacturing, job design, and the relationship between work and nonwork. His current research activities focus on film as a teaching resource.

Carolyn J. Curran is an executive consultant and workshop trainer specializing in values-based organizational development and strategic planning with nonprofit boards and staffs. As a multicultural facilitator, she has worked with over 2,100 community-based organizations in social services and the arts, in the United States and in the Caribbean.

Currently Newsletter Editor of the Organization Development Network of Greater New York (ODN of GNY), Ms. Curran was a contributor to The Independent Sector's Spring 1997 Research Forum, *The Changing Social Contract: Measuring the Interaction Between the Independent Sector and Society,* and was commissioned to write the Effective Administration chapter in the nonprofit management manual, *Taking Charge,* published by the Media Alliance.

Marlene Fox-McIntyre is the principal and owner of Athene, Inc., specializing in the design and implementation of Internet Web sites for nonprofit organizations. Ms. Fox-McIntyre has over 17 years of military, government, and commercial experience in project management and information systems technology, and is a former officer in the United States Army Reserve. Athene's Web sites integrate appropriate technologies for the best results at competitive prices. Athene's client Web sites feature interactive calculators and calendars; online forms and data collection; secure members-only sites; integrated e-mail; integrated databases, original Web art and image processing; digital credit card transactions; and statistics tracking. Athene's nonprofit clients have included the Naval Reserve Association, the Navy Community Service Program, Neumann Medical Center, the Naval Order, the U.S. Environmental Institute, and the Sovereign Military Order of the Temple of Jerusalem.

Suzanne Feeney, PhD, is associate professor and director of the Institute for Nonprofit Management at Portland State University in Portland, Oregon.

Linda L. Graff, MA, is president and senior associate in the nonprofit management consulting firm of Graff and Associates in Dundas, Ontario, Canada. Linda is a policy development and risk management specialist and the author of seven books, including *By Definition: Policies for Volunteer Programs* and the newly released *Beyond Police Checks: The Definitive Volunteer and Employee Screening Guidebook.* She divides her time among consulting and writing projects and the delivery of workshops throughout North America on a wide variety of topics relating to nonprofit management and volunteer management.

James M. Greenfield, ACFRE, FAHP, is senior vice president, Development and Community Relations, at Hoag Memorial Hospital Presbyterian in Newport Beach, California. He is a longtime active member of the Association of Fundraising Professionals (AFP) and the Association for Healthcare Philanthropy (AHP), and is currently on NSFRE's foundation board. He has written several books, including *Nonprofit Handbook: Fundraising,* 3rd edition; *Fund-Raising: Evaluating and Managing the Fund Development Process,* 2nd edition; *Fund Raising Fundamentals: A Guide to Annual Giving for Professionals and Volunteers;* and *Fund-Raising Cost Effectiveness: A Self-Assessment Workbook.*

Adam C. Hart Jr. is the President of NexSys Technologies, LLC *(http://www.NexSys-Tech.com),* a technology business in Cary, North Carolina. A public accountant as well as a Microsoft-Certified Systems Engineer, he has provided extensive design, implementation, and support services to nonprofit organizations as part of his clientele for over 20 years. He is involved in the development and application of cost-effective emergent technologies worldwide, in collaboration with EPower & Associates of Brentwood, Tennessee, and Hayes and Associates of Rural Hall, North Carolina.

Bruce R. Hopkins, JD, LLM, is a lawyer with Polsinelli, White, Vardeman & Shalton in Kansas City, Missouri, where he specializes in the representation of nonprofit organizations. He served as chair of the Committee on Exempt Organizations, American Bar Association; chair of the Section of Taxation, National Association of College and University Attorneys; and president of the Planned Giving Study Group of Greater Washington, DC. He was accorded the Assistant Commissioner's (IRS) Award in 1984. Mr. Hopkins previously practiced law in Washington, DC, for 27 years prior to his move to Kansas City in 1996. Mr. Hopkins is the series editor of John Wiley & Sons' Nonprofit Law, Finance, and Management Series. He is the author of over 11 books, including *The Law of Tax-Exempt Organizations* (7th edition); *The Law of Fund-Raising* (2nd edition); *The Tax Law of Charitable Giving* (2nd edition); *Charity, Advocacy, and the Law; Nonprofit Law Dictionary; A Legal Guide to Starting and Managing a Nonprofit Organization* (2nd edition), and *The Legal Answer Book for Nonprofit Organizations.* In addition, he writes *The Nonprofit Counsel,* a monthly newsletter. Mr. Hopkins earned his JD and LLM degrees at George Washington University and his BA at the University of Michigan.

Eugene M. Johnson, DBA, MBA, is a professor of Marketing at the University of Rhode Island. He has served as a consultant for a large number of businesses and nonprofit organizations and is a frequent lecturer. Dr. Johnson has done extensive research on services marketing and sales management and has published articles in *Nonprofit World, Banking, Journal of Services Marketing,* as well as in a number of other publications.

Richard F. Larkin, CPA, MBA, is technical director for Not-for-Profit accounting and auditing for Lang Group, chartered. Previously he was technical director in the Not-for-Profit Industry Services Group in the national office of PricewaterhouseCoopers LLP, with responsibility for assisting firm partners and staff worldwide with accounting and auditing issues involving nonprofit organizations. He is a certified public accountant with 31 years of experience serving a wide variety of nonprofit organizations as independent accountant, board member, treasurer, and consultant. He teaches, speaks, and writes extensively on nonprofit industry matters and is active in many professional and industry organizations. He was the chair of the AICPA's Not-for-Profit Audit Guide task force and has been a member of the FASB Not-for-Profit Advisory Task Force, the AICPA Not-for-profit Organizations Committee. He is a co-author of the sixth edition of *Financial and Accounting Guide for Not-for-Profit Organizations,* author of *Financial Statement Presentation and Disclosure Practices for Not-for-Profit Organizations* (published by the AICPA), and a contributor to *The Accountants' Handbook.* He is an adjunct professor of nonprofit management at Georgetown University, and as a member of the Peace Corps taught business administration at Haile Selassie I University in Addis Ababa, Ethiopia.

Marci Bernstein Lu, MNO, is a grantmaker for social services and the philanthropic sector at The Cleveland Foundation. Prior to joining the nation's oldest and second largest community foundation, Lu was a legislative assistant to U.S. Congressman Sander Levin and a program coordinator for the Wisconsin Coalition Against Domestic Violence. Lu consulted in strategic planning while earning a Masters degree in nonprofit management from the Mandel Center for Nonprofit Organizations at Case Western Reserve University.

Christine Lucas, MNO, is currently Development Coordinator for Leadership Florida Statewide Community Foundation and Principal, Nonprofit Services of Florida. She has held previous positions as Executive Director of the Cleveland Council on World Affairs and U.S. Coordinator of the Japan Exchange and Teaching Program, Embassy of Japan. She holds a Master of Nonprofit Organizations degree and Certificate of Nonprofit Management from Case Western Reserve University's Mandel Center for Nonprofit Organizations and Bachelor's degrees in Russian Area Studies and Spanish from Wittenberg University. She currently resides in Tallahassee, Florida, with husband Daniel and daughter Virginia.

Suzanne J. Lulewicz is President of SJL Associates, a strategic management consulting firm providing performance consulting services to nonprofit, government, and for-profit organizations. In addition to designing training and leadership development programs with coaching interventions, Lulewicz consults to help improve performance effectiveness in the workplace while maintaining a collaborative operating environment. She has worked with nonprofits as a staff member, vice president of education, director of curriculum, and volunteer leader. She is a past president of the Washington, DC Chapter of the American Society for Training and Development and is currently a member of the Greater Washington Society of Association Executives (GWSAE) Learning Initiatives Advisory Council.

Nancy Macduff is an internationally recognized authority on the management of volunteer programs. She was the executive director of a nonprofit corporation for 14 years, and has written several books, including *Building Effective Volunteer Committees.* She regularly contributes to such publications as *Voluntary Action Leadership* and has worked with such diverse organizations as the American Red Cross and Points of Light Foundation. Ms. Macduff also teaches courses on volunteer management at Lewis and Clark College.

Charles C. Manz, PhD, is an international scholar and consultant on the topics of leadership and self-managing teams. Dr. Manz was a Marvin Bower Fellow at Harvard University, and is currently professor of management at Arizona State University. He was the Charles and Janet Nirenberg Professor of Business Leadership at the University of Massachusetts, Amherst, beginning in the fall of 1997.

Milena M. Meneghetti, CHRP, is Manager of Human Resources with the Bank of Montreal. She is a certified human resources professional with over 14 years' internal and external human resources consulting experience. She is also the vice-president of M4i Strategic Management Consulting. She has served on the executive committee of several nonprofit boards, including as director of ethics for the Human Resources Institute of Alberta, and as the vice-president, support services, for the Canadian Red Cross Sociey. Ms. Meneghetti was involved in the development and implementation of Canadian Occidental's Corporate Integrity Program. She is a regular contributor to John Wiley's nonprofit management series. She is currently pursuing her master's in educational psychology at the University of Calgary, Alberta, Canada.

Marc S. Osten is known for his work as a dynamic motivator, educator, and innovator with non-profit organizations and educational institutions. He currently works as an organizational development strategist and advisor to foundations, management support organizations, and networks of progressive nonprofit organizations. He specializes in strategic use of technology and the Internet to support social change work, enhance organizational effectiveness, and build nonprofit capacity. He is particularly interested in facilitating collaborations within the nonprofit sector, developing peer-assistance programs, and building networks to leverage knowledge and resources for sector-wide impact. He currently is principal of the Summit Consulting Collaborative and holds a master's in education from Wheelock College.

E. Brian Peach, PhD, is an associate professor at the University of West Florida in Pensacola, Florida. His primary teaching areas include strategic management and international business, and he has published in the areas of volunteer motivation, small group performance, performance incentives, and executive pay. He has consulted in the areas of organizational redesign, strategic reorientation, and incentive-based compensation. He works with nonprofit and volunteer organizations as well as for-profit firms.

Craig L. Pearce, PhD, is an assistant professor of management at the Peter Drucker School of Management at Claremont Graduate University. His areas of expertise include leadership, teamwork, and change management. His work has appeared in *Organizational Dynamics, Journal of Management, Strategic Management Journal,* and the *Journal of Managerial Issues* among other publications. Dr. Pearce recently won an award for his research on shared leadership from the Center for Creative Leadership. Dr. Pearce has a breadth of international management consulting experience in the areas of process reengineering, organizational development, and turnaround management. Some of his clients have included American Express; Geico Insurance; Land Rover; Mack Trucks; Nielsen Marketing; and Rayovac. Dr. Pearce serves on the board of directors of Small Potatoes, Inc., an agricultural biotech company. Dr. Pearce received his doctorate in organizational behavior from the University of Maryland, his MBA from the University of Wisconsin–Madison, and his BS in Management (honors) from Pennsylvania State University.

Monica L. Perry, PhD, is currently an assistant professor in the Marketing Department at UNCC, where she teaches marketing concepts, marketing strategy, and Internet marketing. Her industry experience includes significant work in business-to-business marketing. Her areas of expertise are in relationship marketing and Internet marketing. She has consulted with for-profit and nonprofit organizations, such as AMB, BuyManuscripts.com, Mueller and Associates, Ph3 Laboratories, and Charlotte's Web. Dr. Perry's work has appeared in *Great Ideas for Teaching Marketing, Corporate Communications: An International Journal, The Journal of Personal Selling and Sales Management,* and *The Journal of International Marketing.* She has made presentations at regional, national, and international conferences, such as the International Conference on Corporate & Marketing Communications (Salford, England); various American Marketing Association Conferences; and the Marketing Science Institute Conference. Dr. Perry earned her doctorate in marketing with a minor in information systems and logistics at the University of Maryland in 1997, her MBA (honors) from Pennsylvania State University in 1989, and a BS in psychology from the College of William and Mary in 1984.

Richie Platt, PhD, is an assistant professor of management information systems at the University of West Florida in Pensacola, Florida. His primary teaching areas include strategic planning and management of information systems, electronic commerce, information systems analysis, and design and development. He is published in the areas of electronic commerce, competitive uses for information systems and technology, and critical success factors for IS projects. He consults in the areas of database analysis and design, and the planning, design, and development of all levels of information systems in both public and private MS organizations.

Janet Poley, PhD, is president of the American Distance Education Consortium (ADEC) and holds professorships in journalism; human resources and family sciences; and agricultural leadership, education, and communication at the University of Nebraska–Lincoln. She is a well-known international leader in information technology and distance education. Dr. Poley has been named one of the 100 outstanding leaders in business, academia, and government by Federal Computer Week and received the Excalibur Award from the U.S. Congress for her six years of service on the Training for Rural Development program in Tanzania. She has served as Director of Communication, Information, and Technology for the Extension Service and in several international education positions for the U.S. Department of Agriculture. She currently serves on the board of advisors for the Pennsylvania State University World Campus and is a frequent speaker and advisor. She has worked in more than 30 countries and serves on the Program Committee for the International Council for Open and Distance Education.

Elizabeth Power, MEd, principal of EPower & Associates *(http://www.epower-assoc.com)*, is a sought-after business consultant, trainer, and published author in several fields. Her firm's specialty is helping organizations make and manage change through learning and doing. Ms. Power's mastery of diverse interests and innovation has been recognized worldwide. EPower & Associates provides innovative client services in the automotive, telecommunications, mental health, and disability communities. EPower & Associates collaborates with NexSys Technology, LLC, to provide technology services to the NPO sector.

Valerie Raines, MNO, is Senior Director of Organizational Development and Planning at the Catholic Diocese of Cleveland Foundation, where she serves on the senior administrative team. She is in charge of organizational and strategic planning, serves as corporate secretary, and assists with special projects related to education. She holds her Bachelor's degree from Northwestern University and her Master's from Case Western Reserve University.

M. Michelle Regel, BA, is a fund-raising executive with experience in health care and educational nonprofit organizations. Regel is vice-president of development at Junior Achievement of Southern Alberta. She obtained her undergraduate degree from the University of Calgary with a double major in English and Communications Studies. She also earned a diploma in Writing for Children and Teenagers from the Institute of Children's Literature, and is currently working toward her Certified Fund Raising Executive designation in fund raising.

Ruthie G. Reynolds, PhD, CPA, JD, is a Frist professor of Entrepreneurship in the College of Business at Tennessee State University. She has conducted research in nonprofit accounting and management and has published articles in *Nonprofit World, The Woman CPA,* and *The ABC Theological Journal.* In addition, she has conducted seminars and workshops for accountants, board members, and administrators of nonprofit agencies throughout the world.

Keith Seel, MA, is a principal with M4i Strategic Management Consulting, Inc., consulting with corporations and nonprofit agencies in the areas of corporate community investment, board governance, and marketing, as well as volunteer program development and implementation. Keith is the chair for both the Ethics Committee and the Certification Task Force of the Association for Volunteer Administration. He instructs nonprofit management courses at Mount Royal College, where he also serves as the director of the Institute for Nonprofit Studies, and is an avid volunteer.

Henry P. Sims Jr., PhD, is an international scholar and consultant on the topics of leadership and self-managing teams. Dr. Sims is currently professor of Management and Organizations at the Maryland Business School.

Michael Stein is an Internet strategist at CompassPoint Nonprofit Services in California. He is a nationally renowned Internet strategist with a decade of experience working with nonprofit organizations, labor unions, and socially responsible businesses. He is the author of two books about the Internet, including *Fundraising on the Internet: Recruiting and Renewing Donors Online,* with Nick Allen and Mal Warwick, published by Strathmoor Press in 1997. He currently works as a freelance consultant specializing in Internet strategy, marketing, and online fund raising. He has worked with the following organizations and institutions: United Nations World Food Programme, Environmental Defense Fund, Trust for Public Land, Children Now, CompassPoint Nonprofit Services, Service Employees International Union, Independent Press Association, Landmark Education, Family Violence Prevention Fund, Women's Economic Agenda Project, Equal Rights Advocates, New York Committee for Occupational Safety and Health, and California Labor Federation. He has been featured in *The Chronicle of Philanthropy* and *The Industry Standard.*

David A. Pettrone Swalve, BA (University of Kansas), **MPA** (Rutgers the State University of New Jersey), has worked as an International Fellow at the Center for Voluntary Action Studies at the University of Coleraine, Northern Ireland and also a Research Fellow at the United Nations African Institute for Economic Development and Planning, Dakar, Senegal. David is currently an instructor at the Lawrence Career College in Lawrence, Kansas.

Richard L. Thompson, APR, is deputy director for public affairs at the Naval Research Laboratory in Washington, DC; following duties as Director, Congressional and Media Relations, and Space and Naval Warfare Systems Command. In addition, he is a Washington-based business-to-business, business-to-government, and government-to-business marketing, communications, and public relations consultant specializing in contingency and special event planning for the nonprofit, for-profit, and government business sectors. Mr. Thompson is a practitioner accredited by the Public Relations Society of America and has conducted contingency public affairs for more than 23 years as an active-duty and reserve U.S. Navy public affairs officer, and as a senior counselor at a high-technology advertising and public relations agency.

Jon Van Til, PhD, is Professor of Urban Studies and Community Planning at Rutgers University at Camden and is a cofounder of its graduate program of public policy. Mr. Van Til served as editor-in-chief of *Nonprofit and Voluntary Sector Quarterly* and is the author of many books, including *Mapping the Third Sector.* Dr. Van Til has published in journals such as *Urban Affairs Quarterly.* In 1994, he received the Award for Distinguished Research and Service from the Association for Research in Nonprofit Organizations and Voluntary Action.

M. Venkatesan, PhD (University of Minnesota), is a Professor of Marketing at the University of Rhode Island. He has been previously associated with the University of Massachusetts, University of Iowa, and University of Oregon. He has written extensively in the services area and has conducted seminars in Marketing of Services for Nonprofit Organizations, in the United States, Singapore, and Sweden. He is also a contributor to the *Handbook of Marketing* and *Handbook of Service Quality.* He is a consultant to both for-profit and nonprofit organizations in the services marketing area.

Eileen M. Wirth, PhD, is chair of the department of journalism and mass communication at Creighton University in Omaha, Nebraska. She is a former reporter for *The Omaha World Herald* and a former public relations official for Union Pacific Railroad. She has long been involved in freelance public relations writing as well as conducting numerous workshops on media relations for nonprofits. She has written two books and has worked as a volunteer public relations consultant for numerous nonprofit organizations.

John A. Yankey, PhD, is the Leonard W. Mayo Professor at the Mandel School of Applied Social Sciences at Case Western Reserve University, Cleveland, Ohio. He teaches in the area of strategic planning, fund raising, and political processes. Dr. Yankey serves as the Director of Community Services

for the Mandel Center for Nonprofit Organizations and consults with a wide array of nonprofits in strategic planning, board development, and establishment of strategic alliances.

Sally A. Zinno has over 25 years of planning and hands-on management experience in museums and nonprofit institutions in transition. She is a senior program advisor and Director of Evaluation at National Arts Stabilization and works with diverse arts organizations to develop and strengthen the managerial and financial skills they need to thrive.

She directed the administrative and financial operations at the Delaware Art Museum and the Harvard University Art Museums. She was the senior administrative officer at the Boston Museum of Science, where she adapted administrative, financial, and building services during a period of rapid and dramatic growth. Her responsibilities have included the management of financial, human resource, marketing, planning, information systems, board relations, and facilities operations.

She has been active nationally as a board member of the American Association of Museums and immediate past chair of both its Museum Management Committee and the Council of Standing Professional Committees. Currently, Ms. Zinno is a Visiting Professor at George Washington University. She has taught graduate-level courses in nonprofit administration and finance at Harvard University and George Washington University.

Preface

Since the mid-1970s, the number and size of organizations that are public service and tax-exempt have increased substantially. From 1979—when the first nonprofit handbook was published—to 1990, the number of tax-exempt organizations (charitable, religious, and educational organizations)—increased from about 800,000 to more than a million. Between 1975 and 1990, the assets of charitable organizations grew in real terms over 150 percent, to more than $1 trillion. By 1990, when the first edition of the Wiley *Nonprofit Handbook* was published, exempt organizations accounted for over 10 percent of the national gross domestic product in terms of revenue, up from nearly 6 percent in 1975.

The steady growth and expansion of the voluntary sector reflects the fact that contributions by nonprofits are growing in response to the needs of our people. Demands are sharply on the increase for the myriad public services provided by nonprofits. Competition is keen among nonprofits for the human and financial resources needed to provide their essential public services. For many nonprofits today, the search for always-scarce resources is not simply important, it is a matter of survival. For all nonprofits, more effective, economical use of existing resources is essential. Constant attention must be paid to the tools and process improvement techniques needed to ensure organizational efficiency and resource conservation.

It has been 20 years since publication of *The Nonprofit Organization Handbook* (McGraw-Hill). The breakthrough nature of that work lay in its recognition of the fact that regardless of the specific public purpose served by nonprofit organizations, all had much in common when it came to management. Specifically, there were seven areas of management and leadership shared by nonprofits, which, taken together, established that there was an emerging body of professional knowledge and new career fields in something called *nonprofit management.* The management and leadership areas in which nonprofits have such strong commonality include organization and corporate principles; leadership, management, and control; volunteer administration; sources of revenue; communication and public relations; financial management and administration; and legal and regulatory.

Management of nonprofit organizations has steadily become more professional, especially in the last 20 years. Information is shared through a growing number of associations and print and electronic media channels, which alert sector leaders to new developments in management principles, policies, and procedures that help them fulfill the various missions of their organizations. The nature of these channels, however, is that they provide highlights, but rarely depth. Approaches that work are steadily sorted out from those that generally do not. However, this process is often sporadic or subject to chance. The need for a convenient, comprehensive guide to the daily operation and management of nonprofit organizations gave rise to the *Nonprofit Management Handbook* (NPMH) (Wiley). The primary objective of the NPMH was to compile the best of these proven approaches in an accessible, readily adaptable format.

The first edition of the NPMH was completed in the early 1990s and introduced a new management tool called *quality management* as a combination of techniques and approaches to help improve management of nonprofit organizations. The first edition of the NPMH served as a comprehensive reference guide to the policies (guidelines, directives, rules, and courses of action) and procedures (established methods and proven best practices) now shared by a great majority of small and medium-sized nonprofit organizations. The second edition built on that solid foundation, even as it advanced additional key areas of management for nonprofit organizations.

Operational policies and procedures are not static. They cannot be adopted and arbitrarily applied to a particular organization. If they are to be effective, they must be carefully *adapted* to the needs and realities of a specific organization. Second, internal and external environments change, just as the organization itself changes. Operational policies and procedures, once adapted and employed, must be reviewed regularly to ensure that they continue to fulfill the functions for which they were intended.

Within our organizations, the dynamic, evolving nature of all areas of nonprofit management policy and procedures requires constant review, assessment, renewal, and change. Outdated policies and procedures may become impediments to progress and the organization's ability to fulfill its mission. But how and where do we implement changes? In what direction should we move the organization? How do we organize for constant change and also bring about constant improvement in our services, products, and processes? How do we know what we can and should do to fulfill our public services mission in the face of dwindling resources and a more competitive environment?

Timely, rational change is a major benefit gained by those organizations adopting continuous improvement techniques and philosophies. Therefore, a major objective for all of those dedicated to improving excellence in public service is to provide the foundation that nonprofit organizations need to improve and sustain excellence.

Nonprofit organizations, like their corporate counterparts, are affected by global systems of economics and production. Organizations from all sectors of our economy are trying to establish sustainable excellence as their "organizational culture." Nonprofits, like business and government, must adapt the principles and best practices of excellence and continuous improvement, if they are to meet growing public service needs in the face of scarce resources. Because every element of our society is being forced to move in this new direction, excellence is not likely to fade away when organizational leaders change or when press coverage wanes, as it inevitably will. Sustainable excellence must become the basic culture within nonprofit organizations, just as it must become the way all U.S. organizations do business, if they expect to be successful over time.

The "dynamic environment" in which most nonprofits have to operate drives them toward proven approaches to create the self-renewing organization—one not only able to achieve, but also to sustain, high standards of excellence, including the ability to thrive under competitive pressures. The self-renewing organization must simultaneously address such management areas as strategic planning, process improvement, change management, technology application, and resource conservation. Leaders of successful public service organizations find it important to develop a culture and an organizational environment supportive of change. Leaders at all levels of the organization need all the help they can get to ensure that hard-won gains in productivity, effectiveness, mission readiness, and profitability are sustained.

The *Nonprofit Handbook: Management, Second Edition* built on the solid foundation established by the initial work, even as it advanced key areas of management for nonprofit organizations. The second edition for the first time used the Malcolm Baldrige Award and President's Quality Award Criteria as the basis to define and characterize quality performance and achievement in each of seven functional areas common to all public service organizations.

By adapting these national quality standards to the voluntary sector, we gained the ability to benchmark our own organizations against established national criteria and standards. Knowing where our organizations stand in relation to national standards enables us to prepare plans and strategies to help us overcome the "delta" between the next higher level of excellence and the level at which we may now be performing. Making excellence our goal ensures that leaders of nonprofits can maintain the essential balance between effectiveness (vision, customer focus, public need), efficiency (process improvement, resource conservation), and a dynamic organizational environment (change management, transformational leadership).

The second edition of the *Handbook* introduced the *excellence equation for self-renewing organizations* that identified the three fundamental elements necessary for nonprofit organizations to achieve and sustain excellence: *effectiveness, efficiency,* and *organizational environment.* The third edition expands coverage of management areas that most heavily contribute to organizational excellence. It organizes materials into three sections—*effectiveness, efficiency,* and *environment*—each of which includes coverage of management topics reflecting national definitions of excellence. In addition, it emphasizes coverage of the following areas of growing importance for nongovernmental/nonprofit organizations leaders based on reader feedback:

- Identification of emerging management trends and better understanding of ever-changing leadership responsibilities and techniques
- Technology implications and applications for nonprofits
- Understanding of the management context in which nonprofits enter a competitive and challenging new millennium
- Successful governance structures, styles, and approaches within the ever-evolving public service organization
- What nonprofits can and should do to fulfill their public services mission in the face of dwindling resources and a more competitive environment—from commercial ventures to strategic communications
- Second- and third-generation management, organizational excellence–enhancing practices that work
- Self-renewing strategies for achieving both mission effectiveness and efficiency
- Successful management approaches and models used by staff and volunteer managers
- Explanations and examples of proven operational techniques—from distance learning to emergency public affairs
- The importance of maintaining agency integrity to mission and purpose—core values
- Secrets of social entrepreneurism—generating resources while solving social problems
- Sample policies, procedures, reports, and forms designed specifically for nonprofits

In the *Handbook,* we use the excellence equation for self-renewing organizations to establish a straightforward, easily understood "cognitive map" by which to understand the three fundamental and interactive areas in which it is necessary for nonprofit organizations to achieve and sustain excellence.

$$\textbf{N}(ew) = \textbf{E}(nvironment) \times \textbf{E}(ffectiveness) \times \textbf{E}(fficiency)$$

A self-renewing organization is the kind of organization we would all like to be a part of; it is the kind of organization we know would offer us the best opportunity for personal development and to make a meaningful contribution.

When we correlate this "excellence equation" to the functional areas outlined by the national quality criteria in the Malcolm Baldrige Award/President's Quality Award, we see that the following are essential:

Effectiveness…
  Strategic Planning and Development
  Customer Focus and Satisfaction
  Public Service Provider (Business) Results
Efficiency…
  Process Management
  Information and Analysis
Environment…
  Leadership
  Human Resource Development and Management

The excellence equation as explained in Chapter 1, "The Self-Renewing Organization," is an approach that we hope will encourage a deeper appreciation that sustained excellence is the goal we should be seeking—in our public service organizations and in our lives—and that requires the effective application of all three elements of the excellence equation.

The excellence equation helps us better determine and know:

- Where we are going, why we are going, and how we plan to get there
- How to improve constantly in everything we do
- The importance of making it safe to change, to reach, to grow—for ourselves and those for whom we are responsible

Included within Chapter 1 is a comprehensive overview of the chapters in the third edition. Each chapter outline is included within an explanation of the management area to which it pertains. The *Handbook* is basically organized into three areas—Effectiveness, Efficiency, and Environment—which correspond to the three elements of the excellence equation for self-renewing organizations.

Part One, Effectiveness, deals with all of the topics and issues facing a public service organization that must ensure it has a valid purpose—continually adjusted to surroundings and context—to accomplish its customer-focused mission. Subjects and topics in Part One of the *Handbook* and in supporting annual supplements, include:

Management Environment
- Examines the organization's strategy development process, including strategic objectives, action plans, and related human resource plans that strengthen organizational performance and self-sustaining position
- Developing the organization's strategy deployment process, including key short-term and longer-term action plans

Customer, Client, and Public Service Focus
- Determining and targeting customer, client groups, and/or market segments

- Determining and projecting key client/customer requirements and their relative importance/value to customers in terms of marketing, service planning, and delivery
- Determining customer satisfaction and building relationships, including processes, measurements, and data used to determine client satisfaction and how to incorporate this information into strategic decision making

Public Service Provider (Business) Results
- Determining and influencing current levels and trends of customer/client satisfaction and key measures and/or indicators of service performance

Chapters in Part One that address these issues and provide answers on successful approaches to achieving organizational effectiveness include:

Technology and Strategy for Organizational Effectiveness, *Marc S. Osten*

Public Service Provider Results
Managing Organizational Growth, *Carolyn J. Curran*

Part Two, Efficiency, addresses the processes and techniques leaders must use to create an organization that performs well and economically, with reduced waste of time, energy, and materials through efficient resource development, process improvement, and resource conservation. Subjects and topics in Part Two of the *Handbook* and in supporting annual supplements include:

Process Management
- Developing and delivering services that meet changing client/market requirements
- Incorporating new technology into services and systems that improve customer satisfaction and/or efficiency
- Assessing, designing, and improving processes that maximize quality, transfer of learning, cost control, productivity, and other efficiency/effectiveness factors

Information and Analysis
- Designing and installing performance measurement systems that help leaders understand, align, and improve organizational performance at all levels and throughout the organization
- Selection of measures and indicators that track organizational performance
- Linking results of organizational-level analysis to client services delivery and other public service goals

Chapters in Part Two that address these issues and provide answers on successful approaches to achieving organizational efficiency include:

Revenue Generation
Fund-Raising Management, *James M. Greenfield*
Nonprofit Organizations as Entrepreneurs, *Ruthie G. Reynolds*
Commercial Ventures: Opportunities and Risks for Nonprofit Organizations,
Keith Seel

Financial Management
Accounting, *Richard Larkin*
Budgeting Considerations, *Ruthie G. Reynolds*
Unrelated Business Income, *Jody Blazek*

Part Three, Evolutionary Environment, is focused on providing answers on how to create and sustain an organizational environment able to adapt to changing conditions, manage change effectively, transition to new states, and turn in new directions—in short, to constantly evolve. Subjects and topics in Part Three of the *Handbook* and in supporting annual supplements include:

Leadership
- Setting, communicating, and deploying organizational values and expectations
- How senior leaders use organizational performance to improve effectiveness throughout the organization

Human Resource Focus
- Encouraging and motivating staff and volunteers to develop and use their full potential
- Designing, organizing, and managing jobs and services to enhance cooperation, collaboration, individual initiative, innovation, and flexibility
- Staff and volunteer performance management approaches that support high performance
- Recruiting, orienting, and training staff and volunteers using key performance requirements, diversity, and fair work practices
- Education and training approaches that achieve organizational objectives; build staff/volunteer knowledge, skills, and capabilities; and contribute to improved performance
- Creating and sustaining an organizational environment that contributes to the well-being, satisfaction, and motivation of all staff and volunteers

Chapters in Part Three that address these issues and provide answers on how to sustain an evolutionary organizational environment include:

Values
Ethics and Values in the Nonprofit Organization, *Milena M. Meneghetti and Keith Seel*

Leadership
Leadership and the Self-Renewing Organization, *Joseph E. Champoux*
Shared Leadership: Relationship Management to Improve Nonprofit Organization Effectiveness, *Craig L. Pearce, Monica L. Perry, and Henry P. Sims Jr.*
Governance—Creating Capable Leadership in the Nonprofit Sector, *Keith Seel, M. Michelle Regel, and Milena M. Meneghetti*
Self-Managed Teams in the Self-Renewing Organization, *Henry P. Sims Jr. and Charles C. Manz*

Human Resource Development and Management Board of Directors
Board of Directors: Strategic Vision, *Jeffrey L. Brudney*
Strategic Education Planning: An Executive Leadership Tool, *Suzanne J. Lulewicz*
Coping with Change: A Primer for Developing Human Resources, *Elizabeth Power*

Professional Staff
Employment-Related Benefits, *Sally A. Zinno*

Corps of Volunteers
Volunteer Management, *Jeanne H. Bradner*

Policies for Volunteer Programs, *Linda L. Graff*
Risk Management in Volunteer Programs, *Linda L. Graff*
Episodic Volunteering, *Nancy Macduff*
Volunteer Screening, *Linda L. Graff*
Volunteer and Staff Relations, *Nancy Macduff*

Legal & Regulatory
Law and Taxation, *Bruce R. Hopkins*

The *Handbook* is designed for daily use as a guide for nonprofit leaders and managers who seek to achieve and sustain excellence within their organization, update management procedures, and establish more effective management and leadership systems.

Our contributors, representing a wide variety of professional backgrounds, were selected for both their demonstrated knowledge of specialized subject areas and their day-to-day, real-world experience with nonprofits. Their expertise is the cornerstone of this work. While editors have worked closely with our contributors, reviewing and editing their manuscripts, each chapter remains the work and viewpoint of its author.

Our national quality of life, from health care and culture to recreation and religion, depends on whether leaders of nonprofit organizations can achieve and sustain levels of quality and excellence in the future that by today's standards would be considered extraordinary. Making an "enormous difference" has always been the challenge of the dedicated men and women, volunteer and professional, who lead our nonprofit public service organizations. We have tried in this handbook to present the most successful policies and procedures, and to explain and recommend those principles and practices of leadership and management that nonprofit leaders need as tools to meet successfully the challenging demands of an uncertain future.

Tracy D. Connors
Fogland Point
Tiverton, Rhode Island

▼ Acknowledgments

This handbook represents the collective efforts of two groups of dedicated professionals: the authors of its chapters—our contributors—and the staff at John Wiley & Sons who produced this handbook and other works in the Nonprofit Series.

Our contributors represent a wide cross-section of management executives, consultants, and academicians—all highly knowledgeable in their fields. All of us who read and use their chapters are grateful for their willingness to organize their thoughts and materials, and then to spend countless hours in preparing them for publication. Their knowledge, expertise, professionalism, and dedication to improving the overall management of all nonprofit public service organizations were essential to the creation of such a comprehensive handbook in this field. Try as I might, I cannot adequately express my appreciation for their commitment to the betterment of the voluntary sector or my respect for their accomplishments as represented by their chapters. Their friendship and rapport is a major highlight of my professional life.

In over 20 years of serving as executive editor for many editions of nonprofit handbooks, the contributor team for the *Nonprofit Handbook: Management, Third Edition,* is the most knowledgeable and experienced I have seen for any work of its kind. It has been a great personal and professional privilege to work with them to produce this "answer book" of management knowledge and wisdom for leaders of nonprofits.

The Wiley team also deserves our appreciation and thanks. Perhaps mirroring the extra commitment to improving our public services I so often see by professionals in the voluntary sector, the Wiley team also goes the "extra mile" to help ensure that its products and services are steadily improving. As we all know, it is relatively easy to talk "quality," and sometimes quite another to actually achieve and sustain excellence. In my experience, Wiley does both. Of particular importance to the successful completion of the third edition is the leadership and management of the Nonprofit Series by Martha Cooley, whose support and guidance for this and previous works has been essential and deeply appreciated. In addition, Rachel Leiserson, Anne Brunell, and Alexia Meyers played vital roles during preparation and production. Their professionalism and good humor even during "crunch times" were much appreciated.

Other professionals, friends, and family to whom I would like to express my appreciation and gratitude include:

Faith R. Connors
Karen and Jeffrey Henson
Miriam and Dean McCarns
Hon. Karen Heath, Buster Tate, Captain William Hendrix, Dr. Randy Eltringham, and Commander Rudolph Brewington, Office of the Assistant Secretary of the Navy (Manpower & Reserve Affairs)
Colonel James Scott, USA
Ray McBride
Horace Rudisill
Dr. Jan Poley
Richard L. Thompson
Richard Larkin
Charles Grinnell, Esq.
Dr. Joseph Champoux
Ann Richard, Janice Griffin, and Richard Joslin of the Essex Library in Tiverton, Rhode Island
Dr. Seth Hudak

▼ Contents

Part II Efficiency 385

Perform well and economically, with reduced waste of time, energy, and materials through efficient resource development, process improvement, and resource conservation … includes:

Process Management

Developing and delivering services that meet changing client/market requirements.

Incorporating new technology into services and systems that improve customer satisfaction and/or efficiency.

Assessing, designing, and improving processes that maximize quality, transfer of learning, cost control, productivity, and other efficiency/effectiveness factors.

Information and Analysis

Designing and installing performance measurement systems that help leaders understand, align, and improve organizational performance at all levels and throughout the organization.

Selecting measures and indicators that track organizational performance.

Linking results of organizational-level analysis to client services delivery and other public service goals.

Part III Evolutionary Environment 577

Creating and sustaining an organizational environment able to adapt to changing conditions, manage change effectively, transition to new states, and turn in new directions—in short, to constantly evolve … includes:

Leadership

Setting, communicating, and deploying organizational values and expectations.

How senior leaders use organizational performance to improve effectiveness throughout the organization.

Human Resource Focus

Encouraging and motivating staff and volunteers to develop and use their full potential.

Designing, organizing, and managing jobs and services to enhance cooperation, collaboration, individual initiative, innovation, and flexibility.

Staff and volunteer performance management approaches that support high performance.

Recruiting, orienting, and training staff and volunteers using key performance requirements, diversity, and fair work practices.

Education and training approaches that achieve organizational objectives; build staff/volunteer knowledge, skills, and capabilities; and contribute to improved performance.

Creating and sustaining an organizational environment that contributes to the well-being, satisfaction, and motivation of all staff and volunteers.

The Self-Renewing Organization

TRACY D. CONNORS, MA, PRESIDENT
The BelleAire Institute, Inc.

Man's job is to govern the future, not simply be a victim of the wind blowing this way and that way. I know, the best plans are upset. But, without a plan there is no chance. Best efforts will not do it!

W. Edwards Deming

1.1 To Govern Our Future

Without ever having met you, I know that we have at least one thing in common. Way back when we were just sprouts, someone important to us, someone dear to us, who cared about us and what we would become, gave us one of life's great lessons. "Do your best," they told us. It was—and is—good advice. In my case, it was my parents and grandparents. It was one of many terribly important, even vital, lessons in life and living that we learned as children. Simple, straightforward, not terribly complicated, but important, and true—then as children, and even more so, now that we are adults.

Since we already know you remembered that good advice from your childhood and are doing your best, we can go on to some other important questions:

- Do you take joy in your work?
- If not, do you understand why not?
- If you are already doing your best, but there is not enough joy in your work, what else should you be doing to add this vital feeling, to help you "govern" your future?

Robert Fulghum tells us that "all I really need to know about how to live and what to do and how to be I learned in kindergarten."[1] "Share everything," he reminds us. "Play fair. Don't hit people. Put things back where you found them. Clean up your own mess.

Don't take things that aren't yours. Say you're sorry when you hurt somebody. Warm cookies and cold milk are good for you. Live a balanced life—learn some and think some and draw and paint and sing and dance and play and work every day some. When you go out into the world, watch out for traffic, hold hands, and stick together. Be aware of wonder. And then remember the Dick-and-Jane books and the first word you learned—the biggest word of all—LOOK."

He pointed out that everything you need to know is in there somewhere, from the Golden Rule to ecology, politics, equality, and sane living.

We should consider the lessons we learned the earliest as among the most important in our lives. The fact that we learned them as kids does not mean they were trivial. Just because they were basic does not mean they were uncomplicated or even easy to put into practice. "Playing fair" can be a real challenge in a highly competitive environment. The same for "sharing everything." If I share, will they share back, or use my share against me?

Similarly, we should remember that basic truths about achieving excellence can be straightforward and uncomplicated, and yet be critically important. To understand and apply the fundamentals of organizational improvement does not require extensive training in quantitative analysis or statistical theory. It does, however, require an understanding of how excellence is defined within functional areas of management and the basic definitions applied to levels of quality achievement.

"Man's job is to govern the future," Dr. W. Edwards Deming pointed out, "not simply be a victim of the wind blowing this way and that way."

Dr. Deming then went on to tell hundreds of Navy senior leaders: "I know, the best plans are upset. But, without a plan there is no chance. Best efforts will not do it. Is anyone here not putting forth his best efforts? Let him stand." This was followed by silence, then a great deal of laughter.

"I've been inquiring for years, trying to find him who is not putting forth his best efforts," Deming said, with tongue firmly in cheek. "No one has stood up yet. That is our problem! Everyone is putting forth his best efforts—without knowledge, without understanding what his job is, just doing his best. He will not take joy in his work without understanding what his job is. He cannot do his work without understanding why, and who depends on him. Man is entitled to joy in his work."

With apologies to Rev. Fulghum, doing our best is not enough. For us to govern the future, we must do those things that give us knowledge, that bring us to a better understanding of what our jobs really are and how they contribute to the aims of the organization—the customer-focused mission.

1.2 Beyond Quality Management

American organizations in all sectors of our economy struggle constantly to improve, to respond to the demands of operating environments that grow more competitive and challenging every day. Senior leaders have a variety of "tools" available to them, ranging from strategic planning and process improvement to new approaches to leadership and improved communications. Tried independently, these may produce modest improvements in the organization, usually after great investments of time and money. However, these improvements, achieved at great cost, are all too often temporary. Once a high level of excellence is achieved, most organizations find it much harder to sustain.

American leaders need insights to better understand how strategic planning, quality management, and intrinsically motivating leadership can and must work together to help ensure that hard-won gains in productivity, effectiveness, mission readiness, and profitability are sustained.

There can be no "prescription handbook." Like the proverbial lunch, there is no free "prescription" for quality management. "No one can come to your organization and 'install' something and tell you, 'Here, if you do this, this and this, quality is going to emerge everywhere.' That's just mischievous," notes Dr. Curt Reimann, former Director of the Malcolm Baldrige National Quality Award. There is no "instant pudding" for quality. But there is the ability and the need to share those techniques, approaches, principles, and best practices that work—even as we point the way to what lies beyond quality management.

Quality management was believed to be the "secret" behind Japan's come-from-behind international success, when it was "discovered" by American leaders in the early 1980s. Advocates credited its use for major successes in productivity and profitability by some of our organizations. Critics now say that it's not all that it was cracked up to be. Touted as the management miracle that would reestablish America as an international competitor, total quality management (TQM) became a growth industry for gurus and management consultants offering "salvation" to harried American business leaders. TQM spawned a fervent new breed of manager who talked the language of "empowerment" and "profound knowledge."

A new national quality award—the Malcolm Baldrige National Quality Award—was established to mirror a similar award—the Deming Prize—awarded in Japan. Hundreds of thousands of companies sought the criteria, and hundreds applied for consideration. Winning the Baldrige Award was good for morale—and business.

However, mixed signals began to emerge. Many companies that won the Baldrige award appeared to backslide from the high levels of excellence they had achieved. Others announced their commitment to quality with great public fanfare, anointed a guru, and fired up various "quality programs." Later, some of them quietly abandoned many of their "quality programs," but with private doubts as to why they had not measured up to their potential. Articles appeared in the business press criticizing "quality" as not working, or as so much managerial snake oil.

More experience with quality management revealed several contributors to a perceived softening of public opinion toward quality management. After years of highly positive coverage to any topic that claimed kinship to "quality," the press began to tire. "It's been given favorable attention long enough; it's time to be less cheerleader and more analytical," seemed to describe the turnabout in press coverage. More significantly, years of experience have shown the importance of addressing all three components that are essential to achieving—and sustaining—excellence: efficiency, effectiveness, and organizational environment. Organizations that focus too heavily or even exclusively on one or two of these areas may achieve higher levels of excellence for a period of time, but inevitably they are unable to sustain their hard-earned gains.

It became apparent, as shown by the experiences reported in many organizations, that quality management as typically defined, by itself, is incomplete. The primary emphasis is on process improvement and efficiency. While governing our future offers us the means to better our best, it requires that we know where we are going, how to get there, and how to create a climate for "safe change" in our organizations for ourselves and those for whom we are responsible: strategic quality leadership.

Expressed as "great lessons," if we wish to govern our future and that of our organizations, we must:

- Know where we're going, why we are going there, and how we plan to get there.
- Improve constantly in everything we do.
- Make it safe to change for ourselves and those for whom we are responsible.

1.3   *Governing Our Future and That of Our Organizations*

Governing our future and putting joy in our work will take more than simply *improving our processes*—more than focusing on ever-greater efficiencies. We have to *know where we're going*, to define our strategic vision, mission, and guiding principles. We have to have a way as individuals and as organizations to *see where we're going*, even as we try to *get better at what we do*. As Dr. Deming so wisely said, we have to have a plan, a "vision"—a desired future state—of what we desire for ourselves and our organization, and a direction in which to travel. We need some "strategy."

The plan tells us what direction in which to move, and strategy gives us answers about what means we can use to get there. Moving from here to there, however, requires change, *doing some things differently*. When we were little kids, change was fun. We liked to take new routes home from school, to color the sun in the right-hand corner of the picture instead of the left. Before too long, however, we learned that change can be uncomfortable. In most of our organizations, change can be threatening to our power, our authority, our position. Change, we learned, is suspect, perhaps even dangerous. Our path up the organization hierarchy was through management. And managers allocated and coordinated. Most importantly, they controlled. Normally, they resist change unless it is their idea and to their personal advantage.

The essence of management is in its most vital function: dealing with the increased complexity in large organizations. Effective management enables our increasingly complex, far-flung organizations to avoid chaos, by helping impose order and consistency in key functions and operations. Management techniques taught in our business schools stress controlling, planning, and budgeting—setting goals and objectives for the future (usually a not too distant future). Detailed steps are determined to achieve targets, followed by the process of allocating resources—funds and people—to accomplish plans.

Management emphasizes those capabilities and processes needed to achieve the plan—organizing and staffing, creating an organizational structure: job descriptions and qualifications; communicating the plan down the "chain of command"; delegating responsibilities for implementing the plan; and then putting those systems in place that are needed to monitor implementation.

Accomplishing the plan is ensured by controlling and problem solving—comparing results against the plan in great detail—reports, meetings, and inspections. Deviations from the plan are identified. Then replanning and organization take place, focused on solving the problem.

The essence of leadership is coping with change. Leadership has become much more important to all organizations, particularly major U.S. corporations. The world has become much more volatile and competitive. Technological change on the order of exponential, international competition; rapidly fluctuating economic and political developments; and changing demographics is having a major impact on all our organizations because they are all connected in some way to the global marketplace.

The lesson we should take to heart about these global developments is that change is not only necessary, it is inevitable—*change is the only constant.* In addition, major change is increasingly necessary for any organization, large or small, if it is to survive and compete successfully in an always evolving environment. More change inevitably requires and demands more effective leaders—the organization's change managers.

Until recently and in normal times ("peacetimes"), most of our organizations did a relatively good job of managing and administering their product lines, services, and people. However, the overall climate and environments in which most of our organizations must operate more closely resemble that of war—from international competition to galloping technological change in the face of diminishing budgets. A "wartime" organization cannot be successful relying solely on management. A wartime organization needs competent, effective leadership *at all levels.* Over 200 years of our country's military history have taught us repeatedly that soldiers and sailors cannot be managed in battle—*they must be led.* The same can be said for any of us and about almost any of our organizations. Management is important, but effective leaders are required at all levels in our organizations.

The function of leadership is to produce change, not simply to react to forces and pressures as they occur. Intentionally determining and then setting the direction of that change or changes is fundamental to effective leadership, and effective leaders are change agents.

1.4   Palingenesis: Birth Over Again

Birth, growth, maturation, decline, and death—the cycle is ancient and universal. It is the subject of countless fables and myths from distant times. Finding out where the organization must go and how it should get there, constantly studying ways to improve its processes, changing outmoded concepts and approaches to ensure regeneration and growth—the life cycle never ends. If it does, death is the inevitable result. Only one thing holds death at bay: birth. Only birth can conquer death.

As with our bodies, long-term organizational survival depends on a continuous recurrence of birth to nullify the unremitting partial deaths our organizations suffer from competition, technological advances, and market saturation. From victories, the seeds of ruin can spring. Victorious countries continue to prepare for the last war. Organizations continue product lines or services long past their prime. Even organizations that have worked hard to become quality-managed organizations can and have fallen back from hard-gained high ground. When corporate death closes in, there is no salvation except dismemberment (acquisition) and rebirth as a reinvigorated component of another organization.

What is required to stave off inevitable decline or death is birth over again, regeneration, *palingenesis.* Organizational strategic planning is essential but not enough. Continuous improvement of all processes is essential, but leaders who are blind to other life-sustaining essentials can emphasize efficiency to the exclusion of other essential processes. Leaders can bring about change so disruptive or misguided that it destroys even as it breaks free from the outmoded past. Palingenesis requires a fertile organizational environment in which promising concepts and ideas can be conceived and nurtured to maturity. Even as processes and services are honed to ensure they make their strongest contribution to renewed organizational strength, their replacements are taking shape, form, and function behind them.

Two of the first words we ever learned were *old* and *new*. Mostly, we learned that new is good. Old is bad. New has potential—a future. Old is worthless, junk, irrelevant. At the time, we did not realize that new and old are simply at opposite ends of a continuum matrix of two factors: *condition* and *time* (see Exhibit 1.1).

"In mint condition" sums up the highest condition of new—newly minted, shiny, fresh, valuable. At this end, *new* means fresh, recent, vigorous, changed for the better, or reinvented. The opposite end of the condition continuum brings to mind associations of stale, no longer needed, outmoded, antique, obsolete, and disposable—near death.

With it, in step, cool, and *relevant* are terms we associate with things that are current, modern, and in sync with the times. This is the highest value of currency with whatever environment in which we may be operating or have as the center of interest. To be dated is to be totally out of sync, irrelevant, extraneous, and immaterial.

Organizational newness can also be understood in terms of *condition* and *surroundings,* or *ambient,* as seen in Exhibit 1.2. For example, an organization's status or condition can be seen as its readiness to fulfill the mission(s) for which it exists. If an organization lacks purpose, or is not meeting its public purpose, it is tottering on the lowest rung of mission-

---

EXHIBIT 1.1 The New Vector

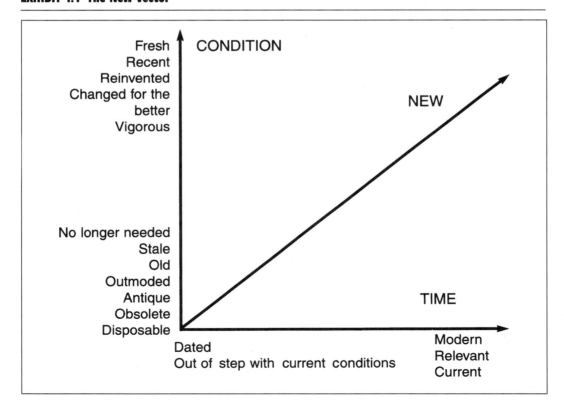

EXHIBIT 1.2 Self-Renewing Organizations in Accord with Mission and Context

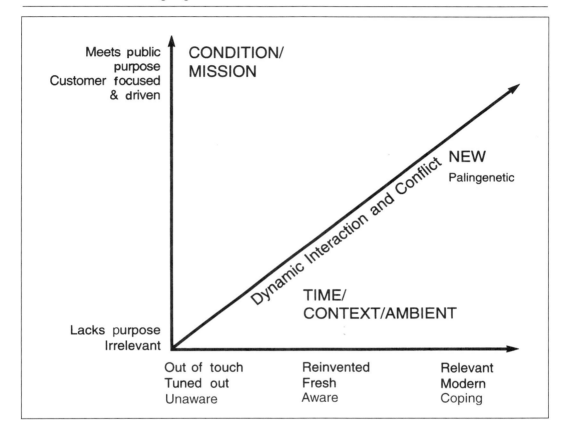

readiness. However, an organization that is customer focused and driven and is meeting its public purposes is fulfilling its mission.

Time and surroundings are closely linked as well. The complex circumstances and ambient in which an organization operates are constantly changing—they are time driven. Those organizations that are in synchronous rhythm with their operating environment(s) are seen to be relevant, modern, coping, fresh, and aware. If they are not, they are tuned out, unaware, and out of touch.

1.5 The Excellence Equation: Key to Sustainability

Organizations that are vigorously proactive in meeting their public purposes, staying mission driven and customer focused, and having synchronized their operations within their surroundings are prime candidates for excellence. Their effective use of strategic planning is the key factor in whether they get there and whether they stay there.

Organizations that can achieve and sustain excellence are rare. Some organizations have worked hard to achieve excellence only to see their hard-fought gains erode as the organization fell back from the pinnacle. They could not sustain their newness. For any organization to achieve and sustain excellence—to be self-renewing—it must understand and exploit the dynamic interdependent relationship among effectiveness, efficiency, and environment—the excellence equation:

$$N(ew) = E(nvironment) \times E(ffectiveness) \times E(fficiency)$$

Self-renewing organizations (SROs) have learned that they must operate at high levels of competence in both the condition (mission/effectiveness) and time (environment/efficiency) dimensions (Exhibit 1.2). In addition, they must create and sustain the enabling organizational environment needed to motivate, empower, and support the people on whom the services and customer satisfaction—results—depend.

Self-renewing organizations are effective (Exhibit 1.3). They use strategic planning to define and accomplish their customer-focused mission. They know they serve valid purposes. They know that they are needed and why. They know their public purpose is valid, and they continually adjust it to environmental conditions to achieve business results. Effective organizations use:

- *Customer focus and satisfaction* as the foundation for setting priorities and focusing improvement activities. Results and trends in this area offer a means to determine the appropriate direction for improvement activities and initiatives. Effective organizations listen to and learn from their customers on a continuous basis, then use that intelligence to determine their current and near-term requirements and expectations.
- *Strategic planning* to strengthen their customer-related, operational, and financial performance to improve customer satisfaction. Planning is essential to help organization leaders use customer and operational requirements as inputs to setting strategic directions. Strategic planning guides ongoing decision making, resource allocation, and organization-wide management.
- *Business results* as the focus for all processes and process improvement activities to assess their progress toward superior value of their offerings as viewed by customers and the marketplace, and toward superior organization performance reflected in productivity and effectiveness.

Self-renewing organizations are efficient. They perform well and economically, with reduced waste of time, energy, and materials (at least in comparison with their competition). We applaud their use of process improvement, information and analysis techniques, and approaches to reduce waste, to streamline their operations, and to make economical use of all resources. They constantly reassess their processes, products, and services to ensure that they meet customer needs while consuming the least amount of resources (money, time, and personnel). Efficient organizations use:

- *Process management* techniques to design and improve their customer/client service design, translating customer requirements into design requirements and into efficient and effective delivery processes. Efficient organizations also maintain process performance systems to ensure that they are performing according to their design and improved to achieve even better performance.

EXHIBIT 1.3 The Interactive Dynamic Among the Excellence Factors of Self-Renewing Organizations

Effectiveness (know and accomplish their customer-focused mission/serve valid purpose)

Efficiency (perform well and economically, with reduced waste of time, energy, and materials)

Environment (use Transformational Leadership to establish and maintain an organizational culture able to adapt to changing conditions, manage change effectively, transition to new states, and turn in new directions, in short, to constantly evolve)

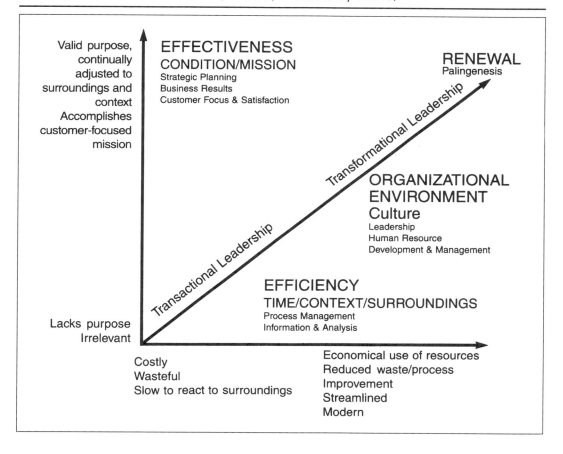

- *Information and analysis* to support overall organizational mission goals and to serve as the primary basis for key decision making.

Self-renewing organizations create and sustain a transformational organizational environment in both leadership and human resource development and management. They adapt to changing environmental conditions and manage change effectively, constantly transitioning to new states, turning as necessary in new directions. They are constantly evolving. Often, we hear the phrase "They reinvented themselves." Organizations having a transformational environment use:

- *Visionary leadership* that establishes strategic directions implemented by a leadership system that fosters high performance, individual development, and organizational learning—a leadership that takes into account all stakeholders, customers, employees, staff, volunteers, suppliers, partners, the public, and the community. Leaders in self-renewing organizations set directions, create a customer focus, establish clear and visible values, and exemplify high expectations.

Leaders in the SRO focus their efforts to ensure the creation of strategies, systems, and methods for achieving excellence, stimulating innovation, and building knowledge and capabilities. The organization's values and strategies should help guide all activities and decisions made by leaders at every level. Senior leaders in the organization should inspire and motivate staff and volunteers while encouraging involvement, development and learning, innovation, and creativity by all members of the organization.

Through their ethical behavior and exemplary personal roles in planning, communications, coaching, developing future leaders, review of organizational performance, and staff and volunteer recognition, senior leaders in the organization will serve as role models, reinforcing values and expectations and building leadership, commitment, and initiative throughout the organization. They use communications and dedicated commitment to realize the organization's values, expectations, and directions. Through transformational leadership, the organization's culture becomes one in which the self-fulfilled individual knows that change is not only safe, but necessary to maintain effectiveness and efficiency.

- *Human resource focus—development and management* practices directed toward the creation of a high-performance workplace, directly linking human resource planning with the organization's strategic directions. Key human resource plans are derived from the organization's strategic and planned planning. The organization's job design, compensation, and recognition approaches enable and encourage all staff and volunteers to contribute effectively, operating within high-performance, empowered work units or teams. In the self-renewing organization, employee and volunteer well-being, satisfaction, and growth potential are based on a more holistic view of them as key stakeholders.

Self-renewing organizations are effective, efficient, and evolutionary. We may find it increasingly difficult to point out future examples of organizations at the lower end of the "in accord with mission and environment" curve. Those that lack purpose are irrelevant, costly, wasteful, and slow to react to their environment—prime candidates for extinction.

Self-renewing organizations gain enthusiasm from their base of intrinsically motivated leadership, reinforcing their desire to excel at ever-higher levels of achievement and comparison with other organizations with reputations for excellence. They have the visionary discipline in their senior leaders to plan and implement long-range strategies; an enlightened commitment to train, nourish, and foster intrinsically motivated "change agent" leaders at all levels of the organization; and the dedication to develop in their team-oriented work groups the tools and approaches needed to continuously improve all major organization processes.

Self-renewing organizations know where they are going, they constantly strive for excellence and improvement in all areas, and their leaders bring about nonthreatening change. An SRO is the kind of organization we would all like to be a part of. It is the kind of organization we know would offer us the best opportunity for personal development and to make a meaningful contribution.

When we use the excellence equation, we establish a straightforward, easily understood cognitive map by which to understand the three fundamental elements necessary for organizations to achieve and sustain excellence. Further, the equation helps us understand the relationship of these three basic elements to the seven fundamental areas of organizational leadership and management, including:

- *Effectiveness:*
  - Strategic planning and development
  - Customer focus and satisfaction
  - Public service provider (business) results
- *Efficiency:*
  - Process management
  - Information and analysis
- *Environment:*
  - Leadership
  - Human resource development and management

In addition, by adapting the Baldrige Award/President's Quality Award Criteria as the basic definitions for these seven functional categories, we now have nationally defined descriptions and characteristics of organizational performance and achievement for each of these areas as well as the ability to benchmark our own organizations against established national criteria and standards. When we are better able to determine where our organizations stand in relation to national standards, we then have the ability to outline plans and strategies to help us overcome the "delta" (or short fall) between the next higher level of quality and the level at which we may now be performing.

The excellence equation is deliberately simplistic. It must be *adapted,* not *adopted,* to meet the assessment and planning needs of each individual organization. Hopefully, explaining and outlining the approach to excellence in this way will encourage others in their efforts to achieve higher levels of quality and improve their ability to do so. In the public service, nonprofit sector, success in quality management by thousands of organizations translates to an overall improvement in our national quality of life.

In addition, the excellence equation approach is intended as a way to encourage a deeper appreciation that sustained excellence is the goal we should be seeking in our organizations and in our lives, which requires the effective application of all three elements of the excellence equation. The excellence equation possibly can be considered a "great lesson," despite its simplicity. It could make a contribution to our collective ability to govern our future and that of our organizations in helping us:

- Know where we are going, why we are going there, and how we plan to get there.
- Determine how to improve constantly in everything we do.
- Impart a better understanding of the importance that we make it safe to change, to reach, and to grow—for ourselves and those for whom we are responsible.

1.6 Description of Categories

The following discussion is adapted for nonprofit organizations from the President's Quality Award criteria and guidelines, in which each of the seven functional areas of excellence is explained and defined for nonprofit organizations. It is doubtful that any single nonprofit organization is currently able to assess itself as having reached these extraordinarily challenging levels of quality and excellence. However, it does illustrate the current "ideal" level of achievement and integration among functional areas toward which nonprofit organizations should be striving. The extent to which these levels are achieved and sustained over time is the measure of the organization's overall health and viability. In addition, it provides its leaders with some idea of the organization's survivability and sustainability in today's challenging, competitive, and fast-changing environment.

(A) EFFECTIVENESS

An effective organization, regardless of the sector in which it operates, has a valid purpose that is continually adjusted to its surroundings and context as it focuses on how to accomplish the customer-focused mission. Management effectiveness includes the overall area of *strategic planning development* that deals with the organization's strategy development process. Strategic objectives, action plans, and related human resource plans that strengthen both organizational performance and help it achieve a self-sustaining position are included, as well as those approaches and techniques used to develop the organization's strategy deployment process, including key short- and longer-term action plans.

Customer, client, and public service focus includes the assessment processes needed to determine and target customer and client groups and/or market segments. As competition for finite resources sharpens, it is increasingly important to long-term survivability for nonprofits to determine and project key client/customer requirements and their relative importance/value to customers in terms of marketing, service planning, and delivery. On the back end of that objective are the techniques and approaches used to determine customer satisfaction and build relationships, including processes, measurements, and data used to determine client satisfaction and how to incorporate this information into strategic decision making.

Public service provider or business results are needed and used to determine and influence current levels and trends of customer/client satisfaction and key measures and/or indicators of service performance.

(i) Strategic Planning

The strategic planning functional area addresses strategic and business planning and deployment of plans, with a strong focus on client/customer and operational performance requirements. For SRO leaders, the emphasis here is that customer-driven quality and operational performance excellence are key strategic business issues that need to be an integral part of organization planning. Specifically:

- Customer-driven quality is a strategic view of quality. The focus is on the drivers of customer satisfaction—a key factor in business success.
- Operational performance improvement contributes to short-term and longer-term productivity growth and cost/price competitiveness. The focus on building operational capability, including speed, responsiveness, and flexibility, represents an investment in strengthening competitive fitness.

An important role for SRO leaders is to ensure an effective focus for daily work, aligning it with the organization's strategic directions. In particular, planning is needed to:

- Understand that key customer and operational requirements should serve as input to setting strategic directions; this will help ensure that ongoing process improvements will be aligned with the organization's strategic directions.
- Optimize the use of resources and ensure bridging between short-term and longer-term requirements that may entail capital expenditures, training, and so on.
- Ensure that deployment will be effective—that there are mechanisms to transmit requirements and achieve alignment on three basic levels: the organization/executive level, the key process level, and the work-unit/individual-job level.

(ii) Strategy Development

Self-renewing organizations develop their view of the future, set strategic directions, and translate these directions into actionable key business drivers, including customer satisfaction. Effective leadership in fulfilling these functions is critical and determines the organization's operational effectiveness.

Every organization is affected by key influences, challenges, and requirements that can alter its future opportunities and directions. Leaders of SROs take as long a view as possible, emphasizing the importance of a thorough and realistic context for the development of a customer/client and market-focused strategy to guide ongoing decision making, resource allocation, and organization-wide management.

Strategy and plans are translated into actionable key business drivers, which serve as the basis for operationalizing and deploying plan requirements. This translation often includes a determination of those activities the organization should perform itself and those for which it might utilize or seek partners. The SRO places a high priority on evaluating and improving its strategic planning and plan deployment processes. This can involve input from work units regarding key deployment factors: effective translation and communications of strategy and plans, adequacy of resources, and identification of key new needs by clients/customers.

SRO leaders are focused on developing a competitive strategy and on operationalizing this strategy. Operationalizing the strategy in the form of key public service/business drivers requires clear and measurable performance objectives. These objectives guide the design and management of key processes. The objectives often align organizational systems (e.g., communications, compensation, recognition) with performance objectives.

SRO leaders place high priority on the organization's key business drivers and how these drivers are translated into an action plan. This includes spelling out key performance requirements; alignment of work unit, supplier, and/or partner plans; how productivity, cycle time, and waste reduction are addressed; and the principal resources committed to the accomplishment of plans (see Exhibit 1.4).

(iii) Customer Focus and Satisfaction

Customer focus and satisfaction is the functional area dealing with the need to understand in detail the voices of customers and the marketplace or operating environment. Much of the information needed to gain this understanding comes from measuring results and trends. Such results and trends provide hard, quantifiable information on customers'

EXHIBIT 1.4 Strategic Planning Characteristics of Self-Renewing Organizations

- Sound, systematic, well-documented, effective process used throughout organization to develop business strategies, business plans, key business drivers for overall operational, financial performance
- All appropriate staff, clients, customers, volunteers, suppliers/partners participate fully in planning process
- Strategy development considers organization's vision, customer-driven values and expectations; includes risk analysis, organization capabilities, supplier/partner capabilities
- Strategies, business plans translated into actionable key business drivers used for deployment throughout organization, to key suppliers/partners; managers, staff, volunteers are held accountable for attaining major targets throughout organization; staff know how their work unit contributes to overall business success
- Systematic procedure used to continuously evaluate strategic planning, plan deployment processes; improvements in processes made on ongoing basis
- Specific business drivers derived from strategic directions translated into actionable plan throughout organization; includes key performance requirements, operational performance measures, productivity improvement, cycle time reduction, waste reduction: work unit, supplier/partner plans fully aligned
- Top priority given to deployment of plans, improvement targets as evidenced by extensive resource commitment to ensuring plan success
- Outstanding product/service quality, operational performance projected for key business areas when compared with key benchmarks

views and their marketplace behaviors. This knowledge then serves as a useful foundation on which SRO leaders can establish priorities and focus improvement activities. Subsequent results and trends offer the means to determine whether or not priorities and improvement activities are appropriately directed.

A quality-focused organization determines current *and* emerging customer requirements and expectations. This is not a one-time process. Many factors may affect customer/client preferences, needs, and loyalty, making it necessary to listen and learn on a continuous basis.

The SRO has established a process to determine current and near-term requirements and expectations of clients/customers. This includes the completeness of the client/customer pool, including recognition of segments and customers of competitors. There is sensitivity to specific product and service requirements and their relative importance to client/customer groups. Validity of the data should be confirmed by use of other data and information such as complaints.

The SRO addresses future requirements and expectations of customers—its key listening and learning strategies. Such strategies depend significantly on the nature of the organization's services or products, the competitive environment, and relationships with clients/customers. The listening and learning strategies selected should provide timely and useful information for decision making. The strategy should take into account the organization's competitive strategy. For example, if the organization customizes its services, the listening and learning strategy needs to be backed by a responsive, capable information system—one that rapidly gathers information about customers and makes this information available where needed throughout the organization. Increasingly, Internet technologies will be used in this process, creating an organizational *intranet.*

Evaluating and improving processes to determine customer requirements and expectations is important. Such an evaluation/improvement process could entail a variety of approaches—formal and informal—that seek to stay in close touch with customers and with issues that bear on customer preference. The purpose of these evaluations is to find reliable and cost-effective means to understand customer requirements and expectations on a continuous basis.

The SRO provides effective management of its responses and follow-ups with customers. Relationship management provides a potentially important means for organizations to gain understanding about, and to manage, customer expectations. Also, frontline staff or volunteers will provide vital information relating to building partnerships and other longer-term relationships with clients/customers. In addition, the SRO provides easy access for customers specifically for purposes of seeking information or assistance and/or to comment and complain. Complaints are promptly and effectively resolved, including recovery of customer confidence. In addition, the organization learns from complaints and ensures that production/delivery process employees receive information needed to eliminate the causes of complaints.

The SRO follows up with customers regarding products, services, and recent transactions to determine satisfaction, to resolve problems, and to gather information for improvement or for new services. The SRO evaluates and improves its customer response management with several types of improvements, including improving service standards, such as complaint resolution time and resolution effectiveness, and improving the use of customer feedback to improve production/delivery processes, training, and hiring.

Satisfaction relative to competitors is determined. Such information can be derived from organization-based comparative studies or studies made by independent organizations. The purpose of this comparison is to develop information that can be used for improving performance. The SRO evaluates and improves its processes and measurement scales that it uses to determine customer satisfaction *and* satisfaction relative to competitors. This evaluation/improvement process draws on other indicators such as customer dissatisfaction indicators (e.g., complaints). The evaluation also considers how well customer satisfaction information and data are used throughout the organization. Usefulness to the leadership can be enhanced if data are presented in an actionable form meeting two key conditions: (1) survey responses tying directly to key business processes and (2) survey responses translated into cost/revenue implications.

Customer satisfaction and customer dissatisfaction are not the same and require different measures. Customer satisfaction measures can include information on customer retention and other appropriate evidence of current and recent past satisfaction with the organization's products and/or services, such as customer awards. Customer dissatisfaction measures and/or indicators depend on the nature of the organization's services or products. For example, an organization's survey methods might include a scale that uses ratings such as "very dissatisfied" or "somewhat dissatisfied."

The reason for including measures of both satisfaction and dissatisfaction is that they usually provide different information. The factors in high levels of satisfaction may not be the same factors as those that relate to high levels of dissatisfaction. In addition, the effect of individual instances of dissatisfaction on overall satisfaction could vary widely depending on the effectiveness of the organization's resolution ("recovery") of a problem.

Customer satisfaction relative to similar providers should be measured and known where possible (see Exhibit 1.5).

EXHIBIT 1.5 Customer Focus and Satisfaction Characteristics of Self-Renewing Organizations

- Comprehensive, documented system for determining current, near-term customer requirements/expectations used throughout organization
- Methods used to obtain knowledge of customer requirements/expectations elicit comprehensive set of quality features for products/services, relative importance of these features; other key data (e.g., complaints) used to support determination of features' importance
- Future customer requirements/expectations addressed throughout organization; listening/ learning strategies used to determine future requirements/expectations
- System, processes for determining customer requirements/expectations evaluated, improved on ongoing basis
- Information readily accessible to all customers to enable them to seek assistance, comment, complain
- Most processes/transactions that bring employees in contact with customers identified throughout organization
- Service standards aimed at exceeding customer expectations; deployed to all employees needing such information, tracked throughout organization
- Effective feedback systems provide knowledge from customers about products/services, recent transactions
- Formal, informal feedback/complaints received by all organization units resolved effectively, promptly; complaint management process ensures effective recovery of customer confidence, meets customer requirements for effective resolution, eliminates causes of complaints
- Organization consistently follows up with customers on products/services and transactions to determine satisfaction, resolve problems, seek feedback for improvement, build relationships
- Customer service standards, including access and complaint management, reviewed and revised on ongoing basis
- Data from customer feedback systems aggregated, evaluated, used throughout organization to improve customer relationship management
- Feedback systems providing knowledge about customers improved on ongoing basis
- Comprehensive set of approaches used to determine customer satisfaction with products/services, their delivery throughout organization
- Comparisons of customer satisfaction for similar providers determined for major products/services, some other products/services
- Methods for determining customer satisfaction and customer satisfaction relative to similar providers evaluated, improved on ongoing basis
- Key customer satisfaction results sustained at very high level, consistent improvement each year for last five years
- Key customer dissatisfaction results sustained at very low levels for last five years
- Customer satisfaction comparisons with similar providers are outstanding

(iv) Public Service Provider Results

Public service provider or business results is the term used to describe another vitally important leadership responsibility in the SRO: ensuring a results focus for all processes and process improvement activities. The objective of this unrelenting focus is to maintain a dual purpose—superior value of offerings as viewed by customers and the public, and superior organizational performance as reflected by productivity and effectiveness indicators. The initiatives included within business results provide "real-time" information (measures of progress or effectiveness) for evaluation and improvement of processes, aligned with overall business strategy.

SRO leaders monitor current levels and trends in product and service quality using key measures and/or indicators of such quality. They select measures and/or indicators that relate to requirements of importance to the client/customer and to the public (marketplace).

Correlation between quality and customer indicators is a critical management tool—a device for focusing on key quality requirements. In addition, the correlation process may reveal emerging or changing market segments, changing importance of requirements, or even potential obsolescence of products and/or services.

Comparative information is developed to enable results reported to be evaluated against competitors or other relevant markers of performance. Some information addresses factors that best reflect overall organization operational performance. Such factors are of two types: generic (common to all organizations) and business-specific. Generic factors include financial indicators, cycle time, and productivity, as reflected in use of labor, materials, energy, capital, and assets. Generic factors also include human resource indicators such as safety, absenteeism, and turnover. Productivity, cycle time, or other operational indicators should reflect aggregate organization performance.

Business- or organization-specific effectiveness indicators vary greatly throughout the sector. However, typical examples include rates of invention, environmental quality, percentage of acceptance of recently introduced products or services, and shifts toward new segments.

Supplier performance results are important considerations. These address current levels and trends in key measures and/or indicators of supplier performance. Suppliers are external providers of materials and services, upstream or downstream from the organization. The focus should be on the most critical requirement from the point of view of the organization—the buyer of the products and services. Data reported and assessed should reflect results by whatever means they occur, via improvements by suppliers within the supply base, through selection of better-performing suppliers, or both.

Measures and indicators of supplier performance should relate to all key requirements—quality, delivery, and price. SRO leaders also develop and use comparative information so that results reported can be evaluated against competitors or other relevant markers of performance (see Exhibit 1.6).

The overall objective of this chapter is to introduce the handbook and to provide some answers to the challenges of achieving and sustaining excellence in our organizations. Previous discussion in this section has focused heavily on defining excellence based on the first of three fundamental categories of organizational management: effectiveness, efficiency, and organizational environment. The remainder of this section moves from "How do we recognize and define excellence?" to "How can we achieve and sustain excellence in our organization?"

(B) EFFICIENCY

Efficient organizations perform well and economically, as evidenced by reduced waste of time, energy, and materials. These objectives are achieved through efficient resource development, process improvement, and resource conservation. Management areas that

---

EXHIBIT 1.6 Public Service Provider Results Characteristics of Self-Renewing Organizations

- Key measures of service or product quality demonstrate exceptional results over past five years
- Current levels of service/product quality are comparable to recognized leaders for similar products/services
- Key measures of operational/financial performance demonstrate exceptional results over the past five years
- Current levels of operational/financial performance are comparable to recognized leaders for similar activities
- Quality performance of major suppliers improving over past five years; performance comparable to recognized leaders

---

contribute to overall organizational efficiency include process management and information and analysis.

Process management ensures that the complex and interactive series of actions needed to develop and deliver our public services do so in ways that conserve resources, satisfy clients and customers, and meet changing client/market requirements. *New technologies* must be continually evaluated; if validated for their contributions to increased efficiency, they should be incorporated into services and systems in ways that improve customer satisfaction and/or efficiency. Throughout our organizations, we need to be continually alert and proactive to assess, design, and improve processes that maximize quality, transfer of learning, cost control, productivity, and other efficiency/effectiveness factors.

Information and analysis approaches help us design and install performance measurement systems that help our leaders understand, align, and improve organizational performance at all levels and throughout the organization. The challenge is to select measures and indicators that accurately track organizational performance. That information, in turn, helps us link the results of our organizational-level analysis to improved client services delivery and other public service goals.

(i) Process Management and Improvement

Effective process management is a critical function for all SROs, requiring effective design, a prevention orientation, evaluation and continuous improvement, linkage to suppliers, and overall high performance (Exhibit 1.7). Virtually all organizations design and introduce products or services. Some do so with great frequency; others, once in the proverbial "blue moon." How the organization goes about designing and introducing products and services says a lot about its health and future prospects in a highly competitive world.

For the SRO, a major focus in this functional area is the rapid and effective integration of production and delivery *early* in the design phase. This integration helps minimize downstream problems for clients or customers and reduces or eliminates the need for design changes that will be costly to the organization. Leaders of SROs pay close attention to three important aspects of this process:

1. The translation of customer requirements into design requirements for products and services
2. How these product and service design requirements are translated into efficient and effective production/delivery processes

---

EXHIBIT 1.7 Process Management Characteristics of Self-Renewing Organizations

- New, improved products/services, processes are designed to exceed customer expectations
- Measurement systems are designed to track process performance throughout organization
- Customer/quality requirements reviewed by appropriate organizational units, suppliers, and partners to ensure integration/coordination/capability
- Initial designs reviewed, validated based on variety of performance, capability considerations throughout organization
- Key designs/processes evaluated to meet customer, quality, and operational performance requirements
- Key production, delivery processes managed throughout organization to meet design plans; measurement plan and measurements used to maintain process performance
- Appropriate analytic methods and measurements used throughout organization to identify, solve problems that disrupt production, delivery processes; corrections systematically verified
- Key production, delivery processes improved throughout organization to achieve better quality, cycle time, operational performance; wide range of techniques used, including process simplification, process research/testing, benchmarking, customer information, alternate technology
- Key support service processes designed and managed throughout organization to meet customer, quality, operational performance requirements; measurements used to maintain process performance
- Support design parameters addressed early in process by appropriate organizational units to ensure integration/coordination/capability
- Appropriate analytic methods used throughout organization to identify, solve problems that disrupt support service processes; corrections systematically verified
- Key support service processes improved throughout organization to achieve better quality, cycle time, operational performance requirements; wide range of techniques used, including process simplification, process research/testing, benchmarking, customer information, alternate technology
- Quality requirements defined throughout organization for expected supplier performance; performance feedback systematically communicated to suppliers
- Quality is primary consideration when selecting suppliers
- Systematic approaches used throughout organization to evaluate and improve supplier performance; supplier abilities, procurement process, inspection/audit costs considered

---

3. How all requirements associated with products, services, and production/delivery processes are addressed early in the design process by all appropriate organization units to ensure integration and coordination. Effective design must take into account all stakeholders in the value chain.

The design of products, services, and processes should meet customer requirements. However, truly effective design must also consider cycle time and productivity of production and delivery processes. This usually includes detailed mapping of service processes to achieve efficiency as well as to meet customer requirements.

Prior to full-scale operation, any product, service, production, or delivery process design should be reviewed and tested in detail. This ensures that all parts of the production/delivery system are capable of performing according to design. This stage is a crucial one. Positive or negative customer reactions and potentially high cost to the organization are virtually assured if preoperation changes are significant.

Following the initial process design, the manner of designing the process should be evaluated and improved to progressively better quality and cycle time. This means that SROs extract lessons learned to build capabilities for future designs. Their evaluation might take into account delays and problems experienced during design, feedback from those involved, and postoperation problems that might have been averted through better design. Evaluation and improvement should strive for a continuous flow of work in the key design and delivery processes.

Another important function is that of monitoring and evaluating process performance to ensure that processes perform according to their design. Leaders require such information as a description of the key processes and their specific requirements and how performance relative to these requirements is known and maintained.

A process performance measurement plan requires the identification of critical points in processes for measurement or observation. Implied in this plan is that measurements or observations be made at the earliest points in processes to minimize problems that may result from variations from expected (design) performance. When measurements or observations reveal variations, a remedy—often called *corrective action*—is required to restore the performance of the process to its design performance.

Depending on the nature of the process, the correction could involve technical or human factors or both. Proper correction involves correcting at the source (root cause) of the variation. *Note:* In some cases, customers may directly witness or take part in the process and contribute to or be a determinant of process performance. In such cases, variations among customers must be taken into account in evaluating how well the process is performing. This is especially true of professional and personal services.

In the SRO, processes are improved to achieve better performance—meaning not only better quality from the customer's perspective, but also better operational performance (productivity) from the organization's perspective. Key support service processes are based on the requirements of the organization's external customers and of other units (internal customers) within the organization—those within the organization who use the output of the process. These processes are also measured, evaluated, and improved.

The performance of external providers of goods and services is another functional area that requires effective management. Such management is increasingly built around longer-term partnering relationships, particularly with key suppliers. Certain basic information on the organization's principal requirements for its key suppliers is required, as are the expected performance and measurements used to assess performance, how the organization determines whether its requirements are being met, and how performance information is fed back to suppliers. Here, SRO leaders evaluate and improve supplier management in three elemental areas:

1. Improving supplier abilities to meet requirements
2. Improving its own supplier management processes
3. Reducing costs associated with the verification of supplier performance

For many organizations, suppliers are an increasingly important member of the complex team needed to achieve not only high performance and lower-cost objectives, but also strategic objectives. For example, key suppliers might provide unique design, integration, and marketing capabilities. Exploiting these advantages requires joint planning and partner relationships to ensure longer-term planning horizons and customer–supplier teams.

(ii) Information and Analysis

Information and analysis includes all key information needed to drive the improvement of overall performance. The objective of this functional area is to bring about the alignment of the organization's information system with its strategic directions. Performance can be improved, if key processes are analyzed and improved. This requires the identification and analysis of key information (Exhibit 1.8). Leaders must ensure that the organization selects and manages key information and data that support overall business goals. Primary emphasis during this process must be on actions and initiatives that support process management and performance improvement.

Information and data are selected for use based on their strategic importance; they are managed most effectively when they can be rapidly accessed and updated; in turn, these factors contribute strongly to their reliability. Leaders of SROs are concerned with how the organization evaluates and improves its selection, analysis, and management of information and data. They ensure an emphasis on alignment with business priorities, support of process management, and feedback from information and data users. Their evaluation should take into account factors such as paths of data use, extent and effectiveness of use, gaps, sharing, and organization of information and data.

EXHIBIT 1.8 Information and Analysis Characteristics of Self-Renewing Organizations

- Criteria for selecting data/information for use in quality, operational performance improvement are integrated and used throughout the organization
- Key data/information relating to key public service/business drivers are used to improve quality and operational performance throughout organization
- Processes and technologies are used throughout the organization to assure that information collected is reliable, consistent, valid, and readily accessible in response to user needs
- Processes are in place to evaluate and improve the information and data system supporting the improvement of organization performance; reviewed on an ongoing basis
- Benchmarking process established based on needs and priorities and aligned with overall organization improvement targets; data used to establish stretch targets and/or support breakthrough approaches throughout organization
- Most areas use benchmark/comparison data, including product and service quality, support service processes, staff, volunteer, supplier-related activities
- Organization evaluates and improves its benchmarking process on an ongoing basis
- Performance, customer/client data aggregated with other key data, analyzed, translated into usable information to support reviews, business decisions, planning throughout the organization
- Performance data aggregated with other key data, analyzed, and related to financial indicators of performance; information used to set priorities for improvement actions throughout organization

---

Information and data are most frequently selected based on their utility to effectively manage performance. However, information, data, and information technology often have strategic significance as well. For example, information technology can be used to build and disseminate vital knowledge about customers and markets—creating the ability to operate more successfully.

Data and information related to competitive position and to best practices serve as external drivers of improvement, giving this information both operational and strategic importance. Of course, the organization should not only select and use this information, but also consider how it evaluates and improves the processes it uses to do so.

The basic premises here recognize the fact that:

- Organizations need to "know where they stand" relative to competitors and to best practice performance for similar activities.
- Comparative and benchmarking information provides the impetus for significant (breakthrough) improvement and alerts organizations to competitive threats and new practices.
- Organizations need to understand their own processes and the processes of others before they compare performance levels.

Carefully selected and analyzed benchmarking information may also be very helpful to support business analysis and decisions relating to core competencies, alliances, and outsourcing.

Organization-level analysis is the principal basis for guiding an organization's process management toward business results. Despite the importance of individual facts and data, they do not usually (in the SRO) provide a sound basis for actions or priorities.

Action should be undertaken only after an understanding has been achieved between cause–effect connections among processes and between processes and business results. Process actions often have many resource implications; results may have many cost and revenue implications as well. Because resources for improvement are limited, and cause–effect connections are often unclear, most organizations face a critical need to provide a sound analytical basis for decisions.

Data and information from all parts of the organization must be aggregated and analyzed to support reviews, business decisions, and planning. SRO leaders ensure that the focus remains on two key areas of performance: customers and operational performance. Analyses use both nonfinancial and financial data, connected to provide a basis for action. For many nonprofits, a particularly important analysis objective is that of linking customer data, improvements in product and service quality, and improvements in operational performance to improvement in financial indicators—guiding the selection of improvement efforts and strategies, to achieve revenue growth, and to reduce operating costs.

(C) EVOLUTIONARY ORGANIZATIONAL ENVIRONMENT

At times, effectiveness versus efficiency initiatives create a push–pull within the organization that can create damaging, even destructive currents. To keep this normal give and take from dividing the organization into "them and us" camps requires an overall organizational environment able to adapt to changing conditions, manage change effectively, transition to new states, and turn in new directions—in short, to constantly evolve. The management areas that deal with creating and sustaining the evolutionary environment include:

- *Leadership,* the setting, communicating, and deploying of organizational values and expectations, including how senior leaders use organizational performance to improve effectiveness throughout the organization.
- *Human resource focus* that encourages and motivates staff and volunteers to develop and use their full potential. This is enhanced by designing, organizing, and managing jobs and services to enhance cooperation, collaboration, individual initiative, innovation, and flexibility.
- *Staff and volunteer performance management* approaches are needed that support high performance. Recruiting, orienting, and training staff and volunteers using key performance requirements, diversity, and fair work practices.
- *Education and training* approaches that achieve organizational objectives, build staff/volunteer knowledge, skills, and capabilities and contribute to improved performance.
- *Creating and sustaining an organizational environment* that contributes to the well-being, satisfaction, and motivation of all staff and volunteers.

(i) Leadership

This excellence category includes the organization's leadership system, strategic directions, and expectations (Exhibit 1.9).

In any SRO, senior leaders fulfill key roles—those that cannot be delegated to others. These vital roles include setting the organization's strategic directions, and building and maintaining a leadership system conducive to high performance, individual development, and organizational learning. Truly effective leaders at all levels of the organization, however, take into account all stakeholders, customers, employees, suppliers, partners, the public, and the community.

Major aspects of leadership include creating values and expectations, setting directions, developing and maintaining an effective leadership system, and building the organization's capabilities. Senior leaders need to reflect these values, and the leadership system needs to include teamwork at the executive level.

Senior leaders within the SRO devote significant time and attention to evaluating and improving the effectiveness of the organization and its leadership system. This function of leadership is crucial, due to the fast pace of competition. A major objective is to create organizations that are flexible and responsive—changing easily to adapt to new needs and opportunities. Both leadership and organization are crucial to high performance. Through their roles in strategy development and review of organization performance, the senior leaders adapt leadership (creation and management of change) and the organization (vision, mission, customer focus) to changing opportunities and requirements.

In the SRO, the leadership system is translated into an effective overall organization structure and management system focused on performance. The SRO's management and work processes support its customer and performance objectives. Senior leaders are alert to identify functional or management barriers that could lead to losing sight of customers or create ineffective or slow decision paths. They take strong measures to ensure alignment of organization units.

The SRO's values, expectations, and directions are "made real" throughout the organization via effective communications. Senior leader communications are necessary for

EXHIBIT 1.9 Leadership Characteristics of Self-Renewing Organizations

- All senior leaders personally, visibly, proactively involved in broad range of quality-related activities; significant time devoted to these activities
- Senior leaders create a vision, quality values, customer focus orientation
- Senior leaders fully participate in setting organization's performance excellence goals through strategic, business planning
- Senior leaders devote extensive time to reviewing organization's customer, operational performance
- Extent to which vision, quality values, customer focus orientation have been adopted is evaluated and improved on ongoing basis
- All senior leaders use a variety of methods to communicate and reinforce vision, quality values, customer focus orientation to staff and volunteers; communication is two-way, clear, open, covers all issues
- Effective strategies involve leaders throughout organization in quality-related activities; roles, responsibilities, accountability clearly defined; extensive cooperation among units encouraged, evident
- Senior leaders, union leaders actively participate in planning, attaining quality goals; mutual support visible throughout organization, reinforced through communications, partnering
- Partnering relationships exist with major customer groups, suppliers, others; number of mutually supportive activities expanding in support of quality, performance goals
- Vision, quality values, customer focus orientation effectively communicated inside, outside organization
- Documented review process of organization's quality, operational improvement plans used throughout organization; results used to implement strategies to improve organization-wide performance
- Quality goals and objectives directly address public health, safety, environmental protection, ethical conduct; accountability for achieving goals, objectives clearly established; improvement efforts throughout organization reflect this commitment; these quality goals, objectives go beyond minimum legal/community standards
- Organization recognized as outstanding citizen in its key communities; senior leaders, staff, volunteers share talents/expertise with community

effective overall communications. Making values, expectations, and directions real demands constant reinforcement and "truth testing," as employees observe whether stated values and expectations are actually the basis for organization actions and key decisions.

Senior leaders review organization and work unit performance and ensure that important work process assessments are included in these reviews. The information they assess addresses important aspects of reviews—types, frequency, content, uses, and who conducts them, which will vary greatly, depending on many factors. Most commonly, the review system blends ongoing (real-time) and periodic reviews.

As the President's Quality Award points out in its award criteria: Reviews offer an effective means to communicate and reinforce what is really important, how performance is measured, and how well business objectives are being met. Important considerations in reviews are the content and organization of information to foster learning and to stimulate action. This means that reviews should include nonfinancial and financial information that together present a clear picture of status and trends relative to the organization's key business drivers. Reviews also provide an effective means to assist units that may not be performing according to expectations.

Public responsibility and corporate (organizational) citizenship are as important to nonprofit organizations as they are to private-sector organizations—how the organization integrates its public responsibilities and corporate citizenship into its business planning and performance improvement practices. Nonprofits, like public- and private-sector organizations, should be concerned about three basic aspects of public responsibility:

1. Making risk and legal requirements an integral part of performance improvement
2. Sensitivity in planning products, services, and operations to issues of societal concern whether or not these issues are currently embodied in law
3. Making legal and ethical conduct visible in the organization's values and performance improvement processes

Fulfilling public responsibilities means not only meeting all local, state, and federal laws and regulatory requirements, but also treating these and related requirements as areas for improvement "beyond mere compliance." This means that all SROs should maintain constant awareness of potential public impacts related to their products, services, and operations. Nonprofits, often the target of legal or regulatory action by public regulators or private corporations, must be diligent in exceeding the average in each of these categories.

SROs serve as a corporate citizen in their key communities. They are productive, reputable, and involved as members of different types of communities and serve as a positive influence on other organizations. They work within and outside their organization to strengthen community services, education, health care, and the environment and improve the practices of trade, business, and other community associations.

(ii) Human Resource Development and Management

Human resource development and management is the functional area and focal point within any organization for all-important human resource practices—those directed toward the creation and sustainability of a high-performance workplace. A vital objective for SRO leaders is to address human resource development and management in an integrated way, aligning them with the organization's strategic directions. Strategic directions should address the development of all those involved in achieving the organization's mission and vision—staff and volunteers—within the context of a high-performance workplace. This requires a coordinated organizational strategy (Exhibit 1.10).

The overall human resource plan should be derived from the organization's strategic and business planning. Primary directions and resourcing must support its overall strategic directions. Senior leaders within the SRO endeavor to develop a multiyear context and guide for human resource planning, management, and evaluation.

As in any values-centered organization, the human resource development area uses the Plan–Do–Check–Act cycle to evaluate and improve overall planning and management. Employee-related and organization performance data and information are tied to overall evaluation of the organization's strategy and business results.

Care is taken to go beyond broad strategy to the essential details of human resource effectiveness. The evaluation needs to provide the organization's senior leaders with

EXHIBIT 1.10 Human Resource Development and Management Characteristics of Self-Renewing Organizations

- Systematic, integrated HR plan is deployed throughout organization to develop workforce potential; it is linked to quality, operational performance improvement plans
- HR plan includes redesign to improve flexibility, innovation, rapid response to changing requirements; staff/volunteer development, education, training; changes in reward, recognition, recruitment
- HR planning is integral, fully aligned part of business planning process; systematically evaluated, improved on ongoing basis
- Employee-related data, organization performance data consistently analyzed, used to assess development, well-being of all categories, types of employees; assess linkage of HR practices to key business results
- Reliable, complete HR information is readily available for use in strategic, business planning
- Unions partner in development, implementation of HR plan where appropriate
- Work, job design promote high performance throughout organization by creating opportunities for initiative, self-directed responsibility; fostering flexibility, rapid response to changing requirements; ensuring effective communication across functions/units
- Working environment throughout organization supports increased empowerment, personal responsibility, appropriate risk-taking, creativity, innovation
- Managers throughout organization support employee contributions, teamwork; managers routinely exhibit coaching and facilitating behaviors, share authority
- Variety of formal and/or informal reward or recognition mechanisms used throughout organization for all levels and types of employees; developed in conjunction with employees; emphasis on recognition of teamwork
- Employees throughout organization provided feedback; evaluated, promoted, provided career opportunities based on personal development, contributions to quality, operational performance goals
- Systematic, documented education, training strategy deployed builds organization, employee capabilities
- Education, training consistently address key organization performance objectives and motivation, progression, development of all employees
- Education, training based on systematic needs assessment; employees, managers throughout organization provide input
- Special education, training designed to enhance high-performance work units
- Knowledge, skills consistently reinforced through on-the-job application throughout organization
- Education, training systematically evaluated, improved on ongoing basis using feedback from employees, customers; appropriate measures of effectiveness, extent of education, training used
- Extensive quality, skills training throughout organization; all employees trained in quality awareness; teams, work groups trained in appropriate quality tools, techniques in support of customer service, continuous improvement; cross-functional training commonplace
- Organization consistently maintains safe, healthful work environment; improvement efforts cover requirements, measures for all employee well-being factors (health, safety, ergonomics)
- Extensive services, facilities, activities, opportunities available to all employees to support overall well-being, satisfaction/enhance work experience, development potential
- Variety of measures used to determine employee satisfaction, well-being, motivation throughout organization; data consistently used to improve employee satisfaction, well-being, motivation on an ongoing basis

information on strengths and weaknesses in human resource practices and development that might bear on the organization's abilities to achieve its short-term and longer-term business objectives. For example, the evaluation should take into account the development and progression of all categories and types of staff and volunteers, including those newly joining the organization.

The evaluation should also monitor the extent to which education and training is deployed throughout the organization, and how well education and training support organization performance improvement. The overall evaluation will rely heavily on well-being and satisfaction factors.

Well-being considerations include the work environment, the work climate, and how they are tailored to foster the well-being, satisfaction, and development of all employees. Long-term well-being and productivity (not to mention legal and regulatory requirements) require a safe and healthful work environment.

SRO leaders' approach to enhance staff and volunteer well-being, satisfaction, and growth potential is based on a more holistic view of the organization's human resources as key stakeholders. They consider a wide variety of mechanisms to build well-being and satisfaction, from development, progression, employability, and external activities, to family or other community service activities.

Many factors might affect employee motivation. Although satisfaction with pay and promotion potential is important, these factors alone are not adequate to assess the overall climate for motivation, morale, and high performance. Therefore, the organization will consider a variety of factors relating to the work environment to determine the key elements of the organization's culture and internal environment. Those factors identified that inhibit motivation will be prioritized and addressed. Additional understanding of these factors is developed through exit interviews with departing staff and volunteers.

In the SRO, job design, compensation, and recognition approaches enable and encourage all employees to contribute effectively, operating within high-performance work units. The latter requires effective work design and reinforcement. The basic intent of such work design approaches should be to enable staff and volunteers to exercise more discretion and decision making, leading to greater flexibility and more rapid response to the changing requirements of the marketplace—in short, to be "empowered" with a combination of authority, responsibility, resourcing, and accountability.

Effective job design and flexible work organizations are necessary but in and of themselves may not be sufficient to ensure high performance. Job and organization design must be backed by information systems, education, and appropriate training to ensure that information flow supports the job and work designs. Also important is effective communication across functions and work units to ensure focus on customer requirements.

Incentives need to be aligned with work systems. Compensation and recognition should be structured and implemented to reinforce high-performance job design, work organizations, and teamwork. These are important considerations because there should be a consistency between the organization's compensation and recognition system and its work structures and processes. Compensation, benefits, and recognition may need to be based on demonstrated skills and evaluation by peers in teams and networks.

The SRO develops human resources via education, training, and on-the-job reinforcement of knowledge and skills. A major objective of "development" is meeting the needs of a high-performance workplace operating in a dynamic, highly competitive environment. Education and training need to be ongoing as well. Education and training serve as key vehicles to build organization and people capabilities. These two capabilities are, in fact, investments the organization makes in its long-term future and the long-term future of people.

SRO leaders pay particular attention to how education and training are designed, delivered, reinforced, and evaluated, with special emphasis on on-the-job application of knowledge and skills. They recognize the importance of involving all levels and categories of people within the organization—staff, volunteers, managers—in the design of training, including clear identification of specific needs. This involves job analysis: understanding the types and levels of the skills required and the timeliness of training.

Evaluation of education and training is vital and should take into account the supervisor's evaluation, employee/volunteer self-evaluation, and peer evaluation of value received through education and training relative to needs identified in design. The evaluation process could also address the effectiveness of education and training delivery, impact on work unit performance, and costs of delivery alternatives.

1.7   Resources

The following is a list of resources found in this, the *Nonprofit Handbook: Management,* Third Edition, and in "sister" works such as its annual supplements and the *Volunteer Management Handbook.* These resources are organized into effectiveness, efficiency, and environmental areas. The descriptions of these "Additional Reading" resources attempt to outline major management issues and understandings that challenge leaders of nonprofits. In doing so, they underscore the complexities and sheer breadth of technical knowledge that face nonprofit organization leaders in today's highly competitive and constantly evolving operating environment.

Management Environment

"Management Context of Nonprofit Organizations in the New Millennium: Diversity, Quality, Technology, Global Environment, and Ethics" by Joseph E. Champoux. All nonprofits operate in one of five critical contexts that will affect them significantly as we move into the next millennium. As we enter the twenty-first century, which is certain to be at least as challenging and dynamic as the last, it is increasingly important to anticipate wherever possible what is ahead for nonprofits and their leaders. As seen by Champoux, nonprofit leaders should pay particular attention to five broad contexts of critical importance: managing for quality, workforce diversity, technology, the global environment, and ethics. He observes, "Each context surrounds modern nonprofit organizations and presents major opportunities for the agile manager as we move into the next millennium." Workforce diversity, for example, will have a major impact on nonprofit operations because (1) managers will have no choice about managing for diversity, and (2) successfully managing for diversity is good business strategy. Another management context, quality management, will bring many benefits to nonprofit organizations that do not directly result from other approaches to management. Managers (executive directors, managers, program directors, administrators, development directors) should be able to use quality management techniques and processes to lower costs of providing a service, conduct research, start a social issues campaign, or manufacture a product. Service processes will function more dependably using quality management improvement techniques. Issues can be targeted and communicated more effectively. Employee, board, and volunteer commitment to continuous quality improvement will increase, Champoux points out, if they perceive benefits or results. The result can be more loyalty to the organization, improved funding potential, easier volunteer and board recruitment, and more lasting social change. Continuous quality improvement can lead to better cooperation and clarity with outside contractors, suppliers, vendors, coalition partners, and the community as well. He concludes with implications that "suggest changing one's thinking about managing a nonprofit organization in the next millennium." Fortunately, his insights offer practical ways in which to guide nonprofit organizations into the twenty-first century. (*Nonprofit Handbook: Management,* Third Edition)

"Goverance Framework for Collaborations and Mergers" by Suzanne Feeney. In recent years, there has been an explosion of interest in nonprofits collaborating. Foundations are encouraging collaborations because they see them as being the answer to most nonprofit problems, that is, organizational inefficiencies, duplication of services, lack of management accountability, and the like. Government contractors are also enamored with collaborations, often requiring that nonprofits collaborate as a condition for receiving public money to deliver services. While the fascination with collaborations and increasingly with mergers continues, they are still not well understood. The collaboration label is no longer sufficient to describe the multitude of multiparty interorganizational relationships that are appearing everywhere in the sector. New labels include strategic alliances, federations, back-room consolidations, joint ventures, restructuring, cooperation, coordination, and mergers. This kind of linguistic alphabet soup has often exacerbated rather than clarified our understanding of collaboration. Most of the books and articles about collaboration focus only on explaining or describing the structures and processes of collaboration. They are helpful in that they provide a framework for thinking about collaborations and how best to engage or not engage in them. Feeney offers a list of "success factors" and a useful template for nonprofits contemplating partnering with other nonprofits to deliver services, consolidate administrative functions, or vie for public dollars to support their organizations' missions. (*Nonprofit Handbook: Management,* Third Edition)

"Change Leadership or Change Management?" by Jon Van Til and David A. Pettrone Swalve. As organizations ebb and flow within the dynamic setting of the third sector, change remains the constant. Change requires organizations to examine the quality and coverage of their existing products and services, reduce their expenses, locate new directions of movement, and develop new relationships, all the while nurturing their environment. Inevitably, organizations face deciding on the main determinant of change—usually, a dichotomous decision—change leadership or change management. Change is often asked for and needed in society and within organizations. Organizations face change from a variety of sources and directions. Forces can originate internally or externally. They include changing technological standards, shifting community needs, increasing client demands, and reduced funds for administrative expenses, as well as changes in the broader social structure. Regardless of its specific origin, change is a constant in the nonprofit world. Boards face a unique responsibility to understand the various relationships the organization maintains. As leaders, boards are challenged to find new directions and lead for positive change. Yet, leaders are found at all levels of the organization, and managers themselves must often serve as proactive change agents. Maintaining and nurturing an effective organization requires all members of the organization to be attuned to potential change, both within the organization and in relation to its clients, community, competition, and the private and public sectors. Leaders and managers that comprehend the change process can foster a "natural state" of change for third-sector organizations. (*Nonprofit Handbook: Management,* Third Edition)

"A Hundred-Year Horizon: Considering Sustainable Development in the Nonprofit Sector" by Keith Seel. The belief that an organization, or any part of our society, including the nonprofit sector, is sustainable is taken for granted. Unless they are in imminent danger of collapse, most organizations anticipate that they will be present and operating in their communities in the future. Many processes, such as strategic planning, scenario planning, forecasting, and the like, are specifically designed to help an organization consider its future and find ways to grow and expand its activities. Yet numerous factors are converging that raise questions about whether current structures—organizations, communities, and economies—are in fact sustainable. For managers in the nonprofit sector, the topic of sustainable development may appear to be better addressed by the corporate sector, particularly large resource companies or manufacturers. Yet at a personal level each of us knows the importance of the 3Rs—reduce, reuse, and recycle—the basic philosophy of sustainable development. If sustainable development concepts have a role to play in the business sector and in our personal lives, there should be elements that also apply to how the nonprofit sector is managed and operates. Seel explores and explains the application of sustainable development concepts to nonprofit sector management and operations. (*Nonprofit Handbook: Management,* Third Edition)

"Using Multisource Feedback to Improve Performance" by Milena M. Meneghetti. Multisource feedback (MSF), the process of gathering information about the work-related effectiveness of an employee from a wide variety of sources, is the important management tool for nonprofit leaders explained and developed by Meneghetti. This important management technique uses a standard behavior-based tool based on a job or role analysis, plus sources of feedback (including peers, professional colleagues, clients, subordinates, team members, and supervisors), a self-assessment, and, finally, aggregated results—to provide comprehensive and more objective, useful performance management results. Today's nonprofit managers, she points out, understand the need to seek out feedback about their employees or volunteers from others. However, they are often unable to gather this feedback effectively. MSF is a critical tool for gathering relevant, valid feedback. Complete or partial ownership of the "results" is handed over to the employee or volunteer, who is in the best position to respond to that feedback constructively. The end result is more effective management of performance. (*Nonprofit Handbook: Management,* 1999 Supplement)

Organizational Identity and Focus

"Ethics and Values in the Nonprofit Organization" by Melina M. Meneghetti and Keith Seel. Nonprofit leaders fulfill vital and complex roles within the nonprofit sector. Often, they are forced to balance interests of staff, volunteers, board, and clients, and in the process face a complex landscape of frequently conflicting values. If they are to meet the challenges of the twenty-first century, they must be equipped with the ethical sensitivity to identify potential issues, the decision-making competency to navigate them, and the conviction to help resolve them. This chapter discusses the unique nature of values and ethics in nonprofit organizations, then moves to more specific areas of managerial concern, including professional codes of ethics, ethics and the management of human resources (including volunteer resources), and ethics as a basis for policy and partnerships. It introduces an ethical decision-making model that will assist the nonprofit leader to resolve even the most complex ethical issues. (*Nonprofit Handbook: Management,* Third Edition)

Customer Focus and Satisfaction
Marketing and Communications

"Marketing" by Eugene M. Johnson and M. Venkatesan. Marketing as a concept and as a management application is steadily broadening and now includes any transaction between an organization and its many publics. Marketing now applies to any social unit that seeks to exchange values with other social units. Products now include organizations, persons, places, and ideas, in addition to goods and services. This broadening concept of marketing includes "social marketing," the use of marketing principles and techniques to advance a social cause, idea, or pattern of behavior. These changes in marketing thought underscore the reality that marketing is applicable to all types of nonprofit organizations. Like all important management activities, marketing must be planned, organized, and controlled. Leaders of nonprofit organizations need to be knowledgeable about many fundamental aspects of marketing, including markets and buyer behavior, marketing intelligence, marketing management, marketing audits, marketing planning, and the marketing mix. (*Nonprofit Handbook: Management,* Third Edition)

"Commercial Ventures: Opportunities and Risks for Nonprofit Organizations" by Keith Seel. Increasing competition for funding, changes in government funding, financial sustainability and flexibility, and corporate marketing initiatives involving a nonprofit partner are some of the reasons that nonprofits are forced to consider commercial ventures. Yet, as Seel explains, nonprofits must be very careful when considering a for-profit endeavor. After outlining the pros and cons of such a venture, Seel provides six steps that help ensure success in commercial ventures. Of particular importance to nonprofit leaders is his review of frequently encountered commercial venture strategies, from strategic philanthropy and sponsorships to premiums, licensing, and sponsored advertisements. His case studies are valuable assessments of what went right and wrong with real-world ventures. He concludes by assessing and reviewing the risks involved for nonprofits. (*Nonprofit Handbook: Management,* Third Edition)

"Strategic Media Relations" by Eileen M. Wirth. Media relations is an integral component of any successful nonprofit's external communications plan. Most organizations believe they are "doing it right" when their staff responds to queries promptly and completely. However, as Wirth points out, "well-intentioned staff members too often confuse effort and output with results." Typically, nonprofits focus on *how* to get coverage and *how* to work with news organizations, but not *why.* Goal setting tends to be in terms of gaining attention, rather than furthering the organization's mission. Dr. Wirth defines the strategic approach to media relations as using those activities to achieve specific public relations goals. These goals, in turn, support the organization's overall mission and communications strategy. Developing a media relations strategy, identifying target audiences, research, media use analysis, message development, visual images, and evaluation approaches are reviewed and helpfully presented. (*Nonprofit Handbook: Management,* Third Edition)

"Contingency and Emergency Public Affairs" by Richard L. Thompson. Many nonprofit organizations, by the nature of their activities, operate in inherently hazardous environments. Other nonprofit organizations conduct "administrative" functions in an office setting. Regardless of the nature of operations, proper response to a contingency or emergency demands mature judgment and appropriate action, taken without hesitation throughout the organization. One vital component of a nonprofit organization's response in a contingency or emergency is communication with concerned stakeholders. Public affairs contingencies and emergencies can include disruption of routine operations, computer failure involving breakdowns or hacking, or an accident involving injury or death. They may also include other occurrences that reflect badly on the organization, such as an employee drug abuse incident, fraud, mismanagement, improper hazardous waste disposal, and the like. The bottom line is that a public affairs contingency or emergency situation can be a real or perceived threat that has the potential to disrupt normal operations, prevent the nonprofit organization from attaining its goals, or cause an adverse reaction among stakeholders. Thompson provides guidance to assist organization leaders, managers, and their public affairs executives in meeting their public affairs responsibilities in a wide variety of contingencies—incidents, accidents, and other emergencies—including the essential "how to's" of surviving a public information crisis: what to do before and after the unimaginable crisis occurs. His point-by-point explanation of this vital skill could help you save your organization's credibility and public support when the worst happens. (*Nonprofit Handbook: Management,* Third Edition)

"Distance Learning for Nonprofit Organizations: Getting Started" by Janet Poley. We are living through a revolution our ancestors could not have imagined—a revolution of information. Many nonprofits are heavily involved in delivering education, training, and information services programs to their members using new and challenging technologies, including those collectively called distance learning (DL) or business television (BTV). For them, as for business organizations, DL/BTV is now seen as a key strategy to improve productivity and competitiveness, just-in-time learning, and communication. DL/BTV helps nonprofits cope with a competitive environment that changes on a daily basis. Poley incorporates her perspective as president of ADEC—A Distance Learning Consortium of state universities and land grant institutions providing high-quality and economic distance education programs and services via information technologies. The various types of distance learning, BTV, or videoconferencing are reviewed, as well as the major applications of these technologies to nonprofit organizations. While major potential benefits can accrue to nonprofits from their investments of money, time, and training in DL/BTV, key decision factors need to be considered before the decision is made to sponsor or participate in DL programs. Major program planning factors are outlined, and key factors in successful DL programs or applications are identified before moving ahead to cover effective marketing strategies and techniques. (*Nonprofit Handbook: Management,* Third Edition)

"Integrated Trade Show Planning and Operations" by Richard L. Thompson. A growing number of nonprofits are using trade shows and exhibits as outreach and marketing tools for their constituencies. Too often, trade show participation was seen as a "stand-alone" activity performed by specialists. Thompson outlines how and why trade show and exhibit operations should be an integral component of the overall marketing communications program, which includes advertising, public relations/constituent outreach, media relations, direct marketing, and trade shows. After outlining the process that successful nonprofits use to research and develop seamless, integrated marketing communications strategies, he moves to the practical aspects of trade and exhibit planning and management, including invaluable checklists for practitioners. (*Nonprofit Handbook: Management,* 1998 Supplement)

Information Management

"Internet Strategy for Nonprofits" by Marlene Fox-McIntyre. As late as 1995, a Web site was a curiosity that few nonprofits were using, outside of the academic community. Since then, however, "the Internet has progressed from a novelty to a necessary business element. Every kind of organization imaginable can make use of the Internet today, not only to get its message out, but to get work done, increase revenues, provide better services to members and constituencies, and streamline day-to-day administrative functions." The question Fox-McIntyre answers is no longer whether nonprofits should go online, but "how to best leverage the Internet to compete effectively for your visitor's time, attention, and money." Thousands of nonprofits are already online. A few minutes of surfing will confirm what a wide range of approaches are being taken by these organizations. Very similar organizations take wildly divergent attitudes toward the purpose and functionality of their Web sites. The result is that some of these sites are showing dramatic successes, while most do little more than consume resources. After reviewing important Internet strategic elements—domain name, Web site presence, secure electronic commerce—she provides important tips on successful Internet marketing approaches that retain existing clients and attract new clients. Nonprofits can increase revenues using the Internet, and Fox-McIntyre offers valuable suggestions for online giving, planned giving, online sales, and other revenue enhancement activities. She concludes by covering Web site design considerations and implementation priorities—from costs and maintenance to common mistakes. (*Nonprofit Handbook: Management,* Third Edition)

"Management Implications and Opportunities of Global Communications" by Janet Poley. One of Theodor Geisel's last books as Dr. Seuss, *Oh, the Places You'll Go!* (1990), took us right into Hakken-Kraks Howl where "the weather is fowl," "enemies prowl," "up many a frightening creek." "Your arms get sore and your sneakers leak." Hakken-Kraks Howl provides an excellent metaphor for some of the murky underside of the Internet issues creating a storm today. Privacy, secrecy, security, and intellectual property are big issues, as Poley outlines. Nonprofit organizational managers, employees, and volunteers can quickly find themselves up to their behinds in alligators if these issues are ignored. Unfortunately, far less important items than these seize the headlines of newspapers and magazines daily. We can expect the weather to get stormier in Hakken-Kraks Howl on the way to development of more common norms, standards, practices, and laws internationally. Sensationalizing the virus du jour probably isn't nearly as important as explaining the messy, slippery processes that could ruin you, your organization, and the vision and mission you are pursuing. Some have called this the Wild West period of the Internet. Poley prefers Hakken-Kraks Howl. You may recall that Seuss took us to Hakken-Kraks Howl after we visited the most useless place of all—"The Waiting Place." Some major corporations and governments have a vested interest in keeping lots of people in the "Internet Waiting Place" because these companies are making money and many people remain ignorant about what the Internet is and how it really works. Nonprofit organizations have a responsibility to understand the big picture Internet world, not just dabble in e-mail, e-commerce, e-learning, or e-"anythingelseyoucanthinkof." When the Internet was simpler, it was referred to as the Information Superhighway, operating much like the nervous system of a vertebrate. Today this Hakken-Kraks Howl has multiple backbones, scattered burrows, ditches, indirect routes, and obstacles. This Internet place is a set of 100 or so long-range global networks that diversely link and transfer messages to and from more than 100,000 local networks. Some of these networks collaborate and share mutual interest;

others are in sharp proprietary rivalry. There are tens of millions of Internet users, including smart instruments that also make cyberspace reports.[2] For-profit companies are certainly going to offer e-sales opportunities in multiple languages. Nonprofits have interesting opportunities and challenges as the Internet becomes increasingly global. (*Nonprofit Handbook: Management,* Third Edition)

"Strategic Planning for Information Systems" by E. Brian Peach and Richie Platt. It sounds like a brand new language—and it is! JAVA. Network computers. Electronic commerce. Firewalls. In the maelstrom of today's digital information age, technological innovations bombard managers nearly as rapidly as the speed of light through a fiber-optic network. How can today's nonprofit leader keep up? How can the organization function competently when technology developments race forward, while the demands mount that budgets shrink almost as rapidly? Harnessing information and the systems designed to manipulate and control information can provide strategic benefits to nonprofits. In their timely chapter, Peach and Platt provide an outline for the nonprofit manager to use to help tame the uncontrolled growth in demand for the latest technology, while building an information systems strategic plan to carry the organization into the twenty-first century. Investment in technology is not a question of whether the investment will be made, and it is not really a question of when. The real question is how much the organization will invest and, more importantly, how it will plan its investment to provide the most strategic benefit. (*Nonprofit Handbook: Management,* Third Edition)

"Nonprofit Success on the Internet: Creating an Effective Online Presence" by Michael Stein. A growing number of nonprofits use the Internet today in unique and powerful ways to reach constituencies and supporters. Through well-crafted combinations of Internet activities, nonprofits are disseminating informational content, news, and alerts, and building a recognizable name online as trusted sources in its various issue areas. "Internet presence" is the comprehensive set of activities that a nonprofit organization engages in to use the Internet to meet its mission and advocacy goals. It can include a range of activities, such as building and maintaining a Web site; writing and distributing an e-mail newsletter; getting a Web site listed with search engines and directories; requesting reciprocal links with other Web sites; getting content placed with Web portals; holding online interactive events, such as chats and threaded discussion forums; running an e-mail "listserv" discussion; using digital audio and video for Webcasting; and more. Stein helps nonprofits think strategically about the complete range of activities that create an effective Internet presence. The traditional nonprofit approach on the Internet is having a Web site, keeping the content up to date, and driving traffic to its site. It has only been in the last few years that a broader definition of Internet presence has been adopted by nonprofits. The reality of the Internet today is far more complex than merely having a Web site and expecting traffic to come to it. This "build it and they will come" mentality has been superseded by a more active and aggressive approach to Internet promotion and marketing. The paradigm of "they will come" is being replaced by "we must go to them." This shift in perspective is a useful one and it works! For many nonprofit organizations using the Internet today, the greatest challenge has been to build, launch, and maintain a Web site. This focus on "Web-centrism" dominates a great deal of conversations at nonprofits. While building and maintaining a Web site is in and of itself not a bad focus of attention, a far greater challenge awaits. That challenge is to strategically integrate the Internet with the rest of the organization's mission and advocacy goals and to publicize and drive Internet traffic to the Web site, and more generally, to get the organization's "Internet presence" into the limelight. Whether you are still in the planning stages or have a well-developed Web site and e-mail outreach campaign, it is never too late to do an Internet tune-up to improve Internet outreach, increase Web site traffic, find new avenues for content dissemination, build e-mail subscribership, and fully integrate the Internet with your organization's activities. A truly effective Internet presence is about bringing the Internet closer to the advocacy goals of the organization and finding ways to use it to communicate with supporters, allies, and friends. (*Nonprofit Handbook: Management,* Third Edition)

Technology

"Emergent Technology and the Nonprofit Organization" by Elizabeth Power and Adam C. Hart, Jr. *Technology* refers to a broad spectrum of devices and processes. Before computers, Power and Hart point out, technology could have referred to an index card system of tracking or hardcopy tickler files. It was the system of communication with distant parties, whether through talking drums or horse-borne messages. With the advent of electricity and ultimately computers, technology has become synonymous with machines, rapid information processing, storage, and distribution. They address the everyday tasks faced by nonprofits in which technology most often supports three primary functions: fund raising, operations, and volunteer management. The same hardware and software may serve these and other functions required to support the organization. Emergent technology can be used and pay for itself in a short period of time, they explain during their assessment of such applications as:

- Satellite-based wide area networks (WANs) when cabling is not the best choice
- Computer-based video meetings for distance use (effective in overseas and domestic work, distance learning, video meetings, and to show marketing videos)
- User-friendly, low-cost telephones and call distribution that reduce dependence on the vendor by relying on plain-English, browser-based interfaces for changes and adjustments
- Wireless intelligent terminals that allow users to send and receive e-mail from a pager with a keyboard
- Voice recognition technology for word processing and other uses; allows input of data using the voice, the other side of text readers for people with visual impairments

Applying these technologies in both for-profit and nonprofit environments, they explain, need not be cost prohibitive, and in fact may result in recovery of investment in a far shorter time than expected. Projections of cost savings can (and should) be part of every technology proposal. The governing body should know when recovery of investment will occur, the projected usage over time, effectiveness, and cost–benefit ratios. Without this information, governing bodies should be reluctant to invest in technology. "It demonstrates to funding sources, persons served, the community of interest, and others that good sense and fiscal responsibility are present." (*Nonprofit Handbook: Management,* Third Edition)

"Building a Knowledge Marketplace: Best Practices to Create Learning Value in Cyberspace" by Janet Poley. Does the proliferation of new nonprofit organizations mean new opportunities for more players or just more weeds among a few flowers? The opportunity,

Poley suggests, is to create a "knowledge marketplace" within the .*org* domain that results in real value for individuals and communities around the world. Other communication media, such as digital broadcast satellite or satellite radio, might also become carriers for quality learning content, but the best current hope is the Internet. In a truly visionary overview, grounded with practical guidelines and pointers, Dr. Poley challenges nonprofit organization leaders to create "a knowledge marketplace rather than just a political cyber-space." Where organizations fit in the knowledge marketplace, including reaching informed nonusers and working in the international marketplace, is followed by a discussion of how to create partnerships with other nongovernment organizations, educational organizations, agencies, foundations, and businesses. After introducing the reader to "portals" and electronic commerce, Dr. Poley summarizes the state of the Internet and concludes with a succinct and highly useful ABCs of best practice. (*Nonprofit Handbook: Management*, Third Edition)

"Technology and Strategy for Organizational Effectiveness" by Marc S. Osten. Strategic technology planning is an ever-important discipline and process that is steadily evolving. Nonprofit organization leaders need to understand how strategic technology planning brings together the broader discipline of organizational planning and assessment with the increasingly important thrust of technology planning. Technology planning is thus fused, informed, and driven by the organizational planning process, resulting in a technology plan that is an authentic reflection of an organization's mission, priorities, and capacity. Several models of planning and evaluation are available to nonprofit organization leaders, each with important pros and cons that can affect organizational efficiency and effectiveness in programs and operations of nonprofit organizations. Strategic technology planning is an integral component of successful technology integration within a nonprofit. Organizations that do not utilize it often waste limited financial and human resources, in addition to not using technology appropriately or to its fullest potential. (*Nonprofit Handbook: Management*, Third Edition)

Public Service (Business Results)

"Managing Organizational Growth" by Carolyn J. Curran. After comparing corporate and nonprofit organizations in terms of their organizational development (OD), this chapter moves to a handy self-diagnosis that provides models of organizational growth, stages of organizational growth combined, a checklist to identify an organization's growth stage and how to move to the next stage, a DNA pattern of organizational growth, and the challenges of one stage leading to solutions of the next. Nonprofits can draw on corporation OD to some extent, if appropriate guidelines are followed. Individual and organizational responses to change and the motivations for change must be balanced against practical discussions of resistances leaders can expect to change opportunities. Potential growth areas are outlined, and a practical prognosis for the effective use of OD approaches within nonprofit organizations is offered. (*Nonprofit Handbook: Management*, Third Edition)

"Lessons in Strategic Plan Implementation" by Marci Bernstein Lu, Christine Lucas, Valerie Raines, and John A. Yankey. Although strategic planning is now widely regarded as standard practice for a self-renewing organization, implementation remains the least understood phase of strategic management. Lu, Lucas, Raines, and Yankey bring together years of experience in strategic planning at the Mandel Center for Nonprofit Organizations at Case Western Reserve University. They address with solid utility the essentials needed for successful implementation, including readiness for strategic planning; developing a sound strategy; using consultants; coordinating strategy with budget cycle; developing an action plan; exercising strategic leadership; mechanisms to control, monitor, and review progress; keeping the plan in front of stakeholders; organizational culture; infrastructure and resources; implications for practitioners; and success indicators. (*Nonprofit Handbook: Management,* Third Edition)

Efficiency
New Revenue Sources
"Nonprofit Organizations as Entrepreneurs" by Ruthie G. Reynolds. Some nonprofit organizations are experiencing the best of times, while others are fighting to keep their doors open. With decreases in contributions and government funding, along with increasing demands to provide additional services, to keep up with technology, and to add new and innovative programs, nonprofit organizations must look to new sources of revenue. Many nonprofits are looking to entrepreneurial ventures to bridge the gap between needed funds and available funds. Entrepreneurial ventures are attractive to nonprofit organizations. The revenue earned can be used to supplement programs, but maybe more importantly, the nonprofit has more control over the revenue than over contributions and government funds. Contributions and government funds carry restrictions. Restrictions limit the use of funds. Earned revenue, however, carries no restrictions. The nonprofits are free to use the funds as they choose, provided they stay within the guidelines of their mission and comply with applicable governmental regulations. (*Nonprofit Handbook: Management,* Third Edition)

Financial Management
"Accounting" by Richard F. Larkin. Nonprofit organization leaders need to understand the duties of the chief executive officer and the basic fundamentals of nonprofit accounting, including cash versus accrual accounting, fund accounting, transfers and appropriations, treatment of fixed assets and contributions, pledges, and noncash contributions. Long-term survivability (not to mention job security) will depend on understanding how to avoid financial problems, including how to establish internal financial controls (receipts/disbursements) and independent audits. (*Nonprofit Handbook: Management,* Third Edition)

"Budgeting Considerations" by Ruthie G. Reynolds. Budgeting is a key to long-term management of any nonprofit organization, with planning and controlling being the two most important components. Projecting and properly allocating resources requires developing a plan of action to guide the management team in applying and tracking these resources. Nonprofit leaders need to understand the links between budgeting and accounting, and budgeting techniques, from line-item budgeting and the Planned-Programming-Budgeting System (PPBS) to zero-based budgeting. (*Nonprofit Handbook: Management,* Third Edition)

"Unrelated Business Income" by Jody Blazek. Regulatory issues are combining with advances in technology to challenge nonprofit leaders, even while offering innovative new approaches. Blazek brings readers up to date regarding "interesting new Unrelated Business Income questions involving the Internet." This topic is particularly important in light of the expansion of exempt organizations into e-commerce. She provides a new and very useful checklist that allows readers to develop an overall evaluation "of the consequences of information contained on an organization's Web site and its links," including a list of issues to consider. (*Nonprofit Handbook: Management,* Third Edition)

Legal & Regulatory

"Law and Taxation" by Bruce Hopkins. Nonprofit organizations in the United States are regulated at both the federal and state levels of government. Hopkins summarizes this extensive body of law and concludes with a checklist that enables nonprofit leaders to review the status of their organization under and compliance with the law. (*Nonprofit Handbook: Management,* Third Edition)

Evolutionary Environment

Leadership

"Leadership and the Self-Renewing Organization" by Joseph E. Champoux. Self-renewing organizations have strong core values that focus the behavior of all organization members. They continually adapt to their environments in an unrelenting pursuit of their mission. Self-renewing organizations have the unique qualities of innovation, growth, and continuous learning. Leadership is an influence process where the leader tries to affect the behavior of a follower or potential follower. Power is a central feature of leadership, with leaders getting power from their organizational positions and personal qualities. Leaders and managers play important but different roles in an organization. Leaders seek change; managers keep a steady direction. Leadership is the driving force that can transform an organization into a self-renewing one. Charisma, self-confidence, and building trust are characteristics that can help a leader energize followers to pursue a vision of becoming a self-renewing system. The continual growth of such organizations requires these and other leadership qualities. Knowledge and vision of the leader, plus the intellectual stimulation of followers, infuses SROs with critical skills to adapt to opportunities in their environment. (*Nonprofit Handbook: Management,* Third Edition)

"Shared Leadership: Relationship Management to Improve Nonprofit Organization Effectiveness" by Craig L. Pearce, Monica L. Perry, and Henry P. Sims, Jr. Sharing leadership within the nonprofit organization can contribute to relationship management and thus effectiveness in nonprofit organizations. Shared leadership is a strategic organizational technique in which multiple members of the team share in the leadership of the team. Pearce, Perry, and Sims explain why shared leadership is highly related to team dynamics and team effectiveness. This chapter defines the concept of shared leadership, explains the likely outcomes of shared leadership in nonprofit organizations, outlines the circumstances under which one would want to develop shared leadership, and describes how to develop shared leadership. (*Nonprofit Handbook: Management,* Third Edition)

"Relational Models of Leadership for the Next Century Not-for-Profit Organization Manager" by Kenneth L. Murrell. The days of the command and control models of leadership are gone, and "with them the myth of the charismatic and great hero leader." All sectors of our economy are exploring new models of leadership that see great potential in the broader concepts of shared and relational leadership. This chapter outlines current thinking, plus explanations and suggestions for why the nonprofit sector in particular needs to give relational models serious thought and more extensive application. It points out the many successful cases now appearing that demonstrate how an empowered workforce is the organization's greatest asset. As that evolves, both the need for liberating structures and organizations as new-styled work communities will be important areas for development. New leadership models will be necessary for developing the nonprofit organizations able to adapt, cope, and survive into the next century. (*Nonprofit Handbook: Management,* 1998 Supplement)

"Governance—Creating Capable Leadership in the Nonprofit Sector" by Keith Seel, M. Michelle Regel, and Milena M. Meneghetti. As we enter the new millennium, the nonprofit sector is under growing pressure to demonstrate effective leadership and accountability. Nonprofits are faced with funding reductions, aggressive competition from other nonprofits, pressure to assume or augment many services traditionally provided by governments, and the challenges of managing their own increasingly complex and sophisticated organizations—usually in the face of different and even conflicting expectations from stakeholders. This chapter outlines three governance models and their operating principles before focusing on the important applications of the policy-governance model and the Deloitte & Touche model. Of particular utility and importance are its guidelines for implementing these models that will no doubt serve as highly useful checklists for nonprofit senior leaders. (*Nonprofit Handbook: Management,* Third Edition)

Human Resource Development and Management

Board of Directors

"Board of Directors: Strategic Vision" by Jeffrey L. Brudney. Providing a mission and vision for the volunteer corps has typically received scant, if any, attention, warns Brudney. The self-renewing organization sought by cutting-edge nonprofit agencies to cope with an increasingly turbulent, interdependent, global environment requires a much more sustained and specific focus on volunteers. To survive and thrive in this competitive marketplace, the SRO must put each of its resources not just to good, but to superior use. The board, he stresses, must seriously consider, appraise, formulate, and support a vision that will galvanize volunteers (and paid staff) toward the attainment of the exciting future conceived for the organization. After explaining how many boards become "mired in unproductive syndromes that stymie attention to the volunteer effort," Brudney turns to developing the mission and vision for the volunteer corps. Finally, he outlines approaches to implement the volunteer corps vision. Specifically, he explains how the board must provide three key elements for the volunteer program, including a basic structure for the program, appropriate policies for governing the program, and risk management and insurance protection for nonpaid personnel. (*Nonprofit Handbook: Management,* Third Edition)

Professional Staff

"Strategic Education Planning—An Executive Leadership Tool" by Suzanne J. Lulewicz. Education and training in the nonprofit organization "is far-reaching in the results it hopes to produce," explains Lulewicz. "Its work reaches out to members to certify them in their professional skills, set work standards, meet regulatory criteria, and, in many cases, ensure that the public health and safety is not compromised through the work of industry and professional members." After contrasting for-profit and nonprofit strategic education planning, she stresses that nonprofits can achieve significant competitive advantages through insights into the marketplace's future. Key trends in the proactive shift to strategic educational planning include advances in technology that will continue to revolutionize the way education and training are developed and delivered, a focus shift to interventions in performance improvement, the proliferation of integrated high-performance work systems, and the transformation into learning organizations. Lulewicz offers highly applicable guidelines on how nonprofits can understand these trends and capitalize on them. She concludes by explaining in straightforward terms how to initiate a strategic education planning process, the strategic analysis, and the strategic education plan. (*Nonprofit Handbook: Management*, Third Edition)

"Employment-Related Benefits" by Sally A. Zinno. During the last half of the twentieth century, the amount spent on employment-related supplements in the United States rose at a rate 11 times faster than that of salaries and wages. Zinno provides the objectives of compensation systems within nonprofit organizations and their financial considerations. She addresses key questions relating to developing and managing the benefits program, including communicating with employees about their benefits. Of particular importance to nonprofit leaders is the understanding she provides regarding the Social Security Act, the Fair Labor Standards Act, the Employee Retirement Income Security Act (ERISA), the Consolidated Omnibus Budget Reconciliation Act (COBRA), and the Family and Medical Leave Act. (*Nonprofit Handbook: Management*, Third Edition)

Volunteers

"Volunteer Management" by Jeanne H. Bradner. Due to changing demographics and a treacherous legal environment, nonprofits are hard pressed to stay abreast of rapid changes in volunteer development, management, and liability. Changes in volunteerism mirror the rapid changes in our society. Identifying, motivating, recruiting, training, orienting, and retaining volunteers is a constant challenge. Even more challenging is staying abreast of developments and trends in the treacherous world of liability and risk management for volunteers. Organizations using volunteers must protect themselves and their leaders from the increasing threat of successful lawsuits and legal actions. Ignorance of risk avoidance and risk management has been disastrous for many nonprofit and public service organizations. Bradner leads the reader phase by phase through the complete cycle of volunteer participation. Of particular usefulness to readers are the many checklists and forms she provides to assist them at whatever stage they may be in the volunteer cycle. (*Nonprofit Handbook: Management*, Third Edition)

"Policies for Volunteer Organizations" by Linda L. Graff. Graff begins with the fundamentals of what and why policies are needed, then takes readers through the development process of how to write policies specifically for volunteer programs. Of particular usefulness are her recommendations relating to policy formulation and compliance issues. (*Volunteer Management Handbook*)

"Episodic Volunteering" by Nancy Macduff, who outlines the nature and importance of short-term volunteering. She identifies barriers to short-term volunteers, and then explains the essential factors needed to recruit and sustain this type of volunteer whose numbers are growing. (*Volunteer Management Handbook*)

"Volunteer and Staff Relations" by Nancy Macduff. A positive relationship between volunteers and staff is essential to a healthy nonprofit organization. However, for too many nonprofits, the tensions that exist between volunteers and employee coworkers can become the "dirty little secret of volunteerism." This chapter outlines the secrets behind a successful volunteer–staff team. Starting with the characteristics of the effective volunteer–staff team and how they are selected, trained, and supported, Macduff explores the three basic types of volunteer–staff teams and how they differ, and assesses their strengths and uses. A volunteer–staff climate audit is another important tool that is explained as a means to monitor changes in the working environment. Negative tensions that can develop between volunteers and staff are usually attributed to three basic causes: professional status, profiting from charity, and delicate management. Each needs a specific strategy that helps ensure that negative tensions are defused before they undermine morale and teamwork. The discussion concludes with an explanation of a successful sequential process to build an effective volunteer–staff team, including practical tips to enhance volunteer–staff relations. (*Nonprofit Handbook: Management,* 1998 Supplement)

"Volunteer Screening" by Linda L. Graff. For nonprofits, ensuring that the best candidates are recruited and placed has always been important. But over the last five years, Graff points out, "volunteer screening has become as much a matter of doing everything reasonable to keep the bad apples out as about achieving a proper fit between the volunteer's skills/interests and the demands of the volunteer position. Screening has become as much about techniques to keep the inappropriate or dangerous candidates out as it is about locating and placing the best candidates for the position." The potential consequences of inadequate screening protocol are all too obvious, including:

- Abuse of clients by volunteers
- Fraud; theft of agency or client resources
- Violence; sexual harassment toward clients, staff, or other volunteers
- Negative public relations for the agency, resulting in a loss of public trust
- Personal or organizational liability resulting in damaging and potentially ruinous lawsuits

After reviewing the legal principles in screening, Graff discusses the "sliding scale of screening," the organization's screening protocol. Of particular usefulness is her inclusion of many checklists and guides to help nonprofits through this vital process. (*Nonprofit Handbook: Management,* Third Edition)

"Risk Management in Volunteer Programs" by Linda L. Graff. Risk realities, are you current? Graff suggests that the fastest way for managers of volunteers to catch up to current risk realities is to engage in an exercise called *disaster imaging.* Consider the range of answers to this question: *What are the worst things that you can imagine going wrong in your volunteer department, or because of the involvement of volunteers at your organization?*

- Think about direct service volunteers and administrative (board and committee volunteers).
- Think about accidents, injuries, and financial and public trust issues.
- Think about personal and organizational liabilities.

Here is a typical list from her workshop participants who answer this same question:

- Accidents
- Injury
- Volunteer stepping outside of job description, exceeding skills or authority
- Substandard performance by volunteers, resulting in harm to clients
- Breach of confidentiality
- Loss or damage to property (physical, financial, electronic, intellectual)
- Theft, misappropriation of funds, fraud

- Abuse of client (physical, emotional, sexual, financial)
- Loss of agency reputation, organizational credibility, public trust
- Loss of ability to raise funds in the future
- Death (of client, volunteer, staff, general public)

One does not have to stretch the imagination to identify multiple disaster possibilities that could happen virtually any day of any week. The risks associated with voluntary action come in many shapes and sizes, but one thing is certain: The risks are both bigger and more prevalent than ever before. This chapter outlines the risk management process and a four-step risk management model, complete with tips on how to put the model to effective use. Following the risk management model should prompt managers to ask not only the right questions, but the right questions *in the right order,* that help to produce risk management solutions throughout the organization. Very few programs involve no risks at all, and very few risky situations are managed with only one risk control mechanism. "Fully evaluating the range of risks that prevail and then systematically exploring all risk reduction mechanisms can generate a properly tailored constellation of mechanisms for each situation. The process will help organizations operate within their own risk tolerance zones. The kind of comprehensive program review that a risk management process entails will often generate more productive and satisfying volunteer involvement, and more effective services to consumers as well," Graff concludes. Not engaging in risk management will not make the risks go away. In fact, not managing and controlling risks will simply increase liability and increase the odds of losing a legal action if, or when, one is launched. Don't find yourself waking up one morning, saying *"If only I had paid more attention to. ..."* Get ahead of risks by learning the lessons and understanding effective risk management techniques. (*Nonprofit Handbook: Management,* Third Edition)

"Training, Education, and Development Management Map (TEDMM): Identifying Learning Needs of Volunteers" by Stephen Hobbs. Volunteers are the backbone for many nonprofits, providing a myriad of services to the organization and its clients. Few would argue the importance of training and education for volunteers; however, determining with relative preciseness what these needs are and how to fulfill them is the challenge addressed by Hobbs in this chapter. Using his volunteer resource management system as a guide, Hobbs outlines the steps involved in the design, development, implementation, and evaluation of a training and education management map to be used by nonprofit managers to identify and meet the learning needs of volunteers. The evolving volunteer resource management discipline is changing "the parental/parochial framework to a collaborative/participatory framework," he explains. Within this framework, volunteers and staff work together in the design, development, administration, and evaluation of organizational programs. Central to Dr. Hobbs's successful volunteer education approach is the creation of a volunteer resource training, education, and development management map (TEDMM). He explains its use and how it provides a systematic approach for staff and volunteers to create a learning strategy that supports the overall volunteer resource management system and the goals of the organization. By adopting and using the TEMM, the organization is better assured of quality services and delivery, plus it gains a significant new recruiting and retention tool. (*Nonprofit Handbook: Management,* 1999 Supplement)

Endnotes

1. Fulghum, R. (1988). *All I Really Need to Know I Learned in Kindergarten.* New York: Villard Books, p. 6.
2. Morrison, P., and P. Morrison. (2000). "Wonders: The Internet as Hardware," *Scientific American* 282(6): 113; *http://www.sciam.com.*

2 Management Context of Nonprofit Organizations in the New Millennium: Diversity, Quality, Technology, Global Environment, and Ethics*

JOSEPH E. CHAMPOUX, PhD
Robert O. Anderson Schools of Management
University of New Mexico

2.1. Introduction

Frances Hesselbein, former executive director of the Girl Scouts of America, moved that organization from a plodding bureaucracy to a responsive, customer-focused organization. During her time as executive director, membership increased to 2.3 million, following eight years of dropping membership.[1] Her first steps focused on reassessing the mission (or vision) of the Girl Scouts. In her words, "We kept asking ourselves very simple questions. ... What is our business? Who is the customer? And what does the customer

---

*Portions of this chapter were adapted and reprinted by permission from Joseph E. Champoux. (2000). *Organizational Behavior: Essential Tenets for a New Millennium,* Chapters 2 and 3. Cincinnati, OH: South-Western College Publishing. Copyright © 2000 by South-Western College Publishing. All rights reserved.

consider value?"[2] Hesselbein is widely credited with successfully changing the Girls Scouts of America by refocusing its mission on its customer.

Frances Hesselbein was operating as a nonprofit organization executive within one of the five contexts that will affect nonprofit management in the future. Her customer focus comes from the context of managing for quality, which carries a heavy customer emphasis. Other contexts discussed in this chapter are workforce diversity, technology, the global environment, and ethics. Each context surrounds modern nonprofit organizations and presents major opportunities for the agile manager as we move into the new millennium.

Much of the research published about organizations in these five contexts comes from studies of for-profit organizations. The discussions of each area draw from this research and include nonprofit organization examples. A final section presents the implications of each context for such organizations and their management. Section 2.7 focuses squarely on nonprofit organizations moving into the new millennium.

2.2   Diversity

Workforce diversity refers to variations in workforce composition based on personal and background factors of employees or potential employees.[3-8] Those factors include age, gender, race, ethnicity, physical ability, and sexual orientation. Other factors include family status, such as a single parent, a dual-career relationship, or a person with responsibilities for aging parents. Exhibit 2.1 shows the dimensions of workforce diversity often discussed by diversity researchers.[9-10] A quick look at that exhibit will show you the complexity and scope of the issues surrounding this topic.

The Bureau of Labor Statistics (BLS) projections of the U.S. civilian labor force growth between 1996 and 2006 show significant changes.[11] BLS projections show civilian labor force growth of 11 percent between 1996 and 2006. The number of women in the labor force is projected to grow by 14 percent, a rate above the total projected growth. Projected growth for men is 9 percent, a rate below the total projected growth. Labor force projections by age show a large increase in those aged 55 and over (44 percent) and much smaller

EXHIBIT 2.1 Dimensions of Workforce Diversity

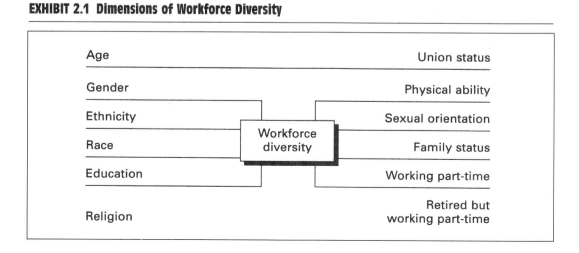

increases for young workers (ages 16 to 24, 15 percent). The race/ethnic projections show a small increase in white workers (9 percent). Most of the projected increase in the labor force by 2006 will come from minority workers.

If the BLS projections hold true, the workforce of the twenty-first century will have more female and minority workers. Age diversity will also continue, with 15 percent of the labor force at age 55 or over in the year 2006. The expected gender and ethnic profile of the labor force in the year 2006 shows 47 percent women and 29 percent minority workers.

Regional variations will also be significant. The projections discussed so far were for the entire civilian labor force. Local population characteristics will affect the workforce from which a specific organization draws.[12] For example, some projections say California's population in 2005 will consist of 50 percent white and 50 percent people of color, speaking 80 languages.[13]

People from different social backgrounds, cultures, and language groups bring different world views to an organization.[14] They view issues and problems at work through different perceptual lenses. If properly managed, these different views present opportunities for organizations, but they also increase the potential for conflict. The challenge for managers is to focus those diverse views on the mission of the organization while managing conflict to keep it at a functional level.

People with different needs and expectations also present challenges to an organization's personnel and work policies. Working parents often require adaptations in work schedules or on-site day care. Single parents may need time off to take a sick child to a physician. Native Americans may need special work schedules during their culture's periods of celebration. A disabled person can require special access to a building and a specially designed work area. Part-time workers may need to arrange job sharing so the organization can get the value of their talents.

There are various definitions of managing diversity.[15] Some organizations and their managers only react to the increasing diversity they see in their workforce. They seek to manage diversity so people of all backgrounds have equal access to employment, promotion, and personnel policies. Other organizations and their managers value diversity. They aggressively embrace it and actively try to build a diverse workforce.[16–17] Such organizations view a diverse workforce as a distinct competitive advantage.

Managing diversity requires a manager to focus on creating an environment that harnesses the potential of all sources of difference within an organization's workforce. Managers can actively tap the diverse perspectives and rethink their approach to tasks and markets. For example, after hiring its first Hispanic female attorney, a small Northeastern law firm discovered a new market because of her unique views. She wanted to pursue English-only employment policies in cases involving immigrants. The previously all-white legal staff had never thought of that market.[18]

Managing diversity is not affirmative action in disguise. Instead, it is managing to get the greatest contributions from increasingly diverse people. It recognizes that a variety of views from diverse peoples enrich organizational life. Managing diversity does not ask diverse people to give up their individuality and take on the values of the majority. It honors differences among people, but also asks everyone to accept the core values of the organization. Ideally, those core values should be related to the organization's mission, such as "an unending pursuit of excellence in customer service." Such a mission statement sets out the organization's goal, not how to reach it. People reach the goal in many different ways because of their diversity.

Why should managers and their organizations care about meeting the expectations and requirements of a diverse workforce? Could they not select people who fit into the organization's existing culture, policies, and procedures? The answer has two parts: (1) managers will have no choice about managing for diversity, and (2) successfully managing for diversity is good business strategy.

The first answer follows from the labor force statistics discussed earlier. Organizations that do not have a diverse workforce now are likely to face one in the future, especially as they pursue scarce skilled labor. Other organizations have followed affirmative action and Equal Employment Opportunity guidelines and directives. Those organizations now have diverse workforces.[19–21]

The second answer implies a more aggressive management position toward workforce diversity. Good business strategy in the changing world of the twenty-first century requires unleashing a diverse workforce's potential.[22–23] The reasons are twofold: (1) the increasing diversity of U.S. society and (2) the need to think and compete globally to remain competitive.[24]

As society becomes increasingly diverse, clients and customers also become more diverse. Having a diverse workforce helps managers attract customers from diverse backgrounds. For example, Pizza Hut found that the presence of Muslim workers attracted more Muslim customers.[25]

As society becomes increasingly diverse, client needs become more diverse as well. Frances Hesselbein noted the changes in the population when she led the development of the Daisy Scout program. More working mothers than ever before needed preschool day care. The program had 150,000 5-year-old girls by 1990, many of whom would continue with other Girl Scout programs at a later age.[26]

The global environment of modern organizations adds another layer of complexity to workforce diversity. Many U.S. organizations sell in foreign markets, operate in countries outside the United States, or enter joint ventures with organizations from other countries. Because U.S. organizations operating abroad often employ native-born people at all levels, managers could interact with employees from other countries. To meet customer expectations in foreign markets, they need to understand local customs and business practices. To be successful, U.S. managers must understand cultural differences around the world and not assume that client and customer requirements in foreign markets are the same as at home.

Organizations face many challenges when managing for diversity.[27–29] The goal of managing for diversity is to unleash the potential of a diverse workforce and channel it toward the organization's goals. The challenge for managers and leaders is to provide vision so everyone understands where the organization is headed. Managers also want to preserve a diversity of viewpoints and help employees get the satisfaction they want from their work experiences.

Managing for diversity forces many organizations to make major changes, such as modifying personnel policies concerning work schedules, personal leave, language training, and other basic skills. Managers must manage for fairness when meeting the diverse needs of their workforce.[30] For example, a day care policy originally created to meet the needs of working women must apply to all employees despite gender and marital status. Managers will also need to learn new skills such as accepting differences, appreciating language differences, and even learning new languages. The latter can include sign language to communicate with hearing-impaired employees.

Other changes touch the heart of an organization's culture by asking for shifts in its values, rituals, and assumptions.[31] Values suitable to a homogeneous white male culture will need to yield to the heterogeneous values of many diverse groups.[32] Social activities that are rituals in male cultures will need to change to allow female managers ready access, or rotate activities to meet the desires of both groups. For example, if social gatherings of managers usually include only male-oriented sports, other activities should be added. Instead of assuming that all managers like a hard game of flag football, the gathering's organizers could poll people for their preferences.

Managing diversity offers the nonprofit leader the opportunity and challenge of creating an organizational environment that harnesses and optimizes the inherent potential of its workforce. A key focus is to progress toward shared goals that channel the "energy" of differences into prideful cohesion, pulling together as a winning team. Nonprofit organizations, with their public service commitment, have some advantages over other types of organizations in this regard.

2.3 Quality*

A major thrust of American management into the twenty-first century is the management for quality of products and services. Although the roots of quality management can be traced to the early 1920s, American organizations did not embrace it until the early 1980s.[33–34] Quality management has many names, including Total Quality Control, Total Quality Management, Total Quality Leadership, Leadership Through Quality, Market-Driven Quality, and Continuous Process Improvement.[35–36] Terms and ideas emphasized in the late 1990s include Robust Design and six-sigma quality.[37] The term *quality management* (QM) embraces all programs of quality management and continuous quality improvement.

Quality management is a philosophy and system of management built on concepts dating back to the 1920s.[38–40] QM includes principles, tools, and techniques that can help nonprofit organizations manage for quality services, products, processes, and relationships. Although its roots are in manufacturing, it is a management system that can result in major improvements for any nonprofit organization.

The focus of QM is the management of quality, although long-term cost reductions and increased profit often result. It readily applies to the management of nonprofit organizations and the internal processes of any organization or group. QM focuses an entire organization on continuous improvement in its product or service.

Effective QM requires a total system view of the organization that reaches well beyond its boundaries. It uses an understanding of interdependence with outside people, outside organizations, and groups within the organization, to better manage for quality. The list of those stakeholders—groups with an interest in the organization's activities—is long. It includes employees, suppliers, donors, board members, volunteers, clients, customers, patrons, constituents, members, the community surrounding the organization, coalitions of which the organization is part, professional or trade associations, chapters of the organization, and competitors for the same funds or clients.

QM can provide many benefits to nonprofit organizations that do not directly result from other approaches to management. Managers (executive directors, managers, pro-

---

* Part of this section originally appeared in J. E. Champoux and L. D. Goldman. (1993). "Building a Total Quality Culture." In *Nonprofit Organizations Policies and Procedures Handbook,* T. D. Connors, ed. New York: John Wiley & Sons, pp. 54–55. Copyright © 1993 by John Wiley & Sons, Inc. Reprinted by permission of John Wiley & Sons, Inc.

gram directors, administrators, and development directors) can expect lower costs of providing a service, doing research, starting a social issues campaign, or manufacturing a product. Service processes will function more dependably. Research will be more focused and cost effective. Issues can be targeted and communicated more effectively. Products will have higher reliability.

Employee, board, and volunteer commitment to continuous quality improvement will increase, if the individuals involved perceive benefits or results. The result can be more loyalty to the organization, improved funding potential, easier volunteer and board recruitment, and more lasting social change. QM's assumption of high interdependence among many system parts to get continuous quality improvement can lead to better cooperation and clarity with outside contractors, suppliers, vendors, coalition partners, and the community.

QM differs from other systems of management in several specific ways. QM emphasizes a long-term commitment to continuous quality improvement. It stresses that quality is everyone's job, not only the job of a hospital's quality assurance department, the executive director of a refugee services center, or the administrator of a cooperative pottery studio. It is intensely client-focused—a focus it requires of all organization members.

This system emphasizes cooperation among people in any unit that has adopted QM and with people outside the unit. QM also emphasizes high involvement in the work process. It assumes that people want high involvement in their work or that managers and supervisors can create that involvement.

QM also emphasizes communication in all directions: top-down, bottom-up, and laterally. This feature follows directly from the requirements of cooperation and high involvement. It also is a way QM generates large amounts of information in the system. Many nonprofit organizations already have such communication systems. Some examples are those with experience using cross-departmental task forces; participative decision making; multicultural staffs, boards, volunteers, or clients; and community and client involvement in policy development; as well as those with a decentralized organization design.

Managers who adopt the QM philosophy develop a long-term orientation, a view to the future. It is not the here and now that is important. The decisions made today by anyone in the organization must be made with the future in mind. Being good now is not enough. Being great is the goal—a passionate pursuit of continuous improvement.

QM's emphasis on continuous improvement of all processes in an organization lets people do more with the same resources. The involvement of everyone in continuous improvement can add challenge to people's jobs. The long-term effect for an organization is a committed corps of people with an impassioned focus on mission, client, and continuous quality improvement.

Peter Drucker's analysis of high-performing nonprofit organizations suggests that they have many features that support a move toward QM.[41–42] The strongest supportive features are a mission focus, a client focus, and self-motivated volunteers.

A mission focus gives people in the organization a clear sense of direction and reason for being. A strong client focus keeps the nonprofit organization focused on client needs. Both foci can remind members of the organization of the need to constantly improve what they offer to their environment. Self-motivated volunteers are a key resource for nonprofit organizations to achieve their mission. They already want to do well. QM can show them how to continuously do better.

Drucker's observations about high-performing nonprofit organizations should have reminded you of the description of QM presented earlier. If your organization is not performing as well as it can, then QM can help improve its performance in several ways.

QM's emphasis on continuous improvement of all processes in an organization will let nonprofit organizations do more with fewer, equal, or new dollars.[43] The agitation to do more for a nonprofit organization's clients is consistent with the philosophies of those organizations and the philosophies of staff and volunteers. The involvement of everyone in continuous improvement can add challenges to employees' and volunteers' jobs. The long-term effect for a nonprofit organization is a highly committed corps of people with an impassioned focus on mission and client.

Moving toward managing for quality typically presents massive change to an organization and its managers. A passionate customer focus, combined with a process view that emphasizes continuous improvement, requires people to reframe the way they think about their organization. Such transformations of thinking are difficult to make and might account for many failures in the journey to quality.[44–48]

2.4 Technology

Massive changes in computing power and computer features, combined with communication technology, will revolutionize much of what organizations will do in the future. Desktop computers with CD-ROM drives, high-speed processors, and large memory capacity will let people create business presentations using three-dimensional animated technology. Laptop and palmtop computers will allow Internet connections using ports in airport telephones, aircraft telephones, or cybercafes.[49] Tracking appointments and staying connected will continue to get easier into the future.

Sweeping changes in communications technology will open unusual opportunities. To better understand these changes, keep in mind that the first transatlantic telephone cable carried only 89 simultaneous calls.[50]

New digital satellite systems will allow handheld digital cellular communication anywhere in the world.[51–52] Lucent Technology's Bell Labs' wave-division multiplexing technology splits a single beam of light into multiple colors. Each color acts as a separate communication channel within an optical fiber, increasing the fiber's capacity.[53] Using the Nokia 9000i Communicator, a manager can send and receive e-mail, talk to a person by telephone, and surf the Web—from anywhere.[54]

Electronically based measurement systems will monitor manufacturing processes in modern factories and collect sales data at store checkout stands. Future computer technologies will digitize information directly from voice interaction and handwriting on a digital tablet. Handheld computers will allow retailers to track inventories and send orders electronically. Navigation satellites will let trucking and shipping firms track entire fleets. Communication satellites will let managers talk to drivers and ship captains anywhere in the world.

E-mail, voice mail, videoconferencing, and teleconferencing are widely used and will increase in use in the future. Videoconferencing adds a two-way video connection to the now-common teleconference.

A revolution in materials technology and engineering is now unfolding and will continue into the future. Some materials already in use are carbon fiber composites and optical fibers, the basis of tennis rackets and communication cable, respectively. Others, such as superpolymers, amorphous metal alloys, and superconductors, will add to a growing list of human-created materials. Innovations in product ideas and technological solutions no longer depend on naturally existing materials.[55–56]

New materials will replace steel and aluminum, making it possible to build lighter cars and trucks that can carry heavier loads. New ceramics technology allows designing jet engines with more thrust. The new engines weigh less than aluminum engines, letting larger planes go longer distances with more people and cargo.

Organizations will increasingly create internal networks called intranets and connect to the Internet.[57] These networks will change the way people interact in the future and change the ways managers should think about their roles. Employees in any part of the organization, even one with wide-ranging global operations, can effortlessly interact.

Manufacturing in the future will feature agile manufacturing processes that keep almost no inventory and use computer-based technology for direct links with customers or end users. These processes will be cost-effective and competitive in producing both single custom-made items and large production runs, all within the same manufacturing plant. The products moving through these processes can differ from item to item.[58–59]

Innovations in manufacturing will occur because of new advances in computer-assisted manufacturing (CAM), computer-integrated manufacturing (CIM), modern materials, robotics, laser methods of cutting and bonding, and the like. The list of changes is almost endless, and no one can predict all the new technologies of the future that will help manufacturing processes.

Internet technology will let suppliers receive parts orders as a manufacturer updates a manufacturing schedule in real time. Ford Motor Company, for example, has built an impressive intranet–Internet system that links 120,000 workstations worldwide.[60] The precision of the system lets a car seat supplier know the color sequence of the next shipment of seats. Workers uncrate the blue seats at the seat installation station as the blue cars reach the station.

Managerial roles will change because a manager might have people in scattered places. The networks, not face-to-face interaction, will act as the coordinating mechanisms. A growing number of employees will telecommute, working from their homes.[61–62]

Flexibility will also be a key feature of new strategies. Such flexibility will permeate the design and response of manufacturing and service operations. It will include a thorough understanding of customer needs and variations among markets. The latter will be especially true for companies that compete globally. Markets in different countries feature high diversity, even between countries that are not far apart. Management must respond to those differences by treating the customers of the different countries in the way they expect.

A decentralized organizational design is needed to attain the goals of a strategy that emphasizes flexibility and customer needs. This organizational design moves decisions down to the lowest level in the organization, where quick responses are needed to meet shifting markets and customer needs. The close ties to both suppliers and customers will require cross-functional teams that tightly integrate many parts of the total business process. Local teams with broad decision-making and problem-solving authority will help even large organizations decentralize. The modern information technologies described earlier will let the most globally dispersed organization reach decentralization on a scale previously not possible.

Organization-wide self-managing work teams will be another management change induced by new technologies.[63–64] An organization forms such teams around a specific client base or product. In the first case, such teams can make all decisions in response to client needs. In the second case, teams can conceive, design, build, and market a service or product. In both instances, the self-managing teams are involved in all parts of a process that affects clients or products. Such teams will also become involved in the hiring process by doing much of the selection and early socialization of new employees completely within the team.

Companies also can link to various partners over the Internet, creating "virtual organizations." Aditi Inc., for example, offers customer support with a twist to software users.[65] Based in Seattle and Bangalore, India, the company provides 24-hour support. After American workers go home, messages transfer over the Internet to Bangalore. The reverse happens at the end of the Indian work day. Customers get almost immediate response, no matter what their time zone.

The Internet is bringing fast changes to worldwide commerce.[66] Forecasters predict $327 billion in Internet commerce by 2002. The biggest growth areas in such commerce are computers, catalogs, books, and software. Amazon.com Inc., the online bookseller, offers 3 million titles, outstripping Barnes & Noble's 175,000 titles. Setting up a commercial Web site is now so simple that observers predict a flood of upstarts will become a new generation of competitors in many industries.

2.5 *Global Environment*

The global environment of organizations demands that modern managers have an international focus that was never required before. Modern managers must begin to think beyond the domestic environment of their organizations. Now the world is their environment, and will become more so in the future. For some organizations, thinking internationally means finding new markets outside the home country; for others, becoming a multinational organization operating in many countries; and for others, becoming a transnational organization whose decisions are not limited by country boundaries. Modern managers must think of the entire planet as a source of labor and materials, places of production, and markets.[67–68] The powerful effects of our highly interconnected world were apparent during the Southeast Asian economic crisis of 1998. Market declines in that part of the world reverberated throughout markets in the United States, Europe, and Latin America.[69]

Modern technology both enables and compels a global view.[70–71] Thanks to modern aircraft, international travel is common and fast. Telecommunication satellites let information in all forms move quickly from country to country. Managers of the same company working in different countries can easily hold videoconferences. Direct computer transfers of information among countries are as easy as using a computer and a modem to dial the telephone number of a computer with a modem in another country.

Advances in technology are not the only reason modern managers are taking a global view. Regional trade agreements are opening vast new markets,[72–73] possibly increasing the competition faced by a firm. The North American Free Trade Agreement (NAFTA) opened the borders of Mexico, Canada, and the United States to easy movement of goods, capital, and services.[74] Europe took similar steps to encourage freer trade among its countries. The movement of 11 European countries to a single currency (the Euro) should enhance freer trade among its users.[75]

The combination of sweeping technological and market changes presents major opportunities to managers with a global orientation. The opportunities are not limited to large organizations. For example, Blue Sky Natural Beverage Company of Santa Fe, New Mexico, has successfully entered markets in Japan, Singapore, and the United Kingdom. Although Blue Sky is a small company without the resources of a multinational giant, its founders saw a new market for their products, worked toward it, and successfully entered it.[76]

Thinking globally raises many issues for managers. An obvious difficulty is the language difference among countries. Forming partnerships with local businesspeople or learning the language oneself can help solve the language problem. More difficult are the issues that stem from the cultural differences among countries. Understanding these differences can be difficult because outsiders are often not even aware of them. Yet cultural differences affect how a company enters markets, the way it markets goods or services, how it deals with labor laws, and how it builds a loyal customer base.

Many cultural differences appear in people's orientation to space and time.[77-78] North Americans ordinarily stand 5.5 to 8 feet apart while speaking. In Latin American cultures, people stand much closer. When a North American speaks to a Latin American in that person's home country, the Latin American moves close to the North American, who then feels uncomfortable and backs away. The Latin American might perceive the North American as cold and distant, an unintended communication of the nonverbal behavior.

Orientations to time and the meaning of time differ among cultures. Latin Americans view time more casually than North Americans. The latter value promptness in keeping appointments, a nonverbal behavior that is even more strongly emphasized by the Swiss. A North American or a Swiss might feel insulted if people were late for an appointment, although no insult was intended.

Egyptians usually do not look to the future, a state they define as anything more than a week away. South Asians think of the long term as centuries, not the typical five- or ten-year view of North Americans. The Sioux Indians of the United States do not have words for "time," "wait," or "waiting" in their native language. You can readily see that misunderstandings about time could arise in a face-to-face business meeting of people from different countries or among people in a culturally diverse workforce.

A major issue faced by managers of multinational organizations is the set of values they want globally dispersed operations to have. Do they want the values of the home country to dominate, or do they want to adopt those of the local culture? Managers who want their international units to hold the values of the home country place people from the home country in charge of those units. Organizations that hire local people for management positions often first socialize them to the major values of the home country organization. Hewlett-Packard has followed this practice for its worldwide operations. Managers know the "HP Way," whatever their national origins or the country in which they work.[79]

Cultural differences also define acceptable management behavior and preferences for organizational forms. One large cross-cultural research program found five dimensions of cultures that imply management and organizational differences in different countries.[80] The five dimensions are:

1. *Power distance:* Degree of inequality among people that a culture considers normal
2. *Uncertainty avoidance:* Value placed on predictability, structure, and stability
3. *Individualism:* Value placed on individual behavior, acting alone and not as part of a group
4. *Masculinity:* Value placed on decisiveness, assertiveness, independence, and individual achievement
5. *Long-term orientation:* Value placed on persistence, status, and thrift[81]

Variations along the power distance and uncertainty avoidance dimensions have especially strong implications for management and organizations. Exhibit 2.2 shows the

EXHIBIT 2.2 Cultural Differences in Uncertainty Avoidance and Power Distance

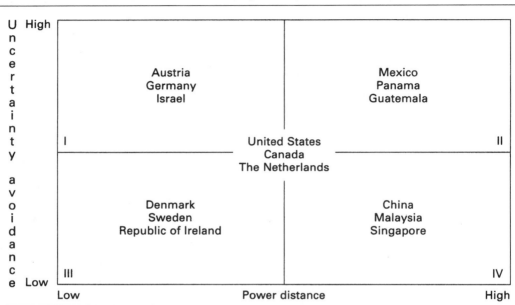

Source: G. Hofstede, *Cultures and Organizations: Software of the Mind.* New York: McGraw-Hill, 1991, Ch. 6.

position of several countries on these dimensions. The countries in each quadrant scored at the low or high ends of the dimensions. Those in the center of the figure had midlevel scores.

People in quadrant I countries prefer well-defined procedures and clear organizational structure. Rules and procedures guide daily behavior, with managers settling only exceptional matters. Quadrant II countries tend to use formal authority for coordination and simple structures that emphasize senior management's role. People in quadrant III countries rely less on formal rules and organizational form and more on direct interpersonal interactions to coordinate work activities. Quadrant IV countries rely on simple organizational forms and the use of direct supervision. The countries in the center of the exhibit rely on middle management to coordinate activities and to specify the desired results.

2.6   *Ethics*

Modern managers will feel growing pressure from the public and the government to behave ethically in all business transactions. This pressure will affect employees of all types of organizations, public or private.

Ethical behavior is behavior viewed as right and honorable; unethical behavior is behavior viewed as wrong and reprehensible.[82–83] These straightforward definitions raise some tough questions for managers and their organizations. First, what standards should they use to judge behavior as ethical or unethical? Second, how should the adjectives used to distinguish ethical from unethical behavior be defined? *Right* and *wrong* may have different meanings for different people. Standards of ethical behavior vary among country cultures. When issues of ethics are combined with the growing opportunities for global activities, the complexity of ethical questions in modern organizations becomes clear.[84]

Questions of ethics abound in organizations and affect management decisions. Is it ethical for an organization to withhold product safety information? Is it ethical for a person to use knowledge about human perception to affect the perception of an organization's customers or employees? Is it ethical for a nonprofit organization to not continuously improve the quality of its programs or services when clients do not demand it? Those are only three ethical questions from an almost endless list that nonprofit managers face.

Only a few in-depth studies of managers and ethical behavior exist. This type of research requires the cooperation of organizations and their managers, which is often hard to get.[85] Robert Jackall's *Moral Mazes* documents the complex and perplexing world of management decision making, where ethics often are not specific decision criteria.[86] Instead, managers find that their decisions are bound by context, leading to a situational form of ethics. Veteran managers navigate such moral mazes in ways that let them survive and succeed in their organizations.

Barbara Toffler's study of ethics and management reinforces this view of ethical ambiguity in management decisions.[87] Her extensive interview data showed that ethical dilemmas are common in management decision making and that the choices between right and wrong are not always clear. Although ethical concerns pervaded management decisions and actions, managers rarely used explicit ethical criteria during the decision process.[88]

Gallup polls taken between 1976 and 1997 found that the public did not view business executives as pillars of ethical behavior.[89] When people were asked which of 26 occupations they believed had "very high" or "high" ethics, pharmacists ranked the highest and car salespeople ranked the lowest. Business executives ranked near the middle, with a 16 to 22 percent endorsement. People in the United States do not have a positive view of ethics and behavior in organizations.

(A) ETHICAL AND UNETHICAL BEHAVIOR

Ethical behavior is behavior judged to be good, right, just, honorable, and praiseworthy. Unethical behavior is behavior judged to be wrong, reprehensible, or failing to meet an obligation.[90–93] The judgment of behavior as ethical or unethical is based on principles, rules, or guides that come from a specific ethical theory, character traits, or social values.[94–95]

The definitions of ethical and unethical behavior pose two nagging issues: the difficulty of finding a standard for judgment on which all reasonable people can agree, and the problem that *good* and *bad* or *right* and *wrong* have different meanings for different people and societies.

More confusion and controversy come from the distinction between what is subjectively and objectively ethical.[96] A person's action is subjectively ethical if that person believes he acted ethically. A person's action is objectively ethical if that person acted according to a rule or law. The same distinction applies to unethical behavior that the person intended (subjectively unethical) and unethical behavior that violates an established rule or law (objectively unethical).

Conflict can arise when a person believes he behaved ethically and other people who observed the behavior believe that person broke a law or rule. For example, doing business efficiently in some countries requires paying bribes. Some firms prohibit such bribes.[97] A manager who pays bribes because he believes it is ethical in a particular country (subjectively ethical) violates his employer's policies (objectively unethical). Conflict can then arise between the employee and the employer over such behavior.

(B)   "IT'S GOOD BUSINESS"

A basic assumption underlying this ethics discussion is that doing business ethically is good for business. That is the position of Robert C. Solomon, a philosophy professor at the University of Texas, Austin, and Kristine Hanson, a New York businesswoman. Together, they have written about business ethics and presented ethics workshops around the country.[98]

Solomon and Hanson argue that ethics is the keystone for smooth, effective, and efficient operation of business organizations. If we could not trust another person's word or feel confident that a person would keep contractual agreements, business as we now understand it would stop. Although some businesspeople behave unethically and do not get caught, unethical behavior can have long-term negative effects on a business. Customers who feel cheated will not return, or will sue, or will report the cheating business to law enforcement agencies. Ethical businesses develop a reputation of fair business dealings and concern for the effects of their decisions on society. They likely will face fewer punitive or regulatory efforts.

Solomon and Hanson take a long-term view of ethical management. They note that behaving ethically can be more costly in the short term than behaving unethically. For example, when a business adds safety equipment not required by law to a manufacturing operation, and another business in the same industry does not, the first company has higher manufacturing costs than the second. Although such ethical concerns can enhance the reputation of the first firm, its higher costs could make it less competitive.

2.7   *Implications for Nonprofit Organizations*

This section discusses the implications of the five contexts for nonprofit organizations and their management. These implications suggest changing one's thinking about managing a nonprofit organization in the new millennium.

The discussion of diversity raises some clear implications for nonprofit organizations concerning clients, volunteers, and marketing strategies. If the organization serves an increasingly diverse clientele, it likely should diversify its volunteer force. This step implies recruiting from places untouched in the past. A nonprofit organization in an area of a diverse minority population can recruit from that group to staff a volunteer force. The recruiting approaches could emphasize how the volunteers will help people similar to themselves.

Diversity implies finding new customers (previously noncustomers) in unusual places and forming unusual marketing strategies. It also requires an openness to difference to avoid the mistake of "righteous arrogance."[99] For example, a young assistant pastor designed a wonderful program for the newly married. He was shocked to find that no newlyweds arrived—only single people living together! They wanted advice on whether to marry. The assistant pastor wanted to remove them from the program. The wise senior pastor decided to press forward with his newfound customers.[100]

Quality management suggests implications for nonprofit organizations in the three areas of quality, customer focus, and continuous improvement. Delivering quality services distinguishes one organization from another, allowing it to draw attention to quality results.[101] Having a customer focus helps clearly define the clients and customers served. It also helps the organization discover the nonclients or noncustomers who could become clients or customers.

Diversity interacts with a customer focus, suggesting that organizations should look for customers in places where they have not looked before. Frances Hesselbein recognized the demographic changes in American society that created a need for the Daisy Scouts program. Five-year-old girls needed this special attention because many parents worked and placed their children in day care centers. Francis Hesselbein wanted those customers, and she got them.[102]

Quality management's continuous improvement emphasis implies that nonprofit managers should repeatedly reexamine the way the organization serves clients and customers. Many types of surgery are now done in day surgery units associated with a hospital. Much dissent centered around creating these innovative units that would not carry the overhead of an entire hospital. The result is the innovative delivery of certain surgeries at lower cost to ambulatory patients.[103]

Modern communication technology offers new ways of communicating with staff, volunteers, customers, and clients. A nonprofit organization can build an intranet (internal network) and connect to the Internet and the World Wide Web.[104] E-mail is a fast and widely used form of communication. A nonprofit organization can quickly disperse messages and updates to volunteers and paid staff. Volunteers and staff who have Internet access from their homes will feel connected to the organization even when they are not there.

The explosion in Internet commerce described earlier has strong implications for nonprofit organizations. Consider setting up a Web page for your organization if you do not already have one. Many nonprofit organizations have Web pages that describe their purpose and the results of their programs. The pages include periodic updates about their programs and plans. They also allow easy access for potential donors, who can donate money using a credit card. Some examples include the American Heart Association and the International Rescue Committee.[105]

Existing software makes Web page development available to nonprofit organizations of any size. The development cost also is not high. A technically experienced volunteer could easily develop a Web page. Costs include the price of the software, the one-time posting fee of about $100, and monthly fees to an Internet service provider.

Nonprofit organization leaders can take a lesson from the for-profits' global orientation. As previously noted, many organizations view the world as their markets and do not limit themselves to the domestic arena. Nonprofit organizations can do the same, albeit with their unique twist.

Fund-raising efforts can now go global. Many American expatriates likely feel committed to the causes of many nonprofit organizations. Citizens of countries outside the United States also can develop a commitment to a cause, especially if it reaches beyond domestic boundaries. For example, the Salvation Army operates in many countries; its reach for donations and volunteers goes well beyond U.S. borders.

Combining technology with a global orientation suggests other possibilities for nonprofit organizations. The World Wide Web is just that—worldwide. If you develop a Web page, you are almost instantly available to the entire world. You can get your message to almost anyone, anywhere, and seek donations from people everywhere.

The earlier observation that "it's good business" to do business ethically holds for nonprofit organizations as well as for-profit organizations, the context within which this view developed. Trust is the major result of ethical interactions within an organization, between the organization and its clients, and within fund-raising efforts. If people feel the organization behaves unethically, they likely will not volunteer. If potential donors perceive the organization engaging in unethical behavior, they likely will not donate. If paid staff view the organization's managers and leaders as unethical, they likely will search for other employment opportunities. The final price of behaving unethically is as high for nonprofit organizations as it is for for-profit organizations.

Ethics or integrity is a key leadership trait,[106] and leadership is essential for managing in the fast-changing environments nonprofit organizations will face in the new millennium. Followers such as paid staff, volunteers, and potential donors will not believe an unethical leader. All forces described in this chapter compel a need for ethical leadership to guide nonprofit organizations into the new millennium.

Endnotes

1. Byrne, J. A. (1990). "Profiting from the Nonprofits," *Business Week* (March 26): 66–70, 72, 74.
2. Id., p. 70.
3. Dass, P., and B. Parker. (1999). "Strategies for Managing Human Resource Diversity: From Resistance to Learning," *Academy of Management Executive* 13: 68–80.
4. Fernandez, J. P. (1991). *Managing a Diverse Workforce.* New York: Lexington.
5. Hayles, V. R., and A. M. Russell. (1997). *The Diversity Directive: Why Some Initiatives Fail & What to Do About It.* Chicago: Irwin Professional Publishing.
6. Jamieson, D., and J. O'Mara. (1991). *Managing Workforce 2000: Gaining the Diversity Advantage.* San Francisco: Jossey-Bass.
7. Rosener, J. B. (1995). *America's Competitive Secret: Utilizing Women as a Management Strategy.* New York: Oxford University Press.
8. Thomas, R. R. Jr. (1991). *Beyond Race and Gender: Unleashing the Power of Your Total Work Force by Managing Diversity.* New York: AMACOM.
9. Jackson, S. E. and Associates (eds.). (1992). *Diversity in the Workplace: Human Resources Initiatives.* New York: Guilford Press.
10. See note 6.
11. Fullerton, H. N. Jr. (1997). "Labor Force 2006: Slowing Down and Changing Composition," *Monthly Labor Review* 120: 23–38.
12. See note 4.
13. See note 6.
14. Bond, M. A., and J. L. Pyle. (1998). "The Ecology of Diversity in Organizational Settings: Lessons from a Case Study," *Human Relations* 51: 589–623.
15. Thomas, R. R. Jr. (1992). "Managing Diversity: A Conceptual Framework," In S. E. Jackson and Associates (eds.), *Diversity in the Workplace: Human Resources Initiatives.* New York: Guilford Press, pp. 306–17.
16. See note 3.
17. Loden, M., and J. B. Rosener. (1991). *Workforce America! Managing Employee Diversity as a Vital Resource.* Homewood, IL: Business One Irwin, pt. III.

18. Thomas, D. A., and R. J. Ely. (1996). "Making Differences Matter: A New Paradigm for Managing Diversity," *Harvard Business Review* (September–October): 79–90.

19. Alster, J., T. Brothers, and H. Gallo (eds.). (1992). In *Diversity Is Strength: Capitalizing on the New Work Force.* New York: The Conference Board.

20. See note 9.

21. Thomas, R. R. Jr. (1990). "From Affirmative Action to Affirming Diversity," *Harvard Business Review* (March–April): 107–17.

22. See note 3.

23. See note 21.

24. Jackson, S. E., and E. B. Alvarez. (1992). "Working through Diversity as a Strategic Imperative." In S. E. Jackson and Associates (eds.), *Diversity in the Workplace: Human Resources Initiatives.* New York: Guilford Press, pp. 13–29.

25. Roth, K. (1998). "God on the Job," *Working Woman* (February): 65–66.

26. Drucker, P. F. (1990). *Managing the Non-Profit Organization: Practices and Principles.* New York: HarperCollins.

27. See note 3.

28. See note 24.

29. Wolf, D. (1992). "Whither the Work Force?" In J. Alster, T. Brothers, and H. Gallo (eds.), *In Diversity Is Strength: Capitalizing on the New Work Force.* New York: The Conference Board, pp. 9–10.

30. See note 24.

31. Gottfredson, L. S. (1992). "Dilemmas in Developing Diversity Programs," In S.E. Jackson and Associates (eds.), *Diversity in the Workplace: Human Resources Initiatives.* New York: Guilford Press, pp. 279–305.

32. Rosener, J. B. (1990). "Ways Women Lead," *Harvard Business Review* (November–December): 119–25.

33. Garvin, D. A. (1988). *Managing Quality: The Strategic and Competitive Edge.* New York: The Free Press.

34. Gehani, R. R. (1993). "Quality Value-Chain: A Meta-Synthesis of Frontiers of Quality Movement," *Academy of Management Executive* 7: 29–42.

35. Rickard, N. E. Jr. (1991). "The Quest for Quality: A Race without a Finish Line," *Industrial Engineering* 23: 25–27.

36. Saylor, J. H. (1992). *TQM Field Manual.* New York: McGraw-Hill.

37. Bylinsky, G. (1998). "How to Bring Out Better Products Faster," *Fortune* (November 23): 238 [B]–238 [E], 238[J], 238[N], 238[R], 238[T].

38. Id.

39. See note 33.

40. Hackman, J. R., and R. Wageman. (1995). "Total Quality Management: Empirical Conceptual and Practical Issues," *Administrative Science Quarterly* 40: 309–42.

41. Drucker, P. F. (1989). "What Business Can Learn from Nonprofits," *Harvard Business Review* (July–August): 88–91.

42. See note 26.

43. Kotler, P., and E. L. Roberto. (1989). *Social Marketing: Strategies for Changing Public Behavior.* New York: The Free Press.

44. Cole, R. E. (1999). *Managing Quality Fads: How American Business Learned to Play the Quality Game.* New York: Oxford University Press.

45. See note 40.

46. Grant, R. M., R. Shani, and R. Krishnan. (1994). "TQM's Challenge to Management Theory and Practice," *Sloan Management Review* (Winter): 25–35.

47. Reger, R. K., L. T. Gustafson, S. M. DeMarie, and J. V. Mullane. (1994). "Reframing the Organization: Why Implementing Total Quality Is Easier Said Than Done," *Academy of Management Review* 19: 565–84.

48. Zabaracki, M. J. (1998). "The Rhetoric and Reality of Total Quality Management," *Administrative Science Quarterly* 43: 602–36.

49. Quain, J. R. (1998). "How to Shop for a Palmtop," *Fast Company* (September): 196–98, 202–203.

50. Cairncross, F. (1998). *The Death of Distance.* Boston: Harvard Business School Press.

51. Freund, J. (1998). "A Global Calling," *Wired* (August): 144.

52. Srinivasan, K. (2000). "Hands-free Net's on the Way," *Business Outlook, Albuquerque Journal* (March 9): 12.

53. Gross, N., and O. Port. (1998). "The Next Wave," *Business Week* (August 31): 80, 82–83.

54. Garfinkel, S. (1998). "Power in Hand," *Wired* (August): 142.

55. Boyd, R. S. (2000). "Next Big Thing in Science Built on Tiny Parts: Nanotechnology Deals with Manipulating Substances at Level of Atoms, Molecules," *Albuquerque Journal* (February 3): A1, A11 (Knight Ridder Newspapers report).

56. See note 53.

57. Zeff, R., and J. Bauchner. (1996). "Navigating the Internet for Nonprofits," In T. D. Connors (ed.), *The Nonprofit Management Handbook: Operating Policies and Procedures, 1996 Cumulative Supplement.* New York: John Wiley & Sons, chapter 28D.

58. See note 37.

59. Schonfeld, E. (1998). "The Customized, Digitized, Have-It-Your-Way Economy," *Fortune* (September 28): 114–17, 120–21, 124.

60. Cronin, M. J. (1998). "Ford's Intranet Success," *Fortune* (March 30): 158.

61. Davenport, T. H., and K. Pearlson. (1998). "Two Cheers for the Virtual Office," *Sloan Management Review* 39 (Summer): 51–65.

62. Nilles, J. M. (1994). *Making Telecommuting Happen: A Guide for Telemanagers and Telecommuters.* New York: Van Nostrand Reinhold.

63. Lipman-Blumen, J., and H. J. Leavitt. (1999). *Hot Groups: Seeding Them, Feeding Them, & Using Them to Ignite Your Organization.* New York: Oxford University Press.

64. Yeatts, D. E., and C. Hyten. (1998). *High-Performing Self-Managed Work Teams: A Comparison of Theory and Practice.* Thousand Oaks, CA: Sage Publications.

65. Vedantam, S. (1996). "Indian Programmers Pick Up for U.S. Counterparts," *Albuquerque Journal* (August 27): B2.

66. Hof, R. D. (1998). "The Net Is Open for Business—Big Time," *Business Week* (August 31): 108–109.

67. Johnston, W. B. (1991). "Global Workforce 2000: The New Labor Market," *Harvard Business Review* (March–April): 115–29.

68. Kirkland, R. I. Jr. (1988). "Entering a New Age of Boundless Competition," *Fortune* (March 14): 40–42, 46, 48.

69. "The 21st Century Economy." (1998). *Business Week* (August 31): entire issue.

70. Boudreau, M-C., K. D. Loch, D. Robey, and D. Straud. (1998). "Going Global: Using Information Technology to Advance the Competitiveness of the Virtual Transnational Organization," *Academy of Management Executive* 12: 120–28.

71. Nulty, P. (1990). "How the World WILL CHANGE," *Fortune* (January 15): 44–46, 50–54.

72. Aho, C. M., and S. Ostry. (1990). "Regional Trading Blocs: Pragmatic or Problematic Policy?" In W. E. Brock and R. D. Hormats (eds.), *The Global Economy: America's Role in the Decade Ahead.* New York: W.W. Norton, pp. 147–73.

73. Ostry, S. (1990). "Governments & Corporations in a Shrinking World: Trade & Innovation Policies in the United States, Europe & Japan," *Columbia Journal of World Business* 25: 10–16.

74. Davis, B., and J. Calmes. (1993). "The House Passes NAFTA—Trade Win: House Approves NAFTA, Providing President With Crucial Victory," *Wall Street Journal* (November 18): A1.

75. Fox, J. (1998). "Europe Is Heading for a Wild Ride," *Fortune* (August 17): 145–46, 148–49.

76. Chavez, B. (1995). "Clear Sky Ahead for Blue Sky Co.," *Business Outlook, Albuquerque Journal* (June 19): 8–9.

77. Hall, E. T. (1959). *The Silent Language.* Garden City, NY: Doubleday.

78. Hall, E. T. (1966). *The Hidden Dimension.* Garden City, NY: Doubleday.

79. Schein, E. H. (1997). *Organizational Culture and Leadership,* 2nd ed. San Francisco: Jossey-Bass, pp. 259–60.

80. Hofstede, G. (1991). *Cultures and Organizations: Software of the Mind.* New York: McGraw-Hill.

81. Hofstede, G., and M. H. Bond. (1988). "The Confucius Connection: From Cultural Roots to Economic Growth," *Organizational Dynamics* 16: 4–21.

82. Brandt, R. B. (1959). *Ethical Theory: The Problems of Normative and Critical Ethics.* Englewood Cliffs, NJ: Prentice Hall, chapter 1.

83. Davis, P. E. (ed.). (1973). *Introduction to Moral Philosophy.* Columbus, OH: Charles E. Merrill, pp. 1–8.

84. Küng, Hans. (1998). *A Global Ethic for Global Politics and Economics.* New York: Oxford University Press.

85. Phillips, N. (1992). "Understanding Ethics in Practice: An Ethnomethodological Approach to the Study of Business Ethics," *Business Ethics Quarterly* 2: 223–44.

86. Jackall, R. (1988). *Moral Mazes: The World of Corporate Managers.* New York: Oxford University Press.

87. Toffler, B. L. (1986). *Tough Choices: Managers Talk Ethics.* New York: John Wiley & Sons.

88. Anderson, C. (1977). "Values-Based Management," *Academy of Management Executive* 11: 25–45.

89. McAneny, L., and L. Saad. (1997). "Pharmacists Strengthen Their Position as the Most Highly Rated Profession," *The Gallup Poll Monthly* (December): 21–24.

90. See note 82.

91. See note 83.

92. "Ethics." (1989). In *The New Encyclopaedia Britannica,* vol. 18. Chicago: Encyclopaedia Britannica, pp. 627–47E.

93. Frankena, W. K. (1973). *Ethics.* Englewood Cliffs, NJ: Prentice Hall.

94. Rosenthal, S., and R. Buchholz. (1999). *Rethinking Business Ethics: A Pragmatic Approach.* New York: Oxford University Press.

95. Werhane, P. H., and R. E. Freeman. (1999). "Business Ethics: The State of the Art," *International Journal of Management Reviews* 1: 1–16.

96. DeGeorge, R. T. (1982). *Business Ethics.* New York: Macmillan, pp. 26–28.

97. Donaldson, T. (1996). "Values in Tension: Ethics Away from Home," *Harvard Business Review* (September–October): 48–49, 52–56, 58, 60, 62.

98. Solomon, R. C., and K. R. Hanson. (1985). *It's Good Business.* New York: Atheneum.

99. See note 26.

100. Id.

101. Id.

102. Id.

103. Id.

104. See note 57.

105. Id.

106. Kirkpatrick, S. A., and E. A. Locke. (1991). "Leadership: Do Traits Matter?" *Academy of Management Executive* 5: 48–60.

3 ▼ Change Leadership or Change Management?

JON VAN TIL, PhD
Rutgers University at Camden

DAVID A. PETTRONE SWALVE
Rutgers University at Camden

3.1 Introduction

As organizations ebb and flow within the dynamic setting of the third sector, change remains the constant. Change requires organizations to examine the quality and coverage of their existing products and services, reduce their expenses, locate new directions of movement, and develop new relationships—all the while nurturing their environment. Inevitably, organizations face deciding on the main determinant of change—usually, a dichotomous decision—change leadership or change management. From this two-pronged examination, other questions naturally follow:

- How does change within society at large affect leadership and management within organizations?
- Under what conditions can leadership affect change? Under what conditions can management affect change?

- When the going gets tough, what is the case for changing leadership? What is the case for changing management?

We write from the premise that change is often asked and needed in society and within organizations. Organizations face change from a variety of sources and directions. Forces can originate internally or externally. They include changing technological standards, shifting community needs, increasing client demands, reduced funds for administrative expenses, and changes in the broader social structure. Regardless of its specific origin, change is a constant in the nonprofit world. Boards face a unique responsibility to understand the various relationships the organization maintains. As leaders, boards are challenged to find new directions and lead for positive change. Yet, leaders are found at all levels of the organization, and managers themselves must often serve as proactive change agents.

Maintaining and nurturing an effective organization requires all members of the organization to be attuned to potential change—both within the organization and in relation to its clients, community, competition, and the private and public sectors. Leaders and managers who comprehend the change process can foster a "natural state" of change for third-sector organizations.

3.2 *Approaches to Change*

(A) MOTIVATION: FEAR AND MONEY

John Kotter, in his influential book, *Leading Change,* provides a blueprint for approaching change.[1] Kotter begins his presentation by citing fear as a primary motivator for change, titling an opening chapter as "Why Firms Fail." The idea that one must change or fail is a theme that resounds throughout the book and throughout much of the current private-sector literature on change. The fear of being left behind, of failing, is often cited as a prime motivator in the market-directed environment.

Change in organizations intensifies as organizations find niche markets, tailoring their purchase of services and goods in an increasingly selective and competitive business environment. The changing boundaries of business through globalization is one of the main concerns Kotter cites for the emerging business leader and manager. Globalization increases competition and pressure on the organization while contributing to the potential demise of an organization through the shrinking market. The language of battle used throughout the book might be a bit strong for many nonprofit managers and a bit stringent for those accustomed to thinking of their work in terms of positively affecting their communities. However, the process outlined by Kotter does provide a road map to potential success for change.

Kotter distinguishes sharply between management and leadership in his book. He explains that managers cope with the complexity of change, the nuances, whereas leadership is about coping with change. More specifically, managing involves planning, budgeting, staffing, controlling, and problem solving, whereas leadership involves a set of processes that create organizations in the first place or adapt them to significantly changing circumstances. Things are to be managed, but people require leadership. Kotter sets a tone of urgency with the idea that managers must create a sense of crisis so that people will understand why they need to change. What the organization requires are people with the attitude that they will never fail or fear being left behind.

The first step of Kotter's eight-stage transformation process is to *establish a sense of urgency.* During this step, while examining the market environment, the leader is instructed to identify and discuss potential crises or major opportunities. A second step involves the leader assembling a team with enough political power within the organization to lead the change effort. Then comes the crucial step of *creating a vision,* followed by the action stages of the process: *communicate the change vision, empower employees, generate short-term and small wins, consolidate change* (and produce more change), and finally *anchoring.* The key to the eight-step process of change occurs in step six. If leaders and the on-board managers can plan for visible performance improvements, create those improvements, and reward those involved, the process will develop a critical mass toward change. During steps seven and eight, the manager is instructed to fire those who are not on board, hire those who will be be players, and assign new projects and themes to change agents, thereby ensuring a leadership succession that will extend the path established by the leader and the coalition.

Kotter's plan is very thorough and is practical in many aspects. But its grounding in the fear of being left behind means that it commits the organization to launching a change initiative in a climate of anxiety and fear. A very different approach to organizational tensions is found in the work of David Cooperrider and associates at Case Western Reserve University. They call it *appreciative inquiry.*

(B) MOTIVATION: APPRECIATION AND CONCERN

The Appreciative Inquiry (AI) approach begins by viewing the organization as a positive force in the dynamic community, evaluating and understanding its strengths and weaknesses, and then preparing a plan to address these weaknesses and enhance the strengths. This method of organizational change is identified as *appreciation,* a means of understanding the organization's position in its community and the importance of its work.

AI is defined by Cooperrider as the art and science of ferreting out the best in an organization through skillful questioning, and bringing key stakeholders together with the knowledge to plan the future or change the present.[2] This process of promoting constant change was discovered by noting when members of organizations felt most alive within the system and when they found themselves most committed to the mission and goals of the organization. Members of an organization, Cooperrider asserts, feel most dedicated when they are moving forward, achieving successes, and advancing with them. Thus, appreciative inquiry was born as a method of finding out how an organization's members feel about the work they do. This approach is particularly significant for the work of third-sector organizations, as many such groups have long held the position that what they do is as important as how they do it.

AI presents five principles to guide the organization confronting change:

1. The *Principle of Constructionism,* which says "you can create our own reality"
2. The *Principle of Simultaneity,* which asserts that inquiry is intervention, that the positive future can be defined
3. The *Poetic Principle,* which explains that organizations are social creations and not machines, and that understanding the human experiences of the organization illuminates the real capabilities of the organization
4. The *Anticipatory Principle,* which assures us that the future we anticipate is the future we create
5. The *Positive Principle,* which asserts that if we can build on the positive of the organization, it will then be possible to move forward without getting caught in the trap of mindset negativity

With its mantra that "imaging a positive future creates a positive future," some may be tempted to see AI as just one more example of the power of "positive thinking" or "accentuating the positive." But the significance of this approach may lie deeper than such cultural platitudes. AI challenges us to look at the organization as a specialist in something rather than a mysterious method for desperately trying to get things right. AI sees the organization as a strong and positive force, which can refine and enhance its already functional positive attributes. If the organization can help to promote positive relationships with stakeholders, positive growth, and positive changes to quality of work, it can address most problems as they occur. The organizational manager, according to AI, has no need to instill fear or "create" a sense of crisis. Rather, one should trust the four Ds Cooperrider identifies—Discovery, Dreaming, Design, and Destiny—and use the process of AI to find areas that might be improved on by existing members of the organization without external stimulus.

3.3 Organizations Involved in Change

Each major force within a nonprofit organization—its board, staff, and members—can play an important role in ensuring that change is productively addressed. Often, of course, change elicits feelings of anxiety. Proactively approached and candidly addressed, however, change can increase the viability of the organization as it challenges the future. And this takes us to the choice we explore in this chapter: change management or change leadership?

When we think of leadership, we often think of executives and board members. When we think of management, we usually think of line managers. This compartmentalized view, although often accurate, is also often incomplete. Herman and Heimovics observe that active nonprofit managers "have discovered that few activities in human endeavor are more fascinating, more challenging, and more rewarding than leading a nonprofit organization with an important mission."[3] Such individuals are what we call *change managers,* and part of their role involves acting also as *change leaders.*

When change is warranted, one must turn to such change leaders and change managers. Together, both sets of organizational actors are needed to address the challenges of change. Leaders must candidly examine goals and stimulate action, while managers must direct and coordinate. The lines between leadership and change, when examined in the context of change, often become blurred.

Ultimately, it is the responsibility of all members of an organization to ensure that the challenges of change are adequately addressed. Nonprofit organizations are rightly advised to incorporate broad-based participation if they are to act effectively, because all members of the organization are affected by change in some fashion. This constant flux requires everyone in the organization to learn new processes, forge new relationships, and discover innovative ways of accomplishing tasks. And so the question remains: change leadership or change management?

(A) CHANGE MANAGEMENT

Organizational development has many facets, none of which is called on more regularly than the refinement and improvement of management skills and structures. Strategic planning, in its attempt to help lay a road map for the organization, is critical to the success of change management. Continually examining the processes of the organization can help to illuminate the need and avenue for change. Implementing new technological applications is another part of change management. As the needs of the community or constituents change, technological advances in telecommunications and information handling can allow an organization to make change more effectively. Also vital, and often overlooked, is the development of an organizational culture and environment that supports change. Such an environment can be created most effectively through communication. With change management, communication is an enabler to changing the culture, behavior, and strategic direction of the organization.

Taken as a whole, the coordinated linkage of culture, behavior, and strategy within a web of communication forms what we call *change management*. Change management uses organizational tools to ensure the continued success and viability of an organization. It not only rearranges established policies, practices, and procedures—it also creates new ones.

(B)   CHANGE LEADERSHIP

The requisites for leadership in a time of change are many. Change leadership requires the ability to communicate, empower, develop mutually beneficial relationships, innovate, learn, teach, and motivate others. Change leadership offers the opportunity to create an organizational culture that learns and a work environment that rewards. The task of the leader is to create a synergy from which perpetual energy can push change to the forefront of understanding for all individuals in the organization.

An example of effective change management in conjunction with change leadership has been the transformation of United Way organizations across the United States.[4] Brian Gallagher, president of the United Way of Franklin County, Ohio, observes that "Our business is community development, quality of life and human development." This rebirth of goals, moving from a collector/dispenser of goods and services to an advocate of quality of life, requires change at all levels. "The new strategy marks a significant attempt to rebuild donor loyalty and break away from an entrenched United Way model of operating."[5]

Following an era of management disgrace in the 1980s under the leadership of former chief executive officer (CEO) William Aramony, United Way of America, the national facilitating organization of United Ways, has created a variety of productive initiatives. Included among these is "Project Blueprint," which seeks to increase the involvement of ethnic minorities as leaders on boards of local United Way agencies. Funded by grants from the W. K. Kellogg Foundation and the Ford Foundation, this project has involved more than 3,000 men and women in 50 communities in a variety of volunteer leadership experiences. Collaboration with key community leaders to help cities determine their most urgent social problems and then come up with the money and ideas to tackle them asks for both change management and change leadership to move to the cusp.

Mark O'Connell, president of the United Way of Metropolitan Atlanta, defines his task as bringing communities together, helping them "agree on what the work is," figuring out how to do it, and then holding "themselves accountable for returns, results and impact."[6]

Change itself is normally undertaken to improve some aspect of an organization. As the organization transforms itself, it ensures its survival and relevance in relation to its community. The origin of change helps to suggest who ultimately has control. If change originates externally, it can dictate urgency. If change originates internally, it can help to nurture the goals that are important to the organization. Managing change is a method through which an organization prevents being managed by change. The issue of change becomes one of proaction versus reaction. Will the organization push itself forward? Or will it instead allow itself to be pushed by the strongest forces at play in the broader society?

An organization is transformed constantly by the dynamic environment in which it operates, but it can shape its responses to those forces.

3.4 The Role of Voluntary/Nonprofit Organizations

Nonprofit organizations have a unique position in society. As both Kotter and Cooperrider assert, *vision,* the stock in trade of the third sector, is a vital means of examining and introducing change. What differentiates AI from the business approach of Kotter is the conception that nonprofit organizations can live without the fear of failure, extinction, or lack of profits that drives Kotter's model. The bottom line for nonprofits, after all, is only partially dollar-based. It is a fuller organizational view, which relates to the widest variety of quality-of-life changes, the positive advances that enhance life opportunities or prevent destructive behavior, keeping the market mindset in an appropriately secondary role. Thus, as the nonprofit organization approaches change, it can move forward with less trepidation and from a different pattern of motivation and commitment.

We do not live in a world where one can assume that all members of the third sector are directed by the desire to serve broader social interests. The nonprofit sector contains too many organizations that basically serve as tax-exempt businesses and that should be from the privileges of tax exemption and the good name of the sector.[7] However, a majority of managers and leaders of the third sector do share a vision that the third sector's role is to serve by articulating and implementing visions of a better society.

Voluntary and nonprofit organizations often work best by promoting systematic change in their own community. Collaboration is key to this effort. By sharing information, ensuring that the necessary processes are available for community change, and making good decisions, the nonprofit organization advances the welfare of the areas it serves. Partnerships can be found through government, through the business sector, and through the obvious collaboration of the nonprofit sector. Change, in the fashion presented here, requires the generation of a vision and applies the elbow grease of motivated action to drive toward implementation.

One of the largest obstacles to change is getting people to change. Organizations, individuals, and communities get caught in "comfort zones" that add to retrenchment and slow change. However, if an organization has been constructed by dedicated leaders and is staffed with competent managers, and if its reason for being has been kept alive in the process, change can be achieved more effectively. We suggest the following five steps in the process:

1. *Engender an organizational culture that builds on the energies of each and every participant.* Open lines of communication, in multiple directions, help nurture organizational culture. Through these lines of communication, issues, ideas, and goals are transmitted, allowing the leadership and management of an organization to shape the message.
2. *Build a collective vision of community development.* By working collaboratively with others, the needs of the community are discovered, and the mission of the organization begins to emerge clearly.
3. *Engender sector growth by staking out the future.* By developing blueprints of collective change that improve aspects of life in the community an organization serves, capacity is built both within the sector and within the organization.

4. *Develop new partnerships that blend service to the community and advocacy of needed change.* Once the vision is defined, the real proof of the pudding emerges from what is accomplished. Serving needs when they are clear and speaking strongly for what needs to be done are the two great tools of nonprofit organizations.

5. *Reinforce positive change and fine-tune activity and process.* Appreciative process mandates one of the oldest principles of voluntary action—to tell the people one works with how important their work is. Giving the further respect involved in fine-tuning that work to help make it even better is another splendid way to make an organization effective.

3.5   *Leadership and Management: Forces in Interaction*

It is time for us to answer the question posed by this chapter: change leadership or change management? Our answer seems clear: not "either–or" but rather "both–and." Change leadership to make it more inclusive, appreciative, and oriented to the advance of mission. Change management to make it support leadership, appreciate participation, and reflect mission.

In addition, develop a style called *change leadership* to continually address the shifting needs of organization and community. Manage the organization with a style called *change management* to keep alert to the constant-newness of the organizational task.

We next present eight cases, some showing how to do things right, others showing what can go wrong. Each of these cases has been developed by this chapter's senior author, and several are reported elsewhere.[8–9] We start with a "pure" leadership case, the structure and process of organizing within the Religious Society of Friends.

(A)   CASE 1: GOOD QUAKER GOVERNANCE

Quakers, as members of the Religious Society of Friends are known, run a low-budget, faith-based organization. Most meetings (what other churches would call parishes) do not hire a minister to manage their affairs and guide their services. Quakers coproduce their own religious services by allowing attenders to rise and speak as they happen to be moved to do so. When no one speaks, the silence that is at the heart of Quaker worship prevails throughout the meeting house.

A Quaker meeting, like the clusters of meetings in regional structures called *quarters* and *yearly meetings,* governs itself by means of a series of working committees. Each member of the meeting assumes a responsibility for governance, and minimal employment is made of paid staffers. Within the Quaker system, with its strong emphasis on service and advocacy beyond the walls of the meeting, leadership is broadly shared and management is largely a matter of voluntary commitment.

Within the various structures of Quaker governance, a number of principles emerge that characterize the process. One list includes the following, asserting that good Quaker governance:

- Joins participants in a shared process of discernment (reflection)
- Inspires a group to the best and fullest use of its members' skills, experience, and wisdom (participation)

- Values and employs effectively the particular contributions of each participant (respect)
- Recognizes the collective advantage that accrues to a diversity of experience, perspective, and personal characteristics (diversity)
- Seeks a sense of the meeting by searching for and developing a substantial unity (consensus)
- Aims toward the achievement of valued actions, decisions, programs, and consequences (proactive)
- Leads and instructs its participants toward clear roles for implementation and follow-through (responsibility)
- Grows and changes dynamically as needs, missions, and environmental constraints emerge and change (flexibility)

The process of good Quaker governance values both process and outcome and is notable for its effort to include the voices of all members in arriving at a consensual resolution. Its polar opposite may be found in a second case, in which the prerogatives of the manager came to run roughshod on both mission and organizational process.

(B)   CASE 2: UNITED WAY OF AMERICA UNDER ARAMONY

Power corrupts, we have been told, and the power of a nonprofit manager who combines his own force into an iron triangle with that of a complaisant board and a fearful staff has few limits. A remarkable book by John Glaser, formerly a key associate of United Way of America's shamed executive, William Aramony, shows how easy it was for a nonprofit manager to forge that iron triangle into a force that provides one with all the wealth, sex, and power that anyone could wish for.[10] (Of course, the downside is that you might get caught, as did Aramony; be tried and convicted; and spend most of the rest of your life in prison.)

Glaser's book is about United Way's head, heart, soul, and various other bodily parts in the Aramony years. Glaser gives us a peek behind the veil of nonprofit piety, beginning with his own initial employment interview with Aramony. Glaser was a community organizer and activist, and Aramony is quoted as saying to him: "Your resume is full of shit, Glaser, but I like your eyeballs."[11] Later on, Glaser recounts, a similar test was applied to the women who worked for Aramony: "(I)t often appeared that raises and perquisites were increased in direct proportion to their attractiveness."

With their pleasing eyeballs and feminine charms, his staff accepted their rewards in higher-than-competitive salary and swallowed the abuse that Aramony dished up on the slightest pretense. The madhouse that was the elegant United Way headquarters in Alexandria is described in a vivid dissection of Aramony's leadership style. The workplace was a roller coaster that shifted rapidly through the ranges of the manic and depressive moods of the leader. Aramony would scream "Fire his ass" about an employee, and then agonize when he learned that his order had actually been implemented. "Only when Aramony was out of town could the staff begin to do productive work."[12]

"Aramony required planning for everyone but himself. … He felt he 'owned' people because of the high salaries he paid them."[13] Glaser presents a powerful recounting of the staff roles made available in Aramony's fiefdom:

- *Chief financial officer,* a friend or long-term associate who "rarely, if ever" questioned Aramony's expenditures
- *Office wife,* the administrative assistant who traveled with the boss, occupied a room connecting to his, and was available for personal service 24 hours per day
- *Bagman,* who handled Aramony's private financial affairs and discharged unwanted employees (a role Glaser apparently played for several years)
- *Court jester,* a male who bonded with the chief and joined him in his favorite pastimes of dining, gambling, and playing the horses
- *Golden boy/girl,* the new member of the team who was counted on to resolve any organizational problem, but then quickly fell from favor[14]

Board roles played during this organizational interlude were no more flattering. Although in daily life they played the game of corporate or nonprofit management with apparent success, board members clearly were invited to check their good judgment at the door when entering United Way meetings. Aramony staged his board meetings with meticulous care, making members as comfortable as he could, and accepting in return their consideration of him as not only "the expert," but also one who embodied "all of the noble virtues of those who spend their lives serving others." Among the board members of United Way of America and its infamous spin-offs were such notables as then Girl Scouts of the U.S.A. executive Frances Hesselbein, identified by Glaser as a "close Aramony colleague."[15]

Readers of Glaser's volume will wonder why he allowed prominent nonprofit attorney Bruce Hopkins to write both an Introduction and an Afterword to his volume. These chapters do offer some comic relief on the matter, especially when Hopkins observes: "Readers will find this statement hard to believe, but I will repeat it: Bill Aramony did not break a single federal law."[16]

In a splendid concluding chapter on "lessons learned," however, Glaser redeems himself by offering the following 13 pieces of advice:

1. A charity is a charity. It is part of the voluntary sector, not the business sector, and must abide by the constraints imposed by the history, ethics, and public perceptions of the sector.
2. Charitable activities must be defensible in the court of public opinion.
3. Charities must represent constituents.
4. Character is more important than administrative ability.
5. Boards must really evaluate staff.
6. Boards must know their legal responsibilities.
7. Boards should have conflict of interest statements.
8. Boards should have viable internal standing committees.
9. Boards should have a risk management plan.
10. Boards should set acceptable salaries and ranges.
11. Boards should enforce equal application of policy.
12. Boards should set terms of office.
13. Boards should bring in outside evaluators.[17]

Glaser suggests that the basic lesson in the United Way fiasco involves the development and sustenance of countervailing points of power and influence within the nonprofit organization. The painful case that he recounts reminds us that there is no special virtue inherent in section 501(c). As a distinguished scholar of nonprofit action, Ralph Kramer has demonstrated in summarizing a quarter-century of comparative research on nonprofit organizations that the legal "ownership" of an organization—whether it is governmental, nonprofit, or for-profit—may be far less important than the quality of services provided by the organization. Form may mean much less than function in assessing the nonprofit world.[18]

The price of effective organization is continuing vigilance, for nonprofit organizations can be useful vehicles in society. When led by someone of dubious will and character, however, they are among the easiest of organizations to corrupt.

(C) CASE 3: THE FOUNDATION FOR NEW ERA PHILANTHROPY

Nonprofit organization executives are often urged to "become more entrepreneurial" by trainers, authors, and other pundits in the field. "Find a service niche, your own place in the nonprofit market, and make it pay for your organization! Don't be so nice about it. Learn to be more aggressive!"

When the scandal at the Foundation for New Era Philanthropy hit the press in 1995, it was clear that Jack Bennett, New Era's founder, was as consummate a nonprofit entrepreneur as the field has ever known. He played every emotional chord perfectly to convince his donors of his personal commitment to the variety of causes, largely religious, to which his foundation was apparently dedicated.

Donors and donees alike were shocked by the revelations, as well they might be, having handed over sums up to the $11 million given by one hapless Rockefeller, and down to the $300 provided by a group of school kids in West Philadelphia, purportedly for the purpose of learning about philanthropy. (What a foundation! Everyone a donor, no one a beneficiary—save for the nonprofit executive himself, of course, and a few family members and friends.)

One disillusioned New Era-ite confessed to his own dismay at judging character when he reflected on Bennett's frequent participation in Philadelphia-area prayer breakfasts. Bennett, this acquaintance noted, "prayed so well." Another New Era broker, a minister, solicited donations from putative "donees" and then had the audacity to invite a further donation in the form of a "thank offering" to his own nonprofit front organization.

How were Bennett and his New Era partners consummate nonprofit entrepreneurs? Let us count the ways. First, they knew how to talk the talk: Their work at the foundation was "pro bono"; they acted as true volunteers; and their work was aimed only at the purposes of doing God's will on earth. Second, they could walk the walk: They knew how to set up for-profits to self-deal with; they fabulously enriched themselves by contracting with their own firms for services; and they knew how to take their pieces of the action.

The word *entrepreneur* is best translated from the French as "the middleman who takes"—*entre* meaning "between"; *preneur* meaning "taker." Bennett put himself between the donor and the donee, and how he did take!

The concept of entrepreneurship was introduced into the social sciences by the Austrian political economist Joseph Schumpeter and has been lionized since in business schools as the answer to a variety of ills: first, the rigidity and bureaucratization of traditional corporate structures and, more recently, the failure of the economy to provide jobs for business school graduates. The rise of nonprofit management as an arena for education and training has moved the concept into our field for similar reasons.

Entrepreneurship without ethics, however, can be a dangerous force. Without a grounding in the traditions, values, and ethics of voluntary action, without a rooting in organizations accustomed to abiding by both the letter and the spirit of the law, the entrepreneur is nothing but another middle person out to grab and take, a broker in it for self-interest, a corrupter of the nonprofit dream.

(D)   CASE 4: THE FETTERSVILLE COLLABORATIVE

The next case involves a gathering of managers—mostly ministers—as well as a number of volunteer participants they designated. This group was organized in 1999 in the Fettersville neighborhood of Camden, New Jersey. Fettersville was developed by Richard Fetters, himself a Quaker as well as a political and civic leader, in the year 1833. In that year, Fetters purchased land from Charity and Grace Kaighn between Line and Cherry Streets and Third Street and the Delaware River and laid it out into lots offered for sale at low rates and easy terms. Among the buyers of these plots were a number of freed slaves, several of whom later joined the ranks of the city's most respected residents. The remarkable past of this area reveals a place of community pride and authentic historical wonder that is today in an active process of rediscovery. Although not much of the physical fabric of Fettersville remains, a group of its citizens are seeking to base the future of the neighborhood on the principles and traditions that shaped its past.

The contemporary neighborhood known as Fettersville consists of about half of Camden's Bergen Square census tract. The boundaries of the neighborhood run from Line Street to Atlantic Avenue and from Broadway west to the Delaware River. These approximately 80 square blocks include a population that is 65 percent African-American and 35 percent primarily Hispanic. The layout of this community is split between residential and industrial uses, which has created a serious land-use dilemma. The residents of this neighborhood find themselves immersed in an area of abandoned buildings, trash-filled vacant lots, open-air drug markets, and industrial excesses such as fumes and other wastes.

Fettersville contains one of the largest numbers of abandoned buildings in the entire city of Camden, and until the recent implementation of a new water main in the area, this neighborhood had not experienced any noticeable development investment in nearly 35 years. Furthermore, the new water main required the tearing up of major city blocks running through the community, which the city has yet to repave. The abandoned building close-up program is no longer in the community, which has encouraged problems of squatters and drug markets. Keeping in mind that these abandoned structures are located directly adjacent to occupied homes, concerns about sanitation and security plague the area. This neighborhood has become a haven for the mentally ill and homeless of the city, while the children who reside in this area have few places to go. Fettersville lacks any public park or open green space in all of its 80 square blocks. In fact, the children of this neighborhood are faced with dangerous elements every day, such as the huge open ditch at the corner of Third and Cherry Streets.

The current reality of industrial uses adjacent to residential uses has caused major problems in the community. Fettersville has several brownfield areas within its boundaries. Industrial companies who have gone bankrupt or simply moved out of the area have left behind contaminated sites. Also, in recent years, there has been a massive encroachment of quasi-public corporations, such as the South Jersey Port Corporation, gobbling up vacant and abandoned property in the neighborhood for nonresidential uses. Meanwhile, Fettersville has not experienced the development of any new housing in nearly 80 years, and very little renovation has been done on existing structures. This neighborhood, like all other areas of Camden, has become a host to the low-income, the elderly, the disabled, the unemployed, and the underemployed.

Over the past half-century, neighborhood residents failed to influence policies of growth-dominated municipal planning within the city of Camden. More recently, a range of nonprofit corporations have proposed and executed several projects involving the development of waterfront lands along the Delaware River. These plans have not brought any significant benefits to the residents of neighborhoods like Fettersville. But there remains in that community a beacon of hope that has shone since the development of this community by Richard Fetters. Contemporary visions being developed from within the neighborhood include the embracing of subcultures and the resolution of ethnic tolerance that could rebuild a sense of community pride. This neighborhood has discovered an opportunity to address its pressing current needs by reinventing its submerged past.

Fettersville began that process of rediscovery supported by a crumbling physical structure, a weakening economic base, and organizational assets primarily consisting of a set of churches and other faith-based organizations. A recent "civil society census" discovered active organizations within the community within only 9 of the 25 possible categories identified by Kretzman and McKnight.[19]

Traditional means of community organization within communities like Fettersville tend to be ineffective in the contemporary city. In Fettersville, a deep sense of distrust, both of established authority and of each other, characterizes many residents. Looking into the future, a group of local residents and organizational leaders that the implementation of state/government-developed initiatives has failed to reach deeply into the community. The interaction among certain residents of the area gave rise to an emergent sense of community and the creation of a grassroots organization, a collaborative of local groups who took upon themselves the power of reinventing a community.

The Fettersville Collaborative seeks to act as a celebration of the meeting of minds, ideas, agendas, and even personalities. The Collaborative has organized itself in the face of the many difficulties and obstacles involved in democratic participation. It embraced its community because Fettersville's residents have nowhere else to go, plagued as they are by handicaps of race, economics, education, and social fabric. The creation of a collaborative marks a sense of hope among a group of low-income urban residents that recognizes the strength of their ties to a community they cannot afford to leave. In that commitment, they are joined by others tied to community through ancestry and belief. Included in the Collaborative's research and activity are several elderly residents, who remember a time when the social fabric was not so torn, and a set of church pastors, tied to the community by the assignment of their ministry. The rediscovered history of this urban space has sparked a resurgence of African-American history and tradition within this bleak Camden urban landscape.

The grassroots neighborhood organization that has developed in Fettersville draws on support from several faith-based groups in the area, as well as from a number of individuals attracted to the process of discovery and organization. Its process is a dynamic and often turbulent one. Meetings of the Collaborative evince the dynamics of group organizing in a raw and diverse urban context. The conflict that inevitably arises is often based in passions radiating within many members of the Collaborative. But the determination of this community to reinstate family history and community pride has revealed a remarkable power found in destroyed areas of urban America. The "end of the line" has stopped in this community at a place where communication and mutual partnership is almost mandatory.

The Fettersville Collaborative experienced a challenge to its viability during the study period (spring 2000), when one of its constitutive members withdrew from participation in protest against what was perceived as inappropriate behavior on the part of representatives of another church. This withdrawal effectively stymied the Collaborative from taking any action because its bylaws require active consent of all members before any action can be taken. Considerable meeting time was consumed during the impasse period by repeated comments from the members whose behavior had been rendered suspect of "negativity," and, at this writing, it remains unclear how and when this particular conflict will be resolved, if at all.

Other differences among participants within the Collaborative were also addressed in a direct fashion with a certain testiness of tone. Usually initiated by the lay representatives of one Collaborative member, these challenges were directed toward city and university resource persons, who were occasionally seen to be lagging in the delivery of information or studies they had promised. The statements were usually explained in terms of "telling truth," and in one case gave rise to a heated back-and-forth exchange of the following sort:

A: You never did the narrative we asked you to do.
B: I am doing it now.
A: We may not want you to do it now.
B: Your demand was for me to start at the beginning.
A: It was a request.
B: It sounded like a demand to me.

Conflict among members of the Collaborative was not all that troubled the effort; occasional conflict within participating member organizations was also evident. At times, the executive of a participating organization was observed to have withheld information from volunteer participants within his own organization, in effect protecting his organization from what might have been perceived as an untimely interest on the part of the Collaborative.

The president of the Collaborative during this period accommodated these various conflicts with considerable tolerance. In his view, the Collaborative's aim was to bring needed development to Fettersville, and if that development was at times a noisy and even sloppy process, it was a process leading to a worthy end.

(E) CASE 5: THE NATHAN CUMMINGS FOUNDATION

Deborah Gardner, in a study of the founding process of the Nathan Cummings Foundation, describes, step by step, the transformation of one man's vision into an effective and humanely administered nonprofit organization.[20] The visionary, a grocer named Nathan Cummings who came eventually to direct the Sara Lee Corporation, established the foundation in 1949. The enterprise moved into high gear when Cummings died in 1985, leaving it assets worth $200 million.

Nathan Cummings hoped his foundation would allow his grandchildren to join in common cause and "accustom them to the understanding that we must contribute to worthy causes, thus sharing our good fortune with those less fortunate than we are." His children and grandchildren pitched in enthusiastically to this task and participated actively as volunteers in building what has become one of our country's most active and enlightened philanthropies.

Gardner's study of the foundation rehearses familiar lessons of organizational development—lessons not always learned or followed by leaders of many nonprofit organizations. She shows how the Nathan Cummings Foundation struggled in its process of growth and ultimately built into its very structure five enduring truths of successful non-profit management:

1. The organization embodies, and does not outgrow, its founding spirit of voluntary concern. In the Nathan Cummings case, family members committed to serve the board without compensation, and that tradition continues to this day as non–family members play increasingly central board roles.

2. Board members are selected with an eye toward the future as well as a respect for the past. Gardner shows how non–family members were carefully selected, with the assistance of a search firm. At the same time, younger family members were groomed for eventual board service by being selected as board associates.

3. The board enables itself to struggle with the definition of its role, its workload, and its relationship to the executive director. In the Cummings case, the board worked hard to shape its own agenda, eventually adopting the practice of a regular retreat session to work through tension and workload issues.

4. The inevitability of board–staff tensions is recognized, confronted, and resolved—at least for the time being. The relationship between an active and vital CEO, like Cummings's Charlie Halpern, and a powerful and committed board, like the one built at Cummings, was never all sweetness and light. Gardner quotes Halpern, a prominent public service lawyer: "The proper line between management and board had to emerge from a process, not start as a given. I started with it as a given." As the organization matured, direct lines of communications were developed and encouraged between board members and midlevel staff, and considerable progress was achieved in developing a sense of "harmonious partnership" among all members of the organization.

5. While the internal organization of a nonprofit is a crucial requisite for its success, its ultimate test lies in the generation of an effective external program to advance its mission and goals. At the Nathan Cummings Foundation, evaluation became a central activity of the Foundation's annual retreat, or "decision-making forum." Gardner writes, "The end result was an entirely new way of evaluating grant programs, proposals and projects, dubbed 'Objectives, Strategies, Outcomes,' or OSOs for short."[21]

These five simple but powerful tests—voluntary concern, quality of board, executive leadership, partnership with staff, and external productivity—can be applied to any non-profit organization. Consider three major Washington-based groups: CIVICUS (the world alliance for citizen participation); America's Promise (the follow-up vehicle to the Presidents' Summit on America's Future); and the National Committee for Responsive Philanthropy (NCRP), a leading advocacy organization in the field—the organizations that are subjects for three final cases presented in this chapter.

(F) CASE 6: CIVICUS

CIVICUS, founded in 1994, was governed in 1998 by a board of directors chaired by the distinguished Indian community developer, Rajesh Tandon. The board is composed of citizens of 19 different nations, working in tandem with Executive Director Miklos

Marschall, the former deputy mayor of Budapest. Its founding board process was a lively one, as members assembled twice yearly from various corners of the earth. In 1997, a board retreat was held, facilitated by an outside expert.

A recurring concern at these meetings has been a choice between organizational models: on the one hand, the traditional North American nonprofit model of a strong director as primary among board equals; on the other, the traditional European model of a strong board chair guiding the efforts of a staff cum secretariat. Marschall, who himself came to see the values of the strong executive model, reports that dialogue on this issue remains lively and that a "hybrid" model has emerged, in which conflicts are frequent but typically resolved by "tolerance and patience."

CIVICUS quite clearly passes the five tests derived from the Cummings experience: Its board members volunteer to gather from the corners of the globe; they have been carefully selected to balance a wide range of diversity concerns; they struggle actively with their role and their relation to the director; they directly face, and seek to resolve, the inevitable board–staff tensions that characterize the modern nonprofit; and, together, board and staff have succeeded in creating an organization that has been extraordinarily productive.

Few organizations so young can point to the range of achievements CIVICUS has amassed in four short years: two highly successful world assemblies, a small bookshelf of useful publications, and policy positions hammered out by widely varying and influential constituent participants. Its current agenda involves a major role in the United Nations' emerging "Millennial Forum," and the creation of a process to strengthen ties between corporations and civil society organizations throughout the world. As board chair Tandon puts it, these efforts are being designed to create a future in which nonprofit organizations will fill "front-row seats" in all aspects of the global development process.

(G) CASE 7: AMERICA'S PROMISE

America's Promise (AP), the second nonprofit we hold to the Gardner tests, has chosen a very different organizational approach than CIVICUS. An important part of the difference reflects AP's founding conception as being a temporary organization, intended to complete its work by the year 2000.

Organized during and immediately after the President's Summit on America's Future of April 1997 as its follow-up vehicle, AP's first year was organizationally turbulent. Within its first year of existence, AP was already under its third executive director; the organization had also experienced a fair amount of turnover among its board of directors, as well.

Applying the Gardner tests, one sees that AP took a few tentative steps (test 1) toward incorporating the voluntary spirit it so vigorously advocates into its own organizational life, particularly if the provision of roles for interns and board spouses are counted as volunteering. Its board, however (test 2), appears to have been selected on the most traditional of grounds from the ranks of corporate and political America. That AP has not chosen to include young persons on its board, including reclaimed youths at risk, seems to counter its elevated rhetoric regarding youth service and empowerment.

As this organization ages, it has yet to demonstrate a maturation of its board (test 3). America's Promise has yet to harness a board fully committed to providing the accustomed work, wealth, and wisdom. Three figures continue to dominate its process: Board Chairman Colin Powell, philanthropist Ray Chambers, and Senior Vice-President Gregg Petersmeyer. The result? An organization that strongly favors the traditional European model (and probably, a wag might observe, its Prussian variation).

Compare (test 4) the CIVICUS board and staff resolving their conflicts through tolerance and patience with the observation of a President's Summit volunteer, there at the founding. She recalls seeing AP's first director completely distraught, having received the order from General Powell to completely reassemble several hundred copies of a press packet because one telephone number listed therein was off by a single digit.

Operating in a mode of continuous short-term, or even crisis, planning, AP is certainly beginning to make its mark within circles of corporate and community life in many American cities (test 5). Its real impact, however, remains to be assessed—the direct impact it will ultimately be found to have had on the quality and quantity of attentive response to the needs of millions of American youth at risk in hundreds of cities and towns.

(H)   CASE 8: THE NATIONAL COMMITTEE FOR RESPONSIVE PHILANTHROPY

The third organization to be held to the Gardner test, the National Committee for Responsive Philanthropy (NCRP), was founded in 1976 out of the Donee Group of the Filer Commission, a major review of philanthropy's structure and process. As the Donee Group, an informal component of the commission's process, those who would come to call themselves the NCRP represented a set of organizations whose interests, they feared, would continue to be ignored by major philanthropic institutions. These interests and organizations represented an array of individuals and groups disadvantaged by structures of privilege and power in American society, a coalition NCRP would come to identify as "disenfranchised" from participation in the recognition and rewards of philanthropic giving.

By 1978, NCRP the group had taken its organizational form and filed an amicus brief in a lawsuit challenging the fairness of the Combined Federal Campaign (the CFC), a struggle it would persist in for two decades. In the following year, the NCRP held its first national conference, on the topic of alternatives to the United Way, another interest it continues to hold until the present day.

As the NCRP developed in its work, a range of issues was addressed, foremost among which were the accountability of philanthropy, the accessibility and monopoly of United Way, the openness of the CFC, the impact of community foundations, corporate giving to racial/ethnic populations, and the emerging role of conservative philanthropy and public policy. By 1998, the NCRP, led throughout its entire organizational life by Robert Bothwell, had become widely recognized throughout the philanthropic world as an important advocate for social justice and fairness in philanthropic practice.

Applying Gardner's tests to the NCRP, we see that the NCRP has sought to build a strong board into its structure (test 1), and to develop a lean staff of persons well acquainted with philanthropic practice into its structure.

Its board (test 2) has been carefully selected to represent the diversity of its principal constituencies: activist organizations, particularly those representing groups disenfranchised from conventional philanthropic process—women, people of color, poor persons, and the like.

As this organization aged, it gradually recognized that its leadership was beginning to "age in place" (test 3). After 22 years of executive service, Robert Bothwell, long perceived as the very spirit and voice of the organization, announced his resignation to assume a three-year research position with the group. The replacement process promised to present severe challenges to the organization, accustomed as it had become to Bothwell's steady and devoted leadership hand.

The NCRP board committed itself to a determined process of governance, decision making, and conflict resolution (test 4). Board meetings were regularly held and occasionally took the form of retreat-type reflection.

As a national advocacy organization, whose recommendations are based on solid research, the NCRP clearly made its mark in circles of third-sector policy and practice. Like the Nathan Cummings Foundation and CIVICUS, it found that a partnership between an able and determined executive and a willing and independent board provided the best path to achieving its organizational goals.

3.6 Leadership and Management: Patterns in Change

The cases we present demonstrate that change is often a difficult process. If an organization does not have steady leadership to provide vision and direction in the dynamic environment in which it exists, it can lose its way, as did the United Way of America under Aramony. Without leaders who can anticipate change, unify forces, and communicate ideas, change is inevitably doomed. Managers must ensure that leaders are kept abreast of environmental changes and changing clientele expectations, even if their role is as constrained as it is within the Quaker meeting. Managers can also ensure that through open communication channels, change is effectively implemented, monitored, and evaluated. Bothwell at the NCRP, Halpern at Nathan Cummings, and Tandon and Marschall at CIVICUS all showed that change can be mastered within the nonprofit organization. Externally driven or internally created, change will have its effect. The question is how it can be shaped to advance the organization's vision and mission.

Let us take a closer look at how the eight nonprofit organizations that are the subject of the cases in Section 3.5 chose to address change. Exhibit 3.1 shows the variety of choices.

The eight cases we present range from the proudest successes to the most shameful corruptions of nonprofit organizations in recent American life. They indicate that both leaders and managers can perform their associational roles successfully or unsuccessfully. The cases suggest the responses that may be taken to reward or correct patterns of leadership and management.

Successful patterns, Exhibit 3.1 suggests, are manifold in the nonprofit world. A leader like the NCRP's Bothwell can shape and manage an organization well over a long period of time. A manager like Nathan Cummings Foundation executive Halpern can perform critical leadership as well as administrative roles.

It is not necessary that either function be filled by a single individual acting alone. A team like CIVICUS's Tandon and Marschall can play the roles of leader and manager, respectively, and build a thriving and productive organization. As the Quaker model suggests, teams of leaders can themselves manage a voluntary organization successfully and productively.

Success, as sweet as it is, is by no means guaranteed to a nonprofit organization. An organization like America's Promise, headed by a beloved national hero, can still perform erratically. On a local level, the effort to create a community collaborative, as in Fettersville, can founder in the face of the seemingly conflicting interests among major nonprofits within the community. Even more discouragingly, charlatans like Aramony and Jack Bennett can corrupt a nonprofit organization to the point that its very viability is threatened.

In these difficult cases, when it is appropriate to change leadership or to change management? We believe that when an organization is struggling, such as America's Promise

EXHIBIT 3.1 Change Leadership? Change Management?

	Successful Responses to Change
Nathan Cummings Foundation	The manager leads for change.
Civicus	The leader teams with the manager for change.
NCRP	The leader manages for change.
Quakers	Leaders manage for change.
	Uncertain Responses to Change
Fettersville Collaborative	Managers frustrate leaders: Change the managers!
America's Promise	The leader frustrates managers: Change the leader!
	Failed Responses to Change
Foundation for New Era Philanthropy	The leader corrupts the organization: Close the organization down!
United way of America under Aramony	The manager corrupts the organization: Fire the manager!

or the Fettersville Collaborative, the proper intervention should take the form of assisting the leader or manager whose actions are most responsible for the organization's distress. Of course, if the leader involved is a retired military hero like Colin Powell, not just anyone can walk into his office to suggest he rethink his ways. Making such interventions, however, is the job of the nonprofit board, difficult as this task can be. If the problem resides with one or more of the organization's managers, the board may find the task easier to address, particularly if its leader can provide direction to the task.

Once an organization crosses the line into wholesale corruption, there is often no viable alternative to the removal of the offending leader or manager. If the board has not been drawn into the corruption, firing the manager may both remove the problem and allow the organization to right itself. Such was the course successfully taken by United Way of America. If the board and its leader are the perpetrators of the offensive activity, however, it may be necessary to dissolve the entire organization, as was done in the case of the Foundation for New Era Philanthropy.

Change, we conclude, is an inescapable reality in nonprofit organization management. We either cope with it or it copes with us. Lead for change, manage for change, or find ways to change leaders or change managers. Firing is the last resort; teaching and learning better ways of leading and managing are far less disruptive and often all that is required. However, the responsibilities of making nonprofit organizations are great, and the potential of this organizational form can easily be wasted. Change must be served.

Endnotes

1. Kotter, J. P. (1996). *Leading Change.* Boston: Harvard Business School Press.
2. Cooperrider, D. L. (ed.). (1999). *Appreciative Inquiry: Rethinking Human Organization Toward a Positive Theory of Change.* Champaign, IL: Stipes Publishing.

3. Herman, R. D., and Heimovics, R. D. (1991). *Executive Leadership in Nonprofit Organizations.* San Francisco: Jossey-Bass.

4. Billitteri, T. J. (2000). "United Ways Seek a New Identity," *Chronicle of Philanthropy* (March 9).

5. Id., p. 21.

6. Id., p. 23.

7. Van Til, J. (2000). *Growing Civil Society: From Nonprofit Sector to Third Space.* Bloomington, IN: Indiana University Press.

8. Id.

9. Van Til, J. and Associates. (2000). *Associations as Assets in the Urban Community: A Study of Two Inner-City Neighborhoods in Camden.* Camden, NJ: Senator Walter Rand Institute for Public Affairs, Rutgers University.

10. Glaser, J. S. (1994). *The United Way Scandal: An Insider's Account of What Went Wrong and Why.* New York: John Wiley & Sons.

11. Id., p. xxiii.

12. Id., pp. 74–75.

13. Id., pp. 81, 91.

14. Id., pp. 104–106.

15. Id., p. 167.

16. Id., p. xix.

17. Id., pp. 235–48.

18. Kramer, R. M. (1998). "Nonprofit Organizations in the 21st Century: Will Sector Matter?" Working paper of the Aspen Institute Nonprofit Sector Research Fund, Washington, DC.

19. Kretzmann, J. P., and J. L. McKnight. (1993). *Building Communities from the Inside Out.* Chicago: ACTA Publications.

20. Gardner, D. S. (1997). *A Family Foundation: Looking to the Future, Honoring the Past.* New York: The Nathan Cummings Foundation.

21. Id.

A Hundred-Year Horizon: Considering Sustainable Development in the Nonprofit Sector

KEITH SEEL, MA, PRINCIPAL
M4i Strategic Management Consulting, Inc.

4.1 Introduction

The belief that an organization—or for that matter, any part of our society, including the nonprofit sector—is sustainable is taken for granted. Unless they are in imminent danger of collapse, most organizations anticipate that they will be present and operating in their communities in the future. Many processes, such as strategic planning, scenario planning, forecasting, and the like, are specifically designed to help an organization consider its future and find ways to grow and expand its activities. Yet numerous factors are converging that raise questions about whether current structures—organizations, communities, economies—are in fact sustainable.

For managers in the nonprofit sector, the topic of sustainable development may appear to be better addressed in the corporate sector, in particular, by large resource companies or manufacturers. At a personal level, each of us knows the importance of the 3Rs—reduce, reuse, and recycle—the basic philosophy of sustainable development. If sustainable development concepts have a role to play in the business sector and in our personal lives, there should be elements that also apply to how the nonprofit sector is managed and operates. The purpose of this chapter is to explore and raise for further discussion ideas related to the application of sustainable development concepts to nonprofit-sector management and operations.

4.2   Background

In general, most people accept that unrestrained, unquestioned, and uncoordinated growth creates excessive burdens on both environmental and social systems—the poor get poorer and environmental degradation increases. Runaway economies of the developed world are having massive impacts on the health of communities both at home and in the developing world.

In 1987, the Brundtland Commission published a groundbreaking report urging both a theoretical and practical response to the emerging development crisis that is directly threatening the global environment and the global economy.[1] In particular, the report discusses the cycle of "poverty, debt, overuse of primary resources, environmental degradation, increased poverty, and increased debt."[2] The Brundtland Commission urged for the widespread adoption of sustainable development. The concept of sustainable development means "a process of change in which the exploitation of resources, the direction of investments, the orientation of technological development, and institutional change are made consistent with future as well as present needs."[3]

Since the Brundtland Commission, corporate North America has been the sector that has made the most moves toward addressing the issue of sustainable development largely by focusing on environmental impacts, mostly from the 3Rs perspective: reduce, recycle, and reuse. The motivators for corporate consideration of the environmental factors associated with doing business include market advantage, regulatory advantage, and organizational and leadership values.[4]

Through the perspective of sustainable development, capitalism and the free-market economy that is in place in much of the world is being questioned.[5] Westley and Vredenburg present the global picture this way: "Citizens of the industrialized countries are dependent on the developing countries for international peace and security because countries that cannot provide basic social services and a minimum standard of living are vulnerable…"[6] Poverty statistics in North America point out that many of our own citizens do not have access to basic services such as health care and live below the poverty line. These people and the communities they live in are also at risk. The successes of a global free market may be creating less sustainable communities in developed, as well as developing, countries.

4.3   Why Look at Sustainable Development?

The free-market economy has produced enormous wealth—for some. It has also created an imbalance in our social fabric. For example, there are clearly issues associated with the observation that roughly 20 percent of the world's population consumes 75 percent of the world's resources. Dalla Costa analyzed corporate ethical performance and suggests that the need for a "global business ethic" is critical because of the "moral inversions" created by a runaway free-market economy. Included in the moral inversions are "personal stress, community dysfunction and ecological breakdown."[7] He suggests that "a global ethic for the global economy is not so much a revolution in values as a return to the genuine human virtues that economic progress has reversed."

Nonprofit organizations across North America know that demands on their services are increasing. This is especially true for core services such as those in the areas of health and welfare, education, crime and violence, and poverty alleviation. Paradoxically, these

EXHIBIT 4.1 Ecological Footprint—One Window on Sustainability

Most of the literature on sustainable development addresses the environment. From the environmental effects, we can begin to understand the impacts that individuals have on their environment. One useful model is the notion of an "ecological footprint."[a] Interesting outcomes of the ecological footprint model include:

- Today, if every human being lived at the current North American standards, we would need two additional planet Earths to provide the necessary resources.
- If the world's population lived at North American standards, then just keeping up with population growth for the next century, five additional planet Earths would be needed.
- Most developed countries require several times their land area to provide the necessary resources. Where is this extra land? In the developing world, where crops are grown and resources harvested and brought back to developed countries.
- Approximately three-fourths of all consumption of resources is by 1.1 billion people who live in affluence. This leaves one-fourth for the remaining 4.6 billion people.
- The average American uses 25 acres (equivalent to 25 football fields) to support his or her current lifestyle. The average Canadian has an ecological footprint that is 25% less and the average Italian 60% less.
- A typical North American city of 100,000 people imports 180 tons of food a day, 900 tons of fuel a day, and 56,000 tons of water a day, and dumps 90,000 tons of garbage a year and 36,000 tons of human waste a year.[b]

[a] Rees, W., and M. Wackernagel. (1994). Ecological Footprints and Appropriate Carrying Capacity: Measuring the Natural Capital Requirements of the Human Economy. In A-M. Jansson, M. Hammer, C. Folke, and R. Costanza (eds.). *Investing in Natural Capital: The Ecological Economics Approach to Sustainability.* Washington: Island Press, pp. 362–390.

[b] FEESA, An Environmental Education Society. (1995). *Sustainable Communities Initiative.* Edmonton, Alberta: Author, 2.

growing needs come at a time of record stock markets and virtually nonexistent inflation. If one listens to the political rhetoric, the citizens of Canada and the United States are doing much better. An examination of some of the facts tells a different story, however.

In Canada, the 1990s saw a one-way trend for all levels of income—families at the richest end of the spectrum barely held their ground, while a growing proportion of middle-income families lost ground. The Centre for Social Justice observes that, "Between 1989 and 1997, the proportion of families raising children who earn less than $35,388 grew from 30 to 35 percent. The very bottom of the income scale grew the fastest. The poorest 10 percent of families earned less than $11,567 in 1989. By 1997, that number swelled to 14 percent. Not only are there more families in the lowest income category but they have also become poorer over time: to belong to the poorest 10 percent of the population meant earning less than $11,567 in 1989. By 1997, it meant earning less than $6,591."[8] To compound the slide in income, governments have undertaken tax cuts as a solution to increase economic prosperity. These cuts "do nothing for the poorest families who have no income to register a tax cut and they erode the public services and supports people rely on in their communities."[9]

In the United States, according to the National Center for Children in Poverty, the young child poverty rate has grown among all racial and ethnic groups, and in urban, suburban, and rural areas. In particular:

- The number of American young children living in poverty increased from 3.5 million in 1979 to 5.2 million in 1997.
- Twenty-two percent of young children in America live in poverty, that is, in families with incomes below the federal poverty line ($12,802 for a family of three in 1997).
- A majority of all poor children under age six (65 percent) live with at least one employed parent. Only one-sixth of poor young children (17 percent) live in families who rely solely on public assistance for income.
- Ten percent of America's young children live in extreme poverty, in families with incomes of under 50 percent of the poverty line. (In 1997, the extreme poverty line was $6,401 for a family of three.) The extreme poverty rate among young children is growing faster than the young child poverty rate. Research indicates that extreme poverty during the first five years of life has especially deleterious effects on children's future life chances compared to less extreme poverty experienced later in childhood.
- Forty-two percent of all children under age 6 live in or near poverty, in families with incomes below 185 percent of the poverty line ($23,684 for a family of three). Many of the concerns of "near poor" families overlap with those of the poor (e.g., the need for well-paying jobs and access to affordable quality child care and health care).[10]

These facts are important reminders to managers in the nonprofit sector that, because the need for their organization's services is real (and growing), they must be conducting long-term, future-oriented planning. In other words, managers in the nonprofit sector need to begin to seriously include sustainable development concepts in their strategic and operational planning. Unfortunately, there is a general lack of awareness and concern regarding sustainable development. In large part, this is because "many organizations in the developed world have been wedded to 'command and control' strategies in which the system is viewed as a machine" and that the strategies they develop are "poorly tuned to adaptive, conservative needs of the larger physical or economic system of which single organizations are a part."[11] In short, the near-total focus of organizations on the mechanics of day-to-day operations has had the consequence of shortening the time frame within which strategic thinking occurs. The result is short-term thinking and a more reactive organizational stance. To be sustainable, organizations will need to push forward the time frame for planning and acting.

4.4   What Is the Sustainable Development Model?

There are three basic elements to a sustainable development model:

1. Environmental objectives
2. Economic objectives
3. Social objectives

Together, the objectives being addressed are intended to lead toward a sustainable future (see Exhibit 4.2). Each of the elements of the sustainable development model are discussed in the following subsections.[12]

EXHIBIT 4.2 The Sustainable Development Model

Economic Objectives
Increase in productive capital
- Growth
- Development
- Efficiency

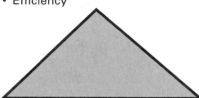

Environmental Objectives
Increase in natural capital
- Ecosystem integrity
- Carrying capacity
- Biodiversity

Social Objectives
Increase in human and social capital
- Poverty alleviation/equity
- Education
- Social and cultural cohesion

Sources: See note 12. Vrederberg, H. (Winter, 2000). Ph.D. Seminar in Sustainable Development Strategies. Reprinted with permission.

(A) ENVIRONMENTAL OBJECTIVES

Environmental objectives aim to increase natural capital, including environmental assets. This means that the activities of an organization should work toward enhancing the integrity of the ecosystem, enhancing the carrying capacity of the ecosystem, and enhancing biodiversity. For an organization, this may mean reducing its ecological footprint (see Exhibit 4.1). Activities here may also include the creation or maintenance of parks or green spaces, planting trees, car pooling, waste management, office recycling programs, purchasing recycled products, and so on.

(B) ECONOMIC OBJECTIVES

Economic objectives are aimed at increasing productive capital, including financial resources, infrastructure, equipment, and other productive resources. This means that an organization is looking for ways to improve its operating efficiency, encouraging sustainable growth and development. In the case of growth and development, this may mean creating partnerships, collaborating with others, or creating new service models.

(C) SOCIAL OBJECTIVES

Social objectives aim to increase human and social capital, including investing in the health, education, and nutrition of individuals as well as investing in formal and informal social institutions. An organization would be looking for ways to address poverty, enhance educational opportunities, build social and cultural cohesion, and contribute to the well-being of the community. The activities within this part of the sustainable development model are largely the responsibilities of the nonprofit sector. Yet, each organization could look for opportunities to provide better-paying or more jobs, encourage workplace volunteering, establish training or personal development opportunities, encourage workplace diversity, support ethical practices, practice philanthropy, and so on.

From a whole-community perspective, the major role of nonprofit organizations is in helping to meet the social objectives within the sustainable development model. Most nonprofit organizations have mission statements that make this clear. Exhibit 4.3 gives some examples of mission statements. Because nonprofit organizations fulfill social objectives, businesses involved in sustainable development initiatives are beginning to seek them out for mutually beneficial partnerships. Knowing the importance of social objectives to sustainable development, nonprofit managers may consider taking a more proactive role in identifying and collaborating with the business community. For managers interested in contacting companies, Exhibit 4.4 provides a listing of corporations that have been recognized for their sustainable development initiatives.

EXHIBIT 4.3 Examples of Mission Statements

AMERICAN RED CROSS—The American Red Cross, a humanitarian organization led by volunteers and guided by its Congressional Charter and the Fundamental Principles of the International Red Cross Movement, will provide relief to victims of disasters and help people prevent, prepare for, and respond to emergencies.

CANADIAN CANCER SOCIETY—The Canadian Cancer Society is a national community-based organization of volunteers, whose mission is the eradication of cancer and the enhancement of the quality of life of people living with cancer.

SALVATION ARMY INTERNATIONAL—The Salvation Army's message is based on the Bible; its motivation is the love of God as revealed in Jesus Christ. Its mission is to proclaim His gospel, to persuade men and women to become His disciples, and to engage in a program of practical concern for the needs of humanity. Its ministry is offered to all, regardless of race, creed, color, age, or sex.

BOYS AND GIRLS CLUBS OF AMERICA—Our mission is the Movement's reason for being: To inspire and enable all young people, especially those from disadvantaged circumstances, to realize their full potential as productive, responsible, and caring citizens.

GIRL GUIDES OF CANADA—Girl Guides of Canada–Guides du Canada is a Movement for girls, led by women. It challenges girls to reach their potential and empowers them to give leadership and service as responsible citizens of the world.

FRIENDS OF RUSSIAN CHILDREN—Friends of Russian Children through innovation, education, and understanding helps badly burned children to a brighter future.

SOUTH AFRICAN NATIONAL COUNCIL ON ALCOHOLISM AND DRUG DEPENDENCE—SANCA has as its overall mission to address chemical dependency through the provision of specialized, accessible, and affordable developmental, prevention, and treatment services to all the people of South Africa, thereby enhancing the quality of life and restoring the self-respect and dignity of persons affected by alcoholism and drug dependence.

AMERICA DIABETES ASSOCIATION—To prevent and cure diabetes and improve the lives of all people affected by diabetes.

EXHIBIT 4.4 Examples of Companies Recognized as Leaders in Sustainable Development

1. The Dow Jones Sustainability Group Index[a] was launched in September 1999 and is intended to track the performance of companies that are leaders in sustainable development. The North American companies on the index are:
   Canada
   Dofasco Inc., Suncor Energy Inc., Enbridge Inc., TransAlta Corporation
   United States
   Bristol-Myers Squibb Co., Honeywell Inc.

2. ConAgra[b] recognizes its operating companies with a sustainable development award. Award winners in 2000 included:
   Butterball Turkey, ConAgra Frozen Foods, ConAgra Malt, ASE Deli/Foodservice Company, Transbas Inc. United Agri Products U.K. Ltd., Lamb Weston Inc., Beatrice Cheese, ConAgra Poultry, ConAgra Signature Meats Group

3. Renew America,[c] a nonprofit organization, recognizes a range of programs that implement sustainable development practices. Recent award winners included:
   Stoneyfield Farm Yogurt, Practical Farmers of Iowa (Iowa State University), The Northeast Pennsylvania Urban Forestry Program, Rensselaerville Institute's Small Towns Environment Program, Gap Analysis Program of the U.S. Geological Survey, New York State's Office of Mental Health, HandMade in America, Purchase of Development Rights Program, Governor Whitman's Sustainable Development Program (New Jersey), Transportation and Air Quality Program (Chicago), Bates College, DaimlerChrysler Corporation—Mack Avenue Engine Plant, Kids Involved in Doing Service as Planners Program, SouthWest Organizing Project (New Mexico)

4. The Manitoba Round Table on Environment and Economy gave the Mennonite Central Committee of Canada an award for outstanding achievement in sustainable development.[d]

---

[a] Dow Jones Indexes. (2000). http://indexes.dowjones.com/djsgi/.

[b] ConAgra Sustainable Development Awards. (2000). http//www.conagra.com/susawrd.html. Within the sustainable development plan, the total reduced environmental impact of ConAgra's companies in 1999 was 9,000 tons less landfill, 293 million gallons of water saved, reduced energy use of 5.6 million kilowatts, and an operational cost savings of $8.25 million. No mention is made of social gains within their sustainable development plan.

[c] Renew America. (2000). http://www.crest.org/environment/renew_america/winrs99.htm.

[d] Mennonite Central Committee. (2000). http://www.mcc.org/pr/1998/06-30/4.html.

4.5 Sustainable Business Practice

The sustainable development model is based on three broad sets of objectives—environmental, economic, and social. Within these objectives occur the day-to-day operations of an organization. If the broad sustainable development goals are to be achieved, then organizations themselves need to consider sustainable business practices. There are three considerations for sustainable business practice: content, context, and process. Content refers to the impacts, both positive and negative, of an organization's activities on the economy, society, and the environment. Context refers to characteristics within the organization that support or resist change, such as structure, governance, or planning. Context also includes external factors such as demographic changes, political climate, and competitive/cooperative actions of others. Process identifies the ways in which values and ideas enter day-to-day operations of an organization. Processes address the complex interactions and interrelationships between individuals and organizations.

Content, context, and process as considerations for sustainable business practice relate directly to a good strategic planning process. In other words, organizations that undertake an effective strategic planning process can, with some small modifications, address sustainable business practices. This is exciting because with a small amount of additional effort, organizations can plan where they want to go and prepare themselves so that they arrive there in good working order. Exhibit 4.5 sketches the linkages between the steps of an effective strategic planning process and sustainable business practices and suggests potentially new emergent issues for managers.

4.6   Reflections on Sustainable Development in the Nonprofit Sector

Nonprofit organizations hold a very special public trust and therefore have greater responsibilities and accountabilities.[13] Accountability can be understood as "the requirement to explain and accept responsibility for carrying out an assigned mandate in light of agreed upon expectations. It involves taking into consideration the public trust in the exercise of responsibilities; providing detailed information about how responsibilities have been carried out and what outcomes have been achieved; and accepting the responsibility for outcomes, including problems created or not corrected."[14] From a sustainable development perspective, simply completing work from day to day is not sufficient, nor is planning from year to year. For example, seeking year-to-year funding for a program means that people who depend on the services provided are at risk of having those services withdrawn the moment that funding comes up short. Meeting a service need is a worthwhile activity, but the moment that people come to depend or rely on the service while at the same time management is looking only one year into the future, both ethical and sustainability issues come up. As holders of a public trust and as providers of services to people in the community, nonprofit organizations must build sustainability into their planning and development frameworks.

Within the various sectors of our community—public, private, nonprofit—pluralism is an important reality. Each sector strives to become more efficient and effective. In practice, this has come to mean that each sector becomes a kind of silo, working within its own boundaries and not seeking opportunities within the other sectors. The challenge is that these silos create an undue burden on the environment, economy, and society. Because a community is actually made up of all the sectors, a change in the role and responsibility of any one of the sectors has a profound impact on the others. Consider the effects of government changing tax rates or off-loading services. Peter Drucker proposes a new pluralism that "requires what might be called *civic responsibility:* giving to the community in the pursuit of one's own interest or of one's own work… There is need for the acceptance of leaders in every single institution and in every single sector that they, as leaders, have two responsibilities. They are responsible and accountable for the performance of their institutions, and that requires them and their institutions to be concentrated, focused, limited. They are responsible also, however, for the community as a whole. This requires commitment. It requires willingness to accept that other institutions have different values, respect

EXHIBIT 4.5 Linking Strategic Planning and Sustainable Business Practices

Strategic Planning Steps	Sustainable Business Practice	Emergent Considerations for Managers—INTERNAL & EXTERNAL
Phase 1—Situational Analysis • Preparing to Plan • Taking Stock	Content—existing impacts Context—internal and external barriers/ supports to change Process—existing values, interactions, and relationships	In terms of environment, economy, and society: • What has our contribution been? • What are our values? • What do we believe is truth, and is that the same as others we work with? • Does our practice reflect our values? • Do we have positive relationships with key stakeholders? • How do we assess/evaluate our practices to date? • From the perspective of different stakeholders, what would be the positives or negatives if the organization ceased to be? • What is our organizational culture and how does that compare with the community around us?
Phase 2—Strategic Framework • Values, Behavior, Philosophy • Vision and Mission • Issue Resolution/Gap Analysis	Content—existing impacts and preferred impacts Context—internal and external barriers/ supports to change and scale of change desired Process—existing and preferred values, interactions, and relationships	In terms of environment, economy, and society: • What values, behaviors, and philosophy does the organization what to create? • Where does the organization want to go and what are the means to get there? • What happens if we consider a 100-year planning horizon? • What are the issues the organization can address on its own, with others, or acknowledge it cannot address? • Who should the organization work with or avoid and why? • Who would be harmed if our plan does not work? • Are our ends ethical?
Phase 3—Operational or Business Plans • Goals, Objectives, Action Plans • Implementation and Evaluation	Content—preferred impacts and evaluation methods or measures Context—realized supports for change, barriers to change addressed	In terms of environment, economy, and society: • Are the means that we will use to achieve our ends ethical? • Does the organization have goals and objectives that directly address how it will be sustainable?

Process—steps to implement or develop values, interactions, and relationships	• How will the organization evaluate its activities? • Is the evaluation process broad enough to consider a depth and breadth of stakeholders? • What role does the community have in implementing or evaluating goals? • What economic credit or deficit does the organization create? • What environmental credit or deficit does the organization create? • What social credit or deficit does the organization create?

for these values, and willingness to learn what these values are. It requires hard work. But above all it requires commitment, conviction, dedication to the common good."[15] Approaches like sustainable development and sustainable business practices can help managers in nonprofit agencies ensure that meeting the common good continues into the future.

4.7   Conclusion

Drucker's call for commitment, conviction, and dedication to the common good is the foundation of sustainable development and sustainable business practices. In the nonprofit sector, we may assume that by virtue of the sector we are in, that we exemplify commitment, conviction, and dedication to the common good. Observation of actual practice may reveal something quite different, however. In our need to secure funding, to undertake reactive instead of proactive planning, and to only rarely cooperate, the nonprofit sector is not addressing sustainability. As poverty and other statistics demonstrate, the role that the nonprofit sector plays will grow. What we need to do is consider the components of sustainable development as new tools to ensure that we are still doing a good job in 100 years.

Endnotes

1. World Commission on Environment and Development. (1987). *Our Common Future.* New York: Oxford University Press.
2. Westley, F., and H. Vredenburg. (1996). "Sustainability and the Corporation," *Journal of Management Inquiry* 5(2): 104–119.
3. See note 1.
4. See note 2.
5. Brown, L. (1995). *Who Will Feed China?* New York: Norton.
6. See note 2.
7. Dalla Costa, J. (1998). *The Ethical Imperative.* Toronto: HarperCollins.

8. Yalnizyan, A. (2000). *Canada's Great Divide: The Politics of the Growing Gap Between Rich and Poor in the 1990s.* Toronto: Centre for Social Justice. http://www.socialjustice.org/java/javaindex_new.html.

9. Id.

10. National Center for Children in Poverty (2000). http://cpmcnet.columbia.edu/dept/nccp/ycpf.html.

11. See note 2.

12. Adapted from Khan, M. A. (1995). "Sustainable Development: The Key Concepts, Issues and Implications," *Sustainable Development* 3: 63–69; Serageldin, I., and A. Steer (eds.). (1994). *Making Development Sustainable: From Concepts to Action.* Washington DC: The World Bank; Munasinghe, M. (1993). *Environmental Economics and Sustainable Development.* Washington, DC: The World Bank, World Bank Environment Paper Number 3.

13. Seel, K., M. Regel, and M. Meneghetti. (2000). Governance—Creating Capable Leadership in the Not-for-Profit Sector. In T. Connors (ed.). *Nonprofit Handbook: Management, 2000 Supplement.* New York: John Wiley & Sons; Seel, K. (1998). Ethics and Values in the Not-for-Profit Organization. In T. Connors (ed.). *Nonprofit Handbook: Management, 1998 Supplement.* New York: John Wiley & Sons.

14. Panel on Accountability and Governance in the Voluntary Sector. (February 1999). Building on Strength: Improving Governance and Accountability in Canada's Voluntary Sector. Final Report. Ottawa: Voluntary Sector Roundtable, p. 118.

15. Drucker, P. (1999). In F. Hesselbein, M. Goldsmith, I. Somerville (eds.). *Leading Beyond the Walls.* San Francisco: Jossey-Bass. *http://www.pfdf.org/leaderbooks/foundation/new-pluralism.html.*

5 ▼ Lessons in Strategic Plan Implementation

Marci Bernstein Lu, MNO
The Cleveland Foundation

Christine Lucas, MNO
Nonprofit Services of Florida
Leadership Florida Statewide Community Foundation

Valerie Raines, MNO
The Catholic Diocese of Cleveland Foundation

John A. Yankey, PhD
Mandel School of Applied Social Sciences
Case Western Reserve University

Little has been written and probably less is understood about successful implementation than about any other phase of strategic management.

James M. Higgins (1983)

5.1 Introduction

In comparison to the amount of literature available on strategic planning, writing on implementation is scarce. Moreover, what is available pertains mainly to the for-profit sector. One reason for the relative lack of information may be the common assumption that good strategic planning will lead to good implementation. However, this is not necessarily the case. Indeed, "practitioners are emphatic in saying that it is a whole lot easier to develop a sound strategic plan than it is to 'make it happen.'"[1]

Most of the literature available on implementation affirms that the executive director is ultimately accountable for translating the strategic plan into reality.[2–3] The shifting of primary responsibility from board to staff occurs because crafting strategy is largely a visionary, creative process, whereas implementing strategy is primarily an internal administrative activity. Thompson and Strickland observe:

Whereas strategy formulation entails heavy doses of vision, analysis, and entrepreneurial judgment, successful strategy implementation depends upon the skills of working through others, organizing, motivating, culture-building, and creating strong fits between strategy and how the organization does things. Ingrained behavior does not change just because a new strategy has been announced. In comparison, implementing strategy poses the tougher, more time-consuming management challenge.[4]

Implementation must be designed to fit the organization's condition, culture, and environmental setting, as well as the type of strategy and the amount of strategic change involved. Implementing a bold new plan, for example, poses different problems than fine-tuning an existing strategy. Nonprofit leaders must understand not only how much culture change is required for goal attainment but also how to manage this change. The executive director's own skills and style of getting things done must also be taken into account.

Although strategic planning is now widely regarded as standard practice for a self-renewing organization, implementation remains the least understood phase of strategic management. In order to prevent strategic plans from collecting dust on a shelf, leaders of nonprofit organizations must address implementation issues throughout the planning process rather than relegating them to afterthoughts. To provide insight into what factors contribute to success or difficulty in operationalizing strategy, this chapter draws not only from the theoretical framework culled from available literature, but also from our own research in the field. Section 5.4 offers practitioners a guide for strategy implementation based on a set of common success indicators.

5.2 Field Study

Our field research was not initially conceived as a scientific study but rather as an independent project following three semesters of graduate-level coursework in strategic planning at the Mandel Center for Nonprofit Organizations at Case Western Reserve University, Cleveland, Ohio. Through our academic work and experience as strategic planning consultants, we observed that many nonprofit organizations devoted a significant amount of time, energy, and resources to strategy formulation. Implementation, however, was not fully discussed. Were nonprofit organizations therefore prepared to translate vision into action? Were they successful in actualizing their newly developed strategic goals? To investigate these questions, we designed a research study to explore:

- Whether nonprofit organizations (NPOs) are successful in implementing strategic plans once developed
- How NPOs move from plan development to action
- What factors and tactics contribute to success or difficulty in implementing strategic goals

(A) DATA SOURCES

We relied on two readily available lists to identify NPOs that had recently undergone strategic planning. The first group had obtained free strategic planning consultation through the Mandel Center of Nonprofit Organizations at Case Western Reserve University. The second was a list of organizations that had financed their planning process, either partially or in full, through grant support from The Cleveland Foundation within the past five years. From this pool of more than 50 organizations, 15 were selected to create a small yet diverse sample set. Although constructed from convenience, the sample represents a range of subsectors, budget sizes, staffing levels, and stages of implementation.

All 15 organizations are located in the Greater Cleveland area. Exhibit 5.1 presents data on the type of subsectors represented in the study. Exhibit 5.2 presents summary data on the organizations' annual operating budgets, which range from a low of $32,000 to a high of $18 million. There is also considerable variety in the organizations' staffing levels,

EXHIBIT 5.1 Type of Subsector

	Frequency	Percentage
Human Services	6	40.0
Cultural	3	20.0
Educational	2	13.3
Health	3	20.0
Volunteer Member Association	1	6.7
Total	15	100.0

EXHIBIT 5.2 Annual Operating Budget

	Frequency	Percentage
$500,000 or less	7	46.7
$500,000–$999,999	0	0.0
$1 million–$10 million	6	40.0
Greater than $10 million	2	13.3
Total	15	100.0

EXHIBIT 5.3 Number of Paid Employees

	Frequency	Percentage
10 or fewer	7	46.7
11–100	5	33.3
101–300	1	6.7
More than 300	2	13.3
Total	15	100.0

which range from one full-time employee to 350 full- and part-time personnel (see Exhibit 5.3). Two of the organizations rely on a large volunteer core to fulfill their mission. All but three of the organizations reported having a previous history of long-range or strategic planning—whether successfully completed or not.

(B) DATA COLLECTION

The findings from our field study are based primarily on semistructured interviews with each of the 15 executive directors. In four cases, key organizational members, such as the strategic planning committee chair, board president, president-elect, chief financial officer, or other senior staff, also participated in the interview. While additional, separate interviews with multiple stakeholders would have enhanced our findings, our focus on executive directors as the key informant group is appropriate because their insights are most important for understanding strategy implementation. Again, it is worth reiterating that responsibility for leading the implementation process ordinarily lies with the executive director.

To guide the interviews, we developed a set of broad discussion questions based on the theories of strategy implementation found in the literature. The questions were designed to gather information on the organization's strategic planning process, the implementation process, monitoring and review procedures, successes and challenges, and outcomes.

Finally, although we recognize the value of a highly formalized, quantitative research design, limited time and resources constrained the scope and method of our study. Notwithstanding the limitations, we believe this project to be instructive to the field. Hence, this study is presented as exploratory research with implications for nonprofit practitioners, funders, and researchers. Further investigation into strategy implementation is recommended.

5.3 Findings from the Field

Although most of the practitioners interviewed reported challenges to strategy implementation, they believe their organizations have been successful in implementing important components of their plans. In all cases, strategic planning was viewed as beneficial. The following 10 key factors that either contributed to or frustrated implementation emerged from the interviews.

(A) ENSURING ORGANIZATIONAL READINESS

One prerequisite for success is that organizations and their members must be ready to undertake strategic planning. Interestingly, this variable was observed by organizations of varying maturity in our study—from a grassroots arts group taking its first step toward professionalization to a highly sophisticated health care organization. For the organization with a staff of one, this meant not embarking on strategic planning until it had engaged in preliminary planning activities, such as board training, made possible by a technical assistance grant. The organization with over 300 staff members believed that several years of deliberate team building and staff education had created an organizational culture open to change. Consequently, staff were prepared to implement strategic changes. (See Redding and Catalanello[5] for a complete discussion of strategic readiness as it relates to an organization's ability to change.)

(B) DEVELOPING A SOUND STRATEGY

It is critical to recognize that plan development and implementation are inextricably linked. Both Brinckerhoff[6] and Bryson[7] note that a well-written plan can serve as a management tool that facilitates implementation. Similarly, respondents in our study indicated that a comprehensive planning process—one that includes both internal and external stakeholders—promotes sound strategy development and helps to ensure success. Although a sound strategy does not guarantee successful implementation, difficulty is more certain without one.

Multiple respondents attributed successful implementation to having involved the organization's leadership and those responsible for implementation in the development process. By doing so, they recognized that implementers must believe in the plan's goals and objectives. Eadie's work, published by the National Center for Nonprofit Boards, underscores this finding.[8] Organizational leaders must know that the process was well coordinated and ably facilitated, that the outcomes were based on organizational and environmental realities, and that the necessary stakeholders were involved. This applies, perhaps more so, to parties not involved in strategy formulation but who are involved in implementation. In such cases, the transfer of responsibility is critical for success.[9]

The interviews further revealed that an effective strategic planning process improved morale, promoted team building, and clarified the institution's mission. Heightened expectations and clearer direction thus served as motivating forces during the implementation stage. Enthusiasm, however, was not enough to ensure successful goal attainment. More than one executive director emphasized that while the plan needed to be challenging and inspiring, it also had to be feasible to be implemented. They noted that a structured planning process helped to create the internal focus and discipline for realistic goal setting. (Research by Khan[10] suggests that in an uncertain environment, flexibility is also a key to realistic goal setting.) Occasionally, we found that implementation preceded the completion of plan development when priorities with sufficient urgency arose during the process.

(C) USING CONSULTANTS

The development of a sound strategy is more likely if the organization engages the services of a consultant who can bring needed expertise and discipline to the process.[11] Consultants can also be retained to help with implementation.

All of the organizations we interviewed reported using consultants during strategic planning, though not all consultants directly aided implementation. Ten agencies used paid consultants, one obtained professional *pro bono* consultant services, and four used teams of unpaid graduate students educated in strategic planning. All organizations credited the consultants with playing a key role in the success of the development and implementation of their strategic plans. Notably, engaging an external consultant provided the incentive for active internal participation and lent credibility to the process and the resulting plan. By investing in a paid consultant or securing the commitment of either graduate students or professionals providing significant *pro bono* time, the organizations felt compelled to commit their staffs and other stakeholders to the process.

The executive directors recounted that past attempts at strategic planning had stalled when they either failed to use a consultant or used one that was not compatible with their organization's culture and values. With regard to the former, the executive directors had learned that internal stakeholders, such as themselves or board members, could not effectively be both facilitator and participant. In the latter case, consultants who did not fit with the organization's culture were not perceived as credible. As a result, implementation was undermined because key stakeholders did not necessarily accept the new strategy.

When respondents had engaged the services of a credible, outside consultant, the momentum for planning was sustained. Using their facilitation skills, consultants kept participants focused, did not allow stakeholders to avoid difficult issues, and kept the process moving along a reasonable timetable even when people experienced discouragement and frustration. The executive directors also reported that their consultants brought key insights into the planning and implementation processes, as well as competitor information and environmental data within the organization's sector or region. Consultants with industry-specific expertise generated added value and helped ensure that newly developed strategies were achievable. Finally, in addition to strategic planning expertise, consultants often provided needed support to organizational leaders or were retained to provide staff and board training. Some also helped with implementation.

(D) COORDINATING STRATEGIC PLANNING WITH BUDGET CYCLE

Timing was also an important factor. Organizations that scheduled strategic planning to coincide with upcoming fiscal year planning were able to proactively create an operating budget supportive of the plan. This deliberate focus on resource management allowed for a seamless flow from planning to implementation. (See Higgins and Vincze,[12] for a discussion of establishing and managing resources to achieve successful implementation.)

(E) DEVELOPING AN ACTION PLAN

Action plans are effective tools for translating strategic vision into tangible steps. At the minimum, such plans should include measurable objectives, time lines, estimated budget requirements, and the person or team responsible for accomplishing each objective. The process of writing an action plan should not be delegated to an external consultant. Although a consultant may assist in the process, assigning this task to organizational members helps to build both internal capability and ownership of the implementation phase.

Several of the executive directors interviewed reported that action plan documents promoted both productivity and accountability among the staff, especially when they were linked to performance reviews. Furthermore, action plans that assigned board responsibilities to strategic objectives resulted in a better understanding among organizational leadership of what it takes to turn talk into action. For example, prior to strategic planning, one board used to set grandiose goals for its executive director to implement. Now that board members have implementation responsibilities, the organization's goals are more sensible and thus more easily accomplished.

(F) EXERCISING STRATEGIC LEADERSHIP

All interviewees cited the importance of process champions (individuals who accept responsibility for keeping the organization focused on goal attainment) for successful plan development and implementation. While process champions are beneficial at all rungs of the organizational ladder, they are critical at the board and executive level. This senior leadership is necessary for galvanizing organizational commitment to the strategy and motivating those stakeholders responsible for implementation. Though cheerleaders of the process, senior leadership must not hesitate to initiate corrective action when resistant employees are disrupting strategy accomplishment.

Through our research, we found that implementation was aided when board leadership set goals for the executive director that were directly linked to the strategic plan. Active board oversight and evaluation of the executive director also helped to promote accountability. Lack of strong board leadership was mentioned as an impediment to effective implementation, particularly in organizations with limited staff. In one case in which board leadership was weak, the planning process did result in an improved board selection process, however. Often, a good strategic plan can be used as a recruitment tool for board and staff.[13]

Executive leadership was pivotal in organizing and motivating staff who were ultimately responsible for executing strategic objectives. When implementation was successful, executive directors made sure their staff members understood that plan implementation meant organizational success. They also made sure that the staff possessed the necessary implementation skills or had access to professional development opportunities in order to acquire them.

In four cases, the executive directors we interviewed were hired after the strategic plan had been developed. The new executives, although not directly involved in plan development, became responsible for implementation. One might expect that this presented problems because they were not involved in determining their organization's direction and were expected to carry out objectives with which they may not agree. Instead, we learned that while this plan might not have reflected their goals for the organization, it provided needed consistency during a critical transition period. In almost every case, the executive directors found that their work was focused and productive in the early months by the existence of the plan. Furthermore, while implementing the current plan, new executive directors were able to become well acquainted with their organizations and could begin framing many of the issues that would need to be addressed in a subsequent plan.

In a case in which an executive director was hired to manage a floundering organization without a plan, the executive director initiated an internal two-year "vision growth plan" instead of undertaking a full-fledged strategic planning process. This approach recognized the urgent need for short-term objectives to address immediate dysfunctions. (In such situations, Migliore et al.[14] provide useful guidelines on the integration of planning and control and performance evaluation procedures.) During this period, the executive director was able to get acclimated and stabilize the organization, which improved its readiness to tackle comprehensive strategic planning at a later date.

(G) INSTITUTIONALIZING MECHANISMS TO CONTROL, MONITOR, AND REVIEW PROGRESS

Goal attainment is enhanced when nonprofit organizations formalize control, monitoring, and review procedures. Ideally, boards should conduct periodic self-appraisal assessments to determine how well they are performing their fiduciary duties. These performance appraisals should also include an assessment of how well the organization is doing in realizing its strategic goals. A board subcommittee should also be established to review progress, perhaps quarterly, and to make policy decisions when strategic adjustments become necessary. In order to make appropriate modifications, however, there must be internal capability to gather environmental data on an ongoing basis that informs whether strategic objectives are still relevant. This responsibility might be delegated to an implementation team composed of staff representing key organizational functions. In some cases, larger organizations have the resources to hire an internal strategic planner charged with managing implementation. Finally, managers might consider linking employee performance reviews to progress made on meeting strategic performance targets.

(H) KEEPING THE PLAN IN FRONT OF STAKEHOLDERS

Below et al. discuss the importance of communicating the strategic plan throughout the organization.[15] Our field study affirmed this finding. Those interviewed offered strategies for keeping the plan and its progress in front of stakeholders. Many spoke of including progress reports on their board's agenda. They also noted the importance of keeping the strategic plan before staff through both verbal and written means, such as updates at staff meetings, and by creating related performance work plans. Also, newsletters and other organizational communications hammered home to stakeholders the goals and objectives of the plan, celebrated the accomplishments, and recognized persons responsible for getting the job done. Finally, a communications strategy should also include informing external stakeholders, particularly funders.

(I) ORGANIZATIONAL CULTURE

Embedded organizational culture is often an impediment to successful strategy implementation. Nonprofit leaders who consciously shape group context and sense making, however, understand that effective leveraging of core traditions can help minimize discomfort with strategic transition.[16] Indeed, the more change, the more traditions need to be emphasized. A well-managed planning process can also help limit opposition to change by exposing underlying fears and tensions in a forum in which constructive dialogue can occur. Our study revealed that implementation was smoother when the strategic planning process included facilitated discussions in which board and staff confronted critical issues and debated sacred cows.

Board and staff were eager to begin implementation when the planning process produced a happier or healthier work environment. In the cases in which this phenomenon occurred, the planning process involved frequent meetings, retreats, and small group projects that allowed for cross-functional interaction and team building. Consequently, the implementation process benefited from the reinvigoration of the agency and its workers. When better morale is not produced through the process, however, there are other options for dealing with culture in strategic reorganizations. Strebel proposes a strategy of exploiting emerging tensions to motivate change for key stakeholders.[17] Additionally, because motivation is predicated on perception of need, implementation is often advanced when the sense of urgency for strategic change is heightened and accepted by organizational members.

Workers who remained out of sync with their organization's new plan often willingly departed or were forced out of the organization. The loss of these resistant individuals resulted in steadier progress of the plan's implementation. Almost without exception, when strategic plans required a fundamental culture change, significant staff turnover transpired. This transformation was observed by respondents across the sectors and in organizations of differing sizes. An incremental strategy, however, seemed to pose fewer personnel challenges for management.

(J)   INFRASTRUCTURE AND RESOURCES

When organizations in our field study encountered difficulties in implementing their plans, there were identifiable consistencies. The challenges most often cited were insufficient infrastructure or resources.

One organization relied on volunteers rather than paid staff to implement its plan, which led to no consistent progress on strategic initiatives. Eight organizations reported that staff members charged with implementation responsibilities were not fully prepared for their tasks and had to be trained or replaced. Five organizations found that staff was adequately trained; however, there was not sufficient staff for the amount of work the strategic plan required. (See Greer[18] for an excellent overview of workforce utilization as it relates to strategy implementation, including employee shortages and surpluses and special implementation challenges. Firstenberg also offers a discussion of downsizing focused specifically on the NPO.[19])

Resource management is often overlooked during the planning phase, yet a careful consideration of what is needed to implement strategy is important.[20] One director recounted that while implementation initially required some risk taking in the form of deficit spending, fund raising was ultimately aided by having a well-articulated plan. The existence of a sound strategy, for example, attracted donors willing to invest in success rather than bail out an organization in crisis. As a result, the organization doubled its income from foundations, increased individual contributions, and balanced its budget.

Many executive directors reported that their organization lacked tools needed by staff members to implement the plan. In most cases, this was technical or communications equipment such as computer software, hardware, multiple phone lines, or fax machines. Only two organizations reported that sufficient hardware and software were in place to carry out their strategic planning goals efficiently. However, one of these organizations noted that the computers needed to be networked and the staff needed to be using the same software in order to share data and access information.

5.4   *Implications for Practitioners*

Nonprofit practitioners must overcome increasingly complex challenges to ensure survival of their organizations into the twenty-first century. Present challenges include, but certainly are not limited to, growing competition from the for-profit sector; cutbacks in government funding; public policy shifts such as devolution, welfare reform, and managed care; and greater public demand for verifiable, measurable outcomes. The effectiveness of the nonprofit sector is further affected by pressures to emulate business sector management practices with limited financial and human resources and outmoded technology. To maximize organizational capacity to respond to such environmental pressures, today's nonprofit leaders must be adept at all aspects of strategic management, particularly with regard to strategy implementation.

Based on our literature review and field study, we offer the following 10 success indicators as a guide for strategy implementation. We recognize that every organization is structured differently, and every strategy has its own set of key success factors and critical tasks. Nevertheless, there is some commonality to successful strategy execution applicable across the nonprofit spectrum.

1. **Determine whether the organization is ready to undertake strategic planning.**
   - Is there a functioning governance structure, or would the organization benefit from preliminary planning activities such as board development and training?
   - Do potential plan implementers, especially at the staff level, understand the environmental factors driving strategic planning? Are they prepared to implement change?
   - Have potential barriers to change been identified? Which stakeholders may be most resistant to change? Is there a strategy in place to manage resistance and build buy-in?
2. **Promote sound strategy development through a comprehensive planning process that includes both internal and external stakeholders.**
   - Was consensus achieved around the organization's mission, vision, and values?
   - Were goals, objectives, and strategies based on information gleaned through an environmental scan, perceptual and competitor analyses, and examination of organizational strengths, weaknesses, opportunities, and threats?
   - Is the plan too risky? Are the goals challenging yet realistic?
3. **Engage the services of a consultant, preferably with industry-specific expertise, to facilitate the strategic planning process.**
   - Besides technical competency, assess whether the consultant is compatible with the organization's culture and values. In other words, will this individual have credibility with key organizational members?
   - If retaining the consultant to help with the implementation phase, do not rely solely on the consultant to develop the operating plan. Staff and board members (the latter in the case of organizations with limited staff) must be actively involved in the formulation of the operating plan in order to internalize ownership of action steps.
4. **Schedule strategic planning to conclude prior to the start of the organization's fiscal year to permit development of a strategy-supportive budget.**
   - Make sure key financial staff are involved in the planning process and are prepared to structure the budget to meet organizational goals.
   - See that each organizational unit has the budget to carry out its part of the strategic plan.

5. **Discuss how the organization will implement the plan during the strategic planning phase, not afterward.**
   - Begin identifying point persons as strategic initiatives are developed.
   - Consider the organization's resources and how they might need to be enhanced to carry out new objectives.
   - Consider retaining the strategic planning consultant to support and facilitate the implementation phase.
   - Form an implementation task force of board and staff members who will be responsible for developing the operating/action plan.
6. **Pinpoint the key tasks requisite for successful strategy execution by developing an operating/action plan that delineates:**
   - Realistic, measurable action steps
   - Board/staff areas of responsibilities
   - Appropriate timelines
   - Estimated budget requirements
7. **Galvanize organizational commitment to the strategy by vigorously exercising strategic leadership.**
   - Create a strategy-supportive organizational culture by leading the process of shaping values, molding culture, and energizing strategy accomplishment.
   - Thoroughly communicate the strategy to employees at all organizational levels.
   - Motivate organizational units and individuals to accomplish strategy through use of both formal and informal controls and incentives.
   - Reinforce that doing a good job equals achieving the target objectives.
   - Deal with the politics of power struggles and consensus building.
   - Initiate corrective actions to improve strategy execution.
   - Keep the organization innovative, responsive, and opportunistic.
8. **Institutionalize mechanisms to control, monitor, and review progress.**
   - Establish a board subcommittee charged with periodic review of goal attainment. Link progress to the board's self-appraisal of its own performance.
   - Establish a cross-functional implementation team to periodically revisit the strategic plan's relevance to the environment and make revisions in the strategy and action plan accordingly.
   - Link work assignments and employee performance reviews, including those of the executive, directly to strategic objectives. Define responsibilities in terms of what is to be accomplished, not just in terms of what duties are to be performed.
9. **Build an organization capable of carrying out the plan by acquiring or nurturing the skills, competitive capabilities, and distinctive competencies in which the strategy is grounded.**
   - Consider professional development and training for existing staff, hiring new talent, and outsourcing projects.
   - Install administrative support systems, such as policies, procedures, and information systems and controls, that keep the organization on its strategic course.

- Create internal capacity to generate strategic information on a timely basis. Implementers should use this information to make necessary modifications to the plan in order to keep it relevant.
10. **Communicate the organization's strategy and progress on implementation to external stakeholders.**
    - Documentation of a strategic blueprint and evidence of progress can be strong incentives for potential donors. Hence, effective communication of a sound strategy can greatly aid resource mobilization to support implementation costs.

5.5 Conclusion

Although our work was conceived in an academic setting, our hope was to give both academics and practitioners access to this research. We believe this work advances the knowledge of strategic plan implementation in the nonprofit sector and is valuable to those in the trenches of nonprofit management: executive directors, managers, board members, researchers, funders, consultants, and others who seek to understand strategic planning and its role in organizational development.

The information in this chapter represents a beginning investigation into the least understood part of strategic planning—implementation. In fact, although our research answers many questions, it raises many more. We imagine and encourage further inquiry into issues such as: How influential a variable was the organization type, the agency size, or the capacity of the operating budget in determining success with strategy implementation? Does linking employee and organizational performance goals fuel success? In addition, we would like to see studies that compare implementation issues between the nonprofit and for-profit sectors to determine if the success tactics or challenges are similar.

There is no doubt that strategic planning is essential to organizations, especially in today's competitive climate. Increasingly, NPOs face greater challenges in seeking support, building collaborations, and incorporating technology. As organizations operating within the public trust, NPOs must also constantly seek creative ways to offer quality services at cut-rate prices. Those organizations that become complacent will fall behind. Those that think strategically must not only plan but also implement with vision, skill, and success. We believe this work will help organizational leaders do so with confidence.

Endnotes

1. Thompson, A. A. Jr., and A. J. Strickland, III. (1989). *Strategy Formulation and Implementation: Tasks of the General Manager,* 4th ed. Homewood, IL: BPI/Irwin, p. 263.
2. Howe, F. (1997). *The Board Member's Guide to Strategic Planning: A Practical Approach to Strengthening Nonprofit Organizations.* San Francisco: Jossey-Bass.
3. Below, P. J., G. L. Morrisey, and B.L. Acomb. (1987). *The Executive Guide to Strategic Planning.* San Francisco: Jossey-Bass.
4. Id.
5. Redding, J. C., and R. F. Catalanello. (1994). *Strategic Readiness: The Making of the Learning Organization.* San Francisco: Jossey-Bass.

6. Brinckerhoff, P. C. (1994). *Mission-Based Management: Leading Your Not-for-Profit into the 21st Century.* New York: John Wiley & Sons.

7. Bryson, J. M. (1995). *Strategic Planning for Public and Nonprofit Organizations: A Guide to Strengthening and Sustaining Organizational Achievement,* rev. ed. San Francisco: Jossey-Bass.

8. Eadie, D. C. (1993). *Beyond Strategic Planning: How to Involve Nonprofit Boards in Growth and Change.* Washington, DC: National Center for Nonprofit Boards.

9. Digman, L. A. (1986). *Strategic Management: Concepts, Decisions, Cases.* Plano, TX: Business Publications.

10. Khan, A. M. (1993). "Realistic Planning for Transportation." In Bryson, John M. (ed.). *Strategic Planning for Public Service and Non-Profit Organizations.* New York: Pergamon Press.

11. Park, D. G. Jr. (1991). *Strategic Planning and the Nonprofit Board.* Washington, DC: National Center for Nonprofit Boards.

12. Higgins, J. M., and J. W. Vincze. (1986). *Strategic Management and Organizational Policy: Text and Cases,* 3rd ed. Chicago, IL: Dryden Press.

13. See note 6.

14. Migliore, H. R., R. E. Stevens, D. L. Loudon, and S. Williamson. (1995). *Strategic Planning for Not-for-Profit Organizations.* Binghamton, NY: The Haworth Press.

15. See note 3.

16. Salipante, P., and K. Golden-Biddle. (1995). "Managing Traditionality and Strategic Change in Nonprofit Organizations," *Nonprofit Management and Leadership* (September): 3–20.

17. Strebel, P. (1992). *Breakpoints: How Managers Exploit Radical Business Change.* Boston: Harvard Business School Press.

18. Greer, C. R. (1995). *Strategy and Human Resources: A General Managerial Perspective.* Englewood Cliffs, NJ: Prentice Hall.

19. Firstenberg, P. B. (1996). *The 21st Century Nonprofit: Remaking the Organization in the Post-Government Era.* New York: Foundation Center.

20. Nutt, P. C., and R. W. Backoff. (1992). *Strategic Management of Public and Third Sector Organizations: A Handbook for Leaders.* San Francisco: Jossey-Bass.

Suggested Readings

Espy, S. N. (1986). *Handbook of Strategic Planning for Nonprofit Organizations.* New York: Praeger.

Higgins, J. M. (1983). *Organizational Policy and Strategic Management: Text and Cases,* 2nd ed. Chicago, IL: Dryden Press, p. 196.

Hussey, D. (ed.). (1996). *The Implementation Challenge.* Chichester, England: John Wiley & Sons, Ltd.

Judson, A. S. (1996). *Making Strategy Happen: Transforming Plans into Reality,* 2nd ed. Cambridge, MA: Blackwell Publishers.

Pearce, J. A. II, and R. B. Robinson, Jr. (1988). *Strategic Management: Strategy Formulation and Implementation,* 3rd ed. Homewood, IL: Irwin Press.

Robert, M. (1988). *The Strategist CEO: How Visionary Executives Build Organizations.* New York: Quorum Books.

6 ▼ Governance Framework for Collaborations and Mergers

SUZANNE C. FEENEY, PhD
Director, Institute for Nonprofit Management,
Portland State University

6.1 Introduction

In the last dozen or so years, there has been an explosion of interest in nonprofits collaborating. Foundations are encouraging collaborations because they see them as being the answer to most nonprofit problems; that is, organizational inefficiencies, duplication of services, lack of management accountability, and the like. Government contractors are also enamored with collaborations, often requiring that nonprofits collaborate as a condition for receiving public money to deliver services. While the fascination with collaborations and increasingly with mergers continues, they are still not well understood. Researchers and practitioner-authors have been caught up in the same collaboration fanfare and have attempted to explain, describe, and advise about how best to do it. The collaboration label, however, is no longer sufficient to describe the multitude of multiparty interorganizational relationships that are appearing everywhere in the sector. New labels include strategic alliances, federations, back-room consolidations, joint ventures, restructuring, cooperation, coordination, and mergers. This kind of linguistic alphabet soup has often exacerbated rather than clarified our understanding of collaboration.

Despite all of the attention to collaborations, most of the books and articles about collaboration focus only on explaining or describing the structures and processes of collaboration. These publications have been helpful because they have provided a framework for thinking about collaborations and how best to engage in them or not engage in them. The early work of the Amherst H. Wilder Foundation, for example, not only provided some definitional clarity about how to think about collaboration, it also isolated 19 success factors of effective collaborations.[1] These success factors, together with clarifying definitions, have created a useful template for many nonprofits contemplating partnering with other nonprofits to deliver services, consolidate administrative functions, or vie for public dollars to support their organizations' missions.

The more recent work of Arsenault on joint ventures[2] and McLaughlin on strategic alliances and mergers[3] have provided detailed step-by-step approaches to developing collaborations and further explaining the complex organizational elements that must be dealt with. These publications, along with the scholarly attention to case study development and analysis, have brought considerable new understanding to nonprofits about what collaboration is, how others have done it, and what nonprofits new to collaboration need to think about when contemplating various kinds of interorganizational relationships.

What is surprising is that none of the literature speaks to the roles of the multiple actors who are involved in collaboration. There is an implicit understanding that chief executives of nonprofit drive, design, and execute these various kinds of interorganizational relationships. The literature is mostly silent on the involvement of governing boards of nonprofits involved in the collaborative enterprise. In the few instances in which boards are mentioned—with the exception of mergers in which boards have clear legal and fiduciary responsibilities—they are marginalized. At least one author has said that boards are resistant to collaborations and mergers because of a fear of change or simply because their egos are wedded to the identity of the organization they govern.[4] In this discussion, executives are admonished to take care of the psychological needs of resistant boards.

While it might serve some useful conceptual purpose to understand just why boards of directors have not been a focus of attention in the literature on collaborations and mergers, this chapter will focus on developing governance-related roles and activities. It will describe board role activities not only for different types of collaborative arrangements but also for different stages of collaboration. Finally, it will describe the need for a new kind of strategic alliance between the board and chief executive.

6.2 *What We Know about Collaborations*

In addition to the popular interest in collaborations in the nonprofit sector, there has been a parallel interest of researchers and academic scholars. One of the early pieces of research on collaboration, *Collaboration: What Makes It Work,* cited earlier, was published by the Amherst H. Wilder Foundation.[5] This very short and to-the-point description of the factors that most contribute to successful collaborations contributed enormously to the thinking and understanding of these nebulous new kinds of nonprofit interorganizational relationships. Mattessich and Monsey researched 133 studies of collaboration in the health, social science, education, and public affairs arenas and found only 18 studies that met their criteria for collaborations. They then were able to isolate 19 factors that influenced the success of the collaborations. They arrayed these 19 factors into 6 principal categories, including environment, membership characteristics, process and structure, communication, purpose, and resources. Each category included a series of factors that describe activities, principles, or characteristics that influenced success. The category, *purpose,* for example, describes the reasons for the development of the collaborative. Important elements in this category are (1) having concrete, attainable goals and objectives; (2) having a shared vision; and (3) having a unique purpose.[6] Throughout the book, the authors carefully describe what each success factor means, provide case illustrations, and then discuss the implications for practice.

Mattessich and Monsey not only provided a matrix of success factors, but they also distinguished among various kinds of collaboration. They found in their original research that many nonprofits used the language of collaboration to describe their interorganizational relationships, but that the degree of involvement with partners and the nature of the agreements varied in significant ways. They found that collaboration was used generically as a label for any kind of partnership, cooperative agreement, or coordination activity. This was an important discovery because when potential collaborators are exploring partnerships with other organizations, or if potential partners come to the table and have a different understanding about what their collaboration is, misaligned expectations can erode the process and undermine trust among collaborating partners.

While the Amherst H. Wilder researchers were among the first to take on the task of defining what is meant by collaboration, successive authors and handbook writers have introduced additional terms and definitions, including alliances, federations, back-room consolidations, joint ventures, and mergers. In each case, writers have attempted to develop helpful understandings, as well as materials, for practitioners about to engage in new multiparty arrangements. What is important here is not that nonprofits adopt any particular one of these definitions but that they come to a shared agreement—and working understanding—about what their collaboration means to them. Following is a glossary of terms.

- **Cooperation.** Informal relationships that exist without any commonly defined mission, structure, or planning effort. Information is shared as needed, and authority is retained by each organization so there is virtually no risk. Resources are separate, as are rewards.[7]
- **Coordination.** Formal relationships between/among organizations with compatible missions. Some planning and division of roles are required, and communication channels are established. Authority still rests with the individual organizations, but there is some increased risk to all participants. Resources are available to participants, and rewards are mutually acknowledged.[8]
- **Collaboration.** A mutually beneficial and well-defined relationship entered into by two or more organizations to achieve common goals. The relationship includes a commitment to a definition of mutual relationships and goals, a jointly developed structure and shared responsibility, mutual authority and accountability for success, and sharing of resources and rewards.[9]
- **Merger.** The generic term for full and final coming together of two previously separate corporations. The legal partnership will persevere only as one corporation. *Acquisition* is another term that means the same thing legally as a merger; however, because there is no ownership of nonprofit organizations, merger is the preferred term.[10]
- **Joint Ventures and Partnerships.** An undertaking of two or more organizations for the accomplishment of a specific purpose. Joint ventures are often time limited and narrowly defined. They may employ different types of legal entities: (1) a contractual relationship; (2) partnership in a limited liability company; (3) a corporation.[11] *Alternative:* A programmatic collaboration between/among two or more nonprofits that involves no consolidation. Joint ventures can change the character or locus of control of nonprofits. Nonprofits involved in joint ventures share risk and reduce interagency competition.[12]
- **Back-Office Consolidation.** An arrangement in which two or more organizations doing similar work share core administrative functions.

Arrangement is generally not apparent to outsiders because it does not affect the delivery of services or products to clients. An increasingly common arrangement among nonprofits.[13]

- **Federation.** Membership group of nonprofits, may begin informally and grow to include formal agreements among members about information sharing, program sharing, and the like. Decision making resides with the members.
- **Alliance.** Generic term for partnership that can be informal or formal.
- **Restructuring.** A new name for various kinds of interorganizational arrangements, replaces the use of the word *collaboration* as the generic descriptor. May have limited usage, particularly by foundations.[14]

While definitions help, there is more than agreed-upon definitions to achieve clarity about the nature of various kinds of interorganizational relationships that we are calling *collaborations*. It is important for all collaborators to understand, both formally and informally, what is meant by sharing and exchanging information, coordinating programs and services, referring and/or sharing clients, and exchanging staff, among other issues. For example, what resources are needed and who will provide them? Who is in charge? Confusion about these matters has frustrated and undermined even the most well-intended and well-motivated collaboration. When it is unclear what is meant by *collaboration,* it is a challenge to figure out who does what when. Many potentially good collaborations unravel at this point.

Thomas McLaughlin's *Nonprofit Mergers and Alliances: A Strategic Planning Guide* is particularly helpful in describing collaborations as arrangements that can involve *parts* rather than *wholes* of organizations.[15] McLaughlin sets up a complex structure of organizational levels in which collaborations might occur. These levels involve the core products or services of an organization, its activities and work processes, as well as its goals and mission. McLaughlin has created a schematic to describe how collaboration can happen at each of four different levels in an organization. He names each level and describes its characteristics. McLaughlin then illustrates how collaborations can start at one level of an organization, stay at that level, or move on to include additional levels or all levels of the organization. The author calls his model CORE, which refers to:

Corporate
Operations
Responsibility
Economic

By *Corporate,* he is referring to the legal entity of the organization itself, including its charter, official purpose, board of directors, and business structure. *Operations* refers to all programs, services, or whatever else the nonprofit might be offering or delivering to its clients. The *Responsibility* level, according to the model, refers to those people and activities associated with getting the work of the organization accomplished. Finally, the *Economic* level refers to all activities that involve cost sharing, bartering, or exchanges of resources.[16]

Like most writers on the subject, McLaughlin believes that most nonprofit collaborations and mergers derive from economic considerations. If the economic motivation is not primary, however, McLaughlin asserts that collaborations can happen on any level of an organization and remain at that level. They can also begin at one level and then move through all four levels, ultimately ending in a merger agreement when the full CORE is involved. His model provides an interesting point of view, as well as a set of strategies for nonprofits engaging at different organizational levels. He urges nonprofit organizations to consider which issues they need to plan for and manage based on which level or levels their collaboration might include.

As detailed as McLaughlin gets about how to do collaborations, alliances, and mergers, he mostly neglects the roles of actors, especially boards of directors. In fact, McLaughlin finds boards of directors to be mostly nuisances. He says that they resist collaborations and mergers and that they are fed by their own fears of change as well as by their ego needs to maintain the status quo.[17] Implicit, if not explicit, in his advice is that boards must be managed if collaborations are going to be successful.

The Mattessich and Monsey approach, while it does not disenfranchise the governing board in the way that McLaughlin's does, simply fails to mention boards at all. That said, their research and listing of collaboration success factors suggests a strong and significant role for boards, which will be evident in the discussion of governance in the following case studies.

(A)   CASE EXAMPLES OF COLLABORATIONS AND MERGERS

The definitional conundrum around collaboration and its multiple organizational arrangements, such as those mentioned by McLaughlin and others, is perhaps best understood by examining real case examples of collaboration. This section presents three different collaborative types and examines the governance issues embedded in these examples.

(i)   Case 1: The Community School Initiative

The Community School Initiative is a collaborative that was formed three or four years ago. There were six lead agencies in the collaboration, including three social service nonprofit organizations and three schools. In addition to the lead agencies, there were 20 other partners, including governments at the city, county, and state levels as well as a number of other nonprofits. The collaboration resulted from two factors: (1) pressures from funders and (2) the natural evolution of work that seemed as though it would benefit from partnering with other agencies.

The partners described the collaboration as one that came about because of political pressure rather than economic necessity. The collaboration was described as programmatic, in which the participating agencies had to give up individual agency autonomy both programmatically and financially. The executives involved indicated that even though the collaboration was programmatic in nature, everyone felt it had an impact on the entire agency, not just the programs.

Another important factor in this collaborative was that the partners involved did not emerge naturally from long-term working relationships. The collaboration actually brought together organizational strangers. As one executive director stated, "The collaboration is forcing me to work with a partner I would not have naturally aligned myself with." This same executive described the collaboration as working well because the key partners believed in it and did not feel that it was forced on them. "Doing mergers and collaboration is scary," she said. "We simply do not understand the institution of mergers. You need a framework to think about them and then be able to have a dialogue that is not laden with emotions. That framework has to apply to every level of the organization so that everyone can talk about it, not just the leaders of organizations."

Discussion.   According to the McLaughlin model, this collaboration would appear to occur at several organizational levels, at both the O and E levels and perhaps at the R level as well. The fact that the partners also felt that the collaboration affected the entire agency suggests that level C is implicitly affected, even though there may have been no formal C-level activities.

Another interesting element in this case is that the partners did not work together or necessarily know each other before coming together in this collaboration. According to the 19 success factors discussed by Mattessich and Monsey, collaborations are more successful when there are strong and trusting relationships with other members to the collaboration. That clearly was not the case in this collaborative.

This case is an example of a mandated collaboration arising from funder (government) pressure to collaborate. Because the partners also experienced a real and palpable evolution in their work programs, it made the collaboration somewhat attractive even if it was mandated.

Governance Issues.   There are several governance issues implicit in this case. One has to do with the boundary-spanning roles involving connecting the nonprofit organizations to the political sphere within the larger community. While boards may not be required to exercise this role, they frequently have excellent access and may be better received than the chief executive. Another issue is that while the collaboration seems to be about programs for which the chief executive is primarily responsible, it was also one in which agencies lost their individual autonomy, both programmatically and financially. The board does have a fiduciary responsibility here for preserving institutional autonomy, overseeing the accomplishment of organizational mission, and monitoring and making decisions about resource commitments that have organization-wide impacts. Thus, this collaboration requires—and clearly could benefit from—the involvement of the board.

(ii)   Case 2: Merger of Two Nonprofit Service Organizations

For many years, two service organizations worked together in the same office, sharing staff and other resources. They did similar work but serviced different populations. A decade or so ago, one of these organizations, Agency A, split off to become an independent organization. Agency A was a federally funded program and was not separately incorporated as a charitable nonprofit with a 501(c)3 designation. Agency A signed an affiliation agreement with a large health corporation and used the facilities and support services provided by the Umbrella Corporation. While remaining largely autonomous operationally, the service organization did not have its own governing board. It did, however, rely extensively on a very active advisory board that acted like a governing board. Their decisions were seldom, if ever, questioned by the Umbrella Corporation. Agency B, however, was a charitable nonprofit organization and therefore had a governing board of directors. An interesting twist in this case was that several members of the advisory board of Agency A also sat on the governing board of Agency B, most likely because of the service overlap.

About five years ago, Agency B ran into serious leadership and financial problems that took it to the brink of closure. For six months to a year, Agency B explored various kinds of partnerships and associational opportunities in the community. After months spent seeking partners, Agency A approached Agency B about a possible merger. Agency B attempted to negotiate a deal with Agency A in order to safeguard programs and staffing. However, because Agency A was not a 501(c)3 organization, it could not officially make any decisions or carry on any binding negotiations with Agency B. The Umbrella Corporation, formerly a silent overseer, became the negotiator. There were not relationships, working or otherwise, between Agency B and the Umbrella Corporation. Having no choice but to move forward with the merger or lose a vital service to the community, Agency B agreed to merge, dissolved its corporate status, and transferred all of its remaining assets to the Umbrella Corporation.

Every attempt was made by the advisory board of Agency A to work out satisfactory arrangements for the program and staff of Agency B, but ultimately they had no authority to make any decisions. A distant board of the Umbrella Corporation, who knew very little about Agency B, made the decisions. Finally, while the two organizations, A and B, had worked together on similar programs for years, the cultures of the organizations were profoundly different. Their work processes and organizational structures also differed. According to board members and staff, the road has been bumpy ever since the merger. Agency B staff and former board members have largely disappeared and with them the culture, work processes, and mission of Agency B.

Discussion.   This is an example of a merger to survive, both economically and programmatically. Mergers always involve all four levels of the McLaughlin model because they involve the legal entity of the nonprofit's corporate structure, governance, mission and purpose, assets, and all programs. The motivation to merge to survive creates organizational anxiety and ambiguity, not only within the organization but also with every key stakeholder group, including funders, clients, and the community.

Governance Issues.   Board members are legally required to be involved in all corporate legal and fiduciary aspects of the organization. Each state has a nonprofit corporation act that sets forth the legal requirements for merging with another nonprofit (nonprofits may not merge with for-profit organizations). The governance duties and responsibilities of board members as well as procedures for mergers are variously stipulated in the revised codes of the several states. In addition to the legal requirements for participation, board members would be involved in seeking out potential partners, protecting the organization's assets, preserving the mission and programs wherever possible, and communicating with clients and other significant stakeholders. In this case, the board was active in a boundary-spanning capacity linking the organization to various potential partners in the community. The board also worked on the merger agreement with the other organization in an attempt to preserve its agency's mission, program, and services in the post-merger organization.

(iii)   Case 3: Four Human Service Agencies Establishing a Federation

Five years ago, four human service organizations came together to sign a letter of agreement to work together in a partnership of equals. The four agencies created a federation because they had a strategic interest in ensuring that each organization would be able to sustain its organizational missions and services to clients over the long term. None of the agencies felt endangered in the foreseeable future—a five-year time horizon—but worried about how stable and enduring they might be in 10 or 20 years. The process to collaborate began with the chief executive of one lead agency identifying potential partners he felt he could work with; that is, these were chief executives he trusted and who shared a strong sense of mission and commitment to their clients. They also were strong and talented leaders who knew their fields and their client needs. This executive approached the other three agency executives to explore partnering in a federation. This led to signing a formal agreement that committed each agency to a long-term partnership built on a shared set of principles and values, as well as to a set of strategic purposes for the collaboration. The partners decided to evolve as a federation after they practiced working together rather than predetermining a more formal model for their collaboration. In the five years they have been together, the partners have achieved service integration and created interorganizational work groups. In the last year or so, they have also created a management service organization in which each of the chief executives serves on the governing board. One of the partners in the original federation left his agency, and his board of directors decided not to hire a replacement. The programs of that agency are now subprograms within the federation. Although there is no merger yet, the federation seems headed in that direction according to some of the partners. The partners still see the relationship as one that is flexible and emergent. They believe that their success can be measured in part because they sought out the collaboration and entered it voluntarily.

Discussion. This is an example of a voluntary and strategic collaboration, one that is future oriented. The motivation to create the collaboration (federation) has been instrumental in determining both the structure and organizational processes involved in the federation. Clearly, issues of policy, mission alignment, program operations, resource commitments, and constituent and stakeholder relations are integral considerations in the evolution of this federation. The McLaughlin model would suggest that the federation involves three, if not four, levels of collaboration. Clearly, there is mission alignment and codelivery, service integration and exchanges of staff and resources, and policy implications and organizational structure as well as business structure considerations. Although the organizations have not merged, they are closely intertwined and interdependent on all four levels.

Governance Issues. While the partners in the federation did not mention board involvement in this process, there are clearly governance responsibilities in this intentionally evolving set of relationships. Formal agreements between/among two or more separately incorporated agencies have governance implications. Sharing staff, programs, and resources requires board monitoring at the least. Supporting and monitoring the executive leadership in interorganizational relationships also requires board oversight and evaluation. There are policy implications for carrying out the organizational mission as well as planning considerations. Because the board is responsible for the planning framework for operations involving the technical core of the organization, there is a clear and particular role for board involvement.

Each of the preceding cases describes a series of governance issues that require or would benefit from board involvement in the collaboratives. Yet in none of them were board members very involved except on a "need-to-know" basis or when they had to approve resource commitments. This is puzzling, yet this lack of inclusion of boards in important interorganizational matters is not inconsistent with a generalized low involvement of boards in the single organizational context. Revisiting the fiduciary responsibilities of boards of directors as set forth in the law may provide clues about how boards will need to practice their fiduciary responsibilities in the new environment of multiparty agreements in collaborations, federations, joint ventures, and mergers.

(B) REVISITING BOARD AUTHORITY AND FIDUCIARY RESPONSIBILITIES

Over the past 10 to 15 years, there has been renewed interest in what might be called the traditional roles that boards of directors play in the organizations they direct. Much of that literature examines boards and responsibilities,[18–23] governance structures,[24–25] and board contributions to organizational effectiveness. Some of the newer thinking suggests that board members should move beyond the strict interpretation of meeting their legal fiduciary responsibilities and become more involved in a shared organizational leadership role with the chief executive. Several recent articles[26–27] suggest a greater strategic and participatory role for boards in the future.

Inglis and colleagues, after conducting research on boards in community-based organizations, suggest that the traditional roles of boards should be reframed into three categories that better represent how boards and executives see the board role: strategic activities, operations, and resource planning.[28] Feeney's approach redefines board roles in the context of a much-changed world for nonprofits. That new world will require the specific expertise, access, and boundary-spanning capacities of board members. This is entirely consistent with the move to recruit more professional boards. Feeney describes an environment in which nonprofits will be more involved with public policy development and implementation, they will be assailed more by the public stakeholders, they will participate in complex interorganizational relationships with profound consequences at the organization and community levels, and they will face increased competition for both public and private dollars.[29] Not all of these are new concerns to nonprofit organizations; however, the pace and complexity of change and the increased scrutiny of nonprofits embedded in communities and governments point to new ways of doing business and new demands for governance and stewardship by nonprofit boards.

The *traditional* fiduciary responsibilities of boards provide a point of departure for considering new and expanded roles of governing boards in an interorganizational environment. Writers variously describe these roles, but they generally include what Brudney includes in his recent discussion of board of director authority and responsibility:

- Overseeing the mission
- Selecting, supporting, and evaluating the chief administrator
- Driving the organization's planning efforts
- Serving as the fiduciary representative of the organization
- Ensuring the financial solvency of the organization
- Serving as the ambassador and spokesperson for the organization
- Evaluating the organization's program regularly
- Communicating the community and lay perspective to the organization as well as the organization's mission to the community
- Serving as a final court of appeals when intraorganizational conflicts arise
- Engaging in periodic self-assessment[30]

While most writers are silent on the role of boards in collaborations, it is not difficult to extrapolate these traditional roles to governance responsibilities in collaborations and mergers. Boards, quite simply, have the ultimate legal responsibility for the health and viability of the organizations they govern. In the case of a merger, no merger can happen without the explicit involvement of the board. The board is the only *actor* that can dissolve the nonprofit corporation and distribute its assets.

There may be a variety of explanations for the neglect and marginalization of boards in the literature on collaborations and mergers. Boards are partly responsible for their own "bad rap" in recent years. The literature is replete with horror stories about nonperforming boards. Popular literature describes boards in the following ways: they are passive rather than active; they leave their business acumen on the hat-rack outside the boardroom door; they are conflict averse; they frequently do not understand the core work of the organization; and, because they are only volunteer and part-time, they are not involved or well informed. These "blame it on the board" topics are well worn in the governance literature. It follows that the *advice* literature on boards focuses on how to manage them, minimize their mistakes, and, where possible, increase their giving and getting. That kind of approach, however, misses the strategic assets that board members bring to the table. There is a need to focus on building on the considerable competencies, expertise, and networks that boards possess to the strategic advantage of nonprofit organizations. This means maximizing board involvement and participation rather than marginalizing and managing the board to do no harm. At no time is this more important than in the context of collaborations and mergers.

It is interesting that since the scandals of Aramony, the Bakkers, and others, there has been increasing pressure on nonprofits to be more accountable, more efficient, and more strategic. In response, nonprofits have systematically gone about addressing some of these problems by developing new kinds of boards. When nonprofit executives are asked about their boards, they talk about filling vacancies with people who can raise funds and otherwise bring new resources—and therefore stability—to their organizations. Executives have also approached board development by recruiting more professionals. Nonprofits need free professionals to assist them with finances and audits, compliance with government regulations, and the legal aspects surrounding personnel and liability issues, for their marketing and fund-raising expertise. Board members are chosen for their strategic connections to a variety of publics in the community who can benefit the organization in its competitive environment. These efforts to attract high-powered experts to the board are what has become known as *professionalizing* nonprofit boards of directors. Some think that this is the only way to develop boards and strong nonprofits. Others believe that professionalizing boards is a dangerous way to proceed because it invokes a for-profit model that might adversely affect mission achievement or undermine nonprofit culture. The fact is, however, those twenty-first-century boards will be more professional than ever before.

Despite the urgency to professionalize boards, these newly recruited boards continue to be underutilized and marginalized. The following discussion reframes the traditional board role in the context of collaborations and mergers. It provides guidelines about how to use governing boards more effectively and how to involve them in strategic ways to achieve organizational success in collaborations and mergers.

(C)   BOARD ROLES AND RESPONSIBILITIES IN COLLABORATIONS AND MERGERS

Building on the work of Inglis et al.[31] and Feeney,[32] this section discusses the five strategic roles that boards can play in collaborations. Their roles naturally evolve from their fiduciary responsibility for their *single* nonprofit organization.

Because collaborations, partnerships, and alliances are conceptually, linguistically, and operationally confusing, multiple definitions make distinctions about complex and dynamic interorganizational relationships difficult to clarify. This makes it especially difficult to develop roles for the various actors who are involved. Many actors play an active role, operating at the strategic, administrative, and operational levels of nonprofit organizations. Because there are also so many external stakeholders to consider, boards may have a special niche of activity.

Building on the collaboration research of the Amherst H. Wilder Foundation and the reconfiguration of board roles of Inglis et al. and Feeney, it is possible to develop new categories of activities for boards in collaborations and mergers. While these categories of role activities are hardly exhaustive, they provide new ways of thinking about how to engage the strategic expertise of boards. There are five general groupings of activities:

- Executive Director–Board Intersect
- Stakeholder Outreach and Boundary Spanning
- Fiduciary and Financial Responsibility
- Policy Development and Monitoring
- Organizational Health

These five groupings can be understood as having specific activities that vary across a variety of types of collaborations, as is shown in Exhibit 6.1.

(i) Executive Director–Board Intersect

One of the primary responsibilities of any board is to hire, fire, monitor, and support the executive director. In traditional approaches to understanding board functions, these activities are usually associated with a series of explicit activities. They concern the board's role within a single organizational context rather than a multiorganizational context. In the collaborative context, boards have an increased responsibility to be involved with the leadership of the collaboration. These role activities might include the following:

- Overseeing, monitoring, and advising the chief executive, who often acts alone in making collaborative agreements with other nonprofit organizations
- Guiding and advising the chief executive, who will work with other organization leaders and governing boards in the development of collaborations
- Determining the reputation and organizational capacity of potential partners in a new collaboration
- Determining the multiple domains, levels, and authority for decision making among partners that affect the organizational health and autonomy of the organization
- Helping to clarify ambiguities about authority in the board–executive relationship in the context of various kinds of collaborations
- Determining the leadership skills and competencies required to participate successfully in collaborations, weighing those against the leadership requirements within the individual nonprofit organization
- Working to clarify ambiguities about authority and expectations within the organization, in the board–executive relationship, and across the collaboration
- Developing strategies to overcome the natural tendency for collaborations or mergers to overtax organizational resources

EXHIBIT 6.1 Board Role Activities by Type of Collaboration

Board Activities	Coordination	Joint Venture	Federation	Collaboration	Merger
Executive–Board Intersect	Assessment and planning	Review/approve contracts/determine locus of control	Assess/approve organizational-level commitments	Hand-in-hand planning	Hand-in-hand, with a clearly defined lead role
Stakeholder Outreach & Boundary Spanning	Little if any activity	Assess partner and stakeholder interests	Sensing/interpreting, gathering information	Assess partners, information gathering, communicating with key stakeholders	Build support with funders and community
Fiduciary & Financial	Assess risk potential and resource commitment	Assess risk and locus of control	Play governance role when formal agreement	Risk assessment, resource commitments, governance issues	Dissolve and transfer assets/ legal compliance issues
Policy Development & Monitoring	Program and mission alignment	Purpose and mission alignment	Mission consistency and compatibility	Mission congruence	State nonprofit corporations act/ compliance
Organizational Health	Monitor staff morale and program delivery	Morale and service delivery	Monitor organi-zational impact/ staff and services	Monitor organizational impact/staff	Support CEO, staff, monitor culture change

(ii)   Stakeholder Outreach and Boundary Spanning

Collaborations by their very nature are about involving other organizations in one's own business. Collaborations involve constituency relationships not only of the individual nonprofit but also the collective constituencies—including the governing boards—of all of the organizations involved in the collaboration or merger. In many cases, collaborations, mergers, and consolidations are the result of funder and/or policy maker pressures. These political and economic players are key stakeholders of all parties to the collaboration. Board members as boundary spanners can play a strategic role in this external arena. Board role activities might include some of the following:

- Monitoring public agency contractor mandates that can often intrude on an organization's autonomy and preferred way of delivering services.
- Monitoring public policy—and policy makers and administrators—when that policy may adversely affect a nonprofit's core mission and goals.
- Monitoring interorganizational relationships so that they do not become coercive.
- Monitoring and engaging in the social–political environment to enhance the probability of successful collaborations.
- Interacting with key constituencies who are involved in or affected by or are influencers of collaborations and their outcomes

(iii)   Fiduciary and Financial Responsibility

Many collaborations involve agreements to share programs, staff, administration, clients, and other organizational resources. While law or regulation may not require these agreements, they do commit nonprofits to a course of action and sets of behaviors that may warrant board attention and monitoring. Collaborations by their very nature tax organizational resources, both human capital and financial. They can affect the financial position of the nonprofit. The costs of designing and implementing an interorganizational agreement may be very significant to the nonprofit. The literature indicates that rarely does the nonprofit fully anticipate or expect the kinds of resource commitments that are often required. Research findings also indicate that collaborations frequently and predictably result in lower productivity and low staff morale. Loss in either of these areas has a financial impact on organizational resources. While many collaborations are perceived to be administrative and/or operational in nature, not requiring the direct involvement of the board, there are still significant, if only implicit, governance issues. Board members may well want to concern themselves with:

- Legal documents and letters of agreement that obligate the nonprofit in some way
- Governance of the collaborative versus governance of the nonprofit
- Reduction of organizational control, increased uncertainty, new accountabilities, and increased organizational risk in mandated collaborations
- Multiple players and potentially multiple authorities and layered authority among partners in the collaboration

(iv)   Policy Development and Monitoring

There are a variety of policy implications attendant to engaging in collaborations, many of them having to do with authority relationships, decision making, commitments of resources, and compliance with laws and regulations. Collaborative agreements at the administrative level may not be consistent with organizational policies but are often not entered into or assessed in a policy context. In addition, public-sector organizations, such as government contractors, are pressuring nonprofit organizations to change their ways of operating to meet their demands. These mandates may also have policy implications at the individual organizational level. Because funder and contractor mandates are most often enacted at the administrative and operations levels, they may escape review for policy consistency. This suggests a clear governance role for boards of directors. Boards may want to particularly consider:

- Communications policy, inside and outside the organization
- Stakeholder and/or client satisfaction/dissatisfaction
- Organizational agreements that do not address authority and policy issues
- Decision-making processes among multiple players

(v) Organizational Health

A review of the literature reveals that collaborations, partnerships, and mergers severely tax the organizational health of nonprofit organizations. Unclear expectations, ambiguity of authority, the unanticipated time commitment involved in coordinating the work of more than one agency, and depletion of resources all contribute to the quality—or lack thereof—of life and work in an organization. First and foremost, the literature speaks to low staff morale and client dissatisfaction. These collaboration side effects can pose significant adverse organizational health issues, sometimes resulting in increased costs of service delivery and decreases in organizational revenues. Organizational operations often have to be adjusted as well, including the deployment of staff and alterations to the usual staff reporting arrangements. When these new organizational arrangements begin to intrude on the overall stability of the organization, there is a clear role for boards of directors. Boards have at the least a monitoring role in the following areas:

- Threats to morale and productivity
- Client satisfaction/dissatisfaction
- Delivery of quality and timely services
- Organizational confusion about who is in charge
- Organizational distraction in general, which threatens standard practices for program delivery
- Continuing progress on organizational goals and priorities
- Possible destabilization of organizational structures and processes

All of these new role activities, described in the five categories preceding, fall within the purview of the standard board governance function. However, there is little, if any, evidence that boards and executives have addressed any of these activities when contemplating, designing, or implementing a collaboration. Because the whole collaborative movement is so recent in the nonprofit sector, it may be that many of these issues simply have not manifested themselves until well into a collaboration. These five categories therefore provide a point of departure for both discussing and framing new role activities for boards of directors in collaborations and mergers.

6.3   Strategic Alliance: Board and Executive

The board and the chief executive should be strategic allies in collaborations and mergers. While books and articles by academics and practitioners traditionally try to separate the functions of each, the board and the executive represent a dynamic duo. Each brings a unique set of skills and competencies as well as stakeholder alliances that complement each other and enhance the capacity of the organization to respond effectively in the changing environment of collaborations and mergers. There are a number of steps boards and chief executives can take in developing this strategic alliance, including:

1. Assessing the strengths and weaknesses, skills, and expertise of the board members and the chief executive that relate to collaborations such as negotiation, environmental assessment, human relations, political connections, and the like
2. Identifying the kind of collaborative the organization is contemplating (coordination, joint venture, federation, merger) and its requirements or organizational demands (financial, legal, program, staff, funding, stakeholders)
3. Identifying the authority and responsibility aspects of the collaboration being contemplated (commitment of resources, deployment of staff, formal agreements, services to clients, etc.)
4. Identifying the stages of the collaboration from exploration through implementation and monitoring along with their associated activities
5. Developing a preliminary plan of the role activities involved in the collaboration based on type of collaboration and stages of the collaboration
6. Arraying role activities by board members alone, chief executive alone, and by shared board–chief executive involvement.
7. Reaching a tentative agreement about who will do what in the collaboration and set a schedule for regular meetings to share information, review progress, and revisit role activity assignments and accomplishments

The first step, identifying the strengths and weaknesses of the board and the chief executive, is really about an assessment of the team strengths and weaknesses in the context of a collaboration. What expertise is needed in multiorganizational relationships? Collaborations involve negotiation, conflict management, frequent and open communication, formal agreements, connections and networks between and among systems of organizations, creating and maintaining a vision, human relations, and so on. Collaborations demand that organizations be able to compromise and work with professionals and non-professionals across organizations and organizational cultures. Do the board and chief executive have the competencies to manage these interorganizational arrangements?

The second step is closely related to the first and requires that the board and the executive consider the kind of collaborative they might initiate. Each kind of collaboration places a different set of demands on participating organizations. Does the organizational team understand the requirements of participating in various kinds of collaborations? Is it in a position to participate in formal collaborations that require shared decision making, some loss of organizational autonomy, and shared staff and financial resources? Collaborations often fail because organizational partners misunderstand the nature of the collaboration.

The third step directs attention to the differing authority and responsibility aspects of collaborations. When collaborations compromise organizational autonomy through shared governance and resources, there are real issues of authority and responsibility that are often not examined. What this means is that the board and the executive need to revisit the fiduciary responsibilities of the board in its traditional single organization situation. Then it must reexamine these fiduciary responsibilities in the context of multiorganizational collaborations.

The fourth step assumes that the board and the executive have completed steps one through three and have determined that the team and the organization are prepared to explore and initiate a collaboration with one or more organizations. At this step, the team needs to focus more particularly on the various stages of the collaboration, which include (1) exploration, (2) decision making, (3) initiation and design, (4) implementation, and (5) monitoring (Exhibit 6.2).

Exhibit 6.3 provides a tighter focus on who does what when. Collaborations and mergers happen in stages, much as we saw it happening in the formation and transformation of Four Human Services Federation. This makes it possible to plot out the kinds of issues that should be addressed at each stage. As the exhibit shows, it is possible to array both the executive and board role activities by stage of collaboration. It provides a template both for discussion and for initiating step five, developing a preliminary plan of role activities based on the stages of collaboration.

In addition to determining role activities by stage, step five also asks that the board and the executive sort out role activities by type of collaboration. If we think about the board's strategic role, according to the Inglis framework,[33] then their community networks—access to political and social circles made up of significant stakeholders—make it easy to develop and assign appropriate role activities to board members. This can be done within the framework of collaborative types as defined earlier in the glossary of terms in Section 6.2 and described by Exhibit 6.2.

The chief executive, however, is almost always the driving force in collaborations because they so frequently happen at the program and administrative levels. The chief executive is most likely to have information about the potential partners, their program competencies and capacity, the alignment of mission, and the depth and capabilities of staff as well as the general resource picture of the other organizations involved. Thus, it is important to think in terms of the team of the board and the chief executive. Exhibit 6.4 provides a general description and small sampling of how the various roles and responsibilities associated with collaborations and mergers might be shared between the chief executive and the board.

The activities of the board represent not only delivery of the professional expertise they are likely to possess in the context of professionalized boards, but also the exercise of their strategic fiduciary responsibilities. The role activities of the chief executive make the highest and best use of his or her information, expertise, and involvement with the administration of programs and connections with potential partners within the collaborative organizational domain.

What is important about using Exhibit 6.4 as a template is not that boards and executives should attend to this particular sampling in a formulaic way, but rather that they should engage in a dialogue and identify the elements of the collaboration by stage and by type. In other words, this is about the board's and the chief executive's building on their distinctive competencies and their role authority and responsibility. This process of arraying role activities completes step six.

The last step in the process, still in advance of negotiating a formal or informal agreement with other partners, is for the board and the chief executive to reach an initial agreement

EXHIBIT 6.2 Stages of Collaborations and Mergers

Exploration	Decision Making	Initiation & Design	Implementation	Monitoring
Seeking and assessing possible partners	Assessing potential partners re: trust, capacity, governance	Develop partnership agreements	Agree and sign partnership agreements	Compliance with agreement
Assessing financial capacity for collaboration	Financial capacity of partners	Develop agreements re: resource commitments	Implement resource commitments; enact policies and procedures	Policy and procedures/funding and financials
Identifying which programs are available for partnerships	Strategic fit of programs and client service	Which programs, how coordinated and delivered; sharing responsibilities	Implement new program delivery, communications, and coordination	Operations, programs, goal accomplishment
Staff ability and capacity to partner	Professional development needs of staff to partner successfully	Mixing and matching staff to program design and delivery	Orient staff, supervise staff, reporting relationships, trainings, communications	Staff morale and performance, organizational health
Assessing environmental support (i.e., community leaders and funders)	Resource commitment of all partners, funders, clients, community	Boundary-spanning assignments with funders, clients; access support	Implement external communications plan: who does what?	External environmental satisfaction
Would collaboration contribute to mission accomplishment?	Leadership, governance, mission congruence	Designing governance, leadership roles	Implement new governance model, new engagements	Mission, leadership, and governance

EXHIBIT 6.3 Board–Executive Roles by Stage of Collaboration

Stage	Board	Executive
Exploration	• Organizational financial capacity • Environmental context • Mission fit	• Seeking and assessing partners • Identifying programs • Assessing staff potential/capacity
Decision Making	• Financial capacity of partners • Strategic fit • Resource commitment • Governance and leadership	• Potential partner capacity • Leadership assignments • Resource needs/client needs served • Staff capacity/support
Initiation & Design	• Decision-making processes • Governance responsibilities • Resource commitments • Leadership assignments	• Program and decision making • Staff assignments/needs • Client needs and services • Resource-sharing design
Implementation	• Governance • Leadership • Resource commitment • Organizational health	• Staff • Program • Clients • Administration
Monitoring & Review	• Governance and leadership • Mission integrity • Support from environment • Funding resources/financial capacity	• Staff morale/performance • Program quality and staff morale • Budget • Partner coordination

about who will do what in the collaboration. Because collaborations are evolving processes, the board and chief executive should set a schedule for regular meetings to share information, review progress, and revisit role activity assignments and accomplishments as well as any unanticipated changes that can be expected to occur on a regular basis. This prepares the organization to engage in formal planning with other potential partners.

6.4   Conclusion

Collaborations occur in complex environments of continuous change. Executives and boards must be able to create a planning framework for collaborations that utilizes the considerable complementary talents of the board and the chief executive. Organizations in which the chief executive and the board work in a strategic alliance will be more assured of success, whether taking a first hesitant step—placing a toe in the water of collaboration—or considering the possibility of a corporate merger.

When we read the appalling stories about nonperforming boards, chief executives often are reluctant to fully engage their board members. The result is that chief executives then

EXHIBIT 6.4 The Board–Executive Intersect: A Sampling

Board	Executive
Assess potential partners	Choose the right partners
Set conditions for negotiations	Conduct negotiations
Set purpose, goals, mission	Share in goal-setting activity; monitor collaborative goals and purposes; execute goals in collaboration
Assess risk and benefits	Provide information re: risks and benefits
Assess organizational capacity	Oversee skills assessment and development for involvement in collaboration
Plan communications at strategic level	Share communications planning at a strategic level; plan administrative and program-level communications
Clarify roles, responsibility, authority	Share role and responsibility clarification
Monitor the "radar screen"	Provide board with feedback about collaboration, clients, staff, and program on continuous basis
Do boundary spanning with key stakeholders	Provide board with information re: stakeholders (political, funder, other)
Monitor organizational capacity and tracking mission and goals accomplishment	Provide information to board re: organizational capacity

focus their energies on managing their boards so they do no harm. Too often, chief executives go it alone and act as lone rangers in the collaboration enterprise. The result has been that the very real talents and expertise of boards have been ignored, dismissed, and lost!

Endnotes

1. Mattessich, P. W., and B. R. Monsey. (1992). *Collaboration: What Makes It Work.* St. Paul, MN: Amherst H. Wilder Foundation.
2. Arsenault, J. (1998). *Forging Nonprofit Alliances.* San Francisco: Jossey-Bass.
3. McLaughlin, T. A. (1998). *Nonprofit Mergers and Alliances: A Strategic Planning Guide.* New York: John Wiley & Sons, 1998.
4. Id.
5. See note 1.
6. Id., pp. 29–30.
7. See note 1.
8. Id.
9. Id.
10. La Piana, D. (1997). *Beyond Collaboration: Strategic Restructuring of Nonprofit Organizations.* Los Angeles: The James Irvine Foundation.
11. See note 2.
12. See note 10.
13. Id.
14. Id.
15. See note 3.

16. Id., pp. 54–56.
17. Id., p. 230.
18. Conrad, W. R. Jr., and W. E. Glenn. (1986). *The Effective Voluntary Board of Directors.* Athens, OH: Swallow Press.
19. Carver, J. (1990). *Boards That Make a Difference.* San Francisco: Jossey-Bass.
20. Herman, R. D., and R. D. Heimovics. (1991). *Executive Leadership in Nonprofit Organizations.* San Francisco: Jossey-Bass.
21. Widmer, C. (1993). "Role Conflict, Role Ambiguity, and Role Overload on Boards of Directors of Nonprofit Human Service Organizations, "*Nonprofit and Voluntary Sector Quarterly* 22(4): 339–56.
22. Brudney, J. (1997). "The Board of Directors: Strategic Vision for the Volunteer Corps." In T. D. Connors (ed.), *The Nonprofit Handbook,* 2nd edition. New York: John Wiley & Sons.
23. Inglis, S., T. Alexander, and L. Weaver. (1999). "Roles and Responsibilities of Community Nonprofit Boards, "*Nonprofit Management and Leadership* 10(2): 153–67.
24. See note 19.
25. See note 20.
26. See note 23.
27. Feeney, S. (1997). "What Do Prisms Have to Do with Governance?" *The Not-for-Profit CEO Monthly Newsletter* 6(7).
28. See note 23.
29. See note 27.
30. See note 22.
31. See note 23.
32. See note 27.
33. See note 23.

Suggested Readings

Feeney, S. (1998). "Authority Dilemmas on a Board in a Multi-tiered Governance Structure," *Cases in Nonprofit Governance* 23 (Program on Nonprofit Organizations, Yale University).

Golensky, M., and G. I. DeRuiter. (1999). "Merger as a Strategic Response to Government Contracting Pressures: A Case Study," *Nonprofit Management and Leadership* 10 (2).

Gray, B. (1989). *Collaborating: Finding Common Ground for Multi-Party Problems.* San Francisco: Jossey-Bass.

Mulroy, E. A. (1994). "Shared Power: How Nonprofit Organizations Collaborate to Reduce Child Abuse Neglect in Poverty Neighborhoods." Paper presented at the Association for Research on Nonprofit Organizations and Voluntary Action, Berkeley, CA.

Oregon Nonprofit Corporation Act. (1997). ORS. Chapter 65.001–990.

Singer, M. I., and J. A. Yankey. (1991). "Organizational Metamorphosis: A Study of Eighteen Nonprofit Mergers, Acquisitions and Consolidations," *Nonprofit Management and Leadership* 1(4): 357–69.

Trist, E. L. (1985). "Intervention Strategies in Interorganizational Domains. "In Tannenbaum, Margulies, Massarik & Associates (eds.), *Human Systems Development.* San Francisco: Jossey-Bass.

Wernet, S. P., and S. A. Jones. (1992). "Merger and Acquisition Activity Between Nonprofit Social Service Organizations: A Case Study, "*Nonprofit and Voluntary Sector Quarterly* 21 (4).

7 ▼ Marketing

EUGENE M. JOHNSON, DBA, MBA
University of Rhode Island

M. VENKATESAN, PHD
University of Rhode Island

There are no magic formulas for successful marketing. The principles and concepts presented in this chapter, however, will help nonprofit directors and managers plan, organize, and control their marketing activities. The key step for nonprofits is to recognize the importance of marketing and to develop a marketing plan. Having a plan will help everyone within the organization focus on what is most important—identifying the needs of clients and supporters and determining the best ways to meet those needs.

7.1 Introduction

(A) MARKETING AFFECTS EVERYONE

Marketing is an exciting, dynamic discipline that affects everyone's life in many ways. Everyone is a consumer, and many people are part of the marketing process, as salespeople, advertising executives, product managers, wholesalers, retailers, and so forth.

For most of its history, marketing has been viewed as strictly a for-profit business function. This is no longer true. Marketing has become a significant activity for nonprofit organizations, with important contributions to make to overall quality improvement. Consider the following:

- A large midwestern hospital conducts inpatient surveys to determine the level of patient satisfaction and to identify suggestions for improved service.
- An art museum uses an "art-mobile" to bring famous works of art to a city's neighborhoods.
- A Roman Catholic religious order employs a national advertising campaign to recruit candidates for the priesthood.
- A public television station features a "900" number during program breaks to request contributions.

These are just a few examples of the many nonprofit organizations that have successfully applied marketing techniques during the past few years. The application of marketing research tools, advertising, personal selling skills, and the like has changed the way many nonprofit organizations operate.

(B)   MARKETING INVOLVES EXCHANGE

Most definitions of marketing refer to marketing as an exchange process. From a business standpoint, this process involves at least two parties—buyer and seller. Each party gives up something of value and receives something of value.

Because marketing activities bring about exchanges, marketing is an essential function in an economic system. In a free-enterprise system, resources are allocated by the interaction of supply and demand in the marketplace. Marketing activities and institutions provide the framework and mechanisms for this interaction and for the exchange that is taking place.

Although business aspects of marketing are very important, business-oriented definitions of marketing have been found lacking in recent years. Critics observe that marketing involves a wide range of activities, and organizations and should be viewed from a broader perspective. They point out that marketing takes place in many nonprofit organizations, such as hospitals, universities, and social and government agencies. These new applications of marketing are further evidence of its growing importance in our society. Any definition must recognize that marketing is a fundamental human activity and that marketing decisions affect everyone's welfare.

The definition of the American Marketing Association provides a description of marketing in its broader context:

> *Marketing is the process of planning and executing the conception, pricing, promotion, and distribution of ideas, goods, and services to create exchanges that satisfy individual and organizational goals.*

While it includes exchange as a key part, this definition expands the marketing process to include all types of organizations. This has been termed the *broadened* or *generic* view of marketing. The importance and application of marketing to nonprofit organizations and problems are recognized. As in business, a carefully planned, coordinated marketing program can help a nonprofit organization reach its goals, whether they are to attract more members, to increase donations, or to provide better client service.

(C)   RELATIONSHIP MARKETING

The 1990s saw the emergence of a philosophy known as *relationship marketing.* This view assumes that an organization wants to form long-term relationships with its customers. Therefore, the focus of its efforts is not on creating transactions, but rather on customer satisfaction and retention, based on developing a relationship with the customer over time. The customer is viewed as a partner who will help the organization achieve its goals.

This approach, which requires extensive knowledge of customers and their needs, has been the basis for the business success of MCI, Lands' End, Compaq, Fidelity Funds, and others. It is also appropriate for nonprofit organizations, since they will benefit from the support of donors and clients who have long-term relationships with the organization. Relationship marketing provides nonprofits with a strategy that helps them build a mutually beneficial partnership with donors and clients, thus increasing loyalty. In addition, the relationship becomes a tangible benefit that offsets the intangible nature of a nonprofit's activities.[1–2]

(D) IMPLICATIONS FOR NONPROFIT ORGANIZATIONS

The changes in marketing thought emphasize that marketing is applicable to all forms of nonprofit organizations. Effective marketing does not just happen, however. There are no magical formulas or secrets to marketing. Nor will nonprofit managers be able to adapt business marketing concepts and practices to their organizations without some difficulty. Like all management activities, marketing must be planned, organized, and controlled. Further, because marketing is new to most nonprofit organizations, it is even more critical that a carefully thought-out, customer-focused marketing strategy be developed and carried out.[3] And it is crucial that nonprofits work very hard to build and maintain long-term relationships with donors and clients.

7.2 *Marketing Concept*

(A) ORGANIZATIONAL PHILOSOPHY

Most businesses—and some organizations—have adopted what has become known as the *marketing concept.* This philosophy, or conceptual framework, has given marketing a much more important role in all forms of organizations, for-profit and nonprofit alike.

Kotler and Andreasen call this the *marketing mindset.*[4] They point out that a nonprofit organization's directors and managers must have a clear appreciation of what marketing is and what it can do for the organization. Most importantly, they must put the customer, or client, at the center of everything the organization does.

(B) MAJOR PROPOSITIONS

As applied to a nonprofit organization, the marketing concept is based on three major propositions: client orientation, coordination of all client-related activities, and goal direction.

(i) *Client Orientation*

As noted previously, this is the key to the marketing concept. Nonprofit managers must shift from an internal organizational perspective to the client's viewpoint. Successful marketing in a nonprofit organization requires a complete understanding of an organization's clients—their needs, attitudes, and buying behavior. For instance, a community agency that provides services to the elderly must know exactly what the needs of the elderly in its community are and must develop programs that meet these needs. *A nonprofit organization must never forget that it exists to serve the needs of its clients.*

When a nonprofit organization does not understand or heed the needs of its clients, marketing can be a dismal failure. The U.S. Treasury Department's introduction of the Susan B. Anthony dollar clearly made this point. Despite research studies that suggested little enthusiasm for a small dollar among bankers and business executives and likely rejection by consumers, Treasury Department officials went ahead with their plan to introduce the Anthony dollar. Almost $1 million was spent to promote and publicize the new dollar, but consumers rejected it. Why? The major reason was that the Anthony dollar was designed poorly and did not meet the needs of businesses and consumers. It was too similar to a quarter in size and appearance. The Treasury Department's promotion effort could not overcome the product's design weakness.

(ii) Coordination

For marketing to be effective in a nonprofit organization, *there must be coordination of all elements of the marketing program.* Because these elements, known as the *marketing mix,* constitute an interrelated system, the program must be viewed and planned as a whole. Marketing itself must be closely interrelated with other activities of a nonprofit organization.

To achieve the desired coordination, there must be close cooperation among all components of an organization. For instance, if the executive director of a health care agency commits the agency to participate in a community health education program, the director must be sure that the agency's education committee supports this activity and that the agency has the resources available to participate.

(iii) Goal Direction

The marketing concept stresses that *the only way an organization can achieve its own goals is by satisfying the needs of its clients (customers).* For example, a college wishing to increase the level of funding provided by the business community must demonstrate to business executives that it is meeting the business education needs of the community. This may require the development of special educational programs and activities for local businesses and their employees.

(C) IMPLEMENTING THE MARKETING CONCEPT

A marketing success story illustrates how a coordinated marketing plan based on meeting clearly understood needs will work. Several years ago, the Dallas Museum of Fine Arts was faced with an urgent need to develop an effective marketing program after its goal of expansion was thwarted. The defeat of a bond referendum for a new museum forced the Dallas Museum's administrators to redefine the museum's goals and its relation to the public. They decided to emphasize that "a great city deserves a great art museum." Through a carefully planned marketing program, they informed the people of Dallas that an art museum is more than a place to store art treasures. They stressed the educational values and the economic benefits from tourists attracted by exhibits and special shows. They developed a model showing the key features, and the corresponding benefits for the public, of the proposed building. Museum officials used this model when they met with public groups. These marketing efforts succeeded, and the second bond referendum passed.

7.3 Unique Aspects of Nonprofit Marketing

(A) PRODUCTS ARE SERVICES

The products of most nonprofit organizations are services, not tangible goods. A service is an activity performed for another person or organization. Johnson and colleagues have identified several characteristics that set services apart from goods and make their marketing more challenging.[5]

(i) Intangibility

Services go out of existence at the very moment they are rendered (e.g., counseling session), although their effects may last for some time. Because of the lack of tangibility, marketers of services find it quite difficult to differentiate their offerings. Their clients see intangible services as abstract and thus difficult to describe and understand.

(ii)   Perishability

Services cannot be stored; they have to be produced on demand. Marketers of services, unlike goods marketers, are unable to manufacture for inventory during slow times and draw on inventory during periods of peak demand. Excess capacity not used in services production is lost forever—for example, empty beds in a hospital or vacant seats in a classroom.

(iii)   Simultaneity

Services are produced and consumed at the same time, in contrast to goods, which are generally produced, then purchased, and then consumed. As a result, a service performer and service buyer usually have to interact and, accordingly, be in the same place at the same time.

(iv)   Heterogeneity

The quality of service performance varies from one service organization to another, from one service performer to another, and from one occasion to another. This variability of service output makes it difficult for a nonprofit service organization to establish and maintain performance standards and thus guarantee quality continuously.

(B)   MULTIPLE PUBLICS

The marketing efforts of business organizations are concentrated on the firm's customers. This is not the case with nonprofit organizations, which must market to multiple publics. As defined by Kotler and Andreasen, a public is "a distinct group of people, organizations or both whose actual or potential needs must in some sense be served."[6] Four types of publics are identified for nonprofit organizations by Kotler and Andreasen:

- Input publics (e.g., donors and suppliers) provide resources.
- Internal publics (e.g., staff and volunteers) convert resources into useful goods and services.
- Intermediary publics (e.g., agents and facilitators) deliver goods and services.
- Consuming publics (e.g., clients and local residents) gain satisfaction from the goods and services provided.

From a marketing standpoint, the key publics are supporters and clients. Supporters (donors and volunteers) provide the key resources to a nonprofit organization, through either their monetary contributions or their time and personal expertise. Clients, who are the primary customers of a nonprofit organization, benefit from its services.

In addition to clients and supporters, a specific nonprofit organization's publics will include many other types of people and groups. A brief review of the important publics of a community hospital illustrates this fact. Its publics include:

- Patients and their families and friends
- Members of the community who aid the hospital through donations, volunteer services, and other forms of support

- Suppliers of goods and services
- Doctors, nurses, administrators, and other employees
- Trustees of the hospital
- Regulatory agencies
- The general public

Because members of each of these publics have different needs and attitudes, marketing concepts must be applied differently.

(C) MULTIPLE OBJECTIVES

Business firms have long-run profitability as their overriding objective. Because they must serve multiple publics, nonprofit organizations have multiple objectives. Sometimes, these objectives may not be consistent with one another. For instance, a community center may wish to provide free family-planning counseling to its clients, but it is limited because a major portion of its funding comes from donors who are opposed to certain forms of birth control.

For many nonprofit organizations, the process of formulating objectives involves compromise and consensus building. This makes marketing more difficult than in businesses because more time must be spent in involving board members, staff, and volunteers, and convincing them to accept the objectives.

(D) PUBLIC SCRUTINY

Many nonprofit organizations provide vital services for society. Because of this, they are often subsidized by government and are given tax-exempt status by government. Their activities are closely watched by government officials, news media, and the general public.

One particular concern is public criticism of the administrative and marketing costs incurred to raise funds. For instance, a newspaper article reported that a charitable organization raised $9 million. After deducting marketing and administrative expenses, about $650,000—less than 8 cents of every dollar raised—was left to assist the needy.

From a marketing perspective, this type of media coverage is harmful to all nonprofit organizations that rely on contributions for a portion of their funding. The negative publicity and possible government intervention related to this situation increase the public pressure on nonprofit organizations. Accordingly, they must be very careful to conduct their affairs in a way that does not result in public displeasure.

7.4 *Buying Behavior for Services*

Buying behavior for services is different than buying behavior for products.[7] Because services are intangible and nonstandardized, it is hard to evaluate services in advance. Only after use or experience can one provide evaluation of services that were experienced. This is not the case with products.

(A) QUALITIES

Since products are tangible things, consumers can specify in advance the *search qualities*, that is, the attributes desired by the consumer. For example, a buyer can specify a desire for carpeting with certain attributes, such as stain resistance, wool blend, green color, and so forth. These attributes can be determined well in advance, and the search for the product or brand having these attributes can begin. Generally, goods are high in search qualities—they can be determined and evaluated before purchase takes place.

Services generally cannot be judged or evaluated until after purchase and/or consumption because of the characteristics (intangibility, inseparability, and nonstandardization) associated with services. Thus, *experience qualities* become more important in evaluating services. Moreover, evaluation made of a service at one time does not guarantee that the buyer will encounter the same experience the next time. For example, the last time a couple vacationed in Hawaii, they experienced complete satisfaction with the facilities, services, and ambience the hotel provided. However, the same kind or level of experience cannot be guaranteed if the couple were to visit the same hotel a year later. In many nonprofit service situations, the services have to be provided day-in and day-out (e.g., in a nursing home), and the service is repeated and experienced every day.

In addition to the experience qualities desired for services, another category of quality becomes important for certain services. It is called the *credence qualities,* or credibility or trust qualities. For example, if an auto mechanic indicates that he has changed a certain part in the automobile, and even if he provides the customer the old part presumably taken from the customer's automobile during the service process, one cannot be sure that the mechanic in fact installed a new part. In most cases, the customer does not have the knowledge to decide whether such a part needed to be changed, and there is no way to check whether that work was really done. The buyer has to take it on faith, based on the credibility or trust, that when the mechanic indicates that certain work was done for the automobile, in fact such work was done. Another example will illustrate the importance of such credence qualities. Even if an appendix is produced in a jar by the physician who performed the surgery, the patient cannot be sure that it is the patient's appendix, nor does the patient have the knowledge to know whether the appendix should have been removed in the first place.

Services provided by nonprofit organizations are high in credence qualities since they are difficult to evaluate. Often, the donor does not know for sure whether such services were provided and, if provided, whether they were provided to the satisfaction of the recipient of the services. The user of such services can experience the service only after it is provided by the nonprofit organization.

(B) PERCEIVED RISK

The second unique aspect of buying behavior for services relates to the concept of perceived risk. Buyers perceive higher risk in dealing with the purchase or use of services than with products. In the case of products, information can be obtained in the prepurchase stage, which might provide information that is likely to reduce the amount of perceived risk. However, the intangible nature of services and the high levels of experience and credence qualities inherent in the evaluation of services increase the nature of perceived risk. Further, because the delivery of many services starts all over again the next day, the perceived risk appears to be present at all times.

In the context of nonprofit organizations, the donors might perceive risk in associating with or providing resources to a particular organization. Similarly, clients may perceive a high amount of risk in receiving services provided by a nonprofit organization. This may be especially true in the case of a nonprofit hospital or other such organization.

The attitudes and demeanor of employees and volunteers will have a major impact on the perception of risk. However, the extent of perceived risk is not equally high for every client or every donor. This depends on the type of nonprofit organization, the nature of service provided, and the type of clientele.

(C) PERCEIVED CONTROL

The third unique aspect of buying behavior for services involves the notion of perceived control.[8] Perceived service quality is related to the perception of perceived control. In the context of a nonprofit organization, if the client or the donor perceive that they do not have much control in the operation or use situation, they are likely to feel uncomfortable. The nonprofit organization should not take away a sense of control (perceived control, not actual control) from their clients or their donors.

7.5 *Information for Marketing*

(A) MARKETING INTELLIGENCE

Marketing intelligence is a broad term used to describe the information-gathering function of marketing. This function may involve informal information gathering, such as conversations with clients in waiting rooms or discussions among nonprofit managers at seminars and conferences. Most often, however, marketing intelligence refers to formal, organized information-gathering activities and subsequent analysis.

The purpose of marketing research and other marketing intelligence activities is to provide information for marketing planning, decision making, and control. For instance, a community service agency carried out a market survey of the attitudes and practices of employers toward hiring people with a mental handicap.[9] The results of the survey were used to develop a marketing program, which involved a job trainer at no cost to the hiring firm, and a promotional program, which emphasized the dependable job performance of employees with a mental handicap.

(B) MARKETING INFORMATION SYSTEM

A marketing information system (MIS) is a set of procedures and methods that provides an orderly flow of relevant information to marketing decision makers. Two types of information are gathered, processed, and analyzed by an effective MIS: secondary data and primary data.

Secondary data are data that have been or are being collected for another purpose and are already in existence. Frequently available from both outside and inside sources, secondary data save a manager time and money. Data from publications, government reports, university studies, and other published sources often provide the information needed for nonprofit marketing planning. Also needed, however, are data about clients and donors, and other relevant data from sources within the nonprofit organization. In particular, a current database of clients and donors is essential to follow up other marketing activities.

Primary data involve the collection of information by the nonprofit organization for a specific purpose. Primary data are needed to fill the information gaps left by lacking, outdated, or otherwise inadequate secondary data. For example, a chamber of commerce knew from its internal records that members were canceling faster than new ones were enrolling. However, there was no information on why the chamber was losing members. To find out, primary data collection was needed. A survey of members who had canceled led to the development of a marketing program to involve inactive members, provide added benefits to members, and offer after-sale service.[10]

(C) DATABASE MARKETING

Computer technology, which developed rapidly during the 1970s and 1980s and is expected to continue to grow during the coming decades, has been the driving force behind the emergence of database marketing. Marketers now have the capability to compile and analyze tremendous amounts of information about individual customers. In addition to the increased sophistication of computers and computer software, the growth of database marketing is also the result of the expanded use of credit cards and toll-free telephone services, the increased availability of ZIP codes and census tract information, and the development of advanced statistical and financial analytical methods.

Many successful business marketers (e.g., L.L. Bean, American Express, and AT&T) have used their ability to store and quickly analyze vast amounts of customer information effectively. They have moved from relying on mass marketing to the use of more targeted and individualized means to communicate with their customers. The key to their success has been the development of sophisticated customer databases.[11]

Nonprofits can also benefit from the development of databases. By compiling information on clients and donors, nonprofits will better understand their constituents on an individual basis. They will be able to target fund-raising and other marketing activities to specific needs of their donors and clients. And the effective use of database marketing information by nonprofits will help them create desired long-term relationships. However, this will not happen if nonprofits do not invest their resources in database marketing information and technology.

(D) MARKETING RESEARCH

As part of an organization's MIS, marketing research is used to collect, process, and analyze primary data. Because marketing research is concerned with helping managers find solutions to marketing problems, there are almost as many uses of marketing research as there are problems.

Many nonprofit marketing research studies are concerned with clients and donors—who they are and what they need; their attitudes and behavior patterns; and so forth. Other projects study marketing activities, such as pricing, service policies, advertising, and public relations. Control and reappraisal of marketing costs, such as promotion expenditures and delivery costs, are the subject of other research efforts. Finally, many nonprofit organizations are concerned with overall marketing strategy considerations, such as the organization's image, marketing policies, and objectives.

Marketing researchers use a number of different techniques and tools to obtain the desired information. Among those that might be used by nonprofit organizations are:

- Informed opinion interviews—asking people with special expertise or knowledge to discuss a problem or to suggest other sources of information

- Focus groups—exploring the feelings and ideas of a small group of people who have similar backgrounds and interests
- Case studies—reviewing, in depth, a few selected situations in order to identify key factors and relationships
- Observation—noting objects or actions through the senses, primarily sight and hearing
- Surveys—obtaining information by asking questions of people (clients or donors, for example) who are affected by marketing activities

7.6 *Marketing Management*

(A) MARKETING MANAGEMENT IN NONPROFIT ORGANIZATIONS

Management is defined as the process necessary to bring the most return from a particular commitment of an organization's resources (technical, financial, human, etc.) when other alternative commitments are possible. The information on which the commitment is made is always incomplete, and the conditions under which the decision will be carried out are uncertain.

Nonprofit organizations feel special pressure because they have limited resources. Cutbacks in assistance from federal, state, and local governments; changes in tax laws that hurt gift giving; and limited growth in corporate giving have combined to place added financial pressure on directors and managers of nonprofit organizations. They must learn to use marketing concepts and techniques to focus their efforts on the needs of their clients.

An overview of the marketing management process is presented in Exhibit 7.1. As suggested by the marketing concept, marketing management is an integrated, interrelated process. The first, very important step is to analyze the marketing situation. This is part of marketing planning, as are the next three steps shown in Exhibit 7.1. In summary form, the critical marketing management tasks are:

- *Planning:* Analyzing the marketing situation, selecting marketing objectives, identifying target markets, and developing a marketing strategy and programs
- *Organization:* Developing a marketing structure
- *Control:* Selecting activities that will ensure that the objectives are achieved

The description of the marketing management process highlights the importance of marketing planning and suggests that marketing planning is a continuous process. Even the most thorough marketing planner realizes that plans cannot be cast in stone. Flexibility is needed. Changes must be made in marketing plans, in order to meet unanticipated market changes, competitive actions, and similar environmental changes. This is why Exhibit 7.1 contains a feedback path from marketing control to the beginning of the marketing management process.

(B) STRATEGIC MARKETING PLANNING

Strategic marketing planning is an essential activity for all nonprofit organizations, regardless of size, location, or function. As shown in Exhibit 7.2, the strategic marketing planning process can be divided into four major steps:

EXHIBIT 7.1 Marketing Management Process

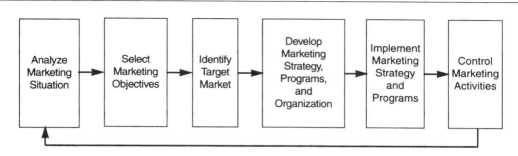

Source: Eugene M. Johnson. (1986). "Marketing Planning for Nonprofit Organizations," Nonprofit World (May–June): 21. Reprinted by permission of Society for Nonprofit Organizations, 6314 Odana Road, Suite 1, Madison, WI 53719 (1-800-424-7367).

1. *Situation analysis* answers the question "Where are you?" by providing a realistic view of the organization's environment, marketing opportunities, and internal strengths and weaknesses.
2. *Identification of an organization's mission and objectives* provides an answer to a second question: "Where do we want to go?"

EXHIBIT 7.2 Strategic Marketing Planning Process

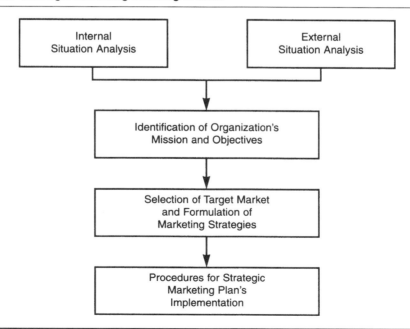

Source: Eugene M. Johnson. (1986). "Marketing Planning for Nonprofit Organizations," Nonprofit World (July–August): 26. Reprinted by permission of Society for Nonprofit Organizations, 6314 Odana Road, Suite 1, Madison, WI 53719 (1-800-424-7367).

3. *Formulation of marketing strategies* is the third step. These strategies answer the question "How do you want to get there?" The answer to this question is dependent primarily on the target market that the organization wishes to serve.
4. Procedures for *implementation of the marketing plan* provide the schedule ("When do you want to arrive?"), organization ("Who is responsible?"), and budget ("How much will it cost?") for carrying out the marketing plan.

7.7 *Marketing Situation Analysis*

(A) COMPONENTS OF SITUATION ANALYSIS

Situation analysis is an assessment of an organization's present position in its current environment. Before establishing its marketing objectives and plans, a nonprofit organization must have a clear understanding of its present situation. This involves the identification of present and potential problems and opportunities. There are two parts to this analysis:

- *External analysis:* Evaluating an organization's markets and publics, market segments, competitors, and environmental trends and issues
- *Internal analysis:* Evaluating critical measures of an organization's performance, resources, strengths, and weaknesses

(B) MARKETING AUDIT

Some organizations use a marketing audit to review their marketing resources and activities and to carry out the situation analysis. Just as a nonprofit organization's financial position is regularly and systematically reviewed, so should its marketing efforts be subjected to regular and systematic evaluation to determine whether the marketing efforts are appropriate and whether they are being properly executed.

A marketing audit is sweeping and comprehensive. Kotler and Andreasen[12] provide a complete guide to the kinds of questions that a marketing audit should consider, as do Lovelock and Weinberg.[13] The nonprofit organization's environment is studied; its policies, organization, methods, and marketing philosophy are reviewed; its programs for reaching its goals are assessed; and its procedures for determining and controlling its marketing efforts are analyzed.

Even the most successful nonprofit organizations should carry out regular marketing audits. Seldom is any organization so good that it cannot be improved. Also, past success may breed complacency and carelessness. Audits that can be conducted easily and inexpensively on certain aspects of the marketing program should be undertaken frequently. In some situations, a checklist can be used to provide a flexible, inexpensive self-study tool.[14]

(C) EXTERNAL ANALYSIS

External situation analysis concentrates on a nonprofit organization's environment. It focuses on external factors that can influence funding and participation.

(i)   Clients and Supporters

The external situation analysis should begin with an assessment of an organization's clients. The key questions are:

- Who are they?
- Who should they be?
- What are they "buying"?
- What could cause this situation to change?
- Why do they "buy" or participate?
- When do they "buy" or participate?
- How do they make decisions to "buy" or participate?
- Where do they "buy" or participate?

The next step is to consider the nonprofit organization's supporters. Unlike business organizations, which are mainly concerned with customer analysis, nonprofit organizations depend on others for support. In particular, a nonprofit organization must answer similar questions about its funders and volunteers.

- Who are they?
- What are they supporting?
- What could cause this situation to change?
- Why do they provide support?
- When do they provide support?
- How do they make decisions to provide support?

Based on the analysis of clients and supporters, several key issues will emerge, including:

- *Market size and growth.* The primary concern here is to determine how large the market is and what potential growth opportunities exist, based on estimates of (1) the potential number of clients and supporters, and (2) the potential rate of participation and/or support.
- *Client/supporter decision making.* An organization must try to understand how clients and supporters (or potential clients and supporters) make decisions regarding the organization; specifically, how do they decide whether to "buy" service and which organization to "buy" from?
- *Market segments.* The organization must identify groups of clients and supporters who are similar in terms of decision making and who might represent specific targets for specialized marketing efforts.

Thorough analysis of clients and supporters will help an organization identify marketing opportunities. This requires taking a broad view of the market and avoiding the limitations of "marketing myopia."

Theodore Levitt, in his classic article "Marketing Myopia," pointed to the shortcomings of major firms and industries that failed to analyze their marketing opportunities correctly.[15] His contention was that top executives in many industries have unnecessarily taken a limited view of the scope of their businesses. They have been product oriented rather than customer oriented. Because of their limited views of marketing, executives in these industries, such as dry cleaning, railroads, electric utilities, and motion pictures, missed marketing opportunities based on changing customers' needs.

Levitt's admonishment is just as applicable today as in the past and is as applicable to nonprofits as it is to businesses. A public library that fails to provide its clients with videotapes, computer software, and other recently developed techniques for making knowledge and entertainment available will soon lose many clients. In contrast, an organization that successfully changed was the March of Dimes. After polio ceased to be a major health concern, this organization switched to birth defects and prenatal care as causes that needed a focal point.

(ii) Publics

In addition to clients and supporters, a nonprofit organization must assess the impact of its other publics. As noted earlier, a nonprofit organization's publics will include many types of people, organizations, and groups.

Key questions that should be asked are:

- Who are the people and/or entities that have an impact on the organization?
- Which are most influential?
- Why do they have an impact on the organization?
- What are their objectives and the reasons for their concern with the organization?
- In what ways do they affect the organization?
- What could cause this situation to change?
- What impact will changes have on an organization's publics and their relationship with it?

(iii) Competition

In recent years, competition has become an important concern for most nonprofit organizations. Not only must an organization be concerned about competition from other nonprofits, but it is also likely to be facing competitive challenges from business organizations. For example: public hospitals compete with for-profit hospitals for patients, staff, and financial support; private and public colleges compete with profit-oriented trade schools, correspondence programs, and business educational services for students; and the United States Postal Service competes with the United Parcel Service, Federal Express, and other businesses for customers.

The key questions to be asked as part of the competitive analysis are:

- Who are the major competitors?
- How do they compete?
- What are their strengths and weaknesses that will pose problems and opportunities? (These may include costs and fees, access to clients and supporters, image, type of client base, personnel, and marketing budgets and other resources.)

(iv) Other External Factors

Nonprofit directors and managers make marketing decisions in a dynamic environment. There are many other external factors over which they have little or no control. Some specific questions that must be considered are:

- What economic factors might influence the attainment of the organization's objectives?
- What national, state, and local regulations affect the organization?
- What are the demographic, social, technological, and other external factors that may affect the organization?

(D) INTERNAL ANALYSIS

The internal situation analysis will help a nonprofit organization identify the internal problems and opportunities that can affect the organization's performance. In particular, what are the organization's marketing strengths and weaknesses? This portion of the situation analysis concentrates on those aspects of the organization that affect its ability to satisfy the clients' needs and influence participation and support.

To assess the marketing performance of their organizations, nonprofit directors and managers must ask themselves questions relating to the following five critical areas of performance:

1. *Trends.* What are the significant trends in the organization's programs, services, participation, and support?
2. *Share of market.* How much of the market does the organization have in relation to competitive organizations?
3. *Stability.* Has the organization demonstrated "staying power"?
4. *Efficiency.* Has the organization been cost effective in its utilization of facilities, personnel, and other resources?
5. *Flexibility.* Has the organization been able to adapt to market and environmental changes?

A second part of the internal situation analysis involves an assessment of the nonprofit organization's marketing efforts (i.e., its marketing objectives, programs, personnel, and practices). The organization must examine its physical, financial, personnel, and other resources used to provide services to clients. The two critical questions are:

1. What key competitive advantages and disadvantages does the organization have?
2. How can the organization maintain its competitive advantages and overcome its competitive disadvantages?

After completing this assessment, marketing planners will have an understanding of what sort of marketing their organization can and cannot do. They will know which of the marketing opportunities can be pursued.

7.8 *Marketing Planning*

The three strategic marketing planning steps are (1) selecting marketing objectives, (2) identifying the target market, and (3) developing a marketing strategy. The planning steps are then implemented through the preparation of an action plan.

(A) SELECTING MARKETING OBJECTIVES

Objectives provide the direction for a nonprofit organization's activities; they answer the question: "Where do we want to go?"

(i) Marketing Objectives and Mission

A nonprofit organization's marketing objectives must be consistent with its mission. If they are not, marketing activities may work against what the nonprofit wants to accomplish.

For example, a medium-size university located in a resort area wanted to upgrade its image as a quality institution with high academic standards. However, the advertising theme used to promote the university to potential students continued to emphasize "sun and fun." Unfortunately, the advertising efforts conflicted with the university's goal.

(ii) Marketing Objectives and Organizational Goals

It is not easy to coordinate marketing objectives and activities with the goals of a nonprofit organization. Unlike a business, which is dominated by the profit motive, nonprofits tend to have multiple goals, such as survival, growth, and social change. As a result, marketing objectives may require modification to adapt them to the varied goals of a nonprofit organization.

(iii) Guidelines for Setting Marketing Objectives

When formulating marketing objectives, there are several guidelines to follow. Most important, marketing objectives must be specific; an objective must be a precise statement of what is to be accomplished by the organization's marketing efforts. Objectives should be stated in simple, understandable terms, so that everyone involved in marketing knows exactly what is to be done. Further, objectives should be measurable; that is, they should be stated in quantitative terms. Finally, marketing objectives should be related to time, so that everyone knows when the objectives should be achieved. Examples of marketing objectives that meet these criteria include the following:

- Church: "To increase average attendance at the Sunday morning worship service from 130 to 150 by the end of one year."
- Senior citizens' center: "To raise $250,000 for a new recreation facility in two years."
- Private college: "To increase enrollment by 10 percent for next year's fall class."

(B) IDENTIFYING THE TARGET MARKET

After formulating its marketing objectives, a nonprofit organization will choose its target market—the specific group of clients and supporters to whom it wishes to appeal. Selection of a target market depends on a careful review of potential clients' and supporters' needs, attitudes, and buying behavior. This analysis will provide nonprofit marketers with the insights needed to develop an appropriate marketing strategy.

There are two prime marketing strategy options: concentrated marketing and differentiated marketing.

Concentrated marketing, also called *targeted marketing* or *niche marketing*, involves focusing on a single, easily defined market segment. This approach is especially appropriate for organizations with limited resources. For instance, a small private college might concentrate its efforts on providing a quality liberal arts education for students from its region of the country.

When a nonprofit organization defines its target market in terms of several market segments, it is employing a differentiated marketing approach. A large state university will offer professional as well as liberal arts courses and programs. It may have several campus locations and will schedule classes at many times of the day and evening. It may offer special courses and seminars to businesses and government agencies for their managers and professional employees.

(C) MARKET SEGMENTATION

In recent years, marketing theorists and practitioners have learned much about buyers' behavior. This new knowledge has led to the emergence of market segmentation as a significant marketing planning and management tool. Market segmentation is the process of dividing a market into separate subsets, or segments, of buyers. The organization can concentrate its marketing efforts on a distinct subset of the market, or it can develop different marketing strategies for each market segment. For instance:

- A college offers classes during the day for its full-time students and at night for its part-time students who work during the day.
- A hospital offers outpatient surgery options for minor operations and traditional inpatient surgery for more serious conditions.
- A nonprofit theater offers matinee performances for senior citizens and school children and evening performances for working people.
- A library provides large-print books for the visually impaired and Saturday morning reading sessions for preschool children.

The most frequently used bases for segmenting consumer markets are demographic, geographic, behavioral, and purchase volume characteristics.

(i) Demographic
A market is subdivided on the basis of age, gender, occupation, income, education, marital status, and other demographic variables. For example, a health care agency might want to concentrate on services for the elderly.

(ii) Geographic
A market is subdivided into different locations, such as states, counties, urban versus rural areas, and so on. For instance, public libraries in rural areas must often use bookmobiles to take books to their distant clients; urban libraries are more accessible to their clients, who may be within walking distance of a branch.

(iii) Behavioral
A market is subdivided on the basis of lifestyle, personality, social class, attitudes, and other behavioral characteristics. Organizations that build housing complexes for the elderly use behavioral characteristics to segment the housing market and develop appropriate facilities. Social service agencies that cater to single parents use lifestyle characteristics to reach those in need of their services.

(iv) *Volume*

A market is subdivided on the basis of usage. Heavy, medium, and light users are studied, to determine whether they have similar demographic or behavioral characteristics. For example, it has been shown that certain segments of the population are most likely to abuse alcohol and other drugs and are therefore the prime target market for rehabilitation programs.

7.9 *Developing a Marketing Strategy*

Strategy, the "how" of marketing planning, is the overall design for achieving a nonprofit organization's marketing objectives. Development of a marketing strategy depends on the target market chosen. The nonprofit marketing planner formulates a marketing approach that will best satisfy the needs of the target market.

(A) CREATING A DIFFERENTIAL ADVANTAGE

When developing its marketing strategy, a nonprofit organization must strive to achieve a differential advantage. This is the "something extra" that makes an organization's marketing efforts just a little better than those of its competitors. Consequently, a particular group of clients (the target market) prefers the organization's services.

A differential advantage can be the result of any part of the marketing effort—price, service uniqueness or quality, psychological benefits created by promotion, and so forth. Consider, for example, the prestigious image of certain colleges and universities, such as Harvard, Yale, and Stanford. When people think of the nation's top academic institutions, they usually think of these universities. As a result, these schools have an advantage when recruiting students and faculty or seeking financial support.

(B) GROWTH STRATEGIES

Because clients' needs are changing rapidly and competition is increasing for traditional nonprofit services and programs, many nonprofit organizations are searching for growth opportunities. Exhibit 7.3 suggests four growth strategy options: market penetration, market development, service development, and diversification.

Market penetration involves an organization's efforts to increase sales and support of its present services to its present markets. The organization may do so by persuading present clients to use more of its services or by attracting clients and supporters from competitors. Aggressive promotion is the approach used most often by nonprofits to increase their market penetration. For instance, college admissions officers are using direct mail, telemarketing, and personal selling to recruit students. On a smaller scale, a minister, priest, or rabbi can increase attendance at religious services and other activities by visiting members and potential members in their homes.

Market development involves selling present services to new markets. This is often done by moving into new geographic markets. Boston's Northeastern University is drawing new students for its specialized, nondegree courses by offering night classes to high-tech engineers and computer scientists in California's Silicon Valley—over 3,000 miles away!

Service development involves creating new services for present markets. In this approach, an organization identifies an unsatisfied need that can be met by introducing a

EXHIBIT 7.3 Growth Strategy Options

	Present Services	New Services
PRESENT MARKETS	Market Penetration	Service Development
NEW MARKETS	Market Development	Diversification

Source: Eugene M. Johnson. (1986). "Marketing Planning for Nonprofit Organizations," Nonprofit World (September–October): 30. Reprinted by permission of Society for Nonprofit Organizations, 6314 Odana Road, Suite 1, Madison, WI 53719 (1-800-424-7367).

new or modified service. Many hospitals, for instance, are developing community "wellness" programs, designed to prevent illness rather than to provide treatment. These hospitals are serving the same clients but in a different way. Another example of service development by nonprofits is the emergence of Christian schools. Sensing a need for a different approach to education, many fundamentalist churches have established their own elementary and secondary schools. Thus, they provide a new service to their present members.

Diversification involves developing new services for new markets. An example is a community service agency that decides to market its internal management development seminars to other local nonprofit organizations. This approach carries the most risk because diversification opportunities are difficult to evaluate. A nonprofit organization must be sure it understands the new markets it wants to pursue.

Many churches, especially those in inner cities, have redefined their markets and become more involved in economic development activities. Some of the business activities are used to help fund social programs. For example, Hartford Memorial Baptist Church in Detroit has opened an auto mechanics training center and leases land to new businesses to promote economic development.[16]

(C) PREPARING AN ACTION PLAN

Implementing marketing strategies ("How do we get there?") requires the preparation of a marketing action plan. The development of schedules and budgets will answer the questions: "When do we want to arrive?" and "How much will it cost?" Marketing organization and implementation plans are also needed.

(i) Schedule

As noted in the discussion of marketing objectives, a marketing plan must have a time frame, a schedule for achieving the plan's objectives. The plan must also include priorities, or a statement of which objectives are to be given the most attention. Marketing planners develop three types of schedules for marketing plans: short-range plans cover a period of one year or less, medium-range plans cover a period of up to five years, and long-range plans are developed for five years or more. Long-range plans are the most difficult to prepare because long-range forecasts of rapidly changing markets and environmental conditions are unpredictable.

(ii) Budget

Because marketing resources are limited, especially in nonprofit organizations, budgets are needed to allocate resources to the desired marketing activities. The budgeted amount for an activity should match its importance to the organization's marketing strategy. For instance, as the number of college-age students has declined in recent years, colleges and universities are spending more of their budgets on direct mail and other techniques to attract students. This reflects the increased importance of recruiting to the growth—and even the survival—of many colleges and universities.

The objective and task approach has become the preferred method for budgeting marketing expenditures. This approach begins with the formulation of specific, measurable marketing objectives. Then the marketing activities, or tasks, required to achieve the objectives are determined. The marketing budget will be the total amount of money needed to accomplish the required activities. The strength of this budgeting approach is its close relationship to the nonprofit organization's marketing objectives.

(iii) Organization

A structure must be established to achieve the nonprofit organization's marketing objectives. If the marketing concept is accepted as a philosophy, the organization must focus itself to reflect its commitment to its supporters and clients. The result will be an expanded policy-making role for marketing personnel.

Because the board of directors is the policy-making body for most nonprofit organizations, its members must include people who have marketing knowledge and experience.[17] It may be wise to establish a marketing committee and to designate specific staff persons to perform marketing tasks such as market research and promotion. Larger nonprofit organizations have created marketing departments with a director or vice-president of marketing charged with overseeing all customer-related activities.[18]

(iv) Implementation

Finally, the nonprofit marketing planner must transmit marketing objectives, strategies, schedules, and budgets to the people who will carry them out. However, communication of marketing plans involves more than informing people of the plans. Nonprofit managers will have to "sell" people on accepting and implementing the marketing plans. People tend to resist change, even a change that may benefit them. They anticipate that new marketing plans and programs will mean more work for them. Management must convince skeptical members of the nonprofit organization that the success of a plan will help them achieve their personal goals.

7.10 Service Marketing Mix

A convenient concept for explaining a nonprofit organization's marketing activities and the decisions made by marketing managers is the marketing mix. Just as a cook prepares a mix of ingredients for a favorite recipe, a marketing manager combines marketing activities to form a satisfactory marketing mix.

The major components of the marketing mix (Exhibit 7.4) are:

- *Service:* The "bundle of satisfactions" provided; the services and ideas marketed to clients and supporters
- *Price:* What is charged for the services and ideas provided; a "price" may be money, time, or something else of value
- *Distribution:* Where and how services are provided; the delivery systems responsible for getting services to clients
- *Promotion:* The organization's efforts to inform and persuade clients and supporters; promotional techniques include advertising, personal selling, public relations, and sales promotion

These four elements are blended together to create a total package that will best satisfy the target market's needs and manage their expectations.

(A) SERVICES

The activities of most nonprofit organizations consist of services, ideas, experiences, and, in some cases, complementary goods. Albrecht and Zemke called this the service package—"the sum total of the goods, services and experiences offered to the customer."[19] They and others[20] pointed out that the service package consists of a core service or idea plus a cluster of supplementary goods and services. The core service or idea is the specific benefit the nonprofit customer wants. For example, a church member will seek spiritual inspiration and guidance. Supplementary goods and services support, complement, and add value to the core service. Examples include a church's newsletter, nursery care during services, and recreational activities for young adults. Developing the appropriate service package requires a clear understanding of the nonprofit organization's mission and the needs of its clients and supporters.

(i) Product Life Cycle

Products and services, like people and other living things, have life cycles. An important managerial planning and control tool, the product life cycle follows a product from birth

---

EXHIBIT 7.4 The Service Marketing Mix

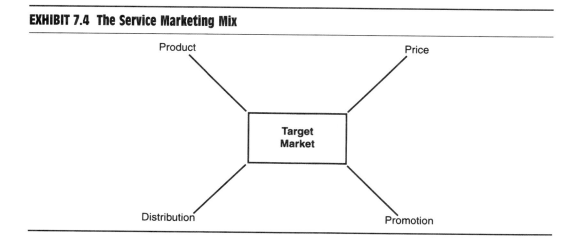

(introduction) to death. It provides a conceptual framework for developing marketing strategies and programs for different stages of a product's life. As shown in Exhibit 7.5, the life cycle of a product or service can be divided into four major stages: introduction, growth, maturity, and decline.

Lovelock and Weinberg, in describing the role of the product life cycle in nonprofit marketing management, noted that public and nonprofit organizations are frequently involved with a product for only a portion of its life cycle.[21] For instance, a nonprofit agency may raise public awareness of a social issue, such as the dangers of smoking or the need for environmental protection, during the early stages of the life cycle. As awareness grows, legislation is passed, public agencies become more involved, and responsibility for the issue shifts to them. At the other extreme are services that have reached the decline stage of the life cycle in the private sector and are then taken over by public or nonprofit organizations. Passenger rail service and urban public transit are historical examples.

During the introductory portion of the product life cycle, the marketer's major task is to create demand. Potential clients and supporters must be told about the cause or service, the need must be demonstrated, and they must be persuaded to make a commitment. In the growth stage, these efforts begin to take effect as support for the nonprofit cause or service increases. However, competitors also emerge during the growth stage.

As the product moves into maturity, support begins to level off as competition becomes more intense. Finally, as the decline stage is reached, the nonprofit cause or service will become out of date and may be eliminated. Some organizations will shift their cause, as the March of Dimes did; others may alter their services, as the Girl Scouts did.

(ii) New Service Development

The needs of a nonprofit organization's supporters and clients are constantly changing. Responding to these changing needs involves the development of new services. This process should be similar to the new product development procedures used by service businesses.[22]

EXHIBIT 7.5 Product Service Life Cycle

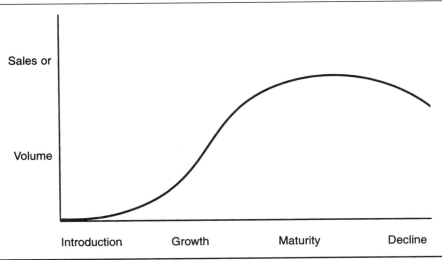

Ideas for new services can come from a variety of sources. Volunteers and staff members may have insights into emerging needs of clients; client surveys, focus groups, and other forms of market research may provide guidance; and secondary sources of information may suggest new service opportunities. For instance, the rapid growth of personal computer sales and use has stimulated many educational institutions to offer new courses and programs to teach people how to use the new technology.

Once an idea for a new service has been suggested, it should be subjected to careful screening and evaluation. This is essential because taking the idea further will usually require significant time and monetary investments. Most ideas are rejected at this point, for reasons of limited resources, unacceptable market potential, inappropriate fit with the organization's mission and objectives, and potentially strong competition.

If the idea passes the assessment step, the development process begins in earnest. The idea is further tested and refined, and the overall marketing strategy is formulated. Frequently, a new service idea is test marketed: it is introduced to a limited market prior to full-scale introduction. This process is very much like a dress rehearsal before a new theater production opens.

Gail L. Warden, chief executive officer of Detroit's Henry Ford Health Care Corporation, has proposed a new-product strategy to provide more facilities for inner-city people.[23] The "Urban Initiatives Program" may include such innovations as storefront clinics to provide health care at lower costs. Warden has been meeting with community leaders and other constituents to test the new program idea.

(iii) Service Differentiation

Many nonprofit organizations use various marketing techniques to differentiate their service offerings. The development of a unique name, symbol, or design, a process known as branding, is one approach. The United Way; March of Dimes; college mascots, like the University of Michigan's wolverine; and the American Medical Association are widely recognized examples. Like business brands, these provide a means of identifying and differentiating one service or nonprofit agency from another.

Services may also be modified, or supplementary goods and services may be provided to differentiate one organization's product from others. A church's special services feature unique forms of music; a public TV station offers local cultural shows to compete with network programs; a civic club sponsors a long-distance bike race. Sometimes tangible goods are used to differentiate. T-shirts displaying the nonprofit organization's name and logo, reproductions of a museum's most famous artwork, and souvenir programs are examples.

Finally, the nonprofit organization's clients or supporters may receive added value from the "packaging" of several services. A community theater offers major donors preferred seating and parking, tickets to social events, and other amenities. A museum includes free parking and a guided tour as a part of its program for selected visitors. A university offers married student housing, a campus child care center, and a family health care program for its students with families. These and many other examples represent ways in which nonprofit organizations can distinguish themselves through product differentiation.

(B) PRICE

Everything has a price, whether price is called *dues, fare, tuition, admission fee,* or something else. All nonprofit organizations must raise revenue to support their activities.

Increasingly, these revenues must come from clients and donors because government sources of funding are becoming restricted.

(i) Fees

Many nonprofit organizations have moved to a membership-based structure. If this is done, it is important that membership fees be reasonably priced for the marketplace.[24] This can be accomplished by establishing several categories of membership, with different fees for various levels of participation and support. Other nonprofit organizations choose to charge program or activity fees above and beyond membership fees. For instance, a YMCA may charge its members for swimming lessons.

(ii) Donations

Most nonprofit organizations receive money, time, and personal effort in the form of donations from members, volunteers, and other supporters. The donation is the price paid by the supporter. Sometimes, the level of donation is set—tithing to a church, or a "suggested" donation to a museum when entering. In many other cases, however, the donor sets the level of monetary support and volunteered assistance. To encourage that assistance, it may be wise to provide guidance by suggesting desired levels of support.

(iii) Service Charges

Faced with rising costs and diminished government support, many nonprofit organizations are charging for services that were once free. This brings up the question: "How much can we charge?"

Ellis has suggested two ways to establish prices for nonprofit services.[25] Both of these approaches require that a nonprofit organization accurately estimate its expenses before establishing a price for an activity or event:

- The *recovery of costs approach* involves determining what the organization's expenses will be and charging whatever is necessary to recover these expenses.
- The *revenue-producing approach* covers all expenses and provides additional revenue for the organization.

Ellis feels that the revenue-producing approach makes more sense because excess revenues from one activity and event may be needed to offset losses from others. To establish a reasonable charge, the nonprofit organization must consider demand and competitive market conditions, in addition to costs. Further, like all other marketing decisions, the decisions concerning price should be based on the target market selected and the organization's objectives.

(C) DISTRIBUTION

Business marketing theory and practice stress the importance of establishing an integrated network, known as a channel of distribution, to transfer goods and services from producers to consumers.

(i) Utilities Provided

Taken together, the components of a channel of distribution comprise a delivery system that makes goods and services available to buyers and creates time, place, and possession utilities, as follows:

- *Time utility* refers to making goods and services available when buyers want them. *Examples:* Hospital emergency rooms remain open 24 hours a day; colleges offer classes during the evening and weekend hours; community centers remain open late in the evening to provide activities for young adults.
- *Place utility* refers to making goods and services available where buyers want them. *Examples:* Storefront clinics and counseling centers provide services in local neighborhoods; emergency hotlines allow people with problems to reach counselors from their homes; colleges have satellite campuses.
- *Possession utility* refers to the transfer of ownership from the producer to the buyer. *Examples:* A college student "owns" the professor's time and knowledge during a class; a patient "owns" a doctor's expertise during a visit; a group of teenagers "own" a community center's playground during a game.

(ii) Service Delivery Systems

Because nonprofit organizations deal mainly in ideas and services, goods distribution concepts and strategies must be modified. Lovelock has suggested that two major questions must be considered, in order to understand service delivery systems:

- Must the customer be in direct physical contact with the service organization or can transactions be completed at arm's length?
- Should a service organization maintain only a single outlet, or should it serve customers through multiple outlets at different sites?[26]

Answers to these questions will help a nonprofit organization develop its distribution approach. For example, community medical care can be provided at a single location (hospital) or at several (storefront clinics). A community visiting nurses' association can visit the elderly and others who need medical attention but are unable to leave their homes for treatment.

For some nonprofit services and ideas, the contact can be completed at arm's length through mailings, written materials, or electronic media. For example, a public TV station's contacts with its clients and donors is usually accomplished through its broadcasts. Likewise, many nonprofit organizations use radio, television, and other nonpersonal media to deliver educational messages to the public. The University of Rhode Island, for example, teaches a literature course via e-mail.

(iii) Intermediaries

Although intermediaries, or *middlemen,* as they were formerly called, are primarily involved in the marketing of goods, they are also becoming important in service and non-profit marketing. Intermediaries make the distribution process more efficient by reducing the number of contacts between producers and their customers. They also perform a number of distribution tasks, such as communication and resource allocation. Applying the concept of intermediaries to nonprofit marketing yields several intriguing possibilities. Some nonprofit organizations, such as the United Way, can serve as clearinghouses for other agencies. They can raise and distribute funds, provide information about other agencies and their services, and suggest appropriate agencies to potential clients. A social worker can serve as an intermediary, guiding needy clients to specific nonprofit agencies and services. This role can also be played by the clergy, doctors, community action agencies, and others. It is important, therefore, that nonprofit organizations establish and maintain relationships with people and organizations that can serve as intermediaries for them.

(iv) Direct Marketing

By far, the fastest-growing form of distribution is direct marketing. As a special kind of delivery system, direct marketing bypasses established distribution channels to deliver goods and services directly from sellers to buyers. The two major forms of direct marketing are direct mail and telemarketing.

Like businesses, many nonprofit organizations have turned to direct marketing for its efficiency as a sales and marketing approach. To date, the major applications have involved fund raising. Direct mail appeals and telemarketing have become commonplace as fund-raising techniques. Organizations as diverse as the American Cancer Society, college alumni associations, and local chambers of commerce use direct marketing to solicit members and contributions.

In fact, almost all fund raisers use direct marketing, and this approach has become the dominant method for distributing fund-raising requests. Major objectives for direct marketing include generating new donors, reactivating lost donors, increasing responses from recent donors, building awareness, maintaining donor relations, and promoting special events. Both large and small nonprofit organizations have found that direct mail, telemarketing, and other direct marketing techniques are key strategic and tactical components of their fund-raising efforts.[27]

Direct marketing has the potential to deliver services to clients. Interactive communication (mail, telephone, or electronic media) can be used to establish direct relationships with targeted clients. For instance, prenatal information and an invitation to visit a prenatal clinic can be sent to young women identified as expectant mothers. Follow-up telephone calls can verify receipt of the information and schedule appointments at a clinic. A video illustrating proper diet, exercise, and personal care programs could be provided.

In an effort to reverse their declines in membership and attendance, some churches have turned to direct mail. This has proven to be an effective way to communicate their messages and inform their target audiences of their activities and services. To make sure their direct mailings succeed, church marketers state specific objectives for their direct mail programs, identify clearly the target audience and develop an appropriate mailing list, prepare compelling messages that will attract people within the target audience, pretest and modify direct mail offerings prior to mailing, and make sure that their mailings are timed properly. When these steps are followed, church marketers have a marketing tool that not only helps them increase participation, but also provides feedback and helps them learn something about their targeted audience.[28]

Another direct marketing tool for delivering nonprofit services and ideas is the advanced telephone technology, specifically "800" and "900" numbers and fax services. These services offer convenient access to a nonprofit organization's staff, information, and expertise. They can be used to provide time and place utility to clients who are unable to visit the organization in person. An example is a university's "answer center" for gardeners and other people who have questions related to their homes, lawns, and gardens.

Finally, nonprofit marketers should consider using e-mail, commercial online services, and the Internet as means of providing access to their services and information. Since half of American households now have personal computers (and the number is growing), electronic commerce has become a reality. The Internet, in particular, has become a major source of information, entertainment, and commerce.

Marketers, such as L.L. Bean, use the Internet and the World Wide Web, its browsing and searching system, as a promotion medium. Nonprofit agencies can do the same. Many nonprofits now have a site (known as *home page*) that includes a history of the agency, descriptions of programs and services, and other relevant information. For example, a university can provide prospective students and their parents with admissions information on its home page.

(D) PROMOTION

No matter how excellent a nonprofit organization may be, how worthwhile its purpose and services, or how dedicated its staff and volunteers, all effort will be wasted unless people are informed and reminded about its availability and persuaded to use its services and support its activities. This is the task of promotion, which involves communication with a nonprofit organization's publics.

The three primary goals of promotion are:

1. *To inform.* As a method of communication, promotion informs people about a nonprofit organization's existence, purpose, services, and capabilities. This is an especially important goal for new agencies, programs, and services. For example, a civic association has decided to offer a late-night basketball program to inner-city youth. To obtain participation in the new program, the association must use promotion to inform the community's young people of the program's availability, time, and location.
2. *To persuade.* Promotion attempts to influence people to do something— support the Easter Seal Society, don't drink and drive, fight illiteracy. Persuasion becomes an important promotional goal as an agency or service enters the growth stage of its life cycle.
3. *To remind.* Promotion is often used to keep an idea, service, or nonprofit organization's name in people's minds. This goal is important during the maturity stage of the life cycle. The Salvation Army, American Red Cross, and The United Way are organizations that stress reminder promotion.

To accomplish these goals, advertising, personal selling, sales promotion, and public relations are combined to form the promotional mix. It is especially important that the promotional mix elements be properly coordinated so that they work together to achieve the same goals.

(i) Advertising

This is the dominant form of nonpersonal promotion. Promotional messages are carried to the public by mass communications media—newspapers, television, and outdoor signs.

There are many forms of advertising and many purposes for which advertising may be used. Product and institutional advertising, the two major forms, are described as follows:

- Advertising designed to stimulate sales of a specific product or service, or participation in a specific activity, is called *product advertising.* Nonprofit organizations use this form of advertising when they feature a specific program or activity—for example, a fund-raising event, a blood donors' day, or a special museum exhibit.

- *Institutional advertising* promotes a concept, idea, image, or philosophy of a nonprofit organization or cause. Anyone who may have an impact on the advertiser, such as legislators, business leaders, or the general public, can be a target of institutional advertising. Much of the advertising done by nonprofit organizations is institutional advertising—for example, the promotion of values and beliefs by the Mormon Church.

(ii)   Personal Selling

In contrast to the impersonal approach of advertising, in personal selling the promotional message is carried by someone who normally communicates with the potential client or supporter face to face. As a result, personal selling can be a highly individualized process that involves complex interpersonal relations.

Kotler and Andreasen observed that almost everyone in a nonprofit organization is likely to have personal contact with persons outside the organization.[29] Salespeople, whose job is to actively influence the behavior of others, will have the most extensive contacts with outsiders. College recruiters, development officers, community organizers, and lobbyists are all contact persons. Service personnel who provide assistance to clients and members of the public will also have personal contacts and must understand the nature of personal selling. Service personnel include receptionists, museum guards, ticket takers, librarians, and the like.

Many observers of service marketing have emphasized the importance of personal contacts to customer satisfaction. Gronroos suggested that service organizations require a different organizational structure, one that integrates the simultaneous production and marketing of a service.[30] This has been called *interactive marketing*. As shown in Exhibit 7.6, the focus is on client–organization interactions.

EXHIBIT 7.6 Interactive Marketing

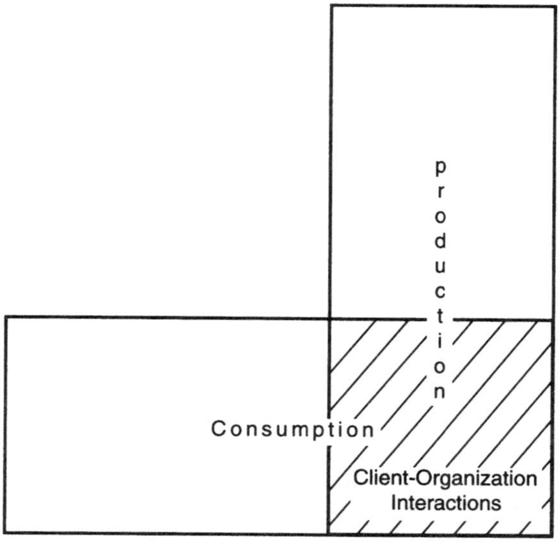

Source: Adapted from Christian Gronroos. (1982). *Strategic Management and Marketing in the Service Sector.* Helsingfors: Swedish School of Economics and Business Administration, p. 137.

These points of interaction have been termed the *moments of truth.* To make sure that its clients are truly satisfied, a nonprofit organization must manage these moments of truth from start to finish. For instance, the receptionist in a health care clinic must greet clients warmly; health care professionals must be friendly and professional; billing and other follow-up activities must be handled effectively. In short, all the contacts with the clinic must make the client feel good about having come there.

Some nonprofit organizations are discovering that they must take personal selling further. They have to continue to provide good service to their clients, but they also have to become more aggressive in their selling efforts. The U.S. Postal Service is an example. To compete against UPS, Federal Express, and other business competitors, the Postal Service has created a 200-person national salesforce to deal with large national and international customers with complex needs and multiple mailing sites.[31]

(iii) Public Relations

These promotion activities play an important role in the marketing programs of most nonprofit organizations. Public relations activities and programs are used to create a favorable impression for the organization and its efforts. Further, effective public relations complement a nonprofit organization's other promotion activities by building credibility. As a result, potential supporters and clients will be more receptive to the organization's ideas and services.

Many nonprofit organizations plan, manage, and coordinate their public relations activities through a director of public relations. This manager is responsible for communicating with an organization's various publics. The media and form of public relations will be adapted to each specific public. Some of the techniques used are press releases speeches by executives, facility tours, annual reports, and community events. The goal of public relations management is to ensure that all contacts with a nonprofit organization's publics support and reinforce the desired image.

Harrison suggested that the most important public relations development for nonprofits is the concept of issue-oriented public relations.[32] This involves positioning an organization as an authority on an issue and as an important part of the solution to the problem. The key, according to Harrison, is to focus on one or two issues that are "hot." By doing this, a nonprofit organization will create an environment in which people are more inclined to respond to its appeals for funds and volunteers, to attend its events, and to support its cause.

A final critical aspect of public relations is dealing with negative events and unfavorable media coverage. In particular, perceived funds mismanagement and other forms of misconduct threaten the credibility of charitable and other nonprofit organization. In the early 1990s, two large national nonprofits, The United Way and the NAACP, suffered a major loss of public confidence and financial reversals because of management irregularities. In both organizations, leadership changes were made and strong public relations efforts were undertaken to regain support.

(iv) Sales Promotion

A variety of promotion activities—other than personal selling, advertising, and public relations—can be used to achieve specific short-term objectives. Business examples include samples, premiums, coupons, demonstrations, contests, sweepstakes, and games.

Because they provide services, many nonprofit organizations are limited in their use of sales promotion techniques, but there are some examples. Fund-raising programs sometimes include a contest or sweepstakes to generate interest and excitement. Contributors may receive tokens of appreciation, and large contributors may be given special gifts. Even clients or customers can be stimulated with sales promotion techniques. For instance, a public transit authority rewards its one-millionth passenger; a museum gives a free bumper sticker to the first 5,000 visitors; a college recruiter gives prospective students a pen with the college logo. The possibilities are endless, and so, it is hoped, are the results.

7.11 *Implementation and Control*

(A) RETENTION

The marketing management process presented in Exhibit 7.1 ends with control of marketing activities. Nonprofit organizations should not focus on a single transaction with their customers/clients. Their marketing objectives are creating and maintaining relationships with their customers. As explained in Section 7.1(c), the focus of nonprofit organizations should be in attracting, developing, and retaining client/customer relationships. Retention of customers depends on the quality of services that were delivered and the level of satisfaction expressed by the users of the services. Retention of donors and volunteers should also be an important part of the retention activities of nonprofit organizations. Volunteers and donors need to be encouraged to stay with a nonprofit organization for many years to come. Further, those impressed with the activities of the nonprofit organization will spread favorable word of mouth, which will attract more donors and volunteers. Retention of donors, volunteers, and clients, therefore, depends on the perceived service quality delivered by the nonprofit organization.

(B) PERCEIVED SERVICE QUALITY

Quality is perceived subjectively by the users of the service. Gronroos indicates that the perceived service quality is the difference between expected service quality and the experienced service quality.[33] When the experienced service quality meets or exceeds the expectations of the customer, good perceived quality is the result, and the benefits for the organization accrue in the form of customer retention. Marketing communication activities by the nonprofit organizations influence the nature of the expectations created among the potential users of services and communicates the image of the organization. The image of the nonprofit organization also plays a significant part in the creation of expectations regarding the performance of the organization. Therefore, it is incumbent on the nonprofit organization to create realistic expectations for their clients, donors and volunteers.

(C) DIMENSIONS OF SERVICE QUALITY

A number of studies have examined the nature of perceived service quality. Parasuraman, Zeithaml, and Berry conducted a study to determine the dimensions that affected service quality.[34] They investigated 10 potential determinants of perceived service quality:

1. Tangibles
2. Reliability

  3. Responsiveness
  4. Competence
  5. Courtesy
  6. Credibility
  7. Security
  8. Access
  9. Communication
 10. Understanding the customer

The final results of this study resulted in these 10 dimensions being reduced into the following 5 dimensions:

  1. *Tangibles:*Appearance of physical facilities, equipment, personnel, and communication material
  2. *Reliability:* Ability to perform the promised service dependably and accurately
  3. *Responsiveness:* Willingness to help customers and provide prompt service
  4. *Assurance:* Knowledge and courtesy of employees and their ability to convey trust and confidence
  5. *Empathy:* Caring, individualized attention provided to customers[35]

The control of marketing activities by the nonprofit organization involves providing the expected experience for its clients, donors, and volunteers and continuous monitoring of the quality of the services provided. The focus should be in incorporating these five dimensions in the delivery of their services. Thus, if the quality of the perceived service is high (meets and exceeds customers' expectations), then customer retention will follow. The nonprofit organization, just like its counterpart in the profit-making sector, should strive to retain its customers, clients, and donors because retention reduces the costs of searching for new clients or recruiting new donors. Sustainable success of nonprofit organizations requires extraordinary leadership, commitment, and determination in everything that they do.[36]

Endnotes

  1. McCort, J. D. (1994). "A Framework for Evaluating the Relationship Extent of a Relationship Marketing Strategy: The Case for Nonprofit Organizations," *Journal of Direct Marketing* (Spring).
  2. Berry, L. L. (1999). *Discovering the Soul of Service.* New York: The Free Press.
  3. Miaoulis, G. (1985). "Nonprofits' Marketing Strategies Begin with Customer Satisfaction," *Marketing News* (March 15), pp. 54.
  4. Kotler, P., and A. Andreasen. (1991). *Strategic Marketing for Nonprofit Organizations,* 4th ed. Englewood Cliffs, NJ: Prentice Hall.
  5. Johnson, E. M., E. E. Scheuing, and K. A. Gaida. (1986). *Profitable Service Marketing.* Homewood, IL: Dow Jones-Irwin.
  6. See note 4.
  7. Zeithaml, V. A. (1981). "How Consumers Evaluation Processes Differ between Goods and Services." In J. H. Donnelly and W. R. George (eds.), *Marketing of Services.* Chicago: American Marketing Association.

8. Bateson, J. E. G. (1985). "Perceived Control and the Service Encounter." In J. A. Czepiel, M. R. Salomon, and C. F. Surprenant (eds.), *The Service Encounter.* Lexington, MA: Lexington Books.

9. Tomes, A. E., and B. Hamilton. (1991). "The Marketing of a Community Service," *Journal of Marketing Management* (April).

10. Nall, J. R., and P. B. Dimsdale. (1985). "Civic Group Adopts Marketing Technique," *Marketing News* (June 21), p. 13.

11. Petrison, L. A., R. C. Blattberg, and P. Wang. (1993). "Database Marketing: Past, Present, and Future," *Journal of Direct Marketing* (Summer), pp. 27–43.

12. See note 4.

13. Lovelock, C. H., and C. B. Weinberg. (1989). *Public and Nonprofit Marketing,* 2nd ed. Redwood City, CA: Scientific Press.

14. Van Doren, D. C., and L. W. Smith. (1985). "Self-Analysis Can Gauge Marketing Orientation." *Marketing News* (December 6), p. 14.

15. Levitt, T. (1975). "Marketing Myopia" (with retrospective commentary), *Harvard Business Review* (September–October).

16. Miller, K. (1993). "More Black Churches Go into Business," *Wall Street Journal* (January 27).

17. Fram, E. H. (1991). "Nonprofit Boards Would Profit with Marketers Aboard," *Marketing News* (April 29), p. 6.

18. See note 13.

19. Albrecht, K., and R. Zemke. (1985). *Service America!* Homewood, IL: Dow Jones-Irwin.

20. Lovelock, C. H. (1991). *Services Marketing,* 2nd ed. Englewood Cliffs, NJ: Prentice Hall.

21. See note 13.

22. See note 5.

23. Byme, J. A. (1990). "Profiting from the Nonprofits," *Business Week* (March 26), pp. 66–72.

24. Temper, R. H. (1991). "Donations Versus Dues," *Nonprofit World* (January–February).

25. Ellis, S. J. (1990). "What Should We Charge for Our Services?" *Nonprofit World* (May–June).

26. See note 20.

27. Peltier, J. W., and J. A. Schibrowsky. (1995). "The Direct Marketing of Charitable Causes: A Study of U. S. Fundraisers," *Journal of Direct Marketing* (Summer), pp. 72–80.

28. Considine, J. J. (1994). "Direct Mail: Can it Work for Religious Organizations?" *Journal of Direct Marketing* (Autumn), pp. 59–65.

29. See note 4.

30. Gronroos, C. (1982). *Strategic Management and Marketing in the Service Sector.* Helsingfors: Swedish School of Economics and Business Administration.

31. Keenan, W. Jr. (1994). "Can We Deliver?" *Sales & Marketing Management* (February). pp. 62–67.

32. Harrison, T. A. (1991). "Six PR Trends That Will Shape Your Future," *Nonprofit World* (March–April), pp. 21–23.

33. See note 30.

34. Parasuraman, A., V. A. Zeithaml, and L. L. Berry. (1985). "A Conceptual Model of Service Quality and Its Implications for Future Research," *Journal of Marketing* (vol. 49, Fall), p. 47.

35. Zeithaml V. A., A. Parasuraman, and L. L. Berry. (1990). *Delivering Quality Service.* New York: The Free Press.

Suggested Readings

Arnott, N. (1994). "Marketing With a Passion," *Sales & Marketing Management* (January), pp. 64–68.

Barbeito, C. L. (1991). "How Researchers Can Make Their Work Relevant to the Needs of Non-Profits," *Chronicle of Philanthropy* (May), pp. 40–43.

Barna, G. (1992). *Church Marketing.* Ventura, CA: Regal Books.

Coffman, L. L. (1986). *Public Sector Marketing.* New York: John Wiley & Sons.

Day, G. S., and R. Wensley. (1983). "Marketing Theory with a Strategic Orientation," *Journal of Marketing* (Fall), pp. 79–89.

De los Santos, G. (1986). "Universities Offer Marketing Research Key," *Nonprofit World* (January–February), pp. 14–16.

DeVos, K. (1986). "Maintaining Support Through Marketing," *Nonprofit World* (March–April), pp. 22–24.

Dickson, J. P., and S. Dickson. (1984–1985). Four-part marketing research series, *Nonprofit World* (November–December 1984 through May–June 1985), pp. 80–88.

Drucker, P. F. (1989). "What Business Can Learn from Nonprofits," *Harvard Business Review* (July–August), pp. 88–93.

Gronroos, C. (1990). *Service Management and Marketing.* Lexington, MA: Lexington Books.

Guy, B. S., and W. E. Patton. (1988). "The Marketing of Altruistic Causes: Understanding Why People Help," *Journal of Services Marketing* (Winter), pp. 5–16.

Kelly, B. (1991). "Cause-Related Marketing: Doing Well While Doing Good," *Sales & Marketing Management* (March).

Kotler, P., O. C. Ferrell, and C. Lamb (eds.). (1987). *Strategic Marketing for Nonprofit Organizations: Cases and Readings.* Englewood Cliffs, NJ: Prentice Hall.

Kotler, P., and S. J. Levy. (1979). "Broadening the Concept of Marketing," *Journal of Marketing* (January).

Lancome, C. (1985). "Strategic Marketing for Nonprofit Organizations," *Nonprofit World* (July–August).

Lauffer, A. (1984). *Strategic Marketing for Not-for-Profit Organizations.* New York: The Free Press.

Laycock, D. K. (1990). "Are You Ready for Strategic Planning?" *Nonprofit World* (September–October).

Muehrcke, J. (ed.). (1989). *Marketing: The Society for Nonprofit Organizations' Leadership Series.* Madison, WI: The Society for Nonprofit Organizations.

Riley, A. L., and M. Bruce. (1992). "United Way: The Fallout After the Fall," *Chronicle of Philanthropy* (March).

Schwartz, K. (1989). "Nonprofits' Bottomline: They Mix Lofty Goals and Gutsy Survival Strategies," *Marketing News* (February 13), pp. 1–2.

Williams, M. J. (1986). "How To Cash in on Do-Good Pitches," *Fortune* (June 9), pp. 71–74.

8 ▼ Management Implications and Opportunities of Global Communications: "Hakken-Kraks Howl" and Global Dot Com: Storm, Norm, Form

JANET POLEY, PhD, PRESIDENT
American Distance Education Consortium (ADEC)

8.1 Introduction

One of Theodor Geisel's last books as Dr. Seuss—*Oh, the Places You'll Go!*—took us right into Hakken-Kraks Howl where "the weather is fowl," "enemies prowl," "up many a frightening creek." "Your arms get sore and your sneakers leak." Yuk![1]

Hakken-Kraks Howl provides an excellent metaphor for some of the murky underside of the Internet issues creating a storm today. Privacy, secrecy, security, and intellectual property are big ones.

Nonprofit organizational managers, employees, and volunteers can quickly find themselves up to their behinds in alligators if these issues are ignored. Unfortunately, far less important items than these seize the headlines of newspapers and magazines daily. We can expect the weather to get stormier in Hakken-Kraks Howl on the way to development of more common norms, standards, practices, and laws internationally.

Sensationalizing the virus du jour probably is not nearly as important as explaining the messy, slippery processes that could ruin you, your organization, and the vision and mission you are pursuing. Some have called this the Wild West period of the Internet. I prefer Hakken-Kraks Howl. As you may recall, Seuss took us to Hakken-Kraks Howl after we visited the most useless place of all—"The Waiting Place." Some major corporations and governments have a vested interest in keeping lots of people in the Internet Waiting Place because these companies are making money and many people remain ignorant about what the Internet is and how it really works. Nonprofit organizations have a responsibility to understand the big picture Internet world, not just dabble in e-mail, e-commerce, e-learning, or e-"anythingelseyoucanthinkof."

In Hakken-Kraks Howl, cluelessness is common. An estimated 113 million people use computers at work and 105 million people use computers at home, but few are truly literate. Research suggests that most people know how to do only one or two things with their computer, and most people surfing the Web are simply wandering aimlessly because they lack the knowledge necessary to conduct targeted searches to find specific things.[2]

When the Internet was simpler, it was referred to as the Information Superhighway, operating much like the nervous system of a vertebrate. Today, this Hakken-Kraks Howl has multiple backbones, scattered burrows, ditches, indirect routes, and obstacles. This Internet place is a set of 100 or so long-range global networks that diversely link and transfer messages to and from more than 100,000 local networks. Some of these networks collaborate and share mutual interest; others are in sharp proprietary rivalry. There are tens of millions of Internet users, including smart instruments that also make cyberspace reports.[3]

When the World Wide Web began to explode in 1994, English was the language and the United States was pretty much the extent of this virtual world. Today, depending on whose numbers you believe, non-English speakers make up from one-third to one-half of the Web's publications. Some are predicting that non-English speakers will surpass English speakers in 2001. For-profit companies are certainly going to offer e-sales opportunities in multiple languages. Nonprofits have interesting opportunities and challenges as the Internet becomes increasingly global.

8.2   From Dr. Seuss to Idiot's Guide to American History

The Dummy's Guide to the Internet has sold in many different flavors. *The Complete Idiot's Guide to American History*[4] may actually be of greater use in sorting out the really important positives and negatives about the digital world. A few facts from the end of that book can provide a perspective. The last chapter is titled "From Leave It to Beaver to Sesame Street to the Internet." It notes that it took a decade to move from a late 1950s and 1960s television image of America as a "collection of ethnically nondescript, vaguely Protestant white people in perfect suburbs" to a Sesame Street urban neighborhood populated with whites, blacks, Hispanics, and Asians, as well as people with handicaps and disabilities.

Their point is that the essence of democracy is *from many, one. The Dummy's Guide to the Internet* hypothesizes that it is this notion that is the real engine driving popular fascination with the Internet. At its best, *The Complete Idiot's Guide to American History* says that the Internet is not democracy but it could become an *expression* of democracy: "a fervent wish to be democratic, to hear and to be heard, to share, to communicate, to connect with one's neighbors-next-door and around the world—and to be at the center of a great web that offers infinite centers."[5]

The book ends with the question: Will the Internet make democracy any easier? The answer: Maybe, maybe not—but it *might* promote and preserve democratic values in this millennium. As a good friend of mine frequently reminds—it is really not about technology, it is about values and ethics.

8.3   More About Democracy, Philosophy, and Philanthropy

In late April 2000, the *Washington Post* headline in the World News section said "Nigerians Await Democracy's Dividends."[6] Nigeria returned to democracy in 1999 after two decades of brutal and corrupt military rule. The article reported that in Nigeria the electricity is seldom on, the telephone system crashes regularly, and ethnic and religious strife continues. Most of the country is in turmoil, with interest groups deeply entrenched in maintaining the status quo. In Nigeria as well as most of Africa, the Internet has little to offer in terms of today's reforms. Less than 1 percent of the population has direct Internet access.

There are possibilities for change, if not in Nigeria, perhaps in other African countries. The presidents of four American foundations just announced a $100 million five-year program to support higher education in sub-Saharan Africa. The Carnegie, Rockefeller, Ford, and MacArthur Foundations will provide aid to countries that have introduced democracy and economic reforms, creating a stable environment.[7] One can guess that higher education reform in Africa will be accompanied by greater Internet connectivity and the possibility of more African countries contributing to the richness in the virtual world as well as taking from the well of cyberspace resources. Some are predicting that it is really knowledge that will increasingly define the ability of any country to do well in the future.

Ironically, it was the late Julius Nyerere of Tanzania who recognized this early. He is often referred to as Mwalimu (teacher in Swahili) Nyerere. A wonderful story about Nyerere's last meeting with World Bank experts in 1998 recently circulated on the Internet. The original story was attributed to Eduardo Galeano, a well-known author from Uruguay. It was reported on the Internet by Silver Donald Cameron in his *Sunday Herald* column.[8] He also tells how he went about verifying that the story was true. Both the story and the verification process have lessons for nonprofit organizations.

Nyerere served as president of Tanzania for 20 years, from its independence until 1985. Socialism and self-reliance, as well as education for all, were key to his policies. "Why have you failed?" the World Bank experts asked him. Nyerere answered:

> The British Empire left us a country with 85 percent illiterates, two engineers, and 12 doctors. When I left office, we had 9 percent illiterates and thousands of engineers and doctors. I left office 13 years ago. Then our income per capita was twice what it is today; now we have one third less children in our schools and public health and social services are in ruins. During these 13 years, Tanzania has done everything that the World Bank and the International Monetary fund have demanded.

And Julius Nyerere passed the question back to the World Bank experts: "Why have you failed?"

Cameron recounts that this story was originally published in Montevideo, in Spanish, on April 2, 2000. He received it in English on April 5 and verified its authenticity by April 11. He followed this with discussion via the Internet—people talking to people and finding one another across oceans and frontiers, around censors, behind corporate spin doctors. He concludes that "we don't need Rupert Murdoch and Conrad Black to tell us what's going on. Information is liberated as never before. We can know the truth, and the truth will make us free."

Not everyone will agree with this position. A vocal but caring skeptic, Neil Postman, boasts of not having a computer and considers the Internet a distraction. In a recent book, he asks that everyone apply a "quiet reason to the fury of technological innovation." He proposes we filter out the jargon of progress, efficiency, and whizbangery and try to perceive the crucial whys, hows, and implications of technology.[9]

- What is the problem to which this technology is a solution?
- Whose problem is it?
- Is it actually a problem at all?
- Who will pay for it?
- Who will benefit from it?
- Who stands to suffer from it?
- What new problems might arise from solving this one?

These are important questions, whether you agree or disagree with his urging that we build a bridge backward from today to the eighteenth century—the home of the Enlightenment.

A different sort of backward look at the eighteenth century has crept into today's lexicon: the concept of *virtual civil society.* Thomas Paine and George Hagel developed the idea of civil society as something positive—separate and parallel to the state. Many ideas that surround discussion of nonprofit nongovernmental organizations today seem linked to the idea that a realm can be created in which citizens associate according to their own interests and wishes. It has been an easy stretch to bridge this philosophy with cyberspace.

Thomas Carothers, Vice-President for Global Policy at the Carnegie Endowment for International Peace, notes that in the 1990s civil society became a mantra for everyone from U.S. citizens tired of their party systems to the developing world as a means of social renewal as governments retract their reach. As the information revolution provides new tools for forging connections and empowering citizens, civil society is part of the post–Cold War zeitgeist.[10]

He urges caution in looking to nongovernmental organizations (NGOs) in developing countries as the heart of civil society. "The burgeoning NGO sectors in many countries are dominated by elite-run groups that have only tenuous ties to the citizens on whose behalf they claim to act, and they depend on international funders for budgets that cannot be nourished from domestic sources," he notes. He concludes that there is potential for a global civil society to rehape the world in important ways, but we must take care not to oversell its strength or idealize its intentions. Nonprofits would do well to consider his "think again" statements:

NGOs are the heart of civil society. *Think again:* NGOs do play important, growing roles in developed and developing countries. They shape policy by exerting pressure on governments and by furnishing technical expertise to policy makers. They can foster citizen participation and civic education. However, in many countries, NGOs are outweighed by religious organizations, labor unions, and other groups that have a genuine base in the population and secure domestic sources of funding—features that advocacy groups usually lack.

Civil society is warm and fuzzy. *Think again:* Civil society everywhere is a bewildering array of the good, the bad, and the outright bizarre. Struggles over the public interest are not between civil society on the one hand and bad guys on the other, but within civil society itself. Also, it is important to note that civil society is very concerned with private economic interests. Although some civil society groups may stand for nonmaterial ("higher") principles and values, much of civil society is preoccupied with the pursuit of private and frequently parochial ends.

A strong civil society ensures democracy. *Think again:* More is not necessarily better—some evidence suggests that a strong civil society can actually reflect dangerous political weaknesses.

Democracy ensures a strong civil society. *Think again:* Societies can have stable democracies with varying amounts of civil society. The United States, Japan, France, and Spain all have varying traditions with respect to the optimal level of citizen engagement. The argument that democracy is not a real democracy unless it has American-style civil society is wrong and dangerous.

Real civil society doesn't take money from the government. *Think again:* Government is almost twice as significant a source of income for American nonprofit organizations as is private giving, despite the presence of large foundations and corporate giving programs.

Civil society has gone global. *Think again:* There are more than 5,000 transnational NGOs—organizations based in one country that carry out activities in others. New information and communications technologies have in part helped to create a fertile ground to widen reach and form multicountry linkages, networks, and coalitions. But transnational civil society is not new, and most of the new transnational civil society actors are Western groups projecting themselves into developing and transitional society. While partnerships are often encouraged, the agendas and values they pursue are usually their own.

Nonprofit organizations constantly encounter ethical dilemmas in working across community and cultural boundaries, including the international arena, whether in person or over the Internet. In fact, the issues may be greater when the rather flat and unrich communication medium of the Internet is the major vehicle for contact. Practitioners can benefit from considering the following:

- Clarify your own values and ethics as a part of international work or work with diverse groups. Carefully consider why you are doing what you are doing, and be particularly careful about anything in the advocacy environment.
- Learn to be a good communicator—the more you can explain your perspective without imposing it on someone else, the better.

- Ask questions more than you make statements. The old journalistic standbys work just as well over the Internet as they do person to person: Who, What, Where, When, Why, and How?
- Recognize that there is much you do not know. Many people have a need to try to control situations. Think about the fact that just because you label yourself as a facilitator does not necessarily mean that you have dropped the "expert" role and really act as a collaborator.

These statements are easy to write and difficult in reality to work through in terms of ethics and values. For example, many of us are working in the nonprofit world because of strong beliefs in certain areas. Take gender issues, for example. It may be very difficult for someone concerned about the gender gaps in school enrollment around the world to easily accept situations that appear wrong and nonequitable. For example, there is a 20 percent difference between school enrollment rates for boys and girls in South Asia and nearly a 10 percent gap in sub-Saharan Africa, Arab states, East Asia, and Latin America, according to Oxfam.[11]

Consider that an educated girl marries later, has fewer children, seeks medical attention sooner for herself and her children, provides better care and nutrition for herself and her children, and has a higher probability of survival for herself and her children, lower total fertility, and better learning and education. (I think this is true and finds a very close match to my values. However, having recently watched *Fiddler on the Roof* for a fifth time, and seeing Tevye examine "tradition"—articulating all the pros and cons of going against "tradition"—it causes one to think carefully about the ramifications of cultural change.)

Although there is not a school enrollment gap in the United States, there is increasing concern about a wide variety of digital divide issues. The American Association of University Women reported recently that there is a large imbalance in the computing and science courses taken by female and male high school students. Female students account for 17 percent of the students who opt to take advanced placement exams in computer science, they earn 28 percent of the computer science bachelor's degrees awarded, and they make up only 20 percent of information technology professionals.

Just as we attributed school enrollment issues in other countries with "cultural" problems, Sherry Turkle, professor of sociology at MIT and co-chair of the commission that wrote the report, states that the lack of participation by females in these areas is not related to a phobia of math or science, but a lack of interest in currently promoted uses of computers. When asked to describe a person who was really good with computers, the girls interviewed often described a man. Parents are also providing boys more opportunities with computers.[12]

These examples are not intended to suggest that nonprofit organizations cease taking stands on important issues. Rather, they suggest that when we take these stands in crossing boundaries, we must carefully examine our understandings, values, and ethics in asking others to make changes. The old "physician heal thyself" adage continues to have merit.

8.4 *Parking Information versus Building Relationships*

A disclaimer on a Web site labeled World Social and Political NGOs[13] is an example of an information parking approach to various perspectives. The list is an excellent and inclusive list of links to international organizations followed by a country-by-country list of NGOs and other resources. The disclaimer states:

> *The following links are provided for information and entertainment purposes only. The sites represent all sides of the political spectrum. Many are biased to the "Left" "Center" or "Right" in terms of political viewpoint. Long Bay Communications, the publisher of this list, does not in any way condone, recommend, or support the content. We are happy to link ALL independent national and international organizations who stand to further the intellectual political discussion in a community.*

This approach is related to the idea of civil society in terms of offering a wide array of resources; however, it does not offer the opportunity for conversation, dialogue, and relationship building. Many are predicting that the next phase of the Internet will be much less about parking information and linking and more about facilitating human interaction and relationship building. The promise of collaborative work tools was made the day we first logged on to primitive e-mail systems. Some are raising questions as to whether the gender gap in the computer science and information technology area may also be slowing the development of collaborative work tools, collaboratories, communities, and "civil" societies.

8.5   *Venture Philanthropy*

An emerging approach to some of the financial issues associated with nonprofits is being called *venture philanthropy*. This idea is developing as government retrenches from the social sector, foundations focus their funding differently with a more business-oriented perspective, and nonprofits seem incapable of scaling. This idea is focused on an Internet-enabled transformation for organizations to create more opportunity in meeting society's vexing and long-standing social problems. The Morino Institute engaged Community Wealth Ventures to see if improved application of investment management practices associated with high-end venture capital and private equity investment firms might be applied to organizations and activities that seek to achieve social change. Terms such as *social venture fund* and *social entrepreneurs* emerge from this model.[14]

The research conducted shows that:

- Current methods of funding and supporting nonprofits can be improved. Nonprofit organizations exist in a "culture of dysfunction." Management and organization issues make success very improbable and call into question the sustainability of organizations unable to adequately capitalize future growth.
- Innovation and new solutions to social problems are not needed, but new ways to fund and support successful nonprofits so they can grow and build on their success are required.
- Present-day philanthropists want their investments in nonprofit organizations to have a broad impact, and they want to be able to measure that impact.
- For-profit organizations understand that strong organizations with well-developed infrastructures will ultimately be more successful, effective, and profitable than their anorexic competitors. The market has rewarded this capacity building, but the nonprofit funding market has yet to sufficiently recognize the importance of this activity.

- New private-sector donors for the nonprofit sector are expert in new technologies. They see it as the backbone of the new economy and believe it will reshape the nonprofit landscape as radically as it has the corporate sector. They predict that the nonprofit sector will use the Internet to build its capacity and transform its operations in ways that will restructure its approach and increase effectiveness. They give examples such as America Online's creating a philanthropic Internet portal; the comprehensive financial disclosure for nonprofits available through Guidestar; and Impact Online's success in attracting new volunteers, mentors, and others.

8.6   The S Word: Secrecy

Back in Hakken-Kracks Howl, enemies prowl. President George Bush declared that the Cold War was over after the fall of the Berlin Wall and the fact that many secrets could no longer be retained in the United States. One of the most accessible discussions of secrecy is the book titled *Secrecy* by Daniel Patrick Moynihan.[15] In this book, Moynihan proposes that governmental secrecy may be the dark thread connecting and explaining some of America's most disastrous Cold War policies. In his introduction of the book (almost as long as the book itself), Richard Gid Powers asks:

- How did the United States develop a secrecy system that still produces more than 6 million classified documents a year?
- Why snoop around to assure that some 3 million citizens are certified to be trusted with papers stamped Confidential, Secret, and Top Secret?[16]

8.7   S Is for Secrecy and Security

In April 2000, the U.S. Environmental Protection Agency (EPA) announced they would not be releasing information about toxic waste sites and dangerous chemicals because federal law enforcement officials (FBI and Justice Department) feared the information could be useful to terrorists. The EPA has been required for years to make information widely available, but these regulations predate the Internet.[17]

A number of senators and congressmen expressed concern that this type of information should not be restricted because the information is critical to public health and safety. Increasingly, it is difficult to sort out legitimate reasons for secrecy, often in the pursuit of national security versus the public right to know. Paul Orun, Director of the Working Group on the Community Right to Know, argues that restricting this type of information will harm the public. He calls this a "know-nothing, do-nothing response to dangerous practices in the chemical industry."[18]

Senator Moynihan argues that secrecy is a form of regulation. He says that much of the U.S. secrecy apparatus is a carryover from the Cold War and is distinctive primarily in that it is relatively unexamined—most of the literature about secrecy remains secret. He states that we should not put an end to secrecy because at times it is legitimate and necessary. However, we need to eliminate the culture of secrecy, instead replacing it with a culture of openness. "A case can be made that secrecy is for losers. For people who don't know how important information really is. The Soviet Union realized this too late.

Openness is now a singular advantage." He states that secrecy has no place in an information age and that it is time to dismantle government secrecy. He contends that *analysis* is really the key aspect of national security.[19]

Given that much of the work of nonprofit organizations involves information—access to it, communication of it, analysis based on it—an understanding of freedom of information and secrecy becomes even more critical in a global environment.

A recent book by Frances Stonor Saundos, *The Cultural Cold War: The CIA and the World of Arts and Letters,* was summarized in the March 31, 2000, issue of *Chronicle of Higher Education.*[20] The book contends that the Central Intelligence Agency (CIA) spread around vast sums of money to advance careers of American and foreign intellectuals it deemed most dependable. Well-known foundations such as Rockefeller and Ford were theoretically used as the conduits for dispensing money to writers and artists expected to express particular views and perspectives.[21] A CIA official quoted in the Saundos book argues that "the finest thoughts were too valuable for a vote. In order to encourage openness, we had to be secret," he said.

Nonprofit organizations can expect to be more drawn into aspects of the escalating conversations about secrecy and freedom of information in the United States and abroad. With the Internet, particularly the person-to-person communication dimension, verifying information is increasingly quick and easy. Nonprofits will need to be very careful that they:

- Are not unwitting propagandists for governments or organizations
- Take the time to verify information and validate sources
- Recognize that increasingly there are no secrets, particularly on the Internet

Use of encryption software has been seen as critical to the growth and development of e-commerce, fostering security as more people send their credit card numbers over the Internet. In September 1999, the Clinton Administration abandoned its push for secret searches of computers. High-tech leaders argue that efforts to deny terrorists encryption tools are futile, given that such software is readily available over the Internet. The discussions of secrecy, encryption, searches, and appropriate legislation and practices is certain to remain an important issue in the next decade.[22]

The question is: How should the Fourth Amendment protect information when it moves from the desktop out into the network? Many nonprofit organization managers should familiarize themselves with the basics related to secrecy and freedom of information. The Freedom Forum is an excellent resource for developing a grasp of freedom of information issues on a global basis.[23]

The enormous growth of Internet communications is creating change in the way government agencies handle and disseminate information. Putting more information online creates a number of new issues—more public and open digital information may ironically create a counterforce to shut down access. The federal Freedom of Information Act (FOIA) requires federal agencies to open their records for public inspection and copying. Government agencies must publish lists of their records, and agencies have 20 days to respond to most FOIA requests, but that deadline is often ignored.[24] "Just as we move into a technological age in which public information can be distributed quickly and easily, we see privacy advocates pushing to keep much of that data secret and governments eager to sell off what's left to the highest bidder," said Kenneth A. Paulson, Executive Director of the First Amendment Center.[25]

Electronic FOIA amendments in the United States now declare that records kept in electronic form are fully covered by the FOIA process. The new law also states that when an agency determines that particular information requested under FOIA is likely to be requested again, it must be put where the public can access it routinely, usually without filing an FOIA request. At the state level, more states have enacted strong public records laws, which call for openness in government, seeking to curtail the government secrecy that creates problems.[26]

8.8   P Is for Privacy

As suggested earlier, privacy and secrecy are often linked. The United States passed a federal privacy law in 1974, and many states have similar laws forbidding snooping and prying into an individual's privacy. The growth of the Internet has created tremendous concerns about privacy—a national and international issue. Protection of children as well as financial, medical, and health information have taken on paramount importance. The Consumers Union has expressed great concern about the way Internet companies collect and use private information. Their study, "Big Browser is Watching You," argues and documents the fact that consumers want greater privacy and won't use e-commerce until they get it.[27]

Interestingly, most personal computer users know little about their machine and take few precautions to protect privacy. In fact, most individuals and organizations leave themselves vulnerable to snooping and unauthorized use of personal information. Privacy law has many unanswered questions, and nonprofits need to develop ethical policies and practices with respect to their partners and clientele. Congress is currently considering legal approaches to protecting privacy. The Federal Trade Commission (FTC) and Federal Communications Commission (FCC) have taken opposite sides on the question.

At the individual level, every computer user should develop a system for creating and changing passwords systematically. Many Web sites offer help in thinking through your particular approach. Many people do not realize that Web browsers have a history feature that can be turned on or off. If used, it can be set for a certain number of days to keep track of all the Web sites and pages visited. If computers are shared, it is a simple matter for a co-user to peek at someone else's history. At a minimum, this could be embarrassing (e.g., a young man visits sites with sexual content or gambling opportunities and a parent checks the history).

Cookies are another issue. Cookies are small programs left on machines from Web sites visited. These cookies can be troublesome in terms of privacy—they constitute another way to track where a computer user has been. These cookies can also slowly fill up the memory of your hard drive. Most of them have expiration dates of more than five years from now.

According to the Small Business Administration, cookies can serve several functions:

- They allow the Web site to identify you as a previous visitor each time you access a site.
- They track what information you view at a site (important to commercial sites trying to determine your buying preferences).
- In the more advanced cases, they track your movements through many Web sites.

- Businesses use cookies for customer convenience to allow them to produce a list of items to buy and pay for them all at one time and to garner information about what individuals are buying at their sites.
- Advertisers use them to determine the effectiveness of their marketing and offer insights into consumer preferences and tastes by collecting data from many Web sites.
- They can be used to help a Web site tailor screens for each customer's preference.[28]

A nonprofit Privacy Rights Clearinghouse home page starts with the following quote:

"The real danger is the gradual erosion of individual liberties through the automation, integration of many small, separate record-keeping systems, each of which alone may seem innocuous, even justifiable." (U.S. Privacy Protection Study Commission, 1977)[29]

The purposes of the clearinghouse are to:

- Raise consumer awareness of how technology affects personal privacy
- Empower consumers to control their own personal information
- Respond to privacy-related complaints
- Document concerns about privacy
- Advocate for consumer privacy rights

(A) HAVE A PRIVACY POLICY

All nonprofits working in the Internet environment must have a privacy policy. The following is the Internet Privacy Policy of the Small Business Administration (SBA), which may serve as a model:

1. The U.S. Small Business Administration provides this World Wide Web (WWW) site as a public service.
2. With the exception of information noted as copyrighted, SBA considers information presented on this Web site as public information, which may be distributed or copied. We request use of appropriate byline/photo/image credits. Copyrighted information falls under all copyright laws.
3. For site management, we use software programs to collect and create summary statistics on the following information for statistical purposes:
   - Date and time
   - Originating Internet protocol (IP) address
   - Object requested
   - Address of the Web site from which you linked to our site
   - Type of browser you use to access our Web site
   - Completion status of the request
4. This government computer system uses these gathered statistics for such purposes as:
   - Assessing what information is of most and least interest
   - Determining technical design specifications
   - Identifying system performance or problem areas

5. For site security purposes and to ensure that this service remains available to all users, this federal government computer system employs software programs to monitor network traffic to identify unauthorized attempts to upload or change information, or otherwise cause damage.

6. Except for authorized law enforcement investigations, this Web site makes no other attempts to identify individual users or their usage habits. We use raw data logs for no other purposes and scheduled these logs for regular destruction in accordance with National Archives and Records Administration General Schedule 20.

7. Unauthorized attempts to upload information or change information on this service are strictly prohibited and may be punishable under the Computer Fraud and Abuse Act of 1986 and the National Information Infrastructure Protection Act.

8. The information we receive depends on what you do when visiting our site —
   a. If you visit our site to read or download information, such as consumer brochures or press releases:
      - We collect and store only the following information about you: the name of the domain from which you access the Internet (for example, aol.com, if you are connecting from an America Online account, or psu.edu if you are connecting from Pennsylvania State University's domain); the date and time you access our site; and the Internet address of the Web site from which you linked directly to our site.
      - We use the information we collect to measure the number of visitors to the different sections of our site, and to help us make our site more useful to visitors.
   b. If you identify yourself by sending an e-mail:
      - You also may decide to send us personally identifying information, for example, in an electronic mail message containing a complaint or compliment.
      - We use personally identifying information from viewers in various ways to further the usefulness and accuracy of the information contained on our Web site or to add new sections and services.
      - Be aware that despite anything we do to protect electronic information, e-mail is not necessarily secure against interception. If your communication is very sensitive, or includes personal information, you might prefer to send it by regular mail instead.[30]

Privacy International (PI) states that with the increasing sophistication of information technology, there is an urgent demand for privacy legislation.[31] Also, new developments in medical research and care and financial transfer have dramatically increased the level of information generated by each individual. Computer linking capabilities also increase concern about privacy violations.

(B)   TRENDS FEEDING PRIVACY INVASION

PI has identified three key trends that contribute to privacy invasion:

1. *Globalization*—The global Internet

2. *Convergence*—Interoperability with other systems and mutual exchange
3. *Multimedia*—Fuses many forms of transmission and expression of data and images so that information gathered in a certain form can be easily translated into other forms

As discussed earlier in this chapter, the global Internet offers tremendous possibility as an open distributed environment. It will be imperative that appropriate laws, practices, and improvements, including appropriate encryption for purposes of privacy and security, are implemented.

The following are key principles agreed upon by a number of countries and in international organizations such as the Organization for Economic Cooperation and Development. Personal information must be:

- Obtained fairly and lawfully
- Used only for the original specified purpose
- Adequate, relevant, and explicit to purpose
- Accurate and up to date
- Accessible to the subject
- Kept secure
- Destroyed after its purpose is completed

"In a networked society, information about us travels at high speeds around the world. Most likely it's being stored in the databases of companies you've never heard of."[32]

8.9 IP Is for Intellectual Property (Not Internet Protocol)

Nonprofit organizations must increasingly be concerned about issues of intellectual property. There are four types of intellectual property recognized by the United States and international law: copyright, patent, proprietary information, and trademarks.

U.S. copyright law gives the owner of a copyright a number of protections. The copyright owner may abridge, expand, revise, or rearrange the copyrighted work. The owner can perform or display the work, the owner has the exclusive right to create decorative works, and the owner can give away or sell all of these rights.[33]

Interesting questions about copyright can arise when organizations use significant taxpayer dollars for development of the "creation." Organizations ethically should determine what constitutes a "significant contribution" of taxpayer funds in determining where the copyright resides. Many nonprofit creations in the Internet world are likely to be "Works for Hire." By definition, these contracted creations belong to the organization, not the individual. However, nonprofits may bump into issues in this area when volunteers, perhaps university faculty members, may develop programs and products on their own using their own intellectual and technical resources. Unless an agreement was first negotiated about copyright, the individual creating the product most probably has the copyright.

In 1998, Congress passed the Digital Millennium Copyright Act, which expanded on the Telecommunications Act. It provides considerable protection for Internet service providers (ISPs) and copyright owners. This was done at the expense of those who post material on the Internet, including nonprofit organizations of a variety of types. This act brought the United States into compliance with the World Intellectual Property Organization treaties. A little material provision gives copyright protection to cookies. Some attorneys tried to argue that it would be a copyright infringement for the computer user to delete these cookies even if they were placed there without the owner's knowledge. The act bans many technologies that try to circumvent encryption and copy-prevention schemes.[34]

At present, the United States is the major victim of international copyright infringement. This is not surprising given the disproportionate number of U.S. creations. When the United States joined the Berne Convention in 1989, as the 79th nation to do so, it gave American copyright owners protection in 24 countries where the United States had no such arrangement.[35]

Some resources for learning more about copyright and intellectual property can be found on the following Web sites:

- American Distance Education Association,
  http://www.adec.edu/online-resources.html
- American Association of University Professors,
  http://www.aaup.org/spccopyr.htm
- Intellectual Property Magazine, *http://www.ipmag.com*

(A) OPEN SYSTEMS AND OBJECTS

In the United States, the National Learning Infrastructure Initiative (NLII) pioneered work with the Instructional Management System (IMS) designed to accelerate cost-effective, reusable, dynamic learning software. The idea is to develop a system for reusable learning content as "instructional objects." International efforts are underway as well. Increasingly, it is recognized that taxonomies and classification systems will be required in all discipline areas. The Dublin Core defines a minimal set of metatags (a standard way to define or tag information). Metatags are words or phrases embedded in Web pages. They are used by search engines to find information on the Internet.

For Internet-based learning to become widespread and cost-effective, issues like platform neutrality and software reusability are essential.[36]

(B) TRADEMARKS AND THE INTERNET

Many organizations want to ensure that the name or trademark of their organization is protected. Nonprofits as well as for-profits in the United States can be registered under the Lanhan Act national registration system. Usually, a search is conducted by an attorney to find out if the selected name or trademark is available for registration. If no one else has registered the name, the organization can follow a federal filing procedure that can be challenged by others wishing to do so. The applicant pays a fee to the U.S. Patent and Trademark Office. Once registered, the trademark must be renewed at the end of 5 years and after that every 10 years.

Obviously, most organizations would like to be able to use their trademark along with their Internet domain as their Web address. For example, the American Distance Education Consortium holds the trademark adec. ADEC was able to also secure the adec.edu, where adec is the specific entity and edu is the generic top-level domain name.[37] By 1999, Network Solutions Inc. (NSI), a Virginia-based company acting as the sole source domain registration entity, had registered 5 million domain names. Some people registered hundreds of names, hoping to sell the Internet domain name to the holder of the trademark for a large profit. Instead of paying, several organizations sued the cybersquatters and usually prevailed based on the proof that they hold a valid trademark of the name. Today, a nonprofit organization, The Internet Corp. for Assigned Names and Numbers (ICANN) is in place, in competition with NSI.

Internationally, the question of domain name registration is also controversial and is likely to take years to resolve, if ever, as the technology stays out in front of the law.

8.10   Conclusion

Large international nonprofit organizations are already aware of the tremendous complexity arising from the uncharted waters of global Internet communication. Tremendous possibilities and daunting challenges are ahead. It is certain that many attorneys will be employed in arguing, tangling, and untangling these overlapping webs.

Will the promise of a global Internet as a tool for collaboration, relationship building, education, democracy, and civil society continue? Probably! Will there be a lot of mistakes, difficulties, and hurt along the way? Certainly. But the world is likely to emerge from Hakken-Kraks Howl one nation at a time. "It's 98 and 3/4 percent guaranteed"!

Endnotes

1. Geisel, T. S., and A. S. Geisel. (1990). *Oh, the Places You'll Go!* New York: Random House.
2. Interactive Week. (March 27, 2000), *http://www.zdnet.com/intweek.*
3. Morrison, P., and P. Morrison. (2000). "Wonders: The Internet as Hardware," *Scientific American* (June), 282(6): 113, *http://www.sciam.com.*
4. Alexrod, A. (1996). *The Complete Idiot's Guide to American History.* New York: Alpha Books, Simon & Schuster Macmillan Company.
5. Id.
6. Farah, D. (2000). "Nigerians Await Democracy's Dividends," *Washington Post* (April 27): A21.
7. Bollag, B. (2000). "4 Foundations Start $100-Million Effort to Help Higher Education in Africa," *Today's News, The Chronicle of Higher Education* (April 24), *http://www. chronicle.com.*
8. Cameron, S. D. (2000). "The Mind of the Planet," (May 8), Column HH0018, Nyerere *http://www.onelist.com/HH0018.*
9. Postman, N. (1999). *Building a Bridge to the Eighteenth Century: How the Past Can Improve Our Future.* New York: Alfred A. Knopf.
10. Carothers, T. (1999–2000). "Think Again: Civil Society," *http://www.foreignpolicy.com/ articles/winter 1999–2000/Thinkagain/carothers.html.*
11. "Education: The Global Gender Gap." (2000). Parliamentary Briefing No. 9 (April), *http://194.200.59.236/policy/papers/gendgap/gendgap.htm.*
12. Woodall, M. (2000). San Jose Mercury Report from American Association of University Women, April 11, 2000. (http://newslibrary.krmediastream.com/cgi-bin/ search/sj).
13. World Social and Political NGOs, *http://www.tampaus.com/main/politics.html.*

14. *Venture Philanthropy: Landscape and Expectations.* (1999). Reston, VA: Community Wealth Ventures for the Morino Institute.
15. Moynihan, D. P. (1998). *Secrecy.* New Haven: Yale University Press.
16. Id.
17. Vise, David A. (2000). "EPA to Limit Web Information," *Washington Post* (April 27): A25.
18. Id.
19. See note 15.
20. Saundos, F. S. (2000). *The Cultural Cold War: The CIA and the World of Arts and Letters,* summarized in *The Chronicle of Higher Education* (March 31), *http://www.chronicle.com.*
21. Sharley, J. (2000). "Tinker, Writer, Artist, Spy: Intellectuals During the Cold War," *The Chronicle of Higher Education* (March 31): A19.
22. Goodman, P. S., and J. Schwartz. (1999). "Curbs on Export of Secrecy Codes Ending," *Washington Post* (September 17): A1, *http://www.washingtonpost.com/wpsrv/ business/daily/sept99/encryption17.htm.*
23. Freedom Forum, *http://www.freedomforum.org.*
24. Overbeck, W. (2000). *Major Principles of Media Law.* Orlando: Harcourt College Publishers.
25. Id.
26. Id.
27. "Big Browser Is Watching You." (2000). *Consumers Union* (May), *http://www. consumersunion.org.*
28. Small Business Administration, *http://www.sba.gov/privacy.html.*
29. Privacy Rights Clearinghouse, *http://www.privacyrights.org/FS/fs1-surv.htm.*
30. See note 28.
31. Privacy International, *http://www.gilc.org/privacy/survey/intro.html.*
32. Electronic Frontier Foundation, *http://www.eff.org/identity.html.*
33. See note 24.
34. Id.
35. Id.
36. Saba, F. (2000). "Next Generation Distance Education Systems," *Distance Education Report* (April 15), 4(8).
37. American Distance Education Consortium (ADEC), *http://www/adec.edu/ online-resources.html.*

Distance Learning for Nonprofit Organizations: Getting Started

JANET POLEY, PhD, PRESIDENT
American Distance Education Consortium (ADEC)

9.1 An Overview of Distance Education

Distance education is today's buzzword, but the idea has been around for more than 100 years. Correspondence courses were born in the late 1800s and worked very well for place-bound learners with motivation. During the 1900s, the technological possibilities for sharing information and education rapidly exploded, including radio, television, and today's Internet. Information technology broadly defined is now the number one industry in the United States, overtaking construction, food products, and automobile manufacturing. Our national well-being depends on developing new uses for technology and a highly trained workforce capable of continuous improvement and innovation.

If one believes management guru Peter Drucker, our national well-being may also depend on answering the question: "Who takes care of the social changes of the knowledge society?" He suggests that the United States needs a new social sector consisting of nongovernmental organizations responsible "to create human health and well-being" and to create "citizenship." He claims that "we do not have even the beginning of political theory on the political institutions needed for effective government in the knowledge-based society of organizations."[1]

The nonprofit organizations could become major partners and players in ensuring that the technology revolution moves the world toward awareness, information, knowledge, empowerment, imagination, cooperation, commitment, and freedom. Many organizations, whether local or global in scope, are looking to participate in distance education, as learners, providers, or marketers. Some organizations see the use of powerful technologies such as the Internet and the World Wide Web as vehicles to draw others to their cause. Some see distance education as part of community building. Other groups are considering offering distance learning programs to raise money or taking training programs to save money. Nonprofit organizations often organize communities of interest to come together for town meetings on key issues delivered via satellite. Whatever the reasons, there is clearly a rush to experiment with developing learning opportunities without increasing budgets.

We recognize that the term *nonprofit* covers a large and diverse set of organizations with the same tax status but different missions. The design and implementation of a sensible distance education strategy at a major public university or for the American Distance Education Consortium (ADEC) will differ greatly from that employed by the National Association of Counties, the League of Women Voters, or the thousands of small, local nonprofit groups. We think that many of the smaller organizations can take advantage of the growing distance learning opportunities via the Internet. We also think that partnerships, collaborations, and networks that include the extensive resources of public educational institutions working with a wide variety of other types of nonprofit organizations could result in a much fuller array of distance learning opportunities. This chapter suggests only a few of the possibilities that could emerge as we understand more about distance learning and how to create it. Building new relationships and communities of interest will be as essential as developing the capacity to build and use new technological applications.

9.2 Getting Started: Key Principles

(A) WHAT DISTANCE EDUCATION IS ABOUT— DISTRIBUTED AND OPEN LEARNING

Distance education is more about teaching and learning than it is about technology. Other terms coming into vogue are *distributed learning* and *open learning*. While some make fine semantic distinctions among distance, distributed, and open education, to be effective they all must focus on learners achieving defined outcomes within a specified time period at a cost that is affordable. Planning is essential, and appropriate technology can be selected only in the context of the program goals, learner needs, and resources available.

Distance education is about providing quality, affordable learning opportunities at a time and place convenient for the learner. Quality distance education creates both access and success. In distance education, technology (data, voice, video, or print) is used to bridge physical and time differences between instructors and learners. Research has shown that distance education can be as effective as face-to-face instruction. Methods and technologies need to be appropriate to the instructional tasks. Learners need to be at the center of the process. Learners can learn from each other as well as from teaching faculty, and timely feedback is important to success.

Task: Clearly define your learners. Who in your organization has assets that could be shared with learners? Who would benefit from information you could make available? How would you describe the target audience—age, education, culture, and so forth? What makes you think that they might be interested in a distance learning opportunity? Will they be able to pay to learn, or will you have to find resources to support the program? What do you know about the learning styles and preferences of your target audience?

(B) THE DISTANCE LEARNING ENVIRONMENT—ANYWHERE

Distance learners may be located anywhere—physical and geographic borders and boundaries will disappear as definers of learning communities.

Increasingly, learning is moving from the classroom to the workplace, the home, and even the automobile. Borders and boundaries are disappearing, offering much greater local and global opportunity. Self-directed learners connected to the Internet are increasingly able to engage in "just-in-time" information seeking and learning with others anywhere in the world. More educated, experienced, mature people are most likely to succeed in this diffuse emerging environment. Potential gaps—haves, have nots, have now, have later—are developing. Large and well-financed organizations can arrange for national, or even international, town meetings, via satellite. Small, relatively poor local groups can engage a volunteer student to create a distance learning opportunity on a Web site. There is a continuum of opportunities available to nonprofit organizations, particularly those willing to learn about the new, change old habits, and seek innovative partnerships.

Task: Clearly define where learners will participate in your offerings—at a community center? at home? at work? Will learners be alone and able to participate "anytime" (asynchronous learning), or will learners need to be with others to discuss the material presented and make decisions for the local community (synchronous learning)? Are you trying to cover a large geographic area and seek national/international input on an issue, topic, or idea? How many learning locations will be necessary?

(C) ACTIVE AND EXPERIENTIAL LEARNING MODELS WORK BEST

Many have had the experience of sitting through a boring lecture delivered in monotone over compressed or satellite video. This lecture would have been bad in person and is made worse by running it through the cool medium of television. While many get excited by "moving pictures," the importance of sound as the element carrying the meaning in a television broadcast is frequently overlooked. Heightened warmth in person and voice can improve teledelivery. But the most important aspect of the design is whether you fully respect the idea that learners have to be engaged actively to learn. The Experiential Learning Cycle is an easy-to-use model for designing learning modules and programs. It is frequently a much better guide for thinking through use of your media tools than thinking about entertainment equivalents. Ideally, learners help to establish the learning objectives so that expectations are clear. Everyone knows that at the end of this training, the learner will be able to X (do, know, list, define, show, value, etc.). This allows for outcome assessment based on mutually agreed-upon goals. Understanding the variation in learning styles is also important—many people like to learn in concrete and active ways, rather than passive, reflective types of activities. The new computer-based tools emerging in the Internet environment offer promise for individualizing instruction by learning style and objectives. They also offer new "doing" possibilities using virtual reality and simulation tools, as well as possibilities for learning by assimilation and analogy. Until we have these tools fully available, most designers will need to work with whatever is available to allow for variations. Some people need to learn step by step, concretely; some need to fully understand the principles and then apply; others like to jump right in and play, then reflect on what they have learned through action.

David Kolb's Experiential Learning Cycle is very useful in planning distance learning modules and events. The chart is not to be used rigidly but is a way to think about all the processes involved in learning—action, reflection and observation, generalization and conceptualization, and experimentation and planning for application.

Step one is to establish learner-centered goals, using the ABCD format: audience, behavior, conditions, and degree:

- *Audience:* List the specific characteristics of the audience.
- *Behavior:* Write down how the audience will behave if it masters the objective.
- *Conditions:* Describe conditions within which the objective will be accomplished.
- *Degree:* Describe an acceptable level of performance.[2]

Don't worry about using this format rigidly—some useful learning goals do not lend themselves easily to measurement. If possible, establish the learning goals and objectives collaboratively with the learners. This is where technology combinations are useful. You can interact with learners on an audioconference or on the Internet and then build their ideas into the production of your national town meeting. Also, remember that engaging learners in establishing goals and objectives is one of the best marketing devices available to you.

Now you have your goals. Start at the top of the chart and decide on the active learning experience for the module. Think about your content—key messages, metaphors, analogies—and in particular, think about the context within which your learners work and live. Your design should relate directly to their lives. This experience should be designed to engage the learner in doing an activity, describing a relevant experience, working on a case study, viewing a videotape, or one of the hundreds of different active learning possibilities. *Teaching at a Distance with the Merging Technologies* by Tom Cyrs includes an excellent list and description of how to use each technique.[3]

During the time for reflection and observation, learners are encouraged to reflect on the experiences identified in the active learning phase. Instructor/facilitator questions should help participants to analyze experiences in a critically reflective manner. Journaling, including online journaling, can be useful at this stage.

Once learners have reflected on the meaning of these experiences, they need to generate theory. Again, questions should be used to assist learners in finding the principles, meanings, and generalizations in the experiences.

Finally, attention should be given to practice and application. Studies have shown that the more time devoted to planning and preparing for application, the much greater the possibility that learning will internalize and change will occur.

Most learners exhibit preferences for one or more of these processes. Some people like to be doing but may need to be helped to reflect on their experiences. Others may enjoy the reflection and observation aspect of the learning process and may need to be urged to action.

These ideas can be applied to groups as well as individuals and can help guide the design of distance learning opportunities from Web-based modules to international town meetings via satellite. You will also want to consider ways to evaluate on an ongoing basis and perhaps consider a larger summative evaluation at the end of a major program.

(D) DISTANCE EDUCATION CAN USE MANY TECHNOLOGIES

Increasingly, all technological options will be digital, and convergence of computer and television assumptions will decrease the clumsiness of today's tools. Today, we are working in a mix-and-match world made up of items from the following menu:

- *Voice:* This includes telephone, audioconferencing, voice mail, Internet phone, short-wave radio, audiotapes, and radio.
- *Data:* Computer applications for distance education include Internet e-mail and World Wide Web applications (digital libraries, warehouse, databases, and learning environments). You will frequently see the following terms:
  - *Computer-assisted instruction (CAI):* The computer works as a teaching machine.
  - *Computer-managed instruction (CMI):* The computer is used to organize instruction and track student records and progress.
  - *Computer-mediated education (CME):* Describes all applications that facilitate the delivery of instruction over a computer.
  - *Computer-mediated communications (CMC):* Describes specific computer applications, including synchronous real-time "chat" as well as asynchronous "threaded" conversations.[4]
- *Print:* While many distance education programs are moving to "print on demand" from the Web, print remains an important part of delivery systems. Print formats often include textbooks, workbooks, syllabi, study guides, and case studies.
- *Video:* Can include slides, videotapes, real-time moving images, and one-way or two-way video with two-way audio. Choice of the videoconferencing delivery mode is usually a matter of numbers to be involved in the session and price. For example, if you have a small number of distance learning sites that are compressed, video may be the best option. If you are doing a national or international videoconference satellite delivery, one-way video, two-way audio may be the only option available, albeit an expensive choice. Improved desktop video options are becoming available, particularly for limited numbers of sites and learners. Digital satellite delivery should result in increased availability of channels for not-for-profit organizational programming at affordable prices. Commercial broadcasters were given a

large amount of "digital spectrum" on the premise that they would need it to introduce high-definition television (HDTV). All studies to date show that there is little or no consumer interest in the "pretty pictures, and pretty sound" at a "pretty price" of HDTV. This "free" gift is likely to be used for very lucrative services, but in return the public should be able to demand greater access to digital channels for public interest and educational purposes.

The *1998 Consumer Reports Buying Guide* has an excellent and readable section on the future of TV. In brief, they suggest the merging of TV/video functions with those of the computer to produce products like WebTV. Consumers are likely to trade up to larger sets. Prices of sets will continue to drop, but HDTV sets will be very expensive, and only people looking for a TV costing more than $2,000 are likely to be a market for this anytime soon.

(E) DISTANCE EDUCATION FOR THE HOME USER

Most distance education programming will be designed for home use, with the exception of just-in-time Internet and desktop-available training in the workplace.

While certain distance learning applications, such as national town meetings, will require people coming together physically in a location outside the home, by far the most frequently used distance education programs will be home based. Women are the largest consumer of distance education, and while price, quality, and convenience are all important factors in decision making about selection of distance learning options, convenience is primary for women who may work and have family responsibilities.

Nonprofit organizations of all types will need to collaborate and work together in order to produce the high-quality programs needed at an affordable price. Institutions of higher education will need to redirect funds from current face-to-face programs and eliminate considerable duplication from state to state, in order to step up to the opportunity and challenge of distance education. Most state universities and land grant colleges have tremendous production facilities and resources for computer and telecommunications, as well as the human capacity to produce programs. Working through organizations like ADEC, they might embrace a much larger array of nonprofit organizations without the capacity and facilities. In addition, foundations could be engaged in this network, increasing effectiveness and efficiency.

The American Society for Training and Development, in its Benchmarking Forum, shows that from 1994 to 1996, companies significantly increased their use of televised distance learning, interactive computer-based training, and Internet/network-based electronic distance learning. They decreased their use of advanced technology classrooms.

Local learning centers will have an important role in providing support for learners, needs assessment, facilitation of library and laboratory access, and marketing. Ideally, community-based nonprofit organizations should work together in designing, staffing, and equipping these centers. Libraries, extension offices, K–12 schools, local media outlets, and others could be brought together in new configurations to develop new relationships.

(F) COOPERATION AMONG NONPROFITS IS ESSENTIAL

Distance education should provide opportunities for collaboration, cooperation, resource sharing, and community building spanning local, state, national, and international boundaries.

Pyramid organizational structures are rapidly losing favor to flat, lean, loosely coordinated structures. Partnerships and alliances among nonprofit organizations should be encouraged as a way to ensure that affordable learning opportunities of high quality are available and accessible throughout the country. The owners of distance education conduits should not be the decision makers limiting programming content to only the "popular," lowest common denominator. Nonprofit organizations will first need to educate themselves about the options, developing a coordinated strategy to ensure that the public interest is represented in a broad array of programs, much of which might be provided by nonprofit organizations.

Distance education programs need to be validated to ensure that they are achieving the goals intended. Validation and evaluation are related but are not exactly the same thing. Today, there is considerable "nonsense" in the air about assessing and testing competency. Differences in philosophy separate these concepts. Distance education focuses on developing the teaching and learning system to ensure that the learner succeeds. Some elements of "succeeding" lend themselves more easily than others to testing.

So what is best? The answer usually is to use an integrated, mixed-media approach designed to meet the learner's needs and accommodate the budget. There are multiple ways to do things, and validation that the system used works for the intended purpose is the most commonsense approach.

9.3 Quality Distance Education Defined

While lists may vary slightly, there is general agreement that important factors for creating quality distance education include:

- Knowing the learners
- Creating confident and committed faculty
- Designing for active and effective learning
- Supporting the needs of learners
- Maintaining the technical infrastructure
- Sustaining administrative commitment
- Evaluating for continuous improvement

The University of Wisconsin–Madison has five video/print modules addressing quality distance education: what it is, factors that contribute to it, case studies in which it is alive and well, and lessons learned about it. Nonprofit organizations can contact UW–Madison or ADEC for details.

Three methods may be used to make judgments about the quality of distance education:

1. A strong student support services model
2. A stakeholder analysis model
3. A qualitative and quantitative evaluation model

Seligman told an international audience that quality distance education is doing the job effectively and appropriately. He says that quality is well thought out, is prepared with care, is implemented with responsibility, has a firm direction, but is flexible enough to cope with contextual variation and is positively responsive to comment and criticism.[5]

Ensuring quality is the number one responsibility of organizations involved in developing distance learning programs. In addition to specific content objectives, distance education programs are increasingly designed to continue to develop independent and self-reliant learners. Techniques for ensuring quality are developing rapidly. The most important thing to remember: Consult with learners and stakeholders and forge consensus about the elements of quality. Find out what works and make it even better. Find out what does not work and eliminate it or fix it.

9.4 Trends and Challenges

Both the public and private sectors are investing heavily in virtual learning, training, and performance support. Recently, J.C. Penney reported that stores with distance learning and videoconferencing capability have consistently sold 5 percent more than those without such facilities. Synergy among information technologies makes human capital a significant factor in productivity—in other words, companies that use technology to improve performance of their employees are ushering in a new era of prosperity.

Distributed and online learning systems are growing in popularity. Working, living, and learning are increasingly blurred, and we are beginning to see profound impacts on all traditional institutions and those involved in educational activities.

Some of the current trends and challenges include:

- Professionalism in distance education will improve. We will no longer see tinkering by people who happen to know something about computers or can get a video signal into a telecommunications network. This is not a business for amateurs.[6]
- Appropriate solutions will be developed for specific distance education problems rather than forcing a favorite distance education model.[7]
- More sophisticated distance education economic models, linking economic analyses with educational analyses, will ensure good fit between needs, solutions, and available money.[8]
- Innovation in support infrastructures is required. Educators must create an environment for distance learners that provides the support they require to succeed. This infrastructure must be reliable and affordable. Today, there are lots of experiments, but too little that is sustained because it is so hard.
- Faculty, teachers, and facilitators for distance education will need different skills and characteristics than required for traditional teaching. There is little room for the individual in distance learning. Distance education is a one-person show, and it is mostly about teachers structuring the learning research, teachers being open to learn from students, and students learning from students. It is also about opening up the learning process. The human and educational resources increasingly available via technology will over time change almost everything about the process.
- Students need new and different skills to succeed in distance education, and distance education may not be the best choice for everyone. How can learners assess their capacity to perform well in this new environment? The notions of "learning how to learn" very early in life and the idea of "lifelong learning" are critical.

- Everybody has to start "Telling the Truth." Because of the long-standing bias against distance education, practitioners must be scrupulously honest in their portrayal of opportunities and benefits of distance education programs. We need wise consumers able to cut through marketing hype and disparaging remarks, able to locate quality education opportunities through a variety of means. There are plenty who would sell equipment, learning systems, virtual universities, and other poor-quality merchandise in this realm. It will increasingly become "Buyer Beware."

- A growing number of professionals are looking to be able to improve and upgrade their job skills in the workplace and *earn* an advanced degree. There is an emerging group of potential students, especially in the high-tech and business arenas, who want and can benefit from graduate programs at a distance.

- Competition in the market is growing incredibly fast, but predictions of large potential profits are exaggerated. So-called "edutainment" is overrated, and there are only so many learning needs common to a very large number of people. There are opportunities, and these systems will change education from top to bottom. Also, there is growing competition in a field formerly defined by geographic regions. People will have a lot more educational choices. Consumer choice will largely be defined on the basis of cost, quality, and convenience—much like other services.

- Curriculum-driven technology decisions will come to the forefront in the next two years. The focus is shifting away from available technology and toward content as the linchpin for distance education delivery mechanism decisions.

- There will be major shifts in who is a teacher, who is a learner, and who is in business. Lines will blur. There is a growing recognition that distance education programs must prepare everyone involved in the enterprise for maximum efficacy.

9.5 Knowledge Management, Electronic Commerce, and E-Learning Systems

The American Society for Training and Development (ASTD) identifies knowledge management as a current hot topic. Knowledge management is the process of creating, capturing, and using knowledge for enhanced organizational performance. Knowledge management must take into account people and learning processes, not just information technology systems. In addition, the knowledge management process may eclipse traditional training programs. Knowledge management is the explicit and organized fashion in which corporations attempt to become smarter. This concept should be of particular interest to nonprofit organizations. They may be able to improve performance by doing a better job of leveraging their resources, including the know-how and experience of the organization's collective memory bank.

Electronic commerce, or e-commerce, is another idea that has reached buzzword status. Defined as buying and selling over the Internet, getting started in electronic commerce is not difficult. Nevertheless, nonprofit organizations need to understand the technology and have a clear vision linked to customer needs and fit with the organization's strategy. Does your organization have a base that is ready and capable of working with you electronically? Will your organization be ready to add electronic commerce features to your Web site, take credit cards to pay for enrollments in training seminars, and order printed materials you may have for sale? The new buzzword is e-learning, and educational providers are being offered a growing number of choices for development of e-learning resources. Most of these products are templates for organizing instructional material, e-mail, conferencing, library resources, evaluation and assessment, administration, calendaring, other instructional tools, and progress tracking. Some products are quick and simple to use with low ramp-up time—others are complex and more difficult.

E-learning is often developed as learning objects or modules or units. Standardized approaches including "meta-data," data about the data in the learning module, will increasingly make sharing, swapping, and mixing and matching of quality materials more possible. Databases will be at the heart of these systems.

More robust e-learning products are in development, and many expect the next "breakthrough" to be powerful computer-based systems for learning of all types. "Next Generation" distance education systems are expected to shift significantly. Farhad Saba wrote in the April 2000 *Distance Education Report:*

> *Marshall McLuhan said the content of a new medium is an old medium. McLuhan's prophecy came true one more time when both the public and private sector put thousands of courses online. These courses, however, are primarily based on the mortar and brick model. They are not individualized, offer very few options for selection of learning goals by students and span 16 weeks or so regardless of the progress of the individual.[9]*

9.6   Realities for Nonprofit Organizations

ASTD reports training expenditures by course type for 1996. This breakdown may provide some help to nonprofit organizations in thinking about categories of distance education that may be of interest to their members and publics:

- New Employee Orientation, 2%
- Basic Skills, 2%
- Executive Development, 3%
- Quality, Competition, Business Practices, 3%
- Enabling Skills, 6%
- Sales, 6%
- Customer Service, 6%
- Management/Supervision, 7%
- Compliance/Regulatory, 7%
- Computer Applications, 8%
- Professional Skills, 19%
- Technical Skills, 30%

Many small, local nonprofit organizations have a need for learning opportunities related to fund raising, legislation, issue development, advocacy, governance, volunteer training, grantsmanship, and overall management. The growing body of material available on the World Wide Web makes it relatively easy for nonprofit organizations to learn from each other, share program ideas, assess competition, communicate with foundation personnel, and establish common databases for recruiting, promoting, teaching, learning, buying, and selling. Most probably, the real power in this sector will only be realized through organized consortia of various types in order to avoid duplication and fragmentation. By working in new collaborative networks, the nonprofit community could play a much greater role in the national conversation on health care, Medicare, water quality, community building, civic responsibility, youth development, consumer rights, conflict resolution, environment, leadership development, and a host of other issues.

Many nonprofit organizations have expertise that could contribute to playing a more active role in distance education programming. It is often a matter of looking at all of the talents of organization members. Increasing numbers of us make our living in one way or another working with information and information technology. Nonprofit organizations may find it easier to ask people to contribute intellectual capital than money in the future. However, organizing and coordinating these types of contributions will require a significant change in the way most of these organizations do business today.

9.7   Ideas that Work

(A)   WORKING THE WORLD WIDE WEB

One of the easiest ways for nonprofit organizations to get involved in the world of distance education is through development of World Wide Web (WWW)-based modules matched to the organization's mission. The Web's success lies in its ability to present information in a nonlinear format. Many nonprofits have home pages and use volunteers and/or students to do the Hypertext Mark-Up Language (HTML) coding. Increasingly, the tools exist for Web creation and composing without knowing HTML.

The Web is a new way of looking at instruction, although the idea was developed in 1945 by Vannevar Bush in a published article "As We May Think" in *The Atlantic Monthly.* Though Bush's prediction of the actual technology involved was incorrect, his ideas about linking information in new ways was extremely powerful. The Web is a delivery medium, content provider, and subject matter all in one.

You should use the Web to explore intellectual and verbal knowledge. At present, video and audio are a problem for most people due to inadequate bandwidth; however, that may soon change with new technologies and convergence. With its versatility and interconnectedness, the Web offers one of the most effective ways to work with learners who are geographically dispersed. Wireless satellite, radio, and asymmetric digital subscriber lines (ADSLs) will increase affordable bandwidth to rural, remote, and underserved audiences.

Obviously, you don't want to use the Web if your learners do not have access to a computer with an Internet connection. Your learners must be literate. Also, because of the current audio and video limitation, it is not good for developing physical procedural skills. This will change as bandwidth options increase and we begin to see work accomplished with virtual reality and simulation tools. So if you need video, it is better to go with videotape, television, or CD-ROM. However, television and Web combinations are immediately on the horizon. One of the most important advantages of the Web is that it can link people from all over the world very inexpensively.

Many nonprofit organizations already have Web pages with information, job listings, and products for sale. Web sites are more powerful when they are worldclass, including information that people and organizations around the world will value. Many Web sites are really cobwebs visited infrequently. Nonprofit organizations in the same mission area might consider working together on distance education offerings, just as they are doing with use of common databases for job listings.

The WWW is just emerging as a marketplace. Some nonprofits may be the best organizations to study the way this market works or doesn't work for various population groups. Some very innovative work is going on within nonprofit organizations such as the Austin Learning Academy, which brings hope, education, and community to kids previously overlooked in the traditional school system. As female entrepreneurs around the world come into the WWW marketplace, nonprofit organizations may be in an excellent position to determine learning assets and needs and develop programs to greatly strengthen these efforts. New ideas about sustainability or programs and projects might emerge. The WWW is also a wonderful place to "surf" around and see what people might want and need. What's already there? What's missing? What might my organization develop?

(B) CREATING INSTRUCTION

Choosing a system for designing distance education depends on the learners and the needs, capabilities, and preferences of the instructor.

Distance education implies that some deliberate thought is given to organizing material and resources to promote specific learning. There are a number of different opinions about how best to do this; however, they all go beyond the idea of creating a Web page. The more traditional instructional design model breaks instruction down into a series of steps that, if followed, are supposed to lead to effective instructional materials. While different experts have various numbers of steps, the sequence looks something like the following:

- Identify behavioral goals.
- Break the behavior down into skills.
- Define what mastery will look like.
- Create tests based on performance objectives.
- Develop the instruction, including media selection, strategy, and production.
- Prepare an evaluation schedule.

This model is very instructor dependent. The model may work well when learners are young and/or immature or when learners come to the setting in agreement about what they want to learn. This model works less well for adults and does not usually handle individual learner differences as effectively as might be possible.

Recently, the Constructivists have come to the fore, working with Cognitive Flexibility Theory. This nonlinear, criss-crossed landscape approach to a multidimensional transversal of complex subject matter fits well with the power for the Web. This Hypermedia Design Model assumes that the instructional medium will serve as the guide rather than a teacher. Another important aspect of this model is *design goals,* which are the knowledge that the designers hope learners will construct from the learning environment. *Learner objectives* are what the learner actually comes to the environment wanting to learn. The Hypermedia Design Model is built on the idea that learner objectives are of utmost importance but that some guidance might help in the achievement of the learner's goals. Aspects of the Hypermedia Design Model include:

- Define the learning domain—how large will the boundaries be?
- Identify cases within the domain—these need to be authentic and represent multiple perspectives.
- Identify themes and perspectives—knowledge that anyone familiar with the domain should have.
- Map multiple paths through cases to show themes.
- Provide learner-controlled access to cases.
- Encourage learner self-reflection.[10]

(C)   SELECTING TECHNOLOGIES

There are many technologies to choose from and to mix and match in developing distance education programs. The merits and demerits of each technology are argued by those who like to engage in "religious" wars. Usually, selection is a matter of knowing what your learners have available and can use conveniently. Price is a major consideration. Also, you will want to consider the quality and capacity of various system mixes to accomplish the learning objectives.

An excellent Web site for learning more about "Selecting Technologies for Distance Education" can be found at *http://labweb.soemadison.wisc.edu/*. This resource helps you analyze use of the following:

- *One-way real-time technology.* This includes real, or central, broadcast technologies, including TV, cable, and radio. These technologies can be motivational if well produced, but they can lack student control and involvement. Unless they are taped, they also lack reviewability. They can be complemented with print to allow reviewability or with teleconferences to allow two-way interaction.

  This has been one of the most popular forms of distance education for training, especially in business and for upgrading professional skills. Budget constraints have limited adoption of this mode in the nonprofit sector.
- *Two-way real-time technology.* This includes videoconferencing, CUSeeMe, teleconferencing, one-to-one telephone, and real-time e-mail chat. Students can use the technologies to communicate with the instructor or other students. Participation may be high, but there is little control over pacing, and everyone must be present to interact.

  One-to-one telephone and audioconferencing are excellent means for people to interact. They lack visualization but may be combined with the Internet. They are usually reasonably affordable when compared with most other methods with the exception of the real winner, e-mail.
- *Two-way asynchronous technology.* People use this technology at different times. Print correspondence, e-mail, listservs, Web boards, and computer mediated communications software such as FirstClass and Learningspace fit this definition. These may be convenient, reviewable, reasonably inexpensive, and interactive.
- *One-way asynchronous technology.* Print, Web sites without Web boards, video- and audiotapes, and CD-ROMS are one-way and asynchronous. They are reviewable and easily controlled by students. They can store large amounts of information and be used when the student needs them. Some one-way

asynchronous technologies permit multimedia. Web sites may contain sound, video, images, and/or animation. CD-ROMs may be programmed with JAVA, Active X, or Shockwave and are interactive in the sense that students may choose a path through the information.

So, what is best? Usually, taking a systematic approach resulting in a mix of media gives the best results. Try combining a course text with online readings and syllabus. Use interactive audio- or videoconferencing for real-time interaction periodically to supplement an online course.

Computer conferencing and electronic mail can be used to send messages, make assignments, give and receive feedback, and direct all types of communication to people in the learning group. Nonprofit organizations also use this strategy for doing "Think Tanks" of all types. Special software, such as Caucus by Screenporch, can be configured to meet the particular need.

Prerecorded videotapes are still an excellent way to present visually oriented content. Whether to feed them over a satellite or mail them is simply a matter of cost. Fax machines can be used to distribute assignments and last-minute announcements. They can also be used to feed questions in to a live videoconference.

(D)   INEXPENSIVE ALTERNATIVES

Audio in combination with the Internet may currently be the least expensive way to get the most out of the options. The majority of learners have telephone access, and increasingly learners around the world are able to get and receive electronic mail and search the Web. Some rural areas still have major difficulties, so this needs to be checked out. People can participate in an audioconference at the same time they are looking at information on one or more Web sites. They can also send e-mail to a listserv or private e-mail to individuals in the conference. It is also possible to send videotapes in advance of an audioconference so that learners can look at the tape ahead of time. These tapes might be trigger tapes designed to produce telephone or Internet Relay Chat discussion. Role plays can be conducted over the phone, as can nearly every type of active learning experience if appropriately designed. It is important to remember that some learners learn more easily from sound and others through visuals—so again, a mix of visuals and graphics on a Web site could be an excellent supplement to an audioconference.

(E)   TOWN MEETINGS THAT WORK

Nonprofit organizations are often asked to become involved in local, state, and national satellite town meetings. This method is particularly useful when you want to involve large numbers of geographically dispersed learners in conversations about issues.

This type of program requires professional expertise, a fully equipped television studio, or an electronic classroom with satellite uplink capability. All participants must have access to a satellite downlink, and the receiver must be tuned to the appropriate transponder to receive the signal. Today, most programs of this type also include "800" numbers for call-in, a fax number, and an e-mail address so that comments and questions can be submitted throughout the real-time program. Also, many of these programs are really "events" promoted over a several-month time period. They will frequently include a special Web site with readings, uniform resource locators (URLs), biographies for participants, a place to submit questions ahead of time, and an online evaluation.

Events of this type vary from a one-time seminar by a nationally recognized expert to a series of adult education programs, to all-day forums on national issues, to organizational change discussions including key personnel from around the United States and beyond.

In addition to the planning, production, and support required to uplink a program of this type, location organization and group facilitation is often required. Often, a national coordinator will be selected to work with the downlink facilitators throughout the country. This person will usually ensure that all the program and technical information is prepared and placed in the Internet for downloading at each site. Often, there will be special training and/or audioconferences to ensure that everything is in place at each location. The downlink coordinator will need to make appropriate arrangements for registration and refreshments if they will be offered. The room arrangement should be comfortable and should have an adequate number of television sets so that all expected participants can see. If the conference will include live call-in, fax and e-mail arrangements should be in place for this as well.

Often, national events of this type will stop and ask participants to hold a discussion at their local site. If you are the local discussion leader, you were probably chosen because you have good facilitation skills. If not, you will want to brush up on the things that you can do to really engage people in discussion by asking questions, paraphrasing, and learning to use a flip chart to record important ideas from the group. There are many good books and references on the WWW that can help you. At one time, a number of nonprofit organizations saw this type of delivery as a money-making proposition. While some of the economic factors might change in the future, it appears that transponder costs are too high and people's schedules too busy to make real-time, synchronous learning at a location outside the home attractive enough that large numbers will pay.

(F) VIDEOCONFERENCING

Compressed videoconferencing allows people at different locations to see and hear each other. While this is not the same as being there, it is often more convenient and less expensive than traveling. Most of this type of videoconferencing today is done over telephone lines. An integrated services digital network (ISDN) line can be dedicated to your videoconference while it is taking place. The hardware that allows the videoconferencing is called a CODEC—short for coder–decoder. It takes the analog video signal and digitizes and compresses it. The CODEC also has to decode, decompress, and undigitize the received transmission. You end up with a jerky picture and some audio delay, but for some situations it may be the best available option.

A broadband satellite connection with studio-quality equipment can produce an excellent full-motion video connection, but the equipment and transmission expense has prohibited widespread use. This may change as satellite systems are changed from analog to digital and more channel space becomes available. These systems can become much less expensive if nonprofit organizations lease transponder space together for their use.

Why consider videoconferencing?

- It can bring together people from all over the world—one-way video with two-way audio, fax, and e-mail can facilitate a national or international town meeting. The compressed two-way video and audio is frequently used with fewer sites and is often used to share learning resources for scattered or rural populations.

- It can enable connections with high-quality external resources—these outside experts can share perspectives with local organizations and agencies.
- Regardless of carrier—fiber, wire, satellite, wireless—these systems are improving and increasing in quality, and will soon be found nearly everywhere. Most of the room systems today include a document camera that allows transmission of a high-quality still image. Some systems allow application sharing so that users at each site can see and edit documents.

The average nonprofit organization (if there is one) will not attempt to do a full-scale national videoconference or town meeting without professional help. This is an area where state universities and land grant colleges and other types of community-based nonprofit organizations might work together because the institutions of higher education have the facilities and expertise available to work in this more complex televisionlike environment.

The less sophisticated two-way compressed systems are usually operated without as much expertise. Although the result is frequently poor, it may be the best available alternative. The following are some key points to consider if you are going to communicate effectively with this type of system:

- Learn the videoconferencing system.
- Maintain eye contact with the video camera.
- Show interest in all your participants.
- Dress appropriately—wear solid-colored clothing.
- Move and gesture slowly and smoothly.
- Learn how to position yourself on camera.
- Be enthusiastic and warm.
- Prepare, prepare, prepare.
- Speak in a strong, clear voice.
- Use the audiovisual aids appropriately:
- Pay attention to the 324 aspect ratio of the screen.
- Use large, bold text.
- Use colors in the middle of the color spectrum.
- Allow time for viewing graphics.
- Obtain authorization to use copyrighted materials.

For more ideas on this subject, see *http://www.kn.pacbell.com/wired/vidconf/description.html*.

9.8   Glossary of Terms

Accessibility   Ability to get a learning resource.

Affective learning   One of the three domains of learning that deals with emotions and attitudes. The other two domains are cognitive and psychomotor.

Algorithm   A step-by-step problem-solving procedure. Transmission of compressed video over a communications network requires sophisticated compression algorithms.

American National Standards Institute (ANSI)   A United States–based organization that develops standards and defines interfaces for telecommunications.

Analog signals   Audio/video signals currently used in broadcasting wherein the signal is represented by variable measurable physical quantities (such as voltage). Current TV and radio signals are analog, as are many telephone lines. (Contrast with Digital.)

Application Function/tasks carried out by computers.

Asynchronous Not at the same time. A form of concurrent input and output communication transmission with no timing relationship between the two signals.

Asynchronous Learning Network (ALN) People networks for anytime, anywhere learning. Combines self-study with substantial, rapid asynchronous interactivity with others. ALNs use computer and communication technologies to work with remote learning resources, including coaches and other learners. The WWW is the most common tool.

Asychronous Transfer Mode (ATM) An international ISDN high-speed, high-volume, packet-switching transmission protocol standard. ATM is the first packet-switched technology designed from the ground up to support integrated voice, video, and data communication applications.

Audience response system Electronic pads with numbers and letters used by distance learning participants. Learners are asked to push the buttons to register answers to questions and opinions.

Audioconference Learners at multiple locations are connected using a telephone bridge. Everyone can hear everyone else and talk together. Speakerphones are often used at group locations. A Meet-Me-Bridge requires all learners to call into a specific telephone number, thus sharing the cost of the call.

Backbone Network of broadband connections between switches.

Bandwidth In casual use, the amount of information that can be transmitted in an information channel. High-bandwidth Internet access means Web graphics load quickly. High-bandwidth videoconferencing means that the picture and sound will be clear and not jerky.

Baud An older term now replaced by bps (bits per second).

Bird Satellite (colloquial).

bps Bits per second (lower case is significant).

BPS (8-bit) bytes per second.

Broadband A high-capacity communications circuit/path. It usually implies a speed greater than 1.544 Mbps. (Contrast with Wideband and Narrowband.)

Browser Software that allows a user to view documents in hypertext on the World Wide Web with the click of a mouse. Common browsers are Netscape Navigator and Microsoft Explorer. The first browser, Mosaic, was developed a the University of Illinois.

Bug A flaw in computer hardware or software functions.

Business television (BTV) Use of satellites, telephone lines, or fiber-optic cable to transmit analog or digital signals to hold meetings or train in a corporate setting.

CALS Computer-assisted learning system.

C-Band Satellite services in the 3.7 to 4.2 GHz (downlink) and 5.975 to 6.425 GHz (uplink) satellite communications band. Most older, nondigital home satellite dishes are C-band.

Coder-decoder (CODEC) The CODEC is required to transmit and receive compressed video signals.

Cognitive learning Means by which a learner gains new knowledge through memory, reasoning, or evaluation.

Compact disc read-only memory (CD-ROM) Very large amount of digital data can be stored on a single disk.

Convergence The idea that all telephone, video, and computer equipment will be based on a digital format and housed into one unit, making their previous distinctions disappear.

Copyright   The legal right of ownership of intellectual property. To register to protect against infringement, write to: Register of Copyrights, Library of Congress, Washington, DC 20559.

CUSeeMe   A computer software package developed by Cornell University to allow audio and video transmission over the Internet.

Database   A clearly defined set of information or data for a specified purpose. Categories are established, and data are entered consistently into these categories.

Desktop video   Camera and software systems that allow videoconferencing among computers on a network.

Digital   Describes electronic technology that generates, stores, and processes data in terms of two states: positive and nonpositive. Positive is expressed by the number 1 and nonpositive by the number 0. Data transmitted or stored with digital technology is expressed as a string of 1s and 0s. Prior to digital technology, analog technology was used to convey data as electronic signals of varying frequency or amplitude that are added to carrier waves of a given frequency.

Direct broadcast satellite (DBS)   Satellites providing direct-to-home transmissions.

Dish   *See* Parabolic antenna.

Distance learning   An instructional setting in which the learner is removed in space and/or time from the source of the instruction.

Distributed learning   Instructors and students are located in different places, and instruction is designed so that learning is independent of time and place.

Downlinking   The retransmission of a signal from a satellite transponder back to Earth, where it is received by ground stations.

Earth station   Ground terminal that includes an antenna and associated electronic components such as a downconverter and low-noise amplifier (used to strengthen the weak signal). Used to receive, transmit, and process communications via satellite.

Electronic commerce   A new way of doing business that includes, but is not limited to, conducting commerce on the World Wide Web.

Electronic mail   Use of computers and network to send messages using standard protocols such as TCP/IP SMTP (Transmission Control Protocol/Internet Protocol Standard Mail Transfer Protocol).

FAQ   Frequently asked questions.

High-definition television (HDTV)   A standard that, if ever achieved, will provide resolution of 35-mm slide on television. Should not be confused with standard digital television (SDTV).

Hypertext Markup Language (HTML)   Used in preparing documents for the World Wide Web.

Integrated services digital network (ISDN)   An international telecommunications standard that will allow telephone lines to carry voice, video, and data.

Internet   A worldwide computer network of networks. It is made up of thousands of separately administered networks of many sizes and styles.

Ka band   Frequency spectrum from 20 to 30 GHz allocated to satellite communications. Mostly used for demonstration or experimental satellite communications.

Ku band   Frequency band from 10 to 20 GHz. Initially used for satellite communications by the European market. Less likelihood of interference from terrestrial microwave communications. However, the Ku and Ka bands are disadvantaged by the fact that rain can wash out or weaken the signal.

LAN   Local area network.

Learner centered　Distance education focused on the learner's needs rather than those of the instructor. It is usually very interactive.

LEO　Low Earth-orbiting satellite.

Lifelong learning　The concept that education is a process that lasts throughout one's lifetime, that there is a need through all stages of one's life to learn.

Listserv　A special interest discussion group corresponding using e-mail or an online learning environment.

Narrowband　A transmission medium or channel with a single voice channel (with a carrier wave of a certain modulated frequency).

Parabolic antenna　Shape of the satellite earth station dish that focuses the weak microwave signal, striking the surface of the dish onto a single focal point in front of the dish (i.e., on the feedhorn). Also called dish.

Passive learning　Learners are viewed as empty receptacles to be filled with knowledge. Instructors speak and students listen.

Point-to-point　Transmission of a television signal from one point to another.

Protocol　A formal set of rules or procedures by which computers communicate with each other and transfer information.

Satellite　An Earth-orbiting device capable of receiving and delivering voice, video, and data over a long distance called footprint.

Search engines　Tools used to search the Internet for information. Different search engines use different strategies for searching. Examples of commonly used search engines are Alta Vista, Lycos, Yahoo!, and Excite.

Synchronous　At the same time.

Teleconference　A multilocation, multiperson electronic conference using one or a combination of audio, computer, or slow-scan video systems. Videoconferencing is a form of teleconference.

Transponder　Collective term for the various components aboard a satellite—receiver, transmitter, and antenna—that form a single repeater channel.

Uniform resource locator (URL)　Standard address used for material located on the World Wide Web.

Uplink　Signal directed from an earth transmit station to a satellite.

Uplinking　Transmission of signals from the ground station to the satellite.

WebTV　Convergence of television with access to the World Wide Web.

Wideband　A transmission medium or channel that has a wider bandwidth than one voice channel (with a carrier wave of a certain modulated frequency).

9.9　Helpful URLs

American Distance Education Consortium, *http://www.adec.edu*
American Center for the Study of Distance Education, *http://www.ed.psu.edu/ACSDE/*
American Society for Training and Development, *http://www.astd.org*
Association for Educational Communication and Technology, *http://www.aect.org*
Asynchronous Learning Networks, *http://www.aln.org*
California Distance Learning Project, *http://www.otan.dni.us/cdlp/*
Commonwealth of Learning, *http://www.col.org*
International Council for Open and Distance Education, *http://www.icde.org*
Interactive Multimedia & Collaborative Communication Alliance, *http://www.imcca.org*

Lucent Technologies—Center for Excellence in Distance Learning, *http://www.lucent.com/cedl/*

Open University, International Centre for Distance Learning, *http://www-icdl.open.ac.uk*

Pacbell Education First, *http://www.kn.pacbell.com/wired/*

Selecting Technologies for Distance Education, *http://labweb.soemadison.wisc.edu/*

Sunsite—North Carolina—The Wonders of Hypertext, *http://sunsite.unc.edu/edweb/web.hypertext.html*

United States Distance Learning Association, *http://www.usdla.org*

University of North Carolina—William Graves Collection in Distance Education, *http://ils.unc.edu/disted/resources.html*

University of Texas Distance Education Sources and Resources, *http://www.utexas.edu/cc/cit/resources/dist_ed.html*

University of Wisconsin—Extension Distance Education Clearinghouse, *http://www.uwex.edu/disted/home.html*

World Lecture Hall, *http://www.utexas.edu/world/lecture*

Endnotes

1. Drucker, P. (1994). "The Age of Social Transformation," *Atlantic Monthly* (November).
2. Heinrich, R. M., M. Molenda, and J. D. Russell. (1989). *Instructional Media and New Technologies of Learning,* 3rd ed. New York: Macmillan.
3. Cyrs, T. E., and E. D. Conway. (1997). *Teaching at a Distance with the Merging Technologies.* Las Cruces, NM: Center for Educational Development, New Mexico State University.
4. Excellent resources for learning more about these tools can be found on the ADEC Distance Education homepage *(http://www.adec.edu)* or within the University of Wisconsin Distance Education Clearinghouse *(http://www.uwex.edu/disted).*
5. Seligman, D. (November 1992). "The Comparative Nature of Quality: Distance Education in the Developing World." Paper presented at the World Conference of the International Council for Distance Education, Bangkok, Thailand.
6. Giltrow, David, educational technology consultant, Santa Fe, NM.
7. Id.
8. Id.
9. Saba, F. (April 2000). *Distance Education Report,* San Diego, CA.
10. Provided by Thomas Fox McManus, mcmanus@mail.utexas.edu.

Suggested Readings

Journals and Newsletters

The American Journal of Distance Education, American Center for the Study of Distance Education, College of Education, The Pennsylvania State University, 403 South Allen Street, Suite 206, University Park, PA 16801–5202.

Distance Education Report, Farhad Saba, 8680 Navajo Road, Suite 102–151, San Diego, CA 92119.

Distance Education & Training National Newsletter, Bob Spencer, Athabassca University, Box 10,000, Athabassca, Alberta, Canada.

Electronic Commerce Advisor, Warren Gorham & Lamont, 31 St. James Avenue, Boston, MA 02116 (published bimonthly)

Journal of Distance Education, CADE Secretariat, 151 Slater Street, Ottawa, Ontario, KIP 5N1 Canada.

Journals in Distance Education, http://www-icdl.open.ac.uk/.

Books

1998 Consumer Reports Buying Guide ("The Future of Television") Yonkers, NY: Consumers Union.

Duning, B. S., M. J. Van Kekerix, and L. Zaborowski. (1993). *Reaching Learners through Telecommunications.* San Francisco: Jossey-Bass.

Donald Hanna & Associates. (2000). *Higher Education in an Era of Digital Competition.* Madison, WI: Atwood Publishing.

Kolb, D. A., I. M. Rubin, and J. M. McIntyre. (1984). *Organizational Psychology: An Experiential Approach to Organizational Behavior.* Englewood Cliffs, NJ: Prentice Hall.

Krebs, A. (1998). *The Distance Learning Funding Sourcebook,* 4th ed. Dubuque, IA: Kendall/Hunt Publishing.

Moore, M. G., and G. Kearsley. (1996). *Distance Education: A System View.* Belmont, CA: Wadsworth Publishing Co.

Moore, M. G., and M. M. Thompson, with A. B. Quigley, G. C. Car, and G. G. Goff. (1990). *The Effects of Distance Learning: A Summary of the Literature.* Research Monograph No. 1. University Park, PA: Pennsylvania State University, American Center for the Study of Distance Education.

Negroponte, N. (1995). *Being Digital.* New York: Vintage Books, Random House, Inc.

Tapscott, D. (1996). *The Digital Economy.* New York: McGraw-Hill.

Verduin, J. R., and T. A. Clark. (1991). *Distance Education: The Foundations of Effective Practice.* San Francisco: Jossey-Bass.

Willis, B. (1993). *Distance Education: A Practical Guide.* Englewood Cliffs, NJ: Educational Technology Publications.

▼ 10 Internet Strategy for Nonprofits

MARLENE FOX-MCINTYRE, PRINCIPAL
Athene, Inc.

10.1 Introduction

Access to the Internet continues to grow. Since the last printing of this book, Internet access is easier, faster, and more ubiquitous than ever. People who use the Internet are becoming much more sophisticated in the way they use the Internet and in the services they demand from it. It is no longer enough to offer static content for larger organizations. Users expect to see custom content based on their roles within the organization. This chapter will delve into some of the ways an organization can meet some of those needs for custom content.

Any organization, no matter how small, should be making use of the Internet to its maximum capability. Larger organizations should use the Internet not only to get their message out, but to get work done, increase revenues, provide better services to members and constituencies, and streamline day-to-day administrative functions. The question is no longer whether to go online, but how to best leverage the Internet to compete effectively for a visitor's time, attention, and money.

There are many exciting new ways Internet technology can be leveraged to maximize your effectiveness and competitive edge in your market area. This is not a "how-to" manual on all the tools available to get you to your goals, although there are a few general pointers on overall design. Rather, this chapter will get you thinking about how you want to direct the development of your Web site from a management standpoint. This edition gives special attention to supporting your volunteers.

Also new this year, a special Web site has been created to collect the perspectives, lessons learned, and opinions of nonprofit organizations. This new site is located at *www.nonprofitsurvey.com.* As the site develops, we will be asking nonprofits to participate in surveys.

10.2 *Internet Components*

(A) DOMAIN NAME

A trademarked domain name reinforces your name recognition and makes it easier for people to find you. An example of an easily recognizable domain name is *www.red-cross.org.* Many people will try to type in your organization name or acronym as a first stab at finding you. Make it easy for them to succeed. You may want to register several versions of your organization name and have them all point to the same Web site. That helps you collect visitors even if they have differing opinions on what should logically be your domain. For example, the Navy Mutual Aid Association is registered as *www.navymutual.org.* However, it can also be found under *www.navymutual.com.* Recently, it was also able to register as *www.nmaa.org* when the previous domain name holder let its registration lapse—intentionally or otherwise. This serves as a reminder to check for availability of desired domains frequently. Even if they are registered to another organization today, they could very well become available at some time in the future. Note that desirable domain names will not be available for long and should be locked down immediately. You should register your domain name as a trademark or service mark, to further protect it from legal challenges.

(B) WEB SITE

This will be your most visible Internet component and require the most effort to manage. However, a Web site alone will not cover all the bases, especially when it comes to getting attention on emerging events. Once your clients come to your site, however, all the information and services they need should be available, in an easy-to-use format.

(C) DISCUSSION GROUPS

Discussion groups are impossible to fully control and should be avoided unless you can assume the risk and commit the staff to monitor all postings as they occur. Discussion groups are generally appropriate only for activist groups.

(D) SECURE ELECTRONIC COMMERCE

Secure online credit card transactions are useful for collecting dues, donations, and other revenues.

(E) AUTOMATED E-MAIL COMMUNICATIONS

Send mass e-mails to your client base to alert them to important emerging events, remind them to renew memberships, or report back on your successes and ongoing needs. Keep your organization visible to your clients, and remind them to visit your Web site often for more complete information and services. Supplemental e-mail reinforces your image as an

Internet resource that is worth visiting. You can create mailing lists from your existing client database or use online services to help you create and manage your mailing lists.

(i) Mass E-Mail Software

Software like Mail King can create customized e-mails for your clients, filter and sort your lists based on your selection criteria, and generate the messages. For under $100, it is a very useful tool to have in your bag.

(ii) Online E-Mail List Services

Online services can help you create and manage e-mail lists. One example is Web Site Post Office. They have a free service that allows you to collect e-mail addresses and other data from visitors to your site. Once they sign up to your mailing list, you can send them monthly newsletters and the like with the confidence that they want and expect your mailings. You can also develop this capability in-house with the proper talent. However, if your organization is small, this free service is a good place to start.

(F) VOICE COMMUNICATION VIA INTERNET ACCESS

Use the Internet to patch through telephone calls to remote sites. The quality is inferior to direct telephone contact in most cases, but it may be a solution to communications needs in locations where telephone calls are expensive and Internet access is available. The Internet is even making inroads to developing nations. Before dismissing the Internet as not applicable to your remote locations, investigate the status of Internet access in your areas.

10.3 Planning the Web Site

(A) BUSINESS PROCESSES

Your Internet presence should support one or more of the following planks of your organization's business processes:

- *Directly accomplish mission objectives.* The Web site could be a vehicle to directly support mission objectives that involve the transfer of information. Examples: public awareness campaigns, lobbying efforts.
- *Market to existing and potential clients.* Example: professional associations.
- *Streamline administrative processes and minimize overhead.* Example: Online forms.
- *Generate revenue.* Examples: fund raising, planned giving, sales drives.
- *Research and information gathering/dissemination.* Example: bills in Congress.

This chapter will touch on all these major areas and go into added depth on supporting the volunteers. Every aspect of Internet implementation should support one of these overarching requirements. Keeping the focus on marketing, mission goals, and reducing administrative overhead will help eliminate fluff and build in the functionality that is the mark of a quality, competitive online presence. This section provides a short list of some of the elements that a Web site might need, depending on the agency's particular mission.

In determining how to use the Internet to support the nonprofit's mission, the place to start is with a review of the agency mission statement and vision statement. The mission statement should be a concise statement that describes the difference the organization intends to make on the outside world, without regard to specific means to the ends. The vision statement expands on the mission statement by describing how the organization will accomplish its mission in the years ahead, and how its place in the world will evolve. Whereas the mission statement provides a clear sense of purpose, the vision statement focuses the efforts of the organization on specific strategies and outcomes.

The way you design your Internet presence should be structured on this foundation. By designing from the mission and vision, the agency is better able to build an integrated Web presence that reflects its character and improves its ability to carry out the mission. The Internet strategy should address all aspects of the Internet, including a Web site, e-mail, bulletin boards, and private intranets. The agency may choose not to implement all elements, but they should be considered for their potential in a systematic way.

(B)   SITE LAYOUT

When planning the Web site, the first step is to clearly define the goals, objectives, and target audience for the site. The site should reflect the organization's identity, philosophy, and message on a deeper level, reflecting the organization's uniqueness and special challenges. An initial "welcome" paragraph helps to set the tone, and tie-ins to this message can be used to knit the various subsections of the site.

The next stage is to identify and prioritize high-level goals for the Web site. It is important to build consensus on these priorities, to ensure that all major departments are accurately represented. As soon as high-level goals have been defined, the Web site look and feel—the style—must be designed. Is it educational? Professional? Upbeat? Friendly?

Based on the top-level goals and look and feel, a style guide should be developed. A style guide might include a color scheme; use of corporate logos, marks, and images; style of graphics art to be developed (line art, photos, nature images, etc.); and type of multimedia that might be appropriate.

Next, content is developed. A well-designed, coherent site structure is a must. The front page of the Web site should be clean and crisply presented, with plenty of white space for easier viewing. Use dark text on light backgrounds—never the reverse. Text should be limited to key ideas and top-level information. Major departments or organization functions should be grouped into site modules with links directly accessible from the front page and from other secondary pages as well. Corporate branding should be reinforced throughout the site, and should be consistent with printed material.

Once basic content has been developed, advanced features such as counters, forms, mapped images, and animated graphics may be added. All advanced features should be carefully crafted to meet organization needs. Appropriate use of advanced features gives the site a polished look but, if overdone, makes a site slow to download and gives it a cluttered look.

10.4   *Mission Accomplishment*

When planning an Internet Web site, keep in mind the organization's mission or goals. Every aspect of its Internet presence should support at least one mission goal, and some elements will cross the boundaries of several organizational goals. Some of the features in the agency's Web site might include:

- A calendar of ongoing and one-time events
- Event registration
- Survey forms and results

(A) CALENDAR

The Web site might need only one calendar or support multiple calendars for local chapters. Small organizations will do fine with a straight HTML (static) calendar, but larger organizations with many events should invest in a more feature-rich calendar. A full-feature calendar software program will allow visitors to search for events by topic as well as location and date. These calendars should be password protected for updates, so only authorized personnel can add or change events. There are several commercial calendar products for sale. One such product is PerlCal, at *http://www.perlcal.com*. This is a very nice package that provides a variety of formats and features, but it does take a small amount of programming to tailor it for the organization use.

(B) EVENT REGISTRATION

If the agency has regular conferences or other events, it should be easy for clients to sign up. The calendar will have basic information about the event's date, location, and purpose, but big events require better publicity and administrative support. Develop a module on each upcoming major event, to include an agenda, a list of speakers with photos and biographies, a description of the locale, directions to the hotel or conference facilities, and spouses' programs. Provide detailed information about all upcoming conferences well in advance, and provide online registration forms for the conference, hotel, and any special trips or outings planned for the group. Take advantage of secure online credit card transaction technology to collect payment in full upon registration. The more an agency's visitors know about an event, the more likely they are to make the right decision and show up!

(C) ADVOCACY AND ACTIVISM

One of the most effective ways the Internet has been used by nonprofits is in the arena of issue advocacy.

(i) Targeted Mass E-Mail

Even a very small organization with a miniscule operating budget can reach thousands—or hundreds of thousands—of potential supporters in a matter of hours. If an agency already has a client database, e-mail addresses can be added to its data collection. Once the agency has collected e-mail addresses, it can send action e-mails to constituents when their direct involvement is needed to support or oppose an issue, such as pending legislation. The following excerpt from the *Congressional Quarterly* illustrates this concept in practice:

> *When President Clinton was deciding whether to set aside 1.7 million acres of federal land in Utah as a national monument in the summer of 1996, a little-known group called the Southern Utah Wilderness Alliance shifted into high gear. Alerting environmental supporters from coast to coast through a World Wide Web Internet site (www.sura.org) and an electronic mailing list, the alliance generated as many as several thousand calls in sup-*

port of the idea to the White House switchboard. Within two weeks, Clinton announced the creation of the Grand Staircase–Escalante National Monument.[1]

(ii) Web Site Advocacy Content

An agency should post updates on its activities, such as national or international conventions, keeping constituents up to date with daily feeds when necessary, and telling them what they can do to help—call their legislator, organize local support, or provide financial or volunteer assistance.

The agency may want to post online surveys, with real-time updates of survey results. This is useful when you are developing consensus on an issue or collecting data to support a position on an issue when advocating for a constituency. Questions asked in your survey might be a combination of general ideas and suggestions, but they should also include very specific questions about the delivery of services and goods. Keep in mind that the longer the survey, the less likely it is that it will be fully completed by all participants. Time to complete your survey should be limited to five minutes or less in most cases. An alternative to a lengthy questionnaire is a single-question survey that changes every month. Place this single-question survey on your front page for maximum exposure. Publishing the results to past surveys in a link from the front page will keep your visitors motivated to continue participating in the surveys. An example of single-question surveys is located on the Fleet Reserve Association homepage at *http://www.fra.org.* Their magazine *On Watch* is published both in hard copy and reproduced electronically on the Web site. This magazine almost always includes one or two questions for members to answer, under the heading "You Said." Results are published in both the hard copy and online versions of the magazine. The Fleet Reserve Association uses the results of these surveys to further lobbying efforts with the U.S. Congress. This is a very easily implemented static survey/results page. However, a little additional up-front design can produce an interactive survey that immediately accepts survey inputs and updates the results.

The agency should consider posting template letters to target legislators for clients to print, complete, and mail. When asking constituents to contact legislators, they should use snail mail, fax, or telephone, rather than e-mail. Many legislators are leery of e-mail because of past experiences with mass-generated e-mail from outside their district or state. Above and beyond this consideration, there is still no substitute for in-person visits, organized events, or the sound of the human voice.

The site should provide visitors with suggestions on how grassroots efforts can be organized and managed and should publish flyers that visitors or local offices can print, reproduce, and distribute.

One of the most famous examples of online advocacy is the anti-landmine campaign. In 1991, the Vietnam Veterans of America Foundation (VVAF) began an effort to ban the production, use, and stockpiling of landmines worldwide. A Vermont woman named Jody Williams was hired to coordinate the effort. Their main communications tools were telephone and fax in the early years of the campaign. When they switched to e-mail as their primary communications tool, the campaign picked up momentum. The coalition grew from 500 organizations in 1996 to over 1,000 nongovernmental organizations in 60 countries in 1997. Ms. Williams spent many long hours sending e-mail to countries around the globe, seeking support for the ban. During the 1997 treaty negotiations, each of the 11 committee members received daily updates, keeping them informed of what was going on in their countries. This helped committee members keep treaty negotiations on track. Updates were also posted to their Web site, helping get the word out to all constituents and possible supporters who were not receiving e-mail updates. As a result, an international treaty banning landmines was signed by 127 countries and became international law in March 1999.

According to Mary Wareham, ICBL Coordinator: "When you look at how far and how fast we've moved in the last year and a half, much of that is attributable to our means of communicating. ... And many people out there maintain their own distribution networks ... They'll forward the [coalition update] releases again" (see *http://cnn.com/ALLPOLITICS/1997/10/13/time/nobel.html*). Robert Muller, president of the VVAF, concurs, "The fact that we can move information around at immediate speed and low cost is the key to moving any massive group of people or organizations." Of course, the VVAF Web site keeps members up to date on the progress of the treaty, complementing the e-mail campaign. During the December 1997 signing of the landmine ban, supporters posted daily updates on the Web site.

(D)   COMBINING ONLINE ADVOCACY WITH TRADITIONAL MEDIA

To get the most out of an online advocacy effort, the agency should combine it with more traditional media. Especially when dealing with time-critical issues, it is useful to complement the online campaign with targeted mass e-mail, television, radio, and printed news. If an agency is advocating for (or against) pending legislation, it should not ask constituents to e-mail their legislators. Instead, they should call, fax, or write to them instead. It is too easy for overzealous organizations to send mass e-mail to Congress using fraudulent return addresses; as a result, many legislators are understandably wary of mass e-mail.

As powerful as online advocacy is, it exacerbates First Amendment conflicts that have plagued television, radio, and newspapers, particularly in the areas of privacy, due process, pornography, and issues of national security. On September 12, 1998, the U.S. Congress posted a devastating report via the Internet. This single document ignited a national moral crisis and led to the unthinkable: impeachment of the president. Although there is violent disagreement on the significance of the document, there is no question that the effect on the nation would have been different if it were not so universally and easily obtainable. It was announced on the television news networks, it was printed in full by major newspapers, and it was available for downloading at dozens of Web sites. CNN announced that its traffic that day was 2.5 times heavier than their previous record. The House Web site was so overloaded with traffic that the server failed and the site was taken down. The Speaker of the House, in a press conference two weeks later, acknowledged that Internet technology made the report available around the world instantly, and said that this pushed Congress to act much more than it would have in a previous age. In his own words, the entire process was forced into fast forward because of the pressure of the Internet.

(E)   EDUCATION

If an organization provides training to clients, it should consider adding distance learning to its Web site. This can be an effective and low-cost solution to training needs. Trainees can register for online courses and proceed through lessons and exams at their own pace or on a predetermined time table. The agency can track each trainee's progress through each course, exam results, classes successfully completed, and more. To combine the flexibility of distance learning with the rigor of monitored testing, the agency can still provide the lessons on the Web site and have the student travel to its testing center only when necessary for the exam.

(F) SPECIAL INFORMATION SERVICES

Many nonprofits contract for specific content tailored to their target market. Mothers Against Drunk Driving, for instance, includes on its Web site a guide to Congress, with tips on how to write to a legislator, an overview of the legislative process, and an online directory of state and national legislators. This congressional tie-in is actually produced by Capital Advantage, an online service that provides tailored Internet content for a fee.

There are a number of specialty information services that an agency can contract with to provide special information to clients. An example of this is FedNet *(www.fednet.net),* an online subscription service that provides streaming video and audio coverage of U.S. congressional events. When Congress is in session, audio transmissions are broadcast live and then archived for one week. Additional information includes congressional schedules, hearing topics, and witness lists.

(G) IMPROVING ACCESS TO SERVICES

One example of client services might be special needs counseling. If an organization provides counseling, either in person or by telephone, it might consider adding online counseling. It can be real-time interactive counseling with a rotating staff, or if resources are limited, it could be as simple as adding a counselor's e-mail address to the Web site.

Another example of online services is the Navy Mutual Aid Association's insurance needs analysis calculator (see *www.navymutual.org/calculator/index.html*). The visitor enters the data requested and the program calculates the amount of insurance needed by that individual. The results are customized with the individual's name and the date, and printed out on a single sheet of paper for later reference.

(H) ACTING AS AN INFORMATION CLEARINGHOUSE

The ability to promote knowledge of your cause or issue can be vastly expanded by providing your users with virtual libraries of issue-specific content. This can be done by building a new online library containing content that the nonprofit controls, building a portal site, or contracting with an existing content provider. Content providers fall into several categories, primarily known as portals and content aggregators.

(i) Portals

A portal is a search engine or Web site that directs visitors to Web sites that contain content relevant to their needs. General-interest portals are fairly nondiscriminating and are funded primarily through advertising on the page: banner ads, targeted messages, and positioning links to paying clients higher on the page. Corporate portals are tailored to the needs of business users and generally charge fees to use the service. These services are used to perform market research, gather intelligence on competitors, and cull large libraries for specific types of information.

The advantage of corporate portals is better search results with little or no advertising. These portals are focused on delivering high-quality content, using specific sources of information, such as periodicals or news archives that might not be easily accessible via the Web. Marginal data sources are generally excluded from these portals.

(ii) Content Aggregators

A content aggregator consolidates information from multiple sources, structures that information into a consistent format, and applies appropriate metatags such as keywords to the content. This value-added data is then resold to end users for a fee. When the user searches on keywords, the results appear consistent regardless of the source or original format of the data. Searches are also more efficient, since the topics and relevant keywords are already linked to each infomration source. Therefore, a search on "Health reform legislation" would return relevant results, rather than an unsorted list of every linked Web page containing that phrase.

The main disadvantage is that many smaller organizations are not able to afford the services. Large nonprofits may find that these content aggregators are worth the investment. A few examples of the many available commercial content providers are Lexus-Nexus, Dialog, Newspage, and Hoovers. Descriptions and Web addresses are provided at the end of this chapter.

10.5 Marketing

No organization can succeed, online or not, if it cannot market its value to the customer. In the case of a professional association, for example, potential members need to know what the benefits of membership are. In addition, members should be able to renew, and prospective members should be able to join, at the instant they make their decision.

The design of the Web site should center around the needs and expectations of clients. Primary marketing elements of a Web site should focus on building the client base, program development, and revenue.

(A) RETAINING EXISTING CLIENTS

The key to retaining an existing client base is customer satisfaction. Web site elements that will help keep a client base include:

- *Current news and information.* An agency's magazine or newspaper should be published online. It is not necessary to post all of it, but it should be current. Stale news is a sure sign of sloppy management. Issues should be archived as they are replaced. Over time, the agency will develop a useful library that clients can use for research into a particular topic. Individual news pages or issues can also be registered with the major search engines to increase visibility. Once several issues are out, a search engine can be added to the site. This helps clients quickly find the information they need and adds a professional touch to the library.
- *Targeted e-mail.* Periodically, perhaps monthly, the entire client base should be e-mailed with the top news of the hour, hot topics, or other information that they want or need. Agencies should not simply wait for them to come to the Web site, but rather go to them. If they have begun to drift away, this can

regain their attention. (*NOTE:* Don't confuse targeted e-mail with spam. Spam is mass e-mail transmitted for the purpose of soliciting, advertising, or harassing recipients. Spam is usually sent through third-party mail servers, that is, not the sending organization's primary mail server. Spam is usually shotgunned out to huge, disreputable mailing lists purchased from list sellers. It is not only a severe annoyance to the recipients, but the Internet service provider may drop the offender's account with no refund, and an organization can even get into legal troubles. Always give recipients a way to opt out of a mailing list. A standard way to do this is to direct recipients to return the e-mail with "remove" in the subject line. If you get these requests, honor them!)

- *Accountability.* Agencies should tell clients about recent successes. A charity should show how the money, goods, and labor donated are used.
- *Recognizing outstanding work.* If an organization gives out awards or recognition for outstanding clients, these should be included in the Web site. People thrive on attention!
- *Keeping track of clients.* There should be a page to allow members to send updated addresses and other contact information so they will not be lost the next time they move!
- *Feedback form.* Right from the outset, the Web site should have a mechanism for clients to let the agency know what they need and expect from that Web site. The feedback page could be as simple as a plain "Questions and Comments" form that generates an e-mail message. It could also be a more complex questionnaire with specific questions on planned or existing programs.

(B)   ATTRACTING NEW CLIENTS

This is the most obvious aspect of marketing and certainly a vital one. The agency's message must get across to clients in a clear and convincing format. An "About Our Organization" page is simply not enough.

(i)   Tour
A "walking tour" through the organization is an elegant way to introduce potential members, donors, or other visitors to an organization. The Web site should include a *brief* history of the organization, a tour of the organization today, and a synopsis of its vision for the future, all made interesting from the client standpoint. These pages should be brief and include a few good illustrations.

(ii)   News
The visitor should have access to some or all of the agency's online publications. The more interested visitors become in an organization, the more likely they are to join or contribute. If the main library is password protected, the most recent issues should be available to the general public. While magazines are a member benefit, they are also a big draw to potential members. When visitors come to a site repeatedly for news, they are much more likely to join because they are convinced that the agency provides a valuable service.

(iii) *Locator*

The site should help visitors locate a chapter near them, if the agency has chapters. The site can choose to use an image map (an image of the United States or globe with hot spots zooming in to local regions). Alternately, the visitor could find a chapter by typing the name of a city, state, or country to find the closest office. A good example of a chapter lookup can be found on the home page of the Salvation Army's Web site. They used a drop-down list of chapters by geographic area. Select the one you want to go to, and you are instantly transferred to that site. This method has an advantage over graphic maps in that it loads much faster and occupies less space on the screen.

(C) PROGRAM DEVELOPMENT

An organization may need to update its programs and services based on the changing needs of customers or to reflect changing laws or other outside factors. One way to determine what clients need most is to publish online surveys or questionnaires. The agency might publish a comprehensive survey or post new single-question polls each month. An example of a single-question poll with immediate feedback is located on CNN's Quick-Vote page, at *http://www.cnn.com.*

10.6 *Streamline Administration*

To make an organization operate more smoothly and efficiently, certain services should be available online to the client base. In addition, the agency may need to create an internal, or private, Web site, to support staff and employees.

(A) CLIENT DATA MANAGEMENT

Traditional administrative tasks such as updating member profiles should be streamlined. The organization can post an encrypted copy of its membership database online and allow members to access the information on file for their accounts: their mailing address, membership expiration date, beneficiaries on insurance plans, and so forth. By using a secure database, the agency can prevent members from accessing data they are not authorized to view. The primary database should not be linked to the Internet, because it is always possible for hackers to damage or destroy data. A copy should be posted instead. When a member updates a record, the online application should transmit or post an update request to the appropriate department for action. There are a number of packages and services available to choose from, with widely varying capabilities and price tags. An agency should shop around before selecting a solution for its needs. Key issues will be security, ease of use, flexibility, speed, and of course, cost.

(B) ONLINE FORMS LIBRARY

Most frequently used forms should be provided in a consolidated location on the Web site. The agency should also link to appropriate forms from any pages that refer to them. A product called Adobe Acrobat Distiller makes it easy to produce read-only forms that the user can complete and fax or mail back. It is also possible, but much more difficult, to post Acrobat forms that can be completed and returned electronically.

10.7   Generate Revenue

(A)   ONLINE GIVING

If an organization accepts donations, it absolutely wants to capture those dollars when the giver is ready to make the contribution. The exchange should not be delayed because of the ever-present threat that the donor will change his or her mind, lose interest, or just forget to follow through. Therefore, the agency should establish a secure means of giving, via credit card, over the Internet. Online giving is already an established feature of quite a few nonprofits. An excellent example is the Red Cross at *http://www.redcross.org*. Virtually every page on its site contains a link to the donations page. It is easy to find out how to donate money or time, and one can make the donation practically the moment the decision to give is made.

(B)   PLANNED GIVING

The Web site can help clients plan for the future by showing them why planned giving is beneficial to them and to the organization. Clients should be able to sign up immediately for a meeting with a representative to assist them in making the necessary arrangements. There could even be a program to show them how a gift made to a trust can grow over time, and how much could be done with their gift. There should be choices (e.g., estate planning, long-term-level giving via automatic bank withdrawals). No matter how large or small their net worth, they can participate at a level that is comfortable for them and can support worthwhile activities.

(C)   ONLINE SALES

If an agency sells goods or services, these should be available online. Memorabilia, holiday greeting cards, and snack foods can all be sold to a much wider market than the agency now has access to. If the agency has annual fund raisers, auctions, sales drives, or telethons, these activities should be integrated into the Web site. People could be encouraged to bid over the Internet, make matching donations, even win prizes online in real time. There is no end to the creative ways to leverage the Internet to enhance sales and revenues.

For a small site or where the agency does not wish to be bothered with the overhead involved in managing an online store, the agency might consider affiliating with an established online merchant. There are several ways for the agency to implement this type of program:

- Create its own Web page with links to specific products on the merchant's site
- Link directly to the merchant site or subject area
- Load the merchant's search engine forms on its own site

The advantage is that the costs, risks, and administrative burden of operating a sales site are eliminated. Typically, an organization is paid a commission on the sales generated from the Web site. Commissions generally range from 3 to 15 percent for bookstores, frequently higher for fund-raising merchandise such as candy. There should be no charge to set up an account with the merchant. The merchant processes the order, ships the merchandise, bills the customer, and pays you the commission. In exchange, they get more sales and better visibility with an agency's customers. Not all merchants have the same capabilities or offer the same percentages, so it pays to shop around. As an example, the Not-for-profit Resource Center publishes a list of recommended references, with links to each book on Amazon.com *(http://not-for-profit.org/books.htm)*. Amazon.com now pays up to a 15 percent commission.

(D)   ADVERTISING

Banner ads and "click-throughs" are frequently used to generate cash for organizations of all sizes. This type of revenue enhancement is generally considered tacky and unprofessional unless properly managed. A more professional approach is to dedicate a page (or module) to "Corporate Sponsors." That page may feature the logos of one or more sponsors with a click-through to their site. It is necessary to obtain the sponsor's permission to use their corporate logo or other branding in order to comply with trademark laws. Also, it is imperative that these linked sites not contain pornography or other unwelcome material and that they not link to any such sites. This does not mean a cursory scan of the site, but a thorough review of all links contained within that site. Even secondary links to degenerate materials on linked sites amounts to condoning that material. That not only reflects very poorly on the organization, but could lead to legal liability as well, particularly in the case of nonprofits that provide services to minor children.

If the nonprofit allows sponsors to provide banner ads, they should be screened for appropriateness. If the unspoken message presented by the banner in any way undermines the organization's image, it should be rejected out of hand.

10.8   Support Your Volunteers

This section applies to nonprofit organizations that use volunteers to deliver services to the client market. Managing an organization that uses volunteers requires that management address their special needs and provide leadership in a meaningful direction. Nonprofit boards too often ignore their volunteer programs. This demeans the importance of volunteers and their efforts and undermines the organization's ability to deliver services in the most appropriate way. Most boards fail to devote systemic attention to service volunteers and the volunteer program commensurate with their actual or potential importance and contribution to the agency.[2]

An organization's Web site can go a long way in providing volunteers with the leadership, tools, skills, and other resources they need to do their best. The volunteer cadre is sufficiently vital to the service/volunteer agency that they warrant their own module within the Web site. As with all major modules, the "Volunteer Web" should be easy to find from the top level of your Web site. The Volunteer Web should be as well thought out, organized, and constructed as the public site. All major sections should be clearly identified at the top level of the site. Additionally, a word-search feature should be provided to help volunteers find the information they need without lost time sifting through the site.

The content and structure of your Volunteer Web can affect not only volunteer morale and a sense of "includedness" but can also increase volunteer effectiveness, supplement training programs, and even help protect the agency from lawsuits brought about by injured volunteers or clients.

(A) VOLUNTEER WEB SITE CORE CONTENT

The volunteer Web site should, at a minimum, contain the following five elements:

1. Mission and vision for the volunteer corps
2. Volunteer opportunities and challenges
3. Volunteer qualification requirements, if any
4. Policies and procedures developed for volunteer corps guidance
5. Volunteer feedback

Additional elements might include:

- Volunteer sign-in
- Monthly message from the Director of Volunteer Services (This might also be e-mailed to all volunteers as an additional way of communicating with the volunteers.)
- Opportunities to volunteer
- Vacancy announcements for hard-to-place volunteer positions
- Event registration
- Online training for volunteers
- Volunteer surveys
- New volunteer sign-up and prescreening
- Volunteer recognition

If the Web site is going to include a login for member volunteers, there should be a public-access volunteer module as well. The public-access portion should include the mission and vision statement, volunteer opportunities, testimonials, top-level screening requirements, and a new-volunteer sign-up form.

(B) VOLUNTEER LOGIN

Volunteers should be required to log on to the Volunteer Web, so that the agency can audit each volunteer's usage of the Web site. No, this isn't 1984. But the agency does have a vested interest in ensuring that all volunteers read key documents, such as the mission statement, standard operating procedures, and applicable policies. Volunteers should read mandatory documents and *confirm* that they have read and understood each document. Volunteers who do not do this electronically via the Web can still sign off on paper that they have read the required documents, but an electronic audit trail is easier to track, back up, and search quickly.

Clear, legally acceptable evidence that you have acted responsibly in training, informing, and supporting your volunteers will be invaluable to the agency in the event of a lawsuit.

(C) MISSION AND VISION FOR THE VOLUNTEER PROGRAM

If an agency has a volunteer program, it should have a written mission and vision for the volunteer corps. This mission and vision statement should be prominently placed within the Volunteer Web. For example, the nonprofit might place a one-sentence synopsis of the mission and a paragraph on the vision, right on the front page of the volunteer site, with links to detailed mission and vision.

If the organization mission statement and vision for the organization and for the volunteer program need to be revised, the input of the board, management, paid staff, and volunteers should be sought. The Web site and mass e-mail is an efficient method of collecting feedback from all participants. Data collected this way can be assimilated into a database for analysis and reporting purposes, or, if there is only a small amount of feedback, responses may be handled individually.

(D) VOLUNTEER OPPORTUNITIES

Both the public and member sections of the Volunteer Web should address opportunities for volunteering within the organization. The public site may have a more general introduction to volunteer work, whereas the member site may have a more extensive listing of where volunteers are needed, specific jobs that need to be filled, and skills/experience required for each. Hard-to-fill volunteer positions are top candidates for posting on the member Volunteer Web for maximum exposure. As part of this section, there should be a volunteer job application form, so that an interested member volunteer can register his or her interest in the job and begin any application process required by the organization.

(E) VOLUNTEER SCREENING REQUIREMENTS

If the organization has special requirements for its volunteers, then it would be helpful to post those criteria on the public portion of the Web site. This may help potential volunteers to self-screen before applying for certain volunteer work. For example, organizations that work with children would likely require a police background check for each application. An applicant with a police record might therefore be persuaded to not bother applying.

(F) VOLUNTEER POLICIES AND PROCEDURES

Many organizations document their standard operating procedures to minimize the exposure to risk factors for their volunteers. These policies and procedures should be a high priority for posting on the Volunteer Web. In some cases, it is necessary to keep a formal record of key policies and procedures that the volunteers have read and understood. If this is the case, then the volunteers should be required to log in to the site to access the library. This will allow the Web administrator to maintain an audit trail of opened documents by user. After reading each key document, volunteers should be prompted to respond whether they have fully read and understood the material.

(G) VOLUNTEER FEEDBACK

Collecting volunteer feedback on programs and services can help the agency find problems and opportunities invisible to senior management. Volunteers on the front line have unique perspectives on how services can be delivered more effectively, what kinds of problems limit their effectiveness, and what kinds of additional or related services would be especially valuable to the client base.

If the organization is large and spread across a wide geographical area, it may be useful to collect input via e-mail or on the agency's public or private Web site. If the agency elects to use the public Web site to gather input, there is also the option of collecting input from the client base or target recipients of the agency's services. In addition to collecting visitor-entered data, the survey form can collect information about the visitor's domain, country of origin, type of browser used, and time of access. This information can prove useful in determining where the agency's services are wanted or needed most.

(H) VOLUNTEER TRAINING

In Chapter 36, "Risk Management in Volunteer Programs," Linda Graff poses the question "What are the worst things that you can imagine going wrong in your volunteer department, or because of the involvement of volunteers at your organization?" It does not take a great deal of thought to come up with past horror stories or possible worst case scenarios. Injury, theft, client (or volunteer) abuse, and damage to the agency's reputation are all possible consequences of deploying ill-prepared volunteers. Some of the examples of "real-life" situations listed in that chapter are quite alarming.

Volunteer training programs, essential in service organizations, can often be supplemented with online training, particularly when the organization is too far-flung to depend on onsite training. Volunteer training and information dissemination can begin with posting current procedures and guidelines on the Volunteer Web, as mentioned above.

A very basic online training program might include electronic versions of all manuals and reference materials in a library module. As the Volunteer Web is further developed, slideshow presentations, video clips, "programmed learning," and interactive quizzes may be added, depending on the level of training required for specific volunteer jobs. Volunteers who complete a set of learning materials or online exams might be recognized on the site as having achieved a higher level of excellence within the organziation, or qualify for higher levels of responsibility.

(I) NEW VOLUNTEER SIGN-UP AND PRESCREENING

Service organizations are constantly on the lookout for qualified volunteers, and the Internet is one way to attract qualified—and not-so-qualified—volunteers. The savvy agency will employ some level of applicant prescreening in conjunction with the standard "feedback form." The volunteer initial interest application form should collect standard data such as the applicant's name, address, and so on. It is a simple matter to add a few questions about the background, skills, goals, and expectations of the potential volunteer. Incomplete or sloppy responses will help quickly weed out less serious applicants. The information provided can be kept on file to assist with the interview or other follow-up processes. It is much more efficient to use this type of online application form than merely requesting potential applicants to e-mail you directly. This is because you control not only the format but also the content that you receive back from the applicant. Incomplete forms may require the applicant to go back to the incomplete fields and fill them in before submitting the application. Direct e-mail has no such error checking.

(J) COMMUNICATING WITH VOLUNTEERS

Volunteers who are spread over a wide geographic area need an efficient, convenient way to communicate with the management, peers, and clients. The way in which this communication is handled may depend on the circumstance. E-mail will probably suffice for most needs. But there may be cases in which a more formal arrangement is needed. Online discussions by topic are frequently useful in problem solving, document revision, and other group efforts.

10.9 Lobbying

(A) MEMBER SURVEYS

Member surveys are a powerful tool to collect and document constituent needs and priorities. Questions asked in your survey might be a combination of general ideas and suggestions, but they should also include very specific questions about the delivery of services and goods. Keep in mind that the longer the survey, the less likely it is that it will be fully completed by all participants. Time to complete your survey should be limited to five minutes or less in most cases. An alternative to a lengthy questionnaire is a single-question survey that changes every month. Place this single-question survey on your front page for maximum exposure. Publishing the results to past surveys in a link from the front page will keep your visitors motivated to continue participating in the surveys. An example of single-question surveys is located on *http://abcnews.go.com*, which posts questions and instantly displays current survey results as soon as visitors submit their votes. They motivate visitors to vote both by providing instant feedback and by wording the questions in a provocative way. For instance, one question asked: "Hillary Rodham Clinton's assertion that her husband's infidelity was due to childhood abuse is … a legitimate explanation … a lame excuse." This is an obvious attempt to grab a visitor's attention by eliciting a strong emotional response, whether in agreement or disagreement.

(B) CONGRESSIONAL DATABASES

Third-party congressional databases provide custom content to support the organization's lobbying and research efforts. CapWeb contains directories of U.S. and state legislators, current and pending legislation, and letter templates that constituents can use to generate printed, faxed, or e-mailed letters to their selected representatives at the national or state level. Examples of congressional resources include CapWeb, Lexus-Nexus, and Thomas.

10.10 Internet Security

Internet security is not taken nearly as seriously as it warrants. According to the Computer Security Research Institute's fifth annual "Computer Crime and Security Survey," 90 percent of 273 corporations and government agencies surveyed had suffered security breaches in the past year.

> *…the Internet suffers from severe security-related problems. Sites that ignore these problems face some significant risk that they will be attacked by intruders and that they may provide intruders with a staging ground for attacks on other networks. Even sites that do observe good security practices face problems with new vulnerabilities in networking software and the persistence of some intruders.*

Some of the problems with Internet security are a result of inherent vulnerabilities in the services (and the protocols that the services implement), while others are a result of host configuration and access controls that are poorly implemented or overly complex to administer. Additionally, the role and importance of system management is often short-changed in job descriptions, resulting in many administrators being, at best, part-time and poorly prepared. This is further aggravated by the tremendous growth of the Internet and how the Internet is used; businesses and agencies now depend on the Internet (often more than they realize) for communications and research and thus have much more to lose if their sites are attacked.[3]

There are *many* ways in which a site, or an entire agency network, can be infiltrated. Examples of system infiltration methods are listed below. Note that this is NOT a definitive list, but only a partial sampling!

(A)   HACKERS

Hackers can and do attack nonprofit Web sites, just as they attack government, academic, and for-profit sites. Computer networks are more often than not attacked from within the organization, but the Internet has opened up whole new worlds of hacking opportunities. Prime examples include Trojan horse shareware programs and e-mail viruses, the like of which indiscriminately attack hundreds or thousands of sites at once, vastly increasing the global threat over the old one-at-a-time attack.

Hackers can be motivated to infiltrate your Web site and connected computers for many reasons ranging from political ideology *(hactivists)*, personal greed, or childish desires for attention. At a minimum, the nonprofit could suffer temporary embarrassment and eroded credibility if the Web site is replaced overnight by dancing monkeys, pornography, or an opponent's political tirade. At worst, you could provide your hacker with detailed confidential information about your organization, staff, and volunteers.

How you protect against hackers will depend largely on the type of information on your Web site and whether your Web site is connected in any way with your offline computer base. If you have only a simple static Web site with no confidential information, simply making your files "read only" is generally sufficient. If you plan to post sensitive information, hire a professional firm to independently test the system architecture to identify weaknesses and make recommendations on protecting it from attack. Your Web developer and service provider should not provide these services directly, because there will be an inherent conflict of interest.

(B)   INTERNAL ATTACKS

The FBI estimates that *insiders* are responsible for at least four out of five hacks in the United States. There are several steps you can take to prevent and address hacks. Mark Grossman, an attorney specializing in computer and Internet law, recommends placing a banner or opening message on all computers warning that employee computer use is subject to monitoring. The purpose is to strengthen your legal position in the event that you have to pursue a criminal charge against a hacker, whether internal or external. This simple action helps to deflect a hacker's defense that he was unaware that his actions were unauthorized and subject to monitoring.

(C) FREE SOFTWARE

Many nonprofits rely heavily on freeware to contain overhead costs. This approach can lead to problems. For example, a popular, freely available file transfer protocol (FTP) server application was discovered to contain a "Trojan horse" that allowed unlimited access to the server running the software.

(D) UNENCRYPTED USER NAMES AND PASSWORDS

Sniffer programs are used by determined hackers to monitor network traffic to obtain user names and passwords transmitted over the Internet or between major gateways. These user accounts can then be used to gain access to network resources.

(E) E-MAIL VIRUSES

Current-technology e-mail programs provide more sophisticated features than ever before, but also provide an inviting target of opportunity for attack. Viruses are easily transmitted via e-mail, self-execute once the mail is read or even previewed, and go on to access the system registry, destroy data, transmit data to outside destinations, and retransmit themselves to all members of the address book. E-mailed viruses and worms are a much more serious threat than traditionally transmitted viruses because of the ease with which they can reproduce and transmit themselves across the Internet.

One of the most highly publicized cases in recent history was the "I love you" virus, which was estimated to have cost between $1 billion and $15 billion in damage worldwide. The young man who stands accused of producing this e-mail virus was apparently disgruntled at the high cost of Internet access—$3 per hour in the Philippines.

(F) SPYWARE

Spyware is any software that uses a personal computer's (PC's) Internet connection in the background without the user's knowledge or consent. Spyware earns its name because of what it does—monitor and transmit back information about the user's browser, installed software, sites visited, and more. This information may be used to defraud the user, resold for profit to marketers, or used for other purposes, all without the user's knowledge.

(G) AUDIT TRACKING

If you have a sophisticated, database-driven Web site, you should implement audit tracking on your site. A good audit-tracking package will monitor logons and logoffs, pages visited, data changes made, and files accessed. Audit tracking will make it easier for you to determine what a hacker has done, so the damage can be repaired more quickly. The audit trail also supports your case in the event you have to prosecute.

A nonprofit organization's sensitive data should be encrypted on several levels. First, your server should support 128-bit encryption if in the United States, and 40-bit if it will be accessed from foreign countries.

To increase a visitor's confidence that you are who you say you are, obtain a signed site certificate from a trusted source such as Verisign *(http://www.verisign.com)*.

10.11 Implementation Issues

(A) INTEGRATING INTERNET SERVICES WITH TRADITIONAL OPERATIONS

The nonprofit Web site cannot stand alone and be entirely successful. Online services are best combined with the nonprofit's traditional operations to get the best results.

Advertise your Web site, e-mail newsletters, and other Internet services on your hard-copy magazines, brochures, and other printed materials. Any advertising should include your Web site address. Printing your Web address is preferred over a generic e-mail address. The reason is that an e-mail address alone will encourage individuals to ask unstructured questions that could often be answered by a visit to the Web site. The Web site will have a feedback form that will collect background information on the writer and structure the e-mail to include the data you need and forward the message to the right department.

Dues notices and other "response requested" mailings should contain a space for the client to write in, or correct, his or her e-mail address. The client should also be able to opt in or out of your electronic newsletters, special offers, and other forms of mass e-mail. Allow clients to be specific as to which lists they want to opt out of, so as not to limit your communications with them unduly.

Telephone support staff should be familiar with the Web site structure and content. Clients who call with questions should be given the opportunity to be directed to the specific location of the Web site that answers their question, as an alternative to, *not in lieu of*, obtaining information via fax, voice, or other traditional means.

(B) WEB SITE DESIGN AND PRODUCTION

The agency Web site should not be managed by short-term volunteers. The workload frequently proves too great for a single volunteer, and site design and production become dependent on the individual's experience and personal preferences. If the individual volunteer is lost to the agency, the impact includes the funding source for the Web site (volunteer effort), the production capability, and perhaps even the procedures for maintaining the Web site.

Agency staff management is needed to ensure that the Web site remains stable and robust over the long term. A better approach to obtaining pro bono Web site support is to find a corporate sponsor to fund professional Web site production for the agency. This ensures that no matter who the sponsor is, the actual production of the Web site remains stable. The organization may contract out the work or hire a professional Web developer. If the developer's work is inferior, they can be replaced. The key is that the source of funding (sponsors versus volunteer effort) is not tied to work performance—either can be replaced without affecting the other.

Your Web designer must have strong graphic skills, solid programming skills, and content development skills. Programming and coding skills should include HTML, Java, and Perl for basic authoring. For more sophisticated sites, your Web master should have experience with online databases, electronic commerce, and security. Web masters should have credentials to prove they have the training they claim, but ask to see their work as well. It is one thing to pass an exam—it is altogether another to have real-world experience. Ask to see Web sites that they have created and maintained over time. Ask to see several sites to see if their approach is strictly boilerplate, or if their designs truly represent the mission and philosophy of the organization. Look at the designer's site, too! An inferior Web site indicates a lack of technical expertise, motivation, and/or organizational skills.

Be wary of Web designers who cannot communicate in "plain English." If they cannot explain most of their work to you in a way you can understand, they lack either competence or good communications skills. Web designers sometimes promise unrealistic results. Building a solid Web site takes time and never occurs without some growing pains.

Watch out for designers plugging every new technology under the sun. There are lots of powerful capabilities that you can build into your site, but most of them will be irrelevant to your needs. Remember that the goal of your Web site is to provide quality services, not feature exciting technologies for their own sake! A nonprofit recently inquired about assigning staff programmers to write pieces of code for a proposed members-only Web site. The assumptions were that leading-edge technology should be used to the maximum extent possible and that in-house programmers were cheaper than contract labor. In this case, the fact that existing programmers were able to generate isolated scripts could easily have lead to major security gaps due to (1) the programmer's lack of experience in the Internet arena, (2) lack of control by a managing Web master, and (3) direct access to corporate network and database resources by the scripts in question. Remember, the goal is not to implement leading-edge technologies, but to provide appropriate services without sacrificing security or wasting resources needlessly.

10.12   Online Resources

Builder.com   News and resources for Web site designers. *http://www.builder.com/*

CapWeb   Provides tailored content on the current U.S. Congress to organizations for a fee. Customized tie-in includes client branding for smoother integration with the client site look and feel. *http://www.capweb.net*

Charities Direct   Provides information on U.K. charities. Limited information freely available, more detailed information for paying clients. *http://www.caritasdata.co.uk*

Compass Point Nonprofit Services   Provides online information to help nonprofits better serve their communities. Although this is a for-profit company, it provides several free services, such as an electronic newsletter exclusively for directors of nonprofits. *http://www.compass point.org*

Computer Security Resource Clearinghouse   Developed to raise awareness of computer security issues and improve information systems security. This site contains an extensive library of information, a calendar of training events, U.S. policy documents, security publications, and links to security-related organizations and online resources. *http://csrc.nist.gov*

The Council on Foundations   A nonprofit membership association of grant-making foundations and corporations. *http://www.cof.org/*

Dialog   Full text search of articles from over 4,000 periodicals. *http://www.dialog.com*

Evangelical Council for Financial Accountability   A self-described "Christian Better Business Bureau," this organization is a member association of Christian nonprofit organizations that adhere to specified accounting standards, including full disclosure. *http://www.ecfa.org*

FBI   Report child pornography, spam, and other Internet abuses. *http://www.fbi.gov*

Hoover's   Corporate information and profiles by company name, symbol, keyword, person's last name, industry, geographical area, type of organization, and more. *http://www.hoovers.com*

InnoNet   Free tools for nonprofits, including program planning, evaluation planning, and fund raising. *http://www.inetwork.org*

International Web Standards Institute   Professional organization that promotes standards of excellence within the World Wide Web publishing community. *http://www.webstandards.com*

Internet Service for Grant-Funded Programs   Fee-based subscription information service for grant-funded organizations. *http://www.gfp.wya.com/*

Internet weather   Measures how reliable connections to primary Name Servers are over 24 hours. *http://www.Internetweather.com*

Lexus-Nexus   Research engine for legal, business, government, and academic sectors. *www.lexis-nexis.com*

Library of Congress   *http://lcweb.loc.gov/*

National Center for Not-for-profit Boards   A nonprofit organization dedicated to building stronger nonprofit boards and organizations. *http://www.ncnb.org/*

National Charities Information Bureau   Promotes informed giving by providing information about the charitable organizations being considered for funding or contributions. *http://www.give.org*

National Council of Not-for-Profit Associations   An alliance of over 20,000 community organizations. *http://www.ncna.org/*

Newspage   News library searchable by keywords, company name, ticker symbol, or general category. *http://www.newspage.com*

Nonprofit Genie   A nonprofit information resource that contains interviews, frequently asked questions, a recommended reading list with book reviews, and more. *http://www.genie.org*

Nonprofit Management.com   A new resource designed to extend the usefulness of this chapter by providing a means for nonprofits to participate in surveys of Internet-related issues and share success stories, problems encountered, and lessons learned. *http://www.nonprofit-management.com*

The Nonprofit Software Index   Software locator resource for nonprofits. *http://pirate.shu.edu/~kleintwi/tnopsi/tnopsi.html*

Not-for-profit Resource Center   A directory of support organizations for nonprofits and boards of directors. *http://not-for-profit.org/supt.htm*

OptOut   This site maintains a list of known and suspected spyware and systems. This site also markets its own spyware detection and removal software. *http://grc.com/optout.htm*

The Society for Not-for-Profit Organizations   A resource for board members, paid staff, and volunteers who lead or help nonprofit organizations. *http://danenet.wicip.org/snpo/*

Thomas   Fully searchable library of current and pending U.S. legislation. *http://thomas.loc.gov/*

Web Site Garage   Web site performance diagnostics. *http://www.Websitegarage.com*

Webwasher   This software is designed to block banner advertisements, pop-up advertisements from browsers, speeding up the download process while eliminating unwanted advertising. *http://www.webwasher.com*

Endnotes

1. Hosansky, D. (1997). "Phone Banks to E-Mail," *Congressional Quarterly, http://cnn.com/ALLPOLITICS/1997/12/01/cq/e-mail.html.*
2. Connors, T.D. (1999). *Nonprofit Handbook: Management* (1999 Supplement). New York: John Wiley & Sons.
3. Wack, J., and L. J. Carnahan. (February 9, 1995). "Keeping Your Site Comfortably Secure: An Introduction to Internet Firewalls," *National Institute of Standards and Technology Special Publication 800-10.*

Suggested Readings

Abel, S. (July 21, 1998). Trademark Issues in Cyberspace: The Brave New Frontier. Fenwick & West LLP, *http://www.fenwick.com/pub/trademark_issues_in_cyberspace.htm*

Adekanmi, O. (1998). Nigeria Gallops into the Internet Race," *On the Internet* (September/October): 35–37.

Bellafante, G. (Oct. 20, 1997). *Kudos for a Crusader, http://cnn.com/ALLPOLITICS/1997/10/13/time/nobel.html*

Bograd, H. (March 27, 1998). *Not-for-Profit Cyber-Accountability, http://www.bway.net/~hbograd/cyb-acc.html*

Cohen, A. (2000). "School for Hackers: The Love Bug's Manila Birthplace Is Just One of Many Third World Virus Breeding Grounds," *Time AsiaNow,* 155(20)(May 22), *http://www.cnn,com/AsiaNow/time/magazine/2000/0522/phil_school-for-hackers.htm/*

FAQ for Not-for-Profit Corporation Board Members, http://www.ncnb.org/askncnb/faq.htm

Gascoyne, R. J., and K. Ozcubukcu. (1997). *Corporate Internet Planning Guide: Aligning Internet Strategy with Business Goals.* New York: Van Nostrand Reinold.

"Government Delay on 'Love Bug' Said to Have Caused Serious Problems." (May 19, 2000). *CNN.com, http://www.cnn.com*

"Interview: Creating Browser-Savvy Sites." (October 6–13, 1998). *Web Site Journal, http://www.Web sitejournal.com/interview/100698_shafer_p.html*

"Interview: Work with Big Brands to Benefit the Site." (September 29, 1998). *Web Site Journal* 1(3), *http://www.WebsiteJournal.com*

Lynch, P., and S. Horton, Web Style Guide *http://info.med.yale.edu/caim/manual/contents.htm/* (This online web development guide provides excellent tips on designing an attractive Web page.)

Millholland, C. D. *Choosing a Professional Web Site Designer, http://www.siteterrific.com/choosing.html* (undated)

"Ninety Percent of Survey Respondents Detect Cyber Attacks, 273 Organizations Report $265,589,940 in Financial Losses." (March 22, 2000). Computer Security Institute, *http://www.gocsi.com/prelea_000321.htm*

"Protecting Your Company from Hackers—Computer Law Tip of the Week," *Mark Grossman's Computer Law Tip of the Week, www.mgrossmanlaw.com*

Rao, M. (September/October 1998). "The National Task Force and India's Internet: Full Steam Ahead?" *On the Internet.*

Web Design: Choosing a Web Designer. (1998). *http://www.techs.co.nz/web_design/choosing.htm*

11 Nonprofit Success on the Internet: Creating an Effective Online Presence

MICHAEL STEIN, INTERNET STRATEGIST
CompassPoint Nonprofit Services

11.1 Introduction

11.2 Overview of Nonprofit Internet Presence
(a) Focus Your Efforts on Audience Interest and Content Development
(b) Maintaining an Organizational Web Site
(c) Using E-Mail Effectively
(d) Outreach to Other Web Sites and Web Portals for Maximum Exposure
(e) Online Fund Raising
(f) Internet Presence and Strategic Planning
(g) Using Access and Referrer Logs for Evaluation and Outreach
(h) Evaluating the Effectiveness of Your Internet Presence

11.3 Focus Your Efforts on Audience Interest and Content Development
(a) Schedule Your Online Content Dissemination and Commit to Timeliness
(b) Drive More Traffic to Your Content

11.4 Maintaining an Organizational Web Site

11.5 Using Appropriate Content Formats on Web Sites
(a) Regular Web HTML Pages
(b) News Headlines and Teasers
(c) Multiple Languages
(d) Visuals, Photos, Maps, Graphics, Cartoons
(e) Search Engines
(f) Adobe Acrobat PDF
(g) Linking with Other Web Sites
(h) Audio and Video Clips
(i) Online Discussion Spaces
(j) E-Mail and Fax Action Systems
(k) Searchable Online Databases
(l) Pop-up Browser Windows
(m) Calendars

11.6 Using E-Mail Effectively

11.7 Getting Linked with Web Sites and Search Engines
(a) Register Your Web Site Content with Search Engines and Directories
(b) Meta-Tags
(c) Registration Services
(d) Organizational Web Links
(e) Link Errors
(f) Link Spies
(g) Link Popularity

11.1   Introduction

Nonprofits use the Internet today in unique and powerful ways to reach constituencies and supporters. Through well-crafted combinations of Internet activities, nonprofits are disseminating informational content, news, and alerts, and building a recognizable name online as trusted sources in its various issue areas. "Internet presence" is the comprehensive set of activities that a nonprofit organization engages in to use the Internet to meet its mission and advocacy goals. It can include a range of activities, such as building and maintaining a Web site; writing and distributing an e-mail newsletter; getting a Web site listed with search engines and directories; requesting reciprocal links with other Web sites; getting content placed with Web portals; holding online interactive events such as chats and threaded discussion forums; running an e-mail "listserv" discussion; using digital audio and video for Web-casting; and more. The purpose of this chapter is to help nonprofits think strategically about the complete range of activities that create an effective Internet presence.

The traditional nonprofit approach on the Internet is having a Web site, keeping the content up to date, and driving traffic to its site. Only in the last few years has a broader definition of Internet presence been adopted by nonprofits. The reality of the Internet today is far more complex than merely having a Web site and expecting traffic to come to it. This "build it and they will come" mentality has been superseded by a more active and aggressive approach to Internet promotion and marketing. The paradigm of "they will come" is being replaced by "we must go to them." This shift in perspective is a useful one, and it works! In my work with dozens of organizations over the past few years, I have witnessed many successful efforts that have come from planned and thoughtful campaigns.

For many nonprofit organizations using the Internet today, the greatest challenge has been to build, launch, and maintain a Web site. This focus on "Web-centrism" dominates a great deal of conversations at nonprofits. While building and maintaining a Web site is in and of itself not a bad focus of attention, a far greater challenge awaits: to strategically integrate the Internet with the rest of the organization's mission and advocacy goals, and to publicize and drive Internet traffic to the Web site, and more generally to get the organization's "Internet presence" into the limelight. In an ideal world, this discussion should have already occurred during the planning stages, but often it does not. As a result, creating an effective Internet presence for the organization is often hampered because the classic Internet "short-cut" is so tempting: build the Web site now, and the rest will fall into place later.

Whether you are still in the planning stages or have a well-developed Web site and e-mail outreach campaign, it is never too late to do an Internet tune-up to improve Internet outreach, increase Web site traffic, find new avenues for content dissemination, build e-mail subscribership, and fully integrate the Internet with your organization's activities. Truly effective Internet presence is about bringing the Internet closer to the advocacy goals of the organization and finding ways to use it to communicate with supporters, allies, and friends.

11.2   *Overview of Nonprofit Internet Presence*

It is certainly natural for there to be some anxiety among nonprofit staff about the institutional and technological demands of building and maintaining an Internet presence. Even today, the Internet is a new medium, with cryptic language and concepts, challenging staffing needs in the areas of information technology, writing, editing, layout, and marketing. I have found nonprofit staff to get quickly overwhelmed by the variety of demands in creating and maintaining an Internet presence. To assist the nonprofit manager in the development of an effective Internet presence, here is my overview of techniques that will guide my discussion through the remainder of this chapter. You can use these brief overviews to get you started or to jump straight to the section of your choice.

(A)   FOCUS YOUR EFFORTS ON AUDIENCE INTEREST AND CONTENT DEVELOPMENT

Internet presence is about understanding the needs of your online audience and developing content to meet their interests. I encourage nonprofits to keep audience and content in the forefront of their efforts online. Section 11.3 explores ways to present content in clear and consistent ways on your Web site and your e-mail newsletter. I also look at the importance of scheduling online content development and committing to timeliness in online publishing. I demystify the issue of "driving traffic to your Web site" by making an appeal to think more broadly about the issue of content development on the Internet. I remind nonprofits that they get "points" every time their content is viewed online, whether it is on their own Web site, via their e-mail newsletter, on someone else's Web site, or on someone else's e-mail newsletter.

(B)   MAINTAINING AN ORGANIZATIONAL WEB SITE

The organizational Web site is the core of an Internet presence, and every nonprofit should have one. Section 11.4 looks at maintaining an organizational Web to store all your Internet content: your boilerplate content about your mission, programs, and history; and the latest news and information about your work and campaigns. Section 11.5 looks at the different Web content formats that are available for the display and archiving of your content: Hypertext Markup Language (HTML) pages, photographs, maps, keyword search, Adobe Acrobat PDF, hypertext links to other Web sites, audio and video streaming, online discussion forums, searchable online databases, and calendars. Each one of these formats has its uses and pros and cons, and while HTML pages are the most common, the others can play vital roles.

(C) USING E-MAIL EFFECTIVELY

I am an avid supporter of using e-mail newsletters to "push" content at your audience and believe that it is an essential component—along with an organizational Web site—to a successful Internet presence. I argue strongly for avoiding "Web-centrism," which is the dependence on an organization's own Web site. E-mail newsletters are the key guarantee that an Internet presence will be effective. People who support your work and believe in your mission will be interested in receiving regular updates about the activities and campaigns in which you are engaged. Section 11.6 looks at e-mail as an ideal technique and technology and reviews issues such as length and frequency of e-mail updates, and the difference between e-mail and junk e-mail.

(D) OUTREACH TO OTHER WEB SITES AND WEB PORTALS FOR MAXIMUM EXPOSURE

Having your own organizational Web site is critical, but of equal importance is working with other Web sites and Web portals for maximum exposure. Other Web sites will be key in making it possible for you to disseminate your content through all available means. You can request reciprocal hypertext links, and you can have other Web sites feature your content as a form of news. Sections 11.7 and 11.8 discuss the specific and powerful role that other Web sites and Web portals can play in your Internet strategy, and ways in which to develop these relationships into ongoing content distribution partnerships.

(E) ONLINE FUND RAISING

Online fund raising should be an essential component of your Internet presence because it allows you to reach out to new audiences and constituencies, introducing them to your issues and campaigns, and asking them to support you. The boom in online fund-raising services on the Internet today offers some promising opportunities to do outreach and build your presence. Section 11.9 looks at options for online fund raising and several strategies for success.

(F) INTERNET PRESENCE AND STRATEGIC PLANNING

The importance of strategic planning is an essential element in all nonprofit work. Section 11.10 encourages nonprofits to integrate Internet presence into their strategic plans. Most strategic plans have a multiyear focus, and with the Internet growing in importance and influence, Internet presence should be part of an organization's plan for outreach and advocacy. Section 11.10 also looks at issues of staffing and volunteer use for Internet-related work.

(G) USING ACCESS AND REFERRER LOGS FOR EVALUATION AND OUTREACH

A commonly held belief is that most of what happens on the Web is anonymous and hard to measure. Nothing could be further from the truth. A huge amount of data is gathered regularly by the Internet company that hosts your Web site and is available to you in the form of access and referrer logs. Section 11.11 looks at how these logs offer tremendously useful information for organizations, not just to evaluate the effectiveness of your Internet presence, but also to design online marketing campaigns.

(H) EVALUATING THE EFFECTIVENESS OF YOUR INTERNET PRESENCE

There is a lot you can learn and understand about the effectiveness of the Internet in your work by careful tracking of Web site usage, the number of links to your Web site, and the pace of subscriptions to your e-mail newsletter. Section 11.12 looks at how to use all the tools at your disposal to help you evaluate your success.

11.3 *Focus Your Efforts on Audience Interest and Content Development*

Internet presence is about understanding the needs of your online audience and developing content to meet their interests. Like written or verbal content, Internet content should be produced with a specific audience or constituency in mind. When developing Internet content for your Web site or e-mail newsletter, keep in mind who will be reading and using it. Design your Web site so that it can easily be explored and browsed by issue or topic. With attention span on the Internet so thin, be sure to maximize your Web visitor's ability to locate content quickly and easily. With e-mail newsletters, use a clear table of contents that lets readers find content easily.

Internet content is what drives people to visit nonprofit Web sites and why they want to be kept up to date with e-mail bulletins. But what is Internet content? Internet content is press releases, news, executive summaries, reports, and statistics—every piece of information developed by your organization should be considered for Internet distribution. Content is the core of the Internet and the Web, so let it drive your online efforts. This is not meant to diminish the importance of technology. But a focus on content will allow nonprofit staff and managers to keep their eye on the prize, which is to disseminate news and information, and engage their supporters and constituencies in the mission and advocacy goals of the organization.

(A) SCHEDULE YOUR ONLINE CONTENT DISSEMINATION AND COMMIT TO TIMELINESS

Similar to the print and media world, content should be scheduled so that it coincides with real-world activities and events. Create an annual calendar that allows you to plan effectively. Note when you are holding events or releasing publications and plan your content development strategy to match. Also, whenever possible, commit to timeliness in your content dissemination. If you are releasing a new report and have planned a big media push, be sure that your Internet presence reflects this. A three-week delay in getting an announced report online will hamper your efforts to build an Internet presence. So be sure your Internet content is developed in a timely manner. Nothing else will make a greater impression on your media contacts, allies, members, and donors than your commitment to timeliness. You will be rewarded with Internet traffic and trust.

(B) DRIVE MORE TRAFFIC TO YOUR CONTENT

We hear much on the Internet today about "driving traffic to your Web site" and "making your Web site sticky." These phrases have crept into our lexicon from the commercial Internet world. "Driving traffic" refers to increasing the number of visitors to your Web site. Making your Web site "sticky" refers to keeping people on your Web site, as if its stickiness prevented people from leaving quickly. I have reinvented those phrases for the nonprofit world as "drive traffic to your content" and "make your Internet content sticky." As a nonprofit that is promoting its mission and campaigns, any means that you can use to do this is acceptable, and any avenues that are available should be used to accomplish it. I remind nonprofits regularly that they get "points" every time their content is viewed online, whether it is on their own Web site, via their e-mail newsletter, on someone else's Web site, or on someone else's e-mail newsletter. The competition for eyeballs on the Internet is so fierce today—and you can expect it to get fiercer—such that driving any kind of traffic to your content should be regarded as a success.

11.4   *Maintaining an Organizational Web Site*

The organizational Web site is the core of an Internet presence, and every nonprofit should have its own Web site. It is used as your home base, a place to store both your boilerplate content about your mission, programs, and history as well as the latest news and information about your work and campaigns.

Building and maintaining an organizational Web site is a considerable challenge. The building phase alone requires money, staff time, patience, and decision making. Once a Web site has been built and launched, it has to be regularly maintained. It is not the intention of this chapter to discuss Web site construction and maintenance, other than to touch on some issues relating to making content selections and choices. An organization will need to make regular and ongoing decisions about putting content on its Web site, usually through an internal discussion and decision-making process. Most organizations doing this effectively have designated a point person (an "Internet Coordinator"), whose job it is to move the content development process forward. Staffing issues will be looked at more closely in Section 11.10, but suffice it to say that staffing for Internet presence is an important consideration for a nonprofit.

Here is an example of maintaining a Web site and making content decisions, from Children Now in Oakland, California.

Children Now is a national children's advocacy organization with special depth in California. They work on issues such as health care coverage for children and coverage of children's issues in the media. In two weeks, they are releasing an important new report documenting the need for increased funding for health care coverage among poor children in California. A press release is being prepared, and the report is also printed and ready. A press conference is scheduled in the state capitol, and a news advisory has been distributed to the media. Ideally, both the press release and the report should be available on the Web site in a variety of formats on the day that the news is publicly released. The job of the Internet Coordinator is to track down the digital versions of the press release and the report and convert them for Web publishing. In this example, the press release was easily available from the organization's designated media person as a Microsoft Word file. The report is more complicated because it was produced by an outside firm in a desktop publishing software program. The report needs to be converted to both HTML and Adobe Acrobat PDF formats. One copy of the report is sent to the office on a zip disk to be converted to HTML by the Internet Coordinator. Another copy of the report is sent to an outside vendor that will convert it to Adobe Acrobat PDF. Both will be uploaded to the Web site by the Internet staff person, the day before the press conference.

Children Now has decided that both HTML and Adobe Acrobat PDF are excellent content formats to disseminate the press release and the report. HTML is an obvious choice since it is the default Web publishing format. Adobe Acrobat PDF is also selected because it is the format of choice for researchers, government, advocacy, and the media. The report itself contains a large number of charts and graphs that will display and print perfectly with Acrobat.

This example is intended to illustrate that an organization should evaluate and choose appropriate Web content formats for the display and archiving of Internet content. Furthermore, format choices will have staffing and cost implications, since some are quite time consuming to produce or require using outside vendors to help with production. Moreover, having an Internet point person on staff coordinating the regular maintenance of your organization's Web site can be an effective strategy for keeping content up to date and integrating the Web site maintenance with the timely release of hard-copy reports and press events.

11.5　Using Appropriate Content Formats on Web Sites

What follows is a review of format options for Web content. Each one of these formats has its pros and cons; while HTML pages are the most common, others can play vital roles.

(A)　REGULAR WEB HTML PAGES

This is the most common format for content on the Web, since all Web pages that contain text and graphics are written in HTML code. This code is, of course, hidden behind the exterior façade of a Web page. Organizations will use regular Web HTML format most of the time for creating the basic structure of a Web site, putting up press releases, boilerplate information about the organization and its campaigns, and so on. Regular HTML page production is usually the most affordable option for Internet content (second only to e-mail). The one exception to this rule is when large reports and documents need to be converted to HTML, in which case production can be lengthy. Shorter documents will be quick and easy to assemble, convert to HTML, and upload to the Web site for instant viewing. Also, regular Web HTML pages can be viewed by anyone with a Web browser, thus requiring no additional software or "plug-ins," which explains why it is the format of choice for Internet publishing. If you want to see this format in action, load your Web browser and visit your favorite Web site; 99 percent of the time you are looking at a regular Web HTML page.

(B)   NEWS HEADLINES AND TEASERS

The practice of creating and using news headlines and teasers does not differ in format from regular Web HTML. However, they are different from a content perspective, because they require the Internet Coordinator to present the content in a unique way, similar to how newspaper and media editors would do it. News headlines and teasers are particularly handy on home pages and secondary-level pages that help steer Web site viewers to content. In reality, a lot of what a Web site contains is navigational cues to help steer people to where they want to go. News headlines and teasers are the bread and butter of navigation.

To see a good example of this format in action, visit the Children Now Web site at *http://www.childrennow.org/.* Each news item has a headline, a teaser sentence, and a hypertext link to take the viewer to the content itself.

(C)   MULTIPLE LANGUAGES

Using multiple languages on your Web site is likely to take place also as regular Web HTML format, but from a content perspective it offers an opportunity for your Web site to be accessible to a wider constituency. If you are already publishing your print content in multiple languages, consider doing the same on your Web site (and in your e-mail). It will also give you an opportunity to be listed in the many language-specific search engines and Web directories.

To see a good example of this approach in action, visit the Planned Parenthood Federation Web site at *http://www.plannedparenthood.org/.*

(D)   VISUALS, PHOTOS, MAPS, GRAPHICS, CARTOONS

As is often said, a picture is worth a thousand words. This is never truer than on the Web, with shortened attention spans and small type on computer monitor screens. Graphic items are important to include on Web sites, to create an elegance in design, illustrate an issue or theme, and to aid in navigation. Photographs are easily acquired, are quickly converted to digital format, and download quickly on the Web when they are of reasonable size. Maps are unique visual aids and can aid in navigation. Other graphics like charts, graphs, or cartoons can also play roles. Think of ways to integrate these items into your Web site. Your visitors will appreciate them.

To see some good examples of visuals, visit the Peninsula Open Space Trust at *http://www.openspacetrust.org/* or David Bacon Photographs and Stories at *http://www.igc. apc.org/dbacon/.*

(E)   SEARCH ENGINES

Most Web site managers do not think of search engines as a form of content, but if your Web site becomes big enough to require installing a search engine, you will find that it quickly goes to the top of the list of the most frequently used pages on your site. From that perspective, your Web site search engine is a gateway to your content and will influence usage patterns and the ability of your Web site visitors to access your news and information. I have one key tip when it comes to search engines on your own Web site: Make sure that you are using consistent and clear "title tags" on all the pages of your site. When someone searches for information on your Web site using your search engine, the search engine is going to display a list of documents that match the search criteria. The document titles in that list are determined by the "title tags" you used for each page on your site. So, think ahead and use consistent and clear tags. Another compelling reason to use good "title tags" is that they will be picked up by other search engines when they index your site. With that in mind, I recommend that you put the name of your organization (or an appropriate abbreviation) at the beginning of each title tag, plus the title of the actual page content.

To see a good example of an organizational Web site search engine, visit Friends of the Earth at *http://www.foe.org/.*

(F)   ADOBE ACROBAT PDF

This Web format allows an organization to put up exact replicas of newsletters, reports, and charts for viewing and printing on the Web. Adobe Acrobat PDF is the format of choice for researchers, government, advocacy, and the media. To produce an Adobe Acrobat PDF file, take a source document such as a report produced with a word processing or desktop publishing software program, and convert it to PDF format through the Acrobat publishing software tool. You will have to either purchase this software tool from Adobe or find an outside vendor in your area that provides this service for a fee. To find an outside vendor, check with businesses that do desktop publishing; they often provide that service or know of other businesses that do. Once you have created a PDF file, you simply upload it to your Web site like any other file and create a hypertext link to it from one of your regular Web pages. For people on the Web to view your PDF file, they will have to have an Adobe Acrobat PDF "viewer," which is conveniently available for free from the Adobe Web site. Most people I know who use PDF viewers will simply print the document out. All your document's original fonts, photos, graphs, charts, and layout will print out perfectly. This Web format has grown remarkably in popularity over the past few years, and many nonprofits make highly effective use of this format as an Internet publishing tool.

To see an example of an organization using Adobe Acrobat PDF, visit Equal Rights Advocates at *http://www.equalrights.org/* and click on "Publications."

(G)   LINKING WITH OTHER WEB SITES

Hypertext links are often not thought of as Web content either, but access logs show that visitors use links as often as other types of content. With the unreliability and overwhelming nature of many commercial search engines, visitors often search through Web links as an effective strategy to search for information and news. Your organization should have a Web Links section on its Web site as a service and courtesy to the community, as a technique for assuring reciprocal links from other Web sites covering similar issues, and finally to attract repeat visitors who will remember that you have a comprehensive and up-to-date list.

To see an example of an organization with good Web links, visit Mothers and Others at *http://www.mothers.org/* and click on "Resources" and "Web Links."

(H) AUDIO AND VIDEO CLIPS

For some organizations, audio and video play central roles in their work and can be an integral component of your Web site content. You might produce a weekly radio opinion piece or have a series of public service announcements on your Web site. The more central these media are in your work, the more you should consider making them available on the Internet. Audio and video clips can be converted easily and inexpensively to digital formats for listening and viewing online. You will likely have to use a vendor or service bureau to help with the conversion, but they are easy to find today. Because it is still a new technology, it has an extra appeal for visitors to the site. Visitors will have to use a "plug-in" to their Web browser to listen or view the clips. Plug-ins are extra pieces of software that work with your Web browser to play audio and video content. The most popular audio and video plug-ins are Real Player from *http://www.real.com/*, Windows Media Player from *http://www.microsoft.com/*, and Quicktime from *http://www.apple.com/quicktime/*. All are freely available for download. I think in general that audio and video clips on the Internet are underappreciated by nonprofits, and that as broadband connectivity becomes more common in workplaces and households, there will be more usage of audio and video. Clearly, nonprofits regularly produce important audio and video content; it is time to take that content to a broader online audience.

To see an example of an organization with good audio and video, visit Talking With Kids About Tough Issues at *http://www.talkingwithkids.org/*.

(I) ONLINE DISCUSSION SPACES

Sometimes called Web forums, threaded discussion, or bulletin boards, conceptually this is an online space for visitors to your Web site to interact with one another by posting messages that create a thread of discussion. A moderator is often needed to keep the conversation flowing. Two other related options are live chat rooms or e-mail listservs. Chat rooms are also discussion spaces, but people have to interact live and in real time, and they are much harder to operate effectively. E-mail listservs are useful in that they can be "attached" to Web forums, so that people can choose to participate in the discussion via e-mail rather than having to return to the Web site. The challenge I want to emphasize from an Internet presence perspective is that creating an Internet discussion space is difficult to sustain effectively because it requires a consistent marketing effort to publicize and also skilled moderation to keep discussion topics interesting and ongoing. I often recommend to organizations that they team up with a commercial or nonprofit Web portal that already has a fully operational online discussion system, rather than building their own from scratch. I do not want to discourage nonprofits from creating online discussion spaces; rather, I am emphasizing that nonprofits plan their resources accordingly.

To see an example of effective discussion spaces, visit ParenthoodWeb at *http://www.parenthoodweb.com/* and click on either "Chat" or "Boards."

(J) E-MAIL AND FAX ACTION SYSTEMS

For organizations that are active in encouraging their members to take action on important issues like legislation, Internet e-mail and fax systems can be valuable tools. By systems, I mean the setup and maintenance of a directory of legislators with draft letters that site visitors can use to send an e-mail message or a fax letter with their own customized message. You could also select any targets, such as a corporate chief executive officer or a city council member, to send e-mail or faxes to. Luckily, a number of excellent vendors have emerged to help organizations set up these types of systems. Be attentive to setup and ongoing costs. Three vendors to consider are Netivation at *http://www.netivation.com/*, Capitol Advantage at *http://capitoladvantage.com/*, and Locus Pocus at *http://www.locuspocus.org/*. There is some research that shows that e-mail actions are not as effective as initially thought, and that faxes (or even mailgrams) may be more powerful lobbying and advocacy tools. I encourage nonprofits to carefully weigh the pros and cons of using these different delivery mediums and to choose those that deliver the most results for the effort and expense invested.

To see an example of an e-mail action system, visit the National Urban League at *http://www.nul.org/* and click on "Contact Congress."

(K)   SEARCHABLE ONLINE DATABASES

It is the dream of almost every organization to offer an online repository of information that can be searched by keyword or phrase. The Internet makes this content offering possible today. It requires an organization to already have a fully operational database in-house, and then to work with an online database expert to put the database into a Web-searchable format. From a cost perspective, this is likely to be expensive to develop, but will likely repay your efforts in the end result. If your organization's mission is based on delivering timely and searchable information, this is a unique opportunity.

To see an example of an online database, visit the Mediation Information and Resource Center at *http://www.mediate.com/* and click on "International Directory of Mediators."

(L)   POP-UP BROWSER WINDOWS

You've seen these "pop-up" mini-browser windows a dozen times when you have visited commercial Web sites. Usually, they are advertising something that is on sale or announcing a contest. You click on the top right corner button and they're gone. Advertising and contests aside, they offer an interesting and creative way to present and highlight content. They have been used effectively in a number of nonprofit venues, and it is surprising how few people are bothered by them once they see that the content is interesting and important.

To see an example of a pop-up browser window, visit Talking With Kids About Tough Issues at *http://www.talkingwithkids.org/* and click on "Violence."

(M)   CALENDARS

From a content perspective, everyone understands calendars because people use them in their daily life. A calendar of upcoming events on a Web site will be intuitive and a perfect way to present information and news to visitors. You can create simple calendars using regular HTML pages, or try out a free commercial online calendar that you can customize for your needs. You can even password protect a calendar for sharing by a group of people. One thing to watch for with calendars is that they are quickly out of date and require regular updating. For an example of commercial calendars, visit *http://calendar.yahoo.com/* or *http://www.when.com/*.

To see a good example of a nonprofit calendar, visit the Feminist Majority Foundation at *http://www.feminist.org/* and click on "Calendar" at the bottom of the page.

11.6 Using E-Mail Effectively

E-mail should be considered a core requirement of an effective and proactive Internet presence. Nothing works more effectively for nonprofits in using the Internet as having an e-mail newsletter that is sent out regularly to members and supporters. Whereas your Web site relies on people themselves visiting you, an e-mail newsletter is something that you send to them. With an e-mail newsletter, you are "pushing" content at your supporters, proactively delivering content directly at people who have given you their e-mail addresses.

If you are starting a new newsletter, pick a publishing schedule that matches your staff's realistic ability to assemble and distribute it. You might try every other month to begin with, and increase the frequency to monthly if you have been successful during your first year.

Select interesting and engaging content for your e-mail newsletter. Combine and coordinate its content with the content on your Web site. Your e-mail newsletter can list half a dozen new content items that are available, and then link directly to your Web site where your readers can obtain the complete item. Generally, you are better off with shorter items in an e-mail newsletter, teasers to the longer pieces that live on your Web site. But this is not an absolute rule; there are excellent newsletters that are stand-alone items, separate from content on the Web.

If you are starting out, one general e-mail newsletter will suffice to keep your supporters updated on your projects and campaigns. Later, as your readership grows and your staff becomes more experienced with Internet publishing, you should consider having a newsletter for each major campaign or project in which you are involved.

One of your most important and challenging tasks will be to build a subscribership. First, be sure to advertise the e-mail newsletter on your Web site, preferably with a subscriber form that people can easily fill out. Put your newsletter subscription form on as many of your Web pages as possible. If you have a Web page that updates people on a campaign, be sure to put the form on that page, so people will have easy access to subscribe. Second, enlist your staff, volunteers, and board in an active campaign to collect e-mail addresses that can be added to your subscriber list. Avoid proliferating e-mail spam by asking people's permission to be added to your list. If you ask people personally for permission, they are likely to say "yes" most of the time. Nominate a specific month as E-mail Newsletter Month and go on an all-out search for new subscribers! Build your readership!

With regard to technology for e-mail newsletter subscriber lists, there are several options at your disposal. The easiest and most low-tech technique is to use an address book in your e-mail software. Netscape Mail, Microsoft Outlook, Eudora, and others all have address books where you can store hundreds of e-mail addresses in one spot using an alias like "Email Newsletter List." When you use this technique, be very careful when you send out your e-mail newsletter to use the Blind Carbon Copy field (BCC) when adding all your subscriber names. That will avoid the annoying practice of receiving a large header of e-mail addresses at the top of an e-mail message. The downside to doing it this way is that you have to manually add and remove subscribers. When your e-mail newsletter has a lot of subscribers, you will not want to keep doing this!

Another, more advanced technique at your disposal is to use one of the free e-mail newsletter services on the Internet. Try Topica *(http://www.topica.com)*, eGroups *(http://www.egroups.com)*, or ListBot *(http://www.listbot.com)* from Microsoft. All offer tools such as easy setup, open discussion or one-way distribution, discussion moderation, and archiving on the Web. The advantage to these services is that they automatically handle all the subscribing and unsubscribing for you. That leaves more time to write interesting content! Also, these services offer snippets of programming code that your Web staff person can add to your Web pages so that new subscribers can sign up quickly.

Maximize your Internet presence by combining your Web site with an engaging e-mail newsletter, and start communicating effectively with your friends, supporters, and allies. For an example of an organization with good e-mail newsletters, visit Compass-Point Nonprofit Services at *http://www.compasspoint.org/* and click on "Board Café" or "Food for Thought."

11.7   *Getting Linked with Web Sites and Search Engines*

The greatest challenge of being on the Web today is not just in having a Web site, but also in driving traffic to your site by making the most of search engines, Web directories, and links with other Web sites. Not enough organizational staff time is spent on this online marketing strategy, which is regrettable because there is a very direct payback to promoting your Web site and e-mail newsletter. It will be a big factor in your success and should be done regularly. Following are some general tips for doing so. Many of these tasks are ideal for volunteers and interns.

(A)   REGISTER YOUR WEB SITE CONTENT WITH SEARCH ENGINES AND DIRECTORIES

Millions of Web surfers use these sites as starting points by using content keywords or by browsing. You cannot afford to be left out. Start with these: Yahoo.com, Hotbot.com, AltaVista.com, Excite.com, Go.com, Lycos.com, NorthernLight.com, and StartingPoint (stpt.com). Visit each site and click on the "Get Listed" button and fill out their forms.

(B)   META-TAGS

Do not forget to add meta-tags (hidden descriptions and keywords) on your home page so that roving search engine robots (sometimes called *spiders*) will catalog you regularly as they visit your Web page periodically. Meta-tags will help you maximize your search engine placement and ensure that people can find you using keywords. Do not hesitate to review your meta-tag keywords several times a year to make sure that you are covering all your issues. Visit the search engines regularly and check that your listing is correct and that you are found in all the right directory categories.

(C)   REGISTRATION SERVICES

Many online companies offer low-cost registration services, and you have probably received a few e-mail solicitations. These services offer to register your Web site with hundreds of search engines and Web directories. These services rarely benefit nonprofit organizations because they are usually designed for businesses. If you want to check out one of these services, visit Microsoft's Submit-It service at *http://www.submit-it.com/.*

(D)   ORGANIZATIONAL WEB LINKS

Just as important as search engines and Web directories are links with other Web sites that are in your issue area. There is a "Web Links" section on organizational Web sites that lists related sites. These Web Links pages are among the most frequently used pages on Web sites. Make sure you have a Web Links page on your Web site. Then, make it a habit to request reciprocal links with other Web sites. Link requests can be general (to your home page) or content specific (a report).

(E)   LINK ERRORS

Pay regular attention to link errors both to and from your Web site. Nothing annoys visitors more than coming to your Web site and getting a "404 Error"—a Web server error that means that the page they were looking for does not exist. If someone e-mails you to inform you about an error, correct it immediately. If your site is particularly large, you might consider subscribing to a service that verifies your links automatically and regularly. One service I recommend is LinkWalker at *http://www.seventwentyfour.com/*, which will check all the links on your site plus links from other sites and tell you about any broken links in a weekly e-mail report. This is useful if you maintain a large directory of links on your site and are tired of manually checking them or if you have a really large site. It is like having a staff person, volunteer, or intern who is constantly checking for errors. It costs roughly between $70 and $100 per year to subscribe.

(F)   LINK SPIES

A variation on this theme includes setting up "link spies." A free service at *http://www.spy-onit.com/* will send you e-mail whenever someone links to your site. You can then go check to see if the link was entered correctly and has a good description. This is a good service to use when you are first publicizing a site and sending out lots of link requests.

(G)   LINK POPULARITY

Finally, another excellent free service that I use regularly is called LinkPopularity at *http://www.linkpopularity.com/*. Enter the address of your Web site, and see how AltaVista, InfoSeek, and HotBot have your Web address listed in their databases. This is a useful tool to identify Web portals and other Web sites that have listed you. Another way you can use this type of service is to visit Alta Vista at *http://www.altavista.com/* and enter URLs of pages that you have recently removed from your site. The syntax for a search would be: "+link:www.myorganization.org/myoldpage.html." It will show you only sites still linked to that old page. You can then contact those Webweavers and ask them to update the link. This is a very useful service.

11.8   *Working with Web Portals*

As Internet institutions go, Web portals are playing increasingly important roles. The rise of media concentration in the industry, the overall growth of Internet traffic, and the specialization of Web sites in specific and narrow issue areas creates opportunities that the nonprofit organization should seek out and use to its advantage. While most would define a Web portal in the strict sense of a "media" portal such as CNN Online (*http://www.cnn.*

com) or MSNBC.com (*http://www.msnbc.com*), I have expanded the definition to fit the non-profit need: A Web portal is any large Web site other than your own that is a gateway to content, is heavily visited, and has the potential to disseminate your content to new audiences and drive traffic to your site. With this definition in mind, your organization should dedicate staff time (or intern/volunteer time) to identify Web portals that can help disseminate your content, particularly a portal that serves your constituency.

(A)   IDENTIFYING WEB PORTALS

Web portals are fairly easy to identify, and here are a few proven techniques. First, do an e-mail survey of a couple of dozen people in your field or issue area and ask them to list their top 10 Web sites that cover your issue. Second, visit the top search engines (Yahoo, Alta Vista, HotBot) and try typing in your issue keywords and see what banner display ads show up; these are often commercial portals paying for advertising space. Third, review your Web site's referrer logs to see what other sites are sending you traffic. (See Section 11.11 for a more detailed description of how to use Web site access and referrer logs.) Fourth, once you have built your list sites, visit them one by one and learn about how they feature content. Also, try to identify e-mail addresses, phone numbers, and the names of editors at these sites that you can contact. Build relationships with editors at Web portals that cover your issues and offer them content on a regular basis. Many Web portals strive to stay current in their issue areas so they can attract repeat visitors and thus sell advertising. They will be generally delighted to receive content submissions from organizations in the field.

Do not forget that in addition to the many commercial portals, there are a large number of nonprofits portals that you should be in touch with for content placement and outreach. Here are just a few examples: HandsNet.com, JoinTogether.org, Alternet.org, Kidscampaigns.org, Mediate.com, MediaChannel.org, IGC.org, Freespeech.org, OneWorld.net, and Idealist.org. There are many more Web portals out there that cover your issues, so go track them down!

(B)   CONTENT COLLABORATIONS

In addition to content placement, valuable collaborations can be created with Web portals to create reciprocal linking and content agreements that drive traffic between Web sites. These strategic agreements are popular on the commercial Internet and are big money deals, and can work well and more affordably for nonprofits and advocacy groups. Since nonprofits want little in return other than exposure, many commercial portals are often delighted to feature your content regularly. It assures their readership that they are plugged into their issue area. Take care to evaluate any reciprocal requirements in the agreement. Some nonprofits are uncomfortable being asked to run commercial banners or put plugs in their e-mail newsletters for commercial products or services. An ideal commercial partner should understand a nonprofit's reluctance and will suggest other options. Do not get locked into a partnership that does not respect your mission and values.

11.9   Online Fund Raising

Online fund raising is an essential component of an Internet presence because you are reaching out to new audiences and constituencies, introducing them to your issues and campaigns, and asking them to support you. Best of all, the boom in online fund-raising services on the Internet today offers some promising opportunities to do outreach and build your presence. Online fund raising must be closely coordinated with an organization's strategic plan. It's not enough to simply put up a "Donate Now" button and hope for contributions to come in. Online fund raising yields few results if it is unplanned and not part of an overall fund-raising strategy. Thus, Internet staff working on online fund raising should work closely with the organization's fund-raising and development staff to coordinate efforts.

(A) CHARITY PORTALS

The first strategy I recommend is to get your organization listed with all the charity portals on the Web today. Charity portals are Web sites that offer a directory of non-profits, of which you would be one of many. Their job is to attract lots of traffic to their site and encourage visitors to make contributions to the nonprofits listed. Often, your listing is free, and the portal accepts secure credit card contributions on your behalf. Some charge a fee when you get a contribution, but usually there are no monthly charges. These portals make their money either from advertising on their site or through the fees they charge the nonprofit. Examples of charity portals include Helping.org, Charitableway.com, 4charity.com, GreaterGood.com, Allcharities.com, eGrants.com, and GiveForChange.com. Individuals interested in donating to charities often use charity portals to help them with their research, so it is important that you be listed and that your listing be up to date.

(B) DONATE BUTTON AND DONOR MANAGEMENT

The second strategy that I recommend is that you have a Donate button on your own Web site. You can either use the donation service of one of the charity portals mentioned previously or you can contract with a vendor known as a payment service provider or donor relationship management service to set one up for you. Using a charity portal is by far an easier and cheaper process, but you will have less control over the branding of the pages and the various administrative and notification tools that accompany the service. Payment service providers are typically more costly, but they will build a fully customized system that meets your exact needs. Examples of payment service providers are Entango.com, SeeUthere.com, DonorNet.com, Acteva.com, and LocalVoice.com.

(C) CHARITY MALLS

Your third strategy might be to work with a charity mall, which is an online fund-raising service that returns a commission to your organization when your members or supporters make online shopping purchases through their network of online stores. Not all nonprofits are comfortable working with charity malls, sometimes feeling that it is akin to a form of advertising or corporate sponsorship or supports consumerism, which may not mix well with your organization's mission. Your staff and/or board should debate the issue and develop a policy. Examples of charity malls are Igive.com, Greater-Good.com, 4charity.com, SchoolPop.com, iReachOut.com, MrGoodBucks.com, and ShopForChange.com.

(D) EVALUATING ONLINE FUND-RAISING SERVICES

Charity portals and malls (as well as other "dot-com" services) have been quite active recently in doing outreach to nonprofits. You should use sound judgment in evaluating their services. Get all the information you can about how their service works. Examine their Web site in complete detail to see how they present their service and how they feature the nonprofits that are signed up with them. Make sure you have a very good understanding of what fees you might have to pay when you receive a donation or any signup or monthly fees. Do not get forced into signing a multiyear contract if you are not comfortable with that. Tell the service that you want a shorter contract so you can evaluate the effectiveness of their service. Get referrals from other nonprofits that have signed up, and try to find out how much money they have raised through the service. Ask about how the service promotes itself through marketing and advertising. You want to know how hard they are working on your behalf. Finally, make sure you understand what the service requires you to do as part of the deal. Some ask for buttons on your home page or announcements in your e-mail newsletters.

(E) RELATIONSHIP BUILDING AND CAMPAIGNS

No matter what strategy you adopt, it is important to remember that online fund raising is just another way to build relationships with your members, potential members, and constituents. In the process of asking for support, you do outreach on your issues and campaigns and stay visible online. It is also important to not have a passive relationship with your online fund-raising efforts. Putting a Donate button on your Web site or signing up with a charity mall is just the beginning of your online fund-raising efforts. Now you have to create a fund-raising campaign that gets people's attention, plugs them into your issues and campaigns in the real world, and makes a clear and determined pitch for their financial support. Combine online fund raising on the Web with your outreach in your regular e-mail newsletter and also with your print material. If you are active at events or in the community, be sure to saturate all these media with your fund-raising message.

    To see two good examples of online fund raising, visit Children Now at *http://www. childrennow.org/* and click on "Support Us," and In Defense of Animals at *http://www.idausa. org/* and click on "Support IDA."

11.10   *Internet Presence and Strategic Planning*

I encourage nonprofits to integrate Internet presence into their strategic plans. With the Internet growing in importance and influence, an Internet presence should be part of an organization's plans for outreach and advocacy. There are two major areas where Internet presence and strategic planning overlap—in fund raising and marketing. Section 11.9 discussed fund raising, emphasizing the importance of integrating Internet fund raising with other fund raising and development campaigns that are underway in the organization. In the area of marketing, it is important to remember that an Internet presence campaign is a marketing campaign that will influence an organization's brand name, its relationship with the media and its supporters, and many other public venues.

In addition to using the online medium effectively to promote your Internet presence, it is important that your organization use every other medium at its disposal. Some ideas for enhancing your Internet presence in your organization's other media include:

- *Print material.* In addition to listing your Web site address in prominent places on your printed document, create an Internet "column" in your hard-copy newsletter that updates readers in a more substantial way about valuable online resources. You can inform people about new documents you have put online or review other Web sites of interest. Always remind people in your print material to subscribe to your e-mail newsletter. You might also consider producing an informational flyer about your Internet presence, describing your Web offerings, your e-mail newsletter, and anything else of interest. This flyer can get distributed at events or go out with regular correspondence and mail that's sent out from your offices.

- *Voice mail.* Make sure your voice mail messages include a mention of your Web site address, particularly around the time when you're releasing a report or organizing an important event. People are often calling to find out more information, so why not direct them to your Web site if they cannot reach you in person?

- *E-mail signature files.* Your organization probably sends out hundreds of e-mails every month. An e-mail signature file can list the person's name and phone, but can also promote the content on your Web site or your e-mail newsletter. Again, this is particularly effective around the time when you are releasing a report or organizing an important event.

- *In-house education.* It is important to regularly educate your in-house team so that everyone's understanding of your Internet presence is consistent. Do regular trainings and updates for staff, board, and volunteers to describe your Internet presence. Print out a hard copy of your Web site front page (and other pages) and distribute them to all staff. Create a wall-size map of your Web site in your office. Send out in-house e-mails to inform people about noteworthy Internet updates. Make regular announcements at staff meetings. Include an item on Internet issues at all board meetings. Make sure all your staff and board recognize the priority of the Internet as a key tool for your organization's goals, mission, and long-term effectiveness.

- *Staffing issues.* Staffing for an effective Internet presence in nonprofits can be a challenging task, given the competing demands for staff time in organizations today. You should expect Internet presence staffing to be somewhere between a part-time and full-time job. The major tasks are to maintain the Web site, do content management, handle occasional technical needs, and do outreach and Internet marketing. Many tasks—as discussed previously—can be accomplished by volunteers and interns, but these people need training and supervision.

11.11   Using Access and Referrer Logs for Evaluation and Outreach

We often think of the Web as a fairly anonymous and mysterious medium, where usage patterns are unknown and people surf around quietly and undetected. Nothing could be further from the truth. When I saw my first access and referrer log report, I was immediately converted to the wonders of logs. Logs offer tremendously useful information for organizations, not just to evaluate the effectiveness of your Internet presence, but also to design online marketing campaigns.

The core information resources at your disposal are Web access and referrer logs. Log files are collected by the Internet company that hosts your Web site and records information such as which page on your Web site has just been viewed and at what time. It records this information continuously in a very long stream of data, with every hit to your Web site meticulously recorded. The two main types of log files that exist are *access logs* and *referrer logs.*

An access log is a record of which page on your Web site has just been viewed and at what time. With this data, you can learn which are the most popular pages on your site, which are least popular, where people enter your site, where they leave, what time of the day or week people visit, and much more. This type of information is critical to understanding usage patterns of your Web content. It should assist you in evaluating your efforts thus far. If several parts of your Web site get little or no traffic, you should consider removing them or reorganizing them. If you are putting huge amounts of staff time into maintaining parts of your Web site, you should see a return on your investment; if not, reevaluate your strategy and priorities. Your Web site access logs are a poll of your readers, so listen up and understand what they want!

Referrer logs record where people have come from before reaching your site, in other words, their originating location. Imagine an airport where you know how many planes are landing and how often. Now imagine you knew what cities all those planes originated from—that is like referrer logs. Referrer logs are extremely valuable tools to understand where your online traffic is coming from. The logs will show which search engines are sending you traffic and what keywords they used to locate your listing. The logs will show the identity of Web portals that have listed you and how much traffic they send your way. The logs will identify any other site that sends you traffic and the precise location of a page where a link to your site is located.

Organizations should use the information about portals and other Web sites to target future marketing and promotion efforts. If you are in the children's advocacy field and you can see in your referrer logs for one month that www.connectforkids.org sent you 80 visitors, then you need to be sure to send those organizations or portals your future news releases—better yet, pick up the phone and get to know that organization better. Little by little, you can build an online promotion checklist that includes many of the Web sites you have discovered by examining your referrer logs. Review your referrer logs each month, and particularly after any news events you have been involved in, and identify new sites that have sent you traffic.

You can use referrer logs to evaluate partnerships with other organizations that have pledged to drive traffic to your site. You can also use referrer logs to evaluate whether your Web advertising banners are delivering traffic to your site.

Take a look at the last quarter of access and referrer log data for Children Now, a national children's advocacy organization based in Oakland, California. The logs are at *http://www.childrennow.org/stats* and are presented here using WebTrends software. WebTrends is just one of several very useful available software programs to help you analyze your hit logs and referrer logs. In Children Now's case, their Web hosting company makes these log files available automatically each month and preformatted in WebTrends software.

The Children Now WebTrends logs reveal the names and Web addresses of search engines, portals, and other Web sites that sent traffic to Children Now's Web site, such as *http://www.childhelpusa.org, http://www.media-awareness.ca, http://www.socialservice.com, http:// www.childrensdefense.org, http://www.child.net, http://www.connectforkids.org, http://www.welfare-info.org, http://child.cornell.edu, http://fdncenter.org,* and more. These Web sites are key partners in Children Now's efforts to do online promotion for its work on behalf of children.

By examining its Web logs regularly, Children Now was able to justify its continued use of Adobe Acrobat PDF files as a format for disseminating reports. In the first quarter of 2000, over 14,000 PDF files were downloaded from the Children Now Web site. Furthermore, each Children Now program was able to monitor access to its material online and add that information to its report to funders and supporters.

If you do not currently obtain access or referrer logs for your Web site, contact the Internet provider that is hosting your site and ask them to help you. If they do not offer logs or are not helpful, consider finding another Internet provider that understands your needs. Some Internet providers can provide you with the software to analyze the data, while others will offer only the raw log files, and then it is up to you to purchase the software and do the analysis on your own.

11.12   Evaluating the Effectiveness of Your Internet Presence

In addition to access and referrer logs for evaluation and outreach, there are other resources at your disposal. One resource at your disposal is tracking the number of subscribers to your e-mail newsletter. Keep track each month of the number of people subscribing, the number of new subscribers, and the number of cancellations. Every quarter, compare Web access levels, e-mail subscription levels, and your organization's activities in the real world. This comparison exercise should help you get a complete picture of the general trends in your Internet presence. Your trends should be toward growth, but can you spot the spikes that help you evaluate what worked best? Did you have an intern one summer that helped boost your traffic? Did the press conference last spring double your e-mail newsletter subscription because you made an extra effort at signing people up?

Another information resource at your disposal is the survey. You can get feedback and opinions from your members about how they understand and interact with your Internet presence by asking them in an e-mail or Web survey. Do they read your e-mails? Do they click through your e-mails to visit your Web site? Do they come back to your Web site, and why? Keep in mind that surveys need careful design and forethought, but when done thoroughly can be effective evaluation tools.

Another resource is one discussed previously, LinkPopularity at *http://www.linkpopularity.com/.* Enter the address of your Web site, and see how AltaVista, InfoSeek, and HotBot have your Web address listed in their databases. They list the total number of links found, which is helpful to use at six-month intervals to look for growth trends in Internet presence.

11.13   Conclusion

Building and maintaining Web sites is just the beginning of the Internet adventure. Much more needs to be done to have a fully effective Internet presence strategy. So much organizational effort is expended in building and maintaining Web sites that the less glamorous activities of doing Internet and non-Internet publicity, reviewing logs, and tracking down Web portal editors is often not recognized. In reality, these important outreach and evaluative activities often are the measure of success of Internet presence. For a field that is constantly expanding and changing, the practice of building an Internet presence is a grounding activity that helps organizations and their staff get a very practical and hands-on grasp of the medium. What was once nebulous and anonymous becomes quantified, measured, and understood.

This chapter began by encouraging nonprofit organizations to keep a focus on content on the Internet, which is another way of saying to keep a focus on their mission and goals. The Internet is full of distractions, seductions, deals, technologies, and offers. But what matters most is that which helps your organization expand your audience, disseminate news and information, and be well positioned to seek financial support. In the past few years, the Internet has become a "dot-com" world, where online malls, media, and Web portals dominate the virtual real estate. But there is plenty of room in this modern cyberspace for nonprofit organizations—the "dot-orgs"—to find their focus. Nonprofits should create an Internet presence that values their nonprofit integrity and their commitment to a mission of social good. With this clear vision and goal, nonprofits are destined to thrive, and the Internet can be a key tool in their success.

Strategic Media Relations

EILEEN M. WIRTH, PhD
Creighton University

12.1 Introduction

The media relations section of a large school district public relations department was terribly busy. Staff members worked 10 hours a day collecting information for news releases and activity calendars, which they distributed to area media. The volume of paper generated was impressive. However, a study of the media relations program determined that the work was mostly wasted. Only a few of the calendar items or news releases ever appeared in news media outlets, and most were inconsequential notices of routine activities.

The district itself made lots of news. However, media relations staff members were so busy compiling calendars and writing news releases about trivia that they had no goals beyond survival. Mostly, they focused on keeping up with their routines and responding to media inquiries. They had no time to think creatively about how to tell their big stories in a way that would positively affect the community's image of their district. They never stopped to ask why they were doing what they were doing. They could document no concrete results from all their work beyond a few news clips.

This office is all too typical of many media relations operations in both the for-profit and nonprofit sectors. Well-intentioned staff members too often confuse effort and output with results. They may have only a hazy understanding of the overall direction in which their organization is moving and how media relations efforts could support it. They feel only loosely connected with its vision. They have no goals or objectives beyond meeting the deadlines that they have set for themselves.

The example illustrates the need for a strategic instead of a traditional approach to media relations. Media relations must be an integral part of an organization's strategic plan. Specific goals and objectives to advance that plan must be developed for media relations efforts. The resources media relations receives must be justified in terms of the contribution to the organization's success. Ideally, a media relations staff should be able to quantify its contribution.

12.2 A Strategic Approach to Media Relations

A strategic approach to media relations may be defined as using media relations activities to achieve specific public relations goals. These goals, in turn, must support the organization's overall mission statement and communications strategy. Such an approach begins with formulating a comprehensive communications plan to help carry out the organization's mission and to bring its vision to life. This linkage of media relations goals to the organization's mission and vision distinguishes a strategic approach from a traditional approach to media relations.

(A) A CONTRAST

A traditional approach to media relations tends to focus on how to get coverage and how to work with news organizations, but not why. Goal setting tends to be in terms of gaining attention rather than furthering an organization's mission. Volume of coverage is perceived as good regardless of whether the content of the coverage is significant or trivial and whether or not the coverage reaches an audience that is valuable to the organization. Organizations often use computerized media services to count usage of particular items. They then measure their success by the growth of these item counts. Success in advancing the organization's overall goals is not a factor to be operationalized or evaluated.

There is extensive literature on how to successfully implement this traditional approach—everything from college textbooks to various handbooks, some of them targeted at certain types of organizations such as libraries or small businesses. This approach is typified by works such as Fraser P. Seitel's popular *The Practice of Public Relations.*[1] The textbook as a whole includes discussions of public relations strategies, but the two chapters on media relations focus on how media groups work handling interviews and press conferences, publicity avenues, placing and producing publicity, public service announcements, talk radio, videoconferences, and so forth. Similar compendiums of advice can be found in a wide range of books and articles. Most of the advice is consistent and useful to nonprofit organizations that have had limited experience in working with media relations. However, nonprofits that follow such advice without first developing a media relations strategy based on advancing the organization's overall mission will not reap the full benefit of their investment.

(B) REASONS FOR DEVELOPING A STRATEGIC MEDIA RELATIONS PLAN

There are numerous reasons to develop a strategic media relations plan. An effective plan enables a nonprofit to:

- Inform and educate target audiences
- Obtain volunteers and contributions
- Recruit members and/or clients
- Promote support for policies and programs
- Counter rumors and misinformation

Media relations personnel who develop and follow a strategic plan are not simply working blindly, wondering if a particular task is worth the effort. They have drawn a road map and developed a rationale for everything they do. Activities can be prioritized depending on their importance in achieving defined objectives. Outputs to the media can be structured in such a way that they reinforce each other. Wasted effort can be reduced.

There are virtually no drawbacks to this approach other than modest investments of time and resources in research, audience identification, media use analysis, message development, and implementation.

12.3   *Development of a Media Relations Strategy*

Development of a media relations strategy involves step-by-step research and analysis of major factors such as audiences, media use, and essential messages. Components need to be examined individually, with findings assembled into a plan that is both feasible and credible. The planning process should begin by examining whether a media relations program will be beneficial to a given nonprofit agency. This "devil's advocate" question may spare some nonprofits needless time and effort.

(A)   DO YOU NEED MEDIA RELATIONS?

Some organizations have mostly internal audiences, which can obtain all the information they need from internal sources such as newsletters or bulletins. Examples are religious congregations and service clubs. Nonprofit organizations should ask themselves if they need to communicate with outside audiences to achieve an organizational goal or if they simply want the visibility and public recognition that come from media coverage. They may find they have been doing media relations work because they thought they should rather than because they needed or wanted to. In these cases, the best strategy might be to eliminate media relations efforts. Most nonprofits, however, will discover that they benefit from a well-targeted media relations effort. Such efforts begin with the identification of target audiences.

(B)   TARGET AUDIENCES

The essence of all public relations is targeting strategic messages to audience segments that the organization needs to advance its goals. This step is relatively simple for most nonprofits. Usually, they target their services toward rather well-defined population subgroups (rarely the general public) and have a fairly good idea of which individuals and foundations are likely to fund them. Current and potential service recipients, volunteers, and funders make up the bulk of most nonprofit target audiences. In addition, some may have important relationships with local, state, and federal government bodies, religious organizations, or ethnic communities. Normally, executives or the program director can easily identify which community segments or entities are most important to target.

(C)　RESEARCH

Once target audiences are identified, representatives of these audiences can be involved in the next step: image research.

- What do target audiences know about a given nonprofit?
- Is the image positive, negative, or blank?
- Where do members of target audiences get their information?
- What forms of media do they use most often?

These are among the fundamental questions that research for developing a media relations strategy should seek to answer. Depending on size and resources, nonprofits can undertake either formal research or "quick and dirty" studies that still provide helpful information.

Nonprofit agencies with extensive resources may wish to hire professional survey researchers to conduct an image research study. Such studies can provide detailed information that can be the basis for developing and disseminating media messages. Small agencies with limited public relations budgets are often tempted to omit doing research because of their inability to hire a research consultant. However, they can learn a great deal by asking representatives of their target audiences questions about their image. A question as simple as "What, if anything, is your image of Midwestern Youth Services?" can uncover valuable information. If 20 of 20 interviewees respond "no image," it is obvious that Midwestern Youth Services has a problem. While such findings might be dismissed as anecdotal, they are infinitely better than guessing, especially if the findings are highly consistent. Interviewing representatives of a target audience also can raise awareness for the contacts that will follow. No media relations strategy should be developed without some research, even research that is subpar by expert standards.

(D)　MEDIA USE ANALYSIS

The research should attempt to discover something about media use patterns of target audiences. The explosion in the number and forms of media outlets has made such information critical. Differences in age, income, occupation, and education can result in startlingly different media use patterns for different audiences. Young people, for example, may be more likely to search for information on the Internet than to read a local daily newspaper. Different radio stations attract different audiences. Newsletters may be effective with some audiences, whereas the same material should be posted on a Web site for others. Sophisticated media relations staff members following a strategic approach will target messages intended for particular audiences to the media outlets such audiences are most likely to use. This results in far greater efficiency and increases the probability that messages will reach and influence their targets.

(E)　MESSAGE DEVELOPMENT

Message development begins with the organization's mission and vision, the research on an organization's current image, and a decision about a desired image. In some cases, an existing image needs to be clarified or refined. The school district that wishes to be perceived as excellent in science education can easily build on an existing image of overall educational excellence, if that is what research demonstrates it enjoys. However, if research shows that the district's image is one of educational backwardness, messages about excellence in science education will need to demonstrate that something specific has changed. For example, a district will need to promote awareness of new facilities, a new curriculum, new programs, or higher-than-expected test scores. A message that the district has outstanding science instruction will not be credible without proof. Even the district that has a reputation for overall excellence will have to document its claims for special excellence in science.

Organizations should formulate an identity message to be included in all news media releases, such as "XYZ Child Care serving Midtown Metropolis since 1958." Identity statements are especially important when research shows that an organization has no image. Constant repetition of the statement should eventually have an impact on target audiences.

In addition to developing an identity message, nonprofits should develop one or two mission or goal messages to which all activities can be related. Media releases should focus on promoting the chosen messages. If an item or an activity does little to promote the organization's central identity or mission, publicizing it should be a low priority.

(F) VISUAL IMAGES

Media relations staff members need to be especially aware that visual images communicate even more powerfully than words. In selecting photos or video for news stories, public service announcements, and the like, organizations should consider whether these also convey the desired strategic message. For example, if a school district wants to be known for promoting technological education, photos should show students in laboratories or computer centers rather than playing basketball or decorating for homecoming.

(G) EVALUATION

Nonprofits should schedule annual evaluations of their media relations programs to test whether media messages are having the desired effect on membership, donations, or other organization goals. Periodic research similar to the initial image research is needed to ensure that the messages being stressed are still top priority, up to date, and needed to achieve an organizational goal. If messages A and B seem to have achieved their goal, this may be an opportunity to develop and communicate additional important messages. If a general favorable image has been created, audiences can be targeted with more specific information. For example, the school district that is perceived as excellent can now concentrate on enhancing its reputation for excellence in science and technology.

Evaluations must consider both the internal and external environments. Consider such questions as:

- Has anything changed that gives a particular message added urgency or appeal with an important target audience?
- Has a major national or local event drawn significant attention to a relevant problem or service?
- Has there been any legislation mandating relevant new programs or providing funding for existing programs?

Keeping pace with developments in the organization and in society is critical for carrying out an effective media relations strategy.

12.4 Media Choices: Impact of a Revolution

Both media relations staff members and target audiences have far more choices for sending and receiving messages than they did even five years ago. Online media have special appeal to educated and young adult audiences. There are more broadcast options than ever before, and even print offers diverse opportunities to target audiences.

(A) BROAD OPTIONS IN PRINT

Many media relations representatives focus mostly on local daily newspapers when smaller, more targeted publications might be more effective in reaching some audience segments. These more highly targeted publications also offer the opportunity to refine messages and offer details that would be of special interest to special audiences but of little interest to the general public. Print options readily available in many communities include:

- Weekly newspapers (including religious papers, neighborhood/suburban papers, cultural and ethnic papers)
- Newsletters
- Church bulletins
- School publications
- Special interest magazines, including trade magazines

(B) BROADCAST OPTIONS

Cable television has greatly expanded broadcast access for nonprofits. Agencies that stand little chance of receiving coverage on a local major station newscast might consider:

- Cable public access channels
- Public television and radio
- All-news radio and television stations
- Public affairs programs on all area channels

(C) ONLINE MEDIA

The Internet offers numerous opportunities for informing the public and has special appeal to audiences under 30 years of age. Growing numbers of business personnel and almost all educators are heavy consumers of information from the Internet. Nonprofits should establish their own home pages and refresh them regularly with news releases, calendars, information about upcoming events, and so forth to reach these prime target audiences.

12.5 Conclusion

A strategic approach to media relations can greatly benefit every nonprofit organization in reaching target audiences with important information. Nonprofits risk squandering scarce resources of time, effort, and money unless they develop an effective strategy, follow it, and periodically evaluate and update it.

Endnote

1. Seitel, F. P. (1998). *The Practice of Public Relations.* Saddlebrook, NJ: Prentice Hall.

Suggested Readings

Caywood, C. (1997). *The Handbook of Strategic Public Relations Integrated Communications.* New York: McGraw-Hill.

Farmer, B. (1995). "A Test and Refinement of the Situational Theory of Publics in Two Key Areas: Media and Demographics." Research paper submitted to the Public Relations Division of AEJMC. Cullowhee, NC: Western Carolina University.

Fombrun, C. J. (1996). *Reputation.* Boston: Harvard Business School Press.

McLoughlin, B. J. (1996). *Encountering the Media: The Strategic Media Communications Tool.* Washington, DC: McLoughlin MultiMedia Publishing Ltd.

Reeder, M. (1998). *The Strategic Communication Plan: Effective Communication for Strategic Leaders.* Carlisle Barracks, PA: Army War College.

Ridgway, J. (1988). *Practical Media Relations.* Cambridge: Gower Publishing Limited.

13 ▼ Contingency and Emergency Public Affairs

RICHARD L. THOMPSON, APR, DIRECTOR OF
PUBLIC AFFAIRS
Naval Research Laboratory, Washington, D.C.

13.1 Introduction

Many nonprofit organizations, by the nature of their activities, operate in inherently hazardous environments. Other nonprofit organizations conduct administrative functions in an office setting. Regardless of the nature of operations, proper response to a contingency or emergency demands mature judgment and appropriate action, taken without hesitation throughout the organization. One vital component of a nonprofit organization's response in a contingency or an emergency is communication with concerned stakeholders.

Public affairs contingencies and emergencies can include disruption of routine operations, computer failure involving breakdowns or hacking, or an accident involving injury or death. They may also include other occurrences that reflect badly on the organization, such as an employee drug abuse incident, fraud, mismanagement, improper hazardous waste disposal, and the like. The bottom line is that a public affairs contingency or emergency situation can be a real or perceived threat that has the potential to disrupt normal operations, prevents the nonprofit organization from attaining its goals, or could cause an adverse reaction among stakeholders.

The purpose of this chapter is to provide basic guidance to assist organization leaders, managers, and their public affairs executives in meeting their public affairs responsibilities in a wide variety of contingencies—incidents, accidents, and other emergencies.

13.2   Public Affairs Practitioner and Staff

During a contingency or an emergency, the public affairs practitioner and staff are key elements of the management team providing direct support to the organization leadership. In the event of a crisis, the public affairs staff should employ a variety of internal information systems—e-mail, faxes, bulletins, intranet/Internet Web pages, and newsletters—to keep staff and stakeholders informed as crisis response proceeds. In a public information capacity, the public affairs staff informs both the internal and external stakeholders of the incident and the organization's actions to control it.

13.3   Public Affairs Contingency Plan

The most effective way to deal with and respond to a contingency or an emergency is to have a public affairs plan in place before anything happens. This plan should, at a minimum, provide the methodology, processes, logistics, and training doctrine to:

- Provide relief and recovery from the contingency or emergency
- Reduce exposure and manage the risk to the organization
- Protect the organization's credibility and image with stakeholders, including the general public

This plan should anticipate and prepare for a wide range of contingencies, up to and including destruction of the organization's facility. Your plan should incorporate communications plans to notify the organization structure (both up and down), local support agencies, customers, stockholders, clients, members, and others in the event of any accident, incident, or contingency.

Employees, clients, customers, members, and the public have a legitimate interest in an occurrence that adversely affects your organization or operations, leading to injury, death, or extensive damage to property. To plan for and to be responsive and forthcoming in such situations:

- The public affairs director should be a participating member of panels, boards, or teams concerned with the planning for and response to crises and emergencies.
- Public affairs should be an element for consideration in all contingency and emergency planning.
- Public affairs actions should be prescribed in all organization contingency or emergency action plans.
- The senior leadership should promptly notify the public affairs director or a designated alternate when any incident, occurrence, or situation develops that has potential for causing a reaction on the part of the news media or the general public.
- The organization's senior public affairs practitioners should be contacted for advice and counsel in an emergency or for contingency planning.

Contingency and emergency planning, like public affairs, is a management function that is coordinated and done in conjunction with other departments within the organization. Organizations should plan for contingencies and emergencies the same way they operate on a daily basis—as a team.

The contingency planning team should include senior members from management, legal, public affairs, operations/customer service, security, finance/supply, purchasing, management information/computer operations, human resources, facilities management, administrative services, in-house and contractor technical experts, and other stakeholders, depending on your organization. Identifying the most appropriate and skilled members for your crisis team is not an easy task. Often, the best team members are not the people with the highest-ranking titles, but those who possess the required skills, talents, and personality to handle each function of crisis management. Carefully screening and selecting individuals who are right for contingency and emergency operation is one of the most critical decisions you can make.

When you pick your team, let your players know. Team members who have a role to play are more likely to prepare for a crisis and take the time to think through potential responses. Depending on the type and magnitude of your crisis, you may need to mobilize your entire team or just a few select members. Be sure you have established a foolproof method of notifying team members for quick response.

Planning for contingencies and emergencies is more than just preparing a written plan. Planning is a process, not a product. Contingency and emergency planning is a dynamic process that must be molded to the organization's changing internal and external environment. Effective contingency and emergency planning requires an active planning and training senior management team. In preparing the public affairs contingency plan, it is useful to have and follow a checklist. The following public affairs contingency checklist can be used as a guideline for planning purposes:

1. Who is the first public affairs official to be notified?
2. Who is notified if that person is not available?
3. Who is responsible for notifying the public affairs person?
4. Who of the public affairs staff is to be notified and mobilized? How will that notification be achieved?
5. Who notifies the public affairs staff?
6. Who is the organization's primary media spokesperson? What training and background do they have in contingency/crisis public affairs?
7. Who is the alternate spokesperson?
8. Who notifies the media?
9. What is the process by which news and information are processed and approved for release?
10. Who notifies employees?
11. Where is the press room? Where is the briefing room?
12. Who will be the secretary in the pressroom?
13. Who will be the messenger in the pressroom?
14. Who will gather factual information and relay it to the pressroom?
15. Who will arrange for food and supplies in the pressroom?
16. Who will arrange for transportation from the pressroom to the site, if not collocated?
17. Who will transport the press from the pressroom to the site?
18. Who in the organization will review and approve information before it is released to the press?

19. What is the senior management team interface process for approval of public affairs policy and release clearance?
20. What statements, if any, will be released by the organization?
21. How will press inquiries to the organization be handled and processed?
22. Who decides if media can visit the site?
23. Who will accompany the media on site visits?
24. Who are the public information officers for area organizations, city, county, state, and so on? How will they be informed?
25. How will your organization coordinate public information operations with other organizations?
26. Who can take photos/video for your organization?
27. Who will maintain a record of press contacts and monitor press coverage?
28. Who will correct the record should incorrect information be communicated by the media?

Keep a folder with incident/accident instructions, local and organization public affairs telephone numbers, and a list of established local organizational public affairs procedures. Include instruction pages from various organization manuals and current policy references that deal with contingencies.

In addition, preformatted contingency press releases that allow the user to either fill in the blanks or mix and match should be included. Update this material periodically. Finally, ensure that the contingency and emergency plans are easily understood so that someone outside the public affairs staff can initiate the plan in the event you are not available.

13.4   Public Affairs Goals During a Contingency or Emergency

Detailed instructions cannot be provided to cover every possible contingency; however, certain general actions are appropriate in most circumstances. Public affairs goals in a contingency or emergency include:

- Safeguarding people and protecting property
- Ensuring that civil authorities are provided with prompt and correct information to enable them to make decisions concerning protection of the public
- Retaining public confidence in the organization
- Respecting the rights of organization personnel to privacy and protecting their welfare and the dignity of the next-of-kin
- Honoring the right of the public to be informed rapidly and accurately of accidents and incidents and the organization's response in emergencies and other contingencies

It is during a time of crisis that your knowledge of the local media is most valuable. Relations with members of the general media in your area, and specific trade media in your business sector, should be constant and ongoing. An organization's working relationships with local media—that is, the ability to contact a media representative who is familiar with your organization—gives a public affairs practitioner a significant head start in solving a contingency or emergency communications situation.

(A) RELEASE OF INFORMATION

Accurate public affairs assessments are essential elements of an organization's evaluation of and report on a crisis or emergency. Public affairs assessments must be included in incident reports to higher levels of authority within your organization. The rapid release of accurate, factual information concerning an accident, incident, disaster, or other emergency is in the best interest of an organization. Speed and accuracy are vital. However, a release containing incorrect or speculative information may create panic and confusion. Conversely, an accurate release that is too late to inform the public is of little or no value. Although most details are unavailable and a comprehensive picture is elusive in the early stages of a contingency, rapid initial release of known, confirmed facts provides valuable information to the community.

When passed to higher elements of your organization, the initial release also alerts a larger public affairs network to render assistance to the local organization involved. If media representatives are at your location or nearby at the time of the accident, full cooperation should be rendered in covering the story, consistent with safety, protection of property and information at the site, and other pertinent requirements. Organizations should modify or expand the following public affairs assessments as required to fit their local situation:

- No media present
- Media present, press release follows
- No media present, media interest expected
- No known press interest
- Public concern anticipated; proposed statement and contingency questions and answers to follow
- Local media on scene, the following statement was made at (date/time): [summary of statement]

When an accident or significant incident occurs, the public affairs practitioner must be notified immediately. Depending on the situation, the public affairs practitioner must have the authority to recall some or all of the staff and prepare, properly staff, and disseminate information to the news media. The organization should draft the initial release and forward it to higher authority for release or release it locally; the information is not held pending inquiry. The goal for initial release should be one hour from the time the public affairs office is first notified of the occurrence and the time information is prepared for initial release. Within the next hour, the majority of local and other interested news media are informed. This is a goal, although situational constraints may cause initial release to take longer. Be right the first time.

During a crisis situation, it is especially important that the organization have only one spokesperson. Establish who that person is in advance, and designate an alternate. If too many individuals talk to the media, conflicting or out-of-date information will be presented, resulting in an impression that information management by the organization is poor and, ultimately, not credible. (This impression will have longer-term impact on overall public support—including funding—on which nonprofits depend.) Strongly suggest to the media that if they have not heard it from the designated spokesperson, they have not heard it correctly. Then "turn off" the unauthorized spokesperson.

The organization spokesperson is the final point of quality control prior to release of information. The spokesperson must ensure that the following six elements are considered and achieved prior to release:

1. Gather and relate accurate information. Consider how the public affairs organization will discover the facts, keep management informed, notify next-of-kin (if a fatality or serious injury is involved), and deal with media.
2. Consider legal aspects carefully. Consider how the organization will determine or be affected by legal liabilities, possible violations, and so on, and delegate this responsibility to a qualified legal counsel early in the public affairs contingency process.
3. Provide full, factual, objective, and truthful information. Resist inclinations—your own or others'—to slant, distort, manipulate, or fragment the truth. Being discovered in a lie will be much more damaging than anything an unfavorable truth might cause.
4. Gather, verify, and complete all units of information before release to the media. Avoid giving out partial, unchecked facts, which could result in repeated media mention with undue emphasis on bad news. Avoid the appearance of noncooperation.
5. Ensure accuracy, thoroughness, and completeness by providing information packages and World Wide Web sites. Press conferences, information sheets, handouts, prepared statements for broadcast appearances, e-mails, Web pages, and (in the final stages) press kits will contribute to effective communication when an emergency requires disseminating information to the media simultaneously.
6. Emphasize perspective by balancing bad news with good. The organization's reputation, earned over the years, should not be forgotten in a crisis.

(B) DENIAL AND ADVERSE INFORMATION

One way to create a public affairs problem for an organization is to deny that a particular event occurred when it did. If an organization has a contingency or emergency situation, either release the information or respond to media query with approved responses. The goal is to keep a one-day news story as just that: a one-day story. Denial or "no comment" on a bad news story will only prolong the issue and reinforce negative impressions among your publics on whom you depend for support, funding, and volunteers.

(C) NEWS RELEASES

Do not eliminate adverse information from a story. Present the facts without opinion and in detail. Your incident/accident story will then be given the treatment it deserves. If you create a situation in which reporters are forced to guess or, even more danger-ous, seek out "a source" (an informer), you can expect inquiries from every level within your organization into the incident, including the information release policies of your office.

The initial release should provide as much information as possible on the key points. It is extremely important that information be released to the public as soon as possible; the rapid release of information prevents or dispels rumors that could easily cause public alarm or promote misinformation in news media reports. Newly arriving media representatives can be updated later.

In general, initial and follow-up releases should include:

- Type of incident, accident, or contingency
- Location and time of the incident, accident, or contingency
- Persons involved. Initially, release number injured and killed, if known, as well as the number of staff and volunteers. Do not speculate—if you don't know, say so. Then find out as soon as possible.
- If a transportation-related incident or accident, the place of departure and destination. This pertains to vehicles, aircraft, vessels, and the like.
- Type of equipment or system involved
- Pertinent facts about activities or operations at the time of the incident or accident
- Investigation. Never speculate about the cause or contributing causes of an accident or the responsibility for the mishap. If the situation warrants, ensure that you release information stating that an investigation into the cause is being conducted by the proper authorities and that corrective measures are being taken. For example, if there is an environmental waste disposal problem, you should be prepared to tell the public what your organization is doing to clean it up and to prevent future occurrences.

(D) RELEASE OF INFORMATION PERTAINING TO EMPLOYEES OR VOLUNTEERS

Whenever possible, the public affairs practitioner must coordinate with the human resources office or other designated organization department prior to releasing information on employees who have been injured or killed in accidents. There are several critical aspects in releasing information pertaining to employees or volunteers involved in accidents:

- Information must not be released to news media until confirmation is received that next-of-kin have been notified. Thereafter, information released to media must agree with that provided to the next-of-kin. This means that the next-of-kin are advised of details before the media are, and that the media are not given any information that is not provided to the next-of-kin.
- Following medical care for the injured, the rights and dignity of the persons involved in accidents and their next-of-kin are of paramount importance. However, the public's right to know takes on new importance in regard to accidents, incidents, and other disasters. Releasing the names of accident victims can relieve the anxiety and concern of relatives and friends of those not injured. Early and ongoing liaison with the human resources office point-of-contact will enable the organization to release names as soon as possible after the accident.
- Should an accident occur off the organization's property but employees are involved, news media on the scene may be able to obtain identification without consulting the public affairs practitioner. Humanitarian considerations dictate that the next-of-kin be notified of the situation before they learn of it through the news media. If it is apparent that news media

know the identity of accident victims and next-of-kin have not been notified, the public affairs practitioner should make a professional appeal to the reporters or editors requesting that they withhold names of persons involved until notification is made. It is critical to inform the human resources office of the results of this appeal and the personnel whose names are likely to be known by the reporters. Knowing and having an established relationship with local and regional editors prior to the occurrence can make the critical difference between success and failure in this area.

(E)   HELPING FAMILY MEMBERS DEAL WITH THE PRESS

During times of crisis, your organization's employees, volunteers, and families may become the targets of news media attention as reporters try to localize or give an emotional edge to the story. It is easy to blame the press for a lack of compassion. But the truth is that many families do not realize that once they are publicly identified, they become targets for other reporters and the general public.

Some important things family members should know about dealing with the press include:

- News is an extremely competitive business, with reporters going to great lengths to get the story before their competitors.
- It is the right of the individual to say no to an interview request. In the past, some reporters have coerced family members into submitting to interviews by emphasizing the public's right to know and freedom of the press, but your right to privacy always takes precedence.
- The individual's home is private property; no one, media or otherwise, has a right to enter your home, or be on your property, unless you grant them that privilege.
- If the subject under scrutiny does decide to talk with the media, ground rules for that protection should be established before the interview. Responsible professional reporters will work to meet reasonable ground rules. These ground rules are often negotiated or brokered by the public affairs practitioner, who represents and provides counsel to the interviewee. The public affairs practitioner will discuss and seek agreement of the ground rules with the media representative prior to any direct contact with the interviewee. Ground rules can include no photos/video of faces, disguising of voices, nonattribution of comments, and the like.
- Family members may not wish to have their full names used, and you should always ensure that the home address is not used. Television pictures of an employee or volunteer's house are usually not a good idea.

13.5   *Incidents or Accidents Outside Your Facility*

Should an incident or accident occur outside your facility, the public affairs challenge becomes more complex. From a logistics standpoint, the public affairs team must then operate from two locations, the public affairs office and the accident site, with public affairs representatives at both locations. This complicates communications, transportation, and public information clearance procedures. This eventuality should be anticipated and addressed in your planning.

Consistent with organizational, legal, and operational constraints, your organization should give maximum cooperation to news representatives covering incidents and accidents. Immediately following an accident or incident, the organization should:

- Take action to minimize further injury and property damage.
- Assist in rescue of survivors and treatment of the injured.
- Report the incident or accident to the proper authority.
- Preserve the accident scene to assist investigators.
- Protect organization files and records.
- Consult with civil authorities if activating public warning or evacuation plans may be appropriate.
- Rapidly meet the need for public information about the accident or incident.

No two contingencies are identical, but public affairs actions at an off-site location should include:

- *Defining the area.* Upon arrival at the accident scene, the senior public affairs official should request that law enforcement or public safety authorities rope off the entire area to protect the public from injury and property from further disturbance.
- *Briefing the reporters.* The organization should prepare contingency questions and answers to respond to likely news media inquiries at the incident or accident scene. Once statements or contingency answers are approved, the senior public affairs official at the scene should be granted permission to release the preapproved information. In addition, reporters should be briefed on safety hazards (if any) and the need to preserve the site for investigators before they are permitted to enter the cordoned-off area. The briefing should be done by the public affairs official at the scene who can get information from others present. If a reporter refuses to cooperate with the ground rules, you have the option to request that security personnel deny access to the individual. Keep in mind that you may not physically restrict the movement of the news media at accident sites, except on your property.
- *Admitting reporters to the area.* After the area is cordoned off, news media representatives are briefed, and law enforcement, public safety, and organization officials advise that an area is safe, the senior public affairs official on the scene may grant permission to enter the accident area.
- *Media identification.* As part of the public affairs office contingency planning, special news media identification badges may be required and should be kept on hand. These may consist of inexpensive plastic badges, arm bands, or other similar devices that conform to the organization's security badging system and are ready for immediate issue in the event of an incident or other emergency. Badges can be prepared in advance, with one or more badges marked and set aside for each local newspaper, several for each television station, and so on. The badges can be taken to the accident scene by the public affairs office member assigned that duty by the organization's

contingency planning. Wearing the badge signifies to the organization and law enforcement personnel that the wearer has been briefed on safety considerations regarding the accident site and the need to preserve the site for investigators. More importantly, the badge system can ease confusion at a busy, crowded site. Reporters' wearing of such identification is voluntary in areas outside your property, but can be required of them when at your facility.

As soon as possible following the conclusion of the event, the public affairs practitioner should develop a narrative summary of public affairs actions taken before and following the contingency, as a training tool to critique the staff and share lessons learned. The summary should be shared with the rest of the organization. A cassette tape recorder is helpful for making notes during fast-moving situations.

13.6   *Contingency Public Affairs Do's and Don'ts*

Do's
- Get the facts before you talk with the press.
- Establish who is going to speak for the organization.
- Get information to the press as quickly as possible and be aware of press deadlines.
- Issue statements in writing if at all possible.
- Emphasize the positive.
- Know to whom you are speaking. Get the reporter's name and get the name and telephone number in telephone interviews. Log all media queries on media query forms.
- Aid media representatives in getting the story.
- Monitor media coverage, including the Internet, and correct errors quickly.
- Say "I don't know" if you don't know. Follow up by taking the question and state that you will try to get the answer.

Don'ts
- Don't say "No comment."
- Don't guess or speculate—ever!
- Don't release damage estimates without double checking for accuracy.
- Don't release names of victims until notification of next-of-kin has been made. Then confirm again that notificiation has been made.
- Don't try to mislead or cover up information. Never lie.
- Don't try to place blame.
- Don't play favorites with the media. Release information to everyone at the same time.
- Don't ever make off-the-record comments. There is no such thing.
- Don't use inflammatory, spectacular terms like "blown to bits," "raging fire," or "torn limb from limb."
- Don't repeat negative or inaccurate statements in answering questions.
- Don't panic, cry, or lose control.

13.7   *Who Has Release Authority?*

Who in your organization has the authority to release news? Important news releases are in effect announcements by the senior administrator concerning major appointments, policy, or matters of sufficient importance that justify release from the highest level in the organization. This also includes news that may affect organization policy or have a political impact.

Information that affects the entire organization may be released by the organization headquarters. The news release and information could be researched and developed by your department or division and provided to the organization headquarters for further staffing and approval prior to release. Depending on the size of the organization, there may be several levels of hierarchy to negotiate prior to reaching headquarters.

Matters concerning an individual organization, such as announcements of limited interest (local achievements, background materials, etc.), may be released at the local level. If you have any doubt about your authority in a given situation, you should contact public affairs officials at a more senior level of your organization before you talk to the press.

13.8   *The Mobile Public Affairs Office*

With the rapidly expanding capabilities of laptop computer technology, increased hard-drive storage, high-data-rate internal modems, increasingly user-friendly software, and the Internet, the mobile laptop office has become a reality. When coupled with a cellular telephone with plug-in modem capability, a pager, and a handheld organizer such as a Palm Pilot™, the nonprofit executive has the capability to set up a mobile office virtually anywhere.

The savvy executive, with some thought and preparation, can load software programs and data that allow the laptop computer to become a multipurpose mobile office capable of not only word processing, desktop publishing, Web page development, database management, and spreadsheet development, but also a powerful communications tool for faxing information to both individuals and groups, and for corresponding directly with stakeholders via e-mail and the Internet.

Due to the rapid evolution of computer technology, particular systems will not be addressed here, except to say that both recent-technology Windows and Macintosh operating system laptops provide more computing power than the average nonprofit executive will ever use. The same can be said for fax/modem, ethernet, and printer technologies.

In the selection of a computer, the same rule that applies to desktop computers applies to laptop computers. Though the circuits, central processing units, and hard drives may be the same from one model to the next, pay close attention to the human/machine interface and ergonomics when purchasing. Of particular importance is determining whether the laptop keyboard (often smaller in size than a desktop computer keyboard) and display are comfortable to you. The best way to determine if you and a laptop are a good ergonomic fit is to perform a number of functions on the keyboard while viewing the screen in varying light conditions. If either your hands or your eyes feel strained, then search for another laptop with a better fit. Other laptop features to look for include random access memory (RAM) expandability, a built-in mouse, infrared communication/networking and file transfer capability, built-in video monitor capability that allows you to connect to an external color monitor, and built-in modem/ethernet capability.

Once you find the computer that suits your specific needs, the next task is selecting software and loading data to make it useful. Regardless of the operating system you use (Windows or Macintosh), there are literally thousands of software products on the market to fill your hard drive. Because you are mobile, it is recommended that you use "industry standard" software for word processing, desktop publishing, database, spreadsheet software, and communications software (for fax/modem and online services). Word Perfect, Microsoft Office, Adobe Pagemaker, Adobe Pagemill and others are widely accepted, and offer a high degree of cross-platform (Windows to Macintosh and vice versa) compatibility. A personal information manager (PIM) that incorporates a calendar, electronic Rolodex, and to-do list is also important. As an example, 3Com's Palm Pilot™ handheld organizers are bundled with the Palm Desktop™ organizer software for the personal computer that incorporates an electronic address book, calendar, to-do list, memo pad, and expense report. This PIM software can be synchronized and updated by pressing one button either by wire connection or infrared file transfer. Many handheld organizers are now available with direct Internet and e-mail connection and transmission capabilities.

What would a nonprofit public affairs practitioner require to operate from a remote site on short notice? From a public affairs standpoint, the well-equipped laptop should include some or all of the following information:

- Executive biographies, history, product, and organization fact sheets (word processing or desktop publishing software)
- Calendar (PIM software)
- Electronic Rolodex (PIM software)
- To-do list (PIM software)
- Organization decision makers and key staff members list with names, addresses, fax, telephone, and e-mail (PIM software)
- Public affairs contingency plan with "fill-in-the-blank" contingency press releases (word processing or desktop publishing software)
- Media list with name, address, telephone, and e-mail (PIM software or database software, tab-separated entry with ability to export to fax/modem transmission software, word processing mail merge for envelope labels, letters/memoranda/press releases, and e-mail)
- Organization membership list with name, address, telephone, and e-mail (PIM software or database software, tab-separated entry with ability to export to fax/modem transmission software, word processing mail merge for envelope labels, letters/memoranda/press releases, and e-mail)
- Organization budget and obligations to date in the event you must operate away from your normal office (spreadsheet software)
- An inventory of supplies required to equip an off-site or remote office (database or spreadsheet software)

Other required equipment includes:

- Backup operating system and software program CDs/diskettes
- Backup CDs/diskettes of program data
- Serial, parallel port printer cables
- Electrical extension cord (batteries don't last forever)
- Spare, charged batteries

- RJ-11 duplex adapter (allows you to plug a phone and a modem into a single wall telephone jack)
- 25 feet of telephone wire
- Ethernet cable for network connections
- Blank diskettes

While operating away from your office, there are normally three options in terms of printing:

1. Use of a printer on site
2. Carrying a laptop portable printer
3. Use of a local fax machine as a printer

Unless you are planning to be off site for an extended period, seriously consider options 1 and 3. "Borrowing" an on-site laser printer when away from your office is a good option, and use of a plain paper laser fax provides high-quality printing. Consider these options before carrying a three- to four-pound portable printer that often provides less quality or speed.

Communicating via fax/modem is now far easier, because many office, hotel, and pay telephones are equipped with data ports. Using a fax/modem allows you to transmit and receive your e-mail messages from your online service mail box or to transmit a fax. Whether operating in borrowed or leased office space, a hotel room, or a pay telephone, with the properly equipped laptop and a fax/modem, the mobile office–savvy public affairs practitioner can communicate efficiently and effectively virtually worldwide.

As an example of this concept, an organization was recently required to evacuate its headquarters facility for several days due to a fire in an adjacent structure. Because of extensive travel requirements, several senior executives were equipped with laptops, cellular telephones, and handheld organizers that allowed them to operate their mobile office while at remote sites. Immediately following the evacuation, these executives organized their staff in temporary quarters at five locations—three of which were in home offices or around dining room tables—and began the process of notifying stakeholders that they were conducting business as usual. Because their laptops and personal organizers used a "standard set" of software programs and could transfer information via infrared link, each team could establish a line-of-site wireless network that sped up the work process.

The displaced crisis team first changed the switchboard voice mail message alerting callers to the emergency situation at their headquarters facility and informing them of a newly established Web site that contained additional information prior to automatically forwarding the call to one of three temporary office sites. Concurrently, the special Web page advising stakeholders of the situation was developed, approved, and uploaded to the organization's Web server. Finally, an initial e-mail was drafted, edited, approved, and released to interested stakeholders and the media. All of these actions were "staffed to approval" via the telephone and e-mail. As the situation changed and more information was available, communication updates were made to the switchboard voice mail message, emergency Web page, and follow-up e-mails to stakeholders.

As the situation dragged on, additional laptop computers, cellular telephones, and telephone lines were purchased to handle the volume of normal business. In addition to the extra telephone lines, conference calling and residential voice messaging services were purchased from the telephone company. After eight days, the organization was able to return to its headquarters facility and resume normal operations.

13.9   Contingency Public Affairs Office Equipment Checklist

The following is a comprehensive supply checklist required to equip a remote public affairs office. This checklist should be used as a "mix and match" to meet the nonprofit organization's contingency or remote requirements. There is also the option of using locally available vendors, public relations/advertising agencies, and other sources to provide some equipment and services required temporarily.

1. Public affairs equipment
   - Audiocassette tape recorder, handheld, with lectret condenser microphone
   - Videocassette recorder ($3/4$-inch or $1/2$-inch VHS)
   - Television receiver/monitor
   - Camera kit (35mm SLR), electronic flash unit, lenses (35mm/50mm/70–120mm zoom, or comparable), appropriate filters, tripod, case
   - Digital camera kit (35mm SLR), electronic flash unit, lenses (35mm/50mm/70–120mm zoom, or comparable), appropriate filters, tripod, case
   - Megaphone/hailer
   - Handheld communications system
   - Automatic broadcast feed unit
   - Cellular telephone
   - Portable lecterns (with built-in microphone/speakers/auxiliary inputs/outputs)
   - Media feed "multiboxes"
   - Portable mixers, extra microphones, power outlets, cables, and connectors
   - VHF/Bearcat frequency scanner
   - Radio, multiband, portable
   - Slide projector
   - Overhead projector
   - Screen
   - Backdrop for briefings
   - Chalkboard/bulletin board
2. Public affairs supplies
   - Audiocassette tapes (C-30 and C-60)
   - Videocassette tapes
   - Film, 35mm (Tri-X/Plus-X/color print/color slide)
   - Nicad batteries for camera and flash unit
   - Nicad batteries for tape recorders
   - Lettering/sign-making kit
   - Photo mailers
   - Cardboard photo protector
   - News release letterhead
   - Media center sign (with Velcro holder)
   - Nicad battery charger
3. Public affairs publications
   - Dictionary (English/Spanish/French/German)
   - Thesaurus (or comparable software program hard copy/floppy disk)

- Public affairs staff directories
- Ayers Dictionary of Publications
- Regulations, instructions, directives (as appropriate)
- Telephone directory
- Maps/charts of area, including road map

4. Office furniture
   - Desks
   - Chairs
   - Computer desk/printer table
   - Filing cabinet, two-drawer
   - Light table

5. Office equipment
   - Laptop microcomputers with hard drive and fax modem
   - Backup system and application software
   - Backup files of all current work
   - Printers with cable connectors
   - Surge protector/fused electric cords
   - Facsimile/fax machine, portable
   - Typewriter, self-correcting electric, with various typewriter balls
   - Typewriter, manual
   - Telephone answering machine with audiocassette and audio patch cords
   - Xerographic copier, portable

6. Office supplies
   - Clipboards
   - Staplers
   - Staple remover
   - Scissors
   - Rulers (12- and 18-inch)
   - Pencil sharpener, electric
   - Pencil sharpener, manual
   - Hole punches (two- and three-hole)
   - File basket
   - Trash baskets

7. Office supplies (consumables)
   - Staples, rubber bands (various sizes), erasers, thumbtacks/push pins, pencils, ballpoint pens, felt tip pens (blue/black/red/green, etc.), waterproof felt tip markers (blue/black/red)
   - Masking tape ($\frac{1}{2}$-inch, 1-inch, 2-inch rolls)
   - Duct tape
   - Nylon filament tape
   - Cellophane tape (clear/transparent)
   - Paper clips
   - Bond paper ($8\frac{1}{2} \times 11$-inch)
   - Writing pads (legal pads, stenograph pads, carbon paper manifold sets, pocket pads, continuous form plain white computer paper, organization letterhead, labels)
   - Business envelopes, white manila ($9\frac{1}{2} \times 12$-inch, 6×9-inch)
   - Computer floppy diskettes (appropriate for type of laptop), hard/protected case labels

- Telephone message pads
- Address labels, gummed, continuous form/fan-folded
- 3 × 5-inch cards
- Post-It™ notes
- Name tags, individual, self-sticking, continuous-form
- Telecopier paper
- Fax paper
- Index tabs
- File folders
- Accordion file folders
- Glue sticks
- Razor blades, single edge
- Ribbons typewriter and computer printer
- Correction tape
- Laser printer toner cartridges

8. Miscellaneous equipment
   - Heavy-duty worklight
   - Flashlights: three-cell, two-cell, penlight
   - Extension cords: 100-foot, 50-foot with multiple outlet strips
   - Coffee pot: 50-cup, including filters, coffee cups, sugar, cream substitute
   - Tool box with standard screwdrivers, Phillips screwdrivers, claw hammer, pliers, assorted
   - Nuts/bolts/nails/screws

9. Miscellaneous supplies
   - Nicad flashlight batteries ("D" and "C" sizes with recharger)
   - Insect repellent
   - Fly swatter
   - Broom
   - Cleaning supplies

10. Temporary shelter
    - Leased office space
    - Home office
    - Mobile home on site (office configuration)
    - Tent (large enough to accommodate 20 people plus equipment)

Note: Quantities of each item and actual items required will be determined by local requirements and expected duration.

Strategic Planning for Information Systems

E. Brian Peach, PhD
University of West Florida

Richie Platt, PhD
University of West Florida

14.1 Introduction

E-mail. Electronic commerce. Digital banking. Wireless communications. Broadband access. Mass customization. ADSL. The digital information age is exploding with over 180 million Internet users expected in the United States by 2004. There is a persistent ratcheting up of the levels of expected service, and technological innovations, opportunities, and expectations bombard managers nearly as rapidly as the speed of light through a fiber-optic network. What is today's information-age, nonprofit manager to do? How is the organization to function competently when technology developments race forward, while the demands mount that budgets shrink almost as rapidly? How can the nonprofit manager improve the organization's strategic focus and position through the recognition that information is an important organizational resource that must be managed (to include strategic planning) just like the organization's capital, equipment, and personnel. How does the nonprofit manager determine which uses of technology best improve the strategic positioning of the organization for success in the digital age?

Harnessing information and the systems designed to manipulate and control that information has the potential to provide strategic benefit to all forms of organizations, including nonprofit organizations. This chapter will provide the nonprofit manager of the twenty-first century with an outline for focusing the use of information technology (IT) and information systems (IS) to improve the strategic positioning of the organization while simultaneously controlling growth in demand for electronic fads and gadgets. Technology investment decisions are not a question of whether the investment will be made and are not really a question of when. The real question is: How much will the organization invest, and more importantly, how will it plan and control its investment to provide the most long-term strategic benefit?

Effective planning requires a clear understanding of what an information system is, and what it is not. This chapter begins by providing a basic understanding of the components and characteristics of an information system. We also clarify some common misconceptions about the difference between information systems and information technology, and about what an information system is or does. We then describe the two critical roles IS should play in organizational goal achievement, and how these dual roles make strategic planning an increasingly important task for IS.

(A) INFORMATION AND INFORMATION SYSTEMS IN THE ORGANIZATION

An information system exists to help provide strategic advantage to the organization by controlling the flow of information within an organization and presenting it to appropriate organizational stakeholders in a timely and useful manner. An IS is a synergistic relationship integrating five components—hardware, software, networks, data, and people—in order to satisfy the information collection, processing, storage, and retrieval requirements of the organization. The key words here are *information* and *system*. Information is data that have been put into some useful and meaningful context to the user/ decision maker. System represents the interaction of these five activities functioning as a single, organized entity. An IS therefore consists of the activities that capture, store, and transform data into the information assets required to support the operational and managerial information needs of the organization, and then disseminate these information assets to where they are needed by the organization.

(B) CLASSES OF INFORMATION SYSTEMS

Successful planning for information systems, specifically strategic planning for information systems (SPIS), requires attention to the alignment of mission and purpose and the inclusion of all five pivotal IS components. This applies regardless of the type(s) of IS used within the organization. Based on the kinds of activities involved and the decisions supported, there are four fundamental types or classifications of IS available to nonprofit organizations.

The first type of activity IS supports consists of the basic operational-level activities performed by transaction processing systems. These systems support the day-to-day business operations and administration activities of the organization (e.g., accounting, payroll, constituent services, customer relationship management). The next three types of activities are a class of IS applications known as management support systems (MSS) and they support managerial information requirements. Each type of MSS satisfies a different category of information need and all can be used as strategic information systems applications. The three MSS types are:

1. *Information reporting systems (IRS),* which supply the regular, recurring types of managerial information often needed by operational-level managers
2. *Decision support systems (DSS),* which address the one-time, *ad hoc* decision problem often best handled by statistical analysis or modeling
3. *Executive information systems (EIS),* which provide senior executives with aggregated presentations while concurrently preserving many levels of supporting detail for display as needed

(C) INFORMATION SYSTEMS VERSUS INFORMATION TECHNOLOGY

Planning for IS requires understanding what you are planning for, and that requires an understanding of the differences between information systems and information technology. Confusing these two related but very different concepts can lead to faulty decisions and wasted resources.

By strict definition, IT represents the most highly visible components of an IS; the hardware, software, and network infrastructure. Examples of IT include personal computers, fax machines, telephone networks, and other physical structures used to physically perform the input, storage, and retrieval operations for an organization's data. Notice, however, that the data and people components of an IS are completely missing from IT. Also missing are the integration and commonality of purpose found in an IS. Although one example of IT is the ubiquitous personal computer that sprouted on every desk in most organizations over the last 10 to 15 years, the technology represented by personal computers does not, by itself, constitute an IS. Neither does building a Web page on the Internet or having a cellular phone. Each of these represents only one of the components required to have an effective, efficient information system. To successfully incorporate IT into organizational information systems, the capabilities of IT must be selected to support the integrated commonality of purpose of the IS and the organization's mission and strategy.

Thus, an IS incorporates not just the technological functionality of IT resources (e.g., hardware, software, and networks); it comprises a synergistic relationship between its five pivotal components that surpasses the capability of each, regardless of the allure and fascination of the latest IT developments.

(D) MISCONCEPTIONS, PITFALLS, AND THE DUALITY OF INFORMATION SYSTEMS

A number of misconceptions and potential pitfalls can hinder an organization's ability to plan for and implement IS as agents for gaining and maintaining strategic advantage. A relatively new source of confusion about the use of IS in organizations is the conflict between the historical role of IS in controlling costs (achieving operational effectiveness) and the contemporary mandate to utilize IS/IT to improve the strategic positioning of the organization.

(i) Confusing Information Technology for Information Systems

If strategic planners are not clear about the difference between IT and IS, there will be a tendency to focus on popular IT hot topics as necessary primary ingredients of SPIS, when in reality these are issues often more appropriately addressed at either the tactical or even the operational level of planning. For example, there are currently two major competitors in the market for providing high-speed, broadband access to the Internet: cable modems and asymmetric digital subscriber lines. A true strategic goal might be to improve the level of access to external communications; thus, SPIS would define necessary infrastructure capacity and capability, but SPIS would not specify which broadband technology to use. Selection of either of these technologies as the backbone for the telecommunications infrastructure is an IT decision.

(ii) Confusing Networks for Information Systems

Another popular misconception is that simply buying microcomputers connected through a network and putting them on desktops is the same as buying an IS for the organization (the need for network connectivity will be addressed later in this section). Microcomputers, even with the latest office application software suite and a high-speed Internet connection, do not inherently constitute an IS. Note the missing commonality of purpose and the absence of any alignment with organizational strategic goals and objectives. However, the same microcomputer network becomes a strategic application of IS if the organization decides to improve the flow of internal information by implementing an intranet and establishing procedures to provide all workers with immediate access to relevant information.

(iii) The Duality of Information Systems: Confusing Efficiency and Effectiveness

Another common source of confusion lies in the dual role for IS within an organization. Historically, most managers viewed IS only as a tool or technique to reduce organizational costs. This view has its origins in the early days of IS when reducing costs was the primary focus of data processing. The cost-cutting view of IS typically worked by reducing the cost to perform simple transactions of existing activity sets by automating them. However, automating a poorly designed process does not affect or improve the process itself and results only in an automated, poorly designed process. This valuable but restricted view limits the full utilization of IS capabilities.

(iv) Information Systems and Strategic Positioning

Today, as organizations position themselves to transition into the next millennium, IS must play a much broader and more involved role within the organization. In addition to its role in improving operational efficiency, IS should also be viewed as a tool to enhance an organization's strategic position by identifying, developing, and implementing value-adding activity sets. Viewing IS solely from a cost-reduction perspective precludes consideration of IS contributions to redefining the organization's strategic positioning. This is not to say that reducing costs or achieving greater organizational efficiency is not part of the role of SPIS. But such techniques as business process reengineering (BPR) focus on using the capabilities of IS to restructure value-adding activities to substantively increase levels of organization performance with existing or reduced asset costs. This is a shift from a purely transactional cost-savings perspective to a strategic perspective that capitalizes on the capabilities of an IS to empower fundamental realignments of organizational activities. The strategic potential inherent in IS underscores the necessity for SPIS to be an integral part of the overall organizational planning effort and thereby altering the strategic posture of the organization.

(E) PRODUCTIVITY PARADOX AND ITS RELATIONSHIP TO INFORMATION SYSTEMS

To reap the full benefit of IS, SPIS has to be involved in all IT acquisitions. In the decade following the introduction of the IBM personal computer (PC) in 1981, organizations invested billions of dollars in computer-related technology, especially desktop microcomputers and the software to operate them, but these investments were made without a rationale based on SPIS. Much of this investment was based on the intuitively attractive belief that providing workers with more powerful tools would improve their productivity. Paradoxically, that appeared to not be the case. In the early 1990s, a common subject for analysis and discussion was the so-called productivity paradox: the apparent lack of measurable improvement in white-collar productivity after a massive investment in technology intended specifically to increase office workers' productivity. This early lack of perceived productivity increases, followed by more recent evidence of productivity increases, gives us insight into the role and importance of IS versus IT.

In the early days of IS, or the mainframe era, all computing was done on the organizational mainframe computer. The importance of sharing data was inherently known from these days of mainframe computers and their proprietary networks. In that environment, organizational databases were readily accessible to all persons who had a terminal connected to the mainframe telecommunications network. Using this network, workers had almost instantaneous access to the most recent organizational data. However, any networking or data sharing had to be done using the mainframe computer's proprietary networking capabilities through terminals connected to the mainframe. In addition, this communications network provided a means for distributed data collection and distribution only. It did not support the collaboration and sharing of ideas directly and immediately.

The introduction of stand-alone microcomputers was an IT decision that did not improve on this model. In fact, they diminished it. Gone was the immediate access to the latest corporate data. The benefits of shareability were lost in the rush to empower workers with their own computing resources. The necessity of sharing data soon became apparent and gave rise to the *sneaker-net* phenomenon: downloading data onto diskettes and walking the diskette to the requesting location. Although this was a slow and cumbersome process, it nonetheless emphasized the dependency on the exchange and sharing of information necessary within organizations. With stand-alone microcomputers, workers had to download a copy of needed data and use the sneaker-net to get it to their office.

Realizing the problems inherent in stand-alone computers, organizations using SPIS began to bring PCs back into organizational-level planning. Beginning with local area networks (LANs) in the late 1980s, organizations have linked their investment in IT into organized, coherent networks that provide two basic capabilities that stand-alone microcomputers did not. First, networks allow workers to share data quickly and easily. Networks once again provide all workers with access to centralized databases.

The second capability of networked computers is their ability to support collaborative work. Networking allows organizations to link their investment in microcomputers into powerful organizational tools that can rapidly exchange data and information among users. They also provided for collaboration and simultaneous work-product sharing, thereby permitting multiple people to work on the same project in parallel by real-time sharing of their ideas and actions. The corresponding increase in worker productivity showed that the paradox of productivity for technology investment was directly related to an organization's ability to successfully incorporate networking as one of the fundamental aspects of SPIS. Although still a subject for discussion and research, the productivity paradox rapidly faded in the middle of the 1990s as measurable productivity began to rise.

14.2 *What Is Strategic Planning for Information Systems?*

(A) STRATEGIC PLANNING DEFINITIONS AND CONCEPTS

Strategic planning is a systematic and iterative process that positions the organization to maximize its continuing ability to effectively respond to the demands its environment (internal and external) places on it. We use strategic planning here in a larger sense (what some call strategic management), where it is an iterative process that constantly assesses, in the words of Peter Drucker, where an organization is, where it wants to go, and how it will get there. Many nonprofit organizations historically occupied protected niches but now find themselves in dynamic, rapidly changing environments that demand new strategies to deal with for-profit invaders, radical changes in the demographics of their sponsors and clients, shifting governmental relationships, and an almost endless variety of new demands.

In Section 14.4, we provide a strategic planning model and an example of developing a strategic plan. In this section, we want to clarify the multiple roles that SPIS must perform if it is to take advantage of the many benefits it can provide.

(i) *Goals and Functions of Strategic Planning*
The goal of strategic planning is to position the organization to adapt to changing environmental requirements and thereby enable the organization to increase the perceived value it delivers to stakeholders. The function of strategic planning is to provide a process and structure for an organization to methodically and consistently apply proven methods and techniques to defining and modifying an organization's internal value-adding activities. Structure helps to avoid overlooking critical steps or considerations and provides continuity of action and a basis for assessing effectiveness. At the same time, to the extent structure ensures inclusion of necessary actions, it defines the process an organization uses and tends to limit planning activities to the identified process. Thus, the planning process itself must evolve over time to provide the appropriate structure and process.

(ii) *Strategic Planning and Operational Effectiveness*
For any organization with finite resources, cost containment is a significant and powerful consideration. A for-profit firm assesses success at cost containment with its profit measure. Nonprofits assess cost-containment success with the additional quality, quantity, and perceived value of the services it provides. Controlling costs has been a major effort for

many firms; Michael Porter, a leading industrial economist, refers to this as operational effectiveness (OE). In its earliest forms, strategic planning was essentially the preparation of budgets to allow organizations to predict and control costs of individual functions or activities. As time passed and the working environment became more complex, strategic planning moved to include more sophisticated techniques to assess and improve on the cost control measures used by organizations. These include techniques such as total quality management (TQM), continuous improvement, empowerment, outsourcing, time-based management, and benchmarking.

Ultimately, however, focusing exclusively on cost control, or OE, may result in undesirable outcomes. One possible outcome is that in its zeal to cut costs, a nonprofit may inadvertently eliminate or curtail services that are viewed as critical by one or more of its stakeholders. This results initially in erosion of perceived value and ultimately in reduction of support. Another possible outcome occurs when different nonprofit organizations cut costs based on comparing themselves against the same benchmarks. This can result in increasing commonality of adopted policies and procedures, reducing differences—real or perceived—among the organizations. Resource support may then erode as sponsors and other constituents perceive no basis for valuing one organization over another. In today's world, OE is a necessary objective for nonprofits, but it is not sufficient by itself to guarantee consistent attainment of organizational objectives.

(iii) Strategic Planning and Strategic Positioning

Strategic positioning is how an organization defines itself to its various stakeholders such that it is perceived as different and valuable. An organization cannot control its image and maintain its strategic position merely through press releases and public statements. True strategic position derives from the unique set of activities the organization chooses to perform. A unique combination and execution of activities provides the organization with a unique position. A first step in strategic planning, therefore, is for the organization to make conscious decisions about how constituent needs and differences will be addressed. An *overly broad* position underserves some clients and overserves others. An *overly narrow* position matches service type and level to a specific client's needs but may exclude all others from the target client base.

As an organization selects and defines its desired strategic position, it should select the set of activities it will perform that will best provide the needed services in support of its strategic position. Defining a strategic position through the selection of activities and establishing synergies and relationships among them is an important process because this is what makes the organization unique and valued. There are three aspects to activity selection: first, selecting the activities themselves; second, defining the internal coordination, communication, and control procedures among them; and third, assessing the level of activity fit. SPIS plays a critical role in all three aspects because it has an organizational view rather than the parochial view of a specific activity, and because it is a major contributor of the enabling mechanisms for activities to function and fit together. Proper activity selection precludes redundant or wasted effort and ensures that the activities fit together. Poor controls and weak communication links dilute the effectiveness of even the best activity set selection.

Activity fit is a key consideration. Activity fit means that attitudes are conceptually consistent across the organization and they are mutually reinforcing in the way they support the strategic position. The tighter and more interlocked activities are, the more they will be able to identify strengths and deficiencies in other activities leading to an improved activity set as well as increased OE. SPIS plays a critical role in devising supportive measures for increasing activity fit by providing information access and sharing and the necessary communication structure.

Proper use of OE and strategic positioning are necessary for an organization to excel. They differ in that OE is typically incremental and focuses on optimizing costs of existing individual activities. Strategic positioning looks at the entire activity set and can create radical change by adding, eliminating, or combining activities into a new set.

(B) STRATEGIC PLANNING FOR INFORMATION SYSTEMS

SPIS is a direct consequence of the philosophy that says that information is an important organizational resource. Organizational resources must, by their very definition, be planned and managed for the success of the organization. Thus, SPIS applies a total organizational perspective instead of a departmental or divisional perspective to planning for the incorporation of IS into the fabric of the organizational mission, strategy, goals, and objectives. This organizational perspective contrasts diametrically with the historical perspective of individual department/division investment in technology.

(i) Early Applications and Uses of IS

Early in the history of data processing, technology resources were often obtained that applied exclusively to individual departmental problems. Economies of scale often dictated that the organization consolidate departmental objectives in the acquisition of hardware, software, and operations personnel, but the resulting transaction processing systems remained the purview of the initiating department. Each department justified its capital investments in terms of increasing operational efficiency without consideration of the impact or usefulness to other organizational departments. Individual systems were oblivious to the requirements of other systems or departments. Further, the concept of a strategic system, from other than a departmental efficiency perspective, did not exist.

SPIS takes control of information systems and technology from individual departments and replaces the departmental owner attitude with an organizational perspective. SPIS looks at the mission and strategy of the organization, contributes opportunities for new technologies to impact organizational strategies, determines the appropriate alignment and role of IS resources in support of the organizational goals and objectives, and then generates the IS mission, strategy, goals, and objectives that directly implement the systems activities to execute organizational strategies.

(ii) Goals and Functions of SPIS

SPIS should take a leadership role in the organization's strategic planning process because it is potentially much more than an avenue for cutting costs and improving operational effectiveness. Its ability to link value-adding activities and leverage their contributions makes it a key player in identifying and enhancing fit between them. SPIS opens opportunities for synergies not otherwise available.

SPIS objectives are different from tactical and operational implementation issues. SPIS objectives do not include topics such as which relational database management system software to choose; whether to use Visual Basic or C++ for developing a new system; or whether to use JAVA or ActiveX to build Internet Web pages. These are operational decisions that derive from strategic objectives. If strategic planners get bogged down in operational decisions instead of planning an organizational strategy, the results are a short-term, *brushfire* mentality that focuses on the technology issues rather than on the organizational objectives and how technology supports them. Brushfire thinking causes lots of little issues to divert strategic focus from aligning uses of technology with organizational mission and strategy.

(iii) SPIS and Operational Decisions

Initial efforts to implement an IS planning and control process often focus on the operational characteristics of the systems, especially operational IS. These operational information systems include the transaction processing and control systems that are highly visible in the day-to-day operations of the organization and are often thought to result in readily identifiable cost savings. In many nonprofit organizations, these initial operational information systems efforts revolve around either accounting activities or customer relationship management. Accounting functions and customer relationship management are important activities for the nonprofit organization, and software for these tasks is widely available. However, focusing solely on the efficiency of operational activities, such as these two applications represent, denies the organization the opportunity to use IS/IT to enhance the effectiveness of the organization; to use IS/IT as a tool to reengineer organizational processes that focus on the core strategies of the organization; and to equitably distribute the organization's technology resources in support of those activities most closely aligned with organizational strategy.

When these types of systems are selected and implemented in response to some suddenly occurring problem arising within the organization, the result is a hurried selection of the system in response to that stimulus. This is analogous to slapping a bandage and antibiotic on a sore before checking to see if it is a skin cancer. Using IT resources solely as reactive solutions to short-term problems may slap a bandage on the immediate problem, but it does not afford the organization the opportunity to examine the ways systems can contribute proactively to the organization's long-term mission, goals, and objectives. For example, implementing a client customer relationship management system may solve a short-term processing need. However, unless the organization plans for the long-term integration of the resulting client history database into the organizational data architecture, the net result will be a very short-sighted approach to information management that misses potentially valuable strategic benefits. If one organizational strategic objective is increasing client retention, then by focusing on the operational effectiveness of the client customer relationship management system, the organization misses the opportunity to use the client history database as a strategic tool in this effort.

Strategic planning allows the organization to examine the role and scope of IS within the organization, align the mission and objectives of IS with those of the organization, and proactively provide a direction and philosophy for the organization's use of technology. Thus, SPIS is directly involved with organizational issues rather than solely with operational issues. SPIS objectives are derived from organizational initiatives and objectives. SPIS focuses on the alignment with long-term tangible and intangible benefits and the impact on organizational function, direction, and success.

(iv) Rapidly Changing, Moving Target

One of the characteristics of IT that makes SPIS so challenging is the dynamics of the IT industry. Beginning with Moore's law and continuing through the evolution of the World Wide Web and electronic commerce, technological developments bombard the chief information officer (CIO) with new alternatives on a daily basis. Some of these alternatives represent opportunities to improve the delivery of existing IS projects. Others represent new technologies that may directly or indirectly impact organizational strategies. Regardless, the pace of change mandates that SPIS be a process of continuous reevaluation and improvement. The normal planning horizon for organizational strategy is two to five years. The planning horizon is the same for SPIS, but concurrently the CIO has to remain alert to new technologies that may provide alternative strategies or new opportunities and necessitate a revised SPIS. In short, no SPIS is cast in concrete, but must remain flexible, able to incorporate new technologies and changes in organizational directions.

(C) ROLE OF MANAGEMENT IN SPIS

(i) *CIO—Planner, Manager, and Educator*

As discussed previously, organizational structure and the nature of people assigned to tasks change as strategies and missions evolve. In the early days when IS was essentially a data processing function, the management structure was a function of the characteristics of early data processing applications, which were primarily financial in nature and focused on controlling and reducing operational costs. Although the data processing department broadened over time to support independent systems designed for individual departments, the senior data processing manager frequently continued to report to the senior financial manager in the organization. IS planning at this point meant that the data processing manager primarily coordinated the activities of the data processing department to achieve economies of scale in hardware and software acquisition. The data processing manager had few planning responsibilities aside from estimating the capacity requirements of the integrated hardware environment. Typically, there were no strategic planning activities involved.

As demands increased for wider access to computing resources, the organizational positioning of the data processing manager position (typically a vice-president for MIS) became a point of contention. Nonfinancial managers perceived the data processing manager as biased toward financial systems requirements since the data processing manager reported to the senior financial manager. Managers in nonfinancial units of the organization wanted systems to do more than simply control costs. These managers forced organizations to became increasingly aware of the potential benefits of viewing data, information, and systems as organizational rather than departmental resources. For these reasons, the data processing manager position was realigned into a position with organization-wide responsibilities for planning and managing the IS and technology resources, creating the position of the CIO. In addition to the IS departmental responsibilities, the CIO also had a new role—technology advisor to the strategic planners of the organization.

As mentioned previously, the rapidly changing dynamics of the IT industry make it impossible for line managers to remain informed on all the latest developments, and especially what the potential strategic implications are for these developments. Therefore, the CIO has an additional task not required of the data processing manager. The CIO must serve as an educational consultant to members of the strategic planning committee. Further, the CIO serves as the lead in envisioning the potential threats and benefits inherent in new technologies, not simply to make operations more efficient, but also to identify opportunities for repositioning the organization in a change of strategic direction.

Earlier, in the data processing era, strategic decisions were not the province of the data processing manager. The strategic planning committee made strategy and policy decisions. Individual departments then determined their own missions, strategies, and policies relative to the organizational decisions. Data processing then designed, developed, and implemented the systems to support the individual departmental decisions. The data processing manager was not consulted on strategy.

This evolution of responsibility played the crucial role in establishing the requirement for SPIS. Today, the CIO has two additional responsibilities not held by the data processing manager. First, the CIO sits as a fully empowered member of the organization's strategic planning committee. In this role, the CIO serves as the liaison between the strategic planning committee and the IS organization, receiving the organizational strategy that forms the foundation for IS mission, goals, and objectives. However, that flow of information between CIO and strategic planning committee is bidirectional (see Exhibit 14.1). Not only does the CIO sit on the strategic planning committee as the representative of the IS department, but the CIO simultaneously has the responsibility to advise and educate the rest of the strategic planning committee relative to the strategic implications of the barrage of technological changes emerging from the external environment. This educational role of the CIO enables the strategic planning committee to incorporate new technologies into a redefinition of the activity set, which represents the execution of organizational strategic positioning, thereby totally changing the organization's competitive position and advantage.

(ii) Participation and Support of Top Management

One of the most frequent topics of IS research is the relationship of senior management support to the success of IS projects. Repeatedly, in all sizes of organizations, IS research demonstrates the significant importance of senior management support to the success of any IS project. Without the unqualified support of top organizational management, IS pro-

EXHIBIT 14.1 Educational Role of CIO

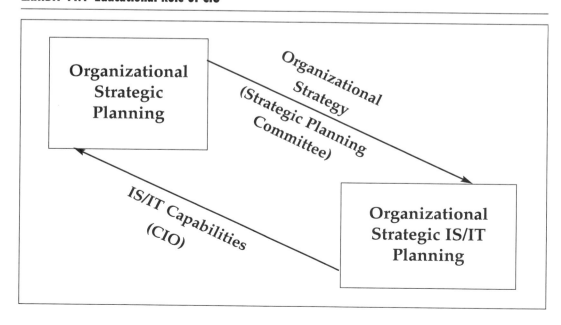

jects—including SPIS—are in dire jeopardy of failure. Anyone in the organization who has any reason for blocking or hindering SPIS will interpret anything less than total support as an opportunity to equivocate on the project and continue the status quo.

Introducing SPIS into an organization that has not previously performed this type of planning will shift the balance of power in the organization, either formally or informally. Few people give up power willingly. Therefore, those who will feel threatened by the loss of control or power due to the SPIS process are prime candidates to attempt to obstruct the process given the opportunity. Less than complete support by top management will provide just that opportunity. Therefore, active participation and complete support to the SPIS process by top management is one of the critical success factors of the SPIS process. Top management must visibly demonstrate its commitment to both the SPIS process and to the philosophy that information belongs to the organization as an organizational resource and will be managed accordingly.

(iii)   SPIS, Strategic Alignment, and Strategic Positioning

In addition to the support of top management, a second important principle of SPIS is the alignment (linkage) of the missions, strategies, and goals of SPIS with the mission, strategies, and goals of the organization. Alignment of IS strategy with organizational strategy ensures that organizational goals drive the SPIS process. In the SPIS process, the organizational strategy set must provide the foundation for deriving the IS strategy set. Only by aligning SPIS with organizational plans can the organization ensure that IS resources are allocated in a manner that best serves the overall organization. This appears to indicate that all SPIS activities come after organizational planning activities. However, that is not entirely the case.

As described earlier, one role of the CIO in the SPIS process is educating the strategic planning committee about the IS/IT capabilities available to the organization. That is informative, not prescriptive. IS/IT is an enabling force within the organization. It is not, and should not, be the primary driving force. As shown in Exhibit 14.1, the relationship between SPIS and organizational strategic planning is circular. As in any circle, there is no beginning and no end, only a continuous process. What is important is the directional flow of information: organizational mission, strategies, and goals flow into the SPIS process. It is capabilities, not plans, that flow from the IS organization back to the organizational strategic planning activity. The educational role of the CIO is to inform the strategic planning committee of the potentials inherent in new technologies. The strategic planning committee then uses that knowledge to examine and refocus the organization's strategic position.

14.3   Purposes and Outcomes of SPIS

(A)   IDENTIFYING PURPOSES OF SPIS

As an organization accepts the philosophy that information and the way it is processed constitute an important organizational resource, then its planning and management of this resource must benefit the organization as a whole rather than be suboptimized as data processing for parts of the organization. In the past, planning for information systems within organizations often focused on a preoccupation with the technology involved: which kind of networking was the organization going to use; which office software suite to choose; what vendor to select for enterprise resource software; and so on. Planners made these decisions without regard for the most important organizational planning issue: how to maximize the overall value to the organization of any incremental decision concerning the organization's essential core activities.

SPIS transforms the organization's perspective for technology planning. Instead of focusing on technology issues, SPIS emphasizes adding value to the organization, regardless of technology implementation decisions. For example, in place of starting with a decision as to which kind of network the organization should select, SPIS looks first at the organizational strategy issues that might lead to identifying a networking requirement. An example would be the issue or objective of improving decision making and improving service to clients. A new computer network might be one alternative to accomplish each of these organizational objectives. After careful examination of the relevant factors involved, if a network was identified as the appropriate approach, the SPIS process identifies the strategic objectives for the new network, and how the network will function to support the organization. Specifying a network solution that will accomplish these strategic objectives then becomes the task of tactical IS planning.

In general, objectives of SPIS include:

- Effectively managing the expensive IS asset, including resource allocation among competing alternatives
- Linking and aligning the IS strategic plan to the organizational strategic plan
- Identifying the information architecture for the organization and specifying its role in organizational strategy
- Planning the flow of information and processes
- Assessing alternative opportunities for strategic information systems
- Effectively allocating IS resources within the organization
- Improving IS response to the dynamic organizational environment

(B)   ASSET MANAGEMENT

Effective management of any expensive asset, including necessary resource allocations among competing alternatives to support that asset, is very important. In most aspects of the organization, management identifies project alternatives that compete for limited resources, evaluates those alternatives, and then allocates organizational resources to the selected projects. The same is true for information systems. However, unless planning is accomplished through a centralized and coordinated approach like SPIS, the true costs of adding new technologies may be underestimated.

For example, while the hardware costs for personal computers themselves shrink on an almost daily basis, the total cost of ownership of personal computers represents a poorly known and frequently misunderstood concept. Total cost of ownership includes not only the direct cost of computer hardware and software, and the cost of activities such as training for personnel on new systems and software, but also lost productivity when one person stops an assigned task to assist a coworker with a technology problem. Such insidious costs can be multiplied when differing approaches to technology or software are executed across an organization. Substantial time can be lost when solutions appropriate to one department are ineffective on a different hardware platform or software in another department. The highly visible decline in hardware costs and consequent anticipated savings in increased productivity can be partially offset or even overwhelmed by the less visible cost increase in indirect salary costs and lost productivity.

If an organization takes the simplistic view that declines in hardware and software costs mean its at-risk investment is also going down, the organization substantively misunderstands the situation, and consequently the size of its investment in technology. From the smallest organization to the largest, expenditures on IT represent an increasingly significant capital investment, both in direct dollars and indirect costs. SPIS assists management to not only understand the strategic significance of IS to the organization, but also evaluate the technology alternatives, and then allocate organizational resources in a consistent and cost-effective manner.

(C) ALIGNING IS AND THE ORGANIZATION

More than anything else, the one concept that differentiates SPIS from earlier forms of data processing planning is the requirement that the SPIS process aligns itself with the strategic plan of the organization. This alignment links the SPIS process and plan to the overall mission, strategies, objectives, and goals for the organization. Without this alignment, departmental- or divisional-level IS planning has no organizational focus and is free to pursue independently determined objectives. This can result in divergent technologies and the attendant costs, as discussed previously. Once in place, IS tends to shape the activities it serves. Therefore, it is incumbent on the strategic planning committee to direct the long-term strategic positioning of the organization from a perspective that proactively examines the alternatives enabled by the developments in systems and technology.

SPIS provides a coherent plan for IS to support the direction of organizational strategy. IS developed without enforcing alignment with organizational goals result in unconstrained technology decisions. Each separate IS may then be supporting a separate rather than a coordinated goal set. This is analogous to a group of horses and a wagon. If the horses do not have a wagon master to guide them, and a harness to control them to pull in the desired direction, there is confusion, misdirection, and a lack of effectiveness regardless how hard each horse pulls.

SPIS is like a team of horses in harness pulling a wagon, with a wagon master in control of driving and guiding the wagon. Technology can help pull the organization toward goals, but the technology itself must not be the motivating force. In an era of scarce resources and expensive technology, only technology and systems that directly support the goals of the organization can be rationalized.

(D) INFORMATION ARCHITECTURE AND ITS ROLE

The information architecture (IA) is the global model for how the organization structures its data resource to meet the information needs of the organization. The IA is a logical depiction that serves as a blueprint, diagramming the structure and organization of the data resource. The IA integrates all the data requirements from the entire organization into one blueprint and associates the building blocks of data on that blueprint to the information requirements of organizational processes. Just as we need to determine the capabilities of different types of required hardware and networking components, SPIS has to determine the objectives and capabilities for the different data necessary for users in the organization. The IA provides the organization a picture showing the integration of all individual data requirements together into one comprehensive logical data model that services the strategic data requirements for the entire organization.

Since the definition of input and output data requirements must precede any process definitions, the organization must design the IA model of the overall architecture for its information resource before it can design the information flows and processes. Linkage of the data building blocks to any strategic processes is paramount in defining the IA. Continuing the client customer relationship management example described earlier, strategically, the organization would be better served to first define the IA required to support the organizational strategic goal of client retention. Defining the IA would force the organization to identify the data necessary to improve client retention and integrate that definition with other required data before implementing any type of transaction system for managing client contacts. After defining the data necessary to support this strategic goal, SPIS has a clear picture of the strategic and operational data requirements that any potential transaction processing system must deliver.

(E) PLANNING THE FLOW OF INFORMATION AND PROCESSES

Historically, the focus of most data processing applications was on improving operational efficiency as a means to control costs. Consequently, organizations developed systems specifically to support the goal of controlling costs through cost reduction. Even today when performing IS planning, many organizations continue to focus on building on the foundation provided by those existing applications, regardless of whether those applications represent the best alignment of technology resources with the organization's current strategic direction.

The organization becomes entrenched, and these systems represent a strong force to continue the status quo. Attempts to expand and modify existing systems that contain intrinsically outmoded processes and procedures leads to several undesirable outcomes. First, it further entrenches the organization in outmoded activities and processes that reduce productivity and increase costs. Second, it prevents the modern organization from fully exploiting the alternatives represented by today's technology. Last, it fails to align IS resources fully in line with the organization's goals and objectives.

One of the alternatives with the greatest potential strategic benefit is the restructuring or reengineering of organizational processes. This is accomplished through a reexamination of the flow of information through the organization's processes, looking at the organization's current strategic goals and objectives, and evaluating if the existing processes represent the best fit with the technologies currently available. Business process reengineering (BPR) has established itself as an effective approach to maximize the capabilities of IS. Unlike TQM, which focuses on incremental improvements, BPR looks for significant improvements through radical redesign of key organizational processes or activities. BPR essentially asks the question: "If we were starting from scratch, how would we organize?" Typically, activities were created or designed given the IS capabilities then in existence. Information flows are often inefficient because they cross many functional lines. Reorganizing along process lines and designing an IS that is supportive requires an SPIS approach. In addition, performing SPIS at regular intervals implies a continuous reevaluation of the information flows and processes, with the goal of always looking for opportunities to create a more effective organization.

(F) ASSESSING ALTERNATIVE OPPORTUNITIES FOR STRATEGIC INFORMATION SYSTEMS

(i) Strategic Information Systems versus Nonstrategic Organizational Support Systems

It is often said that you cannot be too thin or have too much money. A popular corollary to this statement is that an organization can never be too efficient in reducing overhead. In fact, for many organizations, the primary usage of IS/IT is to help manage and reduce the costs of operations—to improve operational effectiveness. They achieve these reductions through the use of transaction processing systems, which automate basic organizational activities. While useful in making the organization more efficient, these operational support systems are rarely strategic in nature. Unless the organization's strategy specifies that success lies in being the low-cost service provider or that staying in operation depends heavily on reducing operating overhead, transaction processing systems are purely a means of reducing costs. One alternative to using IS/IT purely for operational support activities is to consider the development of applications for using IS/IT to implement organizational strategy.

Strategic information systems (SIS) are those systems whose purpose is to increase organizational effectiveness by directly supporting one or more of the organization's strategic goals. SPIS provides the framework for examining organizational strategy and assessing the alternative opportunities available to develop SIS to assist in achieving the organization's strategic goals instead of focusing on IS/IT solely as a cost-reduction tool; in other words, to truly view IS/IT as strategic resources and not merely as a cost of doing business. This viewpoint requires changing the existing cost justification models for evaluating systems proposals. Managing the limited resources available to organizations for technology often means making decisions to pursue one IS/IT project over another. Tangible costs and benefits have traditionally been the primary tools used to aid in making that type of evaluation. The next section discusses the limitations of traditional return on investment (ROI) calculations and how they do not always apply to SIS project evaluation.

(ii) Tangible versus Intangible Costs and Benefits

Just as the strategic focus of IS has changed, so has the way in which organizations evaluate the effect on the organization and the return on the technology dollars invested. Throughout the data processing systems era, ROI calculations based on the value of tangible benefits derived for the cost of the technology dollars invested was the prescribed methodology for evaluating benefits of one IS project against another. The values of the tangible costs and benefits were directly and relatively easily measured, and since most early computer systems were financial transaction systems, this approach satisfied the accountants' perspective of value. However, two important characteristics distinguish these data processing–era applications, and their evaluation, from many of today's information systems projects: focus of the system and who derives the benefit.

In data processing–era systems, the focus of the system was on internal users (e.g., the accounting department). The data processing systems provided a service to users who were internal to the organization. These internal users consumed the service provided by the system, and the organization itself derived benefits from their increased productivity. In these systems, the tangible direct costs (provision of service) and tangible direct benefits (increased productivity) were inputs to the ROI calculations to determine comparative worth of systems projects.

In today's strategic information systems era, the focus of systems has shifted from internal users to external users. For example, if the organization decides to create a site on the Internet to promote services and activities to clients, who is deriving the benefit from this system? The answer is clients, who are external to the organization. The consumer of the system is no longer internal to the organization. Services provided by the system are being consumed by entities outside the organization. For these externally focused systems, the old ROI model for justification and evaluation no longer applies. The consumer of the system's service is external to the organization, and this consumer derives the direct benefit from the system. The benefit to the providing organization is now an intangible one such as increased client satisfaction—not directly measurable, but nonetheless just as valuable as tangible benefits.

As an organization changes the focus of IS, it must develop new measures of effectiveness to evaluate the success or failure of these systems. If an organization mandates strict ROI justification for a system project that has primarily intangible or nondirect cost-related benefits, it will miss valuable strategic opportunities to improve the organization's effectiveness.

(G) EFFICIENT AND EFFECTIVE ALLOCATION OF IS RESOURCES WITHIN THE ORGANIZATION

The resource allocation process is subject to many pressures that can interfere with the proper distribution of critical assets. As needs change and new activities are funded, some activities may receive reduced funding and strong resistance is likely. Entrenched political forces can resist or deflect necessary choices. By centralizing resource allocation decisions for IS projects through SPIS, departmental resistance may be overcome, but powerful champions of outmoded technologies may still attempt to retain funding. Once the decision is made on the direction for IS projects, the SPIS must have the necessary authority to efficiently and effectively allocate the available technology resources to these projects. For example, if a nonprofit organization decides that a key strategic activity is to provide external stakeholders with access to organizational information via the Internet, then the SPIS will define the resources that have to be allocated to the task to accomplish that goal. "Squeaky wheels," especially those with direct telephone lines to top management or IS personnel, often attempt to dictate or influence IS resource allocation. The SPIS document provides the basis for monitoring resource allocations and denying these back-door requests.

(H) IMPROVING RESPONSE TO DYNAMIC ORGANIZATIONAL ENVIRONMENT

Because the SPIS process is linked to the strategic needs of the organization, a substantive benefit is improved understanding. This includes improved understanding of the organization's direction and strategic goals by IS personnel, and also improved understanding by non-IS personnel of the potential contributions to organizational initiatives available through appropriate application of technology. This improved bidirectional understanding between organizational management and IS management directly contributes to more effective use of IS resources. Each group becomes more aware of the ability of technology to make the organization more adaptable to changing needs and conditions in the organizational environment.

(I) OUTCOMES FOR SPIS

Regardless of the size of an organization, the basic steps to SPIS do not vary in method, only in scale. A national organization with multiple organizational divisions may devote several people to the SPIS process, whereas a small, local organization may have all its SPIS activities done by just the part-time efforts of one person. The large organization may require a formal planning process coordinated by senior management and producing a lengthy planning document, whereas the small organization conducts a much less formal, more internalized planning process resulting in a much more modest planning document.

The net result from the SPIS process is a comprehensive planning document to guide the design and use of IT in the organization. The document should clearly define the vision for technology within the organization. The planning document should also contain a mission statement and goals, as well as specific objectives and the necessary strategies for the effective use of IT in the organization. However, the specific document outcomes will vary depending on:

- Degree of existing alignment of technology with organizational strategy
- Level of technical knowledge within the organization
- Focus and sophistication of current systems
- Expectations of senior management for the SPIS process
- Clearly and continuously demonstrated support by senior management; in the case of major projects, this support should include a visible project champion.

14.4   Developing a Strategic Plan for IS

(A)   THE STRATEGIC PLANNING MODEL

Strategic planning is an evolutionary descendant of Drucker's famous three questions: Where are we? Where do we want to go? How are we going to get there? The fundamental premise is that the organization exists in a dynamic environment that is constantly changing. For the organization to survive, it must adapt its product or service to constantly meet the changing needs of its customers. Nonprofit organizations that historically occupied protected niches now find themselves confronted with for-profit invaders, radical changes in the demographics of their sponsors and clients, shifting governmental relationships, and an almost endless series of new demands placed on them. Strategic planning is a systematic approach to positioning the organization to maximize its continuing ability to effectively respond to the demands placed on it.

Today, Drucker's three steps have been replaced by an increasingly sophisticated model of the planning and implementation process. Although various schemas can be found in the strategic planning literature, they all essentially address Drucker's three questions. The following seven-part model effectively captures this process.

(i)   Assessing the Current Situation
This assessment includes analyzing the current level of resources available and the present stated objectives and strategies of the organization. Assessing resources is critical because limited resources limits the options open to the organization, just as bountiful resources support more aggressive options. Strategies and objectives are evaluated to determine how well the organization is accomplishing its current mission. A smooth-running organization executing strategies and achieving stated objectives can focus on new opportunities. Poorly executed strategies and missed objectives likely will require a reappraisal of the organization's current mission and course before engaging in new activities.

(ii) Assessing the External Environment

Often referred to as an *external scan,* this assessment involves gathering data about where the external environment is and where it is going. A number of techniques are available to facilitate this, such as identifying driving forces, assessing the competitive factors facing the organization, and doing a competitive strength analysis. The essence here is to be able to clearly identify how changes in the environment will affect the organization, how the organization can proactively move to modify the environment in its favor, and what changes the organization will inevitably have to make to survive and thrive.

(iii) Assessing the Internal Environment

Often referred to as an *internal scan,* here the organization assesses itself to identify strengths and weaknesses. Again, a number of techniques are available to help accomplish this task.

(iv) Doing a SWOT Analysis

SWOT stands for strengths, weaknesses, opportunities, and threats. Here, the analysis proceeds to summarize all of the data gathered in the external scan and summarize and then distill from all of that data a relevant list of opportunities and threats that exist or are coming in the environment. The organization then matches its strengths and weaknesses against the various opportunities and threats.

(v) Revising Mission, Developing Alternatives, and Selecting Strategies

- *Where do we want to be?* Given all of the data gathering and analysis, the organization then decides if its current mission remains appropriate for guiding the organization into the future environment. Depending on circumstances, it may be necessary to modify or even make fundamental changes in the mission if the environment so dictates. The March of Dimes initially was established to find a cure for polio. When polio was cured, it switched to focusing on children's birth defects.
- *What needs to be changed?* Once the mission is established, the next step is to develop a list of those critical issues that the organization must address to survive and flourish, and devise a set of possible courses of action.
- *Blueprint for success.* From this comprehensive list of possible courses, those specific actions that most appropriately support the mission and objectives of the organization are selected and become the new strategy set for the organization.

(vi) Implementation

New plans imply organizational change. All of the facets of the organization that support the old way of doing things must be modified to support the new strategies. Key parts of the organization to consider include:

- *Structure.* First, structure includes the allocation of new tasks to appropriate activities and elimination of superseded or redundant tasks. Second is the acquisition and disposition of appropriate people to support the strategies. Third is acquisition and assignment of the appropriate skills for the new strategy.

- *Resource allocation.* New strategies inevitably require resources, and this may entail reducing allocations to existing tasks that will engender political resistance from the losing activity. Resources include money, but also include any resource necessary to allow the strategy to succeed.
- *Administrative support systems.* The first part includes policies and procedures. Typically, there will have to be some changes to reflect the new way of doing things. The second part is any necessary operational support system. The third part is information systems. The existing IS will have to be changed to provide the information necessary to support the new strategy, as well as to identify ways to improve the effectiveness of organization.
- *Reward system.* The reward system must be structured to support the new objectives and strategies. Incentives and rewards must be supportive of the current strategies; otherwise, organizational members will resist the changes and support the old strategy.
- *Culture.* An organization's culture can be a strong force in supporting an organization's goal achievement. If new strategies dilute or threaten existing culture, positive steps must be taken to align the culture with the new direction.
- *Leadership.* The organization's leadership must be firmly supportive of any changes for the new strategy to be successful. This would include positive statements and actions as well as active involvement.

(vii)   Evaluation and Control

The environment is constantly changing. Evaluation and control has two purposes: (1) to track the implementation to ensure it is meeting its objectives, and (2) to monitor the environment for changing conditions that would warrant a change in the strategy. For effective evaluation and control, measures of organizational success must be established, and then the strategy's progress monitored for achieving these standards.

(B)   SPIS—APPLYING THE STRATEGIC PLANNING FORMULA TO IS/IT

SPIS is predicated on using the model defined to design and implement an IS for an organization based on the five-part foundation for all IS/IT applications. Just like a fire takes fuel, oxygen, and heat, any SPIS effort requires developing a plan that includes these five critical foundation components:

1. Hardware architecture
2. Software applications
3. Data/Information architecture
4. Network/Communications architecture
5. People

At each step in the SPIS process, the planners must consider each of these five components. Failure to include any one of them in the plan means the plan will fail, just as a fire goes out when you remove any one of its three necessary components. Each step is really part of an overall iterative process—no one step is accomplished without some consideration of the other steps. For example, any recommendations must be done considering whether the organization has the capability to implement it.

(i) Step 1: Situational Analysis

An introspective analysis of the current level of technology absorption in the organization is the first step in the SPIS process. This situational analysis identifies where the organization is today in its technology capabilities. The remainder of the SPIS rests on the foundation established by this initial starting position definition. Overstate capabilities or existing architectures, and the plan outcomes will set impossible objectives and doom the process and subsequent projects to failure. Understate capabilities or architectures, and the plan outcomes will not fully utilize the available resources already in the organization, thereby wasting valuable resources and opportunities. This analysis should separately evaluate each of the five fundamental components relative to the existing status.

The situational analysis also defines existing organizational expectations and constraints on the SPIS process. Expectations come from what the organizational strategic planning group expects from its IS. The results of a situational analysis may also add constraints on alternatives at this time. How the organization perceives and values IS as an organizational resource is determined.

(ii) Step 2: External Analysis

In this step, data is gathered on all relevant technologies that are available. This should include analysis of emerging technologies, changes occurring in the industry, what competitors are doing, and so on.

(iii) Step 3: Internal Analysis

The entire structure of the organization and how IS is configured should be reviewed. How does the current architecture and technology array fit with the organizational mission? What shortfalls, unmet needs, and conflicting technologies are there?

(iv) Step 4: SWOT Analysis

Using the information gathered in Step 3, identify the organization's strengths and weaknesses. What must be fixed? What should be improved? Using the information gathered in Step 2, identify the relevant threats and opportunities the organization faces in the external environment. Are some IS systems becoming legacy systems that even though they accomplish current needs may become unsupportable? What new technologies and other approaches are available that can be incorporated into the IS?

(v) Step 5: Revise IS Mission, Objectives, and Strategies

Where Do We Want to Be?   This is the forward thinking step in the SPIS process. The first factor in defining where we want to be is to look at the organizational mission, goals, and strategy. The organizational mission states why the organization exists. The goals and strategy tell what the organization wants to accomplish and how it intends to accomplish it. This is the first phase in performing the crucial alignment that links the IS/IT strategic plan with the overall organizational strategic plan. From this point forward, all planning activities are done so that the plan is consistent with the organizational strategic plan. This forward thinking includes all five of our fundamental components to ensure that we have a focus for our technology strategies.

The next item to consider in defining where we want to be is to match opportunities provided by new technologies against our strengths and weaknesses. This involves looking at the current organizational strategies, goals, and objectives defined for the organization and matching these with new technologies to identify new ways of achieving these objectives. For example, again using the customer relationship management example and the goal of improving client retention, one new technology alternative might be to make client services accessible through the Internet, such as making appointments via a Web page linked to a calendar database for the organization and its employees.

A properly executed SPIS effort will include the expectations of user departments. For example, if your organization is a foundation that has improved client retention as a strategic objective, then the client relations department should have input as to how they expect to achieve that objective. In addition to capitalizing on opportunities, strategies should be developed to evade threats and compensate for or overcome weaknesses in the organization.

A final item is to define the data architecture to support the activities going into the future. The data architecture conceptual model includes all the databases and other forms of data necessary to support the operational and strategic systems for the organization. The data architecture forms the data foundation on which all systems will build. One tool to use in defining the data architecture is critical success factor (CSF) analysis. CSFs describe the key information needs for the organization. CSFs are those limited number of areas in which results, if they are satisfactory, will ensure successful competitive performance for the organization, but failure will jeopardize mission accomplishment. These are the areas where "things must go right." Using CSF analysis will assist in determining that the overall data architecture includes the data items necessary to support CSF activities.

What Needs to Be Changed?   At this point, the nature of the IS gap and what needs to be changed are determined. We have defined what and how the organization would like to see its systems perform. We have defined the current status of all systems. This step involves a comparison between where the organization wants to be (Step 5a) and where the organization currently is (Step 1). Again, this comparison is done for each of the five fundamental components. It is entirely possible, and even likely, that there will be larger gaps in some components than in others, or for some component there may be no gap whatsoever. For example, during the past year, assume an organization implemented its IS/IT strategic plan, which included the objective to network all desktop computers and install a calendaring system so that everyone can check schedules for meetings and such. The gap last year in the network/communications architecture required totally redesigning and implementing a new communications network. This year, with that new network installed and operational, the gap in the network/communications architecture should not exist.

Blueprint to Bridge the Gap.   This is the strategic planning document for IS/IT. Starting with the mission, the IS/IT strategic plan specifies strategy, goals, and objectives for IS/IT for the planning period. All of these are developed to bring the current state of technology in the organization up to the level necessary to support the organizational strategy, goals, and objectives already defined. Included in this IS/IT strategic plan are:

- *Hardware architecture plan.* What are the hardware infrastructure changes and improvements necessary to implement any new systems or enhancements to existing systems? What is the time frame for completion?
- *Application portfolio plan.* What are the alternative enhancements and additions to the existing applications servicing the organization, including the service levels expected by the departments in the organization? What are the

priorities for these projects? What is the timeline for delivery and implementation?

- *Networking/Communications architecture plan.* What are the changes and enhancements necessary to support the applications defined in the application portfolio plan? What is the time frame for completion?
- *Data/Information architecture plan.* What are the additional data files and databases necessary to support the applications defined in the application portfolio plan? How are these to be incorporated into the existing data architecture?
- *People plan.* What additional staffing is required to implement the previously defined plans? What additional training is necessary for existing staff?

14.5   Conclusion

Nonprofit organizations face an increasingly competitive and demanding environment. The reality of limited resources mandates that each area of the organization must be structured and utilized in a manner that best supports overall organizational goal attainment. Most organizations have adopted some form of planning to aid in positioning the organization to adapt to environmental requirements and maximize resource utilization. But the nature and execution of planning plays a crucial role in its success.

Planning before spending is always the best advice for the nonprofit organization. But for IS, planning is much more than just deciding between two competing hardware or software vendors. Strategic planning for IS means accepting the philosophy that data are an important organizational resource to be managed like every other organizational resource and that IS/IT are organizational data management tools the organization can use to harness its information resources to pull the organization toward its strategic goals. In our modern information age, investment in these tools is inevitable. SPIS furnishes the nonprofit manager with a proven approach to focus that investment on the right tools to maximize the benefits from investments in IS and to IT and to propel the organization successfully into the future.

Suggested Readings

Cassidy, A. (1998). *A Practical Guide to Information Systems Strategic Planning.* Boca Raton, FL: St. Lucie Press.

Frenzel, C. W. (1999). *Management of Information Technology,* 3rd ed. Cambridge, MA: Course Technology.

O'Brien, J. A. (1999). *Management Information Systems,* 4th ed. Boston: Irwin McGraw-Hill.

Porter, M. E. (1996). "What Is Strategy?" *Harvard Business Review* 74(6) (November–December): 61–78.

Rockart, J. F. (1979). "Chief Executives Define Their Own Data Needs," *Harvard Business Review* 57(2) (March–April): 81–93.

Turban, E., E. McLean, and J. Wetherbe. (1999). *Information Technology for Management,* 2nd ed. New York: John Wiley & Sons.

Ward, J., P. Griffiths, and P. Whitmore. (1990). *Strategic Planning for Information Systems.* Chichester: John Wiley & Sons.

Emergent Technology and the Nonprofit Organization

ELIZABETH POWER, MED, PRINCIPAL
EPower and Associates

ADAM C. HART, JR., MCSE, PRINCIPAL
NexSys Technologies, LLC

15.1 The Scope of Technology Usage in the Nonprofit Environment

Technology refers to a broad spectrum of devices and processes. Before computers, technology could have referred to an index card system of tracking or hard-copy tickler files. It was the system of communication with distant parties, whether through talking drums or horse-borne messages. With the advent of electricity and ultimately computers, technology has become synonymous with machines, rapid information processing, storage, and distribution.

In the everyday tasks faced by nonprofit organizations (NPOs), technology most often supports three primary functions: fund raising, operations, and volunteer management. The same hardware and software may serve these and other functions required to support the organization.

Emergent technology includes (and certainly is not limited to) the following applications, each of which can demonstrably pay for itself in a very short time:

- Satellite-based wide area networks (WANs) when cabling is not the best choice (making networking possible between buildings up to 30 miles apart, thus enabling all buildings and users secure access to data)
- Computer-based video meetings for distance communication that use offshore long distance for inexpensive high-compression video with minimal degradation (effective in overseas and domestic work, distance learning, video meetings, and to show marketing videos)
- User-friendly, low-cost telephone and call distribution that reduce dependence on the vendor by relying on plain-English, browser-based interfaces for changes and adjustments as needed

Applying these technologies in both the for-profit and NPO environment, firms such as Jim Hayes and Associates (Rural Hall, North Carolina) continue to prove that emerging technologies need not be cost prohibitive, and in fact result in recovery of investment in a far shorter time than expected. Projections of cost savings can (and should) be part of every technology proposal. The governing body should know when recovery of investment will occur, the over-time projected usage, effectiveness, and cost–benefit ratios. Without this information, governing bodies should be reluctant to invest in technology. It demonstrates to funding sources, persons served, the community of interest, and others that good sense and fiscal responsibility are present.

Other new technologies that may prove to be of use to the NPO include:

- Wireless intelligent terminals that allow users to send and receive e-mail from a pager with a keyboard (*http://www.netsearchllc.com*—of potential use when staff and volunteers are spread out and need to be in contact with each other or a home office, or when the needs of persons served can be communicated by e-mail; a visual means beneficial to the hearing impaired)
- Voice recognition technology for word processing and other functions (for example, DragonSystems of Boston and IBM's Via Voice allow input of data using the voice; the other side of text readers for people with visual impairments)

What makes these technologies emergent is that they are new uses for existing technologies or completely new developments. Although their use is often thought of as limited to the for-profit business world, they have a powerful place in the NPO environment, especially as collaboration among agencies increases and the need for increased communication at lower cost and with less travel occurs.

The use of emergent technology is supported by an effective basic technology—a foundation that allows the NPO to build on a specific platform and set of applications integrated for daily use. There are three basic uses for technology in all businesses: managing money (fund raising in the NPO), daily use (with basic similarities across all business environments), and tasks related to managing people.

(A)   FUND RAISING

This ongoing task involves donor identification, contact, solicitation, tracking of contacts and results, follow-up, and tagging for the next fund-raising event. Whether fund raising targets individuals, corporations, or foundations, or a combination of these, technology plays a critical role, even if only the simplest of technology—paper and pencil—is involved. Whereas only the newest or perhaps smallest organizations may use paper and pencil, the bulk use technology that may include:

- From a single telephone to a multiseat high-tech call center, inbound and outbound call distribution systems support inbound and outbound calls, providing many types of information (much of which may be available on request from your local telephone company). Telethons are a classic example of inbound call center applications in the NPO, such as Jerry Lewis's long-running televised campaign. Other campaigns focus on the outbound calling process, with volunteers calling donor lists and cold-calling prospects.
- Personal computers, mainframe computers, and file servers, with the particular NPO's configuration and software applications installed on them (including those described as follows)
- Fax machines, whether hard copy stand-alone, internal to computers, or vendor-based broadcast systems, can distribute solicitation faxes to many people as well as handle regular faxing operations
- Computer databases and personal information software, used for collecting information, generating documents, tracking donations, scheduling contacts and volunteers, and managing follow-up activities
- Office productivity software used for word processing, bookkeeping and accounting, graphics, and other functions

(B)   OPERATIONS

Most often, the operations of the NPO utilize technology for word processing, bookkeeping and accounting, and again, in the creation and maintenance of databases of information relating to staff, volunteers, and persons served. Contact hours, services provided, needs, and plans for the future are tracked and projected, and reports that provide the organization's governing body with information vital to the future are compiled.

Additional uses that cross the boundaries between fund raising and operations include the generation and production of brochures, flyers, and marketing materials. Specialized graphics packages and skills are required for this kind of work.

(C)   VOLUNTEER AND STAFF MANAGEMENT AND SCHEDULING

In every NPO, staffing is the core of providing services. Whether small or large, the challenge is making sure that volunteers are available to provide services when needed, and that contingency plans exist if volunteers are unable to be present as scheduled. Naturally, there are limits to the responsibility and authority volunteers can accept and exercise; therefore, staff must also be present. Staff, in turn, are responsible to the governing body, and across and up this chain, various reporting requirements exist. The major challenge in terms of people is the maintenance of schedules cross-referenced as needed to skills and abilities.

In all of this, the scope of technology is to be the hub, or central repository, of information. This information is accessed, manipulated, and stored for the purpose of meeting the organization's needs as it provides services. It should do so in a manner that is as efficient and effective as is possible, offering the greatest speed at the least cost. The goal is simple: Reduce the person hours and cost required for the administration of the organization so that more of each hour can be spent in direct service.

15.2 How Technology Serves Customers, Volunteers, Staff, and Board

(A) TECHNOLOGY AND THE CUSTOMERS

While current statistics point out that disadvantaged people are less likely to have access to technology, it is inappropriate to make this generalization in terms of the persons served by NPOs. For example, many people with disabilities are now using assistive technology to improve their quality of life. Assistive technology includes hardware and software in its original configuration as well as adapted to meet physical or cognitive requirements of the user. Persons of all situations may access e-mail accounts in public libraries, and persons in need of information or support may likewise access Internet services in a variety of places at low or no cost.

Because of this, NPOs should suspend expectations and perceptions about technological skill levels of persons served and assume that they may have higher levels of technological skill and access than might seem likely. Suspending assumptions about persons served is critical in any case because the presence of assumptions limits the potential of persons served in terms of options, abilities, and reciprocity with society.

At the same time, it is critical to "learn enough about learning" to be able to assess the level of skill possessed by persons served if they are to interact with technology as part of services received. Few persons respond honestly when confronted with questions about skill levels. No one wants inadequacies or incompetence exposed, as such exposure degrades self-esteem (think about the ability of people who do not read and the efforts made to "pass" as an example).

Knowing how to assess learning style by listening to phrases used and observing interactions with technologies increases the power of what the NPO can offer the people it serves. The person who says "It looks like this" or "See what I mean?" is one who most often learns by seeing and for whom verbal instructions will not be helpful; other cues will inform of the auditory or kinesthetic learner. Simply put, if part of the process of offering services is to educate persons served about how to interact with the world in a different way by increasing access to resources, skills, or other abilities, understanding and leveraging how they learn is a very useful process.

(B) THE WIRED WORLD, STAFF, AND VOLUNTEERS

Likewise, knowing a bit about how staff and volunteers learn makes implementation and adoption of technology far easier. When people are taught or learn in the style most useful to them, learning occurs more quickly and with greater enjoyment.

Staff and volunteers will also adopt technology presented in the organization more quickly when they can clearly identify the benefits to them in terms of their work. The key question is: "WIFM—What's In It For Me?" When answered, it gives direct information about how technology serves.

Today's volunteers are as apt as not to be "wired." Many may have powerful computers with Internet access, e-mail, and perhaps even videoconferencing capability. Some may have restricted their computer interaction to products like Web TV, an add-on technology that requires a television set and telephone line and offers Internet access and e-mail, but not the ability to print or install applications.

Internet access, whether at home or in the NPO, supports volunteers by:

- Increasing access to resources and research
- Increasing the ease with which volunteers can, in turn, communicate with others
- Providing a platform for information sharing and support
- Providing a way to teach persons served how to become more self-determining as part of service provision

As a result, those who have access to different kinds of technology offer the NPO more technologically sophisticated volunteers. When volunteers enter an NPO that has effectively set up its technology (no matter what the level of sophistication), they are in a position to make the optimum contribution at the lowest cost.

(C) STAFF USAGE OF TECHNOLOGY

Staff are responsible for the day-to-day use of technology. As such, they need to possess the highest level of skill in the use of applications relevant to the tasks they perform as well as in maintenance of the operating system and hardware. For tasks they need to remember because they are performed every day, training is in order on those tasks only—not the entire software package. For those tasks performed infrequently, a step-by-step job aid is more appropriate. In either case, validation that the required steps are present, in sequence, and accurately described is critical.

Perhaps the greatest frustration to many computer users is the challenge of performing tasks in a way that prevents computer foul-ups, loss of data, and crashes. To reduce this risk, three simple steps can help:

1. Teach users (through hands-on practice) the basics of operation: powering on, opening specific applications, file retrieval, creation, editing, and closure, and powering down.
2. Set applications to automatically save and create backups of files.
3. Schedule simple maintenance tasks (scandisk, defragmentation, and deletion of temporary files) so that they are routinely performed.

In a networked environment, the network administrator or management information systems (MIS) staff should perform routine defragmentation and disk cleanup, including the deletion of temporary files.

Finally, a coherent file structure should be developed for fund raising, operations, and personnel management. This structure should place most often-used applications and documents in the forefront of the structure. All users should be educated about this structure and encouraged to use it to conserve disk space, support fast run times for the hardware and software, and reduce the risk of user-related downtime.

(D)   TECHNOLOGY AND THE NPO BOARD

The governing body for the NPO may have the least contact with technology as it relates to the organization. Except to see the output, such as reports, or the dollars raised, there will often be no more than e-mail interaction among the board and staff as appropriate.

However, in pursuit of emergent technology applications in the NPO environment, the board may be inclined to polarize along issues of the investment required to acquire the technology. There will be those who oppose it based on cost and the obsolescence issue, and there will be those who oppose it based on the idea that "things work just fine the way they are." Lack of experience, fear of the unknown, and indifference may cause other governing body members to appear neutral.

In any case, governing bodies differ greatly, based on membership and the demographics of the members. This diversity also means there may be varying levels of interest in, experience with, and curiosity about technology and how it can support organizational growth and development despite the natural organizational competition for dollars.

A visionary perspective is required to help NPOs that have been accustomed to pencil-and-paper operations or minimal technology to consider and apply emergent technologies (even if the word *emergent* applies only to the organization rather than to the computer or other technology industries).

15.3   *Technology and the Future in the NPO Environment*

Predictions about technology are difficult to make. There is, however, one prediction that can be made with absolute certainty: technology will continue to change at an ever-increasing rate. The dizzying advances announced almost daily can overwhelm those responsible for determining if, when, and how to use technology, as well as the user.

The appropriate question is how to keep clear vision while technology undergoes constant and often wild changes. The answer is by keeping in mind organizational goals and needs and finding the needs-driven equipment and software, *not* keeping up with what is called "bleeding"-edge technology or blindly following biased advice.

Except on rare occasions, NPOs are not, by design, high-technology organizations fulfilling a need. They are organizations that fulfill a need *using* high technology. Some use technology to manage larger operations; others use it to fulfill specific needs. Some provide assistive technology for people with disabilities, and others use emerging technology (even by short-term "renting") for specific situations such as fund raising. By staying with this approach, the organization, not the technology, remains in charge.

(A)   PERILS

Most perils in applying technology focus on one of the following areas: mission and vision; people issues such as staffing, skills, systems, and supports; organizational structure; and leadership style. In this chapter, four primary perils will be considered that cross these areas of concern.

1. *Obsolescence.* Technology is obsolete before it is even paid for. How do NPOs deal with this peril? Hold to a clear, factual picture of the operation's

technology needs and productivity goals, looking to the future, while at the same time, maintaining current productivity goals in the present.

2. *Lack of self-knowledge.* Technology systems are often based on the personal preferences of management, without consideration for organizational needs and information about how different applications installed on the same system really interact (user versus vendor versus programmer descriptions). The differences between what the organization says about itself and how it works often differ profoundly from what an objective observer would report.

To bypass this peril, the organization must know who it is, where it wants to go, what is needed to get there, and how it intends to do so. This is accomplished by organizational surveys best prepared by human resources (or organization) development professionals and effective strategic planning that involves key stakeholders.

3. *Lack of thoughtful and effective strategic planning.* Organizations often acquire new technology because everyone else has it, someone donates it, or the people who have the authority to make the decision decide that updated technology is necessary. With the results in hand of a fearless self-examination yielding facts with which an outside observer would concur, the process of planning, acquiring, and implementing new technology is far easier.

4. *Buying devices that do not do the job as promised.* Certain basic minimum configurations are required to run specific applications. A program that uses 64 MB of disk space, such as Windows 2000®, requires a minimum of 64 MB of random-access memory (RAM). Does it need to have 128 MB of RAM? Not necessarily. Must it have 64 MB? Absolutely.

(B) POSSIBILITIES

With the aforementioned perils firmly in mind, consider the situation from another perspective—failure to take advantage of new technology is a "lost opportunity" cost, instead of "obsolete equipment money" down the drain. (*Obsolete*, by the way, is a relative term based on the factual needs of an organization.) Some piece of equipment called "yesterday's news" by the latest trade magazines can perform a valuable service to an organization in need of the functions offered by that technology for years to come. What is gained from taking advantage of the increase in productivity afforded by emerging technology easily exceeds the "obsolete equipment dollars paid" costs as measured by an accounting system.

Reconsider the earlier statement about knowing what the need is and where the organization is going in light of purchasing new technology. The fastest way to make any piece of equipment obsolete is to purchase it and not have it perform the job for which it was bought.

This reflects the greatest change in technology in the workplace. In the 1980s, computers were still so expensive that users had to change their styles and habits to work with the equipment because of its inherent ability to increase the productivity of a user who was even minimally skilled. At the end of the twentieth century, technology styles and habits changed so that the technology must do the will of the employee and perform the task for which it was purchased (user skill considered). If it cannot accomplish this reversal, the equipment or technology is of no value to the organization—it is obsolete.

Outside vendors and consultants can be of immense help in clarifying issues surrounding needs and goals. However, a consultant's time is better spent figuring out a way to solve problems the organization's need represents instead of trying to decipher what those needs are. There are product vendors who can offer the products that solve a need, but the systems integrator may be a better choice for a front-end investment. This is the vendor who can consider the current hardware and software, the needs of the organization as the organization defines them, and who can help the organization consider, access, and successfully implement change.

Knowing the organization's needs ahead of time will support the process of determining what emerging technology the NPO may want to consider. This is part of the strategic planning process that follows developing self-knowledge, and when done well, the output can support and shorten the time required of a systems integration consultant.

In taking a different look at the problem, turn the tables on the vendors. State as clearly and concisely as possible the organization's needs and the resources available to satisfy those needs. Then, ask vendors how their products and services can best resolve the gap and differences between those two issues. This reduces or eliminates endless product demonstrations extolling speed, capacity, and technical details. The pitfall to this approach is that without adequate preparation or only a vague idea of the need, it's back to the product demonstrations and being quick overwhelmed.

When an organization does its homework prior to sourcing, this method reduces the blizzard of choices that cloud this critical decision. It is an appropriate, polite demand that the organization be presented with a coherent and readable plan detailing how vendors will respond to create complete satisfaction in terms of the organization's needs and resources, and just exactly how much it will cost for this response.

The ultimate goal of any organization is to satisfy its client's wishes in a profitable and timely manner. While there are many technological advances making offices more valuable and responsive, some are more important than others as foundations for the future.

(i) Communications

Emerging technology is making communications easier, faster, and more efficient than ever before. Twin boons to improving services to clients come with the emergence of call centers and telecommunications technology that makes call-center solutions possible for smaller organizations.

Call centers allow dedicated employees to handle constituent queries with the greatest speed and accuracy, providing "one call does all" service. This increases the organization's value to its clients, increasing constituent satisfaction while reducing the work-flow interruptions to staff that invariably reduce the efficiency of any operation. The dramatic increase in the ease of use and capabilities of telecommunications equipment, coupled with lower prices, enables organizations of virtually any size to take advantage of this increasingly popular technique. Equipment such as the Praxon PDX™ allows NPOs to have larger-operation functionality with user-friendly, lower-cost technology regardless of operating platform. This technology also allows for the user creation of reports for export to popular office productivity software such as Microsoft's Excel™ and allows user configuration through a popular Internet browser rather than through an on-call technical consultant billing at hourly rates. However, the reports such a device generates may only provide rudimentary information.

(ii) Handheld Computing Devices

Now as small as a deck of cards, such as the Palm Pilot™ and Apple's Newton™, these tools permit widely scattered employees to stay in contact with each other and the home office.

Effective telecommunications, smaller communications devices, and wireless communication can prevent either of the twin demons of constituent unhappiness: the failure to deliver services promised or the problem of duplicating costly services. In combination, they permit the rapid dissemination of information, providing an edge for quickly and accurately satisfying clients.

(iii) Software

In the past, organizations had two ways to proceed when it came to software. The first was to buy an off-the-shelf package and adapt their operations to fit the software. Each time software changed, there was the risk of required changes to documents and data—especially if functions used in the prior version were not carried forward to the new version! The second was to pay for extremely expensive custom packages that may be more difficult to modify, placing the organization at the mercy of programmers who may not be around later when changes were needed.

The advent of stable, flexible, and easy-to-comprehend relational database engines has given NPOs a powerful tool. (They are discussed in Section 15.4 as well.)

These database engines can store and retrieve vast quantities of information and yet deliver this information in formats that are easy to use, change, and store and far more secure than earlier software packages. Furthermore, the growing numbers of companies using these tools has spurred a rapid rise in the number of technicians who can work with these relational databases. Should a programmer leave, a suitable replacement can be secured quickly and easily.

Flexibility, speed, strength, and power are hallmarks of today's emerging technologies. The bottom line is that these technologies are slowly swinging the pendulum back toward favoring the users and not the creators of technology. In NPOs, with the potential wide variation in user skill and the potential number of different users over time, robust, stable applications are critical.

(C) PREDICTIONS

Predictions of coming technology may be the most difficult part of any discussion, but the Internet will almost always be involved. The advancements in wireless communications follow as a close second.

The zenith of providing services to constituents or persons served would be to allow access to needed information anytime, day or night, 365 days a year, from a variety of sources. These sources might be free public kiosks, public facilities such as the public library, or even lower-cost commercial facilities such as workstations in coffee houses and photocopy shops or fax-back systems. Users could access text information, in a variety of languages and depictions, and even (if the organization chose to set this in motion) click on an icon and be connected to someone live.

One way to provide that level of service is to staff up for 24/7 support, that is, 24 hours a day, seven days a week. Although not a very practical solution in terms of organizations run by volunteers, it remains a worthy goal. There is an answer, and that answer is the coming of age of the Internet.

It is possible to imagine a time in the not-too-distant future in which information stored on a relational database will be accessible to staff and volunteers via an interactive Web site from handheld computers via wireless communications and perhaps in another form to persons served through kiosks.

This scenario is in operation today on a limited basis, but it may be the wave of the future. One client with whom both authors work is establishing a call center with single-channel portable phones for use with the Praxon PDX to enable agents to travel throughout the association's office as needed. They can gather information not able to be stored on the computer, move among people in the organization, and reduce installation costs—the portable phones eliminate the need to integrate with another vendor's technology, which would add substantial costs. At this time, cost recovery is expected to occur within 18 months.

The future comes one day at a time, and the best way to capitalize on emerging technology is to get a clear picture of where the organization is now and where it wants technology to take it.

15.4 Creating Expandable Systems and Effective Configurations

(A) THINKING THROUGH TECHNOLOGY DESIGN

The technology any organization needs is driven by the needs of the people it serves. Technology exists solely for the purpose of helping organizations to provide services to their customers—as another tool to accomplish the mission and vision discussed earlier.

First, determine the needs of the persons served, making sure to poll both a typical and an extreme population. Then, the organization can explore the information or service required to serve that need. It may be the creation and sharing of an industry's common knowledge base, or perhaps a condensed and clarified information stream of emerging issues and opportunities. Decide what everyone needs to know, and then develop a capture system to locate, analyze, store, and, as required, disseminate that information.

All technology systems should be different if they are to be useful. Every business and every organization is unique, and its requirements will vary across predictable time spans, sometimes as small as hours of the day. Inbound call centers in some industries find that call volume follows a pattern that can be predicted over time in increments as small as 15 minutes, with specific hourly, daily, weekly, monthly, seasonal, and holiday patterns!

(B) BASIC ELEMENTS IN TECHNOLOGY DESIGN

There are basic elements required by all systems in order to function. The initial design of systems even influences how successful pursuit of the mission is. For example, once the process of capturing and storing information has begun, it is very difficult to make many modifications. System design effort should be very heavy in the front-end planning stages, with much testing of samples to ensure the system is optimally flexible, dependable, and able to be successfully modified in the future.

System design should provide relevant information for the widest part of the constituent market. Information not required by that population can be filtered out, but it is impossible to provide information that has not been stored to be available for use. This means that the more well known the needs served by the organization are, the better and more thorough the design responding to that need will be. Above all, system design must be flexible and easy to update and modify by internal staff with minimum training.

The four elements of any good design are:

1. Capture method
2. Storage method
3. Analysis method
4. Dispersal method

(i) Capture Method

For capture method, the most flexible and powerful is the database. Commercial packages that run on a variety of relational database engines, such as Oracle™ and Microsoft's SQL Server™, are often used by organizations that anticipate huge storage needs. If the population served or staff need vast sums of information requiring manipulation in a number of ways, then a relational database is the obvious choice.

Those with more modest needs may find that the flat-file database such as MS-Office Professional's Access™ is suitable. Flat-file databases lack the overall power and flexibility of a relational database but are usually more readily accessible to the average user. This means the capture system can change and grow with the growth of the organization and its clients. To be of best value to an NPO, any technology must be reusable and have the ability to be modified and recycled to continue to change and grow with the needs of the population served.

In this regard, relational databases are superior to flat-file. There is no equal for storing vast quantities of data and manipulating that data to achieve maximum value to the user, and later adding more information and changing the presentation of the data with relative ease. The rise in popularity of relational databases in even small-to-moderate organizations means there is a growing number of consultants and experienced designers working with these advanced databases.

(ii) Storage Method

The second area of design concern is storage of the data. The advent of RAID technology (Redundant Array of Inexpensive Disks) gives the nonprofit unparalleled protection at relatively modest outlays. RAID uses a number of interconnected, inexpensive hard drives, which reduces the cost of storing, retrieving, and manipulating large quantities of data. The RAID 5 system is a forgiving, or fault-tolerant, one and can greatly increase access time over simple mirrored systems while providing the highest level of failure protection in the industry. When teamed with a tape or writeable CD backup, it can prevent virtually any permanent loss of data. This translates to protecting the organization's emerging technology investment from hardware and user failures at a very low cost.

(iii) Analysis Method

Next is the ability to analyze and transform meaningless data into valuable information for use by staff and persons served. There are a lot of commercially available tools to aid organizations of any size with any budget or staff level, ranging from Microsoft Office™ tools (complete with "do-it-yourself" tools) to sophisticated database manipulation and presentation tools such as Crystal Report Writer™. With a little help from a reasonable consultant willing to consider the NPO's specific operation, skill level, and needs, the NPO can get what it needs at a level of investment able to be supported by the governing body.

(iv) Dispersal Method

Last is the method by which information is dispersed. Dispersal relates to how the organization disseminates information to other people. Until the Internet became widely used, this was a paper or video process. Now, clearly, Internet or intranet Web sites (a Web site internal to the organization and not available to persons outside the organization) are the future. Either type of site can contain FAQs (frequently asked questions) and FGRs (frequently given responses), day-to-day updates on programs, eligibility information, data on services provided, and information available only to specific users.

Call centers with staff trained to use relational databases to their maximum and wireless communications can now share data from site to site. In situations in which staff must move throughout a building, using products such as a single-channel portable phone and the Praxon PDX allows this. In situations in which cabling is not effective for creating a WAN, a low-frequency satellite connection can link buildings up to 30 miles away. Think of the information power available among cooperating agencies sharing such a system. In the authors' work with NPOs, such innovative technology has been left out of consideration because of misconceptions about cost and complexity.

Creating open, flexible systems that allow growth and change within the NPO is the boon emergent technology offers. While some of last year's products for the for-profit environment may be emergent for the NPO, there are leading-edge technologies that may make more sense.

15.5 Summary

The key to successful application of technology in the NPO is to figure out what it needs to accomplish—what a "mouse in the rafters" would see if the needs of the organization were being met efficiently and effectively, with all nonproductive activity eliminated, and then seeking help in figuring out what technology will help accomplish that vision. All too often, NPOs (and others) see the technology and attempt to figure out how to use it in their environment, which short-circuits innovation and success.

Consider the future. Project the needs. Identify where waste and nonproductive time and activities exist. Create the vision of the future, letting the low-tech "mouse in the rafters" help. Ask for help, and qualify the effectiveness of that help by how willing the helper is to hear your needs, answer your questions, justify the proposals, and speak to you in plain English about what is recommended.

16 Building a Knowledge Marketplace: Best Practices to Create Learning Value in Cyberspace

JANET POLEY, PhD, PRESIDENT
American Distance Education Consortium (ADEC)

My goal is to make the World Bank the first port of call when people need knowledge about development. By the year 2000, we will have in place a global communications system with computer links, videoconferencing and interactive classrooms, affording our clients all around the world full access to our information bases—the end of geography as we at the Bank have known it.

James D. Wolfensohn, World Bank President, 1997

16.1   Introduction

The number and types of nonprofit organizations (NPOs) are growing. Does this proliferation mean new opportunities for more players or just more weeds among a few flowers? The opportunity is to create a "knowledge marketplace" within the .org domain that results in real value for individuals and communities around the world. Other communication media, such as digital broadcast satellite or satellite radio, might also become carriers for quality learning content, but the best current hope is the Internet.

16.2   Enriching the .org Domain

Today, the .org Web sites are a fragmented collection of little jewels, cobwebs, and clutter. Few NPOs or so-called nongovernmental organizations (NGOs) provide content of sufficient depth and breadth to encourage daily or even weekly return visits. Too often, these sites are shallow and internally self-serving. Typically, they include a mission statement and an overview of the service work of the organization. There will often be an opportunity for the visitor to join a cause or give money. Some sites ask questions and poll visitors on issues related to the money-raising aspect of the organization. In addition to the individual sites, one now finds a variety of portals and gateways designed to cluster the uniform resource locators (URLs) of NPOs for convenience purposes. Usually, these clusters are somewhat mission related and may be operated by national, state, and/or local governments.

Web surfing in the current .org sea makes clear that a much greater richness of ideas, information, learning opportunities, and linkages might be developed and encouraged. Rarely do .org sites come up as the most salient source of knowledge from a search engine; these sites do not often break the mold, innovate, and fill up the market space on even a single issue.

16.3   Political Cyberspace

So who cares anyway? Jessica Matthews, President of the Carnegie Endowment for International Peace, notes that power is increasingly shifting toward NGOs/NPOs in the international arena. She highlights the emergence of the electronic citizen and a network society as key drivers in the demise of the all-powerful state and the rise of a global civil society. She recently said:

The biggest and most worrisome consequence of this trend is a society that is made up of thousands of narrowly defined individual groups and interests—a society that looks, if you forgive the metaphor, more like a Napoleon pastry with thousands of separate layers, instead of a blended soufflé.[1]

Matthews states that even the best NPOs are usually passionately committed to narrow goals. They suffer from tunnel vision, desire to act unilaterally, and one issue-itis. They end up fragmenting perspective and policy. NGOs are often accountable to no one, and sustainable, continuous management is a long-term, well-documented problem.

On the positive side, there is an emergence of a few transnational NGOs in the .org domain, largely coming about in political cyberspace. These organizations cross geographic borders and boundaries and, in a few cases, are succeeding in contributing to more common international perspectives about issues such as environment, human rights, and corruption.

16.4   Why Not a Knowledge Marketplace Rather Than Just a Political Cyberspace?

Matthews states that with all the limitations noted, a few NPOs are creating a "powerful political space."[2] This may continue to be a productive avenue for some of the large, focused, international organizations, but it will be impossible for many smaller NGOs. Their efforts might better be directed toward creating high-quality, Internet-based educational resources in areas where they have a comparative advantage. They must find a niche in the knowledge marketplace.

In the twenty-first century, it will be what people know, more than what they possess, that will define quality of life around the globe. Dr. Thomas Malone, past Executive Director of Sigma Xi, the nonprofit scientific society, argues in an unpublished paper that knowledge should become the organizing principle for the future.[3] Unless NPOs, education organizations, governments, and businesses begin to move in this direction, sustainable development will be impossible to achieve.

As the population increases and resources decrease, human beings will increasingly have to "live by their wits." Many scientists and scholars are arguing that we can no longer predict the future from the past. Rather, the question of whether there is a future will depend on our ability to invent new opportunities and solutions from the global knowledge and research base. Political rhetoric, mindless marketing, and impulsively developed information based only on opinion, even though disseminated via the latest cybertechnology, will do little to serve an organization or larger society in a productive way.

16.5   What Is a Learning Society?

The National Association of State Universities and Land Grant Colleges (NASULGC), in a September 1999 report financed by the W. K. Kellogg Foundation, identifies the key elements of a learning society.[4] They note in introducing the report that we are undergoing change so fundamental and far reaching that a true learning society is within reach. They also note that governors of states are calling for more educational offerings and that learning will rank right up there with money in determining the social and economic well-being of nations into the next century. The key elements of a learning society were identified as:

- Values habits of learning
- Fosters lifelong learning
- Ensures responsive and flexible learning programs
- Fosters learning networks
- Is socially inclusive
- Encourages learning communities
- Recognizes the importance of early childhood development
- Views new information technologies as tools to enrich and tailor learning to societal, organizational, and individual needs
- Stimulates knowledge creation and use
- Values regional and global interconnections and cultural links
- Fosters public policy ensuring equity of access to learning, information, and information technology

The rapid change in knowledge—along with the short shelf-life and quick obsolescence of information and professional knowledge acquisition—requires new approaches. People need to learn how to become critical thinkers and problem solvers. They need to make "just-in-time" learning a lifelong habit. If, as we are told, knowledge becomes increasingly valuable and sought after, it means that NPOs will learn how to be in this marketplace or die.

A study commissioned by the NASULGC/Kellogg project and carried out by the Rutgers Eagleton Institute provided some interesting insights into the reasons people think lifelong learning is important and becoming more of a national priority.[5] This survey included formal and nonformal education administrators and experts, as well as governors and state legislators. It is interesting to note that state legislators responded at a relatively low rate to the survey. There is a growing concern that state legislators are badly in need of lifelong learning in a variety of education- and technology-related areas. This may also be an opportunity for the nonprofit sector. Almost unanimously, the respondents strongly agreed that lifelong learning promotes individual well-being, benefits corporate productivity, is important to a country's economic prosperity, and enhances the quality of community life. More than 8 of 19 respondents also agreed that lifelong learning is important to the security of the nation, is a national priority, and promotes family preservation.

Eighty percent of the respondents thought it was important to advance lifelong learning as a national priority in the United States. Some of the methods suggested for such advancement included:

- Greater commitment of resources
- Reorganization of education and training
- Increased efforts toward equity of access
- Maximum use of new technologies
- Linkage between universal lifelong learning and America's position in the global economy

With the elements identified in this study and the methods they suggest for advancement of lifelong learning, a serious NPO might establish an agenda for evaluation and action. It is important to recognize that it is knowledge and the stimulation of lifelong learning—not the glitz and whirl of the marketplace—that should be the focus.

16.6 Where Does Your Organization Fit in the Knowledge Marketplace?

The level of activity is picking up, and if NPOs want to contribute to the learning rather than the hype, serious analysis is in order. At a recent meeting of the World Campus Advisory Board for Pennsylvania State University (the author is a member), Dr. Gary Miller, head of the World Campus, suggested that there were several key issues requiring attention. These same issues are also important to the nonprofit agenda.

(A) MARKET DIFFERENTIATION

Today's marketplace is very confusing. The upside of the current situation is lots of innovative experimentation. The downside is that no one knows for sure "who is who" or "what is what." NPOs need to consider their place in the lifelong learning market of the future by defining how they want to become known and recognized. Will the narrow, single-issue focus continue? If not, how will it be replaced in a way that NGOs are recognizable as more public and private organizations and agencies crowd into the market?

One characteristic of developing-country open markets is the fact that you might find something of real interest and beauty one day. However, if you did not buy yesterday, you might find tomorrow that the market stall, seller, and "little jewel" you wanted have disappeared forever. NPOs are notoriously good at creating little jewels of knowledge and enterprise from time to time, but historically less good at connecting past knowledge to present and future opportunities. Few have digital libraries, and NPOs often suffer from frequent staff turnover. In short, they frequently lack institutional memory. This is an even more serious challenge in today's environment, where change is a constant, but efficiency dictates that we not constantly reinvent the wheel.

(B) REACHING INFORMED NONUSERS

There is a danger that more and more organizations will rely on Web pages as a primary tool for outreach and dissemination of information and knowledge. Because the most frequent Web page users are those already inside an organization, it becomes more difficult to reach out to informed nonusers of the organization's information, programs, and services. "Push" technology will increasingly be combined with "pull" technology. Many organizations use e-mail and listservs to alert people to something new or important on a Web site; however, the e-mail lists must be kept current, and mechanisms need to be devised to constantly draw in new people and organizations. Satellite radio and television will also become part of "push" information strategies.

The fact that no information business is really yet making money in cyberspace suggests that there remains much to be understood about how to market in this new world. In addition, questions of irritation, information overload, and privacy must be considered.

(C) WORKING IN THE INTERNATIONAL MARKETPLACE

To date, we are largely working in a U.S. marketplace when it comes to knowledge and the just-in-time learning agenda. The really interesting opportunities are beginning to sprout around the globe, and NPOs/NGOs are in an excellent position to help shape this effort from the grassroots. It is very important that organizations identify not just what they want to sell or offer to others through the new environments, but also consider what they need to learn from others. It is also important that the overused phrase *thinking globally* gets into action. The real enrichment of all communities, countries, and cultures can occur only if a much larger number of the world's population becomes engaged in the knowledge marketplace. Just as the World Bank's Knowledge 97 conference began this idea, there is much to be done; unfortunately, much of the doing to date is being approached as a zero-sum game. NPOs, together with other partners, could enliven and recast the parameters of discussion on many of the issues discussed in this chapter.

16.7 *Creating Partnerships with Other Nongovernmental Organizations, Educational Organizations, Agencies, Foundations, and Businesses*

The importance of partnerships has already been mentioned and will be emphasized in other sections of this chapter. The opportunity for impact by NPOs and educational organizations and agencies is perhaps greater in this early stage—the pre–money-making period. Certainly, much of the future well-being of the United States and other countries depends on the economic outcomes of today's experiments. It is also important now to recognize the significance of longer-term social and intellectual considerations. This may ultimately be more crucial than focusing just on short-term gain.

In the long term, quality and depth will be critical to sustainability of the knowledge marketplace. If our livelihoods will be increasingly dependent on quality just-in-time learning, we need to build these systems now and help people begin at an early age to use them. Knowledge has always been important—consider that a small group of engineers failing to make metric conversions brought down a satellite. Precise knowledge (and wisdom) will be the key to the world's future.

(A) PRODUCTION EFFICIENCIES

The United States is such a wealthy nation that it is relatively easy for Americans to be innovative (but often wasteful). As the globe becomes a smaller place and everyone can see what is going on with the "wealthy Joneses" inside the gated community, it becomes very important for us to figure out how to produce efficiently and share the well-being. Many NPOs are interested in the issue of sustainability, and definitions of efficiency will increasingly include not just economic but environmental considerations as well. At the organizational level, the ability of most NGOs to participate in the knowledge marketplace will be dependent on not just creative issues and idea generation, but also an ability to develop a strong, sustainable knowledge production and maintenance system with a memory.

In 1997, the World Bank thought the questions of global knowledge and information technology were so critical to the future that they conducted the "Knowledge 97" conference. International discussants met in Toronto to consider the following seven issues:

1. Empowering the poor with information and knowledge
2. Role of the state for information economy
3. Infrastructure and capacity building
4. Fostering science and technology in developing countries
5. Knowledge flows, civic dialogue, and the informed citizen
6. Distance education and technology for learning
7. Partnerships[6]

This live knowledge market of more than 1,000 international participants was meant to stimulate future connections and relationships among NGOs and others that could be carried into the future via the Internet.

As Michael Schrage stated in an *Educom Review* article, the cyber market might look quite different today if the core design was based on "relationships" rather than the publishing metaphor. Although he expects developments to move beyond the browsing, posting, and listing, little with the exception of an overuse of the word *community* seems to have invaded the English vocabulary.[7]

(B)   THE METAPHOR—KNOWLEDGE MARKETPLACE IN CYBERSPACE

Outdoor open markets, bazaars, flea markets, and even megamalls emerge from small mats, squares, stalls, boutiques, and shops. The thriving, robust market has a personality that overarches the individual sellers and the "stuff" for sale. The character of a market is derived from the structure, the way spaces are arranged, the colors flowing together, the languages that are used, the tones, the shapes, the smells, the human relationships, the chitchat, the business relationships, the exchanges, the bargains struck, and the pace of it all.

Some marketplaces are interesting, diverse, dynamic, and teeming with life. Other marketplaces are boring, shallow, plastic hangouts with little to offer but more of the same—conspicuous consumption. Today, much of what is found on the Internet was created in North America, Australia, and, increasingly, Western Europe. The content is shaped by and for the American market. Much of it is boring. Certainly, bandwidth limits the possibilities for many knowledge providers and customers; however, lack of vision, inadequate creativity, and narrowness and shallowness of content may actually be the greater limitations.

(C)   WILL YOU KNOW A MARKET IF YOU SEE IT?

Many are coming to today's knowledge marketplace—the Internet—with little to sell. Organizations simply announce that they are "number one" and "the best," staking out an audience they hope to capture for the future. In some respects, the seller is like the "flim-flam" artist with smoke and mirrors. The substance, the content, and the product are missing. This shallowness problem abounds in cyberspace as front doors, portals, pages, and promises mark the possible locations for e-education and e-business.

The Internet Nonprofit Center (*http://www.nonprofits.org*) is an example of a cyberspace location established in an attempt to provide an aggregation or gateway to nonprofit resources. The subtitle for the Nonprofit Center is "The Nonprofit FAQ." A little box notes that they receive a royalty on books purchased through Amazon.com. They seem to want to profit in the fashion of others, hoping to be the "portal" to the content provided by others. They ask for feedback, so they in effect get the customers to help maintain this marketspace. The Evergreen State Society in Seattle, Washington, claims copyright over the pages. They use a rather primitive organizing framework, using the following five titles with links to a variety of sites of variable quality. Some links work and others do not. A sort of alphabetic file drawer list of terms is found beneath each of the five major headings. No annotation appears.

1. *Organization*—includes information relevant to mission, purpose, strategy, boards, officers, committees, and business practices.
2. *Management*—is an eclectic mix of topics, including some traditional management subjects and some related to management of information.
3. *Regulation*—provides largely federal and state law and regulation.
4. *Resources*—focuses on information and consulting and includes policies and politics.
5. *Development*—is membership and funding oriented.

Links are those gleaned from other people's sites, e-mail lists, UseNet, and other sources. This is only one example of what NPOs can expect as others point to valuable content on other people's pages. At this stage, it is far too early to know whether "quick and dirty" attempts at marketspace creation add enough value to be sustainable. Because the designated NPO covers a multitude of organizations and interests, it is not clear whether this type of cyber collection is even a community of interest, let alone a market.

One might surmise that these "portals" are simply early crude attempts to capture the lead into the intellectual property of others. They are not rich marketplaces or spaces today, but can they be tomorrow? This is an interesting question. Many of today's marketplaces and portals lack quality content and products and have few vibrant communicators that appeal to diverse market segments. Too often, these places are like an abandoned shopping center or the open marketplaces in developing countries after closing on Saturday afternoon.

16.8   The Portal Question

Nonprofit organizations would do well to watch carefully the work of organizations that are following the development of the knowledge marketplace on a daily basis. Along with the American Distance Education Consortium (ADEC), an outstanding source is the Masie Center (*http://www.masie.com*). Elliott Masie's definitions help carry our thinking beyond seeing *portals* as just another catchy term to be adopted by "wanna-be-rich" organizations looking to dominate a marketplace segment. The following set of definitions comes from his Masie Center newsletter:

- *Portal.* A portal is any site that offers a learner or an organization consolidated access to learning and training resources. Portals can range from a simple page filled with links to a sophisticated virtual classroom and learning center. Most portals proudly announce themselves as portals. Others are more subtle, adding .com, .net, to the end of their corporate name; or a click or two to the front of their name; or starting with the word *my* or *big.* If the site claims to be your single stop for learning, you have stumbled on a portal. Of course, other sites are portals in training and may have the name stamped on the title until we all figure out what a portal is or if anyone will make any portal bucks.

- *Content consolidation portal.* A good number of portals are aiming at the content consolidation and aggregation business. These portals want to give the learner or buyer a simple way to shop for all of their training needs on a single page. The portal gets a cut of the action and allows the buyer to have a consolidated shopping and purchasing plan. Some of these portals are content quality agnostic. They want to be the Amazon.com of learning, so any content can come to their site. Others are claiming to filter content or offer only the best of breed. Still others are "treating" the content so that it can be used interchangeably, mixing and matching training modules from several vendors.
- *Embedded technology portal.* These groups are using the portal as a way of embedding and selling their technology as a component of learning or on a learning service provider basis. For example, you buy a class from the portal and your organization gets all the data it would have collected if it had a training management server. Or the portal supplies free or usage-based access to a virtual classroom with digital collaboration tools. These portals are vending technology more than content.
- *Internal portal.* Why go to the Internet if you can have a portal right in your digital backyard? These companies are offering to build you a branded portal that sits right on your internal server and offers content consolidation and/or embedded technology. These offerings are aimed at allowing the learning or business functions to build a learning site rapidly and often bypass the internal anxieties of an information technology department.
- *Community and collaboration portals.* Other portals are popping up that focus on building a digital community of users. You can recognize these portals with the presence of standard community technologies: chat rooms, what's new in the learning world, threaded discussion, access to coaching, and links to books to buy. We know that learning is a heavily social process, so the community portals will proliferate in the coming months.
- *Affiliation portals.* These portals, popping up in the nonprofit association world, will offer the preceding services, with the "Good Housekeeping Seal" of the association. The affiliation allows for content screening and/or discount buying.[8]

The portal game is new. We will see additional portals based on selling the "eyeballs" of trainees, portals offering to hold the skills portfolios of workers over their lifetimes, portals with live coaching available on a click, and portals to link learning with employment opportunities. Most of the portals are nimbly ready to absorb all of the functions listed and experiment with the widest range of business models.

The portals are hitting the marketplace largely in response to the e-commerce frenzy and to appeal to venture capitalists who love the idea of a single portal for all world learning. Now it is time to see if customers share the enthusiasm for portals and which value propositions work in the marketplace of training buyers. Experimentation in the portal arena is healthy for the industry, creating new offers of capability and pricing. One thing is sure: There will be continuing growth in portals well into the twenty-first century.

16.9   Pipes and Drinking Straws—Knowledge Carriers

A recent *Wall Street Journal* article by Scott Thurm describes the process to hook up one local high-speed Internet connection for a new customer.[9] Technicians at the local phone company make several trips to switch the customer to the new company. Company technicians also make a few trips, and several unsuccessful automated tests happen, along with countless phone calls, before the hookup is complete. This process may take over two months. This does not include the three years the company spent raising money, gaining regulatory approvals, and installing its equipment inside the local telephone company's neighborhood switching office. Companies are building national networks of digital subscriber lines (DSLs) for small businesses, branch offices, and telecommuters. These lines promise Internet connections up to 20 times as fast as a conventional modem. DSLs use special equipment, modems, and traditional copper telephone wires. Ultimately, the DSL firms may lure customers with a low-cost combination of local calling and long-distance service, as well as Internet access. They are not alone—everyone wants to find a way to bring a full pipe into every business and home for as little money as possible. Internet over satellite is another approach to answering the so-called digital divide.

Although there is lots of talk about competition, the so-called Baby Bell operating companies still control 80 percent of the lines. They are very wealthy and like the status quo. The upstart DSLs and satellite providers are also competing with the AT&T/TCI conglomerate running Internet over cable. In terms of numbers, AT&T cable is far ahead, with almost 1 million subscribers. This compares with some 160,000 for DSLs, according to market researchers Kinetic Strategies and TeleChoice, and satellite-based Internet is just coming into the marketplace. In general, NPOs will be wise to let content, programs, and audience access issues guide their strategic technology choices. Cost and ability to migrate to improved systems in the future are also important considerations. Ironically, there are currently too many nonprofit and public-sector organizations casting their missions to the breeze while seriously seeking money. As an individual recently asked, "What good does it do for public universities to be doing distance education programming only to the well-served, well-off, nondistant populations?"

The state of Texas has a large land area with scattered population. It remains unclear whether one phone company's announced plan to bring DSLs to its San Antonio service region by 2003 will change much for rural and underserved populations. Quite possibly, the very technology advertised to reach out may ultimately just enrich the same companies. According to Stephanie Mehta, the Baby Bells were slow to deploy DSL service to consumers, in part because of the expense and logistics of delivering the service.[10] As a result, there are many more cable modems than DSL connections installed in the United States. But with SBC purchasing Ameritech, the company now controls about one-third of the nation's telephone lines that stretch from California to Connecticut. In order to reach all of its consumers with DSL services, SBC will have to spend billions to deploy fiber-optic networks deeper into the communities it serves. If a customer lives far from a Bell switching office or a fiber connection, he or she may not be able to qualify for DSL service. (A DSL connection depends on how far the customer is from the local switching office.) Separately, another Bell telephone company, U S West, is expected to announce that it will test "fixed wireless" service for high-speed Internet access that may be as much as 400 times faster than 56K modems. Fixed wireless, which uses antennas and the airwaves to transmit data, is gaining attention as a third alternative to DSLs and cable modems. The questions about bandwidth availability are very important to NPOs attempting to staff and plan for their Internet strategy. Because many NPOs maintain a strong interest in the educational equity concerns, they will be hesitant to adopt "bandwidth-hogging" applications until access into rural and other underserved communities is improved. The National Telecommunications Infrastructure Administration (NTIA) of the Department of Commerce (*http://www.ntia.doc.gov*) is monitoring the digital divide and issues regular reports.[11] To date, little progress has been made on delivering good Internet access, quickly and cheaply, into rural, poor, inner-city, and minority communities. This is an issue of significant concern to NPOs focused on the knowledge and information needs of these audiences. Also, senior citizens have been lagging behind some other groups, particularly in Internet use beyond e-mail.

16.10   Names/Branding and Your Uniform Resource Locator

It will certainly be difficult to establish identity in the knowledge marketplace if you have to change your name frequently due to copyright claims. Having to change your Internet domain name may be just as bad. The Internet Corporation of Assigned Names and Numbers (ICANN) is currently under heavy criticism from government, business, and consumer advocates.[12] Representative Tom Bliley from Virginia, Chairman of the House Commerce Committee, wrote the following to ICANN Chairwoman Esther Dyson early in 1999: "Rather than promote the Internet's evolution, your organization's policies actually may jeopardize the continued stability of the underlying systems that permit millions of people to use, enjoy, and transact business on the Internet." "ICANN has constructed an edifice of Byzantine complexity (that will) allow a handful of huge corporations to dominate the formerly decentralized entrepreneurial workings of the Internet," charges the *Cook Report*, a newsletter from cyber-gadfly Gordon Cook.[13] Even consumer advocate Ralph Nader has attacked ICANN for a "lack of openness, a lack of accountability, and a lack of membership." Domain names should be considered a right akin to having a phone number, Nader says, with ICANN membership free and open to all.[14] It is in the interest of NPOs to follow these discussions and weigh in on core framework issues of this type.

(A)   ELECTRONIC COMMERCE—SUPPLY AND DEMAND

The Internet is also changing power relationships between buyer and seller. Shifts from vertically linked chains to more horizontal linkages are eroding the old structures for knowledge in the marketplace. Current assumptions are that it will become increasingly difficult to keep knowledge secret to gain and maintain power. This may be only partially true for many years to come given the gaps and fragmentation in the knowledge space within the Internet. These weaknesses are expected to continue indefinitely due to the decentralized nature of the Web and the state of the deployment of search engines and "knowbots" or agents.

However, e-commerce optimists predict that a wider choice of suppliers is just around the corner for consumers. Michael Casey predicts in the *Wall Street Journal* that this could have far-reaching implications for global labor markets and inflation. He states that part of this lies in the Internet's promise to greatly improve inventory systems, with firms being able to link databases via the Internet at a much lower cost.[15] As for consumer buying power, it could strip high-price producers that once relied on geographic advantages for their competitive edge and hand it to their lower-cost competitors. Some consumers are also becoming more efficient spenders, using the Internet to make price comparisons and pool their spending power at "buyer cartel" sites that leverage the power of bulk buying.

(B) FISCAL MOVERS AND MARKET STAKEOUT

So-called first movers are actively engaged in a type of market stakeout. The notion goes that in case there is something valuable in the nonprofit sector, we will try to "claim this chuck of cyberspace" (the something valuable might be content, knowledge, wisdom, solutions to problems, means to other ends such as money, etc.). To date, marketplaces in cyberspace have been elusive. In the physical world of marketplace development, we would ask the geographic location question. Realtors long swore by the admonition location, location, location.

(C) TIMING, INFORMATION, AND KNOWLEDGE COMBINE

Today, some are guessing that timing, timing, timing is the answer to finding cyber markets. One thing is clear: Much remains to be learned about how people will use cyberspace in the future, and many are betting that today's applications of e-mail, the Web, search engines, file transfer protocol, and streaming audio and video on demand will evolve into a much richer array. To date, e-commerce attempts to make money by Internet alone are disappointing with a few exceptions. Small combinations of easily accessible, in-depth Internet content leading to comprehensive understanding of a product, issue, idea, or other intellectual sphere can smartly be combined with face-to-face sales. The role of Internet-based information in selling cars, making airline reservations, voting, and health care selection are interesting examples. They have some similarities and differences. Many people are reluctant to provide personal information over the network, including financial and credit card data as well as individual health status. Irrespective of improved security measures that allow customers to pay for a product or service, it is reasonable to expect that:

- People will become more reluctant, not less, to share personal information via computer networks.
- People are also going to continue to want to kick the tires and see, feel, and smell the product in other cases.
- People will continue to desire human touch and affect in other situations.
- Many people will continue to browse for all possible information before making a decision to purchase a car, a plane ticket, a direction in health care, or a person to vote for.

The Internet as information provider and comparison vehicle is already clear. What is far less clear is how and what types of transactions will be accomplished in cyberspace. The Internet has already demonstrated tremendous power as a knowledge space, but it remains an open question as to how important it becomes as a marketplace.

E-mail has demonstrated its application as a communication vehicle. The World Wide Web brought digital libraries. However, tools to build relationships, close transactions, and verify and validate individual perceptions and transactions are not yet available.

16.11   Relationship Space

In a real marketplace, people sometimes like to go shopping with others. As consumers, we do not always trust what we have been told, what we are seeing, or even our own perceptions about the nutrition or safety of a food product, the color and/or style of a garment, or the reliability of a computer or automobile. In other words, relationships—social interaction of a sort different from e-mail, listservs, and threaded conversations—are critical to decision making.

(A)   WILL I GET SUED?

It is also clear that in a litigious society like the United States, chatting online, brainstorming, or criticizing ideas, issues, and products in cyberspace can lead to subpoenas and lawsuits. Companies are increasingly using subpoenas to obtain the personal information about individuals who might make a derogatory remark about a product online. Although the nonprofit world may be less involved in direct product selling in cyberspace, the same dampers to freedom of expression may quickly arise in a nonprofit world of knowledge, issues, and ideas.

(B)   WHY ANALYZE THE COMMERCIAL SALE?

The knowledge marketplace requires much more understanding from many sources of how or even if these new tools will work well for lifelong learning. Higher education and government have been deeply involved in experiments and analysis for the past 10 years and are just beginning to scratch the surface. NPOs could gain, as could institutions of higher education, by greater collaboration in areas of mutual interest. Businesses have much to contribute to the knowledge stew, the systems for economic exchange and barter, as well as the technologies—hard and soft—they are selling to create such a marketplace. If one considers content, packaging, transmission, and software and hardware integration to be critical to success, it becomes obvious that alliances and porous boundaries among organizations will be essential.

16.12   Market Research: Online Polling Applications to Knowledge Marketplace and Digital Divide

The following comes from Jim Puzzanghera's *San Jose Mercury News* article about Harris Interactive, one of the nation's leading polling firms. Harris is pouring $55 million into recruiting a nationwide panel of 12 to 15 million Internet users for various types of market research. The panel will also be polled on nearly every significant political race, including the U.S. presidential race in 2000. The idea is very controversial among pollsters; some say that Harris's plans to poll by Internet will not yield reliable results. "You are clearly missing people," according to Kathleen Frankovic, director of surveys for CBS News. "It seems to me that moving to an online survey . . . you're giving up half or more of the country to start," she said. According to a U.S. Department of Commerce study, 94 percent of U.S. households had a telephone in 1998, whereas only 26 percent had Internet access. Additionally, Internet users are wealthier than the general population, with minorities and senior citizens particularly underrepresented. "It's saying only some people's opinions matter," said Frankovic.[16]

16.13   Transparency and Taxes

For good or for bad, the only things certain are death and taxes. Now, the detailed tax returns of NPOs are available on the Internet.[17,18] The returns include information such as how much of an organization's money goes directly to charitable services and how much top officers and consultants are paid. Until now, the only way to get copies of returns was from the Internal Revenue Service, which could involve delays of up to six months. "This is, by far, the most important development ever in making charities accountable and making their finances transparent," said Virginia Hodgkinson, a founder of the National Center for Charitable Statistics. The first 140,000 of the 220,000 or so returns are available for free at *http://www.guidestar.org*, and the rest will be posted before year-end.

16.14   Summarizing the State of the Internet

To formulate best practice, it is important to know the environment. Consider the following key facts about the Internet as of late 1999.[19]

(A)   INTERNET USE

- Fifty-six percent of all U.S. adults are online (Harris Poll, December 1999).
- There are 72.4 million host computers (January 2000).
- Sixty percent of the hosts are located in the United States. This is expected to drop to 33 percent by 2002.
- The number of hosts worldwide is expected to reach 100 million by 2001.
- There are 120 million Internet users in North America.
- Thirty-three percent of U.S. households have Internet access today (compared to 5 percent in 1994).
- Fifty percent of U.S. households are expected to have Internet access by 2003.
- The penetration rate of the Internet is moving more rapidly than phone and television.
- 7.7 billion Web pages are expected to exist by 2002.

(B)   E-MAIL

- There were 618 billion e-mail messages sent in 1998 (the U.S. Postal Service sent 101 billion pieces of mail).
- Fifty percent of the population are expected to use e-mail early in the twenty-first century.

(C)   E-COMMERCE

- In 1998, 10 million U.S. households made purchases online.
- By the end of 2003, $1.3 trillion is projected in online purchases.

(D) BROADBAND ACCESS

- Few have access to high-speed Internet, including business.
- Large companies are still connecting at the sub-T1 rate.
- In 2000, an estimated 35.2 million households are connected with copper, 2.2 million are connected with advanced telephony, 2.9 million are connected via cable, and 500,000 are connected through wireless and satellite systems.
- The digital divide will continue well into the next decade.

16.15   The ABCs of Best Practice

Exhibit 16.1 is a set of reminders joined with the alphabet to ease dissemination and memory. Only your organization can define for itself what is really important in terms of strategy, structure, technology, and program—the key elements of living systems. Exhibit 16.1

EXHIBIT 16.1 Best Practices: Alphabet Reminders

	Strategy	Structure	Technology	Program
A	Action-oriented	Affiliative	Access	Audience-focused
B	Balanced	Basic	Bandwidth	Broad
C	Community-oriented	Cooperative	Cost-conscious	Content
D	Dynamic	Distributed	Digital	Deep
E	Equity	Efficient	Easy	Ethical
F	Fast	Flexible	Fiber	First mover
G	Global	Global	Global	Global
H	Humorous	Horizontal	Horizontal	Habit-forming
I	Integrated	Interconnected	Interoperable	Inclusive
J	Just	Journalistic	Judicious	"Just-in-time"
K	Knowledge-based	Knowledge-based	Knowledge-based	Knowledge-based
L	Lifelong learning	Learning organization	Linkages	Learner-centered
M	Multidimensional	Market-oriented	Migratable	Maintained
N	Networked	Networked	Networked	Networked
O	Outreach	Opaque	Operational	Organized
P	Problem-oriented	Porous	Productive	Partnerships
Q	Quality	Quality	Quality	Quality
R	Relationships	Responsive	Reliable	Revered
S	Sustainability-oriented	Sustainable	Secure	Successful
T	Targeted	Transparent	Tailored	Touches
U	User-oriented	Unified	Ubiquitous	Unique
V	Values	Value-added	Verifiable	Valuable
W	Working together	Woven	Web	Works
X	X	X	X	X
Y	Y	Y	Y	Y
Z	Z	Z	Z	Z

is just a start, and we encourage you to make this a dynamic document. You can change the categories, the descriptions, and even the letters of the alphabet into other alphabets used around the globe.

Endnotes

1. Matthews, J. (interview by Stephen Ferry). (1999). "Power Shifts and Citizen Innovation," *Government Technology* (August) Special Issue, *http://www.govtech.net.*
2. Id.
3. Malone, T. F. (March 20, 2000). "Towards a Western Hemisphere Knowledge Partnership." Unpublished, 20 pp. (see p. 1 for statement).
4. NASULGC Report: Returning to Our Roots: A Learning Society. (1999). Kellogg Commission on the Future of State and Land-Grant Universities, 4th Report, Washington, D.C. (September).
5. Id.
6. World Bank Program: Knowledge 97. (1997). Toronto, Canada, June 22–25, *http://www.worldbank.org.*
7. Schrage, M. (1998). "Technology, Silver Bullets and Big Lies: Musings on the Information Age," *Educom Review,* 33(1) (January/February), *http://www.educause.edu/pub/er/review/reviewarticles/33132.html.*
8. Masie, E. (1999). *Masie Center Tech Learn Newsletter* (October 18), *http://www.masie.com.*
9. Thurm, S. (1999). "Phone Upstarts Grab Some Turf in a Wild Race to the Internet," *Wall Street Journal* (B1), http://interactive.wsj.com/articles/SB940194775570100506.htm.
10. Mehta, S. (1999). "SBC Plans to Speed Up Rollout of High-Speed DSL Services," *Wall Street Journal* (B6), *http://interactive.wsj.com/articles/SB940168103379805966.htm.*
11. NTIA. (1999). Falling Through the Digital Divide (July 8), *http://www.ntia.doc.gov/ntiahome/digitaldivide.*
12. Coughlin, K. (Newhouse News Service). (1999). *San Jose Mercury News,* *http://www.sjmercury.com/svtech/news/breaking/merc/docs/icann101699.htm.*
13. Cook, G. (1999). "ISOC's ICANN Coalition Widens Its Control." The Cook Report on Internet (September), *http://www.cookreport.com/isoccontrol.shtml.*
14. Nader, R., and J. Love. (1999). ICANN (June), *http://www.icann.org/nader-questions.htm.*
15. Casey, M. (1999). "Power of Internet Changes Supply and Demand Forever," *Wall Street Journal* (A43C), *http://interactive.wsj.com/articles/SB940193962568568020.htm.*
16. Puzzanghera, J. (1999). "Online Polling Experiment Stirs Excitement, Skepticism," *San Jose Mercury News,* *http://www.mercurycenter.com/svtech/news/indepth/docs/poll101899.*
17. Johnston, D. (1999). *New York Times* (C1), *http://www.nytimes.com/library/tech/99/10/biztech/articles/18give.html.*
18. Rich, M. (1999). "Web Sites to Give Financial Data About Charities and Top Salaries," *Wall Street Journal, http://interactive.wsj.com/articles/SB940196551186180819.htm.*
19. Karle, T. (1999). "Information Supernova," *Government Internet Guide NETG* (October), *http://www.govtech.net.*

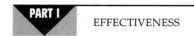

Suggested Readings

The Benton Foundation's Communications Policy and Practice (CPP), *http://www.benton. org/cpphome.html*

Internet Nonprofit Center: The Nonprofit FAQ, *http://www.nonprofits.org.*

Wolfensohn, J.D. (September 23, 1997). "The Challenge of Inclusion," address to the Board of Governors, Hong Kong, China.

17 Technology and Strategy for Organizational Effectiveness*

MARC OSTEN, MED, PRINCIPAL
Summit Consulting Collaborative
www.summitcollaborative.com
www.strategictechnology.net

Author's note: I started working on nonprofit and education technology issues in 1985. My knowledge was built through an embarrassing number of mistakes I made and the work done by many others. Today, a large cadre of individuals and organizations provide technology assistance to nonprofits. A strong spirit of collaboration and sharing permeates this community of which I have the privilege to be a part. This chapter was made possible by the willingness of many of my colleagues to share their experience and resources. Thank you to all of them: Tom Battin, CompassPoint Nonprofit Services; Susan Brown, Evergreen Children's Association; Phil Ferrante-Roseberry, CompuMentor; Andrew Higgins, Summit Intern, MBA Student University of Massachusetts at Amherst; Beth Kanter, *Arts Wire;* Joseph Klement, Summit Intern, MBA Student, University of Massachusetts at Amherst; Denise Joines, One Northwest; Randall Leurquin, Friends of the Chicago River; Joe Matuzak, *Arts Wire;* Justin Maxson, Progressive Technology Project; Marco Paz, Consultant; Catherine Peterson, Arts Boston; Lois Salisbury, Children Now; Jillaine Smith, Benton Foundation; Jon Spear, Handsnet; Rob Stuart, TechRocks; Sheila Tasker, Maine Coast Artists.

17.1   Background

Nonprofit organizations are not currently taking full advantage of advanced technology to improve organizational effectiveness. Nonprofits find themselves ill equipped to handle the technological changes that are occurring. Many executive directors report feeling overwhelmed with the many technology decisions they need to make regarding hardware, software, staff training, and the Internet. The fast-changing landscape is confusing for nonprofits, and many nonprofit technology experts note that decision making needs to move at a pace that matches the pace of technology.

There is incredible untapped potential as the American public embraces the Internet and World Wide Web as a method of communication and interaction. The nonprofit sector has simply not yet found ways to effectively take advantage of the opportunities. A report recently published by Craver, Matthews, and Smith found that there are approximately 50 million Internet users in America who support the work of nonprofits.[1] The report also notes that the potential for online activism and fund raising is vast, and most of this potential is yet untapped. (See Exhibit 17.1.) Careful strategic technology planning can help nonprofits realize this potential.

EXHIBIT 17.1 Internet Users and Nonprofits

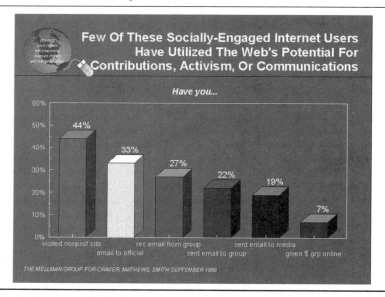

17.2 Technology Use as an Organizational Effectiveness Strategy

Technology has incredible potential to improve the internal efficiency of nonprofit operations and radically improve how organizations connect to their constituency, raise funds, and forward program goals. Consider, for example, the following:

- Hardware and software are as essential today as paperclips, pencils, and paper were in the past.
- Computers provide a common platform for communications and document sharing that makes it possible for many individuals to work together more easily.
- The speed at which electronic information flows radically changes the manner in which people communicate and interact, leading to more timely decision making.
- Powerful communication tools such as e-mail and listservs make it possible for virtually instant communication to take place among staff and colleagues at relatively insignificant cost.
- Software programs make it possible to use data to measure the effectiveness of programs and to communicate about program relevance and effectiveness to the public, government, and private foundations.

Nonprofits that take advantage of technology can expect a variety of positive outcomes, including:

- Improved efficiency of office operations
- Greater productivity from staff
- Cost savings
- Strengthened relationships with constituents
- Improved program outcomes
- Building of organizational capacity
- Enhanced service delivery
- An increase in civic engagement

To take advantage of technology, it is important for nonprofit organizations to carefully set priorities and develop the sophistication to make decisions over time.

17.3 Overview of Strategic Technology Planning

A key to successfully taking advantage of technology is effective planning. As in most nonprofit endeavors, executive managers and decision makers must understand and support initiatives for progress to be made. In many instances, senior nonprofit managers are simply unaware or unsure of how to handle technology deployment within their organizations. When technology initiatives are undertaken, it is often without full benefit of their vision and leadership. When nonprofits do apply technology strategies, they often do so hastily, without careful planning or reference to organizational mission and goals. This usually results in poor use of limited resources and unnecessary disruption within the organization. The bottom line is that most nonprofits lack technology sophistication and are *not* prepared for the major influence that technological innovations will have on their organizations. To help nonprofits grapple with these issues and take full advantage of the transformative nature of technology, it is important to go through a strategic technology planning process.

Strategic technology planning is an effort to move technology use into alignment with an organization's mission. It is a process that clarifies how operations happen, how communication flows within an organization, and how to plan for that logically. Planning therefore relates to the organization's structure, growth curve, and decision-making systems. The focus is not on the technology but on all the implications of technology within your organization in terms of how it affects infrastructure, job roles, and how people interact with your organization.

Strategic technology planning helps an organization appropriately apply technology tools to help meet programmatic goals and improve operational efficiency. During the process, the organization clarifies technology goals and priorities, organizes relevant stakeholders, and creates evaluation systems—all before making hardware, software, or Internet presence decisions. An organization's information and communication flow is taken into consideration, and technology in use is inventoried and analyzed for its effectiveness. Solutions are then developed where technology is not having the desired impact. The result is a technology road map that guides the organization's actions and resource allocations.

Most nonprofit organizations do not have a concrete technology plan. Those that have gone through the process report that it helped them think of creative new ways to do what they do. Strategic technology planning is an ongoing process based on an evaluation of programs and reflection by individuals. Decision makers, staff, and other stakeholders are asked to think about how they do their work and how technology can affect the way things are done. This results in better decision making, saved resources, more effective interaction with the outside world, and more successful and efficient ways to pursue organizational goals. (See Exhibit 17.2.)

17.4   Why Do It?

Strategic technology planning results in a variety of positive outcomes.

- *Technology decisions are in line with an organization's mission and programs.* Technology is a powerful tool. Strategic technology planning will ensure that any technology decisions are in service of your programs.
- *Needs and problem areas are identified.* What does your staff need, and where is technology not currently making the grade in your organization? Answering these types of questions is possible as you go through the planning process. It provides an easier way to prioritize the many choices you have while avoiding costly mistakes.
- *Increased awareness of the expertise needed to implement the plan is achieved.* Technology program implementation can be complex, involving trainers, software developers, and hardware specialists. It is important to know what needs to be done and to identify those individuals within your organization who can take on certain responsibilities. If you are going to outsource some

---

EXHIBIT 17.2 A Few Words on Technology Planning, Phil Ferrante-Roseberry, Executive Director— CompuMentor, http://www.compumentor.org

---

As most people involved in nonprofit technology know, technology dollars spent without some coherent planning are just an invitation to frustration and waste. Funders and the nonprofit sector as a whole seem to be hearing this message in a way they weren't just a couple years ago.

I'm a very strong believer in technology planning. CompuMentor has had to clean up far too many messes for me to believe otherwise. We've worked with agencies that allowed each program to grow a different, stand-alone database, ignoring the fact that other programs in the agency were tracking the very same clients. We've seen agencies pour all their precious technology funding into hardware, software, and fast Internet access, and only then realize that they needed to make a big investment in staff training and technology support. (Or, as we call it, the Humanware aspect of technology.) We've seen agencies become totally crippled when their technology crashed, only then realizing that backups really are an important thing.

Technology Planning Is Simple—Keep It That Way!
Technology planning does not have to encompass six months of near-total attention from everyone at the agency plus an expensive outside consultant. The plain fact is that technology planning doesn't need to be as threatening or as difficult as some "experts" make it out to be. There are a few places where expert advice can be very helpful, but most of the process is just plain old discipline in setting priorities, looking down the road, and writing things down. Consultants who paint technology planning as a cross between rocket science and brain surgery should be avoided at all cost. If you're smart enough to plan your agency's programs and are fairly comfortable with computers, you can do most of the work yourself. By all means, use consultants when you need them; there are countless people with great skills out there ready to assist you. Make sure they understand nonprofit organizations and are there to assist, NOT drive, the process. But remember, your own common sense and planning skills will take you a long way. Don't let the idea of an imposing Technology Plan leave you like the proverbial deer in the headlights.

Where Do You Start?
Fortunately, the World Wide Web is making life easier for nonprofits in all kinds of ways, not the least of which is dealing with technology. To cite one effort I'm very involved in, CompuMentor has launched a Web site called TechSoup.org, which brings technology how-to and expertise to nonprofits nationally. We're gathering the best information we can find, and translating it into language most anyone in a nonprofit can use.

---

parts of the implementation, it is imperative that you know exactly what your needs are before shopping for a vendor or consultant.

- *Financial resources are saved.* A detailed planning process can help you understand exactly what to buy and for what reasons. It is difficult to choose the right equipment, and many organizations have made decisions to purchase hardware, software, or networking tools that were not right for the job at hand. An effective planning process will help you research the correct solutions for your needs. In many situations, this can mean spending less money on hardware or software. Well-developed plans will also help you identify areas in your organization's operations where technology tools can save you money on items such as postage, phone, and transport costs.

- *Organization is positioned for funding.* Foundations are increasingly interested in grant proposals that demonstrate an organization is committed to planning and development of evaluation systems. A strategic technology plan can help nonprofits appeal to funders by demonstrating that careful consideration was given to help the organization make sound decisions.
- *Organization is prepared for new technology innovations.* Technology advances are made at an increasingly rapid pace. Effective planning helps the organization establish systems for decision making on technology choices. These systems are valuable when new technology-related decisions need to be made.

17.5 Principles

There are many ways to begin and complete a strategic technology plan. Regardless of the approach an organization takes, certain key principles should be adhered to in order to develop a well-crafted plan.

(A) LEADERSHIP COMMITMENT

The executive director, board, and other senior managers need to agree that technology planning is essential to the success of the organization. They need to make a commitment to support the people working on the plan with the financial and human resources needed to go through the process and implement the plan. (See Exhibit 17.3.)

What not to do: Move forward with a technology planning process after an informal conversation with a supportive board member. The board member assures you that the board will support the plan's implementation after the plan is written and presented to the board.

On the right track: After an initial presentation to the board about the importance of technology, the board charges the executive director to appoint a technology team to do an initial exploration of the issue. The team presents its initial findings to the board, which then allocates an initial investment of money for the team to hire a consultant to assist in the early phases of the planning process.

(B) THE PROCESS MUST BE MISSION-DRIVEN

Technology is a tool and just a tool. The process and plan should focus on program outcomes, and all discussions and mention of technology should be in service to those desired outcomes.

What not to do: Hire a technology consultant to come in and look at existing hardware and software, who then prescribes a set of new purchases for your organization that will, they claim, solve all your technology worries.

EXHIBIT 17.3 Case Study: A Case of Strong Leadership

Catherine Peterson is executive director of Arts Boston, a marketing and audience development nonprofit serving 165 performing arts groups in the greater Boston area, with 11 full-time and 8 part-time staff. Upon assuming the directorship, she made Arts Boston's technology infrastructure a top priority.

Can you tell me a little about how you got started?

We had received a lot of pro bono help that was not consistent or objective enough. We decided to have an outside consultant come in to help, not come in and do it for us. What I really loved was having the consultant come in and say, "I'm not going to do the work for you, I want you to learn to do this for yourself." She came in and did an audit of where we were and documented it both in a written form and pictorially. It was a very deep organizational audit in terms of what our current needs were and what we needed in order to realize our dreams five years from now. She facilitated a series of meetings with the key staff members to understand what our programs are currently, and what we want to be able to do to better service our member organizations and our constituents. Key to the success of our collaboration was her really understanding what our work is.

How did the consultant get staff included in the process?

She set up a technology team of three of my colleagues across the organization, representing one very technologically astute person who runs two of our programs, a support staff who also has some expertise, and someone from our Bostix booth to keep that part of our team included. They were key to the tasking. They helped to fill out the details of our vision, of what was needed now and what was missing. The team circulated to all of us and asked, "What do you currently need, what are the things you're missing?" So they got the nuts and bolts of that done and it gave us the chance to really think about results.

What were some key steps you took that helped you ensure the plan was on the mark?

We spent a lot of time talking to our prime constituents, which are 165 performing arts groups. We also connected with audience members through a series of surveys and one-on-one interviews. We wanted to know more about how technology is affecting the way people make their entertainment decisions. Our goal was to understand best practices and apply them ourselves. We also made it a point to talk with our 15 or so counterpart organizations across the country to learn from them. We did a lot of sharing of information and ideas.

What were some obstacles you encountered during the planning process?

We hit the bumps in the road in making planning a priority and keeping to a deadline. We developed a very strict schedule for planning, though it had to be adjusted sometimes. The other challenge was the board. I was talking about this stuff for two years, emphasizing the need to get moving on technology, and we were not able to move it up the priority chain until we had the outside consultant come in. She was able to validate to the board how important technology and planning were to our future.

So how are you going to evaluate and keep track of progress?

We are in daily contact with our membership and we hear from them when stuff works and when it doesn't. That's No. 1, which I think is a fabulous way to hear about what's going on. We do written surveys such as our annual surveys in *Arts Mail,* which is our written publication, and also do biannual intensive evaluations of our Bostix audience. We plan to build something onto our Web site as well to gather feedback.

On the right track: Your internal technology team works to analyze your organization's mission, program goals, and the way you currently communicate with your constituency before any discussion of technology starts.

(C) INVOLVE STAKEHOLDERS

Nonprofit organizations are complex, and their success often depends on careful involvement of stakeholders such as staff, board, volunteers, and membership. It is important to solicit input from stakeholders to help identify what types of technology tools they think will forward the organization's mission. By maximizing the level of input from those who will ultimately be affected by technology decisions, an organization will position itself to make appropriate choices. Stakeholders can be involved by working directly on the technology team, being at staff meetings, or through the use of surveys and focus groups to gather opinions and understand the best ways to approach technology deployment.

What not to do: One active volunteer and the management information systems (MIS) staff person sit down to develop a technology plan and then submit it to the board for approval.

On the right track: A survey is sent out to a portion of the membership asking them how they would use an organization Web site. The board of directors is presented with ideas derived from the survey, as well as from several staff meetings and brainstorm sessions on how technology can be used within the organization.

(D) ADHERE TO THE 70 PERCENT TO 30 PERCENT RULE

Technology plans often focus on the financial resources necessary to purchase hardware and software, or build Web sites, and little is allocated to support the people who will put the technology tools into use. The 70 percent to 30 percent rule shifts the focus from machines to the people who design the programs, train staff, and ultimately use the machines. From planning to implementation and evaluation, people determine if technology is put to good use within an organization. Seventy percent of your financial investment should therefore be in staff, consultants, trainers, and the time they need to do the job right.

What not to do: Spend $30,000 on new hardware and software and development of a Web site, and allocate only one day of training for 3 of your 10 staff members.

On the right track: A new Web site is launched. Before the site is developed, there are extensive conversations about the purpose of the site. These conversations reveal that a half-time staff person will have to be hired to maintain the site, and the entire program staff will need training to help learn how to develop content for the Web site that is appropriate.

(E) BALANCE: NOW AND THE FUTURE

Innovations in technology occur so fast that it is difficult to keep up, often making organizations wonder if they are applying technology effectively. During the strategic technology planning process, it is important to think expansively and draw up a creative wish list that represents many options for the future. Once organized, this list of expansive ideas will help guide the organization into the future as it deploys additional technology strategies. Once these ideas have been prioritized, the organization is better positioned to understand realistically what it can deploy in the short, medium, and long term.

What not to do: In one staff meeting, an organization decides it can only buy four new computers and install a new financial management package. Technology planning ceases at that point.

On the right track: Though financially limited, the organization decides to purchase several new computers and implement a training program and institutes a three-year action plan with a goal of additional hardware purchases, training, and launching of a Web site.

(F)   STRATEGIC TECHNOLOGY PLANNING IS AN ONGOING PROCESS AND TAKES TIME

In some cases, it is possible to plan for technology use quickly. Often, however, it takes longer. Regardless of how long it takes, a key to sustaining success with technology is continued review and planning over time. It is an ongoing process, ending in its initial stages in an action plan, and then continuing over years as the organization evaluates and shifts resources to deploy technology effectively.

What not to do: Draft a two-page memo on the organization's use of technology after only two one-hour staff meetings.

On the right track: In its initial meetings, the organization details a six-month timeline for gathering information from stakeholders, assessing the organization's technology infrastructure, and writing a draft plan. The draft is then reviewed by the board and staff before completion of the final plan. The plan specifies technology milestones for every three months that will trigger review and additional planning as needed.

17.6   *Pieces of the Puzzle*

(A)   IS YOUR ORGANIZATION READY?

Before initiating a planning process, it is important to determine whether the organization is ready for it. If an organization does not have a clear vision of where it is going, with established goals appropriate to its mission, moving forward with a strategic technology planning process will not make sense. To begin, consider the following questions to determine your readiness:

- Are communication, information, and decision-making processes operating efficiently within the organization?
- Does your organization already have planning processes and administrative systems that encompass technology planning?
- Will decision makers make the financial commitments necessary to implement the plan?
- Will staff be given the time necessary to do the planning?
- Does the organization have effective leaders who can empower others to champion and lead the process?

(B)   GETTING STARTED

Putting together a strategic technology plan is fairly simple, but it can sometimes take a lot of time. It can be spread out over time and embedded into existing budgeting and planning processes. The challenge is not how much time it takes, but whether the organization is willing to make a commitment to continued reflection and experimentation.

Getting started is often the hardest part of the process and starts with the realization and acknowledgment that technology must be a part of an organization's set of tools. A good place to start is to ask a set of questions.

- In what ways do you imagine your organization can benefit from the use of technology?
- Does your strategic plan currently address technology?
- Who in your organization will be active and support the planning process, and who will not?
- Are there procedures, committees, or decision-making processes already in place that can relate to or take on part of the strategic technology planning process?
- How will you build momentum in order to give the process the early boost it needs?
- How are technology decisions currently made within your organization?
- Will leadership (board, staff, members, etc.) support developing a technology plan?
- What challenges do you anticipate during the technology planning process? How can you overcome these challenges?
- Should you use a consultant to help assist you as you go through a planning process?
- What online tools are available to help you go through the process?

For some organizations, strategic technology planning may mean a long process that is complicated and involves extensive consultant support. For others, it may mean a single-day retreat followed up by a staff committee tying all the pieces together. There are many online resources available to help you in the process. Consultants can be of help as long as they have experience working with nonprofits and are responsive to your working style and needs. Nonprofit technology and management support organizations can provide you with effective planning support at low or no cost. Whatever model you apply, the important thing is to apply the principles detailed earlier. (See Exhibit 17.4.)

(C) STEP BY STEP

It is advisable to complete certain tasks when undertaking a strategic technology planning process. Though each task is important, the order in which they are taken, the emphasis placed on different portions of the process, and the way information is collected will vary. Different organizations will find it helpful to place more or less emphasis on different parts, depending on their existing strategic plan, decision-making systems, and technology sophistication. (See Exhibit 17.5 for a sample sequence to organize your strategic technology planning process.)

Once the leadership is on board, an organization might initiate the strategic technology planning process by getting assistance, often from a management support organization (MSO) or a consultant who understands nonprofits and the use of technology. The MSO or consultant should not be relied on to manage the process and write the plan, but instead should function to support the organization as it goes through the process. This is

---

EXHIBIT 17.4 Strategic Technology Planning Benchmarks for Nonprofit Organizations

These benchmarks were developed as part of the National Strategy on Nonprofit Technology (NSNT) and represent current standards for appropriate, efficient, and sustainable technology use in nonprofit organizations. For more information on NSNT, visit *http://www.nten.org*. For a full list of the NSNT benchmarks, visit *http://208.155.173.227/ nsnt/benchMarks.cfm* or *http://www.artswire.org/spiderschool/workshops/planning/ rubric2.htm*.

Strategic Technology Planning Benchmarks

- Organization has two- to three-year technology plan that is integrated into the overall strategic plan and mission of the organization and is approved by the board.
- Organization involves individuals with both technology and program expertise in the technology planning process.
- Organization has a mechanism through which it keeps current on "best practices" use of technology in nonprofit sector and incorporates this knowledge into the technology planning process.
- Organization has an adequate budget to implement its technology plan or a funding strategy to secure needed funding.
- Organization understands and plans for organizational change implications of technology.
- Organization has primary individual or working group accountable and responsible for implementing the technology plan.

Benchmarks have also been developed for technology use in the following areas: Staff Level, Organizational Business Systems, Internal Networks and Communication, External Communications, Technology Sustainability.

---

important so that the organization develops the skill to do most of its planning and evaluation independently in the future.

Note: You will notice that after each step described as follows there are "Some Questions To Ask." These are a sampling of the many questions that you will need to ask and answer as you proceed with planning and are not meant as a full list to be relied on during planning.

(i) Technology Team

The first step to developing a plan is creating an internal technology team that will guide the process, gather the information, and write the plan. This team should not be made up of only technology-savvy staff, but should include members from different parts of the organization such as program, development, public relations, human resources, finance, and the like. A team that represents different parts of the organization is able to make decisions that will maximize positive impacts on the organization as a whole.

Within the technology team, identify a lead person to organize the planning process. It is also helpful to determine who will be responsible for the different jobs necessary throughout the process. Once the team has been formed, they will need to determine the length of time required to go through the process and write the plan. The technology team

EXHIBIT 17.5 Scope & Sequence

Scope & Sequence

Step 1: Getting Started

Learn about the strategic technology process

Form a cross-program technology team

Get leadership on board

Team collects staff/stakeholder technology attitudes information

Step 2: Grounded in Mission

Review program goals and strategies

Review results from staff/stakeholder attitudes

Prepare for task-tracking and organizational technology assessments

Tech team conducts organization assessment and task tracking

Step 3: Box & Wires Audit and Environmental Scan

Synthesize assessment information

Gain basic understanding of box and wire concepts

Prepare to undertake an environment scan and box and wires audit

Tech team conducts environmental scan

Step 4: Setting Technology Goals

Review box and wires audit and results of environmental scan

Brainstorm technology possibilities as related to existing programs and operations

Tech team conducts staff digital literacy assessment

(Exhibit continues)

should meet on a regular basis during the process and once implementation begins. The team can help assess the training programs and the success of different aspects of implementation and report to the organization on the plan's progress.

Some Questions to Ask

- Who on the team will coordinate its activities?

EXHIBIT 17.5 *(Continued)*

Step 5: The PEOPLE Using Technology

Set technology priorities

Develop technology education programs for staff

Prepare a technical support program

Tech team reviews organization's policies and procedures and budgets

Step 6: Sustainability Planning

Develop technology policies

Consider vendor and consultant needs

Prepare budgets that incorporate technology initiatives

Tech team writes first draft of tech plan using template

Step 7: Writing the Plan

Review all the materials collected through the process

Prepare a first draft of the plan with detailed timelines and milestones incorporated

Tech team gathers feedback on draft plan

Step 8: Finalizing the Plan

Finalize the plan and identify systems to review the plan's implementation over time

Assign primary responsibilities

Prepare for effective implementation (phased implementation/funding, training, redesigns, piloting)

- Who on your staff can be an enthusiastic supporter of technology as you go through the planning process?
- Who has the technical expertise to support the technology team? Will you need help from outside the organization?
- What kinds of different skills, knowledge, and expertise would you like to see represented on your team to make it a good working group?
- How do you envision the team interacting with executive management, the rest of the staff, and the board of directors?
- What level of power will you give the team to make decisions regarding the process and implementation?
- What are the attitudes of staff and other stakeholders about technology?

See Exhibit 17.6 to start the planning process.

EXHIBIT 17.6 Staff Technology Attitudes Survey Form

> **How to Use This Resource** The attached resource is a simple survey that can be copied and distributed to each staff person in order to learn more about his or her technology attitudes. Include a cover memo signed by you, which provides instructions for completing and returning the form. Sample wording is provided below. Use a blank version of this form to tally the results.

Your Name: **Your Department:**

General Attitudes About Technology

1. What was your first experience using a computer like? When was it? Has that experience influenced how you feel or think about computers today?

2. When did you first start using the Internet? What was your first impression? Is it different from your current perceptions of the Internet? How so?

3. What THREE adjectives from the list would you use to describe your current relationship with your computer or technology?

Excited	
Amazed	
Eager	
Pleased	
Great	
Uncomfortable	
Uncertain	
Awkward	
Annoyed	
Self-conscious	
Frustrated	
Nervous	
Dumb	
Overwhelmed	
Upset	

Attitudes about Technology Related to Job Tasks

4. In the table below, describe the technology you use most often for getting your work done. Using the scale below, indicate how efficient each one is.

Indicate efficiency using this scale:
0=Hopelessly Inefficient   1=Barely Efficient   2=Efficient   3=Pretty Efficient   4=Extremely Efficient

Technology	Efficiency	Why Did You Give It This Rating?
Computer		
Productivity software		
Internet software		
Information system		
Internet connection		
LAN		
Phone		
Fax		
Copy machine		

5.   Are there ever times when you are doing a job-related task that you think, "There must be a better, faster, or easier way to do this"? Please describe the task in the space below.

Task	Description

6.   If you could change one thing related to technology use in your job, what would it be?

_____

_____

_____

_____

Attitudes about Our Organization's Use of Technology

7.   How could our organization benefit from the use of technology? What could be the end result? What is the potential impact on our programs, clients, and administration?

8.   What do you think is the biggest barrier to implementing technology within our organization?

9.   At this point in the process, what specific questions, ideas, or concerns do you have regarding the technology plan or the technnology planning process?

10. Do you have any other comments or questions?

©2000 Summit Consulting Collaborative

(ii) Review of the Strategic Plan

Technology strategies chosen by a nonprofit should be in the service of furthering an organization's mission. One way to ensure that technology appropriately supports the organization's programs is to review the existing strategic plan, program plans, budgets, and other visionary documents. Another way to interface technology with organizational mission is to integrate technology decision making with ongoing budget, program planning, and evaluation processes within the organization. Wherever possible, technology planning should be incorporated into the organization's existing decision-making processes. This will make technology a more regular and transparent part of the organization's operations.

Some Questions to Ask
- What are your organization's core objectives, and how are your programs coordinated to meet those objectives?
- How are human and financial resources allocated to help the organization reach its strategic objectives?
- What time frames are specified in the strategic plan for implementation of different programs, and who is responsible for them?

(iii) Research and Assessment

Assessment is an integral part of the planning process. It is important to assess a variety of facets to gain a comprehensive picture of the organization. Internal systems, technology infrastructure, staff attitudes about technology, and the external climate in which an organization functions should all be assessed. There must be an understanding and acknowledgment of the organization's capacity to do certain things, as well as a discussion of the organization's strengths and weaknesses. This will clarify what opportunities exist for technology to help advance program goals.

Internal Assessment.   This research focuses both on the way people do their work and on the technology infrastructure. Examine how the staff does its work, the ways they communicate with each other and the outside world, and how they develop materials. (See Exhibits 17.7 and 17.8 for examples of communication and materials creation assessment tools or see *http://www.strategictechnology.net* for a comprehensive online planning tool.) What problems exist in regard to information or communication flow? Are there unmet needs among staff? Looking at these things exposes opportunities in which the use of technology can have a positive impact. Take, for example, an organization that collects clothing for the homeless and then distributes it to shelters. What happens from the moment a temple calls to donate clothing to the moment it is delivered to a shelter? Charting the flow of processes within your organization will help you identify where technology tools may be of use.

It is very important to understand what staff's needs are in relation to technology. Have staff ask themselves what they would like to accomplish using a powerful technology tool, as opposed to what kinds of equipment they would need to do it. For example, a staff person responsible for inventory control at a food bank may say, "I would like to spend less time doing work to track which organizations are taking which foods from our warehouse. I want a system that makes it easier for me to collect this information. I want to look back and calculate over time how much they have used." This observation leads to an understanding of how a database for inventory tracking and control would be useful. Which database to choose is not important; the point is to identify that this staff person needs a database tool to accomplish her job. (See Exhibit 17.7 for a sample assessment tool used to gather information on an organization's communication flow.)

Internal research also means looking at hardware, software, and other materials to understand the existing technology infrastructure. People often get caught up in deciding what kinds of technology to use based on the equipment on hand. The more prudent approach is to focus on what they are trying to achieve with that equipment. At some point, however, it is important to assess you current infrastructure to understand where you stand. (See Exhibit 17.8 to see a sample infrastructure audit.)

Some Questions to Ask
- How do you communicate with your membership?
- What types of software programs does the staff use?

EXHIBIT 17.7 OneNorthwest: Organizational Technical Assessment *(http://www.onenw.org)*

Communication Strategies: This section assesses how your organization currently communicates (and with whom), and solicits background information about your organizational structure.

Frequency of Communication: How frequently does your organization communicate with each of these groups using the following communication channels?

Indicate frequency using this scale:

0 = Never, 1 = Infrequently, 2 = Monthly, 3 = Weekly, 4 = Daily

	Phone	Conf Calls	Fax	E-Mail	Web	Mail	Overnight Delivery	In-Person Meetings
Membership								
Key activists								
Other nonprofits								
Board of directors								
Elected officials								
Agencies								
Media								
Researchers/Scientists								
Native Alaskans/Native Americans and/or First Nations								
Foundations/Funders								
Other								

With which constituencies would you most like to improve your communications, if any?

When you communicate with other groups and individuals about your organization or your issues, what types of information do you *usually* share, and with what frequency?

Type of Communication	Total Circulation	Electronic Circulation (E-mail and/or Web)	Frequency per Year
Newsletters			
"Action" alerts			
Meetings/Event announcements			
Legislative or regulatory information			
News releases			
Technical data/Research findings/Issue Reports			
Fund-raising appeals			
Other (please specify):			
Requests for organizational information	% submitted electronically	% responded to electronically	

EXHIBIT 17.8 Progressive Technology Project: Organizational Assessment Tool (http://www.progressivetech.org)

Media/Materials Creation
- What media pieces do you create most? (Newsletter, brochure, flyers, etc.)
- How do you develop them?
- Who are your primary audiences?
- What media tools (Web sites, flyers, radio spots, etc.) would you like to be using in your organizing work? Why?

Staff and Members
- Who is most responsible for these activities?
- Do they have the needed skills or access to appropriate training for current systems? How do they get trained?
- Who else needs to be involved? What do they need to contribute effectively?

Types of Media	How are they created?	Who is involved in their creation?	How often" *0 = Never, 1 = Infrequently, 2 = Monthly, 3 = Weekly, 4 = Daily*
Flyers			
Brochures			
Newsletters			
Web sites			
Action alerts			
News releases			
Fund-raising appeals			
Publications/Booklet/Catalog			
Reports			
Radio/Video			
Other:			

Do you keep a copy for your records? Describe:

Based on this assessment, what are the primary strengths and needs of your current approach to media creation?

- What is the current state of Internet access for the staff?
- What are the primary software applications used by the organization for financial management, word processing, databases, and calendar and e-mail management?
- What are the staff's current attitudes regarding their literacy with computers, their training needs, and their need to use computers effectively over time?
- Do you have workstations for every staff person in the organization? What is the status of each workstation in terms of hardware, software, and Internet capabilities?

External Research/Environmental Scan.   This part of technology planning is often over-looked but provides valuable information that can profoundly affect a nonprofit's technology decisions. Doing an assessment of similar organizations and/or your constituency can help you save time and money when choosing technology tools. Take, for example, a theater that needs to sell tickets for dance performances. By surveying audiences the previous year, the organization found that a majority of patrons preferred to buy their tickets online. Getting to the theater was too time consuming, and there often was not a person staffing the phone lines. To remedy the problem, the theater developed a Web site where patrons could buy tickets online. Before doing so, however, the theater contacted several other theaters to find out how they managed online ticket sales. By looking at other organizations with a similar mission and surveying its constituency, the theater was able to be responsive to its market and put into place appropriate technology tools. This process, sometimes known as an environmental scan, can include looking at other organizations' Web sites to see the tools that they are using, conducting phone interviews, or reviewing literature to understand what types of practices are working in the field.

Some Questions to Ask
- What are the social, political, geographic, and/or economic factors that affect your constituency?
- What types of resources, tools, and information are similar organizations providing their constituencies on their Web sites?
- What is the annual budget allocated by similar organizations for technology?
- What types of software have other organizations found particularly useful to track membership and maintain databases within the organizations?

(iv) *Identify Technology Goals and Strategies*

With assessment and research results in hand and a review of the mission complete, the technology team now has the information it needs to identify appropriate technology goals for the organization. This often begins with a brainstorming process to list all of the different things an organization can do to forward its mission using technology. This often results in a long list of technology tools and approaches the organization can take. At this point, it is necessary to look for areas where needs and tools converge. Is there a single technology approach that can help you meet three different needs for the organization? For example, many nonprofits maintain separate databases on members, donors, volunteers, and activists. You may decide that an organizational priority is to better manage all this information. Maybe a database program like eBase (*http://www.ebase.org*) that brings together all the information into one master database is the answer. It is often technology tools that have multiple positive outcomes that make it to top of the priority list.

Some Questions to Ask
- Is it appropriate to develop a Web site for use by your core constituency?
- Does it make sense to invest the time and money necessary to upgrade and integrate your various databases into one master database?
- What types of technology tools will have the maximum impact across different parts of your organization's operations and programs?
- How can using online advocacy tools support the development of your organization financially and politically, and how can it help you meet the program goals of your campaign?

(v) Phased Action Planning

Technology is changing at such a rapid pace that it is difficult to plan for a period longer than three years. Plans should be phased over short periods of time so they can be adjusted as needed. Keep in mind that hardware needs to be upgraded on a regular basis, potentially every two to three years. This must be taken into account when budgeting for technology purchases. Look at your expansive list of ideas brainstormed in earlier meetings and the list of top priorities to develop an action plan that is broken down into short- (six months to a year), medium- (one to two years), and long-term (two to five years) goals. Try to break things into specific projects for which you can use Gantt charts to set target dates for implementation. (See Exhibit 17.9 for an example.)

Some Questions to Ask

- What can you accomplish in the next three to six months with your existing hardware and human resources in place?
- Which technology goals and strategies need to be in place in the short and medium term to help you reach your longer-term objectives?
- What types of technology do you have in place that will work toward your short- and medium-term objectives with slight modifications?

(vi) Technology Infrastructure Decisions

With new technology goals set, it is time to determine whether your existing technology infrastructure can facilitate reaching your goals. If not, it is time to think about new hardware, software, networking systems, and online connectivity. You will need someone with strong technical expertise to help you decide what types of equipment you will need. Many nonprofits have made poor decisions and wasted valuable financial resources due to inappropriate advice from consultants and vendors. Before making any infrastructure decisions, it is imperative that you understand exactly what you need and why. Working with nonprofit technology consultants or support organizations is helpful to ensure that the advice you get makes the most sense for your organization. Online tools can also help you understand what equipment and systems are best suited for your needs. (See Section 17.9.)

EXHIBIT 17.9 Web site Development Timeline

	July	August	Sept	Oct	Nov	Dec
Initial internal planning meetings	--------|					
Decisions on content for site	---------|					
Decisions on graphics elements/feel	--|					
First draft of site complete		--------|				
Review of site by staff		--------|				
Second draft of site complete			----------|			
Usability test by five or more people			-------|			
Third draft of site complete				----|		
Final test by staff				------|		
Final edits to site					------|	
Site goes "live"					-|	

Some Questions to Ask

- What are the choices for high-speed Internet access, considering your current physical location?
- To run your new financial management software, what do you need to do to upgrade your server and workstations?
- Can you continue to utilize donated equipment to help meet your workstation needs, or should you purchase new equipment?
- What are the best requirements for workstations (486, Pentium, PowerMac) needed to ensure that the staff can run the software and have Internet access?

See Exhibit 17.10 for an example of an online hardware, software, and Internet assessment tool.

(vii) Operational Decisions

The use of technology will affect many procedures within your organization. You will need to form policies that respond to these changes. For example, if you decide to install a network that allows staff to access a wide variety of materials online, you will need to think about how you manage confidential documents. How passwords and other security systems are established will have to be discussed. Use of the Internet will also raise many issues. (See Exhibit 17.11.) The technology team, working with staff and decision makers, will need to craft new policies that respond to these challenges. These new policy decisions should be part of the technology plan to avoid confusion as technology use increases within the organization.

(viii) Training and Technical Support

Training is essential to success with technology. Many experts claim that for every $3 allocated for equipment, $7 should be spent on training and support. When staff is trained well, they can take full advantage of the technology, which can save time and money.

Training programs need to be responsive to the needs defined by staff earlier in the planning process. Instead of imposing a training program *on* staff, you involve them *in* development of appropriate training programs. This includes being attentive to the *content* staff want assistance on, but also the type of *training system* that works best for each staff member. For example, some people feel comfortable working in a technology lab with a group of other learners. Other staff may need more one-on-one tutoring with a trainer. There may even be situations in which the best approach is to partner a more technically proficient staff member with a staff person who is less comfortable using technology. Whether you send staff to classes, develop in-house programs, or use online training systems, the key is to make training responsive to the individual's needs.

In addition, for any training program to work, management must allocate time for staff to take the training. Staff need time not only for formal training but also to reflect and share with peers what they have learned. It is often this second layer of reflection and sharing that consolidates the learning done during the training and identifies areas where additional training is needed.

Some Questions to Ask

- What has and has not worked within your organization previously when you attempted training with your staff?
- What types of technical support systems can be built into your existing staff responsibilities, and which need to be provided by experts outside of the organization?

EXHIBIT 17.10 TechRocks: Organization Self-Evaluation Tool, A Project of the Rockefeller Family Fund *(http://www.techrocks.org)*

Hardware

This question lists classes of computers and computer equipment, referring to the categories by their most commonly used names. Please indicate how many of each class your organization *uses*.

____ How many 386s? ____ How many 486s? ____ How many Pentiums?
____ How many Mac Classics? ____ How many PowerMacs/Imacs?
____ How many laser printers?____ How many inkjet or other non-laser printers?
____ How many scanners? ____ How many digital camera devices?

How often does your organization back-up the data on your computers?
____ Daily ____ Weekly ____ Monthly or less ____ Never

Does your organization use a LAN (local area network) to connect your office computers and printers? ____ Yes ____ No

Is your organization's LAN connected to the Internet? ____ Yes ____ No

What LAN software does your organization use?
____ Windows 3.1/95 peer to peer ____ Windows NT client server ____ Lantastic ____ Appletalk ____ Novell ____

What access mechanism does your organization use to connect to the Internet?
____ Modems ____ ISDN line ____ DSL line ____ Dedicated line (56k, 128k, 256k, T1)

For each speed of modem listed, mark the number of computers your organization uses with that speed modem:
____ 14.4k ____ 28.8k ____ 56k or equivalent ____ Faster

How many of your organization's workstations have access to e-mail?
____ All workstations – simultaneous access ____ All stations – shared access ____ Some stations ____ No stations

How many of your organization's workstations have access to the World Wide Web?
____ All workstations – simultaneous access ____ All stations – shared access ____ Some stations ____ No stations

Software

What Software suite(s) does your organization use (e.g., Windows Office '97, WordPerfect)?
_____

What operating system does your organization use (e.g., Windows 3.1/95, Mac OS)?
_____

What database program does your organization use (e.g., Filemaker, Access, Paradox, dbase, etc.)?
_____

What accounting program does your organization use?
_____

Does your organization use virus protection software? ____ Yes ____ No
What virus protection program does your organization use?
_____

How often does your organization update virus definitions? ____ Monthly ____ Less often ____ Never
Does your organization use presentation software (e.g., PowerPoint)? ____ Yes ____ No
Does your organization use GIS/computer mapping software? ____ Yes ____ No

Internet Usage

How often does the staff of your organization use e-mail on average?
____ Several times/day ____ Daily ____ Weekly ____ Rarely

How often does the Executive Director use e-mail on average?
____ Several times/day ____ Daily ____ Weekly ____ Rarely

Does your organizations use any listservs? ____ Yes ____ No
Does your organization sponsor or moderate any listservs? ____ Yes ____ No

How often does your organization's staff use the World Wide Web on average?
____ Several times/day ____ Daily ____ Weekly ____ Rarely

How often does the Executive Director use email on average?
____ Several times/day ____ Daily ____ Weekly ____ Rarely

- How will you schedule training in relation to other staff time commitments?
- What are the three most important training needs identified by the staff?

(ix) Budgeting

Although using technology can help save valuable resources, there are still financial costs associated with implementation of new systems and/or modifying and upgrading existing systems. Funding is needed for ongoing training, systems maintenance, Internet access, and software. Earlier in the planning process, a phased action plan was developed detailing the steps necessary to implement technology strategies. A similar approach should be used when budgeting by identifying short-, medium-, and long-term phases. It is then possible to develop a funding strategy for technology including both internal allocations and additional fund raising to support implementation.

Most nonprofits are already spending money on technology. For example, hardware and software are often purchased under budgets for specific programs, vendors are paid to provide training and support, and electricity is used to run the computers.

Start the budgeting process by identifying all the funds currently associated with technology. Then determine what additional funds will be needed to meet your new technology goals. You will have to consider the following:

- Training
- Technical support
- Hardware
- Software

EXHIBIT 17.11 Establishing an Acceptable Use Policy: Excerpted from HandsNet's *Seven Habits of Web-Savvy Leaders* (http://www.handsnet.org)

It is advisable to establish office protocols and policies about the use of online technology. In doing so, an organization (1) protects against the loss of productivity and (2) possible sexual harassment or other lawsuits, and (3) prevents draining the bandwidth and hardware resources of the organization. The solution to this dilemma may be to implement a policy outlining the permissible parameters of employee Internet use, or an Internet Acceptable Use Policy (IAUP).

An IAUP is a written agreement, signed by employees, which sets out the permissible workplace uses of the Internet. In addition to describing permissible uses, an IAUP should specifically set out prohibited uses, rules of online behavior, and access privileges.

Questions to Ask

➢ Can organizational e-mail be used for personal use? Are employees allowed to check their Web-based personal e-mail during the day? During their lunch hour or on breaks?

➢ Who checks the generic info@nonprof.org e-mail box when the regular employee calls in sick or goes on vacation?

➢ Will employee e-mail be monitored or scanned for inappropriate content?

➢ Are employees allowed to download programs or files?

➢ Will employees be allowed to use chat or instant messaging programs like AOL Instant Messenger or ICQ?

- Internet access
- Personnel
- Building renovation
- Web site development

Note: Do not forget to budget for hardware upgrades (every two years) and build a 10 percent margin into the budget to deal with cost overruns.

Some Questions to Ask
- Will you develop a stand-alone technology budget or incorporate technology costs into different departments?
- How much money do you currently spend on technology?
- How will using technology save resources on postage, phone calls, and other internal operations currently implemented without technology tools?
- What personnel time must be allocated/budgeted to maintain your Web site and/or other technology infrastructure?

(x) Evaluation

Though listed as the final step in the process, development of an effective system to evaluate the success of the technology plan over time is integral. The implementation of technology strategies is an ongoing process that changes constantly with both organizational circumstances and the external environment. Over time, organizational objectives and strategies may change. An effective evaluation system will help the technology team determine how to shift technology resources to relate to those changes. Ongoing evaluation will also help the organization make changes to those parts of the plan that are not working or to place greater emphasis on those areas that are. Some topics that should be regularly evaluated include staff training needs, technical support systems, equipment, and staff usage of software.

There are a variety of ways to evaluate a technology plan. It is necessary to have clear targets set for phases of the implementation that serve as milestones to assess progress. If a certain target is not achieved, determining why will help you make adjustments to move the implementation forward. The method used to collect information will depend on the way your organization operates and the resources allocated to evaluation. In some cases, surveys may be appropriate, whereas in others conducting focus groups or concentrated conversations with individuals may produce more useful information. Anecdotal information collected from staff and other stakeholders who use the technology in the organization can provide great insight into how well things are working. In some cases, you may be able to access statistical data to help you determine if your technology decisions are on track. For example, analysis of Web site statistics can be very useful. Finally, the use of logic models and other evaluation tools can assist organizations as they endeavor to keep their technology plan on track. (See Exhibit 17.12.)

Some Questions to Ask
- What type of internal assessment programs can you set up to evaluate plan implementation?
- Would hiring consultants to evaluate part of your program make sense?
- How can you build technology use evaluation into your existing assessments of staff and programs?

EXHIBIT 17.12 *There's no money in the budget for it. Look Again!* **Parts excerpted from HandsNet's** *Seven Habits of Web-Savvy Leaders*

When you think about how technology might improve all the work that you do, your other department lines can make an investment in technology that they will get back, individually and collectively, over time. For example:

There is a proposal at a national nonprofit organization to pay to get all 15 board members Internet access.

Internet access	15 × $20/month × 12 months	$3,600
Phone lines	15 × $25/month × 12 months	4,500
2-day training		
Travel expenses	15 × $600 travel expenses	9,000
Meeting expenses		2,000
Trainer		1,500
TOTAL		$20,600

Of course, there is no money for this project. But look again. This board meets four times a year, in person.

Current board meeting budget (per meeting)	
Travel expenses	$9,000
Meeting expenses	$2,000
TOTAL	$11,000

In four meetings alone, this group spent $44,000 and a lot of time in transit. With Internet access, proper training, and use of the Internet for much of the board's business, this could result in the board's meeting face to face only two times per year.

- Who will be responsible to collect information to assess the effectiveness of the plan and its implementation over time?

17.7　*Strategic Technology Planning and Outcome Measurement*

(A)　WHAT IS OUTCOME MEASUREMENT?

Outcome measurement is a process that provides specific, concrete information about the effectiveness of a program or organization. For example, outcome measurement tools can help an organization determine whether the Web site they launched a year earlier is having the desired results, or if a new database program improves tracking of donors.

(B)   WHY OUTCOME MEASUREMENT IS IMPORTANT

Outcome measurement allows an organization to understand what the real impacts are from certain programs and strategies. It improves program effectiveness by providing findings that can be used to help shift priorities or direction.

Nonprofits can use outcome data to:

- Strengthen existing services and campaigns
- Target effective programs or strategies for expansion
- Identify staff and volunteer training needs
- Develop and justify budgets
- Prepare long-range plans
- Focus stakeholders' attention on programmatic issues

(C)   OUTCOME MEASUREMENT AND TECHNOLOGY

Financial and human resources are being dedicated by many organizations to build Web sites, develop intranets, and launch online advocacy campaigns and many other technology initiatives. It is important that organizations understand what outcomes they hope to achieve when using technology so they can put the right mix of activities into motion to realize positive results. When developing an intranet, an organization has many choices of tools to put on the system for staff use. Should the tools focus on enhancing document sharing or access to online training modules? An organization trying to build public support for new pollution prevention legislation is launching a Web site. Should it spend its resources on developing applications to link groups working on pollution issues or on creating a detailed database full of information about air and water pollution?

Organizations face many questions as they use technology to forward their mission. By using outcome measurement tools, nonprofits can make more sound strategic decisions, leading to better allocation of resources and more effective programs.

(D)   LOGIC MODELS: HOW THEY WORK

Logic models are useful as evaluation tools, but when used as a planning tool, they can help nonprofits. Their primary value is to clarify the thinking that goes into a program. The logic model describes the reasoning behind the program and explains why and how the program will work. It helps stakeholders (staff, board, members, funders, etc.) understand how the different activities in a program plan will lead to achievement of the goals.

The process used to complete a logic model forces participants to carefully think through, justify, and detail the way a program will fit together. This process leads to more effective planning and establishes criteria the organization can use to judge how a program is going. It gives staff more control and a greater ability to identify weak areas in program delivery. Resources and strategic approach can be modified more efficiently because it is easier to identify what activities are not having the desired outcomes. Conversely, when things are working, it is easier to understand what exactly is working and what the outcomes are. (See Exhibit 17.13.) There are four basic parts of a logic model:

1. *Inputs* include resources dedicated to or consumed by the program—such as money, staff and staff time, volunteer time, policies, facilities, equipment, and supplies.

EXHIBIT 17.13 Sample Logic Model: Intranet to Improve Staff Collaboration

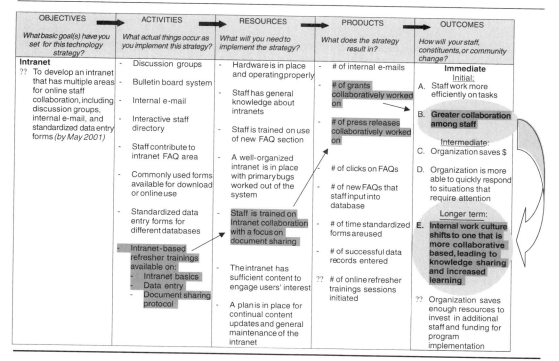

OBJECTIVES	ACTIVITIES	RESOURCES	PRODUCTS	OUTCOMES
What basic goal(s) have you set for this technology strategy?	*What actual things occur as you implement this strategy?*	*What will you need to implement the strategy?*	*What does the strategy result in?*	*How will your staff, constituents, or community change?*
Intranet ?? To develop an intranet that has multiple areas for online staff collaboration, including discussion groups, internal e-mail, and standardized data entry forms *(by May 2001)*	- Discussion groups - Bulletin board system - Internal e-mail - Interactive staff directory - Staff contribute to intranet FAQ area - Commonly used forms available for download or online use - Standardized data entry forms for different databases - Intranet-based refresher trainings available on: - Intranet basics - Data entry - Document sharing protocol	- Hardware is in place and operating properly - Staff has general knowledge about intranets - Staff is trained on use of new FAQ section - A well-organized intranet is in place with primary bugs worked out of the system - Staff is trained on Intranet collaboration with a focus on document sharing - The intranet has sufficient content to engage users' interest - A plan is in place for continual content updates and general maintenance of the intranet	- # of internal e-mails - # of grants collaboratively worked on - # of press releases collaboratively worked on - # of clicks on FAQs - # of new FAQs that staff input into database - # of time standardized forms are used - # of successful data records entered ?? # of online refresher trainings sessions initiated	**Immediate** *Initial:* A. Staff work more efficiently on tasks B. **Greater collaboration among staff** *Intermediate:* C. Organization saves $ D. Organization is more able to quickly respond to situations that require attention *Longer term:* E. **Internal work culture shifts to one that is more collaborative based, leading to knowledge sharing and increased learning** ?? Organization saves enough resources to invest in additional staff and funding for program implementation

2. *Activities* are what the program does with the inputs to reach the desired outcomes—such as developing an online discussion forum, staff sharing of a calendar program, posting notices about a campaign on listservs, or building an online interface that connects volunteers to organizations in need.

3. *Outputs* are the direct products of activities and usually are measured in terms of the volume of work accomplished—such as numbers of clicks on a Web page, new members signed on, or documents collaborated on by staff.

4. *Outcomes* are benefits or changes that occur during or after a technology initiative is put into motion.

(E)   THE WRITTEN PLAN

Throughout the planning process, a great deal of information is collected. The collective knowledge of the team needs to be summarized in a document that facilitates easy review. It is not advisable to include every piece of information into the final plan; instead, craft a summary document. According to CompuMentor's *techsoup.org* Web site, the following key elements should be part of the written plan.

- *Organizational profile.* Who are you and what do you do?
- *Technology vision.* What do you hope to accomplish using technology?
- *Projects.* What projects will you undertake to improve your organization's use of technology?

- *Budget.* What are the costs associated with those projects?
- *Timeline.* What are the phases of work and the deadlines for implementation of your plan?

It is advisable to delineate who will take responsibility for different parts of the plan. If possible, the document should be in a form that makes it easy for anyone interested in reviewing it to quickly get answers to their questions. The use of flowcharts, timelines, and schematic drawings is an excellent way to keep things simple.

17.8   Conclusion

The primary reason to go through a strategic technology planning process is to identify the opportunities in which technology can have a positive impact on nonprofit programs and operations. Strategic technology planning is a simple, mission-driven process based on good communication, research, and recording of ideas. Stakeholders involved from the beginning of the process become invested and understand their various roles as the plan goes into effect. The diversity of their opinions helps balance the plan and makes it realistic. Many technology tools and strategies are considered, and the process helps narrow down those possibilities and focus on the ones that are most appropriate in the long, medium, and short term. A technology road map is now in hand, and the organization has a system for making future technology decisions. Both the planning process and the resulting plan position the organization to take maximum advantage of the power that technology offers.

17.9   Strategic Technology Planning Resources

There are many excellent resources online to assist you. Use the following:
Arts Wire Spiderschool, *http://www.artswire.org/spiderschool/workshops/agendaplanning.html*
Benton Foundation, *http://www.benton.org/Practice/Toolkit/planning.html*
Tech Soup, *http://www.techsoup.org/*
Summit Consulting Collaborative, *http://www.summitcollaborative.com*
Strategic Technology, *http://www.strategictechnology.not*
TechRocks, *http://www.techrocks.org*

Endnote

1. Craver, Mathews, Smith & Co. (1999). *Socially Engaged Internet Users: Prospects for Online Philanthropy and Activism* (September).

Suggested Readings

Anderson, L. S., and J. F. Perry Jr. (March 1994). *Technology Planning: Recipe for Success.* National Center for Technology Planning, Mississippi State University, *http://www.nctp.com.*

Anderson, L. S. (1999). *Technology Planning: It's More Than Computers.* National Center for Technology Planning, Mississippi State University, *http:www.nctp.com.*

Boar, B. H. (August 1993). *Art of Strategic Planning for Information Technology: Crafting Strategy for the 90s.* New York: John Wiley & Sons.

BCC Education Technology Planning Workshop. (December 1996). Bellevue, WA: Bellevue Community College Information Resources, *http://ir.bcc.edc/et.htm.*

Guidebook for Developing an Effective Instructional Technology Plan. (Spring 1996). Graduate Students at Mississippi State University, *http://www2.msstate.edu/~lsa1/nctp/Guidebook.pdf.*

Ringle, M., and D. Updegrove. (1998). *Is Strategic Planning for Technology an Oxymoron? CAUSE/EFFECT* 21(1): 18–23, *http://www.educause.edu/ir/library/html/cem9814.html.*

Sylvia Bodolay's Master Thesis on Technology Planning. South Central Regional Technology in Education Consortium, *http://projects.scrtec.org/%7Etechplan/index.html.*

See, J. *Developing Effective Technology Plans,* Minnesota Department of Education.

The Do's and Don'ts of Technology Planning. Article originally presented at the Florida Educational Technology Conference (FETC) and the National Education Computing Conference (NECC), *http://www.isf.com/services/article1.htm.*

18 ▼ Managing Organizational Growth

CAROLYN J. CURRAN
Executive Consultant, New York, NY

"Be the change you want to see in the world."

Gandhi

18.1 Introduction

(A) ORGANIZATIONS ARE PEOPLE

Corporate management, of which nonprofit management is a relatively recent spin-off, itself evolved from the earliest days of the Industrial Revolution when it was patched together by engineers to meet the needs of mass production. Not surprisingly, these entrepreneurs viewed the organization as a machine and the people in it as cogs in the machine. The cogs approach was found to be more successful (profitable) than previous, less-structured, attempts to get people to work together. For various reasons, including habit, fear of losing control, and lack of exposure to alternatives, too many managers still treat people like cogs. Both corporate and nonprofit management continue to suffer from this legacy.

The next evolutionary step in management acknowledged the cogs as people. It became "common knowledge" that motivational techniques, externally applied to workers, would act like the metaphorical carrot impelling the rabbit forward more quickly. Millions of corporate dollars were spent on developing and teaching these techniques, with mixed results.

Another, more recent stage in management evolution stresses the importance of involving people in decisions that affect their work, addressing their needs to make a meaningful contribution to communities inside and outside the workplace, and providing ladders to learning and achievement that encourage personal growth. These approaches are being touted by most modern management gurus, including the proponents of the increasingly popular total quality management (TQM) and proponents of the "learning corporation," notably Peter Senge, author of the management best seller, *The Fifth Discipline*.[1]

Many innovative corporations are beginning to find that viewing and treating employees holistically pays off in the bottom line. In a PBS program, *The Excellence Files*, Jeff Swartz, CEO of Timberland, said, "We think a whole human beats a fraction of a human; we are working to create the environment where the whole human being can exist and participate," explaining his company's humanistic approach to employee management and community service. Nonprofit organizations (NPOs) on the whole are already predisposed to these values, being service-oriented and inclined toward a humanistic work environment even when the resources and tools to implement it are lacking.

This chapter will lay out an approach to growth and change that incorporates these humanistic values, building on the existing propensities of many NPOs. Theories and techniques offered here will help to take them to new levels of proactivity and productivity. To guide leaders to the next stage of their organization's development, the chapter will first present a global picture of the organization development field, provide a matrix for leaders to identify their organization's stage of development, and then give some tools for moving to the next stage.

(B) CORPORATE AND NONPROFIT ORGANIZATION DEVELOPMENT COMPARED

(i) *Corporate Organization Development versus Nonprofit Organization Development*

Organization development is commonly known in the corporate world as OD. (Ignore all the other connotations of OD.) Contrasting definitions of OD in the for-profit and nonprofit sectors shed light on the gap in awareness, knowledge, and application between the two sectors:

- NPOs have generally defined OD as the stages an organization goes through as its budget size increases.
- Corporate management defines OD as managing organizational change by creating a more humanistic work environment.

The nonprofit version focuses almost exclusively on organizational functions, letting the individual chips fall where they may, whereas the corporate version emphasizes that people are the key to change.

(ii) Historical Time Lag

Why has it taken so long for the corporate version of OD to filter into the nonprofit arena? One answer to this question is history. For-profit or corporate management as a whole is over a century old, whereas nonprofit management is less than a third that age; over three-quarters of all nonprofit organizations have been formed since the mid-1960s.[2] Corporate OD is 30 years old,[3] about the same age as the whole field of nonprofit management.

Early in the history of nonprofit management, there were failed attempts to impose corporate management on NPOs in a blanket fashion. Corporate methods could not be applied instantly and wholesale to NPOs due to differences in organization sizes and their reasons for existence. With regard to differences in size, over 80 percent of NPOs still have budgets under $1 million,[4] whereas a "small business" is classified as having a budget under $5 million. With regard to purpose, corporations exist to make a profit, whereas non-profit organizations exist to provide a service. Sources of income provide another great contrast between businesses and NPOs.

Despite these major differences, slowly, corporate techniques were adapted to the nonprofit field, seemingly one function at a time and almost one-a-decade: first, financial management (audits, fund accounting, cash flow projections, variance analysis), then marketing, strategic planning, human resources management, generating earned income enterprises, and so on.

The first major handbook on nonprofit management[5] was only published in 1979. The breakthrough nature of that work lay in its recognition that "regardless of the specific public purpose served by a nonprofit organization, all had much in common when it came to management."[6] In the handbook, the author, Tracy Connors, covered seven areas of management and leadership, which established that there was an emerging body of professional knowledge and new career fields in something called "nonprofit management." These seven areas are the major management and leadership functions service-oriented NPOs share in common, regardless of their program specialty. They include:

1. Fundamental organization and corporate principles
2. Leadership, management, and control
3. Volunteer administration
4. Sources of revenue
5. Communication and public relations
6. Financial management and administration
7. Legal and regulatory.

Optimistically, now is the time to add OD to these seven nonprofit management cornerstones—now there are eight.

(iii) Why Nonprofit Organization Development?

Nonprofit organization managers face more complex challenges than for-profit organization managers. In addition to dealing with the basic issue they share—producing a quality product or service—NPOs must be extra creative in generating resources, which are usually in short supply. Perhaps because of this, most NPO managers see more money or more control as "magic bullets" to solve any organizational problem. Even when addressing board development, financial and program management, strategic planning, or staffing—core issues involving people—the typical NPO manager will often try to avoid the messy human domain as much as possible, seeking solutions anywhere else. Yet, organizational problems are often solved more easily, quickly, or permanently by addressing people's behavior, individually and in groups.

At the heart of managing people is the challenge to inspire and encourage them to work better, harder, and faster. In this competitive age, both nonprofit and for-profit organizations need to have the most productive workforce possible. When people are not managed with skill and respect, they become discouraged and do not perform well.

(C)   THE TWO DEFINITIONS ARE GROWING CLOSER

There are two reasons why nonprofit organization OD has been largely limited to financial growth: the fast-growing, entrepreneurial nature of NPOs as a relatively new field and the accompanying surge in funding during the 1970s and 1980s. Most repercussions of financial gain, other than in-your-face benefits like salary increases, have been viewed reactively. The focus has been on survival, putting one foot in front of the other, looking only at the ground immediately in front. First, get the money and then solve the management issues that come with it.

This reactive paradigm or model of organizational development tends to let funding sources and their requests for proposals (RFPs) dictate programmatic direction. This survival mode seemed adequate when community needs and funding sources were less challenging than they are now, and when the NPO management field as a whole was less defined.

Fueled in large part by increased financial competition, there are recent signs that the field is moving toward proactive planning to anticipate the consequences of growth. When heads are raised from viewing the ground immediately in front to view the distant horizon, it is possible to anticipate and solve problems before they occur. The growing use of strategic planning is testimony to this shift toward greater self-determination.

The term *growth,* as in this chapter heading, no longer means unilateral or automatic increases in income. Many NPOs have to downsize as they move forward. Therefore, growth no longer means increases in size or funds. *Change* is often a more appropriate term. When organizations change, some take revolutionary giant steps forward. Others prefer to take baby steps and evolve slowly. While both approaches have worked in different circumstances, studies have shown that dramatic change works better in the long run, at least in the initial stages, than incremental change, because slow changes tend to lack momentum and stall.[7]

Too often, the original impetus for change originates outside the organization. Major funding sources drop out or the service environment shifts in surprising ways. Some organizations use this external impetus for change to become more proactive. Being proactive is like a muscle that becomes stronger with use. As proactive planning becomes more habitual, those in the organization become increasingly capable of previously unexplored levels of self-determination. Then, the rich possibilities of transformational change come into view. The more concrete this vision becomes, the closer the organization comes to being a self-renewing corporation. The self-renewing NPO is virtually synonymous with corporate OD.

(D)   THE CHANGING PARADIGM OF NONPROFIT ORGANIZATION DEVELOPMENT

It is becoming possible, advisable, and even necessary, to begin viewing the NPO as a self-renewing entity that operates on a new paradigm. Exhibit 18.1 shows some contrasting assumptions of the old and new paradigms of organization development and growth based on observation and experience.

18.2   *Nonprofit Organization Self-Diagnosis*

(A)   MODELS OF ORGANIZATIONAL GROWTH

A generic, graphic model of stages in an organization's life is illustrated in Exhibit 18.2. This model has been in general use for some time because it provides a quick, visual overview to show, in a very general way, the life stages experienced by most organizations. Some of the existing verbal models of organizational growth and development include:

EXHIBIT 18.1 Changing Paradigm of Nonprofit Organization Development

Characteristic	Old Nonprofit Organization Model	New Nonprofit Organization Model
Modus operandi (MO)	Reactive	Proactive
Locus of control	External	Internal
Engine of change	Money; funding sources	People and planning; environmental changes
Who will fix?	Outside expert	Organizational team, perhaps with outside help
Style of outside help	Analysis, directives	Involvement, analysis, facilitation
What will help?	Magic bullet	We can manage change process
Speed of change	Slow (evolution)	Fast (revolution)
Relationship to environment	Detached, resentful	Involved, responsive
Risk appetite	Try to avoid	Try to encounter
View of constituents	Needy, deficient, helpless	Having assets to contribute
Relationship with constituency	We/they dichotomy, in which "we" the educated, privileged experts are serving the underprivileged, deficient "they"	Servers and servees are partners working together to address the mission

EXHIBIT 18.1 *(Continued)*

Characteristic	Old Nonprofit Organization Model	New Nonprofit Organization Model
Response to conflict	Delay: use procedures and legal recourse	Act quickly: build trust and win–win results
View of mission	One fragment of the problem and solution	Holistic view; one organization is part of a network of other groups improving the whole situation
View of organization	Isolated; many separate parts—staff, board, volunteers, constituents	Organization is a dynamic unit, supports the relationship between internal and external communities
View of staff, board, volunteers	Expendable, interchangeable; selection based on degrees, resume, skills	Valued, nurtured, developed; selection based on accomplishments, problem-solving ability, personal capacities, commitment
Basic belief about people	People are inadequate, need to be directed, and will only change with a blast of dynamite	People possess the innate wisdom to solve their problems and are open to change

EXHIBIT 18.2 Bell Curve of Nonprofit Organization Development

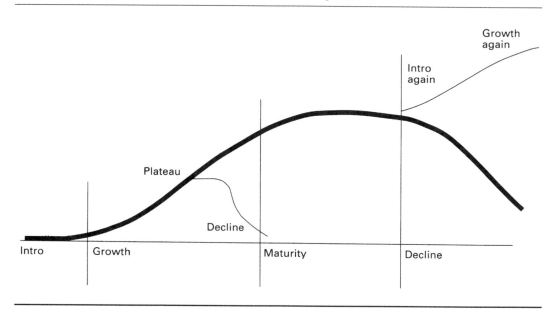

- *Life Cycle Stages*—The Stevens Group
- *PASSAGES: Organizational Life Cycles*—Franco, Gross, Mathiasen, Management Assistance Group
- *The Five Stages of Small Business Growth*—Churchill & Lewis, *Harvard Business Review*
- *Board Passages: Three Key Stages in a Nonprofit Board's Life Cycle*—Mathiasen, National Center for Nonprofit Boards
- *Corporate Lifecycles*—Ichak Adizes, Prentice Hall
- *Developmental Stages and Typical Characteristics*—The Conservation Company
- *Self-Renewing or Palingenetic Organization*—Connors, *The Nonprofit Handbook: Management,* John Wiley & Sons, Inc.
- *Analysis of Client Groups*—The Nonprofit Connection
- *Stages of Nonprofit Organization Development*—Curran

See the Suggested Readings at the end of the chapter to obtain more information on these models.

(B) STAGES OF ORGANIZATIONAL GROWTH COMBINED

The following represents a blending and fusion of these various models, integrated to offer the reader a useful overview. Generally, all of these models depict the organization like any living organism, with these predictable levels:

$$\text{Birth} \rightarrow \text{Growth} \rightarrow \text{Maturity} \rightarrow \text{Decline}$$

and most of them add:

$$\rightarrow \text{Rebirth}$$

They may use different terms that have similar meanings. For example:

Birth	Start-up, creativity, infancy, courtship, emerging, champion
Growth	Take charge
Maturity	Established, prime
Decline	Aristocracy, bureaucracy, death, terminal
Rebirth	Palingenesis (birth over again), self-renewing, turnaround, recycle

Three models divide the *Growth* stage into two stages, as follows:

PASSAGES	Direction and Delegation
Adizes	Go-Go and Adolescence
Curran	Growth/Staff and Growth/Board

(i) Grow or Die

While some of these models are for NPOs and some depict for-profits, they share a basic principle in common: that an organization has a life of its own. The word *organization* shares the same root as the word *organism,* the basis of all life. The root word for *corpora-*

tion is the word *corpus,* meaning "body" in Latin. So, an organization or corporation is a living body, greater than the sum of its parts and with its own characteristics and growth stages, analogous to a person.

In a further extension of this thought, being organic "means that all parts are defined by the whole, thus you cannot take an organization apart to study pieces."[8] While many OD specialists may find this view goes a little too far, the central truth is that organizations are systems, and when one part of the system is altered, all other parts are affected.

Some of the models listed previously take a snapshot of each particular stage, freezing its characteristics in a static frame, whereas others speak of life cycles and describe a dynamic flow of activity; most combine the static and the dynamic. All agree that an organization's very life depends on continuing to grow. At any stage, if an organization stops growing, it "plateaus out" and goes into decline. Following the theme that the organization is like a person, Adizes calls this midcycle decline a divorce. The rebirth cycle can then begin at any of the plateau stages, if and when the group has the energy, will, and resources to regenerate or renew it.

(C)   CHECKLIST TO IDENTIFY AN ORGANIZATION'S GROWTH STAGE

(i)   *At What Stage Is Your Organization?*

The many models listed earlier are integrated in Exhibit 18.3 and Exhibit 18.4. They are an attempt to show both the typical strengths and common pitfalls of most organizations at various levels of development. The checklists in the charts are designed to help the reader pinpoint the development status of a particular organization. After checking the boxes closest to describing the reader's organization, "connect the dots" to see what kind of pattern emerges. Most organizations will be predominantly in one stage, with issues in other stages.

(D)   MOVING TO THE NEXT STAGE

How does the organization move to the next stage? Until OD becomes proactive, the organization has generally been moved by the instinct and skill of the leadership without a detailed map for moving from one stage to the next. Now there is an opportunity to move in a more conscious direction. But how?

Locate the organization's current characteristics in Exhibits 18.3 and 18.4. When the organization's situation resembles the data in a particular frame, observe the qualities described in the frame to its right, representing the next stage. The data depicting the next stage will provide possible developmental goals and potential pitfalls to be avoided.

NPOs are notably resourceful in finding help to improve and develop technical functions such as fiscal management and fund raising, so this chapter does not address those areas. By contrast, as we have noted, there is generally a lack of available resources to improve people-oriented areas such as development of leaders, board, staff, and volunteers. Because people are essential to organizational growth and change, some tools for enhancing the management of people is the focus of Section 18.3.

(E)   DNA PATTERN OF ORGANIZATIONAL GROWTH

Before leaving the subject of classifying organizational growth, Exhibit 18.5 reinforces the idea that organization development is an organic process. The DNA chart is a graphic

EXHIBIT 18.3 Four Stages of Nonprofit Organization Development—Self-Assessment Checklist

	Stage 1: Birth	Stage 2: Growth/Staff	Stage 3: Growth/Board	Stage 4: Maturity
People—Board, Staff, Volunteers	☐ Everyone does everything; board and staff may be the same people ☐ Founders get little or no pay ☐ Personality driven; founder (one or more) vision drives group ☐ Inspiration overcomes all hurdles ☐ Informal structure ☐ Entrepreneurial, risk-taking ☐ Survival mode	☐ Increase in paid staff ☐ Crisis management ☐ Program-oriented board in a state of benign neglect ☐ Confused board/staff roles ☐ Hierarchy begins on organization chart ☐ Both board and staff dependent on too few; a change of leadership would threaten the organization's existence ☐ Still putting out fires	☐ Board wakes up to its responsibilities, diversified skills, and demographics ☐ Board may micro-manage ☐ Executive director (ED) may have trouble letting go; identity crisis ☐ Staff burnout ☐ Staff mostly program + ED; lacks middle management ☐ Growing emphasis on efficiency, control, "take charge"	☐ Staff/Board partnership ☐ Middle-management staff for fund raising, financial, and program management ☐ Board committees are active, especially fund raising ☐ Corporate orientation; hierarchies in communication and control ☐ Procedures dominate relationships
Program and Outreach/Marketing	☐ Mission drives everything ☐ Visionary championing of social issues ☐ Lots of putting out fires ☐ One type of program ☐ Close to clients	☐ Program competency ☐ Plan a whole year of programs; consolidation ☐ Diversify services ☐ Define clients ☐ Public comes to know the organization and its programs	☐ Create service departments ☐ Plan program objectives; emphasis on outcomes ☐ Build on track record ☐ Begin to professionalize marketing; better materials, etc.	☐ Multiyear plan ☐ Targeted marketing and media ☐ May stray from mission
Money— In and Out	☐ Little money—hand-to-mouth ☐ Small-scale community support ☐ Seed grant may be foundation or government ☐ Minimal record keeping	☐ Chase grants and RFPs ☐ Raise funds for programs but not operations ☐ Organization is under-capitalized ☐ Audit but no fund accounting ☐ Cash flow problems	☐ Seek funds for operations and organization capacity building ☐ Expand government, foundations, corporations, special events ☐ Build cash reserve ☐ Increase reports to board: cash flow, budget variances ☐ Extensive internal reporting	☐ Cash reserve leading to endowment ☐ Individual donors → major ☐ Big increase earned income ☐ Expand network, big-time ("friend raising") ☐ Financial management to build capital
Administration and Facility	☐ Office in someone's home ☐ Program space in-kind or rented ☐ No systems; minimal paperwork	☐ Get a proper office and equipment ☐ Consolidate program spaces ☐ Starfish effect—all (program) arms and little central body/infrastructure ☐ Inconsistent quality	☐ Refine administrative systems ☐ Bursting out of space ☐ Emphasis on productivity and task orientation	☐ Use technology to build administrative systems (fiscal, database, mail, clients, etc.) ☐ Own facility

EXHIBIT 18.4 Stages 5a & b of Nonprofit Organization Development—Headed for Growth or Decline?

	Either: Stage 5: Recycle	Or: Stage 5: Decline, Termination
People— Board, Staff, Volunteers	☐ Often has new leadership bringing new energy ☐ Move toward flatter organization chart; network approach to communication, planning, and decisions ☐ Restore entrepreneurial spirit ☐ Emphasis on team building and relationships over procedure ☐ Open to learning ☐ Creative ways of resolving conflict ☐ Able to engage in honest self-evaluation because individuals are valued	☐ Low board turnover; eventually, entropy shrinks size and energy ☐ Lots of staff turnover ☐ Structures and procedures congeal to displace vital relationship energy ☐ Low morale in every group ☐ Internal fighting, back stabbing, acting out ☐ Denial of ineffectiveness ☐ Paranoia paralyzes organization ☐ Urge to abandon ship
Program and Outreach/ Marketing	☐ Revitalize mission; value best aspects of history ☐ Reconnect to constituents' assets and needs ☐ Institutionalize client contact (focus groups, surveys, etc.) ☐ Quantum leap forward in public awareness	☐ Decline in amount and effectiveness of planning ☐ Focus on individual programs instead of mission ☐ Turf wars ☐ Lost touch with client assets and needs
Money— In and Out	☐ Solidify funder relationships and make new ones ☐ Income streams very diverse and continue to grow ☐ Long-term financial stability ☐ Routine, sophisticated financial management as a source of information for planning	☐ Losing credibility with public, funders ☐ Lost funding ☐ Dwindling cash reserves ☐ Increased debt—bankruptcy?
Administration and Facility	☐ If facility is not already owned, will happen now ☐ Sophisticated management information system	☐ Well-developed systems become "red tape" ☐ Departure from systems to crisis management ☐ Deteriorating facility; no maintenance investment ☐ May have energy to close down responsibly

representation of the narrative checklists (previous pages) showing the four basic stages of growth. (The thumbnail sketches provided in the DNA chart are expanded in Exhibit 18.6.)

In the DNA chart, management issues are paired in the same order that they appear in the checklist—staff/board, program/marketing, fund raising/financial management, and administration/facility. Note that each pair of management issues is mated because of what they have in common: the first pair involves people; the second pair, serving the public; the third pair, money; and the fourth pair, infrastructure. When one of the paired functions is projected—for example, staff and board—showing the typical ups and downs of each, they tend to go up and down at alternating times, creating a double helix or DNA effect. This seems to be more than a coincidence.

(i)   What Does the DNA Chart Reveal?

Like biological DNA, each strand in the organizational double helix must continue to spiral around the other to keep life going. Although both positive (growth, solutions, etc.) and negative (challenges, issues to be improved) can be found at every stage, the characteristics shown tend to be the most prominent for most organizations. The negatives/challenges of one stage breed the positives/solutions of the next.

In the DNA drawing, the transitions are shown as smooth lines to carry a graphic message. This gives the illusion that transitions are also smooth, which is far from the truth. Because there are so many ups and downs in an organization's life, a real graphic representation would be jagged lines, some of them extremely uneven. It would be a real graphic design challenge to show *all* of the functions of an organization on one three-dimensional double helix to project how all the functions are interconnected, which they are.

Twenty years ago, Charles Hampden-Turner[9] explored the same double-helix metaphor for the development of a person, pointing out that underdevelopment or overemphasis in one area or another ultimately leads to lopsided development and systems failure. The same could be said of organizational DNA.

(F)   CHALLENGES OF ONE STAGE LEAD TO SOLUTIONS OF THE NEXT

Exhibit 18.6 demonstrates how most organizations move from one stage to the next. In OD, it is more constructive to view "negatives" as "areas to be improved" or challenges, not as weaknesses or issues that cannot be surmounted. That way, there is more hope and opportunity to solve problems, grow, and change.

18.3   Managing People for Change

(A)   NONPROFIT ORGANIZATION DEVELOPMENT CAN DRAW ON CORPORATE ORGANIZATION DEVELOPMENT

When the leaders of an organization decide to embark on the road to greater self-determination and proactive growth, the first hurdle to overcome is to let go of the old paradigm of separate organizational functions and embrace the new paradigm—viewing the organization as a system powered by people. This process can be facilitated by integrating staff development and motivational management techniques with strategic planning to

EXHIBIT 18.5 The DNA of Nonprofit Organization Growth

	1. BIRTH	2. GROWTH-STAFF	3. GROWTH-BOARD	4. MATURITY
BOARD	incorporators	paid-program & ED	management-oriented	gets mid-management
STAFF	unpaid or part-time	program-oriented	lacks mid-management	stagnates
PROGRAM	inspired	formal publicity	get control	formalize marketing
MARKETING	informal outreach	putting out fires	losing touch with grass roots	repetition
FISCAL MANAGEMENT	organize few $	burst into foundations	focus on fiscal infrastructure	diverse streams
FUND RAISING	seed money	systems less than $ capacity	struggle to replace grants	budget "noise"
ADMINISTRATION	simple systems OK	get a proper office	well established administration	get enough space
FACILITY	minimal, borrowed	struggle to develop systems	outgrow space	bureaucracy

EXHIBIT 18.6 Negative Qualities in Any Stage Lead to Positive Qualities of the Next

	Stage 1	Stage 2	Stage 3	Stage 4
Board	Incorporators are a small group of people committed to the mission or the founder or both.	They remain program-focused long after the organization needs more from them.	People with a range of management skills are added. There is a period of vitality.	Insufficient rotation and resting on past success causes a period of stagnation that may lead to renewal or decline.
Staff	Unpaid or part-time staff cannot cover all the work needed.	A paid executive director (ED) and program staff cause an upsurge in productivity.	Dearth of middle-management staff exists long after the organization needs them.	Addition of middle management stabilizes organization and programs.
Program	Activities are new, creatively inspired.	Volume of program exceeds management capacity; crisis orientation.	Program stabilizes through longevity and habit.	Repetition of programs continues long after the need for a fresh approach.
Marketing	Contact with clients is haphazard, informal.	Publicity and communication are formalized—mailings, ads, etc.	Initial closeness between staff and public is weakened as staff grows.	Bonds strengthen again via surveys, focus groups, newsletters, other marketing tools.
Fiscal management	Relatively easy to organize small budgets.	Primitive systems are not adequate to handle growing budgets beyond basic external reports/audits.	Focus on fiscal infrastructure: controls, internal reports, computerization.	Accountability to diverse funding sources and internal management needs leads to clutter and "noise."
Fund raising	Obtain seed money, usually much less than amount needed.	Early foundation support is great—"new kid on the block."	Lifetime contracts are rare. After creaming the top sources, it's a struggle to replace grants.	Diverse funding streams provide stability: individuals, earned income, government, and private sector.
Administration	Simple approaches are adequate.	Struggle to set up systems is reactive and spotty.	Well-established administration makes programs and people easy to manage.	Established systems calcify into unresponsive bureaucracy that needs to be shaken up or it will choke programs and people.
Facility	Space for programs is marginal or borrowed. Office is in someone's home.	Establish proper office and rent program space.	Programs and numbers of people involved grow. Space is too small for the volume.	Move to adequately sized space. May own it.

produce a participatory planning process. Fortunately, people in the nascent field of non-profit OD can draw on the 30 or so years of experience that some in the corporate sector have invested in understanding and promoting organizational change.

Many OD professionals—organization consultants, authors, and psychologists—have already drawn important links between individual and organizational behavior. The corporate OD field is extremely interdisciplinary and eclectic, drawing from early influences such as Maslow's hierarchy of needs; sensitivity training; the work of influential theorist Kurt Lewin; T-groups; quality management; NeuroLinguistic Programming (NLP); facilitation and training techniques fostered by National Training Labs (NTL); and others, to name just a few.[10]

(B) A CONCEPTUAL FOUNDATION FOR NONPROFIT ORGANIZATION DEVELOPMENT: REALITY THERAPY

Another OD resource is reality therapy (RT), a problem-solving method that was developed in the 1960s as a therapy and that has since received wide application for management and education. RT combines theory and practice in pragmatic ways that are relatively easy to learn and apply. Here are a few examples of RT's connections with other powerful management movements, books, and studies:

- Dr. William Glasser's book, *The Control Theory Manager,* demonstrates the links between RT and TQM.
- The essential qualities of excellent corporations in the best-seller, *In Search of Excellence,* are directly analogous to RT.
- The four key dimensions of "empowered employees," identified in a study of 400 top corporate managers,[11] are the same as RT's cornerstone theory, the four basic needs.

One of the central tenets of RT is that of success and failure identities. RT's characterization of "success identity" and "failure identity" is not a classification of a person's worth, nor is it a commentary on a person's status or permanent condition. The terms relate to success and failure only in the outcomes or consequences of particular actions, with examples shown in Exhibits 18.7 and 18.8.

RT proposes the central idea of a manager who has a success identity, is highly productive, produces excellence or total quality, and is empowered and open to change. Many of us yearn to be this person or scarcely dare to believe this person exists. RT provides the building blocks for helping individuals to develop themselves into empowered change agents, and guidance for managers and supervisors to assist this process. RT gives us tools and methods to improve both individual performance and the work climate.

(C) INDIVIDUAL AND ORGANIZATIONAL RESPONSE TO CHANGE

Exhibit 18.7 and Exhibit 18.8 adapt RT's concept of success and failure identities to show characteristic identities of individuals and organizations. The pro-change characteristics represented by the right-hand checklist on both charts depict a "success identity" on the

EXHIBIT 18.7 Individual Person's Response to Change

A person may be resistant to or having difficulty with change when s/he . . .	*A person may be welcoming or coping with change when s/he . . .*
☐ Tolerates a chronic health or family problem for some time without doing much to solve it	☐ Has tried a new type of food, sport, movie, or other experience in the past month
☐ Usually blames others when things go wrong	☐ Practices daily or weekly habits that make her/himself happy
☐ Practices "image management" through fear of looking less than perfect	☐ Tolerates embarrassment without getting mad or depressed
☐ Finds it difficult to say positive things to people, especially when they are experiencing success	☐ Learns from failures and moves on
☐ Makes fun of new ideas	☐ Tries to "see God in the face of everyone" (Mother Teresa)
☐ Rarely tries new things	☐ Smiles and says hello to a stranger occasionally
☐ Spins her/his wheels in resentment when feeling powerless to change someone else	☐ Identifies with other peoples' discomfort and tries to alleviate it where feasible
☐ Gossips, stuffs feelings, or tells person B when person A is doing something irritating	☐ Directly tells a person whose behavior is B when person A is doing
☐ Exaggerates people's flaws to make a point or gain a feeling of righteousness	☐ Holds relatively consistent views about friends and coworkers
☐ Tends to remember slights and dwell on them about self and others	☐ Tells lots of positive success stories about self and others

part of an individual or organization. The success identity list provides a model to work toward.

The premise of Exhibits 18.7 and 18.8 is that the more success-oriented a person or organization becomes, the more open they are to change. These are informal lists, presented to communicate a concept; they are not intended to be definitive or infallible. Feel free to add or imagine additional items.

Each pair of checklists placed side by side represents the two extreme responses to change—resistant and open. Nearly every person or group falls somewhere on the spectrum between the two extremes. By checking off items that apply, it is possible to develop a rough profile for an individual or organization. Once the individual or organization is located somewhere on the spectrum, the "tools" provided in the next section support movement along the spectrum toward the right-hand side. As with individuals, it is possible to reduce organizational resistance and move toward change using various methods provided by RT and other disciplines, most notably appreciative inquiry, an effective OD method emerging on the scene, which shares many of RT's basic assumptions.

These two charts are linked in several ways. People influence and affect what happens in organizations. Organizations are composed of individuals who are, in turn, affected by the forces of organizational change. The group behavior expressed in the organization checklist is a mirror image of the kinds of behavior shown by individuals.

(D) MOTIVATIONS FOR CHANGE: FEAR VERSUS COMMUNITY

(i) *Fear: Incentive or Disincentive for Change?*

Following is an argument for change that seems very compelling. Once upon a time, a community-based organization got a foundation grant when one of the leaders jotted a

EXHIBIT 18.8 Organization's Response to Change

An organization may be resistant to change when people in it . . .	An organization may welcome or cope with change when people in it . . .
☐ Chase RFPs—decide to undertake programs based mainly on funds available "out there" ☐ Have not reviewed its mission statement in more than three years ☐ Make fun of people for deviating from organizational norms—both trivial and large ☐ Have not reviewed its bylaws and other policies in more than five years ☐ Reward people for slavishly sticking to the rules even when it may be destructive ☐ Bad-mouth clients when problems with them become difficult to solve ☐ Conduct most planning sessions by focusing on problems ☐ Habitually criticize each other, thereby reducing trust and community	☐ Have added or subtracted board, staff, and volunteers within the past year ☐ Frequently and publicly acknowledge others' contributions—ideas, skills, money, concern, assistance, etc.—at every level (board, staff, volunteers, clients, peers in the field, community groups, funders, politicians, etc.) ☐ Recently planned and implemented a change in services—added, increased, decreased, or ended—based on internal evaluations ☐ Usually demonstrate affection and respect for clients; solve problems with them ☐ Promote a learning environment—exchange of ideas and skills—by setting aside time, praising those who initiate it, etc. ☐ Have a reputation for being easy to get involved with, not a clique ☐ Hold and express consistently positive views of one another to enhance collaboration and teamwork ☐ Spend considerable planning time exploring what is going well and looking for ways to increase it (i.e., generating the organization's own "best practices")

proposal on the back of an envelope. Another dashed off a quick letter on the foundation program officer's typewriter following a cozy lunch. In those days, the nonprofit sector's response to solving social problems was more spontaneous, haphazard, experimental, and entrepreneurial. In fact, the field as a whole represented many of the "Birth" characteristics in stage 1 of nonprofit OD. Those days are over.

Now, the field as a whole is much more calculated, coordinated, and focused. Perhaps as a group, NPOs are approaching stage 4, Maturity. There are more agencies in existence than ever, competing for declining government support. More professionalism is required to raise funds now; a good program idea is no longer enough. Funding sources want to see a well-managed infrastructure. Does this changing reality mean that fear of lack of funding is a good incentive for change? Yes and no. Fear definitely brings a sense of urgency to organizational change, and urgency is one ingredient needed for success. So much so that "one CEO deliberately engineered the largest accounting loss in the history of the company[12] to shake things up." (The OD approach recommended in this chapter creates a sense of urgency in more positive ways.)

Besides creating a sense of urgency, what other effects does fear have?

- Fear breeds impulsive decisions, created out of an atmosphere of panic or false urgency, preventing in-depth consideration of long-term consequences.
- Fear raises the level of acting-out behaviors, such as being hypercritical, back stabbing, or hoarding vital information, that kill creativity.

- Fear reduces the level of trust and the incentive for learning and taking calculated risks, which in turn has a destructive effect on teamwork and cooperation.

Ultimately, fear is not an effective engine for change, for it can drive people into short-term solutions at the expense of more fundamental and long-term ones. The next section will provide examples of methods that reduce fear to increase trust, teamwork, and cooperation, thus increasing an organization's potential for growth and achieving better results.

(ii) Building Community
In days gone by, people used to live in actual communities that provided safety, nurturance, and support. The OD field has increasing interest in the features of a successful community, with the goal of replicating these features because of the importance of people working harmoniously in groups. Certainly, fear is not a quality that should be cultivated when the goal is to create a more productive working community.

(E) RESISTANCE TO ORGANIZATION DEVELOPMENT

(i) Reasons for Resistance
Even experienced NPO managers and technical assistance professionals usually lack exposure to OD and its potential to help them. The general lack of exposure causes them not to look to OD for solutions, or even to resist some potential OD solutions. Some reasons for the resistance may be:

- The current nonprofit version of OD is task-oriented, and the corporate version is process-oriented. NPO managers tend to be very task-oriented. Perhaps task-oriented people are drawn to the field, or perhaps they become that way from having to cover so many bases with so few resources. Tasks always seem much easier to deal with in the short term, and may in fact be the shortest route to success for many situations. However, in the long run, the task orientation leaves many problems unsolved or worse than before. Tasks are more concrete, therefore easier to communicate. Processes are less quantifiable, therefore more difficult to grasp.
- People who manage NPOs with budgets under $1 million (80 percent of the 1.3 million NPOs nationally[13]) are generally understaffed, overworked, and required to have too many types of skills to run their "mom-and-pop" shops already; it seems like asking too much to add yet another bunch of knowledge, that of understanding better what makes people tick in the workplace and doing more about it.
- Due to lack of exposure, there is lack of awareness of what process-oriented OD can do to help NPOs manage better. When a field is relatively unknown, it can be a little scary, so people invent ways of dealing with it, such as avoidance, denial, control, and so on.
- NPO managers lack access to techniques, skills, and methods for learning process-oriented OD.

(ii) Reducing Resistance to OD
The same personal and organizational qualities depicted in Exhibits 18.7 and 18.8 that are symptomatic of resistance to change may also be the cause of resistance to OD, which is a

new approach, therefore engendering fear of the unknown. Both skeptics and managers seeking new approaches may find useful tools in the next section to help them move incrementally into the new paradigm.

(F) OPPORTUNITIES FOR CHANGE: REALITY THERAPY AND CONTROL THEORY

(i) IALAC Story

The following story illustrates some of the challenges and opportunities for change in management, supervision, and interaction in the workplace. Popular in the 1970s in humanistic education circles, this "IALAC Story" was originally about a little boy, but it adapts well to adults in the workplace.

> *Once upon a time, there was a man named Robert. When he woke up in the morning, Robert had an imaginary piece of cardboard on his chest, held in place by a string around his neck. The cardboard had big letters printed on it: IALAC, which stood for "I am lovable and capable." He bounded happily out of bed. The sign stayed with him as he went to work. Robert dashed into the elevator in his office building, and said, "Good morning. How was your weekend?" to his colleague, Lou, who made a sour face and replied, "Don't ask!" A little corner piece of Robert's sign ripped off and drifted to the floor. As Robert started to work, a coworker snarled at him for asking for information. Another little chunk of Robert's IALAC sign shredded off and fell to the ground. The rest of the morning went pretty much like that. Another coworker was selected for a job Robert knew he had more expertise to do, and so on. The remaining tatters of Robert's sign disintegrated. He had difficulty focusing on his work. He needed to finish two complex projects and wasn't motivated to deal with either one. He walked slowly to the company cafeteria for lunch, dragging his feet, with his head down. In the lunch room, Robert's fortunes began to change. He sat next to Lisa, a colleague from another department. Lisa said, "I've been wanting to talk to you for some time because I have a special project in mind that we could do together." Robert and Lisa tossed around some new ideas about the project and had a few laughs. Robert realized that his contribution was valuable; miraculously, his IALAC sign began to reappear. After lunch, his administrative assistant came over with a belated birthday card, which may have been a response to his hint the day before that he was the only one in the department to have his birthday overlooked. Robert's IALAC sign grew larger with each positive experience. During the afternoon, Robert finished one of the two projects that had seemed so formidable in the morning. With that accomplishment, his IALAC sign grew some more. By the time he left for home, Robert's IALAC sign was intact again.[14]*

Robert is a proactive person attempting to reach out in various ways that are either accepted or rebuffed. His behavior is his "constant attempt to choose what he believes will *best* satisfy his needs."[15] As an adult, Robert is fully responsible for meeting his own needs in his workplace; he is not a victim at the mercy of positive or negative reinforcement from his environment. However, the web of interactions with his coworkers comprises a corporate culture that will either support Robert's productivity or diminish it. The managers and supervisors in Robert's organization can enhance or detract from a productive climate within which Robert is internally motivated to fulfill his own needs.

(ii) Four Basic Needs of Reality Therapy

The IALAC Story contains the elements that reality therapy (RT) defines as the four basic psychological needs.[16] They are listed as follows, along with some interpretations of their meaning:

1. Friendship (also belonging, giving, love)
2. Worth (also achievement, receiving recognition)
3. Fun (humor, creativity)
4. Freedom (self-determination, exercising self-discipline, control over decisions that affect you)

The four basic psychological needs of RT are a useful application to OD because they are relatively easy to learn, remember, and apply. Review the IALAC Story and pick out Robert's experiences that relate to RT's four basic needs and see how they were met or not met. Here is a partial list:

1. Friendship—"Good morning, how was your weekend?" [not met]
    Belonging—"belated birthday card" [met]
2. Receiving recognition—"another coworker was selected for a job" [not met]
    Achievement—"Robert finished one of his two projects" [met]
3. Fun—"Robert and Lisa . . . had a few laughs" [met]
    Creativity—"tossed around some ideas" [met]
4. Freedom, self-discipline—"Robert finished one of the two projects" [met]
    Self-determination, control over decisions that affect him—invitation to develop a project [met]

RT holds that people are internally motivated to meet their needs (in the workplace as well as in their lives outside work) and that it is both possible and advisable to create a work environment to foster this process. RT offers a problem-solving method involving five steps that provides a format for creating this work environment, as demonstrated in Exhibit 18.9. In order to demonstrate how to create such a work environment, it is helpful to understand something about control theory.

(iii) Control Theory

Control theory explains how the four basic psychological needs link up to work performance, and what managers can do to improve it. Unlike the four basic needs, control theory is harder to learn, mainly because it runs counter to the popular psychology that we take for granted and that governs our habitual modus operandi at work.

Common sense has taught us that people in general and workers in particular respond to external stimuli—the above-mentioned rabbit-chasing-carrot syndrome. Called stimulus–response theory, or S-R, it has been popularized and reinforced in the public consciousness by the story of Pavlov's famous dogs, the early behavioral theories of B. F. Skinner, and most management motivation training. The so-called boss style of management is firmly based on S-R. S-R helps create monsters out of managers by making them responsible for everyone else because they have to provide all the "stimulus."

S-R relieves responsibility from employees by allowing them to claim—as did comedian Flip Wilson's "Geraldine"—"The devil made me do it!" If the human brain really worked according to S-R, it would be a stress-free system. However, S-R compounds stress on both managers and employees by setting them up as adversaries and running counter to human nature. Control theory distributes responsibility more equitably among managers and staff, making it easier and less stressful to be a control theory manager (a.k.a "lead-manager" by Dr. Glasser and W. Edwards Deming, originator of quality management).

Recent research, based on the physiology of the brain,[17] has demonstrated that the reverse of S-R is actually true. Dr. William Glasser has combined this research with his earlier findings in practicing reality therapy, resulting in a new explanation for behavior called control theory.[18]

Control theory "is based on the premise that all human behavior is caused by *what goes on inside the heads of each behaving human being.* What goes on outside of us *does not cause us to do anything.* We do not answer a phone because it rings, stop our car because the light turns red. When we choose to answer the phone or choose to do any/all other behavior, it is because this chosen behavior satisfies one or more of the four basic needs that are built into the genetic structure of our brain."[19]

The S-R manager (boss type) thinks he can stimulate the worker into doing what he wants, usually through threats or punishment, regardless of whether the workers' needs are being met. In contrast, the lead-manager gives workers information and creates a work climate that will persuade them that *"expending the effort to do quality work will satisfy them better than anything else they can do at this time."*[20] Therefore, it behooves the manager to know what the worker's needs are.

Control theory provides a theoretical framework for understanding organizational behavior. A simplistic explanation of control theory is that the internal drive to satisfy basic needs causes people to attempt to control their individual universes to get their needs met. The most important things to remember are its applications, especially the four basic psychological needs. (RT identifies five basic needs, but the fifth is physiological, so it is excluded from this necessarily condensed version.)

(iv) Tenets of Lead-Management

Following is an adaptation of the principles of control theory or lead-management for NPO managers, abbreviated for this chapter:

- People are intrinsically, not extrinsically, motivated.
- The manager is a facilitator, creating a friendly, noncoercive, nonadversarial climate within which people can meet their needs, not attempting to meet their needs directly.
- Ninety-eight percent of the success/failure of productivity is with management, not workers, because managers can and should control the environment so that employees are able to meet their own needs.
- Forces that promote productivity:
  - A climate of trust
  - A sense of community
  - Seeing evidence that one's work is useful
- Forces that reduce productivity:
  - Fear and punishment
  - Criticism (expanded explanation in following section)
- Forces that do not affect productivity:
  - Money, as long as it is adequate
  - Empty or irrelevant "strokes"

It should be noted that these tenets useful in management are also true for parenting, teaching, and counseling—any relationships in which the power is inherently unequal.

EXHIBIT 18.9 Network Management Communication Chart

In network management, people work together in groups according to the tasks

Arrows show communication links

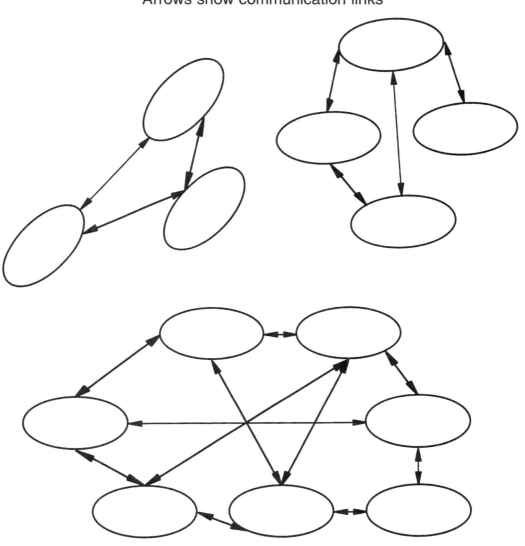

(v) *Power and Communication Relationships in Lead-Management*

Our quasi-egalitarian age has seen a decline in overtly authoritarian leadership. There is often the illusion that managers and workers, teachers and students, parents and children, counselors and counselees, are more or less equal in power, or even that it would be desirable. When the goal is productivity, workplace equality is both impractical and unnecessary.

Lead-management is characterized by a flatter organization chart than the traditional S-R hierarchical style of management. The flatter organization chart is caused by a number of factors, including broader internal communication opportunities offered by the increased use of computer technology and the necessities of operating with far fewer staff due to massive downsizing trends. The previous "silo" approach is being replaced by the "network" approach, which is characterized in Exhibit 18.9. In network management, staff, volunteers, or board members may cluster in groups or teams to accomplish particular tasks, regrouping in different configurations as the challenges of the work change.

This trend toward flatter management hierarchies is likely to evolve at different speeds in different organizations, depending on how effectively managers and teams can develop accountability systems that are responsive to clients' needs and funders' requirements.

Thus, moving away from S-R management is not moving toward a leaderless management model. Lead-management redefines the principles of responsibility and accountability with the goal of making them more effective. Denial of the disparity of authority between leaders and workers actually diminishes the potential for lead-management because denial means that the opportunity to discuss relationships openly is lost. Paradoxically, by accepting managerial responsibility, the manager who desires a more egalitarian environment (as many NPO managers seem to do) can establish it more effectively using lead-management principles.

The lead-manager empowers employees by enabling them to meet their own needs, thus growing in confidence and strength. Empowered employees are an essential component of an egalitarian-style workforce. Empowerment includes four essential elements:

- Authority to implement the organization's mission
- Responsibility for changes identified during fact-based decision making
- Provision of resources needed
- Accountability for performance outcomes

When these four essential elements are present, empowerment of workers in the new lead-management paradigm actually makes them much more responsible than the old, S-R style of management.

(vi) Criticism

Traditionally, managers thought that the only way to keep employees accountable was to criticize them. While positive reinforcement is the cornerstone of S-R management, criticism is the negative side of the same S-R coin. There is an assumption that people will respond to criticism by improving performance. An in-depth understanding of control theory and RT makes it obvious that criticism in any form does not work, and that there are other, much more effective, alternatives.

Criticism can be masked in many ways—using humor and ridicule, so-called constructive criticism, playing devil's advocate, body language, blaming, fault finding, punishing, strategic silences, and so on. Control theory says criticism is in the mind of the beholder; it is anything the employee says it is, because the "employee will act as if it were and quality will suffer. . . . When we are criticized, accurately or not, we feel we have lost power, friendship and the freedom to act as we think best."[21]

Ironically, criticism lowers the stature and esteem of the critic as much as the person being criticized, because criticism is a tacit admission of failure; if more positive ways had worked, the manager would not have had to resort to criticism. Therefore, managers can retain self-respect and the esteem of those for whom they are responsible, while minimizing disruptive negative reactions to criticism by learning new alternatives to its use. Managers are not exempt from the same universal impetus to meet their basic needs in the workplace. Learning to manage without criticism will satisfy their own basic needs—for friendship, accomplishment, fun, and self-determination.

In order to survive in an S-R environment, many managers and employees alike become emotionally shut down, to the point where they either no longer recognize that their own basic needs are not being met, or try to meet them in very convoluted ways. The popular Dilbert cartoons show this dilemma very humorously. It is not easy to develop new skills and behaviors that will effectively replace criticism. The exercises that follow offer some steps in that direction.

(G)   OPPORTUNITIES FOR CHANGE: TWO APPROACHES

Before describing two approaches to meetings (one-on-one and in groups) that will provide hands-on tools for managers to change their techniques and improve their results, it will be useful to set up a context for improved communication and planning.

(i)   Promoting Self-Actualization in the Workplace

One of the tenets of lead-management is the fundamental belief that people have the innate wisdom to solve their own problems, or to seek their own level, like water. When people are functioning at that natural level, they are meeting their own needs, thus working at optimal levels of productivity. One of the most useful techniques for fostering workers' independent problem-solving ability is to use active listening as a communication tool. Active listening is a very effective technique, best described in an inexpensive paperback called *Leadership Effectiveness Training (L.E.T.)*.[22] The listener gives supportive feedback to the speaker so that the speaker solves her or his own problem. The book provides a compelling case for innate wisdom. With practice, implementing active listening techniques can transform the most authoritarian work environment into an empowered, self-actualizing one.

(ii)   Integrating Planning and Self-Actualization

A lead-manager can and must keep the self-actualizing urges of staff moving in the same direction as the priorities of the organization, department, and team. The way to align everyone is to conduct participatory planning, working from the broadest issue (mission) down to the most specific (job goals for individuals), building in evaluation milestones and benchmarks to ensure completion of tasks and accountability. The various layers of planning can be summarized with the mnemonic MOGIER—Mission, Objectives, Goals, Implementation, Evaluation, Recycle.

It is crucial to integrate planning and management functions to gain the optimum results. While limited space prevents describing planning in detail here, it is pertinent that one of the four basic needs identified in RT is "freedom," also defined as "self-determination, exercising self-discipline and control over the decisions that affect you." The essential reason for making most planning participatory and inclusive of those whom it affects is this: When people are included in planning, it will motivate them to carry out the plan. That is because at least one of their basic psychological needs is being met in the process.

(iii)   Trade-off of Control

Promoting self-actualization and empowerment through various lead-management practices and participatory planning will allow the manager to "give up control to gain control." Actually, S-R managers have a great incentive to try lead-management, for there are many benefits awaiting them. Managers who have given up their control (of details, people's behavior, etc.) have found that they actually gain a different kind of control (of productivity, results, and respect). Lead-managers and those moving toward it have already discovered this paradox.

(iv)   Meetings

In the workplace, managers and other staff generally interact in two ways: one-on-one and in groups. Supervision, planning, evaluating, and decision making are accomplished in one of these two formats. Therefore, looking at the ways in which these encounters take place and offering alternative formats for them can substantially change the nature of these contacts.

Characteristically, both one-on-one and group meetings tend to reinforce S-R management, which, as described earlier, provides external controls that are not fully effective. Harking back to old S-R management models, old school models, and even the military, the information flow is usually from the top, down. S-R managers set the standards and the agendas, and control the flow of discussion and results. This reinforces the message that managers have all, or most, of the power, and the other staff has considerably less.

Most modern managers would prefer more initiative, commitment, and the taking of responsibility to come from the bottom, up, and there may be a lot of verbal encouragement along these lines. However, the encouraging words are too often contradicted by the standard meeting environment, which sends a different message, one which says that behaving in an empowered way is insubordinate, or at least unwelcome. Few staff will risk sticking their necks out in an environment permeated with external controls. This imbalance of power may be quite subtle, in an era where informality is the rule.

Just a few ways in which typical meetings exemplify S-R management are:

- Manager sits behind a desk, using it as a "power barrier" between her- or himself and staff.
- Manager sits in his or her "power seat" at a desk, staff person in a less comfortable chair on the edge of the desk or across the room.
- Manager initiates meeting by telling those present what he or she thinks or plans, rather than asking for agenda input.
- Manager asks for input, then makes decisions regardless of input and does not give feedback on how input was used, if at all.
- Group meeting takes place in a crowded space so many present cannot see each other.
- All meetings take place around a table, enabling those present to read, write, and conceal body language rather than interact openly.
- Ratio of positive to negative comments (e.g., criticism, evaluation, etc.) by manager is less than 20:1.
- Manager keeps rescheduling meetings, complaining about them, sending the message he or she does not like meeting with those individuals or groups.
- Manager gives encouragement that is unrelated, or even contrary to, attempts to achieve, belong, and the like.

- Manager rarely or never gives feedback on work that has been successful, only on mistakes (ratio of positive to negative is more like 1:20 than reverse).
- Manager criticizes individuals in front of group (including joking, ridicule, playing devil's advocate, or even temper tantrums).
- Manager is not interested in, or does not allow time for, staff self-evaluation.
- Meeting recorder writes group opinions on chart paper placed so that several in the group cannot see it.
- Meeting facilitator runs meeting with back to certain members, effectively eliminating them from participation.
- Manager relays negative criticism to person *A* from person *B,* who is absent, so that *A* is disempowered with no recourse to his or her "accuser" (triangulated communication).

This partial list of S-R meeting behavior shows that it is heavily reliant upon a meeting environment in which the S-R manager subliminally controls the outcomes, and management styles that are aimed at extrinsically controlling staff. The following exercises will show how relatively easy-to-implement modifications can help managers to achieve their desired results—a staff that is empowered and growing—therefore enhancing organizational growth and development.

Initiative, commitment, and responsibility come from involvement, engagement, and empowerment. It is only possible to foster initiative, commitment, and responsibility in a climate where they have been lacking when there are actual methods and techniques for fostering involvement, engagement, and empowerment. It is not enough to give lip service, exhorting people to behave in a more empowered way while managing them the same as always. As President Clinton quoted his wife, Hillary (at the 1992 Democratic convention): "The definition of insanity is to keep doing the same thing over and over, and expect a different result!"

Much recent literature has focused on the definition of the manager as maintainer of the status quo as differentiated from the definition of the leader as a change agent. A leader, called a lead-manager in RT, actually combines aspects of each, being able to promote stability and flexibility where each is appropriate. It is possible for the lead-manager to straddle this seeming contradiction by learning techniques and exercises that encourage and support staff to exercise internal controls. Learning the following meeting methods allows managers to evolve into leaders, becoming more dynamic and empowered themselves.

(H) CHANGE: ONE-ON-ONE

(i) *Managing for Change*
The following approach to one-on-one meetings could also be called "managing for empowerment, problem-solving, organization development, personal growth," and so on, as all of these things are accomplished in this meeting format. "Managing for change" was selected to communicate that the manager is, or has the potential to be, a change agent for the better, impacting positively on employees' morale and even on their lives in a great variety of ways.

(ii) *Managing for Change Meeting*
Exhibit 18.10 describes a step-by-step method for applying RT's control theory to one-on-one meetings, including supervisions and evaluations. This Managing for Change Meet-

EXHIBIT 18.10 Managing for Change Meeting

Managing for Change: A Two-Person Activity for Improving Staff Performance

1. **SET ASIDE TIME** without interruptions—hold phone calls, schedule from 15 to 60 minutes in a private room where others cannot see or hear the conversation.
2. **WARM-UP ACTIVITY**—spend about 10% of the total planned activity time, divided more or less equally between the two participants, talking about a matter of personal concern. Guidelines: may or may not be work-related; must be positive; preferably in one of these general areas: fun, achievement, belonging, self-determination. Get "involved." **COMMITMENT COMES FROM INVOLVEMENT.**
3. **WORKER REPORTS ACCOMPLISHMENTS**—self-assessment of own work, preferably in relation to a pre-agreed work list or plan.
4. **"SUPERVISOR"** makes *positive* observations—"I agree with . . ." and "I also observe. . . ." (positive bombardment).
5. **WORKER** identifies *one* area of improvement needed. This could be an item from prearranged plan that did not take place as planned or a new problem to be solved.
6. **"SUPERVISOR"** asks worker to make a plan. Supervisor acts as coach and does not help worker unless needed. Details and the "decision to change" come from the worker.
7. **SIGNS OF A GOOD PLAN:**
   - The smaller and more specific, the better.
   - Something doable, with high chances of success.
   - Plan has built-in help from someone else.
   - There is a deadline.
   - There is someone to report to, to be accountable for results.
8. **FOLLOW-UP**
   - Reinforce success.
   - No punishment is allowed.
   - Never give up.

GENERAL GUIDELINES:
   - Ratio of positive to negative is 20:1.
   - Supervisor plays a supporting role, not a directing role.
   - Worker, not supervisor, initiates information.

ing is an adapted version of the RT problem-solving steps.[23] The Reality Therapy Institute provides training and certification in the use of the RT steps for managers, teachers, and therapists, and training is advisable to ensure ease and accuracy of application. However, managers and supervisors are encouraged to use the steps provided here as an outline for their one-on-one meeting agendas. With practice, they will gain positive results.

To prepare for this new meeting format, it may be helpful to work with a peer manager or staff development consultant to plan and even role-play the types of dialogue that will be effective in implementing this method. So much of the ingrained S-R dialogue is directive or even coercive that it will take practice to alter old habits.

On the bright side, mutual openness and empowerment is improved when the manager is vulnerable and secure enough to experiment with a new supervisory approach in concert with staff. In this case, the medium will be the message for movement toward growth and change.

Helpful examples of the lead-manager approach to respectful, positive dialogue between manager and staff may be found in the *One Minute Manager* series of books by Kenneth H. Blanchard and his colleagues. The popularity of these books is testimony to the widespread desire of managers throughout the country to find alternative, positive means of communicating and managing. Although the books are geared toward corporate managers, they are written in a way that is mostly accessible to NPO managers.

(I) CHANGE: GROUPS

(i) *Groups as Systems*

Whenever people work or relate to one another in groups, the group becomes a system. Most managers do not see their departments, teams, organizations, and the like as systems but just as a collection of individuals. It helps managers to see the people they manage as a system because it deepens the manager's understanding of their behavior and creates the opportunity for many more ways to promote growth.

Here are two ways of illustrating how a group is a system: steel bands and families.

1. A steel band is a fun illustration of a system involving a group of people. Steel bands or orchestras can consist of 50 or 60 people playing instruments made from cutoff steel drums that are dented on top or tuned to play certain notes when struck by a drumstick. For those unfamiliar, the size of the drum and the pattern of indentations on top create different qualities of sound—bass, tenor, and so on. A drummer or pannist may play one or more drums or pans at a time, depending on her or his role in the musical spectrum. Collectively, the players are like a giant piano being played by 60 people. When their music is combined, they can play Beethoven like a symphonic orchestra, pop tunes, or the more familiar association, calypso music. While a single pannist can play a tune, the more effective renditions of steel pan are in orchestral formation, which comprises a system. Each player has a distinct role, all of which add up to an organic whole, similar to a staff group, department, team, or organization.

2. Similarly, a family composed of several individual members is a system. Family systems theory holds that different family members are unconsciously assigned roles by the family. Roles that often occur in families have come to be called universal names such as Hero, Mascot, Scapegoat, and so on. These roles may be flexible, changing according to circumstances, or they may become rigid, as in a dysfunctional family that depends for its security on people staying in their assigned roles. Family systems are analogous to groups in the workplace in several ways. Workers take on particular roles in the group, some that may be similar to family roles—Hero, Mascot, Scapegoat, and so on—and some that may be unique to the workplace—Workhorse, Risk-Taker, Malingerer, Boss, Victim, and so on.

One function of the team-building approaches that are coming into vogue is to illuminate and define various roles in working groups. Ideally, people who are different have different strengths that contribute to making a stronger whole, like the steel orchestra. When groups are not viewed as systems, people are often penalized for their differences, thus frustrating attempts to contribute and imprisoning individuals in ill-fitting roles like a dysfunctional family.

The following meeting formats tend to enhance awareness of individual strengths and reinforce the principle of flexible roles within the system.

(ii)   Groups in Action

Since such a large percentage of everyone's work life is spent in meetings, improving meetings is a key to improving performance. The recommendation for drastically changing meeting styles from the familiar, chaired, meeting to the new facilitated meeting covers every type of meeting: board, committee, department, team, whole staff, and so on. Altering the manager's role from chairperson to facilitator and meeting formats from quasi-parliamentary procedure to group participation has a significant effect on motivation, commitment, individual growth, and ultimately, organizational growth and development. Often, this will have to be demonstrated to be believed, so it is advisable to obtain outside help—demonstration meetings and/or facilitation training—from an experienced facilitator.

Following are some of the characteristics and drawbacks of chaired meetings:

- One person, the chairperson, controls all of the information.
- Participation is limited to discussions when discussion time is allowed in the meeting structure.
- Voting generally produces a win/lose result, unless the vote is unanimous, and "losers" are not optimally motivated to carry out the result.
- Parliamentary procedure (e.g., Robert's Rules), the meeting method on which chaired meetings are based, is rather complex and few laypeople know it in enough detail to make it work well.
- Many chaired meetings take place in an environment where some participants' backs are facing other participants, due to overcrowding or ill-planned room setup.
- Chaired meetings are the most familiar kind. This is their main asset. There is no learning curve to learn new skills.
- An apparent asset of chaired meetings is that their familiarity leads participants to expect that the results will be adequate. Managers and employees alike lack awareness of the potential for meetings to meet participants' psychological needs and the impact that can have on organizational growth. The hidden liability inherent in the habitual nature of chaired meetings is that expectations are kept low; no one expects to reach consensus, build community, and so on.
- Chaired meetings generally take place around a board-type table, effectively reducing communication by body language and other nonverbal cues. A study reported in *Psychology Today* magazine in the mid 1970s found that only 20 percent of communication is in the spoken word; the other 80 percent is body language, facial expression, tone of voice, and so on. Even if the percentages are exaggerated, experienced facilitators (such as the proponents of the Interaction Method) agree with the principle. Communication significantly improves when the table is removed. People attending a meeting don't have to be expert interpreters of body language for this to work. It's a case of "try it, you'll like it."

Exhibit 18.11 illustrates the basic approach to facilitated meetings, as compared with the traditional, chaired meeting. Two traditional roles—chairperson and secretary—change into the quite different roles of facilitator and recorder.

EXHIBIT 18.11 Meeting Facilitation Techniques

Facilitation Meeting Style: A Tool for Organizational Growth and Development

1. **SUPPLIES NEEDED**—Pad of large chart paper (18" × 24" or larger) or a roll of white butcher paper. Masking tape. Various colored, water-based magic markers. Identical, comfortable, movable chairs, one for each participant and facilitator. A table is optional (see Item 3.)

2. **ROOM**—A square-ish room with one flat wall, preferably with no windows. For a meeting with 6 to 10 people, room should be approximately 12′ by 12′ or larger.

3. **ROOM SETUP**—Approximately 7 to 10 sheets of chart paper taped to the flat wall at the open end of a U-shaped semicircle of chairs, all placed so that every participant can see one another and facing the chart paper. No table in the middle of the U; table to hold participants' belongings may be placed behind the chairs if needed, if room is large enough. Note: facilitator will remove empty chairs so that every chair in the U-formation is occupied, and will prevent any participant from sitting outside the U-shape.

4. **START THE MEETING**—Facilitator obtains agreement on "house rules" (breaks, refreshments, etc.), announces general purpose of meeting, and obtains agreement on agenda. If agenda was redistributed, review and ask for adjustment. If not, compose it with group. Obtain input on the ending time for the meeting. Ask group to estimate the number of minutes for each agenda item. Ask someone to be timekeeper, announcing when time for each item is nearly up.

5. **WARM-UP ACTIVITY**—Before starting agenda, spend at least two minutes per person having each participant speak on a subject that may be work-related or not. Facilitator goes first, to model the activity. Address one of RT's four basic needs: friendship, fun, achievement, self-determination. For a group new to facilitation, "fun" may be easiest. For a task- and results-oriented group, "achievement" may have more appeal. Many manuals on training contain examples of warm-up activities.

6. **GROUP MEMORY**—It has been estimated that every person brings about five fixed ideas to a meeting. Unless and until a person is assured that others recognize those five ideas, s/he will not let go of them. But unless s/he lets go, s/he can't take in any new ideas. This relatively obvious idea is one of the cornerstones of traditional meeting ineffectiveness. Paraphrasing each participants' ideas on chart paper creates a public record; when a person sees her or his ideas recorded, s/he can let go of them enough to absorb new ones. This is an essential building block for building consensus.

7. **BRAINSTORMING**—Not just a loose, informal method of discussion, brainstorming is actually a technical term with rules: generate ideas with no value judgments; quantity not quality. It is recommended to insert a true brainstorming segment into a facilitated meeting at any point where generating creative solutions would help to reframe a conflict, thus facilitating consensus.

8. **ACHIEVING CONSENSUS**—Arriving at decisions by voting is usually a win–lose situation and should be used as a last resort. In a well-managed group, the vast majority of decisions tend to be consensus decisions. The more adept a group becomes at participating in facilitated meetings, the larger the percentage of group decisions achieved by consensus. Brainstorming and group memory are but two techniques of many for achieving consensus. There are training manuals available to help achieve consensus as a habitual meeting style.

EXHIBIT 18.11 *(Continued)*

Facilitation Meeting Style: A Tool for Organizational Growth and Development

9. **RECORDING DECISIONS**—There are two approaches to producing conventional meeting minutes in a facilitated meeting. One is to have a "secretary" take notes only on final decisions, and another is for the recorder to highlight decisions in the Group Memory in a different color so that decisions can be quickly identified when the chart paper notes are being transcribed. Transcribing the Group Memory is optional. The major pros and cons are that transcription and distribution of chart paper notes promote team building, but it can be time consuming. This decision will depend on the needs of the group.

10. **CLOSURE**—A closing activity analogous to the warm-up activity has a big payoff in group dynamics. Two of the most effective closing exercises are (1) ask each participant to briefly address what s/he learned in the meeting or (2) ask each participant what s/he plans to do as a result of the meeting. This tying together of loose ends will be easier when the facilitator and timekeeper have done their jobs to keep the meeting on focus.

Carolyn Curran created this method by combining RT and *How to Make Meetings Work: The Interaction Method.*

(iii) Roles of Facilitator and Recorder

The role of facilitator is similar to that of a chairperson in attempting to elicit decisions from the group, ideally without predisposing the outcome. Almost everything else about their respective roles is different. The main similarities and differences in style between the two types of meeting leadership (facilitator and chair) are shown in Exhibit 18.12. This distinction is easier to experience than to describe because the meeting environment is also a major factor in distinguishing between the two styles.

(iv) Facilitator Techniques

If the manager plays facilitator, he or must openly indicate when he or she wears the manager hat, thus is promoting a certain point of view. One method of doing this is to step to one side when changing roles from facilitator (neutral) to manager (with a point of view or opinion) and back again. The facilitator will encourage equal participation, encouraging those who speak less and tactfully discouraging those who overstep their "equal time." An experienced and effective facilitator will constantly identify the common threads, building consensus and a positive sense of community in which each participant is a respected and important player.

(v) Recorder Techniques

Starting with the meeting's purpose and agenda (usually prepared jointly by the facilitator and group/team leader), a recorder will write on the chart paper summaries of important observations, conclusions, and recommendations throughout the meeting. There is not enough time or chart paper for the recorder to write every word that is said; therefore, paraphrasing is necessary. It is important and useful for the recorder to use some of each participant's actual words in the summation process, otherwise some attendees might feel manipulated and unheard—defeating much of the good purpose of this structure. (See item 6 in Exhibit 18.11 for further explanation.)

EXHIBIT 18.12 Chairperson and Facilitator Roles

SIMILARITIES OF CHAIR AND FACILITATOR ROLES

Elicit decisions from group.

Maintain order.

Control the flow of discussion.

Help group reach decisions.

Remain neutral or state when an opinion is being expressed.

Learn and implement meeting leader techniques.

Treat people with respect.

Allow fair and equal input.

Do not monopolize the discussion.

Ask for record/minutes of past and present meeting.

DIFFERENCES OF CHAIR AND FACILITATOR ROLES

Chair	Facilitator
• Top manager generally leads meeting	• Top manager generally delegates facilitation so that his or her opinions can be expressed more freely as a group member
• Limits input to format that is often restrictive	
• Promotes an adversarial approach to build issues by emphasis on voting	• Encourages "equal time" by each; more open communication
• Brings discussions to vote, creating "winners," "losers," and divisiveness	• Constantly identifies common threads to build unity, illuminating differences in facts and unity without prejudice
• Prepares agenda	
• Decides how much time to spend on each issue	• Builds consensus, creating unity and motivation
• Expects participants to keep meeting details in their heads or to take notes to help group follow discussion	• Voting can be done as a last resort
	• Prepares an agenda guide; elicits input to finalize
	• Guides group to make a timely meeting plan
	• Provides "group memory" (chart paper notes) which promotes interaction

Facilitation and recording can be done by one person or two people in different roles, with advantages and disadvantages to each choice. One person can create more congruence between leading the discussion and recording it, but time taken to record will slow the action a bit, depending on how fast he or she writes. A separate recorder will speed the action but may be left out of verbal participation or intrude on facilitation. To separate the roles effectively, the two must establish good communication between them.

Meeting facilitation has many practitioners with different ideological and practical variations. The style shown in Exhibit 18.11, used successfully with hundreds of groups for nearly 20 years, is an amalgam of RT and the Interaction Method, a compendium of techniques developed by David Straus and Michael Doyle, authors of the classic *How to Make Meetings Work*, a paperback full of useful tips that will help every NPO manager to improve meetings and, as a result, performance and productivity.

(J) POTENTIAL GROWTH AREAS

The OD field offers a vast amount of resources in addition to these two examples of meeting styles and their conceptual underpinnings from the fields of RT and facilitation. Just a few, brief examples follow.

- Appreciative inquiry, a relatively low-key approach that is apparently seeping into corporate OD while trying not to become trendy, is a wonderful tool for establishing trust and vision in the workplace. It is based, as its title implies, on developing a series of positive questions posed to managers. In seeking to answer the questions, the managers and the organizations they manage are greatly reinforced and validated, preparing a positive foundation for growth. This philosophy for change, as it calls itself, is appealingly described in a small booklet, appropriately called *The Thin Book of Appreciative Inquiry* by Sue Annis Hammond of Kodiak Consulting in Plano, Texas, and may be ordered from her.
- The focus on creating learning organizations that goes way beyond sending staff to the occasional seminar is enthusiastically described in the popular *Fifth Discipline*[24] and its accompanying book of hands-on exercises, *The Fifth Discipline Fieldbook.* Openness to change is at the heart of their concept. The *Fieldbook* defines a learning organization as "groups of people who, over time, enhance their capacity to create what they truly desire to create." It goes on to say that people are changed by this process, often profoundly. As people gain new skills and capabilities, their awareness and sensibilities grow so that they experience the world differently with new beliefs and assumptions. This, in turn, prompts the development of further skills and capabilities. Author Peter Senge calls this the "deep learning cycle" because it results in fundamental shifts of mind, individually and collectively in the organization.
- True creativity is being increasingly sought by corporations and taught by OD practitioners. While many managers may appear to embrace creativity to generate new products and services or find new ways of delivering them, the corporate environment generally does not support the kinds of risk-taking involved because there is a great corporate need to look good, hide failure for fear of repercussions, and so on. This dichotomy was expressed in the 1997 national OD conference, whose theme was "Advancing Our OD Practices Amidst Paradox," meaning the apparent paradoxes inherent in balancing needs for a humanistic workplace and the bottom line. OD consultant firms such as TAI Resources in New York City and Basler Associates in Westport, Connecticut, have built their entire practices on facilitating creativity and openness to change.

(K) PROGNOSIS FOR NONPROFIT ORGANIZATION DEVELOPMENT

(i) *Signs of Growth in Nonprofit Organization Development*

Now is the time for increased attention to OD in the nonprofit sector. Nonprofit organization OD will become more widespread as NPO managers become more aware of OD's potential to foster organizational survival and growth. One good sign is the several workshops on nonprofit OD at the national 1997 conference of Organization Development

Network (ODN), the professional association for OD practitioners, indicating a national presence. Another is the increasing use of facilitation-style meetings for special retreats, strategic planning meetings, team building, and the like. With encouragement, there will be a spillover effect into regular meetings.

Signs of receptivity to OD observed with the author's clients are:

- First responses to new meeting and supervision styles among a range of groups from grassroots to established is generally enthusiastic.
- Once organizations experience good results from several facilitation-style meetings, they tend to automatically continue it themselves without outside help and tend not to return to the old chaired-style meetings.

(ii) Hurdles to Be Overcome

Despite these positive signs, there are conditions working to slow the adoption of OD practices on a broad scale. In addition to some of the general constraints against change mentioned earlier in the chapter, there are additional challenges to be met.

- Nonprofit organization TA generalists think of themselves as being involved in OD, although relatively few have the OD concepts and skills used in the corporate OD field. A small but growing number of TA providers are shifting their perceptions and services, which will open the TA field to new approaches that actually do support OD as a system of change and humanization of work.
- Both the nonprofit and corporate sectors have organizations that represent the full range of corporate cultures and managers, from the most open to the most closed to change. One factor that would promote OD in both sectors is being able to more easily quantify the positive impact of it. This point of view was succinctly expressed on the PBS program, *The Excellence Files,* by Fran Sussner Rogers, CEO and founder of Work Family Directions, a firm that provides family support services for corporations. She said, "The day we put employee commitment on the balance sheet, we will take it more seriously." The nonprofit sector has an additional challenge, that of measuring results other than the financial bottom line.

(iii) Looking to the Future

The nonprofit sector as a whole is approaching its fourth decade as a sizable force in American life. The Independent Sector, in analyzing nonprofit sector trends, predicts that in 10 years, the size of the nonprofit sector may dominate or seriously challenge the other two sectors—government and business.[25] As it is, the nonprofit sector employs more than 10 percent of the national workforce;[26] in New York City, NPO employees outnumber the Wall Street investment community.[27]

This robust picture represents phenomenal growth since the mid-1960s, when there were relatively few NPOs apart from large institutions like colleges, hospitals, and churches, the local Ys, Girl/Boy Scouts, and Red Cross chapters. During the early boom years of smaller NPOs, the resistance to adopting management techniques was quite high. There was a time when grassroots groups said that bookkeeping was an establishment conspiracy to keep minority groups down, and the word "marketing" was anathema to the altruistic values of those dedicated to community service.

EXHIBIT 18.13 Some Perceived Barriers and Facilitators of OD for Nonprofit Organization Managers

Perceived Barrier to OD	Steps That Facilitate OD
Understaffing	• Clarify links between program priorities and job descriptions—an OD systems approach—thus possibly reducing the need for more staff. • Empower present staff with OD-style supervision and meetings to improve productivity and reduce or eliminate the need for more staff. • Envision the ideal staff, develop job descriptions, and raise funds for staff proactively, without waiting for Godot. • Explore innovative ways to budget operating expenses and diversify funding streams to yield a bigger percentage for operating.
Task-orientation, narrow focus	• Apply "appreciative inquiry" to support positive staff development for more equitable redistribution of work. • Strengthen the global picture (the organization's mission) and build a sense of community to allow narrowly focused staff to meet their needs in a broader way. • Re-sensitize staff to their needs by asking more questions and responding in incremental ways. • Encourage staff to support each other; be an example. • Be friendlier.
Lack of time to learn OD	• "Work smarter, not harder"—for example, incorporate new meeting or supervision styles in place of existing meetings rather than adding a big block of extra training. • Calculate current time lost to discouragement, complaining to coworkers to feel better, miscommunication, and so on—compare this time lost to a work schedule without these deterrents—learning OD will provide a net gain of time! • Examine the perceived lack of time and see if it isn't perhaps a displacement issue for fear of change; if so, try to be brave and think about the potential rewards.
Fear of loss of control	• Trade off the appearance of externally controlling staff behavior for the actuality of their exercising internally motivated control to reap the many benefits of a more productive workforce. • Employ an OD professional to help make the transition. • Sometimes, a manager's excess need for controlling others reflects lack of a sense of self-control; if so, the remedy may be finding ways to become more spiritual, get in touch with core values that strengthen the "inner you."
Lack of money to pay OD professionals	• Seek free or low-cost help from the nearest university human resources or OD department. • Ask corporate supporters to supply volunteers from their HR departments. • Write a proposal for capacity-building assistance, including OD, and seek funds for it. • Visualize what you need; it will come.

Government cutbacks and other Darwinian forces have winnowed the nonprofit sector considerably in the past decade, selecting out those with high levels of resistance to the forces of change, and overall, leaving those with more effective management and leadership, more adept at incorporating new survival skills as needed. Increasingly, they will use OD techniques and approaches to obtain a more dedicated, empowered, and motivated workforce of both paid staff and volunteers.

As mentioned earlier, 80 percent of nonprofit organizations nationally have budgets under $1 million. The typically small NPO employs fewer than 20 people, which makes it more flexible to manage, relative to larger institutions with bigger staffs. The flexibility of smaller organizations lends itself to the incubation of more humanistic approaches to management that can prove their value and be adopted by larger institutions. Small- and medium-sized NPOs have the potential to become learning laboratories for OD.

Ultimately, it is up to individuals to promote an OD or systems approach to organizational growth and change. Studies have shown that the most successful change often does not start at the very top. Successful change can bubble up from the bottom, starting at the periphery of power, and succeed when managers of the department or group become involved and lead it.[28]

For those managers who want to find ways to adapt more OD practices to their organization, refer to Exhibit 18.13. It gives an idea of how to cope with some of the most common barriers, most of which boil down to money or apprehension about trying something new.

Endnotes

1. Senge, P. M. (1990). *The Fifth Discipline: The Art and Practice of the Learning Organization.* New York: Doubleday.
2. *Nonprofit Almanac: Dimensions of the Independent Sector.* (1977). Washington, DC: Independent Sector.
3. Burke, W. W. (1992). *Organization Development.* New York: Addison-Wesley.
4. See note 2.
5. Connors, T. (1979). *Nonprofit Organization Handbook.* New York: McGraw-Hill.
6. Id.
7. See note 3.
8. Hammond, S. A. (1996). *The Thin Book of Appreciative Inquiry.* Plano, TX: Kodiak Consulting.
9. Hampden-Turner, C. (1978). *Radical Man: the Process of Psycho-social Development.* Books on demand.
10. See note 3.
11. Quinn, R. E. (1996). *Deep Change, Discovering the Leader Within.* San Francisco: Jossey-Bass, pp. 158–166.
12. Kotter, J. P. (1995). "Leading Change: Why Transformation Efforts Fail," *Harvard Business Review* (March–April).
13. See note 2.
14. Adapted from the Adirondack Mountain Humanistic Education Center.
15. Glasser, W. (1994). *The Control Theory Manager, Combining the Control Theory of William Glasser with the Wisdom of W. Edwards Deming to Explain Both What Quality Is and What Lead-Managers Do to Achieve It.* New York: HarperBusiness, p. 65.

16. Glasser, W. (1965). *Reality Therapy, A New Approach to Psychiatry.* New York: Harper & Row.

17. Powers, W. (1973). *Behavior: The Control of Perception.* Chicago: Aldine Press.

18. Glasser, W. (1984). *Control Theory.* New York: Harper & Row.

19. See note 15, p. 51.

20. Id., p. 52.

21. Id., p. 95.

22. Gordon, T. (1980). *Leader Effectiveness Training (L.E.T.) The No-Lose Way to Release the Productive Potential of People.* New York: Bantam.

23. See note 16.

24. See note 1.

25. Spring Research Conference. (March 1997). "Measuring the Influence and Impact of the Nonprofit Sector on Society." Washington, DC: Independent Sector.

26. See note 2.

27. Newsletter. (1995). New York: Nonprofit Coordinating Committee.

28. Beer, M. R., A. Eisenstsat, and B. Specter. (1990). "Why Change Programs Don't Produce Change," *Harvard Business Review* (November–December).

Suggested Readings

Adizes, I. (1988). *Corporate Lifecycles: How and Why Corporations Grow and Die and What to Do About It.* New York: Prentice Hall.

Bridges, W. (1991). *Managing Transitions: Making the Most of Change.* Reading, MA: Addison-Wesley.

Churchill, N. C., and V. L. Lewis. (1983). "The Five Stages of Small Business Growth," *Harvard Business Review* (May 1).

DePree, M. (1989). *Leadership Is an Art.* New York: Dell Publishing.

Drucker, P. (1995). *Entrepreneurship and Innovation.* New York: HarperCollins Business.

Franco, N. S., S. Gross, and K. Mathiasen. (1982). *Passages: Organizational Life Cycles.* Santa Barbara, CA: Management Assistance Group (May–June).

Gozdz, K. (ed.). (1995). *Community Building, Renewing Spirit & Learning in Business.* San Francisco: Sterling and Stone, Inc.

"Growing Up Nonprofit: An Essay on Nonprofit Life Cycle Development." St. Paul, MN: The Stevens Group.

Jaworski, J. (1998). *Synchronicity: On Leadership.* San Francisco: Berrett-Koehler.

Kelleher, D., and K. McLaren with R. Bisson. (1996). *Grabbing the Tiger by the Tail: NGOs Learning for Organizational Change.* Ottawa, Ontario, Canada: Canadian Council for International Cooperation.

Mathiasen, K. (1990). "Board Passages: Three Key Stages in a Nonprofit Board's Life Cycle." Washington, DC: National Center for Nonprofit Boards.

Sashkin, M., and K. J. Kiser. (1993). *Putting Total Quality Management to Work, What TQM Means, How to Use It and How to Sustain It over the Long Run.* San Francisco: Berrett-Koehler.

Straus, D., and M. Doyle. (1993). *How to Make Meetings Work.* New York: Berkley Books.

PART II Efficiency

Fund-Raising Management

JAMES M. GREENFIELD, ACFRE, FAHP
Hoag Memorial Hospital Presbyterian

19.1 Management of the Fund Development Process
    (a) Mission, Vision, and Values
    (b) Managing Prospects and Donors
    (c) Managing Solicitation Activities

19.2 Revenue Sources
    (a) Annual Giving Programs
    (b) Major Gift and Campaign Programs
    (c) Planned Giving Programs
    (d) Leadership and Voluntary Action
    (e) Cultivation, Solicitation, and Donor Relations
    (f) Building Relationships
    (g) Accountability, Ethics, and Stewardship

19.3 General Areas for Policy and Procedures
Appendix: A Manual of Fund Development Policy and Procedure for Nonprofit Organizations
Endnotes
Suggested Readings

"Hence also it is no easy task to be good. For in everything it is no easy task to find the middle, . . . or to give or spend money; but to do this to the right person, to the right extent, at the right time, with the right motive, and in the right way, that is not for everyone, nor is it easy; Wherefore, goodness is both rare and laudable and noble."

Aristotle (384–322 B.C.)[1]

19.1 Management of the Fund Development Process

The essential characteristic of a successful fund-raising program is quite easy to define—ask for the gift! Were it that simple, no one would need to know anything more about it. What complicates asking is which solicitation method to use, whom to ask and when, who does the asking, what the money is for, who benefits from its use, how much to request, how much is tax-deductible, how much to spend on asking, and many more crucial questions. Asking for gifts is a much more complex and challenging task than many believe and appreciate.

Fund development has been described as "planned promotion for participation, understanding and support."[2] But fund raising is not the mission of nonprofit organizations; it is a means to aid them in fulfilling their mission. Nonprofit organizations are dedicated to public benefit and community service, and philanthropy is the means whereby the public is invited to participate. Philanthropy has been defined as "voluntary action for the public good,"[3] and the scope of fund-raising practices is composed of the methods most often employed in asking people to volunteer their time and money. It helps to remember always that giving is voluntary. Those valued people we call volunteers must be identified, recruited, trained, supported, rewarded, and thanked many times, just as donors also must be cultivated and treated. Fund raising is an action-oriented contact sport and a team effort. It relies on people and depends on their performance (how their time, talent, effort, and money are used), and relies on their confidence and trust perseverance in helping their chosen nonprofit organization to achieve its mission. Success is best measured not in how many volunteers or donors are involved, nor in how much money was raised, but in how their combined efforts and funds were used to benefit others. Outcomes measurement, an inadequate exercise today, is the true test of both philanthropic practice and the mission of nonprofit organizations (NPOs).

To be successful, NPOs must understand the relationship among institutional decisions, as guided by their mission, purposes, goals, and objectives, the quality of the programs and services they offer, and the public's interest and willingness to support their current and future endeavors. Public support is based largely on that same public's confidence in the worth of the organization followed by their trust in its board of directors, in whom their money is invested, to "do the right thing" for the community. The most essential ingredient to successful fund development is a well-founded and well-documented master plan for the NPO. The organization that has carefully evaluated its present ability, measured its capacity against unmet public needs, and defined how it can address these needs successfully provides the best reason for the public to join the effort—because it knows and can document its purpose and can explain exactly how it will use their money. Lacking this essential plan, fund raising is only about asking for money and can never achieve much above "pocket change" from those asked to give.

(A) MISSION, VISION, AND VALUES

A mission statement is a declaration of the organization's cause or purpose for being. It explains why the organization exists and what it is dedicated to accomplish, and identifies its purpose, goals, and objectives. It also is a summary argument that invites the public to participate in a list of community benefit projects that it is dedicated to deliver. In combination, the mission statement is what qualifies this enterprise both as a tax-exempt charitable organization and a public benefit corporation under the law. Mission statements also are required to have legitimate legal structure with a voluntary board of directors who take responsibility for all services provided, commit themselves to be faithful to the mission, and promise that all funds received will be used in fulfillment of that mission and not for the private inurement of any board member, employee, client, or other person involved.

Most mission statements are found in the articles of incorporation. They should be written in simple and precise language with noble aims that promise to deliver defined services of benefit to the community. This text can be quite different from agency to agency, but all must contain a basic charitable purpose to qualify for both federal and state legal standing and to enjoy the privileges of income, sales, and property tax exemption plus deductibility for contributions. Exhibit 19.1 provides an assessment criteria tool to measure success in achieving what the mission declares. To succeed with its mission, every NPO will require public participation at various levels in the form of voluntary service by the board of directors and a fund development committee charged with raising the money it needs to carry out the mission.

EXHIBIT 19.1 Assessment Criteria for the Mission

	Low		Score		High
1. Fulfills a "charitable" purpose	1	2	3	4	5
2. Completes annual public reporting requirements	1	2	3	4	5
3. Provides high quality of service	1	2	3	4	5
4. Offers accessibility to service	1	2	3	4	5
5. Increases public awareness of the cause	1	2	3	4	5
6. Addresses five advocacy measurements	1	2	3	4	5
7. Adequately uses audits and auditors	1	2	3	4	5
8. Is financially accountable	1	2	3	4	5
9. Stimulates innovative ideas	1	2	3	4	5
10. Provides programs of value to the public	1	2	3	4	5
11. Develops new leadership	1	2	3	4	5
12. Is guided by written policies and procedures	1	2	3	4	5

MEDIAN SCORE

Reprinted from "Fund-Raising Assessment," in Greenfield, J.M. (ed.). (1997). *The Nonprofit Handbook: Fund Raising,* 2nd ed. New York: John Wiley & Sons, p. 134.

To be actively engaged as a viable NPO today requires a mission statement that incorporates noble purpose, community benefit, government endorsement, legal structure, voluntary leadership, and stewardship of funds, all of which are to be carried out in the open. There is nothing private about a public benefit corporation. These are the essential components, and all must be in place before an organization can begin to ask the public for gift support.

A *vision* for an organization is a conceptualization of what it aspires to become, even a statement of dreams and aspirations based on the mission. It is equally important that it be written in simple and precise language and capture what the organization's leaders believe are priority community needs, what they care about strongly, and what they perceive is a reasonable and possible plan of action to achieve the mission. At its best, it is a shared vision, a broad consensus of common views held by the board of directors, executive director, top management and professional staff, donors and volunteers, and even the direct recipients of its programs and services. Such a vision can generate enthusiasm and attract others to join the cause, working together as a united front committed to doing the work required that will achieve something of value. Harold J. (Si) Seymour, an early fund-raising professional, wrote that to realize public participation and support, a vision statement should be one that "covers the ground, aims high, catches the eye and ear, warms the heart, stirs the mind, and creates the right mood of relevance, importance, urgency, supported by faith and confidence."[4]

An organization's *values* statements also is essential. Values are a statement of the inner culture and beliefs of the organization. These values are the guideposts for the organization's consistent behavior toward everyone it contacts, serves, and employs. All who are associated with this organization should be informed that these are the values expected to be adhered to in their daily work. Those who are invited to participate as donors and volunteers also will be encouraged to accept these values as a part of their lives as well. For fund-raising purposes, here is where the Donor Bill of Rights should reside as an approved policy statement by the board of directors (see Exhibit 19.2).

EXHIBIT 19.2 A Donor Bill of Rights

A Donor Bill of Rights

PHILANTHROPY is based on voluntary action for the common good. It is a tradition of giving and sharing that is primary to the quality of life. To assure that philanthropy merits the respect and trust of the general public, and that donors and prospective donors can have full confidence in the nonprofit organizations and causes they are asked to support, we declare that all donors have these rights:

I.
To be informed of the organization's mission, of the way the organization intends to use donated resources, and of its capacity to use donations effectively for their intended purposes.

II.
To be informed of the identity of those serving on the organization's governing board, and to expect the board to exercise prudent judgment in its stewardship responsibilities.

III.
To have access to the organization's most recent financial statements.

IV.
To be assured their gifts will be used for the purposes for which they were given.

V.
To receive appropriate acknowledgment and recognition.

VI.
To be assured that information about their donations is handled with respect and with confidentiality to the extent provided by law.

VII.
To expect that all relationships with individuals representing organizations of interest to the donor will be professional in nature.

VIII.
To be informed whether those seeking donations are volunteers, employees of the organization, or hired solicitors.

IX.
To have the opportunity for their names to be deleted from the mailing lists that an organization may intend to share.

X.
To feel free to ask questions when making a donation and to receive prompt, truthful, and forthright answers.

DEVELOPED BY	ENDORSED BY
AMERICAN ASSOCIATION OF FUND RAISING COUNSEL (AAFRC)	(INFORMATION) INDEPENDENT SECTOR
ASSOCIATION FOR HEALTHCARE PHILANTHROPY (AHP)	NATIONAL CATHOLIC DEVELOPMENT CONFERENCE (NCDC)
COUNCIL FOR ADVANCEMENT AND SUPPORT OF EDUCATION (CASE)	NATIONAL COMMITTEE ON PLANNED GIVING (NCPG)
NATIONAL SOCIETY OF FUND RAISING EXECUTIVES (NSFRE)	NATIONAL COUNCIL FOR RESOURCE DEVELOPMENT (NCRD) UNITED WAY OF AMERICA

Reprinted from Greenfield, J. M. (1994). *Fund-Raising Fundamentals.* New York: John Wiley & Sons, p. 363.

Sharing the mission, vision, and values is an essential part of the fund-raising story and provides strong answers to two important questions raised about the organization: "Why do you exist?" and "What's the money for?" Without great answers to these large questions, public participation and support may be inadequate and unsuccessful.

(B) MANAGING PROSPECTS AND DONORS

Every nonprofit organization has friends and supporters, even if it is largely unknown, unpopular, or even unliked. People believe in causes and become advocates for "their" cause. They will join with others to improve the quality of their own and others' lives and to help the cause, be it the environment, animals, or inanimate objects. In all these efforts, they advocate the merits of the cause to others and invite them to join, with the key words being *advocate* and *invite*. Solicitation of their time, talent, energy, and money follows their conviction of the worth, merits, and benefits of the cause itself.

Volunteerism is immensely strong in America and growing worldwide. Research studies by Independent Sector report that one of every two American adults spends 4.2 hours per week in some voluntary capacity.[5] Volunteerism is also a critical factor in gift decisions; individuals who give of their time also give twice as generously ($1,155 compared with $601) as those who do not. And those volunteers who are also regular participants in religious organizations are the most generous of all, with 78 percent making contributions each year.

How much do Americans give and where do they give? Although there is no single authority for such data, the American Association of Fund Raising Counsel[6] has collected and reported giving statistics for more than 40 years. Their most recent annual report reveals that $190 billion in contributions were made to charities in 1999, a significant increase of $16 billion over 1998 (see Exhibit 19.3). That sum is greater than the total annual operating budgets of any state in the union and of most nations around the world. Further, and surprising to some, $144 billion of these contributions were made by living individuals (76 percent), plus another $16 billion (8.2 percent) came in the form of bequests, for a total of $160 billion or 84 percent of *all* contributions. A common misconception is that corporations and foundations are the major sources of annual contributions. Combined, their percentage share in 1999 was 16 percent, for a total of $31 billion. This kind of factual data should be used to help correct assertions made by some, including government officials when considering cuts in social, welfare, education, and health programs, that corporations and foundations can "make up the difference" for government's reduced societal spending.

These generous contributions reflect the giving public's decisions of where they believe the needs are greatest, which may not correspond to government perceptions or decisions. The 1999 distributions were religious organizations (43 percent), human service organizations (9 percent), education (14 percent), health care institutions (10 percent), and the arts and culture (6 percent). To expect an already generous public to increase their support in amounts equal to government devolution is unlikely, if not impossible.

People give for a multitude of reasons (see Exhibit 19.4). Corporations give with an eye toward self-interest goals, and foundations make grants only where projects match up well with their defined purposes and priorities. Matching the priority of needs as well as the mission, purposes, goals, and objectives of NPOs with these three revenue sources is both the art and science of fund development. It is important to appreciate that to succeed

EXHIBIT 19.3 Charitable Contributions

1999 Philanthropy: $190.16 Billion

By Source of Contribution

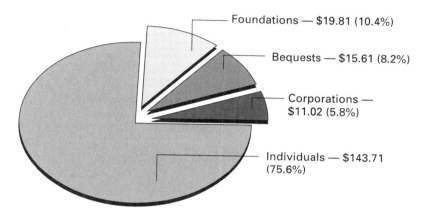

Foundations — $19.81 (10.4%)

Bequests — $15.61 (8.2%)

Corporations — $11.02 (5.8%)

Individuals — $143.71 (75.6%)

By Type of Recipient Organization

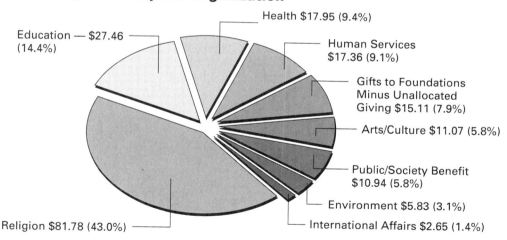

Health $17.95 (9.4%)

Education — $27.46 (14.4%)

Human Services $17.36 (9.1%)

Gifts to Foundations Minus Unallocated Giving $15.11 (7.9%)

Arts/Culture $11.07 (5.8%)

Public/Society Benefit $10.94 (5.8%)

Environment $5.83 (3.1%)

Religion $81.78 (43.0%)

International Affairs $2.65 (1.4%)

Fast Facts about Giving in 1999
- Charitable contributions increased $15.8 billion in 1999.
- Giving as a percentage of personal income has grown steadily from 1.5% in 1995, to 1.8% in 1999.
- Individual giving rose an estimated $11.63 billion last year.
- Individuals account for more than 90% of the total giving each year through outright gifts and bequests.
- Personal giving to foundations has increased more than 10% every year over the last decade.

Source: Giving USA 2000/AAFRC Trust for Philanthropy.

EXHIBIT 19.4 Framework for Determining Why People Give

Internal Motivations	External Influences
Personal or "I" Factors	*Rewards*
Acceptance of self or self-esteem	Recognition
Achievement	Personal
Cognitive	Social
Growth	
Guilt reduction or avoidance	*Stimulations*
Meaning or purpose of life	Human needs
Personal gain or benefit	Personal request
Spirituality	Vision
Immortality	Private initiative
Survival	Efficiency and effectiveness
	Tax deductions
Social or "We" Factors	
Status	*Situations*
Affiliation	Personal involvement
Group endeavor	Planning and decision making
Interdependence	Peer pressure
Altruism	Networks
Family and progeny	Family involvement
Power	Culture
	Tradition
Negative or "They" Factors	Role identity
Frustration	Disposable income
Unknown situations	
Insecurity	
Fear and anxiety	
Complexity	

Source: Reprinted with permission from Mixer, J. R. (1993). *Principles of Professional Fundraising.* San Francisco: Jossey-Bass, p. 14.

in receiving gifts from any individual, corporation, or foundation is a major accomplishment and never accidental.

Because NPOs are not the same in how they define their mission and purposes, in what "their" community's priority of needs may be, and in how they carry out their programs and services for community benefit, such diversity makes for a multitude of challenges to each entity that is engaged in charitable work. They must define their daily activity with great precision in order to reach exactly the people or issues their mission is dedicated to address, or else their impact or ability to solve problems is limited or misdirected. In most instances around the nation and the world, these public needs are obvious—hunger, housing, health, education, not to mention equal access and equal opportunity for all. In other settings, it is less visible or we are just unaware and, as a result, the voice that brings the message to awaken us is not easily heard.

In order to be heard as well as effective in stimulating a response, communications require both funds and expertise when delivering the desired message repeatedly over multiple channels. Another objective of these communications is to reach and stimulate contributor candidates, whether for their time, talent, energy, financial support, or all of these. Not everyone who receives information or even receives a service provided by an NPO is able to help. Certainly those who must use a homeless shelter or soup kitchen, or receive funds to attend college or go to summer camp, are grateful for the service they enjoyed, but they are not likely (at the moment) to do much to help the organization advance its mission—or are they? At another time, they may be better able to help. It is important to remember that those whom you serve also may be able to serve you in the future.

Volunteers and donors are more than valuable partners in the daily operations of an NPO; they are its friends and advocates, its foot soldiers, its "arms and legs," and its "eyes" in the community. The value of their hours of volunteer service alone, estimated to represent half the adult population, if measured by the minimum wage at $4.25, is in the tens of millions. What they permit NPOs to do is to allocate their limited resources to the most critical areas of day-to-day operations. Volunteers and donors also are the most flexible resources an NPO may have because they can respond to new directions, address new challenges, and give with greater generosity (any of these or all) when the need arises. Those who are donors, because of the added dimension of financial accountability, deserve additional consideration. Recognition and reward for sharing their personal resources are always appropriate, but more valuable to both donors and their chosen charity is respect. The Donor Bill of Rights has been prepared to guide nonprofit organizations in their relations with their contributors (see Exhibit 19.2). This text should be formally adopted by the board of directors of every NPO as both its policy and practice with respect to both volunteers and donors.

(C)   MANAGING SOLICITATION ACTIVITIES

Given the value of volunteers and donors and their absolute necessity to every NPO in the successful pursuit of its mission, the methods and techniques that invite public participation should command high attention within each NPO. Too often, fund raising is viewed only as a source of money rather than a carefully managed resource whose full agenda includes constituency building, friend raising, relationship building, marketing and communications, community relations, solicitation activities, recognition and reward, and more.

The best use of the methods and techniques of solicitation is to see them as a continuum of resource development, financial investment, volunteer and leadership development, and institutional advancement. The day-to-day practice of identifying and inviting new prospects to join with others in ongoing annual and major gift support is conducted in conjunction with educating and involving those donors who have already begun their support so that their combined interest and enthusiasm results in faithful giving over many years. This level of commitment has the potential to provide several annual and major gifts and even a portion of their estate in the future. Appreciate this hypothesis: No individual, corporation, or foundation is likely to make their largest gift to a nonprofit organization *first*; but they may make many such gifts over a lifetime if enjoined in a

positive and rewarding relationship by that same NPO. The fund development process is the guidebook for achieving lifetime relationships.

Successful fund development is a planned mix of donor and volunteer contacts, growth, and commitment, as illustrated in the Pyramid of Giving (see Exhibit 19.5). Actual solicitation methods are identified in three groups or tiers, beginning with annual giving at the bottom of the pyramid. Nearly every NPO is or should be engaged in one or more forms of annual giving. As these activities mature on their own, they expand their performance and professionalism to higher levels, where greater sophistication in major and planned gift solicitation and management are required. Those organizations that are most

EXHIBIT 19.5 The Pyramid of Giving

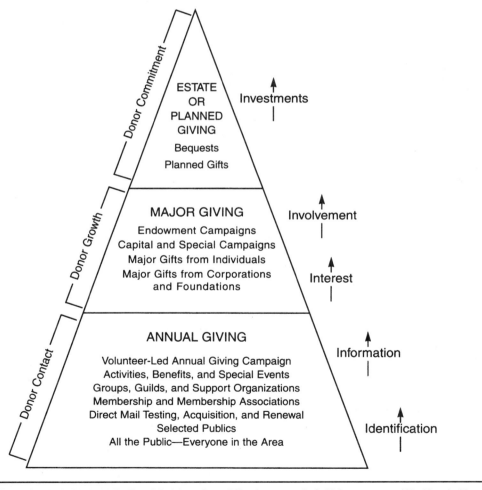

Source: Greenfield, J. M. (1996). *Fund-Raising Cost Effectiveness: A Self-Assessment Workbook.* New York: John Wiley & Sons, p. 132. Reprinted by permission of John Wiley & Sons, Inc.

successful have invested both time and money in building and maintaining the entire pyramid as an organized and structured investment program. A continuous series of cultivation, solicitation, and donor relations activities are well integrated among all three program levels, which concentrates on volunteers and donors as a team, and which is well managed by professional fund-raising executives using principles of coordination, cooperation, and communication.

Annual goals and objectives can be established for each area and useful measurement conducted regularly to monitor performance and progress. NPOs should expect a seasoned fund development program (three to five years of operation) to be effective in carrying out these multiple tasks. Newcomers must invest in the basics of annual giving and grow their programs into a fully integrated pyramid of independent yet coordinated series of activities. Performance measurement tools are available and can be applied to each area to attest to its utility. It is recommended that each solicitation activity be measured using a uniform performance index (see Exhibit 19.6); a minimum of three years is required to achieve reliable performance levels, depending on internal investment and the organization's own ability to deliver valued benefits to the community. Each solicitation activity also has a different performance level. Most are built on the previous support achieved by volunteers and donors, as outlined in the pyramid of giving, plus its own experience in managing each individual method. Fund raising, like the NPO it serves, does not perform the same for every organization. To understand the effectiveness and efficiency of your current solicitation activities, measure each fund-raising program against its own prior performance, *not* against that of other NPOs.

Internal and external factors exert substantial influences over the potential for success in solicitation activities (see Exhibit 19.7). For example, every organization cannot be addressing the most urgent of community needs. Mission statements will differ (education is not health; art and culture are not welfare). The sources of gift support, be they individuals, corporations, or foundations, also have perceptions of issues and causes in need, which differ widely, just as does their individual ability to provide quality voluntary

---

EXHIBIT 19.6 Solicitation Performance Index

Nine-Step Performance Index

1. Participants	=	Number of donors responding with gifts
2. Income Received	=	Gross contributions received
3. Expenses	=	Fund-raising costs (direct, indirect, overhead)
4. Percent Participation	=	Divide participants by total solicitations made
5. Average Gift Size	=	Divide income received by participants
6. Net Income	=	Subtract expenses from income received
7. Average Cost Per Gift	=	Divide expenses by participants
8. Cost of Fund-Raising	=	Divide expenses by income received; × 100
9. Return	=	Divide net income by expenses; × 100

Source: Greenfield, J. M. (1996). *Fund-Raising Cost Effectiveness.* New York: John Wiley & Sons.

EXHIBIT 19.7 Environmental Audit for Fund-Raising Programs

	SCORE				
Group A: External Environmental Factors	low				high
Clear mission, purposes, goals, and objectives	1	2	3	4	5
Competition, image, and market position	1	2	3	4	5
Public confidence in programs and services	1	2	3	4	5
Board leadership and competency	1	2	3	4	5
Management leadership and competency	1	2	3	4	5
Fiscal management and profitability	1	2	3	4	5
Overall economic conditions	1	2	3	4	5
Overall political and government conditions	1	2	3	4	5
Geographic location (urban or rural)	1	2	3	4	5
Accepted style of local fund-raising practice	1	2	3	4	5
Media attention to fund-raising scandals	1	2	3	4	5
Median Scores Subtotal: _____					
Group B: Internal Environmental Factors	low				high
Type of nonprofit organization	1	2	3	4	5
Written long-range and strategic plan	1	2	3	4	5
Board leadership, background, and attitude	1	2	3	4	5
Ethics and professionalism	1	2	3	4	5
Employee wages and benefits	1	2	3	4	5
Status of debt financing	1	2	3	4	5
Pressure for cash	1	2	3	4	5
Commitment to develop an endowment	1	2	3	4	5
Volume and variety of fund-raising practices	1	2	3	4	5
Leadership development program	1	2	3	4	5
Volunteer recruitment and training	1	2	3	4	5
Availability of new prospects	1	2	3	4	5
Existing donors for renewal and upgrading	1	2	3	4	5
Access to wealth	1	2	3	4	5
Focus on major gift cultivation and solicitation	1	2	3	4	5
Professional staff and fund-raising counsel	1	2	3	4	5
Appropriate staff, space, budget, and systems	1	2	3	4	5
Operating donor recognition program	1	2	3	4	5
Median Scores Subtotal: _____					
Median Scores Grand Total: _____					

assistance and strong financial support. A successful fund development program must be designed to address its most likely constituents, must communicate with them in the most effective and efficient ways possible, must invite their support for the most urgent of priorities, and must employ the best and most talented of volunteers and staff that it can recruit and afford. To know what to do, even how to do it, is easy to explain, but in the end, good old hard work wins the day.

19.2 Revenue Sources

NPOs rely on charitable contributions as an essential source of revenue for their annual operations. A generous public will act on factual information and, possessing of confidence and trust, will give their money for good works to benefit others. This revenue enables NPOs to carry out their mission, purpose, goals, and objectives for public benefit.

Public solicitation is carried out by NPOs using several fund-raising methods and techniques, often in combination. Supervision of these interactive and interdependent activities begins with the board of directors because stewardship, the board's chief responsibility, includes developing revenue along with proper investment and management of funds raised. Policy and procedures for fund raising begin with the board and flow to guidelines and operating rules for all elements of the fund-raising enterprise (see Appendix).

There is great breadth to fund development and, given the importance of each of the several forms of revenue it produces, a comprehensive policies and procedures manual for its successful conduct is highly necessary. These will explain direction and purpose for every phase of solicitation activity. A sample of a board-level policy and procedure manual for management of resource development is provided as the Appendix to this chapter and has been written as a comprehensive guide to an overall fund development program.

Fund development is, of necessity, a highly coordinated and cooperative program designed to yield maximum public support for NPOs. The methods and techniques of fund raising are segregated into three broad operating areas: annual giving, major giving, and planned giving, with each built, in pyramid fashion, on the other's success. This structure permits each of the individual fund-raising methods in use to concentrate on three common fund-raising objectives: to acquire, to retain, and to maximize donors. Each fund-raising method, again for simplification, will use three common solicitation techniques for its communications: mail, telephone, and in-person solicitation. The purpose here is not to instruct the reader in detail on how each method of fund raising performs. (See Suggested Readings at the end of this chapter for sources offering instruction on how to conduct the various methods of current fund-raising practice.) Descriptions are adequately explained so that fund-raising policies and procedures, guidelines, and operating rules can be better understood.

Prior to any form of public solicitation, there is the need to prepare (in writing, preferably) the "case for support" as a statement of need. A case statement is the argument, indeed even the validation of the right to ask for support, to enable the organization to continue its work and to fulfill its mission. Henry Rosso describes the language of fund raising as "the gentle art of persuasion."[7] Experienced fund-raising practitioners, both volunteer and staff, realize that money is not given; *it has to be raised.* Harold Seymour's declaration that "fund raising or development is the planned promotion of understanding, participation and support" speaks to the three essential tenets in the fund development process and in the right order of their application based on a well-defined plan of action.[8] Kathleen Kelly incorporated Rosso's and Seymour's time-tested definition of fund raising as "the management of relationships between a charitable organization and its donor publics."[9] Newcomers to the field need to appreciate that asking for money is secondary to what might best be described as a requirement for "friend raising" and "relationship building" among people in the community and the causes and organizations they care about. Indeed, caring is a big factor in most gift decisions and requires that donors need more than casual knowledge to develop an appreciation of the cause that their time, talent, and treasure are intended to address. What each gift decision comes down to most often are the facts of the story itself, as expressed in the case as clear and concise answers to each of the following crucial questions: Why does this organization exist? Whom does it serve? Are these services necessary, perhaps urgently needed, in this community? How do the recipients value these services? Does this organization deliver its programs effectively (with quality) as well as efficiently (by staff and volunteers at reasonable expense)? Each is a tough question; each needs careful preparation of an unequivocal answer in the case statement. Answers help persuade volunteers and donors to join the cause and share their resources.

This "case for giving" is both an intellectual conviction and an actual document to be shared with the public. Its foundation is taken from the institution's master plan, along with its mission, vision, and values statements. The case must contain essential facts about the organization and describe its current programs and services. It also must describe its vision of the future—how it intends to fulfill unmet community needs. The case statement explains how a dedicated staff is prepared to deliver high-quality programs and services according to the institutional values that are part of its culture. Finally, the case describes how each charitable contribution will be used to make a difference to those served as well as benefit the prospective donor whose participation is now requested (see Exhibit 19.8). Finally, the completed case for giving, when it is written, might contain all or nearly all of the following ingredients:

- The problem (or opportunity) to be addressed
- Trends affecting the problem (or opportunity)

EXHIBIT 19.8 Questions to Be Addressed in Creating a Case Statement

- What is the purpose of the organization?
- When was the organization founded?
- What is the structure of the organization? Is it composed of volunteers only, or does it have professional staff?
- What are the key needs that must be met in the community served by the organization?
- What does the organization plan to do to meet these needs?
- How will it accomplish these tasks? Who will carry them out?
- Why is this organization best qualified to undertake these services?
- How do you define success for the program? What criteria will you use to evaluate success?
- How will success enable the organization to continue or to grow?
- What is the funding need for the program? How will the organization meet ongoing funding needs once these dollars have been raised?
- What is expected of donors? How can the donors give?

From Hicks, J. (1997). "Grass-Roots Fund Raising," in J. M. Greenfield (ed.), *The Nonprofit Handbook: Fund Raising,* 2nd ed. New York: John Wiley & Sons, p. 563. Reprinted with permission of John Wiley & Sons, Inc.

- Your response to the problem (or opportunity)
- Role of the prospective donor
- Your mission, vision, and values
- Your history, track record, and marketplace position
- Goals, strategies, and objectives
- Organizational resources
- Accountability and evaluation
- Future organization plans[10]

A brief description of the three broad operating areas of fund raising follows.

(A) ANNUAL GIVING PROGRAMS

Nearly every NPO engages in one or more active forms of solicitation each year. These annual programs have two main objectives: to ask for the money needed to support the urgent priorities in the current operating budget, and to find and retain more donors whose continued contributions will fund future programs with reliability. Annual giving serves as the backbone of fund development because it is designed to produce predictable amounts of gift revenues year after year. Sources for annual gifts include associations and societies, corporations, foundations, government, and individuals. Because the majority of gifts (an average of 80 to 85 percent) are made by individuals each year, solicitation programs for most organizations should concentrate on people most of the time. Each annual giving method is designed to acquire new donors while retaining as many prior donors as possible. Management of annual giving requires careful coordination of each separate method, whether during one year or as part of a multiyear effort, and is essential to increasing performance year after year. Directors and managers of NPOs who fail to understand the need for such coordination also may fail to understand the purpose of annual giving, which is to produce reliable revenue every year. Some may view an annual campaign as only a money-raising activity—a misleading perception that results in accepting quick fixes and easy money ideas for the apparent dollars they promise. These fund raisers fail to appreciate the value of traditional annual giving methods; they have been tested a thousand times and proven to be reliable, cost effective, and highly profitable because they work to build relationships.

Annual giving, the chief means to build relationships between donors and NPOs, will not succeed or long survive if thought of only as a money-raising activity. Donors result from annual investments; their value increases in direct proportion to the care and attention they receive over time. This also means that donor relations programs are an active part of every annual giving activity. Such attention will help ensure that each donor's interest and enthusiasm are retained and that his or her commitment to the organization grows and continues to produce faithful contributions for the future.

NPOs can elect to use one or more annual giving methods during their operating year. The options include direct mail, for acquisition of first-time donors as well as for renewal of prior donors; telephone and public media channels; membership development; special and benefit events; support group organizations; donor clubs; volunteer solicitation committees; and more. The goal of each option is to achieve multiple gifts from the same donors during each year; one gift every 12 months is not likely to provide all the revenue needed to meet annual operating needs. Churches across America invite their members to give weekly; they also raise more money than any other type of NPO. These faithful, committed weekly/monthly/annual donors can and will provide the money needed for operations year after year. These same donors will become the patrons and benefactors of NPOs in the future, provided that the fund development program is designed to this end and not seen only as a money-raising activity within a single year.

A variety of skills are required to manage several annual giving activities at the same time. Coordination and cooperation will help to produce reliable results without causing confusion or "turning off" donors. Written procedures are needed to help guide the conduct of multiple methods of annual solicitation that are performed at the same time with the same audiences. The goals are to increase the pool of suspects and prospects, to increase the number of donors, to retain most prior donors, to upgrade the gift level of current donors, to invite multiple gifts, to encourage active participation, to encourage volunteerism, to offer opportunities for leadership, and to recognize and reward everyone who steps forward to do more. The preservation of goodwill among all who become donors is essential; these same committed friends will faithfully support the priorities of the future with their "time, talent, and treasure."

(B) MAJOR GIFT AND CAMPAIGN PROGRAMS

When a solid base of annual giving activity is in full operation, NPOs are better prepared to engage in more complex forms of solicitation for significantly greater gifts, in size and in donor involvement and participation. Few donors will be engaged at this level as compared with annual givers, but their larger gifts will provide a greater majority of the funds required. The fund-raising techniques used in development of major gifts and grants are usually defined within the context of a special or capital campaign, which is possible only after years of successful annual giving activity. Some history of giving is always necessary before these expanded areas can begin to be successful.

NPOs must prepare themselves for their own future, because their future plans will address the needs of more sophisticated donors. Long-range and strategic plans explain specific directions to be taken, timetables, steps required, estimated costs, opportunities for major gift support, reasoned outcomes, public benefits expected, and more. Major gifts can be solicited separately from annual giving, even in the absence of new institutional plans, in the same manner that government grants may be applied for once a program area is qualified. However, major gift solicitations always will be more successful when included as part of a visibly promoted, multiyear, institutional effort. This is true because the best sources of leadership, commitment, and enthusiasm are assembled in support of the organization to achieve such overall objectives.

The fund-raising method often employed to meet master plan objectives is a major campaign, usually designed to address only the most urgent of priorities. This means that new and higher levels of funding are essential to the organization's future. The campaign is the method to marshall attention to these priorities, presenting them as relevant, urgent, and to be met *now*. Special donor recognition opportunities are offered as added benefits for large gifts, to encourage donors in their generosity. Simply put, it is much more difficult to amass a winning combination for successful solicitation with a single project standing alone than to offer donors the biggest and best ideas the organization has to offer.

(C) PLANNED GIVING PROGRAMS

Donors can be introduced to the special area of opportunity associated with planned giving at any time during annual giving, major giving, or capital campaign programs. In fact, through these communications the idea seeds are planted early and lead to financial and estate-planning discussions. Planned giving is, by definition, a means whereby individuals plan to designate a portion of their estate to be delivered later to the NPOs of their choice. All that is required is a specific instruction written in their will or living trust. Planned gifts are major gifts involving significant assets, which is why they match up well with capital campaigns rather than annual giving programs. The technical complexity of planned giving requires close attention to appropriate policy and procedure by all who would consider this area of fund raising. Planned giving also remains the preferred method to develop the endowment funds that are so essential to financial flexibility and security in every NPO's future.

Planned giving represents final decisions by donors who choose to make arrangements in advance to maintain their personal support of favorite organizations into the future, even after they are deceased. These decisions are guided by their estate plan, prepared alongside their personal financial plan for their retirement years. Planned gifts can be made now, either with (1) benefits from the transfer retained for the donor's lifetime and the asset transferred to the organization after death, or with (2) final assignment, via a will or living trust, of current assets that will flow to the organization after death. Because of their complex technical nature and the permanent obligations of the NPOs that accept them, estate planning and planned giving programs must be guided by clear and complete policies and procedures that address fully the fiduciary, legal, and stewardship responsibilities of the NPO for the life of the donor.

While the balance of this chapter will address fund-raising support, it is helpful to keep in mind three common ingredients. Success in fund raising is always dependent on the interaction of; (1) leadership and voluntary action; (2) cultivation, solicitation, and donor relations; and (3) relationships built between donors and their choices of NPOs. Policies and procedures, guidelines, and operating rules must be designed to match each organization's operating style, taking into account the need to support the professional conduct of fund raising. Such guidelines are seldom a goal unto themselves, however, especially where they would impede fund development operations. These three ingredients for successful fund raising are described briefly in the sections that follow.

(D) LEADERSHIP AND VOLUNTARY ACTION

Nothing much happens in fund raising until voluntary leadership takes charge and provides direction to all other volunteers and staff alike. Leadership, whether it comes from the board or from individuals appointed by the board, is much more than an appointment; it requires dedication, advocacy, personal sacrifice, and serving as an example to others. Among the qualities most often associated with effective fund-raising leaders are: they are rich, have "clout," are generous to lots of causes, are well liked, are true believers in the project, are well-organized, are good speakers, and are fearless.[11] Leaders also have to be trained and aided toward a complete understanding of the mission and purpose, goals and objectives, and personality and operating style of the NPO they serve. Professional staff can assist in many ways, but their chief purpose is to ensure that each leader succeeds in the task he or she is assigned.

Leadership includes providing guidance and direction to others who volunteer their time and energy to the same cause. Volunteers can be asked to perform every task required for successful fund raising; the trick is to pick the right people for the right task at the right time so that the entire program will run smoothly. Although this idea is forever elusive, constant attention to volunteers' training and encouragement of their active support will help achieve success every time. Volunteers are the "arms and legs" of fund raising; no fund development program can expect to be successful without a host of men and women committed to the cause and willing to give of their personal "time, talent, and treasure" toward its fulfillment. Each volunteer must be given adequate time to learn an assignment, allowed to experiment with personal ideas measured against proven methods and prior successes, invited to do more rather than less, given opportunities for growth within the organization, asked for a personal gift early, recognized and rewarded for all that is accomplished, and considered for promotion to leadership assignments, including a seat on the board of directors.

(E) CULTIVATION, SOLICITATION, AND DONOR RELATIONS

Donors and prospects, whether people or institutions, require attention and consideration. Each has potential to assist and, although some can give more money than others, each can give a share of time and a best effort to the cause. Annual giving, by its nature, invites thousands of donors and prospects to participate, and then asks them to do it again. It is not possible to give personal attention to all donors, so the focus must be on those whose prior giving history or potential volunteerism merits added consideration. Annual giving provides the best means to find and develop more qualified candidates. The use of mass communication techniques—for example, mail, telephone, and benefit events—is a bit impersonal, but careful analysis of the results is a means to identify those few-among-many who, by reason of gift size, pattern of support, and commitment, justify more personal attention and further evaluation. Volunteers can help in these final evaluation steps leading to designation of those who will receive more active personal attention, all of which yields cultivation and solicitation of others who will follow.

Volunteer solicitors are pure gold to a fund development program. People who will ask their friends for money for an organization they believe in are indeed beautiful people. It is each organization's duty to train such volunteers in how best to approach others, how to be sensitive when mixing their enthusiasm for the cause with the prospects' potential for present and future support, and how to inform and invite prospects to join worthy programs that will benefit others. Each form of solicitation, whether an impersonal letter, a telephone call, or a personal visit, is an important opportunity for the NPO to make friends. These initial few friends will invite others to join them and, over time, build a cadre of many friends who can be prepared to help the NPO realize its annual priorities and fulfill its long-term aspirations.

Relations with donors, as mentioned earlier, remain highly important for reasons other than just the next gift. As with friendships, time and effort are required of both parties to keep up the contact, show an honest interest in one another, share ideas and goals, and work together whenever possible. Formal recognition programs offer privileged communications for donors; they let them "inside" and include them in "family" discussions. NPOs have an obligation to design donor communications programs and to include public recognition of those whose faithful service and generous contributions have made all the difference in achieving success.

(F)   BUILDING RELATIONSHIPS

The entire purpose of fund development can be captured in the concept of good relations with a community of friends. Opportunities for friends' involvement and active participation exist alongside expectations that these faithful advocates and generous supporters stand ready to assist the organization in achieving its mission to the rest of society. Here, the true purpose of the fund development "process" comes to term: it guides leadership and volunteerism, friend raising and active solicitation, donor relations, and more; it unites *people* with the *purposes* of NPOs.

Relationships take time—often, lots of time—to develop. Multiple opportunities are included in the objectives of annual giving, major giving, and planned giving programs to nurture each individual who chooses to associate with a cause toward achieving the most satisfactory outcomes for both parties, which can be repeated over many years.

(G)   ACCOUNTABILITY, ETHICS, AND STEWARDSHIP

Each NPO holds serious responsibilities in exchange for its multiple privileges. It is obligated to fulfill its mission to the community and to remain true to its vision and values. In the process, it must demonstrate an exacting accountability for delivery of quality programs and expanded services. It must observe ethical conduct in all its relationships, be they with clients or customers, board members or employees, donors or volunteers. It must maintain stewardship of its assets, including all funds raised and invested as well as its people, facilities, and equipment. There can be no substitute for the highest standards of conduct in every area of an NPO's daily activity. In the end, the public's confidence and trust enables the organization to continue to operate. Without such a commitment by the public to give of their own time, energy, talent, and personal funds, an organization cannot long survive.

Therefore, each NPO must operate in full public view, with open and complete disclosure of all its activities and financial affairs, with a commitment to excellence and a dedication to serve every purpose defined in its mission statement. To be accountable to these precepts is also to practice actively, at the minimum, each of the ethical precepts in the Donor Bill of Rights, including its forthright preamble. Each donor's first right is to open and complete disclosure, as described in precept I, "To be informed of the organization's mission, of the way the organization intends to use donated resources, and of its capacity to use donations effectively for their intended purpose" (see Exhibit 19.2). Failure to observe each of these 10 fundamental precepts is a major transgression of stewardship responsibility. Each such blunder or misstep also is a demonstration by those involved—board member or staff manager, employee or volunteer—of a lack of professional conduct and personal commitment to high ethical standards, which cannot be tolerated at any time. Such errors lead quickly to charges of fraud and deception and become scandals as well as illegal acts that affect the confidence and trust of donors to other organizations as well.

What we all have in common is a responsibility to play our roles well. For nonprofit practitioners, conscientious volunteers, and foundation grantmakers, the concept goes to the heart of professionalism. Easy to miss, however, and a source of profound confusion, is the difference between **role** *responsibility and* **ethical** *responsibility—a difference that, as Aristotle suggests, is hardly "an easy matter." The difference is important because of the deceptively easy substitution of role-playing for truly ethical behavior.*[12]

Stewardship includes the obligation to report back to donor-investors on results and performance, which can be measured against the organization's stated mission, vision, and values. It is also a means to preserve or enhance a donor-investor's confidence and trust in the organization's use of her or his contributions. Kay Sprinkel Grace offers an exemplary list of 11 basic principles to guide the preparation and management of a strong stewardship program as follows:

1. Begin involving donors in the stewardship program with their first gift.
2. Alternate messages to your donors.
3. Allocate budget to stewardship activities.
4. Be sure the stewardship practice is appropriate to the amount of the gift and the budget and image of the organization.
5. Determine what kind of involvement your major gift and planned gift donors, some of whom may be very busy with other organizations and their own professions, want.
6. Coordinate stewardship and cultivation outreach, so that current donors have an opportunity to convey their enthusiasm and commitment to prospective donors.
7. Tie stewardship outreach to the organization's mission.
8. Focus on intangible, rather than tangible, benefits.
9. Maintain stewardship with long-time and generous donors, even when their giving flags.
10. Keep all previous large-gift donors informed and part of your database, even those who make what seems to be a "one-time-only gift," unless and until you hear they no longer want to hear from you.
11. Establish relationships between donors and program staff whenever possible.[13]

The final word on these three important obligations—accountability, ethics, and stewardship—and their absolute linkage to professional fund-raising practice is from Rosso:

If we accept the philosophy that stewardship flows from our common value system, then it is clear that ethical fund raising simply surfaces these values and illuminates them. That is why a sensitive presentation with an emphasis on vision and mission will supersede manipulation any day. Sincere passion reflecting the solicitor's commitment and respect for the purpose of the work and its meaning to the civic community will stimulate more interest and desire to give than any contrived maneuvering to induce the gift.[14]

19.3   General Areas for Policy and Procedures

Guidance for daily operations begins at the point of inception of the organization itself. Ownership, legal name, mission and purpose, authority, structure and organization, procedures for dissolution, and more are all defined in the articles of incorporation. The next document, called the bylaws, states the operating rules and procedures for the organization. The bylaws define in detail the process for the election of officers and directors, and their job descriptions; the procedures for the conduct of all meetings; annual operations, including fiscal activities; the process to amend the bylaws; and much more. In combination, the articles of incorporation and the bylaws establish the board of directors as the supreme authority for ownership and operation of the NPO. Federal and state authorities, acting on these texts alone, will charter the organization as a voluntary nonprofit public benefit corporation under the law, by which it is forever bound. Out of these government approvals flow privileges of income, sales and property tax exemptions, and a charitable contribution deduction for all of the organization's donors.

Daily operations remain the responsibility of the board of directors. However, because the board's primary duty is to establish policy and supervise operations, day-to-day tasks are assigned to professional staff whom the board hires and directs through the president/CEO, who also evaluates their performance. Once routine operations are defined and implemented, including the accounting and reporting of all revenue received and spent, the board's attention shifts to supervision of daily activities against stated objectives. A mission statement, drawn from the articles of incorporation, completes the written interpretation of the purposes, goals, and objectives of the organization. Operations are guided through defined programs and services provided through the annual budget and, in time, through long-range and strategic plans designed to move the organization forward toward fulfilling the objectives stated in its articles of incorporation and mission statement.

All of these deliberate activities are necessary and must precede public solicitation activity. When complete, they also provide all the information needed to begin a successful fund-raising program. The board of directors appoints a committee on fund development and authorizes it to supervise all fund-raising activity, including setting annual and multiyear goals matched to the organization's plans and priority funding requirements. The objective is to raise, on schedule, the money for priority needs. The annual budget for fund raising is prepared, reviewed, and approved by the administration and the board. Hiring practices, job descriptions, and evaluation procedures (for programs as well as employees) are used to recruit and supervise professional and support staff hired to conduct fund-raising activities as defined by the committee. Policies and procedures for fund raising, the use of the institutional name in solicitation activities, accounting and reporting for all funds raised and budget expended, honors and recognition accorded to donors—all of these activities are defined, developed, and approved by the committee, administration, and the board. Everyone involved should receive complete information on how each of these activities will be performed and their relationship to all other aspects of the fund development program.

Because fund-raising programs produce cash and other forms of revenue for use by the organization, instructions on their proper disposition are required within the organization's fiscal policy and procedures. Other committees involved in the management of funds raised include the audit, finance, and investment management committees, which ensure accurate accounting for each gift and its appropriate use, investment of funds (including charitable trusts and endowments), and preparation of required audits and public fiscal reports in accordance with accounting standards and in fulfillment of state and federal requirements. Considerable coordination is required to ensure that the board's obligation for fiduciary stewardship of gift revenue is complete. The stewardship includes solicitation practices, fund accounting, budget and expenditures for fund raising, and public reporting of the results, including benefits delivered back to the annuity.

The concluding segment of this chapter gives an example of guidelines, operating rules, and procedures that must be prepared, to cover all aspects of the fund development program. Given the importance of the funds themselves and their value to the organization, the board of directors assigns its active responsibility for this entire area to the committee on fund development. This committee must define the programs of solicitation in the areas of annual giving, major gifts, and planned giving, and then supervise their conduct each year according to policy procedures. The result is a manual such as is shown in the appendix to this chapter.

In addition, direction for organizations that are related to the parent corporation and that also engage in fund raising to support the mission of the parent is required from the committee on fund development. A related organization may be a subsidiary unit, such as a foundation, that is controlled by the parent or acts as its fund-raising arm. Related organizations may also be separate but affiliated groups whose existence, purpose, and franchises to exist originate from the parent corporation and whose own articles and bylaws establish, as their mission and purpose, the provision of financial and other support to the parent corporation. In each instance, operating rules and procedures are valuable and should include prescriptions (often in the form of bylaws) for the nomination and election of officers and directors, the approval of the fund-raising programs employed, the use of the parent organization's name, the accounting required for all funds raised in its name or expended for appropriate charitable purposes, and any other accounting and legal requirements associated with full and proper operation of related organizations.

When all these procedural necessities are in place and well understood by all the participants, a program of fund development can proceed with confidence in its own excellent preparation and with the full support of the board of directors. The community of volunteers and active supporters will be secure in a sound design, will be prepared to follow the organization's leadership, and will be willing to work hard to provide the financial support so necessary to its success.

Appendix: A Manual of Fund Development Policy and Procedure for Nonprofit Organizations*

CONTENTS
A.   Authority for Fund Development
1.   Importance of Philanthropy
2.   Board of Directors

---

* Reprinted from Greenfield, J. M. (1999). *Fund Raising: Evaluating and Managing the Fund Development Process*, 2nd ed. New York: John Wiley & Sons, pp. 381–407.

3. Board Committee on Fund Development
4. Department of Fund Development
5. Related Organizations
6. Role of Volunteers
7. Rights of Donors

B. Management of Fund Development Activities
1. Goals and Objectives Established by the Board of Directors
2. Job Description for Director of Fund Development
3. Public Solicitation Programs
4. Priority and Project Management
5. Procedures for Approval for Gift Solicitation
6. Prospect Reservation
7. Use of Consultants and Vendors

C. Public Solicitation Procedures
1. Correct Legal Name
2. Use of Organization Name for Fund Raising
3. Commercial Coventures and Charitable Sales Promotions
4. Tax Laws and Public Reporting Requirements
5. General Fund-Raising Guidelines
6. Joint Fund-Raising Programs
7. Calendar for Solicitations

D. Forms of Contributions
1. Types of Gifts
2. Unrestricted and Restricted Gifts
3. Appraisal Rules and Procedures
4. Special Handling of Selected Gifts
5. Temporarily Restricted Funds
6. Gifts in Trust
7. Income-Producing Properties
8. Legacies and Bequests

E. Fund-Raising Methods and Techniques
1. Procedures for Setting Goals
2. Annual Giving Activities
3. Procedures for Benefit Events
4. Business, Corporation, and Foundation Relations
5. Special Project Campaigns
6. Multiyear and Capital Campaigns
7. Planned Giving Programs

F. Government Grants and Contracts Administration
1. Authority and Supervision
2. Office of Grants and Contracts
3. Grants and Contracts Officer
4. Institutional Review Committee
5. Manuscripts and Articles
6. Accounting, Reporting, and Audits
7. Royalties, Copyrights, and Patents
8. Nongovernment Grants and Contracts

G. **Gift Processing Procedures**
   1. Checks and Cash
   2. Gifts of Securities
   3. Gifts of Personal Property
   4. Gifts of Real Estate
   5. Gifts-in-Kind
   6. Employee Gifts and Payroll Deduction
   7. Fiscal and Calendar Year-End Procedures

H. **Gift Acknowledgment Procedures**
   1. Official Acknowledgment
   2. Additional Acknowledgments
   3. Time of Acknowledgment
   4. Donor Records and Recognition
   5. Gift Substantiation Rules
   6. Tax Records and Public Disclosure
   7. Gifts Reports on Results

I. **Accounting for Gift Revenue**
   1. Fiduciary Responsibility
   2. Allocation to Restricted Funds
   3. Expenditure Controls
   4. Allocation to Endowment and Investment Earnings
   5. Investment of Funds
   6. Accounting Reports
   7. Audits and Tax Returns

J. **Honors and Recognition**
   1. Policy Concept
   2. Guidelines
   3. Qualifications
   4. Procedure for Approval
   5. Naming of Buildings or Space Therein
   6. Naming of Endowed Chairs
   7. Naming of Departments of Title Positions
   8. Awards or Citations
   9. Process for Recommendation
   10. Public Notice
   11. Forms of Recognition
   12. Graphics Continuity
   13. Renewed Solicitation
   14. Donor Communications

K. **Management of Planned Giving Programs**
   1. Programs for Solicitation
   2. Acting as Trustee
   3. Charitable Trust and Pooled Income Fund Management
   4. Life Insurance Programs
   5. No Commissions or Finder's Fees Paid for Planned Gifts
   6. Wills and Bequests: Probate Procedures

L.   Investment and Endowment Operations
1.   Obligation of the Board of Directors
2.   Selecting Professional Management Services
3.   Short-Term Money Management
4.   Invested Funds Management
5.   Endowment Fund Management
6.   Purposes and Uses of Earnings

M.   Corporate Member: The Separate Foundation
1.   Corporate Member of the Foundation
2.   Routine Operations and Information Reports
3.   Review of Annual Goals and Objectives
4.   Professional Staff Hiring Procedures
5.   Transfer of Funds Raised and Held
6.   Nominations Process for Foundation Directors
7.   Honors and Recognition by the Foundation
8.   Annual Meetings and Annual Reports
9.   Annual Audit Review

N.   Related Organizations: Support Groups
1.   Authorization to Exist
2.   Approval of Operating Rules and Procedures
3.   Use of the Organization's Name
4.   Review of Annual Goals and Objectives
5.   Nominations Process for Officers and Members of the Board of
        Directors
6.   Professional Staff Hiring Procedures
7.   Control of Funds Raised and Held
8.   Annual Meetings and Annual Reports
9.   Annual Audit Review

O.   Department of Fund Development
1.   Areas of Management Responsibility
2.   Approved Fund-Raising Programs
3.   Donor Relations and Communications
4.   Support Services
5.   Job Descriptions and Hiring Practices
6.   Budgets and Accountability
7.   Records and Files

P.   Public Reporting Requirements
1.   Internal Revenue Service
2.   State and Local Agencies
3.   Public Requests for Information

Q.   Approvals, Reviews, and Amendments
1.   Authority of the Board of Directors
2.   Periodic Review and Reissue
3.   Process for Amendment

A. AUTHORITY FOR FUND DEVELOPMENT

1. *Importance of Philanthropy.* The several benefits enjoyed by [name of organization] under the law include active support and voluntary contributions from individuals, corporations, foundations, government, associations, and societies. Positive relationships among all these parties are essential to the mission of this organization, especially its financial stability. Responsibility for preservation and enhancement of philanthropy shall be retained by the Board of Directors and carried out as herein defined.

2. *Board of Directors.* The Board has the authority and stewardship responsibility for all methods and techniques of fund-raising activity; for all forms of contributions received; for professional staff, consultants, and vendors required; for investment and management of all funds raised; and for disbursement of contribution revenues in exclusive support of the mission of this organization.

3. *Board Committee on Fund Development.* This committee of the Board of Directors is charged with leadership and direction of fund raising toward the objectives of (a) defining and developing programs asking for public support, (b) active solicitation in all forms, and (c) maintaining positive relations with donors.

4. *Department of Fund Development.* Under the chief development officer, this department is responsible to the President/CEO and the Committee on Fund Development for day-to-day management of all fund-raising activities. Professional and support staff will provide leadership, management, and direct support to fund-raising programs; acknowledgment of all gifts and maintenance of donor records and recognition; deposit and accounting for all gifts received; supervision of the annual budget; and direction of all employees, consultants, and vendors hired.

5. *Related Organizations.* By authority of the Board of Directors, related organizations whose purpose is to develop gift revenue for this organization shall be authorized to use the name and tax-exempt privileges granted this organization, and shall be subject to the policies and procedures of the Committee on Fund Development. Accounting for all income of and expenses incurred by related organizations shall be made to the Office of Fund Development and leadership of the related organization.

6. *Role of Volunteers.* Active volunteer participation in the fund development program is essential to its success. The roles of volunteers shall be defined as to level of responsibility, period of service, reporting relationships, staff support, and other details as required. A volunteer recognition program shall also be provided to honor the service given by those who lead and assist this organization.

7. *Rights of Donors.* The value of past, present, and future donors shall be preserved and respected at all times in concert with the Donor Bill of Rights. The privileges and benefits accorded donors are defined in Honors and Recognition (Section J).

B. MANAGEMENT OF FUND DEVELOPMENT ACTIVITIES

1. *Goals and Objectives Established by the Board of Directors.* The priorities for public participation and support shall be established by the Board of

Directors and carried out by the Committee on Fund Development and related organizations through the Department of Fund Development.

2. *Job Description for Director of Fund Development.* The Committee on Fund Development and President/CEO shall define the duties and responsibilities of the Director of Fund Development and shall participate in the hiring and performance evaluation of occupants in this position.

3. *Public Solicitation Programs.* All fund-raising activities shall be approved by the Committee on Fund Development and the President/CEO for approved priorities only. Goals and budgets associated with their achievement shall be prepared in advance of active public solicitation.

4. *Priority and Project Management.* Each fund-raising priority shall be managed as a separate fund-raising project. The assistance of volunteers, staff, and budget shall be organized to meet project deadlines and objectives. Fund development volunteers, staff, time, and budget shall be authorized only for approved priorities. Overlapping priorities shall be resolved by the Committee on Fund Development.

5. *Procedures for Approval for Gift Solicitation.* All priorities for fund development shall be defined, within procedures established by the President/CEO, for submission to the Board of Directors for approval, including budgetary authorization. Those programs appropriate for fund-raising support shall be so identified, and evaluation shall be performed by the Committee on Fund Development to assess anticipated public support and budget and staff and volunteer requirements for successful solicitation.

6. *Prospect Reservation.* Prospective candidates deserve considerate treatment at all times. When more than one approved project may qualify for the attention of the same prospect, the prospect reservation procedures shall guide resolution of the timing and period of reservation of its solicitation completion. This procedure will ensure that dual solicitation of prospects will be avoided and that prospects already assigned to approved projects shall have first priority

7. *Use of Consultants and Vendors.* Professional assistance may be retained or purchased to support fund-raising activities. Each such association shall be guided by a written contract or memorandum of agreement in keeping with this organization's policies. The recommendation by the Committee on Fund Development and approval of the Board of Directors shall be required prior to entering into any contract or agreement.

C. PUBLIC SOLICITATION PROCEDURES

1. *Correct Legal Name.* All charitable contributions, regardless of value, form, or designated use, shall be made only to this organization, using the proper legal name of this corporation. Questions about methods of giving, timing, assignment, purpose, or about the value, designated use, and so forth, shall be directed to the Department of Fund Development, as shall all questions about legal forms for gifts, gift substantiation and their tax consequences, and donor recognition.

2. *Use of Organization Name for Fund Raising.* The use of the name of this organization for any fund-raising purpose by any other organization or entity

shall require prior approval of the Committee on Fund Development, acting on recommendations from the Department of Fund Development.

3. *Commercial Coventures and Charitable Sales Promotions.* Joint ventures for public marketing and solicitation with business or commercial organizations shall be defined within applicable state and federal laws and regulations. Each such association shall be guided by a written contract or memorandum of agreement approved by the Board of Directors upon recommendation of the Committee on Fund Development. The commercial partner involved shall disclose all income and expenses associated with each of these promotions. The uses to be made of proceeds from each joint venture shall be in keeping with the mission statement of this organization.

4. *Tax Laws and Public Reporting Requirements.* Voluntary contributions to nonprofit organizations are endorsed by federal and state governments, which provide substantial tax deductions for donors. The Board of Directors will, at all times, comply fully with its obligations to fulfill applicable tax laws and public reporting requirements. Public report documents shall be available the same day a request is made in person, or within 30 days of receipt of a written, e-mail, facsimile, or telephone request, as required by law.

5. *General Fund-Raising Guidelines.* Donors and prospects shall be encouraged to support approved priorities and established programs at all times, in order that the most urgent requirements of this organization may be met to the greatest extent possible. Donor wishes will be considered to the extent possible, so long as their intended use of funds is in keeping with the mission statement. Resolution of donor wishes outside approved priorities and established programs shall be by the Board of Directors upon recommendation of the Committee on Fund Development.

6. *Joint Fund-Raising Programs.* Joint fund-raising activities between programs within this organization shall be encouraged because they provide donors and prospects with more opportunities to address approved priorities.

7. *Calendar for Solicitations.* Each 12-month period contains limited time available for fund-raising activities. Coordination and cooperation are required in planning each solicitation, to respect the rights of donors and to avoid creating the appearance of confusion and competition among the public. Each fund-raising program requires time for its own fulfillment and must also respect the preferred periods when other fund-raising programs shall be scheduled. The calendar for solicitation shall be reviewed and approved by the Committee on Fund Development at the beginning of each fiscal year. Modifications to the calendar will be resolved by the Committee based on recommendations of the Department of Fund Development.

D. FORMS OF CONTRIBUTIONS

1. *Types of Gifts.* Besides *monetary gifts* in the form of cash, checks, money orders, and the like, *nonmonetary gifts* may be accepted, such as (a) bonds and securities, (b) real property, (c) tangible personal property, (d) gifts-in-kind to be used in the form in which they are given, (e) royalties, copyrights, and trademark rights, (f) mineral rights, and (g) insurance policies naming this organization as beneficiary in whole or in part.

2. *Unrestricted and Restricted Gifts.* Gifts with no stipulation by the donor as to their purpose or use are *unrestricted.* Gifts given and accepted for a specific purpose, as designated by the donor as a condition or so directed by this organization, shall be *temporarily restricted.* Such gifts are to be used only for the purpose intended, and their status is to be disclosed in financial and audit statements in accordance with Financial Accounting Standards Board (FASB) and American Institute of Certified Public Accountants (AICPA) accounting standards and guidelines. Gifts given or so directed by this organization to be *retained* are considered to be endowment and are recorded and reported as *permanently restricted,* with only their investment and interest earnings available for use as determined by the Investment Management Committee.

3. *Appraisal Rules and Procedures.* Current Internal Revenue Service (IRS) regulations will be observed when calculating the charitable contribution value of gifts of property, including advice to such donors regarding these regulations and the reporting obligations both parties must observe. A list of qualified professional appraisers will be offered each donor for his or her independent use. Donors are obliged to pay for professional appraisals of their property. The appraised value thus certified will be entered in the donor's gift record and reported in IRS Form 8282 if sold within two years of the date of the gift. Official gift acknowledgment documents will refer only to the object given and appraised value.

4. *Special Handling of Select Gifts.* Commemorative gifts may be received in the form of "in memory of," "in honor of," or "on the occasion of" from any source. Separate gift acknowledgment procedures will reflect the special nature of these select gifts. Unless their use is specified by the donor or the person or family named, they shall be considered unrestricted gifts. Commemorative gifts that qualify for Honors and Recognition also will observe the procedures described in Section J herein.

5. *Temporarily Restricted Funds.* A donor may deliver funds or property as a gift and specify a conditioned use over time, with such funds to be held for a fixed period until the condition is met. Among the conditions may be a specific event, decision, financial transaction, or time-defined future activity. During this interim, the Investment Committee may invest the funds; any earned income is usable by this organization until such time as conditions or maturation are achieved. After the condition has been met and the funds disbursed for the restricted purpose, the use shall be recorded and reported as an unrestricted expense in accordance with FASB and AICPA accounting standards and guidelines.

6. *Gifts in Trust.* This organization may accept gifts in trust, agreeing to hold and manage a donor's principal resources and assets in exchange for life income, after which the principal and future income become the property of the organization for use as designated by the donor. A donor may deliver funds or property in a trust agreement to provide income for his or her lifetime and the lifetime of a spouse or other designated beneficiary, in accordance with the operating procedures of the Planned Giving Program (Section K). Specific details regarding trust documents, tax consequences, and income projections shall be reviewed by legal counsel prior to completion. If this organization acts as trustee, the selection of investment manager and custodian, performance

evaluation, and administrative/ accounting services shall be directed by the Investment Committee and approved by the Board of Directors.

7. *Income-Producing Properties.* In instances where income-producing properties are gifted, the Investment Committee shall determine and report to the Board of Directors, in advance of acceptance, several details including unrelated business income tax implications, environmental analysis and toxic waste potential, operations and maintenance expenses, and salability of the property. If accepted, the Investment Committee shall provide guidance on operations and disposition of the property to resolution.

8. *Legacies and Bequests.* A donor may arrange in a Will or Living Trust that this organization be designated as a beneficiary to receive a direct gift from the Estate. A donor may also arrange, after the death of a named beneficiary, that the principal or some of the surviving Estate shall become the property of this organization. Any restrictions on the use of such income as specified by the donor shall be in keeping with the mission statement. Unless otherwise specified, the Board of Directors, on advice of the Fund Development and Investment Committees, shall consider all other legacy and bequest income as unrestricted endowment.

E. FUND-RAISING METHODS AND TECHNIQUES

1. *Procedures for Setting Goals.* Annual goals and multiyear campaign objectives shall be established by the Committee on Fund Development based on prior years' experience, estimated improvement based on economic conditions and campaign acceptance, established priorities of need, and budget appropriated, with approval by the Board of Directors. Fund development staff, time, and budget are reserved only for established priorities approved by the Board of Directors.

2. *Annual Giving Activities.* The several methods and techniques that solicit donors as well as prospects for support each year shall be coordinated by the Committee on Fund Development. A variety of solicitation programs may be offered, including but not limited to direct mail, memberships, benefit events, telephone and media appeals, personal solicitation, commemorative giving, and more.

3. *Procedures for Benefit Events.* Each special and benefit event shall be approved in advance by the Committee on Fund Development, based on the following criteria: (a) appropriate fit to the existing calendar of fund-raising activities, (b) recruitment of an adequate volunteer committee or sponsoring agency or organization, and (c) a budget reflecting income and expense plans projecting a minimum of 50 percent net proceeds as gift income to this organization. All event funds shall be administered by the Office of Fund Development; so also shall be all contracts and agreements for services required to support any event.

4. *Business, Corporation, and Foundation Relations.* These gift prospects are important resources and deserve careful consideration at all times. Direct contact with any business, corporation, or foundation for any purpose shall be only with prior approval of the Committee on Fund Development. Prospect reservation procedures shall apply at all times.

5. *Special Project Campaigns.* Separate solicitation programs may be developed to meet urgent priorities or to take advantage of unusual opportunities offered by donors that match well with current fund-raising program objectives. Each such special project campaign shall be approved by the Committee on Fund Development prior to initiation, based on (a) appropriate fit to the existing calendar of fund-raising activities, (b) recruitment of an adequate volunteer committee or sponsoring agency or organization, and (c) a budget reflecting the expense required to achieve the income potential proposed with a minimum of 75 percent net proceeds as gift income to this organization.

6. *Multiyear and Capital Campaigns.* The Board of Directors may direct that a major fund-raising effort of a multiyear nature be conducted for urgent priorities, in keeping with long-range and strategic plans. Such campaign plans shall be developed by the Committee on Fund Development in concert with the Finance and Investment Committees and with thorough analysis of leadership and volunteer support, gift potential, internal capability, staff time and expense required, added budget requirements, and other preparations.

7. *Planned Giving Programs.* Public solicitation that offers forms of estate planning and planned giving shall be guided by the Planned Giving Policy (Section K) and administered by the Committee on Fund Development. This organization can act as trustee when accepting gifts in the form of charitable remainder trusts, charitable lead trusts, and pooled-income funds, in accordance with state and federal regulations, subject to approval of each gift by the Board of Directors.

F. GOVERNMENT GRANTS AND CONTRACTS ADMINISTRATION

1. *Authority and Supervision.* The President/CEO and the Sponsored Research Administrator are authorized agents for all grant and contract agreements. Each grant or contract application shall be approved by the President/CEO and Sponsored Research Administrator prior to submission.

2. *Office of Grants and Contracts.* The Office of Grants and Contracts shall provide resource services including the following: details on application requirements, budget preparation with appropriate indirect costs and fringe benefits, application preparation and review, final signature approvals, accounting reports and audits, and liaison to government agencies. Completed applications must be delivered to the Grants and Contracts Office at least five working days prior to the submission deadline.

3. *Grants and Contracts Officer.* The Grants and Contracts Officer is responsible for supervision of all grant and contract applications, including budget review and approval, and for supervision of accounting for funds received and public reports required by these agreements.

4. *Institutional Review Committee (IRC).* An Institutional Review Committee shall be appointed by the President/CEO to be composed of nine members, three of whom shall be laypersons not employed by this organization. IRC duties include oversight and analysis of all work proposed and performed under grants and contracts as well as such other issues of ethics and professional

conduct associated with any activity performed by this organization that is funded by government agencies and other revenue sources.

5. *Manuscripts and Articles.* Manuscripts, articles, and reports based on work performed under a grant or contract awarded this organization, or work identified with this organization by name, shall be reviewed by the Grants and Contracts Officer prior to submission for publication.

6. *Accounting, Reporting, and Audits.* The Chief Financial Officer will establish accounting procedures for administration of all funds received in a grant or contract agreement. Budget changes requested by the Principal Investigator shall be delivered to the Grants and Contracts Officer, who will negotiate with the agency for resolution. Requests for disbursement by the Principal Investigator first shall be directed to the Grants and Contracts Officer, who will verify the fund balance and expense to be in accordance with the approved budget. The Chief Financial Officer will supervise the preparation of all financial statements and public reports, including grant and contract audits, for submission to the granting or contract agency, in accordance with generally accepted accounting principles.

7. *Royalties, Copyrights, and Patents.* All royalties, copyrights, and patentable results from work performed under grant and contract agreements shall adhere to the Royalties, Copyrights, and Patents policy of this organization.

8. *Nongovernment Grants and Contracts.* Funds requested or received from nongovernment sources (e.g., corporations or foundations) that are, in fact, a formal agreement for specific work as defined in the application shall be administered by the Grants and Contracts Office in accordance with its operating policy and procedures, with support from the Fund Development Office as appropriate.

G. GIFT PROCESSING PROCEDURES

1. *Checks and Cash.* All gifts in the form of checks, cash, or credit cards received by any department shall be delivered *on the day they are received* to the Department of Fund Development, which will process the gift. In instances where the use specified by the donor is unclear, these details shall be brought to the immediate attention of the Department of Fund Development by telephone before acceptance of any gift binds this organization to fulfilling the donor's wishes. If none are known, the gift shall be considered to be for unrestricted purposes.

2. *Gifts of Securities.* The transfer of securities certificates or their ownership to the name of this organization is especially sensitive and may only be accomplished as follows: (a) Ask the donor and his or her broker to call the Department of Fund Development for instructions on transfer to our agent, setting up a brokers' account, board authorization action, and other details. In instances where prior securities transfer have occurred with the same broker, the Department of Fund Development will proceed with transfer instructions. (b) Certificates belonging to the donor will be delivered only by certified or registered mail, or by hand. A stock power form, signed by the donor and naming the organization as transferee, shall be in a separate envelope using certified or registered mail. Disposition of the securities will be guided by policies established by the Investment Committee.

3. *Gifts of Personal Property.* Personal property may be accepted when (a) the property can be sold, or (b) the property can be used in keeping with the mission of this organization. Internal Revenue Service regulations require gifts other than cash or publicly traded securities valued in excess of $5,000 to be appraised by a certified professional appraiser, and a copy of the appraisal must accompany the gift. Cost of the appraisal shall be the responsibility of the donor. The gift value shall be the appraised value at the time of the gift. If the property is sold within two years of its receipt, IRS Form 8282 will be completed and submitted to the IRS.

4. *Gifts of Real Estate.* Real estate in the form of a residence, business, commercial building, undeveloped land, etc., may be accepted when (a) the environmental and toxic waste review is completed, *and* (b) the property can be sold in a reasonable time, *or* (c) the property can be used in keeping with the mission of this organization. A certified appraisal performed within 60 days of the gift date shall be provided by the donor. In most cases, real estate will be sold at current market prices through a broker hired by the organization. Properties with mortgages will not be accepted if the mortgage amounts to 50 percent or more of fair market value established in the appraisal. This type of gift will be governed by "bargain sale" rules.

5. *Gifts-in-Kind.* Gifts of material or products may be accepted when the form of the gift can be used immediately by the organization. Contribution values shall be as allowed by IRS regulations. Credit for IRS-approved gift values shall be added to the donor's gift history.

6. *Employee Gifts and Payroll Deduction.* Employees may make gifts at any time and may use payroll deduction to transfer their funds. Arrangements for the amount of the gift, frequency of deduction, and period when deductions are to begin and conclude are made by the employee, who shall be responsible for instructing the Payroll Office of these details in writing. The Department of Fund Development will provide sample language or a proper pledge card for these purposes.

7. *Fiscal and Calendar Year-End Procedures.* Gifts in any form received near the date ending the fiscal or calendar year may be credited to the prior reporting period if there is evidence that the donor intended to make the gift within this period, and the gift is received and processed within 10 days of the closing date for the fiscal or calendar year-end.

H. GIFT ACKNOWLEDGMENT PROCEDURES

1. *Official Acknowledgment.* All gifts, regardless of value, form, or designated use, shall be acknowledged by this organization with official correspondence. Acknowledgment represents to the donor this organization's acceptance of the gift along with its restrictions, and may also serve the donor as evidence to certify a possible tax-deductible event.

2. *Additional Acknowledgments.* Additional "thank-you" messages by volunteers and staff are encouraged and depend on the donor, size of the gift, or purpose, as determined by the Department of Fund Development. Details about the gift will be provided by the Department of Fund Development when additional acknowledgments are appropriate. Copies of additional

acknowledgments shall be sent to the Department of Fund Development for retention in the donor file.

3. *Time of Acknowledgment.* Gifts must always be acknowledged as promptly as possible. Gift processing shall have as its first priority the timely acknowledgment of all gifts within 48 hours of receipt.

4. *Donor Records and Recognition.* The Department of Fund Development shall retain all correspondence regarding contributions, gift records, cumulative gift histories, and other data on donors' activity, which shall be confidential information for use only in support of fund-raising activities. All recognition and reward accorded to donors by reason of their gift frequency, amounts, or cumulative total shall be in accordance with the Honors and Recognition guidelines (Section J).

5. *Gift Substantiation Rules.* The IRS requires nonprofit organizations to disclose to donors of $75 or more *at the point of solicitation (invitation)* when the gift is related to a special or benefit event, the amount of the gift value that is *nondeductible* because of material goods (e.g., food and drink) consumed by the donor in exchange for their gift. Further, the IRS requires of *all* contributions of $250 or more disclosure to the donor of the extent (value) of any benefits, including material goods, due to the donor in exchange for their gift, the value of any such benefits to be reported to the donor as *nondeductible.*

6. *Tax Records and Public Disclosure.* Gift acknowledgment correspondence is useful to donors for tax submission purposes. Donors may request verification of previous gifts for any purpose, which will be documented and released only to donors. Public release of details surrounding individual gifts shall be made only with the express permission of the donor, who shall be appraised of the purpose for such disclosure and given the opportunity for prior approval of the language to be used.

7. *Gift Reports on Results.* Public reports of gift results will not disclose gift amounts for individual donors. Gift reports will tally results by revenue sources, purposes or use, and fund-raising programs employed. Distribution of gift reports shall be limited to those who need to know these results.

I. ACCOUNTING FOR GIFT REVENUE

1. *Fiduciary Responsibility.* Each gift, regardless of value, form, or designated use, shall be accounted for at the time of receipt until used as directed by the donor in support of the mission of this organization. During such time as funds are retained, they shall be actively invested in accordance with procedures of the Finance and Investment Management Committees. The Department of Fund Development shall be responsible for any reports to donors on the use of their funds, to be accomplished in concert with operating managers and the fiscal/accounting department.

2. *Allocation to Restricted Funds.* Gifts received for restricted purposes (either temporarily restricted or permanently restricted) shall be separately accounted for, in order to maintain stewardship of these funds as donors direct. The segregation of these funds is to be performed by the fiscal/accounting department, who shall report to donors on their disposition and use by the departments and managers involved, through the Department of Fund Development.

3. *Expenditure Controls.* The uses of gift revenues, especially restricted gifts, shall be fully accounted for, beginning with their deposit to temporarily restricted fund accounts, stewardship, disposition reports, and with expenditures only as directed by the donor in keeping with the mission of this organization.

4. *Allocation to Endowment and Investment Earnings.* Funds restricted to endowment or so restricted by the Board of Directors shall be invested and accounted for in accord with policies determined by the Finance and Investment Management Committees. Investment earnings shall be used only for the purposes specified by the donor or Board, as directed by the Investment Committee.

5. *Investment of Funds.* All gifts received shall be invested until used in accord with donor wishes, using short-term or long-term investment plans as defined by the Finance and Investment Management Committees. Funds restricted to endowment or so restricted by the Board of Directors shall be invested and accounted for as directed by the Finance and Investment Management Committees. Investment earnings shall be used only for the purposes specified by the donor or Board, with amounts as resolved by the Finance and Investment Management Committees.

6. *Accounting Reports.* Regular accounting reports will summarize the status of all gift money, illustrating their present disposition by source, purpose or use, and fund-raising program originating the gift. These reports shall be prepared monthly and distributed to the Board of Directors and the Finance, Fund Development, and Investment Management Committees, who shall review and approve them. Annual reports will be prepared as a summary of all fiscal-year activity.

7. *Audits and Tax Returns.* The Board of Directors will conduct an audit of all contributions received and held, which shall be conducted in accordance with generally accepted accounting principles. Public reports of financial details shall be prepared as required by federal and state regulations. Public reports of financial details shall be available immediately to the public if request is made in person or within 30 days after receipt of a written, e-mail, facsimile, or telephone request.

J. HONORS AND RECOGNITION

1. *Policy Concept.* Formal recognition of distinguished service to this organization, in the forms of gift support and voluntary time and talent, shall receive official consideration by the Board of Directors. The qualifications, review and decision procedures, and methods of recognition to be followed in regard to gift support in its many forms, and as specified in this Section, are (a) the naming of buildings, property, or any space therein; (b) the naming of departments or titled positions, including chairs within this organization; and (c) the conferring of awards or citations on any individual, institution, association, or society for gift support or services rendered.

2. *Guidelines.* The Board of Directors, in concert with the Committee on Fund Development, shall assess each recommendation for honors and recognition. They shall consider the relationship between the honoree's qualifications and the size and scope of the project supported. Consideration in the

conferral of honors and recognition will include (a) benefit to this organization, (b) visibility and prominence accorded to the honoree, and (c) use of honors and recognition to further the goals and objectives of this organization in financial gain and in public recognition and respect.

3. *Qualifications.* Individuals or institutions that make large contributions shall be qualified for honors and recognition. A gift of $25,000 or higher qualifies for such consideration and may include a single gift received, total giving over several years, or a pledge amount of fund-raising goal achieved. Each such donor may be offered an appropriate form of recognition to be placed in the area selected or in the main donor recognition area, or a suitable dedication ceremony with a tour of the area identified for recognition included whenever possible. Gifts valued under $25,000 shall be recognized at the discretion of the Committee on Fund Development.

4. *Procedure for Approval.* Recommendations for honors and recognition shall be made to the Board of Directors after review and approval by the Committee on Fund Development, with adequate details on the individual or institution to be honored and the reasons for such action by the Board of Directors.

5. *Naming of Buildings or Space Therein.* All areas of this organization are subject to naming. Such identification will be appropriate in light of the gift or gifts received and will be sensitive to function and location and shall be consistent with internal graphics and signage procedure. Buildings, floors, and areas may be named as donors prefer when the extent of service and contribution merits such recognition.

6. *Naming of Endowed Chairs.* Endowed chairs represent another means to recognize major contributions to this organization. Endowed chairs may be named in honor of a present or former staff member, the donor, or someone the donor wishes to honor, and may be either a memorial or a living tribute to the honoree. A financial goal shall be set for each endowed chair that is approved by this organization, and shall be based on a preliminary budget prepared for the use of a portion of the investment earnings in keeping with the mission of the organization.

7. *Naming of Departments or Title Positions.* Professional, scientific, and service departments and their administrative positions represent another means to honor a donor or someone the donor wishes to honor, or a present or former staff member. Such occasions occur especially when the personal contributions, service, and achievements of the honoree have been intimately associated with that department or its service or functional area.

8. *Awards or Citations.* This organization may establish and may confer at its pleasure such awards or citations upon individuals or institutions in recognition for either their voluntary service or contributions or both. These awards or citations may be given at such time and on such occasions as the organization's Board of Directors may determine. Recommendations for conferring an award or citation shall be made as defined in paragraph 9 as follows.

9. *Process for Recommendation.* Recommendations for honors and recognition are directed to the Committee on Fund Development, who shall confer with the Chairperson of the Board of Directors and the President/CEO before action is taken. In those instances where a present or former employee is nominated or a department or title position is proposed, the President/CEO shall confer

with the department head most closely associated with the candidate, or the department head most closely associated with the title position, for advice in advance of forwarding the recommendation to the Board of Directors for its decision. In addition, adequate consultation with the honoree or his or her family or their representative(s) shall be conducted at the same time as other internal consultations, to be concluded to their satisfaction prior to presentation of these recommendations to the Board of Directors for action.

10. *Public Notice.* Honors and recognition decisions represent opportunities for public announcement. Agreement for such public notice shall be requested of each honoree, or his or her family or representative(s), in advance. Honorees shall have the opportunity to notify family and friends, and to invite their participation with the organization in any dedication ceremonies and receptions conducted in connection with the conferring of honors and recognition. Responsibility for coordination of such public notice shall be by the President/CEO and Director of Fund Development.

11. *Forms of Recognition.* Various forms of recognition shall be available in accordance with the wishes of the donor and with the concurrence of the Board of Directors. Details as to form shall be included in recommendations submitted to the Committee on Fund Development. Forms of recognition may be among the following: donor walls, formal dinners, portraits, dedication ceremonies, receptions, plaques, gifts to donors and honorees, photo sessions, reports in the organization's publications, and other forms of recognition.

12. *Graphics Continuity.* Materials, typeface, and presentation forms shall be consistent with graphics standards established by this organization. The application of overall visual aids, signage, and graphics utilization shall be in accordance with graphics standards established by this organization.

13. *Renewed Solicitation.* The resolicitation of donors who have been accorded honors and recognitions shall be reviewed in advance by the Committee on Fund Development, and shall be based on submission of a strategic action plan for continued donor relations and the master gift plan defined for each such donor prior to consideration of another gift that may qualify for added honors and recognition.

14. *Donor Communications.* The Office of Fund Development shall monitor relations with all individuals or institutions accorded honors and recognition, in order to provide continued communications with this organization at a level satisfactory to these donors.

K. MANAGEMENT OF PLANNED GIVING PROGRAMS

1. *Programs for Solicitation.* The types of planned gifts to be offered, minimum gift amount, range for percentage payout, assignment as trustee, and administrative services shall all be defined by the Committee on Fund Development and approved by the Board of Directors, and shall include procedures for preparation and review of performance of planned gifts in force.

2. *Acting as Trustee.* This organization will prefer to act as trustee of charitable trusts, annuities, and pooled income funds with concurrence of the donor(s), and will provide (or arrange to provide) such investment, distribution, income tax, audit, and other administrative services as required of a trustee.

3. *Charitable Trust and Pooled Income Fund Management.* The Board of Directors, acting on recommendations of the Fund Development and Investment Management committees, will administer each charitable trust, annuity, and pooled income fund in which the organization is acting as Trustee in accordance with guidelines established by the trust document, annuity contract, or pooled fund agreement, including investment strategies and payout rates. Investment managers will be selected by the Investment Management Committee, who will perform regular evaluations of investment performance and will report these results to the Board of Directors at least annually.

4. *Life Insurance Programs.* All life insurance programs offered as gift opportunities shall be defined by the Fund Development and Investment Management Committees and approved by the Board of Directors. Selection of agents, performance of due diligence, and supervision of policies in force shall be the responsibility of the Investment Management Committee, acting on recommendations from the Committee on Fund Development. Other life insurance gifts may be accepted, provided the policy is current and designates this organization as owner and beneficiary. If partially paid, the donor will be required to submit a written pledge to complete premium payments within eight years and to provide the original policy to this organization.

5. *No Commissions or Finder's Fees Paid for Planned Gifts.* It shall be the policy of this organization not to pay commissions or percentages associated with negotiation and acceptance of any form of planned gift. Further, the standards of professional conduct in this area shall be as published by the National Committee on Planned Giving.

6. *Wills and Bequests: Probate Procedures.* Sample texts shall be provided to all those who express an interest in naming this organization as beneficiary of a bequest. Sample texts shall be subject to approval by the donor's legal counsel. Donors who name this organization in their Will or Living Trust will be asked to provide a copy of their document or that section wherein this organization is named. It shall be the policy of this organization to closely follow to conclusion all probate proceedings where this organization is a named beneficiary.

L. INVESTMENT AND ENDOWMENT OPERATIONS

1. *Obligation of the Board of Directors.* All gifts to be invested or funds held as endowment shall be managed with professional assistance at all times with the express approval of the Board of Directors. The objectives in management of such funds shall be to preserve their current value and to generate earnings for current use by this organization. Supervision shall be by the Investment Management Committee, who will establish investment guidelines, conduct performance evaluation, recommend distribution of earnings, and submit regular status reports on all invested funds.

2. *Selecting Professional Management Services.* The Investment Management Committee shall interview and recommend to the Board of Directors such professional managers, custodians, and performance evaluation services for

all invested and endowment funds as are required, and shall conduct performance evaluations at least semiannually.

3. *Short-Term Money Management (under two years).* The Investment Management Committee shall recommend to the Board in concert with the Finance Committee how funds to be held for a brief period (under two years) shall be invested and managed, including the selection of professional managers and setting their investment guidelines.

4. *Invested Funds Management (two to five years).* The Investment Management Committee shall recommend to the Board in concert with the Finance Committee how funds that may be held for a period of up to five years shall be invested and managed, including the selection of professional managers and setting their investment guidelines. Funds to be held for more than five years shall observe endowment fund management.

5. *Endowment Fund Management.* Funds restricted to endowment or designated by the Board to observe endowment management shall be invested with professional managers and may include commingling such funds together for maximum benefit. Guidelines for investment shall consider current market conditions, preservation of principal, balanced fund strategies, and the annual income needs of this organization.

6. *Purposes and Uses of Earnings.* Investment earnings shall observe the use designated for any invested or endowment fund at its inception or may otherwise be used at the discretion of the Board of Directors. If a portion of earnings is not consumed or their use is not required, it shall be the policy of this organization to retain and reinvest all such funds.

M. CORPORATE MEMBER: THE SEPARATE FOUNDATION

1. *Corporate Member of the Foundation.* Any organization established in the form of a separate nonprofit corporation in foundation form, whose mission is to assist this parent corporation, shall be as a related organization. The Corporate Member shall be the Board of Directors of this organization, who shall approve the Articles of Incorporation and Bylaws and annually elect the Directors of each such related organization.

2. *Routine Operations and Information Reports.* The routine operations of the foundation shall be guided by its Articles of Incorporation and Bylaws. Information reports shall be made to this organization by the foundation President or other officer, who shall be invited to regular meetings of the Board of Directors of the parent corporation. Reports shall include information about its activities in support of this organization, fund-raising programs, and financial results.

3. *Review of Annual Goals and Objectives.* The foundation shall prepare its annual goals and objectives in concert with the priority needs of this organization. These goals shall include projects identified for fund raising, estimated income, and operating budget and staff required, to be submitted to the Board of Directors of this organization for review prior to inception.

4. *Professional Staff Hiring Procedures.* Professional employees of the foundation, including employees of this organization assigned to foundation work, shall

include in the interview and selection process the Chairman of the Board, Chairman of the Fund Development Committee, Chief Financial Officer, and the President/CEO. All employees shall observe the policies and procedures of the parent corporation at all times.

5. *Transfer of Funds Raised and Held.* The transfer of funds raised and held by the foundation shall be at the request of the President/CEO or Chief Financial Officer of the parent corporation or their delegates. Recommendations shall include the use or disposition of funds to be transferred for reports to donors. Each transfer shall be approved by the foundation board of directors and reported to the Board of the parent corporation.

6. *Nominations Process for Foundation Directors.* The Bylaws of the foundation specify that the Nominations Committee of the Board of Directors of the parent corporation shall identify, recruit, and nominate candidates for service on the Board of Directors of the foundation.

7. *Honors and Recognition by the Foundation.* Honors and recognition accorded to qualified donors and volunteers shall be conducted in concert with the parent corporation at all times, including the naming of any part of facilities, named positions, and the placement of donor recognition materials in or on buildings owned by the parent corporation. Honors and recognition accorded by the foundation shall otherwise be guided by the Honors and Recognition policy of the parent corporation (see Section J).

8. *Annual Meetings and Annual Reports.* The foundation shall conduct its annual meetings and issue its annual reports in concert with the parent corporation at all times. A selection of foundation directors, volunteers, and donors will be invited to attend annual meetings of the parent corporation. Annual reports prepared for the two organizations may be separate or combined, as the two Boards may determine.

9. *Annual Audit Review.* Audits prepared for the foundation shall be conducted in accordance with generally accepted accounting principles. Selection of the firm to conduct the audit shall be made by the parent corporation and the report delivered to the foundation board and the board of directors of the parent corporation. Further, as accounting guidelines may direct, the financial experience of the foundation may also be reported in the consolidated audit of the parent corporation as a related organization.

N. RELATED ORGANIZATIONS: SUPPORT GROUPS

1. *Authorization to Exist.* Support group organizations may be formed either by this organization or its subsidiary foundation only with the approval of the board of directors of both organizations. The purpose of any such support group shall be in keeping with the mission, purpose, goals, and objectives of the parent corporation. Support groups may not be established as separately incorporated associations except in the form of a subsidiary foundation as defined in Section M.

2. *Approval of Operating Rules and Procedures.* Support group organizations formed for fund development purposes shall be guided in their activities by written operating rules and procedures, which shall be approved by the parent corporation or its subsidiary foundation. Their operating rules and

procedures shall include text reporting their formal affiliation, purposes, members, Board of Directors, election of officers and their duties, powers, committees, meetings, receipt of funds and assets and their disposition, rules of order, limitations on political activities, insignia, amendments, and the like.

3. *Use of the Organization's Name.* Support groups may act only in the name of the parent corporation or its subsidiary foundation, use their name in their communications, solicit contributions only for support of their mission and priorities of need, and otherwise support their purposes, goals, and objectives.

4. *Review of Annual Goals and Objectives.* The annual goals and objectives of each support group organization shall be prepared in coordination and cooperation with the parent corporation or its subsidiary foundation. Preparation of annual goals and objectives shall be defined and approved by the Board of Directors of each support group and reported to the Board of Directors of the parent corporation or its subsidiary foundation for review and approval.

5. *Nominations Process for Officers and Members of the Board of Directors.* A nominations committee shall be appointed by the Board of Directors of each support group who will conduct elections to its Board of Directors. Composition of each nominations committee will include the Chairman of the Board, Chairman of the Committee on Fund Development, and President/CEO of the parent corporation, along with similar representatives of its subsidiary foundation. Candidates for election shall be approved by the parent corporation and its subsidiary foundation in advance of their election.

6. *Professional Staff Hiring Procedures.* Professional staff hired to assist support group organizations shall be employees of the parent corporation or its subsidiary foundation. Representatives of each support group will be invited to serve on selection committees for the hiring of professional staff whose duties include staff management and support for these organizations.

7. *Control of Funds Raised and Held.* All funds raised and held by support groups shall be in the name of the parent corporation, or its subsidiary foundation, and shall be delivered to it upon receipt or following completion of the activity for which these funds were raised. Regular reports of funds raised and held shall be made to the Committee on Fund Development of the parent corporation or to the Board of Directors of its subsidiary foundation, which funds shall be included in their regular financial statements and annual audit report.

8. *Annual Meetings and Annual Reports.* Support groups shall conduct their annual meetings and prepare their annual reports as their Operating Rules and Procedures specify. Invitations to annual meetings shall include representatives of the parent corporation and its subsidiary foundation, who shall also receive their annual reports.

9. *Annual Audit Review.* Funds raised or held in the name of the parent corporation or its subsidiary foundation are the property of these organizations and shall be included in their financial statements and annual audit report. If support groups manage their own funds, their books and financial statements will be delivered annually to the parent corporation or its subsidiary foundation for review and to provide such information as is required for preparation of the annual audit statement and IRS return. A report of each review will be delivered to the President of each support group.

O. DEPARTMENT OF FUND DEVELOPMENT

1. *Areas of Management Responsibility.* The Department of Fund Development reports to the President/CEO and is charged with management and staff support to the entire fund development program, including all employees, annual budget, donor records, and files. The definition and direction of fund-raising activities, recruitment and training of volunteers, accounting for all funds raised, and public reports shall be with the approval of the Committee on Fund Development and the Board of Directors.

2. *Approved Fund-Raising Programs.* Only those fund-raising programs and activities approved by the Committee on Fund Development shall be performed by this Department with the use of its employees and their time and with such budget funds as are made available. Any other program must first receive full and formal approval by the Committee prior to its implementation.

3. *Donor Relations and Communications.* This Department is charged with responsibility for the complete supervision of all records, personal relations, and communications with donors, including honors and recognition. This Department shall act as a resource to this organization on its formal obligations to donors at all times.

4. *Support Services.* The organization shall provide this Department with normal and routine support services, such as accounting, financial management, personnel, employee health, engineering, housekeeping, and so on, in the same manner as other Departments and assist in completion of its assigned duties, as appropriate.

5. *Job Descriptions and Hiring Practices.* All employees of this Department shall be guided in their daily duties by a written job description prepared for their position, as reviewed and approved by this organization. Salary levels, pay schedules, benefits, performance evaluations, and other matters relating to full- or part-time employment shall be consistent with personnel procedures of this organization, as shall be all hiring practices. Employees shall observe the same policies and procedures that apply to all other employees at all times.

6. *Budgets and Accountability.* Budget preparation and accountability for funds entrusted to the Department shall be performed by management staff of the Department in accordance with routine procedures of this organization. Departmental managers are responsible for the correct expense of all funds provided for operating purposes in accordance with organization policy, and for verifying these details to the finance division as required.

7. *Records and Files.* All records of correspondence, gift transactions, and their related details will be maintained by the Department as sensitive information for such periods of time and in such form as is appropriate. The use and disclosure of any of this information shall be restricted to Department employees and such others who have a need to know in order to carry out their assigned duties. Donor gift histories shall be preserved for the life of the donor. Any record destroyed shall protect the sensitive nature of the contents until destruction is complete.

P. PUBLIC REPORTING REQUIREMENTS

1. *Internal Revenue Service.* Preparation of Internal Revenue Service Form 990 and other IRS documents associated with the conduct of public solicitation and acceptance of gifts of any type and form shall be completed on schedules provided and in accordance with current IRS regulations.
2. *State and Local Agencies.* Such other reports as may be required by state, county, local community, or other agencies shall be completed on schedules provided and in accordance with current regulations. Such permits, licenses, and fees that may be required, along with public disclosure of tax-exempt certificates, audits, financial statements, and the like, will be completed in accordance with current regulations.
3. *Public Requests for Information.* Any request in writing, asking for copies of public documents so defined by law, such as reports submitted to the IRS and local authorities, will be completed in accordance with current regulations and will be honored the same day a request is made in person, or within 30 days of receipt of a written, e-mail, facsimile, or telephone request, as required by law.

Q. APPROVALS, REVIEWS, AND AMENDMENTS

1. *Authority of the Board of Directors.* This Manual is authorized by the Board of Directors, acting on recommendation of the Committee on Fund Development. It is designed to provide guidance and direction to all areas of fund development activity of this organization. Its contents shall be followed by all who accept appointment to voluntary and staff positions of this organization.
2. *Periodic Review and Reissue.* A review of this entire Manual will be conducted by the Committee on Fund Development every other year, with results reported to the Board of Directors. The purpose of this review will be to maintain an accurate relationship between the current practices of operating programs and the contents of this Manual. Any section or subsection may be examined at any time, as appropriate, with changes and additions proposed in accordance with the amendment procedures.
3. *Process for Amendment.* Changes to this Manual must be approved by the Board of Directors, who will act only on formal recommendations from the Committee on Fund Development. Proposals for amendment may be submitted in writing, at any time, by any participant in the fund development program who shall utilize existing committees, related organizations, or other appropriate and standing leadership structure for prior reviews and approvals leading to submission by the Committee on Fund Development.

Endnotes

1. Aristotle, "Ethica Nicomacea." (1947). Book II, Chapter 9, in R. McKeon (ed.), *Introduction to Aristotle,* trans. W. D. Ross. New York: Random House, p. 346.

2. Seymour, H. J. (1966). *Designs for Fund Raising: Principles, Patterns, Techniques.* New York: McGraw-Hill (paperback edition: Ambler, PA: Fund Raising Institute, 1988).

3. Payton, R. L. (1988). *Philanthropy: Voluntary Action for the Public Good.* New York: Macmillan.

4. See note 2.

5. Hodgkinson, V. A., and Associates. (1992). *The Nonprofit Almanac 1992–1993: Dimensions of the Independent Sector.* Washington, DC: Independent Sector.

6. American Association of Fund-Raising Counsel. (1999). *Giving USA 1998.* A. Kaplan (ed.). New York: AAFRC Trust for Philanthropy.

7. Rosso, H. A. (1996). *Rosso on Fund Raising: Lessons from a Master's Lifetime Experience.* San Francisco: Jossey-Bass, p. 120.

8. See note 2.

9. Kelly, K. S. (1998). *Effective Fund-Raising Management.* Mahway NJ: Lawrence Erlbaum Associates, p. 8.

10. Joyaux, S. P. (1997). *Strategic Fund Development: Building Profitable Relationships That Last.* Aspen's Fund Raising Series for the 21st Century. Gaithersburg, MD: Aspen, pp. 201–202.

11. Warner, I. R. (1990). *The Art of Fund Raising,* 3rd ed. New York: Harper & Row.

12. Anderson, A. (1996). *Ethics for Fund Raisers.* Bloomington: Indiana University Press, p. 1.

13. Grace, K. S. (1997). *Beyond Fund Raising: New Strategies for Nonprofit Innovation and Investment.* The NSFRE/Wiley Fund Development Series. New York: John Wiley & Sons, p. 3.

14. See note 7.

Suggested Readings

Blazek, J. (1999). *Tax Planning and Compliance for Tax-Exempt Organizations,* 3rd ed. New York: John Wiley & Sons.

Brakeley, G. A. Jr. (1980). *Tested Ways to Successful Fund Raising.* New York: AMACOM.

Briscoe, Marianne (ed.). (1994). *Ethics in Fundraising: Putting Values into Practice.* New Directions in Philanthropic Fundraising, no. 6. San Francisco: Jossey-Bass.

Broce, T. E. (1986). *Fund Raising: A Guide to Raising Money from Private Sources,* 2nd ed. Norman: University of Oklahoma Press.

Burlingame, D. F. (ed.). (1992). *The Responsibilities of Wealth.* Bloomington: Indiana University Press.

Burlingame, D. F., and J. M. Hodge (eds.). (1997). *Developing Major Gifts.* New Directions in Philanthropic Fundraising, no. 16. San Francisco: Jossey-Bass.

Burlingame, D. F., and L. J. Hulse (eds.). (1991). *Taking Fund Raising Seriously.* San Francisco: Jossey-Bass.

Carlson, D. M., and W. Freyd. (1997). "Telemarketing." In J. M. Greenfield (ed.). *The Nonprofit Handbook: Fund Raising,* 2nd ed. New York: John Wiley & Sons, pp. 317–328.

Ciconte, B. K., and J. G. Jacob. (1997). *Fund Raising Basics: A Complete Guide.* Aspen's Fund Raising Series for the 21st Century. Gaithersburg, MD: Aspen.

Connors, T. D. (1993). *The Nonprofit Management Handbook: Operating Policies and Procedures.* New York: John Wiley & Sons.

Costa, N. B. (1991). *Measuring Progress and Success in Fund Raising: How to Use Comparative Statistics to Prove Your Effectiveness.* Falls Church, VA: Association for Healthcare Philanthropy.

Council for Advancement and Support of Education. (1994). *CASE Campaign Standards: Management and Reporting Standards for Educational Fund-Raising Campaigns.* Washington, DC: Council for Advancement and Support of Education.

Council for Advancement and Support of Education. (1996). *Case Management Reporting Standards: Standards for Annual Giving and Campaigns in Educational Fund Raising.* Washington, DC: Council for Advancement and Support of Education.

Council for Advancement and Support of Education. (1998). *Fund-Raising Standards for Annual Giving and Campaign Reports for Not-for-Profit Organizations other than Colleges, Universities, and Schools.* Washington, DC: Council for Advancement and Support of Education.

Cutlip, S. M. (1990). *Fund-Raising in the United States: Its Role in American Philanthropy.* New Brunswick, NJ: Rutgers University Press (reprint of a 1965 work).

Day, D. L. (1998). *The Effective Advancement Professional: Management Principles and Practices.* Gaithersburg, MD: Aspen.

Drucker, P. F. (1990). *Managing the Nonprofit Organization: Practices and Principles.* New York: HarperCollins.

Duca, D. J. (1996). *Nonprofit Boards: Roles, Responsibilities, and Performance.* New York: John Wiley & Sons.

Fink, N. S., and H. C. Metzler. (1982). *The Costs and Benefits of Deferred Giving.* New York: Columbia University Press.

Frantzreb, A. C. (1997). *Not on This Board You Don't: Making Your Trustees More Effective.* Chicago: Bonus Books.

Fry, R. P. Jr. (1998). *Nonprofit Investment Policies: Strategies to Grow the Funds of Your Organization.* The NSFRE/Wiley Fund Development Series. New York: John Wiley & Sons.

Golden, S. L. (1997). *Successful Grantsmanship: A Guerrilla Guide to Raising Money.* San Francisco: Jossey-Bass.

Grasty, W. K., and K. G. Sheinkopf. (1983). *Successful Fund Raising: A Handbook of Proven Strategies and Techniques.* New York: Charles Scribners' Sons.

Gray, S. T. (1993). *A Vision for Evaluation.* Washington, DC: Independent Sector.

Greenfield, J. M. (1999). *Fund Raising: Evaluating and Managing the Fund Development Process,* 2nd ed. New York: John Wiley & Sons.

Greenfield, J. M. (1994). *Fund Raising Fundamentals: A Guide to Annual Giving for Professionals and Volunteers.* New York: John Wiley & Sons.

Greenfield J. M. (1996). *Fund-Raising Cost-Effectiveness: A Self-Assessment Workbook.* New York: John Wiley & Sons.

Gross, M. J. Jr., W. Warshauer Jr., and R. F. Larkin. (1994). *Financial and Accounting Guide for Not-for-Profit Organizations,* 5th ed. New York: John Wiley & Sons.

Gurin, M. G. (1991). *What Volunteers Should Know for Successful Fund Raising.* New York: Stein & Day.

Gurin, M. G. (1985). *Confessions of a Fund Raiser: Lessons of an Instructive Career.* Washington, DC: Taft Corporation.

Harris, T. (1999). *International Fund-Raising for Not-for-Profits: A Country-by-Country Profile.* New York: John Wiley & Sons.

Herman, R. D., and Associates. (1994). *The Jossey-Bass Handbook of Nonprofit Leadership and Management.* San Francisco: Jossey-Bass.

Hodgkinson, V. A., and M. S. Weitzman. (1992). *Giving and Volunteering in the United States: Findings from a National Survey.* Washington, DC: Independent Sector.

Hopkins, B. R. (1993). *The Law of Charitable Giving.* New York: John Wiley & Sons.

Hopkins, B. R. (1991). *The Law of Fund-Raising.* New York: John Wiley & Sons.

Hopkins, B. R. (1998). *The Law of Tax-Exempt Organizations,* 7th ed. New York: John Wiley & Sons.

Hopkins, B. R. (1993). *A Legal Guide to Starting and Managing a Nonprofit Organization,* 2nd ed. New York: John Wiley & Sons.

Howe, F. (1991). *The Board Member's Guide to Fund Raising.* San Francisco: Jossey-Bass.

Huntsinger, J. E. (1985). *Fund Raising Letters: A Comprehensive Study Guide to Raising Money by Direct Response Marketing.* Richmond, VA: Emerson.

Johnston, M. (1999). *The Fund Raiser's Guide to the Internet.* The NSFRE/Wiley Fund Development Series. New York: John Wiley & Sons.

Jordon, R. R., and K. L. Quynn. (1994). *Planned Giving: Management, Marketing, and Law.* New York: John Wiley & Sons.

Kihlstedt, A., and C. P. Schwartz. (1997). *Capital Campaigns: Strategies That Work.* Aspen's Fund Raising Series for the 21st Century. Gaithersburg, MD: Aspen.

Kotler, P., and A. R. Andreason. (1987). *Strategic Marketing for Nonprofit Organizations,* 3rd ed. Englewood Cliffs, NJ: Prentice Hall.

Lautman, K., and H. Goldstein. (1991). *Dear Friend: Mastering the Art of Direct Mail Fund Raising,* 2nd ed. Washington, DC: Taft Group.

Levy, B. R., and B. H. Marion. (1997). *Successful Special Events: Planning, Hosting, and Evaluating.* Aspen's Fund Raising Series for the 21st Century. Gaithersburg, MD: Aspen.

Lindahl, W. E. (1992). *Strategic Planning for Fund Raising.* San Francisco: Jossey-Bass.

McLeish, B. J. (1995). *Successful Marketing Strategies for Nonprofit Organizations.* New York: John Wiley & Sons.

Mixer, J. R. (1993). *Principles of Professional Fund Raising.* San Francisco: Jossey-Bass.

Murray, D. J. (1994). *The Guaranteed Fund-Raising System: A Systems Approach to Planning and Controlling Fund Raising,* 2nd ed. Poughkeepsie, NY: American Institute of Management.

New, A. L., and W. C. Levis. (1991). *Raise More Money for Your Nonprofit Organization: A Guide to Evaluating and Improving Your Fundraising.* New York: Foundation Center.

Nichols, J. (1995). *Growing from Good to Great: Positioning Your Fund Raising for BIG Gains.* Chicago: Bonus Books.

Nichols, J. (1998). *Strengthening Fund Raising through Evaluation.* Chicago: Bonus Books.

Nichols, J. (1983). *America's Voluntary Spirit: A Book of Readings.* New York: Foundation Center.

Nichols, J. (1987). *Philanthropy in Action.* Washington, DC: Independent Sector.

O'Neill, M. (1989). *The Third America: The Emergence of the Nonprofit Sector in the United States.* San Francisco: Jossey-Bass.

Pidgeon, W. P. (1998). *The Universal Benefits of Volunteering: A Practical Workbook for Nonprofit Organizations, Volunteers, and Corporations.* The NSFRE/Wiley Fund Development Series. New York: John Wiley & Sons.

Prince, R. A., and K. M. File. (1994). *The Seven Faces of Philanthropy: A New Approach to Cultivating Major Donors.* San Francisco: Jossey-Bass.

Rosso, H. A., and Associates. (1991). *Achieving Excellence in Fund Raising: A Comprehensive Guide to Principles, Strategies, and Methods.* San Francisco: Jossey-Bass.

Scanlan, E. A. (1997). *Corporate and Foundation Fund Raising: A Complete Guide from the Inside.* Aspen's Fund Raising Series for the 21st Century. Gaithersburg, MD: Aspen.

Schmaedick, G. L. (1993). *Cost-Effectiveness in the Nonprofit Sector.* New London, CT: Quorum Books.

Schwartz, J. J. (1994). *Modern American Philanthropy: A Personal Account*. New York: John Wiley & Sons.

Seltzer, M. (1987). *Securing Your Organization's Future: A Complete Guide to Fundraising Strategies*. New York: Foundation Center.

Sharp, R. F. Sr. (1998). *Planned Giving Simplified: The Gift, the Giver, and the Gift Planner*. The NSFRE/Wiley Fund Development Series. New York: John Wiley & Sons.

Shaw, S. C., and M. A. Taylor. (1995). *Reinventing Fundraising: Realizing the Potential of Women's Philanthropy*. San Francisco: Jossey-Bass.

Smith, B., and Associates. (1994). *The Complete Guide to Nonprofit Management*. R. H. Wilbur, S. K. Finn, and C. M. Freedland (eds.). New York: John Wiley & Sons.

Von Til, J., and Associates. (1990). *Critical Issues in American Philanthropy*. San Francisco: Jossey-Bass.

Warwick, M. (1990). *Revolution in the Mailbox*. Baltimore, MD: Fund Raising Institute.

Warwick, M. (1992). *You Don't Always Get What You Asked For: Using Direct Mail Tests to Raise More Money for Your Organization*. Berkeley, CA: Strathmoor Press.

Warwick, M. (2000). *The Five Strategies for Fundraising Success: A Mission-Based Guide to Achieving Your Goals*. San Francisco: Jossey-Bass.

Weinstein, S. (1999). *The Complete Guide to Fund-Raising Management*. The NSFRE/Wiley Fund Development Series. New York: John Wiley & Sons.

White, D. E. (1995). *The Art of Planned Giving: Understanding Donors and the Culture of Giving*. New York: John Wiley & Sons.

Williams, M. J. (1991). *Big Gifts: How to Maximize Gifts from Individuals, with or without a Capital Campaign*. Rockville, MD: Fund Raising Institute.

Young, D. R., and R. Steinberg. (1995). *Economics for Nonprofit Managers*. New York: Foundation Center.

Zeff, R. (1996). *The Nonprofit Guide to the Internet*. New York: John Wiley & Sons.

20 ▼ Nonprofit Organizations as Entrepreneurs

RUTHIE G. REYNOLDS, PhD
Tennessee State University

20.1 Introduction

In today's society, entrepreneurship is seen as a lifesaver to society. Governments promote it as an avenue by which to move the poor away from poverty and toward self-sufficiency, educators see it as a new discipline to offer to their students, and business owners see it as an opportunity to control their own destiny through self-directed employment.

While entrepreneurship is considered a viable career alternative for the private sector, nonprofit organizations (NPOs) have begun to see it as a viable means of support for this operation. Although the U.S. economy is booming, many NPOs continue to see a drop in public support. Therefore, they are forced to seek funding from nontraditional sources. They are being asked to provide more services, while faced with access to fewer dollars. The result has been that many of these organizations have "caught the entrepreneurial spirit." Recognizing that NPOs must be careful to avoid the unrelated business tax on income from commercial activities, this chapter focuses on mission-related activities that can result in additional funds for the nonprofit. The emphasis is on innovative and new ideas, many of which can be used by any type of organization.

20.2 What are Nonprofit Organizations?

The term *nonprofit organization* is used to refer to entities formed to provide social services rather than being formed to seek a profit. These organizations come into existence to meet a need that is not fulfilled by business enterprises or to meet a need that is not completely fulfilled by existing NPOs. The organizations do not have owners, and the ownership interest cannot be sold or traded. While the organization's revenues may exceed expenses, the excess must be used for the common good of society. It cannot directly benefit the members, and it cannot be referred to as profit.

Funding sources for NPOs include contributions or donations from the general public, allocations from governmental units and other NPOs, and service fees. When fees are charged for services, they are usually lower than market value. Often, they are based on need or ability to pay rather than effective demand. Examples of NPOs include colleges and universities, foundations, hospitals, churches, health and welfare agencies, associations, and governmental agencies.

(A)   TYPES OF NONPROFIT ORGANIZATIONS

Basically, there are two types of NPOs: public and private. Public NPOs provide community services to the public. They are sanctioned by laws that grant the approval for them to collect taxes at either the federal, state, or local level. The managers are elected officials, voted into and out of office by the public.

As a result of the growing need in society for services, the budgets of public NPOs have soared. While entrepreneurial activities can be engaged in by all NPOs, the public nonprofit is not likely to use this form of activity because such actions would require the approval of the constituency. Private NPOs are created by members of the general public. Whereas these organizations may be charted by governmental agencies, they cannot levy taxes. Therefore, they rely on voluntary contributions and donations as sources of support.

21.3   *What Is Entrepreneurship?*

There are numerous definitions of entrepreneurship. For the purpose of this discussion, *entrepreneurship* may be defined as the creation of value through idea creation and innovation. Entrepreneurs recognize a need for certain services and create a mechanism by which they can be provided. Entrepreneurs have vision. They are able to take the present and see potential for improvement. They are dreamers, taking actions necessary to ensure the vision.

One of the early forms of entrepreneurship in the nonprofit sector involved the government's acting as an innovator. When the government becomes active in commercializing technology, it is commonly called *technology transfer.* Technology transfer occurs when the government funds research in laboratories that create new products that are then taken to market. This revolutionary process has led to the creation of partnerships or collaborations among scientists in federally funded laboratories and university educators who think entrepreneurially.

The benefits of the collaborations are great. When inventions or developments are created within an organization, revenue is bound to increase. If help is needed to assist in taking the product or service to market, a collaborator can be helpful. The collaborator may have expertise or test the product or service and assist in the further development, if needed. Since the nonprofit entrepreneur is an organization, the attributes and qualities needed for success as an entrepreneur refer to the members of the management team and leaders of the organizations. A list of those characteristics is shown in Exhibit 20.1.

EXHIBIT 20.1 Required Characteristics of Leaders of Nonprofit Organizations Engaged in Entrepreneurial Activities

---

- Accept change as good
- Bold
- Capable of working long hours
- Creative and innovative
- Desire to be a leader in the field
- Dynamic
- Forward-looking
- Persistent
- Possess good organizational skills
- Possess understanding of basic business skills
- Team worker
- Welcome challenges
- Willing and able to negotiate
- Willing to take risk

A disadvantage of NPOs as entrepreneurs is the need for members of the management team and leaders to act as one unit. In business enterprises, the entrepreneur may be a single individual or a small group of individuals who share the same dream. However, in NPOs, certain members of the team may not share the vision. This can present problems for the successful completion of the venture.

(A) STEPS IN THE ENTREPRENEURIAL PROCESS

How does an NPO get involved in entrepreneurial activities? Like anything else, a process should be followed. Exhibit 20.2 shows the steps in the process.

Step 1 calls for idea creation. Often, the idea will result from an existing need, or it can result from a future need. Step 2 calls for studying the idea. This step requires brainstorming. Although the initial idea may be the brainchild of one individual, all members of the management team should be active participants in not only step 2 but all of the remaining steps. Step 3 may require the assistance of business professionals such as accountants, lawyers, market researchers, and computer experts. The business plan must

---

EXHIBIT 20.2 Steps in the Entrepreneurial Process

Step 1: Develop a new idea or expand an old idea.
Step 2: Study the idea.
Step 3: Prepare a business plan, marketing plan, and
         feasibility study.
Step 4: Seek financing.
Step 5: Implement the plans.

---

be completed, even if funds have already been identified for the venture. The business plan is the blueprint showing the future direction of the idea. The market study gathers information on the perceptions of potential customers. The feasibility study determines if the proposed venture is worthwhile. The market study and the feasibility study are often considered integral parts of the business plan.

20.4   Need for Alternative Sources of Revenue

Competition is not peculiar to business enterprises seeking profits. NPOs face competition from within the nonprofit sector as well as from the small-business sector. Like small businesses, NPOs have limited resources. Furthermore, they may have managers with limited management skills and may have to rely on volunteers to provide services usually rendered by paid employees.

NPOs face challenges in raising sufficient revenue. If the organization relies on government funding, it may find that the governmental entity's allocations are decreasing. If the organization relies on charitable giving as its primary source of revenue, it may find that there is a reduction in corporate giving. Another common obstacle is federal, state, and local governments' reduction in tax incentives for charitable giving. There is competition among nonprofit organizations for the pool of limited funds. As a result, NPOs are seeking entrepreneurial activities to increase revenue needed to fund their activities.

The chart in Exhibit 20.3 shows the decrease in private contributions in the nonprofit sector over a 16-year period. While there was an increase in governmental allocations in 1996 (which may have resulted from increases in health care funding from Medicare), the need for alternative financing is clear.

Entrepreneurial ventures are attractive to NPOs. The revenue earned can be used to supplement programs, but maybe more importantly, the nonprofit has more control over the revenue than over contributions and government funds. Contributions and government funds carry restrictions. Restrictions limit the use of funds. Earned revenue, however, carries no restrictions. The nonprofits are free to use the funds as they choose, provided they stay within the guidelines of their mission and comply with applicable governmental regulations.

EXHIBIT 20.3 Decrease in Contributions to Nonprofit Organizations Over the Past 16 Years

	1980	1988	1996
Private contributions: % of total revenue	30%	27%	19%
Government allocations: % of total revenue	34%	27%	32%

Sources: Hodgkinson, V. A., and M. S. Weitzman. (1986). *Dimensions of the Independent Sector: A Statistical Profile.* Washington, DC: The Independent Sector; Hodgkinson, V. A., and M. S. Weitzman. (1988). *Dimensions of the Independent Sector: A Statistical Profile,* interim update, 2nd ed. Washington, DC: The Independent Sector; and Boris, E. T. (1998). "Myths about the Nonprofit Sector." In E. T. Boris (ed.), *Charting Civil Society* (July 1–4). Washington, DC: The Urban Institute.

20.5 Possible Entrepreneurial Ventures for Nonprofits

The type of entrepreneurial venture that a nonprofit engages in may depend on the type of services rendered to the public through its nonprofit status. The following discussion deals with various types of NPOs and the services they may offer.

(A) THE NEED

While some NPOs are experiencing the best of times, others are fighting to keep their doors open. With decreases in contributions and government funding, along with increasing demands to provide additional services, to keep up with technology, and to add new and innovative programs, NPOs must look to new sources of revenue. College and university administrators look to entrepreneurial ventures to bridge the gap between needed funds and available funds.

A good example of the need can be found in the operations of colleges and universities. Increases in cost of educational services provided by colleges and universities come from various sources. Exhibit 20.4 shows that an increase in instruction may arise from many factors, such as lowering class sizes to comply with accreditation standards. In this case, the institution has little or no options but to comply.

The impact of a change can be devastating. Assume that a course currently has 400 students per semester. If the class size is reduced from 40 students to 30 students, the number of sections will increase from 10 to 16. If the average salary of a professor is $60,000 and a professor teaches six sections a year, the cost of instruction is $60,000/6 sections per year = $10,000 per section × 10 sections = $100,000. With an additional six sections needed to service the 400 students, the new cost would be $10,000 × 16 sections, or $160,000. The change in policy results in an increase in cost of $60,000 to service the same number of students. This one change in policy could force the institution to seek alternative sources of funds, such as entrepreneurial activities.

(B) OBSTACLE: UNRELATED BUSINESS INCOME TAX

The major concern NPOs face when choosing entrepreneurial activities is avoidance of the Unrelated Business Income Tax. The Unrelated Business Income Tax is a federal tax imposed by Congress on NPOs that earn profits from the sale of goods or services that are

---

EXHIBIT 20.4 Factors Causing Increase in College and University Education

- Need for advanced technology
- Increase in operations costs
- Reduced teaching loads
- Reduced class sizes
- Salary equities
- Cost-of-living adjustments
- Need for more terminally qualified faculty
- Special accreditation of individual areas of study
- Scholarships to attract outstanding students

---

not related to their exempt purpose. The following discussion assumes that the entrepreneurial activities outlined have passed the test as related exempt activities.

(C)   TYPES OF ACTIVITIES

There is no limit to the types of entrepreneurial activities suitable to the NPO. Selected popular activities are discussed in the following sections.

(i)   Vending Machine Sales

Most nonprofits have some revenues from vending machines as a source of revenue. In the college and university arena, soft drink contracts with vendors have added substantial amounts to operating revenue. Many of the soft drink companies have formed alliances or partnerships with institutions. A major part of these contracts includes the exclusive selling of products of the vendor, preventing competing vendors' products from being sold on campus. It is estimated that the contracts with the two major soft drink companies, Coca-Cola and Pepsi, run into the billions. When the products are sold on campuses of the institutions, the institution receives a commission. The commission may range from 15 percent to 85 percent, depending on such factors as the size and popularity of the sports programs, the location, and the size of the enrollment. The following scenario is a typical example of the impact a soft drink contract has on the revenue stream of a university.

> The Marion Pepsi-Cola Bottling Company of Marion, Illinois, agreed to give $500,000 to the Southern Illinois University at Carbondale's athletic campaign. The University agreed to "use, sell and advertise only Pepsi-Cola products at all athletic events. The University also agreed to that 90 percent of all soft drinks in campus vending machines would be Pepsi-Cola product.[1]

The problem with the Pepsi-Cola scenario is the contractual arrangement was labeled a "gift," and the president of the Marion Pepsi-Cola Bottling Company was also the chairman of the Illinois Community College Board. The president of the company resigned from his board post after the media disclosed the nature of the arrangement. Because of the questionable nature of the "gift" (with all of the restrictions and conditions), the Illinois legislature later passed a law that made it illegal for vendors to make such stipulations.

Vending sales contracts as entrepreneurial activities may be very rewarding financially. However, nonprofits should consider the following three issues before entering into such arrangements:

1. Do not require gifts or any other form of support as conditions of contracts awarded to outside vendors.
2. Exclusive product contracts are not illegal, but carefully consider the ramifications of contracts from vendors who require exclusive contracts, banning all or a substantial number of competitors.
3. Consider the impact of the possible loss of permanent funding due to the presence of these contracts, which may be lost in later years.

For example, government funding may be replaced by revenues from vendor contracts; however, when the government funds are needed in later years, they may not then be available.

(ii) Research and Development

Public and private support for research and development (R&D) is common in today's society. R&D is thought of as a major factor contributing to long-term productivity and advancement in any organization, whether it be for-profit or nonprofit. It improves living standards and adds economic value.

R&D takes place in all sectors of life, including education, housing, technology, and health. In fact, society encourages R&D in many ways. One way is by voting in tax credits for the private sector who undertake projects and by voting in grants for the public sector and other nonprofits.

One of the most heavily funded R&D areas is health care. The R&D activities engaged in by nonprofit hospitals and academic institutions not only meet objectives set by the mission, but also provide needed funding to carry out operations. The organizations, acting through their entrepreneurial arm, receive that alternative source of revenue, which can become an ongoing source of funding.

It is generally accepted that improvements in the health of citizens have a positive effect on the well-being of society and the economy in general. Nonprofit hospitals are major benefactors of funding in this area. For example, it has been said that the development of a new drug costs up to $300 million to move it from the discovery stage to Food and Drug Administration (FDA) approval. Large nonprofit hospitals, which are usually associated with universities, are well equipped to handle such involved research and development. Many of these nonprofits will enter into collaborations with other nonprofits or even private-sector entities to gain a stronger footing in R&D.

Popular sources of R&D funding in the health care area are the National Institutes of Health, the National Library of Medicine, and the Centers for Disease Control and Prevention. Nonprofit organizations can apply for funding in numerous health care areas. Often, the funds are made available to a wide variety of types of nonprofits. For example, the National Institutes of Health recently advertised funding available for R&D in the area of acquired immune deficiency syndrome (AIDS) information outreach. Applications were accepted from universities, colleges, research institutions, hospitals (public and private nonprofit, as well as for-profit), state and local governments and their bona fide agents, and federally recognized Native American tribal governments, Native American tribes, or Native American tribal organizations.

Nonprofits, especially colleges and universities, receive millions of dollars each year from licenses, royalties, copyrights, patents, and other nontangible assets resulting from R&D. Bristol-Myers, a large pharmaceutical company, pays millions to several universities for their inventions or discoveries in drugs designed to treat cancer. Exhibit 20.5 shows sta-

---

EXHIBIT 20.5 1998 Payments to Selected Universities by Bristol-Myers Pharmaceutical

Institution	Award
Florida State University	$29 million in 1997; $45 million in 1998
Michigan State University	$160 million over past 20 years
Montana State University	$10 million annually
Montana Tech University	$10 million annually

Source: Blumenstyk, G. (1999). "How One University Pursued Profit from Science—and Won," *The Chronicle of Higher Education* (February 12): A39–40.

tistics regarding Bristol-Myers's payments to various universities for R&D efforts. Michigan State University is the leader in this field. Inventions by a group of biophysics professors have brought more than $150 million to the university over the past 20 years. Other universities receiving payments for drug inventions include Montana State University, Florida State University, and Montana Tech University.

In addition to universities contracting to have their professors and students perform R&D activities, they also have other R&D arrangements with pharmaceutical companies. For example, a university can turn certain science and technology departments over to outside companies, receiving large of amounts of funds. As a result, the outside firm has all rights or controlling interests in all inventions and discoveries for a stated period of time.

Federal governments made awards for R&D in fiscal year 1998. The Department of Defense awards contracts, grants, and agreements for research, development, testing, and evaluation to NPOs, including federal, state, and local government agencies. There are two broad categories of R&D funding in the Department of Defense: technology base and development. Their technology base research awards were in both areas of (1) basic research and (2) applied research. Most of the technology base awards were made to colleges and universities. The development awards were in the areas of (1) advanced technology development, (2) demonstration and validation, (3) engineering and manufacture development, (4) management support, and (5) operational system development. The development funds were awarded to large nonprofit laboratories administered by or affiliated with institutions of higher education, but organizationally separate and qualitatively distinct from academic departments of the universities. Exhibit 20.6 shows the type and number of R&D awards for fiscal year 1998.

The R&D entrepreneurial activities outlined herein have potential unfavorable consequences to the nonprofit involved. If the university agrees to allow the outside firm to control the operations of its discoveries, the university may lose its ability to meet its educational goals and objectives. The university could find itself restricted by the condition of the outside firm. Although developing close relationships with companies can be beneficial to nonprofits, the nonprofit should be careful to not give up more than intended. Such arrangements could also cause havoc among professors within the university. One of the rights awarded faculty members is academic freedom. If professors are not interested in working on the outside firm's project or do not wish to sign over the rights to their inventions and discoveries, they could view the university's pressure to comply as undue influence.

EXHIBIT 20.6 Department of Defense R&D Awards to Nonprofit Organizations, FY 1998

Type of Nonprofit	Number of Awards	Amount of Award
Technology Base		
Educational Institutions	292	$1,136,000,000
Other Nonprofits	143	397,000,000
Development		
Educational Institutions	149	983,000,000
Other Nonprofits	63	930,000,000

Source: U.S. Department of Defense, 1998.

(iii) Technology Companies

Entrepreneurial opportunities in the form of company start-ups are also available to non-profits. NPOs may contract with outside firms to provide resources to their researchers, who will perform testing needed to develop new products, test new products, and improve old products. The State of Maryland has passed legislation that allows university professors and other state employees to remain with the university while setting up start-up companies. Just as some universities that offer entrepreneurship courses give seed money to students desiring to start a business, universities have also provided start-up funds for faculty and staff. The university does not use its own funds to start the business; it seeks funding from investors.

(iv) Space and Facility Rental

Included in the mission of most NPOs is the goal of serving the community in which it exists. A program that can bring in extra revenue to nonprofit hospitals is clinics served by members of the hospital staff, but outside their regular duties. Physicians who work for a hospital and teach at a related medical school can be provided space to see their patients. A fee is charged for use of the space and other facilities. The benefit to the hospital is three-fold: (1) junior health care providers gain needed experience, (2) the community is provided with health care, and (3) extra revenue is earned.

(v) Community Education

Forms of community education projects include short courses and certificate programs for executives, special adult classes, seminars, workshops, and conferences. Adult education classes are very profitable if the institutions cater to target audiences. Classes could be geared toward professionals who want to be entrepreneurs, new immigrants, or women returning to work after a long absence. The nonprofit must be innovative in developing programs that meet demand. Universities and community organizations can offer English as a Second Language courses for individuals who recently entered the country. One of the benefits accruing to the organization is the possibility that the individuals will sign on for other courses. Courses can be designed to meet the needs of a particular professional group, such as certification programs for teachers or nurses. One caution is for the organizations to make sure regular classes do not suffer for lack of instructors or facilities.

Most community centers increase the number of programs offered to youth in the summer months, but do not consider opportunities that can bring in additional revenue that could result from added adult programs. Generally, the facilities are filled to capacity during day hours, but very few youth programs are offered in the evenings. These nonprofits can survey the needs of the adults in their communities and create evening programs to fit those needs. Likewise, during summer months, colleges and universities either do not offer summer courses to their regular student body or the offered courses are limited. This means that the dormitories, laboratories, and classrooms are vacant. This is a prime opportunity for these institutions to create and sponsor specialty adult programs.

Nonprofits could capitalize on the advent of technological advancements. There are chances for combining technology and education to create an entrepreneurial niche. In-house employee training programs, as well as contracted training programs, could be made available for a fee to other nonprofit or interested parties through distance learning. No longer is it necessary for an individual to physically attend a program. The programs could be made available to organizations all over the world via the Internet.

(vi) Financial Transactions

Many NPOs have developed contractual arrangements with banks and other financial institutions to provide services. Employees of NPOs may receive debit cards from a local bank, and the bank card can be used to make a variety of financial transactions. For example, colleges and universities can make arrangements for their employees, as well as students, to pay for copies, make purchases at the bookstore, pay tuition, or buy books. The institution receives a commission on the use of the cards.

(vii) Consulting

Professors in colleges and universities can secure funding for individual research projects and other funding needs by contracting to perform educational-related services for governmental agencies, corporations, and other NPOs. These opportunities allow professors to have some control of their destinies. At a time when salary raises are decreasing in amount and number, and travel and research funding is scarce, consulting can be a welcome source of personal as well as professional gain. The professor gets additional pay, and the college or university gets the benefit of sponsored research, extra pay for its faculty and students, and real-world experience.

(viii) Other Possible Activities

Following are other possible types of entrepreneurial activities available to NPOs:

- Arts-and-crafts shows
- Bakeries
- Cleaning businesses
- Computer services
- Concessions
- Gift shops
- Housing facilities
- Mail-order businesses
- Printing services
- Thrift stores

20.6 Summary

While the objective of NPOs is not to earn a profit, but rather to provide services or goods to the public, an increasing number of organizations are using mission-related entrepreneurial activities as alternative funding sources. There are possible risks, but carefully designed programs can be operated in a manner that complies with governing regulations. Entrepreneurship is an acceptable and viable alternative source of funding in the nonprofit sector.

Endnote

1. Van Der Werf, M. (1999). "As Coke and Pepsi Do Battle on Campuses, Colleges Find a Fountain of New Revenue," *The Chronicle of Higher Education*, pp. A1–42.

Suggested Readings

Adams, C., and F. Perimutter. (1991). "Commercial Venturing and the Transformation of America's Voluntary Social Welfare Agencies," *Nonprofit and Voluntary Sector Quarterly* 20(1): 25–38.

Blumenstyk, G. (1999). "Research Venture on Umbilical-Cord Blood Proves Costly for U. of Arizona," *Chronicle of Higher Education* (January 29): 44–45.

Boris, E. T. (1998). "Myths about the Nonprofit Sector." In E.T. Boris (ed.), *Charting Civil Society* (July 1–4). Washington DC: The Urban Institute.

Froelich, K. A. (2000). "New competitors for small business: The for-profit mentality of nonprofit organizations," presentation at United States Association for Small Business and Entrepreneurship and Small Business Institute Director's Association Joint National Conference, San Antonio, Texas, February 16–20.

Gronbjerg, K. A. (1993). *Understanding Nonprofit Funding.* San Francisco: Jossey-Bass.

Hodgkinson, V. A., and M. S. Weitzman. (1986). *Dimensions of the Independent Sector: A Statistical Profile.* Washington, DC: The Independent Sector.

Hodgkinson, V. A., and M. S. Weitzman. (1988). *Dimensions of the Independent Sector: A Statistical Profile,* interim update, 2nd ed. Washington, DC: The Independent Sector.

Hodgkinson, V. A., and M. S., Weitzman. (1997). *Nonprofit Almanac: Dimensions of the Independent Sector 1996–1997.* San Francisco: Jossey-Bass.

Hodgkinson, V. A., M. S. Weitzman, S. M. Noga, and H. A. Gorski. (1993). *A Portrait of the Independent Sector: The Activities and Finances of Charitable Organizations.* San Francisco: Jossey-Bass.

Preston, A. (1989). "The Nonprofit Sector in a For-Profit World," *Journal of Labor Economics* 7: 438–63.

Tuckman, H. P. (1998). "Competition, Commercialization, and the Evolution of Nonprofit Organizational Structures," *Journal of Policy Analysis and Management* 17(2): 175–94.

U.S. Department of Defense. (1998). Educational and Other Nonprofit Institutions Receiving DoD Prime Awards of Contracts, Grants, and Agreements for Research, Development, Test, and Evaluation, Fiscal Year 1998.

Walters, M. (1999). "Developing Public Policy for Entrepreneurial Activities in Higher Education," unpublished manuscript. November 29, Nashville, Tennessee.

Weisbrod, B. A. (1998). *To Profit or Not to Profit: The Commercial Transformation of the Nonprofit Sector.* New York: Cambridge University Press.

21 Commercial Ventures: Opportunities and Risks for Nonprofit Organizations

KEITH SEEL, MA, PRINCIPAL
M4i Strategic Management Consulting, Inc.

We are asking more of charities. We are asking them to be efficient, to be more "business-like" and accountable for their actions. Meanwhile, the confluence of cuts in government funding and rising case loads is making many charities look to new sources of revenue.

One potential new source of revenue is a commercial venture—going into business in the expectation of profits to support other charitable purposes.—Judith Maxwell, President (Canadian Policy Research Networks, Inc., 1998, p. xii.)

21.1 Introduction

Four trends are underway that are encouraging nonprofit agencies (both registered charities and other nonprofit organizations serving a public good) to consider undertaking commercial ventures. First, there is an ever-increasing competition for funding within the nonprofit sector. Second, governments are reconsidering or blatantly withdrawing financial support for social programs delivered by such agencies. Third, proactive nonprofit agencies are looking for ways to increase their financial sustainability or their financial flexibility by generating unrestricted funds. And finally, there is a growing interest in corporate marketing initiatives involving a nonprofit partner. These four trends have encouraged experimentation that has resulted in some successes, but often in disappointment as well.

Dennis Young notes that one of the biggest changes in the nonprofit sector has been its commercialization. He adds:

American nonprofits have also been strongly affected by events in the business sector, especially changes that have reinforced their commercial tendencies. The downsizing of large corporations has undermined the viability of United Ways as a mainstay of not-for-profit agency support and has required nonprofits to become more competitive in seeking support from corporations . . . downsizing [has] caused corporations to become more strategic in their giving to nonprofits, less generous with unrestricted cash gifts, but more likely to offer help through workforce volunteering and through strategic alliances or sponsorships that help sell corporate products.[1]

Gregory Dees notes five reasons why commercial ventures have become popular among nonprofit organizations:

1. A worldwide acceptance of capitalism. This acceptance of the "market-driven" society has made commercial ventures by nonprofit agencies more acceptable.
2. Many nonprofit leaders are looking to deliver social goods and services in ways that do not create dependency in their constituencies.
3. Nonprofits are seeking financial sustainability and stability by "self-funding."
4. The sources of funds available to nonprofits are shifting to favor more commercial approaches.
5. Competition between sectors and within the nonprofit sector is forcing agencies to find alternatives to traditional funding sources.[2]

Commercial ventures by nonprofit organizations are relatively new and are, therefore, relatively unstudied. This chapter draws on the author's experience and existing information in the field to outline the opportunities, risks, and considerations that accompany a commercial venture by a nonprofit agency. The information provided is intended to encourage reflection and debate within such agencies considering this strategy to revenue development.

21.2   *Understanding the Trends*

The four trends mentioned previously are discussed in this section. Often, local or regional demographics, legislation, corporate representation, nonprofit representation, and citizen involvement will change the character of these trends. Readers are encouraged to conduct further exploration into how each trend is playing out in their own communities.

(A)   INCREASING COMPETITION FOR FUNDING

Research supported by the Trillium Foundation clearly states that one of the motivators behind nonprofit commercial ventures "is the panic from the environmental shock of radical cuts in government grants to charities in the last few years. Reeling from this shock, charities are looking for methods to quickly replace the lost revenue to continue serving their missions."[3]

(B)   CHANGES IN GOVERNMENT FUNDING

Richard Steckle and Robin Simmons observe that "nonprofits can't do their jobs alone. They need the strength of corporations behind them if they're going to make a difference. They need corporate money to help run their programs because traditional funds are drying up."[4] In Canada, as in other countries, there have been massive shifts in the ways that government funds services provided by nonprofit organizations. A "devolution revolution" is in progress, creating "considerable anxiety as categorical federal programs on which many nonprofits depend are dismantled in favor of 'block grants' that will give state governments less money but more discretion to allocate resources to local priorities."[5]

The Canadian Centre for Philanthropy reports that of the $86 billion that flows through charitable organizations, 56.5 percent comes from government. Furthermore, the Centre contends that for every 1 percent drop in government funding, individuals would need to increase their support to nonprofit agencies by 5.8 percent just to keep funding levels constant.[6]

Faced with that reality, nonprofit organizations (NPOs) anticipating government cuts must either increase donations to their organizations or seek alternatives such as fees for service or commercial ventures. Many are choosing to do both.

(C)   FINANCIAL SUSTAINABILITY AND/OR FLEXIBILITY

Increasingly, donors or grantors are looking to have their particular financial contributions to a nonprofit restricted to a very specific program or project. While this approach creates a close bond between the particular donor, the gift, and services provided to those in need, it often creates a situation in which day-to-day operational costs are left unaddressed. An NPO having large amounts of its budget restricted to specific programs has little or no flexibility to deal with changes in administration costs, repairs, lease arrangements, and so forth.

To give themselves some flexibility, many NPOs have started to charge minimal fees for services. Other groups are looking at earning revenue through a variety of commercial ventures. Because revenue that is generated in either of these ways is not designated for one program or another, it can be spent at the discretion of the agency's management. The flexibility and enhanced sustainability generated by these initiatives is a strong incentive for financially strapped NPOs to consider developing fee structures and commercial ventures.

(D) CORPORATE MARKETING INITIATIVES INVOLVING A NONPROFIT PARTNER

This trend has a number of aspects. First, there has been growth in marketing efforts and strategies involving a nonprofit partner. As Steckle and Simmons put it, through these kinds of marketing initiatives, "capitalism has actually become a philanthropic tool."[7] Likewise, philanthropy has become a marketing tool, as the Market Vision Group's research shows. Their report, "The Not-for-Profit and Private Sectors in the 1990s," points out that traditional brand loyalty is evaporating and that "consumers are much more impressed with business' performance with regard to the relevance of its offering," where being relevant means "being involved in the community with a cause/issue of importance to the customer—an issue high on the customer's personal community or social agenda."[8] The report optimistically reports that "Such a situation represents a significant opportunity to business or the private sector, and the not-for-profit sector."[9]

Second, corporate community relations and corporate community investment programs are increasingly conveying an interest in partnering with the community. In the parlance of The Center for Corporate Community Relations at Boston College, corporations are seeking to become a "neighbor of choice." Indeed, the Standards of Excellence in Community Relations that has been developed by the college include such points as:

- Employee community involvement is encouraged, supported, and recognized through policies and incentives such as release to volunteer, awards and recognition programs, and matching employee gifts.
- Two-way communication with community stakeholders is fostered through consumer advisory panels, policy dialogues, meetings with advocacy groups and neighbors, or similar activities.
- Research and analysis are conducted to determine community needs, characteristics, and trends.
- A community relations strategic plan identifies specific areas of focus that reflect mutual company/community concerns.
- Collaborative efforts are initiated with other companies, government organizations, community groups, advocacy groups, and educational institutions to address issues of common concern.[10]

The collective activities of marketers, community relations personnel, and investment professionals have generated increased activity within such areas as employee volunteerism, gifts in kind, and a host of financial sponsorships. While these are discussed in detail later in the chapter, at this juncture what is important for the reader to understand is the motivations behind many of today's corporate community partnerships.

21.3 Approaches Being Applied to Commercial Ventures

One approach to understanding the trend toward commercial ventures is to outline the expectations of NPOs and corporations. These expectations are numerous and vary widely depending on the organizations involved. Previous work by this author details various aspects of corporate and nonprofit expectations.[11–14] For the purposes of this chapter, Exhibit 21.1 outlines common expectations of the three stakeholders that usually affect

EXHIBIT 21.1 Sample Stakeholder Interests and Expectations

Stakeholder	
Company	• Evaluation assesses changes in public awareness of the company as a result of the sponsorship. • Generates a tangible return such as sales or enhanced image. • Events fit within community investment or marketing policies. • Expects employees' allegiance to company supersedes allegiance to volunteer activity. • Resources to be allocated to the initiatives are clearly defined and for a set period of time. • Expectation that nonprofit acknowledge and recognize the company's participation in the event. • Corporate liability is at a minimum. • A cost–benefit analysis was conducted. • Minimal cost to the company resulting from employee involvement (i.e., time away from work). • Exact cost of additional kinds of support, if any, that are required for the initiative to be successful. • Goals of the initiative align with business goals, values, marketing, or sales objectives. • The initiative is open to all employees who want to participate. • The initiative has a clear reporting and evaluation process.
Nonprofit	• The initiative generated sufficient revenue. • The initiative was well attended by the target audience. • The initiative was successful in finding corporate support of some kind. • The initiative generated a notable public response to the agency. • A client group received better service. • The company and the employees were appropriately recognized. • An evaluation was conducted showing cost, benefit, and outcome. • Opportunities resulted that could lead to a long-term relationship with the corporate partner. • There was no deviation from the organization's mission and values as a result of the initiative.
Employees	• Employees are consulted about the kinds of events the company supports. • Release time from work is given by the company to volunteer at the sponsored event. • The company's support of the nonprofit meets a business objective and a community need. • A good time was had by all. • Employees were recognized by the company for their participation. • The event and the company received positive coverage by local media. • Personal outcomes such as enhanced job security, new networks, and new learning were achieved. • Employees are guiding the development of the program through an advisory group.

EXHIBIT 21.1 *(Continued)*

Stakeholder	
Employees	• Community agencies are willing to help as a partner. • Upcoming events and event summaries can be included in the company newsletter. • The program is being evaluated to improve and enhance its impact on employees, the community, and the workplace.

Adapted from Seel, K. (1995). "Managing Corporate and Employee Volunteer Programs." In T. Connors (ed.), *Volunteer Management Handbook.* New York: John Wiley & Sons, pp. 267–268.

the character of commercial ventures: the NPO, the company, and the employees of the company.

The interests and expectations of each stakeholder in a commercial venture contribute to its success or failure. Being clear about the expectations and interests of your potential partners and your own agency is a crucial first step in the overall strategic planning process that should take place before anyone is irrevocably committed to action.

Exhibit 21.2 presents a very big picture approach to understanding stakeholder interests that can affect any venture. While this is helpful in a general way, depending on the idea being considered, there may be a need to go into greater detail. One way of getting to this more detailed level is to look at what subgroups come together to constitute the broad stakeholder groups mentioned earlier. There is another way of looking at the vested interests affecting a particular venture: who makes up the company, the NPO, and the employees? What are the vested interests of these subgroups? Exhibit 21.2 presents some examples from the perspective of constituents of each of the stakeholder groups mentioned.

When working with very large corporate or nonprofit partners or diverse employee populations, the approach taken in Exhibit 21.2 will likely be more useful in preventure planning. For example, if your organization is looking at a venture involving a multinational corporation with tens of thousands of employees worldwide, you will likely be working with certain subgroups within the broader categories rather than working with the whole company.

Besides ensuring that the interests and expectations of each stakeholder in the commercial venture are understood and addressed, a number of other processes may be needed to collect the right information for the venture to succeed. Processes that may be used to collect the necessary information include:

1. Employee and community surveys to determine values, needs, and priorities around which the venture can be structured or which the venture can address. (For example, M4i Information Industries introduced their "Community Profiler Survey" at the 1998 International Association for Volunteer Effort Conference.[15] This is a standardized yet flexible tool designed for use by corporations and nonprofit agencies to create a succinct profile of community that can be used in commercial ventures.)

   Surveys can be used to collect information in a number of areas, including:
   • Employee values and beliefs
   • Employee perceptions of the company and community
   • Employee perceptions of community needs and social issues

EXHIBIT 21.2 Sample Constituent Interests

Stakeholders	Constituents and Their Interests
Company	**Shareholders** • Return on investment • Solid management and decision-making structure • At minimum risk for legal action **Board of Governors** • Achieving mission and related performance goals • At minimum risk for legal action • Establishing strategic relationships **Public Affairs** • Demonstrating that the company is a "neighbor of choice" • Effective and meaningful distribution of corporate assets into the community **Human Resources** • Employees have training and personal development opportunities • Fair treatment **Legal** • At minimum risk for legal action • Fair exchange of value • Legislated requirements such as licensing are taken care of
Nonprofit	**Board of Directors** • Achievement of the mission • Propriety of any ventures **Staff** • Reasonable workload • Effective service delivery **Volunteers** • Meaningful and reasonable work • Clear indications of need and the impact of services **Funders** • Appropriateness of the commercial venture • Indications of sustainability and community support
Employees	**Union** • Fair treatment of members for flex time to conduct volunteer work • Employee and community well-being **Nonunion** • Balance among work day, volunteer commitments, and family • Ensuring processes are flexible enough to volunteer while being accountable on the job **Management** • Ensuring the job gets done on time and on budget • Balancing employees' requests to volunteer with expected job performance • Improved morale and new skills gained through volunteer experience

- Employee expectations of corporate involvement in the community
- Community awareness of and attitudes about the company
- Community perceptions about priority social issues
- Community social values, needs, and attitudes

2. Market research, including client group demographics, brand equity analysis, communications effectiveness, corporate image assessment, customer satisfaction surveys, positioning and repositioning analysis. (For example, Market Vision Group's research details each of these for use by the stakeholders in a commercial venture.[16])

Qualitative and quantitative research can be combined with a secondary research process that reviews published sources and experts in the field.

Research techniques can be used to address a wide range of strategic and marketing decisions, including:

- Corporate image assessment (internal and external)
- Attitude surveys (internal and external)
- Opinion polling (internal and external)
- Customer satisfaction surveys (internal and external)
- Brand equity analysis
- Competitive analysis
- Positioning and repositioning analysis
- Market segmentation
- Community social priorities

3. Feasibility studies of proposed major corporate–nonprofit partnerships. Much like the feasibility studies conducted by professional fund raisers prior to a major capital campaign, a detailed financial analysis of a commercial venture's likelihood for success may be a key planning tool.

In a major long-term partnership, each partner makes a significant commitment to the relationship, such as:

- Multiyear agreements
- Sharing of markets or customer lists
- Linking brands and images for a joint purpose
- Major financial supports

In these cases, it is important for each partner to be sure that there is a real fit between the organizations regarding issues such as positive community image, mission, vision, values, management style, and shared or excluded publics. A partnership feasibility study would benchmark each organization's qualities and assess the "fit" between those qualities and a potential partner. Examples of qualities that could be examined in the partnership feasibility study include:

- Vision
- Mission
- Values
- Management (board, staff, volunteer)
- Financial stability
- Community image
- Partnership policies
- Licensing policies
- Logo and trademarking policies
- Programs and services

- Communication plans and marketing materials
- Customer loyalty

4. **Establishing expected returns on commercial ventures.** This author's experience has shown that stakeholders—corporate, employee, and nonprofit—often have not spent the time to detail what exactly they expect to see as returns from the commercial venture. While it could be said that if you do not know what you want, it does not matter what you get, in practice there are always expectations, some well beyond what could be reasonably accomplished.

   To all stakeholders, what was known traditionally as philanthropy has significant differences from contemporary approaches, some of which include commercial ventures. New approaches are looking for demonstrable returns on investment such as:
   - Financial sustainability or flexibility
   - Employee skill development
   - Increased market share
   - Greater brand recognition
   - Enhanced awareness of important social issues
   - Real steps made toward creating a healthier community

   The returns on commercial ventures, and other initiatives included within the community investment programs of major corporations, need to be measurable. A phased approach can help ensure that such initiatives show tangible returns. A generic cycle for establishing expected returns on community investment has six distinct steps, as outlined in Exhibit 21.3.

   In complex commercial ventures, there may be multiple strategies under consideration. This typically occurs when one of the partners has any of the following characteristics:
   - Multiple brands, products, service areas
   - Branches or sites across a region or country
   - Corporate and subsidiary or divisional community investment or marketing budgets
   - A large enough budget and supporting resources, such as staff, to address more than one issue effectively

---

EXHIBIT 21.3 Six Steps Toward Ensuring Success in Commercial Ventures

Step 1	Identify expectations, feasibility, and priorities for the venture.
Step 2	Conduct a benchmark survey or research prior to implementing your community investment strategy to gather baseline information on such things as existing community awareness, community needs, employee skills/morale/values, current market share, customer priorities, current brand recognition/differentiation, possible messages.
Step 3	Develop the strategic plan and supporting marketing tactics.
Step 4	Implement the community strategic plan and monitor progress.
Step 5	Conduct a survey to test changes against the benchmark.
Step 6	Reinforce or change the strategy or tactics based on survey results or other validated indicators.

---

5. Collecting a database of information as part of an environmental scan. Knowing who is doing what in a community and to what degree those activities were successful can be a very important piece of planning information. Often, the level of understanding a nonprofit agency has of a corporation (and vice versa) is minimal. (James McPhedran, Director of Membership Rewards, Advertising, and Event Marketing with American Express Canada, has commented, "I am continually amazed that people will just send a package without doing any kind of research into the types of things we've been involved with in the past, and the type of things we'd be looking for.")

   An important part of the planning process may be starting a library of corporate and/or nonprofit annual reports and other documents. This information gives planners a view of the environment in which they will be seeking partners and launching their venture.

6. Affirming your organization's negotiable and nonnegotiable values. Because commercial ventures are a kind of partnership, each partner needs to have a solid appreciation of which points can be negotiated and which cannot. (For example, this author's work in conducting values audits for organizations is a process that, in part, underscores and builds commitment around the key values and principles of an organization. Knowing what these values and principles are and what they mean allows the organization to come to the negotiating table with a clear understanding of what it represents and expects its partner to respect.)

7. Development of a process and criteria with which to review potential ventures. Organizations, both nonprofit and corporate, cannot predict when they may be presented with an opportunity to be part of a commercial venture. By establishing review criteria and a selection process, organizations will find themselves better prepared to address a proposal.

Like the proverbial tail wagging the dog, new sources of revenue can pull an organization away from its original social mission. Consider the YMCA. The association today generates substantial revenues by operating health-and-fitness facilities for middle-class families, but critics charge that the YMCA has lost sight of its mission to promote the spiritual, mental, and social condition of young men.[17]

A commercial venture can be a great deal of work and links stakeholders together for a period of time. For that reason, each partner and stakeholder in the venture is advised to take the time to consider the initiative thoroughly. Following are two simple approaches for considering the suitability of partners to the venture.

The Better Business Bureau is playing a growing role both with business and with nonprofit agencies. In some areas, the Better Business Bureau is starting to collect information not just on businesses but also on NPOs, capital campaigns, and the like. Perhaps because of this, the Bureau suggests using criteria for considering sponsorship requests, one of the approaches involved in commercial ventures. While oriented toward their business members, the following four points also apply to NPOs.

1. Is the program or event compatible with your company product, service, or image? You may choose to lend your support to an event because it is a good

cause; however, it is always advisable to consider how your company's participation will be perceived.

2. Will your participation generate business for your company? Don't confuse a sponsorship with advertising. A sponsorship will not always drive business directly to your organization. Keep your expectations realistic.

3. What is the goal of the event or program? Clearly understand the purpose of your sponsorship. Is it to provide funds to the organization, help offset expenses, underwrite the costs of producing the event, or for other reasons?

4. What is being asked of you and what, if anything, will you receive in return? Ask for a clear, written presentation outlining the program and what you will be expected to provide. Also include anything you can expect to receive in return, such as advertising, tickets, or banners.[18]

Another approach to evaluating sponsorships of NPOs is that detailed by Canadian Tire.[19] This national retailer of automotive, recreational, and home merchandise has developed a four-step, 40-point methodology for evaluating proposals from NPOs. Each of the following elements is scored and gives a comparatively objective reading on the feasibility of the venture:

1. *Selection.* At this step, questions are asked and the decision is made about the fit of a program or an event. An analysis is made of the business area against which the activity is targeted, and the objectives, strategies, and priorities of that business. Selection and fit criteria are established in advance, and each event proposal is evaluated.

2. *Valuation.* At this step, the company considers whether the event's value justifies its cost. Even if a program has "fit," if it cannot deliver value and it cannot be leveraged at a reasonable price, it goes no further.

3. *Development/Implementation/Execution.* At this step, the company considers all the aspects of leveraging and integration against the business, plus the opportunities for effective implementation, management, and follow-through.

4. *Measurement/Evaluation.* Once the decision has been made that the event does fit and it has been developed and executed, it must be measured to determine whether marketing objectives were met. Both qualitative and quantitative measures are used, in addition to benchmarks from previous programs. Three qualitative measures are used in combination with seven quantitative measures.

21.4   Common Commercial Venture Strategies

A range of strategies has been applied to commercial ventures. Commercial ventures initiated by businesses are often easier to understand because they usually focus on obvious marketing goals, namely, increased sales, improved image, repositioning, and aspects related to brand equity and placement in the market. Ventures initiated by NPOs often involve a host of elements unique to such agencies, such as involving volunteers, tax receipts, and the use of donated goods. The most common strategies are outlined as follows.[20]

(A) STRATEGIC PHILANTHROPY

In this approach to commercial ventures, companies use philanthropic dollars to develop new business opportunities (donations to research), develop employees (skill development opportunities), and market (funding customers' key causes). The nonprofit partner in the venture, such as a university, gains funded programs like new research chairs that carry the name of the sponsoring corporation. These programs often generate additional income, either through tuition fees of students entering the sponsored program or by attracting additional corporate sponsorships. This strategy is linked to commercial ventures because both parties are looking for financial gain through such diverse areas as increased public awareness, increased registration, potential employees, market position, image, and research.

(B) CAUSE-RELATED MARKETING

This is becoming a very popular basis for commercial ventures. In a cause-related marketing campaign, a business and a nonprofit agency enter into a joint promotional campaign. Consumers are encouraged to purchase a specific product, knowing that a portion of the purchase price goes to support the NPO. "It happens to have a philanthropic result, but its primary purpose is sales. It requires a consumer to buy a company's product or service in order to benefit the cause."[21] Using this approach, companies like Avon, supporting breast cancer research, and American Express, supporting various programs, have successfully increased sales of their products and services while providing financial benefits to their nonprofit partner(s). (See Exhibit 21.4.)

If the company is uncertain which cause(s) to support through a cause-related marketing campaign, surveying customers on their top community issues may be the solution. For example, in 1987, MasterCard launched a cause-related marketing campaign called Choose to Make a Difference. Each time cardholders used their MasterCard, the company donated money to one of six national NPOs in the United States. MasterCard chose the six agencies that were to benefit from the campaign after surveying cardholders.[22]

(C) SPONSORSHIPS

Sponsorships have a long history in the nonprofit sector. While in the past this strategy was used to some benefit, such as having the costs associated with an artistic performance underwritten, recent sponsorships are much broader in impact. They are also on a much larger scale than ever before because the costs associated with promoting the event through television, radio, or newspaper have soared. Nevertheless, when the sponsorship opportunity meets the requirements (see the Canadian Tire criteria), returns to the corporation and their nonprofit partner can be significant. Sponsorships linked with the Fourth of July, Canada Day, other statutory holidays, or major local events such as the Boston Marathon or the Calgary Stampede, often come with high price tags but can draw large numbers of people to the sponsored event, thus justifying the cost.

The actual numbers associated with sponsorships are hard to come by due to the confidentiality requirements made by many major corporate sponsors. As a commercial venture, sponsorships may require special financial analysis and legal opinion for all parties involved to ensure fair treatment and balanced returns.

EXHIBIT 21.4 TransAlta Sponsorship of the Calgary Zoo Advertisement

Get Ready for
"The Full Monkey"

The Peelers are coming!

The Calgary Zoo is just wild about the 'TransAlta Tropical Africa Pavilion', the exciting new home for our gorillas! Construction will soon be in full swing, and by the spring of 2002 there will be a new habitat for troops of lowland gorillas, colourful mandrills, monkeys, crocodiles and several species of exotic birds and insects indigenous to Tropical Africa. The pavilion will also boast multi-purpose classrooms to educate our children on the role of the rain forest and the need to protect these endangered species. Just imagine wandering wide-eyed through an African rain forest – natural light filtering through the jungle canopy, lush vegetation and thick, warm humidity engulfing you...

The protection of these remarkable and vulnerable creatures is imperative, and if we can do it in a world which satisfies their needs then more power to them.

TransAlta
Boundless energy

calgaryzoo

(D) PREMIUMS

Premiums are quality give-aways that are intended to strengthen a customer's relationship to a particular brand or product. While premiums may be items such as pens, cups, or tickets, very unique premiums can be produced as part of a commercial venture. Using this approach, the business that is intending to use the premium will want to look at customer characteristics, including their perception of social issues and causes. Suppose, for example, seniors are the major purchaser of a product or service and a survey shows that seniors are very concerned about crime or personal safety. Instead of giving a trinket as a premium, the business may look for a nonprofit partner such as Block Watch to produce a small guide filled with tips on home and personal security, key telephone numbers, and the like. The nonprofit would be paid to use its expertise to produce the premium, generating significant revenues.

The Denver Children's Museum partnered with Star-Kist, a company that wanted to boost the sales of its 9-Lives cat food. The company knew its customers were families and veterinarians. The company also knew that the Denver Children's Museum was an expert in innovative children's education. Star-Kist approached the museum to produce a premium educational booklet called *Kids and Pets*. Star-Kist purchased 62,000 copies at $1.25 each. The company gave 12,000 copies of the premium to veterinarians and used the remaining 50,000 copies as a self-liquidating premium on the 20-pound bag of 9-Lives.[23]

Smaller investments can also generate significant results. Novagas ClearingHouse Ltd. (now Dynergy) was looking for a meaningful way to address the stresses associated with a number of major corporate changes. After identifying workplace stress as one of the issues to address, the company formed a small venture with the Canadian Mental Health Association to use that nonprofit's workplace stress materials. Together they also planned and held activities that created a more positive workplace atmosphere while promoting the concept of mental wellness, a major component of the Mental Health Association's mandate.

(E) LICENSING

Major NPOs such as universities have long had licensing arrangements with manufacturers of clothing and other logo-bearing materials. However, for smaller agencies, the concept may be quite new. The power of a logo to generate customer support cannot be overlooked; Shell's logo is perhaps one of the world's most recognized brands, as is the Red Cross. According to the World Wildlife Fund, "At the end of the day it's the power of the panda that counts. The World Wildlife Fund's famous symbol . . . had been used to do everything from creating awareness and building brand loyalty to encouraging trial and increasing sales."[24]

Depending on the nonprofit agency's mission, the value of the logo, and the constraints around its use, significant legal advice may need to be sought. Contracts that lay out the usage period, restrictions, and costs for use should be a requirement for this commercial venture strategy. Successful examples include:

- Spring Industries, Inc., wanting to create a new line of bed linens, went to the Metropolitan Museum of Art and licensed the rights to textile designs in the collection.
- Toys 'R' Us licensed the Sesame Street characters from the Children's Television Workshop, the nonprofit that produces the famous show.[25]

(F)   SPONSORED ADVERTISEMENTS

Traditionally, nonprofit agencies have relied on public service announcements (PSAs) to get media to pick up and promote a message. Unless there is an actual community section in the newspaper, PSAs often fill odd spaces throughout the edition. Radio and television use of PSAs is often similar: to fill gaps in regular programming, often at times when viewership is at a minimum.

Businesses that purchase prime advertising space or time may be looking to connect with their customers in a unique manner, employing a nonprofit cause known to be important to those customers. Agencies that likely could not afford or could not justify the expense of prime advertising have accepted the sponsored ad as a significant commercial venture strategy.

(G)   VENDOR RELATIONSHIPS OR MERCHANDISING

A vendor relationship, sometimes also referred to as *merchandising,* occurs when a business agrees to sell the products or services produced by an NPO. It is not uncommon to find the view both in the business community and the nonprofit sector that the products and services of such agencies are second-rate at best. This misperception is slowly being changed. Businesses are looking to support charities in ways other than donations, and nonprofit agencies are taking their offerings to the marketplace.

Examples of this strategy vary widely. The Developmental Disabilities Resource Centre formed partnerships with a distillery and an oilfield services company to provide wooden containers and stakes, respectively. These quality products were produced as part of job training programs for persons with disabilities. The Children's Cottage, a crisis nursery, produced a cookbook and formed partnerships with many bookstores that agreed to sell it.

(H)   VENTURE ENTERPRISE

Venture enterprises by nonprofits are rare, but they demonstrate what can happen when entrepreneurial ideas are allowed to grow. A venture enterprise is a for-profit enterprise owned wholly or in part by an NPO. The venture enterprise hires its own staff and operates at arm's length from the nonprofit owner.

For example, The Developmental Disabilities Resource Centre (DDRC) reviewed a number of its government-subsidized services, such as respite care and job training, and realized that it had the potential to run at a profit if allowed to. To that end, DDRC turned government-subsidized programs into successful businesses: Bow Catering, which provides job training and a high-quality catering service; Cedar Industries, which provides job training and numerous cedar products; and contracts with other organizations to provide respite care. The case study in Exhibit 21.5 details how the agency thought about and developed its venture enterprises.

(I)   RELATED EFFORTS

A few activities involving businesses and NPOs are related to commercial ventures. These other activities can be used in conjunction with a venture or as a bridge toward building a commercial venture.

EXHIBIT 21.5 Commercial Ventures Case Study

The Experience of Developmental Disabilities Resource Centre

The Developmental Disabilities Resource Centre of Calgary (DDRC) was established in 1952 by a group of parents and community leaders who were determined to provide educational, living support and meaningful employment in the community for children and adults who would otherwise have been institutionalized. It is the oldest and largest organization of its kind in the Province of Alberta, Canada. With a budget of $9 million and almost 400 staff, DDRC serves approximately 1,300 children and adults annually.

A volunteer Board of Directors has always governed DDRC. Historically, the Directors were selected or volunteered because they had a family member with a disability. Coincidentally, in 1991, a majority of the Board members had a strong background in business or financial management and began to place a priority on managing the agency using "good business practices." As Board members' terms expired, new members were increasingly selected for their expertise in business and legal matters.

In 1993, the Government of Alberta announced its intention to eliminate the provincial debt, and nonprofit agencies across the province were advised of a 3.5% cut in funding followed by a 2% cut the following year. The message was clear. Government would no longer "fund everything," and nonprofits were forced to examine the way they delivered service. The DDRC took a multifaceted approach to addressing the cut, including eliminating a number of management and administrative positions. However, the most significant decision was to become more "entrepreneurial," which meant ensuring that programs recovered costs, expanding fund-raising efforts, and establishing independent commercial enterprises.

The idea of commercial enterprise was born out of a number of work contracts that were undertaken in sheltered workshops. Sheltered workshops were becoming increasingly unpopular as a means to provide people with disabilities with meaningful work, particularly since young people and their families expected "normal" life experiences, including employment in community businesses. The work contracts, however, provided a potential source of business ventures. In 1994, the Board of Directors and senior management con- firmed their intention to close the sheltered workshops. Government funding that formerly supported production and management salaries was redirected to increase front-line staff support to clients seeking community employment. The Board of Directors sought the approval of the membership to invest in the business using revenues generated from real estate sales.

Four small business opportunities were identified: industrial sewing, stake and lath, decora- tive cedar box manufacturing, and a catering business. (Later in 1995 a highly successful home care business was also established.) The businesses were given the mandate to firstly be profitable and secondly to train and employ people with disabilities to the same degree as any private sector business (10% of the workforce is disabled). This latter condition was intended to prevent the businesses from redeveloping into sheltered workshops but to ensure that they were still aligned with the objectives of the agency.

Bow Catering

Bow Catering was the creation of an enterprising manager of a vocational training program. It evolved from teaching people with disabilities basic life skills, including cooking. As the skill level of clients improved, the manager began to market simple sandwich trays and

EXHIBIT 21.5 *(Continued)*

sweet trays to internal office meetings and then expanded to larger events in the business community using personal friends and colleagues to establish connections. Eventually, the catering "program" that was part of a vocational training site was serving outside events up to 700 people. All of this was accomplished out of a small kitchen at the site that included two residential stoves, two refrigerators, and one freezer. A neighboring delicatessen generously provided refrigeration for prepared food for large events. Eventually, the size of events being catered grew beyond the capacity of the small kitchen, and as the building itself was in extremely poor condition, a decision was made to purchase a newer facility. The newly renovated building located in a light industrial area of Calgary included office space for agency staff and a large room that was used during the day for on-site activities and training for people with disabilities. The room could also be converted to banquet facilities for 120 people at night because it was connected to a fully equipped commercial kitchen. The new facility was financed from proceeds of the sale of the old building and carried a substantial mortgage.

The agency contracted with an independent consultant to investigate the feasibility of the catering business. The results were not enthusiastic, noting the intense competition from a large number of local restaurants who also offered catering. Despite this opinion, the business opened in April 1995, relying on the considerable entrepreneurial skills of the manager and the existing customer base. Over the previous year, the manager had also begun to develop a gift basket business that quickly moved from individual purchases to executive gifts for various corporations.

Bow Catering opened with a manager, a receptionist who split her duties between the business and the vocational training program, a chef who was a recent graduate and not experienced in costing or purchasing, and one kitchen helper. The manager was responsible for the overall management of the business as well as sales and marketing. Other than the development of business cards and information folders, there was no budget for marketing and advertising. A new delivery van had been purchased through corporate donors who supported the idea of financial independence for a nonprofit organization.

Although Bow Catering, almost overnight, captured a significant portion of corporate catering and executive gift items, tripling sales between 1995–1998, it was a full three years before it achieved profitability.

The industrial sewing, stake and lath, and cedar box businesses were all established in late 1996, operating from the DDRC sheltered workshop/industrial facility and maintaining the name of Advance Industries to preserve recognition with existing customers. (Eventually, the cedar box business was renamed.) They largely followed the same course as Bow Catering, with three notable differences:

1. The manager of Advance Industries was also a former vocational training manager but admittedly lacked the entrepreneurial spirit of the Bow Catering manager.
2. Production staff in these three manufacturing businesses had all been part of the former sheltered workshop and lacked knowledge and experience in a "for-profit" enterprise. Some also lacked "entrepreneurial" spirit and were better suited to careers in human services.
3. The manufacturing businesses achieved profitability in two years because they benefited from the expertise of a cost accountant and the manufacturing expert.

EXHIBIT 21.5 *(Continued)*

What Went Right?

1. An exceptionally entrepreneurial manager who was passionately committed to the mission and objectives of the agency. (The manager eventually became the general manager of the catering and manufacturing businesses and was highly successful.)

2. A Board of Directors with solid business skills and experience, and a commitment to making the businesses successful.

3. Other than the manager (and eventually a salesperson), Bow Catering staff came from the private sector, not from human services.

4. In early 1995, a cost accountant and a manufacturing expert were hired on contract to implement costing systems in all the businesses and to ensure the efficiency of each manufacturing business.

5. In 1995, an enterprising human services staff person identified home care as a potentially lucrative business. It was established and profitable almost from the outset because it capitalized on existing expertise, reputation, and established policies and procedures.

What Went Wrong?

1. Lack of a comprehensive business plan for any of the businesses.

2. Despite exceptional entrepreneurial skills in some individuals, practical business skills were lacking.

3. Failure to provide the necessary resources, such as a budget for marketing, advertising, and training, or adequate capital resources.

4. Due to the "newness" of each business, they were unable to attract (or offer compensation to attract) highly qualified personnel in key positions, i.e., chef and production coordinators in the manufacturing businesses.

5. Following the practice of the sheltered workshops, the newly established businesses continued to generate revenues but did not generate a profit as quickly as they could have because they were lacking costing systems. Key personnel in the businesses were also lacking the fundamental knowledge and understanding of costing systems.

What Would We Do Differently?

1. Management and Directors did not realize at the outset that all the businesses lacked costing systems. An assumption was made that proper costing was in place to bid on contracts in the sheltered workshops. However, generating revenue is different from profitability. There was a misguided belief that increasing sales volumes would eventually result in profitability and, although sales increased dramatically year over year, losses continued to accumulate. As losses mounted, there was a strong reluctance to invest more resources to hire expert advice. In fact, the businesses experienced such a dramatic turnaround when costing systems and manufacturing efficiencies were installed, that the lesson was clear—*"We should have made the investment in expert resources from the outset."*

2. When businesses are established out of nonprofit activities such as sheltered workshops, there needs to be an assessment of which staff have the attitude and interest in making the shift from a nonprofit to a for-profit enterprise.

EXHIBIT 21.5 *(Continued)*

Attitudes and skills will dramatically influence the profitability. This was quickly identified in the manufacturing businesses where some staff were clearly excited by the challenge and others were not only disinterested, but in some cases opposed to the agency owning commercial ventures.

3. On the other hand, the enterprising manager who conceived Bow Catering and eventually became general manager of all the businesses (except home care) was able to capitalize on her extensive experience in rehabilitation and commitment to the mission of DDRC to market the products and raise the profile of the agency in the Calgary community. The manager is also solidly committed to employing and training people with disabilities in all of the businesses.

4. The home care business was a financial success almost from the outset because it capitalized on existing experience, reputation, and policies and procedures. It also had a proven market demand and required no capital investment. It may have been more prudent to develop businesses consistent with our skills as human service providers rather than businesses in which we lacked expertise, such as manufacturing or catering.

Conclusion

Between 1995 to 1997, the business division experienced combined losses of $500,000. In the spring of 1997, costing systems and manufacturing efficiencies were installed, with the result that the business division made a net contribution of $7,000 in the 1997/98 fiscal year. A notable point is that even when sales are lower than projected on a monthly basis, the businesses continue to contain their costs and demonstrate a modest profit.

Author's Note: This case study was written by Pat Fergusson, Executive Director of the Developmental Disabilities Resource Centre in Calgary, Canada. It outlines the experiences of a large nonprofit organization that responded to declining support from government by undertaking several commercial ventures to diversify the revenue base. The information provided and opinions are those of senior management and the Board of Directors, who were closely involved in the development of the businesses.

Reprinted with permission, Developmental Disabilities Resource Centre, 1998.

(i) Employee Volunteering

Employee volunteering has grown remarkably since the early 1990s. Efforts by the Points of Light Foundation, volunteer centers, workplace volunteer councils, corporate or business volunteerism councils, and other organizations have encouraged the development of employee volunteer programs in most of North America's major corporations. (See Petro-Canada's volunteerism advertisement, Exhibit 21.6.) The basic principles behind employee volunteering for corporations are outlined in Exhibit 21.7.

While employee volunteer programs are not of themselves a commercial venture, they can play an important role in creating a relationship between a business and a nonprofit agency. Employees who volunteer may become advocates for expanding the relationship to include commercial ventures. Often, employee volunteer programs have either "Dollars for Doers" or "Matching Grants" programs, through which the company will make cash donations to the nonprofit agency for a certain number of hours contributed to that agency by the employee volunteer.

EXHIBIT 21.6 Petro-Canada's Volunteerism Advertisement

(ii) In-Kind Donations

In-kind donations typically occur when a business donates products, services, or equipment to an NPO. Office furniture, computers, office supplies, technical support, and professional advice are all examples of common in-kind donations by businesses. In some cases, the value of the goods donated can be assessed for the purpose of issuing a charitable tax receipt to the donor company.

Depending on the conditions of the donation, some businesses will allow or even encourage the nonprofit agency to sell the donated service, product, or equipment and thereby generate operational revenue. "Silent Auctions," a common fund-raising event for some NPOs, rely on donated products and services to generate revenue.

21.5 Philosophical Considerations

A commercial venture between businesses and nonprofits may be a new experience for both partners. Some effort should be made to reflect on what the initiative will mean to each organization, what the expected outcome is, what values must be upheld, and what long-term good will be served. Exhibit 21.8 outlines some of the basic questions that should be considered by each partner in the commercial venture.

Businesses interested in becoming partners in commercial ventures with nonprofits have other questions to be answered to ensure that business objectives are addressed, including:

EXHIBIT 21.7 The Principles of Excellence in Community Service

The following Principles of Excellence in Community Service were developed by the Points of Light Foundation to help corporations develop successful employee volunteer programs. The principles are also the criteria for the Awards for Excellence in Corporate Community Service.

1. **ACKNOWLEDGE** that in the corporation's community service involvement and its employee volunteer statements, the recognition that societal and community issues have a direct relationship to the company and its future success.

- Integrate the company's social vision with its business vision, thus making community service and volunteering part of business operations.

- Communicate the corporate social vision and the importance of volunteerism consistently to all of the company's external and internal stakeholders.

2. **COMMIT** to establish, support, and promote an employee volunteer program that encourages the involvement of every employee and treats it like any other core business function.

- Allocate sufficient resources to develop, manage, and sustain successful employee volunteer efforts.

- Manage the employee volunteer effectively, with a business plan.

- Establish policies, procedures, and incentives that encourage optimum employee participation.

- Develop volunteer projects that utilize the distinctive competencies and skills of the company and its employees.

3. **TARGET** community service efforts at serious social problems in the community.

- Survey employees to determine their interests in working on serious social problems.

- Focus employee volunteer programs so that they address serious social problems, efforts contribute to the achievement of its business goals.

- Incorporate in the corporate vision, as expressed through mission statements, credos, or social policy.

- Conduct regular and ongoing evaluations to determine their impact on the company's employee volunteer programs and other community involvement programs on serious social problems.

Source: Points of Light Foundation. (1993). *Principles of Excellence in Community Service.* Washington, DC: Author.

- Is the charity familiar with the participating corporation's subsidiaries, products, and services?
- Is the corporation informed about the participating charity's programs, finances, and other fund-raising efforts?
- Is there a written agreement that gives formal permission for the corporation to use the charity's name and logo?
- Does the written agreement (a) give the charity prior review and approval of ad materials that use its name, (b) indicate how long the campaign will last, (c) specify how and when charitable funds will be distributed, (d) explain any

EXHIBIT 21.8 Basic Philosophical Questions Regarding Commercial Ventures

1. Why are we considering a commercial venture with a nonprofit or business partner?
2. How will a commercial venture help us achieve our mission or goal?
3. What are our values regarding commercial ventures?
4. How will we ensure that we do not compromise our values?
5. How will we protect our reputation?
6. Do we trust our partner to protect our interests and safeguard our mission and values?
7. What is our partner's reputation and does it fit with ours?
8. Who are the people taking responsibility for the venture and do they have the skills necessary to be successful?
9. For what period of time do we commit to the venture and how will we exit it?
10. What are the risks to our clients, our organization, and our bottom line?

steps that will be taken in case of a disagreement or unforeseen result with the promotion?

- Do the joint-venture advertisements (a) specify the actual or anticipated portion of the sales or service price to benefit the charity, (b) indicate the full name of the charity, (c) include an address or telephone number for more information about the charity, (d) indicate when the campaign will end and, if applicable, the maximum amount the charity will receive?
- Does the promotion follow all applicable government regulations in the areas in which the marketing will take place?
- Does the corporation have fiscal controls in place to process and record the monies received to benefit the charity?
- Will more than one charity be involved in the promotion? If so, how will the funds be distributed?
- Will the corporation complete a financial report at the end of the campaign (or annually, if the campaign lasts more than a year) that identifies (a) the total amount collected for the charity, (b) any campaign expenses, and (c) how much the charity received.[26]

21.6 Commercial Venture Business Planning

It is absolutely necessary to have some kind of business plan for the commercial venture in place before any activities are initiated. Each partner should be a full participant in the development of the business plan for the commercial venture. The plan will serve as the fundamental documentation of commitments being made, expectations, deliverables, costs, returns, benchmarks, and so on. The plan may vary in length and detail depending on the complexity and duration of the commercial venture. Additional legal contracts may be required to support the plan.

A basic framework for a business plan includes the following:

1. *Management.* A description of the people behind the venture and their experience with similar situations. Discuss the board of directors or other senior managers and how they will be involved in the commercial venture.

Depending on the venture, a discussion of incorporation, patents, trademarks, and so forth may be important.

2. *The opportunity.* Beginning with a one-sentence description of the purpose of the venture in clear and simple language, expand the description in nontechnical language.

3. *The product or service.* Each product or service involved in the commercial venture should be described with precision. Using nontechnical language, explain the purpose of each product or service and the reason it is being developed. Key questions to consider are:
   - What is the purpose of the product or service?
   - How does the product or service achieve this purpose?
   - What are its unique features (cost, design)?
   - What is its life, and how soon will it be obsolete?
   - What is its stage of development (idea, working prototype, in production)?
   - How will the product be produced (Is it capital intensive, labor intensive, material intensive; Will any part be subcontracted)?
   - Is this an end-use product or service or a component of a larger product?
   - Can your product or service be protected by patent, copyright, or trademark?

4. *The market.* Each product or service involved in the commercial venture will need to be addressed separately. Market research is critical to help partners answer the following questions:
   - Who are your customers (individuals, companies, institutions, government)?
   - Where are your customers (neighborhood, city, state, province, country)?
   - How will you distribute your product or service (direct selling, franchise, networks)?
   - What is the nature of your competition?
   - What will your pricing strategy be (low or high margin, discount policy, credit and collection policies, warranties and guarantees)?
   - What is the "capture potential" of your product and service (total available market, replacement market, incremental market)?
   - What are your market share objectives?
   - What are your estimated marketing costs (head office, selling and travel costs, advertising and promotion)?
   - What are other important factors (seasonality, regulatory requirements, market trends)?

5. *Financial projection.* The nature of your projection depends on the stage of product or service development. Estimates and potential funding sources are necessary if you are in the idea stage. The following areas need to be considered:
   - Project development costs. Phases in development include idea, concept description, design, laboratory model, and production model.
   - Operating projection, including statements of income and retained earnings, balance sheet, changes in financial position, and cash flow projection.

6. *Investment requirements/opportunities.* After plotting time and dollars on a graph using the information in point 5, determine cash needs and payback of the investment. Discuss the total outside investment capital being asked for and the period for which it is required.

21.7 Taking Stock of the Risks

There are risks associated with commercial ventures that NPOs need to be aware of. While there are risks for businesses becoming involved in commercial ventures with the non-profit sector, they are comparatively minor. The business sector has experience with the business process, something the nonprofit sector still lacks. As the reader will note, the following risks are interrelated and therefore may need to be considered as a whole rather than one at a time.

(A) RISK 1: PUBLIC PERCEPTION

How the public views a particular nonprofit agency's role in a commercial venture is important to the long-term viability of the agency. If the public perceives the nonprofit as "profitable," they may no longer see the need to support it as a charity. Some are asking, "Can the public be assured that nonprofits will behave responsibly in their roles as stewards of public resources?"[27] The "public schizophrenia about American nonprofits—their commercial tendencies, unfavorable media attention and unfortunate incidents—is reflected in a new atmosphere of skepticism."[28] This skepticism can have a dramatic negative impact on a nonprofit agency if there is any appearance of impropriety in a commercial venture.

(B) RISK 2: MULTIPLE SOURCES OF ACCOUNTABILITY

NPOs have a complex array of accountabilities. Those that provide financial resources, such as foundations, government, The United Way, and individuals, all expect the agency to be accountable. Clients, staff, volunteers, and board members also have expectations about the agency's accountability. Balancing accountabilities to these diverse stakeholders, a nonprofit agency cannot be seen to be leaning too much in one direction or the other. "While for-profit business can be unequivocally responsive to paying customers to maximize value for stockholders, nonprofits (which also have paying customers) cannot simply be driven by market imperatives."[29]

A commercial venture may strain the public accountability of an NPO by giving the appearance that the agency has sold its neutrality in addressing a social issue to a corporation with a vested interest. For example, if an agency exclusively licenses its logo to a manufacturer of a product, thereby conveying a special endorsement, what kind of accountability does the agency have to customers of competitive products? Does the NPO's endorsement, by virtue of the use of its logo and good name, imply a guarantee about the product? What accountabilities does the board of the agency have to the public after endorsing a product? These questions should be considered before a commercial venture is undertaken.

(C) RISK 3: UNEVEN PLAYING FIELD

As NPOs begin commercial ventures, are they competing fairly with established businesses? The answer to the question will vary depending on the nature of the venture, the competition in the market, and the organizations involved. The issue is not new. In 1988, William Brodhead, former member of the U.S. House of Representatives and the House Ways and Means Committee, addressed competition between for-profits and nonprofits. His fundamental points were as follows:

- The claim that NPOs have an unfair competitive advantage because of their special tax status raises the question of what is special about nonprofit activity.
- Tax exemptions of nonprofit activities by government work on the theory that government is "compensated for its loss of revenue by gaining relief from financial burdens which would otherwise have to be met by appropriations from public funds."
- The exclusive purpose of nonprofit activity is to promote the public good, whereas the for-profit businesses, which underpin the economy, have the principal purpose of making a profit.
- The idea of "profit" to a nonprofit means something different than it does to a business. For the nonprofit agency, the profit will be used to further its charitable activities. For the business, the profit goes to the owners of the business and does not work to serve a public good.
- Nonprofit agencies must pay income tax on all business activities that do not contribute to their tax-exempt purpose. This means that so long as a nonprofit agency aligns its business activities with its purpose, all revenues go to serve that purpose. As soon as the nonprofit's business ventures stray from the exempt purpose, it is treated as a regular business.[30]

Brodhead concluded by stating that "The fairness question raised by the small business community ultimately is the question of fairness to individuals served by not-for-profit organizations. . . . It is clear that nonprofits serve those individuals, their communities, their nation, and the public good in a very special way."

In considering commercial ventures, nonprofit agencies must continue to serve the public good and ensure that their business activities are directed toward achieving the purpose for which that agency was established. To stray too far afield with business ventures could mean criticism from business, government, and the nonprofit sector.

(D) RISK 4: MISSION DRIFT

In considering a commercial venture, the nonprofit agency should ensure that the activity is focused on the purpose or mission. Identifying an unrelated, although potentially profitable, business opportunity and trying to marry it to a nonprofit agency's mission is not a recipe for success. For example, a board member of a crisis line felt that the agency could generate significant profits if it hired street vendors to sell ice cream bars. While the opportunity looked good, the board correctly decided to forego the idea because there was no direct link between ice cream and the mission of the organization. In this case, the board prevented the organization from drifting from being a crisis line to becoming ice cream vendors.

The Canadian Policy Research Network, Inc., notes that "For some charitable organizations, commercial activity may be fundamentally improper because it would distract from the mission or refocus energies away from collective goods and services with long-run impact. For others it may be precisely the lever that triggers useful organization-wide innovation and creativity."[31] For NPOs considering a commercial venture, there must be a clear relationship between business activity and the mission.

From a different perspective, that of the business initiative, the "very values that are central to the charitable mission of many organizations may undermine the potential for successful commercial ventures."[32] In other words, the commercial venture also has a mission: to generate profits. The mission of the venture could be incompatible with the charitable values expressed by the nonprofit partner. Having the mission of the business venture drift would harm the venture.

The examples of mission drift, from either the nonprofit agency or the business venture, highlight how important initial discussions are to the success of the venture. All parties to the venture and the venture itself need to express and uphold their various missions. Compromise at the mission level will not help create long-term sustainability.

(E) RISK 5: OVERDIVERSIFICATION

While diversity is key at community and societal levels, Drucker argues that it should not be the case at an organizational level. "Diversification destroys the performance capacity of an organization, whether it is a business, a labor union, a school, a hospital, a community service, or a house of worship. . . . An organization is a tool. And as with any other tool, the more specialized it is, the greater its capacity to perform its given task."[33] What this means in terms of commercial ventures is that they should be aligned with the purpose and activities of the organizations involved.

Another element of overdiversification is the degree to which commercial ventures will change the character of the nonprofit agency. If an agency appears to be diversifying into business and away from its charitable purpose, the agency runs the risk of losing the community supports that are the foundation of nonprofit activity. The fine line between having a related commercial venture and becoming business-driven should not be crossed.

(F) RISK 6: REPUTATION

"A charity's only true source of capital is its reputation or integrity. This reputation must be protected and enhanced for long-term sustainability."[34] There are certainly examples of the public supporting commercial ventures by NPOs. Indeed, in some cases, the reputation of the organization is enhanced as a result of the venture. For example, gift shops in hospitals are seen to add value, or in the case of the Developmental Disabilities Resource Centre, commercial ventures are perceived to be enhancing the agency's sustainability.

Despite successes, two issues emerge related to the reputation of an NPO becoming involved in commercial ventures:

1. *Community perception.* Depending on what the commercial venture is and how related the community believes it to be to the mission of the nonprofit agency, the community may change its perception of the agency. If the commercial venture is not related and not well understood, the agency runs the risk of losing public support. Funders may interpret unrelated commercial ventures to be evidence of a lack of community support for the agency's activities.
2. *Market perception.* NPOs engaged in business activities have several advantages over businesses. The agency may use volunteers to sell its products or services, it may have tax advantages, and it may have grant subsidies for its administration and management. Businesses may perceive these advantages to be unfair, especially if the commercial activity of the nonprofit is loosely related or unrelated to the charitable mission of the agency. It can be anticipated that to level the playing field, the business sector

would lobby government for changes to tax law and other legislation related to nonprofit activity.[35]

(G)   RISK 7: RESOURCES

Involvement in commercial ventures may change how NPOs view, attract, and retain resources. These resources may be financial, but they may also broaden to include talented staff or community goodwill. The challenge will be for nonprofit agencies to balance "top line thinking" with the "bottom line thinking" of business ventures. "Top line thinking is derived from the history of many charities in which the revenue is relatively inflexible and grants are set ahead of the activities to be performed . . . Bottom line thinking is derived from commercial activities in which costs are incurred with the expectation that they will generate future revenues."[36]

Because of the bottom line approach taken in commercial ventures, the NPO may need to have some kind of risk capital that it can invest in the venture. This risk capital may, if it comes from program budgets, actually have a negative impact on the ability of the agency to provide services. Unrealistic planning of a commercial venture, such as underestimating the costs and overestimating the returns, could have significant negative outcomes for a nonprofit.

(H)   RISK 8: SELF-SUFFICIENCY

"Unless you invent the next pet rock, you are not going to replace your government funding with your business profits. Sorry."[37] Only in rare circumstances have commercial ventures by North American charities generated a significant proportion of total revenue.[38] While commercial ventures hold promise, it is not realistic to expect that they will eliminate NPOs' dependence on government, foundations, and private donors. Commercial ventures may diversify the funding base of an organization, which in itself may be an important gain by a nonprofit agency. Placing too high expectations on commercial ventures is not sound planning and should be avoided.

21.8   Conclusion

Without a doubt, the landscape of the nonprofit sector is changing. The withdrawal of government support, fluctuating corporate support, increasing demand for quality services, and the movement toward more innovative practices have caused nonprofits to consider commercial ventures as a revenue development strategy. Unlike traditional fundraising campaigns and other traditional sources of revenue such as foundation grants, commercial ventures are a foray into the unknown for most NPOs.

The number of different approaches to commercial ventures and the unique skill sets that are required make thorough planning a necessity. The nonprofit agency must be sure that it has the capacity to undertake a commercial venture and that the risks associated with the venture are acceptable.

For the nonprofit sector as a whole, there are also issues to be considered as more organizations launch business initiatives into the marketplace. Because the sector does hold and represent strong values and principles aimed at creating a healthy society, it must ensure that it acts with integrity. For the sector,

. . . expecting the commercial market to fund and support our principles is an unthinking ideology. Panic may lead to short-term solutions with long-term pain. The solution to an unsustainable status quo requires us to broaden our problem definition to include the "work" not just the "workings" of the charitable sector, and to address the protection and promotion of all three dimensions (principles, productivity and policies) of a healthy society.[39]

Commercial ventures are a reality. If done well, they should strengthen the capacity of NPOs and the nonprofit sector to better complete the work it has taken on. The challenge will be to ensure that missions and principles are not sacrificed to market pressures.

Endnotes

1. Young, D. (1996). "Accountability the Key to Keeping the Nonprofit Sector on Course," *Canadian FundRaiser* (August): http.www.charityvillage.com/charityvillage/research/rstew2.htm/
2. Dees, G. (1998). "Enterprising Nonprofits," *Harvard Business Review* (January–February): 55–64.
3. Zimmerman, B., and R. Dart. (1998). *Charities Doing Commercial Ventures: Societal and Organizational Implications.* Toronto: The Trillium Foundation and Canadian Policy Research Networks, Inc.
4. Steckle, R., and R. Simmons. (1992). *Doing Best by Doing Good: How to Use Public-Purpose Partnerships to Boost Corporate Profits and Benefit Your Community.* New York: Penguin Group.
5. See note 1.
6. The Canadian Centre of Philanthropy. (1996). *Creating Effective Partnerships with Business.* Toronto: Author.
7. See note 4.
8. Market Vision Group. (1996). *The Not-for-Profit and Private Sectors in the 1990s . . . or How 'Birkenstock' and 'Pinstripe' Need Each Other.* Toronto: Author.
9. Id.
10. The Center for Corporate Community Relations at Boston College. (1994). *The Standards of Excellence in Community Relations.* Boston: Author.
11. Seel, K. (1997). "Bridging the Sectors: Developing an Effective Workplace Volunteer Council," *The Journal of Volunteer Administration,* XV(4): 5–14.
12. Seel, K., and G. Ramsay. (1996). "Strategic Corporate Community Investment—A New Generation of Social Policy." In *Sustainable Social Policy and Community Capital.* Ottawa: Caledon Institute of Social Policy and the Canada Mortgage and Housing Corporation, pp. 99–108.
13. Seel, K. (1995a). *The Calgary Corporate Volunteer Council: A Community Development Model.* Calgary: Volunteer Centre of Calgary.
14. Seel, K. (1995b). "Managing Corporate and Employee Volunteer Programs." In T. Connors (ed.), *Volunteer Management Handbook.* New York: John Wiley & Sons, pp. 259–289.
15. M4i Information Industries, Inc. (1998). "The Community Profiler Survey—A New Tool for Corporate Community Investments." Paper presented at the world conference of the International Association for Volunteer Effort, Edmonton, Alberta, August 25, 1998.

16. See note 8.
17. See note 2.
18. The Better Business Bureau of Southern Alberta. (1996). Monthly newsletter.
19. *Marketing Magazine* (May 1996): 15–18.
20. See note 4.
21. Id., p. 76.
22. Id., pp. 80–81.
23. Id., p. 99.
24. Id., p. 105.
25. Id., pp. 106–7.
26. Nichols, J. (1995). *Global Demographics: Fund Raising for the New World.* Chicago, IL: Bonus Books.
27. See note 1.
28. Id.
29. Id.
30. Brodhead, W. (May 1988). *Competition Between For-Profits and Nonprofits.* An Independent Sector Occasional Paper.
31. Canadian Policy Research Network, Inc. (1998). *Charities Doing Commercial Ventures: Societal and Organizational Implications.* Toronto: The Trillium Foundation.
32. Id., p. 32.
33. Drucker, P. (1992). "The New Society of Organizations," *Harvard Business Review* (September–October): 94–104.
34. See note 31, p. 30.
35. Id., pp. 34–35.
36. Id., p. 30.
37. Brinckerhoff, P. (1994). "How to Keep Your Funders Happy as You Develop a New Business," *Nonprofit World* 12(6): 18–20.
38. See note 31, p. 19.
39. Id., p. 43.

22 ▼ Accounting*

RICHARD F. LARKIN, CPA, MBA
Lang Group, Chartered

A sound accounting and financial management function is important for every nonprofit organization (NPO). Good financial practices by themselves will not ensure program success, but they will greatly facilitate it. On the other hand, poor financial practices are a certain recipe for organization failure.

---

* Based on chapters from *Financial and Accounting Guide for Not-for-Profit Organizations, 6th ed.,* by Malvern J. Gross, Jr., Richard F. Larkin, and John H. McCarthy (Wiley, 2000).

Responsibility for sound financial management, as for all other operating functions, rests squarely on the senior executive staff. There may be others involved, such as a treasurer/board member, an outside certified public accountant (CPA), and paid or volunteer controller and bookkeeping staff. However, the executive director controls the process.

Specifically, the executive director must determine the kinds of accounting functions the organization needs, hire the senior financial staff, supervise the financial activities on an ongoing basis, ensure that adequate controls are in effect, know when to take action and what action is needed if problems arise, ensure that financial information is received by those who need it (in useful form and on a timely basis), and coordinate the budget process.

All of this sounds like it requires a person with a lot of financial savvy; it does. Yet, very often in the nonprofit sector, senior executives and (most) board members hold the positions they occupy not as a result of extensive training in management or finance, but because of knowledge of a dedication to the program activities of the organization. Thus, these managers (and trustees) have a special responsibility to learn what they need to know to effectively discharge their financial duties.

22.1 *Duties of the Chief Executive*

(A) FINANCIAL RECORDS

The executive director is charged with seeing that the organization's financial records are maintained in an appropriate manner. If the organization is very small, the treasurer will keep the records. If the organization is somewhat larger, a part-time employee—perhaps a secretary—may, among other duties, keep simple records. If the organization is still larger, there may be a full-time bookkeeper, or perhaps even a full-time accounting staff reporting to the executive director. Regardless of size, the ultimate responsibility for seeing that adequate and complete financial records are kept is clearly that of the executive director. This means that, to some extent, this person must know what is involved in elementary bookkeeping and accounting, although not at the level of a bookkeeper or a CPA.

(B) FINANCIAL STATEMENTS

One of the important responsibilities of the executive director is to see that complete and straightforward financial reports are prepared for the board and membership, to tell clearly what has happened during the period. To be meaningful, these statements should have the following characteristics:

- They should be easily comprehensible so that any person taking the time to study them will understand the financial picture. This characteristic is the one most frequently absent.
- They should be concise so that the person studying them will not get lost in detail.
- They should be all-inclusive in scope and should embrace all activities of the organization. If there are two or three funds, the statements should clearly show the relationship among the funds without a lot of confusing detail involving transfers and appropriations.
- They should have a focal point for comparison so that the person reading them will have some basis for making a judgment. In most instances, this will

be a comparison with a budget or with figures from the corresponding period of the previous year.
• They should be prepared on a timely basis. The longer the delay after the end of the period, the longer the period before corrective action can be taken.

These statements must represent straightforward and candid reporting—that is, the statements must show exactly what has happened. This means that income or assets should not be arbitrarily buried in some subsidiary fund or activity in such a way that the reader is not likely to be aware that the income or assets have been received. It means that if the organization has a number of "funds," the total income and expenses of all funds should be shown in the financial statements in such a manner that no one has to wonder whether all of the activities for the period are included. In short, the statements have to communicate accurately what has happened. If the statement format is confusing and the reader does not understand what it is trying to communicate, then it is not accomplishing its principal objective.

It will be noted that the characteristics listed above would apply equally to the statements of almost any type of organization or business. Unfortunately, financial statements for NPOs frequently fail to meet these characteristics.

(C) PROTECTING ORGANIZATION ASSETS

Unless the organization is very small, there will be a number of assets requiring safeguarding and, again, it is the responsibility of the executive director to be sure that there are both adequate physical controls and accounting controls over these assets.

Physical controls involve making sure that the assets are protected against unauthorized use or theft, and seeing that adequate insurance is provided. Internal accounting controls involve division of duties and record-keeping functions that will ensure control over these assets and adequate reporting of deviations from authorized procedures.

Another responsibility of the executive director is to see that the organization's excess cash is properly invested to ensure maximum financial return.

(D) GOVERNMENT REPORTING REQUIREMENTS

Organizations that receive federal government grants above a certain amount are required to have a special audit of the grants and report to the government.

The executive director is also charged with complying with the various federal and state reporting requirements. Most larger tax-exempt organizations, other than churches, are required to file annual information returns with the Internal Revenue Service (IRS), and some are even required to pay federal taxes. In addition, certain organizations must register and file information returns with certain of the state governments even though they are not resident in the state.

All of these requirements taken together pose a serious problem for a person who is not familiar with either the laws involved or the reporting forms used.

22.2 *Understanding Nonprofit Accounting*

Many businesspersons, as well as many accountants, approach nonprofit accounting with a certain amount of trepidation because of a lack of familiarity with such accounting. There is no real reason for this uneasiness because, except for a few troublesome areas, nonprofit accounting follows many of the same principles followed by commercial enterprises.

One of the principal differences between nonprofit and commercial organizations is that they have different reasons for their existence. In oversimplified terms, it might be said that the ultimate objective of a commercial organization is to realize net profit for its owners through the performance of some service wanted by other people; the ultimate objective of an NPO is to meet some socially desirable need of the community or its members.

So long as the NPO has sufficient resources to carry out its objectives, there is no real need or justification for "making a profit" or having an excess of income over expense. Although a prudent board may want to have a "profit" in order to provide for a rainy day or to be able to respond to a new opportunity in the future, the principal objective of the board is to fulfill the functions for which the organization was founded.

Instead of profit, many NPOs are concerned with the size of their cash balance. They can continue to exist only so long as they have sufficient cash to provide for their program. Thus, the financial statements of NPOs often emphasize the cash position. Commercial organizations are, of course, also concerned with cash, but if they are profitable they will probably be able to finance their cash needs through loans or from investors.

NPOs have a responsibility to account for resources that they have received. This responsibility includes accounting for certain specific funds that have been given for use in a particular project, as well as a general obligation to employ the organization's resources effectively. Emphasis, thus, is placed on accountability and stewardship. To the extent that the organization has received gifts restricted for a specific purpose, it may segregate those resources and report separately on their receipt and disposition. This separate accounting for restricted assets is called *fund accounting*. As a result, the financial statements of NPOs can often be voluminous and complex because each restricted fund grouping may have its own set of financial statements.

There are five areas where the accounting principles followed by NPOs often have differed from the accounting principles followed by commercial organizations. The accounting significance of these five areas should not be minimized, but it is also important to note that, once the significance of each is understood, the reader will have a good understanding of the major accounting principles followed by NPOs. The five areas are discussed in the sections that follow.

(A) CASH VERSUS ACCRUAL ACCOUNTING

In commercial organizations, the records are almost always kept on an accrual basis. The accrual basis simply means keeping records so that, in addition to recording transactions resulting from the receipt and disbursement of cash, there is also a record of the amounts owed to and by others. In NPOs, the cash basis of accounting is frequently used instead. Cash basis accounting means reflecting only transactions where cash has been involved. No attempt is made to record unpaid bills owed or amounts due. Most small NPOs use the cash basis, although, more and more, the medium and larger organizations are now using the accrual basis.

The accrual basis usually gives a more accurate picture of an organization's financial condition. Why, then, is the cash basis frequently used for NPOs? Principally, because it is simpler to keep records on a cash-basis than on an accrual basis. Everyone has had experience keeping a checkbook. This is cash-basis accounting. A nonaccountant can learn to keep a checkbook but is not likely to comprehend readily how to keep a double-entry set of books on the accrual basis. Furthermore, the cash basis is often used when the nature of the organization's activities is such that there are no material amounts owed to others, or vice versa, and so there is little meaningful difference between the cash and accrual basis.

Some NPOs follow a modified form of cash-basis accounting: certain items are recorded on an accrual basis and certain items on a cash basis. Other organizations keep their records on a cash basis but at the end of the year convert to the accrual basis by recording obligations and receivables. The important thing is that the records kept are appropriate to the nature of the organization and its needs.

(B)   FUND ACCOUNTING

Although commercial enterprises often do a separate accounting for departments or branches, the term fund accounting is not used by most businesspersons. In fund accounting, assets are segregated into categories according to the restrictions that donors place on their use. All completely unrestricted assets are in one fund, all endowment funds in another, all building funds in a third, and so forth. Typically, in reporting, an organization using fund accounting presents separate financial statements for each fund. Fund accounting is widely used by NPOs because it provides stewardship reporting. This concept of separate funds is not particularly difficult, but it does cause problems in presenting financial statements that are straightforward enough to be understood by most readers. Many organizations now use more simplified reporting formats.

(C)   TRANSFERS AND APPROPRIATIONS

In NPOs, transfers are frequently made between funds. Unless carefully disclosed, such transfers tend to confuse the reader of the financial statements. Some organizations make appropriations for specific future projects (i.e., set aside a part of the fund balance for a designated purpose). Often, these appropriations are shown, incorrectly, as an expense in arriving at the excess of income over expenses. This also tends to confuse. Transfers and appropriations are not accounting terms used by commercial enterprises.

(D)   TREATMENT OF FIXED ASSETS

In commercial enterprises, fixed assets are almost always recorded as assets on the balance sheet, and are depreciated over their expected useful lives. In nonprofit accounting, some fixed assets may not be recorded. Some organizations write off or expense the asset when purchased; others record fixed assets purchased at cost and depreciate them over their estimated useful life in the same manner as commercial enterprises.

(E)   CONTRIBUTIONS, PLEDGES, AND NONCASH CONTRIBUTIONS

In commercial or business enterprises, there is no such thing as a "pledge." If the business is legally owed money, the amount is recorded as an account receivable. A pledge to an NPO may or may not be legally enforceable. Some NPOs record pledges because they know from experience that they will collect them. Others have not because they feel they have no legally enforceable claim. A related problem is where and how to report both restricted and unrestricted contributions in the financial statements. Recently issued accounting standards have resulted in more uniformity of practice in this area. For further discussion, see Gross et al.[1]

Noncash contributions include donations of securities, equipment, supplies, and services. Commercial enterprises seldom are recipients of such income.

(F)   ACCOUNTING FOR INVESTMENTS

Recent accounting standards applicable to NPOs require that all debt securities and all marketable equity securities be reported in the balance sheet at current market value. Businesses follow a different standard in this regard.

(G)   FUNCTIONAL REPORTING OF EXPENSES

Accounting literature applicable to NPOs has long required some degree of functional reporting of expenses—generally into categories of "program," "management," and "fund raising." Business-oriented literature is generally silent on this subject, although many businesses use a form of expense reporting that is partly functional. Recent nonprofit standards require all organizations to report expenses by function.

22.3   *Avoiding Financial Problems*

Some people have the mistaken idea that bankruptcy happens only to businesses. Nonprofits are not immune, and management must work to avoid financial problems that could cause the organization to be unable to carry on its activities. Although final responsibility is the board's, the executive director must watch both the day-to-day and long-term financial pictures. The treasurer, controller, and other financially oriented persons are important resources for management, but they are often either not around every day or do not have the broad perspective of the executive director.

The executive director must monitor the financial progress of the organization with respect to the budget, both as to whether revenue is keeping up with projections and whether expenses are being kept within limits. In particular, the current and forecasted cash position must be watched carefully for any trend that indicates possible future shortages. This monitoring must occur regularly during the year; the more delicate the organization's financial position, the more frequently a "reading" must be taken.

If problems occur or appear imminent, the executive director must alert others in the organization, especially other members of management and key board members, so that a plan of action to deal with the problems can be implemented. It is, however, management's responsibility to decide what needs to be done, and to do it, whether more revenue is needed or expenses must be cut, or some other action is required.

Some possible ways to respond to financial problems include:

- *Increasing contributions.* This is often more easily said than done. It usually requires an up-front outlay of money and/or time, and the results may not be seen for awhile, or at all. An organization in or approaching financial difficulty has an especially hard time convincing donors to support what some may see as a sinking ship.

- *Raising service fees.* By the laws of supply and demand, this may or may not result in an overall revenue increase. Some "customers" will be lost, especially if the organization serves an economically disadvantaged population.
- *Reducing expenses.* This is also easier said than done, because many expenses are relatively fixed, at least in the short term. It is not easy for dedicated staff and volunteers to make decisions that may reduce the entity's services.
- *Borrowing.* This is quick (if a willing lender can be found), but expensive (interest cost). Further, it may merely postpone an ultimate day of reckoning. Borrowing should be undertaken only for long-term projects such as capital assets, where the debt can be repaid over the life of the assets, or as a very temporary short-term measure, when receipts to repay the borrowing are assured in the near future. A grant may be awarded but not yet received, or a firm pledge may have arrived from a reliable donor.
- *Considering whether the needs of the organization's service beneficiaries would be better met by other organizations that have greater financial resources.* This is a euphemism for one of two actions: merging with another entity, or going out of business and turning the organization's remaining resources and clients over to another service provider. These are never easy choices but are sometimes the only feasible alternatives. If one of these options is to be chosen, the decision should be made quickly so that the transfer of services will occur smoothly, before cash is totally depleted and operations become disrupted.

22.4   Staffing the Accounting Function in a Small Organization*

Obtaining the right kind of accounting staff is important to the smooth running of this function. The executive director usually has no training, time, or inclination to do the bookkeeping. Competent professional assistance is needed.

The problem of finding the right bookkeeper is compounded for NPOs because, traditionally, such organizations pay low salaries to all of their staff, including the bookkeeper. The salary level frequently results in the organization's getting someone with only minimum qualifications, which appears to be a false economy. A good bookkeeper can help the organization save money and can free the time of other staff and volunteers.

Often, the other staff members in the organization are extremely dedicated individuals who are interested in the particular program of the organization and willing to accept a lower-than-normal salary. Bookkeepers may not be dedicated to the programs of the organization in the same way. They have been hired to provide bookkeeping services and often have no special interest in the program of the organization.

(A)   FINDING A BOOKKEEPER

The first step in obtaining a bookkeeper is to determine what bookkeeping services are needed. Depending on the size of the organization, there are a number of possibilities. If

---

* This section deals only with the bookkeeping problems of relatively small organizations. Larger organizations are not discussed because, to a very large extent, they are run like commercial organizations.

the organization is very small and fewer than 25 checks are issued per month, a "check-book"-type set of records will likely be all that is required. If so, the treasurer may very well keep the records and not need someone to help.

For many organizations, the number of transactions is too large for the treasurer to handle but not large enough to justify a full-time bookkeeper. If the organization has a paid full- or part-time secretary, often some of the bookkeeping duties are delegated to the secretary. Usually, this means keeping the "checkbook" or perhaps a simple cash receipts and cash disbursements ledger. At the end of the month, the treasurer will summarize these cash records and prepare the financial statements.

Another possibility for the small organization is to find a volunteer within the organization who will help keep the records. While this can occasionally be effective, it often turns out to be less than satisfactory. Keeping a set of books is work, and although a volunteer bookkeeper's enthusiasm may be great at the beginning, it tends to diminish in time. The result is that there are often delays, clerical errors, and, eventually, the need to get another bookkeeper.

Another possibility is a part-time bookkeeper. Some of the best potential may be found among parents with schoolchildren, who were full-time bookkeepers at one time, or, if the organization wants someone at its office for a full day each week or during hours not suitable for a parent with schoolchildren, then perhaps a retired bookkeeper or accountant will be the next best bet.

For larger or growing organizations, there is a point when a full-time bookkeeper is needed. Placing an advertisement in the newspaper is probably the best approach. Alternatively, an employment agency can be used. The principal advantage is a saving of time and effort. The agency will place the ad in the paper and will do the initial weeding out of the obvious misfits before forwarding the potential candidates to the organization for review. Agencies also know the job market and will probably be in a good position to advise on the "going" salary. They should also be able to help in checking references.

If the organization has outside auditors, they may be able to help. Their advice should be requested and, before actually hiring a bookkeeper, they should talk with the candidates.

(B)   ALTERNATIVES TO BOOKKEEPERS

One thing that can be done to reduce the burden on the bookkeeper is to let a bank or a service bureau handle the payroll. This is particularly effective where employees are paid the same amount each payroll period.

Responsibility for bookkeeping, however, cannot be delegated outside the organization. An employee of the organization must continuously monitor and review the work of an outside bookkeeper.

Some banks will handle the complete payroll function. Most will prepare the payroll tax reports. Banks usually have a minimum fee for each payroll. If there are more than about 20 employees, this amount increases. The charge may seem high, but the time saved can be considerable. In addition to the payroll preparation, the bank will keep cumulative records of salary paid to each employee and will prepare the various payroll tax returns, W-2 forms, and similar documents.

Another possibility is to have a service bureau keep all the bookkeeping records. If there is any volume of activity, a service bureau can often keep the records at less cost to an organization than hiring a bookkeeper. For example, some service bureaus will enter information from original documents, such as the check stubs, invoices, and so on. They can then prepare a cash receipts book, cash disbursement book, general ledger, and financial statements, all automatically. The organization only has to provide the basic information.

It is also possible to hire an outside accounting service to perform the actual book-keeping. Many CPAs and public accountants provide bookkeeping services for their clients. Under this arrangement, the accountant has one of the staff do all of the book-keeping but takes the responsibility for reviewing the work and seeing that it is properly done. The accountant usually prepares financial statements monthly or quarterly.

There are still some functions the organization itself usually must perform. The organization will normally still have to prepare its own checks, vouchers, payroll, depositing of receipts, and billings. This means that normally it cannot delegate 100 percent of the bookkeeping to an outside accounting service.

22.5   *Providing Internal Control*

Employee Admits Embezzlement of Ten Thousand Dollars.
Trusted Clerk Steals $50,000.

These headlines are all too common, and many tell a similar story—a trusted and respected employee in a position of financial responsibility is overcome by temptation and "borrows" a few dollars until payday to meet some unexpected cash need. When payday comes, some other cash need prevents repayment. Somehow the employee just never catches up, and borrows a few more dollars, and a few more and a few more.

The reader's reaction may be, "Thank goodness, this kind of thing could never happen to my organization. After all, I know everyone and they are all honest, and besides, who would think of stealing from a nonprofit organization?" This is not the point. Very few people who end up as embezzlers start out with this intent. Rather, they find themselves in a position of trust and opportunity and, when personal crises arise, the temptation is too much. NPOs are not exempt, regardless of size. There is always a risk when a person is put in a position to be tempted.

The purpose of this section is to outline some of the practical procedures that a small organization can establish to help minimize this risk and thus safeguard the organization's physical assets. For purposes of this discussion, the emphasis is on smaller organizations (those with one or two persons handling all the bookkeeping). This would include many churches, country clubs, local fund-raising groups, YMCAs, and other agencies. Internal control for larger organizations is not discussed here because controls for such organizations can become very complicated and would require many chapters. The principles, however, are essentially the same.

Internal control is a system of procedures and cross-checking that, in the absence of collusion, minimizes the likelihood of misappropriation of assets or misstatement of the accounts, and maximizes the likelihood of detection if embezzlement occurs. For the most part, internal control does not prevent embezzlement but should ensure that, if committed, it will be promptly discovered. This likelihood of discovery usually persuades most workers not to allow temptation to get the better of them. Internal control also includes a system of checks and balances over all paperwork, to ensure that there was no intentional or unintentional misstatement of financial data.

There are several reasons for having a good system of internal controls. The first, obviously, is to prevent the loss through theft of some of the assets. A second reason, equally important, is to prevent "honest" employees from making a mistake that could ruin their lives.

Aside from this moral responsibility of the employer, there is a responsibility of the board, to the membership and to the general public, to safeguard the assets of the organization. If a large sum were stolen and not recovered, it could jeopardize the program of the organization. Furthermore, even if only a small amount were stolen, it would be embarrassing to the members of the board. In either case, the membership or the public would certainly want to know why internal control procedures were not followed.

For example, several recent, real, well-publicized situations involving NPOs were all at least partly due to the absence of adequate internal controls:

- The chief executive officer of a major charity misused some of the organization's funds for personal benefit. If this person had been subject to adequate oversight and review by the organization's board of directors, the amount of money that could have been misused probably would have been only a small fraction of what the organization eventually lost.
- The chief financial officer of a national organization embezzled money from the organization's bank accounts and covered up the theft by making improper entries in the books. Had this person been subject to adequate control, including proper segregation of duties, enforced by the organization's board and chief executive, the thefts would likely not have happened at all, or, if money had been taken, the loss would have been evident to others more quickly.
- Another chief executive spent the organization's money on personal expenses and on projects that were not subject to adequate review and approval by the board. Had the board been more aware of what was happening, these wasteful expenditures could have been minimized, or possibly avoided altogether.
- A large religious organization entered into contracts that created liabilities that it had no ability to fulfill. The chief executive did this on his own, without proper board supervision and review.
- (Although governments are not the type of nonprofit mainly discussed in this book, this organization's story could happen in a nonprofit as well.) The treasurer of a local government invested its cash reserves in extremely speculative investments, which eventually turned sour. The government was forced into bankruptcy. If the governing board had exercised stronger controls over the investment activities of the treasurer, the speculative investments would have been much less likely to have resulted in the large losses that occurred.

This is not in any way to condone or excuse the actions of the individuals who did things they should not have done; however, because they were able to do what they did, over a period of time, without being promptly called to account for their actions, indicates that those in position of responsibility over these individuals were not adequately discharging their responsibilities for guarding the organizations' resources. In fact, the very presence of adequate internal controls might have deterred some of these people from even attempting to do anything improper. Note that we are not talking here about taking $50 from the petty cash fund. Of course, a board (or a chief executive) has more important things to do than worry about that (that's the controller's job). These were situations so significant that the very existence of the organizations and their programs were called into question. That is surely a major concern of the very top officials of an organization.

Further, in every case, the ultimate harm to the organization extended far beyond the actual amount of money stolen or wasted. Each situation became a public relations disaster; three ended up in bankruptcy court; some people have gone to jail. When the nonprofit organizations' donors finally became aware of what had happened, contributions dropped significantly. The loss of contributions can never be measured precisely, of course, but it was doubtless many times the actual amount that triggered the donors' reactions. It can take many years for an organization's finances to recover from such a debacle, if they ever do.

(A)   EFFECTIVE INTERNAL CONTROLS

One of the most effective internal controls is the use of a budget that is compared to actual figures on a monthly basis. If deviations from the budget are carefully followed up by the controller or executive director, the likelihood of a large misappropriation taking place without being detected fairly quickly is reduced considerably. This type of overall review of the financial statements is very important, and every member of the board should ask questions about any item that appears out of line either with the budget or with what would have been expected to be the actual figures. Many times, this type of probing for reasons for deviations from the expected has uncovered problems.

A number of other basic internal controls are probably applicable to many, if not most, small NPOs; these controls are discussed as follows. However, it must be emphasized that these are only basic controls and should not be considered all-inclusive. Establishing an effective system of internal control requires knowledge of the particular organization and its operations.

In this discussion, we will be considering the division of duties for a small organization, The Center for World Peace. This organization sponsors seminars and retreats and has a paid staff to run its affairs. The office staff consists of an executive director, the executive director's secretary, a program director, and a bookkeeper.

The officers of the Center are all volunteers and usually are at the Center only at irregular times. The executive director, treasurer, president, and vice-president are check signers. With this background, let us now look at each of eleven controls in detail and see how they apply to this organization.

(B)   CONTROLS OVER RECEIPTS

The basic objective in establishing internal control over receipts is to obtain control over the amounts received at the time of receipt. Once this control is established, procedures must be followed to ensure that these amounts get deposited in the organization's bank account. Establishing this control is particularly difficult for small organizations because of the small number of persons usually involved.

1. *Prenumbered receipts should be issued for all money at the time first received. A duplicate copy should be accounted for and a comparison eventually made between the aggregate of the receipts issued and the amount deposited in the bank.*

The purpose of this control is to create a written record of the cash received. The original of the receipt should be given to the person from whom the money was received; the duplicate copy should be kept permanently. Periodically, the aggregate receipts issued should be compared with the amount deposited. The receipts can be issued at the organization's office, or, if door-to-door collections are made, a prenumbered receipt can be issued for each amount received by the collector.

In our illustration, the Center receives cash at its seminars and retreats on weekends, when the bookkeeper and treasurer are not available. One of the participants, designated as the fee collector for that session, collects the fees and issues the receipts. After all of the fees are collected, they are turned over, with the duplicate copy of the receipts (along with all unused receipt forms), to the program director. A summary report of the cash collected is prepared and signed in duplicate. One copy of this report is mailed directly to the treasurer's home in an envelope provided, and the duplicate is turned over to the program director. The program director counts the money, agreeing the total received with the total of the duplicate receipts and with the summary report. The program director puts the money in the safe for the weekend and, on Monday morning, gives the money, the duplicate receipts, and the copy of the summary report to the bookkeeper for depositing. The bookkeeper deposits the money from each program separately, and files the duplicate receipts and summary report for future reference. Once a month, the treasurer compares the copy of each summary report with the deposits shown on the bank statement.

2. *Cash collections should be under the control of two people wherever possible, particularly where it is not practicable to issue receipts.*

In the illustration in the previous paragraph, control was established over cash collections by having the person collecting at each seminar issue receipts and prepare a summary report. The program director also had some control through knowledge of how many persons attended and comparison of the amount collected with the amount that should have been collected. This provided dual control.

There are many instances, however, where cash collections are received when it is not appropriate to give a receipt. Two examples are church plate collections during worship services, and coin canisters placed in stores and public places throughout the community for public support. To the extent that only one person handles this money, there is always a risk. The risk is not only that some of it will be misappropriated, but also that someone may erroneously think it has been. Therefore, it is recommended that two people be involved.

With respect to church plate collections, as soon as the money has been collected, it should be locked up until it can be counted by two people together. Perhaps the head usher and a vestryman will count it after the last service. Once the counting is completed, both should sign a cash collection report. This report should be given to the treasurer for subsequent comparison with the deposit on the bank statement. The cash should be turned over to the bookkeeper for depositing intact.

This procedure will not guard against an usher's dipping a hand into the "plate" before it is initially locked up or counted, but the ushers' duties are usually rotated and the cumulative risk is low. The bookkeeper and treasurer normally have access to such funds on a regular and recurring basis. Therefore, their function of counting these cash receipts should be controlled by having a second person involved. It is not because they are not trusted; it is to ensure that no one can think of accusing one of them.

Canisters containing cash, which are placed in public places, should be sealed so that the only way to get access to the cash is to break the canister open. Someone could take the entire canister, but if the canister is placed in a conspicuous place—near the cash register, for example—this risk is fairly low. These canisters should be serially numbered so that all canisters can be accounted for. When the canisters are eventually opened, they should be counted by two people using the same procedures as with plate collections.

3. *Two persons should open all mail and make a list of all receipts for each day. This list should subsequently be compared to the bank deposit by someone not handling the money. Receipts in the form of checks should be restrictively endorsed promptly upon receipt.*

Two persons should open the mail; otherwise, there is a risk that the mail opener may misappropriate part of the receipts. This imposes a heavy burden on the small organization with only a few employees, but it is necessary if good internal control is desired. Organizations that have their financial statements audited by CPAs will find that the CPA cannot give an unqualified opinion if internal control is considered inadequate. One alternative is to have mail receipts go to a bank lockbox and let the bank do the actual opening of the mail.

The purpose of making a list of all checks received is to ensure that a record is made of the amount that was received. This makes it possible for the treasurer to later check to see whether the bookkeeper has deposited all amounts promptly.

Checks should be promptly endorsed because, once endorsed, there is less likelihood of misappropriation. The endorsement should be placed on the check by the person first opening the mail.

In theory, if the check has been made out in the name of the organization, no one can cash it. But experience has shown that a clever enough person can find a way to cash it or deposit it in a "personal" bank account opened for the purpose. On the other hand, once the check is endorsed with the name of the bank and the organization's account number, it is very difficult for the embezzler to convert the check to personal use.

In our illustration, the secretary to the executive director of the Center, together with the bookkeeper, jointly open all mail and place the rubber-stamp endorsement on the check. They then make a list, in duplicate, of all checks received; one copy of the list goes to the bookkeeper with the checks for depositing. They both sign the original of the list, which goes to the executive director. The executive director obtains the copy, to see what amounts have been received. At the end of the month, all of these lists are turned over to the treasurer, who then compares each day's lists with the respective credit on the bank statement.

4. *All receipts should be deposited in the bank, intact and on a timely basis.*

The purpose of this control is to ensure that there is a complete record of all receipts and disbursements. If an organization receives "cash" receipts, no part of this cash should be used to pay its bills. The receipts should be deposited, and checks issued to pay expenses. In this way there will be a record of the total receipts and expenses of the organization on the bank statements.

This procedure does not prevent someone from stealing money, but it does mean that a check must be used to get access to the money. This leaves a record of the theft and makes it more difficult for a person to cover up.

(C) CONTROLS OVER DISBURSEMENTS

The basic objective in establishing internal controls over disbursements is to ensure that a record of all disbursements is made and that only authorized persons are in a position to withdraw funds. The risk of misappropriation can be significantly reduced if procedures are established to minimize the possibility that an expenditure can be made without leaving a trail, or that an unauthorized person can withdraw money.

5. *All disbursements should be made by check, or by properly authorized electronic disbursement, and supporting documentation should be kept for each disbursement.*

This control is to ensure that there will be a permanent record of how much and to whom money was paid. No amounts should be paid by cash, with the exception of minor petty cash items. For the same reason, no checks should be made payable to "cash." Checks should always be payable to a specific person, including checks for petty cash reimbursement. This makes it more difficult to fraudulently disburse funds.

At the Center, the bookkeeper prepares all checks for payment of bills. Before a check is prepared, however, the vendor's invoice must be approved by the executive director. If the purchases involved goods that have been received at the Center, the person who received the goods must indicate their receipt, right on the vendor's invoice.

The bookkeeper is not a check signer. If this were the case, this person could fraudulently disburse funds to himself or herself and then cover up the fraud in the books. The check signers are the executive director, the treasurer, the president, and the vice-president. Normally, the executive director signs all checks. Checks of more than $1,000 require two signatures, but these are very infrequent. The executive director carefully examines all supporting invoices, making sure that someone has signed for receipt of the goods before signing the check. After signing the check, each invoice is marked "paid" so that it won't inadvertently be paid twice. The secretary mails all checks to the vendors as an added control over the bookkeeper. By not letting the bookkeeper have access to the signed checks, the bookkeeper is not in a position to profit from preparing a fraudulent check to a nonexistent vendor.

6. *If the treasurer or check signer is also the bookkeeper, two signatures should be required on all checks.*

The purpose of this control is to ensure that no one person is in a position to disburse funds and then cover up an improper disbursement in the records. In part, this recommendation is designed to protect the organization, and in part, to protect the treasurer.

Two signatures on a check provide additional control only so long as the second check signer also examines the invoices or supporting bills behind the disbursement before signing the check. The real risk of having dual signatures is that both check signers will rely on the other and will review the supporting bills in such a perfunctory manner that there is less control than if only one person signed but assumed full responsibility.

7. *A person other than the bookkeeper should receive bank statements directly from the bank and should reconcile them.*

This control is to prevent the bookkeeper from fraudulently issuing a check for personal use and, as bookkeeper, covering up this disbursement in the books. The bookkeeper may not be a check signer, but experience has shown that banks often do not catch forged check signatures. The bookkeeper usually has access to blank checks and could forge the check signer's signature. If the bookkeeper were to receive the bank statements, the fraudulent and forged cancelled checks could be removed and then destroyed, with the fraud covered up through the books.

In most smaller organizations, the bank statement and cancelled checks should go directly to the treasurer, who should prepare the bank reconciliation. In those situations in which the treasurer is also the bookkeeper, the bank statements should go directly to another officer to reconcile. The treasurer should insist on this procedure as a protection from any suspicions of wrongdoing.

In large organizations, the control can be even more effective where the division of duties is such that an employee who is not a check signer *or* bookkeeper can prepare the bank reconciliation. It is possible for check signers to fraudulently make out a check to themselves and then, if they have access to the returned checks, to remove the cancelled check. However, if they do not also have a means of covering up the disbursement, sooner or later the shortage will come out. The person reconciling the bank account is not in a position to permanently "cover up" a shortage, although it could be hidden for several months. For this reason, it is preferable to have neither a check signer nor the bookkeeper prepare the reconciliation.

In the Center's case, the bank statement and cancelled checks are mailed directly to the treasurer's home each month. After receiving the bank statement, the treasurer usually spends half a day at the Center's offices preparing the complete bank reconciliation and comparing the lists of mail and program receipts received throughout the month to the deposits shown on the bank statement.

(D) OTHER CONTROLS

8. *Someone other than the bookkeeper should authorize all write-offs of accounts receivable or other assets.*

This control is to ensure that a bookkeeper who has embezzled accounts receivable or some other assets will not also be in a position to cover up the theft by writing off the receivable or asset. If the bookkeeper is unable to write such amounts off, someone will eventually ask why the "receivable" has not been paid, and this should trigger correspondence that would result in the fraud being discovered.

Generally, write-offs of small receivables should be approved by the treasurer (provided the treasurer is not also the bookkeeper), but if they are large, they should be submitted to the board for approval. Before any amount is written off, the treasurer should make certain that all appropriate efforts have been made, including, possibly, legal action. The treasurer must constantly keep in mind the fiduciary responsibility to take all reasonable steps to make collection.

The Center only rarely has accounts receivable. However, it does have many pledges receivable. Although the Center would not think of taking legal action to enforce collection, it does record those pledges as though they were receivables. Occasionally, the bookkeeper has to call the treasurer's attention to a delinquent pledge. The treasurer, in turn, usually calls the delinquent pledgor in an effort to evaluate the likelihood of future collection. Once a year, a written report is submitted to the board advising it of delinquent pledges, and requesting formal approval to write them off. The board discusses each such delinquent pledge before giving its approval.

9. *Marketable securities should be kept in a bank safe deposit box or held by a custodian in an account in the name of the organization.*

This control is to ensure that securities are protected against loss by fire or theft or from bankruptcy of a brokerage house. Safeguarding investments is discussed more fully in section 22.7, "Investments."

10. *Fixed asset records should be maintained and an inventory taken periodically.*

These procedures ensure that the organization has a complete record of its assets. The permanent record should contain a description of the asset, cost, date acquired, location, serial number, and similar information. Such information will provide a record of the assets that the employees are responsible for. This is particularly important in NPOs in which turnover of employees and officers is often high. It also provides fire insurance records.

11. *Excess cash should be maintained in a separate bank or investment account. Withdrawals from this account should require two signatures.*

Where an organization has excess cash that will not be needed for current operations in the immediate future, it should be placed in a separate account to provide an added safeguard. Frequently, this separate account will be an interest-bearing savings account. The bank or investment manager should be advised that the signatures of two officers are required for all withdrawals. Normally, in such situations, withdrawals are infrequent; when they are made, the funds withdrawn are deposited intact in the regular current checking account. In this way, all disbursements are made from the regular checking account.

In this situation, the officers involved in authorizing a withdrawal should not do so without being fully aware of the reasons for the need of these funds. Approval should not be perfunctorily given.

One final recommendation. Fidelity insurance should be carried. The purpose of fidelity insurance is to ensure that, if a loss from embezzlement occurs, the organization will recover the loss. This insurance does not cover theft or burglary by an outside person; it provides protection only against an employee's dishonesty. Having fidelity insurance also acts as a deterrent because the employees know that the insurance company is more likely to press charges against a dishonest employee than would a "soft-hearted" and embarrassed employer.

There is only one "catch" to this type of coverage. The organization has to have good enough records to prove that an embezzlement has taken place. This means that this coverage is not a substitute for other internal controls. If the theft occurs but the employer doesn't know it or if there is no proof of the loss, fidelity insurance will not help.

Sometimes, employees feel that a lack of confidence in them is being expressed if the organization has fidelity insurance. The treasurer should assure them that this is not the case, and that fidelity insurance is similar to fire insurance. All prudent organizations carry such coverage.

Even the smallest organization should be able to apply the internal controls that have been recommended in this section. The board should insist that these and similar controls be established. It has a responsibility to insist that all practical measures be taken to protect the organization's assets. Otherwise, the board would be subject to severe criticism if an embezzlement were to occur.

The controls discussed in this section are basic ones and should not be considered all-inclusive. A complete system of internal control encompasses all of the procedures of the organization. If the organization is large or complex, or if it has peculiar problems or procedures, the board will want to retain the services of a professional to help set up and monitor the effectiveness of internal control. The next section discusses the services that the certified public accountant can provide, including assistance in establishing internal controls.

22.6 *Independent Audits*

Related to the internal controls discussed in the preceding section is the question of whether the books and records should be audited. Like many other decisions the board has to make, this is a value judgment for which there are no absolute answers. Audits cost time and money, and therefore the values to be derived must be considered carefully.

An audit is a series of procedures followed by an experienced professional accountant to test, on a selective basis, transactions and internal controls in effect, all with a view to forming an opinion on the fairness of the presentation of the financial statements.

Several things should be underscored. Auditors do not examine all transactions. If they were to do so, the cost would be prohibitive. They do look at what they believe is a representative sample of the transactions. In looking at these selected transactions, they are as concerned with the internal control and procedures that were followed as they are with the legitimacy of the transaction itself. If internal controls are good, the extent of the testing can be limited. If controls are weak, the auditors will have to examine many more transactions to be satisfied. In smaller organizations, where internal controls are often less effective, auditors must examine proportionately more transactions.

Another point is that, for the most part, the auditors can only examine and test transactions that have been recorded. If a contribution has been received but not deposited in the bank or recorded in the books, there is little likelihood that it will be discovered. This is why the preceding section emphasized that controls should be established over all receipts at the point of receipt and all disbursements should be made by check. In this way, a record is made and the auditor has a chance of testing the transaction.

The end product of the audit is not a "certificate" that every transaction has been properly recorded, but an expression of an opinion by the auditor on the fairness of the presentation of the financial statements. The auditor does not guarantee accuracy; the bookkeeper may have stolen $100, but unless this $100 is material in relation to the financial statements as a whole, the auditor is not likely to discover it.

(A)   WHY HAVE AN AUDIT?

Audits are not free. This means that the board has to evaluate the benefits to be derived from an audit, and its cost. What are the benefits that can be expected from an audit? There are four: (1) credibility of the financial statements; (2) professional assistance in developing meaningful financial statements; (3) professional advice on internal control, administrative efficiency, and other business matters; and (4) assistance in tax reporting and compliance requirements.

Credibility is the principal benefit of having an independent CPA express an opinion on the financial statements. Unfortunately, over the years, there have been many instances in which NPOs have been mismanaged and the results have been buried in the financial statements in a manner that made it difficult, if not impossible, for the readers of the statements to discern them.

It has been noted that the purpose of financial statements is to communicate in a straightforward manner what has happened. The presence of an auditor's opinion helps in this communication process because an independent expert, after an examination, tells the reader that the financial statements present fairly what has happened. NPOs are competing with other organizations for the money of their members or of the general public. If an organization can tell its financial story accurately and completely and it is accepted at face value, the potential contributor is more likely to feel that the organization is well managed.

Another benefit of having professional help is that the auditor is an expert at preparing financial statements in a format that will be most clear to the reader. All too often, financial statements are poorly organized and hard to understand. The CPA has experience in helping organizations to prepare financial statements in clear and understandable language.

Another benefit is that the CPA will be in a position to advise the board on how to strengthen internal controls and simplify the bookkeeping procedures. The CPA can also assist the board in evaluating the organization's bookkeeper and can help the organization hire someone for this position.

The CPA has had experience in dealing with different types of organizations and is likely to have a number of general business suggestions. Typically, periodic meetings with senior staff or board members will be held to discuss the problems of the organization and business conditions in general. Many boards arrange annual meetings to ask questions and to be sure that the organization has picked the CPA's brain. This meeting also provides the CPA with an opportunity to call any potential problems to the board's attention.

Most NPOs are required to submit some form of report to one or more agencies of a state government and the IRS. These reports are technical in format and, unless the treasurer is an accountant, the assistance of an expert will probably be required. The CPA is an expert and can either offer advice on how to prepare the returns or actually prepare them.

(B) FINDING AN AUDITOR

When it comes time to choose a CPA, discussion should include the organization's banker, attorney, and members of the board. The chances are that collectively they will know many CPAs practicing in the locality and will know of their reputations. Officers of other NPOs should be consulted. They will probably have had some experience that may be of help. One significant criterion in the selection should be the CPA's familiarity with non-profit entities.

As in any professional relationship, the CPA's interest and willingness to serve the organization are among the most important factors to consider when making a selection. It is always difficult to judge which of several CPAs has the greatest interest in helping the organization. In large part, the board will have to make the decision from impressions formed in personal interviews. The appendix at the end of this chapter discusses this subject further.

During this personal interview, the CPA should be asked to take a look at the records, to get a general impression of the amount of time that will be necessary, and thus the fee. For the most part, the judgment should not be swayed significantly by the fee range estimated, unless it is out of line with other CPA fees. Like a doctor or lawyer, the accountant expects to receive a fair fee for services. The organization is largely dependent on the honesty and professional reputation of the accountant to charge a fair fee.

What does it cost to have an audit? This is a difficult question to answer because most CPAs charge on an hourly basis. If the organization's records are in good shape, the time will be less. There is no way to know how much time will be involved without looking at the records and knowing something about the organization.

Sometimes an organization will shop around in an effort to find the CPA that will charge it the least. Because the treasurer is not likely to be in a position to judge the quality of the work, there is a risk in choosing a professional accountant solely on the basis of an estimated fee. Choosing a CPA should be on the basis of reputation, expertise, and willingness to serve the organization.

(C) REVIEW SERVICES

A possible alternative to an audit, for an organization that does not have to submit audited financial statements to a state, a funding source, or another organization, is to have its financial statements "reviewed" by a CPA. A review requires less time, hence incurs less cost; however, it results in a lesser degree of assurance by the CPA. Instead of saying that the financial statements "present fairly," the CPA does only enough work to be able to say, "I am not aware of any material modifications that should be made in order for the financial statements to be in conformity." This is called *negative assurance* and does not give as much credibility to the financial statements as an audit does. Nevertheless, a review may meet the needs of some smaller organizations.

(D) AUDIT COMMITTEES

Many smaller organizations do not feel they can afford a CPA and yet want some assurance that accounting matters are being adequately managed, and especially that disbursements have been made for proper purposes. One solution to this is to set up an "audit committee" consisting of several members of the board or of the membership. The committee may meet on a monthly or bimonthly basis and review transactions since the last meeting. It may also review bank reconciliations; marketable securities bought, sold, and on hand; and any other matter that could be "sensitive."

The advantage of an audit committee is that it strengthens internal control significantly, with little cost. This is particularly important where internal control is weak because it is not practical to segregate duties as much as might be desired.

The institution of external audit committees has now become a common practice for nonprofit organizations. A properly functioning audit committee goes a long way toward demonstrating that the board of trustees has taken prudent steps to perform its administrative and control functions. Thus, with regard to audit committees, the author recommends that:

- Every NPO that raises funds from the general public or that receives grants or membership dues should have an active and functioning audit committee.
- For most effective operation, audit committees should be composed of three to five directors, with the majority (including the chairperson) being trustees who are not employees.
- Audit committees should be responsible for recommending the appointment of the independent accountants and for discussion of their work with them.
- Audit committees should be responsible for the review and evaluation of reports prepared by the independent accountants that contain recommendations for improvements in controls. Audit committees should determine whether management has taken appropriate action on these recommendations.
- Audit committees should be delegated the responsibility to review the annual financial statements with the independent accountants.

22.7 *Investments*

Some NPOs have an investment program to manage, as a result of receipt of endowment funds and other restricted gifts. Some organizations also have excess cash in their unrestricted general fund, which can be invested. Sometimes all of these investment funds can be very sizable. They are usually invested in publicly traded securities, although occasionally a partial amount is invested in real estate or in mortgages.

Where should an organization go to get good investment advice? The answer is clear: to a professional; to someone who knows the market and is in the business of advising others.

Sometimes, a nonprofit's board, recognizing its fiduciary responsibilities, will tend to be too conservative in its investment policy, and will purchase high-grade, low-interest-bearing bonds. This conservatism can be almost as risky as purchasing a highly volatile stock, as many holders of bonds discovered in recent years when high interest rates depressed bond prices. This is why professional advice is needed.

There are a number of places to go for professional advice. If the total investments are relatively small in size (say, under $100,000), many organizations find that a no-load mutual fund or a bank common stock fund is the answer. (If an organization has under $100,000 to invest, the board should carefully consider the nature of the funds being invested before buying common stocks. If the funds available are to be invested for only a short period of time, or if investment income is essential, then the organization should not be investing in common stocks. Instead, a savings account or money-market instrument is probably more appropriate.) In both cases, the organization is purchasing expertise while it pools its funds with those of many other people. Mutual funds offer a convenient way to obtain investment management when the organization has a minimum amount to invest.

Bank-commingled or common stock investment funds are a form of mutual fund. One of the advantages of using a bank fund is that the reputation of the bank is involved and the bank will pay close attention to the investments made. Banks are often more conservative than mutual funds in their investment decisions, but this may be appropriate when one considers the fiduciary responsibility of NPOs.

If the investment fund is large in size, the organization may prefer to select a professional to advise on specific stocks and bonds to purchase for its own portfolio. Most brokers are pleased to offer this service. On the other hand, many NPOs are reluctant to entrust investment decisions to the brokers who handle the actual purchasing, because they are "wearing two hats." This can be avoided by going to one of the many available investment advisory services that does not handle the actual purchasing or selling.

Investment professionals can also offer advice on a type of investment that is frequently not given the attention it warrants by NPOs—short-term investments. Short-term investments are investments in interest-bearing instruments of that portion of an organization's cash balances that is currently inactive but will be needed to fund programs and activities in the near future.

An ordinary savings account is one type of short-term investment of cash balances that are temporarily not deployed. Often, however, it is possible to improve on the interest rate available in savings accounts, without substantially increasing risk, by purchasing "money-market" instruments. These vary in interest rate, risk, minimum denomination available, time to maturity, and marketability prior to redemption; included are U.S. Treasury Bills, "agencies," certificates of deposit, and repurchase agreements.

Treasury Bills are the most marketable money-market instrument. The smallest denomination currently available is $10,000, and the shortest maturity is 13 weeks.

"Agencies" are federally sponsored debt instruments issued by federal agencies or quasi-governmental organizations. Some are explicitly guaranteed by the full faith and credit of the United States Government, but others are not.

Certificates of deposit (CDs) are available directly from commercial or savings banks, or through securities dealers. Only large CDs (over $100,000) are negotiable, and all bear substantial penalties for redemption prior to maturity.

Repurchase agreements are agreements under which a bank or securities dealer agrees to repurchase, at a specific date and at a specific premium, securities sold earlier to an investor. Interest rates on repurchase agreements are often attractive, and a wide range of maturities is usually available.

A list of investment advisory services can usually be found in the classified telephone directory. As with all professionals, the investment adviser's reputation should be carefully checked. The bank's trust department is usually also happy to give advice on investment decisions. The point to emphasize is that investment decisions should be made by professionals in the investment business and not by amateurs (this is as true of investments as it is of medicine!). Even professionals can make errors in judgment, but the risk is lower.

The professional adviser will charge a fee, generally calculated on the basis of a percentage of the monies invested. The larger the investment fund, the lower the rate charged.

The physical safeguarding of an organization's investment securities is as important as making the right decision as to which stocks to buy or sell. This is often overlooked. The board of directors or the finance committee of the board has general responsibility for all investment instruments owned by the organization. Periodic verification of the existence of the securities should be made, either by independent accountants or the board itself. Verification usually involves a physical counting of the securities at the location where they are deposited or, for securities recorded only in electronic form, periodic confirmation with the custodian. Three areas warrant special attention. The first is that stock certificates aren't lost or misplaced through carelessness or poor handling. The second is that they are not lost through misappropriation by an employee. The third is that the stockbroker doesn't lose the certificates or, worse yet, go bankrupt.

If the organization keeps the certificates in its possession, the certificates should be kept in a bank safe deposit box. They should be registered in the name of the organization. The organization should also maintain an investment register that shows the certificate number as well as the cost and other financial information. There should be limited access to the safe deposit box, and it is wise to require the presence of two persons (preferably officers) whenever the box is opened. It is also wise for the board to establish an investment committee charged with the responsibility for authorizing all investment transactions. If an outside adviser is retained, this committee should still review the outside adviser's recommendations before they are accepted. It is not wise to delegate authority to an outside adviser to act except in accordance with an investment policy approved by the investment committee.

An organization must always be concerned that someone having access to stock certificates may be tempted to steal them. Although the certificates may be registered in the organization's name, there is an underworld market for stolen certificates. Furthermore, if the loss is not discovered promptly and the transfer agent advised to "stop transfer," the organization's rights may be jeopardized.

Unless the securities are kept in electronic form by the custodian, the best control is to have the broker deliver the stock certificate directly to a custodian for safekeeping. When the stock is sold, the custodian is then instructed to deliver the certificate to the broker. In this way, the organization never handles the certificate.

Some organizations leave their certificates in the custody of their broker. This has certain risks. One is that the broker will temporarily lose track of the certificates if the back office falls behind in its paperwork or incorrectly records the certificates.

The other risk is the broker's going bankrupt while holding the stock. Provided the broker has not fraudulently hypothecated the stock, bankruptcy should not result in a loss to an organization. However, there could be considerable delay before the stock is released by a court. On the other hand, if the broker has, without the consent of the organization, pledged the stock for personal borrowings, there is a possibility of actual loss. While the organization might be able to take both civil and criminal action against the broker, this would be of little consolation in bankruptcy. The first $500,000 of such losses, however, would be recovered from the federally chartered Securities Investor Protection Corporation.

While these risks might be relatively small, an NPO has a fiduciary responsibility to act with more than ordinary care and judgment. Accordingly, it would be prudent for an organization to have the broker deliver the stock certificates in the organization's name, either to an independent custodian or to the organization.

Appendix: Checklist of Criteria for Selection of a CPA

Not all of these criteria will be relevant in every selection process, and their relative importance will vary for different organizations. The order of the items in the list is not intended to indicate an absolute degree of importance to an organization, but criteria listed in the early part of the list are often considered more important. An organization should set tentative criteria at the start of the proposal process, but should not hesitate to change the criteria or their relative importance if considered desirable. (Criteria that have been disseminated to proposing CPAs should not be changed without notifying the CPAs.)

1. Characteristics of the personnel to be assigned to the engagement:
   - *Experience and expertise in the area of NPO accounting and auditing on the part of the personnel who will be assigned to the engagement.* These are the people who will be directly responsible for serving the organization's needs, and the quality of that service primarily depends on their abilities. The nonprofit environment is different in many ways from that of for-profit organizations; a lack of experience with that environment can be only partly offset by experience with other types of clients, except in the most routine circumstances.
   - *Personal ability of the designated key engagement personnel to relate well to and work effectively with organization staff.* This is a hallmark of any successful professional relationship.
2. *Ability of the CPA to respond quickly, effectively, and competently to the organization's needs.* This is a more general statement of the previous criterion, as well as reflecting other factors such as the ability of the engagement staff to call on other resources if needed. Such resources might include other personnel within a firm, reference material, and other persons with appropriate knowledge and skills. It also encompasses the overall attitude with which a CPA approaches service to clients.
3. *Experience with similar organizations* (e.g., medium-size symphony orchestras, Red Cross chapters, large trade associations, community colleges). A long list of a CPA's present clients can be considered positive evidence supporting an ability to meet criterion 2, but, especially in a larger firm, many of these clients may not be served by the same personnel as would serve your organization. Such a list is certainly a plus but should not be the only basis

for choosing a CPA. An organization may wish to request the proposing CPAs to furnish names of client references who may be contacted.

4. *Reputation.* This includes the two previous criteria, as well as a lot of more intangible factors such as how the CPA is looked upon by others in and outside the nonprofit industry, his or her commitment to serving organizations in the industry, and involvement by personnel in professional activities. (What an organization sometimes means by this criterion is, will the presence of a particular CPA's or CPA firm's signature on our accounts help our fund-raising efforts? The answer is, usually, not much.)

5. *Fee.* This should not be the deciding criterion (although it too often is), unless two or more CPAs are perceived as nearly equal in all other respects. A CPA who proposes a fee significantly lower than others' fees is sometimes: (1) not being realistic about the effort required to complete an engagement or (2) "low-balling" to get the work, and will either give a lower quality of service and/or try to raise the fee significantly in future years. When evaluating a proposal of this type, the organization should question the CPA about the basis for the quoted fee.

6. *Proposed approach to the engagement.* What does the CPA believe needs to be done, and how will the engagement be undertaken? A well-thought-out presentation on this subject improves the chances that the CPA meets criteria 1 and 2. The presentation need not be long but should show evidence that the work will be well planned and tailored to the particular needs and circumstances of the organization. There should also be an indication of the commitment of adequate time to the engagement by more senior personnel.

7. *Closeness of the CPA's office to the organization's headquarters.* (In the case of a multilocation organization; closeness of one or more offices of a firm to the principal operating locations of the organization.) This is really just part of criterion 2. Distance can be a negative factor, but it does not have to be if the CPA can compensate for this.

8. *Size of the CPA's firm and/or local office.* Except for an extremely large and complex organization (which usually does require the services of a large firm), there are no rules on this point. Both larger and smaller firms and individual practitioners can render distinguished service to both larger and smaller organizations, if the conditions of criteria 1 and 2 are well met.

9. *Ability of the CPA to provide other services such as consulting work.* Sometimes this may be important to an organization and sometimes not. An organization should think about this in view of its own current and anticipated future circumstances.

10. *Organization structure of the CPA's firm.* How centralized or decentralized is it? How much authority does the engagement partner have to make decisions? Usually any effect of this factor is far outweighed by criteria 1 and 2, unless a large firm is so centralized that local personnel have little authority.

11. *Continuity of staff assigned to the engagement.* Some amount of staff turnover is inevitable in almost any accounting practice, but excessive turnover is not desirable because it partly defeats the goal of building familiarity with a client. At the same time, some organizations consider orderly slow rotation

of personnel desirable as a way of maintaining the CPA's independence and bringing fresh ideas to bear on the engagement.

Other criteria that are not judgment criteria, but rather should be prerequisites for any CPA to be considered for selection, include:

- Ability to meet reasonable deadlines
- Willingness to furnish recommendations for proposed improvements in internal controls and management procedures identified during the course of other work
- Ability to assign the requisite number and experience levels of personnel to work on the engagement
- Ability to render the desired services in a professional manner

Endnote

1. Gross, M. J., R. F. Larkin, and J. H. McCarthy (2000). *Financial and Accounting Guide for Not-for-Profit Organizations,* 6th ed. New York: John Wiley & Sons.

Suggested Readings

American Institute of Certified Public Accountants, New York:
  Accounting Standards Division, "Accounting for Costs of Activities of Not-for-Profit Organizations and State and Local Governmental Entities That Include Fund Raising," SOP 98-2, 1998.
  Accounting Standards Division, "The Application of the Requirements of Accounting Research Bulletins, Opinions of the Accounting Principles Board, and Statements and Interpretations of the Financial Accounting Standards Board to Not-for-Profit Organizations," SOP 94-2, 1994.
  Accounting Standards Division, "Reporting of Related Entities by Not-for-Profit Organizations," SOP 94-3, 1994.
  AICPA Practice Aid Series, *Financial Statement Presentation and Disclosure Practices for Not-for-Profit Organizations,* Richard F. Larkin, AICPA, New York, 1999.
  AICPA Audit and Accounting Guide, *Not-for-Profit Organizations; A Summary of the More Important Provisions of the Guide.*
  Committee on Not-for-Profit Organizations, "Audits of States, Local Governments, and Not-for-Profit Organizations Receiving Federal Awards," SOP 98–3, 1998.
  Committee on Not-for-Profit Organizations, "Not-for-Profit Organizations," 1996.
  Health Care Committee, "Health Care Organizations." 1996, updated annually.
Anthony, R. N., and D. W. Young. (1984). *Management Control in Nonprofit Organizations,* 3rd ed. Homewood, IL: Richard D. Irwin.
Blazek, J. (1999). *Tax Planning and Compliance for Tax-Exempt Organizations: Forms, Checklists, Procedures,* 3rd ed. New York: Wiley.
Daughtrey, W. H. Jr., and M. J. Gross Jr. (1978). *Museum Accounting Handbook.* Washington, DC: American Association of Museums.

Evangelical Joint Accounting Committee. (1997). *Accounting and Financial Reporting Guide for Christian Ministries.* Diamond Bar, CA: Christian Management Association.

Financial Accounting Standards Board, Norwalk, CT:

Statements of Financial Accounting Concepts:

No. 4, "Objectives of Financial Reporting by Nonbusiness Organizations," 1980.

No. 6, "Elements of Financial Statements," 1985.

Statements of Financial Accounting Standards:

No. 93, "Recognition of Depreciation by Not-for-Profit Organizations," Norwalk, CT, 1987 (amended by No. 99, "Deferral of the Effective Date of Recognition of Depreciation by Not-for-Profit Organizations," 1988).

No. 95, "Statement of Cash Flows," 1987.

No. 116, "Accounting for Contributions Received and Contributions Made," 1993.

No. 117, "Financial Statements of Not-for-Profit Organizations," 1993.

No. 124, "Accounting for Certain Investments Held by Not-for-Profit Organizations," 1995.

No. 136, *Transfers of Assets to a Not-for-Profit Organization or Charitable Trust That Raises or Holds Contributions for Others,* 1999.

Hankin, J. A., A. Seidner, and J. Zeitlow. (1998). *Financial Management for Nonprofit Organizations.* New York: John Wiley & Sons.

Holck, M. Jr., and M. Holck Sr. (1978). *Complete Handbook of Church Accounting.* Englewood Cliffs, NJ: Prentice-Hall.

Hopkins, B. R. (1998). *The Law of Tax-Exempt Organizations,* 7th ed. New York: John Wiley & Sons.

Hopkins, B. R. (1995). *The Law of Fund-Raising.* New York: John Wiley & Sons.

Hummel, J. (1980). *Starting and Running a Nonprofit Organization.* Minneapolis: University of Minnesota Press.

Larkin, R. F. (1994). "Accounting Issues Relating to Fundraising," *Financial Practices for Effective Fundraising* (Chapter 2). San Francisco: Jossey-Bass.

Larkin, R. F. (1998; updated supplement, 2000) *Not-for-Profit GAAP.* New York: John Wiley & Sons.

National Association of College and University Business Officers. (1999). *Financial Accounting and Reporting Manual for Higher Education.* Washington, DC: NACUBO.

National Association of Independent Schools. (1998). *Business Management for Independent Schools,* 4th ed. Boston: Author.

National Health Council, National Assembly of National Voluntary Health and Social Welfare Organization. (1998). *Standards of Accounting and Financial Reporting for Voluntary Health and Welfare Organizations,* 4th ed. Washington, DC: NHC and NANVHSW.

PriceWaterhouseCoopers, New York:

(1992). *The Audit Committee, the Board of Trustees of Not-for-Profit Organizations and the Independent Accountant.*

(1988). *Effective Internal Accounting Control for Nonprofit Organizations.*

(1993). *Not-for-Profit Organizations' Implementation Guide for SFAS Statements 116 and 117.*

Ramanathan, K. V. (1982). *Management Control in Nonprofit Organizations.* New York: John Wiley & Sons.

United Way of America, Alexandria, VA:

(1989). *Accounting and Financial Reporting: A Guide for United Ways and Not-For Profit Human Service Organizations,* 2nd ed.

(1975). *Budgeting: A Guide for United Ways and Not-for-Profit Human Service Organizations.*

Wacht, R. F. (1984). *Financial Management in Nonprofit Organizations.* Atlanta: Georgia State University.

Budgeting Considerations

RUTHIE G. REYNOLDS, PHD
Tennessee State University

23.1 Introduction

As in business enterprises, budgeting is the key to successful nonprofit management. The two most important components of budgeting in business enterprises are planning and controlling. These components are also part of nonprofit budgeting, but a third component—programming—is added. These three components comprise the overall management system.

Budgeting may be defined as the process of projecting future resources to be received and future resources to be used. This process involves the development of a plan of action that will be used to guide the management team in the use of its resources. Quantitative and qualitative data are used in this process.

In addition to planning the use of future resources, budgets are used to plan future programs. Programs are the essence of nonprofit organizations (NPOs). Unlike business enterprises established for the primary purpose of earning a profit, NPOs are established to provide services through programs. The control aspect of budgeting allows management to compare actual results of operations with the budget, gaining feedback that is used to evaluate performance.

This chapter discusses the budgeting process. The discussion includes budgeting techniques, types of budgets, steps in preparing budgets, and the ethical aspects of budgeting. The relationship of accounting and budgeting also will be discussed. The appendix contains sample budgeting forms recommended by United Way of America for human service organizations.

23.2 *Purposes of Budgeting*

The three major components of budgeting summarize the purposes of budgeting: planning, programming, and control.

(A) PLANNING

The planning phase of budgeting is best explained through an organization's mission statement. The mission statement sets forth the vision of the organization and generally is formulated by the founding members. It may, however, be altered or completely replaced over the years.

Economic and social changes are the major reason for changes in mission, goals, and objectives. For example, 20 years ago, day care was not a major community issue. Few mothers worked, and family members were available to assist when needed. Today, a greater number of women work outside the home. There are more single-parent homes than ever before, and the number continues to increase. Therefore, day care for children and senior citizens is a major community concern. Accordingly, an agency with a mission that provides day care services may find it necessary to change or amend its goals and objectives in order to deliver services.

The goals set forth the manner in which the mission is to be accomplished, and the objectives are operational statements of goals. The setting of goals and objectives is outlined for a specified period of time. Goals and objectives set forth the future direction of an organization. Usually, specific targets, dates, and methods of reaching targets are spelled out. The period of time covered by a budget is usually an accounting period, 12 months. However, longer or shorter periods are not uncommon. Exhibit 23.1 shows an example of the relationship among the mission, goals, and objectives of a hypothetical human service organization called American Centers.

EXHIBIT 23.1 Examples of Mission/Goals/Objectives

American Centers Statement of Mission, Goals, and Objectives

Mission:	To provide program services as needed to the citizens of American City, regardless of their ability to pay
Goals:	To assist the citizens in improving the quality of their lives by providing community services, day care, and recreation
Objectives:	To provide community services through an adult tutoring service; to provide day care services for 20 children and 10 senior citizens; and to provide after-school and summer recreation activities for children

Balancing is the key in planning. Strategies must be developed to make the objectives consistent with goals. Furthermore, it is necessary to make sure goals complement the established mission of the organization.

Planning requires cooperation among all members of the organization. The administrator, the staff, and the board of directors must work together to ensure successful planning. The management style of the chief administrator has a bearing on this cooperative effort.

Some administrators and managers prefer a management style in which directives are handed down from the top; others favor a management style in which directives are developed from the bottom. The former style is commonly referred to as *imposed budgeting,* and the latter is referred to as *participatory budgeting.* Governmental units and NPOs, with monetary control and fiscal responsibility as their primary emphasis, have traditionally used imposed budgets. But planning cannot be carried out successfully under imposed budgeting.

Learning from the experiences of business enterprises, NPOs have begun to embrace participatory budgeting. They realize that cooperation and communication among all members of the operation is necessary. Some of the advantages of participatory budgeting are summarized in Exhibit 23.2.

Participatory budgeting is part of a broader concept called participatory management. Both are outgrowths of the behavioral approach to management, which holds that employees' ideas and opinions should be solicited and incorporated into the final budget plans. By soliciting the input of the employees, administrators are likely to have better acceptance of the budget because the employees will feel they are working on a team effort.

During the planning phase, administrators should take a new look at the needs and desires of the group or groups to be served. They should look at past performance by comparing budgeted data with actual results. By looking at past performance, changes in approaches and strategies can be made. Information and opinions should be gathered from the communities served. Surveys of community needs are very helpful in this phase of the process.

(B)   PROGRAMMING

In nonprofit budgeting, programming refers to the execution of the plans developed in the planning phase. During this phase, programs and the staffing of the program positions are the major considerations.

Programming connects the goals and objectives into programs or activity units. As in the planning phase, balancing is a key element as management attempts to design specific

---

EXHIBIT 23.2 Advantages of Participatory Budgeting

- Focuses on teamwork
- Solicits input from workers who are most familiar with operations
- Improves morale of workers
- Encourages acceptance of the budget
- Introduces realism into the process

---

programs within the constraints given. Naturally, resource availability is important; however, management should attempt to concentrate not on the availability of funds, but on the desired results if sufficient resources were made available. In fact, the "desired results approach" is quite beneficial to management because management may use its planned programs in soliciting funding for its operations.

The programming phase begins with a review of the proposed goals and objectives and an evaluation of the existing programs. Old programs are continued, revised, or abandoned. Next, new programs are developed and evaluated as alternatives to existing programs. Finally, the program or programs that best fit the goals, objectives, and mission of the organization are selected. Programs should be the result of fact-finding, not guesswork.

(C) CONTROL

One means of control is comparing actual performance with planned goals and objectives. It calls for monitoring actual activity to ensure that budgeted activity is accomplished in an efficient and effective manner.

Today, most NPOs use many of the same budgeting tools as business enterprises. One of the control tools used is responsibility accounting. As NPOs become larger and more complex, responsibility accounting satisfies the need to communicate results up and down the organizational hierarchy. Program managers are held accountable for use of resources and are required to account for performance of the planned activity. This system produces responsibility reports, which administrators use to evaluate programs and program managers. These reports may contain quantitative and qualitative data. Responsibility accounting requires that program managers and other subordinate managers accept responsibility for their units.

Another common way to use budgets as a control measure is variance analysis. In variance analysis, actual activity is compared to planned (budgeted) activity. The difference between the actual and planned is called a *variance*. Variances are labeled favorable and unfavorable, depending on whether or not the planned activity was achieved. If the variances are significant, they are investigated and subordinate managers must provide explanations.

The explanation should reflect the cause and source of the variance. A common misconception in variance analysis is that only unfavorable variances should be investigated. In most cases, favorable variances should be investigated with equal attention. For example, a favorable expense variance may be the result of the use of inferior goods or services. A favorable revenue variance may be the result of poor forecasting or poor management. For effective control, all factors underlying the variance, both external and internal, must be isolated.

Another misconception about budget variances is that the manager should be "blamed" for unfavorable variances. This belief is in direct opposition to the purpose of variance analysis: to improve decision making by explaining the causes and sources of variances. Often, managers' explanations justify results.

23.3 *Key Participants*

Successful budgeting requires the cooperation of many different people. In light of decreasing sources of revenue and increasing demands for services, NPOs must develop a set of planned programs that will efficiently and effectively utilize the entrusted resources. Accountability is not only expected, it is required.

The major participants in the budgeting process are:

- Board members
- Administrator or executive director
- Controller
- Fund raiser
- Program managers
- Staff members
- Volunteers

The board members set forth the mission, goals, and objectives. In many instances, they comprise the only oversight body for the organization. The administrator or executive director acts as a coordinator of the budgeting process and, with the assistance of the staff and controller and within the constraints handed down by the board, develops the revenue and expense estimates. Staff members' input is often solicited as to daily performance expectations, especially if participatory budgeting is followed. The controller, the chief accountant, provides historical data that are used to form a basis for projected data. Volunteers assist in various capacities, ranging from clerical to administrative.

In many organizations, a budget committee is formed to take on the responsibility for overseeing the entire budgeting process. The committee is composed of selected board members, the administrator or executive director, the controller, and key program managers. The administrator represents the committee on a day-to-day basis, acting as the liaison between the groups.

After all revenue and expense estimates are gathered, the information and data are combined into the final budget documents: the operations budget, the cash budget, the capital budget, and the pro forma statement of financial position. The final budget, also known as the master budget or comprehensive budget, is presented to the board for approval. It may also be presented to various funding sources. Budget presentation can be informal or formal, depending on the audience.

23.4   *Relationship of Budgeting and Accounting*

Budgeting was defined in the introductory section as the process of projecting future sources and uses of resources. *Accounting* is defined as the financial reporting of the historical events of any entity. Accounting provides for the recording, classifying, summarizing, analyzing, and reporting of past financial transactions. Budgeting is future oriented and accounting is past oriented. In addition, budgeting in an NPO involves a great deal of qualitative reporting, whereas accounting deals more with quantitative reporting.

In profit-oriented organizations, budgeting and accounting are reported separately. That is not the case in NPOs. It is not uncommon to see the operations budget as part of the accounting reporting system. For example, some agencies show a comparison of actual operation and budgeted operations as part of their periodic accounting report.

In the traditional sense, accounting provides data for the budgeting process. First, from the planning perspective, historical data provided by the accounting system are the beginning point for forecasting future revenues and expenses. Next, accounting aids in the control phase of budgeting by supplying actual data needed for comparison with budgeted data. Rarely will accounting be the only means of projecting future data or comparing actual data, but it is a very useful and convenient starting point.

23.5 Budgeting Techniques

Numerous techniques have been developed to plan program expenses. Some of the most commonly used approaches in budgeting for NPOs are:

- Line-item budgeting (LIB)
- Planned-programming-budgeting system (PPBS)
- Zero-based budgeting (ZBB)
- Integrated approach (IA)

All four approaches deal with the estimation of expenses because revenue estimation generally does not call for a specific technique. It is based largely on historical costs.

(A) LINE-ITEM BUDGETING (LIB)

Traditionally, the most common type of budgeting in NPOs is LIB. The distinguishing characteristic of LIB is its emphasis on the past. Preparers of the budget look at amounts expended for various program activities in the past. The attempt is made to adjust the amounts upward using a predetermined rate.

Inflation and other sources of increases in expenses may be used to adjust each budget line item upward. Top administrators provide these figures. The projected increases are called *increments*. Thus, LIB is often referred to as *incremental budgeting*. The upwardly adjusted figures are used as estimates of the upcoming year's expenses. The increment adjustment may differ for each line item, or it may be consistently applied to some or all line-item amounts.

Exhibit 23.3 shows a line-item budget for a day care program. The given percentages, representing the increase adjustments, are applied to each line item to arrive at the budgeted amounts for the upcoming year.

EXHIBIT 23.3 Example of Line-Item Budget

American Centers Line-Item Expense Budget for Day Care Program Budget Year 2005

Expense	Actual 2005	Percent of Increase	Budget 2005
Salaries	$155,327	7	$166,200
Employee benefits	7,766	7	8,310
Payroll taxes	15,532	7	16,620
Supplies	62,891	6	66,665
Telephone	2,596	4	2,700
Occupancy	15,472	10	17,020
Total	$259,584		$277,515

The most obvious advantage of LIB is simplicity. Once the percentages are determined, the new budget results from mere mathematical computations. The major disadvantage is that ineffective programs, along with their related costs, are maintained in the budget year after year because of the heavy reliance on historical costs. Despite the major disadvantages, LIB is still widely used in nonprofit budgeting today. It should be kept in mind that LIB does not have to be totally abandoned. When used in conjunction with other techniques, the benefits are retained while the negatives are minimized.

(B) PLANNED-PROGRAMMING-BUDGETING SYSTEM (PPBS)

PPBS was a product of the 1960s. Its popularity was an outgrowth of its use in the Department of Defense. It was abandoned in the early 1970s when zero-based budgeting was introduced. Although the technique has lost its popularity, many of its elements still linger in the budgeting process of many organizations today.

Exhibit 23.4 shows the steps in PPBS. The center of focus is the program. This technique is often confused with the programming phase of the budgeting process discussed in an earlier section. As the steps indicate, PPBS is more extensive than the programming phase of the budgeting process. The latter deals exclusively with the establishment of programs needed to meet the goals and objectives of the nonprofit organization.

PPBS deals not only with the establishment of programs, but also with the evaluation of those programs in terms of cost effectiveness. The advantages of PPBS are (1) it provides an integrated approach to management control and (2) it is somewhat scientific in that it leads to effective and efficient use of resources. The major disadvantages are (1) it requires good coordination of efforts, which is often difficult to achieve, (2) it is political in nature, and (3) it is costly to implement, in terms of both resources and time.

(C) ZERO-BASED BUDGETING (ZBB)

Zero-based budgeting was popularized in the 1970s during Jimmy Carter's tenure as governor of the State of Georgia. Later, when he became president, he took the technique to the White House, where it was implemented in the federal government.

The initial appeal of ZBB was centered around the fact that each program had to justify its existence and costs each year. There was complete disregard for historical costs. As a result, only those programs that were "productive" in satisfying the organization's goals and objectives survived the evaluation process. In a sense, program managers had to "fight" for their programs' existence each time a budget was prepared. Supporters of this technique were quick to point out the fact that it eliminated the ill effects of traditional LIB.

EXHIBIT 23.4 PPBS Steps

---

1. Define the program.
2. Set program priorities.
3. Allocate cost to programs.
4. Evaluate programs in terms of cost effectiveness.
5. Select most cost-effective programs.

The federal government's experience with ZBB, as well as the experiences of many NPOs, proved to be unfavorable. The major disadvantage of ZBB was the excessive amount of time required to implement the technique. Today, ZBB is not as widely used as it was during the 1970s, but certain aspects of the techniques still have possible benefits in the budgeting process for NPOs. This is especially true when used in conjunction with other techniques.

Exhibit 23.5 presents the steps in ZBB. The emphasis in ZBB is on a fresh start each year. Historical costs based on actual performance are disregarded. The process begins with the preparation of decision packages. Each program manager is required to prepare projections of expenses at various levels of effort. These estimates are proposed as alternative ways of accomplishing the goals and objectives of the particular program. Therefore, one program manager's set of decision packages may resemble a complete traditional budget for an entire organization rather than just one program within an organization. This phase results in massive volumes of paperwork.

The greatest time effort, however, is spent ranking the decision packages. Because ZBB requires handling literally thousands of decision packages each year, rarely is there sufficient time in the normal budgeting cycle to accommodate a proper evaluation. Furthermore, it may be necessary to go though the ranking procedures more than once, or even more than twice, which will place additional time pressure on the preparer. The resulting demands on time and resources can be overwhelming, placing a drain on time to perform program services.

(D)   INTEGRATED APPROACH (IA)

Although LIB, ZBB, and PPBS are often thought of as individual budgeting techniques, there is no reason these methods cannot be combined. The integrated approach to budgeting takes the advantages of all budgeting techniques and formulates an approach to budgeting that is tailor-made for the specific organization involved. In reality, this is an ideal approach for NPOs because the unfavorable attributes of the individual methods can be abandoned while preserving the favorable attributes. Therefore, ZBB may be used for some program expense estimates, while LIB or PPBS may be used for others. The obvious benefit of this approach is that the organization gets the best of all worlds.

23.6   *The Budget Process*

Generally, the first phase of the process is the dissemination of the guidelines that govern the budgeting process. If an NPO established a budget committee, the committee will be

---

EXHIBIT 23.5 Zero-Based Budgeting Steps

---

1. Define the decision center (program or activity).
2. Assume that each line item in each program has a zero balance.
3. Develop decision packages for each decision unit.
4. Rank each decision package, first within the decision unit, then within the organization.
5. Allocate the resources to the decision packages.

---

responsible for distributing the guidelines to the appropriate members. This task is usually handled by the committee chairperson or chief administrator.

Guidelines for the budgeting process, formulated by the budget committee or administrator, are passed on to program managers to act as floors and ceilings on program activities. The guidelines set forth all constraints—those on spending, hiring, and government regulations. Other matters covered include budget format, timetable, and feasible assumptions.

Administrators usually estimate revenue, with input from the board and funding sources. Program managers usually estimate the expenses using one or a combination of the techniques mentioned earlier. These figures may go through several revisions before they are accepted. There may be negotiations between the administrator and program managers, and the success of these negotiations is of utmost importance in the overall success of the budgeting process. Even if estimates are in agreement with guidelines, they may be challenged. If so, all or selected budget items may require justification. This procedure strengthens the budgeting process because it increases the probability that only worthy programs survive. The revised data and information are compiled into a single document that has several interrelated parts.

(A) TYPES OF BUDGETS

There are at least four component parts of the final (master) budget: the operations budget, the cash budget, the capital budget, and the pro forma statement of financial position.

(i) Operations Budget

The operations budget is probably the most common in NPOs. It contains the estimates of revenues from all sources and the estimates of expenses for administration and all programs. This budget projects the financial operating activities of the organization for a specified period of time. The period of time is often one year, but annual budgets are also broken down into monthly estimates.

The appendix contains sample budget forms for human service organizations. The operations budget form is labeled Budget Form 1. There are two major sections of an operations budget: revenues and expenses. On Budget Form 1, the human service revenue is called Public Support and Revenue, and Expenses. The form shows that United Way agencies, which are human service organizations, receive their support from the sources appearing on lines 1 through 12.

Sources of revenue differ, depending on the type of NPO. A human service organization such as a neighborhood center may receive contributions, legacies, bequests, and grants. In addition to receiving support from the public, most human service organizations also receive assistance from the federal government, state and local governments, and special interest groups. A governmental agency receives revenue from various types of taxes such as income tax, sales tax, and property tax.

Once a technique has been selected, the budget documents are prepared and presented to the board for approval.

Revenues.   The starting point for the estimation of revenues is prior-year sources. It is not unusual for administrators to receive commitments from former supporters prior to the estimating phase. Grant approval or special allocations from related organizations may be received months before the budgeting process begins. It an advantage for organizations to receive revenue commitments prior to preparing the budget. Government agencies have a different type of advantage. In order to meet revenue requirements, increases in taxes and assessments can be imposed. Therefore, revenue estimation for governmental units may occur before expense estimates are finalized.

When services and products are sold to the public by NPOs, the procedure for estimating revenues to some extent resembles the estimation activity of a profit-making enterprise. The number of service units or products to be sold is estimated, an estimated sale price or rate is applied, and gross revenue is calculated.

Example 1. A neighborhood center may be licensed to provide day care for 20 children. The administrator estimates an average operating capacity of 90 percent throughout the budget year. Assuming that a sliding scale will be used to charge clients and that the average hourly rate is determined to be $5, the estimate of the revenue to be earned by the day care program is:

At 90% capacity:
$$(20 \text{ clients} \times 90\%) = 18 \text{ clients}$$
$$18 \text{ clients} \times 40 \text{ hours} \times 52 \text{ weeks} \times \$5 = \$187,200$$

The day care service fees are not likely to be the only source of revenue for the program. Additional sources of revenue may include grants and contracts from governmental agencies, as well as contributions.

Other forms of revenue can also be estimated. Investment income, for example, can be estimated by applying an expected rate of return to the investment amount.

Example 2. An organization has a portfolio of stocks and bonds of $80,000, and its financial advisor estimates an annual return of 9 percent. The revenue estimate from the investment can be determined as follows:

Expected return of 9%:
$$\text{Investment} \times \text{Expected return} = \text{Estimated investment income}$$
$$\$80,000 \times 9\% = \$7,200$$

Governmental agencies can estimate revenues by applying the tax rate to the tax base.

Example 3. In estimating revenue from property taxes, assume the assessment base is $10 million and the assessment rate is 15 mills per $1:

Assessment base of $10 million:
$$\text{Assessment base} \times \text{Assessment rate} = \text{Estimated tax revenue}$$
$$(\$10,000,000) \times .015 = \$150,000$$

If the governmental agency needs to increase the tax assessments to balance its budgets, it may do so by raising the tax base or the assessment rate. The increase must be approved by the appropriate governmental bodies, but this is an option that no other NPOs enjoy.

Expenses. Estimated expenses for a human service organization appear on lines 14 through 29 of Budget Form 1, which appears in the appendix. A sample program expense budget is present in Exhibit 23.6. The hypothetical organization, American Centers, has three programs. Most of the expenses shown are common to all types of NPOs. One of the largest expense categories is compensation expense, which is the sum of salaries, employee benefits, and payroll taxes. These expenses appear on lines 14, 15, and 16 on Budget Form 1 and appear as the first three line items in Exhibit 23.6.

The estimation of compensation expense requires a personnel budget. Budget Form 5, which lists personnel positions and the related salaries, should be optional only for small agencies. This particular personnel form requires past and present years' data to be presented along with the projected data for budget year.

The personnel budget is usually prepared during the programming phase, when the objectives and goals are defined in terms of programs. Optional Budget Form 5 does not provide for program information; however, the "Account No. Charged" column serves the same purpose. Programs are assigned specific account numbers in the accounting system, to allow each program to be identified individually.

Employee benefits and payroll taxes are usually stated as percentages of salaries. Therefore, if a day care program's annual salaries expense is estimated at $166,200, the employee benefit expense at 5 percent of salaries, and payroll taxes expense at 10 percent of salaries, compensation expense can be projected as shown in Exhibit 23.7.

Salaries expense and other compensation costs for a particular employee may be assigned to one individual program or they may be prorated to two or more programs based on expected time devoted to each program. Consider the salary and related cost for the chief administrator. In addition to the management of the entire organization, assume the position calls for the administrator to tutor adults in reading, through its community service program. If 30 percent of the administrator's time is expected to be devoted to tutoring, 30 percent of the salary, related employee benefits, and payroll taxes should be allocated to the Community Service Program. The remaining time is prorated to other programs and to the management and general function.

EXHIBIT 23.6 Example of Program Expense Budget

American Centers Program Expense Budget for the Year Ending December 31, 2005

	Day Care Services	Recreation Services	Community Services	Management and General	Total
Salaries	$166,200	$124,000	$ 7,200	$40,315	$337,715
Employee benefits	8,310	6,200	360	2,015	16,885
Payroll taxes	16,620	12,400	720	4,030	33,770
Total compensation	191,130	142,600	8,280	46,360	388,370
Professional fees	—	—	—	3,335	3,335
Supplies	66,665	12,500	1,300	7,280	87,745
Telephone	2,700	1,300	400	8,450	12,850
Postage	—	—	—	1,350	1,350
Occupancy	17,020	12,160	2,100	1,475	32,755
Equipment rental	—	11,600	—	—	11,600
Total	$277,515	$180,160	$12,080	$68,250	$538,005

EXHIBIT 23.7 Projection of Compensation Expense

American Centers Estimation of Compensation Expense Budget Year 2005	
Salaries expense	$166,200
Employee benefits (5%)	8,310
Payroll taxes (10%)	16,620
Total compensation expense	$191,130

An important aspect of expense budgeting is making estimates as specific as possible. The type and quality of goods and services to be used should be considered. Future price increases should be anticipated, as well as technological changes that may positively or negatively affect future operations.

Equally important in preparing the operations budget is the need to prepare estimates by months in addition to years. Too often, operations budgets are prepared for the budget year, then divided by 12 months. This approach bears the erroneous assumption that each month will have the same operational level of activity. Nothing could be further from the truth. Rarely will an organization's revenues and expenses be the same each month.

Consider an organization that provides recreational services for youth. Because most students do not attend school during the summer months, recreational services are likely to be in more demand during this time. Thus, the budgets for the summer months of June, July, and August should have provisions for greater operations cost than other months.

Estimating Techniques.   To some extent, the type of budgeting technique (LIB, PPBS, ZBB, IA) influences the type of estimating technique. Various approaches are used, and just as in budgeting techniques, a combination of the individual techniques may be used.

A commonly used technique for estimating revenues and expenses for the upcoming budget year is market survey. An NPO may hire a professional marketing team or may develop its own. The team begins by performing a traditional market survey of the community needs, and then investigates the availability of resources to meet those needs.

Other expense estimation techniques include statistical methods such as regression analysis, probability theory, and modeling. Some preparers have found statistical methods to be reliable; others have not. Generally, the more homogeneous the data and the larger the database, the more reliable the results. Some NPOs still prefer traditional methods such as informed judgment and analysis of historical data.

(ii)   Cash Budget

The cash budget should begin with an estimate of the beginning cash balance for the budget year. Estimated cash receipts are added to the estimated beginning cash balance, resulting in the total cash available for use during the budget year. Cash disbursements expected during the year are estimated and subtracted from the estimated total cash available, resulting in the estimated ending cash balance for the budget year.

The cash budget allows the management team to plan ahead for expected cash shortages. In addition, expected cash overages can be more adequately managed.

Estimated cash receipts may approximate estimated revenues, and estimated cash disbursements may approximate estimated expenses. This is especially true if the organization operates on a cash basis. Cash basis is an accounting method that results in the recognition of revenues when cash is received and the recognition of expenses when cash is paid. In contrast, under accrual-basis accounting, revenues are recognized when earned, and expenses are recognized when incurred. It should be noted that only accrual basis is a generally accepted accounting principle; thus, it is required for most NPOs. Some organizations, however, still may use cash basis.

(iii)   Capital Budget

Capital budgeting in the nonprofit sector may be viewed as fixed asset planning. It differs from capital budgeting in business enterprise in that there is no expected dollar rate of return. The capital budget provides for acquisitions and disposition of property, equipment, and other types of fixed assets. If a fixed asset is to be purchased, the specifications and the funding source are outlined in the capital budget. If an asset is to be disposed of, the selling price and replacement information are also included. Therefore, the capital budget may contain as much qualitative data as it does quantitative.

(iv)   Pro Forma Statement of Financial Position

The pro forma statement of financial position (referred to as a *pro forma balance sheet* in business enterprises) estimates the financial status of the NPO at the end of a budget year. All estimated assets and liabilities are presented. The difference between the two categories is the projected fund (equity) balance. The cash balance appearing in the asset category is the same estimated ending cash balance from the cash budget.

23.7   Ethics in Budgeting

Budget committees and administrators should seek fairness in developing and implementing the budget. To be successful, everyone must "buy into" the budget. If the staff members do not believe that the administrator and board are behind the budget, staff acceptance will be low, and the effectiveness of the budget process will be destroyed.

Also, administrators and program managers should seek to avoid what is commonly referred to as *budgetary slack,* or padding the budget. This is a common problem in NPOs when it is believed that funding sources will automatically reduce revenue request by matching them with estimated expenses. Such practice is counterproductive and leads to distrust.

23.8   Summary

Budgeting is an important but time-consuming part of management. It is used in planning, programming, and controlling an organization's activities. Coordination plays a key role in the process because of the desirability to gather estimates from all levels of the organization. The participants in the process are the board of directors, the administrator, the controller, and program managers. It is desirable for staff members to also take an active role in the budgeting process.

Unfortunately, there is no perfect budgeting technique. The recommended approach is referred to as integrated approach, in which elements of several commonly used techniques are combined. The benefit of this approach is that it minimizes the disadvantages of individual techniques. Three of these individual techniques—LIB, PPBS, and ZBB—were discussed in this chapter.

Four types of budgets were discussed: the operations budget, the cash budget, the capital budget, and the pro forma statement of financial position. These budgets together form the final or master budget, which is used to guide the organization through the process of achieving its goals and objectives.

Suggested Readings

Anthony, R. N., and D. W. Young. (1988). *Management Control in Nonprofit Organizations,* 4th ed. Homewood, IL: Richard D. Irwin.

Apostolou, N. G., and D. L. Crumbley. (1992). *Handbook of Governmental Accounting and Finance,* 2nd ed. New York: John Wiley & Sons.

Adams, R. M., S. H. Denby, and J. C. Zipser. (1996). "A Nonprofit Director's Roadmap for Survival," *Trusts & Estates* (March): 42–54.

Allen, M. B. (1995). "The Ethics Audit," *Nonprofit World* (November/December): 51–55.

Barton, T. L, W. G. Shenkir, and J. E. McEldowney. (1996). "The Case of Dr. Grayson: Fraud and Abuse at a Not For Profit," *CPA Journal* (February): 46–50.

Brinckerhoff, P. C. (1996). "How to Save Money Through Bottoms-Ups Budgeting," *Nonprofit World* (January/February): 22–24.

Covaleski, M. A. (1988). "The Use of Budgetary Symbol in the Political Arena: A Historical Informed Field Study," *Accounting, Organizations and Society* (November 1): 1–24.

Deckard, K. (1996). "A Capital Idea: Linking the Operating and Capital Budgets in Rockville, Maryland," *Government Finance Review* (April): 49–53.

Deshpande, S. P. (1996). "Ethical Climate and the Link Between Success and Ethical Behavior: An Empirical Investigation of a Non-Profit Organization," *Journal of Business Ethics* (March): 315–20.

DioGuardi, Hon. Joseph J. (1995). "Our Unaccountable Federal Government: It Doesn't Add Up," *Accounting Horizons* (June): 62–67.

Douglas, P. (1995). *Governmental and Nonprofit Accounting: Theory and Practice.* New York: The Dryden Press.

Ensman, R. G. (1996). "New Approaches to Accountability," *Fund Raising Management* (January): 58.

Granof, M. H. (1998). *Government and Not-for-Profit Accounting.* New York: John Wiley & Sons.

Gray, S. T. (1995). "Practicing Ethics to Build Public Confidence," *Association Management* (August): 304.

Hayes, R. D., and J. A. Millar. (1990). "Measuring Production Efficiency in a Not-for-Profit Setting," *Accounting Review* (July): 505–19.

Herzlinger, R. E. (1996). "Can Public Trust In Nonprofits and Governments Be Restored?" *Harvard Business Review* (March/April): 97–107.

Higuera, J. J. (1996). "An Ounce of Oversight," *Foundation News & Commentary* (March/April): 36–38.

Jones, L. R., and J. McCaffrey. (1998). "Federal Financial Management Reform," In R. Meyers (ed.). *Handbook of Public Budgeting.* San Francisco: Jossey-Bass.

Lang, A. S. (1996). "Board Primer: Nonprofits Do It Differently," *Association Management* (January): L52–L54.

Leighting, B. (1995). "Nonprofit Groups Need to be Run Like a Business," *Denver Business Journal* (July 14): 11B.

Stevens, S. K. (1996). "Measuring Financial Health in the 1990s," *Foundation News & Commentary* (March/April): 42–45.

Sollenberger, H. M., and A. Schneider. (1996). *Managerial Accounting.* Cincinnati: South-Western College Publishing, pp. 290, 569–570.

Trigg, R., and F. K. Nabangi. (1995). "Representation of the Financial Position of Nonprofit Organizations: The Habitat for Humanity Situation," *Financial Accountability & Management* (August): 259–69.

United Way of America. (1989). *Accounting and Financial Reporting: A Guide for United Ways and Not-for-Profit Human Service Organizations,* 2nd ed. rev. Alexandria, VA: Author.

United Way of America. (1982). *Simplified Budget Forms for United Ways in Smaller Communities.* Alexandria, VA: Author.

United Way of America. (1975). *Budgeting: A Guide for United Ways and Not-for-Profit Human Service Organizations.* Alexandria, VA: Author.

Weidner, D. (1996). "Opportunity to Exercise Professional Judgment," *Pennsylvania CPA Journal* (October): 18.

Ziebell, M. T., and D. T. Decosta. (1991). *Management Control System in Nonprofit Organizations.* New York: Harcourt Brace Jovanovich.

Appendix

The appendix to this chapter contains a set of simplified budget forms prepared by United Way of America for use by United Way–funded agencies. While use of these particular forms is not required, they may be used by most human service nonprofits as guidelines in preparing annual budgets. The forms and chart are presented with the permission of United Way of America, Alexandria, Virginia.

The set contains:

- Summary Information Form—A two-page outline of the agency's mission, services, budgetary requests, and audit comments.
- Budget Form 1—The Support, Revenue and Expense Form which, together with the Summary Information Form, can be used as the basic budget forms for those United Way agencies not using functional accounting.
- Budget Form 2—This optional "spreadsheet" details the income and expense by function. It provides a total agency picture and unit costs of programs where appropriate.
- Budget Form 3—This is an optional form that describes funds that have restrictions placed on their use by the donor.

- Budget Form 4—This is also an optional form. It describes reserve funds designated by the agency's board.
- Budget Form 5—An optional form that lists the personnel positions and salaries of the agency.

UNITED WAY FINANCIAL REPORTING FORMS

AGENCY: _____

Mailing Address: _____

City, State, Zip: _____

Telephone: (   ) _____

For the Fiscal Year

_____ **To** _____

Presented _____ on _____
                          (Name of Funding Body)   (Date)

This budget was considered and approved for submission at the Board of Directors Meeting on _____
                                                                                                            (Date)

_____   _____
       Chief Professional Officer   President or Other Authorized Official

AGENCY: _____   DATE: _____

I. SUMMARY INFORMATION

A. Program Data

1. What is the agency's mission?

_____

_____

_____

2. What programs/services did your agency provide this year?

_____

_____

_____

3. Target population served: (age, sex, special interest, etc.)

_____

_____

_____

4. Number of unduplicated individual units served in United Way area: (3 yrs. ago ____   2 yrs. ago____   last yr.____)

_____

_____

_____

5. Geographic area covered:

_____

_____

_____

6. How are agency programs/services assessed for effectiveness?

_____

_____

_____

7. What are the specific objectives?

_____

_____

_____

8. What new or different programs/services does your agency contemplate providing next year?

_____

_____

_____

9. How will these new or different programs/services be financed?

_____

_____

_____

10. What supplementary fund-raising activities does the agency conduct?

Activity	Net$ Results	Area Covered	Month Conducted

B. Financial Highlights

Financial Highlights	Last Year	This Year	Next Year
Total Expenses (BF 1: Line 35)			
Total Support & Revenue—All Sources (BF 1: Line 13)			
Excess (Deficit)			
Allocation From This United Way Direct to Agency Matching Government Grant Total			
Allocation From Other United Ways to Agency			

FOR UNITED WAY USE ONLY

Audit report has been received by the United Way for the year ending _____.

This audit report was: ( ) Unqualified   ( ) Qualified

If Qualified, explain: _____

_____

_____

_____

_____
(Signature of Chairman of Audit Committee)

AGENCY:

Budget Form: **1**

Support Revenue & Expenses	Fiscal 19 Last Year Actual	Fiscal 19 This Year Budgeted	Fiscal 19 Next Year Proposed
Public Support & Revenue— All Sources [4000-6999]			
1 0000 **Allocation From This United Way**			
2 4000 Contributions			
3 4200 Special Events			
4 4300 Legacies & Bequests (Unrestricted)			
5 4600 Contributed by Associated Organizations			
6 4700 Allocated by Other United Ways			
7 5000 Fees & Grants From Government Agencies			
8 6000 Membership Dues			
9 6200 Program Services Fees & Net Incidental Revenue			
10 6300 Sales of Materials			
11 6500 Investment Income			
12 6900 Miscellaneous Revenue			
13 TOTAL SUPPORT & REVENUE (Add 1 thru 12)			
Expenses [7000-9999]			
14 7000 Salaries			
15 7100 Employee Benefits			
16 7200 Payroll Taxes, etc.			
17 8000 Professional Fees			
18 8100 Supplies			
19 8200 Telephone			
20 8300 Postage & Shipping			
21 8400 Occupancy			
22 8500 Rental & Maintenance of Equipment			
23 8600 Printing & Publications			
24 8700 Travel			
25 8800 Conferences, Conventions & Meetings			
26 8900 Specific Assistance to Individuals			
27 9000 Membership Dues			
28 9100 Awards & Grants			
29 9400 Miscellaneous			
30 TOTAL EXPENSES (Add 14 thru 29)			
31 9691 Payments to Affiliated Organizations			
32 Board Designations for Specified Activities for Future Years			
33 TOTAL EXPENSES FOR BUDGET PERIOD FOR ALL ACTIVITIES (30 + 31 + 32)			
34 TOTAL EXPENSES FOR ACTIVITIES FINANCED BY RESTRICTED FUNDS			
35 TOTAL EXPENSES FOR ACTIVITIES FINANCED BY UNRESTRICTED FUNDS (33 − 34)			
36 EXCESS (DEFICIT) OF TOTAL SUPPORT & REVENUE OVER EXPENSES (13 − 35)			
37 9500 Depreciation of Buildings & Equipment			
38 9900 Major Property & Equipment Acquisition ($ ___1000___ +)			

All Financial Information Rounded to Nearest Dollar

AGENCY:

Proposed Budget for Fiscal 19 ___ By Program & Supporting Functions	Grand Total (2 + 5)	Total Supporting (3 + 4)	Supporting Services		Total Program Services 6 through 12
			Management & General	Fund Raising	
	1	2	3	4	5

Public Support & Revenue— All Sources [4000-6999]						
1	0000	**Allocation From This United Way**					
2	4000	Contributions					
3	4200	Special Events					
4	4300	Legacies & Bequests (Unrestricted)					
5	4600	Contributed by Associated Organizations					
6	4700	Allocated by Other United Ways					
7	5000	Fees & Grants From Government Agencies					
8	6000	Membership Dues					
9	6200	Program Services Fees & Net Incidental Revenue					
10	6300	Sales of Materials					
11	6500	Investment Income					
12	6900	Miscellaneous Revenue					
13		TOTAL SUPPORT & REVENUE (Add 1 thru 12)					
Expenses [7000-9999]						
14	7000	Salaries					
15	7100	Employee Benefits					
16	7200	Payroll Taxes, etc.					
17	8000	Professional Fees					
18	8100	Supplies					
19	8200	Telephone					
20	8300	Postage & Shipping					
21	8400	Occupancy					
22	8500	Rental & Maintenance of Equipment					
23	8600	Printing & Publications					
24	8700	Travel					
25	8800	Conferences, Conventions & Meetings					
26	8900	Specific Assistance to Individuals					
27	9000	Membership Dues					
28	9100	Awards & Grants					
29	9400	Miscellaneous					
30		TOTAL EXPENSES (Add 14 thru 29)					
31	9691	Payments to Affiliated Organizations					
32		Board Designations for Specified Activities for Future Years					
33		TOTAL EXPENSES FOR BUDGET PERIOD FOR ALL ACTIVITIES (30 + 31 + 32)					
34		TOTAL EXPENSES FOR ACTIVITIES FINANCED BY RESTRICTED FUNDS					
35		TOTAL EXPENSES FOR ACTIVITIES FINANCED BY UNRESTRICTED FUNDS (33 − 34)					
36		EXCESS (DEFICIT) OF TOTAL SUPPORT & REVENUE OVER EXPENSES (13 − 35)					
37	9500	Depreciation of Buildings & Equipment					
38	9900	Major Property & Equipment Acquisition ($ ___1000___ +)					

Summary of Program Cost Analysis	
Computation of Per Unit Cost of Agency's Programs	1. Total Program Services Expenses Direct (from Line 33) 2. Total Supporting Services Expenses (Line 33, Column 2 proportionally distributed) 3. Payments to Affiliated Organizations (Line 31, Column 1, proportionally distributed) 4. **TOTAL PROGRAM (1 + 2 + 3)** **PROGRAM VOLUME & UNIT COST** 5. Total Number Program Units 6. Direct Cost Per Unit (Line 1 ÷ Line 5) 7. Total Cost Per Unit (Line 4 ÷ Line 5) 8. Unit Description

All Financial Information Rounded to Nearest Dollar

Budget Form: 2

		Program Services				
6	7	8	9	10	11	12

Optional Budget Form: 3

AGENCY: _____

EXPLANATION OF RESTRICTED FUNDS
(Source Restricted Only—Exclude Board Restricted)

A. Name of Restricted Fund _____ Amount: $ _____

1. Restricted by: _____

2. Source of fund: _____

3. Purpose for which restricted: _____

4. Are investment earnings available for current unrestricted expenses?
   ___Yes ___No   If Yes, what amount: _____

5. Date when restriction became effective: _____

6. Date when restriction expires: _____

B. Name of Restricted Fund _____ Amount: $ _____

1. Restricted by: _____

2. Source of fund: _____

3. Purpose for which restricted: _____

4. Are investment earnings available for current unrestricted expenses?
   ___Yes ___No   If Yes, what amount: _____

5. Date when restriction became effective: _____

6. Date when restriction expires: _____

C. Name of Restricted Fund _____ Amount: $ _____

1. Restricted by: _____

2. Source of fund: _____

3. Purpose for which restricted: _____

4. Are investment earnings available for current unrestricted expenses?
   ___Yes ___No   If Yes, what amount: _____

5. Date when restriction became effective: _____

6. Date when restriction expires: _____

AGENCY: _____

Optional Budget Form: 4

EXPLANATION OF BOARD DESIGNATED RESERVES
(For Funds Which Are Not Donor Restricted)

A. Name of Board Designated Reserve: _____ Amount: $ _____

   1. Date of board meeting at which designation was made: _____

   2. Source of funds: _____

   3. Purpose for which designated: _____

                        _____

   4. Are the investment earnings available for current unrestricted expenses?
      ____Yes ____No   If Yes, what amount: _____

   5. Date when board designation became effective: _____

   6. Date when board designation expires: _____

B. Name of Board Designated Reserve: _____ Amount: $ _____

   1. Date of board meeting at which designation was made: _____

   2. Source of funds: _____

   3. Purpose for which designated: _____

                        _____

   4. Are the investment earnings available for current unrestricted expenses?
      ____Yes ____No   If Yes, what amount: _____

   5. Date when board designation became effective: _____

   6. Date when board designation expires: _____

C. Name of Board Designated Reserve: _____ Amount: $ _____

   1. Date of board meeting at which designation was made: _____

   2. Source of funds: _____

   3. Purpose for which designated: _____

                        _____

   4. Are the investment earnings available for current unrestricted expenses?
      ____Yes ____No   If Yes, what amount: _____

   5. Date when board designation became effective: _____

   6. Date when board designation expires: _____

AGENCY:

Optional Budget Form: 5

Account No. Charged	Position Title and/or Employee Name*	Full-Time Equiva- lent**	19___ Last Year Actual	19___ This Year Budgeted	19___ Next Year Proposed
	TOTAL				

*Denotes position vacant.
**Full-time staff will be noted as 1:00: Halftime as 0.50: Quartertime as 0.25, and so on.
All Financial Information Rounded to Nearest Dollar.

24 Unrelated Business Income

JODY BLAZEK, CPA
Blazek & Vetterling LLP

Exempt organizations receive two types of income: earned and unearned. Unearned income—income for which the organization gives nothing in return—comes from grants, membership fees, and donations. One can think of it as *one-way street* money. The motivation for giving the money is gratuitous and/or of a nonprofit character with no expectation of gain on the part of the giver; there is donative intent.

In contrast, an organization furnishes services and goods or invests its capital in return for earned income: an opera is seen, classes are attended, hospital care is provided, or credit counseling is given, for example. The purchasers of the goods and services do intend to receive something in return; they expect the street to be *two-way*. An investment company holding the organization's money expects to have to pay reasonable return for using the funds. In these examples, the organization receives earned income. The important issue this chapter considers is when earned income becomes unrelated business income (UBI) subject to income tax.

The tax on unrelated business income applies to all organizations exempt from tax under section 501(c) other than corporations created by an act of Congress and also to the following:

- Tax-exempt employee trusts described in Internal Revenue Code (IRC) section 401
- Individual retirement accounts
- State and municipal colleges and universities
- Qualified state tuition programs described in IRC section 529
- Education individual retirement accounts described in IRC section 530

The rules that govern when earned income becomes unrelated business income are complex. The concepts of UBI are vague and contain many exceptions that have been carved out by special interest groups. The House of Representatives Subcommittee on Oversight held hearings and drafted revisions over a four-year period (1987 through 1990). Though proposals to limits deductions and tax a variety of items were not passed, two very important changes resulted from the studies. The Internal Revenue Service (IRS) was directed to expand the Form 990 to report details of revenue sources that now reveals when an organization should file Form 990-T.[1] For-profit subsidiary payments in the form of rent, interest, royalties, or other expense deductible to the subsidiary is taxed to the tax-exempt parent when ownership is 50 percent or more as explained later.

Tax planning of the sort practiced by a good businessperson is in order for organizations receiving UBI. The best method for reducing unrelated business income tax (UBIT) is to keep good records. The accounting system must support the desired allocation of deductions for personnel and facilities with time records, expense usage reports, auto logs, documentation reports, and so on.[2] Minutes of meetings of the board of directors or trustees should reflect discussion of relatedness of any project claimed to accomplish an exempt purpose, if it appears that the activity is unrelated. For example, contracts and other documents concerning activities that the organization wants to prove are related to its exempt purposes should contain appropriate language to reflect the project's exempt purposes. An organization's original purposes can be expanded and redefined to broaden the scope of activities or to justify the proposed activity as related. Such altered or expanded purpose can be reported to the IRS to justify the relatedness of a new activity. If loss of exemption[3] is a strong possibility because of the extent and amount of unrelated business activity planned, a separate for-profit organization[4] can be formed to shield the organization from a possible loss of exemption due to excessive business activity.

Sometimes an exempt organization has facilities that are dually used for exempt and unrelated purposes. If dual-use facilities are partly debt-financed and partly paid for, an organization could purposefully buy the nontaxable exempt function property with debt and buy the unrelated part of the facility with cash available. Or, separate notes could be executed, with the taxable and unrelated property's debt being paid off first.[5]

24.1 IRS Scrutiny of Unrelated Business Income

Beginning in 1989 with the addition of Part VII to Form 990 and Part XVI-A to Form 990-PF, the IRS has a tool with which it can scrutinize the UBI issue. Until this Analysis of Revenue-Producing Activities was added to the forms, UBI was not identified in any special way on Form 990. The UBI was simply included with related income of the same character. The Congressional representatives and the IRS agreed that there was insufficient information to propose changes to the existing UBI rules. Parts VII and XVI-A separate income into three categories:

1. Unrelated income (identified with a business code from Form 990-T that describes its nature)
2. Unrelated income identified by the specific Internal Revenue Code section by which the income is excluded from UBI
3. Related or exempt function income, along with a description of the relationship of the income-producing activity to the accomplishment of exempt purposes

The IRS's first scrutiny of the new information found a 50 to 60 percent compliance rate with UBIT requirements. It found that a large portion of social clubs were failing to file Form 990-T when it took a look in 1997 and 1998.

24.2   History of the Unrelated Business Income Tax

Before 1950, a tax-exempt organization could conduct any income-producing activity and, in fact, many operated businesses and paid no income tax on the profits. Under a destination of income test, the income earned from a business was tax free so long as it was expended for exempt activities. In view of its extensive operations, the IRS tried in the late 1940s to tax New York University Law School's profits from its highly successful spaghetti factory.[6] The court decided no tax could be imposed under the then-existing tax code since the profits were used to operate the school.

In response to pressure from businesses, Congress established the unrelated business income tax in 1951 with the intention of eliminating the unfair competition charitable businesses represented, but it did not prohibit its receipt. The Congressional committee thought that the:

> *Tax free status of exemption section 501 organizations enables them to use their profits tax free to expand operations, while their competitors can expand only with profits remaining after taxes. The problem . . . is primarily that of unfair competition.*[7]

A key question in identifying UBI is, therefore, whether the activity that produces earned income competes with commercial businesses and whether the method of operation is distinguishable from that of a for-profit entity. The Tax Court in one case was of the opinion that "unfair competition plays a relatively insignificant role in the application of the amended unrelated business tax."[8] A Circuit Court expressed the same sentiment in saying that "competition alone does not determine whether an unrelated trade or business should be taxed." The organization had argued that it was not competing with any taxable business, while the government argued that tax on unrelated business income is not limited to competitive business.[9] Another question is, "Does the income-producing activity accomplish the organization's exempt purpose?" These questions are sometimes difficult to answer. The distinctions between for-profits and nonprofits has narrowed over the years as organizations search for creative ways to pay for program services. Consider what the difference between a museum bookstore and a commercial one is, other than the absence of private ownership. Privately owned for-profit theaters operate alongside non-profit ones. Magazines owned by nonprofits, such as *National Geographic* and *Harper's,* contain advertising and appear indistinguishable from *Traveler* or *Life* magazine. The health care profession is also full of indistinguishable examples.

24.3   Consequences of Receiving UBI

There are potentially several unpleasant consequences of earning unrelated income.

- *Payment of unrelated income tax.* Unrelated net income may be taxed at corporate or trust rates with estimated tax payments required. Social clubs, homeowner associations, and political organizations also pay the UBI tax on certain passive investment income in addition to the unrelated business income.

- *Exempt status revocation.* The organization's tax-exempt status could be revoked if the unrelated business activity becomes its primary activity, in which case all income is taxed.
- *Excess business holdings.* A private foundation may not operate a business and is limited in the ownership percentage it can hold in a separate business entity.[10]
- Internal Revenue Code section 501 requires a nonprofit organization to be both organized and operated exclusively for an exempt purpose, although *exclusively* does not mean 100%.[11]

In evaluating the amount of unrelated business activity that is permissible, not only the amount of gross revenue but also other factors may be taken into consideration. Non-revenue aspects of the activity, such as staff time devoted or value of donated services, are factors that might be determinative. The basic issue is whether the operation of the business subsumes, or is inconsistent with, the organization's exempt activities.

A complex of nonexempt activity caused the IRS to revoke the exemption of the Orange County Agricultural Society.[12] Its UBI averaged between 29 and 34 percent of its gross revenue. Private inurement was also found because the society was doing business with its board of directors. In another context, the IRS privately ruled a 50–50 ratio of related to unrelated income was permitted for a day care center raising funds from travel tours.[13] An organization with unrelated income in excess of 15–20 percent of its gross revenue must be prepared to defend its exempt status by showing that it focuses on its mission purposes rather than on its business activities. An organization can run a business as a substantial part of its activities, but not as its primary purpose.[14]

As reflected in the cited examples, the possibility of loss of exempt status when a significant portion, if not all, of an organization's income is unrelated business income is a question with no precise answer. Even if all of an organization's income stems from unrelated sources, continued qualification for exemption may be allowed under the right facts and circumstances.[15] The most important issue is whether the mission is the motivation behind the activity, rather than private or business interests. What is referred to as the *commensurate test* is one method of finding an answer.[16] If most of the organization's income and effort is devoted to charity, the unrelated source of revenues may not be treated as the primary focus.[17]

24.4 Definition of Trade or Business

To have unrelated business income, the nonprofit must first be found to be engaging in a trade or business. *Trade* or *business* is defined very broadly to include any activity carried on for the production of income from the sale of goods or performance of services.[18] The tax court, though, said a trade or business is conducted with "continuity and regularity" and in a "competitive manner similar to commercial businesses.[19] This is an area where the tax rules are very gray. The word *income* does not mean receipts or revenue and also does not necessarily mean net income. IRC section 513(c) says: "Where an activity carried on for profit constitutes an unrelated trade or business, no part of such trade or business shall be excluded from such classification merely because it does not result in profit."

The regulations couch the definition in the context of unfair competition with commercial businesses, saying that "when an activity does not possess the characteristics of a trade or business within the meaning of Section 162," the UBIT will not apply. However, these regulations were written before the IRC section 513(c) profit motive language was added to the code. They are the subject of continuing arguments between taxpayers and the IRS, and the confusion has produced two tests: profit motive and commerciality.

(A) PROFIT MOTIVE TEST

Under the profit motive test, an activity conducted simply to produce some revenue but without an expectation of producing a profit (similar to the hobby loss rules) is not a business.[20] This test is applied by the IRS in situations when a nonprofit has more than one unrelated business. Losses from the unprofitable activity or hobby cannot necessarily be offset against profits from other businesses. Likewise, the excess expenses (losses) generated in fundamentally exempt activity, such as an educational publication undertaken without the intention of making a profit, cannot be deducted against the profits from a profit-motivated project. Social clubs have battled with the IRS about this issue.[21]

(B) COMMERCIALITY TEST

The commerciality test looks to the type of operation: If the activity is carried on in a manner similar to a commercial business, it constitutes a trade or business. This test poses serious problems for the unsuspecting because there are no statutory or regulatory parameters to follow. A broad range of UBI cases where the scope of sales or service activity was beyond that normally found in the exempt setting have been decided by examining the commercial taint of the activity.[22] Exhibit 24.1 highlights situations that may jeopardize an organization's exempt status.

EXHIBIT 24.1 Commerciality Test Checklist

"YES" answers to these questions are warnings signs that signal the exempt organization's exposure to a challenge that the organization operates in a commercial manner and may not be exempt.

☐ COMPETITIVENESS: Does the exempt organization's activity compete with for-profit businesses conducting the same activity? Is there a counterpart for the activity in the business sector, particularly a "small" business?

☐ PERSONNEL MOTIVATION: Do managers receive generous compensation? Is the activity run by well-paid staff members?

☐ SELLING TECHNIQUES: Are advertising and promotional materials utilized? Are retailing methods, such as mail order catalog or display systems, similar to for-profit enterprise used?

☐ PRICING: Is the highest price the market will bear charged for goods and services? There are no scaled or reduced rates available for members of a charitable class.

☐ CUSTOMER PROFILE: Are the organization's services and goods for sale to anyone? Are they available to the general public on a regular basis, rather than only for persons participating in the organization's other exempt activities?

☐ ORGANIZATION'S FOCUS—GOOD WORKS RATIO: Does the organization conduct significant other charitable program activity? Is the income-producing activity its primary focus rather than exempt ones?

☐ CHARACTER OF ORGANIZATION'S SUPPORT: Does very little or none of the organization's support come from voluntary contributions and grants or other unearned sources?

(C) FRAGMENTATION RULE

Further evidence of the overreaching scope of the term *trade* or *business* is found in the fragmentation rule.[23] This rule carves out an activity carried on alongside an exempt one and proves that unrelated business does not lose its identity and taxability when it is earned in a related setting. Take, for example, a museum shop. The shop itself is clearly a trade or business, often established with a profit motive and operated in a commercial manner. Items sold in such shops, however, often include both educational items, such as books and reproductions of art works, and souvenirs. The fragmentation rule requires that all items sold be analyzed to identify the educational, or related, items the profit from which is not taxable and the unrelated souvenir items that do produce taxable income. The standards applied to identify museum objects as related or unrelated are well documented in IRS rulings.[24]

24.5 What Is Unrelated Business Income?

Unrelated business income is defined as the gross income derived from any *unrelated trade or business regularly carried on,* less the *deductions connected* with the carrying on of such trade or business, computed with *modifications and exceptions.*[25] The italicized terms are key to identifying UBI. Exhibit 24.2 shows them graphically. All four prongs of the circle surrounding the circle must be considered to determine what earned income is to be classified as UBI.

24.6 "Regularly Carried On"

A trade or business regularly carried on is considered to compete unfairly with commercial business and is fair game for classification as a taxable business. In determining whether an activity is regularly carried on, the IRS looks at the frequency and continuity of an activity when examined by comparison to commercial enterprises. The normal time

---

EXHIBIT 24.2 Components of Unrelated Business Income

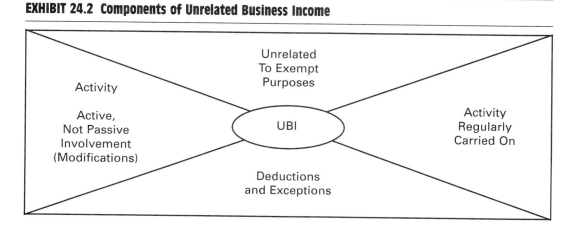

span of comparable commercial activities can also be determinative.[26] Exhibit 24.3 compares regular and irregular activities.

(A) MEANING OF IRREGULAR

Intermittent activities may be deemed *regularly carried on* or commercial unless they are discontinuous or periodic. For example, the revenue from a weekly dance is more likely to be taxed than the profits from an annual fund-raising event. By the same token, ads sold for a monthly newsletter would be classed as commercial; program ads sold for an annual ball might not. Where the planning and sales effort of a special event or athletic tournament is conducted over a long span of time, the IRS may argue that the activity becomes regularly carried on even though the event occurs infrequently.[27] Events held once a year have been the subject of much argument as to their regularity. Congress specifically mentioned *income derived from annual athletic exhibition* in stating that the UBI applies only to business regularly carried on.[28] When the IRS proposed taxing broadcast rights, it argued that preparatory time, not the actual playing time, determines regularity. If an event or program takes the entire year to produce, the span of time spent negotiating contracts and otherwise working on the event is considered. Examples of the arguments follow:

- Time spent by volunteers in soliciting advertisements or sponsorships were to be considered in evaluating the time span of the activity.[29]
- An eight-month concert season program was ruled to be comparable to commercial entertainment operations and thereby regularly carried on.[30]
- The National College Athletic Association (NCAA) convinced the court that an independent company's year-round effort to sell ads for the Final Four championship basketball tournament program was not attributable to the NCAA. The three-week duration of the tournament made it irregular and the program income excludible from UBIT even though the activity was an unrelated business.[31]
- Year-round sales effort for ads in a labor organization's yearbook, in IRS eyes, meant the activity is regularly carried on. The facts indicated that the yearbook had relevance to the members throughout the year and "the vast majority of advertisements carry a definitely commercial message."[32]
- One private ruling, however, said it would be difficult to conclude that an annual ball, which occurs only once each year, is regularly carried on.[33]
- Biannual publication of a business league's directory was also ruled to be a regular activity; the every-other-year publication cycle was regular or normal

EXHIBIT 24.3 Determining Regular Activity

Irregular	Regular
Sandwich stand at annual county fair	Cafe open daily
Annual golf tournament	Racetrack operated during racing "season"
Nine-day antique show	Antique store
Gala Ball held annually	Monthly dance
Program ads for annual fund-raising event	Advertisements in quarterly magazine

in commercial settings. The IRS opined that "continuity" did not necessarily mean "continuously," but rather having a connection with similar activities in the past that will be carried forward into the future.[34]

- Payment made to a statewide farm federation under a nonsponsorship and noncompetition agreement was found to be made in a nonrecurring transaction.[35] Although there was profit motive in making the agreement, no regular trade or business activity occurred when the federation agreed not to compete with the successor to its regional cooperative organization.

- When the Museum of Flight Foundation rented the first Boeing 747 back to the company to use for testing purposes, the IRS contended that the personal property rents paid by Boeing to borrow the plane back for testing purposes was taxable unrelated business income. A court overturned the decision and found that the lease was not a business "regularly carried on" and agreed with the museum that the transaction was a "one-time, completely fortuitous lease of unique equipment."[36]

(B)   SEASONAL ACTIVITY

Activities conducted during a period traditionally identified as seasonal, such as Christmas, if conducted during the season, will be considered regular and the income will not qualify to be excluded from UBIT. Christmas card sales during October or November, or Independence Day balloons sold in June/July, would be regular sales activity.

24.7   *"Substantially Related"*

An activity is substantially related only when it has a causal relationship to the achievement of the organization's exempt purpose[37] (that is, the purpose for which the organization was granted exemption based on its Form 1023 or 1024 and subsequent Form 990 filings). This requirement necessitates an examination of the relationship between the business activities (producing and distributing goods or performing services) that generate the particular income in question and the accomplishment of the organization's exempt purposes.[38]

> *Any business the conduct of which is not substantially related (aside from need to make money) to the performance of an organization's charitable, educational, or other purposes or function constituting the basis of its exemption is defined as unrelated.*[39]

The size and extent of the activity itself and its contribution to exempt purposes are determinative. The nexus (association, connection, or linkage) between the activity and accomplishment of exempt purposes is examined to find relatedness. The best way to illustrate the concept is with examples.

(A)   EXAMPLES OF RELATED ACTIVITY

Related income-producing activities include:

- Admission tickets for performances or lectures
- Student or member tuition or class fees

- Symphony society sale of symphonic musical recordings
- Products made by handicapped workers or trainees[40]
- Hospital room, drug, and other patient charges
- Agriculture college sale of produce or student work
- Sale of educational materials (see Section 24.13 for museum issues)
- College golf course usage by students and faculty[41]
- Secretarial and telephone answering service training program for indigent and homeless[42]
- Operation of diagnostic health devices, such as CAT scans or magnetic imaging machines, by a hospital or health care organization[43]
- Sale of online bibliographic data from exempt organization's central databases[44]
- "Public entertainment activities," or agricultural and educational fair or exposition [Section 24.9(d)]
- "Qualified conventions and trade shows" [Section 24.9(e)]
- Producing tapes of endangered ethnic music[45]
- Birthing center operated as a part of a church in respect of its religious tenets and belief that birth is a sacred and spiritual event[46]
- An "interactive virtual library" selling both access to its collections and staff over the Internet just as if one was visiting the library in person, as well as providing advice based on its expertise in library science (not consultation services) to other libraries, including businesses[47]

(B) SCHOOL ATHLETIC AND ENTERTAINMENT EVENTS

College-sponsored events have traditionally been thought to foster school spirit and advance the educational purposes of the schools. Revenues produced through sales of admission tickets, event programs, refreshments, and similar items have not normally been treated as UBI. Legislative history underlying the UBI provisions states "athletic activities of schools are substantially related to their educational functions. For example, a university would not be taxable on income derived from a basketball tournament sponsored by it, even where the teams were composed of students from other schools."[48]

Payments for radio and television broadcast rights, however, have been controversial. In 1977, the IRS advised Texas Christian University, Southern Methodist University, University of Southern California, and the Cotton Bowl Athletic Association that revenue derived by the universities from the telecasting and radio broadcasting of athletic events constituted unrelated trade or business income. In 1978, the IRS reversed its position after a challenge by the Cotton Bowl and National College Athletic Association.[49] In 1979, the IRS further expanded its position regarding such events and provided a good outline of the issues:[50]

- Sales of broadcast rights were regularly carried on and the activity looked at as a profit-motivated trade or business activity, with extensive time expended training the teams and preparing for the game.
- The events were regularly carried on (systematic and consistent, not discontinuous or periodic).
- Games, however, were related to the Cotton Bowl's exempt purpose. Income from sale of the game broadcast was a by-product because it was presented in its original state and provided a simultaneous extension of the exempt-function game to the general public.

A long series of IRS proclamations on the subject were issued in following years concerning the sale of broadcast rights by colleges, all of which ruled that such sales produced related income.[51] In 1981, the IRS applied the commerciality test[52] to find the promotion of rock concerts in a "multipurpose college auditorium" a taxable unrelated activity. The college's goal to maximize revenue to the exclusion of other considerations indicated that the facility was not operated as an educational program. The nature of the entertainment and the audience were not the criteria used to judge the activity's relatedness; instead, the detrimental fact was the college's selection of events based on their profitability. The facts outlined in the ruling evidencing the businesslike manner of conduct were as follows:[53]

- During the school year, 45 ticket events were held, 44 percent of which were rock concerts.
- Contemporary professional entertainers comprised 40 percent of the concert season.
- The facility was managed by a director with more than 30 years' experience in promoting commercial events.
- The school's fine arts department had no involvement in the selection of events to be held at the center and normally did not participate.
- Twenty-six percent of the tickets were sold to nonstudents.
- Tickets were sold through a commercial ticket service.
- Ticket prices for students were not discounted.
- Concerts were generally indistinguishable by price or type of performance from similar events provided by commercial impresarios.
- Compensation to the performers was negotiated and generally the same as compensation paid by for-profit centers.

Spouses and children of students, spouses and dependents of a university's employees, university alumni, members of President's Club (big donors and guests) were deemed to be unrelated users of a university's golf course. The IRS ruled that only use by full- and part-time students and employees was substantially related and that there was no causal relationship between the university's educational purposes and use of its golf course by any other persons.[54]

24.8 Unrelated Activities

The types of income that can potentially be treated as unrelated income are numerous, as the following controversial types of income illustrate. The examples do not always follow a logical pattern because courts and the IRS do not always agree, and the IRS has not always been consistent in its rulings. Further rules applicable to one type of income are not necessarily applied to another type.

(A) RENTALS

Rentals of equipment and other personal property (such as computers or telephone systems) to others are specifically listed in IRC section 512(b)(3) for inclusion in UBI. Such rental presumably is undertaken only to collect revenue to cover costs, with no direct connection to the organization's own exempt purposes; it *exploits* the exempt holding of the property. However, the following situations should be noted:

- Renting to (or sharing with) another nonprofit (or, conceivably, an individual or a for-profit business) is related if the rental expressly serves the landlord's exempt purposes, such as a museum's rental of art works—that would otherwise be kept in its storage—to other institutions to ensure maximum public viewing of the work or to relieve storage needs.
- Mailing list rentals produce UBI according to the IRS, except for narrow exceptions allowed to section 501(c)(3) organizations for exchanges of lists with other (c)(3)s.[55] A growing number of organizations have successfully claimed that list rentals are excludible royalty income as discussed in Section 24.10(d).
- Real estate rentals are also excluded from UBI under the passive exceptions, but only if the property is unencumbered as discussed in Section 24.12 regarding debt-financed property.[56]

Whether rental charges are at, below, or above cost can be determinative in evaluating relatedness. A full fair market value rental arrangement does not evidence exempt purposes (although the taint can be overcome by other reasons for the rental, such as dissemination of specialized educational information).

(B)   SERVICES

Rendering services by a charitable organization for its exempt constituents—students, patients, the underprivileged, or the parishioners—that accomplish an organization's mission is unquestionably a related activity. Certain types of services are inherently treated as related exempt activities—teaching, healing the sick, feeding the poor, or performing religious rites, for example. Section 501(c)(3) organizations must perform services in pursuit of eight specific exempt purposes.[57] The other types of services a tax-exempt organization is permitted to render in pursuit of its mission are actually narrower. A business league, labor union, social clubs, and others must perform only services that benefit the industry, the union, or the club, not its members as individuals, as discussed later in this subsection.

(i)   Services Provided to Another Nonprofit
Rendering services (such as billing, technical assistance, administrative support) to other nonprofits does not serve the exempt purposes of the service provider and is unrelated, according to the IRS. The fact that sharing creates efficiencies that allow all the nonprofits involved to save money does not necessarily sway the IRS. Only where the services themselves represent substantive programs better accomplished by selling the services to other organizations is the revenue considered related.

Though providing business services, such as accounting, computer services, and management consulting, to an unaffiliated organization is regularly found to be an unrelated activity, such services may be treated as related if provided to an affiliated exempt entity. Affiliate organizations for this purpose are usually referred to as being an integral part[58] of a group or system. Integrated health care delivery systems have lead the way in clarifying this issue.[59] Services rendered to the for-profit organizations in such a group would, however, be treated as unrelated activity.

- The Tax Court sanctioned the sharing of computer database technology for a group of libraries based on the concept that if an activity was a necessary component part of the operation of one library, it served an exempt purpose to provide the service to other exempt organizations.[60]

- Training courses furnished by a university to a business was sanctioned.[61]
- An HMO service provider created to provide management consulting to other exempt HMOs was not itself exempt.[62] Similarly, the exempt status of an organization providing management and administrative services to rural hospitals was revoked although it had been a tax-exempt organization since 1956.[63]

(ii) Cooperative Efforts

Where an organization is created to serve a consortium of organizations with a common building or pooled investment funds, the IRS has generally allowed its exemption when the new organization is partly supported by independent donations. When services are program related, the cooperative performance of charitable or educational functions has generally been acceptable to the IRS.[64]

- Certain cooperative service organizations have been specifically exempted by Congress. IRC section 501(e) grants exempt status to cooperative hospital organizations formed to provide on a group basis specified services, including data processing, purchasing (including the purchase of insurance on a group basis), warehousing, billing and collection, food, clinical, industrial engineering, laboratory, printing, communications, record center, and personnel (including selection, testing, training, and education of personnel services). Note that laundry is not on the list.
- Cooperative service organizations established to "hold, commingle, and collectively invest" stocks and securities of educational institutions are also provided a special exempt category under IRC section 501(f).
- IRC section 513(e) allows a special exclusion from UBI for the income earned by a hospital providing the types of services listed in IRC section 501(e) to another hospital that has facilities to serve fewer than 100 patients, provided the price for such services is rendered at cost plus a "reasonable amount of return on the capital goods used" in providing the service.

Provision of services by one member of a related group of organizations to others in the group is not treated as an unrelated activity if the services rendered are essential to the exempt functioning of the group so as to satisfy the integral part test.[65] In several private rulings, the IRS provided good examples of the types of services and relationships they consider to accomplish tax-exempt purposes. The IRS ruled favorably that a wide range of services, including campus security, telephone and mail service, a central steam plant, financial services, an auditorium, a faculty house used for meals and meetings, a medical center, a library, and an interfaith fellowship center, provided by a graduate school to its related "small colleges arranged around a library," were related to accomplishment of its exempt purposes.[66] Though each entity was legally separate, the graduate school's board of fellows includes the presidents and board chairs of each member of the group; matters concerning central programs and service are subject to a two-thirds vote. The constitution and the college's bylaws provide for a council made up of the presidents of each college in the group to provide policy guidelines on the administration and development of common programs and facilities.

A second ruling considered a hospital support organization created to hold "nontraditional assets." It purchased and operated a computer system for the medical faculty group practice and a motel located a short distance from the medical center.[67] The fact that the computer systems were used in the physicians' private practices was not discussed. Instead, the ruling focused on the need for such doctors as teachers of the medical students and supervisors of interns and residents and stated that the group essentially could qualify for exemption even though it had not sought recognition.[68] The motel operation was deemed a "convenience to the hospital's patients." Because 75 percent of the guests were patients and their families, the facility served an exempt purpose for its supported organization. The public guest revenues (25 percent) were deemed unrelated income under the fragmentation rule.[69]

(iii)   Member Services

Services furnished to members must also accomplish an exempt purpose to be treated as related. Services provided by churches, schools, hospitals, and most other charitable organizations are ordinarily treated as related. Classification of member services by business leagues, labor unions, and other non-(c)(3) organizations is not always clear. The question is whether the service yields private inurement to the individual member or to the profession as a whole and therefore the general public. Excessive unrelated member services can imperil an association's exempt status.[70]

The fact that the services provided to the member cooperatives were "not directly proportional to the amount of the fees paid" also indicated that individual economic benefits were not directly tied to the payments. Educational programs to promote farm cooperatives, information regarding economic and social conditions for farmers and farm products, and other services were found by the Tax Court to be conducted by a statewide federation of local county farm bureaus for exempt purposes.[71] Regarding a payment under a noncompete agreement, the revenue was found not to stem from the performance of services or the sale of goods so as to produce unrelated business income.

(C)   LICENSING USE OF THE ORGANIZATION'S NAME

Licensing the use of an organization's name normally is accomplished by a contract permitting use of the organization's intangible property—its name—with the compensation constituting royalty income that is excluded from UBI.[72] However, such arrangements may constitute commercial exploitation of an exempt asset in arrangements that usually require the nonprofit to furnish its mailing lists, endorse products, distribute materials on behalf of the list renter, and perform other services associated with use of its intangible property.[73] Since 1981, the IRS has been trying to tax organizations on the sale of their names in connection with insurance programs, affinity sales, and other commercial marketing schemes.[74]

To add flavor to the problem, in April 1990, the IRS reversed its position that a *royalty arrangement* licensing an organization's name, logo, and mailing list to an insurance agent (to promote life insurance to its membership) did not produce UBI for the exempt organization.[75] Because of the extensive involvement (active, not passive) of the exempt organization in servicing the membership lists, the narrow exemption of mailing lists,[76] and the agency theory discussed in Section 24.8(h), the IRS ruled that the supposed royalty arrangement produced UBI. The American Bar Association lost a similar battle in 1986, although its case was made more complicated by an arrangement whereby its members made substantial donations of the program profits.[77]

Affinity card revenues are UBI, as far as the IRS is concerned, that do not qualify for the royalty exception. When first ruling on affinity cards, the IRS allowed royalty exclusion for a fraternal order's card income.[78] By 1988, it had reversed this position.[79] While use of the organization's name and logo alone can produce royalty income, the credit card arrangements often depend on an accompanying sale of the organization's mailing list and, in some cases, endorsements and promotion by the organization in its publications and member/donor correspondence. The IRS therefore again applies an agency-type theory to deem that the nonprofit itself, rather than the intermediary organization, performed valuable services that produced unrelated income. Some organizations try to avoid this problem by bifurcating the royalty and mailing list aspects of the contract. The IRS position is to see them as one transaction, in reality, one contract, and apply UBIT.[80] It is the IRS's opinion that Internet service providers most often sell business services and are not qualified for tax exemption.[81]

(D)   ADVERTISING

Sale of advertising in an otherwise exempt publication is almost always considered unrelated business income by the IRS. The basic theory is that the advertisements promote the interests of the individual advertiser and cannot therefore be related to the charitable purposes of the organization. The following examples are indicative of IRS thinking:

- The American College of Physicians was unsuccessful in arguing that the drug company ads in its health journal published for physicians educated the doctors. The college said the ads provided the reader with a comprehensive and systematic presentation of goods and services needed in the profession and informed physicians about new drug discoveries, but the court disagreed.[82]
- A college newspaper training program for journalism students enrolled in an advertising course produced related income.[83]
- Institutional or sponsor ads produce UBI if they are presented in a commercial fashion with a business logo, product description, or other sales information. Only when sponsors are listed without typical advertising copy can the money given for the listing be considered a donation. Different sizes for different amounts of money may not cause the ad to be classified as commercial.[84]
- Advertising revenues received by a police troopers' labor union from sale of business listings and ads in its annual publication were found to be unrelated business income.[85] The firm hired to sell the ads and produce the *Constabulary* was acting on the union's behalf and under its control in an agency relationship[86] similar to that found in the NCAA case.
- Despite classification of ad revenues as UBI, the formula for calculating the taxable UBI sometimes yields surprising results that permit some ad sale programs to escape tax.[87,88] This exploitation formula is discussed in Chapter 27, Section 14, *Tax Planning and Compliance...*

(E)   SPONSORSHIPS

Corporate sponsorships of a wide variety of events—golf tournaments, fun runs, football bowl games, public television, art exhibitions, and so on—are a favorite form of corporate support for exempt organizations. The appeal of wide public exposure for sponsoring worthy causes and cultural programs has gained extensive popularity. The *Wall Street Journal* ran a series of articles during 1991 discussing the extent of such support and reasons why it made good business sense.

The Cotton Bowl Association's payments from Mobil Oil Company were, in 1991 after a lengthy controversy, treated as UBI.[89] The IRS found that substantial benefit in the form of advertising was given to Mobil. After an outcry from the exempt community, and in the face of proposed legislation to exempt such payment, the IRS issued proposed regulations concerning the character of sponsorship payments in 1993.[90] The proposals were said to reflect an IRS policy decision not to be responsible for hampering an exempt organization's need to raise private support. The regulation intended to distinguish between commercial advertising and benevolent payments.

In 1997, the 1993 proposed regulations were codified to delineate between those sponsorship payments that constitute a donation from those that represent payment for an advertisement taxable as UBI. The new tax code provision reduced the uncertainty of reliance on a proposed regulation, but significantly narrowed the definition of an acceptable acknowledgment. The code says the term *unrelated trade or business* does not include the activity of soliciting and receiving qualified sponsorship payments and defines that term as follows:[91]

> *The term "qualified sponsorship payment" means any payment made by any person engaged in a trade or business with respect to which there is no arrangement or expectation that such person will receive any substantial return benefit other than the use or acknowledgement of the name or logo (or product lines) or such person's trade or business in connection with the activities of the organization that receives such payment. Such a use or acknowledgement does not include advertising such person's products or services (including messages containing qualitative or comparative language, price information, or other indications of savings or value, an endorsement, or an inducement to purchase, sell, or use such products or services).*

Note the code only specifically allows the use or acknowledgment of the sponsor's name and logo. Anyone watching public TV or radio sees and hears not only the sponsor's name and logo, but also their address, phone number, and often extensive "value-neutral descriptions" of their business as permitted under the proposed regulations. A typical sponsor announcement says "Black, Brown & White is a 90-year-old plaintiff's law firm with offices around the world serving a broad base of international business clients." The proposed regulations broaden the definition and allow listing addresses and product descriptions in addition to the name and logo.

Unfortunately, neither the new code nor the committee reports explain the meaning of *substantial return benefit.* The House Committee Report stipulates services, benefits, facilities, or other privileges provided to a sponsor in connection with an event have no bearing on the determination of whether the payment is a qualified sponsorship payment. The report essentially says the substantial rules apply to evaluate the value of privileges as a separate transaction. In other words, if a $50,000 sponsor is provided with $1,000 worth of football tickets by a university, the donation is $49,000. This is but one of the many examples of privileges not required to be valued.[92]

Two types of sponsorship payments are subject to the unrelated business income tax rules:

1. A contingent payment, or any payment that is "contingent upon the level of attendance at one or more events, broadcast ratings, or other factors indicating the degree of public exposure to one or more events."

2. Periodical and trade show payments that "entitle the payor to the use or acknowledgement of the name or logo (or product line) of the payor's trade or business in regularly scheduled and printed materials published by or on behalf of the payee organization that is not related to and primarily distributed in connection with a specific event conducted by the payee organization . . . or any payment made in connection with any qualified convention or trade show activity."

The House Committee Report says a payment based on a contingency that the event actually take place does not create unrelated income. The report also permits, similar to the proposed regulations, the display, sale, and free distribution of the sponsor's products at a sponsored event. Again the code contains important new language, the meaning of which is uncertain until guidance is issued.

Reflect proposed sponsorship regulations.   The IRS in March 2000 proposed regulations for new IRC 513(i) to replace the 1993 proposal and elucidate the meaning of terms used to identify sponsorship payments that are treated as contributions from those that are treated as unrelated advertising revenue.[93] Though much of the language contained in the 1993 version was retained, the single paragraph found in the 1993 regulations is replaced with new specific definitions as follows:

Qualified sponsorship Payment.   The term *qualified sponsorship payment* means any payment of money, transfer of property, or performance of services by any person engaged in a trade or business with respect to which there is no arrangement or expectation that the person will receive any substantial return benefit. In determining whether a payment is a qualified sponsorship payment, it is irrelevant whether the sponsored activity is related or unrelated to the recipient organization's exempt purpose. It is also irrelevant whether the sponsored activity is temporary or permanent.

Substantial return benefit.   A substantial return benefit is defined negatively to say it means any benefit other than (1) goods, services, or other benefit of insubstantial value that are disregarded or (2) the use or acknowledgement of the name or logo of the sponsor's trade or business in connection with the activities of the exempt organization. A substantial return benefit includes advertising, providing facilities, services or other privileges to the sponsor or persons designated by the sponsor, and granting the sponsor an exclusive or nonexclusive right to use an intangible asset, such as a trademark, patent, logo, or designation of the exempt organization. Note the regulations clarify that qualifying sponsorships can be received in connection with ongoing activities of an extended or indefinite duration and in support of an exempt organizations operations, not just a single event or special series.

Certain goods or services disregarded.   Goods, services, or other benefits provided to the sponsor or designates that have an aggregate fair market value of not more than 2 percent of the amount of the payment, or $74,[94] whichever is lesser. Token items—bookmarks, calendars, key chains, mugs, posters, or tee shirts—bearing the organization's name or logo that have an aggregate cost within the limit established for low-cost articles[95] can be provided to sponsors. The cost limit can be applied to each of a sponsor's employees or partners. Complementary tickets, receptions for donors, and pro-am playing slots are ignored only if they meet this test.

Use of acknowledgment.   The use of the name or logo (or product lines of the sponsor) in connection with the activities of the exempt organization are not treated as providing a substantial return benefit.

Advertising.   An advertisement is any message or other programming material that is broadcast or otherwise transmitted, published, displayed, or distributed, and that promotes or markets any trade or business, or any service, facility, or product. Advertising includes messages containing qualitative or comparative language, price information or other indication of savings or value, an endorsement, or an inducement to purchase, sell, or use any company, service facility, or product. A single message that contains both advertising and an acknowledgment is advertising.

Exclusivity arrangements.   An arrangement for exclusive sponsorship of an exempt organization's activities or representation of a particular trade, business, or industry generally does not result in substantial return benefit. On the other hand, a sponsorship arrangement that limits the sale, distribution, availability, or use of competing products, services, or facilities in connection with an organization's activity is deemed to be a substantial benefit.[96]

Of most concern to those representatives of exempt organizations that commented on the proposal regulation is the provision that presumes any agreement to allow exclusive use of the sponsor's products at the organization's events or at its facilities yields a substantial benefit. The committee reports, however, specifically say,

> . . . *mere distribution or display of a sponsor's products by the sponsor or the exempt organization to the general public at a sponsored event, whether for free or for remuneration, will be considered to be a 'use or acknowledgment' of the sponsor's product lines (as opposed to advertising), and thus will not affect the determination of whether a payment made by the sponsor is a qualified sponsorship payment.[97]*

Thus it can be argued that the regulation is not in keeping with Congressional intention. Readers must be alert for new proposals and study Section 24.8(i). The proposed regulations say that the revenue received by Georgia Tech in the example found in that subsection would not be treated as a contribution under the sponsorship exception.

(F) INSURANCE

Group insurance programs have been a subject of active litigation among trade unions, business leagues, and the IRS, with the IRS prevailing in classifying revenues produced in an internally managed insurance program for members as UBI.[98] Instead of conducting the insurance program directly, creative nonprofits have instead licensed their membership lists to insurance providers in return for what they hope will be nontaxable royalty income. Similar to the factors considered in affinity card rulings and other mailing list licensing cases, the issue is to what extent the organization renders personal services in connection with the arrangement. It is also important to note in this context that organizations that provide commercial-type insurance cannot qualify for tax-exempt status under 501(m).

The criteria used to evaluate group insurance programs were outlined in a private ruling requested by a business league serving the public health community.[99] The facts leading the IRS to conclude that valuable services were provided, causing the payments to be classified as taxable UBI rather than royalties excluded by section 512(b)(2), were as follows:

- The insurance company acted as the league's agent in choosing suitable policies for its members, marketing the program to members, and performing administrative services such as creation of presentation brochures, seeking enrollments, and handling the premium collections.
- The league agreed to endorse the program and allow the insurance agent to use its logo, name, and membership list to promote the program to its members.
- The league retained the right to approve the form and content of mailings to its members, endorse the plan, and advise its members of its availability, and include plan information in new member packets.
- The league's involvement was direct and extensive and represented the rendering of valuable personal services, so that the so-called licensing payments did not qualify as royalty income.

Careful structuring of the contractual arrangements for such plans can allow the revenues to be bifurcated, resulting in some unrelated taxable income and some nontaxable royalty. Such an agreement would separate the requirements and compensation regarding services to be rendered. Terms for payments due for use of the organization's name can be clearly identified as royalty payments made strictly for use of intangible property, without regard to the service requirements. At best, two separate agreements could be reached to prove that the obligation to pay royalties is dissociated from services required to be performed.

(G) REAL ESTATE

Real estate development projects can be characterized as related (low-income or elderly housing), as a trade or business (subdivision, debt-financed rental, hotel), as an investment (unindebted rental), or sometimes as a combination of all three. Any nonprofit anticipating such a program should study Private Letter Ruling 8950072, in which the IRS outlines the UBI consequences of four different methods of developing an unindebted piece of raw land owned by an exempt organization. Leasing or selling raw land unquestionably produced no UBI because of the passive income modifications. Completion of the preliminary development work of obtaining permits and approval prior to the property's sale did not convert the sale into a business transaction. But total development of the property prior to the sale converts the property into a business asset and produces UBI.

Development of an apartment building and parking garage as a part of an urban renewal effort is a related business for an organization whose purpose is to combat community deterioration. The organization operated to assist the city by encouraging revitalization of its downtown area. While the activity would result in UBI if conducted for investment, in this case the activity served the organization's exempt purposes.[100]

A Catholic religious order received IRS sanction for a UBI exclusion of gain earned in a one-time liquidation of vacant land that had been used as part of its exempt facility. The order proposed to convert the land into 75 or more residential lots. The order obtained the permits, subdivided the land, and made the minimum physical improvements necessary to sell the lots, but an independent broker was to market and sell the lots. As explained in Section 24.10(b), the issue was whether the order was selling property "held for sale to customers in the ordinary course of a trade or business." The fact that the order took the steps necessary to prepare the land for sale and maintained control over the development process did not constitute active business activity.[101]

(H) AGENCY THEORY

An agency theory may be applied to look through certain arrangements. To avoid UBI classification for potentially unrelated activities previously listed, an organization might engage an independent party to conduct the activity in return for a royalty or a rental payment. Inherently passive activities for which compensation is paid in the form of rent or royalty are not subject to UBIT, even if the activity is deemed unrelated. The question is, however, whether the IRS can look through the transactions and attribute the activity of the independent party back to the organization, as it did in the following example.

The National Collegiate Athletic Association (NCAA) hired an unrelated commercial publishing company to produce its tournament programs. NCAA gave the publisher a free hand in soliciting the advertisements, designing the copy, and distributing the programs, in return for a percentage of the advertising and direct sales revenues. Because it had little or no involvement in the activity, the NCAA treated the income as a passive and irregularly carried on activity not subject to the unrelated business income tax. There was no argument that selling the program itself produces related income; nor was there any question that the advertising income is unrelated. The tournament lasts only three weeks.

The issue considered by the Tax Court[102] was whether the NCAA had sufficiently disengaged itself under the contract. Did it sell the right to use its name or did it engage in the ad activity itself? The Tax Court adopted an agency theory and held that because the publisher acted as the NCAA's agent, the activity was totally attributable to the NCAA. The Tenth Circuit Court agreed with the Tax Court but reversed the decision (because the activity was irregularly carried on and not in competition with business); the agency theory was not disputed. The IRS disagrees with the appellate decision regarding irregularity.[103]

Another athletic tournament–sponsoring organization also failed the agency test. The independently hired promoter's efforts during a 15-month ad campaign were attributed to the organization.[104] The agency theory was escaped, however, by an organization that turned over the publication of its monthly journal to a commercial company, retaining one-third of the net revenues from subscriptions and reprints. All advertising income, two-thirds of the circulation revenues, and all the risk of publication expenses were borne by the company. The IRS decided, under the circumstances, that the company was acting on its own behalf, not as agent for the charity. No advertising revenue was allocated to the charity.[105]

Earnings of an ostensibly independent for-profit subsidiary may also be allocated back to the nonprofit parent using the agency theory. The subsidiary's business is treated as separate only if it is managed at arm's length without the parent taking part in daily operations. Additionally, certain factors necessary to prove that the subsidiary's operation is separate must be met accordingly.[106]

(I) EXCLUSIVE MARKETING AGREEMENTS/ COVENANTS NOT TO COMPETE

The Georgia Institute of Technology renamed its sports arena McDonald's Center. The basketball court floor prominently displays a golden arch, and you can guess what kind of food and drink is exclusively served in the facility. The school received $5.5 million in return for agreeing to such actions. How this revenue is classified for federal tax purposes depends on the following medley of unrelated business income concepts and tax rules applied to the proverbial facts and circumstances:

- Is the activity a regularly carried on trade or business? (Does this answer depend on whether annual renewals occur rather than a one-time payment for a longer period of time? [Section 24.6]
- Has the school licensed its intangible property right (its good will and student body) in return for an excludible royalty? [Section 24.10(d)]
- Does the method of acknowledgment constitute a sponsorship payment treated as a contribution? [Section 24.8(e)]
- Has the school rented space for food service? [Section 24.10(d)]
- Is the school required to perform any services in connection with the agreement? [Section 24.10(d)]
- Is the sports arena a student convenience facility provided as part of the academic mission and the school's responsibility to feed the students? [Section 24.9(c)]
- Should the payment be fragmented into difference parts? [Section 24.4(c)]
- Does the outcome depend on the number of nonstudents that patronize the facility? [Section 24.9(c)]

The answer for each institution considering an exclusive-use agreement will depend on its particular set of facts and circumstances.[107] All of the answers to the questions listed earlier must be carefully considered in fashioning agreements that will produce nontaxable income. The proposed regulations on the sponsorship rules discussed in Section 24.8(e) take the position that an "exclusivity agreement" does provide a substantial benefit to the sponsor and disqualifies any revenues for treatment as a contribution under the section 513(i) exception. Several other exceptions, however, might apply. What if, for example, the organization agrees to sell only one vendor's goods to achieve a reduction in the price it must pay for the goods? What if physical circumstances in the cafeteria or stadium dictate that only one type of beverage be purveyed? Due to the significant amount of money involved in these transactions, it is reasonable to expect tax-exempt organizations and their representatives to battle for nontaxable treatment for exclusivity payments.

(J) E-COMMERCE

The character of revenues received from the sales of goods and services on the Internet is an evolving issue, many aspects of which are yet to be considered by the IRS. While there is no question that the law, regulations, court decisions, and rulings that apply to identify and tax unrelated business can be applied to e-commerce activities, certain unique aspects of the Internet prompt new questions.[108] Some practitioners laughingly refer to the one-click rule to suggest that the first click to a linked site may not produce unrelated income, but two clicks might. The following is the author's list of questions that an organization producing revenue from its site should ask, keyed to the portions of this chapter that further discuss the issue.

- *Do the goods and services sold through the site advance the organization's exempt purposes?* This determination is made in reference to the mission and the purposes for which the organization was originally found to be exempt. [Sections [24.7 and 24.8]

- *Does the organization recognize its sponsors or contributors on its Web site? If so, do the IRC section 513(i)(2)(A) rules delineating donor acknowledgments versus advertisements apply to links to business sponsors? Can the one-click rule apply? When does the link represent advertising for the sponsor?* [Section 24.9(j)] A simple banner placed on the organization's site containing whatever information is permitted under the yet-to-be finalized sponsorship regulations should represent a permitted acknowledgment that is not advertising. The difficult issue arises when the organization's links to the sponsor's site contain promotional material beyond words permitted for a donation acknowledgment. One IRS representative opined that any link to a sponsor's site was advertising.

- *What is the character of income received as "referral fees" from online vendors, such as Amazon.com, to their nonprofit associates? Can such payments be characterized as a royalty? Does the result change if the link is established to allow the site visitor to purchase books published by the organization itself?* Creative organizations will compose agreements with commercial distributors that designate such transactions as licensing transactions. Certainly, very little effort on the organization's part is involved, so that arguably the passive "royalty" modification might apply. [Section 24.10(d)] Expect the IRS to say that such fees are unrelated business income.

- *What if the site sells both related and unrelated items and/or both donated and purchased goods?* Relatedness would depend on an ability to identify both the purchaser and the type of goods or services sold. An accounting system capable of tabulating revenues from sale of the purchased, unrelated items separately from the related and donated goods [Section 24.9(b)] would be needed to allow use of the "fragmentation rule" to calculate taxable and nontaxable income. [Section 24.4(c)] The same type of tally would be needed if items were sold both to the general public and to patients, employees, or students. [Section 24.9(c)]

- *How would revenue from licensing the use of the organization's name and logo on some other site be classified? What about sale of the list of visitors to the organization's site?* The royalty exception should apply to exclude revenues from licensing use of the intangible personal property, [Section 24.10(d)] though the IRS may very likely disagree.

- *Is there any circumstance in which the irregular exception would apply?* The continual availability of an organization's Web site to anyone with computer access to the Internet makes any activity pertaining to the site regularly carried on. [Section 24.6]

- *Could the volunteer labor exception be applied?* The value of the volunteers' time in relation to the overall cost of the site would be computed. Will a Web site business be considered a capital-intensive business? [Section 24.9(a)]

- *How are the costs attributable to Web site activity quantified?* All the "ordinary and necessary" expenses[109] of establishing and maintaining the site and handling the revenue-producing activity would be tabulated. Basically, the hardware and software costs (depreciated over three to five years) for computers utilized, Web site design and maintenance fees, access and server fees, cost of personnel involved in maintaining the site, and other direct costs of the activity would be combined. The exploitation rule might apply to allocate a portion of the organization's exempt function costs (such as type 3 costs) to the revenue produced.[110]

24.9   The Exceptions

Despite their literal inclusion in the "unrelated" prong of the UBI rules, certain types of revenue-raising activities are not subject to UBIT, presumably because they are not businesslike and do not compete with commercial businesses. Charitable section 501(c)(3) organizations qualify for all of the following exceptions. Certain exceptions do not apply to non-501(c)(3) organizations, as noted under the particular exception.

(A)   VOLUNTEERS

A business in which substantially all of the work is performed without compensation is excluded from UBI when the labor is an income-producing factor. If the business is capital intensive so that the income is primarily attributable to the investment in property and equipment, such as rental real estate, the fact that accounting and other administrative services are provided by volunteers may not apply.[111] *Substantially* for this purpose means at least 80 to 85 percent of the total work performed, measured normally by the total hours worked. A paid manager or executive, administrative personnel, and all sorts of support staff can operate the business if most of the work is performed by volunteers. This rule is the reason the countless boxes of candy, coupon books, and other items sold by school children to raise funds for parent–teacher organizations do not result in unrelated business income to the school or PTA.[112]

In most cases, the number of hours worked, rather than relative value of the work, is used to measure the percent test. This means that the value of volunteer time need not necessarily be quantified for comparison to monetary compensation paid. In the case of a group of volunteer singing doctors, the value of the doctors' time was considered. Because the doctors were the stars of the records producing the income, their time was counted by the court at a premium, which offset administrative personnel whose time was compensated modestly.[113] Having 77 percent of its labor donated by volunteers, however, was not enough to allow a bingo operation to avail itself of this exception. The 23 percent compensated workforce ratio was substantial enough to cause an Elks Lodge to pay tax on its bingo profits.[114]

Expense reimbursements, in-kind benefits, and prizes are treated as compensation if they are compensatory in nature. Particularly when the expenses enable the volunteers to work longer hours and serve the convenience of the organization, the payments need not be counted in measuring this exception. However, solicitors for a religious organization who traveled in vans and lived a "very Spartan life" were not unpaid volunteers, as the organization had claimed, because their livelihood was provided by the organization.[115]

Similarly, when food, lodging, and other living expenses were furnished to sustain members of a religious group, the members working for the group's businesses were not treated as volunteers.[116]

The court in the Shiloh case found it to be a communal organization that provided for its members' needs. The fact that Shiloh's doctrine expressed a belief that "God commanded them to work," and that members were required, not only to display a willingness to work, but to in fact work convinced the court that the workers were not volunteers. It was also noted that Shiloh's support came primarily from payments for services its work teams performed for a variety of service-oriented businesses.

The result for members of a religious order was different.[117] Under a *but-for* test, it was decided that food, shelter, clothing, and medical care received by brothers in a religious order were paid without regard to whether they worked. The members of the order were under a vow of poverty and were provided necessities by the order without regard to their particular assignment. The court deemed the benefits provided were not compensatory. There was not a connection between the services and benefits because it was not the case that "but for rendering of services, the payments would not have been made." It was also noted that only 14 out of St. Joseph's 167 members worked on the farm and that the court had no doubt that, if the farm ceased to operate, the farm-working brothers would continue to receive their livelihood. The farm revenue was therefore excluded from UBI.

(B) DONATED GOODS

The selling of merchandise, substantially all of which is received by the organization as gifts or contributions, is not treated as a taxable activity. Thrift and resale shops selling donated goods are afforded a special exception from UBI for donated goods they sell. A shop selling goods on consignment as well as donated goods must distinguish between the two types of goods. Under the fragmentation rules,[118] the consigned goods sales would be separated, or fragmented, from the donated goods and any net profit from those sales included in UBI. Note consignment sales by volunteer-run resale shops would be excluded under the volunteer exception.

(C) CONVENIENCE

For section 501(c)(3) organizations only, a cafeteria, bookstore, residence, or similar facility used in the organization's programs and operated for the convenience of patients, visitors, employees, or students is specifically excepted from UBI.[119] Recovery of patients is hastened when family and friends visit or stay with them in the hospital, and the cafeteria facilitates the visits. Museum visitors can spend more time viewing art if they can stop to rest their feet and have a cup of coffee.

When the cafe, shop, dorm, or parking lot is also open to the general public, the revenue produced by public use is unrelated income. It is thought by some that the whole facility becomes subject to UBIT if the facility's entrance is on a public street. Meals served to non–museum visitors responding to advertisements promoting a museum's restaurant produced unrelated income.[120] No exempt purpose was served by selling the meals because the general public had access to the restaurant without having to pay for or visit the museum's art exhibits. If instead the promotion had emphasized the convenience of the restaurant, the result might have been different. A museum cafe is a related facility if it:[121]

- Attracts visitors by providing in-house dining
- Allows visitors to devote more time to the museum's educational facilities than if they had to seek outside eating facilities
- Enhances the efficient operation of the museum by enabling staff and employees to remain on the premises throughout the day

When a museum cafe has customers who are not museum visitors or employees, the fragmentation rules must be applied to separate the related revenues from the unrelated food sales to those who are not museum visitors.[122] It is important to note that the preceding list refers to *visitors,* a term not contained in the tax code. Members, students, patients, officers, or employees are the persons specifically listed in the convenience exception rule. In rulings over the years, the IRS has expanded this group to include visitors. At best, the income from a facility used by both qualified visitors as well as the disinterested public off the street is fragmented. The taxable and nontaxable revenues are identified and tabulated and the net taxable portion is calculated under the appropriate dual use rules.[123]

Parking lots for the exclusive use of participants in an exempt organization's activities can also be excluded from UBI under the convenience exception. A lot open to both visitors and nonvisitors is fragmented into its visitor convenience and nonvisitor parts. If the lot is operated by an independent party under a lease arrangement in which the exempt organization performs no services, the nonvisitor revenue can be classified as rental income excludable from UBI by the passive income modifications. If the organization itself operates the lot, the revenue from general public usage is a trade or business.[124]

The *IRS Examination Guidelines for Colleges and Universities*[125] contains useful criteria for applying the convenience exception for UBI purposes. Most importantly, the IRS admits that the facts and circumstances of each situation are determinative. The items sold to students, officers, and employees in the school book stores are essentially individually judged. First, the relatedness of an item is evaluated. Books and materials required and recommended for classes, supplies such as notebooks, pencils, and computers (one a year), and athletic gear necessary to participate in physical education programs are listed as items that advance the educational institution's exempt purposes. Materials that "further the intellectual life of the campus community," such as books, tapes, records, and compact discs, are also deemed related.

Items considered as unrelated to academic pursuits are those that might be merely conveniences to the students. The unstated presumption is that students or staff can spend more time studying (they need not travel to the mall) if they have toiletries, novelty items bearing the institution's insignia, candy, cigarettes, magazines, greeting cards, film, cameras, and small appliances easily available to them. Sales to alumni, parents, and other outsiders are unrelated and not excludable under the convenience exception.

(D) BINGO GAMES

Bingo games not conducted in violation of any state or local law are excluded from UBI. IRC section 513(f) defines bingo as any game of bingo of a type in which usually (1) wagers are placed, (2) winners are determined, and (3) distribution of prizes or other property is made, in the presence of all persons placing wagers in such game. The regulations expand the definition as follows:

A bingo game is a game of chance played with cards that are generally printed with five rows of five squares each. Participants place markers over randomly called numbers on the cards in an attempt to form a pre-selected pattern such as a horizontal, vertical, or diagonal line, or all four corners. The first participant to form the pre-selected pattern wins the game. Any other game of chance including but not limited to, keno, dice, cards, and lotteries, is not bingo (and will create UBI).[126]

Pull-tabs and other forms of instant bingo are not bingo in the IRS's opinion, and produce UBI despite the fact that such variations of the bingo game are so classified by the state bingo authority. In calculating the taxable income earned from a pull-tab operations, all of the "ordinary and necessary" business expenses are deductible. That portion of the profits from the pull-tabs that is required to be paid out for or dedicated only to charitable purposes under local law is treated as a business expense. During 1990, the IRS aggressively examined non-profits in the Southwest District and assessed tax on any bingo variations not strictly meeting the code and regulation definitions.[127] Publication 3079, entitled "Gaming Publication for Tax-Exempt Organizations," was issued in April 1998 to explain these rules comprehensively.

(E) ENTERTAINMENT, CONVENTIONS, AND TRADE SHOWS

Public entertainment is defined as that traditionally conducted at fairs or expositions promoting agricultural and educational purposes (including but not limited to animals or products and equipment) and does not produce UBI for section 501(c)(3), (4), or (5) organizations. Internal Revenue Code section 513(d)(2) requires that the event be held in conjunction with an international, national, state, regional, or local fair, or be in accordance with provisions of state law that permit such a fair.

A *convention* or *trade show* is intended to attract persons in an industry generally (without regard to membership in the sponsoring organization), as well as members of the public, to the show for the purpose of displaying industry products, or stimulating interest in and demand for industry products or services, or educating persons engaged in the industry in the development of new products and services or new rules and regulations affecting the industry. A "qualified" show is one conducted by section 501(c)(3), (4), (5), or (6) organizations in conjunction with an international, national, state, regional, or local convention, annual meeting, or show. Exhibitors are permitted to sell products or services, and the organization can charge for the display space.

Private Letter Ruling 9835001 should be studied by groups owning exhibition facilities. The IRS found a tax-exempt agricultural fair organization received both taxable and non-taxable rental income from leasing its facilities during its offseason ($10\frac{1}{2}$ months of year). Free admission for its shareholders (essentially members) was found not to result in private inurement because such admissions constituted only 3 percent of the tickets given away.

(F) INDIAN TRIBES

Income earned by a federally recognized Indian tribe from the conduct of an unincorporated business or a corporation incorporated under the Indian Reorganization Act of 1934 (IRA) is not subject to federal income tax.[128] A corporation formed instead under the laws of the state in which the tribe is located, however, would be subject to tax even though it is owned and controlled by an Indian tribe or members of a tribe. The basis of this distinction lies in the definition of an Indian tribe. Section 1 of the Internal Revenue Code subjects individuals, trusts, and estates to tax; Section 11 taxes corporations. A tribe is not such a taxable entity; a separately incorporated business would be.[129]

In 1981, the IRS ruled that a properly established Indian tribal corporation (under the IRA) had the same tax status as an Indian tribe as it regarded activities carried on within the boundaries of the reservation.[130] This restriction to on-reservation activity was reconsidered and removed in the 1994 ruling. The ruling says that because an Indian tribe is not a taxable entity, any income earned by it—on or off the reservation—is not taxable. The ruling states that it applies only to federal income taxes. It does not affect the application of other federal taxes, such as employment and excise taxes (including excise taxes on wagering), to Indian tribes or tribal corporations. A draft of an IRS "Guide to Indian Taxation Issues" was reviewed with tribal representatives on March 3, 1994, but not formally issued. The IRS issued temporary (and has yet to finalize) procedural and administrative tax regulations under the Indian Tribal Governmental Tax Status Act of 1982 that can be studied in this regard. Regulation section 305.7701-1 defines an Indian tribal government, and regulation section 305.7871-1 considers Indian tribal governments treated as States for certain purposes.

(G) LOW-COST ARTICLES

For section 501(c)(3) and veterans groups, gift premiums distributed with no obligation to purchase in connection with the solicitations of contributions are not treated as a sale of the gift premium. The gift must be part of a fund-raising campaign and must cost (not fair market value) the organization no more than $7.20 (during 1999; indexed annually for inflation). The recipient of the premium must not request or consent to receive the premium. Literature requesting a donation must accompany the premium along with a statement that the recipient may keep the low-cost article regardless of whether a charitable donation is made. If the donation is less than $36 (during 1999; indexed annually), the fair market value of the premium reduces the deductible portion of the donor's gift.[131]

The de minimus amount for low-cost articles in 2000 are $7.40 and $37.[132]

A program for distribution of low-cost articles cannot qualify for this exception if it presents unfair competition to nonexempt businesses and is conducted like a commercial enterprise.[133] A religious group's "donation solicitations" in return for caps, T-shirts, and similar items at public sporting and entertainment events was found to be conducted in a profit-seeking fashion in competition with for-profit vendors.[134] For this reason, as well as its failure to prove it distributed the items with no obligation to purchase, the revenues were treated as unrelated business income.

(H) MAILING LISTS

Again for the organizations eligible to receive charitable donations under section 170—primarily section 501(c)(3) and veteran organizations—a business involving the exchange or renting of mailing lists between such organizations only is excluded from UBI classification. This special treatment was added by Congress in 1986 based on IRS recommendation.[135] Sale or exchange of mailing lists by such organizations to others and sales by all other types of section 501(c) organizations ostensibly by omission create UBI. Courts have found, much to the consternation of the IRS, that section 513(h) does not overrule

the passive royalty income exception that modifies revenues from licensing of mailing lists for all types of tax-exempt organizations.[136]

A program allowing credit card holders to direct the bank's affinity card program to pay rebates to named charities is a charitable giving program. When the cardholder voluntarily designated a specific charity, the bank was acting as an agent so that its transfer of the funds to the charity on behalf of the cardholder qualified as a charitable contribution.[137] The furnishing of the charity's mailing list to the card company did not constitute rental of the list because the revenue stemmed from cardholders' voluntary action.

24.10   Income Modifications

For section 501(c) organizations other than social clubs, voluntary employee benefit associations, supplemental unemployment plans, and veterans groups, specified types of investment income are modified, or excluded, from UBI unless the underlying property is subject to debt. IRC section 512(b) excludes "all dividends, interest, royalties, rents, payments with respect to security loans, and annuities, and all deductions, connected with such income." Passive income of a sort not specifically listed is not necessarily modified or excluded from UBI.

(A)   DIVIDENDS AND INTEREST

Dividends and interest paid on amounts invested in savings accounts, certificates of deposit, money market accounts, bonds, loans, preferred or common stocks, and payments in respect to security loans and annuities, net of any allocable deductions, are excluded from UBI.

In 1978, the general exclusion of interest and dividends was expanded to include the words "payments in respect of security loans." For some time there was uncertainty regarding techniques such as "strips," interest rate swaps, and currency hedges. It is now recognized that such investments are *ordinary and routine,* and income earned from such transactions in security portfolios is considered as investment income for section 512 purposes.[138]

When securities producing dividends and interest are acquired with indebtedness, the income is swept back into UBI by IRC section 514. An organization must be careful to use new money to acquire each element of investment in its portfolio. A pension fund owning five-year certificates of deposit (CDs) in 1979 (after interest rates had risen over five points) realized UBI when it purchased new CDs using its old CDs as collateral. Although the fund escaped an early withdrawal penalty and received a higher rate of interest, the new CD was a debt-financed asset purchase. Thus, the fund's original CD produced "modified" or nontaxable income, and the new higher-rate CD acquired with the loan proceeds was held to be taxable as unrelated debt-financed income.[139] The CD switch, incidentally, was not a permissible "payment in respect of a security loan." Such a loan allows a broker to use an organization's securities in return for a fee, not as a loan against which the securities are used as collateral.

The Omnibus Budget Reduction Act of 1993 amended section 512 to provide that gain and loss received from unexercised options on investment assets such as securities and real estate, as well as loan commitment fee forfeitures, are excluded from the UBI.

(B) CAPITAL GAINS

Gains from sale, exchange, or other disposition of property is classified as UBI dependent on the character of the property sold. Generally, the normal income tax rules of IRC sections 1221 and 1231 for identifying capital, versus ordinary income, property apply to identify property covered by this exception. Sales of stock in trade or other inventory-type property, or of property held for sale to customers in the ordinary course of trade or business, produce UBI.

(i) Options/Shorts

Gains on lapse or termination of covered and uncovered options, if written as a part of investment activity, are not taxable.[140] Short-term capital gain from a short sale of publicly traded stock through a broker was ruled not to create UBI. Although a short sale technically creates an obligation for the purchaser to pay for any loss that may occur on covering the short position, this possible loss is not treated as acquisition indebtedness.[141]

(ii) Timber

Timber standing on real estate owned by the exempt organization can be treated as a capital asset if the organization retains an economic interest in the timber.[142] The somewhat complicated rules must be studied for organizations owning such property to ensure proper tax treatment. Percentage depletion may apply, and specific rules for allocating the cost basis of the underlying property between the real estate and the timber are provided.[143]

(iii) Social Club Issues

A gain from the sale of real estate used by a social club in regular club activities (its exempt function) is not classed as UBI to the extent the proceeds are reinvested one year before or three years after the date of the sale.[144] Because social clubs often own valuable and desirable real estate, particularly country clubs and old-line city clubs, this exception can be valuable. When the property is considered as nonexempt function, the club must treat the revenue as nonmember revenue and also face the possibility of failing a so-called 35/15 test necessary to maintain ongoing exemption.

Harvesting pine timber to preserve the usefulness of a club's property as a wildlife habitat was found to further advance the club's exempt purposes. The club, created in 1870, owned a five-square-mile fish and game preserve and historic clubhouse building adjacent to public land areas maintained in a natural state. The club, beginning in 1983, engaged professional foresters to plan timber harvesting to improve the habitat for wild game and to control gypsy moths. Sale of the timber pursuant to the plans did not create unrelated business income.[145]

A Florida club sold a portion of its property to participate in a land price boom and distributed the proceeds to the members. The court said the sale was a "violent departure" from the club's normal behavior and not merely incidental to the regular functions of the club. Because financial gain was the aim, the court revoked the club's exemption.[146]

Property contiguous to a club and held for possible future expansion, or simply protecting the club from the suburbs, is not exempt function property. Only property in actual, direct, continuous, and regular use for social and recreational purposes qualifies. Accordingly, a golf club was taxed on gain from selling off road frontage. The land was originally acquired with the expectation that it would be used for club facilities, but in actuality was not.[147]

Use of vacant land containing no physical improvements but was used for jogging, picnics, kite-flying contests, and other outdoor activities was found to constitute direct use by club members. The court said, "It is certainly conceivable that joggers derive as much pleasure and recreation from that pastime as golfers do from their rounds on the links."[148] A "buffer tract," containing a steep incline and heavily wooded with thick undergrowth, however, was found not to be used directly in exempt functions. Even though it isolated the club from the surrounding developed area and roads, its physical condition indicated it was not devoted to exempt activity. Proceeds from granting a permanent easement for passage and use produced UBI.[149]

(C) RENTALS

Rental income is considered a passive type of investment income that is not modified (excluded) from UBI, except:

- Personal property rentals are taxable unless they are rented incidentally (not more than 10 percent of rent) with real property.
- A fluctuating rental agreement that calculates the rent based on net profits from the property is unrelated income; rent based on gross revenue is not UBI.

When substantial services are rendered, such as the rental of a theater complete with staff or rental of a hotel room complete with room service, the rental is not considered passive.[150]

Sharecrop arrangements for farm land owned by an organization may or may not be treated as excludable from UBI under the rent exception. The method for calculating the rent and risk borne by the organization is determinative. The issue is whether the exempt organization is a joint venturer participating in the farming operations. The following factors were considered in two court cases on the subject.[151]

- Organization is not involved in the day-to-day operation of the farm; it simply provides the land and buildings.
- Organization bears no risk of loss from accidents.
- Organization is not required to contribute to any losses from the operation, but only pays an agreed portion of the operating expenses (in one case 50 percent).
- The rent is equal to a fixed percentage of the gross sale of the crop or a fixed amount, not a percentage of net profits.[152]

Parking lot rental presents a similar situation. Rental of the bare real estate to another party that operates the lot (where the organization has no relationship or responsibility whatsoever to the parkers) clearly produces passive rental income.[153] If the exempt organization provides some services to the operator, UBI taint may occur. The regulations speak of "services rendered . . . primarily for the convenience and other than those usually or customarily rendered in connection with the rental of rooms or other space for occupancy only." Providing maid service, but not trash hauling, in renting a room is the example provided.[154] Operation of a parking lot for the benefit of employees and persons participating in an exempt organization's functions, rather than disinterested persons, should be a related activity.[155] A parking rate structure "not consistent with commercially operated for-profit facilities in the same metropolitan area" was found to reflect an organization's desire to provide a necessary service to the public.

The storage of cars, boats, motor homes, and campers in an agricultural association's fairground facilities for that portion of the year the spaces are not used for its own annual fair was a "mini-storage business" in the eyes of the IRS.[156] Although the ruling noted that no services are provided other than having paid workers to park the vehicles and remove them in the spring, the IRS cited the regulations that say, "payments for the use or occupancy of rooms and other space where services are also rendered to the occupant, such as for the use or occupancy of rooms or other quarters in hotels, boarding houses, or apartment houses furnishing hotel services, or in tourist camps or tourist homes, motor courts, or motels, or for the use or occupancy of space in parking lots, warehouses, or storage garages, does not constitute rent from real property.[157]

Substantial services were provided to corporate and business patrons who rented an educational organization's facilities for receptions in the evenings. The services provided included maintenance and security personnel and liquor service (because the organization held the license). The IRS was not convinced that the rentals served an exempt purpose in finding the programs were primarily social or business oriented and included such items as cocktails, dinner-dances, awards presentations, and holiday celebrations. While there was some educational benefit to the attendees of viewing exhibits, they were ancillary to the events' principal purpose.[158] The IRS noted the holding would be different if the request was for the organization to create an educational event in its space, with the food and services provided only incidentally.

(D) ROYALTIES

The fact that the term *royalties* is not defined under the code or regulations pertaining to unrelated income has caused significant controversy. The IRS and the courts have very different notions about the application of this exception. The IRS insists that a royalty must be received in an activity that is passive to qualify. Most courts have said instead that a royalty paid for the use of intangible property rights is excluded from UBI. The battle has focused on licensing of mailing lists, exempt organization logos, and associated issuance of affinity cards.

The regulations provide that royalties, whether measured by production or by the gross or taxable income from the property, are modified, or excluded from UBI.[159] Income from an oil and gas working interest for which the organization is responsible for its share of development costs is not modified or excluded from UBI.[160]

Initially, the IRS insisted that none of the revenue paid in return for licensing the use of an organization's mailing list is treated as a royalty payment.[161] While agreeing that mailing lists are intangible property, the IRS argued that the activity of exploiting the lists was conducted like an active business. The Tax Court however, ruled in 1993, that it could find no evidence that Congress intended to limit the royalty exception to passively held or investment properties.[162]

The Ninth Circuit Court of Appeals partially agreed with the Tax Court.[163] As to list rentals, the club engaged list managers that marketed the lists and performed all of the necessary services. The club simply provided the lists and retained the right to review rental requests and approve contents. It found that the licensing did not unfairly compete with businesses and that the agreement did not create an agency transaction.[164] When

Sierra licensed its lists to a bank for an affinity card program, however, it agreed to promote the program. The case was remanded to the Tax Court to reexamine "extras" the Sierra Club was required to provide in satisfying provisions of its contract with the bank. The question was whether the club receives compensation for services. The IRS may resume its contest of these court decisions; watch for new developments.

The Tax Court on remand decided that the Sierra Club did not render taxable services when it retained quality control rights over its logo used in a bank affinity card program. The payments received for use of its name, logo, and mailing lists constituted royalties from the licensing of its intangible property rights. Sierra was found not to jeopardize the characterization of income as a royalty when it scrutinized promotional materials to prevent abuse of its logo.[165] From the Sierra Club's and other court battles[166] concerning the royalty exception, guidelines have emerged. Payments that can be treated as royalty income excluded from unrelated business taxable income are distinguishable by the following criteria from those that will be taxable compensation for services rendered:

- Payments are made pursuant to written documents that stipulate the organization is licensing its intangible property.
- The payments are specifically designated as royalties.
- The tax-exempt organization does not participate in marketing the affinity cards, insurance, or other products the commercial company is promoting to the organization's members and supporters.
- When the organization is to participate in the marketing effort, the services to be rendered are clearly defined and compensation for such services set out in the agreement.
- When the organization promotes the program with advertisements in its newsletters or magazines, fees for the ads are separately paid for by the licensee. Net income allocable to the ad revenues is reported as unrelated business income.[167]
- Any retained rights to inspect or manipulate the marketing materials are permitted for reasons of protecting the organization's name and reputation, not required of the organization. If production and design of brochures, letters, and other promotional materials are performed by the organization, compensation for the work should be stipulated.

The IRS announced in December 1999 that it had instructed its agents to cease attempts to tax revenues from affinity card and mailing list rental cases as a result of its losses in the Tax Court in the Sierra Club and other cases.[168] The memo said, "If you encounter a case in which the organization provides extensive services, or the facts indicate a good case of allocating the payment between services and the intangible, call Charles Barrett or Jay Rotz (no longer with IRS) and consider seeking technical advise." In pending examinations, the issue of potential service income was to be considered, but the exclusion of the royalty portion from tax is conceded. However, the IRS continues to consider whether "in some instances it might be appropriate to have an allocation between the name and logo and services provided by the exempt organizations."[169] The IRS sanctioned the bifurcation of an affinity arrangement where the service portion of the arrangement, including personnel and resources to perform the work, was spun off into a for-profit subsidiary. The exempt organization kept the royalty portion of the contract (the profitable portion).[170]

To ensure revenues from licensing its mailing list be treated as nontaxable royalty income, an organization must avoid performing the type of services rendered by the Disabled American Veterans (DAV) in regard to its lists. The DAV lost its battle to escape tax deficiencies of over $4 million based on $279 million of revenue.[171] There was no argument that the DAV managed the activity in a businesslike manner. Several persons worked full-time to keep the list current (not a volunteer operation), the DAV placed conditions on the name usage, required advance approval of the client copy, and had a complicated rate structure that it widely circulated on rate cards. It belonged to the Direct Mail Marketing Association, a trade association composed of organizations using direct mail in their operations.

This issue is of particular interest in the scientific and medical fields, where considerable sums are earned from royalties paid for the use of patented devices and methods. Perhaps because the licensing of intellectual property rights for patents involves complex legal issues and potential for liability, the agreements are very carefully structured. There is usually no question that the exempt organization assigns all responsibility for services performed in developing the patent to the license. Thus the revenue received by the exempt organization is unquestionably passive and eligible to be modified, or excluded from UBI.[172]

What appears from the facts to be the Interscholastic League also failed in its effort to turn advertising revenues into royalties. Under licensing agreements with sporting goods manufacturers and insurance providers, the league was required to perform services and provide free advertising for the commercial concerns.[173] To confuse this issue, IRC section 513(h)(1)(B) excludes revenues attributable to the exchange of lists between entities eligible to receive charitable contributions.[174]

The rule that rent, royalties, interest, and annuities paid by a 50 percent or more owned for-profit subsidiary cannot be modified, or excluded, from the unrelated business income tax "makes no sense."[175] A coalition that includes the National Geographic Society, Children's Television Workshop, NFL Players Association, the American Federal of Farm Bureaus, and others are lobbying to allow such payments to be excluded if they paid at fair market value. The rule seeks to curtail inflation of deductible expenses paid to tax-exempt parent organizations. The coalition questions why rent received from an unrelated tenant is tax-free, whereas rent paid by a related for-profit is taxable. Be on the lookout for new legislation on this issue.

(E) SUBSIDIARY PAYMENTS

Payments of interest, rents, royalties, or annuities excluded under the general rules are includable in UBI if paid by either a controlled taxable subsidiary or a controlled tax-exempt subsidiary. On August 5, 1997, the percentage of ownership constituting control for this purpose was reduced from 80 percent to 50 percent.[176] Specifically, the code now defines control as follows:

- In the case of a corporation, ownership (by vote or value) of more than 50 percent of the stock in such corporation
- In the case of a partnership, ownership of more than 50 percent of the profits, interests, or capital interests of the partnership
- In any other case, ownership of more than 50 percent of the beneficial interests in the entity

The inclusion portion of amounts received is essentially that amount of the payment that would have been taxable to the controlled organization as UBI had it not paid the interest, rent, or royalty that could be claimed as a deductible expense. For a nonexempt controlled entity, the taxable amount is equal to that portion of such entity's taxable income that would have been UBIT had it been a tax-exempt entity.

There are no specifics at this time regarding the meaning of beneficial interests in a nonprofit entity. Under regulations issued before the 1997 amendment to this section, control of a nonstock organization resulted from interlocking directors. If at least 80 percent (now read as 50) of the directors of one organization are representatives of the second organization or have the right to appoint or control the board of the second, control exists.

The attribution rules of IRC section 318 apply for purposes of determining constructive ownership of stock in a corporation. Similar principles shall apply for purposes of determining ownership of interests in any other entity. Before mid-1997, amounts paid by a second-tier subsidiary were nontaxable and not subject to inclusion because this section at that time contained no attribution or indirect ownership requirement that would treat the parent as controlling its subsidiary's subsidiary.[177] Although not a tax issue for the tax-exempt organization itself, a financial issue that arises for an exempt organization owning a subsidiary is the so-called General Utilities doctrine. The transfer of substantially all of the assets of a taxable corporation to a tax-exempt organization (commonly as its parent) is essentially treated as a taxable sale of the transferred assets at their fair market value.[178] The conversion of a taxable entity to a tax-exempt one is similarly treated as a transaction in which gain must be recognized. A transfer of assets that the exempt will use to conduct an unrelated business are not taxed at the time of transfer (because they will be taxed when eventually sold).

(F) RESEARCH

Research income is not taxable if the research is performed for the United States, its agencies, or a state or political subdivision thereof by any exempt organization.[179] In addition:

- A college, university, or hospital can exclude all research income from private or governmental contractors.[180]
- An exempt organization performing fundamental research, the results of which are freely available to the general public, can also exclude all research income.[181]

It has been noted that there is a pronounced distinction between scientific research that is treated as related income and testing that is considered a commercial and unrelated enterprise.[182]

(G) PARTNERSHIPS AND S CORPORATIONS

A tax-exempt organization's share of income from a partnership, regardless of whether distributed or paid to the organization, flows through to the nonprofit partner and retains its character as rent, interest, business, or other type of income.[183] If the partnership conducts a trade or business that is unrelated to the organization's exempt purpose, the organization's share of the business income, less associated deductions, must be reported as unrelated business taxable income. The exceptions and modifications[184] pertaining to passive income apply to exclude the organization's share of interest or other passive income distributed by the partnership. This rules applies to organizations that are general and limited partners.[185]

Until January 1, 1994, distributions from publicly traded partnerships were fully taxable to the tax-exempt partner, including retirement plans. Since 1994, the partnership's income is fragmented to allow each type of income to flow through to the tax-exempt partner according to the general rule outlined previously. Thus, partnership income or loss retains its character as either taxable business income or passive investment income in the hands of the tax-exempt partner.[186] A publicly traded partnership is one for which interests in it are traded on an established securities market or are readily tradable on a secondary market.[187]

Organizations exempt under section 501(c)(3) and 401(a) are eligible, effective for tax years beginning after December 31, 1997, to become shareholders of an S corporation.[188] New IRC section 512(e), however, says that stock in an S corporation represents an interest in an unrelated trade or business. Accordingly, the code now also provides the following:

All items of income, loss, or deduction taken into account under IRC section 1366(a), and any gain or loss on disposition of the stock in the S corporation, shall be taken into account in computing the unrelated business taxable income of such organizations.

Unlike a partnership, all of the income distributed to an exempt organization by an S corporation flows through to it as unrelated business income, including passive income otherwise modified from tax.[189] Gain or loss on the sale of S corporate shares is also treated as UBI. Thus where possible, an exempt organization's investment in an entity that will produce a significant amount of passive income should preferably be held in partnership form.

24.11 Calculating and Minimizing Taxable Income

When an otherwise tax-exempt organization has taxable UBI, the tax is calculated under the normal income tax rules. Gross UBI, minus allowable deductions and exemptions, is subject to tax. As long as the percentage of an organization's UBI is modest in relation to its overall revenues,[190] the only problem UBIT presents is the reduction in profit because of the income tax paid. Maximizing deductions to calculate the income is important. The income tax sections of the Internal Revenue Code of 1986 govern, and the same concepts apply, including:

- *Form 990-T.* The UBIT is calculated on Form 990-T. You may want to take a closer look at a sample of a filled-in form and detailed suggestions for its completion.[191]
- *Tax rates.* The income tax is calculated using the normal tables for all taxpayers, that is, section 1(e) for trusts and section 11 for corporations. For controlled groups of exempt organizations (also including 80 percent owned for-profit subsidiaries), the corporate tax bracket must be calculated on a consolidated basis under the rules of section 1561. The tax liability is payable in advance during the year, as the income is earned, similar to for-profit businesses and individuals.
- *Alternative minimum tax.* Accelerated depreciation, percentage depletion, and other similar tax benefits may be subject to the alternative minimum tax, just as with for-profit taxpayers with certain levels of income.

- *Ordinary and necessary criteria.* Deductions claimed against the unrelated income must be "ordinary and necessary" to conducting the activity and must meet the other standards of section 162 for business deductions. Ordinary means common and accepted for the type of business operated; necessary means helpful and appropriate, not indispensable. The activity for which the expenditure is incurred must also be operated with profit motive.[192] No portion of the organization's basic operating expense theoretically is deductible against UBI because of the exploitation rule. However, when there is an ongoing plan to produce UBI and such revenue is part of the justification affording a particular exempt activity, allocation of overhead is permitted, although it is challenging.[193]

  If the entity that earns unrelated income is required by some law to pay over all of its profits for charitable purposes, the payments may be treated as a business expense, rather than a contribution subject to percentage limitations.[194]

- *Profit motive.* To be deductible, an expenditure must also be paid for the production of income, or in a business operated for the purpose of making a profit. IRC section 183 specifically prohibits the deduction *of hobby losses,* or those activities losing money for more than two years out of every five. The IRS will challenge the deduction for UBI purposes of any expenditure not paid for the purposes of producing the profit.[195]

- *Depreciation.* Equipment, buildings, vehicles, furniture, and other properties that have a useful life to the business are deductible, theoretically over their life. As a simple example, one-third of the total cost of a computer that is expected to be obsolete in three years would be deductible during each year the computer is used in the business. Unfortunately, Congress uses these calculation rates and methods as political and economic tools, and the code prescribes rates and methods that are not so simple. IRC sections 167, 168, and 179 apply and must be studied to properly calculate allowable deductions for depreciation.

- *Inventory.* If the nonprofit keeps an inventory of items for sale, such as books, drugs, or merchandise of any sort, it must use the inventory method to deduct the cost of such goods. The concept is one of matching the cost of the item sold with its sales proceeds. If the exempt organization buys ten widgets for sale and, as of the end of a year, only five have been sold, the cost of the five is deductible and the remaining five are capitalized as an asset to be deducted when those widgets are sold. Again, the system is far more complicated than this simple example, and an accountant should be consulted to ensure use of proper reporting and tabulation methods. IRC sections 263A and 471–474 also apply.

- *Capital and nondeductibles.* A host of nondeductible items contained in IRC sections 261–280H might apply to disallow deductions, either by total disallowance or required capitalization of permanent assets. Again, all the rules applicable to for-profit businesses apply, such as the luxury automobile limits, travel and entertainment substantiation requirements, and the 50 percent disallowance for meals.

- *Dividend deduction.* The dividends received deduction provided by IRC sections 243–245 for taxable nonexempt corporations is not allowed. As a general rule, a corporation is allowed to exclude 70 percent of the dividends it receives on its investments; exempt organizations are not. This rule only presents a problem for dividends received from investments that are debt financed. Most dividends received by exempt organizations are excluded from the UBI under the modifications previously discussed.

(A)   NET OPERATING LOSSES

A loss realized in operating an unrelated business in one year may be carried back for two years and forward for 20 years, for offset against another year's operating income. Gains and losses for different types of UBI earned within any single exempt organization are netted against profits from the various business activities of the organization, including acquisition of indebted investment property. Tax years in which no UBI activity is realized are counted in calculating the number of years for permissible carryovers. Conversely, net operating losses are not reduced by related income.

(B)   EXPLOITATION AND FRAGMENTATION

When unrelated business income is generated in a fundamentally exempt activity, such as a museum gift shop or hospital pharmacy, the revenues and expenses are fragmented into the respective related and unrelated parts.[196] Such revenues are said to exploit the exempt function—the expense deductions are limited and a loss from the exploited activity is limited.[197] A social club, for example, cannot offset losses on serving nonmembers against income from its investments, according to the Supreme Court, which sided with the IRS.[198] There were conflicting decisions among the U.S. Circuit Courts of Appeal for several years, and clubs claiming such losses had to file amended returns to report tax resulting from the loss disallowance.

   In Revenue Ruling 74–399, a museum restaurant was found to be a related activity because it attracted persons to the museum, allowed more time for viewing of exhibitions, and was conducive to efficient museum operative time for the staff. Another museum that allows restaurant customers to eat without paying admission to visit the museum was deemed an unrelated facility. Compounding the problem was the fact that the restaurant was promoted with advertisements in a local monthly magazine and the yellow pages that mentioned the free admission.[199]

   It is extremely important for an exempt organization to file Form 990-T even though it incurs a loss. Reporting the loss allows for carryback or carryover of the loss to offset past or future income. An election is available to carry losses forward and to forgo any carryback in situations where the organization has not previously earned UBI.

(C) $1,000 EXEMPTION

An exemption of $1,000 is allowed.

24.12   *Debt-Financed Income*

The modifications exempting passive investment income, such as dividends and interest, from the UBIT do not apply to the extent that the investment is made with borrowed funds. Debt-financed property is defined as including property held for the production of income that was acquired or improved with borrowed funds and has a balance of acquisition indebtedness attributable to it during the year.[200] The classic examples are a margin account held against the exempt organization's endowment funds or a mortgage financing the purchase of a rental building.

(A) PROPERTIES SUBJECT TO DEBT-FINANCED RULES

Real or other tangible or intangible property used 85 percent or more of the time, when it is actually devoted to such purpose and used directly in the organization's exempt or related activities, is exempt from these rules.[201] Assume a university borrows money and builds an office tower for its projected staff needs over a 20-year period. If less than 85 percent of the building is used by its staff and a net profit is earned, the nonuniversity-use portion of the building income is taxable as UBI.

Income included in UBI for some other reason, such as hotel room rentals or a 100 percent owned subsidiary's royalties, is specifically excluded by the code and is not counted twice because the property is debt financed.[202] Conversely, an indebted property used in an unrelated activity that is excluded from UBI because it is managed by volunteers, is for the convenience of members, or is a facility for sale of donated goods, is not treated as unrelated debt-financed property.[203] Property used in unrelated activities of an exempt organization, the income of which is excepted from UBI because it is run by volunteers for the convenience of members, or sale of donated goods, can be indebted and still not be subject to this classification. Research property producing income otherwise excluded from the UBIT is not subject to the acquisition indebtedness taint. *Future-use land* (not including buildings) acquired and held for use by an exempt organization within 10 years (churches get 15 years) from the date it is acquired, and located in the *neighborhood* in which the organization carries out a project, is exempt from this provision. This exception applies until the plans are abandoned; after five years, the organization's plans for use must be "reasonably certain."[204]

Tax status of the tenant or user is not necessarily determinative. Rental of an indebted medical office building used by staff physicians was found to be related to a hospital's purposes.[205] Although their restoration served a charitable purpose, the rental of restored historic properties to private tenants was deemed not to serve an exempt purpose where the properties were not open to the public.[206] Regulations suggest that all facts and circumstances of property usage will be considered.

Federal funding provided or insured by the Federal Housing Administration, if used to finance purchase, construction, or rehabilitation of residential property for low-income persons, is excluded.

Charitable gift annuities issued as the sole consideration in exchange for property worth more than 90 percent of value of the annuity is not considered acquisition indebtedness. The annuity must be payable over the life (not for a minimum or maximum number of payments) of one or two persons alive at the time. The annuity must not be measured by the property's (or any other property's) income.

Although investment of a pension fund is admittedly inherent in its exempt purposes, debt-financed investments made by such a fund (or most other exempt organizations) are not inherent in a fund's purposes.[207] The Southwest Texas Electric Cooperative's purchase of Treasury Notes with Rural Electrification Administration (REA) loan proceeds represented a debt-financed investment. The loan proceeds were required to be used to pay construction costs. The cooperative's cash flow, however, allowed it to pay part of the construction costs with operating funds. To take advantage of a more than 4 percent spread in the REA loan and prevailing Treasury Note rates, the cooperative deliberately "drew down" on the REA loan. The Tax Court agreed with the IRS that the interest income was taxable debt-financed income.[208]

Indebted property producing no recurrent annual income, but held to produce appreciation in underlying value, or capital gain, is subject to this rule.[209] A look-back rule prevents deliberate payoff prior to sale to avoid the tax. The portion of the taxable gain is calculated using the highest amount of indebtedness during the 12 months preceding the sale as the numerator.[210]

Schools and their supporting organizations, certain pension trusts, and 501(c)(25) title holding companies may have a special exception for indebted real property. If the property is purchased in a partnership with for-profit investors, profit- and loss-sharing ratios must have substantial economic effect and not violate the disproportionate allocation rules.[211]

(B) ACQUISITION INDEBTEDNESS

Acquisition indebtedness is the unpaid amount of any debt incurred to purchase or improve property or any debt "reasonably foreseen" at the time of acquisition that would not have been incurred otherwise.[212] Securities purchased on margin are debt financed; payments for loan of securities already owned are not. The formula for calculation of income subject to tax is:

$$\frac{\text{Income from property} \times \text{Average acquisition indebtedness}}{\text{Average adjusted basis}}$$

The average acquisition indebtedness equals the arithmetic average of each month or partial month of the tax year. The average adjusted basis is similarly calculated using the straight-line method of depreciation.

The proportion-of-use test is applied to identify property used for exempt and nonexempt purposes and can be based on a comparison of the number of days used for exempt purposes with the total time the property is used, or on the basis of square footage used for each, or on relative costs.[213]

Debt placed on property by a donor will be attributed to the organization when the organization agrees to pay all or part of the debt or makes any payments on the equity.[214] Property that is encumbered and subject to existing debt at the time it is received by bequest or devise is not treated as acquisition-indebted property for 10 years from its acquisition, if there is no assumption or payment on the debt by the organization. Gifted property subject to debt is similarly excluded, if the donor placed the mortgage on the property over five years prior to gift and had owned the property over five years, unless there is an assumption or payment on the mortgage by the organization. A life estate does not constitute a debt. When some other individual or organization is entitled to income from the property for life or another period of time, a remainder interest in the property is not considered to be indebted.[215]

It is the IRS's opinion that both debt incurred to acquire a partnership interest and debt incurred by the partnership itself are included in calculating acquisition indebtedness.[216]

(C) CALCULATION OF TAXABLE PORTION

Only that portion of the net income of debt-financed property attributable to the debt is classified as UBI.[217] Each property subject to debt is calculated separately, with the resulting income or loss netted to arrive at the portion includable in UBI. Expenses directly connected with the property are deducted from gross revenues in the same proportion. The capital gain or loss formula is different in one respect: the highest amount of indebtedness during the year preceding sales is used as the numerator.

24.13 *Museums*

Museum gift shop sales and related income-producing activities are governed by the fragmentation[218] and exploitation[219] rules. Since 1973, when it published a ruling concerning greeting cards,[220] the IRS has agreed that items printed with reproductions of images in a museum's collection are educational and related to the exempt purposes so that their sale does not produce UBI. The ruling expressed two different reasons: (1) The cards stimulated and enhanced public awareness, interest in, and appreciation of art; and (2) a self-advertising theory stating that a "broader segment of the public may be encouraged to visit the museum itself to share in its educational functions and programs as a result of seeing the cards."

A second 1973 ruling[221] (still cited today) explored the fragmentation rule and expanded its application to trinkets and actual copies of objects and distinguished items. The IRS felt that educational benefit could be gained from utilitarian items with souvenir value. Since that time, it has been clearly established that a museum shop often contains both related and unrelated items, and the museum must keep exacting records to identify the two.

(A) IDENTIFYING RELATED AND UNRELATED OBJECTS

After the IRS and museums argued for 10 years about the relatedness of a wide variety of objects sold, four exhaustive private rulings were issued in 1983 and are still followed.[222] The primary concern for a museum is to identify the *relatedness* of each object sold in its shops, and to segregate any unrelated sales. The connection between the item sold and achievement of the museum's exempt purpose is evidenced by the facts and circumstances of each object and the policy of the curatorial department in identifying, labeling, and categorizing objects on public view.

The rulings direct that the *facts and circumstances* of each object are examined to prove that the objects being sold have educational value and list the following factors to consider in designating an item:

- Interpretive material describing artistic, cultural, or historical relationship to the museum's collection or exhibits
- Nature, scope, and motivation for the sale activity
- Are sales solely for production of income or are they an activity to enhance visitor awareness of art?
- Curatorial supervision in choosing related items
- Reproductions of objects in the particular museum or in other collections, including prints, slides, posters, postcards and greeting cards, are generally exempt.

- Adaptations, including imprinted utilitarian objects such as dishes, ashtrays, and clothing, must be accompanied by interpretive materials and must depict objects or identify an exhibition. Objects printed with logos were deemed unrelated, although in practice, the IRS has been lenient.
- Souvenirs and convenience items are generally unrelated unless imprinted with reproductions or promoting a particular event or exhibition. Souvenirs promoting the town in which the museum is located are not considered related to the museum's purposes.
- Toys and other teaching items for children are deemed inherently educational and therefore related.

The IRS has refined its blanket approval for teaching items for children. As discussed in the text, the IRS in 1983 said that children's interpretive teaching items with artistic themes furthered the museum's educational purpose. In 1997, the IRS clarified its position by saying "items that develop a child's artistic ability are substantially related to the museum's educational purpose." However, it found that other items, including tot blocks, baby play gyms, cooking utensils, fruit and vegetable playsets, and animal-shaped wagons that generally develop a child's motor skills are not items related to a museum's exempt function.[223]

(B) ORIGINAL WORKS OF ART

Original works of art created by living artists and sold by museums are considered unrelated by the IRS. They think it is inconsistent with the purpose of exhibiting art for public benefit to deprive the public the opportunity of viewing the art by selling it to an individual. This policy can apply as well to deceased artists.

- A cooperative art gallery established to encourage individual emerging artists was not allowed to qualify as an exempt organization because, in the IRS's opinion, the interests of the general public were not served by promoting the careers of individual artists. The art sales served no exempt purpose and constituted UBI. Because the organization was supported entirely by UBI from the sales of art of the artists, it was not exempt.[224]
- A community art center located in an isolated area with no commercial galleries obtained exemption, and the Tax Court decided that its sales of original art were related to exempt purposes. The decision was based on the fact that no other cultural center existed in the county, the art sales were not the center's sole source of support, and a complex of other educational activities were conducted.[225]
- An unrelated gallery managed by volunteers and/or selling donated works of art produces unrelated income, but the income is not taxable because of exceptions. Exempt status depends on whether the gallery is a substantial part of the organization's activities. See Section 24.3 for consequences of receiving such income.

24.14 *Travel Tours*

Museums and other types of exempt organizations sponsor study tours as promotional, educational, and fund-raising tools. The issue is whether such tours advance the exempt purposes of the exempt organization other than its need for funds. Such tours are commonly professionally organized in a fashion similar to those of travel agents and commercial tour guides. To be related to an exempt function, a tour must be educational rather than recreational. The IRS says the crux of the matter is the intent of the tour-sponsoring organization. One must evaluate the difference between "serendipitous acquisition of knowledge" and a deliberate intent to educate.[226] Final regulations were issued by the IRS on February 7, 2000. In evaluating the related aspect of a travel tour, the fact that the tour visits a unique or historic part of the world does not make an expedition an educational one.[227] An absence of a structured educational program with scheduled classes indicates a pleasure tour. The availability of lectures is insufficient; the IRS wants to see course work.

To scrutinize the bona fide educational methodology of the tour, the professional status of leaders and the educational content of the program is considered. Advance preparation, such as reading lists, evidence relatedness. The actual amount of time spent in formal classes and visits to historic sites, mandatory participation for lectures, preparation of reports, and opportunity for university credit are other attributes evidencing the educational nature of a tour.[228] Conversely, a large amount of recreational time allowed to participants, the resort-taint of the places the tour visits, and holiday scheduling suggest predominantly personal pleasure purposes and cause the tour to not qualify as educational.[229] The regulations contain four examples that should be carefully studied by organizations conducting such tours.

The proposed regulations suggest documentation of a trip's relatedness start during its planning stage. The exempt organization's records should indicate how and for what reason the destination(s) is chosen, how guides are chosen, and other information evidencing the educational raison d'être of the trip. Proving the educational nature of a tour may be more difficult for an organization whose sole purpose is conducting tours. An organization that uses professional travel companies to arrange tours also has a burden of proving it was not established to benefit the private operators.

Not only the profit from the tour itself, but also the *additional donation* requested as an organizational gift from all participants in a travel tour program, may be classed as unrelated income if the tour is not considered as educational.[230]

24.15   *Publishing*

Exempt organization publications present two very different exposures to trouble: the unrelated income tax and potential revocation of exemption. As discussed previously, the most universal problem is that publication advertising sales create UBI in most cases. A less common, but more dangerous, situation occurs when the underlying exemption is challenged because the publication itself is a business.

(A)   ADVERTISING

Revenue received from the sale of advertising in an otherwise exempt publication is considered business income by the IRS, and is taxed unless:

- The publication schedule or ad sale activity is irregularly carried on.
- The advertising is sold by volunteers.
- The advertising activity is related to one of the organization's underlying exempt purposes, such as ads sold by college students or trainees.

- The ads do not contain commercial material, appear essentially as a listing without significant distinction among those listed, and represent acknowledgment of contributors or sponsors.

The IRS has continually taken the position that advertising sold using the exempt organization's name is unrelated activity, despite creative contracts attributing the activity to an independent commercial firm.[231]

(B) READERSHIP VERSUS AD LINEAGE COSTS

Even if ad revenue is classified as UBI, the tax consequence is limited by the portion of the readership and editorial costs allowed as deductions against the ad revenue. The important question is what portion of the expense of producing and distributing the publication can be allocated against the revenue.[232] It is helpful first to study Exhibit 24.4, a worksheet reflecting the order in which readership and editorial costs versus advertising costs are allocated.

The formula prorates deductions in arriving at taxable advertising income. Publication costs are first divided into two categories: direct advertising and readership. Because readership costs are exempt function costs, under the *exploitation rule*[233] they theoretically should not be deductible at all against the UBI income. In a limited exception, the regulations allow readership costs, if any, in excess of readership income to be deducted against advertising income. In other words, advertising revenues can be offset with a readership loss. Arriving at a readership loss, however, means the publication's underlying production costs must be more than its revenues.

(C) CIRCULATION INCOME

Circulation income is income attributable to the production, distribution, or circulation of a periodical (other than advertising revenue), including sale of reprints and back issues.[234] When members receive an organization's publication as a part of their basic membership fee, a portion of the member dues is allocated to circulation income. Other types of member income, such as educational program fees or convention registration, are not allocated.[235] When the publication is given free to members but is sold to nonmembers, a portion of the members' dues is allocated to readership revenue. The IRS formula requires allocation of a hypothetical portion of the dues, as described in the calculation.

- Free copies given to nonmembers are subject to controversy with IRS (check for new decisions).
- If the organization has more than one publication, the IRS and the courts disagree on the denominator of the fraction for calculation of allocable exempt function costs.[236]

(D) COMMERCIAL PUBLICATION PROGRAMS

A publication program can be considered a commercial venture, despite its educational content. Distinguishing characteristics, according to the IRS, are found by examining the organization's management decisions.

Characteristics deemed commercial by the IRS include:

EXHIBIT 24.4 Calculating the Taxable Portion of Advertising Revenue

BASIC FORMULA: $A - B - (C - D) =$ **Taxable Income**

A = Gross sales of advertising.

B = Direct costs of advertising:

Occupancy, supplies, and other administrative expenses	$ _____
Commissions or salary costs for ad salespersons	_____
Clerical or management salary cost directly allocable	_____
Artwork, photography, color separations, etc.	_____
Portion of printing, typesetting, mailing, and other direct publication costs allocable in the ratio of total lineage in the publication to ad lineage	_____
Total direct cost of ads	$ _____

C = Readership costs:

Occupancy, supplies, and other administrative expense	$ _____
Editors, writers, and salary for editorial content	_____
Travel, photos, other direct editorial expenses	_____
Portion of printing, typesetting, mailing, and other direct publication costs allocable in ratio of total lineage in publication to editorial lineage (in general, all direct publication costs not allocable to advertising lineage)	_____
Total readership costs	$ _____

D = Readership (or circulation) revenues:

If publication sold to all for a fixed price, then readership revenue equals total subscription sales.	$ _____

or

If 20% of total circulation is from paid nonmember subscriptions, then price charged to nonmembers times number of issues circulated to members plus nonmember revenue equals readership revenues.	_____

or

If members receiving publication pay a higher membership fee, readership revenue equals excess dues times number of members receiving publication, plus nonmember revenue.	_____

or

If more than 80% of issues distributed to members free, readership revenue is the membership receipts times the ratio of publication costs over the total exempt activities cost including the publication costs.	_____

- *Presence of substantial profits.* Accumulation of profits over a number of years evidences a commercial purpose. The mere presence of profits, by itself, will not bar exemption,[237] but other factors will be considered. For what purpose are profits being accumulated? Do the reserves represent a savings account for future expansion plans?

- *Pricing methods.* The method of pricing books or magazines sold yields significant evidence of commercial taint. Pricing at or below an amount calculated to cover costs shows nonprofit motive. Pricing below comparable commercial publications is not required, but certainly can evidence an intention to encourage readership and to educate, rather than to produce a profit.

- *Other factors.* Other factors can show commerciality:
  - Aggressive commercial practices resembling those undertaken by commercial publishers.[238]
  - Substantial salaries or royalties paid to individuals.
  - Distribution by commercial licensers.

- *Nonprofit publications.* By contrast, nonprofit and noncommercial publications:[239]
  - Rely on volunteers and/or modest wages.
  - Sell some unprofitable books and magazines.
  - Prepare and choose materials according to educational methods, not commercial appeal.
  - Donate parts of press runs to other exempt organizations or members.
  - Balance deficit budgets with contributions.

A Christian school publishing program, for example, was treated as an unrelated activity despite the educational nature of the books it sold.[240] Although the program had significant commercial attributes—more than 1,200 titles produced on presses that ran 16 hours a day and sold throughout the world—the IRS said two particular characteristics caused it to consider the activity as unrelated:

1. The methods used in selling the textbooks are indistinguishable from ordinary commercial sales practices.
2. Fifty percent of the schools' highly compensated employees were sales representatives.

The IRS provided some useful criteria for deciding what constitutes a *periodical* in a 1994 private ruling.[241] The definition is important because that portion of membership dues allocated to published periodicals is treated as taxable unrelated income. An educational organization devoted to the study of reproduction distributed a variety of publications, some of which were deemed periodicals and others of which were not. A quarterly newsletter and annual meeting programs distributed to members were periodicals for the following reasons:

- Each was published at regular recurring intervals.
- The right to receive the publication was associated with membership or similar status in the organization for which dues, fees, or other charges were received (even though nonmembers may also).
- Each contained editorial materials related to the accomplishment of the organization's exempt purposes; in this case, publicizing scientific developments in the field, technical articles, and reports of annual meeting.
- The newsletter was part of an ongoing series, with each issue indicating its relation to prior or future issues; it contained a regular feature column, president's message, and reports of organizational meetings and activities.
- With respect to the advertising portion of the publications, the purpose was the production of income, each issue of a periodical indicated a relation with prior or subsequent issues.

Endnotes

1. See Part VII of Form 990.
2. Discussed in Chapter 27, Section 27.14, Blazek, J. (1999). *Tax Planning and Compliance for Tax-Exempt Organizations: Forms, Checklists, Procedures, 3rd ed.* New York: John Wiley & Sons.
3. Discussed in Section 24.3, this chapter.
4. Discussed in Chapter 22, Section 22.4, *Tax Planning and Compliance for Tax-Exempt Organizations* (see note 2).
5. See Section 24.12, this chapter.
6. *C. F. Mueller Co. v. Commissioner,* 190 F.2d 120 (3rd Cir. 1951).
7. House of Representatives No. 2319, 81st Cong., 2nd Sess. (1950) at 36–37.
8. *Smith-Dodd Businessman's Association, Inc. v. Commissioner,* 65 T.C. 620 (1975).
9. *Clarence LaBelle Post No. 217 v. U.S.,* 580 F. 2d 270 (8th Cir. 1978), cert. dismissed, 99 S. Ct. 712.
10. See Chapter 16, *Tax Planning and Compliance. . .,* for rules defining impermissible excess business holdings for private foundations.
11. See Chapter 2, *Tax Planning and Compliance. . .*
12. *Orange County Agricultural Society Inc. v. Commissioner,* 90.1 U.S.T.C. ¶50.076 (2d Cir. 1990), *aff'g* 55 T.C.M. 1602 (1988).
13. Priv. Ltr. Rul. 9521004.
14. Reg. section 1.501(c)(3)-1(e)(1).
15. Gen. Coun. Memo. 34682.
16. Discussed in Chapter 2, Section 2 (d), *Tax Planning and Compliance. . .*
17. Field Service Advice 199910007.
18. Reg. section 1.513-1(b).
19. *National Water Well Association, Inc. v. Commissioner,* 92 T.C. 75 (1985).
20. *West Virginia State Medical Association,* 89-2 U.S.T.C. section 9491 (4th Cir. 1989); 91 T.C. 651 (1988), *Commissioner v. Groetzinger,* 480 U.S. 23 (1987).
21. Discussed in Chapter 9, Section 5, *Tax Planning and Compliance. . .*
22. *Better Business Bureau v. U.S.,* 326 US. 279, 283 (1945); *United States National Water Well Association, Inc. v. Commissioner,* 92 T.C. 7 (1989); *Scripture Press Foundation v. U.S.,* 285 F.2d 800 (Ct.Cl. 1961); *Greater United Navajo Development Enterprises, Inc. v. Commissioner,* 74 T.C. 69 (1980); also see Priv. Ltr. Rul. 9636001 for Christian school's textbook publishing department earning UBI because it was indistinguishable from commercial publishing company.
23. IRC section 513(c).
24. See Section 24.13, this chapter.
25. IRC section 512(a)(1).
26. Reg. section 1.513-1(c).
27. See the NCAA advertising sales discussion following under section 24.8(h).
28. S. Rep. 91-552, 91st Cong., 1st Sess. (1969).
29. Rev. Rul. 75-201, 1975-1 C.B. 164.
30. Rev. Rul. 75-200, 1975-1 C.B. 163. See also *Suffolk County Patrolmen's Benevolent Association, Inc. v. Commissioner,* 77 T.C. 1314 (1981), *acq.* 1984-1 C.B. 2. The fact that the solicitors spent 16 weeks organizing the event makes the activity regular in the IRS's eyes.

31. *National College Athletic Association v. Commissioner,* 914 F.2d 1417 (10th Cir. 1990). The IRS strongly disagrees with this opinion; see Priv. Ltr. Ruls. 9044071 and 9721001.

32. Priv. Ltr. Rul. 9304001.

33. Priv. Ltr. Rul. 9417003.

34. Priv. Ltr. Rul. 9302035.

35. *Ohio Farm Bureau Federation, Inc. v. Commissioner,* 106 T.C. 222 (1996).

36. *Museum of Flight Foundation v. U.S.,* 83 AFTR 2d ¶99,474 (DC W. Wash. 1999).

37. IRC section 513(a).

38. Reg. section 1.513-1(d).

39. Reg. section 1.513-1(a).

40. Rev. Rul. 73–128, 1973-1, C.B. 222; Priv. Ltr. Rul. 9152039.

41. Usage by spouses, alumni, and donors was not considered as related in Priv. Ltr. Rul. 9645004.

42. Priv. Ltr. Rul. 9009038.

43. Tech. Adv. Memo. 8932004.

44. Priv. Ltr. Rul. 9017028.

45. Priv. Ltr. Rul. 9210026.

46. Priv. Ltr. Rul. 925037, citing Rev. Ruls. 80–114, 79–359, and 71–580.

47. Priv. Ltr. Rul. 199945062. The library stipulated it would provide its fee schedule allowed for sliding-scale fees for those that could not afford to pay full – a very important factor in proving the services were purveyed in the public interest. Just selling consulting services to business libraries would be considered as unrelated activity.

48. S. Rep. 2375 and H. Rep. 2319, 81st Cong., 2d Sess. 109 (1950).

49. Priv. Ltr. Rul. 7851004.

50. Priv. Ltr. Rul. 7930043.

51. Priv. Ltr. Ruls. 7851005, 7930043, 7948113; Rev. Ruls. 80–295 and 80–296; and Priv. Ltr. Rul. 8643091. See Section 24.8(e) of this chapter for special consideration of corporate sponsorship of such events.

52. See Section 24.4(b), this chapter.

53. Priv. Ltr. Rul. 9147008.

54. Priv. Ltr. Rul. 9645004.

55. IRC section 513(h).

56. IRC section 512(b)(3).

57. Religious, charitable, scientific, testing for public safety, literary, educational, fostering national or international amateur sports competition, and preventing cruelty to children or animals. These purposes are discussed Chapters 3–5, *Tax Planning and Compliance. . .*

58. Defined in Chapter 2, Section 2 (h), *Tax Planning and Compliance. . .*

59. Discussed in Chapter 4, Section 6(d), *Tax Planning and Compliance. . .*

60. *Council for Bibliographic & Information Technology,* T.C.M. 1992-364 (Tax Ct. 1992). See also Tech. Adv. Memo. 9032005, in which a section 501(c)(6) tourist and convention bureau provided related services to businesses planning conventions but received taxable commissions from hotel referrals.

61. Priv. Ltr. Rul. 9137002.

62. Priv. Ltr. Rul. 9232003.

63. Priv. Ltr. Rul. 9822004.
64. See Priv. Ltr. Rul. 9237034.
65. Discussed in *Tax Planning and Compliance. . .* Chapter 2, Section 2(h).
66. Priv. Ltr. Rul. 9849027.
67. Priv. Ltr. Rul. 9847002; see also Priv. Ltr. Ruls. 9811001, 9711002, and 9641011.
68. See Chapter 4, Section 4.6(c), *Tax Planning and Compliance* . . . medical faculty practice groups can qualify as exempt organizations.
69. See Sections 24.4(c) and 24.11, this chapter.
70. See Chapters 7 and 8, *Tax Planning and Compliance. . .*
71. *Ohio Farm Bureau Federation, Inc. v. Commissioner,* 106 T.C. 222 (1996).
72. Under modifications discussed in Section 24.10(d).
73. In Priv. Ltr. Rul. 9705001 a business league earned royalty income from licensing its name without its mailing list or other services.
74. Rev. Rul. 81-178, 1981-2 C.B. 135.
75. Priv. Ltr. Rul. 9029047.
76. See Section 24.9(h), this chapter.
77. *United States v. American Bar Endowment,* 477 U.S. 105 (1986).
78. Priv. Ltr. Rul. 8747066.
79. Priv. Ltr. Rul. 8747066.
80. Priv. Ltr. Rul. 8823109.
81. See additional discussion at Section 24.10(d), this chapter.
82. Discussed in Chapter 5, Section 5.1(i), *Tax Planning and Compliance...*
83. *American College of Physicians v. U.S.,* 457 U.S. 836 (1986); ads complementing the text concerning developments in manufacturing technology were held to similarly produce unrelated income in Priv. Ltr. Rul. 9724006.
84. Reg. section 1.513-1(d)(4)(iv), Example 5.
85. *Fraternal Order of Police, Illinois State Troopers Lodge No. 41 v. Commissioner,* 833 F.2d 717 (7th Cir. 1987), *aff'g* 87 T.C. 747 (1986); Priv. Ltr. Rul. 8640007.
86. *State Police Ass'n of Massachusetts v. Commissioner,* T.C.M. 1996-407 (Sept. 1996), *cert.denied,* 123 F.3d 1 (1st Cir. 1997).
87. Discussed in Section 24.8(h), this chapter.
88. Discussed in Chapter 27, Section 14, *Tax Planning and Compliance. . .*
89. Priv. Ltr. Rul. 9147007.
90. Prop. Reg. section 1.513-4, entitled *Certain Sponsorship Not Unrelated Trade or Business.*
91. IRC section 513(i)(2)(A) added by the Taxpayer Relief Act of 1997.
92. See Private Letter Ruling 9805001.
93. Prop. Reg. section 513-4(c)(1) and (2).
94. The de minimus rule applicable to premiums and benefits of insubstantial benefit that can be ignored for purposes of determingin the deductible portion of a donation set out in Rev. Proc. 90-12 discussed in Chapter 24, Section 3(a), *Tax Planning and Compliance. . .*
95. IRS section 513(h)(2).
96. See new section 24.8(i), this chapter.
97. Committee reports on Public Law 105-34.
98. *Louisiana Credit Union League v. United States,* 693 F.2d 525 (5th Cir. 1982); *Texas Farm Bureau v. United States,* 93–1 U.S.T.C. ¶ 50, 257 (C.D. Tex. 1993), *rev'd,* 95–1 U.S.T.C. ¶ 50,297 (5th Cir. June 1, 1995).

99. Priv. Ltr. Rul. 9316045.

100. Priv. Ltr. Rul. 9208033; see also Priv. Ltr. Ruls. 9337027, 9616039, and 9619069.

101. Priv. Ltr. Rul. 9337027.

102. *National Collegiate Athletic Association v. Commissioner,* 90–2 U.S.T.C. section 50513 (10th Cir. 1990), *rev'g* 92 T.C. No. 27 (1989). See also Priv. Ltr. Rul. 9137002 and 9211004.

103. Priv. Ltr. Rul. 9306030; see also Priv. Ltr. Ruls. 9721001 and 9712001.

104. Tech. Adv. Memo. 8932004; Priv. Ltr. Rul. 9150047.

105. Tech. Adv. Memo. 9023003; similar result in Priv. Ltr. Rul. 9137002 and 7926003; contrary result in Priv. Ltr. Ruls. 9309002 and 9306030.

106. See Chapter 22, Section 22.4, *Tax Planning and Compliance. . .*

107. Speaking at the Georgetown University Law Center's conference on tax-exempt organizations in May 1999, Jay Rotz of the IRS Exempt Organization Division said, "the agency is likely to view an exclusivity agreement under which a college agrees to grant only one beverage company access to its campus as the sale of a valuable right that will likely produce UBI."

108. As discussed in Chapter 2, Section 2.2(j), *Tax Planning and Compliance . . .* A checklist for Web site exemption issues can also be found as new Exhibit 19-4.

109. See Section 27.14(d), *Tax Planning and Compliance. . .*

110. See Section 27.14, *Tax Planning and Compliance. . .*

111. Rev. Rul. 78-144, 1978-1 C.B. 168; the IRS found that a long-term net lease of heavy machinery that required the lessee to provide insurance, pay taxes, make repairs, and secure and process leases was a capital-intensive business not qualifying under section 513(a)(1) as a trade or business in which substantially all the work is performed without compensation.

112. Priv. Ltr. Rul. 9704012.

113. *Greene County Medical Society Foundation v. U.S.,* 345 F. Supp. 900 (W.D. Mo. 1972).

114. *Waco Lodge No. 166, Benevolent & Protective Order of Elks v. Commissioner,* T.C. Memo 1981-546, *aff'd per curiam,* 696 F.2d 372 (5th Cir. 1983).

115. Priv. Ltr. Rul. 9652004.

116. *Shiloh Youth Revival Centers v. Commissioner,* 88 T.C. 579 (1987).

117. *St. Joseph Farms of Indiana Brothers of the Congregation of Holy Cross, Southwest Province, Inc. v. Commissioner,* 85 T.C. 9 (July, 1, 1985).

118. Discussed in Section 24.4(c), this chapter.

119. IRC section 513(a)(2).

120. Priv. Ltr. Rul. 9720002.

121. Rev. Rul. 74–399.

122. Chapter 27, Section 14, *Tax Planning and Compliance. . .*

123. Gen. Coun. Memo. 39825.

124. Final version contained in IRS Announcement 94–112.

125. Reg. section 1.513-5.

126. See section 24.11 and Chapter 27 section 14.(d), *Tax Planning and Compliance…*

127. *Julius M. Israel Lodge of B'nai B'rith No.2113 v. Commissioner,* 78AFTR 2d ¶96-5482 (5th Cir.), *aff'g.* TCM 1995-439; see also *Women of the Motion Picture Industry, et al. v. Commissioner,* T.C. Memo. 1997-518. *South End Italian Club, Inc. v. Commissioner,* 87 T.C. 168 (1986).

128. Rev. Rul. 94-16, 1994-1 C.B. 19.

129. Rev. Rul. 67–284, 1967-2 C.B. 55, 58.

130. Rev. Rul. 81–295, 1981-2 C.B. 15, relying on *Mescalcro Apache Tribe v. Jones,* 411 U.S. 145, 157 (1973).
131. Rev. Proc. 90–12 (Feb. 1990), supplemented by Rev. Proc. 92-58, 1992-2 IRB 10; and updated annually for COLA, latest revision 98-61, 1998-52 IRB 1. See Chapter 24, section 24.3 *(Tax Planning and Compliance)* for more information about the de minimus rules.
132. Rev. Proc. 99-42, IRB 1999-46 (latest revision).
133. *Hope School v. Commissioner,* 612 F. 2d 298 (CA-7, 1980).
134. Priv. Ltr. Rul. 9652004.
135. IRC section 513(h).
136. See Section 24.10(d), this chapter.
137. Priv. Ltr. Rul. 9623035.
138. Prop. Reg. sections 1.509(a)-3, 1.512(b)-1 and 53.4940-1.
139. *Kern County Electrical Pension Fund v. Commissioner,* 96 T.C. No. 41 (June 20, 1991).
140. IRC section 512(b)(5).
141. Rev. Rul. 95-8, 1995-14 I.R.B. 1; see section 21.12.
142. IRC section 613(b).
143. Reg. section 1.613-2; Priv. Ltr. Rul. 9252028 discusses a private foundation's sale of timber and concludes that the timber sale produces capital gain income not subject to the UBIT and further that the arrangement did not represent a "business enterprise" subject to the excess business holdings rules. See Chapter 16, section 16.1 *Tax Planning and Compliance* . . . See also Priv. Ltr. Rul. 9608002, in which a fishing club's sale of timber was classified as the sale of exempt function property not taxable, except for failure on the club's part to reinvest the sales proceeds in another exempt activity within the four-year period.
144. IRC section 512(a)(3)(D). Priv. Ltr. Rul. 9307004 says it is insufficient that the club bought the land with the intention of using it for club activities. Actual use is required.
145. Priv. Ltr. Rul. 9535051.
146. *Juniper Hunting Club v. Commissioner,* 28 B.T.A. 525 (1933).
147. *Framingham Country Club v. United States,* 659 F. Supp. 650 (D.C. Mass. 1987); IRS Priv. Ltr. Rul. 9307003.
148. *Atlanta Athletic Club v. Commissioner,* 93-1 U.S.T.C. ¶50,051 (10th Cir.), *rev'g* T.C.M. 1991-83, 61 T.C.M. 2011, Dec. 47,195(M).
149. Tech. Adv. Memo. 9225001. See also Priv. Ltr. Rul. 9630001, in which adjacent land was also found not to qualify as exempt function property.
150. While agreeing there was some educational benefit from the site, a museum renting its exhibition halls for private receptions provided substantial services to its tenants that caused the usage fees to be unrelated income in Priv. Ltr. Rul. 9702003.
151. *Trust U/W Emily Oblinger v. Commissioner,* 100 T.C. No. 9 (Feb. 23, 1993); *Harlan E. Moore Charitable Trust v. U.S.,* 812 F. Supp. 130 (C.D. 111. 1993) *aff'd,* 93-2 USTC ¶50,601 (7th Cir.). Similarly, see *Independent Order of Odd Fellows v. U.S.,* No. 4-90-CV-60552 (S.D. Iowa 1993); and *White's Iowa Manual Labor Institute v. Commissioner,* T.C. Memo. 1993-364.
152. IRC section 512(b)(3)(A)(ii).
153. Priv. Ltr. Rul. 9301024.
154. Reg. section 1.512(b)-1(c)(5).
155. Priv. Ltr. Rul. 9401031; also see the convenience exception discussed supra in Section 24.9(c), this chapter.

156. Tech. Adv. Memo. 9853001.

157. Reg. section 1.512(b)-1(c)(5).

158. Priv. Ltr. Rul. 9702003.

159. IRC section 512(b)(2).

160. Reg. section 1.512(b)-1(b).

161. Gen. Coun. Memo. 39827; Priv. Ltr. Rul. 9029047.

162. *Sierra Club, Inc. v. Commissioner,* TCM 47751(M) Dec. 49025 (M) (1993). In 1994, the Tax Court (*Sierra Club, Inc. v. Commissioner,* 103 T.C. No. 17) again ruled in favor of the Sierra Club. The sole issue in question was whether the club was in the business of selling financial services that could produce unrelated business income. The court found no intention on the part of the club to form a joint venture to share in a "mutual proprietary interest in net profits," nor did it bear any risk or loss or expense. The fact that the club was required to solicit members and keep records of their names and addresses did not, in the court's eyes, indicate that the club had control over the financial institution's actions for such actions to be imputed to the club. The Tax Court decision in this case, referred to as *Sierra II; also see Alumni Ass'n of Univ. of Or. Inc. v. Commissioner,* T.C. Memo 1996-63; *Oregon State Univ. Alumni Ass'n Inc. v. Commissioner,* T.C. Memo 1996-34.

163. *Sierra Club v. Commissioner,* 96-2 U.S.T.C. ¶ 503r6 (9th Cir. 1996). Another pair of cases are also on appeal to the 9th Circuit, *Alumni Ass'n of Univ. of Oregon v. Commissioner,* T.C. Memo 1996-63 and *Oregon State University Alumni Ass'n Inc. v. Commissioner,* T.C. Memo 1996-34. The IRS decided not to appeal another defeat in the *Mississippi State Alumni v. Commissioner* (T.C. Memo. 1997-37) case.

164. See Section 24.8(h), this chapter.

165. *Sierra Club, Inc. v. Commissioner,* T.C. Memo. 1999-86 citing Rev. Rul. 81–178, 1981-2 C.B. 135-37.

166. The facts of the *Texas Farm Bureau v. U.S.,* 53 F.3d 120 (5th Cir. 1995) case provides a good example of how they lost the battle; see also *Common Cause v. Commissioner,* 112 T.C. No. 23 (June 1999) and *Planned Parenthood Federation of America Inc. v. Commissioner,* T.C. Memo. 1999-206 (June 1999).

167. Using allocation formulas discussed in Section 24.15(a), this chapter.

168. Discussed in Section 21.10(d), *Tax Planning and Compliance…*

169. According to IRS representative Charles P. Barrett, Senior Conferee-reviewer in the TE/GE Division, speaking at the Georgetown University Law Center's Tax-Exempt Organization conference on May 5, 2000.

170. Field Service Advice 199938041, in which the organization proposed to report back to the IRS annually about its compliance with the plan. Transfer of the entire contract with an agreement that a royalty would be paid to the parent exempt organization would not escape tax due to the rules of IRC section 512(b)(13) discussed in Section 24.10(e), this chapter.

171. *Disabled American Veterans v. Commissioner, rev'g* 91-2 U.S.T.C. section 50.336 (6th Cir. 1991), 94 T.C. 60 (1990).

172. See the fiscal 1999 CPE Text for Exempt Organizations, Chapter B, entitled *Intellectual Property* by Roderick Darling and Marvin Friedlander.

173. Tech. Adv. Memo. 9211004.

174. Discussed in Section 24.9(h), this chapter.

175. According to Celia Roady in "Nonprofits Push Fair Market Value Exception," published in *The Exempt Organization Tax Review,* June 1999, Vol. 24, No. 3, p. 475.

176. IRC section 512(b)(13) as amended by Taxpayer Relief Act of 1997.
177. Priv. Ltr. Rul. 9338003.
178. The February 1999 issue of *The Exempt Organization Tax Review,* p. 259, has a comprehensive article by Mitchell L. Stump, a CPA focused on social clubs, entitled "Final 337 Regulations Bad News for Clubs Wanting to Be 501(c)(7)s."
179. IRC section 512(b)(7).
180. IRC section 512(b)(8).
181. IRC section 512(b)(9).
182. See Chapter 5, Sections 5.3 and 5.4, *Tax Planning and Compliance. . .*
183. IRC section 513(c)(1).
184. Discussed in Sections 24.9 and 24.10. *Service Bolt Nut Co. Profit Sharing Trust v. Commissioner,*724 F.2d 519 (6th Cir. 1983), *aff'g* 78 T.C. 812 (1982).
185. IRC section 513(c)(2), revised effective January 1, 1994.
186. IRC section 469(k)(2).
187. The Small Business Job Protection Act of 1996, section 1316.
188. IRC section 512(e).
189. See note 188.
190. See Section 24.3, this chapter.
191. See Chapter 27, Section 27.14, *Tax Planning and Compliance. . .*
192. Reg. section 1.512(a)-1(a).
193. See Chapter 27, Section 27.14, *Tax Planning and Compliance. . .*
194. See *Tax Planning and Compliance. . .* Chapter 27, Section 14 (b) for a discussion of this tax-saving opportunity.
195. *Iowa State University of Science and Technology v. U.S.,* 500 F.2d 508 (Ct. Cl. 1974); *Commissioner v. Groetzinger,* 480 U.S. 23 (1987); Reg. section 1.513-1(4)(d)(iii).
196. See Section 24.4(f) and Section 24.13(a), this chapter.
197. For discussion, see Chapter 27.14(d), *Tax Planning and Compliance. . .*
198. *Portland Golf Club v. Commissioner,* 90-1 U.S.T.C. section 50,332; *Iowa State University of Science and Technology v. United States,* 500 F.2d (Ct.Cl. 1974); *Groetzinger, supra* n.6. 110 S.Ct. 2780 (1990).
199. Tech. Adv. Memo. 9720002.
200. IRC section 514.
201. Reg. section 1.514(b)-1.
202. Reg. section 1.514(b)-1(b)(2)(ii).
203. IRC section 514(b)(1)(B) & (C)
204. IRC section 514(b)(3)(A)–(E)
205. Reg. section 1.514(b)-(1)(c)(1); Rev. Rul. 69–464, 1969-2 C.B. 132; Tech. Adv. Memo. 8906003.
206. Rev. Rul. 77–74, 1977-1 C.B. 156; Tech. Adv. Memo. 9017003.
207. Section 514(c)(4); *Elliot Knitwear Profit Sharing Plan v. Commissioner,* 71 T.C. 765 (1979), *aff'd* 614 F.2d 347 (3d Cir. 1980).
208. *Southwest Texas Electric Cooperative, Inc. v. Commissioner,* 68 T.C.M. Dec. 50,008(M), T.C. Memo. 1994-363.
209. Reg. section 1.514(b)-1(a).
210. Reg. section 1.514(a)-1(a)(1)(v).
211. IRC sections 168(h)(6), 514(c)(9), and 704(b)(2); Reg. section 1.514(c)-2. The disproportionate allocation rules are discussed in *Structuring Real Estate Investment Partnerships, With Tax-Exempt Investors.* Williams B. Holloway, Jr. in *Exempt Organization Tax Review,* July 2000, Vol. 29. No 1.

212. IRC section 514(c).

213. Reg. section 1.514(b)-1(b)(ii), section 1.512(b)-1(b)(iii) Example 2; Priv. Ltr. Ruls. 8030105 and 8145087.

214. Reg. section 1.514(c)-1(b).

215. Reg. section 1.514(b)-1(c)(3).

216. IRS Tech. Adv. Memo. 9651001.

217. IRC section 514(a)(1).

218. Discussed in Section 24.4(c), this chapter.

219. Discussed in Chapter 27, Section 27.14, *Tax Planning and Compliance. . .*

220. Rev. Rul. 73-104, 1973-1 C.B. 263.

221. Rev. Rul. 73-105, 1973-1 C.B. 265.

222. Priv. Ltr. Ruls. 8303013, 8326003, 8236008, and 8328009; See also Tech. Adv. Memo 9550003, in which the IRS reviewed its rulings and provided an extensive listing of eight categories of items that it considered related to a "living museum's" and six groups of unrelated objects. Importantly, the IRS found off-site sales activity is not, solely for that reason, treated as an unrelated activity, if the museum can show that such sales enhance a broader public appreciation of the art works and encourages visits to the museum facilities.

223. Priv. Ltr. Rul. 9720002.

224. Priv. Ltr. Rul. 8032028.

225. *Goldsboro Art League, Inc. v. Commissioner,* 75 T.C. 337 (1980).

226. Remarks of Marc Owens, Director of IRS Exempt Organization Division, Non-Profits in Travel Conference, on March 9, 1995.

227. Also according to Barrett, supra, note 50.

228. Rev. Rul. 70-534, 1970-2 C.B. 113.

229. Rev. Rul. 77-366, 1977-2 C.B. 192.

230. Tech. Adv. Mem. 9027003.

231. Rev. Rul. 73-424, 1973-2 C.B. 190; IRS Tech. Adv. Memo. 9222001; also see Sections 24.8(d) and 24.8(h), this chapter.

232. Reg. section 1.512(a)-1(f)(6); Rev. Rul. 81-1-1, 1981-1 C.B. 352.

233. Discussed in Chapter 27, Section 14, *Tax Planning and Compliance. . .*

234. Reg. section 1.512(a)-(f)(3)(iii).

235. Tech. Adv. Memo. 9204007; also see Tech. Adv. Memo. 9734002.

236. *North Carolina Citizens for Business and Industry v. U.S.,* 89-2 U.S.T.C. section 9507 (Cl.Ct. 1989).

237. *Scripture Press Foundation v. U.S.,* 285 F.2d 800 (Ct.Cl. 1961), *cert. denied,* 368 U.S. 985 (1982).

238. *American Institute for Economic Research v. U.S.,* 302 F.2d 934 (Ct. Cl. 1962).

239. *Presbyterian and Reformed Publishing Co. v. Commissioner,* 70 T.C. 1070, 1087, 1083 (1982).

240. Priv. Ltr. Rul. 9636001.

241. Priv. Ltr. Rul. 9402005.

25 ▼ Ethics and Values in the Nonprofit Organization

MILENA M. MENEGHETTI, CHRP
M4i Strategic Consulting, Inc.
KEITH SEEL, MA, PRINCIPAL
M4i Strategic Management Consulting, Inc.

The ethical domain for managers focuses on the seam between morality and individual or institutional self interest.[1]

25.1   Why Ethics and Values Are Important

The life of today's nonprofit organization (NPO) managers is increasingly complex. Fulfilling client needs has always been paramount, but now issues like managing diversity, affirmative action, and team-based management change the landscape on which this gets done.

    If you look at management and leadership books today, you will see that values and principle-based management approaches are being promoted as effective ways of dealing with this complexity.[2–3] For example, Senge in *The Fifth Discipline Fieldbook* cites shared organizational values as key to effective total quality management programs,[4] and Covey[5] advocates approaches that are principle centered. These beliefs about effective management stand in stark contrast to decades of "scientific" management theories that are grounded in behaviorism.

There has been a new focus on ethics in management that extends beyond the simplistic legalistic view of ethics. Toffler writes:

Ethical concerns in business are more pervasive and complex than is generally recognized. In fact, ethical concerns are part of the routine practices of management; they are characterized less frequently by legal issues than by concerns about relationships and responsibility.[6]

Managers seem to understand the centrality of values and ethics in their work. The Internet's *Online Journal of Ethics* had 12,965 visitors in just over one year; this is equivalent to 150 visits per week.

How does the NPO manager translate these concepts into action? Max De Pree, the well-known CEO of Herman Miller Corporation, wrote, "I don't believe . . . that ethics is a list of prohibitions. Nor is ethics a list of things we can get away with. I believe that ethical people know what is right and do what is right. The challenge for leaders . . . is how and where to apply our beliefs to the daily stream of interactions with other people."[7]

Mason reflected that, "Ethical lapses in the nonprofit world are like divorces between marriage counselors and bankruptcy by investment advisors. They are incongruous, out of character with the noble spirit of our sector."[8] In calling for managers to build on the "highest and best aspirations," Mason gives a number reasons why ethical behavior should be a priority for those leaders and managers in the nonprofit sector. Some of those reasons are discussed as follows.

1. First, the nonprofit sector has a relatively short history as a sector. While nonprofit organizations such as churches have centuries-long histories providing services to those in need, the collection of organizations that provide charitable services throughout Canada and the United States is new. Evidence for the newness of the sector comes from the number of ways in which it is identified. For economists, lawyers, and accountants, the sector is known as the *nonprofit sector.* For this group, *nonprofit* describes a charitable form of governance with specific fiduciary and regulatory responsibilities and requirements. The term *voluntary sector* is used more commonly by sociologists who see one of the defining characteristics of the sector to be that participation is noncoercive, with volunteer involvement central to accomplishing its purposes. The "third sector" or "independent sector" is used by political scientists to define the group of organizations that operate independently of the business/private sector and the public/government sector. Depending on the definition of the sector, different values, responsibilities, laws, and duties seem to apply. The lack of clarity of what the "nonprofit sector" is has meant that ethical issues held in common by NPOs have been largely undefined.
2. Second, regardless of what the sector is called, it is undeniably made up of diverse organizations. Many of these organizations "enunciate, transmit, and defend ethical values."[9] Different in this regard from the private or public sectors, the nonprofit sector has a duty to do "good" and furthermore, to define what *good* means for our society.
3. Third, because NPOs are part of what Mason calls the "culture of idealism," ethics are an inherent part of the nonprofit sector.[10] Many of the organizations

that make up the nonprofit sector were established on moral and idealistic grounds. The Independent Sector takes the position that "the public expects the highest values and ethics to be practiced habitually in the institutions of the charitable, nonprofit sector. Because these institutions, fundamentally, are dedicated to enhancing basic human values, expectations of them are particularly high. Those who assume the public good assume a public trust."[11] The nonprofit sector has developed its character around founding ideals and values directed at a public good. Payton underscored this point when he wrote, "It is within the philanthropic tradition that the moral agenda of society is put forward."[12]

4. The fourth reason why managers in NPOs should support ethical practice is the foundation of trust that nonprofits have established with the general public. Linked to the foundation of trust is the NPO's accountability to the public that supports it. Voluntary participation and financial support of NPOs depends on the public perception that the organization (and perhaps, indeed, the nonprofit sector) is both trustworthy and accountable. Lawry writes that "a perfectly ethical ideal of accountability implies a willingness to endure public scrutiny, even an invitation for the public to scrutinize the behaviors of the organization's leadership."[13] A concern, according to Milosfsky and Blades is that "[t]he largest charities are beyond accountability."[14]

5. Finally, the ambiguous nature of the nonprofit sector necessitates that a principled approach of addressing issues that exist within the sector be adopted. The rationale for a principled approach is that one of the strengths of the nonprofit sector is its diversity and that diversity must be respected by those within the sector. Within the nonprofit sector are those organizations that have "profoundly different ideas as to what constitutes right and wrong."[15] Part of the rich diversity of the nonprofit sector is that it is made up of "the most uncompromising idealists and advocates of the most extreme positions of their subcultures."[16] This diversity may seem to be similar to the business sector or the public sector, but there is a fundamental difference. Competitors within either the business or public sector can agree on the outcome of their actions—generally speaking, profits for the business sector, and votes for the public sector. No such common agreement about outcome exists in the nonprofit sector—one group's "good" can be another group's "evil." To hold public confidence and support, the nonprofit sector needs to formulate and communicate broad principles. The often competing values within the nonprofit sector make it vitally important that leaders take a principled approach toward working on sector issues. Broad value statements from the sector would go a long way toward creating a perception of sector unity in the public eye.

The issues regarding ethics and ethical behavior in the nonprofit sector are complex and wide ranging. This chapter will begin by discussing the unique nature of values and ethics in NPOs. It will then move to more specific areas of managerial concern, including professional codes of ethics; ethics and the management of human resources (including volunteer resources); and ethics as a basis for policy and partnerships. The chapter will conclude by introducing an ethical decision-making model that will assist the NPO leader in resolving even the most complex ethical issues.

25.2 Ethics in the Nonprofit Organization

As was presented in the introduction, there are several areas in which NPOs differ significantly from their business or government counterparts. O'Neill identifies seven responsibilities unique to NPO managers:

1. Developing, shaping, and articulating values of the members of the organization and the values of the larger society
2. Motivating and managing human resources (voluntary and paid) without using economic incentives
3. Managing organizations frequently made up of professional workers
4. Managing organizations providing services that clients cannot effectively test or monitor
5. Managing organizations in which there is no clear financial or political bottom line
6. Acquiring financial support from widely different sources, such as fees for service, contracts, grants, donations, bequests, and individual gifts
7. Interacting extensively with a board of directors[17]

The relationship between responsibilities and rights of stakeholders, such as clients, staff, board, and management, can be understood only when the values of the organization and of the individuals associated with the organization are discussed and considered. Such discussion and reflection can result in an alignment of values supportive of a common purpose, such as the mission of the organization.

Principles and values are integral to an organization and the individuals tasked with carrying out its mission. As Covey suggests, there are four general areas in which values and principles become evident:

1. Personal—the relationship that one has with one's self in terms of character and competence
2. Interpersonal—the relationships that one has with those around one, including peers, volunteers, managers, clients, and the community
3. Managerial—one's responsibility to accomplish certain tasks toward furthering the mission of the organization
4. Organizational—one's need to organize systems and people, to develop and carry out strategy, and to solve problems[18]

Values and principles are formed, transmitted, and interpreted at and between each of these four areas in a dynamic manner. See Exhibit 25.1. Values are central to how an organization and individuals conduct their business, regardless of which of the four areas one may focus on. Understanding how these areas interrelate becomes fundamental to principled management—another reason why addressing the issue of values should be an ongoing activity for an organization.

25.3 Managing Values and Ethics

"Recently an opportunity was given in the elections for the people to declare their will. They did not declare that will as we know it to be their will." This statement from the late Irish

Prime Minister Eamon De Valera exemplifies the primary issues facing managers of NPOs—who are the people, and what is their will?[19] Values and ethics come from a number of different sources. Exhibit 25.1 suggests a number of pathways for the transmission and interpretation of values. What cannot be shown are the origins of the values that then flow through an organization. Also not shown but implied is the fact that the organization itself is situated in a society that either does or does not sanction the mandates of the organization.

To restate, an organization is made up of values that come from a number of different sources, including:

- Personal—values that each individual learns from birth by exposure to family, friends, school, church, etc.
- Professional—values that professional associations require their members to adopt and live by (for example, code of ethics for fund-raising executives, social workers, and volunteer managers)
- Organizational—values that an organization is formed around, such as caring for the sick, educating children, human dignity, etc.
- Social—values that a community seeks to instate for its citizens (for example, human rights, accessible health care, welfare, etc.)
- Cultural—values that are represented within a culture, such as, in the Western World, the importance of science and monotheism, or as in the Eastern World, the importance of wisdom and pantheism

While full exploration of each of these concepts is outside the scope of this chapter, it is important for managers in nonprofit agencies to recognize that there is no single source or set of values. From a management perspective, values originate, are transmitted, and are interpreted in a number of ways.

O'Neill notes that in general, NPO managers "feel morally bound to exercise justice, honesty, and fairness in their dealings with other people in the organization."[20] He

EXHIBIT 25.1 Values and Relationships Exist and Are Interrelated

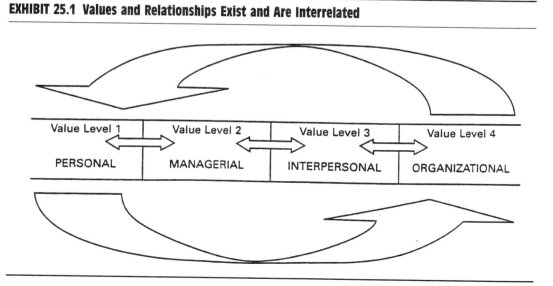

| Value Level 1 | Value Level 2 | Value Level 3 | Value Level 4 |
| PERSONAL | MANAGERIAL | INTERPERSONAL | ORGANIZATIONAL |

continues to explain that while there is nothing particularly unique about these values to managers in nonprofit settings, their general responsibility may take on unique aspects because "of differences in the personnel characteristics of nonprofit organizations." O'Neill puts forward the following example:

> *For instance, in an organization whose work consists primarily of professional services given by the front-line workers (for example, mental health care agencies, hospitals, universities, research organizations), a highly dictatorial management style with frequent overruling of decisions made by the front-line workers could be not only unwise but unethical, since it could easily result in damaging the quality of the organization's professional services and harming the organization's clients.[21]*

Clearly, the makeup of the NPO's human resource base is a matter of not just general management concern, but also of concern from an ethical perspective. Professional values play an especially important role in organizations because these values directly impact job performance, service delivery, and relationships with staff, volunteers, and the board of directors. NPOs often have professionals from several fields working to deliver services to the community. For example, an NPO may have the following professions represented in the volunteer or staff complement:

- Social workers
- Managers of volunteers
- Nurses
- Fund-raising executives
- Human resources professionals
- Lawyers
- Accountants
- Marketers

In each case, the values and ethics of their particular profession will guide the behavior of professional staff and volunteers. How services are delivered, money is raised, volunteers are managed, and care is provided are all guided by the codes of ethics of professional associations much more than by any existing organizational values or codes. For managers, care should be taken to be aware of and to understand the professional obligations of staff whose profession has a code of ethics, standards of practice, or other similar guidelines. Before organizational values, policies, and procedures are developed, every reasonable effort should be made to involve professional staff, if not all staff, in the process.

(A) PROFESSIONAL CODES OF ETHICS

One way for managers to understand the professional responsibilities of front-line workers in NPOs is to become familiar with some of the guiding ethical principles of professions working within the organization. There are many excellent examples of professional codes of ethics, often available from the professional workers themselves. Frequently associated with a profession's code are supporting statements such as ethical principles and standards of practice. These supporting documents should be of additional interest to managers. Following are a few examples of codes of ethics, values, and standards of practice that should assist managers in developing a preliminary awareness of professional ethics influencing service delivery in their organization.

(i) Fund Raising

Fund raising is an activity that most nonprofit organizations engage in. It is an activity that is also under significant public and governmental scrutiny. Exhibit 25.2 is the Association of Fundraising Professionals Code designed to guide the practice of professionals engaged in this key role throughout North America.

EXHIBIT 25.2 Association of Fundraising Professionals Code of Ethical Principles and Standard of Professional Practice

---

Statement of Ethical Principles
Adopted November 1991

The Association of Fundraising Professionals exists to foster the development and growth of fund-raising professionals and the profession, to preserve and enhance philanthropy and volunteerism, and to promote high ethical standards in the fund-raising profession.

To these ends, this code declares the ethical values and standards of professional practice which AFP members embrace and which they strive to uphold in their responsibilities for generating philanthropic support.

Members of the Association of Fundraising Professionals are motivated by an inner drive to improve the quality of life through the causes they serve. They seek to inspire others through their own sense of dedication and high purpose. They are committed to the improvement of their professional knowledge and skills in order that their performance will better serve others. They recognize their stewardship responsibility to ensure that needed resources are vigorously and ethically sought and that the intent of the donor is honestly fulfilled. Such individuals practice their profession with integrity, honesty, truthfulness and adherence to the absolute obligation to safeguard the public trust.

Furthermore, AFP members

- Serve the ideal of philanthropy, are committed to the preservation and enhancement of volunteerism, and hold stewardship of these concepts as the overriding principle of professional life;
- Put charitable mission above personal gain, accepting compensation by salary or set fee only;
- Foster cultural diversity and pluralistic values and treat all people with dignity and respect;
- Affirm, through personal giving, a commitment to philanthropy and its role in society;
- Adhere to the spirit as well as the letter of all applicable laws and regulations;
- Bring credit to the fund-raising profession by their public demeanor;
- Recognize their individual boundaries of competence and are forthcoming about their professional qualifications and credentials;
- Value the privacy, freedom of choice, and interests of all those affected by their actions;
- Disclose all relationships which might constitute, or appear to constitute, conflicts of interest;

EXHIBIT 25.2 *(Continued)*

- Actively encourage all their colleagues to embrace and practice these ethical principles;
- Adhere to the following standards of professional practice in their responsibilities for generating philanthropic support.

Standards of Professional Practice

Adopted and incorporated into the AFP Code of Ethical Principles, November 1992

1. Members shall act according to the highest standards and visions of their institution, profession, and conscience.
2. Members shall avoid even the appearance of any criminal offense or professional misconduct.
3. Members shall be responsible for advocating, within their own organizations, adherence to all applicable laws and regulations.
4. Members shall work for a salary or fee, not percentage-based compensation or a commission.
5. Members may accept performance-based compensation such as bonuses provided that such bonuses are in accord with prevailing practices within the members' own organizations and are not based on a percentage of philanthropic funds raised.
6. Members shall neither seek nor accept finder's fees and shall, to the best of their ability, discourage their organizations from paying such fees.
7. Members shall effectively disclose all conflicts of interest; such disclosure does not preclude or imply ethical impropriety.
8. Members shall accurately state their professional experience, qualifications, and expertise.
9. Members shall adhere to the principle that all donor and prospect information created by, or on behalf of, an institution is the property of that institution and shall not be transferred or utilized except on behalf of that institution.
10. Members shall, on a scheduled basis, give donors the opportunity to have their names removed from lists which are sold to, rented to, or exchanged with other organizations.
11. Members shall not disclose privileged information to unauthorized parties.
12. Members shall keep constituent information confidential.
13. Members shall take care to ensure that all solicitation materials are accurate and correctly reflect the organization's mission and use of solicited funds.
14. Members shall, to the best of their ability, ensure that contributions are used in accordance with donors' intentions.
15. Members shall ensure, to the best of their ability, proper stewardship of charitable contributions, including timely reporting on the use and management of funds and explicit consent by the donor before altering the conditions of a gift.
16. Members shall ensure, to the best of their ability, that donors receive informed and ethical advice about the value and tax implications of potential gifts.
17. Member's actions shall reflect the concern for the interests and well-being of individuals affected by those actions. Members shall not exploit any relationship with a donor, prospect, volunteer, or employee to the benefit of the member or the member's organization.
18. In stating fund-raising results, members shall use accurate and consistent accounting methods that conform to the appropriate guidelines adopted by the American Institute of Certified Public Accountants (AICPA)* for the type of institution involved. (*In countries outside of the United States, comparable authority should be utilized.)

EXHIBIT 25.2 *(Continued)*

---

19. All of the above notwithstanding, members shall comply with all applicable local, state, provincial, and federal civil and criminal law.

Amended: March, 1993; October, 1994

Source: Association of Fundraising Professionals (1991, 1993, 1994). *AFP Code of Ethical Principles and Standards of Professional Practice.* Reprinted with permission.

Money and ethics have always been tied closely together, especially in the charitable sector. Financial accountability as it relates to fund-raising practices increases the public's interest in having opportunities to scrutinize how responsibly NPOs solicit, retain, and expend their monetary resources. The AFP's Code of Ethical Principles and Standards of Professional Practice serve professionals in this field by guiding professional practice. Managers unfamiliar with these principles and standards may unknowingly place professional fund raisers in difficult or compromising positions that cannot be supported by the professionals themselves.

(ii) *Managers of Volunteers*

The Association for Volunteer Administration (AVA) is an international professional association for managers of volunteers and volunteer programs around the world. In 1995, the AVA Board of Directors took the revolutionary step of moving away from a traditional code of ethics. Instead, the AVA developed its Statement of Professional Ethics in Volunteer Administration. What is unique about the Statement is that it is what the author describes as an ethical decision-making tool for AVA members.[22] While an example of one section of the Statement appears later in this chapter, Exhibit 25.3 lists the Statement's core ethical values and ethical principles. These core ethical values are based on the groundbreaking work of the Josephson Institute of Ethics.[23]

The AVA Statement of Professional Ethics serves the Association's membership by providing ethical values and principles to guide work and interaction with volunteers. Like the NSFRE Code, the AVA Statement addresses the relationship of professionals to the organization, to the broader public, to others in the organization, and to their peers in the field. The number and complexity of relationships and roles in which a professional practitioner works in the nonprofit sector is one reason why statements or codes are such important documents. And these documents are important not just for the professional practitioner him- or herself, but also for those managing these professionals within the organization.

As experience with the ethical foundations of different professional practitioners working in their organization grows, managers may find that discussions of professional values are more functional when conducted in day-to-day situations. Many professions organize their codes or statements of ethics around core values as detailed in the previous examples. Two examples of associations that declare their core values are The Canadian Nurses Association and the Manitoba Association for Volunteer Administration, as shown in Exhibit 25.4.

To a manager looking at the core values of the two professions (nursing and volunteer administration) in Exhibit 25.4, several management issues should become apparent. For example:

EXHIBIT 25.3 The Core Ethical Values and Principles of the AVA

Core Ethical Value	Ethical Principle
CITIZENSHIP & PHILANTHROPY	
1. Philanthropy	• **Philosophy of Volunteerism:** The Volunteer Administrator accepts the responsibility for the development of a personal, coherent philosophy of volunteerism as a foundation for working with others in developing volunteer programs.
2. Citizenship	• **Social Responsibility:** The Volunteer Administrator accepts responsibility to help create a social climate through which human needs can be met and human values enhanced.
RESPECT	
1. Autonomy	• **Self-Determination:** The Volunteer Administrator accepts the responsibility to promote the involvement of persons in decisions that directly affect them. • **Mutuality:** The Volunteer Administrator accepts the responsibility to promote understanding and the actualization of mutual benefits inherent in any act of volunteer service.
2. Courtesy, Civility, Decency	• **Human Dignity:** The Volunteer Administrator accepts the responsibility for development of volunteer programs and initiatives that respect and enhance the human dignity of all persons related to it. • **Privacy:** The Volunteer Administrator accepts the responsibility to respect the privacy of individuals and safeguard information received as confidential.
3. Understanding and Acceptance	• **Accessibility:** The Volunteer Administrator will work to understand and treat with respect individuals from a diversity of backgrounds.
RESPONSIBILITY	
1. Accountability	• **Staff Relationships:** The Volunteer Administrator accepts the responsibility to develop a volunteer program that will enhance and extend the work of the organization's staff.
2. Pursuit of Excellence	• **Professional Responsibility:** The Volunteer Administrator accepts responsibility to contribute to the credibility of the profession in the eyes of those it serves. • **Diligence:** The Volunteer Administrator accepts responsibility to be reliable, careful, prepared, and well informed. • **Doing One's Best:** The Volunteer Administrator accepts responsibility to pursue excellence even when resources are limited. • **Perseverance:** The Volunteer Administrator will seek to overcome obstacles to excellence.

EXHIBIT 25.3 *(Continued)*

Core Ethical Value	Ethical Principle
RESPONSIBILITY	
	• **Continuous Improvement:** The Volunteer Administrator commits to improving their knowledge, skills, and judgments.
3. Self-Restraint	• **Self-Disclosure and Self-Restraint:** The Volunteer Administrator commits to reflective decision making with the intent of advancing the long term greater good.
CARING	
1. Compassion and Generosity	• **Compassion and Generosity:** The Volunteer Administrator assumes the responsibility to be kind, compassionate, and generous in all actions so as to minimize the harm done to others in the performance of one's duties.
JUSTICE AND FAIRNESS	
1. Procedural Fairness	• **Procedural Fairness:** The Volunteer Administrator assumes the responsibility for an open and impartial process for collecting and evaluating information critical for making decisions.
2. Impartiality	• **Impartiality:** The Volunteer Administrator assumes the responsibility for having impartial and objective standards that avoid discriminatory or prejudicial behaviors.
3. Equity	• The Volunteer Administrator assumes the responsibility to treat all individuals with whom s/he will work equitably.
TRUSTWORTHINESS	
1. Honesty	• **Truthfulness:** The Volunteer Administrator is committed to the truth and assuring that all interactions with volunteers and other paid staff are founded on the premise of open and honest interaction. • **Sincerity/Nondeception:** The Volunteer Administrator treats all volunteers with sincerity and never operates in a deceptive manner, and will continually promote that principle throughout the organization. • **Candor:** The Volunteer Administrator is committed to fairness and forthrightness.
2. Integrity	• **Principles:** The Volunteer Administrator understands and works to promote the core ethical values. • **Moral Courage:** The Volunteer Administrator will base his/her actions on core ethical values and will not compromise those values for convenience.

EXHIBIT 25.3 *(Continued)*

Core Ethical Value	Ethical Principle
TRUSTWORTHINESS	
3. Promise-Keeping	• **Fair Interpretation of Contracts:** The Volunteer Administrator accepts the responsibility to assure that all mutual contracts or agreements are clearly understood and agreed upon. • **Reasonability of Commitments:** The Volunteer Administrator accepts the responsibility to be reasonable and realistic and professional in determining the appropriateness of expectations or requests. • **Clarity of Commitments:** The Volunteer Administrator accepts the responsibility to assure clear communication regarding commitments made on behalf of the organization, staff, or volunteers.
4. Loyalty	• **Limitations to Loyalty:** The Volunteer Administrator understands the limits of his/her loyalty to his/her volunteers, clients, and organization. • **Prioritizing Loyalties:** The Volunteer Administrator recognizes that they have loyalties to the organization, its staff, volunteers, and to personal relationships and understands how to prioritize those loyalties. • **Safeguarding Confidential Information:** The Volunteer Administrator understands the importance of confidentiality and works to protect confidential information.
5. Avoiding Conflicts of Interest	• Volunteers serving on my Board of Directors clearly understand and have declared possible conflicts of interest. • I am aware of my fiduciary responsibilities to the organization and proactively avoid possible conflicts of interest. • I have a policy or procedure for dealing with gifts (monetary or material) that may be given to me, my volunteers, and fellow staff.

Source: The Association for Volunteer Administration, Statement of Professional Ethics in Volunteer Administration, 2nd ed., 1996. Reprinted with permission.

- What are the similarities and differences in the core values?
- Are there any potential ethical conflicts between the professions?
- How do the core values of these professions fit with the organization's value statements?
- Are there any organizational policies that affect these professions, their values, ethics, and standards of practice?

Developing a functional level of familiarity with the ethical practices expected of diverse professionals in an organization is a core competency of effective NPO managers. The diversity of professionals working in a typical NPO means that a manager may be

EXHIBIT 25.4 Examples of Core Values

Canadian Nurses Association	Manitoba Association for Volunteer Administration
• Health and well-being	• Philosophy of volunteerism
• Choice	• Human dignity
• Dignity	• Privacy
• Confidentiality	• Self-determination
• Fairness	• Mutuality
• Accountability	• Staff relations
• Practice environments that are conducive to safe, competent, and ethical care	• Social responsibility
	• Professional responsibility

Reprinted with permission, Canadian Nurses Association.

Reprinted with permission, Manitoba Association for Volunteer Administration.

mediating among the values of the organization, individual values, client values, and professional values. Understanding and feeling comfortable with the sources of values, their transmission structures, and the need to reconcile different interests to produce the most ethical decision is not easy. The final section of this chapter provides an approach and ethical decision-making model that has been shown to be effective and practicable.

(B) THE PROBLEM WITH CODES OF ETHICS

Most individuals who consider themselves to be professionals adhere to a set of shared ethical standards. As in the previous examples, these ethical standards are generally prescribed in codes of ethics, which must be followed in order to maintain certification or the ability to practice. Often, the existence of a code of ethics is one distinguishing feature of a profession. This is true in the case of older, well-established fields, like medicine and law, as well as in evolving professions, such as accounting, human resource management, and volunteer management. In addition, some nonprofit organizations have begun to develop and publish a code of ethics that is intended to show the organization's commitment to ethical conduct.

There was probably a time when a prepared code of ethics was all that was needed to navigate ethical waters. This would have been a time when the majority of ethical issues and dilemmas could reasonably be foreseen. With the rapid pace of change continuing into the twenty-first century, this is no longer the case. New complex situations that do not fit into the black-and-white world of a code of ethics seem to arise daily. In a study involving in-depth interviews with managers, it was concluded that "the existence of an ethics code . . . do[es] not necessarily represent an awareness on the company's part of how ethical concerns arise for its employees; nor [is it] an effective commitment by the organization to finding ways that allow employees to act with integrity and to solve ethically complex situations."[24] For the NPO manager who oversees the work of professionals from varying fields, a unifying perspective is required. After all, "ethics is not an ideal system that is noble in theory, but no good in practice."[25]

Max De Pree wrote in his book *Leadership Jazz,* "[W]e frequently find ourselves in situations where skill and technique fail us. At times, professional qualifications simply aren't enough. We need to resort to deeper resources beyond techniques and the jargon of seminars, resources [which are] rooted in our beliefs and values."[26]

Instead of looking to a list of predetermined do's and don'ts, we believe the NPO manager is better advised to develop what the authors call an ethical decision-making competency. This competency allows the manager to analyze any complex ethical dilemma as it occurs, and then to make decisions with integrity, from a sound ethical base. The final section of this chapter describes an ethical decision-making process that all managers are advised to study.

25.4   Ethics in Human Resources Management

Any organization is, at its core, simply a group of people formally organized to work toward a common goal. Because ethics has to do with interpersonal conduct, it becomes highly relevant in the approach we take to managing our human resources. In a very interesting study of ethical issues in management, out of 60 ethical situations identified by managers, two-thirds (66 percent) were related to managing human resources processes and personnel.[27]

(A)   TRENDS

There are several emerging realities that make ethics critical in human resource management:

1. The traditional paternalistic culture and hierarchical structure prevalent in many organizations is falling away, as organizations try to deal with new work realities.[28–30] Organizations are changing the nature of jobs, and employees are being asked to take more and more responsibility for managing their own careers. In this climate, organizations need to reevaluate how they view the employer–employee relationship, and what the respective rights and responsibilities are in this new environment.

2. There has been a decreasing distance between personal and professional spheres. People are no longer willing to be two different people, one at home and another at work. They want to be able to bring their values and sense of what is right and wrong to bear on the decisions they make at work. Most employees today believe that the ethics of the work world should be no different than the ethics in one's personal life.[31–32] Yet, in reality, "[w]hen people arrive at work in the traditional organization, they leave most of themselves at the door; their opinions, critical abilities, values, personal beliefs, many of their talents, often their joy—in essence themselves.[33] This incongruity is being tolerated less and less, as employees rethink their commitment to the organizations for which they work.

3. Values and ethics have emerged as a necessary cornerstone of many employee motivation and retention strategies. Organizations are less and less able and willing to promise "work for life." What keeps employees loyal to the organization has more to do with its mission and with quality-of-life issues ultimately rooted in values.

4. There are an increasing number of people-management issues with inherent ethical ramifications. Examples of these are diversity management,

employment equity, and globalization of the workforce. These require greater ethical awareness and sensitivity.

The aforementioned trends underline the fact that, at the center of the organization, "there must be a guiding philosophy that generates a fundamental set of beliefs or assumptions upon which to operate and to guide decisions."[34] Without this underpinning of values and ethics, managers will have a difficult time doing their jobs effectively.

What follows is a discussion of ethical issues within several key areas in the realm of traditional human resource management. Because it is beyond the scope of this chapter to describe human resource management practices and procedures in detail, please refer to Part II of *The Nonprofit Handbook: Management,* second edition for further information, as required.

(B) EXTERNAL EMPLOYEE RECRUITMENT AND SELECTION

A great deal of attention is being paid to equal employment opportunity (EEO) and affirmative action in North America. EEO legislation in the United States and Federal Employment Equity legislation in Canada are clear examples of governmental attempts to realign decades of unethical hiring practices. During the 1990s, much was written about how ethical these mandated programs are in and of themselves.[35-36] In the long term, the authors believe that true change in employment practices will result when we raise the ethical consciousness and ethical decision-making capability of managers and other individuals in our society. Legislation is, at its best, a short-term fix.

The following are key questions to ask yourself to help ensure that you as an NPO manager are recruiting and selecting people in an ethical way. In general, the answers to the following questions should be "yes." (The ethical values noted in brackets in this section are discussed more fully in the section called "An Ethical Decision-Making Model.")

- Is the job for which you are hiring clearly defined and documented prior to the beginning of the recruitment and selection process? [responsibility]
- Are the qualifications for a given position *bona fide?* In other words, is a credential or experience requirement truly necessary for doing the job effectively? [fairness]
- Are any irrelevant characteristics of an individual (e.g., gender, race) being ignored in the recruitment and selection process? [fairness]
- Do all *qualified* individuals within a reasonable geographic area have the opportunity to be considered for a given job? [fairness]
- Is the application and interview process clear to applicants, providing them with every opportunity to succeed? [respect]
- Are the unsuccessful individuals in a competition provided with helpful feedback regarding their skills, qualifications, and interview performance? [honesty, self-determination, caring]
- Are applicants and unsuccessful candidates being kept informed of their status in any given job competition? [respect, caring]

(C) INTERNAL PROMOTIONS AND TRANSFER

Ethical issues seem to arise even more frequently when positions are being filled internally in larger organizations, through transfers and promotions. The previous questions are still relevant, but in this case dilemmas are even more likely to arise. Here, one must consider what are (or appear to be) the sometimes mutually exclusive interests of the employee and the organization. Everyone knows of the case of the excellent employee who a supervisor thinks he cannot afford to lose from one position by promoting her to another position. Whose interests should take precedence? The authors believe that this is an excellent example of a situation that must be considered in context, using the ethical decision-making process described later in this chapter. This will allow you to take into account the long-term interests of the organization.

The previous questions are relevant to internal recruitment as well. The following are some additional questions to ask yourself when promoting or transferring individuals. In general, the answer to these questions should be "yes."

- Is there a clearly articulated and documented process for handling job vacancies, one that is made available to all employees? Is the issue of confidentiality addressed in this process? (In other words, do employees and supervisors know what the organization's stand is on employees applying to positions with or without their supervisor's knowledge?) [fairness]
- Are the unsuccessful employees in a competition provided with helpful feedback regarding their skills, qualifications, and interview performance? [honesty, self-determination, caring]
- Are supervisors sufficiently equipped to respond to career-related inquiries from their employees? [respect, responsibility]

The key to an ethical recruitment and selection process in any organization is open and honest communication.

(D) COMPENSATION

Fairness and equity are the key ethical considerations in the area of compensation and benefit practices in an NPO. Most employees want to trust that they are being compensated fairly given the type and size of organization in which they are employed. They also want to know that they are being remunerated equitably in accordance with standards that are applied to all employees within the organization. Finally, they hope they are being paid in accordance with the value of their work to the organization and to society.

The following are some starting guidelines for developing an ethical compensation and benefits system.

1. A consistently applied, gender-neutral job evaluation system should be the starting point for ascribing value to jobs. Such a job evaluation system clearly sets out standard performance dimensions against which all jobs in the organization are considered. *Education, technical knowledge,* and *independent judgment required* are examples of performance dimensions. Each performance dimension should be weighted according to the value of the dimension to the organization. The result is a system that provides pay scales or ranges for

individuals based on the contribution their job makes to the organization's mission. [fairness]

2. Consideration should be given to ways in which individuals in the organization can be recognized financially and otherwise for their particular contribution. Too often NPO managers will simply decide to live with the fixed salaries that have been the norm in the nonprofit sector. At the same time, they expect more and more of their staff, and are able to take advantage of their increased skills and abilities over time. In much the same way executive directors argue for increased budgets in program areas to their boards and funders, they should also consider arguing for salary budgets that allow for salary increases when merited. [fairness]

3. A clear distinction should be made between a paid employee's duties and any volunteer contributions made by that employee. Effective employees who must work overtime in order to accomplish their jobs should be compensated for that overtime. The blurring of paid and volunteer commitments by employees should not be an expectation of the committed employee. [fairness]

The NPO manager cannot control all of the ethical issues within compensation in the short term. The market value of an information systems specialist, for example, is currently higher than that of a social worker. As a result, the NPO manager may be faced with an apparent or perceived inequity in pay scales resulting from market forces beyond his or her control. Proponents of market-based pay would argue that it is only right that supply and demand should set the relative value of jobs. Critics would say that other systemic forces, such as the tendency for jobs traditionally performed by women to be valued less, are at play in this inequity. Issues such as these will require continued advocacy and research, but may be beyond the scope of an NPO manager's job.

(E) PERFORMANCE MANAGEMENT AND EVALUATION

Current trends in performance management and evaluation have increased the need for ethical sensitivity. For example, practices like 360-degree feedback require attentiveness to issues of confidentiality, honesty, and fairness.[37] Any system that serves as the primary method for planning, monitoring, and evaluating performance has great potential for impacting people's work lives both positively and negatively. The following are some questions that NPO managers can ask themselves about performance management and evaluation systems. In general, the answer to these questions should be "yes":

- Is there a standard process for managing and evaluating all the employees in the organization? [fairness]
- Do all employees and managers know the process? [respect, self-determination]
- Does the process actively involve both the employee and the manager in determining what is expected of the employee? [respect, self-determination]
- Does the process actively involve both the employee and the manager in determining what the employee needs from the manager and the organization in order to do his or her job effectively? [respect, self-determination]

- Is one purpose of the system to help the employee develop his or her knowledge, skills, and abilities over time? [responsibility]
- Does the process actively involve both the employee and the manager in determining criteria for evaluation? In determining success against these criteria? [respect]
- Is the link to compensation (or lack thereof) clear to all employees? [trustworthiness]
- Is there a process in place for appealing performance evaluation results? [fairness]

(F)   TRAINING AND DEVELOPMENT

Training and employee development are often viewed as either a perk proffered to those in positions of power or a slap on the hand to individuals who are not meeting performance expectations. In fact, the training and developing of staff and volunteers is a managerial and ethical responsibility. It allows the manager to ensure that staff and volunteers are able to respond to the changing demands of their jobs.

- One of the key tools for providing effective, relevant training is the training needs assessment. This tool is easily and unintentionally abused, with the results sometimes being used (usually unethically) for purposes other than determining skills or knowledge gaps. (We will examine this issue in detail in the case study found later in this chapter.) In general, there should be full disclosure of the intended purpose of the information gathered during any needs assessment process. [trustworthiness]
- A manager should always think twice about using training as a way to avoid dealing openly and honestly with an employee about performance problems. Sending an employee to a course may be an easy way to deal with a performance problem. However, it is often not the most ethical way. Often, other development approaches, such as on-the-job feedback, are not only more direct, but also more effective. [trustworthiness, respect, responsibility]

(G)   VOLUNTEER RESOURCE MANAGEMENT

Volunteers are a human resource unique to nonprofit organizations. In welcoming members to the profession of volunteer administration, the Association for Volunteer Administration states, "Attention to volunteering has reached an all-time high. . . . Scarcity of financial resources in the face of continued social needs requires that volunteers be mobilized as a source of supplementary time, materials, and expertise. . . . What has been slower to develop is the ability of organizations to utilize the time and abilities of these volunteers creatively and effectively."[38] The observation that the capacity of organizations to utilize volunteers effectively is a slowly developing area raises significant questions both about effective volunteer management and about the ethical treatment of volunteers, including the following:

- What duty of care does the organization owe its volunteers (e.g., training, insurance coverage)?

- What are the roles and responsibilities of line staff, managers, volunteers, and the board of directors (e.g., reporting and supervision)?
- Is the organization operating in a just, fair, and equitable fashion (e.g., nondiscriminatorily)?
- Does the organization encourage citizen participation in a broad range of service delivery and administrative roles?
- Does the organization have a philosophy addressing its responsibility back to the community that supports it (e.g., opportunities for the public to scrutinize its activities)?
- Does the organization, its managers, and board of directors inspire an atmosphere of trust for those internal and external to the organization?

These questions broadly frame an organization's operations in terms of the community it serves, the board that governs, management that works to achieve the mission and goals, the staff who provide services, and the volunteers who enhance service delivery. Within these operations rests volunteer management—a function unique to nonprofit organizations and possessing several unique ethical issues.

(i) Volunteer Management

Many NPOs have been proactive in developing a statement of volunteer rights and responsibilities. In general, these statements address:

- The importance of volunteers to the organization
- What rights the organization extends to the volunteer
- What general responsibilities the organization expects the volunteer to fulfill

For example, McCurley and Lynch provide a generic example of this kind of policy:

Volunteers are viewed as a valuable resource to this organization, its staff, and its clients. Volunteers shall be extended the right to be given meaningful assignments, the right to be treated as equal co-workers, the right to effective supervision, the right to full involvement and participation, and the right to be recognized for work done. In return, volunteers shall agree to actively perform their duties to the best of their abilities and to remain loyal to the values, goals, and procedures of the organization.[39]

What is interesting about this example and others like it is an explicit expectation that volunteers and staff will be loyal to a set of organizational values. In a recent conversation with one of the authors, a manager of volunteers said, "We never talk about values here. I have to do what *I* feel is right. I think maybe our agency's values come from the Board." It is quite common for volunteers and staff to be unaware of the organization's values and to be unable to contribute to discussions about the meaning those values have in terms of behaviors.

As mentioned earlier in this chapter, the AVA has developed a Statement of Professional Ethics for Volunteer Administrators.[40] The authors of this chapter assisted AVA in linking core ethical values and principles to behaviors exemplifying the best practices of a professional volunteer administrator. The resulting Statement of Professional Ethics for Volunteer Administrators (shown in part in Exhibit 25.3) provides a values base for the practice of volunteer administration and furthermore serves as an ethical decision-making tool—the premise of which is discussed later in the chapter. Used by volunteer administrators throughout North America, the AVA Statement serves as an "ethics lens" by focusing the variety of volunteer management activities on ethical outcomes, as shown in Exhibit 25.5.

A practical example of how this lens functions is shown in Exhibit 25.6, which shows the flow from core ethical value of loyalty to program components associated with this value. What is unique about the AVA Statement of Professional Ethics is that a professional can work from core ethical value to program components or vice versa. When an ethical dilemma occurs, the professional can work toward a solution from either perspective. An ethical decision-making worksheet is appended to the AVA Statement to guide ethical decision making.

(H) POLICY AND GOVERNANCE

It is interesting that many organizations set their policies in stone and yet renew their vision, mission, and value statements regularly. In fact, an organization's policies should be just as susceptible to change since they should be a reflection of its values. "Some policies and practices, either in the way they interact or in the way they are implemented, can have effects that are not intended, and produce unexpected outcomes with ethical overtones."[41] For example, an organization may have a stated value of trust. At the same time, it has a policy that all overtime must be approved by one's supervisor. The intention of the policy is to limit the organization's liability and ensure that overtime hours are used only when necessary. However, the employee reads between the lines of the policy and interprets it to mean that the organization does not trust the employee to make the decision him- or herself, given their knowledge of the work that needs to be done and the available time there is to do it. The policy does not reflect the stated value.

EXHIBIT 25.5 The Core Values of the AVA Statement of Professional Ethics as an Ethics Lens

Volunteer Management Activities[a]	Core Values in the AVA Statement of Professional Practice	Outcomes
• Needs assessment and program planning • Job development and design • Recruitment • Interviewing and matching • Orientation and training • Supervision and motivation • Recognition • Evaluation		Ethical decisions Ethical behaviors
	1. Citizenship and Philanthropy 2. Respect 3. Responsibility 4. Caring 5. Justice and Fairness 6. Trustworthiness	

[a] From McCurley, S., and Lynch, R. (1996). *Volunteer Management—Mobilizing All the Resources of Our Community.* Downers Grove, IL: Heritage Arts Publishing.

As another example, many organizations today recognize the importance of teamwork and attempt to foster it by creating multifunctional teams responsible for various aspects of the work. However, these same organizations conduct performance reviews and appraisals that consider only individual outcomes. The employees in these organizations see the inconsistency and feel cheated. The value of teamwork must be reflected in the way work is evaluated, or it is quickly discounted.

Sound policy has at its core an acknowledgment and commitment to a set of values and to ethical practice. Seel writes that the process to arrive at either policy or codes of ethics is dependent on a holistic relationship among:

- *Values*—which come from our life experiences, faith, culture, and so on. Values are our core beliefs that both motivate and guide our attitudes and actions.
- *Integrity*—which is that quality that creates compatibility between our values and actions.
- *Ethics*—which are a particular set of values pertaining to how we behave with others.
- *Collective standards*—which are the particular methods of practice developed by one group within, for example, a community or organization.[42]

Only when the relationships among values, integrity, ethics, and collective standards are understood will policy or codes of ethics be more than ineffectual prescriptive and delimiting statements.

In the ethical decision-making workshops conducted by the authors, it often becomes obvious that life would be much easier for managers if policies and values lined up. One example we often use involves the case of a volunteer director who is asked by the executive director not to inform a volunteer that she is being fired until a suitable replacement is found. In discussing the ethics of this situation, almost everyone presumes that the volunteer has not previously been advised that his or her work is unsatisfactory, and that the whole outcome would come as a surprise to the volunteer. What if, instead, we presumed that an ethical policy was in place that ensured that the volunteer was given every opportunity to succeed? The request could be seen in a much different light, from the perspective of another stakeholder: the client.

For many organizations, policy is a four-letter word. Rather than make managing easier, policies seem to make it more difficult. One of the managers interviewed by Toffler said, "[W]hen it came to dealing with people, there have been vast differences of opinion between what they have set as corporate policy and what I try to do in a lot of cases."[43] If the policies that have been set by the board are consistently ignored by the staff required to implement them, this should be a red flag signaling the need for a values-based policy review.

"Policy is written to express corporate values in a particular area and to set the guidelines for actions relating to that area. But the general nature of a policy cannot take into account all of the possible configurations of events—the exception—that must occur in any organization. The question is: How do you deal with the exceptions?"[44] That is the focus of the next session.

25.5 An Ethical Decision-Making Model: Defining Terms

The ability to deal with real-life ethical dilemmas is necessary in the complex nonprofit environment, which is rich with context and consequence. "While [ethical concerns] deal

EXHIBIT 25.6 Linking Core Ethical Values with Practice—An Example from the AVA Statement of Professional Ethics for Volunteer Administrators

Core Ethical Value	Ethical Principle	Possible Actions	Program Components
4. Loyalty	**Limitations to Loyalty:** The Volunteer Administrator understands the limits to his/her loyalty to his/her volunteers, clients, and organization.	• Clarify limits and boundaries to personal, professional, and community relationships.	☐ I know when I need to make others aware of conflicting loyalties. ☐ I have determined clear boundaries for working with staff, board, volunteers, and any personal relationships that could evolve.
	Prioritizing Loyalties: The Volunteer Administrator recognizes that they have loyalties to the organization, its staff, volunteers, and to personal relationships and understands how to prioritize these loyalties.	• Clear statements of expectations and possible conflicts of loyalty exist and are reviewed periodically.	☐ I know how to determine which loyalties take precedence by considering the greater long-term good.
	Safeguarding Confidential Information: The Volunteer Administrator understands the importance of confidentiality and works to protect confidential information.	• Staff and volunteers have signed confidentiality statements aimed at protecting the organization, its staff, volunteers, and clients.	☐ I have signed confidentiality statements from all staff and volunteers. ☐ Personal and private information is stored in a secure place in my office. ☐ I have a process for responding to surveys. ☐ I know how to protect vulnerable individuals who disclose information that could negatively impact them if disclosed. ☐ The information I collect and have in my files is necessary to the volunteer program. ☐ I have a safe and confidential process for supporting persons with hidden disabilities, including persons with HIV/AIDS, who may not want to make such information public, while still providing a safe workplace for staff and volunteers.

Source: The Association for Volunteer Administration, Statement of Professional Ethics in Volunteer Administration, 2nd ed., 1996. Reprinted with permission.

with right and wrong decisions, they frequently involve factors that make the right and wrong less than patently clear."[45]

An ethical dilemma has five characteristics:

1. It is hard to name.
2. It is embedded in a specific context.
3. It may not be obvious.
4. It addresses the claims of multiple stakeholders.
5. It involves a situation where an individual wants to do the right thing but either does not know what that is or is not able to do it.[46]

The model seen in Exhibit 25.7 is, in essence, a process for working through an ethical dilemma, describing it thoroughly, and then choosing appropriate ethical action. Rather than prescribing what you should do, it helps you decide for yourself what is the right thing to do.

Colloquially, the terms *values, ethics,* and *morality* are used interchangeably. Before describing the model, it is important to agree on the definition for these terms. The authors find the following definitions most useful for our purposes[47] (see Exhibit 25.8).

Values are the strongly held beliefs and attitudes about what is desirable. Examples of values include power, wealth, and fame. Not all values have an ethical aspect to them. For example, power itself is neither good nor bad; it is how you use the power that may have ethical ramifications.

There are two types of values, those that affect our relationships with other people, and those that have primary influence in our personal lives. Values that are private and do not have broad societal implications are called *morals*. These are privately held beliefs and attitudes about what is good and worthwhile and are influenced by culture, religion, and family upbringing. Examples of moral values include beliefs about extramarital sex and drinking of alcohol. On the other hand, public values are called *ethical values.* These values are universally accepted beliefs about what is right and wrong. An example of an ethical

---

EXHIBIT 25.7 Four-Step Ethical Decision-Making Model

Step 1: **Identify the primary stakeholders** in this situation, based on the mission of your organization and its primary clients.

Step 2: **State the problem from each stakeholder's point of view,** identifying the key ethical value(s) being violated.

Step 3: **Determine the actions you could take, given each stakeholder's concerns.**

Step 4: **Make a decision by noting the positive and negative consequences of each action and choosing the option which, on balance, reduces harm and produces the greatest balance of good in the long run.**
Key Principles:
- Always choose a course of action based on core ethical values rather than one based on nonethical values.
- Violating a core ethical value only if it is clearly *necessary* in order to advance another core ethical value that will produce the greatest balance of good in the long run.

EXHIBIT 25.8 Values, Morals, and Ethics

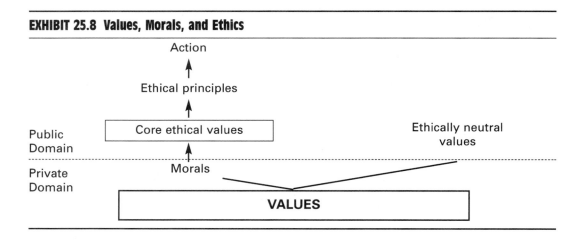

value is honesty. The related ethical principle is "I will be truthful"; and the ethical action is the act of telling the truth.

(A) TOWARD GLOBAL ETHICS

Ethicians have long debated the existence of universal ethical principles. In the late 1980s and the 1990s, there was a particularly strong focus on understanding ethics in a global context. For NPOs, this understanding is critical, because the scope of work in these organizations is often transcultural or intercultural in nature. In addition, the ability to talk about ethics and make ethical choices rests on our ability to cross religious and cultural boundaries. Rachels believes that there are indeed some ethical "rules" that societies will have in common, because "these rules are necessary for society to exist."[48]

In his book *The Ethical Imperative,* Dalla Costa outlines four declarations that have been put forward in an effort to define a "global ethic."[49] They are outlined briefly as follows.

(i) Declaration of the Parliament of World Religions

This declaration arose from the Council for the Parliament of World Religions that met in Chicago in 1993. Developed by academic and spiritual leaders from many religious traditions, the declaration states the belief that "The truth is already known, but yet to be lived in heart and action." It calls for reciprocity of respect and dignity amoung all human beings. The four principles that are the basis for the declaration include:

1. Everyone is responsible for a global ethic.
2. Every human must be treated humanely.
3. Four directives arise out of these principles: respect life, deal honestly and fairly, speak and act truthfully, and ensure equal rights for all.
4. Transforming consciousness is difficult work.

(ii) The Interfaith Declaration

The development of this declaration involved scholars and theologians, as well as business-people and politicians. The focus in this case was to develop a code of ethics for international business. Together, participants agreed on four key concepts that relate to business:

1. Justice
2. Mutual respect
3. Stewardship of nature
4. Honesty of thought, word, and action

(iii) Mutual Responsibility: The Tie that Binds

This document was an ad hoc submission made in 1991 to the Special Joint Committee investigating reform in Canada's Constitution and Charter of Rights and Freedoms. Composed of primarily religious leaders, it proposed the following "fundamental considerations" with a view toward pluralism:

- Human dignity
- Mutual responsibility
- Economic equity
- Fiscal fairness
- Social justice
- Environmental integrity

(iv) The Caux Principles

In an ethical best practices Round Table in 1994, European, American, and Japanese businesspeople sought to provide a forum in which businesses' social obligations could be articulated. The seven principles declared were:

1. Extending the responsibility beyond "shareholders" toward "stakeholders"
2. Orienting the effects of business toward innovation, justice, and world community
3. Moving beyond the letter of the law toward a spirit of trust
4. Respecting rules
5. Supporting multilateral trade
6. Respecting the environment
7. Avoiding illicit operations

Dalla Costa distills the principles uncovered by these various movements, and proposes the following common ethical principles:

- Respect life.
- Be fair.
- Be honest.
- Strive for justice.
- Honor the environment.[50]

These common ethical principles support the groundbreaking work done by Michael Josephson in 1993, when he convened a meeting of a cross-section of people representing a wide variety of cultures and sectors. At a conference, they were able to agree on a list of what he calls "The Six Pillars of Character." These are six broad groupings of ethical values that appear to transcend culture and religion. In the many workshops and seminars lead by the authors in the public and nonprofit sectors, these six ethical values have been confirmed as being held by the vast majority of participants. In addition, they overlap with a set of 10 core values summarized by Guy[51] to be those that many writers see as central to effective relations among people. The six core ethical values allow us to start from a foundation of agreement in order to sort through complex ethical dilemmas.

Exhibit 25.9 summarizes the Six Pillars of Character that Josephson identified.[52]

At first glance, this process may seem too cumbersome to be practical. Many things that we do each day, if described and set out in words, would seem that way. For example, if you were to write a manual describing precisely how to drive a car, it would likely take more than one page to do so. However, once you learn to drive, you rarely have to consult the manual. It starts to become almost instinctual. Similarly, once a manager develops an ethical decision-making competency, the steps in the process become intuitive and second nature.

The following case study will illustrate how to put this model into practice.

(B) CASE STUDY: TRAINING NEEDS ASSESSMENT OR STAFFING TOOL?

You are the executive director for a medium-sized NPO. Recently, your organization has become increasingly complex and differentiated, requiring many new skills of its employees. You have decided to add to the skills of your employees through a formal training initiative.

For the past several months, you have been working closely with a small steering committee consisting of the organization's managers. This steering committee has engaged the services of an experienced consultant to conduct a training needs assessment. You are responsible for managing the consultants. You have distributed memos describing the initiative to all employees. These memos describe the importance of the mandatory one-on-one training needs assessment interviews, which will be conducted by the consultant "for the purposes of customizing a training plan to meet their needs."

The first series of training needs assessment interviews is approaching. You are informally discussing the project at the water cooler with one of the more senior managers. She tells you she is looking forward to having lunch with the consultant to discuss the outcome of the needs assessments: she sees them as an opportunity to gather information about employees in her area. "Some people are just not suited to this new environment. Having that information will really help me make some decisions about how to staff the new department," she says.

You know that this manager has been having problems managing some of her people. You also know that you've given her a new department to manage, and understand how

---

EXHIBIT 25.9 Six Pillars of Character (Core Ethical Values)

Trustworthiness	Truthfulness, sincerity, candor, integrity, promise keeping, loyalty
Respect	Respect, autonomy, courtesy, self-determination
Responsibility	Responsibility, diligence, continuous improvement, self-restraint
Justice and Fairness	Justice, fairness, impartiality, equity
Caring	Caring, kindness, compassion
Citizenship	Citizenship, philanthropy, voting

this information could leverage her ability to manage it more effectively. On the other hand, you can't help but be reminded of the actual purpose of the interviews and the promise of confidentiality that was made in the memo you sent.

What is the most ethical thing for you to do next?

Step 1:	**Identity the primary stakeholders** in this situation, based on the mission of your organization and its primary clients. Yourself (the Executive Director) The Organization and its Clients The Employees The Senior Manager The Consultant
Step 2:	**State the problem from each stakeholder's point of view,** identifying the key ethical value(s) being violated.
Executive Director (ED)	There is a conflict between a promise of confidentiality (trustworthiness) and the ED's responsibility to the organization and its clients. On the one hand, the ED has made a promise that the consultant will keep the results of the interviews confidential, and that only aggregate information will be reported. (trustworthiness) At the time the promise was made, the ED had every reason to believe this would be preferable and possible, given the scope and intent of the needs assessment. On the other hand, the ED has made a commitment to improving the effectiveness of the organization: the ED realizes that staffing the new division with the most capable employees is in the best interest of the organization and its clients. (responsibility) The ED's dilemma is whether to allow the promise of confidentiality to be compromised for the greater good of improved organizational effectiveness.
Employees	Expect to be able to believe promises of confidentiality (trustworthiness).
Senior Manager	Concerned about responsibility to the organization and its clients.
Consultant	Concerned about keeping his promise of confidentiality.
Step 3:	**Determine the actions you could take, given each stakeholder's concerns.**
Executive Director	1. Change the focus of the needs assessment by issuing another memo that restates the purpose of the needs assessment and revokes the promise of confidentiality. 2. Meet with the Senior Manager in private to discuss the situation in their department and to try to assist the Manager with her management problems in isolation of the training needs assessment. 3. Meet with the consultant to ensure his commitment to confidentiality. 4. Some combination of the above. 5. Do nothing at all. Let the situation run its course.

Employees	1. Change the focus of the needs assessment by issuing another memo that restates the purpose of the needs assessment and revokes the promise of confidentiality.
	2. Meet with the consultant to ensure his commitment to confidentiality.
	3. Do nothing at all. Let the situation run its course without intervening.
Senior Manager	1. Change the focus of the needs assessment by issuing another memo that restates the purpose of the needs assessment and revokes the promise of confidentiality.
	2. Meet with the Senior Manager in private to discuss the situation in their department and to try to assist the Manager with her management problems in isolation of the training needs assessment.
	3. Some combination of the above.
	4. Do nothing at all. Let the situation run its course.
Consultant	1. Change the focus of the needs assessment by issuing another memo that restates the purpose of the needs assessment and revokes the promise of confidentiality.
	2. Meet with the consultant to ensure his commitment to confidentiality.
	3. Some combination of the above.
	4. Do nothing at all. Let the situation run its course.
Step 4:	**Make a decision by noting the positive and negative consequences of each action and choosing the option that, on balance, reduces harm and produces the greatest balance of good in the long run.**
Best Alternative? No	1. Issuing another memo would help deal with the issue of confidentiality. However, it would result in a needs assessment that had questionable validity. The consultant had previously informed the ED that confidentiality was required in order to ensure that people were willing to openly discuss their performance problems. In the long term, this action would compromise the ED's responsibility to the organization. (Note: Many managers, at first glance, would consider the new memo a bad option simply because it would make them look bad. It is important to realize that this issue is not an ethical one. Sometimes "changing your mind" is necessary in order to be ethical.)
Maybe	2. Meeting with the Manager may address the issue of confidentiality and it would address the issue of responsibility. Depending on the Senior Manager's respect for your opinion and authority, she may or may not still request specific information from the consultant. However, your action has made it a lot less likely. The training programs that would result from a valid needs assessment would help to increase the proficiency of staff in all parts of the organization, thus meeting the principle of responsibility.
Yes	3. Meeting with the consultant would ensure *confidentiality* and deal with *responsibility.* The training programs that would result from a valid needs assessment would help to increase the proficiency of staff in all parts of the organization, thus meeting the principle of

Best Option

Unethical

responsibility. The consultant could still meet with the Senior Manager for a one-on-one discussion of a more general nature.

4. Meeting with the consultant *and* following up with the Senior Manager separately would also allow you to show the Manager you *care,* and help them deal with the management issues that have arisen for her.

5. Doing nothing is clearly unethical. Some might argue that you are not sure that the Manager would actually carry out her intention to meet with the consultant, so why overreact? This is equivalent to saying that if someone told you they were going to shoot your friend, you wouldn't warn them because it might not happen. It would only be proper to allow someone to violate an ethical value (*honesty*) if it was the only way to ensure that you acted *responsibly,* in the best interests of your clients.

25.6   *Conclusion*

Mason calls on the nonprofit sector, and NPO managers in particular, to put greater emphasis on ethics when he writes:

I vote that between now and the sunset of the 20th century we emphasize ethics as much as we emphasized more intentional management in the past two decades. If we can take the strides in ethics that we have taken in management, the dawn of the next century will reveal the nonprofit sector in magnificent shape.[53]

Clearly, NPO leaders fulfill a vital and complex role within the nonprofit sector—in terms of both internal functions and external community relations. Often in a position to balance interests of staff, volunteers, board, and clients, they face a complex landscape of frequently conflicting values. NPO managers will meet the challenges of the twenty-first century much more effectively once they are equipped with the ethical sensitivity to identify potential issues, the decision-making competency to navigate them, and the conviction to help resolve them.

Endnotes

1. Guy, M. (1990). *Ethical Decision Making in Everyday Work Situations.* Westport, CT: Greenwood Press.
2. Bridges, W. (1994). *Job Shift: How to Prosper in a Workplace Without Jobs.* Reading, MA: Addison-Wesley.
3. Bendaly, L. (1996). *Organization 2000: The Essential Guide for Companies and Teams in the New Economy.* Toronto, Canada: HarperCollins Publishers Ltd.
4. Senge, P., R. Ross, B. Smith, C. Roberts, and A. Klelner. (1994). *The Fifth Discipline Fieldbook.* New York: Doubleday.
5. Covey, S. (1992). *Principle Centered Leadership.* New York: Simon and Schuster.
6. Toffler, B. L. (1991). *Managers Talk Ethics.* New York: John Wiley & Sons.

7. De Pree, M. (1992). *Leadership Jazz.* New York: Doubleday.

8. Mason, D. (1992). "Keepers of the Springs: Why Ethics Make Good Sense for Nonprofits," *Nonprofit World* 10(2): 25–27.

9. Id., p. 26.

10. Id.

11. Independent Sector. (1991). *Ethics and the Nation's Voluntary and Philanthropic Community: Obedience to the Unenforceable.* Washington, DC: Independent Sector.

12. Payton, R. (1988). *Philanthropy.* New York: Macmillan.

13. Lawry, R. (1995). "Accountability and Nonprofit Organizations: An Ethical Perspective," *Nonprofit Management and Leadership* 6(2): 171–80.

14. Milosfsky, C., and S. Blades. (1991). "Issues of Accountability in Health Charities: A Case Study of Accountability Problems Among Nonprofit Organizations," *Nonprofit and Voluntary Sector Quarterly* 20(4): 371–78.

15. See note 8.

16. Id.

17. O'Neill, M. (1992). "Ethical Dimensions of Nonprofit Administration," *Nonprofit Management and Leadership* 3(2): 199–213.

18. See note 5.

19. Bogart, W. (1995). "Accountability and Nonprofit Organizations: An Economic Perspective," *Nonprofit Management and Leadership* 6(2): 157–70.

20. See note 17.

21. Id.

22. Seel, K. (1996). "The New AVA Statement of Professional Ethics in Volunteer Administration," *The Journal of Volunteer Administration* XIV(2): 33–38.

23. Josephson, M. (1993). *Making Ethical Decisions.* Marina Del Rey, CA: The Josephson Institute of Ethics.

24. See note 6.

25. Singer, P. (1993). *Practical Ethics.* Boston: Cambridge University Press.

26. See note 7.

27. See note 6.

28. See note 3.

29. See note 2.

30. Stamp, D. (1995). *The Invisible Assembly Line.* New York: American Management Association.

31. See note 1.

32. See note 6.

33. See note 3.

34. See note 1.

35. See note 25.

36. Rachels, J. (1993). *The Elements of Moral Philosophy.* New York: McGraw-Hill.

37. Edwards, M.R., and A.J. Ewen. *360° Feedback.* New York: American Management Association.

38. Association for Volunteer Administration. (1996). *Volunteer Administration: Portrait of a Profession.* Boulder, CO: Association for Volunteer Administration.

39. McCurley, S., and R. Lynch. (1996). *Volunteer Management—Mobilizing All the Resources of Our Community.* Downers Grove, IL: Heritage Arts Publishing.

40. Association for Volunteer Administration. (1996). *Statement of Professional Ethics in Volunteer Administration,* 2nd ed. Boulder, CO: Association for Volunteer Administration.

41. See note 6.
42. See note 22.
43. See note 6.
44. Id., p. 233.
45. Id., pp. 11, 12.
46. Id.
47. See note 23.
48. See note 36.
49. Dalla Costa, J. (1998). *The Ethical Imperative: Why Moral Leadership is Good Business.* New York: HarperCollins Publishers Ltd.
50. Id.
51. See note 1.
52. See note 23.
53. See note 8.

26 Leadership and the Self-Renewing Organization*

JOSEPH E. CHAMPOUX, PHD
The Robert O. Anderson Schools of Management
The University of New Mexico

26.1 Introduction

Peter Drucker's analysis of high-performing nonprofit organizations pointed to several consistent characteristics.[1–3] They have clearly defined missions that are well understood by all paid and volunteer staff. The clear mission focuses behavior on reaching the organization's goals, often by innovative means.

Frances Hesselbein, former national executive director of the Girl Scouts, used its strong mission focus to energize Girl Scout Councils around the country to try new programs. Under her leadership, the Girl Scouts developed the Daisy Scout program in response to changing population demographics. More women were working mothers who needed preschool day care. By 1990, the program had 150,000 5-year-old girls who likely will continue with other Girl Scout programs as they get older.[4]

The characteristics of high-performing nonprofit organizations (NPOs) are similar to the characteristics of self-renewing organizations (SROs). Frances Hesselbein combined

* Portions of this chapter were adapted and reprinted by permission from Joseph E. Champoux. (2000). *Organizational Behavior: Essential Tenets for a New Millennium,* Chapter 12. Cincinnati, OH: South-Western College Publishing. Copyright © 2000 by South-Western College Publishing. All rights reserved.

her leadership qualities with the self-renewing features of the Girl Scouts to transform it into a high-performing NPO.

26.2 Self-Renewing Organizations

SROs have strong core values that maintain a steady focus for all organization members. They continually adapt to their environments in an unrelenting pursuit of their mission. SROs have the unique qualities of continuous learning, innovation, and growth. These features characterize both individual members and the entire organization.

Exhibit 26.1 summarizes the main features of SROs. Although there is little agreement on an exact definition of SROs,[5] Exhibit 26.1 distills their features from many respected sources.[6–10]

SROs have a strong self-identity. They know who they are and what they are all about. They feature strong cultures with well-defined values, customs, and traditions. These organizations react to their environment based on knowledge of who they are and what they are.

The strong core values of such organizations help sustain a clear focus for everyone in the organization. People have high autonomy but are guided by an unvarying focus on core values and mission. Their focus on a core vision lets them use many routes to reach that vision.

EXHIBIT 26.1 Characteristics of Self-Renewing Organizations

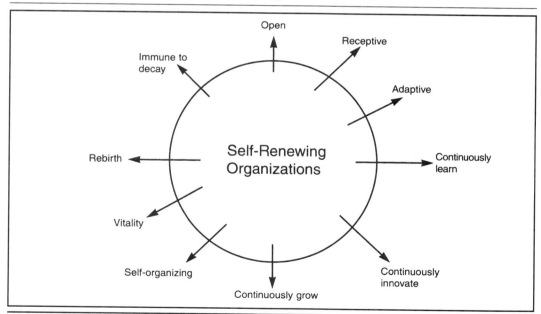

Sources: Developed from Gardner, J. W. (1981). *Self-Renewal: The Individual and the Innovative Society.* New York: W. W. Norton; Lawrence, P. R., and D. Dyer. (1983). *Renewing American Industry.* New York: Free Press; Senge, P. M. (1990). *The Fifth Discipline: The Art and Practice of the Learning Organization.* New York: Doubleday; and Wheatley, M. J. (1994). *Leadership and the New Science: Learning about Organization from an Orderly Universe.* San Francisco: Berrett-Koehler, Inc.

A strong self-identity gives an SRO high autonomy in its environment, although it forges a partnership with its environment. They view their environment as a source of opportunities, not as a source of threats. They have an active exchange with the environment, using it for continual self-renewal. Such organizations aggressively seek feedback from their environment, actively processing such information while remembering who they are and what they are. They use that feedback to shape the future both by changing internal structures and relationships and by changing the environment.

SROs are resilient to environmental disturbances. They do not react with random changes that can disrupt the organization and lead to poor decisions. Leaders in SROs understand that human systems do not maintain an endless state of equilibrium. They view change as both inevitable and desirable—as an important source of growth, development, and self-renewal. The result is a flexible and responsive organization that is paradoxically both a partner with and independent of its environment.

Moving self-renewing values into the culture of an organization is often a major organizational change brought about by a strong leader. The next sections describe leadership from several perspectives. You should find those perspectives useful for understanding the leadership requirements of your organization and assessing the leadership qualities of yourself and others in your organization. For additional sources on leadership, see Avolio[11] and Northouse.[12]

26.3   The Nature of Leadership

Leadership is a social influence process in which the person in a leadership role tries to affect the behavior of another party, a follower or potential follower. The follower must perceive the influence effort as acceptable for it to affect the person's behavior. Power is a central feature of leadership, with leaders getting their power from both their organizational positions and personal qualities.

Leaders can appear at any organizational level. A key position for a leader to affect a self-renewing NPO is the senior executive position. The position can have almost any title—executive director or manager, for example. This senior position is a key one from which a leader can build a self-renewing system.

Leaders and managers play different roles in organizations.[13–17] A simple summary of the differences says: "Leaders change human systems, managers maintain and control them."[18] Leaders form visions, inspire others to chase the vision, take risks, gather and use power, and seek opposing views. Managers build commitment to the organization's goals, use their knowledge of human motivation to guide the behavior of others, solve problems, and pursue an orderly course of action. Managers typically take fewer risks than leaders and do not try to change an organization's direction. Both leaders and managers play important roles in an organization. They are simply different roles. Leaders seek change; managers keep a steady direction.

26.4   Some Views of Leadership

Research and observation over the past 100 years has produced different views of leadership. These views offer different perspectives of leadership that give divers insights about leadership processes. The following describes these views. A later section links them to forming and sustaining an SRO.

(A) LEADERSHIP TRAITS

Leadership researchers have investigated for almost 100 years the types of traits that distinguish leaders from followers or which followers attribute to their leaders. This research consists of survey assessments, interviews, and observations from experience.

Exhibit 26.2 summarizes the results of much of that work. The first two columns list traits from empirical research as found in rigorous statistical summaries.[19–23] The third column shows the traits that over 60 percent of study participants ascribed to their leaders. That series of studies was done in the 1990s with over 20,000 people from Australia, Asia, Europe, and the United States.[24] Column 4 shows many traits that leadership scholar Warren Bennis has uncovered in his 40-year program of interview-based research.[25–27] The last column has John W. Gardner's observations on leadership based on his years of public service.[28] The asterisked traits in the last two columns are similar to traits in columns 1 through 3.

There is a striking pattern and consistency of traits in the exhibit. Leaders have vision, energy, and self-confidence. They are competent and bright, with knowledge that applies to an organization's activities. Leaders have integrity that helps them build trust between themselves and their followers. They can be dominant when they must, such as in moments of decisive action.

The traits in Exhibit 26.2 come from research that is independent of what later sections report. We will see that these traits and related behavior patterns play key roles in leadership processes in SROs.

EXHIBIT 26.2 Comparison of Leadership Traits

Statistical Review 1	Statistical Review 2	Kouzes and Posner	Bennis	Gardner
Dominance	Cognitive ability	Competent	Active listener	Able to build
Energy	Desire to lead	Forward-looking	Articulate	trust*
Intelligence	Drive	Honest	Consistency	Able to
Self-confidence	Honesty/integrity	Inspiring	Controlled	motivate
Task-relevant	Knowledge of		personal	Confidence*
knowledge	the business		ambition	Courage
	Self-confidence		Creativity	Decisive
			Decisiveness	Dominance*
			Dedication	Flexibility
			Humility	Intelligence*
			Inclusive	Need to
			Integrity*	achieve
			Intelligence*	People skills
			Magnanimity	Responsible
			Openness	Stamina*
			Persistence	Task
			Self-awareness	competence
			Self-confidence*	Understanding
			Sense of humor	followers
			Toughness	
			Vision*	

* Similar to traits in columns 1–3.

(B) THE LEADERSHIP MYSTIQUE*

The leadership mystique is a view of leadership developed from observing executives who had made major organizational changes. That research pointed consistently to three dimensions of leadership: a sense of mission, a capacity for power, and a will to survive and persevere.[29–30]

A leader has a sense of mission—a vision of some future state for the organization. The vision is more than a strategic plan; rather, it is a dream about something the leader wants to create. It does not now exist, but it *will* exist. The mission becomes part of the heart, soul, and ego of the leader. It is the leader's heroic vision of the possible. She or he pursues that mission at great personal sacrifice. The leader describes the mission with intense passion, trying to enlist others to pursue it also.

A capacity for power is the ability to get and use power to pursue the mission. Leaders have no fear of power, nor do they believe having power is undesirable. Power—and the capacity to get it—is basic to achieving the mission.

Leaders are often frustrated in the pursuit of their mission. They must have a will to survive and persevere in reaching the mission. This third quality of the leadership mystique deals with impediments to achieving the mission—financial backers, competitors, government restrictions, and so on. A leader has "a will to persevere against a discourteous, unbelieving world of sometimes total opposition."[31]

Frances Hesselbein, former executive director of the Girl Scouts of America, moved that organization from a plodding bureaucracy to a responsive, customer-focused organization. During her time as executive director, membership increased to 2.3 million, following eight years of declining membership.[32] Her first steps focused on reassessing the mission (or vision) of the Girl Scouts. In her words: "We kept asking ourselves very simple questions. . . . What is our business? Who is the customer? And what does the customer consider value?"[33] Hesselbein is widely credited with successfully changing the Girls Scouts of America by repeatedly focusing on its mission.

(C) TRANSFORMATIONAL LEADERSHIP**

Transformational leadership emphasizes charisma, individualized consideration, and intellectual stimulation.[34–37] Charisma is the most important part of transformational leadership because of the power it gives a leader. Followers of charismatic leaders trust them, identify with them, and have high confidence in them. Charismatic leaders often have high self-confidence, self-esteem, and self-determination.

Individualized consideration means the transformational leader recognizes variations in skills, abilities, and desires for growth opportunities among subordinates. The transformational leader knows her subordinates well. The transformational leader also gives

---

* This section originally appeared in J. E. Champoux and L. D. Goldman. (1993). "Building a Total Quality Culture." In T. D. Connors (ed.), *Nonprofit Organizations Policies and Procedures Handbook.* New York: John Wiley & Sons, pp. 65–66, and its *Supplement* (1996), p. 14. Copyright © 1993 by John Wiley & Sons, Inc. Reprinted by permission of John Wiley & Sons, Inc.

** This section originally appeared in J. E. Champoux and L. D. Goldman. (1993). "Building a Total Quality Culture." In T. D. Connors (ed.), *Nonprofit Organizations Policies and Procedures Handbook.* New York: John Wiley & Sons, p. 66, and its *Supplement* (1996), pp. 14–15. Copyright © 1993 by John Wiley & Sons, Inc. Reprinted by permission of John Wiley & Sons, Inc.

individual counseling, guidance, and support and constructively critiques a subordinate's performance. A key part of individualized consideration is the degree to which the leader shows genuine interest in the subordinate.

Intellectual stimulation is the transformational leader's ability to build high awareness of problems and solutions to problems. Such leaders induce changes in the values and beliefs of subordinates. They stimulate subordinates to imagine new and different future states for the group. Intellectual stimulation is more than a change in present direction. It demands a large leap in the values, beliefs, and problem focus of subordinates.

Transformational leaders strive for big increases in performance beyond that needed to reach immediate organization goals. They bring excitement to the workplace and build strong emotional bonds between themselves and their subordinates. Transformational leaders work toward what they believe is right and good for the organization, not its present direction. They often bring dramatic changes to an organization's culture and are remembered long after they are gone.

(D) CHARISMATIC LEADERSHIP*

Charismatic leaders attract devoted followers who energetically pursue the leader's vision. They move their followers to extraordinary heights of performance, profoundly affect their aspirations, build emotional attachment to the leader, and win commitment to the leader's vision. Charismatic leaders win the loyalty of their followers and inspire them to self-sacrifice in the pursuit of a vision.[38–42]

Charismatic leaders see well beyond their organization's current situation and develop a view of the future that is different from the present.[43–44] They develop and widely communicate an inspirational vision—a vision they describe as better in specific ways from the present. Such leaders form bonds of trust between themselves and their followers. Charismatic leaders empower others in their organizations to carry out the vision.

Looking beyond the present situation includes scanning the environment for new opportunities, predicting changes in the environment, and looking for ways to keep their organization aligned with its outside environment. Charismatic leaders are impatient with present conditions and press their organizations to continuously improve. They push their organizations toward a new state by creating dissatisfaction with the present.

Creating and communicating an inspirational vision is a key behavior of charismatic leaders. To communicate, they use all suitable media with which they feel comfortable, including written documents, speeches, conversations with individual employees, television, and direct electronic communication. Charismatic leaders are especially skilled at framing messages that clearly express and support their vision.

Building trust between the leader and her or his followers is a key part of getting commitment to the leader's vision. Charismatic leaders behave in ways that are consistent with statements about the vision. The leader also tries to forge values supporting the vision into the cultural fabric of the organization. For example, Jan Carlzon, the charismatic former chief executive of Scandinavian Airlines System (SAS), reinforced customer-oriented values

---

when he refused to accept a magazine or newspaper while traveling on SAS before all other passengers were offered one.[45]

Charismatic leaders are especially skilled at tapping unused motivational energy in their followers. They rely on empowerment, an approach that helps followers develop self-confidence in their ability to fulfill the leader's vision. Such leaders often design experiences to stretch their followers to new levels of performance. By giving them feedback, charismatic leaders help steer followers in the desired direction and inspire them to higher levels of performance.

(E) SUBSTITUTES, NEUTRALIZERS, AND ENHANCERS OF LEADERSHIP BEHAVIOR*

Substitutes, neutralizers, and enhancers each operate differently in the relationship between a leader and a follower. Exhibit 26.3 shows the different relationships for substitutes, neutralizers, and enhancers.[46–51]

Substitutes for leadership act in place of the leader, making leader behavior unnecessary. The substitute, not the leader, affects subordinate attitudes and behavior. For example, people doing routine and predictable tasks would find directive leader behavior

EXHIBIT 26.3 Substitutes, Neutralizers, and Enhancers of Leadership Behavior

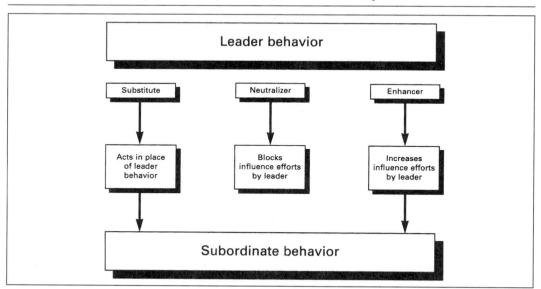

* Modified and reprinted by permission from J. E. Champoux. (1996). *Organizational Behavior: Integrating Individuals, Groups, and Processes,* pp. 338–39. Copyright © 1996 by West Publishing Company. All rights reserved.

redundant. The nature of the task, not the leader, guides the person's behavior. Tasks allowing high levels of intrinsic motivation also substitute for motivational influences from the leader.

Neutralizers prevent leader behavior from affecting the attitudes and behavior of subordinates. A neutralizer breaks the connection between leader behavior and subordinate response. A neutralizer has no direct effect on the subordinate. Instead, it is a block between the leader and the subordinate. For example, work groups often develop norms or rules that control the behavior of group members. If those norms are not consistent with what the group leader wants, the norm neutralizes the leader's efforts to influence the group. People with a professional orientation, such as artists and musicians, often turn to their professional peers for recognition and rewards. That orientation can neutralize supportive leader behavior and any efforts at recognition by the leader.

Enhancers strengthen the connection between leader behavior and subordinate satisfaction and performance. If a leader controls rewards for a subordinate's performance, and the subordinate perceives a direct connection between performance and getting the reward, the reward system enhances the leader's influence over the subordinate. Similarly, organization policies that let the leader hire and fire enhance the leader's influence over subordinates.

(F) LEADERSHIP PERCEPTIONS: "WE KNOW A LEADER WHEN WE SEE ONE"*

The discussions of leadership in this chapter have focused on the traits and behavior of leaders. Human perceptual processes underlie people's observations of leader traits and behaviors. Researchers have developed two different but related views of leadership perceptions. The first view builds on perceptual categories; the second view describes the process of leadership attribution. Exhibit 26.4 shows both views for easy comparison.

(i) Leadership Categorization
According to the Leadership Categorization view of leadership perception, people observe the behavior of another person and then quickly compare those observations to a cognitive category describing a leader. Exhibit 26.4 shows a simplified version of the Leadership Categorization Process.[52–55]

A person's perceptual process helps filter observations from the person's environment. The person compares his or her perceived observations to a cognitive category that is either a leadership prototype or a leadership exemplar. A leadership prototype is a person's cognitive image of the characteristics, qualities, behaviors, and traits that make up a leader. For example, some people might view leaders as intelligent and industrious while others think of leaders as honest and outgoing.[56] A leadership exemplar is a specific person people regard as a leader, such as Margaret Thatcher or Martin Luther King, Jr.

A key step in the Leadership Categorization Process is deciding whether the perceived observations match the leadership prototype or exemplar. If they do not match, the

---

* Modified and reprinted by permission from J. E. Champoux. (1996) *Organizational Behavior: Integrating Individuals, Groups, and Processes*, pp. 339–41. Copyright © 1996 by West Publishing Company. All rights reserved.

EXHIBIT 26.4 Leadership Perceptions

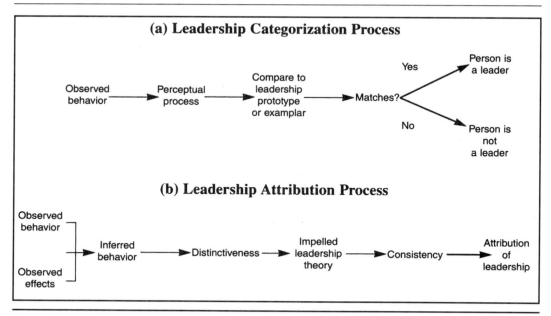

Source: Reprinted by permission from J. E. Champoux. (1996). *Organizational Behavior: Integrating Individuals, Groups, and Processes,* Figure 12–5, p. 341. Copyright © 1996 by South-Western College Publishing, a division of Thomson Learning.

observer decides the observed person is not a leader. If they match, she or he decides the observed person is a leader.

(ii) Leadership Attributions

Attribution of leadership follows the attribution process shown in Exhibit 26.4.[57] Individuals observe the behavior of other people and the effects associated with the behavior. An observer can also infer other behaviors from the observed behavior. For example, an observer might conclude that a talkative person who interacts with many people in a group has much job-related information. The observer made the inference from the talkative and interactive behavior he or she saw.

In the next step in the process, the observer assesses the observed and inferred information for evidence of leadership. A key factor in this step is whether the behavior is specific to one person or is widely shared by other people in a group. An observer accepts only distinctive behavior as evidence of leadership. The observer then compares the distinctive behavior to an implicit leadership theory. Such theories act as perceptual filters and standards of comparison for the leadership qualities a person believes are important for a leader to have. Some people think decisiveness is an important leadership quality. If a leader shows decisiveness, then the person is a leader. The observer now decides whether the behavior is consistent across situations and over time. If the observer sees similar behavior from the same person in different situations and at different times, he or she will build a strong attribution of leadership.

26.5   Leadership and Self-Renewing Organizations

Exhibit 26.5 compares some major characteristics of leadership to the characteristics of SROs. They are open, receptive, and adaptive organizations that continuously learn, innovate, and grow. Such features let self-renewing organizations maintain their vitality and protect themselves from decaying.

Leadership is a driving force that can transform an organization into a self-renewing one. Characteristics such as charisma, self-confidence, and building trust can help a leader energize followers to pursue a vision of becoming an SRO. Perseverance will serve the leader well along the way as he or she meets roadblocks and resistance to the new direction. Empowerment is a leader's important tool to move decision making to the point of contact with clients and to get the adaptability of a self-renewing system.

The continual growth and rebirth of an SRO needs these and other leadership qualities. A leader's knowledge and vision, plus the intellectual stimulation of followers, infuses SROs with critical skills to adapt to opportunities in its environment. Seeing beyond the present supports the organization's rebirth and vitality by finding new ways to serve clients.

Peter Drucker's observations on Willowcreek Community Church suggest that it became an SRO and continues to be one.

Willowcreek Community Church in South Barrington, Illinois, outside Chicago, has become the nation's largest church—some 13,000 parishioners. . . . Bill Hybels, in his early twenties when he founded the church [in 1974], chose the community because it had relatively few churchgoers, though the population was growing fast and churches were plentiful. He went from door to door asking. "Why don't you go to church?" Then he designed a church to answer potential customer's needs: for instance, it offers full services on Wednesday evenings because many working parents need Sunday to spend with their children. . . .

EXHIBIT 26.5 Leadership and Self-Renewing Organizations

Leadership Traits	Leadership Mystique	Transformational Leadership	Charismatic Leadership	Self-Renewing Organizations
Builds trust	Sense of mission	Charisma	Sees beyond the present	Open
Competence	Capacity for power	Individualized consideration	Visionary	Receptive
Dominant	Will to survive and persevere	Intellectual stimulation	Builds trust	Adaptive
Energy			Empowers	Continuously learn
Honest				Continuously innovate
Intelligence				Continuously grow
Knowledgeable				Self-organizing
Self-confidence				Vitality
Vision				Rebirth
				Immune to decay

Hybels continues to listen and react. The pastor's sermon is taped while it is being delivered and instantly reproduced so that parishioners can pick up a cassette when they leave the building because he was told again and again, "I need to listen when I drive home or drive to work so that I can build the message into my life." But he was also told: "The sermon always tells me to change my life but never how to do it." So now every one of Hybels' sermons ends with specific action recommendations.[58]

Mr. Hybels' leadership qualities let him build and maintain Willowcreek Community Church as a self-renewing system.

26.6   Conclusion

Self-renewing organizations have strong core values that focus the behavior of all organization members. They continually adapt to their environments in an unrelenting pursuit of their mission. Self-renewing organizations have the unique qualities of innovation, growth, and continuous learning.

Leadership is an influence process where the leader tries to affect the behavior of a follower or potential follower. Power is a central feature of leadership, with leaders getting power from their organizational positions and personal qualities. Leaders and managers play important but different roles in an organization. Leaders seek change; managers keep a steady direction.

Leadership is the driving force that can transform an organization into a self-renewing one. Charisma, self-confidence, and building trust are characteristics that can help a leader energize followers to pursue a vision of becoming a self-renewing system. The continual growth of such organizations needs these and other leadership qualities. Knowledge and vision of the leader, plus the intellectual stimulation of followers, infuses self-renewing organizations with critical skills to adapt to opportunities in their environment.

Endnotes

1. Drucker, P. F. (1989). "What Business Can Learn from Nonprofits," *Harvard Business Review* 89 (4): 88–93.
2. Drucker, P. F. (1990). *Managing the Non-Profit Organization: Practices and Principles.* New York: HarperCollins Publishers.
3. Drucker, P. F. (1995). *Managing in a Time of Great Change,* Chapter 2. New York: Truman Talley Books/Plume.
4. See note 2.
5. Garvin, D. A. (1993). "Building a Learning Organization," *Harvard Business Review* 71 (4): 78–91.
6. Gardner, J. W. (1981). *Self-Renewal: The Individual and the Innovative Society.* New York: W. W. Norton & Company.
7. Kuhnert, K. W. (1993). "Leadership Theory in Postmodernist Organizations." In R. T. Golembiewski (ed.), *Handbook of Organizational Behavior.* New York: Marcel Dekker, pp. 189–202.
8. Lawrence, P. R., and D. Dyer. (1983). *Renewing American Industry.* New York: Free Press.

9. Senge, P. M. (1990). *The Fifth Discipline: The Art and Practice of the Learning Organization.* New York: Doubleday.

10. Wheatley, M. J. (1994). *Leadership and the New Science: Learning about Organization from an Orderly Universe.* San Francisco: Berrett-Koehler Publishers, Inc.

11. Avolio, B. J. (1999). *Full Leadership Development: Building the Vital Forces in Organizations.* Thousand Oaks, CA: Sage Publications, Inc.

12. Northouse, P. G. (2000). *Leadership Theory and Practice,* 2nd ed. Thousand Oaks, CA: Sage Publications, Inc.

13. Bennis, W., and B. Nanus. (1985). *Leaders: The Strategies for Taking Charge.* New York: Harper & Row, pp. 21, 23, 40–41, 92–93, 218–226.

14. Kotter, J. P. (1990). "What Leaders Really Do," *Harvard Business Review* (May–June) 90 (3): 103–11.

15. Yukl, G. A. (1994). *Leadership in Organizations.* Englewood Cliffs, NJ: Prentice Hall, pp. 4–5.

16. Zaleznik, A. (1977). "Managers and Leaders: Are They Different?" *Harvard Business Review* (May–June) 55 (3): 67–80.

17. Zaleznik, A. (1990). "The Leadership Gap," *Academy of Management Executive* 4: 7–22.

18. Champoux, J. E., and L. D. Goldman. (1993). "Building a Total Quality Culture." In T. D. Connors (ed.), *Nonprofit Organizations Policies and Procedures Handbook,* Chapter 3. New York: John Wiley & Sons.

19. Bass, B. M. (1990). "From Transactional to Transformational Leadership: Learning to Share the Vision," *Organizational Dynamics* (Winter) 18: 19–31.

20. House, R. J., and M. L. Baetz. (1979). "Leadership: Some Empirical Generalizations and New Research Directions." In B. M. Staw (ed.), *Research in Organizational Behavior.* Greenwich, CT: JAI Press, pp. 341–423.

21. Kendrick, D. T., and D. C. Funder. (1988). "Profiting from Controversy: Lessons from the Person-Situation Debate," *American Psychologist* 43: 23–34.

22. Kirkpatrick, S. A., and E. A. Locke. (1991). "Leadership: Do Traits Matter?" *Academy of Management Executive* 5: 48–60.

23. Mann, R. D. (1959). "A Review of the Relationships between Personality and Performance in Small Groups," *Psychological Bulletin* 56: 241–70.

24. Kouzes, J. M., and B. Z. Posner. (1995). *The Leadership Challenge: How to Keep Getting Extraordinary Things Done in Organizations.* San Francisco: Jossey-Bass.

25. Bennis, W. (1989). *Why Leaders Can't Lead: The Unconscious Conspiracy Continues,* Chapter 18. San Francisco: Jossey-Bass.

26. Bennis, W. (1993). *An Invented Life: Reflections on Leadership and Change.* Reading, MA: Addison-Wesley.

27. Bennis, W., and R. Townsend. (1995). *Reinventing Leadership: Strategies to Empower the Organization,* Chapter 2. New York: William Morrow and Company, Inc.

28. Gardner, J. W. (1993). *On Leadership,* Chapter 5. New York: Free Press.

29. Jennings, E. E. (1960). *An Anatomy of Leadership.* New York: Harper & Row.

30. Jennings, E. E. (1974). "On Rediscovering the Leader." In J. W. McGuire (ed.), *Contemporary Management: Issues and Viewpoints.* Englewood Cliffs, NJ: Prentice Hall, pp. 390–96.

31. Id., p. 391.

32. Byrne, J. A. (1990). "Profiting from the Nonprofits," *Business Week* (March 26): 66–70, 72, 74.

33. Id., p. 70.

34. Avolio, B. J., and B. M. Bass. (1987). "Transformational Leadership, Charisma and Beyond." In J. G. Hunt, E. R. Baglia, H. P. Dachler, and C. A. Schriesheim (eds.), *Emerging Leadership Vistas.* Lexington, MA: Lexington Books, pp. 29–49.

35. Bass, B. M. (1985). *Leadership and Performance Beyond Expectations.* New York: The Free Press, pp. 42–43.

36. See note 19.

37. Burns, J. M. (1978). *Leadership.* New York: Harper & Row.

38. Bryman, A. (1993). "Charismatic Leadership in Business Organizations: Some Neglected Issues," *The Leadership Quarterly* 4: 289–304.

39. Fuller, J. B., C. E. P. Patterson, K. Hester, and D. Y. Stringer. (1996). "A Quantitative Review of Research on Charismatic Leadership," *Psychological Reports* 78: 271–87.

40. Gardner, W. L., and B. J. Avolio. (1998). "The Charismatic Relationship: A Dramaturgical Perspective," *Academy of Management Review* 23: 32–58.

41. House, R. J., and R. N. Aditya. (1997). "The Social Scientific Study of Leadership: Quo Vadis?" *Journal of Management* 23: 409–73.

42. Lowe, K. B., K. G. Kroeck, and N. Sivasubramanian. (1996). "Effectiveness Correlates of Transformational and Transactional Leadership: A Meta-Analytic Review of the MLQ Literature," *Leadership Quarterly* 7: 385–425.

43. Conger, J. A. (1989). *The Charismatic Leader: Behind the Mystique of Exceptional Leadership.* San Francisco: Jossey-Bass, pp. 9–10.

44. Conger, J. A., and R. N. Kanungo. (1998). *Charismatic Leadership in Organizations.* Thousand Oaks, CA: Sage Publications, Inc.

45. Carlzon, J. (1987). *Moments of Truth.* Cambridge, MA: Ballinger, pp. 94–95.

46. Howell, J. P., D. E. Bowen, P. W. Dorfman, S. Kerr, and P. M. Podsakoff. (1990). "Substitutes for Leadership: Effective Alternatives to Ineffective Leadership," *Organizational Dynamics* 19 (1): 21–38.

47. Howell, J. P., P. W. Dorfman, and S. Kerr. (1986). "Moderator Variables in Leadership Research," *Academy of Management Review* 11: 86–102.

48. Kerr, S. (1977). "Substitutes for Leadership: Some Implications for Organizational Design," *Organization and Administrative Sciences* 8: 135–46.

49. Kerr, S., and J. M. Jermier. (1978). "Substitutes for Leadership: Their Meaning and Measurement," *Organizational Behavior and Human Performance* 22: 375–403.

50. Podsakoff, P. M., S. B. MacKenzie, and R. Fetter. (1993). "Substitutes for Leadership and the Management of Professionals," *Leadership Quarterly* 4: 1–44.

51. Podsakoff, P. M., B. P. Niehoff, S. B. MacKenzie, and M. L. Williams. (1993). "Do Substitutes for Leadership Really Substitute for Leadership? An Empirical Examination of Kerr and Jermier's Situational Leadership Model," *Organizational Behavior and Human Decision Processes* 54: 1–44.

52. Hall, R. J., J. W. Workman, and C. A. Marchioro. (1998). "Sex, Task, and Behavioral Flexibility Effects on Leadership Perceptions," *Organizational Behavior and Human Decision Processes* 74: 1–32.

53. See note 41.

54. Lord, R. G., R. J. Foti, and C. DeVader. (1984). "A Test of Leadership Categorization Theory: Internal Structure, Information Processing and Leadership Perceptions," *Organizational Behavior and Human Performance* 34: 343–78.

55. Lord, R. G., and K. J. Maher, (1993). *Leadership and Information Processing: Linking Perceptions and Performance.* New York: Routledge.

56. See note 54.

57. Calder, B. J. (1977). "An Attribution Theory of Leadership." In B. M. Staw and G. R. Salancik (eds.), *New Directions in Organizational Behavior.* Chicago: St. Clair Press, pp. 179–204.

58. See note 1.

Suggested Readings

Bass, B. M. (1990). *Bass & Stogdill's Handbook of Leadership: Theory, Research, and Managerial Applications,* Chapters 4 and 5. New York: Free Press.

French, J., and B. Raven. (1959). "The Bases of Social Power." In D. Cartwright (ed.), *Studies in Social Power.* Ann Arbor, MI: Institute for Social Research, pp. 150–167.

27 Shared Leadership: Relationship Management to Improve Nonprofit Organization Effectiveness

CRAIG L. PEARCE, PHD ASSISTANT PROFESSOR
Drucker School of Management
Claremont Graduate University

MONICA L. PERRY, PHD ASSISTANT PROFESSOR
Belk College of Business Administration
University of North Carolina at Charlotte

HENRY P. SIMS JR., PHD PROFESSOR OF MANAGEMENT
University of Maryland at College Park

27.1 Introduction

In this chapter, we define *empowered teams,* describe the shared leadership process within empowered teams, and develop a limited model of conditions conducive for shared leadership. Conditions for shared leadership involve a number of team characteristics and nonprofit organizational characteristics. Increased competition for resources and increasing demands for accountability place nonprofits in a precarious situation in need of innovative strategies. One such innovative strategy is the use of shared leadership in empowered teams to help establish and maintain relationships with key stakeholders. Such teams may include team members from various parts of the organization but may also include members from various stakeholder groups.

The current environment in which nonprofit organizations (NPOs) operate presents ever-increasing challenges. Rapidly changing competitive, legal, demographic, and technological environments, combined with an increased focus on results and accountability, fuel many NPOs' desires to find innovative means to effectively adapt and achieve desired levels of performance.[1] Teams have been suggested as one possible response to this changing environment.[2] Successful nonprofits typically exhibit strong leadership and decentralize decision-making authority (empowerment) to promote and facilitate teamwork.[3–4] Teams can help NPOs build, maintain, and optimize relationships among NPO employees, volunteers, donors, funding agencies, and clients or customers. The process of building and maintaining critical relationships is the cornerstone of relationship marketings.[5] For many NPOs, the combination of empowerment, leadership, and effective teams will turn out to be a necessity in building and maintaining key stakeholder relationships.[6]

While leadership and empowerment are critical to understanding team effectiveness in general,[7,8] trends in the nonprofit environment suggest an even greater need for leadership and empowerment in the team context. As NPOs reduce organizational bureaucracy, nonprofit boards, directors, and managers will ultimately have less time and opportunity to micromanage individuals and teams. Moving toward increasingly fewer layers of management while simultaneously increasing managers' span of control creates an environment in need of the potential benefits of shared leadership in empowered teams.

Empowerment means the team has the authority and power to direct, manage, and lead itself.[9] A fully empowered team possesses the authority to make decisions for which, collectively, the team is responsible. Shared leadership means that the team, as a whole, shares and participates fully in the leadership tasks of the team.[10] If the team has the authority and knowledge of the leadership tasks, team members can accomplish much of the leadership formerly relegated to a manager. For example, team members can actively motivate one another, provide feedback on performance, and direct the activities of the team. Shared leadership is one important way in which a team exercises full empowerment. Providing teams with the power and opportunity to make decisions based on the team's skills makes sense when NPOs use teams to take advantage of the unique skills and talents of individuals not only across the organization but also across a multitude of stakeholder groups.

Making the most of team members' skills may motivate NPOs to organize in teams; however, the ultimate benefit—enhanced effectiveness—appears relatively uncertain and elusive. "Team management is one of the few areas . . . that has yet to receive the full attention of academics, business gurus, management consultants and trainers."[11] Based on a wealth of conceptual and empirical support, however,[12] leadership appears to have a significant relationship with a number of outcomes in all types of organizations and thus may prove a fertile ground for further enhancing team effectiveness.[13]

In the following sections, we develop a parsimonious model of the role of shared leadership in nonprofits. The model is grounded in much of the organizational literature on vertical leadership, as well as the emerging research on alternative sources of leadership in the team context. In particular, we model conditions that are conducive to shared leadership, such as various team and organizational characteristics. Perhaps most importantly, we identify nonprofit characteristics that suggest when shared leadership is likely to be most beneficial.

27.2   Linking Leadership and Teams

Leadership involves the ability and capacity to influence others.[14,15] In the team context, two potential sources of leadership exist: the vertical or appointed leader and the team itself.[16] In NPOs, a vertical leader typically relies on hierarchical authority as the basis for leadership.[17] Undoubtedly, the exercise of vertical leadership ultimately impacts team performance by affecting team processes and functioning along with team member attitudes, beliefs, and behaviors.[18,19]

Although *vertical leaders* have received considerable attention and support in the literature,[20–25] emerging research has brought to the forefront a different source of leadership. The second source of leadership identifies the *team/group* as a potential source of leadership.[26,27] While vertical leadership is an influence on team process, shared leadership is a team process. Shared leadership means the team as a whole, rather than a single appointed leader, engages in leadership.

A wealth of theoretical and empirical evidence supports the important role of leadership in NPOs.[28,29] While there is significant support for the important role of leadership in nonprofits, much of the work has focused on vertical leadership. Teams that use hierarchical or "vertical" leadership are referred to as *vertically managed teams* (VMTs). In VMTs, power and authority are vested in an appointed leader, such as the manager. In this situation, the manager projects downward influence on team members.

Relying solely on vertical leadership in teams would seem "to ignore leadership dynamics within a group context."[30] In particular, in empowered teams, where power and authority are vested in the team itself, the sharing of leadership is a natural outgrowth of vesting power and authority at the team level. Providing the team with the power and authority to lead itself provides the opportunity for shared leadership. While shared leadership can be a natural outgrowth of team power and authority, shared leadership may not simply emerge. The members of the team must be made aware that the team has the responsibility for leading itself; be willing to engage in the sharing of leadership; and, as a team, possess the necessary leadership skills to engage in shared leadership.[31] All three conditions are necessary if shared leadership is to occur.

When shared leadership occurs, what are the likely outcomes? Emerging work on self-managing work teams strongly suggests that group self-leadership,[32] distributed leadership[33] or shared leadership,[34,35] is strongly associated with more effective teams. For example, Katzenbach and Smith's in-depth study of teams[36] showed that high-performance teams actively engaged in shared leadership much more than other teams, and Pearce found shared leadership to be an important predictor of change management team effectiveness.[37]

27.3   Empowered Teams in NPOs

The topic of empowerment and self-management has received considerable attention in recent years.[38–45] Power is a central issue in the empowerment literature.[46] Power relates to influence and the authority to make decisions.[47] Whereas traditional models of management (including nonprofit management) emphasize power and decision-making authority emanating from the top (e.g., directors of NPOs), empowerment emphasizes the *decentralization* of power. The rationale behind the empowering of individual employees is that those dealing with situations on a daily basis are the most qualified to make decisions regarding those situations.

The efficacy of empowered teams is supported by recent work on self-managing work teams (SMWTs)[48–51] and the complexities of addressing issues with multiple stakeholders in an increasingly dynamic environment. A fully empowered team must possess the authority to make decisions for which the team is collectively responsible. Nonprofits may use empowered teams to take advantage of the unique skills and talents of individuals across the organization. Therefore, it is logical to provide these individuals the power and opportunity to make decisions based on the skills they possess.

In a simple transaction in which a nonprofit volunteer or staff member delivers a service, a single person interacts with the client. The person's effectiveness depends on his or her ability to adapt to the client's unique problems and effectively communicate an appropriate solution. Such adaptations cannot always be approved before making them. Multiply this simple interaction by the number of members in the team who will have interactions with clients. The team may have to make specific adaptations, based on client interactions, to establish and maintain effective client relationships. It seems unreasonable to expect each team member to confirm each adaptation with a single vertical leader.

What are the likely benefits of empowered teams? The existing research on SMWTs supports the notion that such teams can yield greater levels of collaboration, coordination, and cooperation, as well as novel and innovative solutions to problems.[52,53] Individuals in empowered teams develop a better appreciation for the interdependencies between their tasks and other team members' tasks, as well as a better appreciation for how their behavior impacts the overall organization.[54] Thus, team members' behavior will reflect a greater understanding of interdependencies. As a result of empowerment, the collective ability of the team can lead to more productive team processes and enhanced performance.

27.4 Shared Leadership in Empowered Teams

While empowerment entails the sharing of power, shared leadership exists only in fully empowered teams in which the team actively engages in the leadership process. Shared leadership is a collaborative process of sharing leadership within the team as a whole. As such, shared leadership is a specific type of team interaction process that involves behaviors in the domain of leadership. The team as a whole must be empowered, or provided the power and authority, to collectively share leadership of the team.

A unique aspect of team functioning is the potential for the team as a whole to share in leadership of the team.[55,56] Shared leadership, as a team process, is likely to affect team responses. In our discussion, we omit the role of vertical leadership for parsimony, but acknowledge that vertical leadership plays an important facilitative role.[57]

Many different types of leader behaviors, such as transactional, transformational, directive, empowering, and social facilitative, can be shared by the empowered team. Given the extensive body of literature that precedes our discussion,[58–62] we will simply provide examples of how these leader behaviors might be shared in empowered teams.

Shared leadership in the team might involve the team's clearly identifying and reinforcing the relationship between the accuracy of handling client requests and the ability to stay within the budget. The team may emphasize the attainment of computer skills to increase a team member's confidence in him- or herself. In this way, the team focuses not just on ways to meet immediate team goals, but also on building the confidence of team members—a higher-order need. The team engaging in directive leader behaviors may meet to organize the topics in an upcoming meeting with a potential benefactor. For instance, the team can identify and assign responsibility for collecting data on the client base, gather information on services provided by competing NPOs, and gather information on foundations' requirements for funding proposals. The team engaging in empowering behaviors may emphasize the importance of each member's setting goals, such as the number of clients served over a given time period. Alternatively, the team might meet to conduct an analysis of why a particular grant proposal did not receive funding—this type of team self-reflection typifies empowering leader behavior.

While we have discussed the importance of empowered teams in NPOs, we also recognize the critical role of different groups of stakeholders. NPOs, when compared to for-profit businesses, must be much more deliberate in their efforts to integrate the views of multiple groups of stakeholders. Thus, one particularly important type of "cross-functional" empowered team in NPOs is an interstakeholder team. Team members in an interstakeholder team might include staff from the NPO, volunteers, donors, government officials, community advocates, and, most importantly, clients or customers of the NPO. Our discussion of shared leadership in empowered teams includes, but is not exclusive to, interstakeholder teams.

27.5   Conducive Conditions for Shared Leadership

Conditions conducive to shared leadership involve two principal aspects: team characteristics and NPO characteristics. Team characteristics have been related to team process and team outcomes.[63–65] The variety of missions for different NPOs suggests that one must account for the nature of differences in NPO characteristics. Therefore, we categorize NPOs and describe how these characteristics also relate to the possible benefits of the shared leadership process.

(A)   TEAM CHARACTERISTICS AND SHARED LEADERSHIP

Empowered teams and shared leadership appear particularly critical in the nonprofit team context for two reasons. First, many NPOs rely extensively on volunteers, and such volunteers often come from a broad cross-section of educational and economic groups.[66] Thus, collectively, such a diverse team can possess the necessary range of potential knowledge, skills, and abilities to effectively lead itself. It seems most efficient and effective to take advantage of the collective skills of the team, rather than to rely on a single, vertical leader.[67]

Second, both volunteers and donors are expecting more from their involvement with NPOs.[68] Volunteers want to be able to apply all of their competencies to their volunteer work and have the opportunity for personal development.[69] Donors are motivated to provide goods and funds to NPOs for a multitude of reasons, from spiritual motivations to achievement motivations.[70] Many donors are motivated to contribute by a multitude or combination of reasons. Engaging in shared leadership can provide volunteers with the chance to exercise a wide range of skills and support donors with multiple reasons for contributing. Thus, shared leadership is likely to enhance volunteers' and donors' personal development.

However, the development of shared leadership does not happen automatically. One set of influences on the emergence of shared leadership relates to team characteristics that describe the compositional attributes of the team. We include the five attributes described as follows because as they have received considerable support in the literature: (1) geographic dispersion, (2) maturity, (3) skill heterogeneity, (4) demographic heterogeneity, and (5) team size.

(i) Geographic Dispersion

Geographic dispersion relates to not only the distance between the vertical leader and the team[71] but also the distance between team members. Pearce and colleagues studied geographically dispersed U.S. government agency teams and found that shared leadership had a greater effect than vertical leadership on a host of group processes, as well as on effectiveness.[72]

In addition to government agencies, many NPOs desire participation from individuals across various locations. For example, nonprofit board members may be spread across a number of towns and cities. As NPOs seek to increase involvement from individuals and organizations across physical locations, the distance between and among team members is likely to increase, rather than decrease. Unfortunately, it may be neither practical nor appropriate to define teams along close geographic lines merely to encourage shared leadership. Thus, when teams are geographically dispersed, all else being equal, we expect to see less shared leadership.

Although the emergence of shared leadership is less likely as dispersion increases, it is precisely these situations in which the need for shared leadership may be the greatest. A single, vertical leader—as the focal and sole source of leadership—may have neither the time nor the opportunity to actively engage in all the necessary leadership when and where the team needs it.[73] When team members are separated from the manager or team leader, shared leadership may in fact ameliorate the potential negative impact of separation from the leader. Because physically dispersed teams will likely engage in less shared leadership, it must be deliberately encouraged by creating teams that possess values or other team characteristics that are most conducive to shared leadership.

(ii) Maturity

Alternative conceptualizations of teams have described how teams develop over time.[74–76] Although there is no universal agreement on the precise number of stages, there is a general consensus that teams go through stages of development. It seems likely that the stage of team maturity would influence the emergence of shared leadership within the team.

In observations of effective and ineffective teams, Barry concluded that in the initial formation stage of the team, effective teams spent much more time on social or interpersonal aspects, like getting to know the skills and preferences of team members.[77] For instance, early in the development of the team, the team can spend time getting to know each member's background, such as accounting, social work, psychology, and so forth.

Without time to mature, team members are unlikely to acknowledge or understand the range of skills of the various team members.[78–81] Without acknowledging or understanding how leadership might be shared among the team members, it seems less likely that shared leadership will develop. A team focusing on maintaining a long-term relationship with a specific foundation or benefactor will have more opportunity to mature because the task has a long-term focus. A team assembled solely to address a natural disaster may be assembled on a temporary basis, therefore having less time to mature. A more stable team would have more opportunity to evolve and mature. Therefore, even though the team may be temporary, combining members who have previously worked together in a team may prove fruitful.

(iii) Skill Heterogeneity

Skill heterogeneity refers to the range and variety of expertise possessed by the team as a whole. As members of a team are more capable, both individually and collectively, traditional vertical leadership becomes less necessary.[82,83] The abilities of the team members may vary with respect to presentation skills, information technology, client expertise, and financial and regulatory knowledge. For instance, one team member may have substantial knowledge of government health care regulations, whereas another may have in-depth knowledge of federal grant requirements, and another may have direct knowledge of services offered by competing NPOs. There is evidence to suggest that such skill heterogeneity results in more innovative solutions.[84] As noted by Peter Drucker, "It is up to community organizations to innovate."[85] Given the importance of developing innovations in nonprofits, skill heterogeneity in teams should be encouraged.

While skill heterogeneity refers to the variety of functional expertise of team members, it also refers to the variety of teamwork skills that exist in the team.[86] Teamwork skills include both interpersonal and leadership abilities.

Why would a team with heterogeneous skills be more likely to engage in shared leadership? Being effective at various stages of team maturity requires teams to vary emphasis on different skills at different stages.[87,88] Therefore, teams with a balance and breadth of teamwork and functional abilities are more likely to be able to appropriately engage in shared leadership over the life of the team.

(iv) Demographic Heterogeneity

Demographic heterogeneity also influences the display of shared leadership. Demographic heterogeneity has been defined in a number of ways, including gender and racial composition in cross-functional teams,[89,90] as well as cultural and educational heterogeneity in top management teams.[91,92] Demographic characteristics, such as education, gender, and race, are important antecedents of shared leadership. The issue of demographic heterogeneity of teams will continue to be important as volunteers increasingly come from across a broad cross-section of the population.[93]

Clearly, demographic heterogeneity is important; however, its impact on teams is not entirely clear.[94] Pfeffer suggested that heterogeneity (diversity) harms team interaction processes, such as communication.[95] If we accept Pfeffer's perspective, then shared leadership, as a unique aspect of the team process, should occur less as with more demographically heterogeneous teams.

However, if diversity affects team process at all, it appears to do so only in early stages of team development. For example, Baugh and Graen found no differences between the quality of diverse and homogeneous cross-functional teams,[96] and similarly Elron found no relationship between cultural heterogeneity and team cohesion.[97] Racially diverse teams have reported less effective team interactions in the initial stages of team development, but over time, processes improve and eventually match racially homogeneous teams.[98] Thus, over time, a team composed of women, minorities, and men may experience initial "bumps" but can be as effective in the long run as a more homogeneous team.

In addition to allowing a diverse team time to work out the bumps, teamwork training may decrease the potential negative effects of demographic heterogeneity. While functional skill heterogeneity can lead to greater conflict and less consensus in top management teams, the negative impact of such heterogeneity on the ability to reach consensus can be ameliorated via the use of agreement-seeking decision-making techniques.[99] Thus, the potential deleterious effect of demographic heterogeneity early in the team's development may be overcome with the use of specific and appropriate team building tools.

(v) Team Size

Team size is another characteristic likely to be associated with the emergence of shared leadership. As team size increases, so should the collective ability of the team. As team size increases, however, it becomes more difficult to manage team interaction processes, as communication among team members becomes more difficult. Several studies have found team size to have a marginal but negative effect on work integration in cross-functional teams.[100–103] These results indicate a potential inconsistency in team size effects. However, given the increasing communication difficulties as team size increases, it seems likely that shared leadership will be negatively associated with team size. It will certainly be more difficult to coordinate communication with a large team than with a two-person team. Thus, to the extent possible, teams should be kept as small as possible to facilitate shared leadership.

(B) ORGANIZATIONAL CHARACTERISTICS AND SHARED LEADERSHIP IN EMPOWERED TEAMS

The costs of developing and nurturing shared leadership in empowered teams are far from negligible. Therefore, it is important that we identify the conditions in which positive net benefits from shared leadership accrue.

One of these conditions is a high level of interdependence. *Interdependence* is defined as the degree to which the accomplishment of goals requires joint contributions and ongoing, mutual collaboration.[104] When tasks are relatively independent (low interdependence), shared leadership may actually result in process losses.[105] Process losses reflect the time and effort needed for the team to initiate and maintain the shared leadership process, and thus represent the incremental costs of working as a team rather than as individuals. Shared leadership, inappropriately applied, may actually hinder accomplishment of relatively independent nonprofit activities. Therefore, we suggest that by defining appropriate NPO characteristics, we can identify conditions, such as a relatively high level of interdependence between the NPO and stakeholder groups, in which positive net benefits of shared leadership accrue.

We have identified three categories of NPOs based on the nonprofit organization typology of Galaskiewicz and Bielefeld that help identify where and when shared leadership would result in a positive net benefit.[106] The three categories are benefit recipients, resource bases, and the type of product offered by the NPO.

(i) Benefit Recipients

The first category, benefit recipients, identifies the recipients of an NPO's products (goods or services). Products can go to the public at large or to members of the NPO (mutual). In mutual-benefit NPOs, the team members are also the recipients of the NPO's goods or services. Therefore, there is considerable alignment between the team's interests and the recipient's interests. Team members appreciate the inherent interdependence in what their team does and its effects on recipients. As a result, perceived interdependence between the team and the recipients is aligned in mutual types of NPOs.

Conversely, public NPOs separate those that deliver and those that receive the products such that an accurate appreciation of interdependence is more difficult. Perceptions aside, it is precisely in the case of public NPOs that high levels of task interdependence actually exist. In order to effectively design and deliver goods and services, public non-profit teams must actively incorporate input from different groups of stakeholders. The coordination of tasks results from individuals recognizing that high levels of interdependence exist.[107] When a team's perception of interdependence is equal to the actual task interdependence, teams are more effective.[108]

Thus, public NPOs have an increased need for shared leadership in interstakeholder teams to align perceptions of interdependence with actual task interdependence. Shared leadership becomes useful in the case of public-benefit teams because the team can be designed to include both recipients and deliverers/designers of goods and services. The interests and issues relevant to a variety of groups of stakeholders can be more meaningfully communicated when shared leadership occurs in such teams. Shared leadership is an interactive team process, and such interaction is needed to encourage cohesion.[109] Cohesion reflects the degree to which the team has a strong desire to remain or stay in the team.[110–112]

Cohesion supports greater and more open communication, greater effort, and better coordination among team members.[113,114] Thus, when shared leadership results in a more cohesive team, team members can more accurately assess interdependence and act accordingly. With public NPOs, task interdependence is high, and shared leadership can contribute by helping to align perceptions of task interdependence with the actual level of interdependence.

(ii) Resource Bases

Similarly, the second dimension for categorization of NPOs, resource bases, also suggests the importance of interdependence as an underlying condition for shared leadership. Resource bases define the inputs required to conduct the organization's operations. There are two aspects of resources. The first, financial resources, concerns the source of funds or products. Financial resources may come from the making and selling of goods or services (products) or from donations. The second aspect, human resources, concerns human inputs or intellectual capital. Human resources may include both paid staff and volunteers. (See Exhibit 27.1.)

An NPO that relies on both donations and volunteers must be able to attract and retain relationships with a multitude of donors and volunteers. The day-to-day survival of such organizations is highly dependent on the organization's ability to do so. Relying on both donors and volunteers increases the possibility of failure because of heightened interdependence between the NPO and its various volunteers and donors. As previously discussed, high levels of interdependence necessitate equally high levels of coordination and collaboration to ensure effective performance.

EXHIBIT 27.1 Resource Bases and Benefits of Shared Leadership

Human Resource Basis	Financial Resource Basis	
	Make and Sell Products	Products or Funds Donated
Staff	Least need for shared leadership	Moderate need for shared leadership
Volunteers	Moderate need for shared leadership	Greatest need for shared leadership

NPO relationships with donors and volunteers must be nurtured with the intent of creating increased commitment from both. One way to help foster increased donor and volunteer commitment is via shared leadership in interstakeholder teams.

Many benefits accrue to donors and volunteers from engaging in shared leadership in empowered teams. First, shared leadership allows individual team members significant opportunity for personal growth. Volunteers have the opportunity to achieve complex (rather than simple) personal growth goals far above and beyond NPO goals. Volunteers expect nonprofit involvement to provide a plethora of benefits and to make choices consistent with greater rather than fewer perceived benefits. The greater the benefits to volunteers, the more committed the volunteers are to the NPO. Similarly, donors contribute to NPOs based on a wide range of motivations or needs, both internal (e.g., achievement) and external. To the degree that shared leadership can satisfy a wider range of donor needs, shared leadership can contribute to an increase in donor commitment. Relevant results of increased commitment include decreased turnover (or stated positively, increased retention), increased satisfaction, and increased effort.[115,116]

The second benefit for donors and volunteers is an increased sense of self-efficacy and collective efficacy. Self-efficacy is an individual's belief that he or she can be effective,[117] while collective efficacy is a belief that the team can be effective.[118,119] Donors rarely have an opportunity to see where their donation goes. Without exposure to the effects of donations, donors may question the true effectiveness of their efforts. However, as part of an empowered interstakeholder team, donors (or representatives of donor groups) can be exposed to the specific results of efforts, including their own. Similarly, volunteers (or volunteer group representatives) who work on teams can also be exposed to the results of efforts, including their own. Thus, if an NPO can encourage shared leadership in interstakeholder teams, there is a greater chance that volunteers and donors will enjoy a greater sense of efficacy, be more satisfied, remain with the NPO longer, and apply greater effort to the task at hand.

(iii) Type of Product Offered

The third dimension for the categorization of NPOs is the nature of the product that the NPO provides. We borrow a conceptual framework from the marketing literature to show how shared leadership can help align the information needs of clients, donors, funding agencies, and volunteers with what an NPO provides. NPOs can provide products that range from tangible goods, like clothing, to pure services, like legal services.

Products can be classified in three categories according to the ease with which quality can be assessed (Exhibit 27.2). The three categories are (1) search, (2) experience, and (3) credence qualities.[120]

EXHIBIT 27.2 Organizational Characteristics and Shared Leadership Benefits

Product Possesses	Product Quality Can Be Assessed	Examples	Need for Shared Leadership
Search qualities	Easily before use or consumption	Sale of used clothing	Low
Experience qualities	Only after use or consumption	Computer training	Moderate
Credence qualities	With great difficulty even after use or consumption	Psychological counseling	High

Tangible goods (or ordinary goods in the parlance of Galaskiewicz and Bielefeld[121]) have considerable search qualities, which means that clients or users of the good can easily assess the quality of the good prior to use or consumption. For example, a consumer can inspect clothing offered for sale before he or she buys the item from an NPO, such as Goodwill Industries. In the case of tangible goods, information about quality can be relatively easily communicated via inspection of the product. Little additional effort is required from the NPO to communicate product quality; thus, the use of empowered teams to develop communications with users is not necessary or particularly efficient.

However, NPOs are likely to offer products that have significant experience or credence qualities (trust-type goods as described by Galaskiewicz and Bielefeld[122]). Products with experience qualities are difficult to assess prior to use such that a client (or user) can assess the quality of the service only after use. For example, a local government agency that provides computer training to displaced workers would be providing a service in which the quality is difficult to assess until after a client has participated in the training.

Products with considerable credence qualities are even more difficult to assess. Credence qualities mean that the quality of the service is difficult to ascertain even after the service has been provided. Professional services, such as psychological counseling, are typical products that have considerable credence qualities and essentially no search qualities.

In the case of NPOs that provide complex services that possess considerable experience or credence qualities, the information needs of stakeholders are high.[123] The NPO must be able to communicate effectively with stakeholders to encourage use of the service and help educate stakeholders about how to accurately assess the benefits or quality of the service. When offering products with considerable experience or credence qualities, an NPO can benefit from empowered teams to help create meaningful communications with clients/users, donors, funding agencies, and volunteers.

Meaningful communication with stakeholders is more likely when interstakeholder teams are responsible for developing and designing communications and engage in shared leadership. Interstakeholder teams, by having members that span stakeholder groups, will have firsthand knowledge of how and what to communicate to stakeholders. However, unless there is cohesiveness and commitment in the team, members are unlikely to openly share their insights with one another. The shared leadership process contributes to the commitment, cohesiveness, and efficacy of such interstakeholder teams such that public relations efforts, advertising, and direct communications with various stakeholders can be more meaningfully designed.

In summary, the net gain from encouraging shared leadership in empowered teams is positive when NPOs serve the public; primarily seek resources from donors, funding agencies, and volunteers; and offer services that have substantial experience and credence qualities.

27.6 Managerial Implications

Highly effective empowered teams require managerial input in their design. Designing the team requires attention to create teams with the right mix of functional and leadership skills. Just as managers take an active role in the recruitment and selection of staff and volunteers, so should they take an active role in the design of teams.

Specifically, managers concerned with developing effective teams must help design teams that have the requisite breadth of leadership skills.[124] The manager can collect information about potential team members' leadership skills via self-report by the potential team member, the manager's past knowledge of the individual, or by observing each potential team member. There is a better chance that shared leadership can occur within the team when the requisite breadth of leadership skills are adequately represented in the team.

Designing teams with the requisite breadth of leadership skills addresses the *ability* of the team to engage in shared leadership. However, ability is only part of the story. The manager must also design teams based on potential team members' *willingness* or predisposition toward sharing leadership in the team. Just as people vary in their need and desire for close supervision by a manager,[125] they also differ in their desire to engage in shared leadership. The manager should assess this willingness based on potential team members' past behavior (including managerial evaluations) and/or by directly addressing potential team members.

27.7 Limitations of Shared Leadership

Shared leadership is not a panacea for ineffective teams or NPOs. Limitations to our model of shared leadership exist. First, because shared leadership is a process that takes time to develop, it is limited in its ability to address situations requiring immediate and swift action. For example, an organization having only one week to develop a grant proposal is unlikely to have the time necessary to design and effectively implement an empowered team. In this situation, it is most expedient to assign a leader and get the team into action quickly.

Another potential limitation of shared leadership can occur if a team attempts to overdevelop its span of influence. An overzealous empowered team may attempt to expand its influence far beyond the team boundaries and create disruptions to other areas in the NPO. For example, an empowered team may have collectively decided that their goal is the achievement of superior client satisfaction in service delivery. As a result of that goal, the empowered team may try to force radical changes to the delivery process. Such radical changes may cause a disruption to the nonprofit with the unintended consequence of preventing others from accomplishing other, perhaps more important, organizational goals.

The idea of empowerment and shared leadership may be at odds with an NPO's organizational culture. For instance, some government agencies place a considerable emphasis on hierarchy via conformance to formal rules and following the chain of command. In a hierarchical culture, other employees may resent a team that no longer "plays by the rules." A nonprofit board member may resent being contacted directly by a team rather than by the NPO director. Those in the organization who resent the empowerment of the team may attempt to thwart the team's efforts.

Finally, although we have emphasized the need to effectively design teams with a balance of leadership skills, this balance may not be attainable. Designing teams with a balance of the leadership skills may be difficult, if not impossible, if the organization cannot identify enough individuals with requisite skills. Achieving the desired balance of leadership skills may be difficult if it requires significant reassignment of individuals or responsibilities. For example, a staff member who has developed a strong reputation with a particular client base may resist being assigned to a new team with a different client base. In summary, while shared leadership can be beneficial in many nonprofit situations, shared leadership is limited in its ability to address time-critical situations and cannot unilaterally overcome organizational and individual employee resistance.

27.8   Conclusion

The trend toward utilization of teams in organizing all types of organizations will continue well into the future. We have expanded the current understanding of team dynamics by investigating shared leadership in empowered teams. Shared leadership, as an important team process, can play a critical role in accomplishing NPO objectives. Encouraging shared leadership requires keeping teams as small as possible while allowing them sufficient time to mature and develop productive working relationships. Shared leadership is most appropriate and useful in NPOs that deliver benefits to the public at large; rely on donors, funding agencies, and volunteers for resources; and deliver services that possess considerable experience and/or credence qualities. Shared leadership, where appropriate, can foster positive team attitudes, beliefs, and behaviors, which can make NPOs more effective. As the importance of teams increases, NPOs that understand the impact of shared leadership on team outcomes will have an advantage in establishing and maintaining successful long-term relationships with key stakeholders.

Endnotes

1. Drucker, P. (1999). "The Discipline of Innovation," *Fund Raising Management* (May): 34–35.
2. Sims, H. P., and C. C. Manz. (1997). "Self-Managed Teams in the Self-Renewing Organization." In T. D. Connor (ed.), *The Nonprofit Handbook.* New York: John Wiley & Sons: pp. 223–42.
3. Osborne, D., and T. A. Gaebler. (1992). "Bringing Government Back to Life," *Governing* 5(5): 46–54.
4. Osborne, D., and P. Plastrik. (1997). "A Lesson in Reinvention," *Governing* 10 (5): 26–31.
5. Gronroos, C. (1995). "Relationship Marketing: The Strategy Continuum," *Journal of the Academy of Marketing Science* 23 (Fall): 252–55.
6. See note 2.
7. Yeatts, D. E., and C. Hyten. (1998). *High Performing Self-Managed Work Teams: A Comparison of Theory to Practice.* Thousand Oaks, CA: Sage Publications.
8. Yukl, G. (1998). *Leadership in Organizations,* 4th ed. Upper Saddle River, NJ: Prentice Hall.
9. Manz, C. C., and H. P. Sims Jr. (1991). "SuperLeadership: Beyond the Myth of Heroic Leadership," *Organizational Dynamics* 19 (Winter): 18–35.
10. Pearce, C. L. (1997). "The Determinants of Change Management Team Effectiveness: A Longitudinal Investigation," unpublished doctoral dissertation. University of Maryland, College Park, MD.
11. Oliver, J. (1996). "New, Improved Salesforce," *Management Today* 82 (December): 82–5.
12. See note 8.
13. Champoux, J. E. (1997). "Leadership and the Self-Renewing Organization." In T. D. Connor (ed.), *The Nonprofit Handbook.* New York: John Wiley & Sons, pp. 99–112.

14. Bass, B. M. (1990). *Bass and Stogdill's Handbook of Leadership.* New York: Free Press.
15. Yukl, G. (1981). *Leadership in Organizations.* Englewood Cliffs, NJ: Prentice Hall.
16. See note 10.
17. Shin, J., and G. E. McClomb. (1998). "Top Executive Leadership and Organizational Innovation: An Empirical Investigation of Nonprofit Human Service Organizations (HSOs)," *Administration in Social Work* 22(3): 1–21.
18. See note 14.
19. See note 15.
20. See note 14.
21. Eadie, D. C. (1996). "Can't Go It Alone: How to Forge the Board-Executive Partnership," *Nonprofit World* 14 (March/April): 16–19.
22. See note 17.
23. Manz, C. C., and H. P. Sims Jr. (1989). *SuperLeadership: Leading Others to Lead Themselves.* New York: Prentice Hall.
24. Burns, J. M. (1978). *Leadership.* New York, NY: Harper and Row.
25. See note 8.
26. Barry, D. (1991). "Managing the Bossless Team: Lessons in Distributed Leadership," *Organizational Dynamics* 20 (Summer): 31–47.
27. See note 10.
28. See note 24.
29. See note 13.
30. See note 26.
31. Id.
32. Manz, C. C., and H. P. Sims Jr. (1993). *Business without Bosses.* New York: John Wiley & Sons.
33. See note 26.
34. Katzenbach, J. R., and D. K. Smith. (1993). *The Wisdom of Teams.* Boston: Harvard Business School Press.
35. See note 10.
36. See note 34.
37. See note 10.
38. Blau, J. R., and R. D. Alba. (1992). "Empowering Nets of Participation," *Administrative Science Quarterly* 27 (September): 363–79.
39. Conger, J. A., and R. N. Kanungo. (1988). "The Empowerment Process: Integrating Theory and Practice," *Academy of Management Review* 13 (July): 471–82.
40. Manz, C. C. (1986). "Self-Leadership: Toward an Expanded Theory of Self-Influence Processes in Organizations," *Academy of Management Review* 11 (July): 585–600.
41. Manz, C. C., and H. P. Sims Jr. (1980). "Self-Management as a Substitute for Leadership: A Social Learning Theory Perspective," *Academy of Management Review* 5 (July): 361–67.
42. Manz, C. C., and H. P. Sims Jr. (1987). "Leading Workers to Lead Themselves: The External Leadership of Self-Managing Work Teams," *Administrative Science Quarterly* 32 (March): 106–29.
43. See note 23.
44. See note 32.
45. Mohrman, S. A., S. G. Cohen, and A. M. Mohrman. (1995). *Designing Team-Based Organizations: New Forms for Knowledge and Work,* San Francisco: Jossey-Bass.
46. See note 39.

47. Hickey, J. V., and J. Casner-Lotto. (1998). "How to Get True Employee Participation," *Training and Development* 52 (February): 58–62.
48. Manz, C. C., D. Keating, and A. Donnellon. (1990). "Preparing for Organizational Change to Employee Self Management: The Managerial Transition," *Organizational Dynamics* 19 (Autumn): 15–26.
49. See note 42.
50. See note 32.
51. Stewart, G. L., and C. C. Manz. (1995). "Leadership for Self-Managing Work Teams: A Typology and Integrative Model," *Human Relations* 48 (July): 747–70.
52. See note 32.
53. See note 7.
54. McCafferty, I., and D. Laight. (1997). "Empowering the Team," *Total Quality Management* 8 (June): S227–30.
55. See note 26.
56. See note 34.
57. See note 2.
58. Bass, B. M. (1985). *Leadership and Performance Beyond Expectations.* New York: Free Press.
59. See note 24.
60. See note 13.
61. See note 9.
62. See note 2.
63. McGrath, J. E. (1964). *Social Psychology: A Brief Introduction.* New York: Holt, Rinehart & Winston.
64. Hackman, J. R., and G. R. Oldham. (1980). *Work Redesign.* Reading, MA: Addison-Wesley.
65. Tannenbaum, S. I., R. L. Beard, and E. A. Salas. (1992). "Team Building and Its Influence on Team Effectiveness: An Examination of Conceptual and Empirical Developments." In K. Kelly (ed.), *Issues, Theory, and Research in Industrial/Organizational Psychology.* New York: Elsevier Science, pp. 117–53.
66. Mackin, J. (1998). "Learning to be an Effective Volunteer," *Human Ecology Forum* 26(3): 10–15.
67. See note 26.
68. See note 66.
69. See note 1.
70. Mixer, J. R. (1993). *Principles of Professional Fundraising.* San Francisco: Jossey-Bass.
71. Kerr, S., and J. M. Jermier. (1978). "Substitutes for Leadership: Their Meaning and Measurement," *Organizational Behavior and Human Performance* 22 (December): 1–14.
72. Pearce, C. L., Y. Yoo, and M. Alavi. (2000). "Leadership in Virtual Teams: The Relative Influence of Vertical vs. Shared Leadership in Technology Mediated, Geographically Dispersed Teams," unpublished manuscript. Claremont Graduate University, Claremont, CA.
73. See note 71.
74. Gersick, C. J. G. (1988). "Time and Transition in Work Teams: Towards a New Model of Group Development," *Academy of Management Journal* 31 (March): 9–41.
75. Jewell, L. N., and H. J. Reitz. (1981). *Group Effectiveness in Organizations.* Glenview, IL: Scott Foresman.
76. Tuckman, B. W. (1965). "Developmental Sequences in Small Groups," *Psychological Bulletin* 63 (December): 384–99.

77. See note 26.

78. Id.

79. Guzzo, R. A., and M. W. Dickson. (1996). "Teams in Organizations: Recent Research on Performance and Effectiveness," *Annual Reviews in Psychology* 47: 307–37.

80. Goodman, P. S., and D. P. Leyden. (1991). "Familiarity and Group Productivity," *Journal of Applied Psychology* 76: 578–86.

81. Watson, W. E., L. K. Michaelsen, and W. Sharp. (1991). "Member Competence, Group Interaction and Group Decision Making: A Longitudinal Study," *Journal of Applied Psychology* 76(6): 803–10.

82. See note 71.

83. See note 41.

84. Banel, K. A., and S. E. Jackson. (1989). "Top Management and Innovations in Banking: Does Composition of the Top Teams Make a Difference?" *Strategic Management Journal* 10 (special issue): 107–24.

85. See note 1.

86. Morgan, B. B. Jr., E. Salas, and A. Glickman. (1993). "An Analysis of Team Evolution and Maturation," *Journal of General Psychology* 120 (July): 277–91.

87. See note 26.

88. See note 86.

89. Baugh, S. G., and G. B. Graen. (1997). "Effects of Team Gender and Racial Composition on Perceptions of Team Performance in Cross-Functional Teams," *Group and Organization Management* 22 (September): 366–83.

90. Nkomo, S. M., and T. Cox Jr., (1996). "Diverse Identities in Organizations." In S. R. Clegg and C. Hardy (eds.), *Handbook of Organization Studies.* London: Sage Publications, pp. 338–56.

91. Elron, E. (1997). "Top Management Teams within Multinational Companies: Effects of Cultural Heterogeneity," *Leadership Quarterly* 8 (Winter): 393–412.

92. Knight, D., C. L. Pearce, K. G. Smith, et al. (1999). "Top Management Team Diversity, Group Dynamics and Strategic Consensus: An Empirical Investigation," *Strategic Management Journal* 20(5): 445–66.

93. See note 66.

94. See note 79.

95. Pfeffer, J. (1985). "Organizational Demography: Implications for Management," *California Management Review* 28 (Fall): 67–81.

96. See note 89.

97. See note 91.

98. Watson, W. E., K. Kumar, and L. K. Michaelsen. (1993). "Cultural Diversity's Impact on Interaction Processes and Performance: Comparing Homogeneous and Diverse Task Groups," *Academy of Management Journal* 36 (June): 590–602.

99. See note 92.

100. See note 89.

101. Campion, M. A., G. J. Medsker, and A. C. Higgs. (1993). Relations between Work Group Characteristics and Effectiveness: Implications for Designing Effective Work Groups," *Personnel Psychology* 46 (Winter): 823–50.

102. Guzzo, R. A., Eduardo Salas and Associates. (1995). *Team Effectiveness and Decision-Making in Organizations.* San Francisco: Jossey-Bass.

103. See note 34.

104. Steiner, I. D. (1972). *Group Process and Productivity.* New York: Academic Press.
105. Id.
106. Galaskiewicz, J., and W. Bielefeld. (1998). *Nonprofit Organizations in an Age of Uncertainty.* New York: Aldine de Gruyter.
107. McIntyre, R. M., and E. A. Salas. (1995). "Measuring and Managing for Team Performance: Emerging Principles from Complex Environments." In R. A. Guzzo and E. A. Salas (ed.), *Team Effectiveness and Decision Making in Organizations.* San Francisco, CA: Jossey-Bass, 9–45.
108. See note 54.
109. Mikalachki, A. (1994). "Creating a Winning Team," *Ivey Business Quarterly* (Summer): 15–22.
110. Bettenhausen, K. L. (1991). "Five Years of Groups Research: What We Have Learned and What Needs to be Addressed," *Journal of Management* 17 (June): 345–81.
111. Holt, D. H. (1990). *Management: Principles and Practices.* Englewood Cliffs, NJ: Prentice Hall.
112. Seashore, S. (1954). *Group Cohesiveness in the Industrial Work Group.* Ann Arbor: Institute for Social Research, University of Michigan.
113. See note 75.
114. Lott, A. J., and B. E. Lott. (1961). "Group Cohesiveness, Communication Level and Conformity," *Journal of Abnormal and Social Psychology* 62 (Fall): 408–12.
115. Meyer, J. P., and J. N. Allen. (1984). "Testing the 'Side-Bet Theory' of Organizational Commitment: Some Methodological Conditions," *Journal of Applied Psychology* 69: 372–78.
116. Porter, L. W., R. M. Steers, R. T. Mowday, and P. V. Boulian. (1974). "Organizational Commitment, Job Satisfaction, and Turnover Among Psychiatric Technicians," *Journal of Applied Psychology* 59: 603–609.
117. Bandura, A. (1986). *Social Foundations of Thought and Action: A Social Cognitive Theory.* Englewood Cliffs, NJ: Prentice Hall.
118. Guzzo, R. A. (1986). "Group Decision Making and Group Effectiveness in Organizations." In P. S. Goodman (ed.), *Designing Effective Work Groups.* San Francisco: Jossey-Bass, pp. 34–71.
119. Guzzo, R. A., and G. P. Shea. (1992). "Group Performance and Intergroup Relations in Organizations." In M. D. Dunnette and L. M. Hough (eds.) *Handbook of Industrial and Organizational Psychology,* 2nd ed. Palo Alto, CA: Consulting Psychologists Press.
120. Thakor, M. V., and L. P. Katsanis. (1997). "A Model of Brand and Country Effects on Quality Dimensions: Issues and Implications," *Journal of International Consumer Marketing* 9(3): 79–100.
121. See note 106.
122. Id.
123. Maute, M. F., and W. R. Forrester. (1991). "The Effect of Attribute Qualities on Consumer Decision Making: A Causal Model of External Information Search," *Journal of Economic Psychology* 12(4): 643–67.
124. See note 2.
125. Moriya, F. E., and J. C. Gockley. (1985). "Grid Analysis for Sales Supervision," *Industrial Marketing Management* 14(1): 235–9.

Suggested Readings

Cox, J. F. (1994). "The Effects of Superleadership Training on Leader Behavior, Subordinate Self-Leader Behavior and Subordinate Citizenship Behavior," unpublished doctoral dissertation. University of Maryland, College Park, MD.

Drucker, P. (1996). "Non-Profit Pioneers," *Executive Excellence* (August): 5.

Guzzo, R. A., R. J. Campbell, J. L. Moses, et al. (1991). "What Makes High-Performing Teams Effective?" unpublished manuscript. University of Maryland, College Park, MD.

Guzzo, R. A., P. R. Yost, R. J. Campbell, and G. P. Shea. (1993). "Potency in Groups: Articulating a Construct," *British Journal of Social Psychology* 40 (November): 87–106.

Hackman, J. R. (1988). "The Design of Work Teams." In J. W. Lorsch (ed.), *Handbook of Organizational Behavior.* Englewood Cliffs, NJ: Prentice Hall, pp. 315–42.

Landy, F. J., and J. L. Farr. (1983). *The Measurement of Work Performance: Methods, Theories and Applications.* New York: Academic Press.

Pearce, C. L., and H. P. Sims Jr. (1998). "Vertical Leadership vs. Shared Leadership: Exploring the Impact of Alternate Sources of Influences in Organizations," unpublished manuscript. University of North Carolina at Charlotte, Charlotte, NC.

Pearce, J. A., and E. C. Ravlin. (1987). "The Design and Activation of Self-Regulating Work Groups," *Human Relations* 40 (November): 751–82.

Shea, G. P., and R. A. Guzzo. (1987). "Group Effectiveness: What Really Matters?" *Sloan Management Review* 28 (Spring): 25–31.

Steiner, I. D. (1976). "Task-performing Groups." In J. W. Thibaut and R. C. Carson (eds.), *Contemporary Topics in Social Psychology.* Morristown, NJ: General Learning Press, pp. 393–422.

Wellins, R. S., W. C. Byham, and J. M. Wilson. (1991). *Empowered Teams.* San Francisco: Jossey-Bass.

Wolff, M. (1999). "In the Organization of the Future, Competitive Advantage Will Lie with Inspired Employees," *Research Technology Management* 42(4): 2–6.

28 ▼ Governance: Creating Capable Leadership in the Nonprofit Sector

KEITH SEEL, MA, PRINCIPAL
  M4i Strategic Management Consulting, Inc.

M. MICHELLE REGEL
  Junior Achievement of Southern Alberta, Canada

MILENA M. MENEGHETTI, CHRP, VICE PRESIDENT
  M4i Strategic Management Consulting, Inc.

28.1 Introduction

Nonprofit organizations (NPOs) fill a complex role in the fabric of communities across North America and in many other countries around the world. Looking back over the history of NPOs in Canada and the United States, one can observe that the elements that made their role complex have been consistent:

- Internal stakeholders such as staff and volunteers
- External stakeholders such as financial supporters (individuals, government, corporations, and foundations) and clients
- A board of directors drawn from the community

The approaches to ensuring that this diverse mix of people and other organizations work well together vary, depending on the resources available to the NPO. Larger organizations such as the Red Cross or the American Cancer Society have long had access to the resources and community profile necessary to afford recruitment of experienced staff leadership, attract large numbers of volunteers, and draw influential board leadership. They have access to the resources needed to set up and maintain a large infrastructure and support systems. Smaller organizations with few resources rely on the passion from individuals committed to addressing a particular issue. Short of resources, these organizations rely on the commitment of volunteers more often than staff to get the work done. Addressing systems and infrastructure are of less concern than addressing the immediate needs of whomever the NPO was set up to serve.

As we enter a new millennium, pressure is being put on the nonprofit sector to demonstrate leadership and accountability. This increased pressure has resulted because NPOs:

- Face reduced funding from governments
- Must compete aggressively with other NPOs for support from funding agencies and private donors
- Are being pushed to assume or augment many of the services traditionally provided by government
- Are themselves increasingly complex and sophisticated entities, with all the inherent challenges of managing large organizations
- Are responsible to a wide variety of stakeholders (unlike profit-oriented companies whose primary responsibility is to the shareholders) who often have different and even conflicting expectations of the NPO[1]

28.2 What Is Governance?

When the executive director of a small rural social service agency was asked how he would define governance, he responded, "Governance is what my board is supposed to do." A senior manager of a large cultural organization defines governance as "a type of management process." These two different perspectives on governance point to the fact that there is a range of understandings within the sector. The perception of governance held by an organization will dramatically affect who is involved, what is done, and the kinds of accountability the organization has to its various stakeholders.

The Panel on Accountability and Governance in the Voluntary Sector defines governance as "the overall processes and structures used to direct and manage an organization's operations and activities."[2] Deloitte & Touche explain governance as defining "the division of power, and establish[ing] mechanisms to achieve accountability between stakeholders, the board of directors and management."[3] These definitions of *governance* bring a degree of clarity to our understanding of what the term means. First, by addressing the processes and structures used to manage and direct an agency's operations and activities, we are asked to dive deeply into the organization to ensure that the organization is truly effective and operating efficiently. This means that governance is not the responsibility of just the board but also includes individuals at all levels in the organization and perhaps external stakeholders as well. From this point of view, governance is the web of responsibilities that binds an organization together and keeps it tied to both those that support it and those that it is intended to serve.

Second, by addressing accountability and the division of power, this definition of governance expands our understanding to include the ethical performance of the organization.

Therefore, an organization needs to develop and articulate proper expressions of how it is accountable to those that support it and those that use its services, but also how it is accountable to its staff, volunteers, and the broader community. In establishing its vision, purpose, and mission statements, an organization should consider how it measures up when "core ethical values" such as trustworthiness, respect, responsibility, caring, citizenship, and fairness are considered in the light of each stakeholder group (see Meneghetti and Seel[4] for a discussion of ethics and nonprofit management). Exhibit 28.1 summarizes a proposed definition for governance based on the ideas discussed previously.

28.3   Governance Models

Within the nonprofit sector, there are a range of approaches to governance—each with its adherents, some with supporting literature and theory. With a couple of notable exceptions, there are no governance models. For the most part, NPOs have created their own ways of linking together the board, the staff, the organization's purpose and activities, and those who support it. Approaches vary widely, as does effectiveness. The United Way of Canada suggests that boards need to consider their structure (e.g., their "model") through three basic questions:

1. Which decisions does the board want to make and which do they want to delegate?
2. How much involvement does the board want to have in the operations of the organization?
3. How will the reporting relationship between the board and its staff be defined?[5]

How the board discusses and implements answers to these questions will determine how it is structured and how it will operate. Three models exist to represent the possibilities, and each model will be discussed later in the chapter:

1. Traditional Board (Policy Board)
2. Policy Governance Board
3. Toronto Stock Exchange Model

(A)   BASIC PRINCIPLES OF GOVERNANCE

Taking our proposed definition of governance (see Exhibit 28.1), some basic principles should be defined before looking more closely at governance models.

EXHIBIT 28.1   Definition of Governance

Governance means the overall processes and structures used to direct and manage an organization's operations and activities. Governance defines the division of power and establishes the mechanisms necessary to achieve accountability among stakeholders, the board of directors, and the management of an organization.

(i) The Board

Boards of directors are the stewards of the organization with specific liabilities and responsibilities pertaining to the operation of the organization. A board of directors may be called by another name, such as a board of governors or a board of trustees. In some situations, a board of governors may exist independently of the board of directors in the same organization and be exposed to similar responsibilities and liabilities. In other situations, a national organization may have a national board of directors and local boards of directors. These local boards may perform more of an advisory role to the national board in that they advise on policy development and operations for the NPO as a whole but still have state or provincial responsibilities and liabilities.

While noting that studies of nonprofit governance are in short supply, Deloitte & Touche draws on its corporate experience to state emphatically that "boards of directors are vitally important to organizations, but they can and should do a better job!"[6] For many nonprofits, the role of the board as well as its structures and processes are not understood by board members nor the staff and volunteers of an organization. Deloitte & Touche propose several reasons for this, including:

- The range of board structures that occur in the nonprofit sector. The incorporation of an NPO under its particular government legislation may require officers, bylaws, and certain reporting requirements. However, when compared to corporate boards, whose role and structure is prescribed by corporate legislation, the board of an NPO is relatively undefined.
- The board of an NPO is made up of volunteers, which, despite their commitment to the cause, can mean that the NPOs often experience high turnover of its board members, resulting in the feeling that it is always going back to "square one." With higher board turnover, the board may lack the ability to grow and evolve its capacity.
- Depending on the board member, there may be very different expectations of their role on the board. For example, clients may bring valuable personal insights to how the agency operates but may have a personal agenda; volunteers who have come to the board via a committee experience have an operational perspective but may not be able or willing to change their role from a service provider to a board member; prominent members of the community may be willing to lend their name to the organization but may have multiple demands and be unable to commit the time necessary as a board member.

Another reason for the confusion is that many of the most recognized NPOs have several "boards" (e.g., local board, regional board, national board, and an international board). For volunteers participating on a board at any level of this progression, confusion around exact roles and responsibilities is commonplace.

Regardless of the source or cause of the confusion surrounding boards of directors, it is advisable that directors and boards strive for the highest levels of stewardship.

(ii) Assumptions

The United Way of Canada has delivered "board development" programs for a number of years and has a reputation of being able to target essential consultation services to boards based on a needs assessment. Interestingly, the assistance, valuable as it is, operates under a set of fundamental assumptions about the governance role of a board. The United Way of Canada's set of basic assumptions about how boards manage organizations is:

- Boards are responsible for *policy* while staff or management are responsible for *operations.*
- Boards have a similar basic structure, including a president or chairperson, officers or executive members, standing committees, and ad hoc committees.
- Boards make decisions by motions decided by a majority vote.[7]

(iii) Accountability

Who is accountable for what in NPOs can be a topic of lengthy discussion. The Panel on Accountability and Governance in the Voluntary Sector narrows the debate by defining accountability as:

> *The requirement to explain and accept responsibility for carrying out an assigned mandate in light of agreed upon expectations. It involves: taking into consideration the public trust in the exercise of responsibilities; providing detailed information about how responsibilities have been carried out and what outcomes have been achieved; and accepting the responsibility for outcomes, including problems created or not corrected.*[8]

Specifically, NPOs are accountable to a range of stakeholders and are accountable at a minimum for:

- Establishing a mission and policies and ensuring that they are relevant
- Scrupulous management of funds, revenues, and expenses
- Effective organizational governance
- The quality, quantity, and range of services and service outcomes[9]

(iv) Elements of Effective Stewardship

The active oversight of organization governance by the board of directors is what we refer to as stewardship. It is the duty of the board to oversee the conduct of the organization's affairs to ensure that an effective team is in place to carry out day-to-day activities, account for its financial and other resources, and ensure that no issue falls between the cracks in steering the organization toward the fulfillment of its mission. Effective stewardship by a board cannot be legislated.[10]

For the board, effective stewardship involves eight core activities, as outlined in Exhibit 28.2.

(B) TRADITIONAL

Not really a model at all, the traditional board evolved out of small groups of volunteers coming together to accomplish a particular task. The board structure grew from ingrained ideas about how meetings should be run (e.g., a chairperson, secretary, etc.) and structures imposed on the organization by government legislation, laws, or demands by funders that a board of directors be in place.

(C) POLICY GOVERNANCE BOARDS

In 1990, John Carver's book, *Boards That Make a Difference: A New Design for Leadership in Nonprofit and Public Organizations,* was released, which advocated that boards reorganize

EXHIBIT 28.2 Dimensions of Stewardship

Dimension	Specific Tasks Involved
Mission and Strategic Planning	• Establish, communicate, and review the mission. • Establish a strategic plan to achieve the mission. • Establish a risk management process. • Establish monitoring processes.
Transparency and Communication	• Establish communications processes and policies to send and receive information, including a process that ensures timely responses to requests for information. • Establish a grievance process and policy that is linked to a code of ethical conduct. • Establish a pattern of regular and effective board meetings. • Establish appropriate documentary and record-keeping processes and policies.
Structures	• Ensure that the board has the capacity and capability needed to provide objective oversight. • Establish an independent nominating committee and board succession policies and procedures. • Establish an audit committee with the responsibility to review the NPO's compliance with all applicable laws and legislation, assess management effectiveness, and supervise the necessary financial audits. • Ensure that appropriate staff and volunteer management processes and policies are in place and effective.
Assessment and Control Systems	• Develop, implement, and monitor a code of ethical conduct for the organization. • Develop, implement, and monitor formative documents such as bylaws, the constitution, and the like. • Complete a compliance audit to ensure that all policies and procedures have been followed. • Conduct an evaluation of the board's performance.
Planning for Succession and Diversity	• Ensure that the qualifications required on the board are identified and then recruited. • Discuss the representation of various constituencies on the board and, if appropriate, work to increase the diversity of representation on the board.

Adapted from "Building on Strength: Improving Governance and Accountability in Canada's Voluntary Sector" in *Panel on Accountability and Governance in the Voluntary Sector* (February 1999, pp. 24–32).

themselves under a policy-governance model.[11] Since its release date, the approach has created a groundswell of discussion as proponents and opponents debate what is widely known as the *Carver Model.*

At its core, the "Policy Governance model takes as its starting point the principle that a governing board is accountable for the organization it governs and that it exists on behalf of a larger group of persons who, either legally or morally, own the organization."[12] This principle causes the most debate within boards considering whether to operate under a Policy Governance model. The reason for this debate is twofold:

1. The concept of moral ownership being external to the NPO turns the board's primary responsibilities away from internal management and operations. For community organizations, the community itself is the owner, whereas for membership organizations, the members are the owners.[13] Many boards have directors that were recruited to manage or work along with staff in a "hands-on" role. The Policy Governance model requires the board to establish its expectations, ends, and limitations; delegate responsibility to the chief executive officer (CEO); and then be "hands off," except for performance monitoring. Individual directors who like to be involved in the details of day-to-day operations may feel that the board is too remote and uninvolved in the Policy Governance model.

2. Under the model, the board must decide to whom and for what it is accountable. Board members may feel that they are advisors to the CEO or even accountable to the CEO. Some board members may see themselves as being partners with staff. The Policy Governance model questions these roles by focusing on the board's accountability to the moral ownership of the NPO. If the moral ownership is the community, for example, the board's role becomes one of ensuring that it is accountable to the community. In terms of what the board is accountable for, the model suggests the board focus on "ends" rather than "means." Put simply, ends can be understood as, "What good? For what people? At what cost?"[14] The emphasis on ends rather than means can be a difficult shift in perspective for many boards.

Boards that adopt a Policy Governance framework must have the resources and commitment needed to address these concerns to the satisfaction of the directors. The discussions that emerge tend to revolve around the flow of responsibility and accountability and the kinds of policies suggested within the model. These are outlined as follows.

(i) Flow of Responsibility and Accountability
Perhaps one of the most interesting aspects of the Policy Governance model is how the flow of responsibility and accountability occurs among the various stakeholders of the NPO. Although specifics may vary somewhat among NPOs implementing the model, in general the flow of responsibility is outlined in Exhibit 28.3.

(ii) Key Policy Types
There are four classifications of policy within the Policy Governance board: executive limitations policies, governance process policies, board–CEO linkage policies, and ends policies.[15] These are outlined as follows.

1. *Executive limitations policies.* Executive limitations policies are "the board's way of telling the CEO the limits of acceptability regarding staff means (methods, situations, circumstances, and practices) . . . these policies are boundary setters."[16] They are written to the CEO, who in turn has the

EXHIBIT 28.3 Flow of Responsibility and Accountability

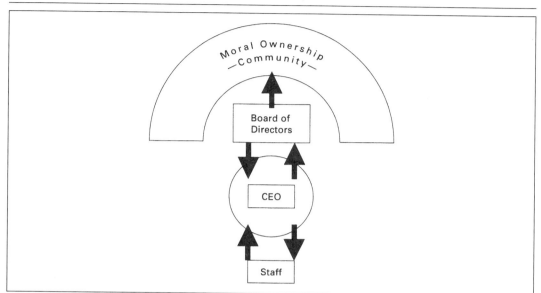

responsibility of ensuring that no aspects of the organization go beyond the limits set by the board.

Phrased in the negative (e.g., "The CEO shall not allow any practices, policies, or procedures that are in direct contravention of existing human rights and employment legislation"), executive limitations policies give the CEO and the board freedom to operate within their prescribed ends and proscribed means without being prohibitive to creativity and innovation.

Typically, the board would identify specific areas of concern, consider any expert (legal or financial) input that may be required, state exactly what is not prudent or ethical, and then draft the policy for discussion and approval. Examples of executive limitations policies are set out in Exhibit 28.4.

EXHIBIT 28.4 Examples of Executive Limitations Policies

- Global executive constraint
- Treatment of consumers
- Treatment of staff
- Financial planning and budgeting
- Financial condition and activities
- Emergency CEO succession
- Asset protection
- Compensation and benefits
- Communication and support to the board
- Ends focus of grants or contracts

Adapted from Carver, J., and M. M. Carver. (1997). *Reinventing Your Board.* San Francisco: Jossey-Bass, p. 190.

2. *Governance process policies.* With governance process policies, the board describes "the standards of group and individual behavior to which it agrees to hold itself [accountable]."[17] This set of policies establishes the way the board will operate, its job description, and how committees will function, and sets forth a code of board member conduct. Examples of governance process polices can be found in Exhibit 28.5.

3. *Board–CEO linkage policies.* This set of policies defines how the board will transfer a portion of its authority to management in the person of the CEO. "These policies deal with the methods and practices (means) of the board that describe not only the nature of delegation but the way in which the proper use of delegated authority is ascertained (monitoring)."[18] Two important concepts underlying board–CEO linkage policies are:

   • The board's single connection to the operations of the organization is the CEO.
   • The board always speaks with one voice, meaning that "decisions or instructions of individual board members, officers, or committees are not binding on the CEO," and the CEO may refuse requests for information or assistance from individual board member or committees.[19] Examples of board–CEO linkage policies are outlined in Exhibit 28.6.

4. *Ends policies.* Ends policies address the relationship between the organization and the world. Ends policies address organizational values and the good that the organization is seeking to produce. The concept of ends can be a challenge to understand and to implement in terms of policy formulation. Carver and Carver define *ends* to be:

   • The impact, difference, change, benefit, or outcome to be obtained in the lives of consumers or consumer-like populations
   • The identity, description, or characteristics of the consumers or populations to receive the results
   • The monetary expense, relative worth, or relative priority of a result or set of results, or the comparative priority of certain recipients rather than getting the results[20]

A shorthand formulation of ends is: what result for which recipients and what cost. Examples of ends policies are outlined in Exhibit 28.7.

EXHIBIT 28.5 Examples of Governance Process Policies

• Global governance commitment
• Governing style
• Board job description
• Agenda planning
• Chairperson's role
• Board members' code of conduct
• Board committee principles
• Cost of governance

Adapted from Carver, J., and M. M. Carver. (1997). *Reinventing Your Board.* San Francisco: Jossey-Bass, p. 190.

EXHIBIT 28.6 Examples of Board–CEO Linkage Policies

- Global board–CEO linkage
- Unity of control
- Accountability of the CEO
- Delegation to the CEO
- Monitoring CEO performance

Adapted from Carver, J., and M. M. Carver. (1997). *Reinventing Your Board.* San Francisco: Jossey-Bass, p. 190.

(iii) Evaluation

Central to the Policy Governance board model is the notion of monitoring. As the board establishes the policies within the four areas outlined earlier, criteria should emerge that will be the basis of CEO reporting as well as the annual evaluation of agency performance. The points that the board wishes to be monitored should be tied directly to an existing policy. This keeps the board in the role of governance (e.g., monitoring policy) and not day-to-day operations. For example, the CEO may report that the investment of new revenue has taken place as per the executive limitations policy on asset protection.

(D) TORONTO STOCK EXCHANGE

The Toronto Stock Exchange (TSE) model as developed by Deloitte & Touche presents what may be the only other formal model available for discussion other than the Policy Governance model put forth by Carver. It is derived from the review of board governance criteria required to be in place for corporations seeking to list on both the Toronto and Montreal Stock Exchanges. As the authors note, "Although designed for publicly listed enterprises, these guidelines are already becoming a benchmark for governance among all publicly accountable organizations in Canada."[21] The 14 guidelines are general enough in nature to have broad international applicability. Exhibit 28.8 details the governance guidelines proposed by Deloitte & Touche.

(i) Considerations for Implementing the Deloitte & Touche Model

The Deloitte & Touche model is not presented with any kind of theoretical framework. This means that for NPOs interested in implementing the model, additional work needs

EXHIBIT 28.7 Examples of Ends Policies

- Vision
- Mission
- Purpose
- Values statement
- Consumer priorities
- Results and priorities

Adapted from Carver, J., and M. M. Carver. (1997). *Reinventing Your Board.* San Francisco: Jossey-Bass, pp. 208–16.

EXHIBIT 28.8 TSE Guidelines for Improved Corporate Governance

1. The board of directors of every corporation should explicitly assume responsibility for the stewardship of the corporation, and, as part of the overall stewardship responsibility, should assume responsibility for the following matters:
   i. Adoption of a strategic planning process
   ii. The identification of the principal risks of the corporation's business and ensuring the implementation of appropriate systems to manage these risks
   iii. Succession planning, including appointing, training, and monitoring senior management
   iv. A communication policy for the corporation
   v. The integrity of the corporation's internal control and management information systems
2. The board of directors of every corporation should be constituted with a majority of individuals who qualify as unrelated directors. An unrelated director is a director who is independent of management and is free from any interest and any business or other relationship which could, or could reasonably be perceived to, materially interfere with the director's ability to act with a view to the best interests of the corporation, other than interests and relationships arising from shareholding. A related director is a director who is not an unrelated director. If the corporation has a significant shareholder, in addition to a majority of unrelated directors, the board should include a number of directors who do not have interests or relationships with either the corporation or the significant shareholder and which fairly reflects the investment in the corporation by shareholders other than the significant shareholder. A significant shareholder is a shareholder with the ability to exercise a majority of the votes for the election of the board of directors.
3. The application of the definition of "related director" to the circumstances of each individual director should be the responsibility of the board, which will be required to disclose on an annual basis whether the board has a majority of unrelated directors or, in the case of a corporation with a significant shareholder, whether the board is constituted with the appropriate number of directors which are not related to either the corporation or the significant shareholder. Management directors are related directors. The board will also be required to disclose on an annual basis the analysis of the application of the principles supporting this conclusion.
4. The board of directors of every corporation should appoint a committee of directors composed exclusively of non-management directors with the responsibility for proposing to the full board new nominees to the board and for assessing directors on an ongoing basis.
5. Every board of directors should implement a process to be carried out by the nominating committee or other appropriate committee for assessing the effectiveness of the board and the contribution of individual directors.
6. Every corporation, as an integral element of the process for appointing new directors, should provide an orientation and education program for new recruits to the board.
7. Every board of directors should examine its size and, with a view to determining the impact of the number upon effectiveness, undertake where appropriate, a program to reduce the number of directors to a number which facilitates more effective decision-making.

EXHIBIT 28.8 *(Continued)*

8. The board of directors should review the adequacy and form of the compensation of directors and ensure the compensation realistically reflects the responsibilities and risk involved in being an effective director.

9. Committees of the board of directors should generally be composed of outside directors, a majority of whom are unrelated directors, although some board committees, such as the executive committee, may include one or more inside directors. An inside director is a director who is an officer or employee of the corporation or of any of its affiliates.

10. Every board of directors should expressly assume responsibility for, or assign to a committee of directors the responsibility for, developing the corporation's approach to governance issues. This committee would, amongst other things, be responsible for the corporation's response to these governance guidelines.

11. The board of directors, together with the CEO, should develop position descriptions for the board and for the CEO, involving the definition of the limits to management's responsibilities. In addition, the board should approve or develop the corporate objectives which the CEO is responsible for meeting.

12. Every board of directors should have in place appropriate structures and procedures to ensure that the board can function independently of management. An appropriate structure would be to: (i) appoint a chair of the board who is not a member of management with responsibility to ensure the board discharges its responsibilities; or (ii) adopt alternate means such as assigning this responsibility to a committee of the board or to a director, sometimes referred to as the "lead director." Appropriate procedures may involve the board meeting on a regular basis without management present or may involve expressly assigning the responsibility for administering the board's relationship to management to a committee of the board.

13. The audit committee of every board of directors should be composed only of outside directors. The audit committee should have direct communication channels with the internal and external auditors to discuss and review specific issues as appropriate. While it is management's responsibility to design and implement an effective system of internal control, it is the responsibility of the audit committee to ensure that management has done so.

14. The board of directors should implement a system which enables an individual director to engage an outside advisor at the expense of the corporation in appropriate circumstances.

Reprinted with permission from Deloitte & Touche. (1995). *The Effective Not-for-Profit Board: Governance of Not-for-Profit Organizations.* Author.

to be undertaken to assess the value of the model for that organization's particular interests. The points that follow discuss the 14 guidelines introduced in Exhibit 28.8:

- **Guideline 1.** This element is crucial for NPOs because it defines the role of the board. Stewardship of an NPO is the most vital responsibility of the directors, and it is imperative that there is agreement among the members as to how stewardship will be established and maintained.

- **Guideline 2.** Although NPOs would not find themselves in a position in which a significant shareholder would be on the board, a similar situation could exist in which either a large stakeholder or donor could also be a director. Therefore, this guideline is important because it stresses the need for objectivity on the board. Any NPO that has a majority of directors who are not free of any interests or partnerships with that NPO needs to ensure that the board is still able to make decisions that are in the best interest of the organization and the majority of its stakeholders.
- **Guideline 3.** This guideline places the responsibility of defining what a related director is in reference to the board and to disclose which of the directors are, in fact, related directors. Usually, an NPO board will have at least one related director who also functions as the CEO of the organization; other related directors on an NPO board may be members of the management team.
- **Guideline 4.** This guideline is probably more important for an NPO board than for the board of a profit-generating corporation. Directors on NPO boards tend to have a higher turnover rate than those of their corporate counterparts and, therefore, have a higher need to ensure that recruiting new board members is an effective function within the board of directors.

Establishing the right criteria for directors of an organization is one of the most important steps in the recruitment process of an effective NPO board. "Aggressive recruiting involves not only selling prospective members on board membership, but excluding those who do not fulfill the requirements . . . Trusting recruitment to a nominating committee can be useful, but integrity is maintained only if the board as a body has decided what types of people it desires. Nominating committees are too often left completely at their own judgement . . . boards would do well to tolerate a few more empty seats instead of rush to fill them. Recruiting will be more diligent if it is made known that membership is an honour."[22]

John Thomas of the Children's National Medical Center in Washington presented a useful recruitment model at the 1997 Third Annual Fund Raising Congress in Toronto. Thomas's recommendations for director recruitment lay the foundation for NPOs to recruit directors who are best suited for their organizations. These eight steps should be followed in the order in which they appear.[23]

1. *Assemble a board development team.* Decide which directors will compose this team. Ideally, the team should include the board chair, who will be responsible for the strategic plan; the CEO, who is the most familiar with the operational plan; the fund development professional, who will detail the fund-raising plan; and possibly two or three other "high-profile," energetic directors. Ensure that the strategic, operating, and fund-raising plans are in place and up-to-date before engaging in recruitment of new directors. Determine the support required for the board development team and enlist NPO staff to assist with clerical and research duties.
2. *Assess and state the needs of the NPO.* Be sure to include the desired skill base and demographics of the board and a brainstorming of potential directors in this assessment. It would be very useful to have some research available on characteristics of different generations so that targeting your approach

to specific candidates would be more successful. There is ample research on demographic and psychographic characteristics of pre-boomers, boomers, busters, and the "X" generation, which would allow a tailored approach for each candidate. (Much of the work by Judith Nichols, PhD, would be helpful in this area of board development.) A board profile grid can be a valuable tool in pinpointing areas of expertise in a current board, and highlighting areas on the board in need of recruitment of directors.[24]

3. *Develop position profiles for directors.*
4. *Script the story to "pitch" the NPO to the prospective candidates.* When writing an NPO's history, remember that a critical element to the NPO story includes listing the benefits of participating on the board of a particular NPO (tailor the benefits based on the generational mindset of the potential candidate).
5. *Research candidate sources.* Be creative when researching for potential candidates. Consider donors, friends, colleagues, associates, foundations, and researched sources.
6. *Develop third-party referral networks.* Developing referral partnerships with groups such as foundations, professional associations, business owners, ethnic groups, and donors will aid the director recruitment process and enlarge the pool of potential candidates.
7. *Contact and meet with candidates.* The most effective approach is to contact the candidates by telephone and then meet with them personally.
8. *Evaluate and select candidates.*

- **Guideline 5.** Although this is a very sensitive issue with NPO boards because it requires the assessment of unpaid volunteers, it is also a crucial element to the success of any board in meeting its objectives. The two things every director deserves from serving on an NPO board are self-satisfaction derived from board participation and personal growth.[25] If board, committee, and individual director evaluations are addressed appropriately, every director would be assured some level of growth suitable to his or her needs and expectations as a volunteer.

    Each of the three levels of assessment (board, committee, and director) would benefit from using a unique evaluation tool; the same evaluation instrument would not be appropriate for all three levels of governance. For example, an annual corporate governance survey could be produced for the board to evaluate itself as a whole and as subunits or committees, but a confidential self-evaluation tool would be the most suitable method to evaluate individual directors. These assessments should not be viewed as a fault-finding measure, but more as an indicator of how to produce a more effective board and offer alternatives to directors who are struggling to fulfill their duties. The director assessment should be used as a tool to define the skills, preferred roles, and level of satisfaction of each director. It is the duty of the CEO to ensure that each director serves the NPO in the capacity most desirable and appropriate to him or her.

- **Guideline 6.** This guideline is one that may be easily overlooked within an NPO organization. Board orientation and development may not be a priority of staff if the NPO is understaffed for its workload or is run mainly by volunteers. A thorough orientation process is time consuming to produce and maintain but is crucial to the performance of the new directors. It should also be performed as a courtesy to recognize the efforts and enthusiasm of new recruits and to motivate and guide them on how to best serve the NPO.

A new director should be given a director's guide, preferably in a three-ring binder, which can be used by the director as a working manual for his or her role on the board. This governance manual should aim to include the following:

- A relevant summary of the nonprofit corporate bylaws
- A copy of the articles of incorporation
- A copy of the certification of approval
- A copy of the Revenue Canada letter of approval and the assigned GST (Goods and Services Tax) and business numbers
- A copy of the board-approved vision, mission, goals, and objectives of a long-term plan
- The description for the operation of a board
- The dated position description of a director
- The dated position description of the CEO
- A brief biography and perhaps a photograph of each director and the CEO
- A detailed chart of the governing board and the organization
- An up-to-date copy of the bylaws as approved, dated, and signed by the board officers
- A chronological fact sheet plus facts of the last fiscal year[26]

Other useful information for the director manuals may include sales and marketing pieces, an annual report, audited financial statements, program or service details, staff contact information, fund-raising tips, and a section that lists upcoming board meeting dates and minutes of past meetings.

In addition, a new director should be invited to become a director-in-residence and dedicate three days to observing the NPO in its daily routines to gain more of an action-oriented training.[27] Directors may also wish to arrange for community members to speak at their meetings for no more than one-half hour about topics of expertise that relate directly to the mission of the NPO. It may also be useful for the board to hold periodic "directors-only" meetings so that they may raise sensitive questions, discuss concerns, and make suggestions off the record.[28] This last suggestion is mentioned in Guideline 12 and may be extremely helpful in allowing board leadership to explore new avenues in growth. In addition to this last suggestion, board retreats are also useful in rejuvenating directors and help to nurture their needs as volunteers.

The orientation process will be different for every NPO, but it is a task that should be adopted as a mandatory part of both board and management's duties. A program that incorporates these recommendations will ensure a comprehensive perspective for new directors that is proactive, exciting, and nurturing.

- **Guideline 7.** This guideline needs to be viewed in a slightly different capacity for NPOs than for corporations. Most NPOs welcome new directors and are rarely concerned about board size because, typically, it is assumed that a larger group of directors translates into a higher level of revenue generation. However, going back to Guideline 5 and the importance of board assessment, it is imperative that NPO boards run effectively and that all directors have assigned roles to fulfill.

This guideline also raises the sensitive issue of how to persuade a nonperforming director to resign voluntarily from the board without feeling animosity for the NPO or its remaining directors. Several options can be used to alleviate the angst of this situation. First, an alumni or honorary board of directors can be created and populated by former directors or potential directorial candidates who wish to serve the NPO but for various reasons cannot dedicate the resources expected from an active director.[29] Second, a slow but relatively painless removal process can be put into place whereby a director's lack of performance is addressed by the CEO or chairman using objective criteria, and the director is then sent an "outreach" letter.[30] This letter can serve a dual purpose—it can be a beacon to a floundering director in search of extra guidance and also the signal of the first phase in the removal process.

Other methods to remove (or avoid) the nonperformance crisis are to ensure that a proper job description is given to all directors, assign a probation period or trial assignment to new directors, have a rotation policy in place so directors are given the opportunity to try different roles on the board, and institute a fair and objective assessment policy.[31]

Although addressing nonperformance will never be enjoyable, it is important for a board to commit itself to this guideline if it is to reach peak effectiveness. Whatever option is chosen to remedy the nonperformance dilemma, it will be an effective method to maintaining a healthy board as long as courtesy, honesty, and respect for each director are maintained.

- **Guideline 8.** This guideline covers three issues surrounding NPO director compensation. First, because NPO board members are unpaid volunteers, it is essential for NPOs to address their volunteer recognition policies and ensure that they are suitable for each level of volunteer within the organizations. Directors choose to serve on an NPO board because they believe in the mission of that organization; therefore, their compensation is derived from ensuring that the organization reaches its goals and from being properly recognized for their participation in that success.

  Second, liability insurance is an important issue for NPO directors. It is the responsibility of an NPO to ensure that it carries enough coverage. Ideally, each director should have a predetermined amount of coverage that is deemed appropriate by the board, and the organization itself should have its own coverage. The organization's insurance should be incorporated into the operating budget; the directors may choose to pay their own insurance or have it covered under the NPO's budget as well. Typically, NPOs will cover all insurance expenses related to operations and directors.

  Last, but certainly not least, a volunteer and/or client protection policy should be in place to protect both the volunteers (directors are included in this group) and the clients served by the NPO. This interpretation of this guideline is especially relevant to NPOs whose volunteers come in direct contact with residents of the community being served. This protection policy may also need to address such items as health coverage, immunizations, and life insurance if the volunteers, in the course of their duties, are exposed to a certain level of personal risk.

- **Guideline 9.** Issues to be considered here are similar to those outlined in Guideline 2. This guideline stresses the importance of having a high level of objectivity within the board and its committees.
- **Guideline 10.** NPOs are not legally bound to disclose their governance practices as publicly traded companies are.[32] However, if an NPO board objective is to ensure that an effective governance structure is in place, it would be prudent for a selected group of directors to commit themselves to periodically reviewing and challenging the governance policies of the NPO.
- **Guideline 11.** The single most important relationship in any NPO is that between the CEO and the board of directors. This relationship needs to be nurtured and monitored if the organization is to flourish. If the CEO–board relationship is dysfunctional, so too will be the governance and management of the entire organization.[33] Carver defines the CEO–board relationship as:

More than a mere coordinator, the CEO is accountable for all the parts coming together in an acceptable whole. The board is therefore able to govern by dealing conceptually only with the whole and personally only with the CEO. The CEO becomes the board's bridge to the staff, a role more distinct than merely lead staff member. A powerfully designed CEO position is key to board excellence. It enables a board to avoid the intricacies and short-term focus of staff management and to work exclusively on the holistic, long-term focus of governance.[34]

Guideline 11 is a strong example of being simply good business practice. If the board sets clear objectives for the CEO, then the CEO can in turn set objectives for the staff. Director and CEO position descriptions may be supplemented by a visual organization chart that shows each of the positions in reference to the governance structure of the entire NPO.

Director and CEO position descriptions should contain the following information to ensure that each member has a clear document stating expectations, including:
- The scope of each position
- The experience and skills required for each position
- The key duties that need to be performed for each position
- The expectations of each position
- The priorities for each position, laid out in a chronological fashion[35]

Additional expectations of the directors, such as fiduciary responsibility, attendance at meetings and events, active and meaningful participation on the board, and personal giving, should also be included in the position description.

Directors should have the position descriptions for both directors and the CEO included in the appropriate section of their directors' manuals. Board committee mandates would also be useful supplements to the position descriptions.

- **Guideline 12.** This guideline expresses the need for NPO management to distinguish between their operational duties and their responsibilities on the board. If a related director also has a management position in the NPO, then he or she should not hold an executive position on the board. For example, the vice president of an NPO should not also hold the position of chair of the board because this would distort the leadership hierarchy between the chair of the board and CEO, who would normally manage the vice-president in daily activities but would take guidance from the vice-president in a board capacity.

Alternatively, a bylaw should be created if any director performs operational, nonmanagement duties at the NPO—often referred to as "two hat" syndrome.[36] The leadership hierarchy should be clear in the bylaws: The CEO guides the NPO staff, and the board as a whole guides the CEO. Any misinterpretation of this hierarchy will cause mayhem in the organization because the staff will become confused about whom to seek guidance from— the CEO or the director. When performing operational duties, directors should respect the leadership of the CEO with the staff and not cross the boundaries of the decision-making process.[37] In other words, "When offering themselves as volunteers in tasks for which the CEO is accountable, 'board members, now wearing volunteer hats . . . are subject to the direct supervision and control of the [CEO] or the responsible staff person.'"[38]

- **Guideline 13.** NPOs should follow this guideline to the letter. The audit process is a very valuable tool in evaluating the performance of an organization, and the government is getting stricter about regulating NPOs and their reporting procedures. A current development that emphasizes the importance of proper NPO audits (and donor-relations procedures) is the government's designation of NPO surveillance to the Better Business Bureau. Although this arrangement is too complex to address in this chapter, it does demonstrate the transition to an era of higher accountability expected from NPOs.

  An offshoot of this guideline is that NPOs are currently struggling with professional ethics codes and federal regulations that are sometimes at odds with one another. The National Society of Fund Raising Executives (NSFRE) has a code of ethics and a donors' rights document to which members must adhere. The Canadian Centre for Philanthropy (CCP) has also produced a document outlining ethical fund-raising standards. Neither the NSFRE nor the CCP document currently addresses the details of acceptable accounting methods; however, both address donors' rights to honest disclosure of spending practices.

  An annual audit of an NPO should enhance transparency as well as make disclosure easier. The information gathered can help with such things as grant proposals in which foundations insist on seeing methodical and accurate financial records before awarding funds.

- **Guideline 14.** This guideline may not have as much relevance to an NPO board as it does to a corporate one, but it cannot be overlooked. Occasionally, an NPO director may require outside guidance to ensure that due diligence is applied to a particular situation.[39] It is a director's privilege to secure appropriate professional guidance when necessary.

  Adherence to Guideline 14 need not be a costly affair for an NPO. Organizations such as the Centre for Non-Profit Management make it possible for NPOs to match their needs for professional advice with business volunteers who possess such skills for nominal fees that are considerably lower than industry standards. NPOs should honor directors' requests for outside assistance because it will empower the board and result in a more satisfied group of directors and a higher caliber of stewardship for the organization.

28.4   *Common Board Member Frustrations*

It can be useful to look at some of the common frustrations of board members in order to get clear on what a board governance model needs to take into account:

- *Which hat?* Because board members often wear more than one hat, many find it difficult to determine which one to wear, and when. When board members are also chairpersons of committees, for example, they sometimes find their thinking split between doing what is best for the organization as a whole and what is best for the committee in particular. Consequently, board meetings can seem to be more about advancing individual group interests and/or personal opinions rather than thinking strategically about the future of the organization.
- *What role?* This problem is a variation on "which hat?". Despite all that has been written on the subject, most board members receive little or no orientation regarding the scope and mandate of their role as a board member. Although volunteer position descriptions are often prepared for committee members and chairpersons, rarely do board members have a clearly outlined set of expectations available to them.
- *Who's got the time?* Because of the multiple roles most board members have, many find that there simply is not enough time to adequately fulfill all of their duties. Many board members may have paid employment responsibilities. The 80/20 rule seems to apply here: Twenty percent of the people attempt to do 80 percent of the work, and it seems more common than not for board members to be overcommitted. The result is that something has to give, and it is usually some of the board commitments that are often less tangible or more frustrating.
- *Why am I here?* Board members join in order to make a real difference but sometimes find that their experience falls short of their expectations. Partially because of lack of role clarity, boards can sometimes get caught up with issues that are nonstrategic. Examples include the time-consuming discussions around minutiae of budgets or parking spaces. The work of the board is to ensure the fulfillment of the organization's mission. Those board members who joined to do that level of work will find anything less to be frustrating and disappointing.

28.5   *Issues in Governance*

A number of issues are evolving that could have serious impacts on board effectiveness. Some of these are outlined in this section.

(A)   EAGLE VISION

Issues that can dramatically impact an organization can come from anywhere—government changes in legislation or funding, demographic shifts, media comments, loss or gain of a major donor, client attitudes, and so forth. In order to govern an organization effectively, boards need to develop "eagle vision"—the capacity to see the big picture and focus in on the details that make sense. Sources of risk and opportunity for an organization are found in this way. Boards that operate in a "head in the sand" or "tunnel vision" manner may not be aware of risks and opportunities that could make or break the organization.

(B) SHOW ME . . . OR ELSE

There has been a marked increase in the demands for organizational transparency and board accountability. Foundations and government funders have increased the amount of information they want on the operations of NPOs applying for grants. Private donors are also looking for evidence that an NPO is credible before making a donation or volunteering. The Better Business Bureau has begun to collect information on NPOs in order to meet the people's demand for proof of charitable status, board accountability, services offered, and so on. It is not uncommon to see NPOs cease operations because the board lapsed in its accountability to funders, legislators, the community, or its staff and volunteers. With the number of NPOs from which to select increasing every year, donors and volunteers are very quick to move their support to organizations that can demonstrate their effectiveness through transparent processes and board accountability.

(C) ALTERNATIVE FRAMEWORKS

Jane Arsenault notes, "As many nonprofits have discovered to their cost, an organization's own structure—its corporate identity—can impede its ability to compete for the resources necessary for survival. . . . As I see it, the task of managing a nonprofit is becoming so complex that small, locally based organizations will not be able to compete for resources or consumers."[40] Alternative frameworks to deliver services and attract resources need to be considered. Arsenault proposes five new structures for NPOs to consider: joint ventures, partnerships, management service organizations, parent corporations, and mergers. Although many of these frameworks are common in the private sector, they are still uncommon in the nonprofit sector. Each of these alternate frameworks requires forethought and strategic planning on the part of the board. Knowing about different frameworks will become an important strategic skill for nonprofit boards.

28.6   Conclusion

It is the intent of the authors to set forth in this chapter a set of different board governance models for boards of directors to consider. Fundamental to everything in the chapter is the belief that governance does not just happen. It is a strategic activity that requires commitment from the directors and sufficient time and resources to plan and implement. As most directors know, the final responsibility for the organization rests with them. Board governance is the process to help directors understand and manage that responsibility.

Endnotes

1. Deloitte & Touche. (1995). *The Effective Not-for-Profit Board: Governance of Not-for-Profit Organizations.* Author, pp. 1, 3, 4, 24, 25, 119.
2. Panel on Accountability and Governance in the Voluntary Sector. (February 1999). *Building on Strength: Improving Governance and Accountability in Canada's Voluntary Sector.* Final Report. Ottawa: Voluntary Sector Roundtable, pp. 11, 23, 118, 119.

3. See note 1.
4. Meneghetti, M., and K. Seel. (1998). "Ethics and Values in the Not-for-profit Organization." In T. Connors. (ed.). *The Nonprofit Handbook: Management,* 2nd ed., 1998 Supplement. New York: John Wiley & Sons, pp. 1–30.
5. United Way of Canada. (1995). *Board Basics Kit for Volunteer Organizations.* Manual, p. 1D–2.
6. See note 1.
7. See note 5.
8. See note 2.
9. Id.
10. Id.
11. Carver, J. (1990). *Boards That Make a Difference: A New Design for Leadership in Nonprofit and Public Organizations.* San Francisco: Jossey-Bass, pp. 109, 110, 127, 201.
12. Carver, J., and M. M. Carver. (1997). *Reinventing Your Board.* San Francisco: Jossey-Bass, pp. 15, 16, 18, 57, 113, 135–136, 205.
13. Id.
14. Id.
15. See note 11.
16. See note 12.
17. Id.
18. Id.
19. Id.
20. Id.
21. See note 1.
22. See note 11.
23. Thomas, J. W. (November 14, 1997). "Getting and Keeping a Great Board." Presentation notes distributed at the 1997 Third Annual Fund Raising Congress in Toronto.
24. Swanson, A. (1984). *Building a Better Board: A Guide to Effective Leadership.* Washington, DC: Taft Corporation, pp. 20–21, 32, 43.
25. Id.
26. Frantzreb, A. C. (1997). *Not on This Board You Don't: Making Your Trustees More Effective.* Chicago: Bonus Books, pp. 11–12.
27. Id.
28. Id.
29. See note 23.
30. Id.
31. Id.
32. See note 1.
33. See note 11.
34. Id.
35. See note 23.
36. See note 24.
37. Id.
38. See note 11.
39. See note 1.
40. Arsenault, J. (1998). *Forging Nonprofit Alliances.* San Francisco: Jossey-Bass, pp. xi–xiii.

Self-Managed Teams in the Self-Renewing Organization

HENRY P. SIMS JR., PhD, PROFESSOR OF
MANAGEMENT AND ORGANIZATION
University of Maryland at College Park

CHARLES C. MANZ, PhD, CHARLES AND
JANET NIRENBERG PROFESSOR OF BUSINESS
LEADERSHIP
University of Massachusetts

The leader looked out at the eyes around the campfire. Slowly, he picked up a stick, and snapped it in a second. Next, he picked up a bunch of sticks together, and attempted to break them. They bent, but did not break. "A stick by itself," he said, "can be broken easily. But if all the sticks stay together, they will not break." Slowly he smiled. "The same is true of us."[1]

29.1 Introduction

Self-leadership is the capacity of individuals to influence their own behavior in the absence of external influences. Fundamentally, self-leadership is an attribute of an individual. That is, each person in an organization has both an opportunity and a responsibility to develop his or her own self-leadership capabilities. Also, leaders have the responsibility of developing and encouraging individual self-leadership. Essentially, developing individual self-leadership is a form of employee empowerment. In fact, much of our previous writing has been concerned with the challenge of how individuals can lead themselves, and how leaders can lead others to become skilled self-leaders.

But few of us work in isolation. For most of us, our work has some degree of interdependence with others. In fact, in today's increasingly complex environment, the opportunity and requirement for working together is stronger than ever. The "lone wolf" is gone. Much of our work involves working together, and today, working together means teams and teamwork. In this chapter, we extrapolate the concept of individual self-leadership to self-managing teams, and how these teams have become a critical factor in sustaining a self-renewing organization (SRO).

Empowered teams are the cutting edge of the SRO. The essence of self-renewal lies in the capacity of each individual and groups of individuals to create a bottom-up culture of renewal. Renewal is possible only through empowerment.

Recent years have brought many challenges for Western organizations—intense international competition, a workforce that now demands more than simply making a living, and the increasing complexity of technical knowledge and information flows. As a result, companies are pressured to explore more effective ways of using human resources. Among the more noteworthy and promising is the concept of empowered teams.

Teams are the focus of this chapter. In fact, in today's contemporary organization, teams are the most common vehicle through which self-leadership is expressed. Empowerment typically relies on team structures. Thus, teams are a critical element of the organizational self-leadership system. For most organizations, teams are the *springboard* to self-leadership. In this chapter, we address the idea of self-managed and empowered teams, and how these teams can enhance service, quality, productivity, and innovation. And most of all, we emphasize how leaders can encourage self-leadership through empowered teams. The team becomes the unit of self leadership. Team self-management is the essential building block of a self-renewing organization.

29.2   What Is a Team? What Do Teams Do?

Work designs based on self-management tend to give employees a high degree of autonomy and control over their immediate behavior. Teams are one of the many forms of employee participation that have emerged in the United States. Not all teams are empowered, however. Indeed, the traditional sports team is seldom a participatory unit. In fact, a team can function well under the thumb of a strong-minded leader—we think of the late Vince Lombardi (coach of the champion Green Bay Packers) as an example of a successful boss-type coach who demanded compliance from his players. His teams were definitely *not* self-managed. But the teams of today's contemporary business sector in the United States are *not* like the Lombardi teams.

In contemporary empowered teams, employees are typically organized into units that complete a whole or distinct part of a product or service. They make decisions on a wide range of issues, often including such traditional management prerogatives as who will perform which task, solving quality problems, settling conflicts between members on the team, and selecting team leaders. The story of the Fitzgerald Battery Plant of General Motors Corporation is an example of the many activities that self-managed teams have taken on in many work organizations (Exhibit 29.1).

Team designs have varied across companies, and it is difficult to find a single commonly accepted definition of what the team approach really is. It seems to be more of an overall philosophy and approach to work design rather than a tightly defined set of rules. In fact, part of the essence of teams is to encourage each set of employees to find their own

EXHIBIT 29.1 Team Roles and Responsibilities at Fitzgerald[a]

Here, we describe some of the self-management practices at the Fitzgerald Battery Plant of General Motors Corporation. Our main purpose is to use this concrete, specific example to demonstrate the typical roles and responsibilities of self-managing teams. We derived this information from interviews and observations that we conducted several years after startup. Thus, the plant was at a relatively "mature" stage, rather than a startup stage. Following are some more specific details, in no particular order, that describe how the teams actually handled responsibilities that in other organizations are typically performed by traditional "bosses."

Establish Relief and Break Schedules

Teams had great discretion in establishing their own schedules. Since most of the teams were "buffered" by short-term in-process inventories, breaks could be scheduled at their own discretion. Did teams handle this authority in a responsible way? Yes! Often, breaks are scheduled to facilitate production. For example, a short tool or process change might be undertaken while the team is on their break.

Select and Dismiss Leader of the Group

Teams elected their own team leader, who was a member of the team. Elections were conducted whenever a current leader resigned, or was challenged by another team member. A few teams had the same team leader since the startup of the plant. Other teams had experienced several team leaders over the years. At first, "popular" individuals tended to be elected team leader. However, teams soon found that the leaders who had organizing and planning skills, who also possessed interpersonal and conflict resolution skills, were more effective. So-called popularity diminished as a criterion for election to team leader.

In addition, management appointed people to fill the role of "coordinator," which was a leadership role external to the team—that is, the coordinator was not a team member. In other plants, this person might be called a "facilitator" or a "counselor." Each coordinator had responsibility for one to three teams. While the coordinator filled the space in the organizational hierarchy typically occupied by a foreman or general foreman, their behaviors were quite different. Many of the coordinators at Fitzgerald had previously served as team leaders.

Finally, while teams technically had the authority to dismiss a team leader, this was virtually never done. Instead, an ineffective team leader might be encouraged to resign, or might be challenged by another potential leader.

Initiate Minor and Major Equipment and Machinery Repair

Overall, team members might carry out minor repairs themselves, in order to keep production flowing. Major repairs were carried out by the maintenance department, but were frequently initiated by team members. We recall the statement of a team member in a weekly team meeting: "They better get that bearing replaced this weekend, or that machine will break down next week, and we'll lose a day's production!" Most of all, team members seemed to take an unusual degree of psychological "ownership" in their production equipment. They were very concerned about making the equipment work in the right way.

Make Specific Job Assignments within Work Group

Each team made their own job assignments, and the practices were quite different across teams. One team might rotate jobs every hour, whereas another team would make assignments strictly on a seniority basis. Overall, teams seemed to find a way to satisfy individual preferences within the team without compromising productivity goals.

---

[a] These roles are taken from Chapter 2, "The Day-to-Day Team Experience: Roles, Behaviors, and Performance of Mature Self-Managing Teams," in C. C. Manz, and H. P. Sims, *Business Without Bosses*. New York: Wiley, 1993. Copyright © 1993 by C. C. Manz and H. P. Sims. Reprinted by permission of John Wiley & Sons, Inc.

EXHIBIT 29.1 *(Continued)*

Train New Members of Work Group

This was a responsibility that was carried out by all teams. Occasionally, the external coordinator would pitch in or conduct some special training. Of course, other more formal training programs were also conducted for the team members. Training was also important in terms of developing the wide range of skills required for each new member to advance along the pay scale.

Make Sure Needed Production Materials Are Available

In many traditional plants, workers will allow a production material to deplete, in order to take an unauthorized break. At this plant, responsibility to make sure production materials were available was vested in the team itself. Team leaders, in particular, spent a great deal of their time ensuring that proper materials would be available to meet production requirements.

Keep Record of Hours Worked for Each Group Member

Each team member kept a record of their own number of hours worked—the plant had no time clocks. Weekly time records were turned in to their team leader and then to the coordinator. When asked "Don't they cheat?," one team member replied, "Who do they cheat? Other team members! You may be able to get away with it once or twice, but that's all. You can't fool your teammates."

Make Sure Spare Parts Are Available

Team members accepted the responsibility for keeping track of minor spare parts that were required to run their own operation.

Perform Quality Control Inspections and Compile QC Data

For the most part, teams did their own quality inspections and compiled their own quality statistics. One team member might typically be assigned this responsibility. A separate quality control inspector did not exist. However, occasionally, team quality data would be audited by a small central quality control department.

Prepare Material and Labor Budgets

On an annual basis, teams undertook a planning exercise in which they prepared a budget for their team. Budgeting was also done independently, in parallel, by accountants from the office. In general, team budgets were at least as demanding and as stringent as the accounting budgets. Differences were discussed and reconciled in order to arrive at a final budget. Of course, team members required training and appropriate information to carry out this planning exercise.

Prepare Daily Log of Quantity Produced and Amount of In-Process Inventory

For the most part, teams compiled their own in-process inventory records, subject to occasional auditing from production scheduling. Teams knew their own production schedule, and kept their own records of how much they produced and the quantity of their in-process inventory.

Recommend Engineering Changes for Equipment, Process, and Product

As they worked with equipment, teams would occasionally request changes that would lead to significant process or product improvements. One engineer at the division level expressed a preference for placing new or experimental equipment at Fitzgerald. "They make it work!" he exclaimed.

Select New Members for Group; Dismiss Members from Group

Teams had considerable, but not total, discretion over who would join or leave a group. Most intergroup mobility was facilitated by the coordinator, who would use interpersonal skills to explore new assignments to different groups. Great effort was made to match the preferences of individuals with teams. Employees would move from one team to another for any

EXHIBIT 29.1 *(Continued)*

of several reasons. Some wanted to earn the higher pay rate. Others preferred a different type of work. Others would move because of interpersonal preferences.

Evaluate Group Members for Pay Raise

The plant used a "pay for knowledge" system, where an employee was paid according to the tasks he or she was qualified to do, rather than being paid a rate for a particular job that he or she was performing at the moment. To gain the highest pay rate, an employee had to pass performance tests for all tasks on two different teams. These performance tests were conducted by a coordinator, team leader, and senior team member. Thus, part of the evaluation of whether an employee could perform a specific job or not was performed by a teammate.

Conduct Safety Meetings

Safety meetings were conducted on a scheduled basis—normally by the team leader, or perhaps by a coordinator or other technical person. During the early stages of the startup of the plant, safety performance of the plant was poor. However, the safety record had continuously improved, and during the time of our visits, Fitzgerald's safety performance was in the top quartile of all General Motors plants.

Shut Down Process/Assembly if Quality is Wrong; Stop Production to Solve Process or Quality Problems

Teams had the authority to stop production without necessarily asking permission from a representative of management. Typically, this authority would be rarely exercised, and almost always to solve a serious quality or process problem. Of course, this authority would be used with great discretion, since a shutdown decision might have ramifications for other teams.

Conduct Weekly Group Meetings

Usually, a weekly half-hour meeting was conducted on company time. In addition, shorter ad hoc meetings would be conducted on almost a daily basis. Also, on occasion, a more lengthy problem-solving meeting might be conducted to work on special production or quality issues.

Review Quarterly Performance of Company, Plant, and Group

Each quarter, the plant manager met separately with each team, and reviewed company, plant, and team performance with the team. These occasions provided an opportunity for an exchange of communication between the plant manager and team members. The communication exchange went both ways.

Discipline Group Members for Absenteeism or Tardiness

Theoretically, this authority was vested within each team, but some teams utilized the authority, others did not. Coordinators said this was the most difficult responsibility to get the team to undertake.

Select New Employees for the Plant

Employees were selected into the plant through an assessment center process. An evaluation team observed employee candidates during interpersonal exercises and provided ratings and final judgments. The plant evaluation team consisted of one manager, one coordinator, one team leader, and two members of different teams.

Summary

Of course, all of these responsibilities are appropriate to the specific site of The Fitzgerald Battery Plant. Other sites will undoubtedly be different in the specifics of the roles and responsibilities expected of each team. In each case, however, roles and responsibilities must be specified in advance, with a sequenced timetable of implementation, and a substantial degree of flexibility to take advantage of the learning as team implementation proceeds.

way, their own kind of group self-leadership that best fits their own situation and team members. But most of all, the team approach represents an attempt to more fully utilize the organization's human resources—especially those at the lowest levels.

A typical objective of an empowered team system is to simultaneously *improve productivity for the organization as well as the quality of working life for employees.* Sometimes the dignity and freedom workers receive is especially publicized, but the drive toward productivity and competitiveness is always there, whether stated openly or not.

Typically, teams have some common characteristics: a distinct recognizable task that employees can identify with; members with a variety of skills related to the *group* task; discretion over such decisions as work methods, task scheduling, and task assignments; and compensation and performance feedback for the group as a whole.

The team concept has emerged as a distinctly Western phenomenon (teams have been used in the United States, Canada, Europe, and Mexico, to name just a few locations) although it's frequently confused with so-called Japanese Management. While both are often associated with the idea of participatory management, each approach is targeted at a quite different population, with distinct cultural values. In our attempts to understand the team system, we have traveled to Japan and read extensively about Japanese management systems. But teams in Japan are quite different from U.S. teams.

Our main conclusion is that we would be better served by attempting to learn from successful experiences with empowered teams in the West rather than looking to the Japanese for innovative organizational philosophies. The rationale and early successes with team designs originated in the United States and Europe, and better fit Western cultures. The unique defining characteristic of U.S. teams is that they promote a high degree of initiative, and a sense of responsibility, creativity, and problem solving from within. When teams live up to these ideals, they are uniquely self-reliant.

29.3 Why Teams?

The challenge of competitiveness is upon us. The emergence of the global marketplace has placed a new premium on productivity and quality. Business and nonprofit organizations around the world are struggling to find ways to deal with increasing interdependence, complexity, and uncertainty. In the face of these pressures, the team concept is beginning to show proven worth for improving productivity, quality, and employee quality of work life, among other payoffs. It is an approach that is designed to take advantage of the strengths of Western culture and history.

Teams have emerged as a potent weapon in the competitiveness wars. In fact, we suspect that the notion of teams has reached the stage of the recurring management "fads" that we often encounter in the United States. Therefore, some team applications are being undertaken simply because "it's the thing to do," with little thought given to how the approach fits with the needs of the organization. We deplore this justification, and strongly believe it's a sure recipe for failure. Nevertheless, there are some solid reasons why teams make good sense. From a management viewpoint, *productivity* and *quality* are typically the main reasons to implement a team system. Teams are a way to undertake "continuous improvement" to enhance productivity. Today, teams are often seen as a critical element within a total quality management (TQM) program. And of course, the real issue is whether teams actually work as well as they're supposed to! (See Exhibit 29.2.)

EXHIBIT 29.2 Are Teams Effective? The Bottom Line[a]

Do self-managing teams really produce superior results? *BusinessWeek* claims teams can increase productivity by 30 percent or more, and can also substantially improve quality (Horr, 1989). Other examples reported in the press include an ALCOA plant in Cleveland, where a production team came up with a method for making forged wheels for vans that increased output 5 percent and cut scrap in half. At Weyerhaeuser, the forest-product company, a team of legal employees significantly reduced the retrieval time for documents. At Federal Express, a thousand clerical workers, divided into "superteams" of five to ten people, helped the company reduce service problems by 13 percent in 1989. At Rubbermaid, a multidisciplinary team from marketing, engineering, and design developed the "auto office" in 1987, and sales exceeded projections by 50 percent in the first year (Dumaine, 1990).

Corning Glass eliminated one management level at their corporate computer center, substituting a team adviser for three shift supervisors, producing $150K annual savings and *increasing* quality of service. Perceptions of autonomy and responsibility among workers increased because they felt they experienced more meaningful and productive work (Weiss, 1989). In an insurance firm, change to automation led to a shift from functional organizational design to self-managed teams. A 24-month follow-up found improved workstructure, flows, and outcomes (Frederiksen et al., 1984).

Also, in our previous book, *Business Without Bosses,* we describe several organizations that have enjoyed impressive payoffs with teams in both the long and short term. For example, in Exhibit 29.1 we tell a more detailed story of the mature General Motors automobile battery plant organized around teams in which company officials reported productivity savings of 30 to 40 percent when compared with traditionally organized plants. Teams helped Lake Superior Paper Company enjoy possibly the most successful startup in the history of the paper industry. We describe the very beginning adjustments of management to the team approach that a few short months later was credited with productivity improvements of 10 percent per year, cost savings of 10 to 20 percent of earnings, and customer service quality levels of over 99 percent.

Considerable data indicate the effectiveness of teams, but perhaps the difficulty of evaluating the team concept in terms of any hard scientific data was best expressed by Miner (1982):

> The results are often positive. It is hard to predict whether the outcomes will be greater output, better quality, less absenteeism, reduced turnover, fewer accidents, greater job satisfaction, or what, but the introduction of autonomous work groups is often associated with improvements. It is difficult to understand why a particular outcome such as increased productivity occurs in one study and not in another, and why, on some occasions, nothing improves. Furthermore, what actually causes the changes when they do occur is not known. The approach calls for making so many changes at once that it is almost impossible to judge the value of the individual variables. Increased pay, self-selection of work situations, multiskilling, with its resultant job enrichment and decreased contact with authority almost invariably occurs.

[a] This section is adapted from a similar section in Manz and Sims' *Business Without Bosses.* New York, John Wiley & Sons, 1993. Copyright © 1993 by C. C. Manz and H. P. Sims. Reprinted by permission of John Wiley & Sons, Inc.

EXHIBIT 29.2 *(Continued)*

One of the more revealing scientific studies of the bottom-line effect of teams is contained in a paper from Dr. Barry Macy and associates at the Texas Center for Productivity and Quality of Work Life (Texas Tech University) (Macy and Izumi, 1994). Their analysis contrasted the success of various changes involving human resources, work structure, and technology, for example, training, reward systems, work teams. Very strong effects, especially in terms of financial outcomes, were observed with team applications. The Macy study is one of the first rigorous scientific efforts that shows the clear financial effect of the team approach.

In another, more recent study, Lawler, Mohrman, and Ledford, at the Center for Effective Organizations, investigated financial effects of employee involvement programs (which, in many cases, consist of empowered teams). They found significant relationships between usages of employee involvement and firm financial performance.[b]

Are teams *always* successful? Clearly, the answer is no. In our previous book, *Business Without Bosses,* we reported on a team implementation at an insurance company that was clearly a failure. Indeed, we believe that team success depends much on implementation. For example, we continue to hear tales of companies removing a supervisor and precipitously declaring that a work group is "a team." We call this the "team alone" syndrome, where a group of employees suddenly finds itself with much larger responsibility, but without the training and resources to handle this responsibility.

Those close to the self-management movement informally report substantial productivity gains and cost savings that typically range from 30 to 70 percent when compared with traditional systems. Clearly, self-managing teams have the potential to exert substantial effects on the bottom line. Perhaps the notion was captured best by the following quote from Charles Eberle, a former vice president at Procter and Gamble. He speaks with the advantage of years of practical experience.

> At P & G there are well over two decades of comparisons of results—side by side— between enlightened work systems and those I call traditional. It is absolutely clear that the new work systems work better—a lot better—for example, with 30 to 50 percent lower manufacturing costs. Not only are the tangible, measurable, bottom line indicators such as cost, quality, customer service and reliability better, but also the harder-to-measure attributes such as quickness, decisiveness, toughness, and just plain resourcefulness of these organizations.[c]

[b] See Part III, Section 13 of Lawler (1995).

[c] Interview originally published in *U.S. News and World Report* (August 31, 1981): 66–67.

On occasion, the implementation of teams is motivated by a humanistic ideology. That is, teams are seen as an important way for people to find satisfaction and dignity in their work—in essence, an *enhanced quality employee of work life.* Other reasons are also occasionally cited: better *innovation* and *adaptability,* and also *reduced turnover, absenteeism, and conflict.*

While we are sympathetic with all of these reasons, as researchers and authors we believe that issues of productivity and quality—the important elements of competitiveness—are the more important drivers. In the end, more teams will be adopted only if teams really do work.

For a time—when international competition was not strong, when employees were more accepting of no power and fulfillment—top-down control was sufficient for organizational success. More recently, however, employees have changed—people expect growth, fulfillment, and dignity from their work. Most of all, the emergence of the global marketplace has forced organizations to consider alternative ways of dealing with the competitive challenge. Flexibility, speed, quick response, and short cycle time have become extremely important performance criteria. Many organizations are moving toward flat, flexible organizations, including sophisticated structures such as virtual teams.

After more than 15 years of studying teams, we are convinced—teams do work! Moreover, there is something exciting about the challenge of bringing a group of people together to combine their abilities and coordinate their efforts to excel.

29.4   The Historical Emergence of Teams—Where Have Teams Been Applied?

According to a study by the Center for Effective Organizations at the University of Southern California, 68 percent of the *Fortune* 1000 companies were using self-managed or high-performance teams in 1993, but they had been applied to only a small percentage of the work force.[2] This data does show a significant increase from 28 percent in 1987, and 47 percent in 1990. In essence, there's a whole lot of experimentation going on out there, but it's touched only a minority of employees. In the early 1980s, Edward Lawler, Director of the U.S.C. Center, estimated that about 150 to 300 work sites were using teams. Clearly, the number of companies using teams has grown considerably. We believe that nearly every major U.S. company is currently trying or considering some form of empowered work teams somewhere in their organization.

Procter & Gamble is generally considered an important U.S. pioneer in seriously applying teams to their operations. Their work began in the early 1960s, although it was not publicized and virtually escaped media attention. P&G saw the team approach as a significant competitive advantage, and up through the 1980s, attempted to deflect attention away from their efforts. The company thought of their knowledge about the team organization as a type of trade secret, and required consultants and employees to sign nondisclosure statements. Other companies have had team-oriented plants for years, but have also considered their team approaches to be proprietary.

Despite their obsession with secrecy, Procter & Gamble's successes with teams received considerable informal "off-the-record" attention from a small group of in-house and external consultants across the country who were inspired by the P&G experiences, and who learned techniques through an informal network. Many of them originally worked at P&G and were attracted away to other companies by lucrative job offers because of their unique knowledge and expertise.

Through the 1970s and 1980s, General Motors was a locus of active experimentation with teams, and was significantly less secretive than Procter & Gamble. Many of the GM team implementations have been very successful, and have served as models for other changes around the country.

General Motors remains an interesting enigma, however—they are a textbook case of how success with teams at one location does not necessarily transfer to another location within a huge corporation. (Further, teams are not the sole answer to the competitiveness challenge.) We suspect the "not-invented-here" syndrome to be rampant at GM. Also, while specific GM manufacturing plants have been on the cutting edge of employee self-management, many would suggest that the corporate level has maintained a more traditional top-down, control-based management mentality. Despite the problems of diffusion of their successes with self-management, General Motors should be credited with their leadership in active exploration of the team concept.

Other prominent companies have been active with teams. These include the early work with teams at the Gaines dog food plant in Topeka (incidentally, this is another case where diffusion of a successful change did not occur). Other companies include Cummins Engine, Digital Equipment, Ford, Motorola, Tektronix, General Electric, Honeywell, LTV, Caterpillar, Boeing, Monsanto, AT&T, Texas Instruments, and Xerox, to name just a few. In manufacturing, we now have extensive experience with self-managing teams, starting in the 1960s. Today, teams in manufacturing are a proven system. It's no longer a question of why, but now only a question of fine tuning to specific sites.

In the past few years, the use of teams in the service sector has been the most exciting area of application. Service teams, such as office teams at IDS (now American Express) (Sims et al., 1993), are now well past the experimentation phase, although we still have much to learn.

Perhaps the most promising area of team development will be empowered professional and middle-management teams. These include teams like concurrent engineering teams, cross-functional teams, product improvement teams, task force teams, ad hoc teams, and, as discussed later, new venture teams.

Teams in government is the most rapidly changing area of application. Until a few years ago, there was very little interest in empowered teams in government agencies. Now, however, driven by the "reinventing government" thrust, and the stark reality of government downsizing, experimentation with teams in government seems to be very active indeed. It remains to be seen, however, whether teams in government will attain the same success seen in manufacturing and service.

29.5   Team Leadership: Roles and Structures

The key to team success is team leadership. Team leadership comes in all forms, starting with the traditional director, who exercises his or her power through authoritarian behaviors. But in this chapter, we are concentrating most on self-managed or empowered teams. The fundamental question we wish to address is: What type of leadership is most appropriate for empowered teams that are vested with a high degree of power, authority, and self-responsibility? First, consider the four archetypes of leadership that are likely to be found in today's contemporary organizations (Exhibit 29.3).

Before we consider the *behavior* of team leaders, we should first consider the *structure of team leadership.* By structure, we mean the question of how the leader is appointed (and, perhaps unappointed), whether the team leader is a member or co-performer of the team, and the degree of formal authority that is vested to the leader versus the team itself.

As a part of this discussion, we also raise the philosophical issue of whether formal leaders are really necessary. After all, if teams are really to be "self-managed," then why do they need a leader? Occasionally, one hears the term *leaderless teams,* which usually means that a team does not have an appointed leader. This is somewhat of a paradox, because, in reality, no team is ever truly "leaderless"—at least no *effective* team is leaderless. Some form of lead-

EXHIBIT 29.3 The Four Archetypes of Leadership: Strongman, Transactor, Visionary Hero, and SuperLeader

There is an old Norse word, *Laed,* meaning "to determine the course of a ship." We can easily see how our modern word *lead* comes from this ancient expression. And we can even visualize the modern version of a *leader* as the person who guides the course of an organization. But in today's contemporary world, how should this guidance take place?

Fundamentally, leadership means influence—the ability to influence others. But this influence can be carried out in different ways. Here, we present a simplified historical perspective on different approaches to leadership. We focus on four leader *archetypes:* The Strongman, the Transactor, the Visionary Hero, and The SuperLeader.

The *Strongman* pattern of leadership concentrates on command and instruction to influence followers. A strongman's source of power is the coercion that stems from the authority of his or her position. It is a top-down type of leadership that produces a fear-based compliance in followers. The behaviors most frequently used by this leader are instruction, command, assigned goals, threat, intimidation, and reprimand.

The *Transactor* leader enters into an exchange relationship with followers. Rewards are the major source of influence, with the follower entering into a calculating compliance with the wishes of the leader in order to secure rewards that are controlled by the leader. The behaviors most frequently used by this leader are the dispensation of personal and material rewards in return for effort, performance, and loyalty to the leader.

The *Visionary Hero* leader is a source of inspiration to the follower. This leader uses a top-down vision, to inspire and stimulate followers, who make an emotional commitment based on the vision and charisma of the leader. This leader uses behaviors such as communicating a vision, exhortation, inspiration and persuasion, and challenge to the status quo. Other terms that describe the visionary hero are "transformational leader" and "charismatic leader."

The *SuperLeader* is the only leader who focuses primarily on the development of the follower. Sometimes called an "empowering" leader, this leader is "super" because he or she is strengthened through the strengths of followers. This leader leads others to lead themselves. The SuperLeader encourages follower initiative, self-responsibility, self-confidence, self-goal-setting, positive opportunity thinking, and self-problem-solving. Power is more balanced between the leader and followers. SuperLeadership is a perspective that reaches beyond visionary leadership. In the past, the idea of a leader implied that the spotlight was on the leader. This alternative viewpoint places the spotlight on the follower. In return, followers experience commitment and psychological ownership. For the SuperLeader, the essence of leadership is the challenge to lead followers to discover the potentialities that lie within themselves.

ership is always necessary for a team to function (for example, team-member self-leadership will exist within the team). In the absence of some form of *formal* external leadership, then, at least some degree of *emergent* leadership will always be present. Thus, so-called *leaderless* teams really do have leadership, but it typically is exercised by leaders that emerge to de facto leadership without being assigned this role by upper management.

In general, we are not in favor of trying to create leaderless teams. Most of the time, particularly in organizations, we believe some type of recognized leadership should be established, especially at the inception of the team. However, a team leader certainly need not be a traditional directive. And, we believe that a high degree of empowerment of the team itself, rather than primarily relying on the leader, is typically most effective over the long run.

There are various structural alternatives through which team leadership can be expressed. The most common and well known is the traditional external supervisor or foreperson. Typically, this person is appointed by management and has traditional powers that stem from the position itself. This person usually has the authority to make job assignments, give instructions and commands, and allocate some rewards and/or reprimands. Control over the team's activities are mainly vested in this appointed leader rather than the team itself. We think of this person as a "boss." Usually, this person is *not* a team member, and is at least one step removed from actually carrying out the work tasks themselves.

Interestingly, a natural pattern of leadership of an external appointed leader is often to act as a directive leader who directs and commands compliance from the team. Other leadership options, however, are more appropriate. Indeed, even under a traditional system, a supervisor might voluntarily choose to *act* as a SuperLeader, and encourage considerable self-leadership-based empowerment in the group. The main point, however, is that often situations are structured via an external leader appointed by management who retains a high degree of control and decision making that is typical of a formally appointed position.

Other types of structures are possible. For example, leadership may be expressed through an appointed external leader, often called a "facilitator," who is purposefully intended to facilitate empowered workers. Other terms that are sometimes used to label this position are "coordinator," "counselor," or "coach." A facilitator is usually *not* a part of the team—that is, he or she does not actually carry out team tasks, but offers advice and counsel on how the team itself might perform their duties. A facilitator is usually appointed by management, similar to a supervisor, but the expected behavior or "role" of the facilitator is quite different. While a supervisor retains a high degree of control and decision making, a facilitator typically attempts to encourage a team to undertake self-control activities such as self-assignments, self-goal-setting, and so on. In other words, the expected role and pattern of leadership of an external facilitator is to assist a team to become empowered.

Again, the actual behaviors of this role might vary from person to person. However, generally, we would expect the role of an external facilitator to be consistent with Super-Leader-type behaviors that facilitate and influence team members and the team itself to act more as self-leaders. Directive-type behaviors are quite incompatible with this facilitator role.

Other types of structures might be utilized for team leadership, including the internal elected team leader. This type of leader is usually an actual team member and engages in most of the typical day-to-day activities of the team in addition to leadership responsibilities. This leader frequently comes to his or her position as a result of some type of team election (or, even team leader rotation), and thus might be considered more of an emergent leader. Of course, if there is an election of the team leader, there must be some method of replacement to deal with turnover within the leadership role. This might be accomplished by invoking a specified "term of office," at the end of which the leader may or may not be reelected. Other mechanisms might include a "runoff" to choose between alternate candidates, or a "vote of confidence" in which a leader might be unelected or deposed. (We have found this to be quite unusual. Typically, an elected team leader in difficulty with his or her team will voluntarily step down before an "unelection" is necessary.)

A fellow-worker who is also a team leader will have advantages and obstacles in terms of group norms, interpersonal relationships, and so on that are not shared by external team leaders. For example, *internal* team leaders may be in a better position to contribute to the social well-being (group maintenance) of the group, but may face difficulties in emphasizing task performance because of personal relationships with other group members.

We like to think of an elected team leader as being "empowered from below." That is, this elected leader acts to organize, motivate, and influence the team, but the power and authority to do so comes from the very people the leader is attempting to influence. Note that the team itself may have been "empowered from above" to carry out this and other self-management responsibilities.

Clearly, the leader behaviors of an elected team leader are most consistent with the philosophy of a SuperLeader—that is, a leader who attempts to influence the team to lead itself. Conversely, directive behaviors tend to be highly incompatible with the role of elected team leader. An elected leader who behaves as a directive is likely to incite a rebellion among team members.

To summarize, at least three types of structures might be possible to express team leadership:

1. Foreperson or Supervisor
2. Appointed External Facilitator
3. Elected Internal Team Leader

These structures provide considerable variance in terms of direct control that is vested in the team itself, versus direct control retained by management. In the care of the traditional foreperson or supervisor, virtually all control is retained by management, since most of the power is vested in the supervisor, who represents management. At the other end of the spectrum, a great deal of control is vested in the team itself, which, in turn, "delegates upward" to the elected team leader.

The appointed external facilitator is a role that is somewhere in between in terms of empowerment, although the philosophy and practice typically is moving in the direction of greater team control. A facilitator attempts to move more control into the hands of the team, but in reality, management retains a great deal of control through the power to appoint or remove the facilitator.

In our own experience, we have seen all of these structural forms at one time or another. Of course, the traditional supervisor is the usual baseline or beginning point, and remains the most common structural form of leadership of work groups in the United States today. Nevertheless, we have seen many successful teams that use the elected team leader concept. We believe that for a team to be fully and *truly* empowered, team members should have a significant role in deciding who the team leader should be. However, the use of external facilitators and coordinators is probably the most frequent approach to team empowerment, and indeed can work very well, especially in a transition mode. Also, we have found the use of external facilitators to be most common when management has lingering doubts, or is not 100 percent convinced about team empowerment.

We also wish to note that while the behavior of leaders is *correlated with* the structure of the leadership position, structure and behavior are not necessarily the same. For example, as we mentioned before, a supervisor has a wide range of leadership patterns to select from, ranging from directive to SuperLeader. Facilitators are more likely to behave as SuperLeaders, although we have seen a few that have difficulty in refraining from giving orders and instructions. Also, we would clearly expect elected team leaders to act more like SuperLeaders, or face considerable displeasure from their constituency.

Finally, consider once more the notion of "leaderless" groups. Again, we don't believe there are any truly leaderless groups in formal organizations. Leadership always exists, and the question is how leadership is structured and how leaders behave. The effectiveness of any work group or team is highly dependent on how the leadership function is designed, and we recommend almost any other alternative rather than a "leaderless" group.

29.6   Behaviors of Team Leaders

The role of an external formal leader establishes an apparent paradox or conceptual inconsistency relative to the *ideal* concept of self-managing teams. The leader is charged with the responsibility of leading teams that are philosophically designed to be *self-led*. How can they lead when the team is supposed to lead itself! What is the appropriate role and behaviors for these leaders? Why should such a leader be necessary?

In the organizational hierarchy, this external leader—facilitator or coordinator—has replaced roles traditionally referred to as foreman, general foreman, or supervisor. However, under a self-managing concept, the nature of the authority and responsibility of the leader can become an issue of considerable confusion. To what extent should the leader give direction and evaluate performance yet be a facilitator and communicator? To what degree should he or she directly invoke authority? What are the behaviors that differentiate effective from ineffective facilitators? These questions become particularly challenging when one considers the ideal—that these work teams are supposed to be self-managing. The question "how does one lead employees who are supposed to lead themselves?" establishes a paradox and exemplifies this dilemma.

In our own research about self-managing teams, we have found widespread ambiguity and confusion about the role of appointed external leaders. We believe this issue is commonly a very troublesome point of implementation. While executives and workers who have direct experience with self-managing teams are generally pleased with the results, questions about the role of the external leader continue to be particularly bothersome. For managers who must select, train, counsel, and evaluate these external leaders, the questions are not ones of leisurely theory, but of immediate pragmatic application.

Consider the case of the coordinators at the Fitzgerald Battery Plant. The coordinator behaviors presented are clearly consistent with our earlier definitions of SuperLeadership (Exhibit 29.4).

29.7   The Transition: How Do We Get to Team Leadership?

Let's begin with an assumption that an organization wishes to implement some form of self-managed or empowered work team. Examples of such teams might be: (1) blue-collar manufacturing self-managing teams; (2) white-collar office-worker teams; or (3) cross-functional professional product improvement teams. Whatever the type of team, the tran-

EXHIBIT 29.4 What Do Coordinators Do?

In part of our early research on self-managing teams, we investigated team leadership at a manufacturing site with mature self-managing teams. In this section, we describe the results of this elicitation, which was conducted at the Fitzgerald Battery Plant of General Motors Corporation.[a] The particular role that was the target of this elicitation were the coordinators, or external team leaders.

What do "coordinators" do? What are the behaviors and actions of effective coordinators? If employee work teams are supposed to be "participative," or "self-managed," then why are coordinators necessary? There are no formal guidelines regarding what a coordinator actually does, and coordinator behaviors seem to be loosely defined according to social convention rather than according to any structured set of rules and regulations. There is no "job description." At the time of our research, the ambiguities about this position were still an unresolved issue.

The inquiry was intended to answer the question: "What important behaviors can coordinators use in their work?" We asked this question many times, using a focus group technique. A summary of their answers is listed as follows.

Coordinator Behaviors Identified by Top Management

- Try to get a team to solve a problem on its own.
- Ask for solutions to problems.
- Facilitate a team's attempt to solve conflict within its group.
- Tell people (teams and individuals) when they do something well.
- Tell the truth even when it may be disagreeable (painful).
- Encourage team members to openly discuss problems.
- Ask for a solution to a problem rather than proposing (telling) a solution—people promote what they create.
- Encourage teams to set performance goals, such as scrap rates, efficiency, quality control index, safety. Provide teams with information they need to "run the business."
- Anticipate future problems or situations (planning).
- Encourage team self-evaluation.
- Train teams in the philosophy of the plant.
- Be a resource to a team.

The list provides some interesting insights. First, several of the behaviors, including the behaviors obtaining the highest importance ratings, reveal an emphasis on getting teams to manage their own efforts, for example: "Get a team to solve a problem on its own," "Ask for a solution to a problem rather than proposing (telling)," and "Encourage teams to set performance goals."

Another major theme is a focus on some form of communication. Examples include "Tell people when they do something well," "Tell the truth even when it may be disagreeable," "Encourage team members to openly discuss problems," "Communicate plant needs," and "Act as a communication link."

Several behaviors indicated the role of the coordinator as a facilitator rather than a director. This perspective was indicated in such descriptions of behaviors as "Facilitate a team's attempt to solve conflict," "Be a resource to a team," and "Provide teams with information they need to 'run the business.'"

EXHIBIT 29.4 *(Continued)*

A general view understood in the plant was that teams resented overly *directive* coordinator behavior, for example, a coordinator giving orders to a team regarding solutions to problems.

We concluded that there is a fine line between overdirection and underdirection on the part of coordinators. While team members placed a high value on independence to manage themselves, they also wanted guidance and assistance when needed. It's important for a coordinator to be there, but not with a heavy hand. Consequently, coordinators must make a decision regarding the appropriate level of involvement based on the nature of each unique situation.

Overall, these results show a strong degree of similarity with the notion of SuperLeadership—leading others to lead themselves. Most of all, both sources of data emphasize the potential of unleashing the power of team self-leadership.

[a] See "The Day-to-Day Team Experience: Roles, Behaviors, and Performance of Mature Self-Managing Teams," Chapter 2 in C. C. Manz, and H. P. Sims, Jr., *Business Without Bosses: How Self-Managing Teams Are Building High-Performing Companies.* New York, John Wiley & Sons, 1993. Copyright © 1993 by C. C. Manz and H. P. Sims. Reprinted by permission of John Wiley & Sons, Inc.

sition to teams should always begin with three questions: (1) Where are we now in terms of team capability and team leadership?; (2) Where do we want to get to in terms of team capability and team leadership?; and (3) How long do we want this transition to take?

In this section, we concentrate on the issue of establishing empowered team *leadership.* That is, how do we manage the transition to empowered team leadership? Typically, an organization begins with one of two situations: either (1) a new *startup* (sometimes called a "greenfield"), or (2) a *redesign* of an existing organization (sometimes called a "retrofit" or a "brownfield"). In a startup, the organization begins with essentially a blank slate, with no existing personnel or organization. Conversely, in a redesign, an organization is currently in existence, with personnel currently in place. Often, these personnel may be individuals with considerable seniority and experience. In actual practice, these situations share many issues that must be considered and dealt with as a part of the transition. Let us begin with a startup situation, and we will later extend these ideas to a redesign situation.

29.8   *Developing Team Leadership in a Startup Situation*

Typically, a startup is the creation of a new organization. In manufacturing, a startup is often called a "greenfield." We will begin with the assumption that this organization has already developed several important elements for the startup, such as a mission, strategy, physical location, logistics, a human resources system (including selection of new personnel), a production or service delivery system, a marketing system, and so forth. In addition, we will presume that the organization has made a decision to implement an empowered "team" organization, where the organization structure will mostly consist of small groups of employees who are empowered to carry out many of the day-to-day responsibilities associated with their job duties and responsibilities. The issue we wish to address here is concerned with the design of the leadership of these teams. What kind of leadership do we want? How can we get there?

Actually, we are faced with a rather daunting task. We can select and assemble groups of employees into teams that have logically defined boundaries and at least some initial idea of what their team responsibilities should be. Should we appoint a supervisor or team leader? Should we require the team to elect a team leader?

Also, the question of technical development is important—that is, the employees' need to learn the technical or task performance aspects of the particular process or service they perform. Who will teach these task performance skills to new employees?

We should first recognize that in the beginning there is no formal leadership, and typically very little informal leadership. Management must do something to create this initial form of leadership. At this stage, we recommend that a team leader be *appointed* by management *to a defined term of service.* This term might be six months; it might be a year. We would not recommend an initial term of longer than a year.

At first, this appointed leader frequently needs to behave in ways that are similar to a traditional supervisor. For example, most employees will not be fully trained in the tasks that are necessary to carry out their work. Further, employees are likely to have little experience at group self-leadership. They will probably be used to having others tell them what to do. Unfortunately, their lack of technical experience means that they will likely be highly dependent on their appointed leader in this early stage.

But soon, the team must be weaned off this dependency. Step by step, they must be introduced to team self-leadership. Concurrently, the role and the behavior of the leader must change. At first, the leader provides a significant amount of task instruction, assigned goals, and direct reinforcement for task accomplishment. After all, this is what good "traditional" leaders do. But then, gradually, team members must learn to lead themselves. That is, the leader becomes more concerned with stimulating and reinforcing team self-leadership instead of dealing *directly* with work behavior and team performance. For example, it is not difficult to imagine a team leader encouraging a team to define their own goals.

From a process viewpoint, a leader can (1) model the specific self-management strategies; (2) provide encouragement and guidance for teams to use them; and (3) provide reinforcement when they are used. A leader could facilitate the use of team goal setting, for example, by displaying it in his or her own behavior, providing guidance (e.g., suggesting that specific and challenging goals are especially effective), asking for and encouraging the *team* to begin using self-goal-setting, and then praising team members when goal-setting behavior is observed.

As time goes by, the focus of goal setting and administration of consequences will logically and significantly change. That is, the team leader becomes more concerned with stimulating and reinforcing self-managing behavior than dealing *directly* with work behavior and performance. For example, eventually the team leader will want to facilitate the team in defining its own goals. There may also be occasions of blatant worker misconduct that necessitate the use of punishment, but we have observed team self-discipline to be a most effective alternative in our own research—a process we suspect a leader would be wise to encourage at a reasonable level. The point is, *the leader's primary task becomes helping the team to manage itself.* External modes of influence should mainly be devoted to developing team self-management capabilities, especially in the early team development stages, and also in providing the external guidance needed when team self-management breaks down.

Finally, the culture that surrounds team leadership is critical to success, especially in the early stages. First, the culture must reward leaders for team development, rather than

EVOLUTIONARY ENVIRONMENT

short-term performance. A focus on short-term performance is dysfunctional because team implementation is sometimes accompanied by an initial temporary drop in performance. Leaders who are rewarded solely for performance will abandon their patient development of team self-leadership and instead return to older supervisory behaviors of instruction and command. While short-term productivity is always a matter of concern, it should not overwhelm the objective of developing team self-leadership capabilities for the long term.

29.9   *Developing Team Leadership in a Redesign Situation*

The term *redesign* typically means converting an existing organization from a "traditional" to a team system. Sometimes the term *brownfield* is used. In redesign, a critical question arises in terms of the role of existing supervisors. Can supervisors who have been trained to command and direct change their behavior to team leader behaviors?

According to Kim Fisher, who has extensive experience with conversion to teams at Procter & Gamble, many supervisors become extremely frustrated when asked to convert from a supervisory role to a team leader role. Here are the four most common reasons he gives for difficulty in the supervisor transition:

- It is frequently seen as a net loss of power or status.
- The team leader role has not been well defined for them.
- Some are concerned that they will lose their jobs as a result of the transition to teams.
- Many supervisors are asked to manage in a way that is quite different from the way they are managed themselves.[3]

We have encountered similar situations in our own experience. One supervisor in the midst of a transition to a team organization stated that "the atmosphere rewards a high profile (by leaders) and getting personally involved in everything, not in recognizing people who support others."

Some are not very confident about the potential to convert supervisors to facilitators. At the Texas Instruments Malaysia Plant, A. Subramaniam (usually called "Subra") recounts how one manager could not make the transition to teams.[4] According to Subra, this manager "completely dominated his team, with his self-centeredness. He never was able to adapt to the give-and-take of the team system and the sharing of authority. He wanted to make all the decisions himself." Eventually, this manager left the organization for another. "From a technical viewpoint, we regretted his loss," says Subra. "He was excellent at the technical side, but he was never able to accept the team system. I've talked to him recently, and he's much happier in a traditional management setting."

In the end, however, many can make this transition, and the problems seem to solve themselves once the supervisors are truly in the new role of team leader. Our own viewpoint is this: We do not believe that every supervisor can successfully make this transition (at least not in a reasonable time frame). However, we know of no reliable way of predicting who will make it, and who will not. We have seen the most intense "bull of the woods" foreman become the most passionate advocate of the team system. We believe that every supervisor deserves a chance to change, and most of all, should be given the training and modeling necessary to make the transition. But in the end, some will not succeed. Even those who do successfully make the transition are aware of the challenge. Consider the comments from former supervisors at IDS Corporation who undertook the transition to team facilitator, presented in Exhibit 29.5.

29.10   Teams, Leadership, and the Self-Renewing Organization

When contrasting a traditional organization with a team organization, leadership roles are the most critical element that changes. The main purpose of the team leader is to create a positive atmosphere for exercising team self-management. More specifically, he or she acts as a SuperLeader by stimulating the use of the follower self-leadership. Some of the particularly important elements in this role are (1) the evaluative and reinforcement functions are gradually shifted from external sources to the work team itself; (2) the progress made in a team's self-leadership behavior is encouraged; and (3) increased emphasis is placed on the goals and expectations of team members themselves rather than external sources (e.g., external leaders).

EXHIBIT 29.5 On the Transition from Supervisor to Facilitator

Following are quotations taken from supervisors experiencing a transition to team facilitators at the IDS Corporation.[a]

- In the traditional system it was clear that I had the final word, and right now it is not clear. That's different. Another thing that's different is that we have changed the tasks. It's one thing to be self-managing in your old room and doing the same function, but now we've put together 20 other types of jobs that we didn't know anything about, so instead of having one set of goals and objectives, we've got a variety of them.
- It's frustrating because you feel like you should be knowing it, but you don't, and yet we know it's unrealistic for us to think at this point that we can know everything. We make it a learning experience, and it takes a lot of time to do that.
- The thing I've been struggling with is that there's nothing to call my own. Eventually, if they're truly self-managing, it's going to be the team that gets most of the recognition. Now, I get more satisfaction out of helping someone to do something on their own rather than telling them to do it.
- In the traditional structure of supervision, you'd have goals and objectives: It was laid out. I always felt I knew what part of the path I was traveling on. Here as a team facilitator, so far I haven't felt that clarified yet, so I don't quite know where we're going.
- The reorganization of the task and the structure of the task are one dimension, and the management style or the division of authority is a different dimension.
- Weekly, we just feel more and more comfortable with it. The pilot team is working. They're getting work done. Things are going fine. I'm delighted. I think that it's going to make jobs a lot more interesting for people. There will be a lot more buy-in to decisions if it's a group decision than if it's mine.

---

[a] Taken from Chapter 4, "The Early Implementation Phase: Getting Teams Started at the Office," in C. C. Manz and H. P. Sims, Jr. *Business Without Bosses: How Self-Managing Teams are Building High-Performing Companies.* New York: John Wiley & Sons, 1993. Copyright © 1993 by C. C. Manz and H. P. Sims. Reprinted by permission of John Wiley & Sons, Inc.

As the leader shifts to this supportive and facilitating perspective, changes will take place in team-member motivation, satisfaction, effort, flexibility of response and, ultimately, performance. Most important, this provides a *process* by which external leaders can develop and enhance, over time, the team self-management. Team leadership can create a foundation for true empowerment.

Our years of studying teams had convinced us of their tremendous potential. We were gratified that finally, at the beginning of the 1990s, the topic of teams had reached the front page. *Fortune* magazine featured a cover story—"Who Needs a Boss?"—about teams in the May 7, 1990 issue. *BusinessWeek* also featured a cover story about teams in their July 1989 issue. Even Dan Rather spoke about "self-directed" teams.

Although it's taken some time, the topic of teams has clearly reached the stage of becoming a popular fad with all the accompanying advantages and disadvantages, but we believe teams will pass the test of time and prove to be enduring. We think that teams are here to stay, and that they constitute a fundamental change in the way we go about work. We suspect the label and approach will evolve and perhaps pass—like all fads—but the fundamental ways that teams do business will remain with us for a long time—mainly because teams are effective. Teams may represent a whole new management paradigm. Perhaps they reflect a new business era as influential as the industrial revolution and are destined to revolutionize work for decades to come.

Self-managing and empowered teams are a natural extension of self-leadership. Teams are a type of collective or group self-leadership. The SuperLeader makes it happen by initiating, encouraging, and supporting empowered teams. Indeed, teams are a critical ingredient in creating a company of heroes.

Most of all, self-managing teams are the day-to-day mechanism through which the self-renewing organization is actually implemented on the firing line. Teams promote self-renewal by influencing both the effectiveness and the efficiency factors of the self-renewing equation (see Chapter 1). Through myriad small decisions and actions, teams keep the organization focused on both doing things right (efficiency) and doing the right thing (effectiveness). In today's contemporary organizations, teams are the essence of self-renewal.

Endnotes

1. This story is inspired by one told by Kelvin Throop, III in *Analog,* May 1994, p. 81.
2. See Part I, Section 4 of Lawler (1995).
3. For further development of these ideas, see: Fisher, K. (1993). *Leading Self-Directed Work Teams: A Guide to Developing New Team Leadership Skills.* New York: McGraw-Hill, p. 48.
4. Cheney, A. B., H. P. Sims Jr., and C. C. Manz. (1993). "Teams and Total Quality Management: An International Application." In C. C. Manz and H. P. Sims Jr. (eds.), *Business Without Bosses: How Self-Managing Teams Are Building High-Performing Companies.* New York: John Wiley & Sons.

Suggested Readings

Dumaine, B. (1990). "Who Needs a Boss?" *Fortune* (May 7): 52–60.

Frederiksen, L. W., A. W. Riley, and J. B. Myers. (1984). "Matching Technology and Organizational Structure: A Case in White Collar Productivity Improvement," *Journal of Organizational Behavior Management* (Fall–Winter): 59–80.

Horr, J. (1989). "The Payoff from Teamwork," *Business Week* (May 7): 56–62.

Lawler, E. E. III, S. A. Morhman, and G. E. Ledford Jr. (1995). *Creating High Performance Organizations: Practices and Results of Employee Involvement and Total Quality Management in Fortune 1000 Companies.* San Francisco: Jossey-Bass.

Macy, B. A., and H. Izumi. (1994). "Organizational Change, Design, and Work Innovation: A Meta Analysis of 131 North American Field Studies—1961–1991," *Research in Organizational Change and Development,* vol. 7, JAI Press, pp. 235–313.

Miner, J. B. (1982). *Theories of Organizational Structure and Process.* Hinsdale, IL: Dryden, pp. 110–111.

Sims, H. P. Jr., C. C. Manz, and B. Bateman. (1993). "The Early Implementation Phase: Getting Teams Started at the Office," Chapter 4 in C. C. Manz and H. P. Sims Jr., *Business Without Bosses: How Self-Managing Teams Are Building High-Performing Companies.* New York: John Wiley & Sons.

Board of Directors: Strategic Vision

JEFFREY L. BRUDNEY, PhD
Department of Political Science
University of Georgia

30.1 Introduction

Boards of directors of nonprofit organizations (NPOs) seldom occupy themselves with discussions of the volunteer corps. In the academic literature on nonprofit boards as well, providing a mission and vision for the volunteer corps has received scant, if any, attention. Apparently, this function—if indeed it has been taken to be a function of the nonprofit board—does not rank high in importance. In Barbara Burgess Soltz's chapter on "The Board of Directors" in nonprofit organizations,[1] which appeared in the second edition of *The Nonprofit Handbook*,[2] setting a vision for the volunteer corps is not among the responsibilities identified for the board. Two classic books on boards by Cyril Houle[3] and John Carver[4] are, likewise, silent on this issue. Perhaps one might read into these and other treatments of the nonprofit board a concern with volunteers: Authorities concur that the board of directors has ultimate legal, financial, and policy responsibility for the NPO, and for bringing all aspects of its operations, which would include the volunteer component, to bear on its mission. Yet, to the extent that this concern has been manifested at all, it has been implicit, rather than explicit. The relationship of the nonprofit board of directors, who are volunteers, to the service-delivery volunteers has not been clarified, and the task of establishing and implementing a mission and vision for the volunteer corps has been largely overlooked.

To achieve the self-renewing organization (SRO) sought by cutting-edge nonprofit agencies (as well as for-profit businesses), the board of directors will need to maintain a much more sustained and specific focus on volunteers. To cope with an increasingly turbulent, interdependent, global environment, these stewards of the organization's future must put each of its resources not merely to good use but to the most efficacious use. This process begins with the board of directors developing a mission and vision for the volunteer corps. The board must seriously consider, appraise, formulate, and support a mission and vision that will galvanize volunteers (and paid staff) toward the attainment of the exciting future conceived for the NPO.

This chapter elaborates how the board of directors of an NPO can create and sustain a motivating vision to invigorate its volunteer corps. It first explains why, despite the manifest importance of volunteers to most NPOs, the volunteer program typically does not rank high on the list of board priorities. The chapter proposes that many boards become mired in unproductive syndromes that stymie attention to the volunteer effort; it describes the syndromes and why they occur, and provides effectual means to overcome them. The chapter then turns to the development of a mission and vision for the volunteer corps. The mission should briefly articulate the organization's philosophy and purpose in having volunteers; the vision is a more complete statement that delineates the positive changes that the NPO seeks to bring about in the environment and the leadership role to which it aspires. Next, the chapter discusses the implementation of the vision for the volunteer corps. It argues that mission and vision statements alone are ineffectual without the active support of the nonprofit board of directors. To actualize the vision, the board must provide three key elements for the volunteer program, which are explained fully in the chapter: (1) a basic structure for the program consisting of leadership positions and a budget, (2) appropriate policies for governing the program, and (3) risk management and insurance protection for nonpaid personnel. By overcoming board syndromes regarding volunteers, creating a stimulating mission and vision for their involvement, and affording the necessary support to this effort, the board of directors brings the SRO closer to fruition.

30.2 Surmounting Board Inattention to the Volunteer Program

As Ellis correctly observes, "While the vast majority of nonprofit organizations involve volunteers in direct service and support roles, the subject of volunteers is rarely raised in the board room."[5] Although this oversight is more than a little ironic—the board is composed of volunteers—boards of directors might give comparatively little attention to service volunteers for a variety of reasons. The different reasons or explanations constitute a series of syndromes that the board must surmount if it is to create the self-renewing organization. The particular syndrome afflicting a nonprofit board can vary from one agency to another, but the result is always the same: to deter meaningful consideration of the volunteer program and, consequently, to limit the opportunity to integrate the program more completely with the rest of the organization, improve its performance, and think strategically about its contribution to organizational goals. Exhibit 30.1 briefly describes four board syndromes that produce these deleterious consequences.

EXHIBIT 30.1 Board Syndromes that Inhibit Attention to the Volunteer Program

- *The Micromanagement Syndrome.* Nonprofit boards with this syndrome do not devote systematic attention to the volunteer program because this activity strikes board members as meddling in agency management.
- *The Discomfort Syndrome.* Nonprofit boards with this syndrome do not devote systematic attention to the volunteer program because this activity could expose status differences between board and service volunteers uncomfortable to board members.
- *The Overgratitude Syndrome.* Nonprofit boards with this syndrome do not devote systematic attention to the volunteer program because this activity could result in a new arrangement in which not all citizen contributions could be accommodated or welcomed.
- *The Devaluation Syndrome.* Nonprofit boards with this syndrome do not devote systematic attention to the volunteer program because this activity implies and could reveal the value and usefulness of volunteers to the organization.

(A) THE MICROMANAGEMENT SYNDROME

Probably the greatest reluctance and obstacle to board involvement with the volunteer corps is the seemingly benign desire or intention to stay out of areas of day-to-day organizational management. No board wants to be accused of micromanagement, that is, infringing on the legitimate prerogatives of the chief executive officer (CEO) to administer the nonprofit agency according to its charter, mission, and general policies. Contemporary treatments strongly encourage the board to "govern" rather than to "manage" the affairs of the organization, to "steer" rather than to "row."[6–8] Among its major responsibilities, the board must review and protect the agency mission; act as fiduciary authority for the organization and ensure its financial solvency; and serve as spokesperson and ambassador for the organization externally and represent the viewpoints of the community and stakeholders internally. From this perspective, the volunteer component shrinks in significance to a managerial matter in which program purpose, design, and execution can be safely and appropriately left to the discretion of organizational staff. This tendency is exacerbated by the limited time, personnel, and resources available to the nonprofit board to dispatch its important, primary duties.

(B) THE DISCOMFORT SYNDROME

In NPOs, the board of directors consists of citizens who are not compensated financially for their efforts. So, too, does the corps of volunteer service providers, who are often identified simply as the *volunteer program*. While both groups are volunteers, status differences between them are apparent, though usually submerged in the daily crush of organizational activities. It should not be surprising, then, that when the roles of volunteer board member and volunteer service provider are mixed, the result is often conflict and confusion.[9] Some boards fear that if the differences between these roles were to be raised explicitly—for example, through the creation of mission and vision statements for the volunteer corps and deliberate attention to the policies necessary to support and govern them—this airing would lead to debilitating resentment and discord among nonpaid personnel. As a result, these boards choose the path of least resistance and avoid matters of governance for the volunteer program.

The positions occupied by board and service volunteers have many differences. As discussed previously, the board exists to attend to significant matters of organizational mission, policy, finances, and community representation; by contrast, the volunteer program provides assistance in day-to-day service delivery and organizational maintenance activities. The nomination, recruitment, and turnover of the small number of board members is normally quite selective and celebrated; given the heavy demands placed on them, NPOs cannot afford to be nearly as particular in attracting the numerous service volunteers needed, and fanfare is notably absent from their entry into (and exit from) the agency. The actions of the board are highly visible to the organization and often the community; the important work of the volunteer program on behalf of the agency is typically carried out in relative obscurity. Board expert John Carver summarizes that service volunteers play a helping role in the organization, whereas board members have an *"ownership interest* rather than a *helpfulness interest."*[10]

On one level, board and service participants are equally volunteers, who seemingly should be given the same respect, appreciation, and treatment in the NPO. On another level, distinct functions and responsibilities are held by the two groups, a factor that gives rise to differences in the status and recognition accorded them. Some boards are uncomfortable with this tension and prefer to shy away from it. They fear that conscious attention to the volunteer program will expose a "two-tier" or "two-caste" system that could provoke resentment and antagonism among service-delivery volunteers and, quite possibly, anxiety for themselves.

Graff similarly describes a tension between "equality or elitism" that confronts the board of directors, consisting of volunteers, should they try to devise organizational policies to apply to other, service-delivery volunteers: Should the same rules and provisions apply to them as to service volunteers?[11] This tension can be debilitating: Carver warns that "some connotations of voluntarism can *detract* from the board's job, severely reducing its ability to lead."[12] Concerned about unleashing new problems on the organization, these boards avoid reflective examination of the service volunteer effort. Their discomfort with one group of volunteers overseeing or dictating to another stymies the creation of a mission and vision for the volunteer program.

(C) THE OVERGRATITUDE SYNDROME

The overgratitude syndrome occurs in NPOs in which members of the board of directors view having volunteers as a sufficient goal or end in itself. The degree to which the skills, talents, abilities, and labor of the volunteers are actually utilized to meet the needs of clients and the agency is secondary, if considered at all. Organizations and boards lacking a history or culture of volunteer involvement or expertise in volunteer program management can easily fall prey to this syndrome.

Rooted in incorrect stereotypes regarding volunteer participation, overgratitude is manifested in counterproductive organizational attitudes and behaviors. Brudney provides a review of these stereotypes or "myths," as he calls them, that interfere with effective management and strategic thinking concerning volunteers.[13] They include a reluctance to evaluate the performance of volunteers or the volunteer program as a whole (evaluation is "threatening") or to sanction or discipline volunteers when appropriate (one cannot "fire" a volunteer). The organization need not insist on adequate record-keeping for volunteers (it smacks of "bureaucracy" and takes time away from "helping") or enforce standards of appropriate conduct on the job (the volunteers may leave). The message conveyed by such policies is that volunteers come first, and that any participation by them is to be valued, regardless of its impact on quality or cost to the nonprofit organization or its clients.

In an era in which the recruitment of service volunteers has become a major obstacle to an effective program,[14] the spread and influence of the overgratitude syndrome are understandable, if regrettable. In such an organizational climate, the board of directors will almost surely eschew proper oversight and direction-setting for the volunteer program. Board members would not want to appear to question in any way the nature, extent, or effectiveness of the involvement of service volunteers. Instead, having volunteers is the goal.

(D)   THE DEVALUATION SYNDROME

At the opposite end of the spectrum from the overgratitude syndrome lies the devaluation syndrome. Instead of appreciating whatever contribution volunteers might make as in the former conception, in NPOs in which the latter syndrome has taken hold, the volunteer corps is not viewed as sufficiently important to occupy the time or attention of the board of directors. Here, the volunteer program suffers from "benign neglect" from organization management and the board of directors.[15] Nora Silver asserts, "By their actions, *boards establish an attitude toward volunteerism in their organizations.* Even by doing 'nothing,' they are saying something. In this situation, neutrality is akin to indifference and promotes the message that volunteerism is unimportant in the organization."[16]

Other observers, too, lament the prevalence of the devaluation syndrome in the nonprofit world. According to Graff, "For so long, volunteer programs have gone under-recognized and under-valued. . . . Managers of volunteer programs are often at the bottom of the organizational hierarchy, under-paid, over-worked, and taken for granted. Boards and senior management have lost touch with how important volunteers have become to service delivery and to the community life we all have come to enjoy."[17] The result of this syndrome is to diminish the present involvement of volunteers in the organization and to slight their future potential in helping the agency to achieve its goals.

(E)   STRATEGIES FOR OVERCOMING NEGLECT OF VOLUNTEERS IN THE BOARDROOM

Regardless of the syndrome that may grip a particular nonprofit board of directors, or the organizational culture that gives rise to it, the consequence is the same: Most boards fail to devote systematic attention to service volunteers and the volunteer program commensurate with their actual or potential importance and contribution to the agency.[18] This scenario represents opportunity and capacity foregone, and is inimical to the achievement of the SRO.

The nonprofit board of directors bears final responsibility and authority for allocating all organizational assets to their best use, whether paid staff members, revenue or endowment, agency facilities, or productive capacity. Volunteers constitute one of these assets. To create a strategic vision for the volunteer corps, the nonprofit board must realize that nonpaid staff are part of this resource mix. The SRO must learn to mobilize its volunteers to help in meeting the challenges of a dynamic, competitive environment. A necessary first step is to give serious consideration to the volunteer program.

Exhibit 30.2 lists a number of measures that boards can take to internalize this new perspective on volunteers. These recommendations will help alleviate the board syndromes that otherwise undercut appreciation of the present role and future potential of

---

EXHIBIT 30.2 Overcoming Board Syndromes: Steps toward Taking a Strategic View of the Volunteer Program

- Set aside time at board meetings to discuss the volunteer program.
- Call for reports from organization staff describing the membership and performance of the volunteer corps.
- Invite representatives of the volunteers to some board meetings.
- Address the volunteer program in orientation sessions and related materials.
- Visit the organization periodically to observe the activities of volunteers and take part in them.
- Attend recognition events for volunteers.
- Recruit former service volunteers to some positions on the board.

---

volunteers in the organization. Although the suggestions are eminently practical, for many boards they represent a change in culture, so that full integration will likely take some time and effort to develop. Where the syndromes are entrenched particularly deeply, use of board change techniques, such as those developed by Holland and colleagues,[19] may prove advisable.

Short of the need to effect a change in its culture, the nonprofit board of directors can begin to embrace a new outlook on volunteers by setting aside time at its scheduled meetings to discuss the volunteer program. On a regular basis, the board should call for reports from organization staff describing the membership of the volunteer corps (for example, demographic information), the divisions and departments in which volunteers work (and those in which they are not involved), their job responsibilities within the agency, and any data on their performance (including feedback from clients). Second, the board should periodically invite spokespersons from the volunteer program to attend its meetings; the official with responsibility for the volunteers (for example, the director of volunteer services or the volunteer coordinator) is probably the most appropriate representative. Third, orientation sessions and related learning materials for new board members should be revised to include treatment of the volunteer corps, including such facets as the goals underlying citizen participation, the size and scope of the volunteer program, oversight arrangements, and rights and responsibilities. Fourth, a further idea to stimulate awareness and knowledge of the volunteer program is to convene some orientation sessions jointly for volunteer board members and service providers.

The board of directors can also engage in activities that signal to the rest of the organization their endorsement of a new perspective on volunteers. For instance, from time to time, the board might visit the agency during its hours of operation to observe the work of service volunteers and, perhaps, participate with them. Board members should attend recognition events for the volunteer program; by doing so, they build greater understanding of the contributions of service volunteers and, simultaneously, convey formal organizational appreciation. Finally, when vacancies occur on the board of directors, recruitment might sometimes come from the ranks of those who have formerly assisted the organization as service volunteers. A nonprofit board might engage in a frenetic search for new members who possess extensive background and knowledge concerning the agency, when seasoned, former volunteers with the desired attributes are often close at hand and eager for a different type of involvement in the organization.

30.3 Creating a Mission and Vision for the Volunteer Program

Once the nonprofit board of directors has embraced this new perspective on volunteers as a valuable resource to harness in pursuit of organizational goals, it is ready to turn its attention to a crucial task: conceiving a mission and vision for the volunteer program. Because these terms are interrelated and have similar meanings, it is easy to confuse them.

(A) DISTINGUISHING MISSION AND VISION

Most authorities describe the mission as a succinct statement of the purpose of a group or organization, its *raison d'etre*. "A mission statement constantly reminds us of our basic purpose."[20] Were this ultimate goal to be achieved, the organization would have no further reason for remaining in existence.[21-23] The mission statement should be clear, concise, and memorable, briefly describing the difference an organization intends to make in the world outside its doors. In a highly compact manner, it crystallizes the central purpose of the agency.

Mission statements should neither be overly narrow nor focus on the technology currently employed by the group or organization. For example, a library volunteer program with a mission to "read books for children" is fixed on the technology (reading) and would likely overlook other educational modalities, such as use of computer instructional programs or the Internet. This mission statement also fails to identify the goal(s) the volunteers are trying to accomplish—literacy, lifelong learning, and so forth—so that it cannot inspire volunteers to search for new, better options, approaches, or innovations to achieve the desired outcome. A better mission statement in this case would be "to stimulate learning and curiosity at the earliest possible age." The mission seeks results (here, child learning and curiosity), leaving the choice and development of methods open to healthy exploration and experimentation.

Another example of a mission statement that could bear improvement along the same lines is a nonprofit agency that exists "to provide exceptional day-care to the elderly." Even "exceptional" day care may fail to inspire volunteers, and in any case, this agency is again fixed on the technology, day care, rather than on its intended results, for example, "to improve the living standards and personal well-being of older people." Such a change in mission alters the focus of organizational activity to achieving desirable outcomes for the elderly. It opens the door to consideration of a variety of means, including not only day care but also transportation, recreation, learning, and nutrition, as agency interests, funding, and circumstances warrant.

Analogous changes to organizational mission statements found in other social policy domains illustrate possible improvements. For example, many agencies exist to "promote animal rights," when a mission statement to "protect the lives and natural habitat of animals" would offer both greater flexibility of means and measurability of results. Although most schools strive toward the goal to "provide quality education," that mission has an internal focus; a change to "prepare students for fulfilling lives and careers" would shift the perspective externally to the possible impacts of formal education. Most volunteers would find a mission to "staff the museum" mundane and uninspiring, a means to the real goal, to "enrich cultural understanding and awareness"; the latter mission would invite healthy discussion and questioning concerning possible methods. Similarly, a volunteer program that exists to "counsel young people on drug abuse" misses what is likely the larger mission, "to create a drug-free environment for young people," a goal that might be pursued through a variety of means, including counseling. A government-sponsored volunteer program to "offer recreation services" should be more concerned with end results captured in a mission to "raise the physical health of the community."

Closely related to the mission is the vision statement, which expresses the future the organization sees (and sets) for itself. Much more lengthy and detailed than the mission statement, it describes the organization—and world—the agency hopes to create and the leadership role to which it aspires.[24,25] McCurley and Lynch explain that the mission is a short statement of purpose that provides the "skeleton" upon which the "flesh" of the organization's more elaborate vision statement is hung.[26] The vision should portray a vivid, desired future and, in this way, provide motivation and meaning for members of the organization. "A vision represents the highest aspiration of the organization. It must challenge and inspire its members."[27]

(B) DEVELOPING THE MISSION AND VISION

As Brudney elucidates, to begin the process of crafting a mission statement and a vision statement for the volunteer program, the nonprofit board of directors and other agency leadership must grapple with the fundamental question, "Why have volunteers?"[28] In response, the mission statement will briefly describe what the organization is trying accomplish, the positive difference it proposes to make in the external environment with and through the participation of volunteers. With respect to the vision statement, Fisher and Cole state that the vision for the volunteer corps is a beacon intended to guide the nonprofit organization toward its future purpose while simultaneously amplifying the meaning of its present activities.[29] The vision "articulates an organization's values, communicates its priorities, and inspires behavior that reflects them." The vision statement will elaborate the role of volunteers in bringing about the desired future sought by the organization.

In discussing and formulating the mission and vision statements for the volunteer program, board members need not—and, almost certainly, should not—act alone. Enlisting the input and counsel of agency management, paid staff, volunteers, and the director of volunteer services (see following section) will not only yield fruitful ideas and directions but also help to generate acceptance and a sense of ownership of the program. In addition, fostering widespread participation in the visioning process can help the board to air and resolve differences with respect to organizational purpose; identify possible obstacles to accomplishing the mission; develop strategies to overcome them; set goals and time lines to implement these strategies; and perhaps most important, create a galvanizing sense of purpose, excitement, and idealism that provides direction and meaning for all participants.[30]

Involvement in mission setting is not without cost, however. Participants often have different interpretations of organizational purposes and values, which they assume implicitly are shared by other members and lie beyond questioning. When these views are brought to the surface in the mission-setting process and treated there, instead, as possibilities rather than certainties and the subject for serious discussion rather than tacit acquiescence, it can be extremely unsettling to some participants. Reaching agreement on such profound matters as the mission of the organization and its vision for the future can be a tense, arduous process: Weiss describes several cases of mission setting in public organizations in which the process was contentious, protracted, and exhausting—yet well worth the effort.[31] Many organizations, both nonprofit agencies and commercial businesses, have found a trained facilitator useful in this process.

While diverse participation in arriving at a mission and a vision for the NPO offers many benefits, involvement should not be mistaken for board leadership. The mission and vision statements constitute agency policy and aspirations regarding its future and the role to be played by volunteers in it at the highest level and, therefore, should emanate from final deliberation and approval at its apex, the board of directors. "As the board is ultimately legally responsible for the agency program, it is also responsible for the volunteer component. . . . This is one of the tasks that legitimately falls to the board, and the board must assume ultimate responsibility for the volunteer program in the agency."[32]

When the board of directors has acted, the focus for the volunteer program has been legitimately established. Should the board later decide to revisit the mission and vision, it is, of course, free to do so. In fact, reflection—and re-reflection—on the purpose and rationale for the volunteer corps is precisely the change in mindset required by the self-renewing NPO.

(C)   A FOCUS ON TWO DIMENSIONS

Although the specific content and presentation format vary dramatically across NPOs, a vision statement typically will communicate a value or ethical dimension for volunteer participation and an instrumental or strategic component. Sometimes the value or ethical dimension is given a name of its own, such as a "values statement" or "statement of principles." In the end, the vision statement should convey organizational purpose (mission), principles (values), and future path (vision).[33,34]

With regard to the values dimension, the vision should articulate why the nonprofit organization esteems volunteers as well as the principles governing their participation in the organization. The rationale often turns on the intangible qualities that the board of directors believes citizens can infuse into an agency, such as a more human touch and individual dignity in dealings with clients, enhanced input from and access to the community, and greater public awareness, commitment, and ownership of agency programs. Principles undergirding volunteer involvement might include statements that volunteers and paid staff work as partners to create meaningful jobs for both, and that even were sufficient material resources available to meet all demands on the program, the organization would still seek volunteers for their unique contributions.

With respect to the instrumental dimension, the vision "will provide a quick and clear understanding of what benefit the organization thinks will be derived from engagement of volunteers, and provide a sense of purpose for the volunteer program. In essence, it should answer the question, 'Why are we doing this?'"[35] One of the most attractive features of volunteer programs is that the answers are manifold and robust. They range along a broad continuum from decidedly economic motivations (e.g., the potential for cost savings, increased productivity, more organizational capacity, and greater innovativeness) to noneconomic motivations (e.g., enhanced agency responsiveness, better client outcomes, stronger issue and client advocacy, and greater credibility with policy makers and other organizational stakeholders).[36]

In sum, the vision statement should express the reasons that the organization values the participation of volunteers, the benefits to be gained through their involvement, and the bright future they will help the organization to attain. Exhibit 30.3 presents an example of a vision statement for a volunteer action center focusing on youth.

EXHIBIT 30.3 Sample Vision Statement for a Volunteer Action Center Focusing on Youth

- Mission: Many young people in our community want to make a difference and do not know how, and many adults want to help them to succeed. Our mission is to provide volunteer opportunities for, and on behalf of, young people. Through service today, the Volunteer Action Center creates satisfying, fulfilling lives for the adults of tomorrow.

- Values: Volunteering builds commitment and community. It facilitates greater outreach to citizens and input from them. It stimulates a sense of ownership of programs and responsibility for the larger community. Volunteering allows people, young and old alike, to learn more about themselves and others. Volunteer service generates the self-confidence, personal satisfaction, and understanding that encourage people to become active citizens and successful in other areas of their lives.

- Vision: The Volunteer Action Center envisions a future in which every young person will have readily available to her or him the opportunity to volunteer. Young people will understand the importance and benefits of volunteering for themselves and the community and will participate avidly. Adults will be aware of volunteer opportunities as well and will be eager to serve young people. Intergenerational volunteering will be the norm, a practice that will spread mutual appreciation and understanding. The spirit of participation will invigorate all aspects of community life, enriching existing institutions and programs and inspiring new ones, so that our community will become an even more desirable place to live. As a result of its leadership, the Volunteer Action Center will come to be recognized as the foremost agency in our region for fostering volunteer activity for, and on behalf of, young people. Other volunteer action centers with a youth orientation will look to us first for ideas, stimulation, and assistance.

(D) FROM BOARD SYNDROMES TO STRATEGIC VISION

As explained previously, the influence of the micromanagement, discomfort, overgratitude, and devaluation syndromes deters many nonprofit boards of directors from serious consideration of the volunteer program necessary to achieve the SRO. The process of deliberating and creating a mission and vision for the volunteer corps moves the nonprofit board of directors beyond these counterproductive syndromes.

First, crafting a vision for the volunteer corps cannot be confused with the agency micromanagement most boards would like to avoid. The vision expresses the general values and ambitions that the board holds for the volunteer program: It is meant to capture what the organizational leadership hopes to accomplish with and through volunteers. The actual follow-through—the day-to-day (micro) management—is left to the agency staff. Ellis explains that "the board's role is not to focus on details, but to provide an outline for the staff to fill in. Your dreams set the direction for everyone to follow. . . . The organization's staff will consider the management details . . . but the board sets the framework for volunteer involvement."[37]

Second, creating a strategic vision calls for the nonprofit board to appraise the present state of volunteer involvement with the goal of bringing about a more fulfilling and productive future. The evaluative nature of this undertaking dictates that the board cannot be satisfied with merely having volunteers—the overgratitude syndrome—but must consider seriously their most appropriate and effective uses in the organization. As Fisher and Cole point out, "The vision challenges the status quo and makes complete contentment with the present unthinkable."[38] The emphasis changes from the existence of the volunteer program to program results.

In developing the vision, too, the board cannot persist in overlooking the contributions of volunteers—the devaluation syndrome—but is made to see them as a strategic asset to the organization. The visioning process calls for board members to assess critically the status and role of the volunteer program and to weigh this judgment against their aspirations concerning what the program could be, and should be, into the future. Their evaluation is most likely to be mixed: Almost certainly the board will encounter negative aspects of the program that should not have been condoned, let alone appreciated, as well as positive elements that should not have gone overlooked, let alone demeaned. Based on this careful appraisal, the board can chart novel directions for further volunteer participation.

Finally, developing a strategic vision for the volunteer corps is part of the responsibility for governance of the NPO held by the board of directors. The board should certainly solicit the input and assistance of diverse participants in this process (see previous section). In the end, though, the vision calls for board (policy) volunteers to formulate goals and expectations for the involvement of other (service provider) volunteers that, in the judgment of the board, are in the best interest of the organization. Their responsibility for organizational governance requires board members to confront and overcome the discomfort syndrome that might otherwise inhibit them as volunteers from establishing goals, policies, and standards for the volunteer service corps. In the self-renewing NPO, board governance encompasses the volunteer program.

30.4   *Supporting and Sustaining the Vision*

As challenging as it may be for the nonprofit board of directors to develop a meaningful mission and vision for the volunteer corps, the conception of purpose is not the end point in the process. The board must also see to supporting and sustaining the vision. These tasks have an external (environmental) and internal (operational) component. Externally, the board will need to identify impediments and hurdles in the environment to accomplishing the mission; develop strategies to surmount the obstacles; and establish milestones for implementing the strategies. Depending on the mission of the agency and the environment in which it operates, the strategic plan to attain these objectives will differ markedly across nonprofit organizations and contain highly idiosyncratic elements. (A full discussion of these techniques can be found in McCurley and Lynch.[39]

Internally, the demands on the board of directors for supporting and sustaining the mission and vision for the volunteer corps are much more generic across NPOs. To meet this responsibility, the board must (1) provide a basic administrative structure for the volunteer program; (2) determine policies to govern the program; and (3) furnish risk management and insurance protection for the volunteers.

(A)   PROVIDING AN ADMINISTRATIVE STRUCTURE TO SUPPORT THE VISION

The two primary factors necessary to support the vision for the volunteer corps consist of establishing (or approving) positions of leadership for the volunteer program, and authorizing a budget for the program commensurate with its goals and objectives. Absent such backing from the top of the organization, even the most radiant of visions is destined to tarnish and fade. Failure of the nonprofit board to provide this follow-through can breed cynicism regarding the credibility of the vision and the rationale for volunteer involvement in the organization. This result would undermine not only the operation of the volunteer program but also the delivery of services to clients and the prospects for the SRO.

(i) Leadership Positions for the Volunteer Program

Experts agree that a successful volunteer program requires a leader, here called the Director of Volunteer Services (DVS).[40-43] As detailed in Exhibit 30.4, the DVS position bears a number of key leadership responsibilities.

Most important among them, the DVS is responsible for guiding the volunteer program toward fulfillment of the vision. Given this primary obligation, he or she should participate actively with the board in development and refinement of the mission and vision statements. The charge to the DVS is to implement the view of the future encapsulated in the vision—to effect the difficult translation from rhetoric to organizational reality. To do so, he or she will need to communicate the vision throughout the organization; persuade staff, paid and nonpaid alike, to accept it; and inspire them to work toward its achievement.[44] In this manner, the DVS endeavors to align present practice of the volunteer program with the nonprofit organization and outcomes sought for the future. By establishing this position, the board of directors lodges accountability for the volunteer program and its results squarely with the DVS and, thereby, demonstrates its seriousness of purpose.

The DVS is the focal point for contact with the volunteer program for those outside the organization seeking to donate their time, as well as for employees inside who may wish to enlist volunteers or to involve them more productively. The DVS represents the volunteers to other departments and the organization as a whole and promotes their achievement and satisfaction on the job. As the chief advocate of the program, the incumbent works not only to express the volunteer perspective and advance useful policies (see following section) but

---

EXHIBIT 30.4 Leadership Responsibilities of the Director of Volunteer Services (DVS)

- Guide the volunteer program toward fulfillment of its vision (for example, communicate the vision, persuade staff to accept it, and inspire them to work toward its achievement).
- Serve as the focal point for contact with the volunteer program for both potential volunteers and employees.
- Represent the volunteers to the organization and facilitate their achievement and satisfaction on the job.
- Act as chief advocate of the volunteer program (for example, express the volunteer perspective, advance useful policies, facilitate collaboration between paid and nonpaid staff).
- Promote the volunteer program in the community through publicity, outreach, and recruitment.
- Promote the volunteer program internally (for example, work with departments and employees to meet their needs for volunteers, expand areas of volunteer participation, prepare job description for nonpaid positions).
- Educate, orient, and train paid and nonpaid staff for volunteer involvement.
- Coordinate, evaluate, and recognize all facets of the volunteer program.

---

also to allay any apprehensions of employees concerning volunteers and to facilitate collaboration between paid and nonpaid staff.

The DVS is responsible for volunteer recruitment and publicity, a critical function requiring active outreach in the community and highly flexible working hours. The incumbent communicates with department and organizational officials to ascertain workloads and requirements for voluntary assistance and takes the lead in preparing job descriptions for volunteer positions. Assessing agency needs for volunteers, enlarging areas for their involvement, and educating staff to the approach are not a one-time exercise but an ongoing responsibility of the DVS. The DVS interviews and screens applicants for volunteer positions, maintains appropriate records, places volunteers in job assignments, supervises them (or assists employees in this task), and monitors performance. The office coordinates the bewildering array of schedules, backgrounds, and skills brought by volunteers to the agency. The DVS bears overall responsibility for orientation and training, as well as evaluation and recognition, of volunteers; training for employees, too, regarding volunteer services emanates from the position. Given the breadth and importance of these responsibilities, other positions of program leadership to support the DVS are likely to prove advisable and necessary.[45]

The board of directors should establish the DVS position but not infringe upon its prerogatives. The DVS must have the authority and creative license to guide the volunteer program toward the exciting future envisioned for it. To achieve the mission and vision, the board must also provide the incumbent with a budget for the volunteer program.

(ii)   Budget for the Volunteer Program

Ellis notes that when it comes to fund raising, the nonprofit board of directors is accustomed to discussions of whether "it takes money to make money."[46] Unfortunately, when it comes to "people raising"—the equally vital task of recruiting, retaining, and invigorating volunteers—the adage is not nearly so well-known or accepted.

Because the term *volunteer* connotes free labor, the board and other organizational members are often unaware of the support costs that make a thriving program possible. In a study of a large sample of volunteer programs representing all levels of government, for example, less than half of the volunteer coordinators (47.9 percent) reported that they had a budget for the program.[47] Although a well-conceived and -managed volunteer program will generate a return in dedicated labor, talents, and caring (and often fund raising) many times greater than the budget invested in the endeavor, it still "takes money to make money," that is, to attract and maintain a committed corps of volunteers. Here, the monetary investment underwrites the design and delivery of essential program activities through volunteer participation. Without an adequate financial base, progress toward attainment of the vision for the volunteer corps is put in jeopardy.

Some of the more notable expenses incurred in an effective volunteer program include the salary of the DVS (usually a paid position in larger NPOs) and orientation and relevant training for both volunteers and employees. Major program components, such as promotion and outreach, recruitment and retention, screening and interviewing, evaluation and recognition, and administration and supplies, add to these costs. Extending organizational liability insurance to cover volunteer personnel is normally an additional expense (see following section). In addition, reimbursement for work-related expenses can quickly mount with the size of the volunteer contingent and must be accounted for in the budget of the program.

The board's job is not to prepare the budget for the volunteer program or to undertake a detailed review or audit of expenditures (unless circumstances should warrant). Instead, the obligation of the board is, first, to authorize a budgetary line for the program. The DVS should not have to implore other organizational units with different objectives for funds to sponsor her or his own unit. Absent an independent source of financial support, the incumbent cannot be held accountable to the vision. Second, the board should ensure that the amount of funding allocated is commensurate with the scope of the present volunteer effort as well as the future expectations held for it.

In most organizations, the budget is a reflection of priorities. When the nonprofit board of directors grants financial status as well as fiscal accountability to the volunteer program, it affirms the rightful place of the program among competing agency goals. Conversely, a lack of budget (or leadership positions) dedicated to the volunteer corps transmits quite a different message to the organization and its members concerning the importance of volunteers. This action (or lack of it) imperils achievement of the vision.

(B) DETERMINING POLICIES FOR THE VOLUNTEER PROGRAM

John Carver writes, "To the extent a board wishes to provide strategic leadership, it must clarify policies and expect organizational activities to give them life."[48] No less than in other areas of organizational operations, the board should exercise policy leadership with respect to the volunteer program. Inevitably, policies express values and perspectives binding on the organization. The board of directors has the ultimate authority to render these judgments, for this body bears primary responsibility for governance of the agency.

Although policies for the volunteer program may strike some as confining, Carver argues that a good policy is actually liberating.[49] Well-crafted policies clarify what is, and what is not, acceptable in controversial domains of organizational activity where debilitating uncertainty, confusion, and even conflict might otherwise predominate. A clear policy from the board will answer myriad operational questions, thus reducing delays and the need for repeated checks with higher-level officials. Thoughtful policy will identify those areas in which the board reserves final control and decision-making authority, and those in which discretion by agency staff is not only allowed but also encouraged in pursuit of organizational goals. In short, the policies established by the nonprofit board of directors can empower the volunteer program: They spell out the boundaries within which participants can move freely and energetically to achieve the strategic vision.

(i) Policies for Sharing the Workplace

With regard to volunteers, the initial and most fundamental policy issue facing the board of directors concerns the positions volunteers are to occupy in the agency. What types of functions will volunteers perform, which are reserved for paid staff, and what job protections are afforded to each group? One reason the creation of a strategic vision for the volunteer corps is so important is that it provides a rationale for volunteer involvement that can frame the process of job creation and eventual work assignment in the agency: In general, volunteers should be enlisted for the purposes enunciated in the vision statement. Although the statement will be too broad to dictate specific jobs for volunteers, it offers a touchstone for determining the types of responsibilities they are to have in the organization, and which belong to paid staff.

Because no job is inherently "volunteer" or "paid," the process by which the NPO determines a suitable arrangement of work duties is crucial.[50] Depending on the vision statement, and such other factors as the culture, history, and environment of the organization, employees and volunteers might share the workplace in a number of productive and mutually satisfying ways. In determining policies for sharing the workplace, the board should seek active participation from agency management, the director of volunteer services, employees, and volunteers.[51] Based on this process, the realization of the vision for volunteer involvement might take a variety of forms.

Many strategies for involving volunteer workers lie open to nonprofit agencies. For example, an agency may choose to recruit volunteers with specific expertise to complement the talents of paid staff or, conversely, to attract citizens to perform more general work tasks. While boosting the former might broaden the skill base of the agency, enlisting the latter might free employees to spend more time on those job activities for which their professional background and training qualify them. Alternatively, an agency may resolve to enlist volunteers in order to enter a new service domain or to take on new projects that present circumstances and resources will not allow. Or, the board may decide to expand the pool of volunteers to heretofore untapped populations to enhance the responsiveness and representativeness of the agency in the community. The board may also decide to enlist volunteers for purposes of fund-raising or policy advocacy. Depending on the mission and vision conceived for the volunteer corps, the nonprofit board may utilize a variety of staffing options for integrating citizens into the organization.

A host of other basic policy issues await deliberation by the board of directors.[52] The board will need to clarify the rights and responsibilities of volunteer workers. For example, will the agency allow court-mandated (community service) volunteers, youth volunteers who are minors, and other special groups of volunteers? The board will need to set basic requirements for entering volunteer service (interviews, background checks, references, etc.) and for meeting standards of appropriate behavior and performance on the job. These standards provide the framework for counterpart policies covering grounds for discipline and termination, a regrettable necessity in volunteer (and employee) programs no matter how worthwhile the endeavor or adroit its leadership. Policies for adjudicating disputes or grievances involving volunteers are another consideration. The nonprofit board of directors can determine general policies in these and related domains and leave the specifics to a competent director of volunteer services. Without policy guidance from the board, however, the volunteer program lacks coherence and can easily founder.

(ii) Comparable Policies for Employees and Volunteers

Authorities in the field of volunteer administration advise organizational leadership to enact policies as comparable as possible for paid and nonpaid personnel.[53,54] They argue that by setting standards as high for volunteers as for employees, the agency engenders trust and credibility, increased respect and requests for volunteers from paid staff, a healthy work environment, an avoidance of stereotyping (for example, volunteers labeled and resented as "second-class" workers and organizational citizens), and high-quality services. These attributes advance dramatically the prospects for achieving the SRO.

(C) FURNISHING RISK MANAGEMENT AND INSURANCE PROTECTION

Developing policies for the nonprofit organization can be an arduous task for the board of directors. Although the board should "speak with one voice" with regard to final policy,[55] to reach that point members may have first had to engage in lengthy discussion and debate and to revisit "first principles"—that is, the rationale for the existence of the agency and the philosophy and vision that should continue to animate it. Ignoring the need for policies to guide the volunteer program (or other important aspects of the organization) is a far worse option, however. Not only does this course mire the board of directors in the dysfunctional syndromes elaborated earlier (and, in the process, sacrifice the benefits of good policy), but it also courts severe risk management problems. As Graff counsels, "There is no more pressing reason to develop policies for volunteer programs than the role that policies play in an overall risk management system."[56]

In many, if not most, NPOs, volunteers carry out mainstream work activities, from client service and outreach to clerical work and support of employees to project management and highly technical duties, such as legal, accounting, and marketing functions. As a result, volunteers can put themselves, clients, and the agency at risk. Such responsible and complex work also heightens the liability of the agency to volunteers (for example, for protection from harm in the course of their work and the right to fair treatment in employment practices). As the final authority, the board of directors is legally responsible for all operations carried out under the auspices of the agency, including the volunteer component; an aggrieved party initiates legal action, the board will be served. The board can be held accountable for the mistakes, accidents, and negligence of volunteers acting on behalf of the organization. Under certain conditions, in fact, individual board members can be held legally liable, for example, for failing to exercise reasonable oversight and due diligence over the agency.[57]

No institution or person can guarantee that a nonprofit organization will be able to avoid accidents or mishaps (or legal action) totally. Nevertheless, "policies can reduce an organization's exposure to liability in the event that a law suit is launched . . . there is no better proof that an agency has acted prudently and responsibly in attempting to reduce the likelihood of injury or loss than a full set of current, comprehensive policies and procedures, clearly in place, and consistently communicated to all relevant parties."[58] By contrast, a nonprofit board of directors that fails to exercise its policy-making authority and, in the breach, leaves its nonpaid (or paid) staff members and clients exposed to needless risks or potential harm will have a difficult time convincing litigants or a court of law that it has acted responsibly. Much less will such an agency be in a position to attract and retain volunteers, motivate and sustain them toward the strategic vision, or achieve the SRO.

To protect the organization and themselves as individuals from liability for the risks that volunteering can potentially entail and to avert possible legal action, the board of directors should see to the development of a comprehensive plan for risk management.[59,60] Given the breadth of information needed, the amount of study entailed, and the far-reaching ramifications of the decisions taken, the board should appoint a committee with wide organizational representation to formulate the risk management plan. Risk management comprises four steps:

1. Identification and evaluation of risks
2. Development of strategies for controlling or reducing risks
3. Implementation and reassessment of the risk management plan
4. Provision of liability insurance protection as needed[61]

Exhibit 30.5 summarizes the steps in creating a risk management plan for the volunteer corps.

(i) Identify and Evaluate Risks

The first step in the risk management plan consists of identifying and evaluating potential risks encountered in the volunteer program. Kahn recommends that the risk management

---

EXHIBIT 30.5 Steps in Developing a Risk Management Plan for the Volunteer Corps

- Identify, evaluate, and prioritize the potential risks encountered in the volunteer program.
- Develop strategies for reducing, or possibly avoiding, the risks identified.
- Implement and periodically reassess the risk management plan.
- Provide liability insurance protection for volunteers as needed.

---

committee examine the activities of each volunteer position and list all the ways that the volunteer could cause injury to others, and all the ways in which the volunteer could be personally injured. Given this identification of the possible risks, the committee should evaluate which can be expected to occur most often, which might cause greatest damage or harm, and which are most likely to result in liability for the organization. In this evaluation stage, risks are prioritized.[62] Brainstorming and other group development techniques can be especially useful for identification and evaluation of risks.

(ii) Develop Strategies for Reducing Risks

The second step in the risk management plan consists of developing strategies for reducing, or possibly avoiding, the risks identified. One alternative is to cease agency activities that are deemed excessively risky. The risk management committee may conclude that in certain areas the risks are too great and recommend that the board make a policy decision for the organization to discontinue these activities. Examples might include handling toxic materials, staffing a suicide hotline, or mediating disputes among rival gang members.

In other areas, the committee may determine that the organization can and should continue the activity but must impose safeguards to limit risk to an acceptable level. Policies enacted by the board can be a powerful tool for minimizing the chances that accidents and organizational exposure will occur. Policies that authorize standards and procedures for conducting a risky activity, mandate requisite training for paid staff and volunteers, or require screening of prospective volunteers (and employees) for a particular job(s) are a potent means to do so.[63] Such policies can help to reduce, but not eliminate, risk and potential exposure.

For example, board policies specifying that a criminal records check and further inquiries must be performed before a volunteer is allowed to work with children (or other vulnerable clients) will markedly decrease the chances of an ill-advised job placement. Board policies requiring general orientation for volunteers as well as training appropriate to particular positions will cut down on mistakes and accidents. A board policy stating that a job description must accompany each volunteer position, which describes the backgrounds and skills necessary for the job as well as the duties and means of supervision, should have the same effect. Policies that clarify how various activities are to be performed (for example, agency vans must be used for all transportation of clients; client counseling is to be performed only by certified personnel, whether paid or nonpaid) also lessen agency risk and potential exposure. Well-designed board policies in the context of risk management not only limit the probability that accidents will occur but also help ensure that volunteer jobs are staffed and functions are performed as effectively as possible.[64] In short, they are good volunteer administration practice.

(iii) Implement and Reassess the Risk Management Plan

The third step is to implement and periodically reassess the risk management plan. Implementation will proceed more smoothly and gain greater acceptance to the degree that leaders and managers are convinced that the risk management plan will help to decrease mishaps and organizational liability and improve the operation of the volunteer program. To this end, involving representatives from throughout the organization in a risk management committee is a highly recommended strategy (see previous section). Although the present discussion has centered on the volunteer program, the board should see to risk management for all organizational operations and agency staff, paid and nonpaid; the same four-step procedure can be used for employees.[65] Because agencies, services, activities, personnel, and information all change with the passage of time—possibly raising new or unforeseen hazards and risks as well as offering novel solutions to address existing or emerging problems—periodic reassessment of the risk management plan is highly desirable.

The pursuit by NPOs of important missions in dynamic social policy domains often entails some degree of exposure to risk and potential liability. Recognizing the possible ramifications of this problem for volunteer recruitment and retention, every state has some form of liability protection legislation for volunteers; in 1997 the U.S. Congress passed the Volunteer Protection Act (PL 105-19) to offer some uniform provisions. Nevertheless, the protection legislation does not provide blanket immunity to volunteers, and even when the board of directors of an NPO has invested substantial time, effort, and care in formulating and implementing a risk management plan, accidents involving volunteers (or employees or clients) as well as lawsuits can still occur. These occasions afford a good opportunity to reevaluate the risk management plan to see what changes might be warranted to prevent reoccurrence in the future. They also point up the need to provide liability insurance protection for volunteer workers.

(iv) Provide Insurance Protection

The risk management plan is a complement, not a substitute, for insurance coverage for volunteers. The risk management plan incorporates a sensible series of steps to identify, evaluate, and limit the risks and hazards associated with volunteer service in the organization. It cannot eliminate risk altogether, but it does afford an "eyes open" approach to the problem. After the plan has been formulated and implemented, the nonprofit agency will continue to perform some activities that entail (reasonable) risk; in these areas, the board of directors will have determined that the risk must be accepted in order to maintain the integrity of the organizational mission and vision. For those risks it has judged reasonable and necessary for the effective performance of the agency, the board needs to make sure that the organization's liability insurance coverage embraces volunteers as well as employees. The board can also consider other possible means for transfer of liability, such as seeking a waiver of responsibility from clients.[66]

Insurance companies tend to be apprehensive about providing liability coverage for volunteers. The development of a comprehensive risk management plan endorsed by the board of directors can help to assuage any doubts an insurance carrier may harbor concerning a nonprofit agency that utilizes volunteer workers.[67] A nonprofit board of directors that can show, in addition, that it takes the volunteer corps seriously enough to create a mission and vision for the program and to bolster it with leadership positions, its own budget, and judicious policies will encounter much less difficulty in securing the desired insurance protection for volunteers. More importantly, by investing this level of commitment and support in the strategic mission and vision, the nonprofit board will also find that its volunteer program is likely to garner success in all the other ways identified in this chapter.

30.5 Conclusion

NPOs are continually buffeted by the demands and vagaries of a complex, dynamic environment. They are hard-pressed to make effective use of every available resource, including volunteers. Yet, most nonprofit boards have not given on their volunteer programs the systematic attention necessary to evaluate how this component might most productively contribute to the future they envision for the organization, nor given them the support necessary to enact this pivotal role. This situation represents resources and opportunity foregone and undermines prospects for the self-renewing NPO.

This chapter proposes that the influence of one or more deleterious syndromes regarding volunteers (micromanagement, discomfort, overgratitude, and devaluation) diverts nonprofit boards from this important work. The chapter provides effectual methods to overcome the syndromes, such as soliciting regular reports concerning volunteer participation, inviting the director of volunteer services periodically to board meetings, addressing the volunteer program in orientation and training sessions, and recruiting former service volunteers to vacancies on the board. When the board comes to recognize this new, strategic role of volunteers in the agency, it is ready to turn to the crucial task of developing a mission and vision for the volunteer corps. As the chapter shows, progress toward the vision will also require support from the board, including leadership positions and a budget for the volunteer program, policies to govern the program, and risk management and insurance protection for volunteer workers.

Creating and supporting a strategic vision for the volunteer corps should rank as a priority in the self-renewing NPO. This responsibility rests with the board of directors, with widespread participation from other organizational members. As Silver maintains, *"The commitment of the administrative leadership of an organization is necessary to raise the volunteer program to priority status.* Without the leadership behind it, a volunteer program—no matter how well organized and potentially viable and valuable—simply will not have the organizational power necessary to progress and develop."[68] When the nonprofit board of directors empowers the program in this fashion, not only the volunteer corps but also organizational clients stand to benefit.

Endnotes

1. Soltz, B. B. (1997). "The Board of Directors." In T. D. Connors (ed.), *The Nonprofit Handbook: Management,* 2nd ed. New York: John Wiley & Sons, pp. 195–227.
2. Connors, T. D. (ed.). (1997). *The Nonprofit Handbook: Management,* 2nd ed. New York: John Wiley & Sons.
3. Houle, C. O. (1989). *Governing Boards: Their Nature and Nurture.* San Francisco: Jossey-Bass.
4. Carver, J. (1990). *Boards that Make a difference: A New Design for Leadership in Nonprofit and Public Organizations.* San Francisco: Jossey-Bass.
5. Ellis, S. J. (1995). *The Board's Role in Effective Volunteer Involvement.* Washington, DC: National Center for Nonprofit Boards.

6. See note 1.
7. See note 4.
8. See note 3.
9. Widmer, C. (1996). "Volunteers with the Dual Roles of Service Provider and Board Member: A Case Study of Role Conflict," *Organization Development Journal* 14 (Fall): 54–60.
10. See note 4.
11. Graff, L. L. (1995). "Polices for Volunteer Programs." In T. D. Connors (ed.), *The Volunteer Management Handbook*. New York: John Wiley & Sons, pp. 125–55.
12. See note 4.
13. Brudney, J. L. (1995). "The Involvement of Volunteers in the Delivery of Services: Myth and Management." In S. W. Hays and R. C. Kearney (eds.), *Public Personnel Administration: Problems and Prospects,* 3rd ed. Englewood Cliffs, NJ: Prentice Hall, pp. 319–30.
14. Brudney, J. L. (1990). *Fostering Volunteer Programs in the Public Sector: Planning, Initiating, and Managing Voluntary Activities.* San Francisco: Jossey-Bass.
15. Ellis, S. J. (1996). *From the Top Down: The Executive Role in Volunteer Program Success,* revised edition. Philadelphia: Energize.
16. Silver, N. (1988). *At the Heart: The New Volunteer Challenge to Community Agencies.* Pleasanton, CA: Valley Volunteer Center.
17. Graff, L. L. (1993). "The Key to the Boardroom Door: Policies for Volunteer Programs," *Journal of Volunteer Administration* 11(4) (Summer): 30–36.
18. See note 5.
19. Holland, T. P., D. Leslie, and C. Holzhalb. (1993). "Culture and Change in Nonprofit Boards," *Nonprofit Management and Leadership* 4(2) (Winter): 141–55.
20. Jones, B. E. (1996). "Strategic Planning in Government: The Key to Reinventing Ourselves," *Program Manager* 25(1) (January/February): 12–16.
21. Van Wart, M. (1995). "The First Step in the Reinvention Process: Assessment," *Public Administration Review* 55 (September/October): 429–38.
22. McCurley, S., and R. Lynch. (1996). *Volunteer Management: Mobilizing all the Resources in the Community.* Downers Grove, IL: Heritage Arts Publishing.
23. Sheehan, R. M. Jr. (1996). "Mission Accomplishment as Philanthropic Effectiveness: Key Findings for the Excellence in Philanthropy Project," *Nonprofit and Voluntary Sector Quarterly* 25 (March): 110–23.
24. See note 21.
25. See note 22.
26. Id., p. 13.
27. See note 20.
28. See note 14.
29. Fisher, J. C., and K. M. Cole. (1993). *Leadership and Management of Volunteer Programs: A Guide for Volunteer Administrators.* San Francisco: Jossey-Bass.
30. See note 22.
31. Weiss, J. A. (1997). "Managing the Mission." Paper presented at the National Public Management Research Conference. Athens, GA: University of Georgia, October 30–November 1.
32. See note 16.
33. Fairhurst, G. T., J. M. Jordan, and K. Neuwirth. (1997). "Why Are We Here? Managing the Meaning of an Organizational Mission Statement," *Journal of Applied Communication Research* 25 (November): 243–63.

34. See note 21.
35. See note 22.
36. Brudney, J. L. (1995). "Preparing the Organization for Volunteers." In T. D. Connors (ed.), *The Volunteer Management Handbook.* New York: John Wiley & Sons, pp. 36–60.
37. See note 5.
38. See note 29.
39. See note 22.
40. See note 29.
41. See note 14.
42. See note 15.
43. See note 22.
44. See note 29.
45. See note 15.
46. Id., p. 14.
47. Brudney, J. L. (1999). "The Effective Use of Volunteers: Best Practices for the Public Sector," *Law and Contemporary Problems* 62 (Autumn), 219–255.
48. See note 4.
49. Id.
50. See note 14.
51. See note 36.
52. See note 5.
53. See note 22.
54. See note 36.
55. See note 4.
56. See note 17.
57. See note 11.
58. Id., p. 131.
59. See note 22.
60. See note 11.
61. Kahn, J. D. (1993). "Legal Issues in the Involvement of Volunteers." In T. D. Connors (ed.), *The Nonprofit Management Handbook: Operating Policies and Procedures.* New York: John Wiley & Sons, pp. 907–19.
62. See note 22.
63. See note 61.
64. Id., pp. 912–13.
65. Id., p. 913.
66. See note 22.
67. See note 61.
68. See note 16.

Suggested Readings

Hodgkinson, V. A., and M. S. Weitzman. (1992). *Giving and Volunteering in the United States: Findings from a National Survey.* Washington, DC: Independent Sector.

Hodgkinson, V. A., M. S. Weitzman, C. M. Toppe, and S. M. Noga. (1992). *Nonprofit Almanac 1992–1993: Dimensions of the Independent Sector.* San Francisco: Jossey-Bass.

Strategic Education Planning: An Executive Leadership Tool

Suzanne Lulewicz
President, SJL Associates

31.1 Introduction

Every effective nonprofit organization (NPO) needs to be proactive in dealing with its future and the future of the community that it serves. Facing tremendous structural change, uncertainty, and decisions with huge opportunities and risks, an NPO's survival requires that it must anticipate what it needs, rather than responding reactively. When an NPO does not articulate a strategic outlook for itself, or think strategically as it operates in today's world, its leadership may find itself, to paraphrase Oscar Wilde, knowing the value of everything and the price of nothing. Anticipating the future in this volatile environment calls for more than systematic analysis; it also demands creativity, insight, and intuition.

The perspective of stewardship—the degree to which we feel ownership and responsibility for the success of our organizations, our society, and our lives[1]—has become a necessary component of strategic planning in the twenty-first century. It is this concept that can help NPOs determine what from their organizations they must save and what they must abandon. The decisions that NPOs make to enact change within their structure and operations can have a momentous impact on the society's future and the quality of life. Well-conducted and soundly built strategies can align an NPO's leadership and staff toward making decisions that make the best use of not just the resources they have at their command, but, more importantly, to reenergize the values important to sustain the lives of generations to come.

Decisions based on these strategies allow an NPO's staff to operate within a framework that guides choices of action and allocation of resources. They give others guidance on how to positively impact the work of the NPO. While an NPO's staff tends to be primarily concerned with the operational improvement of their departments—spotting problems and putting out fires—it is becoming imperative that they must now be involved in the development and implementation of the strategic elements of the organization. The time has come when their reward for work is not for working hard and putting in long hours, but for clear thinking and for being visionary. Now more than ever, an NPO's staff must clearly recognize the difference between the strategic and operational aspects of their job.

31.2 *Strategic Thinking and Planning Skills*

To understand the larger context in which the NPO operates, staff must know something about where the organization is heading. While the leadership of the NPO has to think strategically, others within the organization have to be able to support that strategic thinking. To effectively anticipate where an NPO is going and being prepared to support it when it gets there requires special thinking skills and tools when developing strategies.

To develop strategic thinking skills that can implement an organization's strategic plan, an NPO's staff must begin seeing the organization from a more global perspective—in terms of overall services, priorities, and strategic rather than operational needs. It becomes necessary for all involved in developing, implementing, and supporting strategy within the organization to know the business of the NPO. This means they must know more than just the mission of the organization, but how each department functions to serve its member and community's needs. Additionally, an NPO's staff needs information about the world in which the organization operates and that impacts it either directly or indirectly. This gathering of information, both external and internal to the organization, is critical.

Strategic thinking addresses competing goals within an organization. To develop an NPO whose staff think and plan strategically, an NPO needs to become aware of the connection between the organization's vision and values and the visions and values of the people who make up its staff and membership. Senge identifies vision (taken from the Latin word *videre,* meaning "to see") as an image of an NPO's desired future: Values (taken from the French word *valoir,* meaning "to be worth") describe how an NPO's staff intend to operate on a daily basis as they pursue and enact their vision. It has become generally recognized that when the operating values of the staff and/or membership of the NPO are ignored, a large part of the energy and vitality of the organization is cut off.[2]

Shared values relate to strategic thinking and planning. They do this by making individual operating values a central part of the NPO's vision. When this occurs and when the organization's vision and values are discussed and shared by all members and staff of the NPO, they become a guiding symbol of behaviors that will help people move toward the larger organizational vision. As a result, it becomes easier for staff to think, speak, and act in alignment with the organization's strategies. Some examples of individual and organizational values are:

- Learning and growth
- Self-expression
- Freedom and independence
- Innovation and creativity
- Partnership and collaboration

It is vital that an NPO identify the role of shared vision and values. Because these values are necessary to planning the future direction of an organization, the NPO's performance will be better when its vision, values, goals, and objectives are linked to those of its staff and members. Too often, the planning process of an NPO ignores the future people truly want to create and focus merely on financial and business objectives.

31.3 The Use of Story as a Strategic Thinking and Planning Tool

Developing story plots can be an effective way for an NPO to develop the skills of strategic thinking and to create strategies to meet its future more effectively and with greater success. The development of story plots is also known as *scenario planning*.

Stories are an old way of organizing knowledge. They can be an effective planning tool because they encourage a willing suspension of disbelief. It has been frequently said that we do not describe the world we see; we see the world we know how to describe.[3] This statement highlights the fact that as human beings, we tend not to see patterns in our environment about which we have not even thought or to which we have given little relevance. As a result, stories can bring vital information to the attention of an NPO and its leadership that they would not ordinarily stop to consider as strategically important and relevant to the NPO's future.

Stories are also able to express a diverse number of perspectives on complex events, while giving meaning to those events. This perspective provides the opportunity to include the views of many layers of stakeholders in the story development. The reliability of the futures they describe is less important than the types of conversation they will spark among an organization's staff and members.

(A)   SCENARIO PLANNING

Scenario planning uses stories to identify future worlds and prepare an NPO's staff to develop strategies for meeting those varied futures. Each scenario developed—and there are generally no more than four, so that their plots can be remembered and discussed— represents a distinct and plausible world that an NPO may find itself caught up in at some point in the future. The stories' perspectives are external to the organization, but their plots will have an impact on the organization's success.

The purpose of developing these future scenarios is not to predict the future, but rather to show how different forces can manipulate the future of the NPO in different directions. It is very important to realize this, because the process of developing scenarios will help an NPO identify forces over which it has no control and provide opportunities for it to develop organizational strategies to respond to them if and when these forces occur. The benefit of developing these scenarios lies in their giving the NPO an ability, both in terms of speed and resources, to better anticipate the future.

According to scenario planning experts, scenario planning is particularly effective when:

- The environment in which planning occurs is complex, chaotic, and uncertain.
- Decisions need to be made that have long lead times but significant consequences.
- Warning signals or red flags that provide insight into possible subsequent events need to be identified.
- Organizational mental models need to be articulated and assumptions and information gaps need to be exposed.

- Solid and well-founded strategies that play well against a range of possible and diverse outcomes need to be generated.
- A strategic discussion about the future is to be stimulated throughout the organization.[4]

Conventional planning that most NPOs go through to get the work done generally ignores the future people truly want to create. The combination of strategic thinking, scenario planning, and shared vision can bring into relief the choices facing an NPO and the impact those choices might have on the organization's future and its members.

In his *The Art of the Long View*, Peter Schwarz gave an example of strategic scenario thinking. In 1983, Royal Dutch/Shell (the company that first pioneered the use of scenario planning) undertook a study to determine the impact of the Soviet Union on future oil and gas supplies. The Soviet Union was one of the natural gas suppliers to Europe, but for political reasons, was limited to only 35 percent of the European market. However, in an effort to determine Royal Dutch/Shell's future economic and marketing opportunities, they began to develop stories that centered on answering the following question: "Under what conditions might the Soviet Union open its most treasured resources for development by such multinational giants as Shell and Chevron?" Schwartz and the other Royal Dutch/Shell planners developed a scenario that forecasted normalized relations between the Soviet Union and the NATO countries of Europe and the West. They identified an unknown person at the time—Mikhail Gorbachev—as a likely leader of economic reform.[5]

Within two years of creating the scenario, Gorbachev became premier of the Soviet Union, announced a new series of economic reforms, and signaled more to come. These reforms led to widespread liberalization within Russia and a significant drop in the price of natural gas to Western Europe. While the fall of communism stunned the rest of the world, Royal Dutch/Shell was not surprised.[6]

(B)   WHERE SCENARIO PLANNING CAME FROM

Scenario planning first emerged following World War II as a method for military planning. In the 1960s, Herman Kahn (who had been involved with the military's efforts at scenario planning) refined it as a tool for foretelling business futures. Scenario planning, however, reached its pinnacle in the work of Pierre Wack, a planner in the London offices of Royal Dutch/Shell, the international oil enterprise.[7] Wack and his planners were looking for events that might affect the price of oil, which had been steady since World War II. Scenario planning is now recognized as a fundamental tool for thinking strategically about the future.[8]

Scenarios—stories about possible futures—combine predetermined elements and identifiable trends with critical uncertainties: they form a foundation that can help an organization create robust strategies in response to potentially unexpected change. The test of a good planning scenario or story is not whether it portrays the future accurately but whether it enables an organization to learn, adapt, and create an ongoing strategic conversation within the organization.

Strategic conversation is an ongoing process that brings a deeper understanding of how the external environment affects an NPO's business, its ideas, and its competence. A scenario can spark this conversation by organizing an NPO's perceptions about alternative futures in which the decisions its staff and leadership make today may play out. In practice, scenarios resemble a set of stories, written or spoken, built around carefully constructed plots of the future.

Scenarios are not predictions. When we are making predictions, we tend to look for evidence that confirms our beliefs and discount evidence that does not. Because scenarios are possible futures, not predictive futures, this gives them one of their great strengths: the ability to engage a diverse group of people in thinking about multiple possible futures. As a result, good scenarios will challenge tunnel vision by instilling a deeper appreciation for the various elements and uncertainties that can shape our future. This process of tapping the knowledge of a group of people's diverse perspectives will yield breakthrough insights and innovations. Throughout any organization, many people have ideas about where the future may be heading, but there is generally no established process for gathering such knowledge and putting it to good use. Scenario planning can provide a framework for sharing the insights of a broad cross-section of people.

Once scenarios have been fleshed out and woven into a narrative, the NPO (through its strategic planning team) then identifies the scenarios' implications for the organization. They work out the various possible actions within each scenario. Then, looking across the set of three or four scenarios, the team identifies strategies that would lead to success no matter what the future may hold. From there, the team identifies leading indicators that the organization will monitor on an ongoing basis. These will be the events the NPO will watch for that will indicate which future (or combination of futures) may actually be unfolding.

By rehearsing the future in this way, the scenarios enable an NPO to adapt more quickly to what is actually happening and to anticipate better what could happen. In the face of some major new development, the organization does not have to spend months trying to understand what is happening, and then many more months developing options and marshalling resources.

(C)   BENEFITS OF SCENARIO PLANNING

Generating scenarios can help alert an NPO to developments in the present that are pointing to particular futures that would have been missed by conventional strategic planning processes. They are powerful planning tools precisely because the future is unpredictable. Unlike traditional forecasting or planning tools, scenarios present alternative images instead of extrapolating current trends from the present.

By recognizing the warning signs and the story that is unfolding, an organization can avoid unsettling surprises, adapt their strategies, and act effectively. The end result of scenario planning is not a more accurate picture of tomorrow, but implementing better decisions today.

According to Kees van der Heijden, the process of scenario planning serves a number of objectives:

- It creates a more robust generation of projects and decisions.
- It develops better thinking about the future.
- It enables leadership to be more perceptive about events, recognizing that they are part of a pattern and able to realize the implications.
- It enables management to influence not by means of directives, but by using scenarios to set the context within which decisions are made by others.
- It provides leadership to the organization.[9]

Additionally, scenario planning is especially useful to prevent tunnel vision. At times nearly every organization becomes so bogged down in the daily business of just getting by that people can lose sight of their larger sense of purpose and lose touch with subtle changes taking place in the world outside. Scenario planning involves taking a big step back from these daily concerns for a moment and "lifting our heads above the clouds," to see the landscape from a fresh perspective and deeper sense of purpose.

(D) THE PROCESS OF ORGANIZATIONAL STORY TELLING/SCENARIO PLANNING

While the number of steps the scenario planning process follows may differ among proponents, there is a sequential series of steps that an NPO engaging in scenario planning needs to follow:

1. Articulate the business idea.
2. Identify the focal issue or decision and the time frame.
3. Identify the major stakeholders.
4. Identify the primary driving forces or basic trends.
5. Identify key uncertainties.
6. Construct initial scenario themes.
7. Check for consistency and plausibility.
8. Identify research needs.
9. Evolve toward decision strategies and tactics.
10. Select and define strategies and tactics.

(i) Step 1—Articulate the Business Idea

The business idea is the organization's mental model of the forces behind its current and future success. The business idea is embedded in the language of the organization, and as such is a rational explanation of why the organization has been successful in the past, and how it will be successful in the future.[10] "It is the perception within the organization as to why success will occur, how the organization will compete successfully, and what forces and assets will factor into their success."[11]

When an NPO's business idea is combined with its distinctive competencies (institutional knowledge, such as organizational know-how, shared assumptions, and values; embedded processes, such as leadership style, internal communications, systems, and culture; reputation and trust, such as its brand and financial clout; legal protection, such as ownership of patents and prime sites; and activity-specific assets, such as investments in market share), the result is the NPO's competitive advantage.[12] Competitive advantage is not the same thing as an organization's strengths. "Any government or public institution that offers value that can be matched elsewhere runs the risk of being devolved or eliminated. Any corporate entity without a competitive advantage is not capable of competing."[13]

By understanding how the NPO sees the world, the planning team undertaking the scenario planning can identify key assumptions, shared expectations, beliefs, and blind spots in the organization's collective perception. This knowledge will help them shape scenarios or stories that are provocative and plausible.[14]

(ii) Step 2—Identify the Focal Issue or Decision and the Time Frame

In this step, the question under discussion, time frame and scope of analysis, is defined. Earlier in this chapter, the question Royal Dutch/Shell posed for one of their analyses was "Under what conditions might the Soviet Union open its most treasured resources for development by such multinational giants as Shell and Chevron?"[15] The time frame for them would have very likely been measured in decades, because of the long lead times necessary to plan and develop projects.

Once the time frame has been determined, then it is necessary to ask what knowledge would be of greatest value to the organization that far down the road. It is useful to look at the past and think about what you wish you had known then that you know now. If the time frame for your story analysis is 10 years, then look back over the past 10 years at the changes that have occurred in your organization, industry, and society at large. You should anticipate a similar amount of change or even more over the next 10 years.[16]

(iii)   Step 3—Identify the Major Stakeholders

At this point, the planning team identifies who will have an interest in the issue under analysis. Questions to determine the major stakeholders include: Who will be affected by it? Who could influence it? The more obvious stakeholders generally include membership, suppliers, politicians, government, the general public, and so forth. During the process of this step, it is important to identify the current roles, interests, and power positions of these stakeholders. For example, in an NPO that is prominent in environmental activism, judges, politicians, developers, lawyers, journalists, and regulators may be powerful stakeholders.

(iv)   Step 4—Identify the Primary Driving Forces or Basic Trends

After defining the scope, time frame, and stakeholders, the planning team needs to ensure that the following questions get asked: What political, economic, societal, technological, legal, and industry trends are shaping the NPO's future? For example, a historical preservation society might identify environmental regulation, continuing growth of urban development, increase of political involvement in urban redevelopment, architectural advances, or an increasingly liberal/restrictive political environment.

The predetermined factors that affect these trends are identified. "Predetermined elements do not depend on any particular chain of events. If it seems certain, no matter which scenario comes to pass, then it is a predetermined element."[17] As an example, for over a decade, the presence of the U.S. budget deficit in any scenario was considered a predetermined element.

During this step, each trend is briefly explained, including how and why it exerts its influence on the issue. It may be helpful to list each trend on a chart to identify its impact on your present strategy as positive, negative, or uncertain. Everyone participating in the process must agree that these trends will continue. Any trend on which there is disagreement (within the time frame) would generally be identified as a key uncertainty.

(v)   Step 5—Identify Key Uncertainties

This step identifies those events whose outcomes are still uncertain and that will significantly affect the issue under analysis. Uncertainty continually plagues our future so that our plans break down. At this step, again, the planning team considers economic, political, societal, technological, legal, and industry factors. Questions that identify uncertainties may include:

- Will the next political leader, mayor or president, be a Republican or Democrat?
- Will a particular piece of legislation be passed?

- Will a new technology be developed?
- What will the public and/or community value in the future?

During this step, the planning team identifies what knowledge would be of greatest value to the NPO that far down the road. In other words, if they could know just two things about the future that would enable them to create sound long-term strategies on the issue under discussion, what would they like to know?

Then, create a matrix of these two future issues that would be of the greatest value to know. This then becomes the basic plot dynamic of the stories that the planning team chooses to develop. Here, the basic idea is not to look at the NPO itself in any of the scenarios. The whole idea of these stories is to present some very different ways in which the outside world might change during this time, whether the NPO likes it or not. The point of telling these stories in such detail is that they lead us to one question: If this particular scenario were the future, then what should the NPO do?

Exhibit 31.1 is an example of a scenario plot matrix. In this particular example, the NPO's two key uncertainties were whether there was a situation of free or restricted trade markets and the presence of a boom or bust economy.

The basic plots that then would unfold into scenarios for these two key uncertainties would be:

- *Scenario Plot A:* NPO member activity occurs in a boom economy with a free and open international trade market.
- *Scenario Plot B:* NPO member activity occurs in a boom economy with strict international trade barriers.
- *Scenario Plot C:* NPO member activity occurs in a poor economy with a free and open international trade market.
- *Scenario Plot D:* NPO member activity occurs in a poor economy with strict international trade barriers.

Three major plot types tend to consistently occur in modern-day scenarios:

1. *Winners and Losers.* Stories that have this plot generally center on conspiracy theories. Conflict is an inevitable fact of life. Only one candidate can win the election; only one country can dominate the economy; only one industry can dominate the market. This type of logic leads to war and persistent conflict.
2. *The Heroic Challenge and Response.* This plot refers to the adventure stories in which an individual faces one unexpected test after another. Mark Twain's hero Huckleberry Finn is a good example of a character who undergoes this test. After each test, the tested person (or organization) emerges differently

---

EXHIBIT 31.1 Scenario Planning Matrix

	Free and open international trade market	Strict international trade barriers
Boom economy	Scenario Plot A	Scenario Plot B
Poor economy	Scenario Plot C	Scenario Plot D

from the way he or she was before. Overcoming the test, passing the test, is important—not for its credential, but for its effect on the hero's character.

3. *Evolution.* Evolutionary changes are always biological in nature. They involve slow change in one direction—either growth or decline. They are hard to spot if you are not attuned to them because they occur so slowly. Once spotted, however, they are easy to manage, precisely because they do not suddenly leap upon you. Technology falls into this plot dynamic. New innovations grow in a biological fashion, sprouting slowly from earlier technologies, gradually ripening and then bursting upon the world. It is an evolutionary dynamic because it fits within an existing system.[18]

(vi) Step 6—Construct Initial Scenario Themes

Once the stakeholders, key trends and uncertainties, and the basic plots using the scenario matrix have been identified, the planning team has the main ingredients to construct the scenarios. The next activity then is to choose one of the plots from the matrix and write a story combining the driving forces and key uncertainties identified.

For example, an organization concerned with its future trade with China might construct four scenarios. Political forces and key uncertainties surrounding political stability may get more play in one scenario, whereas legal trends and the health of the economy may feature more prominently in the other two scenarios. Naming the scenarios is also important. A scenario is a story; by capturing its essence in a title, you make the story easy to follow and remember. At this stage, you have learning scenarios, which are tools for research and study rather than for decision making. The titles and themes are focal points around which to develop and test the scenarios.

(vii) Step 7—Check for Consistency and Plausibility

The simple worlds you have just made are not yet complete scenarios because they probably have internal inconsistencies or lack a compelling story. There are three tests for internal consistency and a fourth that also should be considered:

1. Are the trends compatible with the chosen time fame?
2. Do the scenarios combine outcomes of uncertainties that indeed go together? For example, full employment and zero inflation do not go together, so eliminate any possible scenario or pairing of uncertainties that would not likely occur.
3. Are the major stakeholders placed in positions they do not like and can change? For example, an exporting country may not tolerate low prices on their high-demand products for very long. If so, your scenario will evolve into another one. It is important to try to describe this end scenario, which is a much more stable story.[19]
4. Are the scenarios relevant? To have impact, they should connect directly to the concerns of the NPO.

(viii) Step 8—Identify Research Needs

At this point, the planning team may need to do further research to flesh out their understanding of uncertainties and trends. The initial story themes should help find the organization's blind spots. For example, is it clear how a key stakeholder in this future story will behave? Often, organizations know a lot about their own sector, but little beyond the fringes from which the innovations may come. New technologies that create new products and markets fall into this category.[20]

(ix) Step 9—Evolve toward Decision Strategies and Tactics

At this step, the scenarios become tools to determine strategies and tactics for effective decision making. There are four steps to follow when working with the scenarios that have evolved in order to begin developing effective strategies:

1. Brainstorm possible strategies operating under one or more of the scenarios.
2. Sort the possible strategies into categories or clusters.
3. Vote on the importance of the proposed strategy clusters.
4. Brainstorm tactics that might improve chances for success under each of the scenarios.

(x) Step 10—Select and Define Strategies and Tactics

In this final step, measure the potential strategies against the following success criteria and choose those strategies to which all of the criteria can be applied:

- The strategies are consistent with the core values and culture of the organization.
- The strategies draw on the core competencies and strategic assets of the organization.
- The potential strategies strike a reasonable balance between risk and return that is consistent with the organization's culture.
- The strategies can be sustained financially in the long run.

Now, the planning team can define the tactics and next steps that will support these proposed strategies.

If the stories are to function as planning tools, their focus must be based on issues critical to the success of the decision under consideration or to the organization. Only a few scenarios can be fully developed and remembered, and each should represent a plausible alternative future, not a best case, worst case, or most likely story. Once the scenarios have been fleshed out and put into a narrative form, the planning team can then identify the implications of these future forces and determine what leading indicators need to be monitored on an ongoing basis.

31.4 Conclusion

The vitality and benefits that scenario planning bring to an NPO's preparations to deal with the future are best summed up by former Royal Dutch/Shell planner, Kees van der Heijden. Scenario planning is vital to a staff's day-to-day management tasks. Organizational management is a way of thinking that penetrates the institutional mind, affects all activity, and is based on a number of basic assumptions:

- Possessing sound organizational strategies reduces the complexity of the management task rather than adding to it.
- Discussing strategy is a natural part of any management talk, and not the exclusive domain of specialists.

- There is nothing unusually difficult in good strategy: It is based on commonsense thinking.
- Investing time in structuring the strategic debate will pay off many times over in increased efficiency of dealing with the day-to-day issues managers face.[21]

Endnotes

1. Block, P. (1993). *Stewardship*. San Francisco: Berrett-Koehler Publishers, Inc.
2. Senge, P., et al. (1994). *The Fifth Discipline Fieldbook*. New York: Currency/Doubleday.
3. Id.
4. Willmore, J. (1998). "Scenario Planning," *Info-Line* (September): 3–5.
5. Schwartz, P. (1996). *The Art of the Long View*. New York: Currency/Doubleday.
6. See note 4.
7. Wack, P. (1985). "Scenarios: Shooting the Rapids," *Harvard Business Review* (November/December): 139–50.
8. See note 5.
9. van der Heijden, K. (1996). *Scenarios: The Art of Strategic Conversation*. West Sussex, England: John Wiley & Sons Ltd.
10. Id.
11. See note 4.
12. See note 9.
13. See note 4.
14. Id.
15. See note 5.
16. Shoemaker, P. J. H. (1996). "Scenario Planning: A Tool for Strategic Thinking." *Strategies for Success: Core Capabilities for Today's Managers*. Sloan Management Review, 41–55.
17. See note 5.
18. Id.
19. See note 16.
20. Id.
21. See note 9.

Suggested Readings

de Geus, A. (1997). *The Living Company*. Boston: Harvard Business School Press.
Garvey, D. (1997). "Boston Scenarios," *The New England Nonprofit Quarterly* (Fall/Winter): 24–31.

Coping with Change: A Primer for Developing Human Resources

ELIZABETH POWER, MED, PRINCIPAL
EPOWER & ASSOCIATES

32.1 The Power of Change

Individual people, at the micro level, are the actors in the drama of change. How we understand it, manage it ourselves as we experience it, and model it for others is profoundly influential. This does not mean that anyone will serve their own best interests to grin and bear it through hard trauma or that hard times should be sugar coated. It does mean that having a way of understanding what change does to us and how to do something different with it is important. Choices equal power, and in the face of change, power counts.

Why is this important in the nonprofit organization (NPO) environment? Most people think of NPOs as agencies that work with people who are "down and out." In this view, NPOs support the victims of natural disasters, crime, economic misfortune, and life's hardships. In reality, NPOs function across a very broad span of needs that focus not only on the down and out but also on the up and coming and the already arrived. The common denominator for everyone who works for or who is served by an NPO is change.

So, the better equipped to cope with change the people who work for the NPO are, the more effective they may be in helping others, no matter their station in life. Everyone needs help with change, and the world needs more people who can manage it with more skill.

Why is the need so great? As the speed with which communication occurs increases, as the borders of the world shrink, the rate of change and the speed with which we know about it increases. Change was once the exception rather than the norm. We operated on an agrarian cycle. Seasons came and went, and the events in our lives were fairly knowable and predictable. Neighbors and religious institutions helped people through the changes that occurred by providing food, support, and sometimes shelter. With the Great Depression in the 1930s, that changed. The volume of people needing help was so great because of the change brought by the financial collapse that there were not enough neighbors and religious institutions to help all who needed help.

Now, while technology has taken us to edges of intellect and experience we never thought possible, we have not expanded our ability to cope with change. We can replace body parts, we can travel to distant planets, even clone animals. But most of us cannot deal with change any better than our ancestors a few generations back. And the changes we face are just as challenging, if not more so. Their speed and impact outstrip our ability to incorporate them into our lives. In this chapter, we will start with a very personal look at change and how to cope with it, and extrapolate from there.

32.2   How Change Affects Us

Do you enjoy change? Welcome it? Seek it out? Chances are, your experience of change is like that of the many people I have worked with as they face change. These people have been employees of companies undergoing organizational change as a result of anti-trust cases or transformational start-ups, survivors of trauma and torture, and people recently diagnosed with life-changing and sometimes terminal illnesses. A few anticipated a change they engineered or were consciously executing a redirection of their lives.

Most of you who read this use computers. Those of you who are younger cannot remember a time without computers; those of you who are older can remember the IBM Selectric® and before that maybe the Olivetti® manual typewriter. Do you use a personal digital assistant? Can you remember when they didn't exist? Do you remember when "portable computer" meant a "luggable" machine that weighed about 25 pounds?

Think about the very first time you sat down in front of a computer. The very first time you turned it on to learn to use it. After about 45 minutes, how did you feel? Between 1984 and 1999, eight out of ten people who were asked this question in the course of learning to cope with change answered the same way.

The feelings they reported were unpleasant: discomfort, anxiety, fear, terror—irritated, annoyed, angry, full of rage—incompetent, dumb, inadequate. After about 45 minutes, people learning to use a computer for the first time (especially if they were older when they began to learn) wanted to shoot the computer right between its disk drives. The experience of learning how to use it was embarrassing. The fact that it would announce their errors with beeps loud enough for everyone to hear exposed feelings of inadequacy and incompetence that are normal during learning.

Only a few new learners reported feeling excited or challenged. They *wanted* to learn computer skills. The change was something *they* sought, not something they felt compelled to do or felt coerced into doing. They felt control over the process.

The feelings people report in the face of change are normal. They are not fun, and they make change even tougher. But they are normal. It does not matter what the change is—those same feelings come with all kinds of change. They come with the changes you face, that the NPO you are associated with faces, and that the people served by the organization face.

32.3   Coping Mechanisms for Change: Fight or Flight

What happens when these powerful feelings rise up? It is interesting how the mind works. It remembers what feeling threatened feels like. It remembers how it felt to be charged by a saber-toothed tiger or a dinosaur. It has no interest in learning anything new; it is interested only in survival. Survival at the physical, mental, and emotional level means protecting you from threat. Rather automatically, the two options become fight or flight.

Fight or flight are appropriate, on-target responses in the face of a saber-toothed tiger. They are not, however, particularly helpful in the face of learning a new skill. As strategies they don't work particularly well in the face of many changes, only prolonging inevitable adjustments that must occur. In extreme expressions of fight or flight, we see behavior that is self- and other-destructive—the addictions. Depression may be a form of behavioral flight that becomes physiological. Dissociation—separating oneself from one's experiences—is a form of flight.

Unfortunately, sex, drugs, work, shopping, food, depression, dissociation, or even psychosis will not result in the altered behavior that is required by change. Each of these represents yet another change, one that takes us farther from the results we need to help create to manage the change we face.

Everyone knows people who decide they need to overhaul their lives. So they change cars, houses, addresses, hairstyle, spouse, or maybe job. But have they overhauled themselves? The outward changes can be very significant; the real issue is often inward changes in how a person thinks and feels. Change—especially self-directed change—from the inside out is a powerful form of self-directed behavioral change that transforms the individual and results in outer differences.

Unfortunately, it evokes the same feelings as being laid off, divorce, or learning a new skill. Emotionally, it feels safer to change the trappings of life instead of changing one's interior. What would happen if you used a simple model to make it easier to make change, or to go through changes that come before you? After all, you may not be able to choose the changes you face, but you can choose how you handle them.

32.4   *An Option: Separating Facts from Feelings*

All of the events of change described to this point have a common denominator: They are facts; they can be made objective; they can be measured and counted and their existence validated by scientific methods. These events generate powerful feelings. It is fact that we have feelings, and in this context, the goal is to decouple feelings from facts for the purpose of mastery (not denial).

When change occurs, feelings occur. However, the feelings (fear and anger in their various forms, for example) are not the facts (marriage, divorce, birth, death, layoff, new procedures, a surge in clients, applying for funding). In today's culture, these two are often so very linked that they are treated as if they are the same.

Feelings are subjective. Each person's experience of emotion is unique to him or her. Have you ever tried to measure someone else's feelings? Have you ever tried to get two people to agree on a feeling, what it is, how to describe it, how to measure it? They might say they feel "angry," but what makes them angry will be different. How they describe their "anger" will vary.

How does this relate to change? Change evokes unpleasant feelings for most people. If the natural reaction to these feelings is to avoid them, the implication is that the change is something to be resisted. It is problematic, something to which we should say "no." (In fact, we act out our no rather loudly.)

Consider it this way. A change occurs. The feelings come up. They are powerful enough that we completely miss the change, and begin to yell "No!" to it with our very lives. We react, doing the same things we have always done—gravity drags us downhill into looking at and experiencing the change as a problem, something that we should resist, and we go into either fight or flight.

The option? To recognize that the speed with which we go from *recognizing* a change to *feeling* an emotion is incredibly fast. It is so fast that it requires a conscious effort to decouple these two steps from the next step: acting on either one (and we will usually act on the feeling first!). Increased personal power comes from choosing to make the choice to decouple these two steps. It also sets you up for even more power in the form of added options.

32.5 The "No" and the "Yes" of Change

The "No!" of change is a natural effect of learning that change may well mean separation from something familiar. To symbolically roll downhill into a no-based, problem-focused view of change and reacting to it the way we always have creates the inevitability of fight or flight. Depending on the psychological defense mechanisms we are most comfortable with, our behavior could be anything from relapse into addictive behavior to avoidance, denial, displacement, or numbness. Each person learns to cope (and fight or flight are coping mechanisms, no more) and then applies what works. Enough said. What about the other side?

If you are willing to recognize that the feelings of change are a cue—and nothing more at this point—to the fact that a change has occurred, you automatically increase your options. Imagine that they are a flag, and when the flag pops up, it is time to identify the change and chose how to frame it. As a "No," the outcomes are clear.

What about the "Yes" frame? When the flag pops up, choosing the "Yes" frame means you choose to consider that there may be opportunity in the change. This is thinking again before acting, that is, choosing to respond instead of react.

What changes with this one choice? The feelings will be the same, regardless of which option you choose. Chose no, choose yes, the normal feelings of change will be there. The outcome is what changes. With the no, it's fight or flight. With yes, interrupting the automatic brings the ability to engineer personal growth and gain.

In the NPO environment, think about the difference it could make if volunteers, staff, board, and persons served could choose to look at the "Yes" of change. It is a learned skill, one that helps relegate emotions to their rightful place. It does not encourage anyone to ignore their feelings, and it does not minimize them. It only says that regardless of which way a person chooses to consider a change, the normal feelings of change will be there. Remember, sometimes it is not possible to choose the change you face, only to choose how you handle it. You might as well get what you can out of the change.

Exhibit 32.1 provides a visual model for how these options look.

32.6 Change and the Failure–Success Issue

No model can account for all situations. The dynamics of human behavior are too complex—the multiple changes some people face are too overwhelming and the consequences too big. However, a general model such as this one can address some of the issues and perhaps help you open the door for yourself or others in the area of taking charge of changes

EXHIBIT 32.1 Choosing Change

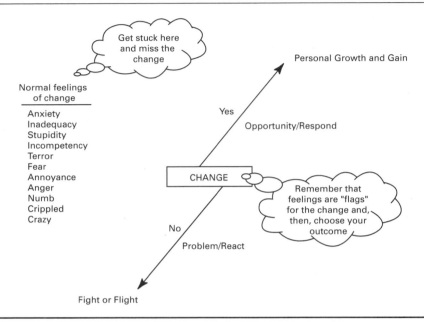

that occur. Some of the changes may take years to finish engineering and finalizing. It is never too late to start or start again. It is never too late to resume practicing behavior that can lead to a different outcome through accumulating different behaviors on top of each other.

What is failure? Simply, it is anything that moves us significantly away from something we believe we deserve, feel entitled to, or have worked hard to attain that results in our feeling "less than." It does not matter if it is in the area of career, health, relationships, education, finances, status, spirituality, physical condition, or some other part of our life. You want good things, you plan for good things, you take the actions you know how to take, you do the best you can, and then suddenly it's gone.

Gone. Change has given you a whack on the side of the head. If change is the constant for all of us, why do some of us act in ways that are resilient? How are some people able to work their way back from events that level others? Even in the face of events such as victimization by violent crime, loss of job, divorce, death, disease, mental illness, or natural disaster, some people seem able to keep going (feelings and all) and capitalize on their lives.

Culturally, each of those events is in some way classified as failure. We all know that it is not appropriate to blame the victim, but we all think we could have done something differently. "If only" and "Maybe if" become the key phrases that inform us of the regret (perhaps subtle guilt or even shame) at being party to such events.

What do people say to us at these times? "Oh, honey, I'm so sorry! I can't believe that so-and-so did such and such!" or "Can you imagine? The nerve of them! Do you have a lawyer?" and similar phrases abound. Even if the words vary, the message is often one of sympathy and comfort. Sympathy and comfort do not come your way unless something bad happens.

That which we call failure evokes the need for pity, sympathy, comfort, and attention. These are the positive benefits of failure. Failure feels bad, and nobody likes feeling bad. We do not like it when others feel bad, either. We try to comfort them, make them feel better in the face of their situation. Is it appropriate? You bet. Can it also backfire over time. Absolutely.

Every position has both positive and negative benefits, even failure and success. Failure brings with it the *positive* benefits of pity, sympathy, comfort, and attention. The *negative* benefits of failure are losses in self-esteem and self-respect, lowered expectations, smaller rewards, less access to what is desirable, and limits in earning and future.

What about success? What is it? Isn't success moving toward your desires, fulfilling your dreams? Does it have benefits? Yes. When you look at Exhibit 32.2, you can see how the benefits of failure and success take some interesting twists when you look at them from a larger, generic level.

Ironically, the negative benefits of success represent the loss of the positive benefits of failure. The positive benefits of change are the opposites of the negative benefits of failure. Can your limbic system make sense of this change in perspective? Let's make it a little tougher. Look again at Exhibit 32.2. What do you go through when you begin to move from failure to success, however you define them for yourself?

You go through change. How does it feel? Pretty unpleasant, as a general rule. Certainly uncomfortable as you try new behavior and do things you have never done before. Think about the number of times people in abusive relationships attempt to leave before they actually make it. It is said that we prefer the familiar hell to the unfamiliar paradise. The safety and comfort of the known are almost always a stronger pull than the fear and discomfort of the unknown. In many ways, the feelings that change brings up prevent us from being instigators of change in our own lives. It also impairs others from instigating change in their own lives.

EXHIBIT 32.2 The Benefits of Failure and Success

Failure Failure Failure	Failure Failure Failure
Positive Benefits Pity Sympathy Comfort Attention Less responsibility	**Negative Benefits** Loss of self-esteem Loss of self-respect Lowered expectations Smaller rewards Less access to what is desirable Limits in earning and future
Success Success Success	**Success Success Success**
Negative Benefits Loss of pity Loss of sympathy Loss of comfort Change in attention Loss of less responsibility	**Positive Benefits** Increase in self-esteem Increase in self-respect Increase in expectations Bigger rewards More access to what is desirable Fewer limits in earning and future

Change

If you want the positive benefits of success, be prepared to go through change. Avoid getting trapped in failure-oriented behavior just because it brings sympathy and comfort. You can still have empathy and comfort when you succeed, but the outcome will be different. How do you help yourself practice new and different behavior—even if it is something as simple as recognizing a flag and making a choice—over and over again?

32.7   Self-Discipline and Discipling the Self through Change

Most people use self-discipline to help them achieve their goals. It is the process of deciding the new behavior and then training yourself to perform that behavior over and over again, whether it is not eating chocolates or eating more vegetables. How do you develop self-discipline? How did most of us?

Generally speaking, self-discipline starts at home with discipline by parents. It is what parents help children learn as early as children begin to learn language. The process goes something like this:

"'Tove, mommy?" As the little one points up at the stove.

"Yes-honey-that's-a-stove-no-don't-touch-it-you-might-get-burned." And the mommy turns back to her work, assured that her child has not reached up to touch a hot stove. All goes well, and then a few minutes later:

"'Tove, mommy?"

"Yes-honey-that's-a-stove-no-don't-touch-it-you-might-get-burned." This time mommy sounds a little harried. It's obvious that her little darling is learning a new word, but this is a time when learning by experience is not something to foster. She goes back to the task at hand.

By now, it's a litany. "'Tove, mommy? Mommy? 'Tove?" Mommy's had it. "Yes-honey-that's-a-stove-no-don't-touch-it-you-might-get-burned." She's tired, worn out, and about the umpteenth time that precious little darling says "'Tove, Mommy?", she loses her ability to separate how she feels (completely worn out and frustrated) from the fact (all that precious darling is doing is learning what a stove is) and whacks the child on the behind.

"Yes, that's a stove! Now stay away from it!!" she shrieks. And the child, stunned by this reaction, squalls and runs, confused by the sudden change from acceptance to rejection. This is the beginning (however you rewrite it) of self-discipline. Early childhood methods of helping children learn self-discipline focus on "yes–no–whack," although "whack" may have changed over time. It becomes very apparent to children early on that "no" and "whack" are more powerful and important—they mean separation from what is desirable.

"Yes–no–whack" carries over into school years, when parents and teachers try to get children to exhibit socially acceptable and desirable behavior, ranging from doing assignments to playing nicely with others. In every generation, the methods change according to cultural dictates, even though the principles are the same. There are four basic methods parents and educators alike use to help kids do what is right: punishment, monitoring, restriction, and restraint. Exaggerating a bit for the sake of illustration, let's explore how that might look. Imagine that fourth-grade school teacher you had—the one who looked perpetually unhappy. She wore the same style suit every day, only each day it was a different dark, modest color.

"James, I can see you. I have eyes in the back of my head, and if I catch you doing that again, you will write 500 sentences. Is that clear?" And she would imperiously continue screeching the chalk across the blackboard in that neat, precise cursive writing. That's punishment, all right.

"Young man, you know perfectly well that you may not shoot spit wads in class. I'll be watching you for the next 10 years [that's the exaggeration part!], and you'd better not get caught again." Well, they really couldn't monitor that long, but it sure seemed like it. Those baleful old lady eyes seemed to be everywhere.

Chris got the restraint threat if he didn't adjust his behavior to conform. "Christopher! You have gotten up out of your seat for the last time. If I catch you up again without permission, I will glue you to your seat. Is that clear?"

Later, it's "Margaret, it is not all right for you to chew gum. I'll give you one more chance—and if I should catch you chewing gum again, you will not go out for play period for the rest of the week. You will be restricted to this classroom." That settled it—restriction was too tough an option. No more chewing gum; who cared about getting glued to the seat, it was the potential loss of time outside and having to think one more minute about that teacher that was the real threat! It was easier to comply, to blend in through obedience.

It does not matter if these threats are all bogus, what matters is that they are stereotypic illustrations of how everyone begins to learn how to generate the kind of behavior that is supposed to help us get ahead in life.

Now come forward in time. How do you talk to yourself when you go off of a diet? When you spend money you meant to invest in retirement? What do you say to yourself when you do something that disrupts a relationship? Which set of phrases do you use when you find yourself having lost your keys, job, or temper? Are the words and tone of voice you use nice? Chances are, they are a lot like what you think would come out of that grouchy teacher's mouth (if not worse). "I can't believe how stupid I am! I'll never drop that 10 pounds. I must just want to be a fat pig." Or maybe it's "I deserved it. I've never been anything except a failure, and I shouldn't expect myself to do any better."

How do these ways of thinking and acting toward yourself help you when you face change? They don't. When you are abusive in this way to yourself or others, the feelings that you evoke in reaction to your perceived failure are not good. They require a certain degree of resolution, which comes through receiving sympathy, pity, attention, and comfort. They are a form of self-hatred.

Sound familiar? There you are—or your client population, your staff, volunteers, or board—again, caught up in trying to get relief from the pain of events that have occurred, or events that need to occur, working to be effective initiators of change. You may also be the target of the change or the change agent, depending on the situation. Maybe overwhelmed and overloaded, your first-line response may be "Why? We don't need to change. We've always done it this way, and it's worked fine. We don't need to change a thing." In this response, change is seen as a problem. There is no invitation to understand the reasoning behind the change, and there is certainly a focus on fight *and* flight.

The alternative is to reframe how we can deal with ourselves around self-discipline. The root word for discipline is the same as the root word for disciple, *discipulus*. This Latin word encompasses meanings of teaching, following, and being a pupil, according to Webster's New Collegiate Dictionary. Most often, the process of "discipleship" is used in the context of religion, spirituality, or politics. The most familiar examples are in the Islamic, Christian, Jewish, Buddhist, and Hindu spiritual traditions; one can also look to political traditions such as fascism and communism. In all cases, there are four common steps that apply:

1. Recognizing the "teacher"
2. Choosing consciously to follow

3. Progressive learning of the new
4. Being taught and learning through acceptance rather than condemnation and punitive process (judgment)

How can you follow someone or something you haven't recognized? In all cases in which discipleship is a process, recognition of that person identified as the "teacher of the faith" is key. A conscious choice to follow is also a key: after all, you would want to know you chose to follow unless you are comfortable not knowing how you end up somewhere! Third, progressive change is crucial. After all, turning away from one way of being and toward another requires unlearning and relearning as well as practice. Seldom do people make a choice and get the new behavior right the first time and every time afterward. Only robots can do that, and even then, their programmers must test the program and tinker with it now and then.

Finally, the fourth step is being taught and learning through acceptance instead of through condemnation and punitive processes. In the Christian tradition, Peter was a professional fisherman who became a disciple of Jesus. It is written that in the Garden of Gethsemane, when Jesus was praying and the disciples were sleeping, the servants and soldiers came to arrest Jesus. Peter is alleged to have drawn his sword and cut off the servant Malchus's ear. In this tradition, Jesus could have turned to Peter and declared him unfit for discipleship and about to become a pile of ashes. Jesus could have condemned Peter to a life of fishing and punished him any way he saw fit. What Jesus did instead, according to the story, was put Malchus's ear back on and remind Peter that while he, Jesus, could call down a legion of angels to handle the situation, it was simply what was next on his journey. He accepted Peter instead of condemning him.

Even so, Peter stumbled significantly after this. According to the story, he denied Jesus three times, swore by the fire, doubted his choice to follow, and ended up going back to his previous occupation. The new behavior was not "cemented" well enough in Peter's life to be his new habit.

Few children are born able to walk. They go through a process of neurological and physical development, and in their efforts to walk, they stumble and fall. Do their parents criticize and condemn them for mistakes and stumbles? Generally not. But how do we as adults deal with ourselves and others as we try to change our own behavior or guide others through changing their behavior?

To reframe self-discipline away from the traditional potentially abusive notions most of us grew up with to a frame that focuses on learning and development offers a degree of graciousness that we all need. It makes it easier to consider how everyone involved with the NPO may be affected by change and changes.

Combining the three models presented—separating fact from feelings, redirecting effort from the benefits of failure to the benefits of success, and addressing self-discipline as a process of discipling—offers the NPO a comprehensive framework for planning and initiating change. When taught to persons who receive services, and supported in the agency's relationship with them, it makes service delivery easier. (See Exhibit 32.3.)

32.8   *Change and the NPO*

This chapter has been presented as a personal imperative on coping with change. Truthfully, it does not matter what your position in the organization is if you become an advocate of effective change management: you still have to do it for yourself. What does matter is the frame of reference you use with change as it relates to others. Think now about the services you offer. Are the people you serve coming to you because of change in their lives?

EXHIBIT 32.3 The Stages of Self-Discipline

Self-Discipline → Self-Discipling		
Root word for "disciple" is Latin "discipulus," which means to follow		
Learning Self-Discipline in Early Childhood	**Self-Discipline from School Years through Adulthood**	**Discipling the Self as Conscious Practice**

• Safety-focused
• Yes–no–whack!
	• Socialization-focused
	• Four primary methods:
	  1. Punishment
	  2. Monitoring
	  3. Restriction
	  4. Restraint
	• Often abusive in application as a form of self-hatred
		• Personal growth and development focus
		• Four steps:
		  1. Recognizing teacher
		  2. Choosing to follow
		  3. Progressive change
		  4. Learning through acceptance instead of judgment

May be appropriate for children learning language and personal safety; can become abusive if it is the only method known or used	Inappropriate in adulthood if pursuing "success" unless success includes self-hatred as operational condition	Appropriate in adulthood, has positive and negative spiritual, sports, and political examples

If so, and the answer is almost certainly "yes," can you see how these models apply to them? They have the same experience you do—and how you respond enables them in continuing in either failure- or success-oriented behavior. Does it alter how you view them? They may not be the inappropriately angry people they have looked like; they may be dealing with a normal reaction to change, one that staff need to be able to handle, even perhaps educating about these models a bit at a time. Can you understand why they may have become passive, quiet recipients of service? The politics of caring can cause a service receiver to become what the prevailing culture defines as a "good client" to increase the risk of continued services: quiet, compliant, and passive.

How about volunteers and staff? What model of caring is in operation? Does the agency subtly require people who are "victims" instead of "people who have been victimized," or does it have people who are okay who need to help people who are not okay? What is rewarded and reinforced by staff and volunteers? Would it help if they too understood and applied these models in their own lives?

Where do the board and donors stand relative to change and the organization? Are you supported in making the changes required by the times as you forge ahead in your work? When organizational change occurs, do you have a model for helping people cope, and for planning and implementing effective change? Effective organizational change requires understanding these very personal models first. It requires incorporating that understanding into action plans that focus on communication, schedule, strategy process, outcomes, and impact.

Resources

Elizabeth Power, M.Ed., *http://www.epower-assoc.com*

33 Employment-Related Benefits

SALLY A. ZINNO
National Arts Stabilization

33.1 Overview of Employment-Related Benefits

A universal goal for self-renewing organizations (SROs) is attracting and keeping skilled and motivated staff members. In order to achieve that goal, the organization has to provide its employees with a work environment, motivators, and compensation that encourage job satisfaction. A carefully designed employee benefits program is a key contributor to a strong compensation package and a work environment that supports productivity.

Employees and potential employees have become much more aware of their total compensation, including employer-paid benefits as well as salary and wages. Before making the decision to accept a position, candidates now want to know what benefits are offered. In order to recruit and maintain quality staff, nonprofit organizations (NPOs) have to provide a package of benefits that allows them to compete with businesses and the larger nonprofits, such as hospitals and universities, which offer benefit packages that are more competitive with the business community.

The new technology-based economy creates additional pressure for NPOs. They compete for young employees who were much less concerned about employee benefits in the past and now seek stock option benefit packages. At the same time, employees are struggling to balance family and work life issues. Employers now have a workforce that includes a growing number of families with two working parents, single-parent families, and employees caring for elderly relatives. Dealing with personal and family issues can affect employee productivity. As a result, the most significant changes in employee benefits plans today are not coming from revisions in the laws, but from responses to these changes in the workforce needs.

NPOs have been known as family-friendly workplaces because traditionally many offered a more flexible work environment than for-profit businesses. In order to maintain that competitive edge, NPOs must review and update their employee benefits plans and work life policies continually to ensure that they meet both the needs of their employees and potential employees.

(A)   OBJECTIVES OF COMPENSATION SYSTEMS

The primary objective of a compensation system is to attract and retain employees who meet the organization's needs and help it to achieve its mission. The total compensation package consists of the salaries and wages and the employee benefits, which are the services or benefits purchased or provided by the employer for the employee. These include mandated coverage, such as the employer contribution to Social Security benefits, and voluntary programs, including medical insurance, group life insurance, disability coverage, and a retirement plan, as well as paid leave time including holidays, personal and sick days, and vacation.

The organization needs to offer a benefits package that is competitive with external organizations and meets internal needs. Meeting these objectives requires an awareness of two types of equity:

1. *External equity,* a condition existing when the compensation is competitive with those of similar organizations
2. *Internal equity,* wherein individuals feel that differences in compensation within an organization are justified by differences in job requirements, length of service, or both

The NPO manager must address both types of equity while coping with numerous constraints, including:

- The organization's financial resources
- The internal labor market (including present and proposed positions, their relationships, and the existence of unions)
- The external labor market (particularly the number and compensation patterns of competitors for employees)
- Employment-related laws, for example, the Fair Labor Standards Act, the 1964 Civil Rights Act, and relevant state laws
- The requirements of the Internal Revenue Code and Regulations (the IRS Code)

As employers balance both concerns for equity and constraints, their ultimate goal is to design a benefits program that is simple and clear and, as a result, easy to administer and explain.

(B)   FINANCIAL CONSIDERATIONS

The cost of employee benefits packages has been among the fastest-rising portions of employers' budgets in recent years. Employers are balancing the growing mix of compensation options, the changing needs of an increasingly diverse workforce, and management requirements to contain costs.

EXHIBIT 33.1 Benefits Budget

Total annual salary costs for the organization	$1,000,000
Benefits target at 25% of annual salary costs	$250,000

(i) *The Benefits Budget*

In order to design a package that meets these competing demands, the governing board has to determine a target dollar amount for benefits expenses as a percentage of the total salary cost. For example, an organization may determine that an amount equal to 25 percent of the total annual payroll cost will be allocated to pay for all employee benefits. This target figure is used by the manager responsible for selecting the benefits and the providers. (See Exhibit 33.1.)

In this example, the 25 percent figure is an average. It does not mean necessarily that each employee will receive 25 percent of his or her salary in benefits. The level of the employee's salary, the eligibility requirements, the options the employee selects, and other factors will make the percentage vary for each individual. (See Exhibit 33.2.)

Management will need to consider three cost elements in calculating how much it has to spend on benefits:

1. *Costs of benefits mandated by law.* These include Social Security and Medicare, generally listed as Federal Insurance Contribution Act (FICA) deductions; workers' compensation; and unemployment. Individual states may also have mandated programs such as temporary disability insurance.
2. *Costs of discretionary benefits paid directly by the employer.* These may include coverage such as health, life, and disability insurance and the employer's pension plan contribution.
3. *Employees' payment toward benefits.* Some employers may ask employees to contribute an amount for the cost of benefits. Most often, employees contribute toward medical or dental insurance, although some employers' insurance plans allow the employees to pay directly for increased coverage beyond what the employer provides.

EXHIBIT 33.2 Comparison of Benefit Costs for Two Employees

Example using hypothetical costs:		
	Employee A	**Employee B**
Basic annual salary	$20,000	$50,000
Mandatory benefits		
Social Security and Medicare @ 7.65%	1,530	3,825
Unemployment insurance, workers' compensation @ 3.35%	670	1,675
Other employer-paid benefits:		
Individual health and life insurance, pension	4,100	6,050
Total benefits and salary	$26,300	$61,550
Benefits as % of salary	31%	23%

The costs for most benefits that are mandated by law are fixed. The employer has to pay the amount specified by the federal government for Social Security and Medicare, and the state for unemployment. Insurance companies provide state-defined insurance coverage for workers' compensation, with costs that vary depending on a number of factors. Workers' compensation programs are managing costs by increasing control of the process and by monitoring those who receive compensation payments.

The employer can take actions to control the cost of discretionary benefits and the employees' contribution. Normally, benefits insurance carriers review and, if necessary, revise prices once each year on the policy anniversary date.

(ii) How Can the Employer Offer the Best Package for the Dollars Available?

The cost for insurance-related benefits is lowest if the organization has an employee base large enough to spread out the risks. Large NPOs go to insurers directly to get competitive bids on their packages.

Many NPOs that seek insurance on their own may be too small to qualify for rate discounts. As a result, organizations have begun to collaborate in order to achieve the benefits of large-group rates. For example, the Greater Philadelphia Cultural Alliance and the American Association of Museums offer their member organizations benefits options with lower negotiated rates than many members could get on their own. State collaboratives such as the independent associations in 40 states that are members of the National Council of Nonprofit Associations or the local Chambers of Commerce do the same for their members. Such organizations also make it possible for NPOs to offer their employees additional types of benefits that are not usually available to companies that have few employees. Employers need to seek out such collaboratives among their peer organizations as they create or revise benefits packages.

Some NPOs work with insurance brokers or insurance consultants who assist them with technical advice. The insurance professionals will also seek the best price through market competition by asking several companies to bid on the organization's insurance package. Usually, the competitive process results in lower costs. Brokers can also assist the organization with claims and policy-related issues. The insurance brokers are paid a fee by the insurance company. The fee is most often a small percentage of the insurance premium.

(C) KEY QUESTIONS IN DEVELOPING AND MANAGING THE BENEFITS PROGRAM

Defining and maintaining an effective benefits program is an ongoing process. The employer must develop strategies to respond to a constantly changing environment and a number of issues:

- *Benefits design*—developing packages that meet both the employees' and the employer's needs, particularly in view of changing family patterns and resource constraints
- *Benefits communication*—involving employees in the process of assessing their needs, letting them know the details of their compensation, and enlisting their aid in managing costs
- *Government requirements*—complying with frequently changing state and federal laws
- *Group size*—finding insurance companies that will provide coverage to organizations with a small number of employees

- *Rising costs*—developing procedures and identifying options to deal with the continuing increase in benefits costs; for example, exploring medical insurance cost savings using higher deductibles and second opinions before costly procedures are done

An organization regularly has to answer some key questions about needs, options, and constraints whether it is developing a benefits program for the first time or is involved in the continuous process of self-renewal.

(i)   *What Benefit Options Are Available?*

The benefits package consists of the coverage mandated by federal and state law, and an ever-growing list of discretionary benefits.

The mandated benefits include:

- Social Security retirement and disability payments for those who meet the guidelines [see Section 33.2(a)]
- Medicare insurance coverage for the elderly and disabled [see Section 33.2(a)]
- Unemployment benefits [see Section 33.2(a)]
- Workers' compensation, required by the states, which provides payments to employees who are unable to work because of a job-related illness or injury
- Programs mandated by the individual states, such as temporary disability insurance
- Leave time mandated by the Family Medical Leave Act [see Section 33.2(f)] for covered employees

The employer has a wide range of discretionary benefits available. As a general rule, the employer is not required to provide these benefits; however, the employer must make a selection based on criteria that meet the employees' needs, the organization's values, the employer's constraints, and community norms. Some of the more popular options available include:

- *Accidental death and dismemberment insurance coverage* offers additional payments for accidental death or the loss of a limb, sight, or hearing due to injury. It is often added to the life insurance policy.
- *Employee assistance* provides counseling to employees for serious job-related or personal problems that are interfering with their work performance. Programs offer referrals for a range of other issues, including substance abuse, finances, and family difficulties. This does not duplicate services covered by medical insurance.
- *Life insurance* is usually based on the employee's salary level. Under the IRS Code, any premium payment for life insurance coverage in excess of $50,000 is considered income to the employee and is taxable. Some plans enable the employees to purchase additional life insurance at a favorable rate.
- *Long-term care insurance* covers some of the costs related to care in nursing homes or similar institutions.
- *Long-term disability insurance* provides partial replacement of income during a period of total disability when the employee is unable to work (usually after a defined waiting period).
- *Medical and dental insurance* for the employees and, if the employee chooses, for their eligible dependents. Employers have to explore a variety of insurance coverage packages, managed care options, and employee copayment alterna-

tives so that they can offer their employees the widest choice for the lowest cost. Plans usually allow the employer to purchase additional coverage for services such as vision services and prescription drugs.

- *Medical/dental and child care/dependent care accounts* allow the employee to pay for certain medical and dental expenses not covered by their insurance plans, and child care or dependent care expenses with funds that are not taxed. Employees state once per year how much of their expected earnings, up to a defined limit, they want placed in these accounts. If these funds are not used during the year, they revert back to the plan and may be used to pay the plan fees.

- *Paid leave time benefits* include sick leave, vacation, paid holidays, family leave to care for a new or adopted child or a sick family member, personal leave (the employee does not need to specify the reason), sabbatical, and professional development leave. Employees may also be concerned about the amount of unused leave time that they can accumulate from year to year. Often, the employer allows the employee to accumulate up to a defined amount of unused vacation and/or sick leave. Sick leave often is allowed to accumulate until it reaches the number of days required in the waiting period for short- or long-term disability insurance. Some employeers allow employees to convert a portion of their unused leave time into additional paid salary.

- *Retirement plans* provide income after an employee retires. Defined benefit plans provide an annual pension usually based on years of service and salary level. Defined contribution plans generally offer a lump-sum payment based on the employer's contributions and a matching employee's contribution. The employeer's contribution is typically a percentage of the eligible employee's annual salary.

- *Short-term disability insurance* provides partial replacement of income during a period of total disability when the employee is unable to work (usually after sick leave is exhausted and before a long-term disability plan takes over).

- *A 401(k) plan* is a defined contribution retirement plan that enables employees to choose between receiving current compensation and making pretax contributions to an account through a salary reduction agreement. Employers may also make contributions to the employees' accounts.

- *A 403(b) tax-deferred annuity plan* is designed specifically for employees of NPOs. Current regulations allow the employees generally to save up to 25 percent of their annual salary up to $10,500 (indexed for the year 2000) per year exempt from federal income tax. Funds are taxed only when they are withdrawn, usually after retirement. Penalties apply if funds are withdrawn before retirement.

- *Transportation benefits plans* enable employers, who offer plans that qualify under IRS provisions, to exclude from the employee's gross income the dollar value of the benefits up to an amount specified by the IRS. Covered costs include parking, mass transit passes, and automobile and van service.

- *Travel accident insurance* covers employees when they are traveling on business.

- *Tuition assistance plans* reimburse employees for some portion of the cost of courses they take in accredited programs. This benefit may be taxable to the employee.

Employees are often able to balance family needs and work needs more easily if the employer offers benefits that cost nothing but provide flexibility. Flex time lets employees adjust their work schedule to meet personal needs while allowing the employer to achieve its goals. Job sharing has two or more individuals do one job on a regular schedule.

NPOs also have a unique opportunity to enhance their employee benefits package with low- or- no-cost options that relate to the services they provide. For example, institutions offering classes can let employees and their families take, at no cost, the classes that are not filled. Membership organizations like museums can provide each employee with a family membership. Day care centers can offer reduced rates to employees. Available seats for events or performances can be offered to employees as well.

Unique benefits such as these enhance the NPO's ability to recruit and retain skilled employees, to make employees more productive, and to compete with other organizations.

(ii) What Do the Employees Want?

The typical benefits package was developed for a stereotypical family structure that no longer represents the majority of households. Although the *Year 2000 Value of Benefits Survey* showed that the benefits employees rank as most important are health care coverage and retirement plans, an employer cannot hope to know what employees value and what motivates them without asking the employees themselves. Employee input into the creation and restructuring of a benefits plan can be solicited in several ways:

- Written survey of employees
- Focus groups in which representative employees are asked to define their needs and to react to options
- Employee participation on an advisory committee that assists management as they consider benefit options

(iii) How Can the Needs of the Employer and the Employee Be Met at the Same Time?

Answering these questions requires a balancing act. For some, the solution is to provide a flexible plan wherein everyone receives some core benefits such as individual health insurance and has some choice about the others. For others, the best approach is to increase salaries enough to offset higher taxes and let employees make their own purchases. For still others, the preferred approach is to offer a set package and give employees the right to refuse all or some of the items they do not need or want. In all cases, the package that works for an organization is one that considers its unique history and is tailored to the values of the employer and the lifestyle of the employees.

(D) COMMUNICATING WITH EMPLOYEES ABOUT THEIR BENEFITS

Often, the success of a benefits program depends on how effectively the organization explains the package to the employees. Benefits descriptions can be vague, and the procedures required in order to receive benefits can be complex. The employer has the responsibility to set up a system that both delivers the benefits and provides information in a clear and timely manner. Four communications tools can assist the employer in carrying out these responsibilities:

- A key person who acts as the source of information for the employees and a communications link to the benefits provider. This person should be able to answer questions or know who can.

- Summary plan descriptions are the descriptions of the benefit plans that the employer is required to provide for employees. The employer must ensure that each employee is given an up-to-date description of each benefit program.
- Benefits update meetings should be held before any new benefit is introduced and periodically thereafter. A key time to schedule the meeting is during an "open enrollment" period prior to the start of a new benefit year. The meetings allow employees to ask questions and comment on the services provided. Presentations need to be made by individuals who know the plans and procedures thoroughly. The employer could ask representatives of the insurance carriers or brokers to make presentations.
- A personal statement of compensation and benefits, distributed annually, lists the total value of benefits and compensation the employee receives and the actual cost of the benefit to the employer. The statement serves both to summarize the major benefits the employee receives and to share what it actually costs the employer to provide the benefits. Regulations require that this information be provided annually for retirement plans, but it is an advantage to the employer and the employee to include all benefits, as shown in Exhibit 33.3. Some statements include the cost of leave time allowed as well as other benefits.

EXHIBIT 33.3 Sample Personal Statement of Compensation and Benefits

Dear (employee name):

This confidential report has been prepared to acquaint you with the total compensation including benefits which you receive from your employer. Total value of the compensation package including leave time is 45% above your base salary. The level of benefits the organization provides represents our strong commitment to you and to all of our employees.

This report is issued annually with the aim of keeping you informed about the nature and value of your benefits. Where estimates were required, certain necessary assumptions were made based on the information available. We urge you to review it carefully and keep it as a guide for your personal planning.

	Benefit Level	Annual Cost
Salary	$30,000	$30,000
Life insurance	Two times annual salary, $60,000	200
Long-term disability	$1,500 per month after 6 months total disability	2,000
Medical insurance	Individual coverage fully paid by employer	3,500
Dental insurance	Individual coverage, employer pays 50%	300
Social Security and Medicare	7.65% of annual salary	2,300
Pension	5% of annual salary	1,500
Workers' compensation	Benefit level defined by a formula if you are disabled due to a work-related accident or illness	200
Total cost for your compensation and benefits		$40,000
In addition, your annual leave time including vacation, holiday, and sick leave, if taken, costs		$3,500
Total including leave time		$43,500

33.2   *Compensation- and Benefits-Related Laws*

The framework for compensation in this country was provided in the 1930s by the Social Security Act and the Fair Labor Standards Act, both of which have been amended several times. The landmark benefits-related law remains the Employee Retirement Income Security Act of 1974 (ERISA), which established the basic requirements for tax-qualified pension plans. In recent years, Congress has accelerated the pace of benefits-related legislation as it responds to issues related to taxation and retirement plans and the changing workforce.

(A)   SOCIAL SECURITY ACT

(i)   *Overview*
The country's most comprehensive piece of social legislation, the Social Security Act created the social security program, the federal–state unemployment insurance system, and various other governmental programs. The social insurance portions are funded through payroll taxes.

(ii)   *Major Provisions*
The following comments concern only the programs funded through payroll taxes:

- Employees are exempt from overtime pay obligations if their job meets the requirements for an exempt position. First, they must hold bona fide executive, administrative, or professional positions or work as outside sales representatives. Second, the exempt-level work must be paid on a salaried basis, which is defined as the same amount of pay per pay period regardless of the quality or quantity of work performed.
- Retirement benefits (income and Medicare coverage) are funded through provisions of the Federal Insurance Contribution Act (FICA), with each employer and employee paying the same percentage of the salary or wages received.
- Unemployment benefits are funded through a payroll tax paid by the employer. Some states also require that the employee contribute. Because the unemployment program is managed on a state level, amounts and duration of payments vary.

Details on program eligibility, rates, and benefits are too numerous for this chapter.

(iii)   *Implications for Nonprofit Organizations*
- Payroll tax amounts must be withheld from employees' wages, supplemented by the employer's share, and deposited in the appropriate account in a timely fashion. Failure to do so results in penalties.
- Employees must be given an accounting of the amount withheld for their FICA share. This must be done on the annual W-2 form given to employees for income tax purposes.
- NPOs generally may choose, once a year, whether to pay the unemployment amount (1) as a flat tax on a defined amount of each person's wages or (2) as a dollar-for-dollar reimbursement of amounts paid to former employees collecting benefits. An employer with high turnover would choose the former; an employer with little or no anticipated turnover would choose the latter.

- Another reality is that the program's old-age benefits were never intended to provide an adequate income for retirement. Thus, as NPOs (and their employees) mature, the importance of having some type of pension plan increases.

(B) FAIR LABOR STANDARDS ACT (FLSA)

(i) *Overview*

The FLSA established the minimum wage, maximum work hours, child labor standards, and overtime pay requirements.

(ii) *Major Provisions*

- Employees are exempt from overtime pay requirements if they hold bona fide administrative, managerial, or professional positions or if they work as outside sales representatives. Nonexempt employees must be paid at 1.5 times their normal hourly rate when they work more than 40 hours in a given workweek.
- Employees must be paid the federal minimum wage unless the state minimum wage is higher, in which case the latter applies. A student or "learner" wage may also be paid in some circumstances, after the employer has received the appropriate certificate from the Department of Labor.
- Children between the ages of 14 and 16 may be employed if the work is other than mining or manufacturing (which are not areas known for NPOs) and if the work does not interfere with their education, health, or well-being. Many states have their own child labor laws. An NPO employing children needs to review both the state and federal laws and adopt the provisions that offer the greatest amount of protection for their employees.
- Independent contractors are exempt from FLSA provisions.

(iii) *Implications for Nonprofit Organizations*

- State and local governments have the option of granting nonexempt workers compensatory time instead of paying overtime. Private employers do not have a similar right. Also, the government views the workweek as the unit of measurement: Overtime is earned for each week separately. It is not legal to average a 30-hour week and a 50-hour week, declare them two 40-hour weeks, and thereby avoid paying overtime.
- To support decisions about overtime pay, employers must keep sufficiently accurate records of time worked. If these records are incomplete or missing, the employee's memory may be deemed sufficient to win a claim.
- The label of "independent contractor" or "consultant" cannot be used to avoid compliance with FICA and FLSA. Among the factors examined are the contractor's economic ties to the employer and the permanency of the relationship. In recent years, the Internal Revenue Service has looked much more closely at the use of such arrangements in the nonprofit sector. They apply a 20-factor test to the situation. The IRS looks at the contractors' ability to perform work according to their own methods without being subject to the control of the employer except for the results.
- The nonprofit sector is not exempt from scrutiny for FLSA violations. In the past few years, libraries have been prosecuted for child labor violations (too

many hours), and even the Salvation Army has been accused of violating the minimum wage provisions.

(C) EMPLOYEE RETIREMENT INCOME SECURITY ACT (ERISA)

(i) Overview

ERISA is the major law governing the establishment, operation, and administration of employee benefit plans, specifically those concerning pensions and welfare (including health care, vacation benefits, dependent care, prepaid legal services, and educational assistance). It also covers the requirements for informing employees of their benefits and rights.

(ii) Major Provisions

ERISA is a lengthy, highly complex piece of legislation. It does not require that any employer offer a pension or welfare benefit plan. Should an employer choose to offer a plan, however, that plan is subject to ERISA. In general:

- The act covers requirements for reporting and disclosure, participation, vesting (the right to receive a benefit), funding, and fiduciary standards. It also covers tax provisions, presented as amendments to the Internal Revenue Code.
- ERISA is enforced by the Treasury Department (for participation, vesting, and funding matters) and the Labor Department (for reporting, disclosure, and fiduciary matters).

(iii) Implications for Nonprofit Organizations

- Pension and welfare plans cannot be established or operated for the exclusive or disproportionate benefit of highly compensated or "key" employees. (The complexity of the nondiscrimination rules precludes their presentation here.)
- Employers must give employees understandable information about their plans and benefits.
- Employers must file annual IRS reports on forms from the 5500 series.

(D) CONSOLIDATED OMNIBUS BUDGET RECONCILIATION ACT (COBRA)

(i) Overview

Essentially, this act, referred to as COBRA, amended ERISA and the IRS Code to require that employees and their dependents (current and former) be allowed to continue group health insurance coverage after certain qualifying events occur by reimbursing the employer for the amount of the coverage plus an additional 2 percent as an administrative fee.

(ii) Major Provisions

- An employee who leaves or loses a job (for reasons other than gross misconduct) may continue group health insurance for up to 18 months by electing to continue and making the payments mentioned previously. An employee whose hours are reduced to a level below that at which eligibility for coverage begins may continue the coverage in the same way. Someone

ruled disabled under the Social Security Act is eligible for 29 months of continuation after job loss or reduction of hours.
- Some dependents are eligible for 36 months of continuation if certain events occur, such as divorce or legal separation from the covered employee.

(iii) Implications for Nonprofit Organizations
- Employers must amend the summary plan descriptions of their health insurance plans to advise employees of their COBRA rights. In addition, there are several notification requirements.
- Employers with fewer than 20 employees are exempt from COBRA but may be liable under COBRA-like state laws.

(E) OTHER RECENT BENEFITS LEGISLATION

Since ERISA was passed in 1974, the pace of legislative action on compensation and benefits issues has quickened. Four major trends are discernible:

1. An increasing interest in ensuring that taxpayers will not subsidize the wealthy, evidenced in the requirements that benefit plans seeking tax breaks in turn not discriminate in favor of owners or the highly compensated
2. Changes in regulations concerning the establishment and funding of individual retirement accounts (IRAs) and pension plans for small employers
3. Expanded requirements to help ensure solvency of pension plans
4. Response to changing workplace and family needs by providing leave for the employee who cares for family members and enabling employees to maintain benefits when they change jobs

Many changes have been designed to expand coverage and benefits; all have increased the system's complexity. This section highlights the major pieces of legislation and summarizes their main features.

(i) Tax Reform Act of 1976
A worker with a nonworking spouse can set aside $2,250 a year in an IRA.

(ii) Revenue Act of 1978
The simplified employee pension (SEP) was created for small employers. It also allowed employers to establish what became known as 401(k) plans, named after their relevant section in the Internal Revenue Code.

(iii) Economic Recovery Tax Act of 1981 (ERTA)
The maximum deductible limit for an IRA was raised to $2,000, and IRAs were extended to all workers, even those covered by an employer-provided pension plan. ERTA also doubled the amount that could be contributed to an SEP or a Keogh plan.

(iv) Tax Equity and Fiscal Responsibility Act of 1982
This act restricted the maximum contribution and benefit limits for pension plans, permitted partial rollovers between IRA accounts, and limited the kinds of loans people could get from their pension plans without tax consequences. Keogh plans became subject to the same minimum age and service requirements as other pension plans.

(v) Deficit Reduction Act of 1984

Intended to close tax loopholes, this act limited flexible benefit plans ("cafeteria" plans). The only benefits that could be included in a cafeteria plan without tax consequences were those specifically excluded from gross income by the Internal Revenue Code. These included health care benefits, group term life insurance, prepaid group legal services, dependent care, and educational reimbursement.

(vi) Retirement Equity Act of 1984

Designed to improve women's pension opportunities, this act lowered the age at which an employee must be allowed to participate in a pension plan and lengthened the acceptable "break in service," the period during which one may leave work without losing pension credits. The law also specified that a worker could not waive survivor benefits or designate a nonspouse beneficiary without the spouse's written consent. (The intention here was to constrain a worker from choosing higher benefits during his or her own lifetime in exchange for coverage as long as either spouse survived.) It also added provisions allowing pension benefits to be paid to a former spouse in certain circumstances in connection with a divorce.

(vii) Tax Reform Act of 1986 (TRA 86)

TRA 86 shortened vesting periods (generally to five years); restricted the ability of workers covered by an employer-sponsored pension to make tax-deductible contributions to an IRA; dropped the annual employee deferral in a 401(k) to $7,000 (indexed to $10,500 as of 2000); allowed small employers to defer part of a salary to an SEP; imposed a 10 percent penalty on funds withdrawn from an IRA before a person reaches age $59\frac{1}{2}$; and increased nondiscrimination rules.

(viii) Omnibus Budget Reconciliation Act of 1986

The Age Discrimination in Employment Act was amended to require employers to continue pension benefit accruals for workers over 65.

(ix) Omnibus Budget Reconciliation Act of 1987

Pension contributions for employers having defined benefit plans were increased, and restrictions on pension plan terminations were tightened.

(x) Unemployment Compensation Amendments of 1992

These amendments modified the rules relating to withholding from pension distributions and tax-free rollovers. For distributions made on or after January 1, 1993, any part of a taxable distribution from a tax-qualified plan or tax-sheltered annuity (other than one requiring minimum distribution) can be rolled over tax free to an IRA or other eligible retirement plan, unless the distribution is one of a series of substantially equal installments made over the participant's (or the participant and his or her beneficiary's) life expectancy or over a period of 10 years or more. An "eligible rollover distribution" that is not transferred directly to an IRA or other eligible retirement plan is subject to 20 percent withholding.

(xi) Retirement Protection Act of 1994

This act changed the rules relating to funding of defined benefit pension plans in an effort to ensure adequate funding of pension benefits.

(xii) Health Insurance Portability and Accountability Act of 1996

This act amended ERISA, the Public Health Act, and the Internal Revenue Code to improve the portability and continuity of health care coverage. The law limits the circumstances under which health insurance coverage may be excluded for medical conditions present before an individual is enrolled in a health plan. It also provides credit for prior health coverage and entitles the individual to a certificate that shows evidence of prior health coverage. The certificate may help the individual to receive coverage without preexisting condition exclusion.

(xiii) Small Business Job Protection Act of 1996

Provisions of the act extend to NPOs the option of structuring a pension plan using a 401(k) plan. Between 1986 and 1996, only for-profit organizations could establish 401(k) plans. Employers who are choosing between a 401(k) and a 403(b) plan format need to check the provisions of each carefully before making a decision. Each has different features that could be beneficial to the employees and the employer. The employer needs to weigh the benefits and administrative requirements of each before making a decision.

(F) FAMILY AND MEDICAL LEAVE ACT (FMLA)

(i) Overview

The FMLA entitles eligible employees to take up to 12 weeks of unpaid, job-protected leave each year for specified family and medical reasons. The law, which went into effect in 1993, contains provisions relating to employer coverage; employee eligibility for the benefits; entitlement to leave, maintenance of health benefits during leave, and job restoration after leave; notice and certification of the need for FMLA leave; and protection for employees who request or take FMLA leave. The law also includes certain employer record-keeping requirements.

(ii) Major Provisions

- Unpaid leave must be granted for any of the following reasons: to care for the employee's child after childbirth or placement for adoption or foster care; to care for the employee's spouse, son or daughter, or parent who has a serious health condition; or for a serious health condition that makes the employee unable to perform the employee's job. At the employee's or employer's option, certain kinds of paid leave may be substituted for unpaid leave.
- Upon return from FMLA leave, most employees must be restored to their original or equivalent positions with equivalent pay, benefits, and other employment terms.
- The law applies to all public agencies and local educational agencies as well as private-sector employers who employ 50 or more employees for at least 20 workweeks in a calendar year.

(iii) Implications for Nonprofit Organizations

- Employers must amend their policies and procedures and employee handbooks to reflect the provisions of the law. In addition, the employer is required to notify employees of the provisions of the law.
- Employers with fewer than 50 employees are exempt from FMLA.

33.3   *Benefits-Related Resources*

Given the rapidly changing nature of employment-related benefits, a resource listing needs updating almost as soon as it is printed. Nonetheless, this section presents major types of resources that may be useful to NPOs.

(A)   ASSOCIATIONS AND ORGANIZATIONS

(i)   *American Association of Health Plans (AAHP)*

A national association representing prepaid health care programs (meaning health maintenance organizations [HMOs]), the AAHP provides information through publications on industry trends, regulatory trends, and legislative issues. Its library provides research help on matters concerning managed care plans. For more information, contact:

AAHP Information Services
1129 20th Street, NW
Washington, DC 20036
(202) 778-3268
http://www.aahp.org

(ii)   *American Law Institute–American Bar Association (ALI–ABA) Committee on Continuing Education*

ALI–ABA provides numerous short courses throughout the year to inform both lawyers and managers about changes and proposed changes in the laws and regulation. A number of the courses are related to NPOs and employee benefits.

ALI–ABA
4025 Chestnut Street
Philadelphia, PA 19104
(215) 243-1630
http://www.ali-aba.org

(iii)   *Association of Private Pension and Welfare Plans (APPWP)*

With members from large and small benefits consulting firms, investment firms, accounting firms, insurers, utilities, law firms, and other businesses, the APPWP is a national association that lobbies Congress on benefits issues. It also helps members deal with governmental agencies and elected officials. In addition to an annual conference, it offers members a newsletter and a report on legislation and regulation. For more information, contact:

Association of Private Pension and Welfare Plans
1212 New York Avenue, NW
Washington, DC 20005
(202) 289-6700
http://www.appwp.org/appwp/

(iv)   *Business Group on Health*

Such groups can be found variously on state and city levels. They exist to share information and sometimes to lobby. Probably the best known is the Washington Business Group on Health, which produces *Business and Health,* a monthly journal. For more information, check local information or Web-based sources.

(v) The Conference Board

One of the most widely known providers of information about employment-related issues, the Conference Board bases its reports and conferences on actual practices. Representatives of over 2,500 organizations from business, academia, and government are connected through Conference Board activities. The organization has produced reports on such issues as retiree health care, family issues, and flexible benefits. One regular publication is *Across the Board.* For more information, contact:

The Conference Board
845 Third Avenue
New York, NY 10022
(212) 759-0900
http://www.conference-board.org

(vi) Employee Benefit Research Institute (EBRI)

A "nonprofit, nonpartisan, public policy research institution," EBRI sponsors policy forums and produces research reports and other publications on benefits-related issues. Its monthly report, *EBRI Issue Briefs,* examines benefits issues and trends. Of its many publications, one is particularly noteworthy: *Fundamentals of Employee Benefit Programs,* now in its fifth edition. This is an excellent primer on the subject. For more information, contact:

Employee Benefit Research Institute
2121 K Street, NW, Suite 600
Washington, DC 20037-2121
(202) 659-0670
http://www.ebri.org

(vii) Health Insurance Association of America (HIAA)

A major trade association of commercial health and life insurers, HIAA provides information on cost-containment approaches, benefit plan designs, financing insurance, and insurers that write policies for small employers. For more information, contact:

Consumer Affairs
Health Insurance Association of America
1025 Connecticut Avenue, NW
Washington, DC 20036-3998
(202) 824-1849
http://www.hiaa.org

(viii) International Foundation of Employee Benefit Plans

Founded to foster an exchange of information about benefits, the Foundation sponsors conferences at the introductory and advanced levels; programs leading to certification as an employee benefits specialist (CEBS designation); books on such topics as cost containment and ERISA; research reports; the quarterly *Employee Benefits Journal;* and various other publications on legislation, regulations, and benefits. The Foundation also has an extensive library on benefits-related topics. For further information, contact:

International Foundation of Employee Benefit Plans
18700 West Bluemound Road, P.O. Box 69
Brookfield, WI 53008-0069

(262) 786-6700
http://www.ifebp.org

(ix) National Council of Nonprofit Associations

Association members provide a variety of services for NPOs through member associations established in 40 states. Member benefits include group rates on a variety of employee benefits plans and services. Contact information for the state associations is available from the Council.

National Council of Nonprofit Associations
1900 L. Street, NW, Suite 605
Washington, DC 20036
(202) 467-6262
http://www.ncna.org

(x) Practising Law Institute (PLI)

Among PLI's many courses and conferences are several each year concerning employee benefit plans. The materials for these sessions are published in compendia for general purchase. In the 18-title tax law and estate planning series, for example, PLI offers a two-volume set, *Employee Welfare Benefit Plans.* Because the laws and regulations change so rapidly, the PLI publications are valuable for timeliness. For more information, contact:

Practising Law Institute
810 Seventh Avenue
New York, NY 10019
(212) 824-5700
http://www.pli.edu

(xi) U.S. Chamber of Commerce

Of this organization's services, two seem particularly useful to NPOs: (1) the annual survey on employee benefits (quantity discounts available), and (2) the syndicated television show, "It's Your Business." For more information, contact:

Research Center, Economic Policy Division
U.S. Chamber of Commerce
1615 H Street, NW
Washington, DC 20062
(202) 659-6000
http://www.uschamber.com

(B) PUBLICATIONS AND PUBLISHERS

Specific topics vary with journals and issues. Following is a sampling of the available publications.

- *Benefits Quarterly*—A publication (with refereed articles) of the International Society of Employee Benefit Specialists, through the International Foundation of Employee Benefit Plans.
- *Business and Health*—A monthly publication of Health Learning Systems, in consultation with the Washington Business Group on Health.

- *Compensation & Benefits Management*— Quarterly journal of articles and columns directed to those in charge of designing or managing compensation programs.

  Panel Publishers, Inc.
  36 W. 44th Street
  New York, NY 10036

- *Compensation and Benefits Review*—Published bimonthly by the American Management Association.

  American Management Association
  1601 Broadway
  New York, NY 10019-7420

- *Employee Benefits Journal*—Published quarterly by the International Foundation of Employee Benefit Plans; free to members of the IFEPB.
- *Employee Benefits News*—A monthly publication that provides comprehensive reports on industry trends, benchmarking data, case studies, news, and commentaries.

  Employee Benefits News
  1165 Northcase Parkway, NE
  Marietta, GA 30067
  http://www.benefitsnews.com

- *Employee Benefit Plan Review*—Monthly digest of developments concerning employee benefits; summarizes legislation, speeches, consulting firms' studies, court cases, and trends.

  Charles D. Spencer & Associates, Inc.
  222 West Adams Street
  Chicago, IL 60606

- *Pension World*—Monthly directed toward pension plan sponsors and investment managers; understandable by people other than actuaries.

  Pension World
  6255 Barfield Road
  Atlanta, GA 30328

(C)   WEB SITES

- *BenefitsLink, http://www.benefitslink.com*—Clearinghouse for information about employee benefits that includes message boards, white and yellow pages, and an extensive guide to Web resources.
- *Employee Benefits General Information, http://www.employee-benefits.com*— Comprehensive sumary of current issues and portal into benefits-related sites.
- *Employee Benefits News, http://www.benefitnews.com*—News service offers daily news updates, articles on current topics, a conference calendar, product and service information, and research links. Some portions require payment.

- *Employee Benefits Research Institute, http://www.ebri.org*—Site focuses on advancing the public's, the media's, and policy makers' knowledge and understanding of employee benefits. It includes research results and extensive links to other employee benefits–related sites.
- *Employee Benefits Software, http://www.benefitslink.com/software.shtml*—Provides a description of software and the ability to download from a collection of benefits software for employees and employers, including a 401(k) contribution calculator.
- *Employee Benefits Survey—Department of Labor Statistics, http://www.bls.gov/ebshome.htm*—Offers news, statistics, and related documents in text and pdf formats.
- *International Federation of Employment Benefit Plans, http://www.ifebp.com*—Site provides benefit information to companies and employees, including details on its programs and services, job postings, and industry news.

33.4 Benefits-Related Terminology

The glossary entries in this volume have been selected to provide a basic working vocabulary, but by no means are they the only terms with which a benefits manager would have to be familiar.

Accidental death and dismemberment insurance   Coverage is usually added onto the life insurance policy. It offers additional payments for accidental death or the loss of a limb, sight, or hearing due to injury.

Accrual   The accumulation and crediting of benefits to an employee by virtue of his or her participation in a compensation plan. Accrued benefits may be forfeited unless they are vested.

Actuarial equivalent   Amount of equal present value. An amount to be received in the future is the actuarial equivalent of another if they have the same present value, determined by using the same actuarial assumptions (such as rate of return and retirement age). See *present value.*

Age Discrimination in Employment Act (ADEA)   Prohibits discrimination in conditions or termination of employment because of age (protecting those over age 40). Mandatory retirement for employees eligible to receive pensions violates ADEA.

Annuity   A contract for the periodic payment of specified or objectively determinable amounts over a specified period or over the recipient's lifetime.

Beneficiary   The person eligible for benefits or payments upon the death of a plan participant.

Bonus   A lump-sum payment to an employee in recognition of some achievement. Because a bonus is not added to the employee's base pay, some employers use this approach to limit compensation and taxation growth as well as to recognize achievement.

Break in service   A year in which an employee is credited with no more than 500 hours of service. If an employee has such a break, he or she may lose credit for service before the break, unless he or she returns to service and works another year. A qualified maternity or paternity leave may not be counted as a break in service but may be treated as a neutral year.

Cafeteria plan   A plan in which participants can choose from among two or more options consisting either of tax-qualified benefits or of a combination of cash and tax-qualified benefits.

Cliff vesting   A schedule for vesting in which accrued benefits become nonforfeitable after a specified period of service, such as five years.

COBRA   Consolidated Omnibus Budget Reconciliation Act of 1985.

CODA   Cash or deferred tax arrangement, as a 401(k) plan.

Coinsurance   Payment by employees for part of the benefit being provided. A common approach is for a health insurer to pay 80 percent of a health service while the employee pays the remaining 20 percent.

Contributory plan   A plan to which contributions are made in part or whole by participants rather than (or in addition to) their employer.

Coordination of benefits   Procedure whereby two insurance companies share information to limit their individual liability for expenses. This may arise when spouses have insurance from different employers or when someone is covered by both Medicare and an employer-provided policy.

Coverage test   Requirement that a plan benefit a minimum number or percentage of employees, with the aim of avoiding discrimination in favor of highly compensated employees.

Deductible   Expense amount that an employee must pay before other sources (insurance company or employer) assume liability for payment. Deductibles are seen as cost-saving measures by employers and insurance companies.

Defined benefit plan   A pension plan that pays a specified benefit at retirement, often keyed to average salary over the last few years of employment and to years of service. Contributions to the plan vary according to the amount needed to provide the projected benefit. In this instance, the employer bears the risk and must set aside enough now to make the payments later.

Defined contribution plan   A pension or profit-sharing plan to which the contributions are specified amounts and the participants have a right to receive benefits contingent on the accumulated value of the total contributions. In other words, the benefits may vary according to the investment expertise of the plan's trustee; the employee, therefore, bears the risk under this plan.

Dependent care assistance programs   A plan whereby the employer helps employees with services for dependents, which the employee needs in order to earn a living. The employer may provide the needed services, pay the service provider directly, or reimburse the employee for the expenses incurred. If the employer gives the money to the employee, the funds are treated as regular compensation and the employee seeks tax relief under Internal Revenue Code Section 21, dependent care tax credit. If the employer provides or subsidizes the benefit, up to $5,000 per year may be excluded from gross income ($2,500 each, for married individuals filing separately).

Direct compensation   Pay received in the form of cash or cash equivalents (generally, wages and salaries).

Discrimination   Favoring of highly compensated employees, owners, or officers by the operation or terms of a plan.

Disqualified person   Someone who has a specified relationship to a plan, such as the fiduciary, the employer, officers, directors, and highly compensated employees.

Educational assistance program   A plan whereby an employer provides instruction for or pays educational expenses of an employee. The plan must be written and must not discriminate in favor of officers, owners, highly compensated employees, or their dependents.

Employee   One who performs services for compensation and whose working conditions are set by the employer.

Employee assistance   Provides counseling to employees for serious problems that are interfering with their work performance. Usually, services are for substance abuse; however, referrals may be provided for other problems, including financial and marital. This does not duplicate medical insurance–covered services.

Employee Retirement Income Security Act of 1974 (ERISA)   Public Law 93-403, the law that established the basic requirements for tax-qualified plans. ERISA covers pension and welfare plans, both of which must comply with provisions concerning reporting and disclosure, fiduciary responsibility, and enforcement. The former are also subject to detailed regulations concerning coverage, funding, and vesting. ERISA does not cover federal or state governmental plans for public workers, unemployment insurance, workers' compensation, church plans, excess benefit plans, or plans maintained outside the United States.

Entry date   The date on which an employee must be allowed to participate in a plan. The Internal Revenue Code requires that a tax-qualified plan admit an employee who has satisfied the age and length-of-service requirements no later than the earlier of these dates: (1) the first day of the first plan year beginning after the date on which the employee first satisfied the requirements; or (2) the date six months after the date on which the employee satisfied the requirements. Multiple dates (as many as 366 in a leap year) may be used when employers want to cover employees as soon as possible.

ERISA preemption   Explicit preemption by ERISA (in Section 514) of state laws concerning employee benefit plans, except those laws regulating insurance, banking, and securities.

Excess benefit plan   A plan that provides benefits beyond those in a tax-qualified plan and therefore is not covered by ERISA.

Executive perquisites ("perks")   Special benefits made available to top managerial employees. These are becoming more and more likely to represent taxable income to the employee receiving them.

Federal Insurance Contributions Act (FICA)   The source of social security withholding requirements.

Forfeiture   Loss of benefits caused by leaving employment before all accrued benefits have been vested.

Forward averaging   Procedure of computing tax on a lump-sum distribution whereby the tax is determined as if the money were received over a period of years. This application of Internal Revenue Code (IRC) Section 402(e) avoids combining the total distribution with the taxpayer's other income for a tax year, thereby lowering the overall effective tax rate.

401(k) plan   A defined contribution retirement plan that enables employees to choose between receiving current compensation and making pretax contributions to an account through a salary reduction agreement. Employers may also make contributions to the employees' accounts.

403(b) plan   Tax-deferred annuity retirement plan for employees of tax-exempt IRC section 501(c)(3) organizations. The same nondiscrimination rules apply here as to section 401(a) plans, including minimum participation rules. In addition, a section 403(b) plan can be considered discriminatory in terms of elective deferrals unless all employees have an opportunity to make the deferrals. (These deferrals are amounts shielded from current taxation through a salary reduction agreement.) An employee's annual deferral is generally limited to $10,500 for 2000, a limit higher than those for CODAs or SEPs.

Frozen plan   A plan in which benefit accrual has stopped but existence continues to distribute assets to participants and beneficiaries.

Graded or stepped vesting   A schedule whereby an increasing percentage of accrued benefits become vested, until 100 percent is reached. The 1986 Tax Reform Act replaced earlier forms with seven-year graded vesting: A plan must provide at least 20 percent vesting after three years, 40 percent after four, 60 percent after five, 80 percent after six, and 100 percent after seven years.

Highly compensated employee   One who, in the current or previous plan year, (1) was a 5 percent owner; (2) received more than $80,000 in compensation; and (3) was in the most highly paid 20 percent of employees of the organization when ranked on the basis of the previous year's compensation.

Hour of service   An hour for which an employee is paid or entitled to be paid for performing duties, exercising excused absences, or meriting back pay.

Indirect compensation   Pay received in the form of benefits or services.

Individual retirement account (IRA)   A trust organized and created in the United States for the exclusive benefit of an individual and his or her beneficiaries. The limit on contributions for a tax year is $2,000, except for rollover contributions. An IRA may not be invested in insurance contracts or in "collectibles" (such as stamps or rare coins) and must provide for mandatory distributions. Under Internal Revenue Code section 408(c), employers and employee associations may establish IRAs for employees. Distributions from both types are taxable in the year paid.

Integration   Reduction of pension benefits or contributions to take into account Social Security benefits to which a participant is entitled. Some pension plans are designed to yield a retiree a certain amount when combined with Social Security. In such cases, the contribution or benefits will vary according to the amount being paid into or received from Social Security.

Joint-and-survivor annuity (J&S)   Upon the participant's retirement, a J&S lasts for his or her lifetime and then provides an annuity for the lifetime of the surviving spouse.

Key employee   One who is an officer of the employer or who meets one of several ownership tests. "Key" and "highly compensated" are not synonymous.

Leased employee   Someone who is not an employee yet provides services usually provided by an employee, but does so under contract with a leasing organization and on basically a full-time basis for over a year.

Life insurance   Usually based on the employee's salary level. Under the IRS Code, any premium payment for life insurance coverage in excess of $50,000 is considered income to the employee and is taxable.

Long-term disability insurance   Provides partial replacement of income during a period of total disability when the employee is unable to work (usually after a defined waiting period).

Lump-sum distribution   Distribution of the entire balance of an employee's account within the same tax year as a triggering event (retirement, death, disability, termination of service, or reaching age 59 $1/2$).

Mandated insurance benefit   A benefit that a state requires in an insurance package or plan if the insurer is to operate within the state. The most commonly mandated benefit is mental health care within employee health plans.

Medical and dental care accounts   Allow the employee to pay for certain medical and dental expenses not covered by their insurance plans, with funds that are not taxed. Once per year the employee elects how much he or she wants placed in these accounts, up to a defined limit, Any funds that are not used during the year revert back to the plan.

Minimum accrual standards Established by ERISA's section 204, these reinforce the vesting requirements. Section 204 describes three formulas to prevent backloading, or the limiting of generous accrual until later years. Accrued benefits may not be reduced because of increased age or years of service. Also, pension plan assets or liabilities cannot be transferred, merged, or consolidated unless each participant receives benefits at least equal to those to which he or she would have been entitled before the transaction. Still, someone may transfer enough assets to meet this stipulation and then keep the rest, a phenomenon increasing in recent years.

Minimum funding standards Guidelines for the minimum amount an employer must contribute to a plan, to cover all liabilities and operating costs. A plan is underfunded when the market value of its assets is less than the present value of vested deferred benefits. Sections 301 to 306 of ERISA specify funding requirements for pension plans.

Minimum vesting standards Requirements for the points at which benefits become nonforfeitable. Benefits derived from employee contributions are fully vested immediately. Employer contributions may meet one of three standards: (1) 100 percent vesting after five years (cliff vesting), (2) seven-year graded vesting, or (3) ten-year cliff vesting under multiemployer, collectively bargained plans.

Money purchase plan A defined contribution plan.

Normal retirement age The earlier of (1) the age specified in the plan, or (2) the latest of (a) the participant's 65th birthday, (b) the fifth anniversary of plan participation, for someone who began participating within five years of the plan's stated normal retirement age, or (c) the tenth anniversary of someone's initial plan participation.

Participant Someone entitled to receive benefits under an ERISA plan. A former employee is a participant if he or she has been vested and has yet to receive all accrued benefits under a plan.

Participation Taking part, or allowing one to take part, in a plan. Generally, the maximum required waiting period is one year if the employer wants to retain tax qualification; an employer may allow employees to participate immediately. The usual minimum age requirement is 21, although tax-exempt educational institutions may use age 26.

Pension Benefit Guarantee Corporation (PBGC) An entity operated under the Department of Labor to administer pension plan insurance and termination provisions. The PBGC may terminate a plan experiencing financial difficulty; it might also assert claims against an employer filing for bankruptcy.

Pension plan A plan providing for definitely determinable retirement benefits over a period of years for participants or their beneficiaries. A tax-qualified plan must be in writing, be established by an employer, be communicated to employees, be a permanent rather than a temporary program, and exist for the exclusive benefit of covered employees and their beneficiaries.

Plan year Any 12 consecutive months specified in a plan, not necessarily the calendar year or the employer's fiscal year.

Present value Value in today's terms of money to be received in the future. Because money has a time value, a dollar today is not the same as a dollar received in a year. Present value calculations are used to translate future benefits or income to today's terms for ready comparison and to determine the amount of money one must put aside or invest to yield benefits of a certain amount in the future. Consider, for example, a sweepstakes awarding the winner $1 million to be paid at the rate of $25,000 a year for 40 years. Assuming a 6 percent inflation rate, that award is worth only $542,000 in today's dollars. Clearly, then, there is a substantial difference between a benefit promised in nominal dollars and one promised in current dollars.

Prohibited group   That group in whose favor a tax-qualified plan must not discriminate.

Prohibited transaction   One that is not allowed for a plan. For example, a plan fiduciary may not buy, sell, or exchange property or services with the plan; also, there must be an arm's-length relationship between the employer and the plan.

Prototype plan   A master plan operated by a mutual fund or financial institution and adoptable by an employer upon execution of a participation agreement. (By using such an approach, an employer does not have to create its own legally correct plan language.)

Qualified plan   A plan that meets IRS requirements and therefore receives favorable tax treatment.

Retirement Equity Act of 1984 (REA)   Noteworthy for requiring that married vested participants retiring under a plan must receive joint-and-survivor benefits (rather than having the employee exhaust all benefits and leave the surviving spouse without income) unless both participant and spouse consent in writing to a different option.

Rollover   Reinvestment in a tax-qualified plan of funds or property received from a non-required distribution of another tax-qualified plan. If done within 60 days of the distribution, the transaction is not taxed.

Short-term disability insurance   Provides partial replacement of income during a period of total disability when the employee is unable to work (usually after sick leave is exhausted and before a long-term disability plan takes over). A 401(k) plan is a defined contribution retirement plan that enables employees to choose between receiving current compensation and making pretax contributions to an account through a salary reduction agreement. Employers may also make contributions to the employees' accounts.

Simplified employee pension plan (SEP)   Essentially, an individual retirement account of annuity established by an employer, often under a model or prototype arrangement with a bank or other financial institution.

Summary plan description (SPD)   Summary of each plan that must be given to all participants and beneficiaries. It must be written in language that the average participant can understand while at the same time covering the plan's provisions. ERISA requires that the plan administrator file the SPD with the Labor Department and file an update every fifth year thereafter. (Employers adopting a prototype plan avoid this requirement because the operator of the master plan does the filing.) Among the items that must be included are the plan sponsor's name and administrative type; the name and address of the plan administrator; the requirements for eligibility, benefits, and vesting; the source of funding; the procedures for claiming benefits and redress; and the dates of the plan year. Failure to supply a participant or beneficiary with the SPD (or a summary of material modification when a major change is made) within a month of plan adoption or amendment can result in a fine of $100 a day.

Tax-deferred annuity   An investment method used to fund retirement plans of tax-exempt employers or their employees. See *403(b) plans.*

Tax Equity and Fiscal Responsibility Act of 1982 (TEFRA)   Regarded by some as the beginning of the trend toward nondiscrimination rules; this act applied nondiscrimination rules to group term life insurance plans. When an employer pays the premium for more than $50,000 in group term life insurance for an employee, the amount in excess of the premium for $50,000 of coverage is taxable income to the employee.

Top-heavy   Giving disproportionately more benefits to key employees.

Transportation benefits plans   Enable employers, who offer plans that qualify under IRS provisions, to exclude from the employee's gross income the dollar value of the benefits up to an amount specified by the IRS. Covered costs include parking, mass transit passes, and automobile and van service.

Travel accident insurance   Covers employees when they are traveling on business.

Tuition assistance plans   Reimburse employees for some portion of the cost of courses they take in accredited programs. This benefit may be taxable to the employee.

Unemployment insurance   Combined federal and state program (administered by each state) that is intended to provide financial security to jobless workers. Program is financed by an employer-paid tax on the first X dollars of each worker's pay; in a few states, a small employee contribution is required as well. Nonprofits may have the option of paying the tax (at a rate determined by employer age and experience) or of paying no tax but reimbursing the system for all unemployment benefits claimed. Such a choice can be made only once a year.

Vesting   Acquiring the right to receive benefits; reaching the point at which benefits become nonforfeitable.

Welfare benefit plan   Any plan or program to provide participants (and beneficiaries) with benefits for health care (medical, surgical, dental, hospital coverage), sickness, accidents, disability, death, unemployment, vacation, training, day care, educational assistance, or prepaid legal services.

Workers' compensation   Employer-paid insurance program regulated by each state and designed to protect employees from financial loss as a consequence of a work-related injury or illness.

Year of service   Any 12-month period during which an employee has at least 1,000 hours of service.

34 Volunteer Management

JEANNE H. BRADNER
CONSULTANT AND AUTHOR

34.1   The Self-Renewing Volunteer Program

(A)   CONSTANCY OF CHANGE

John Gardner, cofounder of Independent Sector, said "micromanagement is not the function of leaders. The task of leaders is to have a sense of where the whole system should be going and to institutionalize the problem solving that will get it there. *And the pace of change is such that they will find themselves constantly rebuilding to meet altered circumstances"* (emphasis added)[1]. To be effective, to serve the community, to take maximum advantage of volunteer time and talents, yesterday's volunteer programs must be constantly evaluated and reworked in the light of today's needs and today's volunteer force.

(B)   ASSESS AND REASSESS

The Metro Chicago Volunteer Coalition, a voluntary group of leaders of volunteer recruiting and volunteer-involving agencies, came together in 1995 to create a strategic plan for enhancing volunteerism in the Chicago metropolitan area. Through focus groups, open meetings, and surveys, the group discovered that only 42 percent of nonprofit organizations (NPOs) did assessments to make sure that the current ways volunteers were involved were still the most meaningful to the agency's mission in the community.

Many volunteer managers become so immersed in micromanagement that it is tempting just to continue doing the volunteer program the way it has always been done. They need to have opportunities to step outside the day-to-day activities to determine, with the aid of other staff, volunteers, and board, the priority areas for involving volunteers. They need to make sure that their program is meeting the needs of their customer: the community they serve.

An organization cannot be self-renewing without realizing that the volunteer program is critical to renewal and community outreach. Therefore, it is important for the volunteer manager to be part of the agency planning process and for evaluation of the program, the volunteers, and the effects of the program on the community to be performed on a regular basis.

(C)   HAVING A SUCCESSFUL PROGRAM

In 1993, The Points of Light Foundation embarked on a study to determine the factors that facilitate or inhibit the effectiveness of volunteering in nonprofit and public sector human service organizations. They found that successful organizations could differ widely in their approach, but they shared "a commitment to continuous improvement and to challenging current practice in light of changing conditions."[2] Volunteer managers need evaluations as a key to continuous improvement, and they need to be partners in the agencywide planning process to open the door and their imaginations to change and renewal.

(D)   IMPORTANCE OF VOLUNTEERS TODAY

Volunteers are too important an asset to be taken for granted. They need to be viewed as central to the agency's mission. Volunteers today are of all ages, all races, and all ethnic backgrounds, and contribute time to agencies that the Independent Sector/Gallup Survey of 1998 estimates to be the equivalent of 9 million paid staff![3]

The opportunities for involving people are manifold: senior citizens, early retirees, families, young professionals, executives, middle management, labor unions, small business, homemakers, religious institutions, college service learning and intern programs, school community service classes, service clubs, fraternal organizations, and stipended programs such as Foster Grandparents, Senior Companions, VISTA, and AmeriCorps.

Volunteers are important not only in the United States and Canada; there is growing interest and activity in volunteerism throughout the world. The International Association for Voluntary Effort that began in 1970 as a small group has now held 16 biennial world conferences, and over 100 countries participated in the most recent one.[4]

The United Nations, with the support of 123 governments from Andorra to Zimbabwe, has declared the year 2001 as the International Year of the Volunteer, and December 5 of each year has been set aside as International Volunteer Day. A world conference is set for the year 2001 in Amsterdam.[5]

In the United States, the Independent Sector/Gallup Organization survey of volunteerism in the year 1998 (published in 1999) states that 55.5 percent of those interviewed volunteered.[6] This is the highest percentage of volunteerism indicated in the six surveys that Independent Sector has conducted since 1987. This compares to 45.3 percent in 1987; 54.4 percent in 1989; 51.1 percent in 1991; 47.7 percent in 1993; and 48.8 percent in 1995.

However, in 1998 the average number of volunteer hours contributed per volunteer weekly was 3.5 hours. This is the lowest it has been. The average for the preceding five surveys was 4.2 hours a week. Independent Sector points out that "the average number of hours volunteered may have declined due to the broader participation of individuals who did not regularly volunteer." For example, 41 percent of the volunteers said they contributed time sporadically and considered it a one-time activity, and 9 percent reported volunteering only at special times of the year such as during a religious holiday.

Independent Sector assigns a dollar value of $225 billion dollars to the volunteer time given in 1998 and states that volunteers in addition contribute over two and a half times as much money as those who do not volunteer.

The necessity of building communities from within and the belief that problems are best solved when the community assesses its own needs and organizes to help meet those needs have placed greater emphasis and hope on volunteerism. Yet there is concern that America's civic involvement has been declining over the last 20 years.

A Nation of Spectators is a report issued by the National Commission on Civic Renewal,[7] a project funded by the Pew Foundation. In the report is an Index of National Civic Health (INCH) measuring civic involvement. This includes voter turnout and other political activities from writing a letter to one's congressperson or a newspaper to holding political office; trust and confidence in others and the federal government; membership in religious or local organizations; charitable contributions; security; and family components, including divorce and nonmarital births. While the index released in 1998 showed a 20 percent decline in combined elements between 1984 and 1994 with a slight upswing in 1996, the 1997 figures (released in 1999) show "a significant improvement," according to the Commission. This improvement is largely in the areas of trust of other people and reduced fear about personal security, probably due to the reduction in reported crimes. However, the Commission also points out that "a return to the level of civic health last seen in 1984 is not sufficient. Our best estimate shows that INCH was far higher in the previous decades." The 1997 figures show only an average 42.5 percent voter turnout and a 38.0 percent trust in the federal government.

When *Habits of the Heart*[8] was published in 1985, the authors discussed Americans' commitment to community and citizenship as an antidote to individualism, or "radical individualism," as they termed it. When the book was published again in 1995, Robert Bellah said that "the consequences of radical individualism are . . . more evident today than they were a decade ago."

In his 1995 article, "Bowling Alone: America's Declining Social Capital,"[9] Robert Putnam reported that between 1980 and 1992 the total number of solitary bowlers in America increased by 10 percent, whereas league bowling decreased by 40 percent. He stated that the number of Americans who said they attended a public meeting on town or school affairs had fallen by more than a third since 1993.

This research indicates not only that today's volunteers should be treasured and involved in meaningful ways, but also that there is a challenge to involve more people in volunteering so that they build trust in themselves and others, exercise their civic responsibility, and learn that they can make a difference in their communities.

(E) IMPORTANCE OF BOARD AND CEO SUPPORT OF VOLUNTEERISM

A volunteer program cannot be central to the mission of the agency, or self-renewing, if it does not have the support of the board and the chief executive officer (CEO). Board members, who are volunteers themselves, need to encourage the involvement of the direct service volunteers. A board member should have the assignment of liaison to the volunteer program; consult with the volunteer manager; be a member of the volunteer advisory committee; and represent the board's active interest in the volunteer program. Volunteers should be invited to the board meetings from time to time to share their firsthand experiences in the community.

CEOs need to include reports on the in-kind contributions made by volunteers along with the financial report, and need to regard the manager of the volunteer program as an important part of the Resource Development Department. The value of the time volunteers contribute is great and, in addition, as the Independent Sector survey points out, volunteers give over two and a half times as much money to charity as people who do not volunteer.[10]

(F) IMPORTANCE OF THE MANAGER OF VOLUNTEERS

Effective volunteer programs need to be led by a skilled manager of volunteer human resources. Various titles are used: Director of Volunteers, Volunteer Manager, and Volunteer Coordinator. But meaningful programs that have a solid impact do not happen without the leadership of a person who can keep one eye on the mission and another on making maximum use of the talents volunteers have to offer while smiling encouragingly and moving ahead. The following is a slightly tongue-in-cheek want ad for a skilled volunteer coordinator, but it gives some notion of the skills required:

WANTED: A manager and developer of resources valued at millions of dollars. Good communication skills, oral and written, are required, as well as thorough knowledge of community needs and services. Applicant must have an understanding of marketing principles to promote exchange of implicit and explicit benefits. Applicant must have the ability to work with people from all racial, economic, ideological, age, and social backgrounds. Applicant must have a knowledge of psychology, participatory planning, motivation, and human values. Applicant must possess the ability to lead and motivate others, be able to delegate authority, survive ambiguity, and be innovative and creative. Applicant must strive for the highest standards in preservation of human dignity, personal privacy, self-determination, and social responsibility.[11]

The profession of volunteer administration is commanding new respect as people realize its significance and its complexity.

A recent United Parcel Service (UPS)[12] study demonstrates the importance of a well-trained, professional volunteer manager. UPS wanted to find out why people volunteer, why they do not, or why they quit. Over 1,000 people were interviewed through a telephone survey, and 1,400 interviews were conducted in major cities in the United States. The reason most people gave for not volunteering was that they are "too busy." When asked what would make them more likely to volunteer, 58 percent said they would be very to somewhat likely to volunteer *if good use were made of their time;* 52 percent would be very to somewhat likely to volunteer *if the organization had a reputation for being well managed;* and 50 percent would be very to somewhat likely to volunteer *if the organization made better use of volunteer talents.* Among the poor management practices that caused two out of five volunteers interviewed to resign from their volunteer assignments were *not a good use of time* (23 percent), *not a good use of talents* (18 percent), *tasks not clearly defined* (16 percent), and *not thanked* (9 percent).

Good volunteer managers make sure that people are making good use of their time and talents, that tasks are clearly defined, and that volunteers are recognized and thanked for their efforts.

Today's effective volunteer managers are realizing that they are community collaborators, focusing not merely on their own organization but also on the possibility of forming synergistic relations with other community groups.

While volunteer managers still count the hours their volunteers contribute, they are now involved in measuring the outcomes that those volunteers produce, a much more useful way to show volunteers, paid staff, and the community how valuable the volunteer efforts are, as well as a guide to make needed program changes.

Volunteer managers are increasingly involved with computers and the Internet. Computers are not just useful for keeping track of volunteers, but there are numerous technical assistance Web sites for volunteer managers as well as sites that match willing volunteers with needy agencies. In addition, virtual computer-based volunteerism is a new opportunity for people to assist from their homes or offices.

Volunteer managers may be paid or unpaid; they can work for organizations or for ad hoc community groups; but all can be professional in their work, taking advantage of certificate programs offered by some colleges and the certification program of the Association for Volunteer Administration (AVA). Also available to them are such materials as the AVA Statement of Professional Ethics in Volunteer Administration[13] and the AVA Portrait of a Profession.[14] The Points of Light Foundation and the AVA sponsor yearly volunteerism conferences, and many states hold smaller conferences. Local organizations of directors of volunteers exist in many communities throughout the United States and provide support and training for volunteer managers.

However, despite the importance of volunteer managers, salaries of volunteer managers in agencies are low, according to a February 1999 survey issued by the *Nonprofit Times*.[15] The average salary for a volunteer manager is $32,707, whereas the average for a director of development is $46,695.

34.2 Steps in a Volunteer Program

(A) THE CONTINUUM

The following steps represent a volunteer program continuum:

1. Needs assessments
2. Mission
3. Policies
4. Budget
5. Risk management
6. Position descriptions
7. Recruitment
8. Interviewing/Screening
9. Orientation
10. Training
11. Guiding/Retraining
12. Recognition
13. Evaluation
14. Reassessment, and then follow steps 1 through 13 once again

34.3 Needs Assessments

(A) INVOLVING STAFF AND BOARD

Needs assessments help the volunteer manager find out what tasks the paid staff needs help with; but, equally important, they allow the staff to be a partner in determining how volunteers will be involved.

Exhibit 34.1 is a very simple needs assessment to circulate to staff. However, even more effective may be conversations at staff meetings, the strategic planning meetings where staff and board articulate their hopes and dreams for the agency and the volunteer manager's own observations of needs. Essential, however, to involving volunteers meaningfully is having staff and board view them as partners.

(B) WINNING STAFF SUPPORT

Staff will resist volunteers if they do not see them as genuinely helpful to them. "They're too much trouble; they won't show up on time; you can't fire them" are ways staff will indicate their unease about volunteers. The volunteer manager must show by word and practice that the volunteers in the agency will be regarded as unpaid staff; that there will

---

EXHIBIT 34.1 Staff Needs Assessment

What are some things you would like to see this agency doing for its clients and the community that it is not currently doing?

What parts of your job responsibilities do you wish you could delegate to someone else in order to free up your time for higher priority tasks?

What are those things you would like to have done, but that you don't have the skills and training to do yourself?

Do you have any concerns about involving volunteers in your work?

What assistance would you need before involving volunteers in your work?

---

be expectations that the volunteer will honor; and that staff will not be expected to continue working with volunteers who are not helpful to them.

CEOs can be helpful by articulating their commitment to the importance of the volunteer program; making sure that staff are rewarded for working effectively with volunteers; and stressing to staff the importance of the management experience they gain by working with volunteers.

34.4 *Mission Statement*

(A) REASONS FOR A MISSION STATEMENT

A mission statement for the volunteer program helps paid staff, policy volunteers (the board), and direct service volunteers understand the importance of the program. Just as the organization mission testifies to why the community needs the agency and what is special about it, the volunteer program mission should state why the volunteer program is important to the agency and what is special about it.

(B) IMPORTANCE OF VOLUNTEERS

Think about why volunteers are important to the agency. They:

- Amplify services
- Represent the community
- Are credible in the community in volunteer recruitment, fund raising, and advocacy because they are not paid for their work
- Often are more effective than paid staff with clients because they are working with them voluntarily

(C) A GOOD AGENCY–VOLUNTEER PARTNERSHIP

Think about the relationship the organization wants to have with volunteers. For example:

- Regard them as partners.
- Respect them.
- Involve them in ways that are meaningful to them, the agency, and the community.
- Help them grow and learn.
- See them as resources that are as valuable to the agency as money.

(D) SAMPLE MISSION STATEMENT

Hammer out the wording until you and everyone who reads it can say, "yes, that's why we have a volunteer program; that's why it's important; that's why people will want to be involved." For example: "In this community, many young people need role models to expand their horizons and help them make decisions about their future. Volunteers are integral to the XYZ agency's efforts to meet this need. Part-time, trained volunteers can make a difference in young people's lives. The volunteer human resources are welcomed. They permit the XYZ agency to expand and amplify the services it provides in the community."

34.5 Policies

(A) IMPORTANCE OF POLICIES

Policies will be constantly changing to meet new circumstances and will differ among agencies, depending on the agency mission. But it is important to start a program with some statements that reflect the values and principles of the organization, the expectations of volunteers, their expectations of the agency, and the parameters within which they will work. Clear policy guidelines help management make equitable decisions, and set a framework within which people can operate.

Policies are essential to good risk management of a program, and as the manager defines the risks present in the various volunteer jobs in the agency (see Section 34.8), the manager will expand the policy statements to encompass them.

Volunteers should be given a copy of the policies at their orientation and asked to review them and to sign a paper indicating that they have reviewed them.

(B) AGENCY EXPECTATIONS OF VOLUNTEERS

Policies vary from agency to agency depending on demands and priorities. The following are a few areas to consider. Policies should be no harsher for volunteers than they are for paid staff:

- Professional attitude (e.g., confidentiality, notification of absence)
- Faithfulness to the position description
- Adherence to agency rules and regulations
- Participation in training
- Criminal records checks (when working with vulnerable populations)
- Reference checks
- A valid driver's license and car insurance (when driving as an agent of the agency)
- Trial periods
- Drug-free workplace
- Dress
- Use of telephone
- Health tests, if needed

(C) VOLUNTEERS' EXPECTATIONS OF AGENCY

- Orientation and ongoing training
- Guidance
- Evaluation
- Participation in decisions affecting their assignments
- Equal employment policies
- Expense reimbursement
- Insurance
- To be treated as unpaid staff
- Suitable assignments
- Personnel file

- Grievance procedures
- To know the reasons a volunteer can be dismissed

(D) SAMPLE POLICY

Policies are broad statements of belief and restrictions that serve as guidelines for administration. For example:

It is expected that all volunteers in this agency will keep in confidence any information learned about clients during the performance of their volunteer duties. Failure to do so can be a reason for dismissal of the volunteer.

34.6 Budget

Volunteers are very cost effective, but they are not free. A budget will be needed in most agencies for:

Salaried Personnel
- Salary and benefits for a skilled volunteer manager with excellent people skills
- Salary and benefits for an administrative assistant to keep records and generally assist the manager
- Professional development (e.g., volunteer management conferences, subscriptions, memberships)

Volunteers
- Reimbursement of volunteers' expenses (e.g., parking and carfare)
- Recognition events (e.g., lunches, dinners, coffees, awards—from coffee mugs to plaques)
- Training
- Insurance for the volunteers (see Section 34.8)
- Uniforms, if required

Operating Expenses
- Printing
- Administration (e.g., computer, fax, telephone, postage, supplies)
- Space

34.7 Position Descriptions

(A) NEW VOLUNTEER POSITIONS

When volunteer managers review suggestions made by staff for new positions, they need to analyze whether they are appropriate for volunteers to do. Some of the questions to consider are:

- Is it something that can be done on a part-time basis?
- Is it cost effective to supply the necessary training for a volunteer to do this job?
- Is it something a volunteer would want to do?
- Is it worthwhile?

(B) PREPARING THE POSITION DESCRIPTION

If you do not know what you want the volunteers to do, how will they know? Therefore, as in all human resource management, the volunteer needs a position description that spells out responsibilities. The position description (see Exhibit 34.2) is the volunteer manager's blueprint to designing a recruitment strategy to find people who are interested and able to do the task (see recruitment, Section 34.9).

(C) POSITION DESCRIPTION AS RISK MANAGEMENT

The position description is an absolutely essential risk management tool. It clarifies what the volunteer should do and protects the volunteer and the agency. Once the volunteers are recruited and accepted, they and the volunteer manager should sign the position descriptions, demonstrating that they have read and understood it.

EXHIBIT 34.2 Volunteer Position Description and Contract

Position title:

Supervisor: Location:

Objective: (Why is this job necessary; what will it accomplish?)

Responsibilities: (What specifically will the volunteer do?)

Commitment: (Short term; long term; hours)

Qualifications: (What special skills are needed? Can all ages do it? Does it
                               require any particular educational background?)

Policies: (e.g., confidentiality, criminal records check, code of behavior,
                               prohibited activities)

Training provided:

Benefits: (Transportation, insurance, parking, expenses)

Trial period (probation):

References required:

Other:

Signatures to be added at time of mutual agreement:

Date:

Signature of volunteer:

Signature of supervisor:

34.8   Risk Management

(A)   VOLUNTEER MANAGEMENT AND RISK MANAGEMENT

Good volunteer management is good risk management. Interviewing, screening, orientation, training, guidance, and policies are part of the risk management process.

The volunteer manager should analyze the position descriptions prior to recruitment and determine what risks are involved to the volunteer and to the agency. (See Exhibit 34.3.) The manager should then decide how to manage the risks or reluctantly decide to avoid the risks by not involving volunteers in that particular work.

(B)   PROTECTING THE VOLUNTEERS

Managers of volunteers must remember that volunteers:

- Must have a safe working environment
- Should not be asked to do tasks paid staff would not be asked to do
- Should not be asked to do tasks paid staff are doing without equal training

In 1997, the Volunteer Protection Act was passed by Congress and signed by the president (Public Law 105-19) to limit the personal liability of volunteers in 501(c)(3) and governmental organizations to actions that were not willful or criminal misconduct, gross negligence, reckless misconduct, or a conscious, flagrant indifference to the rights or safety of the individual harmed by the volunteer. The legislation states that "The volunteer must be acting within the scope of the volunteer's responsibilities in the organization" and that the limitation does not cover harm caused by the volunteer operating an automobile or another vehicle.

(C)   PROTECTING THE AGENCY

Many states today have legislation limiting the liability of volunteers to acts that are willful and wanton, that is, with a deliberate intent to cause harm. But agencies must be care-

---

EXHIBIT 34.3 Targeted Volunteer Recruitment Analysis

What do I need? (Skills and commitment required. Would the ideal person be motivated by affiliation, achievement, or power?)

Who could do this job? (Flexibly evaluate the times and places the commitment could be fulfilled, the training you will offer, and the diversity of volunteer resources available to you.)

What do they need and want from me? (Training, child care, flexible time commitment, experience, affiliation, achievement, power?)

How can I reach them? (Where do they live, work, go to school, worship?)

What should be my message? (Consider program mission and the motivation of potential volunteer.)

---

ful to make sure that volunteers are well trained and have clear position descriptions so that the difference between willful and wanton and specified duties is clear. By so doing, the agency is also protecting itself.

For example, a telephone reassurance program for latchkey children states clearly in its position description and policies that volunteers are to have no personal contact with the children beyond the telephone. Clearly, a volunteer who violates this is "willful and wanton" and not acting as an agent of the program.

(D) INSURANCE THAT COVERS VOLUNTEERS

Agency umbrella liability policies can be expanded to cover both paid staff and volunteers as named insured. In addition, inexpensive liability and excess automobile and accident insurance is available for volunteers.

34.9 Recruitment

(A) UNDERSTAND VALUES EXCHANGE

The closer a manager of volunteers can come to meeting the needs of the volunteers while *at the same time* meeting the needs of the program, the more successful he or she will be. Therefore, starting with the development of the recruitment strategy, the successful volunteer recruiter tries to match the needs of the program with the needs of the volunteer. Questions the recruiter must keep in mind continuously are: What can a volunteer get out of the volunteer experience? Who are the people most likely to find satisfaction in the opportunity? How can the program give them a motivational paycheck that will keep them interested?

If the manager worries only about the needs of the program, the volunteers are likely to feel unappreciated and quit. But equally important, if the manager worries only about the needs of the volunteer, the program will suffer. Balancing these needs is essential to good volunteer management.

(B) WHO VOLUNTEERS

The Independent Sector 1998 Survey states that as the level of education and household income increase, so does volunteering.[16] In 1998, 42 percent of the households with an average income under $20,000 reported volunteering, whereas 68 percent of those with an average income of $40,000 and $49,999 did so. In addition, college graduates were between 50 and 60 percent more likely to volunteer than people with only a high school diploma. In 1998, volunteerism among women was up 10 percentage points; among African-Americans up 11 percentage points; among Hispanics up 6 points; among persons between the ages of 35 and 55 years of age up 12 points; divorced or separated individuals and those living with a partner was up 12 and 16 points, respectively; part-time workers was up 13 points; and individuals who were not employed was up 10 percentage points.

Independent Sector suggests that organizations give more attention to the potential of the 55 to 64 age group who are about to retire and can be moved by understanding the value of the volunteer assignment not only for the needy but for themselves as well. They also stress making a personal "ask" [see Section 8.9(d)] and using the Internet as an educational and marketing tool.

Independent Sector points to a strong relationship between religious involvement and volunteering. Among people who attend religious services regularly, 76 percent report volunteering. Independent Sector also points out that 69 percent of people whose parents volunteered are now volunteers themselves.

The most frequent kinds of volunteering, according to the survey, are direct service (food, transportation, etc.), 23.6 percent; fund raising, 16 percent; giving advice or counseling, 10.5 percent; organizing an event, 9.8 percent; visiting people, 8.6 percent; administrative or clerical work, 7.4 percent; board membership, 4.5 percent; and advocacy 3.4 percent. (Remainder is "don't know," 12.2 percent; and "other," 3.4 percent).

(C) FINDING POTENTIAL VOLUNTEERS

Sources from which to recruit volunteers include:

- Volunteer centers, which will try to match prospective volunteers with an agency and job description appropriate to their talents
- Retired and senior volunteer programs, which involve almost half a million people age 55 and above in volunteer opportunities
- School, college, and university service learning and community service programs
- Service clubs, such as Rotary, Kiwanis, and Altrusa
- City Cares programs, which involve young professionals in projects in major urban areas
- Corporate, business, and labor volunteer programs
- Senior centers and retirement homes
- Religious groups
- Professional organizations (e.g., accountants, lawyers)
- Executive Service Corps for management volunteers
- National Retiree Volunteer Coalition (groups of retired employees who volunteer under the auspices of their former employer)
- American Association for Retired Persons
- Alumni groups
- Sororities and fraternities
- Stipended programs (e.g., VISTA, AmeriCorps, Foster Grandparents, Senior Companions)
- Open houses
- Volunteer fairs
- The Internet

(D) DEVELOPING STRONG AND DIVERSE VOLUNTEER SUPPORT

(i) Ask Them

The Gallup Survey tells us that people of all ages are nearly four times as likely to volunteer if someone asks them . . . particularly someone they know. Fund raisers have known for years that "you don't get if you don't ask," and a person the potential donor respects is the most effective person to do the asking.

In his 1986 book *Designs for Fund Raising* (so effective that it was reprinted in 1988 by the Fund-Raising Institute), Harold Seymour posits two hypotheses that are equally important for managers of volunteers, who, after all, are also in development work:

1. The most universal and deep-seated fear that people have is xenophobia—fear of the stranger.
2. We all aspire to be sought out and to be worthwhile members of a worthwhile group.[17]

This is why person-to-person recruitment works so well. Because someone who is known to potential volunteers is doing the asking, volunteers are assured that they are not getting involved in something strange or unsavory. Volunteers also know that the group must be worthwhile because the person doing the asking is worthwhile.

(E) PLANNING FOR CULTURAL DIVERSITY

In our society, however, person-to-person asking sometimes breaks down when programs want, as they should, to involve a cross-section of the community and need to recruit for ethnic, racial, age, and economic diversity that is not already present in the program. Here setting up an advisory group made up of leaders from the groups the program wishes to involve can be helpful in learning whom and how to target. Sometimes cultural sensitivity training is necessary for both current paid staff and volunteers.

Many programs fail to be as effective as they might because recruiters or volunteer managers have a limited notion of whom to involve. In addition to the diversity mentioned previously, think about involving:

- People with disabilities
- Unemployed people
- Former clients
- Families of clients
- Donors
- Interns
- Offenders sentenced to community service
- Displaced homemakers

When recruiting any groups, however, one must again think of what they need from the program. People with disabilities, unemployed people, former clients, and displaced homemakers, for example, might like to work as volunteers for a limited period of time in exchange for some job training, a personnel file, and a letter of recommendation. Donors might enjoy hands-on experience and some involvement with people rather than always being viewed as writers of checks. Interns might work for college credit or for experience in the area in which they have concentrated. Offenders, while required to serve, might consciously or unconsciously be looking for something they can care about.

(F) PLANNING FOR DIVERSITY OF COMMITMENT

As managers think about their needs, they are likely to think that those needs can only be met between the hours of 9:00 A.M. and 5:00 P.M. on weekdays. This can seriously limit volunteer resource potential and, more important, the potential to help the community.

Volunteers today can be short term or long term; they can work every Tuesday for a year or more; or they can handle a project that lasts just a few weeks or even just a day. Some might prefer a project they can do at their offices, others will want to do something with their families; some want to work in the evenings, some want to work on the weekends; some want to do something in their area of expertise; some want to develop a new skill; and others want to do something from home.

Although it may not be possible to meet all of these personal desires in any particular program, a wise manager will evaluate whether the job can be done under circumstances different from those envisioned originally.

(G) PLANNING FOR DIVERSITY OF SPECIAL VOLUNTEER NEEDS

Besides understanding the need for cultural diversity and the volunteers' diversity of commitment, managers must understand the special needs that may make it impossible for people to volunteer. Some volunteers may be able to help if the agency can provide child care. A busy program during the day at a Champaign, Illinois, hospital provides baby sitting while young mothers satisfy their needs for affiliation and outreach by working together at the hospital. Families can offer their help on weekend and evening projects if their younger children can be taken care of.

Programs should offer to reimburse volunteer out-of-pocket expenses (e.g., car fare). Many volunteers will not turn in their expense lists, but for some, car fare may be the difference between involvement or staying at home. Transportation or parking for volunteers can also be helpful. A hospital parking lot for volunteers at a Connecticut hospital carries a sign "Volunteer Lane."

People with disabilities also have abilities that can benefit programs, but the agency needs to make "reasonable accommodation" for the disability—perhaps supplying a tape recorder for someone who is legally blind or understanding that people with mental retardation are pleased to be involved as volunteers. A program in Chicago involves young adults with mental retardation as ushers in neighborhood theaters.

(H) UNDERSTANDING MOTIVATIONS

Gallup Survey results show that most people volunteer to be helpful and become involved as a direct result of their religious beliefs. However, there are many additional reasons: need to be needed, desire for sociability, interest in a particular area, curiosity about a particular program, job experience, and boredom with a paying job . . . the list can go on and on.

For the purposes of volunteer management, one of the most valuable tools on motivation is the work done by David McClelland and John Atkinson, referred to by Marlene Wilson.[18] McClelland and Atkinson conclude that all people are motivated by three things, but most strongly by one more than the others. These motivations are:

1. *Affiliation*—the need to be with other people and enjoy friendship
2. *Achievement*—the need to accomplish goals and do one's personal best
3. *Power*—the need to have influence on others.

In 1970, McClelland defined power as having two faces:

1. *Positive power*—socialized power: I win/you win
2. *Negative power*—personalized power: I win/you lose[19]

People motivated by socialized power internalize the *raison d'être* for volunteerism: We can't change the world by ourselves, but if we can involve enough other people in socialized power, we can change the world (or our community or a block). Socialized power people understand that when we improve a community for others, we can also improve it for ourselves. A wise volunteer manager can use affiliation, achievement, and power (negative or positive) to understand volunteers and to match them with the right assignment.

(I) RECRUITMENT TECHNIQUES

To be successful and to protect the agency, client, and volunteer, recruitment techniques need to be matched to the challenges, complexities, and risks of the job.

- *Generic* (for mass events and low-risk and unskilled jobs). "Volunteers Wanted" on posters, newsletters, and public service announcements can be effective for assignments that anyone and everyone can do. For example, Hands Across America, a 1986 campaign to raise consciousness about hunger and homelessness by an unbroken line of Americans holding hands, was something in which everyone could be involved. It took no special skills, and the only limitation, for some, was transportation to a site. Therefore, an open invitation was all that was needed.
- *Specific* (for medium- or high-risk and skilled jobs). Targeted recruitment is usually the more effective method since "volunteers wanted" does not work when the recruiter has specific skills in mind, just as "paid staff wanted" would not work when an agency wants to hire someone with the ability to do a specific job.

The recruiter should review the position description and ask: What is the mission of the position (why is it important); what is the commitment (long term, short term, evenings, at home, in the office, or ongoing); what skills would the volunteer need; what will be required of the volunteer; what benefits, psychic and tangible, will the volunteer receive from the assignment; and finally, who might have the necessary skills and be attracted by the mission, commitment, and benefits? (See Exhibit 34.2.)

(J) OFFERING THE OPPORTUNITY

After this exercise, the volunteer manager will begin to focus on a recruitment strategy; targeting individuals and groups who might be interested in the program. The manager will then ask: "How can I reach them, and what should the message be?"

There are many ways to reach prospective volunteers, but the wise recruiter needs to decide which techniques might be most effective for the job in mind:

- Soliciting names of individuals from current volunteers, board members, and staff and having the most credible person ask them to be involved
- Contacting volunteer centers or organizations (religious, professional, educational) that include the targeted population
- Distributing targeted flyers (consider multilingual material)
- Distributing targeted brochures

- Giving speeches to targeted organizations (most successful when given by a volunteer who is a member of that organization)
- Putting public service announcements on television or radio on stations to which the targeted population listens
- Placing classified ads in newspapers that prospects might read (include free shoppers and neighborhood papers)
- Posting your volunteer needs on Web sites formed for the purpose of connecting willing volunteers with tasks

It is important that the promotional message emphasize the need your program hopes to remedy: "Two million people in this state can't read above a fourth-grade level"; "One out of every three children in this country is living in poverty." People want to do worthwhile work, and even though the job may be administrative in nature, prospective volunteers will be more involved if they share the mission that the work is advancing.

The promotional message should also speak to the needs of the people who could potentially be most effective in the job: If they are affiliators, being with others and helping others will be motivating; if they are achievers, concrete accomplishments will be enticing; and if they are power people, a task that has significant impact will attract them. Remember, affiliators are concerned about relationships; achievers look for goals and objectives; and power people demand them. If the program does not have them, they will create them or leave!

34.10 Interviewing and Screening Volunteers

(A) THE APPLICATION FORM

Prospective volunteers should fill out an application form. Exhibit 34.4 is a sample, but many agencies use the same form that they use for their paid staff. The application form should include information relevant to the work that is to be done. It should ask for at least two references (not relatives); and it should require the driver's license number and insurance source for volunteers who will drive in the course of their duties. If the volunteer will be working with vulnerable populations, it should ask for permission to do a criminal records check. If health or drug tests are required, it should so state.

A confidentiality agreement may also be required in certain agencies. For example, agencies that work with people with disabilities will require this. Some people will suggest that volunteers cannot keep information confidential. That, of course, is nonsense. It is the personal integrity of a person, not a salary, that determines his or her ability to keep a pledge. Agencies for whom confidentiality is important will often state in their policies that a breach of confidentiality is regarded as a reason for dismissal.

(B) THE INTERVIEW

(i) Ask Open-Ended Questions

As the volunteer director interviews potential volunteers and works to make sure that the job and the volunteer are a good match, McClelland's affiliation, achievement, and power motivations are extraordinarily helpful. Open-ended questions—What are your goals? What do you hope to get out of your volunteer involvement? What kind of work envi-

EXHIBIT 34.4 Application for Volunteer Position

Name:

Current address:

Telephone Number:　　　　Home:　　　　　　　Work:

Current employment:

Volunteer experience, current and past:

Skills:

How did you learn about our program?

Educational background: High school graduate: ＿＿＿ Some college ＿＿＿ College degrees: ＿＿＿
Have you had any previous experience working with our cause (or population)? Give specifics:

References: (List two people whom we may contact, and include addresses and telephone numbers. These should not be relatives but should be teachers, employers, or other community members.)

When (days, hours, seasons) would you prefer to volunteer?

In case of an emergency, whom should we notify?

For high-risk programs, add any of the following that are appropriate:

Since driving is part of the volunteer job for which you are applying, we need your driver's license number and your proof of insurance.

License number:　　　　　　　　　　　　Insurance carrier:

State:　　　　　　　　　　　　　　　　 (Please attach a copy of your certificate)

Since the volunteer job requires working with children, people with disabilities, the dying, or the frail elderly, we will need to do a criminal records check.

Permission granted ＿＿＿ yes ＿＿＿ no

All volunteers (and paid staff) are required to sign a confidentiality agreement. By signing on the space below, you agree that you will keep confidential all information you learn about clients or families if you perform volunteer duties for this agency.

Signature ＿＿＿＿＿＿＿＿＿＿＿＿＿＿＿＿＿＿＿＿＿＿＿

ronment do you like? What job have you had that you enjoyed the most?—can all help the interviewer understand the prospective volunteer and make an effective match.

The volunteer manager should clarify that:

- An interview is necessary to make a proper placement.
- Both volunteer and the program should benefit from the match.
- This is an opportunity for the manager and the prospective volunteer to explore whether the position is appropriate for the volunteer's skills and interest.
- Everyone who is interviewed is not appropriate for the program.

When interviewing, remember that the same rules apply that cover equal employment practices. Questions about race, religion, sexual preference, national origin, age, and marital status should not be asked.

(ii) Tailor Depth of Interview to Risk of Program

Programs that serve vulnerable populations and where the volunteer is directly involved with clients—children, people with disabilities, the homebound, and the dying—will want to explore the motivations of the volunteer for the interest in this particular population; and a second interview, after applications are processed and references checked, may be required.

Although good interviewers listen more than they talk, they know that the interview is the time to review the position description and to pay particular attention to policies that cover agency attitudes and volunteer behavior. It affords an opportunity to listen and observe carefully and to assess volunteers' reactions to these policies. Cover all items appropriate and necessary for the program: confidentiality, contracts, probation, health and drug tests, and criminal records checks.

While it is only fair to ask the same questions and make the same general statements to all prospective volunteers, the less comfortable the interviewer is with the volunteer's reactions to policies, the more the interviewer should emphasize the policies in order to probe the volunteer's attitudes.

Interviews should also cover required training. Some agencies that offer intensive and often sought-after training (e.g., negotiation skills, HIV prevention, or crisis intervention) ask prospective volunteers to commit to six months or more of volunteerism once training is completed.

(iii) Explore Volunteer's Special Needs

During the interview, managers should be sensitive to accommodations that the agency might make to the volunteer (e.g., transportation, parking, car fare, planned leave of absence, flex time, shared jobs, or disability-related accommodations). Exhibit 34.5 is a sample form on which to record interview impressions.

(C) SCREENING

(i) The Interview

Preliminary screening starts with the application and the interview. At the end of the interview, one of three things will happen:

EXHIBIT 34.5 Interviewer's Report Form

Name of prospect: Date:

Background relevant to placement:

Does this person have a special reason for wanting to be involved with your population or cause?

Did the person understand your requirements: probation, training, contract, confidentiality, criminal records check, health tests? (Use those appropriate to program and add others.)

Times available for volunteer job:

Strengths of the person:

Weaknesses you perceived:

Special needs:

References checked: _____ Satisfactory   _____ Unsatisfactory

  Date:

(If appropriate, add space for receipt and status of health or drug tests and/or criminal records check.)

Second interview to be scheduled? _____ yes   _____ no

  If "yes," date:

Accept _____ yes   _____ no

Person notified: Date

---

1. The manager of volunteers is convinced that the job is not appropriate for the prospective volunteer and suggests another assignment in the agency or refers the volunteer to a local volunteer center or an agency with a more compatible program.
2. The potential volunteer realizes that the job is not appropriate and says so. It is helpful to the manager to say at the end of the interview, "Are you still interested in this job?" This gives the prospective volunteer a graceful exit, if desired.
3. The interview is satisfactory enough that it leads to the next step. . .

(ii)   The Reference Check

The reference check should be conducted, and Exhibit 34.6 is an easy way to contact the references. If the references are satisfactory, the manager will proceed. If not, the manager will follow suggestion 1 above.

(iii)   Special Requirements

The volunteer manager institutes the criminal records check. There are usually two forms this check can take: a check of conviction records based on date of birth and name or a more expensive but surer check based on fingerprints. The latter is recommended for especially sensitive cases, such as screening for possible pedophiles.

    In 1998, the National Child Protection Act of 1993 was amended by the Volunteers for Children Act. This amendment provides qualified entities the ability to request finger-

---

EXHIBIT 34.6 Volunteer Reference Form

The person named below wishes to become a volunteer in our program. This person has indicated that you would be able to evaluate his/her qualifications. This form is confidential and voluntary; but we would appreciate having it returned as soon as possible.

Name:

How long have you known this person?

In what capacity have you known the person?

In your opinion, is this person responsible?

In your opinion, can this person work well with others?

Are you aware of other volunteer work in which this person is involved? (If so, please name it.)

Please tell us about any special talents you believe this person has.

Additional comments:

Your name: Address:

  Phone:

MANY THANKS FOR YOUR HELP

---

print-based national criminal history background checks of volunteers and employees. A qualified entity is "any business or organization that provides care, treatment, education, training, instruction, supervision, or recreation for children, the elderly, or individuals with disability—whether public, private, for-profit, not for profit, or volunteer." Qualified entities are asked to contact their state law enforcement identification bureau, which will in turn contact the FBI.

If the volunteer is required to have a health test (e.g., a tuberculosis test is required for some schools, and drug testing for some correctional facilities), the volunteer should take responsibility for making sure that the manager receives the results.

(iv)   Second Interview

In especially sensitive work, a second interview is usually required; and sometimes it is needed in other instances just to verify impressions. If (iii) and (iv) are not satisfactory, the next step is rejection.

(D)   REJECTING APPLICANTS

Managers of volunteers should remember that in all personnel work, the most important decision made is whom to hire. This is no less true for volunteer positions. To involve someone about whom one has real misgivings is not fair to the person and not fair to the program. Refer them to another position, another agency, or a volunteer center. It is good to pay a sincere compliment to the prospective volunteer, such as, "You have wonderful writing skills, but as I mentioned to you, our needs are limited in that area. I would like to keep you in mind for the future, but meanwhile, you might call. . ."

34.11   Orientation

The volunteer has been invited to join the program and has been accepted. The next steps are important to maintain enthusiasm and momentum.

(A)   SIGN A CONTRACT

The simplest form for a contract is the position description, which the volunteer manager shared at the interview. Any additional items agreed upon can be added to the position description (length of probation period, for example), and then it can be dated and signed by the volunteer and the manager. The manager can also make the program policies part of the contract.

The contract can be signed before, during, or after the orientation. The volunteer should be given a copy and the original should go in the office personnel file. (See Exhibit 34.2 for a sample position description and contract.)

(B)   WHAT THE VOLUNTEER NEEDS TO KNOW

Orientation to the program is a process to familiarize volunteers with the broad mission and function of the agency so that the volunteer sees his or her position as an important part of that mission. Orientation can be individual, in small groups, or in large groups. Large-group orientations usually happen when a significant number of volunteers are brought into a program at almost the same time. But whether the orientation is held in a classroom setting with videos and speeches, a small group around a conference table, or individually through appointments with relevant personnel, the agenda must be set to meet the volunteer's needs to know.

Do not bore them with information that may be important to agency operations but is not necessary for them to know to perform their duties. However, do share with them exciting plans for new buildings, new programs, breakthroughs in technology, and recognitions of agency excellence. These make the volunteers feel that they are respected new members of the staff and are learning some things that only "insiders" would know. Exhibit 34.7 is a sample agenda for one-person or a large- or small-group orientation.

(C)   QUESTIONS

A special packet should be prepared for volunteers. It should include a welcoming letter, an annual report, newsletters, an organizational chart, a list of staff and board, and any other information that might be helpful. If the agency is holding a large-group orientation, make sure that it is lively, friendly, and energetic. Ask only those people who are enthusiastic and mission driven to make presentations. Start with coffee and cookies, have attractive name tags (perhaps permanent ones that the volunteer can use consistently), make sure in advance that audiovisual equipment works, and encourage questions, participation, and evaluation. Send out invitations a month in advance and follow up with phone calls.

34.12   Training

Review Section 34.8 concerning risk management. This will point out some of the areas where training is needed in a program. Necessary training varies from job to job.

EXHIBIT 34.7 Sample Orientation Agenda

I. Greetings from the boss: the executive director or board president, who acknowledges how integral volunteers are to agency operations.

II. A review of the history and organizational structure of the agency. This could be a role for a staff member who has been with the agency a long time, or perhaps the agency has a good video.

III. Introductions of staff to volunteer(s).

IV. An overview of the population or cause for which the volunteers are working. Experienced and enthusiastic program persons who do not use acronyms and jargon can do this.

V. Expectations of volunteers: a review of important policies and behaviors.

VI. Volunteer expectations of agency (e.g., benefits, insurance, parking, expenses, training).

VII. A presentation from an enthusiastic volunteer about what the agency has meant to him or her.

VIII. A tour of the facility.

In-service training is important for volunteers. In-service training also serves as a reflection experience where volunteers can debrief about their experience and share with each other. Some volunteer positions, like serving on a crisis line, can be quite lonely, and volunteers worry that they are not providing the right answers. Giving them a chance to exchange ideas and problems at an in-service training can be rewarding in terms of improved morale and service.

Frequently it's a good idea to take volunteers to a volunteer management conference or to send them to a workshop on a subject that they are working on. Just as paid staff needs to improve its skills, so do volunteers.

(A) HOW ADULTS LEARN

When working with adults, trainers need to remember that adults, according to Ron and Susan Zemke, learn best:

- When they feel a need for the information or learning experience. Keep in mind that adults have a natural motivation to learn at certain points in their lives—a window of opportunity—when they perceive a need to learn something new or different. If the window of opportunity is missed or delayed, however, the impact of the learning is greatly lessened.
- When the learning experience is problem centered—when it helps them cope with life-changing events—a new job, a new position, a challenging assignment. The more they perceive that the learning opportunity will address the changes that face them, the more motivated they become to participate.
- When the learning experience builds on the learner's personal goals for the program, and when their own experience is incorporated.
- When their curiosity about the subject is stimulated and the utility of the learning is emphasized—and the experience is designed as low risk for the learner.

- When the learning design promotes information integration. Training designers should expect slower integration of information that conflicts sharply with what learners already hold to be true—forcing them to rethink and reevaluate the old material. Similarly, information is acquired more slowly if it has little conceptual overlay with what is already known.

Adult learners prefer:

- Exercises and cases that have fidelity—that ring true to their life experiences
- Activities that are realistic and involving, that stimulate thinking, and that have moderate challenge
- Active to passive learning—exercises, cases, games, and simulations—incorporating reflective elements
- Planned feedback and recognition — "what we are trying to accomplish and how we're doing"
- Curriculum designs that account for learning-style differences.
- Straightforward how-to content
- Learning designs that accommodate their continued growth and changing values
- A safe and comfortable environment
- Facilitation over lecture presentations[20]

Frequently, training is done too early, before the adults have an opportunity to know what information they need. That's why it's better to do training in short sessions spread over a period of time rather than heaping all of the information on the volunteers at once.

Adults want to participate in the training. They come with life experiences of their own, so it's important to give them an opportunity to share and problem solve.

(B) WAYS TO COMMUNICATE INFORMATION

Because people learn in different ways, an entire training should not be a lecture. In fact, the lecture pieces should be short, 10 minutes or so at a time, and broken up with some of the following:

- Video
- Peer presentations
- Role play
- Discussions
- Panels
- Site visits
- Case studies
- Questionnaires
- Stories
- Interactive groups

Interactive groups are effective because after adults hear about concepts, they need to process them, practice them, and experience them.

(C)   ORGANIZE YOUR TRAINING

Trainers need to ask themselves:

- What is the purpose of this training?
- What do I want the volunteers to know and feel when they have completed the training?
- What are the three major concepts I want to get across?
- What variety of techniques can I use to make the training varied, lively, and interesting?
- How will I get the group to know each other (e.g., introductions, icebreakers)?
- How will I get them involved in an interactive way?

Allow for breaks during the training; encourage questions; and ask for evaluations at the end so that the next training can be even more successful.

34.13   Guidance/Retention

Effective programs, according to the Points of Light New Paradigm project, "were effective simply (because they) saw volunteers in a different way, a way that was empowering and encompassing."[21]

Managers of volunteers need to provide mission-focused leadership, letting the volunteers know how important they are to making a difference in the community. They need to help volunteers develop their talents; discover new challenges; and feel good about their successes. Volunteer managers need to provide prompt feedback about better ways of attacking problems. They need to solicit the advice of volunteers and involve volunteers as middle managers. After all, if the volunteer manager could do all the work alone, there would not be a need for the volunteers. The manager who does not delegate and does not empower others is performing a disservice to the volunteers and the program.

One hundred percent retention of volunteers is an unrealistic goal. As with paid staff, there are sometimes people who need to be outplaced (yes, volunteers can be dismissed when they consistently do not honor their contract). In addition, new jobs, moves, lifestyle changes, and new interests are bound to take their toll on the volunteer program. However, volunteer managers can do many things to help their volunteers keep their enthusiasm and interest in the program. Some ideas are listed as follows:

(A)   OPPORTUNITIES FOR EVALUATION

There should be opportunities for mutual evaluation of the volunteer experience. Evaluation can take a very informal tone. Ask "How's it going?", and if the response or body language is negative, invite the volunteer in for a chat. Certainly evaluation is required at the end of a probation period, and managers should provide a chance for discussion about the volunteer commitment at least twice a year. Questions that can be asked are:

- What do you like most about your job?
- What do you like least?
- Was your training sufficient?

- Are there other programs in this agency in which you would like to be involved?
- What can we do to make your time here more fulfilling for you?

In addition, the volunteer manager needs to provide honest feedback on the volunteer's contribution.

(B) VOLUNTEER VACATIONS AND LEAVES OF ABSENCE

Sometimes good volunteers like to take the winter off, they may become deeply interested in another volunteer assignment, their paying jobs may become overwhelming, or they suffer from burnout. Offer them a volunteer leave of absence or vacation rather than losing them. Keep in touch with them; send them newsletters, an annual report, and a birthday card; and if you don't hear from them, call and invite them back.

(C) VOLUNTEER PROMOTIONS

Few people want to do the same job endlessly, even when they are good at it. Consider offering good volunteers a promotion—perhaps as a manager. Be creative about restructuring your program to make the most of their talents. How about a volunteer as an assistant to the volunteer manager, or as an assistant fund raiser or marketing person? The possibilities are endless, depending on the talents of the volunteers and the needs of the community.

(D) STAFF MEETINGS

Include volunteers at staff meetings; if this is not possible, create team meetings. Volunteers need to have a voice in their own assignments, and they can contribute good ideas. Good ideas are not restricted to those who get paid for their work.

(E) PRESENTATIONS

Invite volunteers who are involved in interesting projects to make presentations at a board meeting. The enthusiasm and interest of the unpaid staff person can frequently be more inspirational than that of a paid staff member.

Also, involve volunteers in radio and television interviews. It is tempting for staff to want to take center stage, but volunteers speak engagingly about a program since they are involved only because they want to be.

(F) ADVOCACY OPPORTUNITIES

Invite volunteers to advocate with governmental agencies. Volunteers are often much more credible witnesses, simply because they are not paid to advocate.

(G) VOLUNTEER ADVISORY COUNCIL

Form a volunteer advisory council to discuss the policies and procedures of the program; develop new ideas for volunteer recognition; and assess additional needs for volunteer involvement. Rotate the membership among the volunteers by having terms of office, and always include some members of the board of directors so that policymaking and direct-service volunteers have a chance to interact.

(H) EXPENSE REIMBURSEMENT

Volunteers should be reimbursed for out-of-pocket expenses such as carfare or parking. Volunteers are not free, but a very small budget yields remarkable cost benefit.

(I) BENEFITS

Volunteers need a cup of coffee or a soda; a safe working environment; and liability, accident, and excess automobile insurance (if they drive as part of their volunteer job description). They also need to be regarded as an important part of the staff.

(J) PERSONNEL FILE

A volunteer should have a personnel file that contains a record of involvement. This is very useful when the volunteer needs a reference or the manager has to be reminded of good performance to be recognized.

(K) GRIEVANCE PROCEDURES

It is good for volunteers to know that there is a process for settling grievances—perhaps first with the manager of the program, second with the advisory committee, and finally with the executive director.

(L) INTERESTING TASKS

Volunteers want to do interesting and meaningful work. Routine tasks have to be done sometimes, but vary the work that volunteers are given.

(M) RESPECTING VOLUNTEERS

No one is "just a volunteer"; volunteers deserve respect and work that takes advantage of their skills and interest. If one agency is not right for them, they should be referred to another.

(N) PROFESSIONALIZING THE PROGRAM

Volunteer managers are professionals in the area of human resource development. They must respect their own professional development. They must regard their volunteers as professionals, too, and expect professional behavior from them. The more respect volunteers receive, the more they will contribute. Think every day: "There is no task in this agency that the *right* volunteer can't do."

(O) VOLUNTEERS AS TRAINERS

Volunteers can be very helpful in training other volunteers, and they will appreciate being tapped for this kind of responsibility.

(P) VOLUNTEER SOCIALIZATION

Create opportunities for volunteers to celebrate success.

(Q) STAFF APPRECIATION

Recognize and commend staff who work particularly well with volunteers. When staff see that their management skills are recognized, they are much more apt to welcome volunteers as part of their team.

34.14 Recognition

Recognition is something that starts the minute a volunteer enters the program, when the program in all that it does recognizes its volunteers as partners doing significant work in an effective way, and the manager sets high standards and encourages and supports the volunteers.

Recognition is remembering people's names, their birthdays, their needs, and their motivations, and giving them honest compliments for their good work. Recognition can be formal or informal, public or private; it can be tailored to suit the person's individual needs for affiliation, achievement, or power. For example:

- Recognition for people motivated by affiliation:
  - Public: Balloons tied to their desks
    A recognition lunch, tea, or dinner and a corsage or coffee mug
    Their pictures on the bulletin board
  - Private: A personal note
    A birthday card
    An invitation to have coffee, one on one
- Recognition for people motivated by achievement:
  - Public: A report with their byline
    A letter to their boss recognizing their achievements
    A promotion
  - Private: A letter from the executive director
    A letter from the chair of the board
- Recognition for people motivated by personalized power:
  - Public: Their pictures in a metropolitan newspaper
    An interview on radio or television
    Their picture with the president, governor, or mayor
  - Private: A letter from the president, governor, or mayor
- Recognition for people motivated by socialized power:
  - Public: Acknowledgment that some important legislation would not have passed without their lobbying power
    Acknowledgment that the fund-raising goal would not have been reached without their organizational skill
  - Private: Observing that they are developing other leaders in the organization besides themselves
    Encouragement and respect of peers

Many agencies give annual dinners for their volunteers and find that all volunteers do not attend. That is simply because that kind of recognition does not appeal to everyone: It does not meet their needs.

Pins, mugs, and certificates are all pleasant ways to recognize volunteers, but there is a great deal of debate about recognition that takes the form of choosing "the best volunteer." Those in favor of choosing an outstanding volunteer say that it is an inspiration to other volunteers and gives them something to strive for. It also can create good media coverage, particularly if the best volunteer is honored by the president, governor, or mayor.

Those opposed to such awards say that it is impossible to choose the best volunteer and that for every volunteer that is happy to be chosen, at least 20 who believe they are just as outstanding feel hurt and unappreciated. They suggest that it is better to choose the "most exciting new idea," the "most interesting project," the "best team"—or, don't worry about the "best"; just celebrate the program and treat everyone equally. If a program does decide to give "best" awards, it should choose an objective committee so that the decision is not attributable to anyone who manages the program or the agency.

34.15 *Evaluation*

(A) EVALUATING THE PROGRAM: TYPES OF EVALUATION

(i) *Process Evaluation*
Most programs calculate the number of volunteers involved in the program and the number of hours they volunteered. They will also ask themselves if they went through all the proper steps to create the program (see Section 34.2). Good programs will have a mutual evaluation with the volunteers to talk about the quality of their work. These are "process evaluations." They are looking at the *means* through which the program was accomplished. It is essential to measure process, but too many managers stop there, evoking the very natural questions, "That's fine that you did all of those things; but what did the volunteers accomplish; what was improved because of this program?"

(ii) *Outcome-Based Evaluation*
Outcome-based evaluation answers the most important question: What did the volunteer program accomplish? It is an absolutely essential question so that volunteer managers can assure themselves, their boards, CEOs, funders, and volunteers that something significant happened. But even more important: *It is the way volunteer managers can decide if the result was worth the effort put into the program and, if not, determine how they will change the program to make it more effective.*

(iii) *What Is Success?*
Outcome-based evaluation concentrates on *ends*, not means. Volunteer managers need to ask themselves the following question at the beginning of the program: What will be successful outcomes of this program to:

- The agency?
- The volunteers?
- The community?

Successful outcomes for the agency could be:

- The agency's ability to meet client needs successfully will be enhanced by 50 percent.
- There will be a 30 percent increase in funds contributed because of the agency's increased presence in the community.
- Paid staff will undertake a new program (name it) because volunteers have successfully taken over major operations of the current program.
- There is increased CEO, board, and staff commitment to the volunteer program.

Successful outcomes for the volunteers might be:

- Volunteers are excited about the impact they are making.
- Volunteers want to continue in this program.
- Select volunteers are able to serve as middle managers in the program.
- Volunteers have met some of their personal needs by being involved in the program (e.g., experience that has led to a paying job or credit in a college course, knowledge of a particular field).
- Volunteers were involved in this program who might not have been able to be involved in other programs because of flex-time, family volunteering, or other innovations.

Successful outcomes for the community might be:

- Increased percentage of clientele served
- Percentage of clientele able to do something they were not able to do before program started
- Community involvement in program (e.g., collaborations with other agencies, involvement of community leaders, involvement of community as volunteers)

(iv) How to Measure Success

Starting simply, the volunteer manager can put in place some useful ways to measure outcomes. In some instances, there will be comparable data already available. In others, the wise volunteer manager will need to accumulate some information at the beginning of the program. The following are ways to measure:

For the Agency
- Client surveys of satisfaction with the volunteers
- Fund-raising reports before and after program
- New program undertaken by staff and its impact on agency's ability to deliver services
- Board attendance at volunteer recognitions; budget for volunteer program; involvement of volunteer manager in planning before and after program. Staff involvement of volunteers and level of satisfaction with volunteers indicated in staff survey before and after program

For the Volunteers
- Surveys of volunteer satisfaction
- Volunteer retention

For the Community
- Client surveys
- Surveys of community people involved with clients (e.g., parents, teachers)
- Pre- and post-tests of skills attained
- Survey of community leaders regarding involvement in program

Community measurements will be different depending on the nature of the program, but the community is the most important measuring stick. They are the agency's prime customer.

If the program rehabilitates housing, it is quite simple to measure the number of houses rehabilitated and the families having better housing. It is more difficult to measure some other programs, such as neighborhood safety or self-esteem building. But surveys and pre- and post-tests can tell a lot about attitudinal changes. These attitudinal results can show more concrete results in the second year of the program. The following are some measurement devices to consider:

- Pre- and post-tests
- Focus groups
- Questionnaires
- Customer satisfaction surveys
- Tests of a "control group," a group not involved in the program evaluated in contrast to a group that is involved in the program
- Job placements (for a jobs program)
- One-on-one interviews

(B)   DISMISSING VOLUNTEERS

The policies for the volunteer program should contain the reasons that volunteers might be dismissed, for example, failure to adhere to the rules of the organization or inability to fulfill the position description. (See Section 34.5.)

Some things like breach of confidentiality or abuse of drugs or alcohol (rules of the organization) can lead to immediate dismissal. But when a volunteer is obeying agency rules but seems unable to do the task needed, the volunteer manager needs to let him or her know the areas for concern; make some suggestions and follow up with coaching and/or training to give the volunteer an opportunity to improve. Many times, just a careful review of the position description can be helpful. Sometimes a situation can improve by assigning the volunteer to another position. Occasionally, a diplomatic referral to another program can "outplace" a problem volunteer to a more appropriate situation. The manager should keep a record of the conversations with the volunteer, the efforts made to help the volunteer do a better job, and the volunteer's improvement or lack thereof.

However, when all reasonable efforts are exhausted to help a volunteer become more effective and the volunteer has been made aware of his or her problems, the volunteer may have to be dismissed. If the efforts to discuss the matter with the volunteer in advance and provide some assistance to him or her have been clear and honest, many times dismissal of the volunteer will not be necessary because the volunteer will realize the situation is not appropriate and will leave the program voluntarily. But when dismissal is required, if the volunteer manager has followed the necessary steps, dismissal should be straightforward and not argumentative, since the volunteer has been made aware previously of the concerns and has had sufficient opportunities to overcome them. A simple grievance procedure should be in place if a volunteer believes dismissal is not just and wishes to contest it.

34.16 Conclusion

Volunteers are important resources to meet community needs. They are too important to be taken for granted or patronized. Good volunteer programs demand the best of each person involved. This builds self-esteem and continuing involvement.

Good volunteer programs demand the best of the agency. This builds capacity, collaboration, and community presence.

If programs are to be good for the community, the agency, and the volunteers, they must follow the steps of good human resource management. But having position descriptions, training, and recognition are not enough by themselves. Programs must make sure they are not just continuing to do things the same way because that is the way they have always done them. They must continuously ask themselves: "How can we do it better?"

The need for volunteers changes as the needs of the community change. The needs of volunteers themselves change as their lives change. The effective leader understands the constancy of change and accepts it as a challenge and an opportunity.

Endnotes

1. Gardner, J. H. (1988). *The Changing Nature of Leadership.* Washington, DC: Independent Sector.
2. The Points of Light Foundation. (1993). *Changing the Paradigm.* Washington, DC: Points of Light.
3. Independent Sector/The Gallup Organization. (1999). *Giving & Volunteering in the United States, 1998.* Washington, DC: Independent Sector.
4. International Association for Voluntary Effort Web site, *http://www.unv.org/projects/iyv2001/ iave.html.*
5. International Year of the Volunteer Web site, *http://www.unv.org/projects/iyv2001/index.html.*
6. See note 3.
7. National Commission for Civic Renewal. (1998 and 1999). *A Nation of Spectators.* School of Public Affairs, University of Maryland.
8. Bellah, R. N., Madsen, R., et al. (1985). *Habits of the Heart.* Berkeley: University of California Press.
9. Putnam, R. (1995). "Bowling Alone: America's Declining Social Capital," *Journal of Democracy* (January).
10. See note 3.
11. Bradner, J. H. (1986). "Strengths and Weaknesses of Volunteerism in Illinois and What it Means to Those Who Lead Volunteers," *Volunteer Illinois* (Winter).
12. United Parcel Service, Community Relations Report. (May 1988). *UPS Study Finds That Poor Management Turns Off Volunteers.*
13. Meneghetti, M., and K. Seel, "Ethics and Values in the Not-for-Profit Organization." In T. D. Connors (ed.), *The Nonprofit Handbook, 1998 Supplement,* New York: John Wiley & Sons, p. 1.

14. Association for Volunteer Administration, P.O. Box 32092, Richmond, VA 23294.

15. *Nonprofit Times,* 240 Cedar Knolls Road, Cedar Knolls, NJ 07927.

16. See note 3.

17. Seymour, H. J. (1988). *Designs for Fund Raising.* Ambler, PA: Fund Raising Institute.

18. Wilson, M. (1976). *The Effective Management of Volunteer Programs.* Boulder, CO: Volunteer Management Associates.

19. Id.

20. Adapted in part from Zemke, R. and S. Zemke. (1995). "Adult Learning: What Do We Know for Sure?" *Training* (June): 31–40.

21. See note 2.

Suggested Readings

Bradner, J. H. (1993). *Passionate Volunteerism.* Winnetka, IL: Conversation Press.

Bradner, J. H. (1999). *Leading Volunteers for Results.* Winnetka, IL: Conversation Press.

Bradner, J. H. (1998). "Strengths and Weaknesses of Volunteerism in Illinois." *Journal of Volunteer Administration,* Association for Volunteer Administration (Fall).

Graff, L. L. (1993). *By Definition: Policies for Volunteer Programs.* Volunteer Ontario.

Internet Sites of Interest

Provides an online newsletter called Board Café, as well as technical assistance papers on their Nonprofit Genie.

CYBERVPM: *http://www.cybervpm.com*

Virtual university on volunteer management.

ENERGIZE: *http://www.energizeinc.com*

Site on volunteer management.

GENIE.ORG: *http://www.genie.org*

HELPING.ORG: *http://www.helping.org*

Information on volunteering and volunteering opportunities. Information on how to set up a nonprofit organization.

INTERNATIONAL YEAR OF THE VOLUNTEER: *http://www.iyv2001.org*

Information about the international year, sponsored by the United Nations.

IMPACT ON LINE: *http://www.volunteermatch.org*

Provides an opportunity for nonprofits to list their volunteer needs and connect with interested volunteers.

LEGAL HANDBOOK FOR VOLUNTEERS: *http://www.ptialaska.net/~jdewitt/vlh/*

Online edition of the Volunteer's Legal Handbook.

NATIONAL FOUNDATION TO PREVENT CHILD ABUSE: *http://www.childsexualabuse.org*

Information on criminal records checks.

RISK MANAGEMENT: *www.nonprofitrisk.org*

Information and publications

VIRTUAL VOLUNTEERISM: *http://www.serviceleader.org*

Information on volunteering via computer.

VOLUNTEER TODAY: *http://www.voluntertoday.org*

Monthly Web magazine on volunteer program management.

Policies for Volunteer Programs*

LINDA L. GRAFF
Graff and Associates

* This chapter is adapted from the monograph *By Definition: Policies for Volunteer Programs* (Graff, 1992), used here with the generous permission of the publisher, Graff and Associates; it originally appeared as Chapter 7 in Tracy Daniel Connors (ed.). *The Volunteer Management Handbook.* New York: John Wiley & Sons, 1995.

All of this is a far cry from the days when an agency staff member would pick up the phone periodically and call in some friends and neighbours to help with the task at hand—Nora Silver[1]

35.1   Introduction

There are many excellent reasons to write policies around voluntary action in nonprofit organizations (NPOs). Policies can be used to establish continuity, to ensure fairness and equity, to clarify values and beliefs, to communicate expectations, to specify standards, and to state rules. There is no more compelling reason for immediate policy development, however, than fear of the consequences of not doing so.

Consider this situation: Sandy, a volunteer friendly visitor in a program for isolated seniors, arrived for her regular shift at her client's house to find the client quite unwell. The client, Mrs. Fritz, didn't want to make a fuss and tried to keep Sandy from notifying anyone, but finally allowed her to call the family doctor. The doctor said, "Bring her in." While driving wasn't really part of the volunteer job, Sandy thought it important to get help right away and drove Mrs. Fritz over to the doctor's office.

The doctor thought that Mrs. Fritz might have had a mild heart attack, scheduled some tests, and told Sandy to take her home. Sandy objected, but when the physician insisted, Sandy helped Mrs. Fritz into the car and they headed off home. On the way, Mrs. Fritz cried out, put her hands to her chest, and slumped forward. Sandy reached over to hold Mrs. Fritz up, and drove into a tree.

If this happened in your volunteer program, you would probably be wringing your hands, rushing to check your insurance coverage, and wondering where things went wrong. The fact is that this kind of example, and thousands like it, describe accidents waiting to happen in volunteer programs all over North America. And while there is nothing anyone can do to guarantee that injuries and loss will not occur as the result of volunteering, there are many steps that agency administrators and managers of volunteers can take to help prevent serious incidents, and to minimize harm and reduce liability when they do occur. Policy development is one of the most critical of those steps. This chapter will define policies and procedures, discuss how policies fit into an overall risk management program, and outline four important types and functions of policies. Included are descriptions of the policy development process, how to write policies, and how to increase compliance with policies.

35.2   What Are Policies?

(A)   DEFINITIONS OF POLICY AND PROCEDURE

The word *policy* is one with which we are all familiar, yet for most people it is difficult to identify exactly what it means in the context of our agencies and programs. It is difficult to sort out what a policy is, how it differs from a procedure, and the respective roles of each. The very word policy can be intimidating. Few people work with policies on a regular basis. Most do not have the opportunity to understand policy or to feel at ease with it.

There are a variety of perspectives on what policy is or should be. A number of definitions of policy are presented here, because each offers different elements of what policies are and what they can achieve. *Webster's New World Dictionary* (Second College Edition) defines policy as "a principle, plan, or course of action." Two distinct themes emerge from this definition:

1. Policy, in the sense of a principle, implies that some kind of position is being taken, that a value or belief is being stated.
2. Policy, in the sense of a plan or a course of action, would include specific steps, procedures, or perhaps a method.

Both of these aspects of the definition of policies are relevant because nonprofit organizations need to articulate their values and also need to have procedural guidelines in place to instruct staff (paid and unpaid) on what to do or not to do.

Shaw adds some thoughts on the nature of policies:

- They apply to everybody associated with the organization: its directors, staff, volunteers, and clients.
- A policy states a boundary: inside the boundary, things are acceptable; outside the boundary, things are not.
- It is also in the nature of a policy that violations make one liable for consequences; in that sense, a policy is tough.[2]

Paula Cryderman, who has written a manual on how to write policy manuals, helps clarify the difference between policies and procedures. She says policies tell people *what* to do:

Policies form the written basis of operation secondary to legislation and the organization's bylaws. They serve as guidelines for decision making; they prescribe limits and pinpoint responsibilities within an organization. Policies can be viewed as rules or laws related to the facility's overall mission, goals and objectives. They are usually broad statements that are general in content. Despite this, policies may be detailed and particular if appropriate to the subject matter.[3]

On the other hand, procedures tell people *how* to do what they must do. According to Cryderman:

Procedures give directions according to which daily operations are conducted within the framework of policies. They are a natural outgrowth of policies, supplying the "how to" for the rule. Procedures describe a series of steps, outline sequences of activities or detail progression. Thus the procedure manual is operational and is usually best expressed in a directive tone.[4]

Cryderman says that the terms policy and procedure should not be confused, yet in practice it is often difficult to distinguish between types of policies, or between policies and procedures. The distinction drawn previously—policy as *what* and procedure as *how*—seems straightforward, but in reality the distinction blurs.

35.3   Why Policies Are Written

(A)   WHY NOW?

The convergence of several key trends in the voluntary sector compels us to develop policies for volunteer programs. Among these trends are the:

- Changing nature of volunteering
- Increasing degree of risk associated with volunteering
- Deficit of organizational and administrative support for volunteer programs
- Increasingly litigational nature of our culture

Volunteer work is increasingly responsible, sophisticated, and complex. It constitutes the "real work" of voluntary organizations. In fact, a great many voluntary organizations would see their operations grind to a halt without the contributions of volunteers. Volunteers themselves are increasingly skilled and educated, and looking to apply their expertise through voluntary action.

Simply put, the more responsible and complex the work, the greater the risks associated with its completion. If volunteers are rolling bandages, for example, dangers are minimal. But consider these actual examples:

- Volunteers providing home support for the disabled are helping to transfer patients in and out of the bathtub without training.
- Volunteer counselors staff a suicide prevention hot line with little training, and they have no professional backup while on duty.
- A volunteer friendly visitor drives his client to the grocery store each week to help her do her shopping. If he were to be stopped, his car would be pulled off the road for noncompliance with safety regulations.
- A volunteer at the local senior citizen center has some first-aid training and has been helping seniors make some decisions about which of their prescription medications they should and should not bother to take.
- An elderly woman who has been a volunteer escort at the cancer treatment center for over two decades is beginning to lose her faculties. Last week she took a patient in a wheelchair to the wrong clinic, where he waited for three hours before staff were able to locate him.
- Female volunteers are sent out to deliver parenting education classes to single mothers in low-income housing projects. The volunteers go alone, according to their own schedule, often at night. The agency has no record of who is going where or when.
- Volunteers for the local environmental cleanup agency have been disabling the chain brake safety mechanisms on chain saws because the brakes make this already hard work even more arduous.

Rapid change and growth, combined with chronic underfunding of volunteer programs, have produced a gap between the real complexity of volunteer involvement and the ability of organizations to understand and manage the valuable resource they have mobilized. As Nora Silver puts it:

The future of community organizations, and the independent sector as a whole, depends on the future of our volunteers. Right now that future is at risk. It is not for want of volunteers. It is not for want of good organizations providing good services. It is for want of the capacity of these good organizations to utilize people well.[5]

In contrast to the stereotype of volunteering held by the general public, and even by some agency managers (paid and unpaid), volunteering has developed into important work that deserves profound and immediate administrative attention. Unfortunately, administrators in many voluntary organizations do not understand that their attention is needed. Ellis puts it this way:

After years of training and consulting with so many leaders of volunteers, I have become convinced that many of their concerns stem directly from a lack of substantive support from their agencies' top administrators. This lack of support is not due to malice or unwillingness to be of help, but is rather due to the failure of executives to understand what is really needed from them.[6]

As a consequence, many large-scale, complex volunteer programs operate in a policy void, and, ironically, remain virtually invisible to the very people who will be held accountable when something goes wrong.

That someone will be held accountable for errors, omissions, accidents, injuries, or loss grows more certain every day. In this increasingly litigational culture—the "suit society," according to Conrad and Glenn, where people "sue anybody for anything"—voluntary organizations, and the good people who are ultimately responsible for the work undertaken in the name of the organization (themselves volunteers), simply cannot afford to ignore such exposure to liability.[7] As O'Connell indicates: "There have been several legal cases where board members were held legally accountable, largely because they had failed to exercise reasonable oversight and objectivity . . . the trustees had not taken responsibility for knowing what was going on."[8]

In the courts, in the press, in the public mind, boards are being held accountable for mistakes, accidents, and negligence on the part of volunteers acting on behalf of the organization. "Not knowing" simply is not a good enough excuse—legally or morally. The matter of policy development for volunteer programs has become urgent. The formula is quite simple: The greater the degree of responsibility of volunteer work itself, the greater the need for rules to govern and regulate its accomplishment; the greater the need for guidelines to ensure safety; the greater the need for policies.

(B)   LEVELS OF POLICY

When we think about the term *policy*, we usually think about statements issued from the highest levels of the organization in terms that are both general in nature and broad in scope. Proclamations issued from senior administration often take the form of policy statements. In fact, John Carver, who writes about policy governance by boards of directors, says "Conventionally, policy has referred to any board utterance."[9]

Policies from the top of the organization typically have organization-wide applicability. For example, organizations develop board policy statements on philosophy, values, and beliefs that apply to all aspects of the organization. Here is an example from the Volunteer Centre of Metropolitan Toronto that has implications for both external programming (who is eligible for service) and internal operations (who is hired as paid staff, who is recruited as a volunteer, how promotions are determined):

> *The Volunteer Centre of Metropolitan Toronto is committed to ensuring that its mission and operations embrace the community. It actively encourages the community to partici-pate fully and benefit fully from its services. The Volunteer Centre . . . is committed to racial equality and the elimination of racism in Metro Toronto. It strives to reflect the com-munity in its structure (volunteer and staff) and to promote equal access to its services.[10]*

Typically, policies at this level will be the responsibility of senior administration, both paid and unpaid. Input from staff, direct-service volunteers, and other organizational stake-holders may be invited, but the board is the key player in this kind of policymaking.

Many policies are much more specific and much more limited in scope. For example, organizations write policies about whether or not the newsletter volunteers in the home sup-port program must pay for the coffee they drink while on duty. This too is a policy matter, but with limited applicability, influence, and import. Policies of this nature are less likely to receive board and chief executive officer (CEO) attention. Rather, they are more likely to be the responsibility of departmental staff or program committees, although in smaller organi-zations, boards will sometimes involve themselves in policy matters of this sort.

(C) POLICY AND RISK MANAGEMENT

There is no more pressing reason to develop policies for volunteer programs than the role that policies play in an overall risk management system. There are several simple, straightforward risk management models that managers of volunteers can consult.[11–15] While each of these models is slightly different from the others, a key theme found in all of them is the need for policy development as a critical component of a comprehensive risk management program.

Policies supply rules. They establish boundaries beyond which volunteers should not wander. They specify what is and is not expected, what is and is not safe. To take the story about Sandy and Mrs. Fritz, there were several points at which the presence of policies could have prevented the tragedy that occurred. For example:

- What is the agency policy regarding volunteers who are tempted to exceed the limits of their job description?
- What is the agency policy regarding volunteers who encounter a situation with which they feel they cannot cope or in which they feel uncomfortable making decisions?
- What is the agency policy regarding volunteer backup? Is there someone in authority on call at all times that volunteers are on duty—staff who can take over when the situation exceeds the limitations and responsibilities of the volunteer's role?
- What is the agency policy about friendly visiting volunteers driving their clients? Is it allowed? Is there a full set of policies regarding such volunteer transportation service? What is the agency policy regarding insurance coverage for nonowned automobiles?

If policies such as these had been in place and well known to Sandy, the story would most certainly have had a different outcome. The conclusions to be drawn here are obvious: Policies can play a major role in preventing accidents; and policies can serve to minimize the harm that can result from accidents. Although there is nothing that any agency can do to guarantee that accidents will not happen, policies can reduce an organization's exposure to liability in the event that a law suit is launched. For example, there is no better proof that an agency has acted prudently and responsibly in attempting to reduce the likelihood of injury or loss than a full set of current, comprehensive policies and procedures, clearly in place, and consistently communicated to all relevant parties.

(D)　POLICIES AS EMPOWERMENT (GAINING ACCESS TO THE BOARD)

Volunteer programs are typically underrecognized and underresourced. Boards and senior management have lost touch with the expansion in scale and significance of voluntary action, even in their own organizations. As Nora Silver points out, a gap has been created between the ability of managers of volunteers to create volunteer programs—to recruit, place, and supervise volunteers—and the organization's development of administrative, communications, and accountability systems to support those volunteer programs.[16] Ellis calls this "benign neglect."[17] Silver calls it "benign indifference." Silver says:

> The Board of Directors provides leadership to the organization: it sets overall agency policy and assumes fiscal responsibility for the organization. As the board is ultimately legally responsible for the agency program, it is also responsible for the volunteer component. The board has the power to authorize the construction of a volunteer program, and it has the responsibility to ensure the effectiveness of that program. The board can—and should—call for program objectives, established policies and procedures, professional management, involvement and recognition of volunteers, and adequate budget for the volunteer program.[18]

The question arises: "But how do we get the attention of senior management and boards of directors?" The answer may be: "Policies, in the context of risk management."

When something goes wrong in the volunteer program, the ultimate responsibility will not fall to the manager of volunteers. As Silver notes, the board is ultimately legally responsible for all that occurs under the auspices of the agency, and hence the law suit, when it arrives, will settle on the board table.[19] And board members, in general, are becoming increasingly aware of their own vulnerability to liability:

> Board volunteers are suddenly realizing that not only can the voluntary organization they serve be sued; but there are instances in which volunteers themselves can be sued—as individuals.[20]

It is suggested, then, that the best way to get the attention of senior management—boards and CEOs—is to alert them to the potential risks and hazards embodied in volunteering. In this view, policy development for volunteer programs is the key to the boardroom door.[21] Some would suggest this to be fear-mongering, or manipulation by fear. In fact, managers of volunteers have an obligation to alert their supervisors to risks and liability. Not doing so is irresponsible. Only when risks are fully identified and assessed can they be managed properly.

But alerting management to the dangers is only half of the task. As we have seen, policy development is a key component in risk management. Boards generally concur that policy development is within the realm of board mandate, and they can, therefore, be counted on to pay attention when someone exclaims, "We need a policy on that!" The comprehensive strategy might be to:

- Identify the risks.
- Draft policies and procedures that minimize the risk and/or limit the organization's liability.
- Take these, together, to the board table.

When the board realizes that the activity being undertaken in the volunteer department is significant enough to create liability exposures for both the organization and board members personally, the volunteer program will be seen in a different light. Suddenly, it will become a department worthy of board time and attention. From here, the manager of volunteers can build a case for adequate resources (budget, space, staffing) and agency support services (supervision, direction, insurance, policy and procedure development). Here is a concrete tool to accomplish what Scheier calls on all managers to do: "Insofar as volunteer administration continues to see itself as derivative, passive and dependent, others naturally tend to see us that way too. Beginning to define ourselves as powerful, active and autonomous is the first step in becoming more so."[22]

Policy development via risk management may be the most productive route for managers of volunteers to empower their volunteer programs. As Silver found in her research on organizational factors that engender effective volunteer programs:

> *The commitment of the administrative leadership of an organization is necessary to raise the volunteer program to priority status. Without the leadership behind it, a volunteer program—no matter how well organized and potentially viable and valuable—simply will not have the organizational power necessary to progress and develop.[23]*

35.4 Where Policies Are Needed

With the possible exception of policies about confidentiality, a great many volunteer programs operate in a policy vacuum. Managers of volunteers ask anxiously, "What policies do I need?" and "What if I miss something really important?" The answer to these questions varies from program to program and inevitably hinges on the nature of the volunteer program, the kind of work done by volunteers, the nature and complexity of the organization, and the amount of resources available for policy development. In a recent manual on policy development for volunteer programs, sample policies are presented on more than 70 different topics that would be applicable to most types of volunteer programs.[24] Nearly as many again could be added to cover the unique dimensions of any specific program.

(A) FUNCTIONS OF POLICIES

There is a way of conceptualizing policies according to their function that can be used to determine which policies any specific program needs to develop. There are four general functions served by policies in volunteer programs:

1. Policies as risk management
2. Policies as values and belief statements
3. Policies as rules
4. Policies as program improvement tools

Each is explored in some detail as follows.

(i) Policies as Risk Management

As discussed earlier, policies are a critical component in an agency's overall risk management program. Through policies, boundaries can be established to delineate what is and what is not safe. Consider these examples.

On waivers:

All new clients must sign a liability release form as a standard component of the "application for service" procedure.

On agency backup for volunteers on duty:

It is important that all direct service volunteers have backup from the agency in the event that they encounter trouble in the course of their volunteer duties. An identified staff member or other agency representative will be on duty and accessible at all times when agency volunteers are on assignment.

On volunteers driving:

While on duty, volunteer Friendly Visitors for the Acme Home Support Agency will not use their own personal vehicles to transport agency clients.

The procedure to follow such a policy might look like this:

Should an emergency arise in which a client requires immediate transportation, and time permits, the volunteer will contact his or her manager of volunteers or agency backup at Acme for direction. If the circumstance is more urgent, the volunteer may use his or her own judgment regarding whether an ambulance or other emergency service is required. Immediately after an incident of this sort, the volunteer must notify Acme of the situation and of the actions the volunteer has initiated.

Here is a final example of a policy established primarily for risk management purposes regarding the agency's obligation to inform volunteers of risks associated with volunteering, and the right of volunteers to refuse assignments:

The safety and well-being of all volunteers serving Acme is of paramount importance, and every effort will be made to eliminate all hazards related to the performance of volunteer duties. In circumstances where some element of risk remains beyond our control, volunteers will be informed, in advance, to the best of our knowledge and ability. This includes, but is not limited to, notification of any hazardous material, practice or process that volunteers may encounter while engaged in Acme business. Volunteers are entirely within their rights to refuse to perform volunteer assignments that appear to pose unacceptable risks.

Using this particular policy function as a guide to determining which policies a volunteer program needs to develop, the manager would:

- Look around the volunteer program.
- Better still, walk around the volunteer work site(s).
- Watch out for risks, hazards, and dangers.
- Play the "What if?" game, trying to identify what could go wrong under a series of different circumstances. What would this room look like if it were filled with smoke? How would this activity look from the perspective of a wheelchair? Would this activity be more dangerous in cold temperatures? in high winds? in the middle of an ice storm?

This, in fact, is a common first step in the risk management process. Called *disaster imaging,* it allows the manager to determine where policies might prevent accidents and injuries, to minimize the likelihood of accidents and injuries, and to minimize the harm should an accident happen. For example:

- If the manager, in walking around the day care center, spots a skateboard in the toy box, she may very well go back to her desk and issue a policy to the day care staff that prohibits use of skateboards on agency property.
- When the trail maintenance supervisor accompanies her volunteers on a shift and notices that they have disengaged the chain saw brake mechanism, she might very well write a new policy about *all* equipment safety features and be certain that this new policy is highlighted in all volunteer training programs from here on.

This technique is proactive and, of course, takes place under ideal circumstances. In reality, we often cannot foresee accidents. We are alerted to dangers only after an incident or a near miss. So write a policy that requires all staff and volunteers to report all accidents and other serious occurrences to you. Make it a practice to think in detail about policy development whenever a serious incident report arrives on your desk. Accidents are bad enough. Reoccurrences because of inaction are inexcusable.

(ii) Policies as Values and Belief Statements

Every organization builds a web of values and beliefs about the world in which it works, the nature of the problem(s) it seeks to address, and the way in which it operates. Some of these are subtle and rarely discussed. Many are unwritten but nonetheless well known and clearly understood. In addition, agencies often take positions on questions and issues related to their services, as well as to their own internal operations. Policy statements are a mechanism for both articulating and communicating such values, beliefs, and positions. Following are some examples.

On antidiscrimination and affirmative action:

The Centre will not permit discrimination against applicants or employees (paid staff/volunteers) on the basis of race, religion, age, gender, sexual orientation, disability, socio-economic background or ethnicity. This applies to all areas of employment (paid staff/volunteers) including recruiting, hiring, promotion, assigning of work . . . provided the individual is qualified and meets the requirements established by the Centre for the position.[25]

Equal opportunity practices and affirmative action techniques relative to minority involvement, training, development, recognition, and retention will be incorporated in volunteer recruitment efforts. Established affirmative action targets will be met within a specified time frame, tailored to local demographic realities, and include formalized, periodic evaluation.[26]

On the importance of volunteers to the organization:

The achievement of the goals of this agency is best served by the active participation of citizens of the community. To this end, the agency accepts and encourages the involvement of volunteers at all levels of the agency and within all appropriate programs and activities. . . [27]

Volunteers, and the contributions they make through volunteering, significantly enhance the quality of life, community spirit, and leisure time opportunities in Burlington. Volunteers are a valuable human resource requiring and warranting support and encouragement to maintain and develop their skills and to ensure their continued involvement in the provision of leisure opportunities throughout the City. The Parks and Recreation Department will continue to develop and provide support for volunteers and volunteer groups to ensure their continued involvement in leisure services and to develop this resource to its fullest.[28]

On the agency's right to fire volunteers:

The agency accepts the service of all volunteers with the understanding that such service is at the sole discretion of the agency. Volunteers agree that the agency may at any time, for whatever reason, decide to terminate the volunteer's relationship with the agency.[29]

Values embodied in acceptable terminology:

. . . greater policy direction be given and attention be paid, in both speech and the written and printed word, to the appropriate and accepted vocabulary in describing the Red Cross work force. This is always "paid and volunteer staff" or "paid and volunteer consultants" or "paid and volunteer instructors," etc., and never "professional staff and volunteers."

. . . The entire organization, including volunteers themselves, are to be encouraged to think of volunteers as staff members, with all the organizational support and personal responsibilities which this implies. Such phrases and attitudes as "I am just a volunteer" or "he is just a volunteer" are to be strongly discouraged.[30]

The technique to identify policies of this sort involves thinking through the values, beliefs, and positions held by the organization. Answer these questions:

- What do we hold as important? What do we value that volunteers need to know about? What is our philosophy about volunteers, about the work we do, about how we do business around here?
- What positions has the agency taken on issues, questions, or problems?
- What does the organization believe regarding good and bad, right and wrong, proper and improper, ethical and unethical?

The answers to many of these questions might be substance around which policies should be written and communicated.

Frequently, the most difficult policies to write—the ones around which there develops the greatest debate—are the policies that derive from values. Often, where disagreement surfaces in policy development, conflicting values will be the cause. In the examples in Exhibit 35.1, policy development will be difficult because the values that underpin the policies are both complex and not necessarily congruent with one another.

These are values in conflict. Profound beliefs that run to the very heart of organizational existence can sometimes be found to clash with one another. In these circumstances, it is first useful to recognize that the source of disagreement is values in conflict. Having identified the problem, the organization must engage in a *values sort*, a process whereby values are prioritized, with those that emerge on top serving as the basis for policy development.

(iii) Policies as Rules

Policies can be employed as rules to specify expectations, regulations, and guides to action. The distinction between policies as rules and policies as risk management often blurs. That is, a policy written to eliminate or reduce a specific risk might sound like a rule. A policy written because a rule is needed to guide a particular action may reduce a specific hazard.

EXHIBIT 35.1 Examples of Conflicting Values

Values Conflict 1

✓ We believe that volunteering is about caring for others, about simple motives to do good and help one's neighbors in times of need. It should not be overbureaucratized and overorganized.

✓ We also acknowledge that rules and regulations around volunteer involvement—rules on topics such as application processes, thorough screening, and discipline and dismissal—have become necessary to protect the well-being of both volunteers and clients.

☛ Will the volunteer screening policy require a personal interview, reference checks, and criminal records checks for all volunteers?

Values Conflict 2

✓ Like many voluntary organizations, our mission is based on the struggle to obtain and preserve the values of inclusivity, individual rights and freedoms, and antioppression in all of its manifestations. We believe that we have an obligation to extend those values both to our programming (outreach and equality of access, for example) and to our internal operations (hiring and promotions practices, for example).

✓ We also believe that clients have the right to demand from us services of the highest quality. Yet what is our response when a client refuses to accept the services of a volunteer on grounds typically prohibited by human rights legislation (the volunteer is the "wrong" age, the "wrong" gender, the "wrong" color, the "wrong" sexual orientation . . .)?

☛ Will we comply and find another volunteer and thereby collude with beliefs and behaviors that contradict our deeply held values regarding antioppression, or will we stand firm and refuse to reassign a volunteer, thereby failing to fulfill our mission to deliver services?

The solution to this seeming confusion is this: Don't worry about it, because it simply does not matter. The point is that one develops whatever policies are needed; if some policies serve more than one function, all the better. The following example of a conflict of interest policy is a good illustration of a policy as a rule:

> *Any possible conflict of interest on the part of a director shall be disclosed to the board. When any such interest becomes a matter of board action, such director shall not vote or use personal influence on the matter, and shall not be counted in the quorum for a meeting at which board action is to be taken on the interest. The director may, however, briefly state a position on the matter, and answer pertinent questions of board members. The minutes of all actions taken on such matters shall clearly reflect that these requirements have been met.[31]*

On the use of organizational affiliation:

> *Volunteers may not use their organizational affiliation in connection with partisan politics, religious matters, or community issues contrary to positions taken by the organization.*

On volunteers and picket lines:

> *In the event of a union-initiated work stoppage or legal strike, volunteers will not cross the picket line.*

On paid employees as volunteers:

> *Paid employees may not serve in governing, policy-making or advisory roles while employed by the organization, or within one year of terminating their paid employment with the organization. Paid employees may, however, serve in direct-service volunteer roles which are outside the scope of their paid work within the organization and which take place outside of usual working hours.[32]*

On family members as volunteers:

> *Family members of employees are allowed to volunteer but they may not be placed under the direct supervision or within the same department as other members of their family who are employees.[33]*

To determine required policies of this sort, review existing rules, both written and unwritten. Review past records such as memoranda, volunteer job descriptions, and volunteer performance review documentation to identify where rules have been articulated or directives issued. Also think about advisements or directives issued verbally to volunteers that have never been written down anywhere, but that nonetheless reflect "how we do things around here."

(iv) Policies as Program Improvement Tools

On occasion, it may be useful to upgrade an expectation, a protocol, or a standard to the level of a policy, to give it more authority and import. This technique is useful where an activity is important but is perhaps not seen to be important by, or at least warranting the attention of, those expected to comply. Time sheets are an excellent example:

Volunteers will mail or deliver their activity logs to the manager of volunteers within five working days of month-end.

Sometimes policies can be used to ensure that a program operates smoothly or to improve the effectiveness of a program or service. This policy on expectations of volunteers will enhance the service delivered:

Volunteers are expected to work within the parameters of their own volunteer job description while on duty with the agency. However, regular contact with clients can allow volunteers to make important observations about changes in the health and well-being of clients. Agency policy requires volunteers to report such observations to the Manager of Volunteers who will take appropriate action.

Implementing a policy that speaks to the operation of the program does not, of course, guarantee compliance, but the weight or import of stating an expectation in the form of a policy can help. It will also provide a basis for pursuing consequences in the case of noncompliance. To pinpoint which policies of this sort are required, the manager can simply consider aspects of the volunteer program that are not operating as effectively or as efficiently as desired. Having identified these, one might consider whether the additional weight of a policy pronouncement would encourage improvement.

(B) EQUALITY OR ELITISM? POLICY FOR DIRECT-SERVICE AND ADMINISTRATIVE VOLUNTEERS

It is rarely the case in agencies where policies have been written to guide the volunteer component that policies apply equally to direct-service *and* administrative (board, committee, advisory) volunteers. In the same way that so many board members refuse to consider themselves as volunteers (is it because they consider the label below them?), board members often think of themselves as outside (above?) the scope of policies written for volunteers. This type of two-tiered elitism among volunteer ranks has left administrative volunteering beyond both the control of, and the protection afforded by, risk management programs and policy development. The consequences of this pattern are dangerous. Consider these examples:

- Board members are rarely screened; formal application and interview procedures are rarely required.
- Reference checks on board members are rarely required, even of those board members who have significant financial responsibilities—treasurers and comptrollers, for example.
- The involvement of board members is rarely monitored, even though their actions and decisions are among the most important and influential in the organization.
- Board members are rarely disciplined or dismissed, even when clear cause exists.

It is recommended that policies written for volunteer programs include, in their scope, *all* volunteers, equally. Exceptions need to be identified clearly, and only with justification.

35.5   *Policy Development Process*

(A)   WHO SETS POLICY?

The precise way in which policies are drafted, reviewed, revised, approved, and implemented varies a good deal from agency to agency. In some agencies, the board will hold within its own mandate anything that even remotely resembles a policy. In other agencies, the executive director (CEO, administrator, or other senior staff member) may determine that drafting policies for board approval is his or her own responsibility. Some agencies may have, or decide to create, a policy committee that will oversee all matters of policy for the agency. In other agencies, senior administration (paid and unpaid) will welcome the research, advice, input, and drafts from front-line staff regarding policies with broad applicability, allowing more specific policies or policies with limited scope to be developed and implemented by department staff. Although none of these development systems is inherently right or wrong, it is probably best if organizations develop an internal culture that welcomes notification of the need for policy development, review, or revision from all agency personnel, paid or unpaid. It is not helpful for front-line workers to think of policy as out of their realm, or somehow "above them." People actually doing the work are often those most likely to identify risks, the need for improvements, or the need for rules or changes in rules.

(B)   ROLE OF THE MANAGER OR DIRECTOR OF VOLUNTEERS

It is important for the manager of volunteers to determine how policy development is typically handled in his or her organization. The manager will thus be able to determine just what role he or she can play in policy development for the volunteer program. There is no question, however, that the manager of volunteers is primarily responsible for identifying policy issues within the volunteer department and for bringing those to the attention of senior staff and administrators. At a minimum, it would be unethical not to report hazards or risks and to do everything possible to ensure the safety and well-being of all volunteers.

With few exceptions, senior administrators, paid and unpaid alike, have little knowledge of the details, the complexities, or the scale of volunteering as it actually occurs within their organizations. This makes getting the attention of senior administrators more difficult, to be sure, but it is all the more reason why the manager of volunteers must take the initiative in policy development for volunteer programs. The process may have to include a good deal of education regarding the true dimensions and significance of volunteer work. Some mention of personal and collective liability exposure will often motivate board members and senior staff to listen more closely.

(C)   ASK FOR HELP

As volunteer programs grow larger, as risks and liabilities grow, and as volunteers become engaged in increasingly sophisticated and even technical work, managers of volunteers have more and more complexities to manage. And changes and growth outside the volunteer department create new demands on the manager of volunteers. As Vineyard says:

*All of the trends that surround us as a nation have an impact on the work of directing vol-
unteer efforts. As the rapid pace of change escalates in the wider world, we find ourselves
having to adapt to the impact of those changes on our daily work and the roles we play in
leading volunteer energies.[34]*

It is simply unreasonable to expect any single individual to have expertise in all the areas
in which volunteers are engaged, especially in large organizations or organizations with
large volunteer programs. Developing policies for volunteer programs can require skills
and background in a wide range of fields, including:

- Human resource management
- Labor law
- Contract law
- Human rights legislation
- Risk management
- Statistics
- Insurance
- Information management
- Athletics
- Fund raising
- Planning
- Occupational health and safety
- Systems analysis
- Liability
- Accounting
- Education and training

How many managers of volunteers who do not work in health care settings know
enough details about communicable diseases and universal precautions to develop policies and procedures in this area? How many managers of volunteers know enough about
liability and insurance to guarantee maximum coverage and protection?

No one can be expected to know enough to develop all policies alone, so ask for help.
People from all walks of life are generally willing to volunteer for short-term positions as
consultants. Ask them to prepare a draft policy, to work with you and/or other agency
representatives to draft a policy, or to review or edit an existing draft. After all, managers
of volunteers are experts at volunteer recruitment—they just do not think, as often as they
might, about recruiting volunteers to help with their own work.

35.6   *How to Write Policies for Volunteer Programs*

(A)   SIX PRINCIPLES OF WRITING POLICIES

(i)   *Be Concise*
Write as much as is required for the policy to be clear and comprehensive. Remember,
however, that the longer the policies and the thicker the policy manual, the more intimidating it will be and the less likely that it will be read and used regularly.

(ii) Be Clear

Policy writers must take great care to ensure that the policies they develop convey precisely and completely what is intended. Do not assume that the people reading and applying policies will understand them to mean what was originally intended. Avoid technical terminology and jargon. Where it is necessary to use technical terms, explain them, either in the text or in an attached glossary.

(iii) Be Direct

Policies should very clearly tell people what is expected. Although one would hope for complete compliance with all policies, it is obvious that compliance with some policies is much more important than compliance with others. It is appropriate, therefore, that some policies be more strongly worded and more authoritative than others. For example, there are some policies for which the imperative mood—a command—is entirely proper:

- Volunteers will not give patients anything to eat or drink before patients' surgery.
- Volunteers will not disengage or otherwise tamper with any safety mechanisms on any equipment entrusted to their use.

In all cases, remember that policies are policies. They must be directive and they must articulate, as Cryderman says, the *what*.[35]

(iv) Round the Edges

Without diminishing the importance of the three preceding principles, one must not lose sight of the fact that the subject of the policy development being discussed here is the work of volunteers. Therefore, it is suggested that the tone of many policies in the volunteer department very consciously be softened to be as palatable and inoffensive as possible. Here are some sample policies to illustrate how rounding some of the rough edges of policies can make a big difference in tone.

On conflict of interest:

No person who has a conflict of interest with any activity or program of the agency, whether personal, philosophical, or financial shall be accepted or serve as a volunteer with the agency.[36]

An alternative might read something like this:

Many volunteers are very busy people who often have many connections and who sometimes volunteer for more than one organization at the same time. It is, therefore, not unusual for volunteers to find themselves in a conflict of interest situation, regardless of whether they do administrative (board or committee) or direct-service volunteering. Any volunteer who suspects that he or she may have a conflict of interest must notify his/her immediate supervisor in order to discuss application of the conflict of interest procedure, a copy of which is available from . . .

On turning volunteers away:

The agency reserves the right to decline involvement in its volunteer program by anyone it assesses to be unsuitable. The decision of the agency is final in these matters.

Versus:

While the agency may need to decline offers of involvement by prospective volunteer applicants, every care must be taken, in turning such applicants away, to leave intact the applicant's sense of self-confidence and dignity. In the process, emphasis must remain on the absence of a match between the gifts that the volunteer has to offer and what the position requires at the present time. Alternate placement opportunities or referral to the Voluntary Action Center will be offered wherever possible. (See also the Anti-discrimination Policy, outlined on page . . .)

The following series of policy statements regarding volunteer placement also conveys a deep respect for the rights and dignity of volunteers:

In determining suitable placements for volunteers, equal attention will be given to the interests and goals of the volunteer and to the requirements of the agency and of the position(s) in question.

No volunteer will be placed in a position for which s/he is not fully qualified or for which the organization could not provide adequate training.

Volunteers will be fully and honestly informed of the expectations and responsibilities of their volunteer position, along with any risk or liability that the position might entail.

Volunteers will be made to feel comfortable in declining a suggested placement or in requesting changes to the position expectations at any point in their involvement with the organization.

Volunteers have the right to expect work that is meaningful and satisfying.

No position is too high in the organizational structure or too skilled for a volunteer, assuming appropriate background and time commitment.

No position should be considered too tedious or unskilled as long as volunteers are given a clear understanding of the nature and importance of the work to be performed.

(v) Emphasize the Positives

Whenever possible, policies should enable, motivate, and inspire. They should articulate outside limits, leaving as much room as possible for flexibility and creativity. The presence of supportive and enabling policies can provide the encouragement and recognition that volunteers require to maximize their potential. Policies can demonstrate just how important the work is and the very real consequence of error when standards are not attained or guidelines are not followed. As Lynch points out, *we should never be surprised at the lack of results we get from volunteers if we never give them results to achieve.*[37]

(vi) Illustrate

Do not hesitate to draw pictures, illustrate steps and sequences, or sketch methods or techniques. Diagrams and other graphic additions make the manual more pleasing to read, and they convey specific details that words sometimes cannot.

(B)   WHICH POLICIES? WHICH ONES FIRST?

Policy development for volunteer programs can seem completely overwhelming, particularly for those who are starting with few or no policies. The panicky question, "Oh dear! Where do I start?" is both typical and understandable at this stage. Given that developing a full set of policies for the volunteer department might take two or three years of fairly steady work, the task is to outline the range of possible policy topics and then be certain that the most urgent are developed first. Following is a simple, two-step process that is equally useful to managers of volunteers who are just getting started and to managers who already have many policies in place.

(i)   Which Policies?

Developing a list of possible policy topics is the first task. Using the policy checklist in Exhibit 35.2, the manager of volunteers can begin the process by listing all the items that he or she can think of. Consult the table of contents of Linda Graff's *By Definition: Policies for Volunteer Programs,* which lists over 70 generic volunteer program policy topics.[38] The brainstorming process can be prompted at this point by segmenting the policy checklist into separate sections for risk management policies, values and belief statement policies, policies as rules, and policies that will enhance the program's effectiveness. See Section 35.4 for guiding questions.

Since this is a brainstorming exercise, no possibility should be ruled out at this point. It is also appropriate to include on this list those policies that are already in place. As possible policy topics arise, list them in the left-hand column. Complete the other columns for each topic as appropriate, indicating whether the policy exists, is in progress, or needs to be developed. It is suggested that the manager of volunteers begin this process by listing the policies identified initially. More than one page may be required to contain the growing list of topics. When the manager has listed all that he or she can think of for the moment, the checklist can be circulated so that others—staff, volunteers, clients, supervisor, board members, colleagues, outside consultants—may add to the list. They use the bottom portion of the checklist, and since they are less likely to know what does and does not already exist, they do not need the additional columns. There should be no censoring at this point, although the right-hand column does allow anyone to register an opinion on the applicability of any policy topic(s) already on the list. The manager of volunteers can pursue these notations in more detail with the people involved.

(ii)   Which Ones First?

If this process generates an enormous list, there is no reason to panic. Remember that the goal is to prioritize so that the most urgent and/or most important policies are being developed at any given time. What needs to be done is to rank each prospective policy topic on an urgency scale, from which can follow the list of policies in order of greatest to least urgency. To assess urgency and importance, the manager of volunteers can again refer to the questions itemized in Section 35.4 on functions of policies. Each policy can be

EXHIBIT 35.2 Policy Checklist

POLICY TOPIC	DEVELOPED: Date Of Last Review	IN PROGRESS	TO DO	NOT APPLICABLE
1. Volunteer Screening			✓	
2. Recruitment			✓	
3. Anti-Discrimination			✓	
4. Crossing Picket Lines			✓	
5. Probation			✓	
6. Recruitment of Minors			✓	
7. Volunteer–Paid Staff Relations			✓	
8. Confidentiality	January '92			
9. Sexual Harassment		✓		
10. Conflict of Interest	September '90			
11. Discipline			✓	
12. Dismissal			✓	
13. Immediate Dismissal		✓		
14.				
15.				
16.				
17.				
18.				
19.				
20.				

Additional Policies Our Organization Should Develop

1. Professional Development/On-going Training for Volunteers
2. Police Checks
3. Volunteer Recognition
4.
5.
6.
7.
8.

rated on its importance within each function. Exhibit 35.3, the priority scale, can be used to facilitate the process and record the results. To use the priority scale, transfer the policy topics that were itemized on the policy checklist (Exhibit 35.2) to the left-hand column of the priority scale. Taking each policy topic in turn, assess its urgency on a scale of 1 to 5 (1 meaning not very urgent, it can wait; 5 meaning very urgent, needs development immediately) with respect to each of the four possible functions: risk management, values and belief statements, rules, and program improvement aides. Follow through this illustration on volunteer screening, asking the following questions about the urgency of need for policy statements:

Risk Management
- Are there risks associated with volunteer screening?
- Do we expose ourselves, our clients, or the organization to liability by not having a volunteer screening policy?
- Are our screening policies and procedures thorough enough to screen out dangerous candidates?
- Are our screening policies and procedures so extensive that they infringe on the privacy and/or the legal rights of prospective volunteers?
- How great are those risks?

Allowing for some variance depending on the nature of the work done by volunteers, the vulnerability of clients, and so on, it is likely that the risks surrounding volunteer screening will be quite high because of the need to strike a proper balance between agency responsibilities and the rights of volunteers. Consider the implications of a violent offender or a pedophile being recruited into a day care center because "He was such a *nice* man!" or the ramifications of accepting an expert in fraud as the treasurer for the board of directors. Consider as well the indignation of a well-meaning candidate when confronted with unnecessarily probing questions. To complete the priority scale for the policy on volunteer screening, the score under the heading "level of risk" would be 5 for most programs.

Values and Belief Statements
- Do we have values or beliefs about volunteer screening that need to be articulated?

There are always certain beliefs and positions held by organizations about volunteer screening that may seem self-evident to those in the field but that are completely unknown to the general public. For example, many citizens still believe that seeking to do good unto others is the only criterion one must meet to become a volunteer. Being refused would be a shocking offense. It is therefore quite important for the agency to be clear about its beliefs about volunteer screening, including messages about the agency's right to decline offers of involvement; the belief that the screening interview is an opportunity for mutual information exchange and assessment; that antidiscrimination and affirmative action principles will guide assessments of suitability. The score for volunteer screening in the "need value statement" column would also be high: 4 or 5.

Rules
- Do organizations need to identify rules around the volunteer screening process?

EXHIBIT 35.3 Priority Scale

POLICY TOPIC	← ASSIGN RATINGS* →					
	Level of Risk	Need Value Statement	Need Rules	Need to Improve	Other	Totals
1. Volunteer Screening	5	4	5	3	—	17
2. Recruitment	2	4	3	1	—	10
3. Anti-Discrimination	3	5	4	0	—	12
4. Crossing Picket Lines	5	5	5	2	5	22
5. Probation						
6. Recruitment of Minors						
7. Volunteer–Paid Staff Relations						
8. Confidentiality						
9. Sexual Harassment	3	5	5	5	5	23
10. Conflict of Interest						
11.						
12.						
13.						
14. Enabling Funds	1	4	4	2	4	15
15.						
16.						
17. Free Coffee For Volunteers	0	2	3	0	—	5
18.						

Notes in margin:
- Strike Imminent (→ row 3/4)
- Incident Reported Last Week (→ row 9)
- Funder Demands Clear Policy (→ row 14)

Rules regarding interviews, police checks, and references are very important. Additionally, agencies need to state their policies that detail what will be done with, and who can gain access to, confidential information obtained through the screening process; and what constitutes grounds for nonacceptance. The score in this column, headed "need rules" would be 5 for most programs.

Program Improvement Tools

Each agency needs to assess its own functioning in this regard, but here is an example of a policy that could improve the recruitment success rate: Undue delay in following up with volunteers after the screening interview regarding their acceptance is both disrespectful and potentially damaging to volunteers' motivation. A policy that commits the organization to contacting the volunteer within a specified number of working days of the screening interview could significantly alter the proportion of volunteers who are still willing to volunteer when the agency is able to confirm acceptance. How well the screening program is currently functioning will be a major determinant of how high the score will be in this column for screening policy.

To summarize, screening would rate high to very high in all four columns. It is a policy topic that requires thorough attention. In contrast, the policy on whether volunteers should or should not pay for their own coffee while on duty is a policy issue that would rate fairly low on the urgency scale.

The fifth column on the priority scale, "other," is there for use at the manager's discretion. There may be additional reasons for work on a specific policy to begin sooner rather than later: the organization just had a serious incident in an area where policy could prevent reoccurrence; the funder is insisting that all its member agencies implement a specific philosophy of service; the manager's supervisor just came back from a course on safety in the workplace and is requiring immediate policy development on sexual harassment. This column allows the manager to assign urgency bonus points in these kinds of circumstances.

To complete the priority scale, rate each policy topic in each of the five columns, add across each row to obtain a total score for each topic, and place that total in the right-hand column. Those topics with the highest scores need to be dealt with first. Those with lower scores can wait. Transfer the list of policy topics to a separate list in order from highest to lowest score, and consider this the "policy to-do list" for the foreseeable future.

(C)   TRACKING DRAFTS AND INPUT

Once the policy development agenda has been established, the manager can actually begin the process of researching, drafting, and revising policies. Some policies will be relatively easy to write; others will be extremely complex; some will demand input from outside experts; others will involve lengthy processing and values clarification. Work on a wide range of policies can proceed simultaneously, particularly if a policy development team, a policy committee, or a collection of consultants/resource persons is recruited to assist with the task. Depending on the number of policies needing to be drafted and the number in progress at any given time, tracking where each policy is in its development may become cumbersome.

Exhibit 35.4 can be used as a tool to track the progress of policies as they are being researched, drafted, revised, and approved. Use one of these forms for each policy that needs to be tracked. Track development by indicating who needs to be involved and/or consulted and who is responsible for each stage of the policy's evolution. The form allows

EXHIBIT 35.4 Tracking Policy Development

POLICY ISSUE: _____

POLICY NUMBER: _____

WHO WILL BE INVOLVED?

- ❏ **Manager of Volunteers**
- ❏ **Staff Department Head**
- ❏ **Staff** _____
  _____
- ❏ **Volunteers** _____
  _____

- ❏ **Board of Directors**
- ❏ **Executive Director**
- ❏ **Policy Committee**
- ❏ **Legal Counsel**
- ❏ **Insurance Advisor**
- ❏ **Others** _____
- ❏ **Others** _____

VERSION	WHO IS RESPONSIBLE	DUE DATE	COMPLETE (✓)
First Draft			
Second Draft			
Third Draft			
Approval			
Review/Revision			

the manager to note due dates and completion dates for various activities. Use the two blank lines at the bottom to add other policy development activities that may need to be accomplished: external reading and editing; vetting by head office, staff, or union.

(D) EDITING POLICIES

Careful review of policies after they have been drafted is a critical step that is often overlooked. It is recommended that at least four people read a newly drafted policy. Readers and editors from both within the field of volunteer management and from outside it will round out the editing team. Different readers can be asked to attend to different aspects of policies. For example, legal counsel or insurance advisors can be asked to review from their professional point of view. Other readers may be asked to concentrate on meaning; others may attend to mechanics and sequencing, or terminology and grammar.

35.7 Compliance

A great deal of time and resources can be wasted on policy development if policies are not understood and followed. Although there is nothing one can do to guarantee absolute compliance, there is a good deal that one can do to increase the likelihood of compliance. Here are some suggestions.

(A) SENSITIVE WORDING

The way in which policies are worded can significantly enhance compliance. As noted previously, rounding rough edges of policies can make them both more understandable and more palatable to volunteers who might otherwise be hurt or offended by apparent absence of trust or appreciation (review Section 35.6a(iv) for examples).

(B) STATE THE WAY

Including in the policy statement the reason for its existence reminds volunteers that policies do not exist just to make volunteering more bureaucratic for those engaged in it. This is not to say that agencies must justify every sentence of policy they write, or that the rationale for every policy statement must be an integral part of the policy itself. However, the rationale for some policies may not be immediately apparent to volunteers. In such cases, reference to reasons such as the well-being of clients, the importance of efficient expenditure of precious resources, the furthering of the mission of the agency, or the safety of volunteer workers will certainly clarify the policy's purpose and reinforce the importance of volunteers' compliance with it. Here is an excellent example:

> Volunteers in this program are considered as nonpaid, part-time staff and it is expected that volunteer relationships with clients will have the same boundaries as those of paid staff. Our role is therapeutic in nature. It is not appropriate to become friends with clients. This is not to say that volunteers cannot be friendly, caring, or supportive. On the contrary. The reason that relationships with clients should not lead to friendships is because the relationship is not equal. Volunteers are privileged to more power by virtue of their position with the organization. Hence, clients are in a more vulnerable role. It is normal for clients to want to establish friendships with volunteers. They perceive volunteers to be caring individuals who pay attention.

The procedure that accompanies this policy is:

1. When "turning a client down" in terms of a friendship role, volunteers will do this in a supportive manner giving the basis of this policy as a reason.
2. Volunteers will notify the Coordinator of Volunteers whenever the nature of the friendship with a client is in question.[39]

This policy clearly outlines the "why." It is unlikely that a shorter version of the same policy that reads, "Volunteers are prohibited from developing social or friendship relationships with clients" would engender the same level of compliance, simply because it does not communicate sound reasons for doing so.

(C)   MAKE COMPLIANCE EASY

The preceding sections notwithstanding, the shorter, more concise, more clear, and more straightforward that policies are, the greater the likelihood of compliance. Policy writers need to strike a balance between policies that are short and to the point, and policies that are more involved and detailed. Without trying to be facetious, the lesson here might be: Write as many and as much as you need to ensure understanding and compliance, and not one word more.

(D)   MAKE POLICIES ACCESSIBLE

Produce policies in a format that makes them easily accessible to volunteers. For example, produce a complete manual of policies and procedures for the volunteer program and make it accessible to any volunteer who wishes to see it. Extract the most critical of all policies for reproduction in a smaller handbook for each type of volunteer position or for volunteers in each department. Make certain every volunteer has his or her own copy. Print a subset of the most critical policies in a pocket- or purse-sized summary for day-to-day use. Distill these even further and print the policies about emergency situations on a card the size of a credit card, have it laminated, and ask volunteers to post it near the phone at the worksite, carry it in their wallets, and/or carry it in the glove compartments of their automobiles. Printing the latter on the reverse of the photo ID badge ensures that volunteers have critical policies with them while on duty.

(E)   COMMUNICATE POLICIES AT EVERY OPPORTUNITY

Create and take every opportunity to communicate with, and remind, volunteers about policies and procedures.

- Begin to make reference to policies in volunteer recruitment publicity by mentioning agency efforts to make volunteering safe and satisfying.
- Notify volunteers at the initial screening interview that there are policies— rules, beliefs, and ways of doing things—that are integral to volunteering with your agency.
- Include detailed coverage of agency policies and procedures in volunteer training and ongoing training sessions.
- Be certain to assess compliance with policies and procedures as a regular component of volunteer supervision and evaluation sessions.
- Post relevant policies and procedures as reminders around the worksite.
- Write articles about policies and procedures in newsletters and other communication vehicles, giving background, rationale, and implications.

(F)   SIGNED CONTRACT

As part of their acceptance into service with the organization, require volunteers to sign a contract. This type of document, alternately called an *agreement* or a *memorandum of understanding* to soften its image, requires volunteers to sign their commitment to following policies and procedures. Signing such a contract lends greater significance to the promise of compliance. Typically, the commitment to compliance with agency policies and procedures is one of several items included in an initial volunteer/agency contract. The sample drafted by McCurley includes other agreements: to serve as a volunteer, to perform volunteer duties to the best of his or her abilities, to meet time and duty commitments or provide adequate notice, as well as a section on adherence to rules and procedures.[40] It is suggested that a paragraph such as the following be included in the signed agreement:

> I, (volunteer's name), affirm that I have read, understood, and agree to comply with the policies and procedures of the (name of agency) as they are outlined in the attached job description, and in the volunteer (handbook/policy manual . . .).

An optional paragraph such as the following may be considered:

> I understand that compliance with these policies and procedures is important to preserve the quality of service offered to our clients, and critical to the safety and well-being of (agency) volunteers, clients, staff, and the general public. Further, I understand that any breach of agency policies and procedures will be taken seriously, and could be cause for discipline, up to and including dismissal.

(G) FOLLOW THROUGH

Consistently monitor compliance. Ensure that compliance with policies is a routine aspect of the volunteer performance review system. Offer speedy reinforcement, including awards for superior performance. Write newsletter articles about positive outcomes that have resulted from volunteers following policies and procedures. Act quickly when policies are breached. Clarify what the consequences of failure to comply will be (e.g., reminders, verbal or written warnings, suspension, dismissal, immediate dismissal). Do not hesitate to follow through on their implementation.

35.8 Resistance to Policy Development

Near the end of a recent workshop on risk management and policy development in which most administrative leaders of an environmental conservancy organization had begun to recognize the full range of risks being undertaken by volunteers in service to their organization, a participant stood up and exclaimed: "I just don't see why we have to worry about all these things now. We've been operating this organization since 1953 and not one single person has ever been seriously hurt!" The kind of resistance to policy development embodied in this remark is prevalent throughout the voluntary sector. Ellis anticipated similar resistance to her call for senior management to recognize their own responsibilities in volunteer program success:

> Some readers may be feeling a bit uncomfortable in the suspicion that I am going to suggest lots of structure to bureaucratize volunteerism. The fact is that successful volunteering does not come from spontaneous combustion. Most of our organizations today are already rather complex and, unless we develop clear ways for volunteers to participate in our activities, people really do not know how to become involved. This is true whether the organization is an "agency," an "institution," or an all-volunteer association.[41]

By clinging to outdated stereotypes and myths about volunteering, people—paid staff and volunteers alike—have lost touch with the reality of volunteering as it really is in the twenty-first century. It is understandable to wish to preserve a simpler time when volunteering to help your neighbor required only that you show up with the desire to do good. But denying the complex, sophisticated, demanding, and risky nature of volunteering as it is today exposes both organizations and individuals to liabilities that are simply too great to bear.

It *is* important to preserve what we can of volunteering's essential quality of altruism. But as long as we expect volunteers to do real work, volunteers deserve real management. Silver puts it this way:

> *Coming into their maturity, volunteer programs are being challenged to socialize their volunteers into increasingly complex organizations, to formalize their policies and procedures and yet to maintain a humane and personalized character . . . to construct a volunteer program that is at the same time highly organized and highly flexible.*[42]

The challenge is to craft policies and procedures for volunteer programs that ensure the safest, most satisfying, and most productive experience without kicking the heart out of volunteering. And while continuing to ignore the need for policies in volunteer programs might put off for a little bit longer the realization that volunteering now is not what volunteering was 40, 30, 20, even just 10 years ago, we run the risk of allowing endless accidents, injuries, and tragedies, to transform volunteering into a movement people are simply too afraid to join. How you decide to manage that risk is up to you.

35.9   Conclusions

Now is the time to engage in policy development for volunteer programs. Because our expectations of volunteers have become more complex and more demanding, the practice of voluntary action involves more risks and creates greater exposure to liabilities both for volunteers and for the voluntary agencies through which they volunteer. Policy development is a crucial risk management tool that simply cannot be put off any longer. In addition, policies help volunteer programs to communicate values and beliefs to guide action, articulate rules, and develop guidelines that increase service effectiveness.

The development of a comprehensive set of policies for a volunteer program may take two to three years of concentrated effort. It is not unusual for managers of volunteers to feel overwhelmed by the magnitude of the task or by the fear that crucial policies will be missed. This chapter has outlined useful techniques for segmenting the policy development process into a manageable plan, including guidelines for determining which policies are required. Concrete suggestions have been offered regarding how to write policies and how to increase compliance with policies. Readers are urged to overcome resistance to policy development since further delays can only mean increased risks and dangers for volunteers, clients, staff, agencies, and the general public.

Endnotes

1. Silver, N. (1988). *At the Heart: The New Challenge to Community Agencies.* Pleasanton, CA: Valley Volunteer Center.

2. Shaw, R. C. (1990). "Strengthening the Role of the Voluntary Board of Directors." Excerpts reprinted in G. Johnstone (ed.), *Boards of Directors' Resource Binder.* Etobicoke, Ontario, Canada: Volunteer Ontario.

3. Cryderman, P. (1987). *Developing Policy and Procedure Manuals,* rev. ed. Ottawa: Canadian Hospital Association.

4. Id., p. 10.

5. See note 1.

6. Ellis, S. J. (1986). *From the Top Down: The Executive Role in Volunteer Program Success.* Philadelphia: Energize Associates.

7. Conrad, W. R., and W. E. Glenn. (1976). *The Effective Voluntary Board of Directors.* Athens, OH: Swallow Press.

8. O'Connell, B. (1985). *The Board Members' Book: Making a Difference in Voluntary Organizations.* New York: The Foundation Center.

9. Carver, J. (1990). *Boards That Make a Difference: A New Design for Leadership in Nonprofit and Public Organizations.* San Francisco: Jossey-Bass.

10. Volunteer Centre of Metropolitan Toronto. (1993). *Administrative Manual.* Toronto, Ontario, Canada: Volunteer Centre of Metropolitan Toronto.

11. McCurley, S. (1993). "Risk Management Techniques for Volunteer Programs," *Grapevine* (September/October): 9–13.

12. Minnesota Office on Volunteer Services. (1992). *Planning It Safe: How to Control Liability and Risk in Volunteer Programs.* St. Paul, MN: Minnesota Office on Volunteer Services.

13. Tremper, C., and G. Kostin. (1993). *No Surprises: Controlling Risks in Volunteer Programs.* Washington, DC: Nonprofit Risk Management Center.

14. Vargo, K. S. (1995). "Risk Management Strategies." In T. D. Connors (ed.), *The Volunteer Management Handbook.* New York: John Wiley & Sons.

15. Graff, L. L. (1997). "Risk Management." In G. Johnstone (ed.), *Management of Volunteer Services in Canada: The Text.* Carp, Ontario: Johnstone Training and Consultation (JTC), Inc.

16. See note 1.

17. See note 6.

18. See note 1.

19. Id.

20. See note 7.

21. Graff, L. L. (1993). "The Key to the Boardroom Door: Policies for Volunteer Programs," *Journal of Volunteer Administration* 11(4) (Summer).

22. Scheier, I. (1988). "Empowering a Profession: Seeing Ourselves as More Than Subsidiary," *Journal of Volunteer Administration* (Fall): 29–34.

23. See note 1.

24. Graff, L. L. (1992). *By Definition: Policies for Volunteer Programs.* Dundas, Ontario: Graff and Associates.

25. See note 10.

26. American Red Cross. (No date). *Volunteer 2000 Study.* Washington, DC: The American Red Cross Society.

27. McCurley, S. (1990). *Volunteer Management Policies.* Downers Grove, Ill.: VMSystems and Heritage Arts Publishing.

28. Parks and Recreation Department, Burlington, Ontario, Canada. (No date). Brochure.

29. See note 27.

30. See note 26.

31. See note 7.
32. Canadian Red Cross—Ontario Division. (1992). *Human Resources Policies & Procedures Manual.* Mississaugo, Ontario, Canada.
33. Id.
34. Vineyard, S. (1993). *Megatrends and Volunteerism: Mapping the Future of Volunteer Programs.* Downers Grove, IL: Heritage Arts Publishing.
35. See note 3.
36. See note 25.
37. Lynch, R. (1983). "Designing Volunteer Jobs for Results," *Voluntary Action Leadership* (Summer): 20–23.
38. See note 24.
39. Psychiatric Day Programme. (1992). *Volunteer Policy and Procedure Manual.* Hamilton, Ontario, Canada: Psychiatric Day Programme, St. Joseph's Hospital.
40. McCurley, S. (1988). *Volunteer Management Forms.* Downers Grove, IL.: VMSystems and Heritage Arts Publishing.
41. See note 6.
42. See note 1.

36 Risk Management in Volunteer Programs*

LINDA L. GRAFF
Graff and Associates

36.1 Introduction

I have come to an important realization after more than a decade of presentations across North America and into Europe: There are still a good many well-meaning people, some

---

* This chapter appeared as Chapter 10 in Tracy Daniel Connors (ed.). *The Nonprofit Management Handbook*, 2nd ed., 1999 Supplement. It was adapted from an article entitled "Risk Management," which originally appeared in *Management of Volunteer Services in Canada: The Text*, Ginette Johnstone (ed.). Carp, Ontario: Johnstone Training and Consultation (JTC), Inc., 1997. It is adapted and reprinted here with the permission of the author.

Readers are cautioned that this is an introductory review only. It is not intended as a comprehensive guide to risk management. The author recommends that additional material and expertise be consulted to implement an effective risk management process. The Endnotes and Suggested Readings include a number of excellent risk management resources.

of whom are in positions overseeing volunteer work, and some of whom are ultimately responsible for the work done by volunteers, who still believe that volunteering is about lady bountifuls with bonnets and baskets administering unto the sick and the orphaned, rolling bandages, and serving tea!

36.2 Disaster Imaging

The fastest way for members of boards of directors and managers of volunteers to catch up to current risk realities is to engage in an exercise called disaster imaging. Consider the range of answers to the following question: What are the worst things that you can imagine going wrong in your volunteer department, or because of the involvement of volunteers at your organization?

- Think about direct-service volunteers and administrative (board and committee) volunteers
- Think about accidents, injuries, and financial and public trust issues
- Think about personal and organizational liabilities

Following is a list of typical responses from workshop participants in answer to that same question:

- Accidents
- Injury
- Volunteer stepping outside of job description, exceeding skills or authority
- Substandard performance by volunteers resulting in harm to clients
- Breach of confidentiality
- Loss or damage to property (physical, financial, electronic, or intellectual)
- Theft, misappropriation of funds, fraud
- Abuse of client (physical, emotional, sexual, or financial) by volunteer; vice versa
- Loss of agency reputation, organizational credibility, or public trust
- Loss of ability to raise funds in the future
- Death of client, volunteer, staff, or member of general public

It does not require a great stretch of the imagination to identify multiple disaster possibilities that could happen virtually any day of any week in volunteer programs across the continent. The risks associated with voluntary action come in many shapes and sizes, but one thing is certain: they are both bigger and more prevalent than ever before.

In anticipation of the critics who caution us not to engage in, or to be ruled by, "worst-case thinking," the problem is that there are still too few managers of volunteers in the field right now who consider the extent of risk that exists in voluntary action. True, some practitioners may feel overwhelmed, or even immobilized, by the potential for disaster, but they are outnumbered by those who still ignore the risks that volunteer involvement generates for clients, staff, volunteers, and the organization. Risk management, reasonably applied, is not a function of worst-case thinking. It is not excessive or incompatible with the work of charities and nonprofit organizations (NPOs). It is responsible and contemporary best practice that places due and appropriate priority on personal safety, program effectiveness, and organizational well-being.

The underlying assumptions to the application of risk management in any setting are as follows:

- There are no absolutes and no guarantees in risk management. No risk management system in the world can prevent all risks. Things can, and do, go wrong.
- Ignoring the potential for trouble never makes it go away; inattention to risks can exacerbate the harm, and increase the liability attached to it.
- Facing risks head on and making every effort to control them will often avert disaster and/or minimize the magnitude of harm that results.
- If something does go wrong, any attempts that have been made to anticipate and prevent the loss or tragedy through a risk management process will constitute concrete proof of diligence, and consequently reduce personal and organizational exposure to liability.

36.3   Change as the Context to Understanding Risk

It is almost trite these days to say that things are changing, but change is perhaps the most significant factor to consider in constructing a context for risk management in volunteer services. The kinds of changes that were experienced in the human and community service system in the 1990s surpass any other period of change in the history of service provision. Fundamental shifts have permanently altered health care, education, social services, and other aspects of community life. All of these changes have direct consequences for the work of volunteers, and for the volunteer movement itself.

Not all that long ago, organizations needed to be encouraged to consider involving volunteers at any level beyond the legally necessary board of directors. Now, it is difficult to identify NPOs that do not involve volunteers at all organizational and program levels, in both administrative (board/committee) and direct-service positions. Volunteering has grown to enormous proportions and now hardly resembles what it was as recently as a decade ago.

As governments withdraw funding for services, and as other funding sources also experience campaign shortfalls, nonprofit and charitable organizations, often in desperation, say "Let's get a volunteer to do it!" There is no question that volunteers are being engaged in direct-service delivery in ways that just five years ago would have been considered inappropriate or even unethical.

Both positive and negative consequences follow from such changes. For the purposes of this chapter, the key consequence is the dramatic increase in risk that has accompanied the new, more sophisticated, more responsible, and often more risky, volunteer positions that volunteers are now being asked to fill. Volunteers are not only in boardrooms making the critical financial and service decisions, they are also on the front lines in our neighborhoods and in our agencies, often side by side with paid staff, doing "real work," and working directly with clients and program participants. As Marlene Wilson said more than 20 years ago, and clearly it is even more true today: "What we are just beginning to realize is that as our communities grow and the problems increase and become more complex, helping one's neighbour becomes more complex as well."[1]

Existing risks and liabilities are exacerbated by two associated trends. First, society has become significantly more litigious. This is true now in both Canada and the United States. People are suing others more often, and nonprofit organizations are far from immune from legal accountability. Sometimes suits are launched specifically because of the activities of volunteers.

Second, as resources are stretched to their absolute maximum, which is more and more often the key reason why volunteers are invited to take on increasingly responsible positions in the first place, there are fewer supervisory staff to ensure adequate performance standards among volunteers. Less supervision invites greater risks. In some settings, the very position that should be considered indispensable, the manager of volunteers position, is being cut to solve budget problems.

The consequence of these trends is obvious: The risk of injury/malpractice/accident increases directly, and the likelihood of legal action is greater. As long as volunteers are confined to simple and routine chores, away from direct contact with clients or the public, agency administration has little risk with which to concern itself. As soon as an organization chooses to assign demanding, responsible, and direct-service work to volunteers, the consequence of error multiplies, and an obligation arises to responsibly manage volunteers as the real workers we ask them to be. As employers, organizations have corresponding ethical and legal obligations to ensure that volunteers work in the safest manner possible, in the least hazardous environment that can reasonably be created.

36.4   Are You Working in "Silver's Gap"?

Many managers of volunteers feel a sense of unease about some of the positions their organizations have required them to create for volunteers. Others suffer a well-formed, full-blown dread of injury, harm, and loss that appears altogether too likely to result from the placement of volunteers in positions of great risk. Too often, when managers of volunteers try to respond appropriately to risk identification, when they try to advise their administration that placement of volunteers in certain positions is too risky, or when they request the time and resources for policy development and risk management, they are met with comments from administration such as, "Don't worry about that. They're just volunteers," or "Why are you always waving red flags and looking for trouble?"

At some point, the lag created by rapid and radical change catches up. As Silver points out, the result of rapid growth and change in volunteerism has been the creation of a gap between the real complexity of volunteer involvement and the ability of *organizations* to understand and comprehensively manage the valuable resource they have mobilized.

> *The future of community organizations, and the independent sector as a whole, depends on the future of our volunteers. Right now that future is at risk. It is not for want of volunteers. It is not for want of good organizations providing good services. It is for want of the capacity of these good organizations to utilize people well.*[2]

Managers struggle to do the best they can, but for many, support from their organizations is absent.[3] Organizational systems such as the following are not in place for volunteers:

- Communication systems
- Reporting systems

- Accountability systems
- Policies and procedures
- Resource planning and development
- Insurance
- Risk management systems

A few recent high-profile cases of abuse by volunteers in positions of trust have served to dramatically raise legal standards and demands for public accountability. These changes have arisen so quickly that managers who have not significantly increased their attention to risk management in volunteer services in the last two to three years are very likely exposing both volunteers and clients to greater risk of harm, and their organizations to greater liability.

It is critical that we begin to acknowledge the complexity and significance of the work that is mobilized in volunteers and that is required in the managers of volunteers position. Risk management has become an indispensable function in the management of volunteer resources in the twenty-first century.

36.5 *The Risk Management Process*

(A) THE AIMS OF RISK MANAGEMENT

There is no risk management model that comes with a guarantee. There is nothing that anyone can do to absolutely guarantee that nothing will go wrong, short of stopping services and closing the doors. There is no way to completely eliminate the element of risk from voluntary action. That is, the possibility of accident, injury, loss, or damage is always present. But this is the case in nearly everything we do, all of the time. It is important not to ignore risks, but it is equally important not to become immobilized by them. What is needed is a rational, systematic approach to risk management that reduces and controls risks as much as is reasonably possible.

There are two central and distinct aims of every risk management process:

- Prevention of harm and loss must always be the first priority of every risk manager. It is clearly preferable to keep things from going wrong in the first place than it is to deal with the consequences of tragedies and disasters.
- Liability reduction is a close second aim of every risk manager. Given that things can and do go wrong, even with the best prevention mechanisms in place, it is entirely appropriate to undertake measures that reduce personal and organizational liability exposure.

(B) RISK MANAGEMENT IS NOT DIFFICULT OR MYSTERIOUS

Risk management may sound complicated and highly technical, but the reality is that in most circumstances, it is neither. In fact, we all engage in risk management all of the time; we just do not label our actions and decisions as such, and we are not as systematic about our efforts as we probably should be.

Risk of any sort may not be the primary consideration in the hundreds of small and large decisions faced every day, but risk is a subtheme that runs at or near the surface of most daily activities. When one considers that all avenues of human endeavor bring some measure of risk, from stepping out of bed in the morning to finding one's way back there at night, all that goes on between is about risk management.

We constantly engage in often barely conscious risk management:

- Testing the temperature of the water before stepping into the shower
- Eating fresh fruit and low-fat cottage cheese for breakfast rather than bacon and eggs to reduce the risk of heart disease
- Using an umbrella to protect that new suede jacket from the rain in the forecast
- Using the car instead of public transit because a late meeting tonight means a walk from the bus stop after dark
- Deciding which route to take (the highway may be faster but is definitely more dangerous); accepting the risks of driving by the highway route; making decisions about which lane to drive in, when to pass, what speed to drive, whether to let a transport truck pull in front
- Making investment decisions (whether to reinvest with low risk and low return, or go for equity funds)

We engage in risk-related decision making virtually all of the time; we just do not recognize it as such, label it as such, or approach it systematically. For these reasons, the following comment about risk management offered by Tremper and Kostin makes good sense:

At its heart, risk management is not a new trick, and it's not something mysterious. It's an orientation to everything you do that is highly consistent with every charitable mission. Risk management is not just looking for trouble, it's looking for solutions that make your organization more effective.[4]

Risk management does not have to be difficult. One does not need a college certificate in risk management to substantially reduce and control risks in most volunteer programs.

(C)   RISK MANAGEMENT IS A PROCESS

In an organization or a volunteer department, one does not "go and do" risk management and then say, "there, that's done" and forget about it. Doing so would be comparable to attempting to anticipate all of the risks that might surface in a day, making decisions and choices among options, setting a plan, and then going through the remainder of the day with no consideration to any of the hundreds of big and small risks that might surface unanticipated.

Risk management needs to be integrated into existing systems: program planning, cost–benefit analyses, program evaluation, performance reviews, agency governance, and so forth. This is not to say that risks govern all, but rather, that risks need to be considered along with any number of other variables in actions and decisions throughout every organization, on a regular, if not continuous, basis.

36.6 The Risk Management Model

The essence of risk management is planning and prevention. The aim is to anticipate risks in advance and then take deliberate and appropriate measures to control or reduce those risks to a tolerable level. The risk management model presented in Exhibit 36.1 is a four-step planning process that leads the manager systematically through a series of questions, allowing and encouraging consideration of a range of action and decision alternatives. It may look complicated at first, but it works quite simply.

The internal workings of the flowchart are reviewed first so that the reader gains a sense of the overall system, and how decision making should progress in a systematic fashion. When the model has been outlined, a more detailed discussion of how to implement each of its components is presented.

This model works equally well with paid and unpaid workers, and at every level in the organization, including governance, administration, support services, maintenance, and delivery of services to clients. Start the risk management process by choosing a subsection of the organization to work on: any program or service; any job description, task, or position (board functioning, direct-service volunteer involvement, or paid staff role). The area or function to be investigated can be large or small. It is advisable, however, to break the agency into component parts and engage in the risk management process with each part in turn, rather than trying to apply the model to the whole agency at one time.

(A) STEP 1

All risk management begins with the question, "Are there any risks here?" Consider the component of the agency under examination and ask that question. It will be a very rare agency or service in which the answer is "no." However, if an agency is examining a service where there are no detectable risks, the diagram points to the left side of the "Identify Risks" box, and drops down the left side to the "Review" box. This reflects the fact that there are no current risks detectable, but given that things are continually changing, the model suggests that the agency periodically re-ask the "Are there any risks here?" question. If, in answer to the "Are there any risks here?" question, a risk is detected, of any sort or magnitude, then the model points out the right side of the "Identify Risks" box, and on to the next box below.

(B) STEP 2

The second step in risk management involves evaluating the risks identified so far. The question to be applied to all of the risks on the list at this point is: Is this a high risk or a low risk? The distinguishing factor between "high" risk and "low" risk lies in the answer to this question: Can we live with this risk without any further action to reduce or control it? As much as we might wish for unequivocal direction about risk management, final decisions will often come down to a matter of judgment. One cannot be more technical or scientific than this: Each organization must locate its own "risk tolerance zone," within which it is comfortable with the level of risk and liability exposure, and outside of which it feels compelled to take some form of risk management action.

Those risks that fall within the risk tolerance zone direct the manager out the left side of the "Evaluate Risks" box and once again drop to "Review," indicating that while there may

EXHIBIT 36.1 Risk Management Process

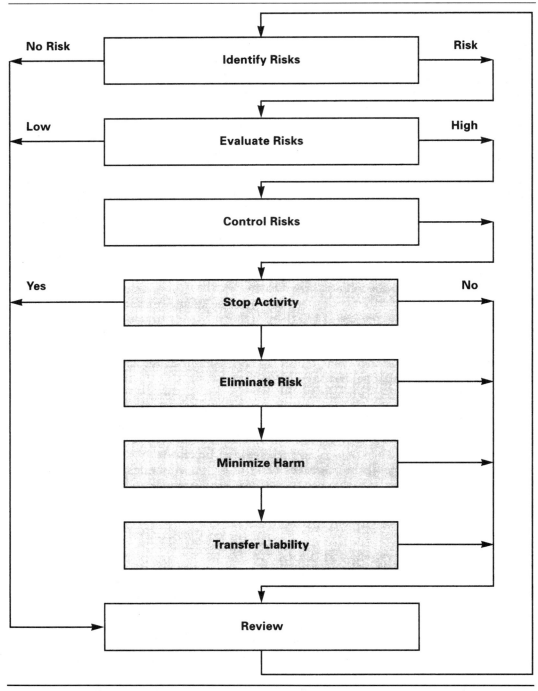

This diagram has been adapted from McCurley, S. (1993). "Risk Management Techniques for Volunteer Programs," *Grapevine* (September/October):9–13.

be comfort with no additional action on these risks at this point, things change, and it is advisable to re-examine risks again in the not-too-distant future. Those risks that are rated outside the risk tolerance zone, those that are assessed to be "high," point out of the right side of the "Evaluate Risks" box and direct attention downward to the next box in the model. ("High" in this instance does not necessarily mean an enormous risk. It simply denotes a risk that requires some form of risk management action. The action may turn out to be minimal.)

(C)   STEP 3

The risks still on the list are those that require some kind of control action. This step of the model directs the user through a range of four control options. These are the four grey boxes on the model diagram.

The first risk control mechanism (the first action) to consider is to stop engaging in the risky activity. Ask the question: Is this the kind of risk, or a big enough risk, that the appropriate risk management response would be to quit the risky action, extract the organization and its personnel from the risky situation, or at minimum, cease involvement in its riskier elements? If the answer is that the agency should stop the activity, the diagram leads us out to the left and down to the "Review" box, indicating that once the activity is stopped, no further control actions need be taken (at least for the time being) because there is no involvement in the risky activity. However, it is recommended that the situation be reviewed periodically, because things change. If the answer is that the agency should not stop the activity, the model points down to three other possible risk control mechanisms: eliminate risk, minimize harm, and transfer liability. Each of these options is discussed in more detail as follows.

(D)   STEP 4

Ultimately, all arrows lead to "Review," reinforcing the critical point that risk management is never finished. The arrow from the "Review" box leads up to the top of the flowchart, where one begins again. Agencies need to continually engage in risk management, scanning for risks and changes in both the environment and the organization's risk threshold that would recommend changes in policy and procedures and that would bring actions, decisions, personnel, and services back to within the risk tolerance zone.

36.7   *Operationalizing the Model*

(A)   STEP 1: IDENTIFYING RISKS

The agency should brainstorm a list of possible dangers, situations, or problems that might occur in the operation of programs or the governance of the organization. Tremper and Kostin suggest there are four main classifications of risk to look out for: people, property, income, and goodwill.[5] An agency might use the Risk Identification Checklist shown in Exhibit 36.2 as a tool in risk identification. The agency should invite participation from others who are familiar with the volunteer department and the various roles and responsibilities assigned to volunteers, and also ask for help from those who are completely unfamiliar with the operation of the organization. Both will identify risks.

It is also wise for the organization to review both current and past operations and occurrences, as well as reviewing existing policies, procedures, personnel, and operating

EXHIBIT 36.2 Risk Identification Checklist

PROGRAM: _____ **DATE:** _____

RISK TYPE	NO APPARENT RISK	RISK PRESENT	COMMENTS
PEOPLE:			
Clients	( )	( )	
Volunteers	( )	( )	
Paid Staff	( )	( )	
Board	( )	( )	
General Public	( )	( )	
Other			
PROPERTY:			
Real Property: Buildings, Equipment, Vehicles, etc.	( )	( )	
Financial Property: Operating, Capital, and Reserve Accounts, etc.	( )	( )	
Electronic Property: Databases, Donor Lists, Client and Personnel Records, etc.	( )	( )	
Intellectual Property: Manuals, Books, Training Modules, Documents, Forms, etc.	( )	( )	
Other			
INCOME:			
Contracts, Licensed and Mandated Services	( )	( )	
Donations, Grants, etc.	( )	( )	
Other			
Goodwill:			
Agency Reputation, Credibility, Stature	( )	( )	
Agency Profile	( )	( )	
Public Trust	( )	( )	
Other:			

manuals. These should comply with all relevant legislation, regulations, codes, licensing agreements, and so on, and need to be considered from the perspective of risk and hazards.

The organization should examine each aspect of service delivery and all job descriptions, disassembling them into component parts and considering what might go wrong in the various pieces and steps.

The agency should not conduct its own risk management efforts from behind a desk. Those identifying the risks should go to the locations where clients receive their services, go to all of the sites, floors, wards, and branches where volunteers perform their duties. It is necessary to walk the premises and try to pinpoint risks and dangers, considering the safety of the work site and the state of working conditions. Equipment should be examined; buildings inspected; staff–client and collegial relationships observed. Questions to ask include:

- Do people know where the emergency exits are?
- Do people know where the fire extinguishers are?
- Do people know where the first aid supplies are?
- Do people know who to call in an emergency?
- Do people know what priorities should prevail (for example, always the safety of persons first) in the event of a threat or disaster?
- Do volunteers know that they have the authority to act in such a way as to protect themselves and others when in danger, and equally, what the limits of that authority are?

The examiners should try to imagine the setting in emergency situations and ask: What would need to be done and who should do it? Safety records, workers' compensation claims, and serious incident occurrence reports are good sources of past dangers that may need additional attention.

A "near miss" procedure should be instituted through which staff and volunteers are required to report any potentially serious events that nearly materialized so that administration has the opportunity to implement preventive measures before the next "near miss" becomes a tragedy. The agency should develop a positive organizational culture about risk management that both empowers and rewards all personnel for risk identification, reporting, and control initiatives. Risk management should never be considered "squealing" on a colleague.

These techniques will assist in the creation of the master list of risks. At this stage in the risk management model, all risks, no matter of what magnitude, should be recorded. Even risks that are currently assessed to be "under control" should be included on the list.

(B) STEP 2: EVALUATING RISKS

When the master list of risks is compiled, each item will need to be evaluated. The agency should ask these questions:

- Is this a "high" risk or a "low" risk?
- Does this risk fall within our risk tolerance zone and is it a risk that we can comfortably live with without any (further) form of risk reduction attention?

There are two key perspectives from which to evaluate each risk: likelihood of occurrence and magnitude of harm.

(i) Likelihood of Occurrence

To assess whether the organization can "live with" a risk at its current level, it must first consider the potential for the risk to materialize. It is impossible to apply a mathematical equation, and pure science should not be the aim. Consider what the odds might be of each specific risk materializing into actual loss or harm. An informal rating system like the Risk Rating Scale in Exhibit 36.3 can prompt a systematic approach. It also gives organizational personnel a tool by which to compare and discuss their respective "guestimates" and to pinpoint divergence. This might be a particularly useful tool to work through with, or at least share with, a board of directors that is reluctant to acknowledge the existence of risks in the volunteer department, or that will not authorize the development of risk management policies and procedures for the volunteer department because "they are just volunteers, after all."

It will be obvious that risks that have a large or moderate chance of materializing will need some form of risk control treatment. Risks that exist, but that are very unlikely to materialize may, at first, seem to require no further attention. An organization might be tempted to dismiss them as "nothing to worry about" and set them aside for no further attention. However, it is recommended that even risks that are rated at the lowest end of the "likelihood" scale be examined from the second perspective, "magnitude of harm," before being dismissed.

(ii) Magnitude of Harm

The second perspective from which to evaluate each risk on the master list of risks is "magnitude of harm." Here the evaluator considers the range of possible consequences in the event that the risk actually materializes, asking these questions:

- How significant might the injuries, losses, harm, or liabilities be?
- Are the potential consequences something the organization should pay attention to, or are they something that can be lived with? For example, children at the day care center play. It is inevitable that a good number of them will fall down and, predictably, routinely, hurt themselves.
- How big might the hurt be?

EXHIBIT 36.3 Risk Rating Scale

Risk	Likelihood of Occurrence (Rate 1 to 5)*	Tolerance Zone		Comments
		We Can Live With It	**We Cannot Live With It**	

* Assign a "likelihood rating" such as:
1 = Very unlikely that this risk will materialize into harm, loss, or liability.
3 = Somewhat likely that this risk will materialize into harm, loss, or liability.
5 = Very possible that this risk will materialize into harm, loss, or liability.

To illustrate: Take the case of the day care center that has paid attention to the safety of its grounds and premises with regard to children at play. It has ensured, for example, that there is no particularly risky playground equipment on site, there are no sharp edges to tables or furniture in the playroom, children are well and continuously supervised, all rambunctious players are attended to quickly, and so on. That day care center might determine that even though the likelihood of a bump or bruise to children at play is quite significant, the magnitude of the harm of such occurrences for both the children and the center is something the center can live with.

Consider the same illustration at a day care center where skateboards are a routine fixture in the toy box, cleaning supplies are kept on the bottom shelf of an unlocked cabinet, the swing set is never inspected for wear, and funding cutbacks have reduced the children-to-adult ratio to below safe levels. Children in this setting may play just the same as in the first example, but both the likelihood of occurrence and magnitude of harm are probably much greater in the second example.

Those risks that fall within the risk tolerance zone—risks that are assessed to be among those that the organization can live with without additional risk control measures—can be set aside at this point in the process, and targeted for review at some identified point in the future. Those risks that, because of the likelihood of their occurrence, magnitude of harm, or a combination of the two, fall outside of the risk tolerance zone, will be targeted for further control treatment. Risks that involve a significant degree of harm—even those risks that are less likely to occur—may require immediate risk management attention.

Remember that all risk management decisions have implications for more than personal safety and organizational well-being. They also have ethical implications and consequences. It is useful for the evaluator to apply the "headline test" to risk management activities: consider how the risk management decisions taken today will look as the substance of a headline in the local paper the morning after a tragedy at the site. The agency should try the "hindsight test," asking the question: If we are ever looking back at our risk-related decision making in the wake of a tragedy, will we feel we implemented proper and sufficient risk management protocol? Will we be perceived by the public and our peers as having done enough? Risk management almost always forces organizations to identify and explore their ethical obligations and their organizational values as well as their organizational liabilities.

(C) STEP 3: CONTROLLING RISKS

Risks that cannot be tolerated must be reduced. A range of mechanisms exists, and the risk management model directs us to consider one or more of these, in the following order.

(i) Stopping the Activity
Certain risks are best controlled by simply stopping, or ceasing involvement in, the risk-producing activity. This may sound like a radical solution, but it need not mean canceling the service or the program, or closing the doors of the agency. Stopping the activity might mean terminating an action or service that has come to be increasingly unsafe, suddenly or gradually, over time. For example:

- Not allowing children to spend considerable time in the company of just one person in an isolated setting; dropping the overnights from the program and finding another way to teach leadership, self-esteem, competence, or whatever the aims of the canceled activity were.

- Revising the volunteer application form and deleting all sections that would now be considered discriminatory under human rights legislation.
- Elaborating on client eligibility criteria and refusing to deliver a service to violent and abusive clients who pose a danger to staff and volunteers.

Stopping the activity might mean postponement to a safer time or place. For example:

- Postponing the picnic when it begins to storm; canceling the ski trip when there have been a few inches of freezing rain the night before.
- Waiting until a second camp counselor is available before conducting tent checks after lights out.
- After the tree in the backyard is damaged in a windstorm, keeping the children inside until the debris can be cleared away and the stability of what remains is assessed.

Stopping the activity might mean cutting out a portion of it that is most dangerous, leaving the remainder to operate within risk tolerance boundaries. For example:

- Palliative care volunteers never accept gifts of any sort from clients and never involve themselves in clients' financial affairs.
- The friendly visitors are prohibited from driving their clients because driving is not an essential function of the friendly visitor job description, and all of the appropriate driver's records checks, insurance checks, and vehicle inspections will require more effort and expense than the agency is willing to expend.

In practice, managers of volunteers "stop the activity" frequently because of risk. This step does not necessarily mean termination of an entire service, or cancellation of the whole volunteer program. However, managers will, from time to time, identify a volunteer position, or a specific service or activity that has, indeed, become too risky. When the magnitude of the risk warrants it, radical action should not be avoided.

(ii) Eliminating the Risk

In this step of the risk management model, when the decision has been taken to proceed with the activity in question, and a significant (that is, intolerable) risk exists, the agency should consider changing the operation of the program to reduce the likelihood of risk occurrence. This step, in essence, is about prevention. The action taken should be reasonable to keep the identified risk from materializing; for example:

- Changing procedures, updating equipment, implementing new rules, setting additional boundaries to keep volunteers safe.
- Paying closer attention to personnel requirements, increasing the minimum qualifications for the position, upgrading screening protocols.
- Hiring security guards or off-duty police officers to guard fund-raising events where there is a lot of cash on hand (e.g., bingos, carnivals, charity casinos).
- Having staff, rather than volunteers, feed those patients who are at greatest risk of choking.

- Insisting that volunteer activity take place on site or only in the presence of others; increasing training and supervision for volunteers; implementing a performance review system that promotes early detection of errors or other substandard performance.
- Removing the skateboards from the equipment boxes at the after-school program.
- Installing handrails on all stairs and grab bars in all showers.
- Moving the petty cash box from the shelf in the main office and placing it in a locked cabinet to which only two people have a key.
- Partitioning databases, instituting a password system, and limiting access to sensitive or vital agency records.

In reality it is virtually impossible to eliminate all risk, but this step in the risk management model encourages consideration of all reasonable mechanisms that will reduce the likelihood of loss, injury, or liability.

(iii) Minimizing Harm

Even where all reasonable risk elimination mechanisms have been implemented, it is likely that some measure of risk will still be present because it is virtually impossible to eliminate risk entirely. In recognition of ever-present risk, the next risk control mechanism directs attention to reducing the degree of harm that might result if the risk materializes. Following are examples of techniques that help to minimize the magnitude of the harm that might result from a "go wrong":

- Training fund-raising staff and volunteers thoroughly. If the casino is held up, the protocol is "hit the dirt and let 'em have the cash!"
- Insisting on protective clothing, special equipment, safety boots, and so forth wherever appropriate.
- Allowing the resident who is unsteady on his feet to walk on his own if that is important to his independence and rehabilitation, but insisting that he wear a helmet so that if he does fall, his injuries will be less.
- Allowing residents to smoke if they must, but only outside. All matches, lighters, and cigarettes are to be handed in at the front desk before bedtime. Installing extra-sensitive smoke detectors in all bedrooms.
- Keeping no more than $50 in the petty cash box at any given time; if it does sprout legs and take a walk, the loss is minimized.
- Keeping detailed files on all risk management deliberations, and maintaining up-to-date agency policies and procedures, so that if something does go wrong and a legal action is launched, the organization has tangible proof of all it has tried to do to control risks and prevent harm.
- Allocating responsibilities in such a way that only staff and volunteers who are calm, stable, and reliable are assigned to positions of first response in the event of a calamity.
- Regularly and frequently backing up all sensitive and vital data so that little is lost in the event of a power failure, fire, flood, or other peril.

(iv) Transferring Liability

Increasing numbers of charitable organizations across the United States, and more recently, in Canada as well, are facing legal action because of accidents, injuries, and abuse, and the allegations of negligence that typically follow. When all other avenues have been pursued and every reasonable effort has been made to reduce risks and minimize harm, when the organization believes that it has met its ethical obligations and satisfied its duty of care, when all of these measures have been implemented and some measure of risk still exists, it is entirely appropriate for the organization to consider its own liability in connection with its operations. Note, however, that it is neither legally nor ethically defensible to identify a risk and then move automatically and directly to liability reduction, thereby bypassing all attempts at prevention and control. Everything reasonable should be done to prevent and reduce harm before attention and resources are devoted to liability reduction.

This is not to say that responsible organizations are not obliged to tend to their own liability exposure. On the contrary, this "transfer liability" step in the risk management process directs the organization to move remaining liability to another party, via mechanisms such as memoranda of agreement, save harmless agreements, waivers,[6] contracting out, and/or insurance policies. Some suggestions for transferring liability are to:

- Transport the really ill client by ambulance, not by volunteer driver.
- Hire a company to clean the outside of the windows on all floors above the first floor.
- Hire a moving company when the agency moves.
- Fully investigate insurance needs. Because there are many kinds of insurance products available, organizations need to read and research about insurance, and consult an insurance advisor concerning insurance requirements.
- Institute waivers and save harmless agreements.
- Contract the most risky activities to another organization or company that is better qualified, better prepared, or is a specialist in that field.

Whenever liability is transferred to another party, credentials must be checked thoroughly. When an organization transfers a liability, it retains an accountability to have done so responsibly. It should be certain the other organization, firm, or individual is appropriately screened, licensed, insured, bonded, or whatever other qualifications are fitting.

A caution is offered about overdependence on insurance, since one so often hears managers, executive directors, and board members all make the leap from "Are we at risk?" to "Are we insured?" Insurance, like waivers, is useful, and maybe even essential, but unfortunately, insurance cannot be relied on as total protection. There are at least three important reasons not to rely on insurance:

- Insurance does not cover everything. For example, no insurance policy can repair damaged organizational reputation or the shaken faith of supporters after a disaster or an incident of abuse. Insurance will not restore lost public trust, or heal the negative publicity wounds that so often follow tragedies, accidents, and disasters. Insurance cannot recover the time and anguish spent defending against a claim.
- Depending on the circumstances and the nature of the insurance coverage, protection may be void in the presence of a finding of negligence.
- The payout of all insurance policies is limited, and there is always the potential that the judgment will be for a sum greater than the insurance provides.

There is no question that insurance is an important part of risk management, but smart managers know that insurance covers only a small portion of the loss. It should be purchased, but not considered a shield.

(D) STEP 4: REVIEW

Risk management is a process, a way of thinking. That means it needs to be continuous. It should never be considered finished. Risk management can be kept alive by:

- Building a review of the risk management system into the annual evaluation, policy review, and personnel appraisal systems.
- Keeping an eye open for changes in legislation, bylaws, community standards, and legal precedents that may alter organizational responsibilities and/or liabilities.
- Contracting the (volunteer) services of a lawyer who agrees to watch out for legal decisions that might have an impact on the standards that apply to the organization, reviewing jobs carefully to ensure that conditions have not changed, or new hazards emerged.
- Making certain all equipment and facilities are checked regularly and procedures are updated accordingly.

These questions should be asked: How effective are the controls the organization put in place? Is it still willing to bear the burden of risk it thought acceptable the last time?

36.8 *The Connection Between Risk Management and Policy Development*

The reader may have recognized the integral link between risk control and policy development. Policies and procedures are indispensable in all risk control steps. Policies set the rules and the guidelines about what will be done and how it will be done. They establish the boundaries beyond which volunteers should not stray. They define what is, and what is not, acceptable, and specifically what to do in the event of trouble.

Policies, therefore, are critical to risk management as a preventive device. They are as important with respect to reducing liability exposure. They are concrete evidence of all the agency has done to try to identify risks and prevent harm. A comprehensive set of policies demonstrates that the organization has been prudent in assessing risks, setting safety limits and standards, and generally and specifically attending to the health and well-being of those connected to agency services. They are tangible proof of attempts to be diligent and to attend to the duty of care. Policies and procedures are indispensable to risk management.

36.9 *Conclusion*

Risk management may sound like a lot of work, and it can be. Remember that organizations and their personnel are actually doing much of it all the time, anyway, just not systematically. Following the risk management model outlined in this chapter prompts managers to ask not only the right questions, but the right questions *in the right order,* that help produce risk management solutions throughout the volunteer department, and indeed, throughout the agency.

Remember that very few programs involve no risks, and very few risky situations are managed with only one risk control mechanism. Fully evaluating the range of risks that prevails and then systematically exploring all risk reduction mechanisms can generate a properly tailored constellation of mechanisms for each situation. The process will help organizations operate within their own risk tolerance zones. The kind of comprehensive program review that a risk management process entails will often generate more productive and satisfying volunteer involvement, and more effective services to consumers as well.

Not engaging in risk management will not make the risks go away. In fact, not managing and controlling risks will merely increase liability, and increase the odds of losing a legal action if, or when, one is launched.

Endnotes

1. Wilson, M. (1976). *The Effective Management of Volunteer Programs.* Boulder, CO: Volunteer Management Associates.
2. Silver, N. (1988). *At The Heart: The New Challenge to Community Agencies.* Pleasanton, CA: Valley Volunteer Center.
3. For managers who are working in "Silver's Gap" and need help to convince their administrators, executive directors, or board members of the necessity of risk management in volunteer services, three resources are recommended. Tremper and Kostin's *No Surprises* (1993) is an excellent primer for agency administration (paid and unpaid) because it makes a strong case for risk management for both direct-service and administrative (board and committee) volunteering. For those administrators who are not likely to read a book, or who might be persuaded to at least listen to a tape on the way to and from work one day, consider the author's *AudioWorkshop™ Policy Development for Volunteer Services.* It describes the need for policies in risk management and makes a strong case for policy development as an essential risk management device (1996). The third resource to help administrators understand their role in effective volunteer services is Susan Ellis's *From the Top Down,* written specifically for executive directors and board members (1996).
4. Tremper, C., and G. Kostin, (1993). *No Surprises: Controlling Risks in Volunteer Programs.* Washington, DC: Nonprofit Risk Management Center.
5. Id., p. 5.
6. For a decade or more, prevailing advice suggested that waivers provided little, if any, protection from liability and were not worth the bother. Current wisdom recommends reconsideration of waivers and other save harmless agreements. They are not guarantees against suits, but they serve as one piece of tangible evidence of informed consent. Best practice recommends use of waivers but further recommends full application of all other reasonable risk management techniques. In brief, implement waivers where useful, but do not rely on them.

Suggested Readings

Ellis, S. J. (1996). *From the Top Down: The Executive Role in Volunteer Program Success,* rev. ed. Philadelphia: Energize Associates.

Graff, L. L. (1997). *By Definition: Policies for Volunteer Programs.* Dundas, Ontario: Graff and Associates.

Graff, L. L. (1996). *Policy Development for Volunteer Services.* AudioWorkshop.™ Dundas, Ontario: Graff and Associates.

Lai, M. L., T. S. Chapman, and E. L. Steinbock, (1992). *Am I Covered For. . . ? A Comprehensive Guide to Insuring Your Non-Profit Organization,* 2nd ed. San Jose, CA: Consortium for Human Services, Inc.

Minnesota Office on Volunteer Services. (1992). *How to Control Liability & Risk in Volunteer Programs.* St. Paul: Author.

Patterson, J. (1994). *Staff Screening Tool Kit: Keeping the Bad Apples out of Your Organization.* Washington, DC: Nonprofit Risk Management Center.

Patterson, J. (1995). *Child Abuse Prevention Primer for Your Organization.* Washington, DC: Nonprofit Risk Management Center.

37 Episodic Volunteering

NANCY MACDUFF
Macduff/Bunt Associates

37.1 Introduction

In 1989, a study on volunteering was conducted by The National VOLUNTEER Center and J.C. Penney Company. They asked those not volunteering what it would take to get them to volunteer. Seventy-nine percent of those asked said they would be inclined to volunteer if the positions were short in duration.[1] Ten years ago, this survey was an early warning for what is reality in the twenty-first century. The Independent Sector's most recent study of volunteers reports that fully 41 percent of all those volunteering are doing it episodically, or short term.[2] The wishes of the survey respondents in 1989 are a reality for close to half of the millions of volunteers in the United States.

An understanding of the nature of short-term volunteering begins with an understanding of terminology. Not all volunteers who provide "short-term" service disappear at the end of their duties. Some volunteers provide assistance annually for events or one-time tasks. They might work at the registration table at a statewide Special Olympics track and field event, serve as auctioneer for a gala fund-raising dinner for a symphony orchestra, or coordinate cookie sales for the local Girl Scout Council. They are reliable long-term volunteers, but they do their work in an episodic fashion.

Other volunteers more aptly fit the description *short term*. They may be students who need real-world experience outside the classroom for the subject they are studying, a busy professional person who has an interest in the service provided by the organization but can work for only one Saturday on a special project, and sometimes they are a relative or friend of a staff member who is looking for something to do for a few hours. All of this service is also episodic.

The Oxford Dictionary and Thesaurus (American Edition) defines the word *episodic* as follows: 1: sporadic; 2: occurring at irregular intervals. Synonyms are *occasional* and *temporary*. The term *episodic* is a more accurate description than short term of what volunteers do in their service.

To develop effective strategies to both recruit and sustain volunteers, it is essential to understand what "episodic volunteering" is and how it differs from the type of volunteering that has been the norm. The dictionary definition outlines the two most predominant types and kinds of episodic volunteer opportunities. A *temporary* episodic volunteer gives service short in duration, and the *occasional* episodic volunteer is one providing service at regular intervals for short periods of time. Another form of episodic volunteering is the interim volunteer: someone who gives service on a regular basis for less then six months. A student who interns at a social service agency for a semester, to gain experience and college credit is an *interim* episodic volunteer. A rule of thumb is that the episodic volunteer rarely serves longer than six months. Someone serving on a committee that meets once per month all year long is not an episodic volunteer. His or her service is continuous.

Temporary, interim, and occasional volunteers are familiar to the volunteer program manager. Informally, most volunteer programs or organizations accommodate individuals who wish to serve in short-term assignments. In many cities, organizations recruit people who are interested only in episodic assignments.

Traditionally, many volunteer programs organized their positions for volunteers around the "continuous-service" volunteer. Recruiting, screening, management, and recognition activities were for the person who continued to serve the organization for a long time on a regular schedule. The episodic volunteer was welcome, but had to fit into the existing systems for long-term, continuous-service volunteers.

This strategy is accurate and well conceived, but totally inappropriate for the episodic volunteer. In fact, short-term volunteers may question the validity of the volunteer assignment if they are forced to sit through an orientation designed for continuous-service volunteers. Designing volunteer tasks to attract episodic volunteers requires a fresh look at the elements of managing volunteers. Taking a position description written for the continuous-service volunteer and applying it to someone serving for a short term is not developing positions for those wishing to give episodic service. A program to attract those who want to give episodic service requires the establishment of a separate program with its own recruiting, screening, supervision, training, recognition, and evaluation. There are no shortcuts to developing an effective and quality program to attract those who will serve volunteer programs in small chunks of time.

37.2 *Barriers*

Some organizations with volunteer programs are still quite resistant to the incorporation of an episodic volunteer program. The need for services and activities has them continuing old practices hoping to find sufficient long-term volunteers. Rarely is that the case. Other volunteer programs have a seemingly ample supply of retirees to fill their needs. They often avoid reorganizing their program to accommodate episodic volunteers because there is no pressing current need. The future may prove them to be shortsighted.

In some cases, short-term assignments are already provided for volunteers in an informal and unstructured way. People rarely see the need to formalize what appears to be working. In any organization wishing to build the strength of its commitment to episodic volunteering, the barriers must be addressed first. What are those barriers that keep volunteer programs from implementing that which is needed and wanted?

- *Current volunteers and staff may see little value in the use of episodic volunteers.* Undoubtedly, the single largest barrier to starting a formalized episodic volunteer program exists in the current workforce—paid and unpaid. Volunteers expect other volunteers to have "paid their dues" or have the same level of time commitment. Professional staff often feel the supervision of episodic-service volunteers challenging and the idea of training and supervising someone who is present only for a short time as inefficient. There has always been tension between volunteers and staff. Volunteers are sometimes seen by staff as potential usurpers of their jobs; staff work can be misjudged by volunteers as being easy and something they could do. These attitudes are by no means universal, but they exist when volunteers and paid staff have worked together for years. Introducing the idea of "office temporary" types of volunteers can be a cause for both anxiety and resistance.
- *There has been little use of episodic volunteers in the past.* Institutional knowledge frequently overlooks the fact that episodic volunteers have been around forever. Those inside the organization tend to remember the people they see on a daily, weekly, or monthly basis. This perception of episodic volunteers as different from continuous-service volunteers can create a lack of confidence in the ability of the organization or agency and its staff and volunteers to cope with a "new type" of volunteers.
- *Allegiance to volunteer positions/tasks as they are currently designed is strong.* Church and synagogue teachers used to come in the "year-long" variety. Girl Scout leaders signed on for several years. Ten years ago, leaders in youth organizations did not envision shared leadership teams or other ways of delivering their program to children. Today, those same organizations offer and promote a variety of ways to make programs available without adults having to "sign on for the rest of their natural lives or the lives of their children." One barrier to an episodic volunteer program may be resistance to changing traditional positions descriptions or the way service is delivered. Some volunteer tasks can be refocused into smaller pieces, redesigned, or organized for a team rather than an individual. Staff and volunteers need assistance and guidance to develop tasks specifically for those wishing short-term service. Resistance is often due to inexperience or lack of knowledge, not just a desire to be difficult.
- *Energy and resources are focused on the volunteer who stays.* Training sessions for hospice volunteers can be as long as 40 to 80 hours. Formal recognition for most volunteers comes during the spring celebration of National Volunteer Week. For the episodic volunteer, the message is clear: The people who count here are those who stay. A caste system among volunteers is created. This is a barrier to attracting those who want to give episodic service but receive a clear message that it is insufficient. The energy of staff and current volunteers is placed on keeping the continuous volunteer happy, not on meeting the needs of the person with short-term service. This is a double-barreled barrier. It has the potential to immobilize the staff and current volunteers by restricting their focus to one type of volunteer, and it can turn off people who do volunteer for a short-service assignment. Those who are unhappy share it

with their friends and colleagues. Thus, recruiting for episodic positions (and sometimes continuous positions) might become difficult.

- *Legal liabilities can be a barrier.* Some programs require volunteers to complete screening procedures that are costly and time consuming. For example, many hospitals require volunteers to have medical tests prior to beginning their work. Since these tests are provided at no cost to the volunteer, recruiting episodic volunteers is expensive when the time and charges for the tests are considered. However, exempting episodic volunteers from this requirement could put the organization in a legally tenuous position. Similarly, screening for volunteers who work with children, the developmentally delayed, or fragile elderly is often extensive. Doing the same type of screening for someone who is giving only four or five hours of services hardly seems worth the effort. The reluctance of many organizations to formally organize an episodic volunteer program is based on the legal liability issues. Addressing the legal liability issues with those in charge of risk management is critical for some programs.

- *Episodic volunteers can face rejection.* Some volunteer managers are reluctant to put volunteers in "harm's way." They sense that the person giving short-time service will be treated shabbily by those who work in the program for a longer time, both staff and volunteers. What if the volunteer administrator organizes an episodic volunteer program, recruits new people, and orients them to their position, only to have them rejected by staff or continuous-service volunteers? It is easier to avoid the issue by not formally organizing the volunteer program. Episodic volunteers continue to be used informally, thus sidestepping the issue of the acceptance or rejection of those giving short-term service. Allowing this situation to continue means that a "class" system of volunteers is created. Those with the highest status are those giving continuous service.

These barriers can be reduced or eliminated by the organization through a formally established episodic volunteer program with clear lines of authority and responsibility. This is best done by involving continuous-service volunteers in the planning process and creating a trained and supervised corps of volunteers to serve as middle managers, monitoring the work of episodic volunteers. The process begins with understanding where the organizations stands now in its use of episodic volunteers and how it might better organize that effort.

37.3   *Recruiting the Episodic Volunteer*

Formal or informal episodic volunteer positions already existing in an organization can be the foundation on which to develop a full-fledged episodic program. To do that requires planning and implementing an organized volunteer recruitment and support initiative specifically designed for the episodic volunteer opportunities in the organization. There are nine steps included in the development of an episodic volunteer program.

(A)   THE NEEDS ASSESSMENT

Any new program or service begins with a needs assessment. "A needs assessment is an excellent means of involving the volunteers and staff in problem solving and developing local goals. The tendency to resist change is frequently caused because people have inadequate information, or are not involved in the decision-making process."[3] Increasing the acceptance of current staff and volunteers to the use of episodic volunteers is achieved by involving them in the needs assessment process. As full participants in identifying potential positions, surveying others about the need for episodic volunteers, determining resources available, and delineating the current use of episodic volunteers, they become owners of the outcomes.

A needs assessment for the episodic volunteer program should include, but is not limited to:

- Identifying the current quality and quantity of service by episodic volunteers in the last three to five years
- Surveys identifying areas in which episodic volunteers might be helpful
- Resources needed to support episodic volunteers (human and financial)
- The perceived need for episodic volunteers in areas where they are not now serving or to increase service in underutilized areas (See Exhibit 37.1.)

EXHIBIT 37.1 Are We Ready for an Episodic Volunteer Program?

DIRECTIONS: Organize a group of volunteers and staff to help assess the readiness of the organization for an Episodic Volunteer Program. Begin by using this questionnaire to list the current episodic volunteer opportunities available in your organization. Be careful. Remember the definitions!

1. What type of episodic volunteer positions/opportunities do we currently have? List all the different types of episodic positions/tasks you have accommodated in the last three years. Remember to list those in all three categories.

     a. Temporary (short in duration):

     b. Occasional (occurs at regular intervals):

     c. Interim (short duration, usually less than 6 months, but on a regular schedule):

2. In your view, will short-term or episodic volunteers be accepted as members of the volunteer and staff team? Why or why not?

3. Are there adequate human and financial resources to launch an episodic volunteer program? How do we know? Who can do it? How long will it take them? Is there financial support for their work? Will management support the work of volunteers and staff to establish an episodic volunteer program?

4. How can you document the need for episodic volunteering in your program, organization, or agency? For example, are there episodic positions available? Have volunteers and staff been surveyed about the availability of episodic tasks/positions?

5. Are partners in the organization prepared to support the development of a dual-focused volunteer program? Conceptually this means thinking in new ways about volunteer programs. For example, the establishment of an episodic volunteer program means promoting continuous-service volunteers into positions of manager or supervisor. Who will train them to carry out the management functions? Who will supervise them? (Macduff, 1985)

The results of the questionnaire are compiled, published, and then provided to anyone interested in the development of the episodic volunteer program. It is also a useful document to provide a board of directors or advisory committee who are considering financial or programmatic support to an episodic volunteer program. When you have competed this self-assessment, it is clear whether your program, organization, or agency is ready to move to the next phase of developing the episodic volunteering program.

(B) THE PLAN

Following the needs assessment, if an affirmative decision is made to develop and implement an episodic volunteer program, the next step is to establish a plan to accomplish the task. This includes setting an overall goal and smaller objective statements that describe in measurable increments the steps to be taken to implement the episodic volunteer program. This planning process also serves as the foundation to evaluate the success of the total program.

"Planning is a disciplined effort to produce fundamental decisions and actions that shape and guide what an organization is, what it does, and why it does it."[4] Many episodic volunteer positions/tasks are arrived at by accident. Someone calls and asks for a short assignment, he or she seems sincere, there is an immediate need, and so the person participates for two weeks.

Individuals deserve respect for their volunteer service, regardless of its duration This requires a team effort to plan the organization of an episodic volunteer program similar to the way in which the program for continuous-service volunteers is organized. Plans address the areas of task or position development, descriptions for them, recruitment strategies, methods to screen, training plans, supervision strategies, evaluation, and recognition techniques.

A key to the success of the episodic program is the organization and staffing of the planning team. "The best examples of planning . . . demonstrate effective, focused information gathering; extensive communication among and participation by key decision makers and opinion leaders; the accommodation of divergent interests and values; the development and analysis of alternatives; an emphasis on the future implications of present decisions and actions; focused, reasonably analytic, and orderly decision making; and successful implementation."[5] Assembling the right people to serve on the planning team is key to achieving these objectives. Success or failure of an episodic program initially rests with this important group of people.

The episodic planning team should include current continuous-service volunteers, paid staff, and selected episodic volunteers from the past. It is also useful to include representatives from support staff. Many times, clerical or maintenance support staff observe the work of volunteers, know where good short-term positions are located, and are often put in the position of supervising episodic volunteers. Rarely are they included in the decision-making process related to something that will affect their job.

It is also helpful to have "outsiders" sit on the committee. These can be individuals from organizations with experience in episodic volunteering or a person who is interested in the mission of the organization and is an effective planner. Outsiders frequently challenge those "inside" the organization to do their best work.

The committee chair should be an individual who supports the idea of a formally organized episodic volunteer program and has good leadership skills. The volunteer program manager serves as staff support for this group.

The group's responsibility typically begins with the needs assessment and then proceeds with establishing goals and objectives that address the issues of position or task development and position descriptions, recruitment, screening, training, supervision, evaluation, and recognition.

(C) POSITION/TASK DEVELOPMENT AND DESCRIPTIONS

Frequently, short-term volunteers are assigned tasks usually done by a continuous-service volunteer. Often, they perform poorly or do not complete the task. This has the effect of reinforcing all the barriers and stereotypes mentioned earlier. It is a mistake to take current positions for volunteers and assume they can be done by episodic volunteers, as is! A primary task for the planning team is to identify new tasks that can be performed on a short-term basis and/or redesign traditional volunteer tasks or positions so they are more appropriately assigned to the short-term volunteer. Once this position/task development process is completed, then position descriptions are written.

Marlene Wilson, in *The Effective Management of Volunteer Programs,* refers to this as "job design." She says position development is "to plan and fashion artistically and skillfully."[6] Task and position development includes gathering information from staff and other volunteers about specific tasks that can be accomplished by those giving short-term service. The form shown in Exhibit 37.2 is designed to collect information needed to design positions for episodic volunteers.[7]

Distributing the form to staff and volunteers helps to identify positions ideally suited for the person wanting to give short-term service. Members of the planning team or the volunteer manager need to be available to assist those who have never completed a position development form.

Another way to develop episodic tasks/positons is to review the tasks currently done by continuous-service volunteers. Being a Girl Scout leader does not require someone to sign on for 12 years. The scouting organization has adapted to the needs of the modern volunteer by allowing and encouraging leadership of troops to take a variety of forms. There are teams of parents or adults who work with large groups of more than one troop, but the actual time of service is only two or three times per year. In other cases, leadership is rotated every few months through the parents of girls in the troop. In some cases, the troop meets less often than in the past. These are creative solutions for busy parents and children.

The challenge to altering the way current volunteer positions or tasks are developed is the strength of the commitment to the current way of doing things. If the program is delivered effectively, there is a natural reluctance to changing it. However, many continuous-service volunteers can have their service or experience enhanced by the participation of an episodic volunteer. As an example, hospice friendly visitors (volunteers who provide direct patient visits to an individual with a terminal illness) can be assisted in their work with terminally ill patients by an episodic volunteer. The episodic volunteer might make library trips for the patient, thus allowing the continuous-service volunteer to spend more quality time with the patient rather than driving around picking up books. Episodic volunteers need clearly defined parameters for their tasks, which might mean not seeing the patient except with staff or a volunteer from hospice present.

EXHIBIT 37.2 Episodic Volunteer Request Form

DIRECTIONS: Some volunteers like to provide their service to (name of organization or agency) with short-term or episodic service. These are positions/tasks that can be completed in one day, over a short period of time (less than three months), or occur only once in a given year. Complete the following form and deliver the completed copy to _____.

DATE: _____ Phone/EXT: _____

Name of Person Making Request: _____

Department or Division: _____

Brief Description of Position/Task:

_____

List briefly the skills/abilities required to do this position/task:

_____

Can this postion/task be accomplished by using the Internet or e-mail?

_____

Who will supervise the work of this volunteer? _____

Has this supervisor worked with volunteers before and, if so, how long?

Yes _____ No _____   How Long? _____

Where will the individual work? _____

List the minimum and maximum amount of time you think this work will take? If the individual is needed on specific days of the week or times, please list those.

Minimum _____   Maximum _____

Any other requirements: _____

When do you need the volunteer to start on this task or position? _____

Is this a position that could be done by different episodic volunteers on a regular basis?

Yes _____ No _____

Return this form to: _____

Position/Task development forms are also available in the book *Volunteer Management Forms* by Steve McCurley.

This adaptation of a long-term position requires some flexibility and creativity. The value is to the organization, the individual receiving the service or program, and the volunteer who has the opportunity to give without guilt. Their position is prescribed. They know they are needed and providing a valuable service.

A new and exciting type of volunteering is *virtual volunteering,* wherein volunteers provide their service via electronic mail or the Internet. For example, some volunteers are tutoring students via computer. Just as long-term, continuous-service positions/tasks are available online, so too are episodic. Episodic volunteers can design brochures, flyers, and documents; set up record-keeping systems for special events; and assist in cleaning donor or member databases. These are all examples of tasks that can be accomplished in a short time by a "virtual" episodic volunteer.

"All volunteer positions within an organization should have position descriptions. We tell volunteers how we feel about their position by the professionalism we display in regard to that position. If we want to attract energetic, busy, professional people to our organization, we must send a message loud and clear that we take the volunteer role seriously."[8] The haphazard way in which episodic volunteers are often fit into an organization can influence that organization's ability to attract more volunteers. People talk. They tell their friends and colleagues about their experience on a volunteer task. The organization that treats them with respect and professionalism is miles ahead of the one in which the volunteer manager says, "Gosh, I'm sure I can find a task for you somewhere. Just give me 10 minutes."

The task/position description should provide basic information about the task and time required, and it should be portable. The requirements for the hospice friendly visitor mentioned earlier would be much longer than their "aide-de-camp" who is only going to work two hours per week for three months. The form illustrated in Exhibit 37.3 gives an idea of what an episodic volunteer position description might look like.

The planning team working with the staff can use the task development forms to write a description. Notice that the sample would easily fit on a 5″ × 8″ index card. That needs to be the rule of thumb! KISS: Keep it simple, sweetheart.

EXHIBIT 37.3 Position Description

Position Title: *Hospice Aide-de-Camp*   Supervisor: *Friendly Visitor*

Description of Duties: *Run errands for hospice client at the direction of the friendly visitor; includes but is not limited to: library services, VCR pick-up and delivery, mail service, supplies pick-up and delivery, incidental grocery shopping, etc.*

Qualifications: *Must be 18, have valid driver's license and insurance, have reliable vehicle, an interest in the work of hospice, patience, and sensitivity to the needs of those who are critically ill.*

Time Required: *2 hours per week for a minimum of two months*

Training: *30-minute orientation by director of volunteers, training as needed by friendly visitor*

(D) RECRUITMENT

The recruitment process begins with the needs assessment, plan, task/position development, and finally, task/position descriptions. Without this preliminary work, recruitment efforts are wasted.

Episodic volunteers have different needs than those of continuous-service volunteers. Information to episodic volunteers should be aimed very directly at them. In marketing terminology, the product (the volunteer position) is priced (cost of doing the tasks for the volunteer—financial, emotional, and personal) within reach. Then a promotion strategy (brochures, public service announcements, TV ads) is selected to attract those who are likely "buyers" of the product. The promotional material is placed where it can be most easily accessible to the potential customer.

For example, suppose the organization is sponsoring a fund-raising "fun run." Many episodic volunteers are needed at the various checkpoints during the race. Flyers asking for volunteers might be placed in stores carrying running equipment.

Marketing strategy insists that when you sell you must consider product, price, promotion, and placement. These are the infamous 4 P's of marketing. They apply in the volunteer sector as well. "Develop the right *product*. Support it with the right *promotion*. Put it in the right *place*. And at the right *price*."[9]

Vineyard suggests four methods to recruit. First is the one-to-one or "in-person" method. Studies of volunteers from a variety of sources reinforces the fact that the majority of people become volunteers "because someone asked them."[10] Episodic volunteers who are recruited by other volunteers or representatives of the organization will have a better sense of the needs, develop a relationship with someone inside the organization, and have the opportunity to have their questions answered directly.[11]

The second recruiting technique is an individual's asking a group. "The asker explains the need, shares their own commitment, tells the group what they can do to help and what is being asked of them."[12] Many clubs and organizations are interested in episodic volunteer opportunities for their members. The group request is an effective means to provide information to a large number of people at the same time. To be effective, this technique should include such resources as client-oriented audiovisuals, colorful and informational written material, and more than one person to answer questions informally at the end of the presentation.

The third recruiting technique is the telephone contact. Consider the various types of calls: The person making the call knows the callee and that he or she knows about the organization; the caller knows the person being called, but that individual knows little or nothing about the organization; the person being called knows about the organization, but not the caller; and finally, the person being called does not know the caller or the organization.[13] As you might expect, the first type of call has the greatest chance of success and the last one the least. Colleges have increased the likelihood that calls made on their behalf are successful by using students to call alumni during their fund-raising drives. In this case, the people do not know each other, but they know the institution.

The fourth method of recruiting is the printed appeal. Broadly defined, this would include such things as flyers, print and media ads, billboards, brochures, window displays, bus/subway cards, handbills, posters, or want ads. This passive method of recruiting is the least personal, and therefore has the least likelihood of success.

All volunteers are making a "consumer" decision when they agree to take a position. The volunteer task is the product. That product requires them to exchange some of their leisure time to meet a personal need. It is an exchange. Although the terms of exchange are often not discussed, it is an exchange, the same as the purchase of a new shirt or blouse is an exchange. "Exchange is the act of obtaining a desired object from someone by offering something in return."[14] In the case of a volunteer, the "object" is an intangible need.

Episodic volunteers do not respond favorably to appeals directed at those expected to give long-term service. To build the episodic volunteer program, the recruiting effort must treat the potential volunteer with the same respect as those giving longer service. By creating and developing recruiting techniques and strategies aimed at episodic volunteers, the organization signals respect for the individuals and tells them emphatically that the work they do is valuable enough for the organization to have expended time and effort in finding the right people for the position. Merely finding places for episodic volunteers who stumble into the organization means that the work they do is not very important to the mission. It also sends a clear message about how seriously volunteers should take their task with respect to such things as being on time, dressing appropriately, observing safety and health rules, and completing assigned duties.

(E)   SCREENING

Screening episodic volunteers is similar to screening for long-term volunteers. Screening, both episodic and continuous, includes written position/task descriptions, applications, and interviews.

The difference between episodic volunteers and continuous-service volunteers is the extent of the scrutiny.[15] For example, hospice friendly visitors are quite closely screened. They are often asked to complete a "grief or loss history," which is a document that helps them focus on their experiences with loss. This seems sensible given the sensitivity of the work they do with terminally ill individuals and their families. An episodic volunteer who is running errands for a client at the request of the friendly visitor might not be required to complete such a history. Each organization must decide the extent of the screening absolutely essential for volunteers. It is good practice to review screening procedures every two years.

Another way to deal with the issue of screening is to establish policies regarding the types of positions that might be performed by episodic volunteers. Suppose a hospital has stringent screening requirements for volunteers giving continuous service, including an overall requirement that all volunteers complete an expensive health screening. A policy is established that no episodic volunteer position is created that has direct patient contact. Volunteers work in administrative offices, the volunteer office, or with external educational programs, but they do not work with patients. Thus, the screening requirements are targeted at the task being performed and might therefore reduce barriers, costs, and time needed for the potential episodic volunteer.

Once the policies are established and minimum requirements determined, then the three areas of screening are put in place:

1. *Task/position descriptions* are a means by which a person can self-screen. If someone calls and says he or she has two Saturdays available and would like to volunteer for the organization, the next step is to use the mail service or refer them to the organizational Web site. Send a task/position description of the area of interest and an application. A phone call from the organization in a few days may find that the person does not meet the requirements or is not

interested in what is available. Time of the volunteer or staff overseeing the episodic volunteers is saved, and the potential volunteer has self-screened.

2. *Applications* for episodic volunteers should be edited to fit on a 5″ × 8″ index card.[16] It contains only the essentials. Be sure to have emergency contact phone numbers. A filing system can be a labeled box.

3. *Interviews* for episodic volunteers can be conducted via phone. This means that there should be a standardized interview process and script that is the same for every applicant. In some cases, it is necessary to interview applicants. This is done most effectively by specially trained volunteers.

Some barriers to starting an episodic volunteer program are the potential legal liabilities. Interviews are an effective way to screen out the volunteer who may be inappropriate for the task. When a volunteer is going to serve for only several hours on one day, it may seem like a waste of time to interview them. From there, it is easy to think that the entire idea of short-term volunteers is a big "time guzzler." Creativity is demanded to surmount this barrier.

The 1988 Calgary Winter Olympics is a case in point. Forty thousand volunteers were needed at various locations around the city and in the mountains of Alberta. A paid staff of five trained a score of volunteers to interview the thousands of Albertans who completed the application process. From those interviews came the corps of episodic volunteers, some of whom worked only a few hours at a particular location. While the interviews were being conducted, the staff moved ahead with other tasks. It was efficient, effective, and frugal. Does this technique work? If you saw the 1988 Olympics on television, you already know the answer to that.

(F) THE RECRUITING TEAM

The use of a recruiting team could ease the burden of work on the volunteer director or program manager. The team can set numerical targets for recruiting, design the screening process, review position descriptions, and design and carry out advertising and recruiting strategies. The volunteer program manager has a "workforce" to implement the new program. Members of the planning team, supplemented with additional workers, can make up a volunteer recruiting team.

Those who recruit are members of the organization or, at a minimum, people who believe in the work of the organization, but may not currently be members; parents, partners, or relatives and friends of the clientele of the organization are ideal recruiters.[17] Avoid recruiting currently active volunteers to serve on this team—they already have volunteer assignments. If you want to avoid burnout, concentrate instead on people who have recently retired from volunteer positions in your organization.

Recruiters need to develop specific campaign plans based on the goals and objectives established by the planning committee. These include guidelines (the position description for a committee) for the work of the recruiting team, including such things as the type and number of people serving on the recruiting team. If the planning committee has not developed this information, the recruiting team starts by laying out their tasks.

The tasks of the recruiting team include:

- Setting goals for the number of people to be recruited
- Establishing timelines to meet the goals

- Dividing duties or tasks among members
- Assigning each member a "territory," much like a salesperson, in which to carry out recruiting

The team also is instrumental in designing tools for recruiting: brochures, ads, media material for radio and TV, or posters. Their involvement in the decision-making process allows them to clearly understand their task and the "product" they are selling and to whom. Recruiters are motivated and energized by ownership over the process and the procedure they must carry out.

The team needs a packet of information about the organization and all its activities. If the organization provides any service that is controversial or misunderstood by the public, the team needs special information to help individuals answer any questions they might encounter. The last thing a volunteer recruiter should do is inadvertently misrepresent a position of the organization to a potential volunteer. The recruiting team must manage its recruiting effort within the constraints of the resources available: It must have a budget.

Once the mechanics of the recruiting team effort are in place, the last step before it begins its work is training. Areas in which the recruiting team needs training include:

- Brief history of organization and the place of episodic volunteers within it
- The benefits of volunteering to the prospective volunteer
- Details of the various types of episodic volunteer opportunities available, including copies of position/task descriptions
- How the organization and its various volunteer opportunities (continuous, episodic, intern, etc.) are different from those of other similar organizations or agencies
- Review of all recruiting campaign material (literature, deadline, publicity, goals, physical territory, etc.)
- A system for reporting results
- How progress will be measured and shared by the team (meetings, reports, phone calls, e-mail, etc.)
- How to deal with "no" as an answer

37.4 *Sustenance*

(A) PROVIDING SUPPORT FOR THE EPISODIC VOLUNTEER

The development of a short-term volunteer program does not end with bringing the recruits through the door to an organization, agency, or program. An episodic volunteer program also includes strategies to sustain and support volunteers during their service.

Notice that the word used to describe support for the episodic volunteer is sustain. *Sustenance* is "something that sustains, strengthens, or supports."[18] The process of supporting the long-term volunteer is best described as maintenance. This is "to carry on; continue."[19] The difference between sustenance and maintenance is a subtle but significant one for the short-term volunteer.

(B)   TRAINING

The best place to begin the process of sustaining the volunteer is with training. The episodic volunteer does not have time to attend lengthy training sessions. Fortunately, appropriate positions for episodic volunteers rarely require a significant investment in training. One effective method to develop and design training is to invite experienced volunteers plus some experts in adult education to serve on a volunteer training committee.

Training for episodic volunteers needs to be concentrated. This is the time to think about stand-alone types of training: a video, a self-study guide, training delivered via telephone, e-mail instructions, a page on the organization's Web site. Episodic volunteers need the basics—"Do this! Do not do this!"—and they need the information quickly!

The orientation process for episodic volunteers should help dispel anxiety or confusion.[20] It should help the volunteer feel comfortable and a part of the organization. It needs to send a clear message that *all* volunteers are welcome and needed—regardless of their length of service. Sending that message helps volunteers generate a stronger commitment to complete the assigned tasks and makes them more effective at their tasks.

Deciding on the type of training needed begins with the planning committee. It establishes the learning criteria for what episodic volunteers must know before they begin their service. The committee then decides on the most appropriate training delivery approach.

For example, a volunteer working a four-hour shift on an event might receive the following training:

- When a completed application is received and the volunteer is accepted, he or she receives the following in the mail: a brochure on the organization; a brief, one-page history of the event (this information is likely available on the organization's Web site) and contribution of the episodic volunteers (numbers participating, money raised, clients served, etc.); copy of the position description; and the name and phone number or e-mail address of the person who will be supervising.
- Depending on the number of volunteers and the size of the event, the supervisor—volunteer or staff—calls the volunteer to review the duties and any other things needed to make him or her more comfortable (e.g., parking, clothing, costs, identification, on-site training). This is also the time to find out what the person already knows about the tasks ahead.
- When the new volunteer arrives at the service location, there should be an orientation to the actual duties. This often can be conducted by another episodic volunteer who returns from one year to the next and is willing to work longer hours. The person responsible for the work area prepares a written list of responsibilities. This ensures that the training is consistent from one person to the next. Refinements can be made in the basic list, if needed.
- Volunteers need to know how they will be evaluated. Share with them the standards of performance for the work they are doing. Explain how their performance will be reviewed and discussed with them.

(C)   SUPERVISION

Supervision of short-term volunteers can be done quite effectively by long-term volunteers. A large, national volunteer organization is exploring the idea of designing programs to recruit a small number of long-term volunteers who agree to serve 15 to 20 hours per week for a minimum of three to five years. The agency will dramatically change the support and education provided to the continuous-service volunteers who then become key players as supervisors and planners of the greatly expanded episodic volunteer corps. This makes the volunteer program director the "supervisor of volunteers who supervise other volunteers." This intriguing idea is best done in a field-study situation, but it has extremely interesting possibilities for such organizations as Hospice, the Humane Society, orchestras, hospital volunteer programs, youth agencies, and so many more.

Supervision in many volunteer programs is haphazard at best and damaging in the worst cases. Volunteer satisfaction is influenced by adequate supervision and assistance. Effective work is done by those who know clearly their roles and responsibilities and receive support and monitoring to do the task more effectively. Yet, few organizations provide formal training for paid staff or volunteers designed to enhance skills they need to supervise the continuous volunteers, let alone the episodic volunteers. As with any volunteer program, training to work with volunteers is essential. Volunteer managers and administrators need to lobby for in-service time with paid staff to teach the skills needed to effectively oversee the work of volunteers. Volunteer managers also prepare training programs for volunteers who supervise other volunteers.

Fisher and Cole[21] outline the skills that a supervisor of volunteers needs to be successful. They suggest that a *supportive environment* is made up of elements designed to enhance the workers' ability to perform and be satisfied with that performance. This includes such things as "training, a clear understanding of job assignments, information about standards, expected levels of performance, and instruction in how to do the job. Resources necessary to do the job are provided and conditions harmful to performance are corrected."[22] With an episodic volunteer, this communication must be immediate and helpful in order to bring about effective performance immediately. Some supervisors are better at building long-term relationships with volunteers over time. The episodic volunteer has no time for that. Direct information is what is needed. Skill-building workshops can teach techniques to supervisors so they can do this without offending the volunteer.

Creating an environment in which volunteers and staff work together on a "team" is desirable. Learning the skills to *build teams* includes knowing and communicating the reasons for working together, a personal commitment to the fact that teamwork is the most effective means to work, developing strategies to bring about accountability from members of the team, and understanding skills necessary to build work teams with diverse membership (age, sex, cultural diversity, income, motivations, and pay).[23] Episodic volunteers often work with people who have vastly greater experience and history with the organization. It is easy for that group to dismiss the skills of the short-term volunteer. The supervisor's job is to help the more experienced volunteers respect the ideas of the newcomer and for short-term volunteers to not act as if they have all the answers. Training sessions using a case-study format can help supervisors develop specific strategies to deal with these types of situations.

The ability to *delegate* responsibility to volunteers is a skill supervisors must have. Delegation is assigning tasks and activities to volunteers and giving them real responsibility to carry out those tasks. It is not giving them a task and then making them do it the way you would do it. Delegation also does not mean giving assignments to volunteers and letting them sink or swim alone. A supervisor must "choose the right task, choose the right person to do it, give clear instructions, turn the task over to the worker but stay in contact, give authority, and review results with the worker."[24]

Supervisors are in a perpetual situation of needing to monitor and improve the effectiveness of their *communication skills*. Verbal and written skills are essential facets of being in any type of management or administrative position. Supervisors must strive to achieve "accurate and mutually understood communication."[25]

Written communication, especially the new forms of electronic communication, is sometimes as important as verbal communication in the case of the episodic volunteer. Preparation of episodic volunteers through written material can save time when the volunteer arrives to perform the tasks. Five-page memos that are single spaced may be thorough, but it is unlikely they will be read by the episodic volunteer. The volunteer program manager for a senior-serving program prepares written material using all the principles of good graphic design—lots of white space, bold typeface to highlight that which is important, cartoons to break up written monotony, and humor. Her materials are so inviting it is hard to resist reading them.[26]

Similarly, verbal communication is critical to bring the episodic volunteer up to performance standards as quickly as possible. Practicing direct, clear communication can be learned in skill-building workshops. Active listening is essential in any relationship, but particularly important when working with someone with whom there is little time or opportunity to develop good communication. Two-way communication is particularly important between episodic volunteers and supervisors to ensure the volunteers understand the requirements of the position.

Feedback is an essential element of effective supervision. Feedback provides a continuous circle of communication from the volunteer to the supervisor and back again. It is informal and is provided on a regular basis. Volunteers need to know about their work on a regular basis, not just when things are going wrong. Feedback can take a variety of forms, including verbal praise, suggestions for improving performance, written outlines of information to help performance, a postcard saying "thanks" after the task is complete, or sharing the work done by episodic volunteers with others in the organization, making sure the volunteers get the credit.

For episodic volunteers, the evaluative behavior mentioned above is usually the only type received. They are rarely given an annual performance evaluation. The person-to-person information about performance is immediate and designed to enhance. This is not the time for personal criticism; rather, it is specific to the task or service being performed. "It is descriptive rather than judgmental"[27]; praise is essential. Models or samples of work can be used so volunteers can measure their performance against them.

Self-assessment is a useful technique to use with episodic volunteers. It can be as simple as "How do you think you are doing with this task?" or asking volunteers to describe which tasks they are doing well and which tasks they would like to do better. In this way, the volunteer is telling the supervisor where help is needed. An effective supervisor can guide volunteers in learning what they want to learn and interject other areas where improvement is needed. "The guidance and support an organization provides to its volunteer staff are essential to their successful performance and to the achievement of organizational goals."[28]

(D) RECOGNITION

Recognition is awareness. It is seeing something and acknowledging it. The most effective recognition for volunteers is that which is directly related to the work the volunteer has done. The outward manifestation of the recognition is personal. Recognition initiatives are part of an ongoing, year-long process, not just an annual event that happens in the spring. Records should be kept of awards presented. There should be both formal and informal recognition.[29]

Evaluation is one way to recognize volunteers. For example, auction volunteers might receive a short report on the results of the event and thus their work. The supervisor could include total receipts, attendance, net receipts, and the money earned and its relationship to client services. This short report and a thank-you letter can be a powerful way to acknowledge the volunteer's position and reinforce the agency's mission.

The *sustenance* of episodic volunteers does not happen accidentally. Like the recruitment, selection, and screening of short-term volunteers, it is best done in a planned and organized manner. The planning committee develops the strategies to implement those things needed to sustain episodic volunteers.

37.5 Launching the Program: Field Tests

Too often in nonprofit and voluntary organizations, administrators and leadership volunteers rush to implement new programs or services only to have them fail. The notion of field testing is often ignored. Field testing includes organizing a program or service for a small group and then implementing it. The testing period involves close scrutiny of every aspect of the program. "Market testing [field testing] is the stage where the product and program are introduced into more authentic consumer settings to learn how consumers react to use . . . and how large the market is."[30]

The director of volunteer services at a large performing arts center decided to implement an episodic volunteer program. The episodic planning team completed all the steps listed in this chapter. At the advice of the director, it was decided to field test the program and evaluate the results. The performing arts center was located in a large city with many colleges and universities. The planning team decided to target colleges with performing arts or theater arts programs. For three months, they coded advertising for episodic volunteer positions and used it only at the selected schools. They were seeking volunteers for assignments of one week or less, with a minimum of four hours per day. The episodic volunteers were to work in administrative offices throughout the building.

By starting small, using current volunteers to develop the program, and gradually building the confidence and trust of the staff, this organization was able to launch a successful episodic volunteer program. It took less than six months from the first committee meeting to the launch of the field test. The volunteer administrator saw her role as supportive and advisory. It was a new volunteer opportunity for the continuous-service volunteers who had created the program. Its chances of long-term success were improved by that ownership.

Within a month of the launch, over 30 volunteers had been placed, and paid staff and continuous-service volunteers were clamoring for more help. The episodic volunteer planning committee knew which of its advertising and promotional techniques had been the most effective. The field test allowed them to increase the scope of the program and reach out to a greater pool of episodic volunteers. They avoided making large and very public mistakes. The field test also afforded the opportunity to refine various aspects of the volunteer opportunities: advertising and promotion, position descriptions, and the screening process.[31]

The 1999 study by Independent Sector of volunteering in the United States tells us that episodic volunteering is a reality.[32] Organizations and programs that diversify the way in which people can serve will flourish, like their brothers and sisters in the for-profit sector, who have changed the ways in which people can work: full-time, part-time, job-sharing, telecommuting. Episodic volunteering is only one means to offer the opportunity to serve. National community service programs such as Americorps and Retired Senior Volunteers, positions to attract volunteers who are disabled, and youth volunteer initiatives are all effective means to diversify and reach out to new markets of volunteers. Like episodic volunteering, they require new management strategies for the volunteer administrator.

Endnotes

1. National Volunteer Center, 1989
2. Independent sector, 2000
3. Butler, 1980
4. Bryson and Einsweiler, 1988
5. Id.
6. Wilson, 1976
7. McCurley, 1988
8. Macduff, 1996
9. Vineyard, 1984
10. Pearce, 1991
11. See note 9.
12. Id.
13. Id.
14. Kotler, 1983
15. Macduff, 1991
16. Id.
17. See note 8.
18. Riverside Webster's II Dictionary, 1996
19. Id.
20. Ilsley and Niemi, 1981
21. Fisher and Cole, 1993
22. Gidron, 1983
23. See note 21.
24. Fisher, 1993
25. Id.
26. Dalton, 2000
27. See note 24.
28. Id.
29. MacKenzie and Moore, 1993
30. See note 14.
31. Shapiro, 1992
32. See note 2.

38 Volunteer Screening*

LINDA L. GRAFF
Graff and Associates

* This chapter appeared as Chapter 5 in Tracy Daniel Connors (ed.). *The Nonprofit Management Handbook,* 2nd ed., 1999 Supplement. It was adapted from an article entitled "Selection Screening and Placement," which originally appeared in *Management of Volunteer Services in Canada: The Text,* edited by Ginette Johnstone. Carp, Ontario: Johnstone Training and Consultation (JTC), Inc., 1997. It is adapted and reprinted here with the permission of the author.

38.1 Introduction

There is perhaps no aspect of volunteer program management that has changed as dramatically or as quickly as screening. I remember talking about screening in a workshop for managers of volunteers in the mid-1980s in which a participant remarked, in public, with full comfort, "Screening! We don't screen. We're too desperate for volunteers!" She worked in a residential facility for people with severe physical disabilities. It was only a short time ago that the typical answer from most managers of volunteers to the question "Do you screen your volunteers?" would be something like, "Yes, we interview them."

Screening has typically been conceptualized as a single-action task that helps the manager place candidates in the proper positions. However, with recent high-profile cases of abuse by staff and volunteers in positions of trust,[1] the field has quickly come to understand that screening is a much more serious and complex matter.

The potential consequences of inadequate screening protocol are all too obvious:

- Abuse of clients by volunteers
- Fraud; theft of agency or client resources
- Violence; sexual harassment of clients, staff, or other volunteers
- Negative public relations for the agency resulting in a loss of public trust
- Personal or organizational liability resulting in damaging and potentially ruinous lawsuits

Ensuring that the best candidates have been recruited and placed has always been important. But over the past five years, screening has become as much a matter of doing everything reasonable to keep the bad apples out as about achieving a proper fit between the volunteer's skills/interests and the demands of the volunteer position. Screening has become as much about techniques to keep the inappropriate or dangerous candidates out as it is about locating and placing the best candidates for the position.

It is important to clarify two parameters of screening at the outset. First, there are no foolproof screening techniques that can guarantee that all "bad apples" will be detected and excluded. No screening device in the world comes with a guarantee. Prospective volunteers who are ill-suited or ill-intended can occasionally slip through even the most intensive screening protocol. Managers of volunteers and agency administrators are advised to recognize this critical point. Second, there are no absolutes in screening. That is, even the most experienced, skilled, and knowledgeable manager of volunteers will still need to exercise his or her best judgment about the specific set of screening devices to be used for each volunteer position.

It is equally important for managers of volunteers to recognize that there is a wide range of screening mechanisms available, and that when they are used in the appropriate combination, volunteer screening can be highly effective in lessening the likelihood of harm and decreasing organizational liability even if a "bad apple" does slip through.

For screening to be as effective as possible, organizations must acknowledge that things can go seriously wrong when volunteers are inappropriately placed, or volunteers with criminal or sinister intent slip through the screening protocol. Only when the worst is faced can managers be freed to construct reasonably thorough screening systems that will generate volunteer placements that are both safe and productive.

38.2   Volunteers and Paid Staff: Parallel Systems Advised

Unless otherwise stated, all of the following discussion applies equally to paid and unpaid staff. It is now widely acknowledged that the work of volunteers increasingly approximates that of paid staff. Volunteer work has become more complex, responsible, and sophisticated. In many settings, it is the "real work" of the organization. Volunteers are routinely placed in direct service activities. They are "on the front lines," working directly with clients, consumers, participants, and the general public, often right alongside paid staff. Volunteers are no longer relegated to the menial, routine chores in back rooms.

Reflecting these changes in volunteering, precedent-setting cases have established that legal systems in both Canada and the United States are beginning to consider volunteers as employees, making them subject to much of the same legislation and standards that apply to paid workers. For more on Canadian laws that relate to screening, see Street[2]; for examples of U.S. case law related to screening, see Patterson.[3] Volunteers need to be managed in almost all respects as if they were paid staff. Volunteers, too, require organizational systems and management practices. In this sense, the same principles of screening that apply to paid staff should be applied to volunteers. (The reverse also applies. In some settings, the manager of volunteers begins to apply more rigorous screening techniques with volunteers than the personnel department uses when hiring paid staff, and soon they find their counterparts borrowing volunteer department policy and protocol to upgrade paid staff hiring practices.)

39.3   Conceptualizing Screening: Perception and Understanding Shape Behavior

It seems obvious to say that how a situation is perceived will shape how one responds to it. One might see an object with four legs, a seat, and a back, understand it to be a chair, and therefore sit on it. One might see the very same object being wielded above a person's head in a menacing fashion, perceive it as a weapon, and run from it. How screening is conceptualized shapes how screening is operationalized, the kinds of information sought, and the kinds of screening mechanisms deployed.

Because there is a tendency to think of volunteering in the context of nice people doing good deeds, an extra effort may be necessary to acknowledge that there are dangerous candidates out there. This is not to say that the nonprofit world is populated by dangerous and nefarious characters intent on doing harm to the weak and defenseless. But it is equally inaccurate to think that there are no dangerous characters targeting volunteer work as the perfect access point to particularly vulnerable people. Volunteer screening protocol must be fact-based and grounded in an often-regrettable but nonetheless realistic view of the world. Denial has no place in screening system design. As Street wrote:

> It is a sad truth that individuals who prey on the vulnerable often seek out opportunities in the voluntary and public sectors, as paid or unpaid staff, looking for positions which provide significant access to the person and property of such individuals.[4]

A failure to detect critical information in the screening, selection, and placement process that results in the placement of an otherwise good person in the wrong job can have equally disastrous consequences. Hence, screening needs to be constructed to ever-higher standards. The reliability, trustworthiness, skills, and qualifications of volunteers are so critical, and the work that volunteers now do is so important, that there can be no substitute for careful, effective, thorough, and at times, tough screening procedures.

38.4 Limitations to Screening Intensiveness

The mission or other organizational variables may limit the extent to which some agencies want to, or are able to, preclude certain individuals from volunteer involvement. For example:

- An organization that works in the criminal justice system may deliberately set out to recruit volunteers who have come into conflict with the law. Ex-offenders may have the most appropriate background to work with high-risk youth.
- Persons who have survived their own ordeals within mental health systems may be ideal candidates for facilitating self-help groups of other survivors.
- Persons who have lost their licenses because of drunk driving may be perfect in public education, providing testimonials regarding the consequences of such behavior.

Some organizations will have screening limitations embedded in their constitutions. For example, organizations that have municipal politicians or other delegates appointed to their boards by outside bodies find themselves in an awkward position if they decide to implement, for example, reference checks, credit bureau checks, and/or police records checks on all incoming board members. This is not to suggest that any appointed volunteer should be exempted from the screening protocol, but rather that organizations may find it awkward or strategically difficult to apply the same standards to all. None of this is inherently right or wrong, but circumstances such as these bring a unique context to the screening enterprise. Organizations must work within their own parameters, their own value systems, and their own ways of doing business. It is recommended, however, that barriers and limitations to otherwise reasonable and appropriate screening policies be carefully scrutinized for their implications for safety and effectiveness.

Organizations must be alert to the dangers they choose to live with and to those that can be reduced either through screening or any number of other risk mitigation techniques such as teamwork, increased supervision, and buddy systems. Unfortunately, there are no definitive rules about how thorough is thorough enough without being too intrusive. No one can say with any certainty or authority: "With volunteers doing this kind of work, with this kind of consumer, in this kind of setting, with this kind of supervision and support, here are the five techniques that must be used in the screening protocol." Much remains a matter of circumstance, judgment, and which lawyer is consulted for advice!

38.5 Legal Principles in Screening

Screening appropriately and thoroughly will, in most cases, mean finding a fine legal balance point between screening adequately to protect the well-being of clients, other personnel, and the general public, and respecting the legitimate legal rights of applicants.

Screening too much or too little can result in real injury and loss, in addition to very expensive and time-consuming legal action.

The key question—the essential question at the heart of all screening system design—is this: *How is a manager of volunteers to determine with any certainty just how to screen for any given position?*

Should the screening protocol include a police records check or not? Should it include reference checks? If yes, how many, from whom? Is it sufficient to take notes from a reference check done by phone, or should the reference be asked to sign off on notes taken from the phone conversation with him or her? If a candidate says he or she has a certificate in early childhood education, is it enough to believe the claim, or should the candidate be asked to show the original and permit a copy to be kept on file?

However, there are two general sets of legal rules that should guide screening decisions. The first pertains to the rights of the individuals being screened; the second to the organization's responsibility to screen thoroughly enough to protect volunteers, clients, staff, and the general public from harm and the organization and its personnel from liability.

(A)   THE LEGAL RIGHTS OF CANDIDATES

For the most part, the legal rights of candidates that pertain to screening are those protected by human rights legislation. While the human rights legislation that influences volunteer screening is set by states and provinces and varies by jurisdiction, in general it prohibits discrimination with respect to employment on a number of specific grounds such as race, color, ethnicity, gender, sexual orientation, and so on. It is recommended that all volunteer screening protocols comply with relevant legislation, even in jurisdictions where volunteer work is not explicitly named as covered by the legislation. (Organizations are advised to consult the legislation in their own province or state for the specific grounds that apply to them. National organizations that deliver programs in more than one provincial, state, or territorial jurisdiction will need to ensure that their policies are adjusted to comply with all relevant legislation. For an overview of human rights and other types of legislation in Canada that pertain to screening, see Street[5]; for an overview of legislation that pertains to screening in the United States, see Wendover[6] and Deblieux.[7])

Human rights legislation instructs employers not to refuse to accept a candidate because of any characteristic not directly related to the work that person is applying to do. Most managers of volunteers are familiar with this legislation and understand that for both legal and ethical reasons, volunteer screening policies should comply with it. But many managers do not understand that this prohibition is only half of what the legislation typically says.

If we cannot use the variable of a candidate's age in the selection process, how do we avoid an accusation of discrimination from the 13-year-old applicant not accepted as the new board chair? How might we avoid legal action for discrimination from the male candidate who is not accepted as a volunteer in the shelter for abused women even though he appears to meet the minimum requirements of the position? The answer lies in the other half of the legislation, which generally states "unless the reason for rejection is directly related to a bona fide (in good faith) occupational requirement (BFOR)." If gender, physical ability, age, *or any other characteristic* is a bona fide requirement of the position, it is a legitimate line for inquiry in the screening process and can be considered in the screening decision. Whatever is outside of the requirements of the position is out of bounds to the screening process.

To illustrate, when screening candidates for the volunteer gardener position at the local day care center, asking about a candidate's expertise and experience handling money, or checking a candidate's credit bureau rating would not only be inappropriate, but it could also possibly be construed as an invasion of privacy. The reason is simple: There is no connection between that line of inquiry and the BFORs. In contrast, ensuring that gardener candidates have the physical strength and stamina to rake leaves, turn sod, and mow grass in the weather conditions that typically prevail would be entirely appropriate. Asking about a candidate's experience handling other people's money, or indeed, uncovering a history of fraud, embezzlement, and/or even a bad credit rating, might be entirely appropriate as screening mechanisms for candidates applying to be the treasurer of a board of directors, or the bookkeeper for the local theater troupe.

The *requirements of the position* establish what should and should not be investigated as part of the screening process. They dictate what questions can be included in the application form, what questions can be asked in the interview, what topics can be discussed with references, and on what basis the final hiring decision can be made. The screening rule that emerges is this: The screening protocol for any position must be directly connected to, and is determined by, bona fide occupational requirements.

(B) SCREENING IS NOT A EUPHEMISM FOR DISCRIMINATION

While screening is an admitted mechanism for exclusion, screening should never exclude anyone just because that person does not fit the recruiter's notion of the "ideal" volunteer. Mere ideas or beliefs should not be used to screen applicants out, unless a particular approach, philosophy, or belief system is integral to the way the work is to be done and therefore constitutes a BFOR Even then, one must be cautious to separate a candidate's personal beliefs from his or her ability to perform the job as described. One might be totally repelled by the practice of tobacco smoking but still be able to volunteer in the rehabilitation wing that requires helping patients get to the smoking room. *Conduct* should be the basis for exclusion.[8] The underlying principle is that "difference" or "diversity" should never be considered a disqualifier. Screening thoroughly is not a license to discriminate, nor will it be found so by a court of law.

(C) SCREENING THOROUGHLY ENOUGH

Determining how thoroughly volunteers should be screened to satisfy the courts should something go wrong and a subsequent allegation of negligence be leveled is perhaps the most difficult assessment that any manager of volunteers will face on the job. There are no absolutes and few guidelines.

Although human rights legislation establishes certain boundaries of legal inquiry in screening, it does not clearly specify which types of screening should be deployed, or identify how thorough the screening system should be. That is, such legislation speaks to how much screening is too much, but it does not speak to how much is enough. In this regard, managers of volunteers must take into consideration not only what screening mechanisms they believe will elucidate the appropriateness of applicants, but also what the courts might consider to have been adequate if a volunteer ends up causing harm.

The manager of volunteers who does not screen adequately, does not pursue all reasonably appropriate lines of inquiry, or fails to detect indicators of unsuitability in volunteer applicants risks not only inappropriate or substandard performance from volunteers, but, indeed, may endanger the well-being of consumers, staff, and others connected to the organization, as well as expose the organization to liability.

The manager of volunteers must ask:

- How thoroughly should volunteers be screened?
- What screening mechanisms are available?
- Which screening mechanisms should be deployed for various volunteer positions?

(D)   HOW THOROUGH? THE DUTY OF CARE

While there is no legislation about volunteer screening that defines precisely what each party is expected to do in every eventuality, there is a general principle in law called the "duty of care," which bears on the question of legal responsibility in screening. The duty of care, which an organization owes to its clients, staff, volunteers (including the board), and to some extent, members of the general public who come into contact with the organization's services, requires the organization to do everything it reasonably can to deliver its programs and conduct its affairs in a safe, adequate, and well-managed manner. Organizations must tend to the safety and well-being of persons in their care as well as to that of their staff, volunteers, and the community in general.

For screening, this means that organizations have a legal, as well as an ethical, responsibility to screen and place carefully all of the paid and unpaid staff they engage. The legal rule is that an organization must take reasonable steps to protect others from harm. Where an organization's clients are vulnerable, there is a correspondingly greater burden to protect them from harm,[9] and the growing trend is toward more sophisticated investigation of the applicant's background and qualifications.[10]

Ignorance is neither morally nor legally defensible. The organization that fails to screen thoroughly enough or that fails to pursue information that was available runs the dual risks of causing harm to clients as well as exposure to allegations of negligence.

(E)   CREATE PROOF

If an allegation of negligence in screening is brought against an organization, that organization will be faced with the task of proving that it was not negligent, that it acted with reasonable care in its screening practices. The lesson here is that it may not be sufficient to be thorough. The best-practice model dictates that organizations must create proof that they have exercised reasonable diligence.

Documentation of screening policies and procedures is mandatory. Ensure that a paper trail records all screening actions and their results. Retain application forms, notes from interviews, notes from reference checks, and so on, and take copies of all other position-related materials such as driver's licenses and certificates of qualifications.

38.6   The "Sliding Scale of Screening"

So what should an organization's screening protocol look like? How does a manager of volunteers decide what specific screening devices should be used? Perhaps the most important point about volunteer screening is that the specific set of screening devices to be deployed must be determined by the demands—the BFORs—of the position. Pursuing information not related to the position risks allegations of discrimination or invasion of privacy. Not pursuing information related to the position brings the risk of substandard performance, danger to clients, and the allegation of negligence, if harm, loss, or damage result.

The only way to determine what screening devices should be used is to consider very carefully the nature and demands of the work that volunteers will be asked to perform. This process is called the *sliding scale of screening:* The kind and extent of screening required should be determined by the characteristics and demands of the work to be done. The more demanding, complex, risky, responsible, dangerous, and/or direct the work, the more thorough the screening protocol should be. If volunteers are to roll bandages, hand out programs, or stuff envelopes, the screening protocol can probably be minimal. If volunteers are to work with children or other vulnerable populations, perform physically or intellectually challenging functions, or engage in any otherwise risky or demanding work, screening must be correspondingly more thorough.

How does one determine the relevant nature and characteristics of the job? The basic premise is that the key elements of each position need to be assessed. Three broad aspects of assessment should be considered:

1. The vulnerability of the client
2. The requirements of the position
3. The directness of the relationship between the volunteer and the client[11]

Each aspect is examined as follows in reference to the sliding scale concept.

(A) THE VULNERABILITY OF THE CLIENT

Assess the vulnerability of the clients with whom the volunteer will work directly or come into contact. Consider factors such as age, language and communication skills, maturity, disability, isolation, dependence, history of abuse, powerlessness, and so on. The principle is that the more vulnerable the clients, the greater the obligation on the part of the organization to more carefully attend to their well-being. In some positions, the "client" with whom the volunteer works might be the organization. For example, members of boards of directors and administrative volunteers such as bookkeepers, fund raisers, and committee members serve the organization. In such instances, consider the vulnerability of the organization to exploitation, criminal action, or any other form of abuse.

(B) THE REQUIREMENTS OF THE POSITION

Consider the demands of the position, including dimensions such as:

- Complexity
- Responsibility
- Degree of risk (to the volunteer, client, staff, agency reputation, property, and general public)

The premise is that the greater the demands of the position, the more rigorous the screening ought to be.

(i) Degree of Supervision

Consider the following questions:

- How well are volunteers supervised: regularly, thoroughly?
- Are volunteers continually or regularly observed while at work?
- Is feedback on volunteers' performance frequently sought by the supervisor from coworkers or clients?

(ii) Degree of Isolation

Consider the following questions:

- Do volunteers work off site? Are they located in a different office from the supervisor? in a remote setting?
- Do volunteers have unsupervised contact with a vulnerable client?
- Do clients ever visit volunteers' homes?
- Do volunteers ever visit clients' homes?

(iii) Degree of Physical Contact

Consider the following questions:

- Does the position, by definition, involve physical contact between the volunteer and the client/participant?
- Is this a coaching position where the coach needs to physically demonstrate or position a student or program participant?
- Is there a rehabilitation component to this position in which volunteers are required to mobilize limbs or physically support the movements of patients?
- Does the position involve working with young children in a setting where touching, hugging, lifting, toileting, and so forth are not only inevitable but intrinsic aspects of the position?
- Is this a residential setting for clients that presents greater opportunity or likelihood for physical proximity and/or intimacy?
- Does the position require volunteers to help clients change clothes, bathe, or accomplish other personal activities?

(iv) Degree of Physical Demands

Consider the following questions:

- Does the position require extreme physical exertion, significant physical strength, or endurance?
- Is a specialized physical ability or skill required to successfully fill this position, such as helping a client transfer from a wheelchair, athletics, coaching, or carrying and operating a chainsaw?
- Might the position subject the volunteer to extremes of heat or cold?
- Is this a position in which the volunteer will experience stress, emotional strain, or burnout?

(v) Degree of Trust/Degree of Temptation

Consider the following questions:

- Will the volunteer have access to confidential client or organizational information?
- Will the volunteer be expected to handle or manage the organization's or the client's funds?
- Will the volunteer come into regular contact with other financial instruments or resources such as a checkbook or donations in the mail?
- Are volunteers working at a fund-raising event (e.g., bingo, charity casino, carnival, garage sale) at which cash transactions are commonplace?

(vi) Degree of Risk Inherent in the Task
Consider the following questions:

- Does the position involve transportation of clients, and in particular, vulnerable clients?
- Is there potential for the volunteer to come in contact with bodily fluids or infectious diseases?
- Does the position require the volunteer to assume personal safety or liability risks such as in fighting fires, working on a construction site, or being on the board of an organization faced with a funding shortfall?

(C) DIRECTNESS OF RELATIONSHIP BETWEEN VOLUNTEER AND CLIENT

How direct is the relationship between volunteers and the people with whom they work? What is the nature of the contact? Patterson advises managers of volunteers to consider the relationship along the following dimensions:

- Will the volunteer spend solitary time with the client when there is a likelihood that no one else is nearby?
- How much dependence does the relationship involve between the volunteer and the client? Is this, for example, a friendly visiting or companionship kind of position, in which the relationship might grow intense and somewhat exclusive?
- What is the frequency of contact between the client and the volunteer and how much time do they spend in each other's company when they are together? A server with a meal delivery program might see a client four times each week, but only for three or four minutes each time. Contrast that with a volunteer assistant who spends 24 hours a day with children on a week-long canoe trip in a wilderness environment.
- How long is the relationship expected to last? In some positions, the ideal volunteer/client match could last a decade or more.[12]

All of these considerations should influence screening tool choices. The underlying premise is that the thoroughness of the screening process should increase with the demands of the position.

38.7 Screening Tools

Screening should not be considered a single-task activity. In fact, a full range of screening tools is available to managers of volunteers. Every screening tool has inherent advantages and limitations. Each tool allows the manager of volunteers a limited window on a specific aspect of a candidate's qualifications and character. No single screening mechanism, alone, can reveal complete or sufficient information on which to base the final selection decision. Regardless of the intensiveness and thoroughness of the screening process, a leap of faith is always required regarding whether a volunteer is qualified and appropriate for the position. The challenge is to do as much as is possible, reasonable, ethical, appropriate, and legal to achieve an organizational comfort level with information gathered and decisions taken.

For every position, an appropriate *set* of screening devices should be used that, together, provide enough information to make the final selection and placement decision. The requirements of the position will point to the kinds of information that are required and the kinds of screening tools that produce those kinds of information. The key concept here is that different sets of screening tools should be used for different positions.

A large set of screening devices is available to managers of volunteers. Fourteen of the most widely used, practical, and readily available have been selected for review here:

1. Job descriptions
2. Preapplication devices
3. Application forms
4. Interview
5. Reference checks
6. Qualifications checks
7. Police records checks (criminal records checks)
8. Driver's record checks
9. Credit bureau checks
10. Performance assessments
11. Home visits
12. Medical/psychological/drug testing
13. Orientation and training
14. Probation

(A) JOB DESCRIPTIONS

Written job descriptions, for both paid and unpaid staff, are powerful risk management tools, as well as being the personnel management tools they are usually understood to be. A written job description defines what the volunteer is supposed to do and *not* supposed to do. The duties specified in the job description guide both the *nature* and *extent* of screening required. Here is how we define *bona fide* in human rights terms. The expectations of the position form the basis on which qualifications for the position are determined and, therefore, they also form both the legal and ethical foundation for the screening process.

If the position calls for the candidate to work directly with clients, the areas to screen may include:

- How well the person relates to others
- Indications of a history of abusive behavior
- The candidate's ability to relate to persons of diverse cultural or racial background

The nature of the work also has implications for the extensiveness of the screening process to be applied. For example, if the volunteer is to have contact with clients only in group settings under direct supervision, then screening may need to be less exhaustive than if the position requires the volunteer to visit isolated clients in their own homes. If the gardener's assistant will never be expected to operate a chainsaw, a power take off, or a backhoe, *and* if he or she will never be in a position to spend time alone with clients in an isolated area of the grounds, then screening may need to go no farther than assessing relevant knowledge (Does the candidate know the difference between a canna lily and a dandelion?) and physical ability (Does the candidate have the physical strength and stamina to use tools such as shovels and rakes for two to three hours at a time?).

It is critical that the specifics of the tasks and the associated qualifications be outlined in the job description. If the position on the board requires good decision-making abilities, the job description should ask for more than Tuesday night availability. Because the job description provides the legal basis for screening inquiries, there must be clear and defensible continuity between what the job description specifies and the types of screening techniques applied in the selection and placement process. Screening more or less intensively than the job description calls for can be dangerous and illegal.

(B) PREAPPLICATION DEVICES

Helping prospective volunteers to screen themselves out is the most effective and humane screening device available. Whatever can be done early on to help volunteers understand the nature of the work, its demands, and its requirements will go a long way to reducing the number of inappropriate applications in the first place and the number of times the manager will have to decline candidates' offers of assistance.

Following are three examples of preapplication screening devices.

(i) Recruitment Publicity
It is important to recognize that screening begins before candidates even make contact with an organization. How the work of volunteers is portrayed, how the position is advertised, and how detailed the information provided about minimum qualifications is all help volunteers to determine whether a position sounds attractive, interesting, and appropriate. If volunteers are to perform important, demanding, or risky work, then position requirements must be portrayed accurately in recruitment publicity. This is not intended to discourage good candidates from applying, but rather to help inappropriate candidates to self-identify.

(ii) First Contact
When a candidate has made the effort to make contact about volunteering, the very first message that person receives can be a powerful screening mechanism. Consider the two different messages from the organization's receptionist outlined in Exhibits 38.1 and 38.2.

The message about how the organization values volunteers and their work starts here. It is important to be clear about what the agency's needs are, whether applications are being accepted (and if not, other agencies the volunteer may contact, including the local volunteer center), what the application process is, and what the next step is.

The requirements of the job should never be minimized or undersold. It is tempting to do so to avoid scaring away prospective volunteers, but full disclosure is always the best practice for three reasons:

EXHIBIT 38.1 First Contact

"Hello, Acme Home Support Agency.

"Oh, gee, thanks for calling. Yes, we are looking for new friendly visiting volunteers. In fact, we're running our volunteer orientation session this week and I know it isn't full yet. Are you available to join us at 7:00 Thursday evening? I'm sure the Volunteer Coordinator would be delighted to have you involved in the program."

EXHIBIT 38.2 First Contact

"Hello, Acme Home Support Agency.

"Thank you so much for your interest in our friendly visiting program. Our volunteers do such important work for seniors in our community. Have you ever had any contact with our organization before? No? Well, let me give you a bit of information about the position. That will give you a better idea of how we do things around here, and what the position entails . . . before you go to the trouble of starting the application process since we are not always able to accept the offer of volunteer time from all of our applicants.

"The reason that we carefully consider every volunteer application is to make sure that Acme provides the very best service possible to every senior we work with. I am sure that you would want to make sure that we did the same if one of your family members was receiving service from us, wouldn't you?. . ."

- Clarifying the importance of the work and the significant responsibilities placed on the volunteer simply reveals the truth.
- To mask or diminish the seriousness of the volunteer contract is to do a disservice to all.
- If expectations are not articulated, how can volunteers be expected to meet them?

Provide as much information as possible and appropriate at the outset. Many volunteers who would be "unsuccessful applicants" to the program will screen themselves out if given sufficient information.

(iii) Applicant Response Letter

Follow up on all first contacts with a response in writing. Send to all who express interest a brochure describing the organization and the position, including minimum requirements. Be sure to indicate that acceptance as a volunteer with the program is not automatic, and that the screening process is an occasion for mutual assessment. Provide full information about which screening procedures will be followed for each position. The general rule here is one of no surprises. All volunteers should know from the outset precisely what the screening protocol will involve, before they begin any part of it.

(C) APPLICATION

All candidates should complete a written application form, which will be the basis of their "personnel file" with the organization. A wide range of information can be obtained through the application form, including:

- Identifying information (name, address, telephone number)
- Qualifications (relevant skills, education, training, licenses, equipment/vehicle specifications, computer experience ([operating system, IBM/Apple])
- Car (year, make, model, ease of entry, carrying capacity) (if driving is part of the job)
- Availability (day of week, time of day, frequency, length of shift)
- Preferred working conditions or limits (likes working with children; does not want to work with children; likes working outside; prefers inside work; likes to work alone; is pursuing volunteer work to meet and socialize; feels comfortable driving on highway/country/city roads in bad/only good weather; will/not drive at night)
- Reason/motivation for volunteering
- How the applicant heard of the position
- Relevant paid and unpaid work history; other skills (cardiopulmonary resuscitation [CPR], first aid, driver education, defensive driving). Include dates of service, description of duties, name of employer and immediate supervisor with addresses and telephone numbers to facilitate verification of the information.
- Background (any other relevant experience that relates to the position in question)
- References (Best practice suggests wherever the names of references are requested, one must also require the candidate to provide explicit [signed] permission for the organization to actually contact those references in connection with the current application.)
- Authenticity (a signed statement indicating that the applicant certifies that the information provided is true and accurate)
- Authorization to verify (a signed statement indicating that the applicant grants permission to the organization to verify the information included on the application form)
- Signature and date

Please note that not all agencies will seek all of these types of information; not all of it will be relevant to all positions. Some information gathering may wait until the personal interview or be obtained on separate forms (insurance, medical, references, and so forth).

It is recommended that the draft application form be reviewed by legal counsel to ensure compliance with all relevant legislation.

(D) INTERVIEW(S)

The personal interview has traditionally been the cornerstone of most screening processes. While a personal interview may not be possible or practical in the selection of volunteers for some of the shorter term and/or special events positions, most volunteer departments will include personal interviews in the screening protocol for most volunteer positions.

The personal interview allows a face-to-face interaction, often the first opportunity for the candidate and the manager of volunteers to meet. This meeting allows the interviewer to pick up on all sorts of verbal and non-verbal cues, and to assess manner of personal presentation, style of relating, verbal communication skills, and non-verbal communication characteristics.

The interview permits in-depth exploration of position-related attitudes, perspectives, and issues. Here is a chance for truly mutual exchange, an important point in the screening process because up to this point, the agency has typically been doing all the asking. Here, too, is the opportunity for candidates to check out the site, the organization, and its setting and culture, and ask for all of the information they need to make their own decisions. (For more information on the specifics of interviewing, see Patterson,[13] Street,[14] Deems,[15] or Crowe.[16])

While details about how to conduct a proper interview are beyond the scope of this chapter, three key thoughts about the personal interview are offered here. First, keep the importance of the personal interview in perspective. Certainly, this is an opportunity to obtain more information, and different kinds of information, than will have been gathered to date, but remember that the interview is just *one* element in a much lengthier and more complex screening process. Resist the temptation to put too much emphasis on the interview results. Do not use them as the sole basis for applicant selection. As Patterson cautions, "Keep in mind the interview represents one brief exposure to an applicant who may not have developed good interview skills or may just be having a bad day."[17]

Second, a good personal interview is a two-way process. It is the primary opportunity for mutual exchange and mutual screening. Do not become so focused on the organization's need for information that the needs and rights of the candidate are ignored.

Third, every screening mechanism has its limitations, and the personal interview is no exception. Do not further limit its potential by thinking of the interview only in terms of a one-to-one encounter. There are different interview models available:

- First interview (the interviewer and candidate only)
- First interview (more than one interviewer and the candidate)
- First interview (more than one interviewer and a group of candidates)
- Second and subsequent interviews with any of the above variations
- Second and subsequent interviews with different organization representatives than those who participated in the first interview

Each of these options brings its own opportunities and limitations. Each allows a different angle on candidates' qualities. Consider designing an interview protocol that mixes these models at various stages of the screening process. Do not limit your options!

(E)   REFERENCE CHECKS

Reference checks are a fundamental feature of most screening protocols. Of course, there is no way to guarantee that references will provide complete or fully candid details. But several references, particularly when the different types that are reviewed as follows are used in combination, can often reveal useful, and often surprisingly candid, information. Be certain that the candidate's *written permission* to contact referees is obtained in advance.

Best practice indicates that the mere inclusion of the name of the referee on an application form or resume does not constitute permission to contact. There are three different types of references to consider in the screening protocol:

(i) Professional References

These references are provided by referees who have known the candidate in a work (paid or unpaid) capacity. Typically, these references are provided by a supervisor or manager of volunteers from a candidate's previous employment or volunteer placement. They are most useful when provided by someone who directly supervised the candidate, rather than by someone from the personnel department whose only contact with the candidate has been through a file.

(ii) Personal/Character References

These references add another piece of useful information to the decision regarding candidate suitability. The referee is typically someone who has known the candidate for some time and is in a position to speak to the volunteer's character, other (always job-related) personal characteristics, and general appropriateness for the position. Potential sources of character references would include teachers, ministers/rabbis/priests, and physicians.

(iii) Family References

References from members of the candidate's family have traditionally been considered inappropriate and worthless. Current wisdom suggests reconsideration of this form as a potential screening device. Family members are in a position to know things about a candidate that no one else does. (Remember, it was the Unabomber's brother who was in a position to identify the culprit when years of intensive investigation by multiple law enforcement agencies came up empty-handed.) When such knowledge pertains to job-related characteristics, it can prove invaluable.

Family members, more than anyone else, may have a personal interest in the success of the candidate. They, more than a previous employer, for example, do not want the candidate to be placed inappropriately or in a position from which that person could cause harm. This factor may, in fact, compel family members to be more candid (rather than less candid) than other referees. Family members also will likely be the least concerned about an allegation of slander or defamation by the candidate.

Choose the number and type of reference checks according to the requirements of the position and the kinds of characteristics of candidates that need investigation. Document all reference notes thoroughly, and keep them on file. (For more information on how to conduct references checks, see Graff.[18])

It is advisable that any negative information received from a referee be checked out with the candidate. There may be legitimate reasons for discrepancies that are not immediately apparent or that may be legitimately beyond the control of the candidate. (This advice has been reinforced by several participants in my workshops who have disclosed that they had been sexually harassed by previous employers or supervisors. Because they launched complaints, they fully expect references from harassers to be less than glowing. However, since the position was an important element of their employment history, and/or since not listing the position for a reference would have left an obvious hole in their employment record, they felt compelled to list the position and the referee in their application efforts. It is only when the prospective employer gives candidates the opportunity to explain the less-than-glowing reference that they feel released to speak of the incidents.) Discuss the findings with the candidate and give him or her a chance to explain.

(iv) On Confidentiality

Wherever possible, do not promise confidentiality to the referee. If an organization promises to safeguard the source of reference information (and this is particularly pertinent to negative information about a candidate that influences the decision not to accept the application), it may be forced at some time in the future to either break that pledge of confidentiality or justify a not-to-hire decision without apparent grounds. Either way, the promise of confidentiality can mean trouble.

(F) QUALIFICATIONS CHECKS

This is a screening tool that is very often overlooked, but which should be considered an essential component of most screening protocols. A qualifications check simply involves obtaining proof of a qualification(s) claimed by the candidate. Many human resource professionals, whether hiring paid or unpaid staff, simply accept as truth candidate claims regarding all kinds of qualifications. Candidates are believed when they claim to have:

- A valid driver's license of the class required by the vehicle they would drive as a volunteer
- Valid auto insurance with the minimum amount of protection specified by organization policy
- A professional license, certificate, or academic degree
- Proof of immunization

Best practice dictates that when a specific qualification is essential to the position, and the candidate claims to have the qualification, ask for proof. Ask for a transcript of grades, or to see the original degree or certificate, and request a photocopy of same for the volunteer's personnel file. This is a simple, unintrusive, and probably too often overlooked screening tool.

(G) POLICE RECORDS CHECKS

Increasing numbers of agencies are using police records checks as one measure of candidate acceptability. These checks provide information on the individual's previous contacts with the criminal justice system. Police records checks were relatively rare as recent as a decade ago. For a few years now, many organizations have been turning to the police records check as "the solution" to volunteer screening, assuming that a clear police records check guarantees suitability, or at least, harmlessness. Many organizations have been requiring police records checks on all candidates for all positions, often regardless of the nature of the work and the relevance of previous criminal activity to candidates' suitability.

Most recently, the severe limitations of the police records check have been acknowledged and more widely publicized.[19,20] Yes, there are dangerous individuals in the world, and some of them do target volunteering as an easy access point to vulnerable populations. But many have not yet been caught and therefore have no criminal record, and many others know only too well how to avoid detection through a police records check.

No organization should expect to turn up dozens of pedophiles, gerontophiles, and other convicted felons in its police records checks on volunteer candidates.

Nevertheless, police records checks are still an important element in the screening protocols of many organizations, and it is true that the very fact that an organization does police records checks deters some inappropriate or dangerous candidates. The best reason to conduct police records checks as part of the screening protocol is not so much that they provide good information about the acceptability or suitability of candidates, but rather, that if a police records check is not conducted on a volunteer who ends up causing harm, the organization's degree of exposure to an allegation of negligence is enormous. Conducting a police records check, particularly in combination with several other screening devices, will go a long way toward demonstrating that an agency has not been negligent in its screening practices, even if a volunteer does cause harm, injury, or loss at some point in the future. Hence, the police records check is at least equally useful, if not more useful, as a liability reduction tool than as a hiring and screening device.

Current wisdom strongly recommends the use of police records checks whenever volunteers work directly with (particularly vulnerable) clients, or whenever volunteers are placed in positions of trust. But the results of a police records check should not be relied on alone. In particular, beware of false negatives. Use police records checks only in combination with other screening techniques. Finally, because the actual data set searched, the specific protocol required, and the kind of information revealed through police records checks vary from community to community, and from police department to police department, managers of volunteers are advised to contact their own local, state, or provincial police departments to determine the process in operation in their vicinity. In some locations, child abuse registries exist and are accessible as a screening device. Check with authorities in your area to determine if this mechanism is available to you.

(H)   DRIVER'S RECORD CHECKS

Managers sometimes mistakenly assume that a police records check includes a driver's record check. This is not necessarily so. If driving a vehicle is part of what volunteers will be expected to do in their position (whether the volunteer drives an agency vehicle or his or her own is usually immaterial), it is advisable to investigate the candidate's driving history for significant and relevant offenses. Depending on the jurisdiction, driver's records checks are launched through the appropriate provincial/state transportation department, or as part of a police records check.

Keep in mind that these checks cover a limited period of the driver's history, and like police records checks, are accurate only up to the date they are conducted and are not necessarily proof that past history is an accurate indicator of future behavior. Like all screening devices, the driver's record check has limitations, but it nonetheless constitutes one more piece of information to be considered in the overall selection process.

(I)   CREDIT BUREAU CHECKS

Credit bureaus are private companies that collect enormous quantities of data on citizens. They collect information from sources such as:

- Major department stores
- Major credit card companies

- Banks (regarding loans and mortgages)
- Court records of lawsuits, charges, convictions, bankruptcies, and liens on cars and other property
- Collection company files

Credit bureaus typically know what a person owes, how much, and what the monthly payments are; they can know what one's financial position is regarding debt and credit, and one's legal position in relation to finances. For a fee, and with the candidate's written permission, a credit bureau check can be supplied almost immediately. The credit bureau check is of most utility when screening for positions that involve financial trust, such as bookkeepers, treasurers, fund raisers, collections personnel, and special events volunteers, who come into contact with significant quantities of cash or other hard-to-track financial instruments.

As with other screening devices, it may be wise to share with the volunteer any negative information gathered through a credit bureau check. This not only provides candidates with the opportunity to explain their situation but also allows the manager the opportunity to ensure that the credit bureau has provided information about the right person.

(J) PERFORMANCE ASSESSMENTS

Some positions require very specific skills, abilities, or specialized knowledge (e.g., typing speed and accuracy, computer skills, ability to lift a certain weight, driving, or working with young children or persons with specific kinds of disabilities). In these cases, it is entirely appropriate for the employer to ask the candidate to demonstrate his or her ability. There are two kinds of performance assessments: the test run and the observation period.

(i) The Test Run

The typing test is a classic example of the test run form of the performance test. Others include:

- Having the candidate demonstrate (to someone who knows enough about the job to be an accurate assessor) that he or she can turn on a computer, use the main menu, get to the specified program application, and do some actual work
- Having the person demonstrate (on a well/able person) knowledge of how to transfer patients from a wheelchair to a car
- Taking the groundskeeper applicants out to the garden and asking them to identify the plants, shrubs, trees, and insects
- Asking the volunteer driver to take you for a test drive in the vehicle (or type of vehicle) to be used on the job, in the city or highway conditions volunteers typically encounter on that job

Including a performance assessment in the screening protocol is not meant to suggest that skills cannot be learned in training, but if a candidate claims a certain knowledge or skill, the performance test allows measurement of both the skill level and the degree of truth of the claim.

(ii)   The Observation Period

The second kind of performance test is the observation period. If the position requires working with specific populations, such as adolescents, seniors, young children, persons with learning disabilities, or persons with physical disabilities, an observation period can be a useful element of the screening process. During an observation period, the applicant is asked to work with, and interact with, clients while being observed. Patterson suggests looking for factors in candidates such as (1) has realistic expectations of the capabilities of the clientele; (2) demonstrates comfort/familiarity with clients and/or the setting; (3) exhibits interest, warmth, enthusiasm, patience, sense of humor; and (4) interacts appropriately with, and supports, other staff.[21]

(K)   HOME VISITS

This screening technique is a special kind of interview that might be used in situations such as the following:

- Where the employee is to engage in a close, long-term relationship with the client
- Where it is anticipated that the client will be taken home by the volunteer (for example, Big Sisters, Leisure Buddies, mentoring programs)
- Where it can be anticipated that the client might come in contact with members of the employee's household

Home visits provide a sense of the living conditions of the prospective candidate and the setting into which the client may be taken, as well as an opportunity to meet, and to some extent assess, other people that the client may come in contact with in the volunteer's home. Patterson offers an important caution about home visits: Screening, by necessity, always involves some measure of judgment, but in perhaps no other screening device is the temptation to be judgmental as great as in the performance of a home visit. The home visit should be as objective as possible, based on a checklist of clear criteria that are related to bona fide occupational requirements, and conducted by someone who is capable of both objectivity and sensitivity to the privacy rights of the candidate and his or her household members.[22]

(L)   MEDICAL/PSYCHOLOGICAL/DRUG TESTING

Organizations have several types of medical tests at their disposal, to be deployed only when legitimated by the bona fide requirements of the position. Where appropriate, agencies may require any number of the following medical tests:

- Immunization or proofs thereof
- Medical certification of physical fitness to drive an automobile or other specified vehicle
- Medical certification of hand–eye coordination, or fine motor coordination
- Medical certification of fitness to operate other kinds of machinery or perform particularly arduous physical chores

In certain, albeit rare, circumstances, organizations might even consider personality inventories, psychological testing, honesty testing, or certification of candidates' mental health as a prerequisite to acceptance. These latter screening techniques are, of course, at the far end of the continuum with regard to intrusiveness, and their use should be considered only in the most special circumstances. An exception to this rule is immunization, or proof thereof, which, in the case of tuberculosis (TB) testing, is a typical prerequisite for workers in settings such as hospitals and day care centers. Since a positive TB test would be an immediate disqualifier from service, it is a screening device that ought to be applied sooner rather than later. Why waste time on more intensive, costly screening procedures such as interviews and reference checks if the TB test, when done early, provides advance notice of unacceptability?

The arsenal of screening tools includes drug testing and even various forms of electro-mechanical devices such as lie detectors and psychological stress evaluators. One could also add handwriting analysis to the list, although it would seem that all of these latter devices would rarely, if ever, be deployed with volunteers.

(M)   ORIENTATION AND TRAINING

Volunteer acceptance can be delayed if more time or information is needed before the final hiring decision is made. This is particularly applicable in the volunteer situation, where provisional acceptance is granted while the volunteer completes orientation and training program(s). This trial period offers the organization an opportunity to spend more time with the candidate and determine what skills exist and can be acquired. In particular, using the orientation and training period as part of the screening protocol provides an opportunity to observe other characteristics, such as interpersonal style, communication capabilities, and attitudes. In return, the volunteer has an opportunity to spend some time on site, meeting other staff and volunteers. He or she can gain a sense of the organizational culture and, in particular, a sense of what the organization's treatment of volunteers actually feels like. This technique presents an excellent opportunity for more meaningful investigation and more mutuality in the screening process than many of the other techniques discussed so far.

To maximize the potential of orientation and training sessions as screening devices, include in them some of the following:

- Role plays
- Exercises
- Values activities
- Relating/relationship experiences

These mechanisms are particularly useful when the position calls for an assessment of candidates' work-related beliefs, values, biases, attitudes, and judgments.

If acceptance is delayed while both the agency and the volunteer check each other out, be certain that the volunteer knows that the final acceptance has not yet been granted.

(N)   PROBATION

As with paid staff, conditional acceptance can be granted through a probationary period for volunteers. This practice gives both the candidate and the agency an opportunity to test each other out in the real-life setting. It allows either or both parties to change their minds within a certain, set period, without penalty, and with limited explanation.

As with training, build into the probation period a range of mechanisms to check performance, such as:

- A buddy system through which an experienced volunteer trains and monitors, and provides feedback about the new recruit
- More frequent and thorough supervision and monitoring
- Using this time to deliver ongoing or additional training if that might make the difference to the volunteer's acceptance

38.8 The Balancing Act: Putting the Pieces Together

When the demands and requirements of each volunteer position have been fully assessed, the manager of volunteers is in a position to consider which constellation of screening tools will supply the necessary information to make selection and placement decisions. This process requires a careful balancing of a number of considerations.

Different positions have different requirements, producing the need for different types of information about candidates. Given that the application of each screening device will take time, effort, and in some cases money, the challenge is to carefully choose the right number and type of screening devices that will supply the appropriate kind of information needed, and no more.

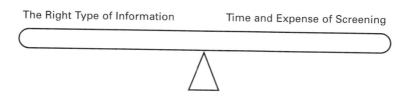

Information sought must be related to bona fide occupational requirements. The balance here is between what the organization legitimately needs to know to make the selection decision and the candidate's right to privacy.

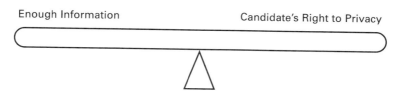

Another consideration in the choice of screening tools involves balancing the organization's need for sufficient detail to satisfy its duty of care against making the application process so complex and intrusive that prospective candidates simply decide not to bother.

Making the Application
Process Too Intrusive   Sufficient Detail

Unfortunately, there are no absolutes to assist managers of volunteers in this complex decision-making process. At this point in time, when standards are shifting constantly, it is impossible to say with any certainty which set of screening tools is the right set for any given position. There are, however, several points that managers might consider while designing the screening protocol.

- Standards are generally increasing. At the present time and, in particular, in light of recent high-profile cases of abuses by volunteers in positions of trust, the expectation is that organizations will be much more thorough in their volunteer screening practices than might have been imagined as recent as five years ago.
- The more complex and demanding the work required of volunteers, and the more vulnerable the clients and others with whom the volunteer will make contact while volunteering, the more thorough and intensive the screening protocol must be.
- Managers are advised to regularly consult with their colleagues who work in similar organizations or who manage volunteers in similar positions because the standard of care is, in part, a community standard, established by current practice throughout the field. What is generally practiced and considered reasonably appropriate and sufficient in the field will, to a great extent, influence legal decisions about whether particular actions or inactions were suitably diligent or, on the other hand, negligent.
- Because standards in volunteer screening are continually changing and, in general, increasing, it is critical that managers of volunteers *keep* talking with their colleagues about their screening practices, and keep current with the literature in the field of volunteer management. Only in this way is it possible to stay current with best-practice models.
- Managers should seek legal opinion from time to time on what the standard of care might be as it develops in case law across the country. Ask someone with expertise in nonprofit law, someone who is keeping watch for cases that might bear on the work of organizations like yours.
- Managers must remember to document all screening efforts, leaving a paper trail of all screening activities, and ensuring that appropriate documentation is retained in volunteers' personnel files.

Exhibits 38.3 and 38.4 are sample checklists that might assist with the documentation process. When the decision has been made regarding which screening tools to use for a specific volunteer position, create a custom checklist like those illustrated. Two key benefits are generated. First, a checklist like this provides clear documentation of the full set of screening tools that need to be used in each position. Having a custom set of screening practices for each position demonstrates diligence in planning and management. Second,

EXHIBIT 38.3 Volunteer Screening Checklist, Sample 1

Position: Volunteer Driver

Screening Device	What Documentation on File	Date Completed	Initial
Application form			
Personal interview			
Reference checks			
— Personal			
— Work (paid or unpaid)			
Valid driver's license			
Driver's record check			
Auto insurance verification			
Physician's verification of fitness to drive			

EXHIBIT 38.4 Volunteer Screening Checklist, Sample 2

Position: Camp Counselor

Screening Device	What Documentation on File	Date Completed	Initial
Application form			
Personal interview			
— Individual			
— Group			
TB test			
Reference checks			
— Personal			
— Work (paid or unpaid)			
— Family member			
Valid driver's license			
Driver's record check			
Police records check			
Probation			

the checklist serves as a prompt to both complete all screening tasks and acquire all the necessary documentation for each task in the set.

38.9 Conclusion

Volunteering and volunteer work have changed dramatically in just the past few years. With the increasing responsibilities that have been assigned to volunteers have come increasing responsibilities on organizations to manage well the human resources they have mobilized. As volunteers perform more sophisticated duties, and as they work more directly with increasingly vulnerable populations, there is a direct increase in the dual burdens of responsibility and liability on organizations that deploy volunteers. As a result, volunteer screening needs to be ever more thorough to protect clients from harm, to ensure the safest and most productive volunteer experience for volunteers, and to fulfill legal and ethical responsibilities that require each organization to do everything reasonable for the safety and well-being of all those to whom it owes a duty of care.

Until very recently, screening was viewed as a single-task activity that is done and, in essence, forgotten. Best practice now dictates that screening be a multi-task effort that balances the sometimes competing factors of duty of care with candidates' rights. A wide range of screening devices is available; fourteen have been briefly reviewed here. The challenge is to construct the right constellation of devices, based on the bona fide requirements of each position, that in combination generate reasonably sound and defensible screening and placement decisions.

As yet there are no definitive rules about which specific tools are appropriate and sufficient for each type of volunteer position. This chapter proposes application of a concept called the "sliding scale of screening," which dictates that the nature and extent of the screening protocol be determined by the work that the volunteer will be doing. As a general rule, the more demanding the position and the greater the vulnerability of the client, the more intensive and thorough the volunteer screening needs to be.

It is no longer sufficient to be appropriately diligent. One must also create proof that one has been so. Full documentation must be gathered and carefully stored in comprehensive personnel files for all volunteers.

Endnotes

1. Street, L. (1996). *The Screening Handbook: Protecting Clients, Staff, and the Community.* Ottawa: Volunteer Canada.
2. Id.
3. Patterson, J. (1994). *The Staff Screening Tool Kit: Keeping the Bad Apples out of Your Organization.* Washington, DC: Nonprofit Risk Management Center.
4. See note 1.
5. Id.
6. Wendover, R. W. (1996). *Hand Picked: The Complete Guide to Finding and Hiring the Best Employees.* Shawnee Mission, KS: National Press Publications.
7. Deblieux, M. (1996). *Legal Issues For Managers: Essential Skills For Avoiding Your Day in Court.* West Des Moines, IA: American Media Publishing.
8. See note 3.

9. See note 1.
10. See note 3.
11. Id.
12. Id.
13. Id.
14. See note 1.
15. Deems, R. S. (1994). *Interviewing: More Than A Gut Feeling.* West Des Moines, IA: American Media Publishing.
16. Crowe, R. (1994). *Resource Kit For Interviewing Volunteers.* Vancouver: Volunteer Vancouver.
17. See note 3.
18. Graff, L. L. (1999). *Beyond Police Checks: The Definitive Volunteer and Employee Screening Guidebook.* Dundas, Ontario: Graff and Associates.
19. See note 1.
20. See note 3.
21. Id., p. 86.
22. Id., p. 42.

39 ▼ Volunteer and Staff Relations

NANCY MACDUFF
Macduff/Bunt Associates

In *Volunteers: The Organizational Behavior of Unpaid Workers,* Jone Pearce devoted a section to the research data on the relationship between volunteers and staff. In an early draft, she referred to those relationships as "the dirty little secret of volunteerism." Regrettably, the editors of her book sanitized it to read, "The tension that can exist between volunteers and employee co-workers remains one of the unpleasant secrets of nonprofit organizations."[1]

It is unfortunate her original statement did not survive the editor's blue pencil. A positive relationship between volunteers and staff is essential to a healthy nonprofit organization. As Pearce discovered, the research data on the state of relationships between volunteers and staff is not voluminous, despite the apparent severity of the problem.[2]

Books on volunteer management and administration have little information on volunteer and staff relations. They do, however, carry admonitions to guard against "poor volunteer-staff relations," with advice that everyone work happily together. There is little information to describe the characteristics of a healthy volunteer–staff partnership, the symptoms of poor relations, how to assess the state of the relationships, or what to do to improve the situation if it is bad.

More than ever, the relationship between volunteers and staff can influence the success or failure of a program, fund-raising event, changes in leadership, and the ability to make positive organizational changes. When people work together as a team, at all levels of an organization, agency, or program, efficient and effective services are delivered to clients, patrons, or members. Harmony is achieved not by accident but by attention to the needs of both sides of the volunteer–staff equation.

39.1 Volunteers and Staff: A Team

A set or group of people who work together for a common goal is a team. In this context, the "team" is a thing—a group, an association, an entity. Change the grammatical usage, however, and team becomes the willingness of someone to act for the good of the group rather than one's self, as in "teamwork."

In selecting members for a board of directors, one issue considered by those recommending names is the ability of the individual to rise above the single issue to look at the "big picture" and thus the welfare of the entire organization. Sometimes volunteers are asked to set aside ways in which they have operated for years and move into a new mode. Those who do have subordinated what is good for them personally and put the organization's needs first. The good of the team takes precedence.

Team is a word also used to describe transport or conveyance. The Teamsters Union was founded to represent those workers providing transport of goods. An effective team in a voluntary setting is also in the business of transport. The joint working relationship between volunteers and paid staff produces different results; in the Girl Scouts, it allows children to build their citizenship skills; in orchestras, it brings music to the community; in Hospice, it provides skilled and sensitive support to those who are dying and their families; in libraries, it fights censorship; and in humane societies, it supports the work of caring for a community's unwanted and unloved animals. Volunteers and staff have the capacity to transport and "carry over" the cares and concerns of other people into creative solutions.

"A team's performance includes both individual results and what we call 'collective work-products.'"[3] Those work products reflect the joint contributions of the members. The effective volunteer–staff team is greater than the participation of any one member.

The following are characteristics of an effective volunteer–staff team:

- *Teams are a manageable size.* "Virtually all effective teams we have met, read or heard about, or been members of have ranged between 2–25 people. The majority of them have numbered less than 10."[4] In most nonprofit organizations (NPOs), this means that the large group of 100-plus volunteers and 12 staff operate in subgroups or teams. Those serving on the board of directors are one team, the people who work "every other Thursday" in the organization's office are another team, the committee that plans the annual "fun run" fund raiser is yet another team.
- *People are appropriately selected to serve on a team.* Putting together the right combination of volunteers and staff in terms of personality, skills, influence, communication styles, and ability to perform is important. The more time and care spent in selecting the right combinations for the team, the greater the chances of success.
- *Team leaders are trained.* Whether the team leader is an unpaid volunteer or paid staff, he or she deserves and should be required to receive training in completing his or her tasks. Leaders who think they must do all the jobs or have little capacity to delegate make poor team leaders. Find a "Tom Sawyer"—someone who knows how to paint the fence, but gets others to do it. This person has the makings of a team leader—planning, delegating, motivating.
- *Teams are trained to carry out their tasks.* The board of directors or advisory board is a team. They need training on how to carry out their responsibilities and tasks. For example, they must understand the fundamental differences in governance and administration. Volunteers serving as school aides need to understand appropriate and inappropriate behavior in relationship to the children. The teacher (staff) and volunteer aide need to have an understanding of the same set of expected behaviors. Differences between

volunteer duties and those of the teacher are negotiated within a uniform framework.

- *Teams are the foundation of the organization.* Voluntary organizations, whether staffed by paid personnel or not, are founded on the notion of people working together for a common good or joint effort. That foundation means everyone affiliated with the organization is in some way connected to everyone else. Working together effectively and efficiently is the foundation that builds and strengthens the organization or agency. For example, suppose volunteers and staff are working on a capital campaign. If the staff makes all the decisions, then tell the volunteers to make phone calls or stuff envelopes, they might find less than enthusiastic workers. Participation in joint decision making increases commitment.

- *Volunteers and staff are supported by administration.* Managers and administrators of NPOs need to understand the importance of their commitment to the working team—volunteers and staff. Any program is enhanced through a formal policy statement that outlines the role of volunteers and explains the nature of the volunteer and staff relationship. It continues with support that is both personal and financial.

- *Teams have goals and objectives.* Effective volunteer–staff teams have a vision of the mission that is the same. Usually they develop a plan with purposes, goals, objectives, and work plans to guide their efforts. "Effective teams develop strong commitment to a common approach, that is, to how they will work together to accomplish their purpose."[5] Trust cannot be ordained. It develops when people work together successfully. Having a plan helps to build the mutuality of experience that builds trust over time.

- *Volunteers and staff trust and support one another.* People come to trust each other when they have shared positive experiences. In a voluntary organization, this means everyone knows the purpose of the organization and the tasks at hand. Goals are arrived at by members of the team who work together. Some orchestra boards of directors, for example, decide how much money is to be raised by a volunteer guild or association during their budget-building process and do not consult with the volunteers whose responsibility it is to raise the money. This undermines trust and support between governance volunteers and fundraising volunteers, and the staff who must work with both.

- *Communication between volunteers and staff is both vertical and horizontal.* The common notion about communication deals with the sending and receiving of messages. Communication is really about sending *meanings*.[6] It is less a language process and more a people process. It involves the active and continuous use of such things as active listening, feedback, e-mail messages, telephone "trees," short one-page memos -FYI-, clarifying perceptions, reading body language, and noticing symbols that communicate meaning. It also travels in all directions. Leadership volunteers communicate with direct service volunteers. Staff communicate with volunteers all the time. Hierarchical blocks to communication are bridged when volunteers and staff are working together effectively. It is also true that working together is best facilitated by good communication.

- *The organizational structure promotes communications between volunteers and staff.* Volunteers and staff need policies, procedures, and structure that permit and encourage them to communicate. A group of volunteers who raised substantial money for an organization and led educational programs had a small office [read: closet] in the administrative offices of a large nonprofit group. In a management shuffle, the new executive director saw no reason why these women (the group was largely female) couldn't work out of their homes so he could use the small office for storage. Volunteers who could formerly walk down the hall and talk with paid staff colleagues about their plans and activities were now forced to deal with the telephone voice mail and to make appointments to share information. This is an example of the organization creating roadblocks to effective communication and sending a message that volunteers are unimportant.

- *The work of volunteers and staff has real responsibility.* Millions of volunteers stuff envelopes each year for NPOs. This seems like an unimportant job except that it provides information, education, and news to constituents, clients, or members. Most volunteers know this and willingly fold and stuff for hours because it is a real job with real responsibility. All volunteer jobs need to be as clear as this one to the people doing them—whether volunteer or staff.

- *Volunteers and staff have fun while accomplishing their tasks.* Harmonious relationships between volunteers and staff are readily apparent in the amount of fun exhibited during planning meetings, at activities, or during evaluation sessions. A group of volunteers and staff recruiting parents to serve as leaders of youth clubs heard many "no's" before someone would agree to serve. Reporting meetings were sometimes quite grim. A volunteer came to a meeting and said, "I think I have heard the worst excuse yet for not volunteering. A woman told me yesterday she couldn't be a leader of her son's club because she ironed." This brought laughter all around and generated other "best excuse" stories. Someone produced a notebook, and the stories were recorded. The recording of "best excuses" was institutionalized by the group. It went on for years. New members—volunteers and staff—were indoctrinated with readings by returning members from the "best excuse" book. The humor and affection exhibited by the group while finishing a task built a sense of fun and reinforced the concept of mutual responsibility.

- *There is recognition for the contributions of volunteers and staff.* Volunteers publicly recognize the work of staff. Staff publicly acknowledge the efforts of volunteers. There are both formal and informal expressions of appreciation for the work accomplished by groups. Management or administration encourages this and organizes ways to make it easy for the recognition to occur. This effort at recognition is consistent, public, and visible.

- *Volunteers and staff celebrate their successes.* Celebrations with food, frivolity, and friendship are a hallmark of effective volunteer and staff relationships. These activities are often spontaneous and inexpensive. They are encouraged by the leadership of the organization and might often be led by them. Budgets in NPOs are planned to pay for celebratory events to herald the effectiveness of the volunteers and staff who work together to achieve the mission of the organization.

- *The entire organization sees itself as promoting and encouraging the health of volunteer and staff teams.* Building effective volunteer and staff relationships works only when everyone in the organization sees him- or herself as part of a volunteer and staff partnership and actively promotes it.

39.2   Types of Volunteer–Staff Teams

There are many different types of teams. The three basic teams have variations, but the following descriptions give some idea of how they are similar and how they are different.

(A)   VOLUNTEER AND STAFF TEAMS WHO MAKE OR DO THINGS

These are groups of people who provide the most direct service; they stuff envelopes, visit shut-ins, deliver library books, walk dogs, take someone's blood pressure, lead a Girl Scout or 4-H club, teach nutrition, weigh rice into one-pound sacks, and make soup for the homeless. These teams can be long term or short term. Managers need to assess the volunteer and staff relations in these teams. By measuring productivity and performance on a regular basis, alterations can be made in how work groups are organized; the training they receive; and client, member, or patron responses. Feedback from these groups is quick, clear, and concise.

(B)   VOLUNTEER AND STAFF TEAMS WHO RUN THINGS

The board of directors or a group overseeing some functional activity of the organization or agency is a team that is in effect governing. The key here is to help the team avoid just being a "working group" and to keep output high. If the volunteers and staff want to organize as a team, they must have goals and objectives separate from the mission of the organization. Boards of directors often focus their planning on accomplishing the mission of the organization, to the exclusion of the development of their own skills as decision makers. These teams need separate and distinct goals and objectives, different from the organizational goals and objectives. Time constraints of busy people in leadership positions may preclude the entire group—for example, the board of directors—from operating as a team. However, two or three people on an executive team provide effective leadership and vision for others in the formalized structure of the organization. It works best as an openly acknowledged team, with the aim to empower others.

As executive director of an NPO for almost 15 years, the author developed a team relationship with five succeeding presidents of the board, and in several cases the team was enlarged to include other officers. This small team of volunteers and staff influenced creativity in problem solving, leadership development of others, program innovation, policy direction, and organizational change. Small teams do not operate to exclude others, but rather to develop the plans and strategies to enable other volunteers and staff to perform as effectively as possible.

(C)   VOLUNTEER AND STAFF TEAMS WHO RECOMMEND THINGS

Nonprofit and voluntary groups rely heavily on the task force, advisory panel, and project groups. These are groups with an assignment to accomplish tasks or solve a problem. This type of group might start as a task force. Usually they must get off to a fast start and meet deadlines for recommendations or activities.

The key component of building "teams who recommend" is an early and clear role definition, and the opportunity for volunteers and staff to create their own goals and objectives. The relationship between volunteers and staff can be enhanced by the careful selection of members. This is often the time to put people together who have a track record of working effectively. It is also critical to include among the volunteers and staff those who have the responsibility of implementing the recommendations. There is a far greater likelihood it will happen.

Building effective volunteer teams involves more than implementing training programs on communication. It includes knowing the types of teams, what skills are needed, how to match tasks with skills and interpersonal style, and how to address the challenges faced by teams of volunteers and staff.

During an open-air concert at a country fair, a band had several members who sang, played, and worked the front of the stage. Additional musicians behind them served in a more supportive role. The obvious harmony of this team of musicians came from their agreement about programming, communication while on stage, the fun they had with each other, and a willingness to listen to support players to further enhance the concert. This "musical team" is delightful to watch. "Usually when this occurs it is that the unique and separate talents of all those involved were somehow blended into a whole that was greater than all of its parts."[7] It is also the ideal to which all volunteer and staff teams should subscribe.

39.3 Symptoms of Poor Volunteer–Staff Relationships

In some organizations, a lack of communication can and does influence the very survival of the institution. Volunteers and staff are locked in adversarial roles detrimental to the health of the entire organization. This situation usually begins gradually and is noticed by few staff or volunteers.

Symptoms include the increasing use of "us and them" language. Volunteer managers hear things like, "They always do things like this to us." "We would never do something like that to them." There is uncertainty among volunteers and staff about roles and responsibilities. Individuals are often uncooperative in working on projects. They do not communicate directly, but rather go around each other to get questions answered and to solve problems.

Volunteers and staff often carve out territory and guard it tenaciously. For example, programs become the sole property of staff, volunteers stake out a fund-raising event and won't entertain suggestions from staff, or board members go into secret meetings to establish budgets and do not consult direct-service volunteers or paid staff.

When volunteers and staff have poor relations, there is little information sharing. In a territorial environment, information is seen as power. "Withhold information and you are in control" is the philosophy. A large city orchestra had to cancel its concert season due to a severe money shortage. Leaders of the orchestra asked preseason ticket holders to donate the purchased tickets and not request refunds. Several months after this dramatic action, the president of the volunteer association knew little about the plans to improve the financial situation, although the volunteer association was expected to raise several hundred thousand dollars to help balance the budget. That withholding of information is a way for the board and senior staff to demonstrate their ownership of the budget. It is also a bright road sign that the relationship between volunteers and staff is not healthy.

How can management and volunteer leaders determine the current state of volunteer–staff relations? What can they do to develop strategies to improve the staff and volunteer work environment to increase productivity?

The first step is to conduct an audit of current volunteer–staff relations, and the second is to implement appropriate steps or strategies to improve the relationship between the two groups.

39.4   *The Volunteer–Staff Climate Audit*

The Volunteer-Staff Climate Audit assesses the current state of volunteer–staff relations and provides a way to monitor changes in the working environment. It is distributed to randomly selected members of staff, volunteers, clients/patrons/members, and perhaps people outside the organizational "family" who regularly interact with staff and/or volunteers (only if "outsiders' perspectives" are needed).

Begin the process by organizing a volunteer and staff Audit Committee. The committee is led by a volunteer and staff team. Members include volunteers from all areas of the organization and representatives of staff (including individuals who do staff support work). The person who coordinates or manages volunteers is a likely candidate to provide staff support to this committee. The Audit Committee needs the support of management and administration in the form of a budget and resources to carry out its work. The commitment of leaders in the organization to an assessment of volunteer and staff relations will be judged not just by words, but also by the actions taken to support the efforts designed by the Audit Committee.

The Audit Committee should follow all the recommendations for effective teams listed in Section 39.6, which describes steps to building effective volunteer and staff relationships. The work begins with a purpose statement and then goals and objectives that are measurable, achievable, demanding, flexible, and observable.

A random sample of volunteers, staff, and clients receive the survey in one-third proportions. For example, if you want to survey 30 people, each group receives 10 surveys. If you add "outsiders" to the group, they receive half the amount distributed to the three main groups. The number distributed depends on the size of the organization and its various programs that use volunteers, the time needed to compile the results, and the cooperation expected from those completing the form.

The audit is distributed with a cover letter explaining (1) the purpose of the activity, (2) who is conducting the survey, (3) how confidentiality is maintained, (4) when the results are available, and (5) how the respondent can learn about the results. If the survey is mailed, it should include a stamped return envelope.

The Audit Committee tabulates the responses and prepares a statistical report on responses for its deliberation. The first step in the deliberation is to have the person who was responsible for tabulation explain or clarify statistics. This is not the time for opinions. That is the next step. The group should discuss conclusions they can infer or draw from the statistics provided. Recommendations are based on the conclusions of the group.

The final report is a copy of the statistics, the conclusions, and the recommendations. The cochairpersons are responsible for delivering written copies of the report to those in leadership positions. They can also present an oral report to interested groups within the organization. The results of the audit are shared with the leadership of the organization, volunteer leaders, and staff management team.

People participating in the audit may want to see the results. A decision on the wider distribution of the results of the audit is made jointly by the members of the organizational leadership team. (See Exhibit 39.1.)

The director of volunteer services at a large institution felt that the relationship between volunteers and staff was less than desirable. There had been reports by both volunteers and staff criticizing the others' work, turnover seemed on the increase, and there was some "us and them" language used by volunteers and staff. A study was conducted to evaluate the attitudes of volunteers and paid staff toward each other as employer and unpaid worker.[8] The result of the attitude survey questionnaire was that "paid staff and volunteers generally have positive attitudes toward one another's performance."[9]

The use of a quantifiable measure of attitudes of staff and volunteers provided information for a volunteer advisory committee and the director of volunteers to enhance what was essentially a healthy situation. She discovered, for example, that the turnover was with volunteers assigned to one area with an untrained (and sometimes unresponsive) supervisor. Supervisors were less sure than volunteers about the "performance standards"[10] for their jobs. There are easy remedies for these two things.

This experienced and capable volunteer manager misread cues on the state of volunteer and staff relationships. It is easy to do. The use of the Volunteer–Staff Climate Audit is a method to reduce overreaction, identify specific areas of concern, and develop a plan to improve relationships throughout the organization.

39.5 *Causes of Poor Relationships*

Pearce suggests three causes for the negative tension that can exist between volunteers and staff: professional status, profiting from charity, and delicate management.[11] Paid staff have a higher status than unpaid staff. The status is greater in proportion to the degree of specialization in training for the occupation.[12] For example, paid staff in social service who have social work degrees can be resentful that volunteers with no college training are permitted to work with clients. Pearce found the tension caused by the difference in status was reduced in several of the studies she reviewed when volunteers were in the position of "office-holders" and there was "a careful deference on the part of paid [staff] members."[13]

The notion of profiting from charity is twofold. First is the idea that once there are employees in an organization, you have the volunteers and staff working at cross-purposes. The volunteers are raising money to fund worthwhile causes, and employees are working to earn money. Second, volunteers are perceived by some employees as being a direct threat to their livelihood. For example, in the mid-1970s, New York City had a budget crisis, and 40,000 city jobs were lost. The solution by the mayor was to enlarge the volunteer contingent. Despite the mayor's pledge that no volunteers were to substitute for public employee positions, some departments did just that. "Incidents like these can do little to reassure public employees that volunteers pose no threat to their livelihood."[14] Pearce's review of the research backs up the notion that some hostility between volunteers and staff can be traced to job threat. She found that "those employees who were most hostile to volunteers were the ones most threatened by them."[15]

EXHIBIT 39.1 The Volunteer–Staff Climate Audit

DIRECTIONS: Read each situation and decide how frequently it occurs. Check the appropriate box. Try to respond to each "situation."

SITUATIONS	Usually	Sometimes	Rarely
1. "They never" or "we always" are words heard when staff refer to volunteers.	1	2	3
2. Volunteers ask for credits or measures of their worth. Example, paid parking, discounts, mileage allowance, etc.	1	2	3
3. Volunteers and staff both use words like "together," "we," "our project" (meaning staff and volunteers), etc.	3	2	1
4. Reports on volunteer activities during management meetings come from other staff, not just the person responsible for volunteer coordination.	3	2	1
5. Volunteers are visible on Board of Directors or Advisory Board committees.	3	2	1
6. Decisions affecting volunteers are made by staff without consulting the volunteers.	1	2	3
7. Decisions affecting staff are made by volunteers without consulting the staff.	1	2	3
8. Volunteers say "thank you" to staff publicly.	3	2	1
9. Staff treat volunteers who serve on the Board of Directors or Advisory Board with more respect than other volunteers.	1	2	3
10. Projects are planned collaboratively between staff and volunteers.	3	2	1
11. Volunteers focus on the past rather than on future possibilities.	1	2	3
12. Volunteers jump appropriate organizational structure lines to get answers to their questions from staff.	1	2	3
13. Staff are too busy to explain the "rules of the game" to volunteers.	1	2	3
14. The leaders of the organization (staff and/or volunteers) are visible at volunteer events.	3	2	1
15. Volunteers are asked to give input and assistance in most organizational projects, not just fund raising.	3	2	1
16. Staff says "thank you" to volunteers publicly.	3	2	1
17. "They never" or "we always" are words heard when volunteers refer to staff.	1	2	3
TOTALS			

SCORING: Add the numbers in all the boxes you checked. If there are situations for which you did not check any boxes, add 2 points for each situation. Then add the three numbers for your Grand Total. 38–51 means you have excellent volunteer–staff relations (but don't let up!); 28–37 means you are doing some things right, but could use some tuning up in some sections (the situations can help you identify those areas); 17–27 means you have a serious problem and need to take action immediately.

GRAND TOTAL

Are you?   Volunteer   Staff   Other   Date

The third cause of tension between volunteers and staff falls in the lap of management systems. It appears that blurring the lines between volunteers and staff is a way to reduce the potential damage from hostility. This is especially true when paid staff leave their positions only to return to the organization or agency as a volunteer. It is as if neither volunteer nor employee sees the work as "just a job," but rather as a calling.[16]

Susan Ellis, in her book *From the Top Down: The Executive Role in Volunteer Program Success*, discusses the refusal of an employee to accept an assigned volunteer as a symptom of poor relations. "As long as salaried staff are given the choice or act as though they have the choice of accepting volunteers as co-workers, top administration is sending messages about volunteers."[17] This is a management problem. Sometimes the refusal to work with volunteers is based on inaccurate stereotypes. No one wants to work with a person who is incompetent, whether paid or unpaid. Ellis contends that in a well-managed volunteer program, recruiting the right people for the right jobs should be an expectation of management. Staff are encouraged to see volunteers as coworkers.

Pearce concludes a comments section on volunteer and staff relations by saying there is a better chance of improved relations "when volunteers become more employee-like."[18] This includes organizing the selection, orientation, training, and supervision of volunteers to standards similar to those for staff.

Despite the lack of abundant hard evidence on the causes of tension, it seems clear that management strategies can help reduce some tension. Building teams of volunteers as coworkers is a successful strategy to enhance communication and thus effectiveness.

39.6 A Sequential Process to Build the Volunteer–Staff Team

Volunteers and staff who work together to achieve the mission of the organization are a team. The committee that plans a fund-raising event, the executive committee of the board of directors, individuals who work with staff to deliver direct service to clients, members, or patrons, and those who provide support services are all part of smaller teams that make up the organization. All the small teams working together make up the organizational team.

To build the effective and efficient volunteer team requires a sequential process. Attention to each of these steps can enhance the opportunity for volunteers and staff to work together more effectively.

1. Begin the process of building effective relationships by allowing members of the work teams to develop their own goals and objectives. People who have a hand in defining outcomes are generally more committed to seeing that they happen. A fund-raising team can establish a time line, target financial goals, or benchmarks for measuring success. The goals belong to the team and are arrived at by volunteers and staff working together.

   Once a work team of volunteers and staff has determined goals and objectives, they are written and distributed to all members. These become tools to evaluate progress. Each member of the volunteer and staff team makes a personal commitment to the goals by agreeing to take some responsibility for their completion.

2. Internal role expectations are those written and unwritten "rules" that describe the appropriate behavior of both volunteers and staff. For example, many boards and committees have an established internal expectation that members may have three excused absences from regularly called meetings. After the third absence, their membership in the group is called into question. Some groups enforce this rule, others do not. By clarifying the role expectations, ambiguity is reduced and each half of the equation—volunteer and staff—knows what is expected. It is also important to address the issue of multiple expectations and possible overload. For example, the secretary to an executive director was asked to represent support staff on a volunteer planning committee. Her job was to participate in committee deliberations, not take notes and type up the minutes. That role had to be clarified for her. She did volunteer to do much of the written requirements of the group. The chair of the committee was careful to ask if it was too much or if she was feeling the group expected her to do this. As time passed, other members of the team picked up the message from the chair, and both volunteers and staff agreed to do the work of the "scribe" for the group. Staff and volunteers working together clarified her role in the group as different from her "job" and helped her avoid role conflict.

   Another type of potential role conflict is when board members are also direct-service volunteers. Sometimes they forget which hat they are wearing. "As association members, they are 'owners' of the organizations; as 'direct service volunteers' they are workers obligated to perform in accordance with directives and subject to performance surveillance."[19] Role confusion can result if a volunteer or staff member also receives the services of the organization or agency. Clarity and conscious attention to the roles for volunteers and staff keeps it clear in everyone's mind. Thus, it is more likely each will carry out the assigned job.

3. External role expectations need to be addressed. Volunteers and staff need to know with whom it is appropriate to share their concerns, praise, suggestions, or turmoil. Are they only allowed to talk to an immediate supervisor? That is an unrealistic expectation. It is better to help both volunteers and staff understand the importance of knowing the limits and scope of their own influence and how using it will affect the team with which they work. A persistent problem for NPOs is when one spouse is a direct-service volunteer and the other serves on the board. The board spouse frequently brings direct-service concerns to meetings dealing with governance issues. Likewise, the direct-service spouse may share with friends information on new policy directions when no firm decisions have been made. Helping people deal with their loyalties and appropriate avenues of communication is important to positive relationship between volunteers and staff.

4. Communication between volunteers and staff is critical. Are two newsletters produced to keep people informed about the organization—one for staff and one for volunteers? Could they be folded into one? The volunteer manager can map the flow and frequency of communication between and among volunteers and staff. This helps identify areas of weakness. It is also critical that all volunteers and staff are participants in the information flow. That flow should also cross status and authority lines.

5. Decisions made by effective work teams are uniform in the manner in which they are determined. The group needs to decide on a process for decision making. Leaders should not assume that everyone wishes to use a consensus model. Discuss alternatives and let the group make a conscious decision. The discussion also includes who is involved in the process of making decisions. Many people might be consulted, but only a few might make the "final" decision. There are two other important issues to address before beginning work on a project:
   - Problem-solving techniques to be used by the group.
   - The way conflict is managed.

   If volunteers and staff have been working together on a team for years, this information should be reviewed annually, whether there are new members or not.

6. Leaders of volunteers and staff must be skilled. This means appropriate training for staff who supervise volunteers *and* for volunteers who supervise other volunteers. It also is not optional. Leaders need skills as facilitators, meeting managers, problem solvers, and conflict resolvers. Volunteers and staff work harmoniously when they are led by people with good skills.

7. All groups have norms, whether they acknowledge them or not. These are the unwritten rules that guide organizational and personal behavior. The best norms are those that encourage the positive relationships between volunteers and staff. For example, the way volunteers and staff greet newcomers is often an indication of the state of volunteer and staff relationships. There are rarely policies about greetings, but having one in place can immediately tell volunteers and staff whether a "team spirit" exists in a group. New volunteers arrive at a meeting with all paid staff. No one greets them or attempts to find seating appropriate to the reason they are attending the meeting. A paid staff person attends a meeting of all volunteers. The staff person is not included in the discussion or consulted about decisions that must be carried out by other staff members. Inclusion or exclusion is the basis of many organizational norms. If the organization runs on staff "in-groups" or volunteer "in-groups," then others can be excluded, and that does not build effective volunteer and staff teams.

39.7   Tips to Enhance Volunteer–Staff Relations

The following are tips to enhance volunteer–staff relations.

- The position of the volunteer manager is challenging, time consuming, and vital. Coordination of volunteer programs is a complex professional job requiring a variety of skills and strategies. The person doing this job needs to commit no less than three to four hours per day to its duties. The person also needs to attend training for professional volunteer managers and to read books and magazines on the topic.
- Most organizations are in "hot" competition for qualified volunteers. Recruiting and retaining volunteers is a key factor in overall organizational success. It is also a major challenge. Building a strong volunteer and staff

team means delegation of tasks and responsibilities. An effective volunteer manager learns to delegate to others because it results in efficiency, productivity, and highly motivated people.

- Training on "team building" enhances volunteer–staff relations. Knowledge of team-building strategies helps both volunteers and staff manage more effectively. Sending volunteers and staff together to a "team-building" workshop sends a clear message about the goals of the organization.

- Volunteers find alternate lines of communication in an organization when they don't get their questions answered. Staff and volunteers in leadership roles need to constantly monitor the types, forms, and frequency of communication to members of the work team.

- Open, honest evaluation of tasks and positions, both volunteer and staff, within the organization should be undertaken on a regular schedule. Volunteers need to evaluate their own efforts, including making assessments about the staff who work with them. This is a joint effort and not a session where staff outlines a list of transgressions. Volunteers can improve only if *they* identify and plan to correct weaker elements of their performance. Similarly, when a staff member works on an event or program, the evaluation process is done jointly.

- Volunteers and staff are evaluated on supervision and management competencies. The organization's performance appraisal form or process includes an area that assesses staff ability to work effectively with volunteers. If a staff member does not work with volunteers, that portion of the performance appraisal is marked "Not Applicable." If management does not take volunteer–staff teamwork seriously enough to evaluate staff on a regular basis, why should the staff? Likewise, volunteers in leadership roles are evaluated on how they might enhance their skills. The person conducting the assessment for the volunteer is the paid staff or volunteer to whom the person reports. For example, a board of directors' president and the chief executive officer (CEO) of an agency meet annually to discuss their respective performance as it relates to the management of volunteers and staff. A standardized management competencies form is completed by each individual regarding his or her own performance. During the meeting, the individual shares the form and make adjustments based on the other person's observations of the individual's work. This is not part of the formal evaluation for the CEO, but an evaluation by the person who most closely observed the work of the other.

- Clear communication means:
  - Straight talk from both volunteers and staff
  - Active listening by volunteers and staff
  - Emphasis on building a teamwork environment
  - Volunteer work areas in close proximity to staff
  - *Payment* for volunteers in the form of a constant flow of information
  - Staff working continuously with volunteer leadership to understand the larger needs and goals of the organization
  - "Thank you's" coming often to volunteers—publicly, even when volunteers contributed only part of the total job.

- Monitor how often the volunteers are included in planning for new projects. For example, a director of volunteers in a large urban setting uses as one measure of volunteer–staff relations how consistently the volunteers are invited to participate in discussions of service goals or projects. This means everything from determining the means to stuff envelopes to meeting with the director of development at a problem-solving session on reaching a targeted group for contributions. This volunteer manager knows things are okay if requests increase for the special "expertise" that volunteers bring to the team.
- The volunteer coordinator is seen by both volunteers and staff as fulfilling a key linking role. One important responsibility is to communicate the views of volunteers to the paid staff and explain the roles and responsibilities of paid staff to the volunteers. The person who coordinates volunteers for the organization *never* bad-mouths volunteers or staff.
- Mutually define roles and responsibilities.
- Paid and unpaid staff relations are often improved through training and orientation on working in an NPO. The training session might focus on the concept of "paid and unpaid" staff to begin to reduce barriers that might exist between volunteers and staff.
- Volunteers can sometimes see themselves as operating to the side or "off in a field" from the organization. A team approach to volunteer–staff relations means that everyone works *together* to further the mission. Decisions that affect the volunteers and the service they deliver or the money they raise are arrived at jointly with paid staff. Volunteers consult staff as they make decisions about how they will carry out an event or activity.
- Staff should be represented on the volunteer committees, and the volunteers should be represented on the board of directors. Paid and unpaid staff also make good contributing members of management committees.

Every volunteer program or NPO faces unique problems and challenges in building an effective team. The efforts to bring about positive relationships have a practical and powerful payoff. Teams can deliver results efficiently and effectively. The power of the team is in creating the kind of environment that enables individuals and organizations to perform at their peak. The relationship between volunteers and staff in an NPO can be the glue that holds the programs and services together or that which pulls it apart.

Endnotes

1. Pearce, J. (1993). *Volunteers: The Organizational Behavior of Unpaid Workers.* London: Routledge.
2. Id., p. 142.
3. Katzenbach, J. R., and D. K. Smith. (1993). "The Discipline of Teams," *Harvard Business Review* (March–April).
4. Id., p. 112.
5. Fisher, J. C., and K. M. Cole. (1993). *Leadership and Management of Volunteer Programs.* San Francisco: Jossey-Bass.

6. Wilson, M. (1976). *The Effective Management of Volunteer Programs.* Boulder, CO: Management Associates.

7. Id., p. 181.

8. Macduff, N. (1991). "Attitudes of Volunteers and Paid Staff on Job Performance," *Conference Proceedings: 1991 Association for Research on Nonprofit Organizations and Voluntary Action (ARNOVA),* "Collaboration: The Vital Link across Practice, Research and the Disciplines." Chicago.

9. Id.

10. Id.

11. See note 1.

12. Id., p. 143.

13. Id., p. 144.

14. Brudney, J. (1990). *Fostering Volunteer Programs in the Public Sector.* San Francisco: Jossey-Bass.

15. See note 1.

16. Id., p. 146.

17. Ellis, S. (1986). *From the Top Down: The Executive Role in Volunteer Program Success.* Philadelphia: Energize Associates.

18. See note 1.

19. Id., p. 178.

40 Law and Taxation

BRUCE R. HOPKINS, JD, LLM
Polsinelli, White, Vardeman & Shalton

Nonprofit organizations (NPOs) in the United States are regulated at both the federal and state levels of government. The purpose of this chapter is to summarize this body of law, which largely is federal tax law.[1]

Each segment of this chapter is followed by a brief checklist, enabling an organization to review its status under and compliance with this body of law. An organization may wish to photocopy these checklists, complete them, and keep the information as part of its minutebook or other organization document file.

40.1 Nonprofit Organizations: The Legal Definition

United States society is comprised of three sectors. In one sector are the federal, state, and local governments. For-profit entities comprise the business sector. NPOs constitute the third of these sectors, which is often referred to as the "independent sector" or the "voluntary sector."

The concept, in the law, of a *nonprofit* organization is best understood through a comparison with a for-profit organization.

In many respects, the characteristics of these two categories of organizations are identical: both require a legal form, have a board of directors and officers, pay compensation, face essentially the same expenses, are able to receive a profit, make investments, and produce goods and services.

A for-profit organization, however, has owners—those who hold the equity in the enterprise, such as stockholders of a corporation. The for-profit organization is operated for the benefit of its owners; the profits of the enterprise are passed through to them, such as the payment of dividends on shares of stock. This is what is meant by the term *for-profit* organization; it is one that is intended to generate a profit for its owners. The transfer of the profits from the organization to its owners is the inurement of net earnings to the owners.

Like the for-profit organization, then, an NPO is able to generate a profit. Unlike the for-profit organization, however, a nonprofit entity generally is not permitted to distribute its profits (net earnings) to those who control and/or financially support it. A nonprofit organization usually does not have any owners (equity holders). Consequently, the private inurement doctrine is the substantive dividing line that differentiates, for law purposes, between nonprofit organizations and for-profit organizations. (The private inurement doctrine is discussed in Section 40.7.)

A *tax-exempt* organization is a subset of NPOs; that is, not all NPOs qualify as tax-exempt organizations. The concept of an NPO usually is a matter of state law, whereas the concept of a tax-exempt organization is principally a matter of the federal tax law. Nonetheless, nearly all of the states have some law pertaining to one or more tax exemptions.

40.2 Role of State Law

The rules concerning the creation of NPOs are essentially a subject for state laws. A few NPOs are chartered by the U.S. Congress, but nearly all are formed under state law. An NPO must be created in one of three forms: a corporation, an unincorporated association, or a trust. The document by which these organizations are established is the *articles of organization*.

Today, most NPOs are established as corporations. This is the case because of the limitation on personal liability that the corporate form generally provides and because of the substantial body of law that defines the operations and duties of the organization and its directors and officers.[2] A corporation is formed by filing a set of articles of incorporation; the document containing its rules of operation is generally termed the *bylaws*. (See Exhibit 40.1.)

An unincorporated association is formed by the execution of a constitution. Again, its rules of operation are contained in bylaws. A trust is created by the execution of a trust agreement or a declaration of trust. A trust can, but infrequently does, have bylaws.

An NPO's articles of organization and/or operational rules should contain provisions stating the organization's purposes and addressing the organization's structure and administration. These elements include the origin and composition of the board of directors (or board of trustees), the origin and types of officers, whether there is a membership, and the nature of the organization's committees. (See Exhibit 40.2.)

State law also addresses matters such as the extent of personal liability for the directors and officers of nonprofit organizations, the deductibility of charitable contributions (under state law), the imposition of or exemption from several taxes (such as income, sales, use, and property taxes), and the extent to which fund-raising by the organization is regulated.[3] (See Exhibit 40.3.)

State law may require an annual report. If an organization has operations (is *doing business*) in a state other than the one in which it is based, it must comply with the corporate and other laws of that state. This situation can arise where the organization has an office and/or conducts programs in the other state (as to which it is a *foreign* organization). Some states regard the maintenance of a banking account or fund raising in the state as sufficient nexus to constitute doing business in the jurisdiction. (See Exhibit 40.4.)

40.3   *Federal Taxation System*

Generally, every person is subject to income taxation. The term *person* includes individuals and entities (corporations, unincorporated associations, trusts, partnerships, and estates).

EXHIBIT 40.1 Checklist for Incorporation

Form of organization:
 _____ Corporation
 _____ Unincorporated association
 _____ Trust
 _____ Other
Types of articles of organization:
 _____ Articles of incorporation
 _____ Constitution
 _____ Declaration of trust
 _____ Trust agreement
Date organization formed _____
Place organization formed _____
Date(s) of amendment of articles _____
Date operational rules (e.g., bylaws) formed _____
Date(s) of amendment of rules _____

EXHIBIT 40.2 Checklist for Articles of Incorporation

Fiscal year _____

Membership   Yes ____   No ____

   If yes, annual meeting date _____

   Notice requirement _____

Chapters   Yes ____   No ____

Affiliated organizations _____

Board of directors (or trustees):

   Origin _____

   Number _____

   Quorum _____

   Voting power _____

   Terms of office _____

   Annual meeting date _____

   Notice requirement _____

Officers:

   Origin _____

     Titles:

      _____ President

      _____ Vice President

      _____ Treasurer

      _____ Secretary

      _____ Other _____

      _____ Other _____

     Terms of office _____

Committees:

      _____ Executive

      _____ Nominating

      _____ Development (or Advancement)

      _____ Finance

      _____ Long-range planning

      _____ Other

Registered agent _____

Some organizations are exempt from federal and state income taxation; these are known, as noted, as *tax-exempt organizations*. The categories of organizations that are eligible for tax exemption include those that are charitable, educational, scientific, and religious, as defined under the law framed by Internal Revenue Code (IRC) section 501(c)(3).

Charitable organizations include those that have the following purposes:

- Relief of the poor and distressed or of the underprivileged
- Advancement of religion
- Advancement of education
- Advancement of science
- Lessening the burdens of government
- Community beautification and maintenance

EXHIBIT 40.3 Checklist for Liability and Tax Concerns

Does organization have officers' and directors' liability insurance?	Yes ____	No ____
Is organization eligible to receive contributions that are deductible under state law?	Yes ____	No ____
Is organization exempt from state taxation?		
Income tax	Yes ____	No ____
Sales tax	Yes ____	No ____
Use tax	Yes ____	No ____
Tangible personal property tax	Yes ____	No ____
Intangible personal property tax	Yes ____	No ____
Real property tax	Yes ____	No ____
Other taxes:		

EXHIBIT 40.4 Checklist for Reporting Requirements

State annual report due _____

State in which organization is qualified to "do business" _____

Registered agent(s) in other state(s) _____

- Promotion of health
- Promotion of social welfare
- Promotion of the arts
- Promotion of environmental conservancy
- Promotion of patriotism
- Promotion of sports
- Local economic development
- Advancement of public safety

Educational organizations include:

- Formal educational institutions, such as schools, colleges, universities, and museums
- Organizations that instruct individuals for the purpose of improving or developing their capabilities
- Organizations that provide instruction of the public on subjects useful to the individual and beneficial to the community

The concept of education does not include propagandizing, which is the propagation of particular ideas or doctrines without presentation of them in any reasonably objective or balanced manner. The Internal Revenue Service (IRS) utilizes a *methodology test* to differentiate between educational activities and propagandizing.

Scientific organizations include:

- Research organizations
- Publishing organizations

Religious organizations include:

- Churches
- Conventions and associations of churches
- Integrated auxiliaries of churches
- Religious orders

Tax-exempt organizations, however, include organizations other than those that are charitable and the like. Other types of organizations that are exempt from federal income taxation include:

- Title-holding organizations (IRC section 501(c)(2))
- Social welfare organizations (IRC section 501(c)(4))
- Labor organizations (IRC section 501(c)(5))
- Professional, business, and trade associations (IRC section 501(c)(6))
- Social clubs (IRC section 501(c)(7))
- Fraternal organizations (IRC sections 501(c)(8) and (10))
- Employee benefit funds (IRC sections 501(c)(9), (17), and (21))
- Veterans' organizations (IRC section 501(c)(19))
- Farmers' cooperatives (IRC section 521)
- Political organizations (IRC section 527)
- Homeowners' associations (IRC section 528)
- State tuition plans (IRC section 529)

The concept of *tax exemption* does not necessarily mean a total exemption from taxes. Thus, nearly all forms of tax-exempt organizations are taxable on their unrelated business income. Also, political organizations, social clubs, and homeowners' associations are taxable on their investment income.

Public charities can become taxed if they engage in an excessive amount of lobbying activity or in any political campaign activity. The taxes on lobbying expenditures, which are technically cast as *excise* taxes, can also be imposed on the directors and officers of these organizations.

Private foundations are taxed on their net investment income. Private foundations (and others) can also be taxed, again in the form of excise taxation, if they engage in self-dealing with disqualified persons, fail to make adequate grants and other distributions for charitable purposes, have excess business holdings, make jeopardizing investments, or make various forms of taxable expenditures (such as lobbying or political expenditures, or certain grants to individuals).

40.4   Applying for Recognition of Tax Exemption

To be exempt from federal income taxation, an NPO must fit within at least one of the categories of tax-exempt organizations (see Section 40.3). Once this classification is achieved, and assuming it is maintained, the organization generally is tax-exempt by operation of law.

Two categories of NPOs, however, to be tax-exempt, are required to have their tax exemption *recognized* by the IRS. These categories of organizations are subject to this "notice" requirement:

- Charitable, educational, scientific, religious, and like organizations
- Certain employee benefit funds

The other types of NPOs may apply for recognition of tax-exempt status if they wish. Charitable and like organizations make application for recognition of tax-exempt status on IRS Form 1023. Nearly all other nonprofit organizations make this application on Form 1024. Farmers' cooperatives and like associations apply by means of Form 1028.

(A) CONTENTS OF APPLICATION

When an NPO seeks to be recognized as a tax-exempt charitable or like organization, it also seeks to be classified as a charitable organization for purposes of the income, estate, and gift tax charitable deductions. Moreover, if the organization has a basis for avoiding classification as a *private foundation,* it makes this claim as part of this filing. All three of these statuses are retroactive to the date the organization was formed if the application is filed within 15 months (and, where an extension is necessary, up to 27 months) of the end of the month in which the organization was created. (See Exhibit 40.5.)

(B) EXCEPTIONS

Certain organizations are exempt from the general rule of mandatory application for recognition of tax-exempt status. These organizations are churches, associations and conventions of churches, integrated auxiliaries of churches, and charitable and like organizations (other than private foundations), the gross receipts of which do not normally exceed $5,000.

40.5 *Organizational Test*

Most forms of tax-exempt organizations must meet an *organizational test.* This test is a set of rules containing certain requirements as to the contents of the document by which the organization was created. As noted, this document will be articles of incorporation, a constitution, a trust agreement, or a declaration of trust. The organizational test requirements are the most refined in the case of charitable, educational, scientific, religious, and like organizations.

The organizational test for charitable and like organizations requires that the articles of organization limit the organization's purposes to one or more exempt purposes and do not expressly empower it to engage (other than in substantially) in activities that are not

EXHIBIT 40.5 Checklist for Application

Is organization tax-exempt under federal law?	Yes ____	No ____
If yes, IRC section: _____		
Has organization received IRS recognition of tax exemption?	Yes ____	No ____
If yes, date of determination letter _____		
Descriptive IRC section	IRC section 501(c) (_____)	
Other IRC section	IRC section _____	

in furtherance of exempt purposes. These articles of organization may not authorize the organization to devote a substantial part of its activities to legislative purposes or any of its activities to political campaign purposes. Moreover, these articles of organization must provide that, upon dissolution or liquidation, the organization's assets and net income will be distributed for exempt purposes.

Additional requirements are imposed for the governing instruments of supporting organizations and private foundations.

40.6   Operational Test

Most forms of tax-exempt organizations must meet an *operational test*. This test is a set of rules containing certain requirements as to the nature of the activities in which the organization can engage. Basically, the operational test requires that a tax-exempt organization engage primarily in exempt purposes. The operational test requirements are the most refined in the case of charitable, educational, scientific, religious, and like organizations.

The operational test for charitable and like organizations focuses on the activities of these organizations in view of their stated purposes. It also embraces the proscriptions on private inurement, substantial legislative activities, and political campaign activities. Organizations of this nature that engage in excessive lobbying activities or any political campaign activities are considered *action organizations* and, for that reason alone, cannot qualify as tax-exempt charitable organizations.

The federal tax law provides that an NPO, to be tax-exempt as a charitable or like organization, must be organized and operated *exclusively* for exemption purposes. The courts have converted the term *exclusively* to the term *primarily,* with the Supreme Court stating that the presence of a single nonexempt purpose, if substantial in nature, will destroy the exemption regardless of the number or importance of truly exempt purposes. The term must be interpreted in this manner, if only to accommodate the existence of some unrelated business activity (see Chapter 24).

Thus, tax-exempt organizations, particularly charitable ones, must adhere to a *primary purpose test,* by which a substantial part of its activities must be in furtherance of exempt purposes. A charitable organization may not be organized or operated for the primary purpose of carrying on unrelated business.

40.7   Private Inurement Doctrine

An NPO, to be tax-exempt as a charitable, educational, scientific, religious, or like organization, must be organized and operated so that no part of its net earnings inures to the benefit of any private shareholder or individual. This is known as the *private inurement doctrine.* This doctrine also applies with respect to other categories of tax-exempt organizations.

The concept of private inurement is broad and wide-ranging. Essentially, the doctrine forbids ways of causing the income or assets of a tax-exempt organization (that is subject to it) to flow away from the organization and to one or more persons who are related to the organization (*insiders*) for nonexempt purposes. The Office of Chief Counsel of the IRS has stated the doctrine quite bluntly: "The inurement prohibition serves to prevent anyone in a position to do so from siphoning off any of a charity's income or assets for personal use."

The essence of this concept is to ensure that a tax-exempt organization is serving a public interest and not a private interest. That is, to be tax-exempt, it is necessary for an organization subject to the doctrine to establish that it is not organized and operated for the benefit of private interests, such as designated individuals, the creator of the organization or his or her family, shareholders of the organization, persons controlled (directly or indirectly) by such private interests, or any other persons having a personal and private interest in the activities of the organization.

In determining the presence of any proscribed private inurement, the law looks to the ultimate purpose of the organization. If the basic purpose of the organization subject to the doctrine is to benefit individuals in their private capacity, then it cannot be tax-exempt even though exempt activities are also performed. Conversely, incidental benefits to private individuals, such as those that are generated by reason of the organization's program activities, will usually not defeat the exemption if the organization otherwise qualifies under the appropriate exemption provision.

The IRS and the courts have recognized a variety of forms of private inurement. These include:

- Excessive or unreasonable compensation (the most common form of private inurement)
- Unreasonable or unfair rental arrangements
- Unreasonable or unfair lending arrangements
- Provision of services to persons in their private capacity
- Certain assumptions of liability
- Certain sales of assets to insiders
- Certain participation in partnerships
- Certain percentage payment arrangements
- Varieties of tax avoidance schemes

The reach of the private inurement doctrine may be somewhat circumscribed by reason of the advent of the intermediate sanctions rules (see Section 40.8). These rules are likely to be imposed in instances of private inurement transactions, rather than revocation of tax-exempt status. The IRS has discretion in this field, however, and has the authority to impose the intermediate sanctions penalties and revoke tax-exempt status in instances wherein the private benefits were egregious.

There is a separate but analogous body of law termed the *private benefit* doctrine. This doctrine is a derivative of the operational test and is potentially applicable with respect to all persons, including those who are not insiders. Thus, it is broader than the private inurement doctrine and, in many respects, subsumes that doctrine. The private benefit doctrine essentially prevents a charitable or like organization from benefiting private interests in any way, other than to an insubstantial extent.

More specific rules are applicable to private foundations in the form of prohibitions on self-dealing. (See Exhibit 40.6.)

40.8   Intermediate Sanctions

The intermediate sanctions rules are designed to curb abuses in the arena of private inurement using a mechanism other than revocation of the charitable organization's tax

EXHIBIT 40.6 Checklist for Self-Dealing

Has the organization identified its insiders?	Yes ____	No ____
If yes, identify them _____		
Is organization engaging in transactions with these persons?	Yes ____	No ____

exemption.[4] These sanctions are applicable with respect to all public charitable organizations and tax-exempt social welfare organizations. These two categories of organizations are termed *applicable tax-exempt organizations.*

In the past, revocation of the tax-exempt status of a charitable organization, which has provided an unwarranted private benefit, has not solved the problem. The person receiving the undue benefit continued to retain it and the beneficiaries of the charitable organization's program were the ones who were damaged or otherwise disadvantaged in the aftermath of loss of exemption. Intermediate sanctions are *intermediate* in the sense that they are imposed on directors, officers, key employees, or other types of disqualified persons who engage in inappropriate private transactions.

The heart of this body of tax law is the *excess benefit transaction.* A transaction is an excess benefit transaction if an economic benefit is provided by an applicable tax-exempt organization directly or indirectly to or for the use of a disqualified person, if the value of the economic benefit provided exceeds the value of the consideration received by the exempt organization for providing the benefit. An immediate focus of intermediate sanctions will be unreasonable compensation—where a person's level of compensation is deemed to be in excess of the value of the economic benefit derived by the organization from the person's services. In that regard, an economic benefit may not be treated as compensation for the performance of services unless the organization clearly indicated its intent to so treat the benefit.

The concept of the excess benefit transaction includes any transaction in which the amount of any economic benefit provided to or for the use of a disqualified person is determined in whole or in part by the revenues of one or more activities of the organization, where the transaction is reflected in tax regulations and it results in private inurement.

A *disqualified person* is any person who was, at any time during the five-year period ending on the date of the transaction, in a position to exercise substantial influence over the affairs of the organization, as well as a member of the family of such an individual and certain controlled entities.

A disqualified person who benefited from an excess benefit transaction is subject to an initial tax equal to 25 percent of the amount of the excess benefit. This person, moreover, will be required to *correct* the matter by returning the excess amount to the tax-exempt organization. An *organization manager* (usually a director or officer) who participated in an excess benefit transaction, knowing that it was such a transaction, is subject to an initial tax of 10 percent of the excess benefit. An additional tax may be imposed on a disqualified person where the initial tax was imposed and the appropriate correction of the excess benefit transaction did not occur. In this situation, the disqualified person is subject to a tax equal to 200 percent of the excess benefit involved.

If a transaction creating a benefit was approved by an independent board, or an independent committee of the board, a presumption arises that the terms of the transaction are reasonable. The burden of proof would then shift to the IRS, who would then have to over-come (rebut) the presumption to prevail. This presumption may cause a restructuring of the board of directors or trustees of many charitable organizations.

In many respects, the concept of the excess benefit transaction will be based on exist-ing law concerning private inurement. The statute expressly states, however, that an excess benefit transaction also includes any transaction in which the amount of any eco-nomic benefit provided to a disqualified person is determined at least in part by the rev-enues of the organization. These transactions are referenced in the legislative history of the intermediate sanctions as *revenue-sharing arrangements.*

40.9   *Legislative Activities Limitation*

For charitable organizations, considerations as to whether to engage in lobbying can be paramount. Often, what ultimately is at stake is their federal income tax exemption. That is, for some entities, too much lobbying can mean payment of a tax or even loss of exempt status.

Nonprofit organizations, to qualify as charitable or like organizations, are subject to a rule of federal tax law, which is that no substantial part of the activities of the organization may constitute carrying on propaganda or otherwise attempting to influence legislation.

The term *legislation* is broadly construed and includes bills, resolutions, appropria-tions measures, treaties, and Senate consideration of presidential nominations. The term *propaganda* is discussed in Section 40.6, in the context of educational activities.

Attempts to influence legislation—or lobbying—are of two basic types. One is *direct lobbying,* which includes the presentation of testimony at public hearings held by legisla-tive committees, correspondence and meetings with legislators and their staffs, and pub-lication of documents advocating specific legislative action. The other is *grassroots lobbying,* which consists of appeals to the general public, or segments of the general public, to con-tact legislators or take other specific action as regards legislative matters.

As to the meaning of the term *substantial* in this context, there are two sets of rules. One is the *substantial part test,* which is a vague requirement limiting allowable lobbying (both direct and grassroots) to insubstantial lobbying. Insubstantiality in this setting can be measured in terms of expenditures, time, or influence. The IRS, however,—supported by the courts—refuses to be constrained by any specific formula. A charitable or like orga-nization that exceeds the bounds of insubstantiality is considered an action organization (see previous discussion) and may lose its tax-exempt status as a result.

For organizations that are governed by the substantial part test, some legislative activ-ities are excluded from the concept of lobbying. These include responding to a request from a committee of a legislature to testify on a technical matter and engaging in nonpar-tisan analysis, study, and research.

Organizations that are under the substantial part test and engage in excessive lobby-ing are subject to an excise tax in the amount of 5 percent of the excessive lobbying expen-ditures. A like tax may be imposed on the directors and officers of an organization who agreed to the making of the excess lobbying expenditures, unless the agreement was not willful and was due to reasonable cause. The IRS has the discretion to revoke an organi-zation's tax-exempt status for undertaking excessive lobbying.

The other set of rules, which is the *expenditure test,* must be affirmatively elected by eli-gible public charitable organizations. These rules measure allowable lobbying in terms of percentages of total expenditures (other than certain fund-raising expenses). Direct lobbying expenditures may be up to 20 percent of the first $500,000 of expenditures, 15 percent of the next $500,000, 10 percent of the next $500,000, and 5 percent of the balance, with no more than $1 million expended for lobbying in any one year. These percentages are measured over a four-year average. Maximum allowable expenditures for grassroots lobbying are 25 percent of the allowable expenditures for direct lobbying.

This test exempts a wide range of legislative efforts from the concept of lobbying. These are:

- Making available the results of nonpartisan analysis, study, or research.
- Providing technical advice or assistance to a governmental body or legislative committee in response to a written request.
- Communications to a legislative body with respect to a possible decision by that body that might affect the existence of the organization, its powers and duties, its tax-exempt status, or the deduction of contributions to it.
- Communications between the organization and its members with respect to legislation of direct interest to it and them.
- Routine communications with government officials or employees.
- Examinations of broad social, economic, and similar problems, even if the problems are of the type with which government would be expected to deal ultimately.

An organization that exceeds the lobbying expenses tolerated by the expenditure test is subject to a 25 percent excise tax on the excess lobbying expenditures. Where the lobbying expenditures exceed 150 percent of allowable lobbying outlays, the organization may lose its tax-exempt status.

Private foundations (see Section 40.11) are essentially prohibited from engaging in any lobbying activities.

Most other categories of tax-exempt organizations—such as social welfare organizations, membership associations, and veterans' organizations—may freely lobby without concern as to their tax-exempt status. Indeed, the primary purpose of some exempt organizations is lobbying; this is primarily the case with social welfare organizations and some membership entities. There usually is no business expense deduction for the costs of lobbying; however, legislative efforts by business and professional associations can cause a portion of the members' dues to be nondeductible.

Where a charitable organization wishes to engage in a substantial amount of lobbying, it may be advisable to place the activity in a tax-exempt social welfare organization. (See Exhibit 40.7.)

EXHIBIT 40.7 Checklist on Lobbying

Does organization engage in lobbying?	Yes _____	No _____
Percentage of funds or time devoted to lobbying _____		
Has expenditure test been elected?	Yes _____	No _____
Does organization utilize a related lobbying entity?	Yes _____	No _____

40.10 Political Campaign Activities Limitation

Nonprofit organizations, to qualify as charitable or like organizations, are subject to a rule of federal tax law, which is that they must not participate in, or intervene in (including the publishing or distributing of statements), any political campaign on behalf of or in opposition to any candidate for public office.

This prohibition is deemed by the IRS to be absolute, that is, not underlain with an insubstantiality threshold (as is the case with respect to the lobbying rules, as discussed in Section 40.9). Recent court opinions, however, suggest that there is some form of a de minimis standard in this context. In general, this rule of federal tax law is considerably undefined, although it is clear that public charities may not make political campaign contributions or endorse political candidates.

The political campaign activities prohibition embodies four elements, all of which must be present for the limitation to become operative. These elements are:

- A charitable or like organization may not *participate* or *intervene* in a political campaign.
- The political activity that is involved is a *political campaign*.
- The campaign must be with respect to an individual who is a *candidate*.
- The individual must be a candidate for a *public office.*

A charitable or like organization may not establish and maintain a *political action committee* to engage in political campaign activities.

There are a variety of activities that may be considered political but are not political campaign activities. These activities include lobbying, action on behalf of or in opposition to the confirmation of presidential nominees, litigation, boycotts, demonstrations, strikes, and picketing. Tax-exempt organizations may not, however, engage in activities that promote violence, other forms of law breaking, or other activities that are contrary to public policy.

A tax-exempt organization (other than a political organization) that engages in the type of political activity embraced by attempts to influence the selection, nomination, election, or appointment of any individual to any federal, state, or local public office will not lose its tax exemption but will become subject to a 35 percent tax. This tax is imposed on the lesser of the organization's political expenditures or its net investment income.

Charitable and like organizations that engage in political campaign activities are subject to an initial excise tax in the amount of 10 percent of the political campaign expenditures and perhaps an additional 100 percent tax. Like taxes, in the amounts of $2^1/_2$ and 50 percent, may be imposed on the directors and officers of an organization who agreed to the making of the political campaign expenditures, unless the agreement was not willful and was due to reasonable cause. The IRS has the discretion to revoke an organization's tax-exempt status for undertaking political campaign activities.

The IRS has the authority, in the case of a flagrant violation of this prohibition against the making of political expenditures, to immediately terminate the organization's tax year and assess the tax(es). If the organization flagrantly persists in the participation or intervention in political campaign activity, the IRS may commence an action in federal court to enjoin the organization from making further political expenditures.

Private foundations are essentially prohibited from engaging in political campaign activities.

Most other categories of tax-exempt organizations—such as social welfare organizations, membership associations, and veterans' organizations—are not subject to specific rules concerning political activity. Often, they do not directly engage in political campaign activities but utilize political action committees for that purpose. Political activity is the exempt function of these committees. By the use of them, the parent organizations can avoid payment of the tax on political activities. (See Exhibit 40.8.)

40.11   Public Charities and Private Foundations

The federal tax law differentiates between charitable, educational, scientific, religious, and like organizations that are *public* and those that are *private*. The latter type of organization is termed a *private foundation*. Since there is no advantage as a matter of law to being a private foundation, charitable and like organizations usually strive to be classified as public entities. The private foundation distinction does not apply with respect to any other categories of tax-exempt organizations.

The law does not define what a private foundation is; it defines what it is not. Generically, however, a private foundation essentially is a charitable or like organization that is funded from one source (usually, an individual, family, or corporation), that receives its ongoing funding from investment income (rather than a consistent flow of charitable contributions), and that makes grants for charitable purposes to other persons rather than conduct its own programs.

In defining what a private foundation is not, the federal tax law presumes that all charitable and like organizations are private foundations. It is, therefore, the responsibility of the organization to (if it can) rebut this presumption by showing that it is a public organization.

(A)   PUBLIC CHARITIES

There are four basic categories of public charitable organizations:

1. Institutions, such as churches, universities, colleges, schools, hospitals, and medical research organizations
2. Organizations that are publicly supported, because the support is substantially in the form of contributions and grants (*donative* charities)
3. Organizations that are publicly supported, because the support is substantially in the form of contributions, grants, and revenue from the performance of exempt functions (*service provider* charities)
4. Organizations that are organized and operated exclusively for the benefit of, to perform the functions of, or to carry out the purposes of one or more public organizations (*supporting organizations*)

EXHIBIT 40.8 Checklist on Political Activities

Does organization engage in political campaign activities?	Yes _____	No _____
Does organization have a political action committee?	Yes _____	No _____
Does organization engage in any advocacy activities?	Yes _____	No _____

The donative publicly supported charity is one that receives at least one-third of its support, directly or indirectly, from the public. This support ratio is measured over a four-year period. Support from any discrete source is public support to the extent it does not exceed 2 percent of the entity's total support over the measuring period. Certain related persons are considered single sources of support for this purpose. Support from other donative charities is considered public support for this purpose, without limitation. A *facts and circumstances test* allows for qualified charitable organizations to be considered donative publicly supported charities where the public support ratio is as low as 10 percent; this test is often used by museums, libraries, and other heavily endowed charities.

The service provider publicly supported charity is one that receives at least one-third of its support from the public. This support ratio is measured over a four-year period. Support must come from permitted sources, which cannot be disqualified persons. Thus, large gifts or grants may not count as public support (if they are derived from substantial contributors). Relatively small amounts of fee-for-service revenue can constitute public support. These entities cannot receive more than one-third of their support as investment income.

A supporting organization is a charitable entity that would be a private foundation but for this exception. A supporting organization must support or benefit one or more public charities; an eligible supported organization must be a donative publicly supported charity or a service provider publicly supported charity. Support may be provided as grants or by the conduct of programs that advance the supported organization's purposes. There are several allowable relationships between these organizations, with a common one being a parent–subsidiary model. A supporting organization may not be controlled by disqualified persons (other than its directors and officers). Tax-exempt social welfare organizations, labor unions and like entities, and business and professional associations may maintain supporting organizations.

(B) PRIVATE FOUNDATION RULES

Organizations that are classified as private foundations are subject to a battery of rules and requirements:

- A private foundation must, at all times, know the identity of persons who have special relationships to it (such as directors, officers, and their family members, and major [*substantial*] contributors); these persons are termed *disqualified persons.*
- A private foundation may not engage in acts of *self-dealing* (such as sales, rental, or lending transactions, or the payment of excessive compensation) with one or more disqualified persons.
- A private foundation must annually pay out, in the form of grants for charitable purposes (termed *qualifying distributions*), an amount equal to at least 5 percent of its investment assets (termed *minimum investment return*).
- A private foundation may not hold more than 20 percent (sometimes 35 percent) of an active interest in a commercial business (with impermissible interests termed *excess business holdings*).
- A private foundation may not invest its income or assets in speculative investments (termed *jeopardizing investments*).
- A private foundation may not make expenditures for purposes that are noncharitable, lobbying, or political, nor make grants to individuals or

organizations that are not public charities without complying with certain rules (termed *taxable expenditures*).

- Private foundations that make grants to organizations other than public charities must exercise *expenditure responsibility* with respect to the grants.
- A private foundation generally must pay a 2 percent tax on its net investment income.
- A private foundation must file an annual information return (see Section 49.12) that is more complex than that required of other charitable and like organizations.
- Contributions to private foundations may be less deductible than contributions to public charities.

See Exhibit 40.9.

Some organizations are not "standard" private foundations and thus are treated differently under the federal tax law. A private foundation that conducts its own programs is a *private operating foundation;* it is treated in certain ways as a public charity. Private foun-

---

EXHIBIT 40.9 Checklist for Private Foundations

If IRC section 501(c)(3) organization:
   Public _____ Private _____
If public IRC section 501(c)(3) organization:
   Church _____
   University _____
   College _____
   School _____
   Hospital _____
   Medical research organization _____
   Donative publicly supported charity _____
   Fee-based publicly supported charity _____
   Supporting organization _____
   Other _____
   Date ruling issued _____
If private IRC section 501(c)(3) organization:
   Standard private foundation _____
   Private operating foundation _____
   Exempt operating foundation _____
   Other _____
   Date ruling issued _____
If publicly supported organization:
   Date advance ruling period (if any) ends/ended _____
   Date definitive ruling (if there is one) issued _____
If supporting organization:
   Name(s) of supported organization(s) _____
   Nature of relationship _____
   Date definitive ruling issued _____

dations that are exempt from the investment income tax and that can receive grants that do not require expenditure responsibility are *exempt operating foundations.* Foundations that are supportive of governmental colleges and universities are regarded as public charities, as are community foundations. A *conduit* private foundation is one that makes qualifying distributions, which are treated as distributions out of its assets, in an amount equal to 100 percent of all contributions received in the year involved.

A private foundation may convert to one of the four forms of public charities. To do this, it must terminate its private foundation status, following one of a variety of procedures.

As noted, a charitable organization is classified as a public or private charity as part of the process of applying for recognition of tax-exempt status. An organization that qualifies as an institutional public charity or a supporting organization is categorized as a nonprivate foundation by a *definitive ruling* from the IRS. If an organization is seeking to be categorized as one of the two types of publicly supported charities, and it has been in existence for at least one full tax year, it may acquire nonprivate foundation status by means of a definitive ruling; otherwise, it will receive an *advance ruling* for a period during which it obtains the requisite public support (if it can), with that ruling subsequently ripening into a definitive ruling. This intermediate period is the *advance ruling period.* (See Exhibit 40.9.)

40.12   Filing Requirements

Nearly every organization that is exempt from federal income taxation must file an annual information return. This return is one of the following:

- Most tax-exempt organizations—Form 990
- Small (see following) tax-exempt organizations—Form 990-EZ
- Private foundations—Form 990-PF
- Black lung benefit trusts—Form 990-BL

The annual return for political organizations is Form 1120-POL and for homeowners' associations is Form 1120-H.

The annual information return filed by tax-exempt organizations must include the following items:

- The organization's gross revenue (such as contributions, grants, program service revenue, and investment income) for the year
- Its disbursements during the year for program services
- Its management and fund-raising expenses for the year
- A balance sheet showing its assets, liabilities, and net worth
- The total of the contributions received by it during the year, and the names and addresses of all substantial contributors
- The names and addresses of its directors, officers, and key employees
- The compensation and other payments made during the year to each of its managers and key employees
- Information concerning lobbying and political campaign activities
- Information with respect to direct or indirect transfers to, and other direct or indirect transactions and relationships with, other tax-exempt organizations (other than charitable and like organizations, and political organizations)

(A) FORM 990

The annual information return that is required to be filed by most tax-exempt organizations is Form 990. The general contents of this return are stated in the preceding paragraph. In addition, an organization must describe its *program service accomplishments*. Expenses must be reported on a functional basis, that is, allocated to program, management, and fund raising. Revenue-producing activities must be detailed. Business activities must be categorized using various codes.

A tax-exempt organization must report certain other information, including:

- Taxable subsidiaries
- Changes made in the organizing or governing instruments
- Receipt of unrelated income (see Section 40.15)
- Ownership of an interest in a partnership
- Liquidations, dissolutions, terminations, or substantial contractions
- Relationships with other organizations
- Receipt of nondeductible gifts
- Requests to see an annual information return or application for recognition of tax exemption
- A reconciliation of revenue and expenses as shown on the audited financial statement

In addition to filing the annual information return, a charitable or like organization must file an accompanying schedule containing additional information. This is Schedule A of Form 990.

Schedule A is the document by which charitable and like organizations report on the compensation of the five highest paid employees, the compensation of the five highest paid persons for professional services, eligibility for nonprivate foundation status, and information regarding transfers, transactions, and relationships with other organizations.

Charitable organizations that elected the expenditure test with respect to their lobbying activities must report their lobbying expenses, including those over the four-year averaging period. Organizations that have not made this election, and thus remain subject to the substantial part test, are subject to other reporting requirements.

(B) FORM 990-EZ

The annual information return for smaller tax-exempt organizations is the two-page Form 990-EZ. This return may be used by tax-exempt organizations that have gross receipts of less than $100,000 and total assets of less than $250,000 at the end of the reporting year.

An organization can use this annual information return in any year in which it meets these two criteria, even though it was, and/or is, required to file a Form 990 in other years. Form 990-EZ cannot be filed by private foundations. A charitable or like organization filing a Form 990-EZ must also file a Schedule A (see Section 40.10).

(C) FORM 990-PF

Private foundations must file an annual information return. This return is on Form 990-PF.

EXHIBIT 40.10 Checklist for Filing IRS Form 990

Is organization required to file return with IRS?	Yes ____	No ____
If yes, identify form Form _____		
Date annual return due _____		
Is form 990-T required?	Yes ____	No ____

On this return, private foundations must report their revenue and expenses, assets and liabilities, fund balances, and information about trustees, directors, officers, other foundation managers, highly paid employees, and contractors. Private foundations must report on qualifying distributions, calculation of the minimum investment return, computation of the distributable amount, undistributed income, and grant programs and other activities.

A private foundation must calculate the tax on its investment income (unless it is an exempt operating foundation). A private foundation must provide certain information regarding foundation managers, loan and scholarship programs, grants and contributions paid during the year or approved for future payment, transfers, transactions, and relationships with other organizations, and compliance with the public inspection requirements.

In addition to reporting on its activities in general, like nearly all tax-exempt organizations, a private foundation must also report on any self-dealing transactions, failure to distribute income as required, excess business holdings, investments that jeopardize charitable purposes, taxable expenditures, political expenditures, and substantial contributions. Additional reporting requirements are applicable to private operating foundations.

(D)   DUE DATES

The Form 990, 990-EZ, or 990-PF is due on or before the fifteenth day of the fifth month following the close of the tax year. Thus, the return for a calendar-year organization should be filed by May 15 of each year. Extensions of time for filing can be obtained from the IRS.

The filing date for an annual information return may fall due while the organization's application for recognition of tax exemption is pending with the IRS. In that instance, the organization should nonetheless file the information return (rather than a tax return) and indicate on it that the application is pending.

(E)   PENALTIES

Failure to file the appropriate information return, or failure to include any information required to be shown on the return (or failure to show the correct information), absent reasonable cause, can give rise to a $20 penalty for each day the failure continues, with a maximum penalty for any one return not to exceed the lesser of $10,000 or 5 percent of the gross receipts of the organization for one year. In the case of organizations having gross receipts in excess of $1 million in a year, however, the per-day penalty can be $100, with a maximum penalty of $50,000. An additional penalty may be imposed, at a rate and maximum of $5,000, on the individual(s) responsible for the failure to file, absent reasonable cause, where the return remains unfiled following demand for the return by the IRS. An addition to tax for failure to file a federal tax return on time may also be imposed.

(F) ESTIMATED TAX PAYMENTS

As noted, private foundations are required to pay an income tax on their investment income. This tax is paid on Form 990-PF. Form 990-W is used to compute a foundation's estimated tax liability; the tax must be paid four times a year. A foundation that does not pay the estimated tax when due may be charged an underpayment penalty for the period.

(G) EXCEPTIONS

Certain categories of organizations are excused from the filing of an annual information return with the IRS. These include:

- Churches, and associations, conventions, and integrated auxiliaries of churches
- Religious orders
- Organizations (other than private foundations), the gross receipts of which in each year are normally not more than $25,000
- State entities and affiliated organizations

(H) UNRELATED BUSINESS INCOME TAX RETURN

A tax-exempt organization that is required to report unrelated business taxable income (see Chapter 24) does so by filing a tax return. This return is Form 990-T.

40.13 Disclosure Requirements

The most recent three annual information returns and the application for recognition of tax exemption of an exempt organization must be made available during regular business hours for public inspection.

Also, in general, these documents must be provided to requestors for them to keep. In the case of an in-person request, the copies must be provided on the day the request is made, absent unusual circumstances. Generally, document requests made in writing must be responded to within 30 days. A reasonable fee for photocopying may be charged. There are two exceptions to these rules: copies of the documents need not be provided where (1) they are *widely available* (which means accessible without charge by means of the Internet) and (2) the request is in the context of a *harassment campaign*.

The penalty for failure to provide access to copies of the annual return is $20 per day, absent reasonable cause, with a maximum penalty per return of $10,000. The penalty for failure to provide access to copies of the exemption application, payable by the person failing to meet the requirements, is $20 per day, absent reasonable cause, without any limitation. Any person who willfully fails to comply with these inspection requirements is subject to a $5,000 penalty with respect to each return or application.

The application for recognition of tax exemption and any supporting documents filed by most tax-exempt organizations are open to public inspection at the National Office and regional offices of the IRS.

A charitable organization must, for the donor to obtain the contribution deduction, *substantiate* the gift, if it is $250 or more, by means of a contemporaneous written acknowledgment. This document must state the amount of money and/or the description of property contributed, and whether the donor was provided any goods or services (and, if so, an estimate of the value) in consideration for the gift.

A charitable organization may receive a *quid pro quo contribution,* which is a payment made partly as a contribution and partly in consideration for goods or services provided to the payor by the charity. If this contribution exceeds $75, the charity must inform the donor that any charitable contribution deduction is confined to the amount in excess over the value of the goods or services provided and provide the payor with an estimate of the value of the goods or services.

A tax-exempt organization must pay a penalty if it fails to disclose that information or services it is offering are available without charge from the federal government. The penalty, which is applicable for each day on which the failure occurred, is the greater of $1,000 or 50 percent of the aggregate cost of the offers and solicitations that occurred on any day on which the failure occurred and with respect to which there was this type of failure. (Exhibit 40.11)

40.14   *Commerciality Doctrine*

The IRC and the accompanying tax regulations contain rules concerning the eligibility of NPOs for tax-exempt status. The courts have engrafted onto these rules additional requirements for obtaining and maintaining exempt status. These rules include those of the *commerciality doctrine.*

In essence, the doctrine holds that a tax-exempt organization is engaged in a nonexempt (taxable) activity when that activity is conducted in a manner that is considered *commercial.* (To date, this doctrine has been applied only with respect to public charities.) If a tax-exempt organization engages in an activity that is comparable to the way a for-profit entity would conduct it, the exempt organization is operating in a commercial manner. If an activity is, or combinations of activities are, nonexempt in nature and substantial, the organization cannot be tax-exempt. Otherwise, the nonexempt activity is treated as an unrelated business (see Section 40.15).

Several factors can trigger application of the commerciality doctrine. They include:

- Sales of goods or services to the general public (this factor can raise a presumption that the activity is commercial)
- Operation in direct competition with for-profit organizations

---

EXHIBIT 40.11 Checklist on Disclosure Requirements

Does organization make its exemption application available to the public?	Yes ____	No ____
Does organization make its annual return available to the public?	Yes ____	No ____
Does organization comply with the substantiation requirement?	Yes ____	No ____
Does organization comply with quid pro quo gift rules?	Yes ____	No ____
Does organization make disclosure concerning information or services?	Yes ____	No ____

- Setting of prices using a formula that is common in the realm of commercial business
- Sizable profit margins
- Utilization of promotional materials and other forms of advertising to induce sales
- Hours of operation similar to those in for-profit setting
- Payment of employees and lack of use of volunteers
- Charitable contributions not part of the revenue base

Somewhat related to the commerciality doctrine is the *commensurate test*. This is a standard articulated by the IRS in 1964 and not vigorously applied until recently. The commensurate test is used to determine whether an exempt organization (particularly a charitable one) warrants ongoing tax-exempt status. This is done by comparing the amount of exempt activity in relation to the organization's available resources. (Exhibit 40.12.)

40.15   *Unrelated Income Taxation*

The unrelated business income rules are an integral part of the law of tax-exempt organizations. While discussed more fully in Chapter 24, a brief overview is warranted here.

(A)   OVERVIEW

Taxation of a tax-exempt organization's unrelated business income is based on the concept that the approach is a more effective and workable sanction for authentic enforcement of this aspect of the law than denial or revocation of exempt status. This body of law is fundamentally simple: The unrelated business income tax applies only to business income that arises from an activity—technically known as a *trade or business*—that is *unrelated* to the organization's tax-exempt purposes. The purpose of the unrelated business income tax is to place tax-exempt organization business activities on the same tax basis as the nonexempt business endeavors with which they compete.

The term *unrelated trade or business* means any trade or business, the conduct of which is not substantially related to the exercise or performance, by the tax-exempt organization carrying on the trade or business, of its exempt purpose or function. The conduct of a trade or business is not substantially related to an organization's tax-exempt purpose solely because the organization may need the income or because of the use the organization makes of the profits derived from the business.

Absent one or more exceptions, gross income of a tax-exempt organization subject to the tax on unrelated income—and most exempt organizations are—is includible in the computation of unrelated business taxable income if three factors are present:

EXHIBIT 40.12   Checklist on Commerciality

Does organization have a for-profit counterpart?	Yes ____	No ____
Does organization operate in a commercial manner, using the aforementioned criteria?	Yes ____	No ____
Does organization satisfy the commensurate test?	Yes ____	No ____

- The income is from a *trade or business.*
- The trade or business is *regularly carried on.*
- The conduct of the business is not *substantially related* to the organization's performance of its tax-exempt purposes.

(B)   TRADE OR BUSINESS

Generally, any activity that is carried on for the production of income from the sale of goods or the performance of services is a trade or business for purposes of the unrelated income tax. Some courts have added another criterion, which is that an activity, to be considered a business for tax purposes, must be conducted with a *profit motive.*

The IRS is empowered to fragment a tax-exempt organization's operations, run as an integrated whole, into its component parts in search of one or more unrelated businesses. This *fragmentation rule* enables the IRS to ferret out unrelated business activity that is conducted with, or as a part of, related business activity. The rule is intended to prevent exempt organizations from hiding unrelated business activities within a cluster of related ones.

(C)   REGULARLY CARRIED ON

In determining whether a trade or business from which a particular amount of gross income is derived by a tax-exempt organization is regularly carried on, regard must be had to the frequency and continuity with which the activities that are productive of the income are conducted and the manner in which they are pursued. This requirement is applied in light of the purpose of the unrelated business income tax which, as noted, is to place tax-exempt organization business activities on the same tax basis as the nonexempt business endeavors with which they compete. Thus, specific business activities of a tax-exempt organization will ordinarily be deemed to be *regularly carried on* if they manifest a frequency and continuity and are pursued in a manner generally similar to comparable commercial activities of nonexempt organizations.

Where income-producing activities are of a kind normally conducted by nonexempt commercial organizations on a year-round basis, the conduct of the activities by a tax-exempt organization over a period of only a few weeks does not constitute the regular carrying on of a trade or business. Where income-producing activities are of a kind normally undertaken by nonexempt commercial organizations only on a seasonal basis, however, the conduct of the activities by a tax-exempt organization during a significant part of the season ordinarily constitutes the regular conduct of trade or business.

Traditionally, in assessing regularity, only the time of the actual event was taken into account. Thus, for example, a special event over a weekend would amount to two days a year, which is not an activity that is regularly carried on. Recently, however, the IRS has been including the time expended in *preparing for* the event—which, of course, can significantly augment the total time involved and convert what may otherwise be irregular activity into one that is regularly carried on.

(D) SUBSTANTIALLY RELATED

Gross income derives from unrelated trade or business if the conduct of the trade or business that produces the income is not substantially related to the purposes for which tax exemption is granted. This requirement necessitates an examination of the relationship between the business activities that generate the particular income in question—the activities, that is, of producing or distributing the goods or performing the services involved—and the accomplishment of the organization's tax-exempt purposes.

Trade or business is related to tax-exempt purposes only where the conduct of the business activity has a causal relationship to the achievement of a tax-exempt purpose, and it is substantially related only if the causal relationship is a substantial one. Thus, for the conduct of a trade or business from which a particular amount of gross income is derived to be substantially related to the purposes for which tax exemption is granted, the production or distribution of the goods or the performance of the services from which the gross income is derived must contribute importantly to the accomplishment of these purposes. Where the production or distribution of the goods or the performance of the services does not contribute importantly to the accomplishment of the tax-exempt purposes of an organization, the income from the sale of the goods or the performance of the services is not derived from the conduct of related trade or business.

Whether activities productive of gross income contribute importantly to the accomplishment of any purpose for which an organization is granted tax exemption depends in each case on the facts and circumstances involved.

In determining whether activities contribute importantly to the accomplishment of a tax-exempt purpose, the size and extent of the activities involved must be considered in relation to the nature and extent of the tax-exempt function that they purport to serve. Thus, where income is realized by a tax-exempt organization from activities that are related to the performance of its exempt functions but that are conducted on a larger scale than is reasonably necessary for performance of the functions, the gross income attributable to that portion of the activities in excess of the needs of tax-exempt functions constitutes gross income from the conduct of unrelated trade or business. This type of income is not derived from the production or distribution of goods or the performance of services that contribute importantly to the accomplishment of any tax-exempt purpose of the organization.

Ordinarily, gross income from the sale of products that result from the performance of tax-exempt functions does not constitute gross income from the conduct of unrelated business if the product is sold in substantially the same state it is in upon completion of the exempt functions. However, if a product resulting from a tax-exempt function is utilized or exploited in further business endeavors beyond that reasonably appropriate or necessary for disposition in the state it is in upon completion of tax-exempt functions, the gross income derived from these endeavors is from the conduct of unrelated business.

An asset or facility necessary to the conduct of tax-exempt functions and so used may also be utilized in a commercial manner. This is a *dual-use* arrangement. In these cases, the mere fact of the use of the asset or facility in exempt functions does not, by itself, make the income from the commercial endeavor gross income from related business. The test, instead, is whether the activities productive of the income in question contribute importantly to the accomplishment of tax-exempt purposes.

There is an emerging view that, where the stated primary purpose of an organization is a charitable one, the operation of one or more unrelated businesses can still be activities that are *in furtherance of* exempt purposes in the context of determining eligibility for tax exemption. One way in which a business may be in furtherance of exempt purposes is to raise money for the exempt purposes of the organization, even though the business may be taxable. Under this view, the majority of an organization's activities can be unrelated, taxable ones, yet the organization continues to be eligible for exemption because of the financial support provided by the unrelated businesses.

(E) EXCEPTIONS

Certain types of income or activities are exempt from taxation under these rules. These exemptions include:

- Interest, dividends, royalties, rents, annuities, and capital gains
- Income derived from research for government
- Income derived from research performed by a college, university, or hospital
- Income derived from a business in which substantially all of the work is performed by volunteers
- Income from a business conducted by a charitable or like organization primarily for the convenience of its members, students, patients, officers, or employees
- Income from a business that is the sale of merchandise, substantially all of which has been received by the organization as contributions
- Income from the conduct of entertainment at certain fairs and expositions
- Income from the conduct of certain trade shows
- Income from the provision of certain services to small tax-exempt hospitals
- Income from the distribution of certain low-cost articles incidental to the solicitation of charitable contributions
- Income from the exchange or rental of mailing lists with or to charitable organizations

Current issues of the day, concerning the business activities of tax-exempt organizations, include the operation of fitness centers, the conduct of travel tours, the receipt of corporate sponsorship payments, exclusivity arrangements, sales by health care providers to those who are not patients, activities conducted by means of the Internet, the scope of the convenience doctrine, and the definition of a tax-excludable royalty.

In computing a tax-exempt organization's unrelated business taxable income, there must be included with respect to each debt-financed property that is unrelated to the organization's exempt function—as an item of gross income derived from an unrelated trade or business—an amount of income from the property, subject to tax in the proportion in which the property is financed by the debt.

Unrelated business taxable income is reported to the IRS on Form 990-T. This tax must be paid on an estimated basis four times each year; the installments are calculated using Form 990-W. In computing taxable unrelated income, an organization can utilize all related deductions and is entitled to a specific deduction of $1,000. (See Exhibit 40.13.)

40.16 Combinations of Tax-Exempt and Nonexempt Organizations

One of the most striking and significant practices of contemporary tax-exempt organizations is the structuring of activities, which in an earlier era were or would have been in a single tax-exempt entity, so that they are undertaken by two or more related organizations, either tax-exempt or taxable.

EXHIBIT 40.13 Checklist on Unrelated Business Income

Does organization engage in any unrelated business activities?	Yes ____	No ____
If yes, identify activities _____		
Does organization rely on any exceptions from unrelated income taxation?	Yes ____	No ____
If yes, identify exceptions _____		
Does organization have unrelated debt-financed income?	Yes ____	No ____
Is organization paying related income tax on an estimated basis?	Yes ____	No ____
Is organization timely filing Form 990-T?	Yes ____	No ____

For example, there are several common categories of combinations of tax-exempt organizations. These include a tax-exempt organization that utilizes a tax-exempt title-holding organization, a tax-exempt charitable organization that has an affiliated tax-exempt social welfare organization that engages in substantial lobbying, a professional association with a related foundation, and a business association with a related political action committee. Another illustration of this type of bifurcation is the use of a supporting organization. Hospital systems generally represent the largest of the clusters of related tax-exempt organizations.

There are combinations of tax-exempt organizations and nonexempt organizations as well. Thus, tax-exempt organizations often utilize for-profit subsidiaries. Where this relationship is properly structured, the activities of the subsidiary will not be attributed to the parent tax-exempt organization for tax purposes. Revenues from the subsidiary to the parent tax-exempt organization may be taxable as unrelated business income, where a control test is satisfied. Where all of the entities are bona fide ones, revenues from a second-tier for-profit subsidiary (a subsidiary of the first-tier for-profit subsidiary) are not taxable to the exempt parent.

Another combination of exempt and nonexempt entities involves a partnership. It is the position of the IRS, however, that a charitable or like organization will be denied or lose its federal income tax exemption if it participates as the, or a, general partner in a limited partnership, unless the principal purpose of the partnership is to further charitable purposes. Even where the partnership can so qualify, the exemption may be revoked if the charitable organization/general partner is not adequately insulated from the day-to-day management responsibilities of the partnership and/or if the limited partners are to receive an undue economic return.

A business that is unrelated to the purposes of a tax-exempt organization may be conducted by a partnership, which has the tax-exempt organization as a general or limited partner. The revenue from the partnership to the exempt organization is likely to be taxable, as the consequence of a *look-through rule,* which treats—for tax purposes—the business as if it were conducted directly by the exempt organization.

A tax-exempt organization may enter into a joint venture with a for-profit organization without adversely affecting its exempt status. One situation where tax exemption would be revoked for participation in such a joint venture is likely to be where the primary purpose of the exempt organization is to participate in the venture and if the function of the venture is unrelated to the exempt purposes of the tax-exempt organization. (See Exhibit 40.14.)

Another instance in which tax exemption can be imperiled is where the tax-exempt organization places itself, in its entirety, into the joint venture, under circumstances where

EXHIBIT 40.14 Checklist on Partnerships

If organization has any of the following, identify:
Taxable subsidiary   _____
Participation in partnership as general partner   _____
Participation in partnership as limited partner   _____
Participation in joint venture   _____
Other affiliations with other exempt organizations   _____
Other affiliations with nonexempt organizations   _____

the exempt organization loses control over its assets and income flow. The best illustration of this is the *whole hospital joint venture,* wherein a tax-exempt hospital joint ventures with a for-profit entity (with the venture vehicle often being a limited liability company) and thereby loses control of its resources. These principles, emanating from the health care setting, are spreading to other aspects of charitable operations.

40.17 Other Legal Matters

There are a variety of other matters of law with which a nonprofit organization should be concerned. Some of these are referenced in Exhibit 40.15.

EXHIBIT 40.15 Checklist on Other Related Legal Matters

County tax exemption information _____
City tax exemption information _____
Tax returns due:
State _____
County _____
City _____
Other _____
Payroll taxes filings _____
Lobbying registration(s) (nontax):
Federal _____
State _____
Insurance information _____
Leases _____
Other contracts _____
Names and addresses of:
Accountant   _____
                 _____
                 _____

[a] A separate checksheet in the fund-raising context is in Greenfield, *The Fund-Raising Handbook,* Chapter 32 (New York: Wiley, 1997).

EXHIBIT 40.15 *(Continued)*

Chief executive officer

Chief financial officer

Fund raiser[a]

Lawyer

Insurance representative

President

Registered agent(s)

Endnotes

1. Hopkins, B. R. (1998). *The Law of Tax-Exempt Organizations*, 7th ed. New York: John Wiley & Sons.
2. Hopkins, B. R. (1996). *The Legal Answer Book for Nonprofit Organizations.* New York: John Wiley & Sons.
3. Hopkins, B. R. (1996). *The Law of Fund-Raising*, 2nd ed. (and annual supplements). New York: John Wiley & Sons.

4. Hopkins, B. R., and D. B. Tesdahl. (1997). *Intermediate Sanctions: Curbing Nonprofit Abuse.* New York: John Wiley & Sons.

Suggested Readings

Blazek, J. (1999). *Tax Planning and Compliance for Tax-Exempt Organizations: Forms, Checklists, Procedures,* 3rd ed. New York: John Wiley & Sons.

Gross, M. J. Jr., R. F. Larkin, R. S. Bruttomesso, J. J. McNally, and Price Waterhouse LLP. (1995). *Financial and Accounting Guide for Not-for-Profit Organizations,* 5th ed. New York: John Wiley & Sons.

Hopkins, B. R. (1999). *The Second Legal Answer Book for Nonprofit Organizations.* New York: John Wiley & Sons.

Hopkins, B. R. (2000). *Starting and Managing A Nonprofit Organization: A Legal Guide,* 3rd ed. New York: John Wiley & Sons.

Hopkins, B. R. (2000). *The First Legal Answer Book for Fund-Raisers.* New York: John Wiley & Sons.

Hopkins, B. R. (2000). *The Second Legal Answer Book for Fund-Raisers.* New York: John Wiley & Sons.

Hopkins, B. R. *The Nonprofit Counsel* (monthly newsletter). New York: John Wiley & Sons.

Sanders, M. I. (2000). *Joint Ventures Involving Tax-Exempt Organizations,* 2nd ed. New York: John Wiley & Sons.

Index